AS PER THE LATEST REDUCED
SYLLABUS ISSUED BY **ICSE**

CHAPTERWISE
LAST YEARS
SOLVED PAPERS

CLASS X

2022 EXAMINATION

ENGLISH-I | ENGLISH-II | HINDI | HISTORY & CIVICS
GEOGRAPHY | MATHEMATICS | PHYSICS | CHEMISTRY
BIOLOGY | COMPUTER APPLICATIONS

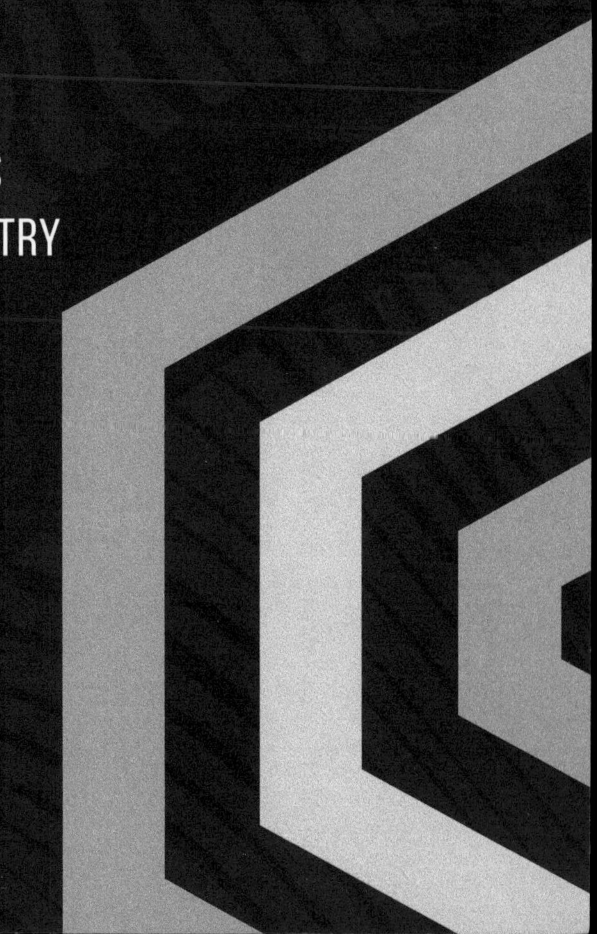

BY PANEL OF AUTHORS

DISCLAIMER

With the ambition of providing standard academic resources, we have exercised extreme care in publishing the content. In case of any discrepancies in the matter, we request readers to excuse the unintentional lapse and not hold us liable for the same. Suggestions are always welcome.

ISBN : 978-93-91184-54-4

PUBLISHED BY

 OSWAL PUBLISHERS

 1/12, Sahitya Kunj, M.G. Road, Agra - 282002

 (0562) 2527771-4, +91 7534077222

 info@oswalpublishers.in

 www.oswalpublishers.com

The cover of this book has been designed using resources from Freepik.com

Printed At Upkar Printing Unit, Agra

In accordance with the latest syllabus prescribed by the Council for the Indian Certificate of Secondary Education Examination, New Delhi.

 # PREFACE

Board exam is a crucial milestone for every student. Therefore, in order to score and perform well in this exam, we have introduced ICSE Chapterwise Solved Papers for class X. Considering the need to succeed in the examination, we have designed the book accordingly, so that students can attempt questions at any changing scenarios and exam patterns. The content of the book has been updated according to the latest reduced syllabus issued by the board. These solved papers by Oswal come in handy while understanding the variations of the board question patterns, so that students can manage their time efficiently.

This book contains matter collaborated by highly proficient teachers and subject matter experts across the country. Questions are segregated as per their respective chapters, by which students can concentrate on all questions from one chapter at a time, before they move on to the next.

This book is compiled in accordance with Marking Schemes given by the board to help understand the criteria used for marking in the board exams. Additionally, with humble representation and simple usage of language, we cater to the requirement of easy comprehensibility for the students.

We hope you will find this book helpful in your preparations for X board examinations. We would advise you to stay calm and manage your time efficiently. Do not get overwhelmed with too many resources and study guides, be selective and settle with the best ones.

—The Publisher

HOW TO SAVE WATER AT HOME

Turn off the tap when you have wet the toothbrush or while applying soap to the dishes.

Take shorter showers. Prefer bucket-bath over shower one.

Soak your dishes first in warm water before cleaning them in running water. This will make the dirt come out much faster.

Leaky faucets can waste upto 20 gallons of water. Keep a close eye on them. Turn them off tightly.

Use broom instead of pipes to clean sidewalks or driveways.

Try watering plants during the early part of the day. Avoid watering them when it is too sunny or windy.

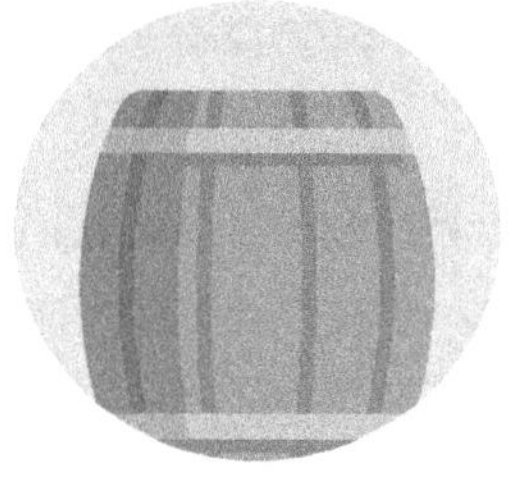

For harvesting rainwater use barrels or drums at the rooftop.

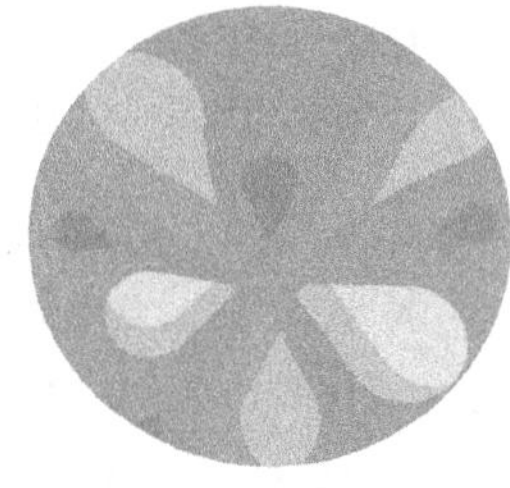

Avoid unnecessary throwing or splashing of water. Drink it upto the very last drop.

Wash your car manually instead of using a pipe.

Be conscious of the leaky washbasins/sinks.

Make use the waste water for cleaning floors.

Collected rainwater can be used for plants as it is rich in minerals.

CONTENTS

STUDY LOG

1. Divide lengthy topics into smaller chunks and work on understanding one sub-topic at a time.

2. At the end of each study session, make short notes for quick revision.

3. Revisit previously learnt topics regularly from self-made notes.

4. Try to understand the topic than just mugging it up. It will stay in your memory for longer.

ENGLISH-I

Story Writing

Q. 1. Write an original short story entitled 'The Secret'. **[2020]**

 Marking Scheme

> The short story must be centred around something that was kept a secret for a long time and was later revealed. The revelation should include an element of surprise or suspense. A touch of humour must be given merit.

Ans.
THE SECRET

It was a normal day in Mrs Ray's life. The clock struck twelve at noon and her house was looking as prim as it always did. The blankets were folded neatly, the bedsheets were crisp, the kitchen slab was nicely scrubbed to clean away the remnants of the morning breakfast, the plants were watered, the mats were dusted and the furniture was wiped.

Everything looked in order but the look on Mrs Ray's face contradicted the orderliness of the atmosphere. Something was disturbing her. And that was a delayed payment. She worked as a translator for an organisation and did freelance work to utilise her time in a productive manner. But for this particular project, her expected payment was to be delayed due to shifting of the office premises. Or so she was told.

She was banking on this money to buy a watch for her husband's birthday that was in the following week. He had admired the watch from a distance on their last outing to the shopping mall and she had understood his desire to own it. But what was she to do now? She had really wanted to treasure the expression on his face when he wore it. When he came back home from work that day, he noted the grim expression on her face and asked her about it. He was very calm about the situation and asked her to be patient about the money. He also reassured her that he wasn't expecting any gift from her and wanted only a quiet dinner.

These words touched her and now she was all the more determined to buy that gift for him. So, she decided to shell out the money she had been saving up for a gold bangle that she had liked. She thought it to be worth the sacrifice. Her husband was delighted to see the surprise and asked her where she had managed it from. 'It's a secret!' she replied with a smile.

Q. 2. Write a composition (300–350 words) on the following:

Write an *original* short story in which two children and their Grandfather are the main characters. **[2019]**

 Marking Scheme

> The story must be original. The Grandfather and the two Grandchildren form the main characters. All three characters must be part of the plot. The story may be in first or the third person and could take any form – i.e. comic, tragic, dramatic or a mystery.

Ans.
INSPIRATION

On a bright Sunday afternoon, my little sister Khushi and I were playing in the garden. "Please stop, Rahul! I am tired of running now. Let us go inside and have something to eat", said Khushi. I agreed with her and we went inside the house to have our favourite drink, *Aam Panna.*

The temperature during summer touched new heights every year in Amravati. Our grandfather was delighted to welcome us to his house there during the summer vacation and we had made it a ritual to visit him every year in Amravati.

That afternoon, when we were relishing our delicious *Aam Panna*, grandfather called out to us, "Hey kids! Please come here once you are done. I need to show you something". We immediately gulped down the rest of the drink and went running to him.

His room resembled to the ones designed in ancient India, where the huge bed occupied major portion of the room, there were niches in the wall and the ceiling laid low. Being an ex-army officer, his room was very neat and tidy. Every object was in its perfect place.

As we approached our grandfather, who we called Naanu, we saw him sitting on the bed with an opened box. It was the trunk that he used to carry to his camp during the service. Naanu asked us to sit and started taking out objects from the box. We watched him with amazement.

He began telling us the importance of the army uniform. How the colour, the fabric and the design of the uniform speaks loudly of our nation's strength, prestige and courage. He showed us the photos of his friends from the army and told us how all of them fought for the nation's pride and only three of them survived the battle.

As Naanu spoke, we could see different emotions in his eyes. As Naanu concluded, we ran up to him and gave him a tight hug. Khushi said, "We are so proud of you Naanu!". I said, "Even I want to be like you one day. Serve the nation and die for it!" Naanu with teary eyes said, "Youth like you are the building pillars of India. I am sure you will take us forward, towards a better future. I am really happy to see the spirit within you".

Q. 3. **Write an original short story entitled 'The Gift'.** [2018]

Ans.
THE GIFT

Aniket was in a fix. It was his parents' anniversary and he had forgotten to wish them. At work, he was contemplating about finding a suitable gift for them to surprise them in the evening. However, it was easier said than done. His father had a keen interest in books and arts while his mother was the quintessential Bengali housewife who only wanted utility stuff as gifts. He just couldn't buy something like a watch, or jewellery, for the risk of being scolded for spending hard-earned money without consulting them first. Being in the fag end of the month, Aniket had to even look at his stretching expenditures before deciding to buy something. He spent the whole day thinking about the gift options while pretending to look busy at work. He also searched online for ideas, for something financially viable, an attractive yet a utilitarian thing, something that brings a smile on his parents' faces, but in vain.

Finally, at around 4 p.m., Aniket decided that it is best to get down to the market and look for a gift himself rather than thinking around in circles. He left office early, and about an hour later found himself roaming around the busy roads of Karol Bagh market looking at the colourful stores and stalls. He walked around for nearly an hour, only to get confused at the end.

At last, swallowing his pride he dialled his father, "Hello Baba, is Ma around? Yes, well I forgot to wish you guys happy anniversary today. I was feeling bad about it. So I am here at the market looking for a gift but as always I am totally confused as to what to buy. Can you help me out, please?" He heard a chuckle at the other end. "Where are you? At the market? Well, come home first, we'll decide on the gift later". With that, his father disconnected the line. "Well at least they are

not angry," thought Aniket as he walked back home somewhat relieved.

As he rang the bell and walked in, he found his father at his desk, working on some project files while his mother was tinkering something in the kitchen. Aniket touched their feet and sought blessings from them and it hit him at that moment. The best gift he can give them is his love and respect which are much more valuable and priceless than any material gift. While the blessings he received from them were by far the best gift he could ever get in return.

Q. 4. **Write an original short story that begins with the words: "It was raining hard that night. In my hurry to get into the house, I didn't notice the black car parked across the road. I realized something was wrong when........."** [2017]

Ans.
IT WAS RAINING HARD.........

It was raining hard that night. In a hurry to get into the house, I didn't notice a black car parked across the road. I realized something was wrong when an arm pulled me into the bush next to the door. I tried shouting but another big palm landed on my mouth. I struggled with my legs but soon felt a fistful blow that made me unconscious.

I woke up to loud voices of men and women screaming around me and the heat made me squirm uncomfortably. I opened my eyes, feeling dizziness in my head and coughed. There was smoke all around me. I heard the loud sound of a fire engine and found myself in a house that was on fire.

It was not my house, the things lying there were not mine. It was an unknown place.

I was scared. In order to look for a way out I pulled myself up and started moving towards the door. I touched the doorknob and 'aeww!', it was hot. It then struck me, the house was on fire.

I didn't know what to do. The coughs became frequent and it was difficult to breathe. I didn't realize when I fell down unconsciously. I could feel nothing, but faintly heard a door break open and I was being covered and carried away.

The cool breeze on the skin and faint voices calling out my name, brought me out of the deep slumber. I opened my eyes to white walls and lights around me. I felt a warm hand on my palm and heard exciting words. 'He is awake now!' Moving my head towards the right, I saw the most beautiful face, my mother was there in front of me and tears welled up in my eyes. Feeling safe, I drifted peacefully into sleep again.

My parched throat forced me out of sleep. I mumbled softly, 'water', 'water!' I drank some and opened my eyes, feeling a lot better. It felt like a rebirth.

Q. 5. **Write an original short story that begins with the words:"The day started off well enough, whoever thought it would……………"**
[2016]

Ans. **THE DAY STARTED OFF WELL ENOUGH……**

The day started off well enough, but whoever thought it would be a bad one were partly mistaken. This day was to become a life-changing one for Astrid. He woke up at five as usual, just in time to catch the rising sun that appeared red in the horizon, and to breathe in the fresh morning air amidst the musical chirping of the birds flying in the air. The grass beneath his bare feet was wet with dew and it gave him a strange sensation. This was the only peaceful moment of the day that Astrid would enjoy. Hereafter, every morning begins a mad rush for the numerous trips to tutorial classes, libraries, book stores and college. But today would be different because he would be going home after exactly one year.

Astrid was secretly preparing for the entrance examinations for the National Defense Academy and had cleared the written examinations as well. Although his family had opposed his idea, determined Astrid went ahead with a crash course in preparation for the Services Selection Board that he was to face later that month. In fact, he planned to leave for the SSB centre right from his home town.

After almost an hour's jostle in the heavily crowded bus during peak Kolkata traffic, Astrid managed to reach the station. After another gruesome war at the ticket counter of the perennially crowded Sealdah Station, he managed to secure a seat in one of the superfast trains that would take him to his destination in three hours' time. He enjoyed gazing out of the windows of moving trains and buses and was caressed to sleep by the soft wind fanning his face and hair.

Four hours later, he was walking along the alley that led to his house but from afar he was quite surprised to find a small crowd gathered in front of his house. As the people became aware of his approach, he was quite puzzled with their expressionless looks. Astrid entered his house only to find his father's lifeless body, enshrouded in a piece of white cloth, lying on a plank on the floor. There were two injury marks on his forehead. His mother, sister and some neighbours were sitting around the body with expressionless faces.

Within a matter of a few minutes, his life changed forever. It made Astrid stronger and more resolute, and he did go on to join the Indian Army.

Q. 6. **Write an original story that begins with the words: "He was the funniest boy I had ever met. He would make everyone laugh……………"**
[2015]

Ans. **HE WAS THE FUNNIEST BOY I HAD EVER MET.
HE WOULD MAKE EVERYONE LAUGH……**

He was the funniest boy I had ever met. He would make everyone laugh with his witty remarks, quirky explanations or plain tomfoolery. He was my best buddy and his name was Satya. He was a lover of fun which could be at anybody's expense, even at his own. He did not mind being made the butt of a joke now and then.

Satya was in the habit of chewing gum and once a nosy old man asked him, "Why do you keep chewing gum all the time? It's like patronizing western consumerist policies."

As is typical of Satya, he replied coolly, "Well, Uncle, I do that simply to contribute to India's economic growth. When I chew a pack of gum, I actually spend money to buy it from the local *paanwallah* and he must be making a profit out of it, even if small, isn't it? In his turn, the *paanwallah* buys it from the wholesaler and distributor who again make profits from the gum. At the same time, the delivery agent makes money in transporting it and is able to hire a helper who would otherwise be unemployed and take to petty theft to feed his family. The manufacturer of the gum sells it to the wholesaler and distributor, making a neat little profit of his own. Likewise, as the demand for gum increases, he is able to hire more people and enables them to lead dignified lives through honest labour. These employees are then able to spend on things beyond the bare necessities enabling people in other sectors, to lead dignified lives again. Gradually, because of the constant demand and supply, businesses expand and hiring continues. This enables people like us to get work and a chance at dignified existence. You see, it is all about a continuous cycle of existence!"

Till today, that nosy old man is unsure whether to feel enlightened or to feel humiliated! And Satya continues to be loved because of his witticisms and quirky explanations.

Q. 1. **"A family without pets is an incomplete family". Express your views either *for* or *against* this statement.** **[2020]**

📋 **Marking Scheme** --------------------------

Argumentative essay: Views for or against the motion are to be accepted. Credit is to be given for a cohesive, well-constructed, logical argument, ideas and reasoning based on personal experience. Candidates must establish why pets are or are not important for the wellbeing and happiness of the family. Examples should be given to prove their argument. Candidates must take a clear stand and give valid reasons for their opinion. [2 to 3 points]

Ans. **A FAMILY WITHOUT PETS IS AN INCOMPLETE FAMILY**

(1) FOR THE MOTION

It is rightly said by James Cromwell that, 'Pets are humanizing. They remind us we have an obligation and responsibility to preserve and nurture and care for all life.'

First of all, keeping pets is a great antidote for loneliness. Pets instantly brighten up the atmosphere of the house. You take care of them like your own kids and with the same love and affection. No matter how low you feel or lonely you are, a pet will always be there for you. Whether you want to pour your heart out to them or tell them your secrets, you can be sure that you have a listener!

Secondly, pets can give you unconditional love and are always faithful in return. It has been proven that pets can help reduce stress and anxiety levels. Moreover, several studies have also revealed that people who tend to spend their time with pets are more likely to live longer than people who don't.

Moreover, a pet such as a dog can help you maintain the safety of your house. Dogs are known to help around with thieves and strangers coming in as they have sharp hearing and smelling senses.

Also, activities related to pets like feeding, bathing, playing and cleaning are also good ways to exercise yourself and keep fit and active.

Surprisingly, having a pet can also help you make friends. The pet-owner communities both online and offline are huge and organise regular meetups. You can go to these with your pet and meet pet-owners who are like-minded. You can discuss pet care tips and other stuff. Having pets is an excellent way to initiate small talk, make lasting friendships and bond with different people.

Finally, they teach you important life skills such as responsibility, empathy, affection and practicality as you nurture your pet through the years. So, a family is really incomplete without a pet.

(2) AGAINST THE MOTION

Having a pet such as a cat, dog, rabbit, bird or any other animal as a companion may seem like a wonderful idea at first but it comes with great responsibility.

There are many things that do not go in favour of this statement. First, keeping a pet comes at a cost. There are many

expenses related to a pet. For instance, you have to feed it special food, take it to the vet regularly for check-ups and vaccinations, make a special place for it to sleep, eat, invest in a good collar and a coat for winters, get it trained by a trainer, etc. Also, as pets age, they are prone to developing medical conditions requiring additional vet visits, testing, medications and medical procedures, which can add up to considerable expense.

Secondly, pets bring a lot of additional responsibility with them. It is like practically raising a child. You need to feed them on time, play with them, make sure they are sleep well, take them to the doctor if they are unwell, and ensure that they exercise enough. Also, you cannot leave them alone at home and go out for long periods of time, stay on vacations as they may develop some infection or can even die being left unattended.

Thirdly, there is a lot of time commitment involved with pets. For instance, dogs need to be walked and cleaned up after; a cat needs its litter box cleaned and changed; and small animals, such as rabbits and hamsters, require regular housekeeping. In fact, small animals require additional care because their living spaces need regular cleaning and maintenance, such as removing all bedding and washing the cage. Fish tanks require regular water changes and water quality monitoring to ensure that fish live in a safe and healthy environment.

So, keeping a pet could be very inviting, but it's a very big decision. Remember that your family is complete without a pet too.

Q. 2. **Write a composition (300–350 words) on the following:**

Closed Circuit Television (CCTV) must be installed in every class room. Give your views either *for* or *against* this statement.
[2019]

 **Marking Scheme**

Views for or against the motion are to be accepted. Credit is to be given for a cohesive, well-constructed, logical argument and ideas and reasoning based on personal experience. Candidates must establish why CCTV cameras are necessary or not in the Classrooms/ schools of today. Candidate must *take a clear stand* and give valid reasons for the stand taken.

Ans. **CLOSED CIRCUIT TELEVISION (CCTV) MUST BE INSTALLED IN EVERY CLASS ROOM**

(1) FOR THE MOTION

CCTV serves as a helpful medium to observe the movement and activities of the people wherever it is installed. Taking increased number of accidents and mishappenings into consideration, CCTV installation is essential in public places and areas sensitive for children and women. It not only gives the citizens, a sense of protection but also helps to prevent crimes and nab the criminals otherwise.

Installation of CCTV should be mandatory in every classroom not only from the security point of view but it will also help to monitor the activities of the students as well as the teachers during the lectures, breaks and otherwise. Any kind of mishap can be easily monitored and prevented by CCTV surveillance.

CCTV will help to monitor any malpractices or misbehaviour carried out during the classroom lectures by the students. It will prevent malpractices during examinations and theft of any kind. Students will be aware of being monitored and hence will follow discipline even in the absence of a teacher in the classroom. It will help to identify the cause behind any kind of accidents in the classroom.

Unacceptable behaviours such as bullying and intimidation can be prevented under CCTV surveillance. False accusations pretentions and other such incidents can also be avoided. Students shall be under safe, protected and comfortable environment, if CCTV is installed in classrooms.

Misbehaviour of the staff members with the students, undesirable gestures and child abuse of any kind can be easily prevented. Observation of lectures, body language of the staff members and child behaviour can be monitored. Classroom management and planning can be efficiently done with the help of CCTV footage. This will also help to develop a sense of security amongst the parents.

(2) AGAINST THE MOTION

A waste of resources and energy, CCTV is an inessential component in the school classroom. It shall pose a serious threat towards the trust, privacy and performance of the teachers and students.

CCTV installation in the classroom will be an infringement of both the teacher's and student's privacy. An unintentional act can prove to be an embarrassment before the school management which breaches the human rights and it shall affect the psychology of the child.

A clear message of lack of trust will be sent between the principal, teachers and students, if CCTV installation is carried out in the classroom. An unnecessary fear may develop within the teachers and the students before entering the classroom.

Parents who are picky may tend to get pickier due to CCTV installation and may demand to see the footage often. This shall cause an unnecessary waste of time of both the parties.

Constant monitoring may affect the performance of the students and the flow of the lectures. The teachers also may feel cautious and may not be able to deliver their best in the class.

CCTV installation may encourage bad behaviour of students due to constant monitoring for it is said that forbidden fruits taste the sweetest. They may practise this in areas that do not cover the CCTV observation. This completely defeats the purpose of the device and may reap detrimental effects.

Nevertheless, CCTV footage cannot be considered as the ultimate observation of a classroom. Technical glitches and lack of clarity may reflect a different image than the reality. It also fails to cover the dimensions such as force or pressure by which a person comes in contact with the other person or object in case of accidents or feuds. If a case arises to measure these, CCTV shall fail the test.

CCTV installation is a futile attempt to monitor classroom activities. However, installing them in corridors and staircase of the school can be considered as an optional remedy for security reasons.

Q. 3. **"Money is important for happiness." Express your views either *for* or *against* this statement.** **[2018]**

Ans.

MONEY IS IMPORTANT FOR HAPPINESS

Money holds an important place in our day-to-day lives. We need money for most things we are required to do. From education to travel to household expenses, man needs money. Without money, life becomes difficult or at times impossible.

(1) FOR THE MOTION

Money makes one powerful, wealthy, respected, and stylish, enabling him/her to live a lavish and comfortable life without any trouble or botheration. Many people believe that if one has money then he/she can get anything. All his needs and demands can be fulfilled with money. Perhaps they are right. In today's world, your social status is measured by your bank balance, your posh house and swanky cars that you possess. Your status is measured by the number of clubs that you are a member of or how many parties you throw to your friends and admirers during the week or month. If you have ample money, you will always be surrounded by many people who pose or feign to be your admirers and well-wishers. The fact that money can buy anything in the world justifies it to be the ultimate source of happiness in life. People consider themselves very lucky if they have got enough money to live a lavish life and spend that money in any manner they may deem fit. Thus, for them it is the most important thing to get happiness, well being and almost anything under the sun.

(2) AGAINST THE MOTION

Money is definitely a source of happiness to mankind. But this happiness is not permanent since money is not likely to stay with you forever. People think that money can buy anything they need and is a guarantee for a good life. It is true to some extent but not entirely. Money does not guarantee peace of mind and tranquillity since superfluous money gives birth to greed, arrogance and lust to have more. This desire is endless and invariably causes mental tension and health problems like high blood pressure, heart ailment and many more complications. Money is thus said to be a 'necessary evil' in today's life. In general, people having more money, have a rather narrow mindset and they would not like to part with their money. So they cannot be generous and are unwilling to help others.

We should be able to draw a distinct line between the good effects and bad effects of having money. Those who have more money should have a broader mind to help those who need money for living. A wealthy person can easily pay for the education of a meritorious student who does not belongs to a wealthy background. The concerned person would remain ever grateful to him for his act of kindness. The future of a bright student will be secured. A person with limited resources may be happier than a person with unlimited resources because the former has faith in himself and in God. He is happy with whatever God has given him and does not hanker after more.

Too much money for one and no money for another is a perennial problem. As a consequence nobody is happy; the one with no money wants to earn some and the one with more money hopes to earn even more and enhance his treasure. Therefore, money cannot be considered as a lifelong source of happiness.

Q. 4. **"School days are the happiest days of our lives." Express your views either *for* or *against* this statement.** **[2017]**

Ans.

SCHOOL DAYS ARE THE HAPPIEST DAYS OF OUR LIVES

(1) FOR THE MOTION

School was like my second home, my teachers and friends were my family! I still remember my first day in school.

None of us was crying, but playing happily and taking turns on the slide. Those were some carefree days with no worries. Learning alphabet and numbers was not a big deal. Although the best part was shouting our lungs out while telling the rhymes. My favourite time was spent in the little garden that had slides, merry-go-round and other fun rides. Soon time flew and we all were in the primary section. I still remember those moments vividly, all that fun while sneaking around the corridors, playing in the rains, stealing mangoes from the mango tree in our school garden and watching our playground turn into a swimming pool.

One incident that I can never forget, is "The Rat's Day Out." Our science teacher Mrs. Kamath was taking our class, when suddenly someone from the corner of the class screamed "Eekkkss! There is a rat here", so we all jumped on our bench-tops, more shouting and screaming followed, but somehow Mrs. Kamath convinced and made us sit at our places so that she could proceed, but we were not in the mood to listen, and in every five minutes someone would shout that there is rat here and there to which finally, Mrs. Kamath got annoyed and called the peons. The class was vacated and the peons went on a 'Rat Hunt'. Finally, after 15 minutes, the rat was caught, but the moment we stepped inside, the bell rang to which we all heaved a sigh of relief!

One more incident that I can recall is when we were in the 10th standard, our principal decided to take our History Classes (normally Principal ma'am never took classes). For a week we did succeed in trying hard to act decent in front of the principal, but soon got bored, moreover we were frustrated by the way our principal taught. Every day she would revise whatever she taught the day before and then start afresh. Then one day we observed that when one of our classmates was coughing, Madam would stop until he stopped coughing. There, our devil brains started working again. So from the next day, we began our daily ritual of coughing our heart out. Our Principal tried to adjust for a week with our persistent coughing but ultimately she complained to our class teacher. So the next day, our teacher distributed Halls tablets to the whole class and warned us all that we should not catch cold.

Seriously I enjoyed school days a lot. Whenever I meet my old school mates, such beautiful memories flash again and bring back smiles and tears of joy and I miss my school all the more, the place where I spent the happiest days of my life.

(2) AGAINST THE MOTION

It's not necessary that the school days are always the happiest days of our lives as we generally think. They sometimes appear to be a nightmare. Some people don't even want to dream of their school days as they bring fear to their mind. The first thing that terrorizes the children is getting up early in the morning when the rest of the world is sleeping. The anxiety begins at night only when one has to prepare the bag according to the timetable, gets his or her uniform ironed and polish the shoes. They enter the bathrooms yawning and unwantedly when it's still dark in the morning. After which, waiting at the bus stop

in the early morning hours on the lonely roads adds one more tag to the boring routine life.

In the class again the teachers are aggressive who pressurize the children for completing work on time. These teachers, scold and punish the children for negligence and thus develop a kind of inferiority complex in them. Such students feel insulted in front of the other students if the work remains incomplete. Howsoever genuine reasons the students give, the teacher would not listen. It seems as if the teachers have descended from some other planet or as if they are from the army who still hold the strict army rules. They are dried, rude, rough and bitter and that may be due to their job demand as they have to face the class of mixed children but children don't understand their limitations.

Then there are boring school uniforms for continuous many years. The same colour, same pattern, same hairstyle and same footwear. It's difficult to see the so-called uniformity daily. Everything becomes so monotonous that children lose charm in attending the classes. Apart from this, there are daily morning assemblies which children usually hate and try to avoid. They find different excuses to sit in the class. Sometimes they get a diary note to be shown to the class teacher or the monitor to sit in the class during assembly.

It's not necessary that all the subjects are interesting for all the children. Some may find Biology interesting, while others may find English or Math more interesting. So what happens is that, the uninterested children create chaos in the class and disturb other students as there is no such system in our country to provide only those subjects to the children in which they are interested.

So I can say that, there is one or the other anxiety always during the school time. One has to be time bound and cannot live the life of a free bird.

Q. 5. **"The use of Mobile Phones must be allowed in schools." Express your views either *for* or *against* the statement.** **[2016]**

Ans. ### THE USE OF MOBILE PHONES MUST BE ALLOWED IN SCHOOL
(1) FOR THE MOTION

The above is a highly debatable topic and there can be numerous arguments and counter-arguments related to it. On my part, I feel that children should be allowed to use mobile phones in school but with a great deal of caution.

With the infiltration of mobile phones, human life has become both easy and complex. In fact, today the phone does not serve merely as a device for making calls to friends and distant relatives, but it also serves as a computer device through which we can check our emails; social and professional networking profiles, surf the net, download movies, songs and books, and do online shopping. It can also guide us when we are visiting or are lost in unknown places. In short, a mobile phone is not a mere device any longer, it is an indispensable virtual world that has become part and parcel of our lives.

There are many instances of little children missing their buses and vans while on their way home from school. They can be traced easily if they have their mobile phones with them. Also, if some students are absent from school and home at the same time, then both the school authorities and parents can keep track of their whereabouts. There are frequent reports of children being kidnapped from school for different reasons. Such incidents can be avoided if there are mobile phones with them.

School authorities often complain that children use mobile phones to play games or surf sites and indulge in other inappropriate activities in class than paying attention. However, these can be prevented by laying down strict rules. For example, schools can specify that children are allowed to carry only basic JAVA sets, without cameras, audio and internet surfing facilities. Also there should be provision to submit the phones to the teacher before beginning the class, restricting the use to only before and after school or during breaks. There should be frequent and surprise checks to ensure that students comply with these rules.

In fact, if children learn to use mobile phones responsibly in school, then they will be able to do so in their later lives as well. Also, it will give them the idea that they can be and are trusted by their elders on such important issues. This will help them to develop as responsible individuals.

(2) AGAINST THE MOTION

Although there has been a rapid increase in technology, particularly in communication technology, and children have adapted to them much better than adults, yet the question that arises in my mind is, do children really need mobile phones in school? Many generations of school students have completed their schooling, even their higher education without a mobile phone, so why is there a need for school students to carry such devices, all of a sudden?

In school, the child really needs to learn and play, so how can mobile phones come with handy in these two activities? In fact, children will grow a tendency to fiddle with their devices and thereby disturb themselves and their classmates as well. The teachers will also be wasting valuable time and energy just to ensure that children are not texting or playing video games in class.

Moreover, those children who are hooked on to mobile games actually might use them as a pretext for avoiding outdoor games and sports. Consequently, this will prevent them from being fit and healthy and will also not help them to understand the concept of team-spirit as all such children would be busy playing games by themselves. It will also lead them to be addicted to online games and therefore lose their focus on constructive activities.

Some parents argue that carrying mobile phones to school provides additional safety to children. But that can be equally taken care of by a planned and systematic approach for handling children. This methodology has been used successfully, all the while.

Mobile phones are also responsible for scandalous video clips, especially in co-educational schools, causing much embarrassment and pique to girls' families. Such nuisance can be avoided if mobile phones are banned within school premises.

Lastly, there might be enviousness among students concerning whose mobile phone has more features and this might lead to unnecessary acts of crime like theft, vandalism and even fights. All such petty issues can be avoided by banning mobile phones in schools.

Q. 6. **All Girls or all Boys Schools provide a better learning environment than co-educational schools. Express your views either *for* or *against* the statement.**   **[2015]**

Ans.   **ALL GIRLS OR ALL BOYS PROVIDE A BETTER LEARNING ENVIRONMENT THAN CO-EDUCATIONAL SCHOOLS**

(1) FOR THE MOTION

All girls or all boys schools definitely provide a much better learning environment.

The growth of an individual lies upon the basic foundation which is laid down in a school, and having girls and boys in the same school cannot cater to the proper development of either, as they have different requirements..

Moreover, the competition between the genders can result in an unequal learning environment, and the inclination towards a subject can also be highly hampered.

The biggest fear for students in a co-education is the fear of being laughed upon, and this fear deteriorates the confidence level to a great extent. While in a gender-specific education, this fear is less, maybe because one may feel that everybody present around them is cut from the same cloth. Hence, it leads to a great sense of comfort.

It is vital that boys and girls learn how to work together, so a completely gender-specific school is believed to be counterproductive. They learn to work in unity, have confidence and then whenever required, they are very well qualified to work without having any feeling of inferiority or superiority amongst each other.

Many researchers have proved that single-gendered education helps the student to excel in all aspects of their life. They teach the students to focus and set their priorities in life, and they eventually emerge out as successful human beings, with flying colours.

(2) AGAINST THE MOTION

Many arguments, have been put forward so many times in favour of boys and girls studying in separate schools. It is believed that they are able to concentrate more on studies in such schools. They feel more comfortable dealing with the students of the same gender. "When girls go to all girls' schools, they stop being the audience and become the players" is the opinion of two American professors. Well, I have my reservations about these well-deliberated observations. I think I'll always remain an advocate of co-educational schools.

There are many reasons why I prefer co-educational schools. The foremost reason being that the school is a world in miniature and all rudiments of life are learned from here. In the real world, both the genders have to mingle and interact with each other. So, these basic lessons have to be learnt in school.

Secondly, there is no superiority or inferiority as far as intelligence is concerned. A girl is as skilled as a boy in intellectual spheres, so every competition is fair and equal. If boys and girls grow up in the same environment, having the same exposure, then there is no question of feeling odd or shy in front of each other. It rather inculcates confidence for the future and also enhances their personality.

A research conducted at Arizona State University in 2011 shows classes that separate boys and girls can be detrimental to the personal and social growth of both. Children spend their formative years in the classroom developing skills that will help them in maintaining relationships throughout their lives. If a child has little exposure to the opposite gender, then building meaningful relationships can be difficult for him/her.

In a nutshell, everything boils down to the fact that gender diversity suffers at a single gender school. In addition, even if it is easier for students to participate actively and do well academically at a coed institution, the real world is not gender-specific. It may prove difficult for students from gender-specific schools to adjust to a coed work atmosphere after they graduate. A real life atmosphere makes children accept the other gender and interact with them normally. This will drive away the belief that boys are from Mars and girls are from Venus.

Narrative Composition

Q. 1. **Which do you prefer—morning, afternoon, evening or night?**

Describe your favourite time of the day. What are the sights, sounds, smells and feelings that you associate with your favourite time of the day? Why do you like this part of the day better than the others. **[2020]**

 Marking Scheme ------------------------

This is descriptive composition, and the candidate must choose the best part of the day. A brief description of the time and reasons for the choice must be given.

Ans. **DUSK—MY FAVOURITE TIME OF THE DAY**

Nicholas Sparks has poetically captured my favourite part of the day, dusk, by saying that, "Dusk is just an illusion because the sun is either above the horizon or below it. And that means that day and night are linked in a way that few things are; there cannot be one without the other, yet they cannot exist at the same time."

Dusk is a very special part of my day. I love how it paints the sky in vibrant hues – fiery orange with blue tones on some days, sometimes royal pinks, sometimes fierce purples and also sometimes inky shades of blue spread all over.

There is something special about the sky during that hour of the day as it bids adieu to the Sun and says hello to the Moon.

The flowers still linger on their fragrances as they are watered during this time. The wet soil emits a wonderful smell of its own, uplifting the mood of all and sundry.

The weather too is pleasant and amiable at this time of the day. It is not too hot as it is when the sun is shining bright in the afternoon and neither is it chilly cold like it is during winter nights. I feel very calm and relaxed at this time of the day.

I usually like to spend this time on my balcony, gazing at the sky and journaling while sipping coffee. This time of the day triggers my brain in a positive manner and gets my creative juices flowing. I usually spend this time of the day alone and write what I feel. It helps me vent out my stress, clear my head and compose myself for the tasks ahead. This 'me time' of the day is very important for me and I like to spend it fruitfully.

Q. 2. **Write a composition (300–350 words) on the following:**

Your class had to conduct a Morning Assembly. Write an account of how you prepared for it, what your role was and what you gained from the experience.

[2019]

Marking Scheme ------------------------

This is a personal account of 15-year-old child of the Morning Assembly in each School. The composition must include planning, motivation and the role played by the students. The composition should also indicate what lessons are learnt through this exercise and why these lessons are so important.

Ans. **A TRIBUTE TO OUR REAL HEROES**

This monday morning at school was not an ordinary monday morning. A plethora of emotions were arising within me including nervousness, anxiety, excitement and everything else because it was the turn of our class, class X – B to conduct the morning assembly. Being the monitor of the class, I had to choose students as well as make arrangements and execute practises. After discussing with my classmates we decided to perform a small but special act to pay tribute to the martyrs who sacrfice their lives protecting their nation.

I decided to make a chair group of give students to sing the famous song. 'Aey mere watan ke logon'. Further five boys will be dressed as soliders and will be shown leaving their homes while girls will be acting as mothers, sisters, wives for daughters of the soliders sending them to the border with teary eyes. They will bravely fight and get shot, creating an environment of mixed feelings, of both sorrow and pride.

I took the responsibility to narrate the act. After an extensive practice, we were finally ready. On Monday as the clock struck 07:45 AM, all the students started gathering in the assembly hall.

The morning prayer ended and we were called for our performance. The choir group gave a mellifluous performance whereas the theatrical act engaged the attention of one and all. As I began my narration, the entire school went into silence and I could see the visualization of my words in their eyes.

Stories of brave soldiers and their families, their sacrifices and courage gave gooseflesh to one and all. As I concluded my speech, the entire school shouted, '*Jai Hind! Bharat Mata ki Jai!*'. Our Principal, all the teachers and students appreciated our efforts.

Q. 3. Narrate an incident from your own experience when you helped to prepare a meal. Explain what you did and what you gained from the experience. **[2018]**

Ans.

MY EXPERIENCE WHEN I HELPED TO PREPARE A MEAL

Once when I was in school, my mother was taken ill. We were shocked and very disturbed since it was the first time that I saw my mother in bed late in the day, many hours after her usual rising time, early in the morning.

However, one morning the scene was different. My father was sitting by her side while my elder sister was preparing tea in the kitchen. Amongst the four siblings, I was closest to her. Even today, we are very close though living far away from each other.

My sister was in the kitchen, getting the meal ready for the day. Father had to go to the office and my elder brother was sent to school. I went to the kitchen and asked her if I could help her. She was very happy and her face beamed with joy. I sat by her and helped her by peeling the potatoes first and then chopping other vegetables. Although the chopping was not as good as hers but she was happy. I washed the vegetables and kept them aside for the next step. She was planning to make Dal. So, I washed it and kept it ready for boiling. Lastly, rice had to be washed. I did that too and kept it in a bowl. Later, I poured water to soak the rice well so that it takes less time to boil. While working with her, she kept asking me to be careful with the knife and the stove in order to avoid any accident.

It was my first time in the kitchen, but I thoroughly enjoyed the work. I was happy that I could help her and also learnt to cook dal. It was a good experience which helped me immensely later.

Q. 4. Narrate an incident from your own experience when you helped a friend who was in trouble. Explain what happened. What did you do to make the situation better? **[2017]**

Ans.

FRIENDSHIP

Haroon and I were best friends long since we met in grade 5. He was the only friend I had when I moved to England with my family. We had studied in the same school and college but our path diverged as we grew up and followed our own ambitions. Haroon became a radio jockey and I became a lawyer. Though we were far apart, yet we would never miss an opportunity to meet each other and help each other in times of need.

One day he called me that he had been arrested and I went to rescue my best friend. I bailed him out of jail and then he told me that the previous evening when he was returning from his work, he had stopped at a nearby mart to buy some food items, when he saw a black man beating up a teenager. Being a good Samaritan, he went to help the teenager and knocked out the man. The teenager ran away.

Haroon called the police and after investigation, it was found that the black man was the owner of the shop and was beating the robber (the teenager). Even though Haroon tried his best to explain to the police, what the misconception was, but no one was ready to listen to him and it appeared as he had accompanied an armed robbery and assaulted a civilian, and consequently he was arrested and taken to the jail.

Haroon was confused and shocked at what was going on and suddenly realized that he had actually saved the robber! I believed my friend as I knew he could never do such a misdeed and as he couldn't afford a lawyer, so I insisted him on keeping me.

Haroon had to appear in front of a court to explain his actions. The police had caught the thief who was involved and he blamed Haroon for being the mastermind of the plot, even though Haroon had no idea of who he was. The video of the fight going outside the mart was shown which made Haroon look as the criminal. I argued that the tape of inside the mart shall also be seen to prove that Haroon was innocent. Though the judge had made his decision, yet he ordered the tape to be shown and it seemed obvious that Haroon had helped the robber unintentionally. The judge saw this as a case of misconception and apologized for the problems caused. Overjoyed, Haroon and I congratulated each other.

Q. 5. Narrate an incident from your own experience when you expected to do very well, but for some reason were unable to do so. Explain what happened and why it happened. What lesson did you learn from it? **[2016]**

Ans.

AN EXPERIENCE

Even though it is important to prepare well yet at times we do experience failure in spite of the best preparations. Such things can happen due to many reasons and one of them is over-confidence or underestimating the opponent. A similar incident happened to me, which earlier I did regret, but admittedly, it gave me a lesson for a lifetime.

I had received the Best Athlete Award for three consecutive years from my school for performances, not only in the Annual School Sports but also in the Interschool Athletic Meet. Considering the fact that I hardly met any tough opponent in the 100 m, 200 m, 400 m relay and 100 m hurdles races, success had actually gone to my head and I had grown to be proud and egoistic, sure to remain undefeated. Although I never had tantrums or showed disrespect to anybody, yet at times I considered people to be inferior to me and formed poor estimates of them.

That was the reason for my undoing and the lifelong lesson.

Two years ago, I was representing my school in the All-India ICSE School Sports Event in Shillong and many of the participants were already aware of my presence. They considered me to be a formidable competitor who could not be defeated. But, there was one person, who did not think so.

Hailing from one of the smaller towns in the tribal belt of Jharkhand, Samson was a dark and lanky fellow who was lucky to have been taken in by the missionaries and given a proper education. His tribal instincts, inherited from his ancestors, made him tough.

We cleared our qualifying heats easily, though, never pitted against each other during the initial stages. But, the finals were a different ballgame altogether. In spite of my reputation and consistency, there was always a chance for somebody else winning the race, though I dismissed such thoughts summarily. Consequently disdainful of the others, I took a day off from practice just ahead of the finals and went sightseeing.

As the whistle blew, we darted for the finish line of the 100 m event and in a few seconds, I was far ahead of others. But Samson overtook me by a fraction of a second just at the finishing line. It was too late but I did realize the importance of assessing opponents thoroughly to understand their strengths and weaknesses.

Q. 6. **You had booked a ticket on an early morning train. However, you woke up late and missed it. You then decided to run to catch a bus to the next station where you hoped to catch up with the train. Narrate the entire event, how you felt, the effort you made and how you finally caught the train. What did you learn from this stressful experience?** **[2015]**

Ans.

MISSING THE TRAIN......

In India, punctuality is a rarity. Everything here is said to happen in 'five minutes', but nobody knows what would be the actual duration of those 'five minutes'. In government offices, they can extend up to some hours as well. Trains are the biggest defaulters! A delay of 15 to 20 minutes is quite normal and timely, especially for commuter trains. Consequently, daily commuters adjust their time-tables accordingly. In fact, problems arise when they start running in time, all of a sudden and the regular routines get disrupted, inconveniencing office-goers, students and a host of others.

I am also one of the billions of Indians who depend upon the Indian Railways for commuting to and fro from my office daily. It is cheap, comfortable and a lot less time consuming than any other form of transport. Moreover, I get to meet so many people on the way. Subsequently, like the rest of my brethren, I am too in the habit of catching a particular train everyday that runs late by about 10 to 15 minutes. But sometimes, my routine gets disrupted like it happened yesterday!

As usual, I reached the railway station at 8:05 a.m. to board the passenger train scheduled at 7:50 a.m. but departing regularly at 8:10 a.m. However, it was a shock for me to learn that the train had left on time leaving, most of my fellow commuters stranded. The next best option to be in office right on time for the scheduled meeting was to take the town service bus to the inter-city bus depot. That's what I did.

The scene at the depot made me almost fall on my knees because it seemed all those unfortunate souls who missed the train had the same bright idea as I did and ended up occupying every conceivable square inch of the bus! After a great deal of acrobatics, I managed to get a foothold and hung on to the overly of the overcrowded bus. My intention was to get down at the next railway station, which was on the way and catch the elusive train. I only hoped that the others did not have the same bright idea flashing in their minds.

Luckily for me, nobody did. I got down at the next station only to learn that my train was actually delayed by an hour because of some technical reasons! You can well imagine how the rest of my day went.

4 Descriptive Composition

Q. 1. **Have you ever said or done something that changed the life of another person?**

Give an account of your words or actions that led to this change and describe how the experience made you feel. **[2020]**

 Marking Scheme

A brief account of words or actions. The impact on the other person, the effect on the narrator. This is a first-person account. 'I' must be the protagonist. [Action/impact can be positive or negative]

Ans. **A LIFE CHANGING EFFORT**

Khalil Gibran has famously said that, 'The smallest act of kindness is worth more than the greatest intention.' I understood the real meaning of this statement last week. My friend, Raj, was diagnosed with a severe bout of chickenpox and was missing from the school for a good whole week. The poor thing was weak, frail and had very limited energy due to the dose of antibiotics that he was on. I was missing his presence tremendously in class that week. We literally spent all our time in school together. We sat together, ate together, played together and even did our classwork together.

Every day, I would ritualistically call him after coming back home from school to update him on all that had happened during the day. We were a group of three friends, Raj, Rahul, and I. We would connect on a conference call sometimes. Today was one of those days as we three had been assigned a science project which we had to work on together. After we discussed, it was my idea to help Raj by sending him the relevant links to help him understand the concept and to type some portion of the assignment using the reference material. On the other hand, Rahul had the greatest intentions about Raj. He would talk about him every day and it was clear that he missed him. But of what use was all this concern?

When Raj re-joined school after 10 days, he was beaming and had the project assignment in his hands. He had used all the links that I had sent to him and completed his assignment on time and escaped the teacher's scolding too. He was really appreciative and thankful to me for my help. This was when I realised that a small act of kindness can really bring a difference to a person's life and it is even more important than having good intentions sometimes.

Q. 2. **Write a composition (300–350 words) on the following:**

Summers are becoming hotter with each passing year. Write a description of one such very hot day. What did you see and hear as you walked outside? How were birds and animals affected? **[2019]**

 Marking Scheme

The candidate must give a detailed description of hot summer day. The heat, rising temperatures, humidity or aridity must be included. Images of animals and birds seeking shade and water should make up a part of this composition.

Ans. **A HOT SUMMER AFTERNOON**

I called for another glass of chilled water as I wiped the sweat from my forehead. Summer that year felt quite rageful. The temperature was oscillating between 45°C–50°C. Even the air conditioner inside our rooms could not provide any relief. Life for us had truly become difficult in Ahmedabad. My mother made sure to keep us hydrated by making us drink lemonade and water regularly.

Mornings weren't pleasant enough and evenings became enjoyable only hours after sunset. Sun was shining to its brightest and the heatwave had trapped the land and water alike. As I was walking through the shade of the trees in our verandah, trying to enjoy the shadow, my eyes got stuck on the ground where I saw a little bird. It was lying on the ground with minimal movements. I understood its plight and rushed inside the house to fetch a bowl of water.

I lifted the bird and held its beak near the water. The poor bird tried to drink water but to no avail. It died within a few minutes in my hands. I could not hold back my tears and broke down. After some time, I dug a pit nearby and buried the bird there.

As I walked back to the house, the thought struck me, "If this poor little bird died due to lack of water in this scorching heat, what about others?" I looked around at the dryness, a mosaic of broken ground was created under my shadow, and relief was nowhere to be found.

I promised myself that no animal shall henceforth suffer the same fate as the bird did. I went to the terrace, got an earthen pot, filled it with water and placed it on the parapet of the roof. Soon crows and pigeons started coming and drinking water from it. I used the same idea and put an earthen pot outside the compound wall of my house wherein dogs, cats and cattle could come and quench their thirst.

After that day till date, I make sure to keep the earthen pots filled with water so that no animal or bird suffers due to lack of water. The death of that little bird changed my perspective and approach towards animals forever.

Q. 3. **You had been waiting outside the examination hall. Describe what you saw and the sounds you heard when you arrived at the place. What were your feelings? Describe how the scene changed once you entered the hall and the examination started.** **[2018]**

Ans.

WAITING OUTSIDE THE EXAMINATION HALL

I was waiting outside the examination hall of Harcourt Butler School, on the first day of our Higher Secondary examination. It was my first experience of sitting in an exam hall outside my school. There was a strange feeling. I was apprehensive but not nervous.

This is the first step in any student's life to enter a bigger life outside his school where he has spent many years preparing himself for this day. Today was English Paper I. It was my favourite subject.

There were so many other students from my school as well as some other schools too. Different types of noises were coming from everywhere. Some were frantically checking their notes for the final time before the first bell was to ring. Some were rehearsing lines mutely, but with their lips moving. Some of my classmates were also busy, the same way avoiding the eyes of their friends. Some parents had also come and were seen giving last minute tips to their children.

I stood in a corner, silently, not trying to remember or recollect anything in particular. I was so lost in my own thoughts that I missed the first bell, but suddenly found the other children hurrying towards the exam hall. When I began moving, one of my classmates with whom I used to share a desk in class came by and both of us moved towards the hall.

At the entrance, a teacher asked for the admit card which we showed and he asked another person to lead us to our designated seats. We were asked to keep any books, notes, mobiles and other things near the door and collect them on our way out. Only pens, pencils and erasers were allowed inside the hall.

It was a big hall which could accommodate about 50 boys at a time. There were four rows of single desks in the hall. My seat was in the middle of the second row while my friend was seated in the fourth row.

Suddenly all the noise and turmoil was replaced by absolute serenity and silence. We all then, joined our hands to praise to the almighty, seeking his blessings and recited our prayer.

As we got seated, the invigilators started giving us the answer sheets and we were asked to put our name, roll number and subject on top of the sheet. At exactly 9 a.m., the question papers were distributed to us. I sat composed and after a few seconds, opened the paper and started reading it. I was happy. It was an easy paper and I went through it twice, choosing five best questions which I had prepared well. It was a great experience.

I did moderately well in the exams passing with a good second division and scored the highest marks in English in my class.

Q. 4. **There has been heavy rain in your city/town. You went to school but found that it was closed because of the rain. Describe the sights and sounds near the school and narrate how you finally reached home and spent the rest of the day.** **[2017]**

Ans.

MY EXPERIENCE ON A RAINY DAY

My experience on 'A Rainy Day' gives me sour memories. It's true that rains are blessings but sometimes they are a curse. If we could control rains and bring them wherever we are, or keep them off as long as we desire them, of course rains would be a blessing. But as we all know that elements of nature are not under human control, they are sometimes not to our liking. There was a day when it rained and I did not like it.

It was a usual day and I went to school but it was closed due to rain. I regretted for not having checked any message or notification from school about the holiday. Though I was also a little happy for not having school that day. Thus, I started for home. Even at that hour, I could see bad weather ahead. Dark, smoky clouds gave the warning of rain. I thought I would be safe if I got into a bus.

I was getting into the bus when it started raining and it rained the way as it had never rained. Within a few minutes, everyone was drenched to the skin. No one got the time to get shelter. In a very short time, the roads were flooded and the traffic came to a standstill.

Visibility was reduced to a few meters. It poured so heavily that even the headlights could not pierce the thick sheet of water pouring from the sky. Water collected more speedily on roads than it went down the drains.

The stalls and the temporary structures of the shops at the bus stop dripped. Those inside the shops and buses were in no way better than those outside on the road, who were getting wet in utter helplessness. It soon became worse. The stools, benches, chairs and small tables, outside the shops and stalls began to float in the rising streams of rainwater. It was a pity to see people running after their articles.

A man running to catch a bench fell into a drain. He might have been swept away by the strong current but the water itself threw him out. The poor man stood for a moment looking dazed at the rushing water.

It rained continuously for four hours and during this period all activities came to a halt. When at last the rain stopped, I was hardly in shape to carry on my journey. I longed to be at home in my comfortable bed.

Finally, I reached home sick and sad.

Q. 5. **You walk home from school one afternoon to find the door unlocked and on entering you are shocked to see the house in total disarray. You call out but get no answer. Describe in detail what you saw, the reason behind your house being in total disarray and how you found your family. Mention also how the experience ended and what impact it had on your life.** **[2016]**

Ans.

A CHAOTIC SITUATION

This afternoon, as I came back home from school, I had the most anxious moment of my life. In fact, I was quite surprised to see the front gates wide-open and a lot of tyre marks criss-crossing on the lawn that did not resemble the tyre marks of our car. Even the front door opened by a mere turn of the knob. But what I saw after that left me stunned and immobilized for a few seconds. Everything was in disarray—cupboards and drawers pulled open, broken flower vase on the floor, the covers of the sofas and other furniture ripped open.

My first reaction was to shout out for my mother and grandmother and next for James, our Alsatian dog. When there was no answer, I ran to my mother's bedroom. The condition of that room was also the same and both my mother and grandmother were firmly tied and taped on the bed. James was lying lifeless in the balcony and there was blood all around him.

I grabbed a pair of scissors, freed the two women and helped them recirculate their blood. Grandmother was too shocked to speak and mother said haltingly that three gun-toting hooded men entered the house all of a sudden and ordered them into that room. Then they tied them up firmly and began to thoroughly search the house. They were not looking for money or jewellery, but they were after some drawings or plans that my father had made. Hearing this, I rushed to my father's study and found all the things scattered as usual and the cabinets broken open. Papers and drawings were scattered all over the room.

Next, I called up the police and then my father. The police came in twenty minutes and my father, a little later. My father felt relieved that both mother and grandmother were unhurt except for the bruises on their wrists because of the tight tapes. The intruders were actually looking for some drawings that father had made for building a new missile system for our defence forces. It is a well-known fact that my father always keeps a backup of his work on his home PC. He suspected that this was the work of enemy spies who were desperate to get the plans to improve their own missile systems.

After taking stock of the situation and making some further inquiries, the police left.

Strangely, my father had remained calm all along. He said that in every drawing there was some object which was wrongly positioned deliberately. This had been done to hoodwink people like these and it was a technique that had been perfected by Leonardo da Vinci.

Q. 6. **Describe in detail the view from your bedroom window. Does your room overlook a park? A busy street? What are the sights, sounds and smells that you would typically see, hear and experience at different times of the day? When do you most enjoy the view? Early in the morning, in the evening or late at night? [2015]**

Ans.

FROM THE BEDROOM WINDOW

Staring out of bedroom window lazily is a luxury that can hardly be afforded by people these days. Either they are leading a typical life of cash-crunching robots, with hardly any time to catch two winks throughout the week or there is hardly any space available to see anything worthwhile because of the rapid developments all over the country and the huge number of buildings that are coming up every other day. Even getting a glimpse of sunshine amongst the clusters of skyscrapers is a matter of luck.

Still, there are people who do find the time and opportunity to enjoy the finer things of life. I am one such person who is very particular about what I want. For me, a spacious apartment in a posh locality is not the criteria. I would gladly settle for a small house at the fringes of the city, offering me plenty of sunshine and surrounded by greenery.

When I moved to Pune, my search for the ideal apartment led to the discovery of a small one-storied house, bordering a lake on one side and the fringes of the Western Ghats on the other, fresh air, plenty of sunshine and the chirping of birds. Every morning, I woke up not to the ringing of the alarm clock but to the chirping of the exotic migratory birds that flocked the lake. As the place was on the outskirts of the city, there was hardly any noise of vehicles and consequently, even lesser smoke and dust. I was greeted by the sweet smell of different trees and plants around the house and the rays of the glistening sun.

However, the evenings were even more fascinating. Bright lights dotted the banks of the lake and it resembled a golden sun eclipsed by the moon. The birds would return to their nests and the air would be full with the sounds of the chirping of crickets and cicadas. Also, a cool breeze would blow and reduce the stress of the frayed nerves. It was a little paradise of my own because it had remained untouched by civilization for the two whole years that I spent in Pune.

Chapter 5
Picture Composition

Q. 1. **Study the picture given below. Write a story or a description or an account of what it suggests to you. Your composition may be about the subject of the picture or you may take suggestions from it; however, there must be a clear connection between the picture and your composition.** **[2020]**

Ans. **NAIVE INTENTION**

The picture shows exactly what is wrong with society these days. The 'selfie' culture has taken on everyone's minds and people are becoming more and more addicted to the craze of self-publicity on social media by way of posting selfies and check-ins. This concept is problematic especially for young minds as they can get deeply influenced by this kind of negative culture.

In the picture, we can clearly see this in little kids who perhaps cannot even afford a cell phone or are mimicking their elders and posing, for a selfie as a game. The innocence in the eyes and the way that they are smiling and posing, speaks volumes about their naïve intentions as they have converted posing and getting clicked to a mere game play. Perhaps the children are of the opinion that they are in their imaginary world and the slipper is actually a camera. This is very typical of children in that age. They constantly live in worlds of their own to escape their reality.

The cell phone is replaced by a slipper and is enough to evoke sympathy in the eyes of the viewer on the one hand as we are forced to think that the children are creating their own happiness in absence of having the means to afford a real phone. The picture also ignites deep thought on the other hand as we are forced to think about the kind of upbringing and education we are imparting to the future generations. Are we teaching them only to be self-absorbed and rely on social media and materialistic things for their happiness?

On a lighter note, the warm smiles of the children in the picture state their innocence clearly and remind us of the simple joys in life.

Q. 2. **Write a composition (300–350 words) on the following:**

Study the picture given below. Write a story or a description or an account of what it suggests to you. Your composition may be about the subject of the picture or you may take suggestions from it; however, there must be a clear connection between the picture and your composition. **[2019]**

Ans. **A HEALTHY MIND RESIDES IN A HEALTHY BODY**

I was walking back to my home from my office, when I saw a group of very young students gathered near the local confectionary store, buying something. They were from the nearby school. Few of them were buying chocolates, few were buying some chips while few were engrossed in thinking about what to buy. They were no more than 7-8 years old. I walked past them and continued my journey.

On the way, I began contemplating the view I just witnessed. I thought and thought, about who gave them the money to buy chocolates? Why were they alone and not supervised by their parents ? What if the shopkeeper conned them? What if they fell sick after eating something unhealthy and why was such junk and unhealthy food so important and apparently delicious for them?

Kids should be well educated by elders on how to manage money and put it to best use. They should be also be taught about the health and hygiene and how they should avoid eating outside. Parents should be vigilant enough not to give unnecessary cash to the kids because it may lead them into harmful indulgence. Also, a clear understanding of importance of healthy food and balanced diet should be given to the kids so that they avoid eating unhealthy food outside.

This does not suffice the issue. It is also very unsafe to allow kids to shop alone from unknown shops. Taking into consideration the growing crime rates against children, kids should be strictly warned to return home immediately after school and accompany an adult if something essential needs to be purchased.

I had already reached the gate of my building by the time I finished thinking about it. As I entered my building, I heard some chattering behind me. I turned around and saw the same kids walking along the road. They were maybe returning to their homes. They were enjoying their cups of ice-cream as they walked and teased each other. I took a sigh of relief after seeing all of them happy, safe and together. However, the fear of them falling sick due to unhealthy diet had still not left my mind.

Q. 3. **Study the picture given below. Write a story or a description or an account of what it suggests to you. Your composition may be about the subject of the picture or you may take suggestions from it; however, there must be a clear connection between the picture and your composition.** **[2018]**

Ans.

THE GAME OF CRICKET

The picture here depicts three village girls on a rough ground with one of them holding a cricket bat. The idea is perhaps to show the wide popularity of cricket in India, in the villages and towns apart from the metropolis.

Men have been performing well in cricket for many years now. Of late even the Indian Women's Cricket team is doing well in the domestic and the international circuit. In the last ICC Women's World Cup, the Indian women team led by Mithali Raj narrowly missed the cup and ended as runners-up. Captain Mithali Raj was the top scorer while medium-pacer Jhulan Goswami became the first-ever woman cricketer in the world to beg 200 ODI wickets. Thereafter, the team toured South Africa and played five ODIs and three T20 matches there, almost simultaneously with our Men's team. They returned home triumphant, winning both the ODI and T20 series. BCCI has recognised the talent of women cricketers and has brought the players under a central contract scheme like their male counterparts. Some outstanding cricketers amongst them are Mithali Raj, Harmanpreet Kaur, Jhulan Goswami, Rumeli Dhar, Ekta Bisht and Veda Krishnamurthy.

Women's cricket in India is slowly gaining prominence and popularity among the public. To popularise the game further, the BCCI must take more initiative. Publicity of Women's Cricket needs a big boost. There should be regular telecasts of women's cricket matches. These telecasts will boost the players' morale and consequently, people will be drawn towards the game. With more viewers, advertisers will also show interest to sponsor women's cricket team as they do for men's cricket now. Cricket academies for budding players should be set up throughout the country and scouting should be done to find future cricketers from schools and colleges. If BCCI starts taking concrete steps in earnest, women's cricket in India will flourish in no time.

Q. 4. **Study the picture given below. Write a story or a description or an account of what it suggests to you. Your composition may be about the subject of the picture or you may take suggestions from it; however there must be clear connection between the picture and your composition.** **[2017]**

Ans.

PICTURE COMPOSITION

We have evolved from animals and since then, we humans do have a connection with them. Animals have been man's best friends and companions as they understand us so well that we don't even have to say what we don't want or feel. It is said very often that a Dog is a man's best friend.

The relation that you develop with an animal is lifelong and rigid unlike that which you build up with another person.

The people who have pets would be able to explain better, the relation they hold with these animals. Animals respond back with all their love and affection and would make sure that no harm reaches us. Whether it is a bird or an animal, pets have a special bonding with their masters.

Apart from the bonding, they also provide great services to their masters. For example, cats and dogs are the most common pets found. Cats help in keeping the house clean by killing rodents and insects and dogs safeguard the house and keep strangers away. The sensitivity to smell in dogs has been the greatest tool used to hunt down criminals. Apart from them, even birds form a great company. Parrots are wonderful pets and they talk so much that it is real fun to be with them. They also inform the owner when strangers are around.

Apart from cats and dogs, horses, elephants, donkeys and camels can also be tamed and used by man for his needs. These animals help a man in several ways and have been of great help to man for several decades. Animals also rescue men from danger. There have been instincts where dogs have saved small kids or old men from dangerous situations like drowning or an accident.

The help that these animals give can not be measured by any means and animals and man do share a special kind of bonding. Rather than seeing the commercial side with animals, if a man tries to be more compassionate with them, they would do anything for him and will maintain an everlasting relationship.

Q. 5. **Study the picture given below. Write a story or a description or an account of what it suggests to you. Your composition may be about the subject of the picture or you may take suggestions from it; however there must be clear connection between the picture and your composition.** **[2016]**

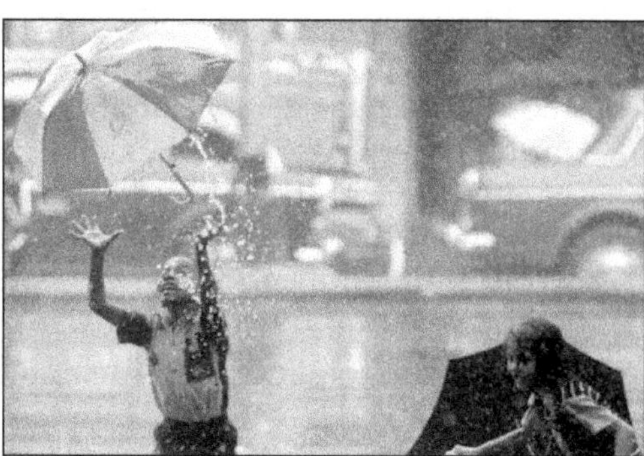

Ans.

PICTURE COMPOSITION

The picture reveals the relief brought to the city by the first showers of the season. For the past few weeks, the city was enshrouded by the sweltering heat and it was becoming unbearable for most of the people, especially the pavement dwellers.

These showers did have a cooling effect because the mercury dipped by almost six to seven degrees and the day was cloudy overall. The Meteorological Department had predicted that the rains will continue for another forty-eight hours. That meant that the people will be able to relax for some more days.

However, the brief spell was also enough to cause waterlogging in some parts of the city and if the rains continue then greater parts of the city would soon become waterlogged. This is a perennial problem and nothing concrete has been done over the years to improve the situation. This water-logging also marks the onset of some of the most common water-borne diseases like cholera and dysentery because the water enters the sewers and water reservoirs. Consequently, the first showers are always dangerous because of the threats to the outbreak of diseases.

However, most people prefer to soak themselves in these showers because of the relief they provide. Men and women, old and young, all seem to come out of their homes and enjoy themselves. Also, huge crowds flock towards the seafront to enjoy the lashings of the seawaters. Young children enjoy the most, especially those living on pavements. They troop to the fields and play football and other games. For once, cricket takes a back seat.

Q. 6. **Study the picture given below. Write a short story or description or an account of what the picture suggests to you. Your composition may be about the subject of the picture or you may take suggestions from it; however, your composition must have a clear connection with the picture:** **[2015]**

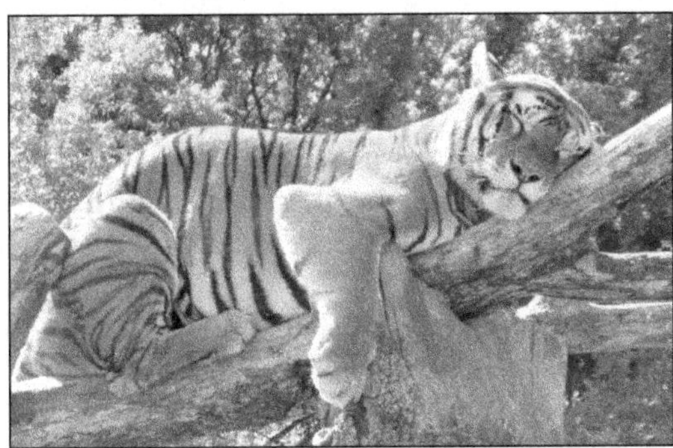

Ans.

PICTURE COMPOSITION

Such a beautiful sight of a tiger sleeping blissfully may not be seen any more in reality because of the rapidly dwindling of tiger population all over the world. Most of the decline is due to the rampant poaching because of the huge demand for tiger skin and claws. It is also because of massive human encroachment into the natural habitat of the tigers, upsetting their eco-system and leading to a decline in their breeding.

However, the Indian government has done a commendable job in protecting tigers and contributing to their increase in population by almost 30% in just 3 years. It is the outcome of a meticulously planned approach towards tiger conservation, using all our knowledge about their behaviour patterns, food habits and everything else that has seen a rise in the number of tigers from 1411 in 2008 to 1706 in 2011 to 2226 in 2014. Consequently, India is now home to almost 70% of the world's tigers. Considering the above, the country can now play a prominent role in helping other countries in their tiger conservation efforts.

The secret behind these figures is designated areas for tiger conservation in the country. These are manned by forest rangers who have actively worked towards the reduction in the number of poaching incidents. In India, the total area dedicated to tiger conservation is almost around 53547.5 sq. km or 20674 sq. miles. Altogether, there are 48 tiger reserves that are looked after by the National Tiger Conservation Authority (NTCA) and the Wildlife Institute of India (WII).

Such sincere acts of tiger conservation will ensure that posterity is not seen only in books and digital media but also in real life. Tigers are here to stay!

Notice & Email

Q. 1. Your school is organising a fete/carnival to raise funds for victims of the recent floods in your State. Write a notice to be put up on the school notice board giving details of the event. **[2020]**

 **Marking Scheme** - - - - - - - - - - - - - - - - - - -

Creative Title – e.g. Carnival, Fun time, Care and Share, Helping hands, etc. [English words only.] …School helps flood victims.
Date – Any date in March (date + month + year)
Time – accept any time - a.m./am/A.M
Venue – smaller to bigger place
Invite participation, to whom to apply to, etc. [Target audience]

Ans.

HANDOUT TO SUPPORT

HANDOUT TO SUPPORT

The Fundraising Carnival for Flood Victims

Date: 8th February 20xx
Time: 9.00 a.m. to 5.00 p.m.
Venue: The Big Field, St. Louis School

The carnival schedule is as follows:

- Speech by the principal followed by the lighting of the lamp.
- Pre-lunch activities such as a treasure hunt, mini golf, bowling, karaoke, etc.
- Science exhibition, painting and other art pieces exhibition.
- Lunch around 1 pm.
- Post-lunch arrangement for drama and dance performances.

All pupils from Classes IV to XII who wish to participate are to give their names to Mrs. Charu Shankar on or before 1st February 20××. The entry tickets will be ₹ 100/- per person. All collections from this event shall go to the flood victims in the state.

Q. 2. Write an e-mail to the principal of a neighbouring school, inviting him/her to send their students to attend the fete/carnival. **[2020]**

Marking Scheme - - - - - - - - - - - - - - - - - - -

E-mail – id [No name to be used in the email id]
Subject: Invitation + for the event
Salutation [As in formal letter]
Opening sentence
Closing sentence
Subscription [As in formal letter]
Expression – All details of the notice are to be included in full sentences in the e-mail. [Date/time/venue should be included.]

Ans. principalbluebellschool@gmail.com

A charitable carnival for victims of recent floods.

Dear Sir,

St. Louis School is organising a fundraising carnival for the victims of recent floods. Therefore I write to you to invite the students of your school to attend the carnival, going to be held on Saturday, 7th February 20xx from 9.00 am to 5 pm at the Big field, St. Louis School.

The schedule for the day would start with a speech by the principal followed by the lighting of the lamp. Then, we have arranged for pre-lunch activities such as ring toss, a treasure hunt, mini golf, bowling, karaoke, face painting and many other exciting activities for students as well as teachers and parents. We also have an exhibition put up by the students of their Science models, paintings, coursework and other art pieces.

Then at around 1 pm we would proceed for lunch. We have a pre-set selection of healthy yet delicious food items.

Post-lunch we have arranged for a drama and some dance performances.

The day will end with multiple photos on our very special photo booth so that we all are able to preserve these happy memories forever.

I hope that you will accept this invitation and allow the students of your school to participate in the event wholeheartedly. We look forward to welcoming them.

Thanking you,
Yours faithfully,
Alia Kapoor Secretary,
Student Council, St. Louis Sc

Q. 3. **Your school is hosting an Inter-School Quiz Competition. Write out a notice to be displayed in your school giving all details for the event.** **[2019]**

 Marking Scheme

Creative Title - e.g. Question Hour, Quizzitica!, Brain Storm etc.[English words only]

Inter-School Quiz - e.g. Annual Inter school Quiz, Bradley Memorial Inter-School Quiz etc. Date - any date after 22nd February and before 28th March.

Time - accept any time - a.m./am/A.M.

Venue - smaller place to larger.

Invite participation, to whom to apply to, etc.

Ans.

Young Chanakya
Inter-school Quiz Competition

on 10th March 20XX
from 10:00 a.m. to 3:00 p.m.

at Auditorium, St. Francis High School

All the students from Classes VI to X who wish to participate are to give their names to Mr. Thomas on or before 1st March 20XX.

Q. 4. **Write an e-mail to the Principal of a neighbouring school requesting him/her to send a team of three members to participate in the Quiz Competition.** **[2019]**

 Marking Scheme

E-mail id
Subject
Salutation
Opening sentence
Closing sentence
Subscription
Expression/Body

Ans. principal.globalschool@gmail.com

Inter-school Quiz Competition

Dear Sir,

Our school is celebrating its Silver Jubilee this year. As a part of the celebrations, we are hosting a series of competitions beginning with 'Young Chanakya', the Inter-school Quiz competition.

It will be held on 10th August 20XX from 10:00 a.m. to 3:00 p.m. in the auditorium of St. Francis High School.

Please do send a team of three members from Class IX/Class X of your school to participate in the competition.

The quiz will be based on Current affairs, Indian history, Indian Geography and General knowledge.

We look forward to enthusiastic participation from your school in the competition.

Thanking you,

Yours faithfully,

Meghna Roy
Academic Coordinator

Letter Writing

Q. 1. **(a) You have changed your school recently. Write a letter to your friend in your old school telling him/her what you like about your new school but also what you miss about your old school.** **[2020]**

 Marking Scheme

Informal Letter: Format, Content, Expression
Body
Two or three reasons about why you like the new school.
Two or three reasons why you miss the old school.
Explanatory Note:
1. Friend's name should be mentioned in the salutation.
2. In the content there must be a total of five points between like and dislike.

Ans.

B-1/404, Green Avenue
New Delhi – 110090
3rd February, 20××

Dear Reena,

Hope this letter finds you well. You will be happy to know that I am comfortably settled in my new school. Although, I terribly miss you and our school as well.

My new school is really big. It has a sports arena, a swimming pool, two auditoriums, and a big garden. We even have a solar water heating unit and lots of green plants all around. The school offers plenty of exciting activities such as sports, art, music, drama and debate. I want to participate in tennis and painting. Wish you were here, and we could do it together, like old times! Anyway, I have made new friends and they both are locals from this town. We go cycling in the evenings together. The teachers are really nice and have welcomed me into their class warmly. My friends and teachers are helping me catch up with my studies and by the end of this month I hope to be at par with the rest of my classmates. The best thing about the school is that it fosters a positive learning environment and makes us learn by the practical way instead of simply rote learning to clear exams.

I really miss you and my old school. I can never forget our morning assembly gatherings and daily words of wisdom from our Principal. But my most cherished memory stays to be stealing lunch from your tiffin during break time!

Please keep writing to me so that we can discuss everything that happens in our lives.

Yours lovingly,
Priya

(b) **Some taps in your locality are left open all day resulting in a tremendous waste of water. Write a letter to the Municipal Commissioner of your town/ city, complaining about the problem. Suggest ways in which this waste of water can be prevented.** [2020]

 Marking Scheme ----------------------

Formal Letter: Format, Content, Expression
Complaints: water wastage / dirty / slippery / unhealthy / stagnant water / causes severe shortages. (Any two complaints)
Suggestions: Call the plumber / repair / install tank / change valve / frequent monitoring / shut off the mains / helpline/ any other suggestions. (Any two suggestions)
Explanatory Note: Designation and name of the city should be mentioned in the 'To' address.

Ans.

Flat 22, Block E
Sitaram Apartments
Rajpur Road,
New Delhi

3rd February, 20××

The Municipal Commissioner
Modern Town,
New Delhi

Dear Sir,
This is to bring to your attention the problem of water wastage in our colony. Recently, I noticed that a lot of water is being consumed rather than wasted in our colony since the past few days. This is because some common taps in the locality are left open throughout the day and are left unattended.

This causes a lot of freshwater to be wasted. We all must be sensitive to the problem of water wastage as water is a precious resource.

Everyone across the globe is talking about the issue of water conservation as it is critical for the environment. So, as world citizens, we must treat the issue of water conservation with respect and follow some simple steps in this direction. I would recommend that the common taps in the locality are monitored for usage by the staff to avoid wastage. Also, each resident should be encouraged to reuse the water used to wash vegetables and pulses to water their plants, take shorter showers, use a bucket and mug instead of a pipe, check their toilets for leaks, harvest rainwater and use a high efficiency washing machine.

I request you to take the necessary steps in this regard and help initiate a water conservation drive in our locality so as to ensure that all residents are alerted to this issue and act accordingly.

Thanking you,

Yours faithfully,

Rita Joshi

Q. 2. **(a)** **You want to start a new club in your school. Write a letter to your Principal requesting permission to start the club, explain your role in it and give reasons to prove that the club will be beneficial for the school.** [2019]

 Marking Scheme ----------------------

Informal Letter	Formal Letter
Address	From address
Date	Date
Salutation	To address
X	Salutation
Subscription	Subscription
First name	Name + surname/initial

(a) Formal Letter: Format, Content, Expression
Body:
Kind of club
Your role/Your duty (*Any 1*) Head/President/leader/
Plan/organize/carry out activity/motivate
Reasons – Why you want a club? (*Any 2*)
Give skills/Spot new talent/exposure/team building/extra activity/improve campus/help others/All-round development

(b) Informal Letter: Format, Content, Expression
Expressing concern (*Any 1*)
Sorry/worried/upset/anxious/concerned Advice - (*Any 2*)
Plan proper study timetable/use study notes/ seek teachers' help/pay attention in class/practice frequently/proper food/rest/relaxation.
Help - (*Any 2*)
Take my notes/I shall sit with you/I shall help you/I shall take up your work – "I" must be there.

Ans.

15, Kushal Paradise,
Magadi Road,
Bengaluru

22nd February, 20XX

The Principal,
St. John's School,
Wilson Garden,
Bengaluru

Dear Sir,

I write on behalf of all the students of class X-B to seek your kind permission to start a 'Consumer Club' in our school. With a vision to create awareness about Consumer Rights, Consumer Forum and Consumer Activities within the society, we wish to take the initiative of beginning this club in our school.

As the prospective President of the Consumer Club, I assure you to carry out activities that shall spread awareness amongst the consumers of our society to the best of my capabilities.

A few proposed activities are quizzes, competitions-both written and activity type, seminar, conferences etc.

Kindly permit us to begin the club in the school from the last Friday of the month i.e. 28th February 20XX. The club shall carry out its activities on every Saturday of the week from 10:00 AM to 4:00 PM.

Please consider my request.

Yours faithfully,
Divya Pawar

(b) Your friend has not fared well in the recent examinations. Write a letter to him/her expressing your concern. Give him/her some advice on how to score better marks and offer to help him/her to improve his/her performance. **[2019]**

📋 Marking Scheme ------------------

Informal Letter: Format, Content, Expression
Expressing concern (Any 1)
Sorry / worried / upset / anxious / concerned
Advice -(Any 2)
Plan proper study timetable / use study notes / seek teachers' help / pay attention in class / practice frequently / proper food / rest / relaxation.
Help -(Any 2)
Take my notes / I shall sit with you / I shall help you / I shall take up your work – "I" must be there.

Ans.

10, Shanti kunj,
Pathardi Road,
Lucknow.

12th January, 20XX

Dear Karishma,
Hope this letter finds you in the best of your health and spirits. I have been meaning to write to you but have been occupied with my office work and hence the delay. I got to know about your results and I am really concerned.

I heard that you could not perform your best in the recent examinations. But it is completely alright and you need not to lose hope. You are definitely a very talented girl and a little focus and non-diverted concentration will help you to pass the examinations with flying colours.

You can get up early in the morning instead of late-night studies as early morning is the best time to study. Also, revise the concepts and practise math regularly. However, if you face difficulty in understanding any topic, please feel free to write to me. I shall be more than happy to help you.

All the best for the upcoming examinations. I know you will make us all proud.

Yours lovingly,
Deepak Raj

Q. 3. (a) Your uncle has offered to get you a pet for your birthday. Write a letter to him telling him what you would like, give reasons for your choice and tell him how you would take care of your pet. **[2018]**

Ans.

A/13 Himgiri Apartments

Kalkaji, New Delhi

19th March, 20XX

My dear uncle,
I received your letter a few days back. I am sorry for my late reply. I was busy with the sports event in my school which ended yesterday. You will be glad to know that I have won three prizes at the event.

I must thank you for asking my opinion about my favourite pet, which you propose to gift me on my forthcoming birthday. I would love to have a small puppy since dogs are said to be 'a man's best friend.' I want a puppy not only because all of my friend possess one but also because it's a great companion. I assure you that I shall fully take care of it. Once I get it, the first thing I will do is to take him to a vet and get him a thorough checkup. I will clean and bathe him regularly and take him out to the park every evening.

He will be fed as per the vet's prescription. I will also take care of his regular checkups and preventive medicines and injections that will be needed to be given to prevent any infection or disease. I shall give him the training to behave with people and whenever guests visit. This pet will live with us in our home just like another member of the family. Everyone at home is excited at the prospect of having a pet or rather, having another new member in the family. Give my regards to aunty and love to Rohan.

Your loving nephew,
Aniket

(b) **The traffic outside your school is very heavy and chaotic. Write a letter to the Deputy Commissioner of Police (Traffic) pointing out the danger of such heavy and chaotic traffic in a school zone. Suggest possible solutions for the problem.** **[2018]**

Ans. St. Joseph School,
Ferozeshah Road, New Delhi

23rd May, 20XX

The Deputy Commissioner of Police
Office of DCP Traffic Control
Police Headquarters, New Delhi

Subject: Regulation of traffic outside St. Joseph School, Ferozeshah Road

Respected Sir/Ma'am,
I am writing this letter to you on behalf of my school, St. Joseph School. This letter intends to inform you about the chaotic situation of traffic just outside our school and some possible solutions for controlling the same.

First of all, I would like to bring to your kind attention, the traffic light at the three-way intersection on the main road in front of our school, does not function properly. Out of 30 days of a month, it is malfunctioning for most of the days. Secondly, the traffic pyramid situated there for the traffic policeman is seldom manned by anyone, resulting in even more chaos on the road. All these factors together pose a serious threat to the safety of school children. Such uncontrolled traffic may lead to life threatening accidents also. It gets extremely congested here, creating a situation of rush. This in turn, serves as a potential opportunity for anti-social elements promoting activities of child abuse. However, there are some feasible solutions to these problems.

- To start with, I would request you to kindly get the traffic light repaired or replaced immediately so that it can function smoothly.

- Deploy a traffic policeman at the intersections, especially during morning hours when the school children are arriving and in the afternoon when the school closes for the day so that he can regulate the traffic and ensure that the school buses are not hindered by the passing traffic.

- In case if it is possible, try and divert the afternoon traffic from the main road to the auxiliary road, next to the school lane so that the buses are able to move without hindrance.

Thanking you

Yours truly,

Aniket Sharma

Q. 4. **(a)** **A number of loose electric wires are hanging from a lamp post near the main gate of your school. Write a letter to the Municipal Commissioner explaining the problem, the danger it poses and suggest a quick solution.** **[2017]**

Ans. Tarangi nagar, M.G. Road,
West Bengal

23rd March, 20XX

The Municipal Commissioner,
Bidhannagar Municipal Corporation,
Kolkata

Subject: Hanging live wires in front of the School Main Gate

Dear Sir,
I would like to bring to your kind notice, the miserable condition caused due to the hanging of live wires in front of our school's main gate. Our area is Salt Lake City Sector-1, Kolkata. Although we have made repeated complaints to the Municipalities at repeated intervals, yet they have paid a deaf ear to our complaints. These wires have been causing havoc among kids who get dispersed in an attempt to safeguard themselves. It has been a persistent issue for long now. Also, these wires can prove to be life-threatening.

We would, thereby, like to call for your immediate attention for the said problem without any further delay.

Yours sincerely,
Sannidhya Datta

(b) **You were a part of an organizing committee for an inter-school event which was very successful. You and the other committee members were congratulated and praised at the school assembly by the Principal. Write a letter to your grandmother telling**

her about the event and your feelings at **being recognized and praised in front of the school.** **[2017]**

Ans.

Plot no: 137
M.G. Road
Agrapath
Hyderabad

23rd March 20XX

Dear Grandma,

I hope that this letter finds you in the best of your health and spirits. Recently, I had the opportunity to organise the annual cultural fest in my school- 'Ullas'. It was a three-day long inter-school cultural fest with a huge number of events ranging from painting to writing to spell bee to dance and so on. We had a huge participation from schools across the city and it was a huge success. However, our school came second in the fest overall. Next day, in the morning assembly, all my team members and I was appreciated for organising the event so well. It was indeed a great learning experience for all of us. This event helped us a lot to develop our sense of team spirit, working as a group hence we had a lot to take back. However, when the principal praised us in the assembly it was a great experience for all of us. I could not refrain myself from sharing tis moment of glee. Hope to hear from you soon.

With love,
Sunny

Q. 5. **(a)** **Your class wants to visit a well known historical monument in a nearby town. Write a letter to your Principal seeking permission and say why you would benefit from the visit.** **[2016]**

Ans.

Flat 236, Block C,
Hill Great View Apartments,
Salam street,
West Bengal

28th February, 20XX

The Principal
St. Patrick's H.S. School
Asansol, West Bengal.

Subject: Permission for educational trip to The Indian Museum, Kolkata

Dear Sir,
Through this letter, we seek your permission for a one-day educational trip to the Indian Museum in Kolkata. Built in the British era, the Indian Museum is one of the largest museums in the country and is a huge storehouse of artefacts. A visit to this place will be beneficial for us because of the numerous scientific instruments and specimens that can be seen there. It will also provide us with a clear idea about the process of evolution that is beautifully explained through numerous figurines and skeletal displays. Also, we will have an opportunity to learn about the different rock-formations over the ages, the implements used by early human beings and numerous fun-filled aspects of science.

Our science teachers will accompany us on this trip. We propose to start early in the morning so as to be able to return on time the same day.

I request you to please grant us the permission for the trip.

Thanking you,
Yours faithfully
Students of Class Xth

(b) **Your school recently held a jubilee celebration. Write a letter to your friend who was unable to attend, giving details of the function and your role in it.** **[2016]**

Ans.

D. K. Road
Durgapur
West Bengal

February 26th, 20XX

Dear Rima,
It was indeed unfortunate not to have you amongst us during the Golden Jubilee celebrations of our school, Carmel Convent, Kolkata. Had you not met with the accident, probably you could have also shared the fun. However, I have taken it upon myself to give you at least a glimpse of it through this letter.

The Principal of our school, in the presence of the Chief Guest and other dignitaries, delivered a fine speech, narrating the initiation of the Carmelite Order and their motto. He also narrated how the Carmelite Nuns came to India and started different schools in the country and how, over the years, the students have upheld the dignity and prestige of the institution.

The celebrations began with a song and a dance presentation. It was choreographed entirely by the students of the senior section and had almost thirty participants. It was followed by poetry recitals, debate and quiz contests.

On the second day, an exhibition-cum-fete was organized within the school premises where the students had displayed their drawings, handicrafts and scientific models. The ceremony came to an end with another stellar song and dance performance. All the present and past students, parents, guardians, teachers and staff members enjoyed immensely. The Principals of all the other Carmelite institutions across the country were in attendance.

Hope I have enabled you to enjoy a small part of the fun and festivities. Get well soon.

Yours affectionately,
Paromita

Q. 6. **(a)** **Break time (recess) at your school is only for a duration of fifteen minutes. Write a letter to your Principal requesting an extension in the breaktime from fifteen minutes to half an hour. Give reasons for your request and explain in what way an extended break would make a difference to you as a student.** **[2015]**

Ans. Jingle Bells, Residency
Porur, Chennai

30th March, 20XX

The Principal
Millennium School
Porur,
Chennai - 600 089

Subject: Extension of Recess Period at School

Sir,
We the students of the Millenium School, would like to earnestly request to add 15 minutes to the existing time for the recess. Currently, we are getting a lunch break of only fifteen minutes. We find it considerably less. We are not able to have our lunch properly in this short span of time. Moreover, there is a long wait near the water dispensers. Eventually, most of the time we have to go without water.

In addition to that, we do long for a few minutes to relax and enjoy with our friends. This will be a great stress buster for all the students.

We request you to kindly look into the matter at the earliest and allow us to have a half an hour of break.

Thanking you,
Yours faithfully.
Students of class 10th, section B

(b) **You are to be awarded a Special Prize at the Annual Prize Day ceremony of your school. Write a letter to a lady relative giving her the news. Be sure to include details of the prize that you are to receive and tell her why you have been chosen for this honor.** **[2015]**

Ans. 23, Bhana Vihar
M.G. Road
Pune

30th December, 20XX

Dear aunt,
I hope that this letter finds you in the best of health and spirits. Mummy informed me that you have returned from your trip and I'm sure you must have enjoyed your trip to Ooty. It must have been a welcome escape from this terrible heat of the summer.

I have some terrific news to tell you. Today, my class teacher told me that I'm going to receive an award for the 'Best Interact Club Member' of this year. This is in view of my contribution to community welfare and the project on preserving the environment.

With the help of the Moderator of the club, I took the initiative to teach the underprivileged children of the nearby locality of our school after school hours. Along with my friends, I collected books, notebooks and other writing material for them. I made interesting Powerpoint presentations to spread awareness among them.

As far as my eco-development project is concerned, I motivated my class to plant trees all over the campus, initiated a rain harvesting system, and also hung pitchers of water for birds during the summer.

Altogether it was a delightful experience. I felt I was contributing something for the good of the other fellow beings and the environment. The fact that I'm going to be awarded for my initiative is the crowning glory. The Principal told me that no one has so far taken such interest in the club activities, that too, without my studies getting affected by it; so they have added a new category of awards this year and I will be the first recipient of this! My project on rain harvesting system will get a special mention on this day.

You have always taken a keen interest in what I do in school; so I felt like sharing the news with you. Please come to my Annual function so that you can see in person, your favourite niece receiving the award.

Looking forward to see you and uncle.
Yours lovingly,
Alia

Comprehension

Q. 1. **Read the following passage carefully and answer the questions that follow:** [2020]

Attending classes inside a railway carriage seemed unusual enough, but the seating arrangements turned out to be unusual, too. At Totto-chan's previous school each pupil was *assigned* a specific desk. But here they could sit anywhere they liked at any time.

The most unusual thing of all about this school, however, was the lessons themselves.

Schools normally schedule one subject, for example history, during the first period, when everyone in the class just did history; then say arithmetic in the second period, when you just did arithmetic. But here it was quite different. At the beginning of the first period, the teacher made a list of all the problems and questions in the subjects to be studied that day. Then she would say, "Now, start with any of these you like" 10

So, whether you started on history or arithmetic or something else didn't matter at all. Someone who liked composition might be writing something, while behind you someone who liked chemistry might be boiling something in a flask over an alcohol burner.

This method of teaching enabled the teachers to observe–as the children progressed to higher grades– what they were interested in as well as their way of thinking and their character. It was an *ideal* way for teachers to really get to know their pupils. 20

As for the pupils, they loved being able to start with their favourite subject, the fact that they had all day to cope with the subjects they disliked meant they could usually manage them somehow. So, study was mostly *independent* , with pupils free to go and consult the teacher whenever necessary. Then pupils would be given further exercises to work at alone. It was study in the truest sense of the word, and it meant there were no pupils just sitting inattentively while the teacher talked and explained.

The first-grade pupils hadn't quite reached the stage of independent study, but even they were allowed to start with any subject they wanted. Some copied letters of the alphabet, some drew pictures, some read books, 30 and some even did physical exercises.

Just then the boy sitting behind her got up and walked toward the blackboard with this notebook, apparently to consult the teacher. Totto-chan stopped looking around the room and fixed her eyes on his back as he walked. The boy dragged his leg, and his whole body swayed from side to side, Totto chan wondered at first if he was doing it on purpose, but she soon realized the boy couldn't help it.

The boy said brightly, "My name's Yasuaki. What's yours?"

She was so glad to hear him speak that she replied loudly, "I'm Totto-chan". 40

Adapted from Totto-chan

(a) Give the meaning of the following words as used in the passage:
One-word answers or short phrases will be accepted.
  (i) assigned (line 3)
  (ii) ideal (line 19)
  (iii) independent (line 24)

(b) Answer the following questions briefly in your own words.
  (i) What was unusual about the seating arrangement?
  (ii) How did the method of teaching help the teacher?

(iii) Why did the pupils enjoy their lessons at this school?

(iv) What different things did the first-grade pupils do?

(v) Which sentence in the passage tells us that the boy had difficulty in walking like other children?

(c) In not more than 50 words, describe how the children were taught.

📋 Marking Scheme

(a) Give the meaning of the following words as used in the passage. One-word answers or short phrases will be accepted.

  (i) assigned - allotted, to give for a particular purpose, given, allocated

  (ii) ideal - perfect, the best possible, appropriate, flawless most appropriate. most suitable, excellent

  (iii) independent - free, not needing or wanting help, separate, self-directed, without any help, self-reliant, without assistance.

(b) (i) The children were allowed to sit / anywhere they like.

  (ii) Enabled the teacher to observe / what were they interested in / their way of thinking / their character.

  (iii) They loved starting with their favourite subject / had all day to cope with what they didn't like / could work independently. [any two points]

  (iv) They copied letters of the alphabets / drew pictures / read books / did physical exercises.

  (v) "The boy dragged his leg and his whole body swayed from side to side." (Entire sentence to be quoted exactly).

(c) Points to look for:

How the children were taught

1. Teacher makes a <u>list</u>

2. Children could choose to do first <u>they liked to best/choose</u> favourite subject/ start with any subject. (Any one point)

3. Would do later (cope up with) what they disliked

4. Children worked independently

5. They could approach/consult the teacher when they needed help / free to go to.

(Any one point)

6. Further exercises were given as homework. /to work at (alone)

Ans. **(a)** **(i)** to give a particular job or piece of work to someone.

  (ii) perfect or best possible.

  (iii) not influenced or controlled in any way by other people, events or things.

(b) **(i)** The seating arrangement was unusual because first it was inside a railway carriage and second because although each student was assigned a specific desk, the students were allowed to sit anywhere their liked at dry time.

  (ii) The method of teaching enabled the teacher to observe the interest of each student as well as gave the teacher more insight into their characters and thought processes.

  (iii) The pupils enjoyed their lessons at this school because they could start their day with what they liked. Also, they studied independently and called approach their teachers whenever needed.

  (iv) The first grade pupils were involved in multiple activities. Some of them copied letters of the alphabet, some got busy in making drawings, some read books, while some even did physical exercise.

  (v) The statement which tells us that the boy had difficulty in walking is: "The boy dragged his leg and his whole body swayed from side to side.

(c) The students were taught innovatively. The teacher started by making a list of all the subject problems. The pupils could begin their day with any subject and cope up with the remaining subjects later. They studied independently and could reach the teacher anytime in case of doubts. Further exercises were given as homework. **(52 words)**

Q. 2. **Read the following passage carefully and answer the questions that follow:** [2019]

Billy Weaver had travelled down from London and by the time he arrived it was nine o'clock in the night and the moon was coming up.

''Excuse me,'' he asked a porter. ''but is there a cheap hotel nearby?''

''Try The Bell Hotel,'' the porter answered, pointing down the road.

Billy thanked him, picked up his suitcase and set out to walk the distance to The Bell Hotel. He had never been to Richmond before. But the man at the Office had told him it was a *splendid* city.

Billy was seventeen years old. He was wearing a new navy-blue overcoat, a new brown hat, and a new brown suit, and he was feeling fine. He walked briskly down the street. He was trying to do everything briskly these days. The big shots up at the Head Office were fantastically brisk all the time. They were amazing.

The road was lonely and dark with a few scattered houses.

Suddenly, in a downstairs window Billy saw a printed notice propped up against the window glass. It said Bed and Breakfast.

He moved a bit closer and peered through the window into the room, and the first thing he saw was a bright fire burning in the hearth. On the carpet in front of the fire, a little dog was curled up asleep with its nose tucked into its belly.

The room in half-drakness was filled with pleasant furniture. There was a piano and big sofa and several plump armchairs; and in one corner he *spotted* a large parrot in a cage. Animals were usually a good sign in a place like this, Billy told himself and it looked to him as though it would be a pretty decent house to stay in.

Then a queer thing happened to him. He was in the act of stepping back and going away from the window when he felt a strange urge to ring the bell!

He pressed the bell. He heard it ringing, and then at once the door swung open and a woman was standing there.

She gave him a warm welcoming smile.

"Please come in," she said pleasantly. Billy found himself *automatically* moving forward into the house.

"I saw the notice in the window," he said, holding himself back.

"Yes, I know."

"I was wondering about a room."

"It's all ready for you, my dear," she said. She had a round pink face and very gentle blue eyes.

"How much do you charge?"

"Five dollars a night, including breakfast."

It was fantastically cheap. He could easily afford it.

(a) Give the meaning of the following words as used in the passage.
One-word answers or short phrases will be accepted.
   (i) splendid (line 7)
   (ii) spotted (line 20)
   (iii) automatically (line 29)
(b) Answer the following questions briefly in your own words:
   (i) How did the porter assist Billy?
   (ii) Why did Billy want to everything briskly?
   (iii) Why did Billy think animals were a good sign in a place like this?
   (iv) Which sentence tells you that something strange happened to Billy?
   (v) How much did the room cost?
(c) In not more than 50 words, give a brief account of what Billy saw as he looked through the window of the room.

📋 Marking Scheme -------------------------------------

(a) Give the meaning of the following words as used in the passage. One word answers or short phrases will be accepted.
   (i) splendid - very good, wonderful, majestic, magnificent, impressive.
   (ii) spotted - saw, sighted, noticed, caught sight of.
   (iii) automatically- by himself, mechanically, with no outward force, instinctively, involuntarily, spontaneously
(b) (i) Gave him information/about the Bell Hotel/ (cheap, nearby)
   (ii) Wanted to become/(like the big shots in the office, they were fantastically brisk/they were amazing) any one from within the brackets.
   (iii) Proof that the people were good/they loved and cared for animals. (anything that implies love and care)
   (iv) "Then a queer thing happened to him." (Quote exactly the entire sentence).

> (v) Five dollars a night with breakfast.
> (c) Points to look for:
> 1. Bright fire in the hearth
> 2. Little dog (on the carpet)
> 3. Pleasant furniture
> 4. Piano
> 5. Sofa and stuffed armchairs
> 6. Parrot in a cage
> **All Nouns.** Implied meaning/the words may be placed in any order/only a description of the room is required. (*six things in the room + expression*)

Ans. **(a)** **(i)** very impressive, magnificent
(ii) found, noticed
(iii) involuntarily
(b) **(i)** The porter suggested Billy to try 'The Bell Hotel' when he asked him about cheap hotels in the locality.
(ii) The senior officers of the Head Office where Billy worked were fantastically brisk all the time. They were amazing in their work. This influenced Billy to do everything briskly.
(iii) Animals were a good sign in a place like this because it showed the compassionate and loving attitude of the owners of the place.
(iv) The sentence that tells us, something strange happened to him is ''Then a *queer thing happened to him*''.
(v) The room costed only five dollars a night including the breakfast.
(c) As Billy looked through the window, he saw a bright fire burning in the hearth. A dog was sleeping on the carpet in front. The room was half dark with pleasant furniture including a piano, a big sofa and plump-sized armchairs. He also spotted a large parrot in a cage. **(50 words)**

Q. 3. **Read the following passage carefully and answer the questions that follow:** [2018]

Granny knew I'd been in the train for two nights, and she had a huge breakfast ready for me.

Later she told me there'd been a letter from Uncle Ken.

"He says he's the manager in Firpo's hotel in Simla,' she said. 'The salary is very good.

It's steady job and I hope he keeps it.'

Three days later Uncle Ken was on the veranda steps with his bedding roll and *battered* suitcase.

'Have you given up the hotel job?' asked Granny.

'No,' said Uncle Ken. 'They have closed down.'

'I hope it wasn't because of you.' 10

'No, Aunt Ellen. The bigger hotels in the hill stations are closing down.'

'Well, never mind. Come along and have your lunch.'

Over lunch, Uncle Ken talked very seriously about ways and means of earning a living.

'There is only one taxi in the whole of Dehra,' he *mused*. 'Surely there is business for another?'

'I'm sure there is,' said Granny. 'But where does it get you? In the first place, you don't have a taxi. And in the second place, you can't drive.'

'I can soon learn. There's a driving school in town. And I can use Uncle's old car.'

'I don't think it will run now,' said Granny.

'Of course, it will. It just needs some oiling and greasing and a spot of paint.' 20

'All right, learn to drive.'

so, Uncle Ken joined the driving school.

After a month Uncle Ken announced that he could drive and that he was taking the car out for a trial run.

'You haven't got your license yet,' said Granny.

'Oh, I won't take it far,' said Uncle Ken. 'Just down the road and back again.'

He spent all morning cleaning up the car. Granny gave him money for a can of petrol.

After tea, Uncle Ken said, 'Come along, Ruskin, hop in and I will give you a ride. Bring Mohan along too.' Mohan and I needed no urging. We got into the car beside Uncle Ken.

'Now don't go too fast, Ken,' said Granny anxiously. 'You are not used to the car as yet.' 30

Uncle Ken nodded and smiled and gave two sharp toots on the horn. He was feeling pleased with himself.

Driving through the gate, he nearly ran over a cat.

Miss Kellner, coming out for her evening rickshaw ride, saw Uncle Ken at the wheel of the car and ran indoors again.

Uncle Ken drove straight and fast, tootling the horn without a break.

At the end of the road there was a roundabout.

'We'll turn here,' said Uncle Ken, 'and then drive back again.'

He turned the steering wheel, we began going round the roundabout, but the steering wheel wouldn't turn all the way, not as much as Uncle Ken would have liked it to…So, 40
instead he went on–and straight through the Maharaja of Jetpur's garden wall.

It was a single-brick wall, and the car knocked it down and *emerged* on the other side without any damage to the car or any of its occupants. Uncle Ken brought it to a halt in the middle of the Maharaja's lawn.

Running across the grass came the Maharaja himself. When he saw that it was Uncle Ken at the wheel, the Maharaja beamed with pleasure.

'Delighted to see you, old chap!' he exclaimed. 'Jolly decent of you to drop in again. How about a game of tennis?'

(a) Give the meaning of the following words as used in the passage.
One word answers or short phrases will be accepted.
   (i) battered (line 6)
   (ii) mused (line 14)
   (iii) emerged (line 42)

(b) Answer the following questions briefly in your own words:
   (i) Why did Granny hope Uncle Ken would keep his job at Firpo's hotel?
   (ii) When Uncle Ken arrived with his luggage, Granny remarked that she hoped the hotel had not closed down because of him. What does this remark tell you about Uncle Ken?
   (iii) Why did Uncle Ken think, that driving a taxi in Dehra would be profitable?
   (iv) Which sentence tells you that the narrator and his friend were waiting to be invited for a drive in a car?
   (v) Why did Miss Kellner run indoors when she saw Uncle Ken at the wheel of the car?
   (vi) What was Uncle Ken's intention at the roundabout?

(c) (i) In not more than 60 words, describe what happened after the car went through the wall.
   (ii) Give a title to your summary in 3(c)(i). Give a reason to justify you choice of the title.

Ans: **(a) (i)** damaged /old and overused
   (ii) thought aloud
   (iii) got out/stepped out

(b) (i) Granny hoped that Uncle Ken would keep his new job because the salary was good and it was a steady job.
   (ii) It tells that he was an irresponsible man and had a history of causing problems for his employers.
   (iii) There was just one taxi in the town and so there would be huge possibility of business for another.
   (iv) "Mohan and I needed no urging."
   (v) Miss Kellner run indoors when she saw Uncle Ken at the wheel of the car because she was frightened and was aware of Uncle Ken's rash driving.
   (vi) Uncle Ken wanted to turn around and head back home.

(c) (i) Once the car went through the wall, it got out on the other side where Uncle Ken brought it to a halt in the middle of the Maharaja's lawn. The Maharaja himself came running across the lawn and looked very happy to see Uncle Ken. He also invited to a game of tennis.

          (53 words)

   (ii) 'An Eventful Drive'. This drive was certainly eventful for most of the participants involved: Mohan and Ruskin got to go on a drive; Uncle Ken understood that he still needed to work on his driving skills; and the Maharaja got to see his friend.

Q. 4. **Read the following passage carefully and answer the questions that follow:** [2017]

Every Monday, on his way back from work, Bipin Chowdhury would drop in at New Market to buy books. He had to buy at least five at a time to last him through the week. He lived alone, was not a good mixer, had few friends, and didn't like spending time in idle chat. Those who called in the evening got through their business quickly and left. Those who didn't show signs of leaving would be told around eight o'clock by Bipin Babu that he was under doctor's orders to have dinner at eight-thirty. After dinner he would rest for half an hour and then turn in with a book. This was a routine which had *persisted* unbroken for years.

Today, Bipin Babu had the feeling that someone was observing him from close quarters. He turned round and found himself looking at a round-faced, meek-looking man who now broke into a smile. 10

"I don't suppose you recognize me."

Bipin Babu felt ill at ease. It didn't seem that he had ever encountered this man before. The face seemed quite unfamiliar.

"Have we met before?" asked Bipin Babu.

The man looked greatly surprised. "We met every day for a whole week. I arranged for a car to take you to the Hudroo falls. My name is Parimal Ghose."

"Ranchi?"

Now Bipin Babu realized this man was making a mistake. Bipin Babu had never been to Ranchi. He smiled and said, "Do you know who I am?"

The man raised his eyebrows, and said, "Who doesn't know Bipin Chowdhury?" 20

Bipin Babu turned towards the bookshelves and said, "You've making a mistake. I've never been to Ranchi."

The man now laughed aloud.

"What are you saying, Mr. Chowdhury? You had a fall in Hudroo and cut your right knee. I brought you iodine. I had fixed up a car for you to go to Netarhat the next day, but you couldn't because of the pain in the knee. Can't you recall anything? Someone else you know was also in Ranchi at that time. Mr. Dinesh Mukherjee. You stayed in a bungalow. You said you didn't like hotel food. I'll tell you more; you always carried a bag with your books in it on your sightseeing trips. Am I right or not?"

Bipin Babu spoke quietly, his eyes still on the books. 30

"Which month in Nineteen fifty-eight are you talking about?"

The man said, "October."

"No, sir," said Bipin Babu. "I spent October Nineteen fifty-eight with a friend in Kanpur. You're making a mistake. Good day."

But the man didn't go, nor did he stop talking.

"Very strange. One evening I had tea with you on the verandah of your bungalow.

You spoke about your family. You said you had no children, and that you had lost your wife a *decade* ago."

When Bipin Babu had paid for the books and was leaving the shop, the man was still looking at him in utter disbelief. 40

Bipin Babu's car was safely parked in Bertram Street. He told the driver as he got into the car, "Just drive by the Ganga, will you, Sitaram." Driving up the Strand Road, Bipin Babu regretted having paid so much attention to the *intruder*. He had never been to Ranchi. He had an excellent memory.

Unless he was losing his mind!

(a) **Give the meaning of the following words as used in the passage.**
One word answers or short phrases will be accepted.
  (i) **persisted (line 7)**
  (ii) **decade (line 38)**
  (iii) **intruder (line 43)**

(b) **Answer the following questions briefly in your own words:**
  (i) **How did Bipin Chowdhury find time to read five books a week?**
  (ii) **How did he get rid of visitors who stayed late?**

    (iii) **Which sentence tells you that Bipin Babu was uncomfortable?**

    (iv) **What strong argument did Bipin Babu give to prove that he was not in Ranchi at that time?**

    (v) **What does Bipin Babu regret?**

    (vi) **What are Bipin Babu's feelings at the end of the passage?**

(c) (i) **What memories of the trip does Parimal Ghose evoke to prove that Bipin Babu was indeed in Ranchi? Answer in not more than 60 words.**

    (ii) **Give a title to your summary in 3(c) (i). Give a reason to justify your choice.**

Ans. **(a)** (i) continued

    (ii) a period of ten years

    (iii) encroacher

(b) (i) Bipin Chowdhury had a few friends and he didn't socialize much. Moreover, he always took his dinner at 8:30 p.m. after which he devoted all the time to reading books.

    (ii) If any visitor stayed back late and didn't show any signs of leaving Bipin Babu used to tell the visitor at 8'o clock that he was under doctor's orders to have dinner at eight-thirty. Also, he had to rest for half-hour after dinner and then read his books.

    (iii) "Bipin Babu felt ill at ease."

    (iv) Bipin Babu said that in the October of 1958, he was in Kanpur with his friend and this was the strongest argument that he gave.

    (v) Bipin Babu regretted having given so much of attention to the intruder and for having answered all his questions diligently.

    (vi) Bipin Babu felt that he should not have given so much of importance to the intruder. He knew that he had an excellent memory unless he was loosing his mind.

(c) (i) Parimal Ghose in the beginning told Bipin that when the latter had cut his right knee, he was the one to get iodine. He reminded that how allergic Bipin was to hotel food and that he carried a bag of books. He added that Bipin had stayed in a bungalow and had also spoke about his family. **(58 words)**

    (ii) **The Persuasive Man:** This is because Parimal Ghose by all means tries to pursue Bipin Chowdhury to believe in the fact that he had been to Ranchi before.

Q. 5. **Read the following passage carefully and answer the questions that follow:** [2016]

For some time Mother had greatly envied our swimming, both in the daytime and at night, but as she pointed out when we suggested she join us, she was far too old for that sort of thing. Eventually, however, under constant pressure from us, Mother paid a visit into town and returned to the villa coyly bearing a mysterious parcel.

Opening this she astonished us all by holding up an extraordinary shapeless garment of black cloth, covered from top to bottom with hundreds of frills, pleats and tucks.

'Well, what do you think of it?' Mother asked.

We stared at the odd garment and wondered what it was for.

'What is it?' asked Larry at length.

'It's a bathing-costume, of course,' said Mother. 'What on earth did you think it was?'

'It looks to me like a badly-skinned whale,' said Larry, *peering* at it closely.

'You can't possibly wear that, Mother,' said Margo, horrified, 'shy, it looks as though it was made in nineteen-twenty.'

'What are all those frills and things for?' asked Larry with interest.

'Decoration, of course,' said Mother indignantly.

'What a jolly idea! Don't forget to shake the fish out of them when you come out of the water'.

'Well, *I* like it, anyway,' Mother said firmly, wrapping the monstrosity up again, 'and I'm going to wear it.'

'You'll have to be careful you don't get waterlogged, with all that cloth around you,' said Leslie seriously.

'Mother, it's awful; you can't wear it,' said Margo. 'Why on earth didn't you get something more up to date?'

'When you get to my age, dear, you can't go around in a two-piece bathing suit…you don't have the figure for it.'

'I'd love to know what sort of figure that was designed for,' remarked Larry.

'You really are hopeless, Mother,' said Margo despairingly.

'But I like it…and I'm not asking you to wear it,' Mother pointed out angrily.

'That's right, you do what you want to do,' agreed Larry; don't be put off. It'll probably suit you very well if you can grow another three or four legs to go with it'.   30

Mother snorted indignantly and swept upstairs to try on her costume. Presently she called to us to come and see the effect, and we all tropped up to the bedroom. Roger the dog, was the first to enter, and on being greeted by this strange apparition clad in its voluminous black costume rippling with frills, he retreated hurriedly through the door, backwards, barking *ferociously.* It was some time before we could persuade him that it really was Mother, and even then he kept giving her vaguely uncertain looks from the corner of his eye. However, in spite of all opposition, Mother stuck to her tent-like bathing-suit, and in the end we gave up.

In order to celebrate her first entry into the sea we decided to have a moonlight   40 picnic down at the bay, and sent an invitation to Theodore, who was the only stranger that Mother would tolerate on such a great occasion. The day for the great *immersion* arrived, food and wine were prepared, the boat was cleaned out and filled with cushions and everything was ready when Theodore turned up.

(a) **Give the meaning of the following words as used in the passage. One word answers or short phrases will be accepted.**
   (i) peering (line 12)
   (ii) ferociously (line 36)
   (iii) immersion (line 42)

(b) **Answer the following questions briefly in your own words:**
   (i) Why did mother not join the swimming in the beginning?
   (ii) Briefly describe her swimming costume.
   (iii) What did Larry think it was?
   (iv) Which sentence tells you that Margo thought it was old fashioned?
   (v) What was Leslie's concern?
   (vi) Why did mother think it was suitable?

(c) **(i) In not more than 60 words describe what happened after mother went upstairs to try on her costume.**
   (ii) Give a title to your summary in 3(c). (i) Give a reason to justify your choice.

Ans. **(a)** **(i)** looking closely
   (ii) fiercely
   (iii) dipping something into a liquid

(b) **(i)** Mother did not join the swimming in the beginning because she considered herself to have grown rather old for that sort of thing.

   (ii) Mother's swimming costume was an extraordinarily shapeless black garment that was covered with hundreds of frills, pleats and tucks from top to bottom.

   (iii) Larry thought that Mother's swimming costume was a badly-skinned whale.

   (iv) 'You can't possibly wear that, Mother', said Margo, horrified, 'Why, it looks as though it was made in nineteen-twenty'.

   (v) Leslie was concerned that all the cloth on the costume might actually trap enough water to waterlog their mother.

   (vi) Mother thought it to be suitable for an aged lady like herself.

(c) **(i)** The children trooped upstairs to scrutinize Mother in her costume. Roger, the dog, entered first. He saw an apparition and came out barking ferociously. After sometime Roger was persuaded that it was actually Mother but he kept giving her vague uncertain looks. However, Mother stuck to her bathing suit adamantly. The children surrendered to her opinions. **(56 words)**

(ii) The above summary can be entitled **'Roger Sees an Apparition'**. This title is appropriate because the summary actually describes Roger's first reaction upon seeing Mother in a swimming costume. He felt as if he had seen some apparition.

Q. 6. **Read the following passage carefully and answer the questions that follow:**   **[2015]**

Lying in bed, Swami realized with a shudder that it was Monday morning. It looked as though only a moment ago it had been the last period on Friday; already Monday was here. He hoped that an earthquake would reduce the school building to dust, but that good building—Albert Mission School, had withstood similar prayers for over a hundred years now. At nine o'clock Swaminathan wailed, "I have a headache." His mother said, "Why don't you go to school in a bullock cart?"   5

"So that I may be completely dead at the other end? Have you any idea what it means to be *jolted* in a cart?"

"Have you any important lessons today?"   10

"Important! Bah! That geography teacher has been teaching the same lesson for over a year now. And we have arithmetic, which means for a whole period we are going to be beaten by the teacher … Important lessons!"

And Mother generously suggested that Swami might stay at home.

At 9:30, when he ought to have been lining up in the school prayer hall, Swami was lying on the bench in Mother's room. Father asked him, "Have you no school today?"   15

"Headache," Swami replied.

"Nonsense! Dress up and go."

"Headache."   20

"Loaf about less on Sundays and you will be without a headache on Monday."

Swami knew how *stubborn* his father could be and changed his tactics, "I can't go so late to class."

"I agree, but you'll have to; it is your own fault, You should have asked me before deciding to stay away."   25

"What will the teacher think if I go so late?"

"Tell him you had a headache and so are late."

"He will beat me if I say so."

'Will he? Let us see. What is his name?"

"Mr. Samuel."   30

"Does he beat the boys?"

"He is very violent, especially with boys who come late. Some days ago a boy was made to stay on his knees for a whole period in a corner of the class because he came late, and that after getting six cuts from the cane and having his ears twisted. I wouldn't like to go late to Mr. Samuel's class."   35

"If he is so violent, why not tell your headmaster about it?"

"They say that even the headmaster is afraid of him. He is such a violent man."

And then Swami gave a lurid account of Samuel's violence; how when he started caning he would not stop till he saw blood on the boy's hand, which he made the boy press to his forehead like a vermilion marking. Swami hoped that his father would be made to see that he couldn't go to his class late. But Father's behavior took an unexpected turn. He became excited. "What do these people mean by beating our children? They must be driven out of service. I will see…"   40

The result was he proposed to send Swami late to his class as a kind of challenge. He was also going to send a letter with Swami to the headmaster.   45

No amount of protest from Swami was of any *avail*: Swami had to go to school.

By the time he was ready Father had composed a long letter to the headmaster, put in an envelope and sealed it.

"What have you written, Father?" Swaminathan asked apprehensively.   50

"Nothing for you. Give it to your headmaster and go to your class."

Swami's father did not know the truth, that actually Mr. Samuel was a very kind and gentle man.

(a) **Give the meaning of each of the following words as used in the passage. One word answers or short phrases will be accepted.**

   (i) jolted (line 9)

   (ii) stubborn (line 22)

   (iii) avail (line 47)

(b) **Answer the following questions briefly in your own words:**

   (i) **What did Swami wish for on a Monday morning? Why was his wish unlikely to be answered?**

   (ii) **Which sentence tells us that Swami's father was completely unsympathetic to his son's headache?**

   (iii) **In what way was Swami's mother's response different from his father's?**

   (iv) **Why did Swami give a colorful account of Mr. Samuel to his father?**

   (v) **In what way did Father's behaviour take an unexpected turn?**

   (vi) **What was Swami finally ordered to do by his father?**

(c) **(i)** **In not more than 60 words describe how Swami tries to prove that Mr. Samuel is a violent man.**

   (ii) **Give a title to your summary in 3(c). Give a reason to justify your choice.**

Ans. **(a)** **(i)** jerked

   (ii) obstinate

   (iii) use

(b) **(i)** Swami didn't want to go to school as he was having 'Monday blues'. He wished that his school would be razed to the ground by an earthquake. He knew that it was an impossible wish as his school, Albert Mission, had survived many prayers like this for over a century.

   (ii) Swami's father's sarcastic remark "Loaf about less on Sundays and you be without a headache on Mondays" shows that he was unsympathetic towards Swami. He knew his son was pretending.

   (iii) Swami's mother was convinced of her son's arguments and allowed him to stay at home. In her simplicity, she believed that her son really had a headache, whereas, his father was shrewd enough to understand his son's tactics and so he insisted that Swami should go to school.

   (iv) Swami started giving a colorful description of Mr. Samuel's violent behavior thinking that his father would be more sympathetic towards him and would allow him to miss his school.

   (v) Swami's father was taken aback listening to his son's description of the violent behavior of his teacher but he took it as a challenge and insisted that his son should go to school and also take the letter written by him to the Principal. Swami had thought that his father would take pity on him so that he would not have to face the wrath of the teacher but this reaction was totally unexpected.

   (vi) Swami was ordered to give the letter written by his father to his Headmaster and go to his class.

(c) **(i)** Swami told his father that his teacher Mr. Samuel was very violent especially with the boys who are late-comers. He would beat, twist the ears and cane the palm till it would bleed, and then pressed it against the forehead of the student like a vermilion mark. Even the headmaster was afraid to intervene.

   (54 words)

   (ii) Title - **'A Pack of Lies'**. Swami tells a lot of lies to restrain himself from going to school but they don't work out. In fact, they fell like a pack of cards; flimsy and without any solid base.

Chapter 8 — Verb Forms

Q. 1. **Fill in each of the numbered blanks with the correct form of the word given in brackets. Do not copy the passage but write in correct serial order the word or phrase appropriate to the blank space.** **[2020]**

Example :

(0) taught

By the time she was three, Matilda had **(0)** ________ (teach) herself to read by **(1)** ________ (study) newspapers and magazines that **(2)** ________ (lie) around the house. At the age of four, she could **(3)** ________ (read) fast and well and she naturally began **(4)** ________ (hanker) after books. The only book in the whole of this enlightened household was something called Easy Cooking **(5)** ________ (belong) to her mother, and when she had read this from cover to cover and had **(6)** ________ (learn) all the recipes by heart, she **(7)** ________ (decide) she **(8)** ________ (want) something more interesting.

Marking Scheme

0. taught	1. studying
2. lay	3. read
4. hankering / to hanker	5. belonging
6. learnt/learned	7. decided
8. wanted	

Ans.

(1) studying	**(2)** lay
(3) read	**(4)** hankering
(5) belonging	**(6)** learnt
(7) decided	**(8)** wanted

Q. 2. **Fill in each of the numbered blanks with the correct form of the word given in brackets. Do not copy the passage, but write in correct serial order the word or phrase appropriate to the blank space.** **[2019]**

Example:

(0) roamed

Once upon a time in the days when genies and giants **(0)** ________ (roam) the land, there **(1)** ________ (live) a farmer **(2)** ________ (name) Baba Ayub. He lived with his family in a little village by the name Maidan Sabz. Because he had a large family to feed, Baba Ayub **(3)** ________ (see) his days **(4)** ________ (consume) by hard work. Every day, he **(5)** ________ (labour) from dawn to sundown, **(6)** ________ (plow) his field and **(7)** ________ (turn) the soil and **(8)** ________ (tend) to his meagre pistachio trees.

Marking Scheme

0. roamed	1. lived
2. named	3. saw
4. consumed	5. laboured
6. plowing/ploughing	7. turning
8. tending	

Ans.

(1) lived	**(2)** named
(3) saw	**(4)** consumed
(5) laboured	**(6)** ploughing
(7) turning	**(8)** tending

Q. 3. **Fill in each of the numbered blanks with the correct form of the word given in brackets. Do not copy the passage, but write in correct serial order the word or phrase appropriate to the blank space.** **[2018]**

Example:

(0) beginning

Alice was **(0)** ________ (begin) to get very tired of **(1)** ________ (sit) by her sister on the bank and of having nothing to do: once or twice she had **(2)** ________ (peep) into the book her sister was reading, but it **(3)** ________ (have) no pictures or conversations in it, "and what is the use of a book," **(4)** ________ (think) Alice, "without pictures or conversations?"

Alice wondered whether the pleasure of **(5)** ________ (make) a daisy-chain would be worth the trouble of getting up and picking the daisies, when suddenly a White Rabbit with pink eyes **(6)** ________ (run) close by her. Alice did not think this was very remarkable, until the Rabbit actually **(7)** ________ (take) a watch out of its waistcoat-pocket, and **(8)** ________ (look) at it, and then hurried on.

Ans.

(1) sitting	**(2)** peeped	**(3)** had
(4) thought	**(5)** making	**(6)** ran
(7) took	**(8)** looked	

Q. 4. **Fill in each of the numbered blanks with the correct form of the word given in brackets. Do not copy the passage, but write in correct serial order the word or phrase appropriate to the blank space.** **[2017]**

Example:

(0) started

My mother **(0)** _______ (start) school when she **(1)** _______ (be) six and **(2)** _______ (stop) the same term. She was unusual in the village as she had a father and brother who **(3)** _______ (encourage) her to go to school. She was the only girl in a class of boys and claims she was brighter than the boys. But every day she **(4)** _______ (will) leave behind her girl cousins **(5)** _______ (play) at home and she **(6)** _______ (envy) them. There **(7)** _______ (seem) to be no point in **(8)** _______ (go) to school just to end up doing housework.

Ans.
(1) was	**(2)** stopped	**(3)** encouraged
(4) would	**(5)** playing	**(6)** envied
(7) seemed	**(8)** going	

Q. 5. **Fill in each of the numbered blanks with the correct form of the word given in brackets. Do not copy the passage, but write in correct serial order the word or phrase appropriate to the blank space.** **[2016]**

Example:
(0) He had been **(0)** ... (sit) on the bank of a small irrigation canal.

Answer: sitting

He was **(1)** _______ (gaze) at a couple of heron **(2)** _______ (fish) in the muddy water, when he **(3)** _______ (feel) something bump his elbow. **(4)** _______ (look) around, he **(5)** _______ (find) at his side a little goat, jet black and soft as velvet with lovely gray eyes. Neither her owner nor her mother **(6)** _______ (be) around.

She continued to **(7)** _______ (nudge) Mukesh, so he **(8)** _______ (look) in his pocket for nourishment.

Ans.
(1) gazing	**(2)** fishing	**(3)** felt
(4) looking	**(5)** found	**(6)** was
(7) nudge	**(8)** looked	

Q. 6. **Fill in each of the numbered blanks with the correct form of the word given in brackets. Do not copy the passage, but write in correct serial order the word or phrase appropriate to the blank space.** **[2015]**

Example:
(0) One morning I **(0)** _______ (see) the python curled up on the dressing table.

Answer: saw

It was **(1)** _______ (gaze) at its own reflection in the mirror. I **(2)** _______ (go) for grandfather but by the time we **(3)** _______ (return) to the room, the python **(4)** _______ (move) on. He was seen in the garden and once the cook saw him **(5)** _______ (crawl) up the ladder to the roof. Then we **(6)** _______ (find) him on the dressing table again **(7)** _______ (admire) himself in the mirror. "He's trying to look better for Aunt Mabel" I said. I **(8)** _______ (regret) this remark immediately because grandmother overhead and held up my pocket money for the rest of the week!

Ans.
(1) gazing	**(2)** went	**(3)** returned
(4) had moved	**(5)** crawling	**(6)** found
(7) admiring	**(8)** regretted	

Q. 7. **Fill in each of the numbered blanks with the correct form of the word given in brackets. Do not copy the passage, but write in correct serial order the word or phrase appropriate to the blanks space.** **[2014]**

Example:
From his perch behind the clock, Hugo could **(0)** _______ (see) everything.

Answer: see

He rubbed his fingers nervously against the small notebook in his pocket and **(1)** _______ (tell) himself to be patient. The old man in the toy booth **(2)** _______ (argue) with the girl. She **(3)** _______ (be) about Hugo's age and he often saw her go into the booth and **(4)** _______ (disappear) behind the counter. The old man **(5)** _______ (look) agitated today. Had he figured out some of his toys were **(6)** _______ (miss)? Well, there was nothing to be **(7)** _______ (do) about that now. The old man and the girl argued some more and finally she closed her book and **(8)** _______ (run) off.

Ans.
(1) told	**(2)** was arguing	**(3)** was
(4) disappear	**(5)** looked	**(6)** missing
(7) done	**(8)** ran	

Q. 8. **Fill in each of the numbered blanks with the correct form of the word given in brackets. Do not copy the passage, but write in correct serial order the word or phrase appropriate to the blank space.** **[2013]**

Example:
A woman **(0)** _______ (wait) at an airport one night, with several long hours before her flight.

Answer: was waiting

She **(1)** _______ (hunt) for a book in the airport shops, **(2)** _______ (buy) a bag of cookies and found a place to sit. She **(3)** _______ (engross) in her book but happened to see that the man sitting beside her, bold as could be, grabbed a cookie or two from the bag in between, which she tried to ignore to avoid a scene. So she **(4)** _______ (munch) the cookies and watched the clock, as the gutsy thief diminished her stock. She **(5)** _________ (get) more irritated as the minutes ticked by, thinking, "If I wasn't so nice, I **(6)** _________ (black) his eye." With each cookie she took, he took one too. When only one was left, she wondered what he would do. With a smile on his face, and a nervous laugh, he **(7)** _________ (take) the last cookie and broke it in half. He offered her half, as he ate the other. She had never known she could be so angry and turned to gather her belongings. As she reached for her baggage, she gasped with surprise, there was her bag of cookies, in front of her eyes. If mine are here, she moaned in despair, the others were his, and he **(8)** _________ (try) to share.

Ans.
(1) hunted   (2) bought
(3) was engrossed   (4) munched
(5) was getting   (6) would have blackened
(7) took   (8) was trying

Q. 9. **Fill in each of the numbered blanks with the correct form of the word given in brackets. Do not copy the passage, but write in correct serial order the word or phrase appropriate to the blank space.** **[2012]**

Example:
My guide **(0)** _________ (tell) me if I wanted to meet these people I would have to walk two miles.

Answer: told

We finally **(1)** _________ (reach) a village where I **(2)** _________ (meet) a lady whose age I **(3)** _________ (can) not immediately make out. My translator **(4)** _________ (find) it difficult to interpret the lady's words because her dialect was quite different. She **(5)** _________ (is) a dark-skinned and dark-haired lady. She must have been around seventy years old but there was no grey in her hair. She obviously could not afford to dye her hair. So what was her secret? Nobody **(6)** _________ (know). It must have been a 'secret' common to all for not one person in that whole village **(7)** _________ (has) a trace of grey hair! I **(8)** _________ (think) about it for a long time.

Ans.
(1) reached   (2) met
(3) could   (4) was finding

(5) was   (6) knew
(7) had   (8) had been thinking

Q. 10. **Fill in each of the numbered blanks with the correct form of the word given in brackets. Do not copy the passage, but write in correct serial order the word or phrase appropriate to the blank space.** **[2011]**

Example:
We were not **(0)** _________ (allow) to talk during the lecture.

Answer: allowed

The children **(1)** _________ (sit) in a neat circle and **(2)** _________ (begin) **(3)** _________ (copy) their multiplication tables. Most **(4)** _________ (scratch) in the dirt with sticks they had **(5)** _________ (bring) for that purpose. The more fortunate **(6)** _________ (has) slate boards that they **(7)** _________ (write) on with sticks **(8)** _________ (dip) in a mixture of mud and water.

Ans.
(1) sat   (2) begun   (3) copying
(4) scratched   (5) brought   (6) had
(7) wrote   (8) dipped

Q. 11. **In the following passage, fill in each of the numbered blanks with the correct form of the word given in brackets. Do not copy the passage, but write in correct serial order the word or phrase appropriate to the blank space.** **[2010]**

Example:
(0) given

But just when I had almost **(0)** _________ (give) up hope, I was **(1)** _________ (strike) with a brilliant idea: my birthday was due fairly soon, and if I **(2)** _________ (deal) with the family skillfully, I **(3)** _________ (feel) sure, I could not only get a boat but a lot of other equipment as well. I **(4)** _________ (suggest) to the family that, instead of **(5)** _________ (let) them choose my parents, I **(6)** _________ (may) tell them the things that I **(7)** _________ (want) most. In this way they could be sure of not **(8)** _________ (disappoint) me.

Ans.
(1) struck   (2) dealt   (3) felt
(4) suggested   (5) letting   (6) might
(7) wanted   (8) disappointing

Prepositions

Q. 1. Fill in the blanks with appropriate words. **[2020]**

(i) It has been raining _________ two hours.

(ii) He just scraped _________ his examination.

(iii) Mrs. Kapoor was bent _________ attending the meeting.

(iv) She is proud and looks _________ on her colleagues.

(v) Rahul plays football _________ his grandfather.

(vi) The mother was sitting _________ the sick child all night.

(vii) Monica is leaning _________ the wall.

(viii) Rosie is very good _________ art and craft.

Marking Scheme

(i) for	(ii) through
(iii) on/upon	(iv) down
(v) with	
(vi) beside / with / near / by	
(vii) against	(viii) at / in

Ans.

(i) for	(ii) through
(iii) on	(iv) down
(v) with	(vi) beside
(vii) against	(viii) at

Q. 2. Fill in each blank with an appropriate word: **[2019]**

(i) The puppy was hiding _________ the sofa.

(ii) Stop worrying _________ your future.

(iii) When I stepped _________ the lift, I found it had stopped working.

(iv) We had to use a bridge to go _________ the river.

(v) I have lived in this town _________ ten years.

(vi) Please switch _________ all lights and fans when you leave the room.

(vii) Ronnie is married _________ my cousin.

(viii) The gift came _________ a birthday card.

Marking Scheme

(i) under/behind/beside	(ii) about
(iii) into	(iv) across
(v) for	(vi) off
(vii) to	(viii) with

Ans.

(i) underneath/under	(ii) about
(iii) into	(iv) across
(v) for	(vi) off
(vii) to	(viii) with

Q. 3. Fill in each blank with an appropriate word: **[2018]**

(i) The poet's mother was stung _________ a scorpion.

(ii) "Please write _________ what I tell you otherwise you will forget," the teacher said.

(iii) The dog was hiding _________ the bed, barking at the stranger.

(iv) Sheila's grandmother found it difficult to climb _________ the steep staircase.

(v) The soldier fought bravely _________ his country.

(vi) There is no use crying _________ spilt milk.

(vii) I don't know what they were arguing _________ but I could hear angry voices.

(viii) The school playground is out _________ bounds for the pupils of the primary school.

Ans.

(i) by	(ii) down
(iii) under	(iv) down
(v) for	(vi) over
(vii) about	(viii) of

Q. 4. Fill in each blank with an appropriate word: **[2017]**

(i) She shouted angrily _________ the disobedient boy.

(ii) I asked them to provide us _________ a guide.

(iii) The tree grew at a dangerous slant and had to be cut _________

(iv) My daughter believes _________ fairies.

(v) He drew a beautiful diagram _________ the board.

(vi) She battled her way _________ the crowd.

(vii) We were asked to gather _________ the teacher.

(viii) They had to climb _________ the steep pathway to reach the top.

Ans.

(i) at	(ii) with	(iii) down
(iv) in	(v) on	(vi) through
(vii) around	(viii) up	

Q. 5. Fill in each blank with an appropriate word: [2016]

(i) There was a steep rise _________ onion prices.

(ii) Air pollution is responsible for the spread _________ bronchitis.

(iii) He was _________ pressure to complete the work.

(iv) Joan jumped _________ the river to rescue the child.

(v) His teacher is very pleased _________ him.

(vi) Ali took _________ his cap and wiped his face.

(vii) The old woman could not get _________ the shock.

(viii) He should not get _________ with such rudeness.

Ans. (i) in   (ii) of

(iii) under   (iv) into

(v) with   (vi) off

(vii) over   (viii) away

Q. 6. Fill in the blanks with an appropriate word: [2015]

(i) He found the key just _________ the front door.

(ii) I could not accompany my cousin _________ the trip because I had fever.

(iii) The noise prevented us _________ sleeping.

(iv) The young man put the flute _________ his lips and began to play.

(v) Ashok leaned _________ the wall tiredly.

(vi) The paper dart went gliding _________ the air.

(vii) The cyclist rode quickly _________ the path.

(viii) The young child carried the heavy bucket _________ the stairs.

Ans. (i) outside/near   (ii) on

(iii) from   (iv) to

(v) against   (vi) through

(vii) along   (viii) up/down

Q. 7. Fill in the blanks with an appropriate word: [2014]

(i) The teacher spoke _________ for Raju when he was wrongly accused of stealing money.

(ii) We can visit her in the hostel _________ 3pm and 5pm on Saturdays.

(iii) The Sinhas have lived in new Delhi _________ 1943.

(iv) Little children are often afraid _________ the dark.

(v) Sneha has applied _________ a scholarship.

(vi) It look Ahmed many months to get _________ the loss of his friend.

(vii) She turned _________ the generous offer made by the manager.

(viii) We were asked to take _________ our footwear as we were entering a place of worship.

Ans. (i) up   (ii) between

(iii) since   (iv) of

(v) for   (vi) over

(vii) down   (viii) off.

Q. 8. Fill in the blanks with an appropriate word: [2013]

(i) She takes a lot of trouble _________ her work.

(ii) Our English friends have taken _________ Indian food quite quickly.

(iii) He got an A _________ the Mathematics test.

(iv) He jumped _________ the river to save his friend from drowning.

(v) Always be prepared _________ a surprise test.

(vi) She hid _________ the cupboard and gave everyone a fright.

(vii) She is fond _________ pets.

(viii) The brothers quarreled _________ themselves for their father's property.

Ans. (i) with/towards   (ii) to

(iii) in   (iv) into

(v) for   (vi) inside

(vii) off   (viii) amongst.

Q. 9. Fill in the blanks with an appropriate word: [2012]

(i) He was touched _________ pity when he heard the tale.

(ii) There is always a demand _________ good tailors.

(iii) The mother prevented her child _________ going out in the rain.

(iv) The baby crawled _________ the table and hid there.

(v) Once upon a time the great King ruled _________ all these villages and towns.

(vi) She is the smarter _________ the two.

(vii) Sheila insists _________ wearing that dress, although her mother thinks it is too short for her.

(viii) The teacher complained _________ him when she met his mother in the market.

Ans. (i) by   (ii) for
(iii) from   (iv) under
(v) over   (vi) of
(vii) upon   (viii) against

Q. 10. **Fill in the blanks with appropriate words:**
[2011]

(i) He congratulated me ________ my great achievement.

(ii) The poor man is afflicted ________ arthritis.

(iii) She is blind ________ the faults of her husband.

(iv) The boss had many complaints ________ Shyam.

(v) You must prepare ________ the examination.

(vi) She is not aware ________ the danger.

(vii) Ravi was accurate ________ his calculations.

(viii) They hid the money ________ the carpet.

Ans. (i) for   (ii) with
(iii) to   (iv) against
(v) for   (vi) of

(vii) in   (viii) under

Q. 11. **Fill in the blanks with appropriate words:**
[2010]

(i) I refrained ________ telling Reeta the truth.

(ii) The leader counted ________ the cooperation of his colleagues.

(iii) The public was cautioned ________ pickpockets.

(iv) Janaki escorted her daughter to the cinema theatre as she was anxious ________ her safety.

(v) Their path was beset ________ difficulties yet they succeeded.

(vi) The mouse crept stealthily ________ the cheese.

(vii) It was good ________ you to invite Sheila for the picnic.

(viii) Smoking ________ public places is now banned.

Ans. (i) from   (ii) on
(iii) of   (iv) about
(v) with   (vi) towards
(vii) of   (viii) in

Removing Conjunctions

Q. 1. Join the following sentences to make one complete sentence without using *and*, but or *so*: [2020]

(i) Sarah and Tyra are twins. They look exactly alike.

(ii) Rohan does not like to play cricket. He does not like to play hockey either.

(iii) Sania pushed as hard as she could. The door would not open.

(iv) The school bus drove through the gate. The clock was striking eight at that moment.

Marking Scheme

(i) Sarah and Tyra who are twins look exactly alike.
Sarah and Tyra are twins who look exactly alike.
Sarah and Tyra, who look exactly alike are twins.

(ii) Rohan neither likes to play cricket nor hockey.
Rohan likes to play neither cricket nor hockey.
Rohan does not like to play either cricket or hockey.

(iii) Although / Though / Even though Sania pushed as hard as she could, the door would not open.
In spite of/ Despite Sania pushing the door as hard as she could, it would not open.
Sania pushed as hard as she could,[yet/ however/still/nevertheless] the door would not open.

(iv) The clock was striking eight when the school bus drove through the gate./
The school bus drove through the gate when the clock was striking eight./
When the clock was striking eight the school bus drove through the gate./
When the school bus drove through the gate, the clock was striking eight at that moment.

Ans. (i) Sarah and Tyra are twins, who look exactly alike.

(ii) Rohan neither likes to play cricket, nor hockey.

(iii) Although Sania pushed as hard as she could, the door would not open.

(iv) When the school bus drove through the gate, the clock was striking eight at that moment.

Q. 2. Join the following sentences to make one complete sentence without using *and, but* or *so*: [2019]

(i) He was very ill. He did not take any medicine.

(ii) You come back from your holiday. We will discuss the problem.

(iii) He remained absent on Friday. It was foolish of him.

(iv) Rahul ran all the way to the bus stop. He missed the bus.

Marking Scheme

(i) Although / though/ even though he was very ill, he did not take any medicine.
In spite of being / Despite being/ very ill, he did not take any medicine
He was very ill, yet/still/ he did not take any medicine. (if the words- 'very' 'any' missing - no penalty)

(ii) After you come back from your holiday we will discuss the problem.
We will discuss the problem after/ when /you come back from your holiday. (After/ when can be in the beginning or in the middle of the sentence.)

(iii) It was foolish of him to remain absent on Friday.

(iv) In spite of /Despite/ running all the way to the bus stop, Rahul missed the bus. Although/ though/ even though Rahul ran all the way to the bus stop, he missed the bus. Rahul ran all the way to the bus stop yet/still he missed the bus.

Ans. (i) In spite of being ill, he did not take any medicine.

(ii) We will discuss the problem once you come back from your holiday.

(iii) It was foolish of him to remain absent on Friday.

(iv) Although Rahul ran all the way to the bus stop, he missed the bus.

Q. 3. Join the following sentences to make one complete sentence without using *and, but* or *so*. [2018]

(i) They have to go to bed early every night. They are allowed to stay up late on Saturdays.

(ii) The children were delighted. The exams had been cancelled.

(iii) We are not allowed to play in the sun. We are not allowed to play in the rain.

(iv) This is the place. The dog was rescued from its cruel owner.

Ans. (i) Although they have to go to bed early every night, they were allowed to stay up late on Saturdays.

(ii) The children were delighted since the exams had been cancelled.

(iii) We were not allowed to play either in the sun or in the rain.

(iv) This is the place where the dog was rescued from its cruel owner.

Q. 4. **Join the following sentences to make one complete sentence without using** *and, but* **or** *so.* **[2017]**

(i) **This is the hospital. I was born here.**

(ii) **The children have been sick for a week. They were unable to go to school.**

(iii) **Mrs. Kumar has been a teacher for thirty years. She will now retire.**

(iv) **We have had to respect for nature. Now we are suffering from the effects of global warming.**

Ans. (i) This is the hospital where I was born.

(ii) Having been sick for a week, the children were unable to go to school.

(iii) Mrs. Kumar who has been a teacher for thirty years will now retire.

(iv) Since we have no respect for nature, we are suffering from the effects of global warming.

Q. 5. **Join the following sentences to make one complete sentence without using** *and, but* **or** *so.* **[2016]**

(i) **My grandfather is very old. He is very active.**

(ii) **Mala is not in the classroom. Mala is not in the library.**

(iii) **She was so excited about her performance. She could not sleep at night.**

(iv) **Mumbai is densely populated. It is one of the major cities in the country.**

Ans. (i) Although my grandfather is very old, he is very active.

(ii) Mala is neither in the classroom nor in the library.

(iii) She was so excited about her performance that she could not sleep at night.

(iv) Mumbai, one of the major cities in India, is densely populated.

Q. 6. **Join the following sentences to make one complete sentence without using** *and, but* **or** *so.* **[2015]**

(i) **He has learnt cycle. He has yet to learn to swim.**

(ii) **The child helped her mother to make breakfast. She washed the tomatoes.**

(iii) **They bought a new car. They can travel long distances.**

(iv) **Sunita opened her purse. She found the money missing.**

Ans. (i) Although he has learnt to cycle, he still has not learned to swim.

(ii) The child helped her mother to make breakfast by washing the tomatoes.

(iii) They bought a new car to travel long distances.

(iv) When Sunita opened her purse, she found the money missing.

Q. 7. **Join the following sentences to make one complete sentence without using** *and, but* **or** *so.* **[2014]**

(i) **He is good at gymnastics. His handwriting must improve.**

(ii) **Her grandfather gifted her a paint box. He knew she was good at art.**

(iii) **Ravi fractured his arm. He insisted on playing the match.**

(iv) **Mona has been ill for a month. She stood first in the examination.**

Ans. (i) Though he is good at gymnastics, yet his handwriting must improve.

(ii) Her grandfather gifted her a paint box because he knew she was good at art.

(iii) Though Ravi fractured his arm, yet he insisted on playing the match.
Or
Ravi insisted on playing the match despite having fractured his arm.

(iv) Mona stood first in the examination despite being ill for a month.

Q. 8. **Join the following sentences to make one complete sentence without using** *and, but* **or** *so.* **[2013]**

(i) **We had better get ready now. We may not have time to reach the airport.**

(ii) **Mr. Liew has been sick. He has been so since he came back from Japan.**

(iii) **The debating teams were very happy. Both were declared joint-champions.**

(iv) **He escaped from the prison. He looked for a place where he could hide.**

Ans. (i) We had better get ready now else we might not have time to reach to the airport.

(ii) Mr. Liew has been sick since he came back from Japan.

(iii) Both the debating teams were very happy as they were declared joint-champions.

(iv) Having escaped from the prison, he looked for a place where he could hide.

Q. 9. Join the following sentences to make one complete sentence without using *and, but* or *so*. [2012]

(i) He lived in the city for many years. He could not find his way about.

(ii) She complained that her brother did not know anything. Her brother claimed he knew everything.

(iii) The coffee isn't strong. It won't keep us awake.

(iv) I finished my homework. I switched on the TV.

Ans. (i) Although he lived in the city for many years, he could not find his way about.

(ii) She complained that her brother did not know anything whereas her brother claimed he knew everything.

(iii) The coffee isn't too strong to keep us awake.

(iv) I switched on the T.V. as soon as I finished my homework.

Q. 10. Join the following sentences to make one complete sentence without using *and, but* or *so*. [2011]

(i) The minister was wise. The king did not trust him.

(ii) We reached the port. The storm came on.

(iii) One should not borrow money. One should not lend money.

(iv) She will win the prize. She deserves it.

Ans. (i) Although the minister was wise, the king did not trust him.

(ii) As soon as we reached the port, the storm came on.

(iii) One should neither borrow nor lend money.

(iv) She deserves to win the prize.

Q. 11. Join the following sentences to make one complete sentence without using *and, but* or *so*: [2010]

(i) You will surely be late. Hurry up!

(ii) The trekkers got lost due to the heavy fog. They had misplaced their map as well.

(iii) She has to apologize. He will not meet her again if she does not do so.

(iv) I wear this expensive outfit very sparingly. I bought it last month.

Ans. (i) Hurry up, or else you will surely be late.

(ii) The trekkers got lost due to the heavy fog since they had misplaced their map as well.

(iii) He will not meet her again unless she apologizes.

(iv) I wear this expensive outfit which I bought last month, very sparingly.

Connectors

Q. 1. Re-write the following sentences according to the instructions given after each. Make other changes that may be necessary, but do not change the meaning of each sentence. **[2020]**

(i) The librarian orders books for the school library every year. (Begin: Books...)

(ii) No one will deny that the children have worked very hard this year. (Begin: Everyone....)

(iii) As soon as the teacher enters, she is greeted by her students. (Begin : No sooner.....)

(iv) She is so busy that she finds no time to entertain her friends. (Rewrite using 'too')

(v) In spite of the very hot weather, Kevin stepped out to buy some bread. (Begin : Despite....)

(vi) Sheela will be selected for the competition only if she goes for the auditions. (Begin: Unless....)

(vii) I would rather eat fruit than a lot of unhealthy junk food. (Begin: I prefer...)

(viii) The tree was cut down ruthlessly. (Begin: They...)

Marking Scheme

(i) Books are ordered for the library every year by the librarian. / Books are ordered by the librarian for the library every year.

(ii) Everyone will agree/admit/affirm/ accept that the candidates have worked very hard this year.

(iii) No sooner does the teacher enter, than she is greeted by her candidates. /

(iv) She is too busy to find time to entertain her friends.

(v) Despite the very hot weather Kevin stepped out to buy some bread.
Despite the weather being very hot, Kevin stepped out to buy some bread.
Despite the fact that the weather was very hot, Kevin stepped out to buy some bread.

(vi) Unless Sheela goes for the auditions she will not be selected for the competition.

(vii) I prefer eating fruit to a lot of unhealthy junk food.

(viii) They cut down the tree ruthlessly. / They ruthlessly cut down the tree.

Ans. **(i)** Books are ordered for the library every year by the librarian.

(ii) Everyone would agree that the children have worked very hard this year.

(iii) No sooner than the teacher enters, she is greeted by her students.

(iv) She is too busy to find time to entertain her friends.

(v) Despite the very hot weather, Kevin stepped out to buy some bread.

(vi) Unless Sheela goes for the auditions, she will not be selected for the competition.

(vii) I prefer eating fruit than a lot of unheathy junk food.

(viii) They ruthlessly cut down the tree.

Q. 2. Re-write the following sentences according to the instructions given after each. Make other changes that may be necessary, but do not change the meaning of each sentence. **[2019]**

(i) The old woman said to Arun, "Can you help me to cross the street?"
(Begin: The old woman asked Arun .....)

(ii) As soon as the sun rise over the hills the fog disappeared.
(Begin: No sooner ....)

(iii) It rained so heavily that they could not go for the picnic.
(Rewrite: Using 'too .... to')

(iv) If your friends get here before 7 o'clock we can take them out for dinner.
(Rewrite: Using 'unless'.)

(v) The school captain was elected by the students of classes XI and XII.
(Begin: The students ....)

(vi) Greenland is the largest island in the world.
(Begin: Using 'larger'.)

(vii) How cruel Shylock was to demand his pound of flesh!
(Begin: It was cruel ....)

(viii) Arun was asked by his mother to explain the missing buttons on his shirt.
(Rewrite: Using 'explanation')

Ans. (i) The old woman asked Arun whether he could help her to cross the street.

(ii) No sooner did the sun rise over the hills, than the fog disappeared.

(iii) It rained too heavily for them to go to the picnic.

(iv) We can not take your friends out for dinner unless they get here by 7 o'clock.

(v) The students of classes XI and XII elected the school captain.

(vi) No other island in the world is larger than Greenland.

(vii) It was cruel of Shylock to demand his pound of flesh.

(viii) Arun was asked for an explanation by his mother about the missing buttons on his shirt.

Q. 3. **Re-write the following sentences according to the instructions given after each. Make other changes that may be necessary, but do not change the meaning of each sentence.** **[2018]**

(i) **She laid the table after she had finished the cooking.**
(Begin: When ....)

(ii) **He is old but still he works hard.**
(Begin: Despite ....)

(iii) **The delivery boy was requested to bring the parcel the next day.**
(Rewrite using direct speech)

(iv) **I prefer playing a game to watching television.**
(Begin: I would rather ....)

(v) **Every family has a black sheep.**
(Begin: There is no ....)

(vi) **I have never worn a more ill-fitting suit.**
(End: .... ever worn)

(vii) **Anil is too fast a runner not to come first in the race.**
(Begin: Anil is so ....)

(viii) **As soon as the sports meet ended, the children ran on the field.**
(Begin: Hardly ....)

Ans. (i) When she had finished the cooking, she laid the table.

(ii) Despite being old, he works hard.

(iii) "Please bring the parcel tomorrow," he said to the delivery boy.

(iv) I would rather play a game than watch television.

(v) There is no family that does not have a black sheep.

(vi) This is the most ill-fitting suit that I have ever worn.

(vii) Anil is so fast a runner that he cannot but come first in the race.

(viii) Hardly had the sports meet ended, when the children ran on the field.

Q. 4. **Re-write the following sentences according to the instructions given after each. Make other changes that may be necessary, but do not change the meaning of each sentence.** **[2017]**

(i) **Not many people read for pleasure these days.**
(Begin: Few ....)

(ii) **Since her childhood Meera has been good in Mathematics.**
(End: .... childhood)

(iii) **"We have had no rain since January", Ramu said.**
(Begin: Ramu said that they ....)

(iv) **It is dangerous as well as illegal to drive a motorcycle without a helmet.**
(Begin: It is not ....)

(v) **He had plenty of wealth but he was not happy.**
(Begin: In spite ....)

(vi) **He was so tired that he could not stand.**
(Use: too ....)

(vii) **Every one of them was an experienced mountaineer.**
(Begin: There was no ....)

(viii) **I have never seen a film as bad as this.**
(Begin: This is ....)

Ans. (i) Few people read for pleasure these days.

(ii) Meera has been good in Mathematics since her childhood.

(iii) Ramu said that they had had no rain since January.

(iv) It is not only dangerous but also illegal to drive a motorcycle without a helmet.

   (v) In spite of the plenty of wealth he had, he was not happy.

   (vi) He was too tired to stand.

   (vii) There was no one who was an inexperienced mountaineer amongst them.

   (viii) This is the worst film I have ever seen.

Q. 5. **Re-write the following sentences according to the instructions given after each. Make other changes that may be necessary, but do not change the meaning of each sentence.** **[2016]**

   (i) The book was so interesting that I could not put in down.
(Begin: The book was too ....)

   (ii) The Principal said, "All the prizes will be distributed tomorrow."
(Begin: The principal said that ....)

   (iii) Last night's dinner was cooked for us by father.
(Begin: Father ....)

   (iv) If Mary catches the first bus, she will be on time for school.
(Begin: Unless ....)

   (v) In spite of having high fever the girl came to school.
(Begin: Despite ....)

   (vi) I prefer going out with friends to staying alone at home.
(Begin: I would rather ....)

   (vii) Hardly had the teacher left the room, when all the children started making a noise.
(Begin: No sooner ....)

   (viii) This is the funniest movie I have ever seen.
(Begin: Never ....)

Ans. **(i)** The book was too interesting to be put down.

   (ii) The Principal said that all the prizes would be distributed the next day.

   (iii) Father cooked last night's dinner for us.

   (iv) Unless Mary catches the first bus, she will not be on time for school.

   (v) Despite having high fever, the girl came to school.

   (vi) I would rather go out with friends than stay alone at home.

   (vii) No sooner did the teacher leave the room than all the children started making a noise.

   (viii) Never have I seen a funnier movie than this.

Q. 6. **Re-write the following sentences according to the instructions given after each. Make other changes that may be necessary, but do not change the meaning of each sentence.** **[2015]**

   (i) Arun gave Ramesh some excellent advice.
(Begin: Ramesh was ....)

   (ii) As soon as Sania sat down to study, the lights went off.
(Begin: No sooner ....)

   (iii) Has Alia written to you?
(Begin: Have you ....)

   (iv) As soon as the function got over. The crowd dispersed.
(Begin: Hardly had ....)

   (v) The monsoon is the best season in our country.
(Rewrite using 'good')

   (vi) Harish was so tired that he could not keep his eyes open.
(Begin: Harish was too ....)

   (vii) Father said to Sunil, "I can help you with your homework."
(Begin: Father told Sunil ....)

   (viii) Naresh goes to a school which has over a thousand students.
(Begin: There ....)

Ans. **(i)** Ramesh was given some excellent advice by Arun.

   (ii) No sooner did Sania sit down to study, than the lights went off.

   (iii) Have you heard from Alia?

   (iv) Hardly had the function got over when the crowd dispersed.

   (v) No other season in our country is as good as the monsoon.

   (vi) Harish was too tired to keep his eyes open.

   (vii) Father told Sunil that he could help him with his homework.

   (viii) There are over a thousand students in the school to which Naresh goes to.

Q. 7. **Re-write the following sentences according to the instructions given after each. Make other changes that may be necessary, but do not change the meaning of each sentence.** **[2014]**

   (i) As soon as we lit the candle, the power supply was restored.
(Begin: No sooner ....)

   (ii) The bee is more industrious than all other creatures.
(Use 'most industrious')

   (iii) The old woman was too slow to catch the bus.
(Begin: The old woman was so ....)

   (iv) "I'll do it tomorrow," he promised.
(Rewrite in indirect speech)

   (v) Though Reema got an expensive gift she was not happy.
(Begin: In spite ....)

   (vi) I prefer reading a book to watching a movie.
(Begin: I would rather ....)

(vii) I have never seen Mr. Roy   lose his temper.
(Begin: Never ....)

(viii) She found your keys in the garage.
(Begin: The keys ....)

Ans. **(i)** No sooner did we light the candle than the power supply was restored.

(ii) The bee is the most industrious of all creatures.

(iii) The old woman was so slow that she could not catch the bus.

(iv) He promised to do it the next day.

(v) In spite of getting an expensive gift, Reema was not happy.

(vi) I would rather read a book than watch a movie.

(vii) Never have I seen Mr. Roy lose his temper.

(viii) The keys that belong to you were found in the garage by her.

Q. 8. Re-write the following sentences according to the instructions given after each. Make other changes that may be necessary, but do not change the meaning of each sentence.   [2013]

(i) These windows need cleaning again.
(Begin: These windows will ....)

(ii) My mother said I could go with you only if I returned home by five o' clock.
(Use: as long as)

(iii) It doesn't matter which chemical you put into the mixture first, the results will be the same.
(Use: difference)

(iv) Who does this pen belong to?
(Begin: Do you know ....)

(v) Heavy rain has caused the cancellation of the outdoor garden party.
(Begin: Due ....)

(vi) I've never seen so many people in this building before.
(Begin: This is ....)

(vii) If we light the fire, the rescuers will see us.
(Begin: We will ....)

(viii) Only a few books were remaining on the shelf when we left.
(Begin: Most ....)

Ans. **(i)** These windows will have to be cleaned again.

(ii) My mother said I could go with you as long as I returned home by 5 o' clock.

(iii) Putting either of the chemicals in the mixture first will not make any difference, the result will be the same.

(iv) Do you know to whom does this pen belong?

(v) Due to heavy rain, the outdoor garden party has been cancelled.

(vi) This is the first time I have seen so many people in this building.

(vii) We will light the fire so that the rescuers will see us.

(viii) Most of the books were removed from the shelf when we left.

Q. 9. Re-write the following sentences according to the instructions given after each. Make other changes that may be necessary, but do not change the meaning of each sentence.   [2012]

(i) My mother left a month ago.
(Begin: It has ....)

(ii) Anil was wrong to lose his temper.
(Begin: Anil ought ....)

(iii) As soon as the Chief Guest had seated himself the play began.
(Begin: No sooner ....)

(iv) Rajiv said to Arjun, "Is this the book you were reading yesterday?"
(Begin: Rajiv asked Arjun if ....)

(v) Only a foolish person would be taken in by this trick.
(Begin: None ....)

(vi) Everybody has heard of Gandhiji.
(Begin: Who ....?)

(vii) He will issue the cheque only when he hears from the head office.
(Begin: On ....)

(viii) Father will send you a message if his flight is canceled.
(Begin: Should ....)

Ans. **(i)** It has been a month since my mother left.

(ii) Anil ought not to lose his temper.

(iii) No sooner did the chief guest seat himself, than the play began.

(iv) Rajiv asked Arjun if that was the book he had been reading the day before.

(v) None other than a foolish person would be taken in by this trick.

(vi) Who has not heard of Gandhiji?

(vii) On hearing from the head office he will issue the cheque.

(viii) Should the flight be canceled, father will send you a message.

Q. 10. Re-write the following sentences according to the instructions given after each. Make other changes that may be necessary, but do not change the meaning of each sentence.   [2011]

(i) This horse is better trained than yours.
(Begin: Your ....)

(ii) The children will sit out in the garden, if the weather is cool.
(Begin: The children won't ....)

(iii) The thief ran so fast that the police could not catch him.
(Rewrite using: too ....)

(iv) Her attitude often annoys me.
(Rewrite using: annoyance ....)

(v) The child disappeared as soon as the bus stopped.
(Begin: Hardly ....)

(vi) There is no success without effort.
(Being: Whenever ....)

(vii) "Please teach me to cycle" she asked her brother.
(Rewrite in indirect form)

(viii) The peasants regarded him as a thief and called him a villain.
(End: .... the peasants)

Ans.

(i) Your horse is not that well trained as this one.

(ii) The children won't sit out in the garden unless the weather is cool.

(iii) The thief ran too fast for the police to catch him.

(iv) Her attitude often causes annoyance to me.

(v) Hardly did the bus stop, than the child disappeared.

(vi) Whenever there is effort, there is success.

(vii) She requested her brother to teach her to cycle.

(viii) He was regarded a thief and was called a villain by the peasants.

Q. 11. Re-write the following sentences according to the instructions given after each. Make other changes that may be necessary, but do not change the meaning of each sentence. **[2010]**

(i) Unless Ria takes care of her health, she will not be able to look after her family.
(Begin: Ria must ....)

(ii) His arrogance was the cause of his losing the election.
(Rewrite the sentence using "arrogant")

(iii) If you are not a member you cannot borrow books.
(Begin: Only ....)

(iv) It is a pity our vacation is not longer.
(Begin: I wish ....)

(v) Raju did not complete the exercise on time.
(Rewrite the sentence adding a question tag)

(vi) Rohan was so terrified of being left alone in the house that he started screaming.
(Begin: So ....)

(vii) The teacher asked, "How many of you think the answer is correct?"
(Rewrite the sentence using indirect speech)

(viii) Sunil is the fastest runner in the school.
(End: .... as Sunil.)

Ans.

(i) Ria must take care of her health, otherwise she will not be able to look after her family.

(ii) He lost the election because he was arrogant.

(iii) Only members are allowed to borrow books.

(iv) I wish our vacation was longer.

(v) Raju did not complete the exercise on time, did he ?

(vi) So terrified was Rohan of being left alone in the house that he started screaming.

(vii) The teacher wanted to know how many of us thought the answer was correct.

(viii) No one in school can run as fast as Sunil.

ENGLISH-II

Drama

The Merchant of Venice: Shakespeare

Q. 1. Read the extract given below and answer the questions that follow :

Launcelot: But, I pray you, ergo, old man, ergo, I beseech you, talk you of young Master Launcelot?

Gobbo: Of Launcelot, an't please your mastership.

Launcelot: Ergo, Master Launcelot. Talk not of Master Launcelot, father; for the young gentleman, according to Fates and Destines, and such odd sayings, the Sisters Three and such branches of leaning, is indeed, deceased; or as you would say in plain terms, gone to heaven.

(i) What information does Gobbo seek from Launcelot at the beginning of this scene?

What does Launcelot say has happened to Gobbo's son?

(ii) Who are the 'Sisters Three'?

What role were they thought to play in the lives of humans?

(iii) Who was Launcelot's master?

What gift had Gobbo brought him? What does Launcelot want him to do with it?

(iv) What reasons does Launcelot give for wanting to leave his present master's service?

Whom does he wish to serve instead ?

(v) Why does Gobbo have trouble recognising Launcelot?

What purpose does this scene serve in the context of the play? **[2020]**

📋 Marking Scheme

(i) • The way to Shylock's OR master Jew's house OR does Launcelot live with him.
• had died (deceased) / gone to heaven.
(ii) • Greek mythology three sisters = three Fates / Destinies/ Clotho, Atropos, Lachesis
• Controlled the destiny of humans / had power of life and death over humans/ Clotho spun the thread of life/ Lachesis measured [gave] the thread of life/ Atropos cut the thread.

(iii) • Shylock or the Jew
• dish of doves
• give it to Bassanio instead
(iv) • He is starving / famished / "you may tell every finger I have with my ribs."
• Launcelot fears that he will become a Jew if he served Shylock (a Jew) for much longer./ He is ill-treated / Shylock is the Devil incarnate / He is the very Jew, or typical Jew
• Bassanio
(v) • Launcelot is dressed well / like a gentleman.
• Launcelot speaks with the air of a gentleman.
• Gobbo cannot see very well or sand blind or half blind
• Launcelot has grown a dense, bushy beard.
• Serves to provide comic relief / reveals Shylock's nature as cruel master / conflict between good and evil / Bassanio is a kind person / good master/Bassanio is leaving for Belmont/ Launcelot's attitude towards his master

Ans. **(i)** Old Gobbo asks the way to Shylock's house because he wants to meet his son Launcelot who is working there. The young man says that Gobbo's son is deceased or in simple terms gone to heaven.

(ii) According to Greek mythology, the three sisters represent fate or destiny. They were Clotho, who spins the thread of life, Lachesis, who measures the thread of life and Atropos, who cuts the thread of life. They were regarded as the decider of the course of the human's life. The belief is the three sisters of fate after every birth, visit the child and determine their fate to see how to spin their lifeline.

(iii) Launcelot's master is Shylock, the Jew. The present is a dish of doves. Launcelot wants the gift to be given to Bassanio, a gentleman, whom he wants to serve.

(iv) Launcelot's main objection in working for Shylock is that he is a Jew. Since a Jew is miserly, Launcelot is famished throughout the day so much so that his ribs can be counted. Another reason is that he has met Bassanio, a Christian gentleman who provides handsome liveries. He also feels Bassanio has God's grace.

(v) Gobbo cannot recognise his son as he is sand-blind. Besides, it has been a long time since he has seen his son who is now grown up with a beard and hair on his chest. Also, Launcelot was dressed very well and spoke with the air of a gentleman.

(vi) After the serious scene at Belmont, comes the comic scene of Launcelot and his father. This works as dramatic relief and adds fun to the play. Launcelot fooling his blind father and also using impressive words that do not match the context evoke pure laughter. First, he tells Gobbo in a witty manner that his son is dead and then announces he is alive. Gobbo touches his face and compares his beard to the tail of a horse. Most of his jokes are meant to entertain the groundlings but he also cracks witty comments that can be appreciated by the more intellectual ones. He also throws light on Shylock's miserly character by saying that he does not get enough to eat. A sense of racial prejudice is also introduced through his words as his main reason to leave is that Shylock is a Jew.

Q. 2. **Read the extract given below and answer the questions that follow:**

Shylock: **To bait fish withal. If it will feed nothing else, it will feed my revenge. He hath disgraced me and hindered me half a million, laughed at my losses, mocked at my gains, scorned my nation, thwarted my bargains, cooled my friends, heated mine enemies-and what's his reason ? I am a Jew. Hath not a Jew eyes ? Hath not a Jew hands, organs, dimensions, senses, affections, passions ? Fed with the same food, hurt with the same weapons, subject to the same diseases, healed by the same means, warmed and cooled by the same winter and summer as a Christian is? If you prick us, do we not bleed?**

(i) **Who is 'He'?**

What does Shylock want from him?

What does Shylock mean by 'to bait fish withal'?

(ii) **Explain in your own words any three ways in which 'he' had wronged Shylock.**

(iii) **According to Shylock, in what other ways did Jews resemble Christians?**

(iv) **How does Shylock use Christian example to justify his desire for revenge?**

(v) **The given extract reveals two distinct emotions that Shylock experiences.**

What are they? Give one reason to justify each of these emotions. **[2020]**

Marking Scheme

(i) • Antonio or the merchant of Venice
   • A pound of flesh / revenge
   • To use as bait to catch fish/ use the flesh to catch fish/ use for fishing/ nobody should question him / sarcastic / satisfy his thirst for revenge

(ii) *Any three* of the following:
   • He hath disgraced me (Shylock) / hindered me (Shylock) half a million
   • laughed at my (Shylock's) losses / mocked at my (Shylock's) gains / scorned my (Shylock's) nation / thwarted my (Shylock's) bargains / cooled my (Shylock's) friends / heated mine (Shylock's) enemies.
   • Spat on gaberdine/ spat on beard / gives money gratis/ calls him a misbeliever/ hates the Jewish race / kicked him like a cur / Shylock hates Antonio because he is a Christian.

(iii) Jews are like Christians:
   • laugh when tickled
   • die when poisoned
   • seek revenge when wronged   *(Any two)*

(iv) Shylock argues that:
   • When a Jew wrongs a Christian, the Jew is humiliated in revenge.
   • Therefore, following **the example set by Christians**.
   • If a Christian were to wrong a Jew, then it is appropriate that the Jew take revenge on the Christian.

(v) Emotions: Anger / thirst for revenge / Hurt / pain / bitterness / pain / malice / suffering / sadness; sorrow/ jealousy /
   • caused by humiliating treatment at the hands of Christians.
   • caused by insensitivity, unfair treatment of Jews by Christians (any two reasons from the play)

Ans. **(i)** 'He' is Antonio, the merchant of Venice. Shylock wants a pound of flesh to be cut from any part of his body which pleased Shylock, as per the forfeit. "If it will feed nothing else, it will feed my revenge". He would use Antonio's flesh for baiting fish, showing his complete disdain for the corpse of his enemy. If the fish aren't interested in eating the "bait," Antonio's death will feed Shylock's dire need for revenge against him.

(ii) He had disgraced Shylock, prevented him from earning half a million through usury, laughed at his losses, mocked at his gains, scorned his nation, thwarted his bargains, turned his friends against him, riled up his enemies—just because he is a Jew.

(iii) According to Shylock, Jews and Christians have similar eyes, ears and other organs. A Jew bleeds just as a Christian when wounded. In the same way, a Jew has feelings just as Christians. They also laugh when they are ticked. They are fed with the same food, hurt with the same weapons, subject to the same diseases, healed by the same means and warmed and cooled by the same winter and summer as a Christian is. They also die when poisoned or seek revenge when wronged.

(iv) Shylock feels deeply pained by the inequality. He says when a Jew offends a Christian, the Christian's kind and gentle reaction is revenge. So, if a Christian offends a Jew, the punishment that the Jew will come up with, if he follows this example of the Christian, is revenge. Shylock says that Christians have set up examples of wickedness and cruelty. He has followed the same example and wishes to take a greater revenge upon the Christian, Antonio.

(v) Shylock is gripped with feelings of revenge. He feels angry with Antonio as he had been instrumental in causing loss to Shylock at Rialto. Also, the Christian has insulted by calling him a dog and spitting on him. He has lost friends and gained enemies because of Antonio and he cannot ever forget the mockery and insults he has undergone. On the other hand, he is pained by the feeling of anti-semitism prevalent during the times. He feels Antonio hates him because he is a Jew. So, he expresses his anguish through his monologue in which he says there is no difference between a Christian and a Jew physically or emotionally. Both feel pain and anger and react similarly to changes of weather. He seems to be really pained by this social inequality.

Q. 3. **Read the extract given below and answer the questions that follow:**

Portia: **The quality of mercy is not strained;**
It droppeth as the gentle rain from heaven
Upon the place beneath : it is twice blessed;
It blesseth him that gives and him that takes :
'Tis mightiest in the mightiest', it becomes
The throned monarch better than his crown :

(i) **Where does this scene take place?**
Why is Portia here? Why does Bassanio not recognise her?

(ii) **To what is mercy compared in these lines?**
Why is mercy said to be 'twice blessed' ?

(iii) **Explain the lines:**
'Tis mightiest in the mightiest; it becomes
The throned monarch better than his crown?

(iv) **Later in her speech Portia mentions a sceptre. What is a sceptre?**
How, according to Portia, is mercy above the 'sceptred sway'?

(v) **To whom are these words addressed?**
What does the person say in response to Portia's words?
Portia is seen as the dramatic heroine of the play. Using references from the text mention any two aspects of her character that appeal to you most. **[2020]**

📋 Marking Scheme --

(i) • A court of justice OR Venice
• To resolve the case / save Antonio / help Bassanio's friend escape from the Jew's clutches. / to be the judge, lawyer / to act on Bellario's behalf
• She is disguised / in lawyer's robes / dressed as a man.

(ii) • To gentle **rain**
• It blesses the giver
• And the recipient

(iii) • Mercy in a powerful man makes him more powerful.
• Mercy is the most powerful weapon a powerful person can possess
• Mercy suits a king far better than a crown does.
(Synonyms of mightiest and becomes; explanation)
Becomes – looks better; attractive; suits

(iv) • Sceptre – a staff (rod; baton) held by a monarch/ symbol of his authority/ temporal power
• A Sceptre is a symbol of a ruler's earthly / worldly power - it inspires fear and dread/ symbol of awe and majesty.
• But mercy is an attribute of God / a Divine quality/ so when a ruler shows mercy, he is elevated above the level of earthly kings / raised to the level of God/ mercy has a seat in the hearts of Kings

(v) • To Shylock

• "My deed upon my head! / I crave the law ready to face consequences /

The penalty and forfeit of my bond/ let me have the penalty."

• Personal Response: Accept any two plausible traits

E.g.:

Obedient daughter - was willing to abide by father's casket test to choose life partner.

Clever / Quick Witted - At Antonio's trial... outwits Shylock using his own logic.

Sense of humour - the ring episode.

Tactful / wise / helpful / ingenuity / understanding / intelligent

(2 adjectives or 2 examples, or 1 adjective and 1 separate example).

Ans. **(i)** The scene takes place in the courtroom in Venice. Portia is here to argue the case on behalf of Antonio. Bassanio cannot recognize her as she is dressed as a lawyer, hiding her feminity.

(ii) Mercy is compared to the gentle rain from heaven. It blesses the person who shows mercy by way of getting happiness in the generous act, and the one who is at the receiving end, also benefits from the act. So, it is 'twice blessed.'

(iii) Portia says it is the best quality of a human. The powerful ruler becomes more powerful if instilled with this noble quality. It is the most powerful weapon that a powerful person can possess. It suits the king better than his crown which is the symbol of sovereignty. In fact, he acquires the status of God, the supreme power.

(iv) Sceptre is the insignia of kingship. It represents power. But the quality of mercy can sway power more effectively since it appeals to the heart of the subjects which make them love the ruler and owe allegiance to him without fear or compulsion.

(v) These words are addressed to Shylock who refuses to take back his claim. He says the law is on his side and he need not give any reason for his refusal. He insists on the justice of his cause. On the contrary, he is determined to ensure that the terms of the contract he made with Antonio are fulfilled to the letter.

Portia is gracious, with all the noble qualities a woman should have which endear her to all. She has tremendous love in her heart that prompts her to do everything that can make her husband Bassanio happy. It is her love and faithfulness which makes her follow the instructions of her father. Another quality that makes her stand out is her extraordinary intelligence which makes her quick-witted enough to win the case for Antonio. Her argument that Shylock can take a pound of flesh without dropping a drop of blood is a clever argument that turns the forfeit in favour of Antonio.

Q. 4. **Read the extract given below and answer the questions that follow:**

Bassanio: **To You, Antonio,**

I owe the most, in money and in love;

And from your love I have a warranty

To unburden all my plots and purposes

How to get clear of all the debts I owe.

Antonio: **I pray you, good Bassanio, let me know it;**

(i) Describe Antonio's mood at the beginning of this scene. State any two reasons that Antonio's friends, who were present, gave to explain his mood.

(ii) What promise did Antonio make to Bassanio immediately after this conversation?

(iii) What did Bassanio say to Antonio about 'a lady richly left' in Belmont?

(iv) Why was Antonio unable to lend Bassanio the money that he needed?

(v) What does the above extract reveal of the relationship between Antonio and Bassanio? Mention one way in which this relationship was put to the test later in the play. [2019]

Marking Scheme

(i) • Antonio's mood: sad/despondent/gloomy/depressed/melancholic/weary of the world, etc.

(Accept any word synonymous with the above) Salerio and Solanio say that Antonio's mind is on his rich merchant ships/tossing on the ocean

• Antonio was concerned/worried about possible misfortunes - Fear of tempests/mudflats/dangerous rocks that could wreck his ships

• Antonio must be in love

• Not happy because he was sad

• Antonio deliberately wants to appear wise/grave/philosophical *(Any two)*

(ii) • His 'purse' (wealth)/unlock wealth/resources
- His 'person' (himself)
- His 'extremest means' (every last resource in his possession)
- Extend every help he could (to help Bassanio as long as Bassanio's plans were as honourable as he himself was)

(iii) The 'lady richly left' in Belmont is described by Bassanio as:
- Beautiful (fair/fairer than the word)
- Virtuous (of wondrous virtues)
- Called Portia
- He had received 'fair speechless messages' sometimes from her eyes
- Her worth and fame attracted renowned suitors   *(Any three)*

He compares her to the golden fleece and her suitors to Jason(s) from Classical mythology.
- Sunny locks
- Not inferior to Portia – Cato's daughter/ Brutus' wife
- The world is not ignorant of her worth

(iv) • All his 'fortunes were at sea' (invested in his many merchant ships)
- Antonio has no money
- Has nothing of value (commodity) which he could sell to raise the money needed

Antonio proposes
- that both he and Bassanio should make enquiries among the wealthy merchants
- to see if they can borrow the money –
- (try what my credit in Venice can do)

(v) • Shows that Antonio and Bassanio were very *good* friends
- That Bassanio has always relied on Antonio both for financial (money) as well as emotional (love) support.
- Bassanio is assured of Antonio's love and care. Confides all his plans in him – clear all his debts with Antonio's help.
- Bassanio exploits Antonio's love/trust
- When Shylock demands his pound of flesh and Antonio is willing to sacrifice his life for Bassanio.
- When Bassanio receives Antonio's letter in Belmont, he is willing to drop everything – go to Venice
- When Bassanio agrees to give away the wedding ring given to him by Portia – and sacrifice his love (Portia) for Antonio.
- (Any mention of Antonio/Bassanio being willing to sacrifice anything for the other … wife/life, etc.)

Ans. **(i)** At the beginning of this scene, Antonio appeared to be sad and despondent. But he did not know the reason for his sadness. He said that he had no idea how he caught it, found it, or came by it, or what stuff it was made of and how it originated. This sadness had made him such an idiot that he had much trouble to know himself.

Salerio said that Antonio's mind was troubled with the thoughts of his ships that were being tossed on the ocean. He said that Antonio must be worried about the fate of his argosies that sail like signiors and rich burghers in the sea, overpeering the petty traffickers. Solanio further added that if he had such ships venturing at sea, the better part of his concerns would be hoping about his commercial gains from his trade with foreign countries. He further added that Antonio must be in love. Hence, he was sad.

(ii) Antonio requested Bassanio to tell him everything and promised him that if his plan was as honourable as him, his money, pursue he as a person, his uttermost resources-extremest means, all would lie unlocked for Bassanio. All his resources would be available for his dearest friend's disposal.

(iii) Bassanio said that there was a 'lady richly left' or inherited a big fortune in Belmont. She was beautiful, and more so because of her wondrous virtues. Sometimes, he had received speechless messages from her eyes. Her name was Portia and she was in no way inferior to Cato's daughter and Brutus' wife, Portia. The whole world was aware of her worth since renowned suitors set sail from the four directions to seek her hand. Praising her beauty, he said that her sunny locks hung on her forehead like the Golden Fleece.

So her house in Belmont can be suitably compared to the coast of Colchis to which many men used to sail in ancient times in quest of the golden fleece. He said that if he had enough wealth, he would have undoubtedly proved to be her successful suitor.

(iv) Antonio was unable to lend the money to Bassanio because all his fortunes were invested in the cargoes which his ships were carrying upon the sea. He neither had money, nor commodity to raise the present sum. He was as poor as Bassanio. Antonio asked Bassanio to go to Venice and contact some other merchant or money lender and borrow the required amount of money in the name of Antonio. Antonio was certain that Bassanio would be able to borrow the money through his trust or his sake.

(v) Antonio and Bassanio shared a deep bonding and their friendship was beyond measure. They both were loyal to each other and their relationship was based upon mutual trust and respect. Basanio has always relied on Antonio both for financial (money) as well as emotional (love) support. There was selfless love between the two.

The relationship was put to test later in the play when Antonio failed to repay the money that he borrowed from Shylock and was tried in the court of law. Antonio had made the bond for Bassanio's sake, putting his life at risk willingly just to lend him some money. Shylock wanted to extract a pound of flesh from Antonio's body as per the condition in the bond in case of failing to pay him back. Bassanio blamed himself for putting his friend in such a poor condition as Antonio had borrowed money for his dear friend. However, Portia intervened as the witty lawyer and saved his life.

Q. 5. **Read the extract given below and answer the questions that follow:**

Bassanio: **A gentle scroll. — Fair lady, by your leave; (Kissing her)**

I come by not, to give and to receive.

Like one of two contending in a prize,

That thinks he hath done well in people's eyes

Hearing applause and universal shout

Giddy in spirit, still gazing, in a doubt

Whether those peals of praise be his or no;

(i) **Where did Bassanio find the 'gentle scroll'? What 'prize' had bassanio just won?**

(ii) **Explain why Bassanio said he felt 'Giddy in spirit, still gazing, in a doubt'.**

(iii) **Shortly after this exchange, Portia gave Bassanio a ring as a token of her affection. What did the gift symbolise?**

(iv) **What assurance did Bassanio give her when he accepted the ring?**

(v) **What did Portia urge Bassanio to do when she learnt that his friend Antonio was in trouble? What aspect of her character is revealed through her words?**
[2019]

Marking Scheme

(i) • Inside the leaden Casket/the casket that contained Portia's portrait.
 • Portia's hand in marriage

(ii) Bassanio felt
 • 'Giddy'/light headed with relief/delighted/excited/happy that he had chosen the right casket.
 • 'Still gazing in a doubt' – dazed/not able to believe that he had made the right choice and won Portia
 • He had succeeded in a 'competition' where many had failed.
 • It had still not been validated/confirmed by Portia.
 (*Alternately* a paraphrase of the lines in the extract.)

(iii) The ring was symbolic –
 • a token that said that she was giving Bassanio control over her house/her servants/herself
 • Portia's trust/love/commitment/loyalty/possession/bond of marriage
 • If Bassanio loses the ring it means he does not love her (*Any three*)

(iv) Bassanio promises
 • When the ring parts from his finger
 • then his life would leave his body
 • Bassanio could be declared dead
 Or
 Bassanio + would die + before he parted with the ring.

(v) • Pay off the bond/offer twice or three times the sum to the Jew/pay 6000 and deface the bond/double 6000 and treble that/pay the debt 20 times over
  ▪ Marry her
  ▪ Leave for Venice immediately
  ▪ Use her wealth to pay off the debt and
  ▪ save Antonio from Shylock
  ▪ Bring Antonio back with him to Belmont.
  (*Any three*)
 • Personal response – any plausible trait e.g. loving wife/trusting/compassionate/willing to share her wealth helpful/caring, etc.

Ans. **(i)** Bassanio found the 'gentle scroll' in the leaden casket. He had just won Portia's hand in marriage as the 'prize', by choosing the right casket that contained Portia's portrait.

(ii) Bassanio felt 'Giddy in spirit, still gazing in a doubt' because he could not believe his fortune. He felt like one of the two people competing for a prize, and like the successful competitor, he thought that he had done well in people's eyes. However, hearing their applause and universal shout, he wondered if their praise was for him. He was doubtful if what he saw in front of his eyes was true until confirmed, signed, and ratified by Portia herself.

(iii) The ring had great significance between Portia and Bassanio because it was a symbol of their marriage. It not only symbolised trust and commitment between the two but also gave Basanio the authority over her house, her servants and even her own self. Portia gifted Bassanio the ring and asked him not to part with it. If he ever parted with it, or lost it, or gave it away, it would indicate that his love for her has come to an end.

(iv) Bassanio accepted the ring from Portia and assured her that if the ring parted from his finger, he would part from life. Then, she might be bold to say that Bassanio had ceased to live in this world. He assured her that he would never part with the ring unless death was the reason.

(v) Portia urged Bassanio to pay Shylock six thousand ducats and nullify the bond. In fact, he should pay shrewd Shylock double that amount; even triple it, before Bassanio's friend loses a hair because of him. She suggests him he should first go to the church and solemnize the marriage with her and then go to Venice to help his friend for he would have enough gold to pay such a petty debt twenty times over. She even requested Bassanio to bring his friend to Belmont after the debt is paid.

Portia was a woman of great strength and integrity. She valued love and friendship more than anything else. Her words revealed her kind and generous nature. She had immense capacity for love and human compassion. We could notice her sympathy towards Antonio through her words. Her love towards Bassanio made her surrender all her property to him spontaneously.

Q. 6. **Read the extract given below and answer the questions that follow:**

Duke: You hear the learn'd Bellario, what he writes:
And here, I take it, is the doctor come.
[Enter Portia, dressed like a Doctor of Laws]
Give me your hand. Come you from old Bellario?

Portia: I did, my lord.

Duke: You are welcome; take your place.
Are you acquainted with the difference
That holds this present question in the court?

(i) **Where is this scene set? Why was Portia there?**

(ii) **What reason had Bellario given for his absence? Whom had he sent in his stead?**

(iii) **Bellario's letter stated that he had taken some measures to prepare the 'young and learned doctor' to deal with the case. What were they?**

(iv) **What was the 'difference' between Shylock the Jew and Antonio the merchant that the Duke was unable to resolve?**

(v) **How does Portia succeed in saving Antonio? What does this reveal of her character?** [2019]

Marking Scheme ----------------

(i) A *court* (of justice)/in **Venice**
- To assist at Antonio's trial/to save Antonio from Shylock/from the bond he had signed with Shylock/to act as a lawyer/to help her husband save Antonio *(Any three)*
- he was very sick/ill
- Balthazar/a young doctor of Rome/Portia in disguise

(iii) • explained the details of the 'controversy' between Antonio and Shylock
- they had studied many law books together
- Bellario had given Balthazar his opinion/advice

(iv) • Antonio had borrowed three thousand ducats from Shylock for a period of three months.
- Antonio's ships had been lost at sea – he was bankrupt and unable to repay the debt.
- Shylock was adamant in demanding his pound of flesh – refusing all offers of money.

(v) Portia grants Shylock his bond but says:
- that not one drop of Antonio's blood must be shed – if it were then all his land and goods would be confiscated by the laws of Venice
- Shylock had to cut out exactly one pound of flesh – if he cut even the smallest bit in excess of pound Shylock would be put to death.
Personal Response: Any plausible answer such as - Portia proves that she is clever/quick-witted etc.

Ans. (i) The scene is set in the court of justice, in Venice. Portia was there disguised as the young lawyer, on behalf of the learned Bellario, to save Antonio from Shylock.

(ii) Bellario had given the reason of sickness for his absence. He wrote in the letter that he was very sick so he was sending a young doctor of Rome whose name was Balthazar.

He further wrote that he acquainted the young doctor with Antonio's case and they have consulted many law books and he had also told him his point of view about the case. In reality, Balthazar was none other than the mistress of Belmont, Portia herself, disguised as a young lawyer.

(iii) Bellario's letter stated that he had acquainted the young doctor of Rome, Balthazar with the cause of controversy between Shylock and Antonio. Moreover, they had consulted many books on law together. Balthazar was furnished with Bellario's opinion, bettered with his own learning. He requested the Duke to let the young doctor come in his place and told him not to let his young age be an obstacle in receiving a respectful consideration from him and his court for he had never known so young a person to be so intelligent.

(iv) Shylock had lent Antonio three thousand ducats on the condition that if he failed to repay the amount within three months, he would extract one pound of flesh from Antonio's body. Unfortunately, Antonia's ships got lost at the sea. He turned bankrupt and was unable to repay the debt. Despite several requests and pleadings, Shylock was determined to extract the flesh and hence Antonio was tried at the court of law. The Duke was unable to solve this 'difference' as Shylock was not ready to listen. He had requested Shylock to lose the forfeiture and moved by human gentleness and kindness, forgive Antonio's portion of the principal amount, on 'glancing an eye of pity on his losses'. He asked Shylock to draw compassion seeing Antonio's poor condition. However, Shylock had sworn by their holy Sabbath to have the penalty of the bond which was the pound of flesh and if the Duke denied justice, he threatened that the privileges enjoyed by his city and the freedom of his city would suffer much damage.

(v) Portia succeeds in saving Antonio by asking Shylock not to shed a single drop of blood while extracting the pound of flesh since it is not written in the bond. But if he sheds one drop of the Christian's or Antonio's blood, his lands and goods, by the laws of Venice, would be confiscated by the state of Venice. Also Shylock had to cut out exactly one pound of flesh. If he cut even the smallest bit over a pound, Shylock would be put to death. This made Shylock finally lose the trial.

This reveals Portia's immense courage and wisdom. Without being afraid, she bravely fights the trial and releases Antonio from the clutches of Shylock. She was no more the meek wife of Bassanio, but a fearless woman, full of wit and presence of mind.

Q. 7. **Read the extract given below and answer the questions that follow:**

Portia: Go draw aside the curtains, and discover
The several caskets to this noble prince—
Now make your choice.

Morocco: The first, of gold, who this inscription bears,
"Who chooseth me shall gain what many men desire".

(i) Who is Morocco? How did he introduce himself to Portia when they first met in an earlier scene?

(ii) How would Morocco know that he had made the right choice? What would his reward be?

(iii) Which casket did Morocco finally choose? What reasons did he give for rejecting the casket made of lead?

(iv) What two objects does Morocco find in the casket of his choice? What reason does he give to Portia for leaving in haste?

(v) How does Portia respond to Morocco's parting words? What does this reveal of her nature? **[2018]**

Ans. **(i)** Prince Morocco is a dark-skinned, boastful warrior of African origin, who seeks the hand of fair Portia. He introduces himself as a person who lives near the equator, where the exposure to sun rays have to be blamed for his complexion and Portia should not dislike him for it. He even says that his blood is as red as that of 'the fairest creature northward born'–that 'the best regarded virgins' of his land find him most attractive and his outward appearance inspired fear in the most courageous of men.

(ii) Morocco would know he has chosen the right casket, if he finds Portia's portrait in one of them. His reward would be Portia's hand in marriage.

(iii) Morocco chooses the golden casket. He says lead is of lowly origin and the portrait of a lady as great as Portia cannot be placed in it. He reads the inscription, "He who chooses me must give and risk all he has." This makes the lead casket too threatening. He wonders why should anyone risk everything for lead and that men would be prepared to take a risk only if there was a chance of winning 'fair returns'. He also feels that a golden mind like his should not bow down to choose something worthless. So, he will not risk anything for lead.

(iv) Morocco finds 'A Carrion Death', — an empty human skull and a scroll in the gold casket, which he chooses. Morocco says he is moved and that he does not want to make his departure a painstaking process and he wants to leave immediately without revealing his emotions. He is sad, disappointed and says, 'labour lost... farewell heat and welcome frost'.

(v) Portia is relieved that Morocco has left without making any scene. It was a gentle riddance and all like him should go in a similar manner. This shows that Portia has a kind heart and does not want anyone to be hurt. Her love for Bassanio overrides her passion that makes her wish that only he should be able to make the right choice. She also judges a person by outward appearances and does not wish to marry Morocco because of his dark skin and vain boastful attitude.

Q. 8. **Read the extract given below and answer the questions that follow:**

Bassanio: **Were you the doctor, and I knew you not?**
Gratiano: **Were you the clerk?**
Antonio: **Sweet lady, you have given me life and living;**
For here I read for certain that my ships
Are safely come to road.
Portia: **How now, Lorenzo!**
My clerk hath some good comforts too for you.

(i) **Where does this scene take place? What had Portia directed Antonio to give to Bassanio, just moments before the above words were spoken?**

(ii) **Portia had just given Antonio, Bassanio and Gratiano a letter to read. Who had written this letter? What does Bassanio learn about Portia from this letter?**

(iii) **What good news does Portia have for Antonio? How does he respond to it?**

(iv) **To whom does Portia refer as 'My clerk'? What 'good comforts' does the 'clerk' have for Lorenzo?**

(v) **How was Bassanio persuaded to give away the ring that Portia had given him at the time of their marriage? What does this reveal of Bassanio's relationship with Antonio?** **[2018]**

Ans. **(i)** The scene takes place in the avenue outside Portia's house in Belmont. Portia gave Antonio the ring she had given to Bassanio at the time of marriage. She had made him promise that he would not part with it on any account but her husband had given it to the lawyer who saved his friend Antonio from death.

(ii) Portia says the letter that came from Padua was written by Bellario, a lawyer. Bassanio learns that it was his wife who had pretended to be a lawyer and saved Antonio.

(iii) Portia gives the good news that Antonio will find three of his argosies at the harbour laden with rich cargo and hearing this, Antonio is too surprised to react. Antonio says, 'You have given me my life and my livelihood.'

(iv) Portia refers to Nerissa as 'My Clerk'. She says that she has a special gift for Lorenzo and Jessica, from the rich Jew. It is a special deed of gift which makes clear that after his death, all his possessions will be inherited by Jessica and Lorenzo.

(v) Portia who had played the role of a lawyer defending Antonio, had asked for the ring that Bassanio had received from her earlier as an appreciation of her role in saving his friend. Bassanio, at first refused to part with it saying his wife would be upset if he gave the ring away. He was supposed to keep it as a token of faith. Portia said, he was giving a lame excuse as all husbands do and pretended to be disappointed when Bassanio did not part with it even after she had saved his friend from the clutches of death. Antonio also persuaded him in the name of friendship and for the lawyer's service. Bassanio valued Antonio's friendship highly and could not refuse him. He was prepared to risk Portia's anger as Antonio was his dearest friend.

Q. 9. **Read the extract given below and answer the questions that follow:**

Why, look you, how you storm!
I would be friends with you and have your love,
Forget the shames that you have stain'd me with,

Supply your present wants, and take no doit
Of usance for my moneys, and you'll not hear
me:
This is kind I offer.

(i) Where does this scene take place? Who is the speaker? To whom is he talking?

(ii) What are the 'shames' which the speaker says have stained him?

(iii) What are the 'present wants'? Who is in need of the 'present wants'? Why?

(iv) Explain "This is kind I offer". What does the speaker propose to do immediately after this?

(v) What do you think of Antonio and of Shylock with regard to the signing of the bond? [2017]

Ans. (i) The scene took place in Venice. The speaker is Shylock. He was talking to Antonio.

(ii) Shylock says so because Antonio called him a non-believer, merciless dog and spat on his long Jewish robe. He had also mocked and abused him at the Rialto for the practice of charging interest.

(iii) The 'present wants' were a sum of money of three thousand Ducats. Bassanio was in need of them because he wanted to go to Belmont to present himself as a worthful suitor to woo Portia.

(iv) Assuring Antonio that he means to be friends, Shylock offers to make the loan without interest. He proposes to go to the notary and get Antonio to sign a single bond.

(v) Shylock is cunning, cautious and crafty. He belongs to a race which has been persecuted since its beginning. Antonio is easy-going, trusting, slightly melancholic, romantic and naïve.

Shylock trusts only in the tangible – that is, in the bond. Antonio trusts in the intangible, that is luck. Here, Shylock seems almost paranoid and vengeful, but on the other hand, Antonio seems ignorantly over-confident rather stupid because he is lacking common sense and maturity while dealing with such a large sum of money.

Q. 10. Read the extract given below and answer the questions that follow:

Portia: To these injunctions everyone doth swear

That comes to hazard for my worthless self.

Arragon: And so have I address'd me. Fortune now

To my heart's hope! – Gold, silver and base lead.

(i) Who had tried his luck in trying to choose the correct casket before the prince of Arragon? Which casket had that suitor chosen? What did he find inside the casket?

(ii) What are the three things Arragon was obliged by the oath to obey?

(iii) What was the inscription on the golden casket? How do the actions of the martlet illustrate this inscription?

(iv) Which casket does Arragon finally choose? Whose portrait does he find inside? Which casket actually contains Portia's portrait?

(v) Who enters soon after? What does he say about the young Venetian who has just arrived? What gifts has the Venetian brought with him? [2017]

Ans. (i) The Prince of Morocco tried his luck in choosing the golden casket before the Prince of Arragon.

He finds an empty human skull with a scroll in its hollow eye in which it is written that those who are attracted by the glittering outside of things are always deceived.

(ii) He promises Portia that he will abide by her father's rules, that:

He must never tell anyone which casket he had chosen. If he fails to choose the right casket, he will never court another woman; and he will leave Belmont immediately.

(iii) The inscription on the golden casket was, "Who chooseth me shall gain what many men desire".

The martlet is like the many men who choose by outward show or appearance; they do not see the inner worth of things.

(iv) Arragon chooses the Silver Casket.

He finds the portrait of a blinking idiot – a picture of a fool's head.

The lead casket contains Portia's portrait.

(v) After the departure of the Prince of Arragon, the servant announces that a young Venetian named Gratiana has arrived in order to announce the approach of his master Bassanio who has sent warm greetings and rich presents to Portia.

Q. 11. Read the extract given below and answer the questions that follow:

Portia: **As from her lord, her governor, her king.**

> **Myself and what is mine to you and yours**
>
> **Is now converted: but now I was the lord**
>
> **Of this fair mansion, master of my servants,**
>
> **Queen o'er myself; and even now, but now,**
>
> **This house, these servants, and this same myself,**
>
> **Are yours, my lord:**

(i) Where are Portia and Bassanio? What has just taken place which makes Portia to speak these words? What was the inscription given in the lead casket?

(ii) What does Bassanio say in praise of Portia's portrait?

(iii) What news saddens Bassanio on this happy occasion? What does Portia ask him to do?

(iv) Who is Balthazar? What was the work assigned to him by Portia?

(v) Where does Portia really plan to go? What similarity do we find between Portia and Antonio? What does this scene reveal about the character of Portia? Give a reason to justify your answer.   [2016]

Ans. **(i)** Portia and Bassanio are in a room in Portia's house, in Belmont.

Bassanio had selected the right casket, the lead one and had won Portia's hand in marriage.

The inscription given in the lead casket was:

'Who chooseth me must give and hazard all he hath.'

(ii) Bassanio feels that the picture is so lifelike that only a demi-god could have painted it. He looks at the portrait and exclaims, "Fair Portia's counterfeit!" He wonders if her eyes are moving or if they seem to move along as his eyes move. He notices that her sweet breath forces her lips open a lovely divider of lovely lips. He then says that the painter was like a spider in creating her hair that looks like a golden mesh to trap the hearts of men, like little flies in cobwebs. Furthermore, he wonders how could the painter kept looking at her eyes for so long while painting them. Bassanio would have expected that when the painter finished one of them, it would have enraptured him and kept him from painting the other. Then he realizes that he is giving only a faint praise to the picture, just as the picture itself, as according to him it is just an imitation of the real woman herself.

(iii) The news of Antonio's failed ventures saddens Bassanio. He receives a letter from Antonio stating that all his ships had got lost at sea. He had turned bankrupt and was unable to repay the debt. Despite several requests and pleadings, Shylock was determined to extract the flash and hence he was to be tried at the court of law.

Portia asks Bassanio to haste to the rescue of Antonio after solemnizing their marriage. She asks him to pay as much gold as possible to nullify the bond and then bring back Antonio to Belmont after everything is settled.

(iv) Balthazar is a servant in Portia's household.

Portia assigns Balthazar the task of carrying a letter to her cousin, Doctor Bellario, in Padua with all haste and to bring back at the earliest whatever the papers and clothes the latter gives him. Finally, he was to meet her at the common ferry that would carry her to Venice.

(v) Portia plans to go to Venice.

The similarity between Antonio and Portia is that they both love Bassanio unconditionally and can go to any extent to help him whenever he is in distress. Portia is graceful throughout the play with her poise, nobility, presence of mind, courage to execute plans and elegance. From this scene, it is revealed that Portia is a very practical and intelligent woman who is also concerned about the well-being of others. We see that she is able to take quick decisions and dares to act in a way which a normal lady would not even think about. She is not ready to sit back and see actions happen around her, rather, she becomes the centre of actions.

Q. 12. Read the extract given below and answer the questions that follow:

But mercy is above this sceptred sway;

It is enthroned in the hearts of kings,

It is an attribute to God himself;

And earthly power doth then show likest God's

When mercy seasons justice.

(i) **Name the speaker. Why did the speaker appeal to the Jew for mercy? Earlier who else in the play appealed for mercy?**

(ii) **What are the three qualities of mercy which the speaker has stated just before the extract?**

(iii) **Give the meaning of 'But mercy is above this sceptred sway'. How does Shylock turn down Portia's plea for mercy? What does he insist on?**

(iv) **What is Bassanio ready to do for Antonio in the court? Why is Bassanio snubbed immediately by the disguised Portia?**

(v) **Mention two prominent character traits of Shylock as highlighted through the scene from which the extract has been taken. Substantiate your answer with examples from the text.** **[2016]**

Ans. **(i)** The speaker of the above lines is Portia, disguised as a 'doctor of law'.

Portia appealed to the Jew for mercy in order to save the life of Antonio, her husband's friend. Shylock asks why he must show mercy towards Antonio, to which Portia responds that 'the quality of mercy is not strained' but is a blessing to both; those who provide and those who receive it. She further says that mercy is an attribute of God, and humans approach the divine when they exercise it.

Earlier in the play, the Duke also begged for mercy.

(ii) Just prior to the extract, the three qualities of mercy that Portia speaks of are that the quality of mercy is not strained; mercy drops from heaven just like the gentle rain; and that mercy is twice blessed.

(iii) This line means that mercy is much more powerful than the power wielded by the swords of kings and monarchs.

Shylock remains deaf to reason and turns down Portia's plea for mercy by insisting that justice should be given to him by extracting the penalty for the forfeiture of the bond executed by him.

(iv) Bassanio is ready to give twice the sum or ten times over the sum. He says that he is ready to sacrifice his life, and even his wife Portia for Antonio.

The disguised Portia snubs Bassanio because with his declaration, he had hurt her feminine sentimentality.

(v) The scene shows that Shylock has an obstinate mindset and is not ready to make any compromises when the question of taking revenge arises. He is, therefore, a vindictive person who is bound to take revenge at any cost. He is pitiless and evil in his thirst for revenge.

In this trial scene, Shylock's cruel mind finds its expression not only in demanding a pound of flesh of Antonio, but also in the way he whets his knife.

Q. 13. **Read the extract given below and answer the questions that follow:**

Portia: ....**But this reasoning is not in the fashion to choose me a husband. O me, the word "choose"! I may neither choose whom I would, nor refuse whom I dislike; so is the will of a living daughter curbed by the will of a dead father. Is it not hard, Nerissa, that I cannot choose one, nor refuse none?**

(i) **What test had Portia's father devised for her suitors? What oath did the suitors have to take before making their choice?**

(ii) **Who is Nerissa? What does she say to cheer up Portia?**

(iii) **Why does Portia disapprove of the County Palatine? Whom would she rather marry?**

(iv) **How, according to Portia, can the Duke of Saxony's nephew be made to choose the wrong casket? What do these suitors ultimately decide? Why?**

(v) **Whom does Portia ultimately marry? Who were the two other suitors who took the test? Why, in your opinion, is the person whom she marries worthy of her?** **[2015]**

Ans. **(i)** Portia's father, the Lord of Belmont, devised the scheme of the three caskets of gold, silver and lead for her suitors. There were inscriptions on all the three caskets. The one who chooses the right casket, could marry Portia.

The oath which the suitors had to take before making the right choice was that they will not reveal it to anyone, which casket they had chosen and also they will not woo any other woman for the purpose of marriage in their life.

(ii) Nerissa is Portia's lady-in-waiting.

To cheer up Portia, Nerissa states that her father was a very virtuous man. She added that such Holy men have divine guidance on their deathbeds and so he had devised the will of three caskets. She further assures Portia that the right casket will be chosen by the person who loves her and not her money.

(iii) Portia disapproves of the County Palatine by describing him as sullen and morose. She further says that he listens to jovial stories without a smile. She is afraid that he will become a sad philosopher like Heraclitus, when he grows old because he is so unusually gloomy at his young age. Also, he has an abrupt manner when he speaks. Portia would rather be married to a grinning skeleton with a bone in his mouth.

(iv) Portia tells Nerissa to place a tall goblet of Rhenish wine on the wrong casket, that is, the casket which does not contain her picture. Portia is sure that the German suitor will not be able to resist the temptation of this national drink even if the picture of the Devil himself is within.

These suitors ultimately decided to leave Portia and go back home, and not press their courtship further, unless her father's decree concerning the caskets can be set aside, and they may woo her in an ordinary way.

(v) Portia will ultimately get married to Bassanio.

The other two suitors who took the test were the Prince of Morocco and the Prince of Arragon.

Bassanio is worthy of Portia because he was truthful and was not swayed by external appearences, moreover, she was already in love with Bassanio.

Q. 14. Read the extract given below and answer the questions that follow:

Duke: **What, is Antonio here?**

Antonio: **Ready, so please your grace.**

Duke: **I am sorry for thee: thou art come to answer**

A stony adversary, an inhuman wretch

Uncapable of pity, void and empty

Form any dram of mercy.

(i) What are the terms of the bond that Antonio has signed?

(ii) Why does the Duke call Shylock 'inhuman'? What does the Duke expect Shylock to do?

(iii) What reason does Shylock give for choosing rotten flesh over money? What are the things hated by some people?

(iv) State three examples Antonio gives to illustrate Shylock's stubborn attitude.

(v) How is Shylock's property distributed at the end by Antonio?

Do you think Shylock deserves the punishment given to him?

Give a reason to justify your answer.
[2015]

Ans. **(i)** The terms of the bond that Antonio has signed were that, if Antonio is unable to repay Shylock three thousand ducats within three months in an agreed place, the forfeit to be paid will be an exact pound of Antonio's flesh which Shylock will be at liberty to take from any part of his body which pleases him.

(ii) The Duke calls Shylock 'inhuman' as in spite of Duke's attempt to make Shylock show mercy on Antonio, Shylock intended to keep up this show of severity and hatred until the last stage of the case. To kill Antonio ruthlessly, Shylock keeps demanding a pound of his flesh as per the bond.

The Duke expects that Shylock will give a sympathetic reply to his appeal. He makes fun of the Jew and pays him a compliment that he possesses a 'gentle' heart and not a stony heart like the 'stubborn Turks and Tartars'. His object is to pacify him.

(iii) When Portia tells Shylock that thrice his money has been offered to him, Shylock tells her that he has sworn an oath before God to have nothing but his bond. He cannot commit the sin of breaking the oath, nor for the whole wealth of Venice will break his oath. He further says, he has fancy for the rotten flesh, that should satisfy him.

There are some people who cannot tolerate the sight of an open-mouthed roasted pig. Some people get almost frantic by the sight of a cat. Still others feel infuriated to hear the scream of the bag-pipe. These are the things hated by some people.

(iv) Antonio tells Bassanio that if he is hoping to soften Shylock's heart, he might as well stand on the seashore and ask the tide not to rise so high as usual. Further, he may as well ask the wolf why he has made the mother sheep to mourn for the lamb he has devoured. Furthermore, he may as well expect the tall pines in the hillside not to wave their high tops and not to make a noise when they are disturbed by the gales of Heaven.

These three examples clearly prove that if Bassanio tries to melt the hard heart of the Jew, his pleas will stand ineffective.

(v) Antonio distributed Shylock's property by asking if the Court remits the fine in place of one half of Shylock's goods which comes to the state; provided that, Shylock draws up a will leaving this half, which he retains during his lifetime, to Lorenzo and Jessica after his death and that he must convert to Christianity.

Antonio will hold the half awarded to him in trust also for the benefit of Lorenzo and Jessica. He will give them money regularly until Shylock dies. Then he will give it all to them.

Yes, Shylock deserves the punishment given to him as he was surrounded by so much malice and hatred that he was ready to take Antonio's life to satisfy himself. Shylock's obsession with revenge breaks down only when his intention to kill Antonio is thwarted and utter destitution threatens him. His sense of reality returns. He exclaims that there is no point in pardoning his life if the wealth and property that sustains it, is taken away. He also becomes greedy for money and asks for his three thousand ducats.

Q. 15. **Read the extract given below and answer the questions that follow :**

Bassanio: **Be assured you may.**

Shylock: **I will be assured I may; and that I may be assured, I will bethink me. May I speak with Antonio?**

Bassanio: **If it please you to dine with us.**

Shylock: **Yes, to smell pork; to eat of the habitation which your prophet the Nazarite conjured the devil into. I will buy with you, sell with you, talk with you, walk with you, and so following; but I will not eat with you, drink with you, nor pray with you. What news on the Rialto? Who is he comes here?**

(i) **Where are Bassanio and Shylock at this time?**

What is the purpose of their meeting?

(ii) **Why does Bassanio say, "Be assured you may?"**

What has Shylock said earlier about Antonio's ventures?

(iii) **What reply does Shylock give to Bassanio's invitation?**

(iv) **What does Shylock say 'aside' about Antonio when he enters the scene?**

(v) **What biblical allusion does Shylock make while speaking to Bassanio in the extract?** **[2002]**

Ans. **(i)** Bassanio and Shylock are in a public place in Venice. Bassanio has come to ask Shylock whether he would lend three thousand ducats for which Antonio would stand as surety.

(ii) Bassanio asks Shylock to be assured of the return of his loan, as a guarantee from Antonio. Shylock is hesitant and says that since Antonio's merchandise is in various ships, and anything may happen to the ships.

(iii) Shylock replies to Bassanio that he cannot accept the invitation because it is the principle of Jews not to dine with the Christians. They eat pork which is forbidden for Jews.

(iv) Shylock hates Antonio and says in the aside that he looks like a fawning tax-collector. He hates him because he is a Christian and also because he foolishly lends money without interest thereby affecting his business in Venice. He has now got a chance to catch Antonio upon the hip if he fails to pay the borrowed money in time.

(v) Shylock narrates a biblical story which says that when Jacob, the prophet, goes to look after the sheep of his uncle Leban, an agreement is made between the two. It is decided that Jacob would receive all the lambs born with spots and stripes. During breeding season, Jacob places wooden rods on the ground, so that their shadows would fall on the sheep. Almost all the lambs are born with spots and stripes and Jacob profits by his trick. He does this in order to justify his practice of charging.

Q. 16. **Read the extract given below and answer the questions that follow :**

Shylock: **My deeds upon my head ! I crave the Law,**
The penalty and forefeit of my bond.

Portia: **Is he not able to discharge the money ?**

Bassanio: **Yes, here I tender it for him in the court;**
Yea, twice the sum :..............
..............And, I beseech you,
Wrest once the law to your authority:

> **To do a great right, do a little wrong,**
> **And curb this cruel devil of this will.**

(i) **Where are Shylock, Bassanio and Portia at this time? Why are they there? Why does Shylock say, "My deeds upon my head!"?**

(ii) **What does Bassanio go on to say immediately after "Yea, twice the sum"?**

(iii) **What does Bassanio mean by, "Wrest once the law to your authority; to do a great right, do a little wrong"? What reply does Portia give?**

(iv) **How does Shylock react to Portia's reply? Who reacts in a similar way as Shylock, later in the scene? What does that person say when Portia asks Shylock to "Down therefore and beg mercy of the duke"?**

(v) **What is your opinion of Shylock in this scene?** [2002]

Ans. (i) Shylock, Bassanio and Portia are at the trial court of Justice in Venice. Shylock is there to make sure that the penalty of a pound of flesh is levied on Antonio. Bassanio is there to save his friend Antonio by paying three times the actual amount taken and Portia is in the court in disguise of a lawyer to defend Antonio in the case.

Portia tells Shylock the importance of mercy and how it is a quality of God. She also tries to convince him to give up the case and consider being merciful. On this, Shylock tells her that 'his deeds are upon his head' which means that he alone is responsible for whatever he does.

(ii) Immediately after Bassanio says to Shylock that he is ready to pay twice the sum, he adds that if that doesn't suffice him, he is ready to pay ten times the actual amount and sign a contract by giving his hands, head and heart as security. And even if that doesn't appeal to him then it is evident that he is malicious.

(iii) Bassanio requests the Duke of Venice to use his authority to alter the law in this case. He pleads mercy for Antonio from the Duke and requests him to do a great right by doing a little wrong. To this, Portia replies that it can never happen as no power can change the already established law. She also tells him that even if it is recorded as precedent, the repercussions would set a bad example in the state.

(iv) Shylock is all in admiration for Portia in disguise. He calls her Daniel because to him she is fair.

Gratiano reacts in a similar way later when Portia warns Shylock that if he takes even a strand of hair more than what is in the contract, he would lose all his property.

Gratiano tells Shylock to beg to be hung by the state because he wouldn't be left without money to buy a rope for himself.

(v) This scene begins with Shylock's mercilessness towards Antonio. He is shown as a ruthless man and how much he hates Antonio. He is often labeled as a wretch and inhuman and these words seem to befit him. Later, when Portia announces that he would have to pay half the property to Antonio and the other half to the state, we find him left all alone among his enemies and a victim of prejudice.

Q. 17. Read the extract given below and answer the questions that follow:

Portia: **But mercy is above this sceptred sway,**
> **It is enthroned in the hearts of kings,**
> **It is an attribute to God himself;**
> **And earthly power doth then show likest**
> **God's**
> **When mercy seasons justice.**

(i) **Why does Portia speak about mercy in the extract?**

(ii) **Give the meaning of the following:**
But Mercy is above this sceptred sway,
It is enthroned in the hearts of kings.

(iii) **Who else had appealed for mercy earlier? What was the outcome of the appeal?**

(iv) **One should stand for justice. Referring only to the extract, state why, according to Portia, mercy should season justice.**

(v) **When Shylock refuses to show mercy, what legal tactics does Portia use to free Antonio?** [2001]

Ans. (i) Portia finds Shylock's case the most unusual one. She tells Shylock to show mercy as a first step before arguing the case for Antonio. Portia finds there is no logical reason behind the bond. However, Shylock is adamant on having the bond fulfilled to satisfy himself and his thirst for revenge. Therefore she gives Shylock an opportunity to alter the bond.

(ii) A King's sceptre is a symbol of authority and power but mercy is greater than the King's sceptre. Mercy occupies a lofty place in the hearts of kings. It is an essential quality of God. So, the king then acquires a divine quality when he gives mercy.

(iii) Bassanio had appealed for mercy earlier. He tried to reason out and negotiate with Shylock by saying that he could not kill just because he disliked someone. He also explained that disliking and hating were entirely different. But Shylock was least affected by all that and it only added fuel to the fire. A little later, Bassanio also offered double the amount of the loan but that too did not soften Shylock's heart and he impatiently awaited for his joyous moment of taking a pound of flesh from Antonio's heart.

(iv) According to Portia, Mercy is an attribute of God himself. One must stand for justice because it is right. When a king adds the flavour of mercy to his justice, he acts in accordance with the God's will and nature. Therefore, she says that "mercy seasons justice".

(v) When Shylock refuses to show mercy, Portia examines the contract and announces that no law could stop Shylock from taking a pound of flesh from Antonio's heart. She further tells Shylock to arrange for a surgeon so that Antonio's wounds are dressed immediately and he may not die. Shylock is slightly perplexed at this and declares that it has not been written in the bond. Later, Portia also demands that not a drop of blood must ooze out of Antonio's body. She uses this tactic to throw Shylock in a fix and free Antonio.

Q. 18. **Read the extract given below and answer the questions that follow:**

Lorenzo: **Madam, with all my heart,**

> **I shall obey you in all fair commands.**

Portia: **My people do already know my mind,**

> **And will acknowledge you and Jessica**

> **In place of Lord Bassanio and myself.**

> **So fare you well till we shall meet again.**

(i) **Where are Lorenzo and Portia at this time? What 'fair commands' are given to Lorenzo?**

(ii) **How does Lorenzo describe Portia in the beginning of the scene?**

(iii) **What does Portia say to Lorenzo about the place where she is going? Where is she actually going and why?**

(iv) **What order does Portia give to Balthazar a little later?**

(v) **What information does Portia give to Nerissa? (In what mood is Portia when she is speaking to Nerissa?)** **[2001]**

Ans. **(i)** Lorenzo and Portia are at Belmont.

Portia reveals to Lorenzo that she has sworn to contemplate in prayer at a monastery around two miles away, until her husband returns from Venice. She tells him that Nerissa would accompany her and asks him to manage the house with Jessica till things are settled. In response, Lorenzo tells her that he would be obliged to do whatever she asks him to do.

(ii) After Bassanio departs to rescue his beloved friend, Antonio, Lorenzo tells Portia that he stands in admiration for her noble respect for friendship and the way she has perfectly understood the bond of friendship between Bassanio and Antonio.

(iii) Portia tells Lorenzo that she would live a life of contemplation and pray at a monastery which is two miles away from their place. But in reality, Portia plans to go to Venice in disguise with Nerissa and argue the case in defence of Antonio. She is very sure that her plan would succeed.

(iv) After asking Lorenzo to manage the house, Portia orders her servant Balthazar to go to Padua, as quickly as possible, where he is supposed to meet her cousin Bellario, a doctor of law by profession. She tells him to bring them clothes and letters which he would give him on the ferry that goes to Venice without wasting any time.

(v) Portia informs Nerissa that they would see their husbands at the trial without their knowledge. She also tells her of her plan to go in men's disguise and follow Bassanio and Gratiano to Venice.

While speaking to Nerissa about her plans to argue the case in Antonio's defence, Portia is excited. She is also in a mood of adventure and is thrilled to flaunt her capability in presenting her arguments for a fair trial.

Q. 19. **Read the extract given below and answer the questions that follow:**

Portia: **O me the word 'choose' ! I may neither choose who I would nor refuse who I dislike; so is the will of a living daughter curbed by the will of a dead father.**

(i) Where are Portia and Nerissa? Why are they there?

(ii) Earlier, in what way did Nerissa try to cheer Portia? What was Portia's reaction to what Nerissa had said?

(iii) State in your own words what Portia means by 'the will of a living daughter curbed by the will of a dead father.'

(iv) Immediately after this extract, what reasons does Nerissa give to Portia to justify 'the will of a dead father'? Do you think that the justification proved correct? Give reasons for your answer.

(v) Towards the end of the scene, Portia affirms that she must abide by 'the will of a dead father'. What does she say? From what she says, what opinion do you form of her? **[2000]**

Ans. **(i)** Portia and Nerissa are in Portia's house in Belmont. Portia does not like any of her suitors and they are in the room to discuss the events of the day and evaluate each suitor.

(ii) When Portia complained that she was tired of that world, Nerissa told her that 'being tired' was for those whose luck was bad and with all the wealth and good luck, Portia shouldn't be tired at all. Nerissa also told Portia that too much of anything was bad as they suffered more than those who did not have anything. She advised Portia that one could seek happiness if they had enough to live longer.

Portia was pleased with Nerissa's attempt at cheering her up. She saw a point in what Nerissa said and appreciated her for the way she tried to uplift her spirit.

(iii) Portia's father made a will for her daughter which states that she cannot marry a man of her choice but the one who chooses the right casket from among the three caskets of gold, silver and lead. It is her father's wish that Portia should abide by the will.

Since Portia cannot choose her husband and can only go by her luck with the caskets, she exclaims that her will to choose her partner was curbed by the will written by her late father.

(iv) In order to justify 'the will of a dead father', Nerissa explains to Portia that her father was a virtuous man and such people who are inclined to religion acquire odd ideas on their deathbeds. Nerissa justifies that her father's idea behind such a game is to select the right man for Portia. She also assures Portia that only the one who deserves her love would be able to choose the right casket. This actually proves true as Bassanio who is a true lover chooses the right casket while others due to their self-love and vanity fail to win her.

(v) When Nerissa tells Portia not to worry about the suitors as they have preferred to stay from her unless there is another way of marrying her, Portia feels that even if she lives like Sybil who has been granted eternal life, she prefers to die a virgin like Diana. There is no option for her but to abide by her father's will, if at all she has to marry.

This shows that Portia is an obedient daughter and is respectful towards her father. This decision of hers tells us that she is loyal in her relationships and law-abiding. Her conversation with Nerissa also throws light on her capability to reason out things and be practical.

Q. 20. **Read the extract given below and answer the questions that follow :**

Shylock: **How now Tubal ! What news from Genoa ? Hast thou found my daughter ?**

Tubal: **I often came where I did hear of her, but cannot find her.**

(i) Who is Tubal? What has been said about him a little earlier in the scene?

(ii) What does Shylock say in response to Tubal's words: 'but I cannot find her'?

(iii) What information does Tubal now give to Shylock concerning Antonio? State what Shylock tells Tubal expressing his reaction to what the latter has said.

(iv) What instructions does Shylock give to Tubal at the end of their meeting?

(v) What is your impression of Shylock as a father? Give reasons to justify your answer. **[2000]**

Ans. **(i)** Tubal is a wealthy Jew and a friend of Shylock's. A little earlier, Tubal enters the scene wherein Salerio, Solanio and Shylock are in a discussion. As soon as Solanio sees Tubal entering in, he comments satirically that one cannot find another Jew like these two unless the devil himself turned into a Jew. His comment implies that together they made themselves the worst of Jews, Shylock being a moneylender and Tubal being a loyal friend to him.

(ii) Tubal tells Shylock that he could not find Shylock's daughter, Jessica, in spite of tracing her to Genoa and other places where he has heard about her. In response, Shylock speaks about his losses. He considers the material loss such as the diamonds and ducats more significant than his daughter. He also wishes to see his daughter dead with those jewels. Shylock's response throws light on his mindset and his obsession for material wealth.

(iii) Shylock is grieving over his loss when Tubal informs him that even Antonio has got bad luck and that his ship is wrecked which was returning from Tripolis. On hearing this, Shylock is excessively relieved and with a revengeful laughter, thanks him for the good news.

(iv) At the end of the meeting, Shylock instructs Tubal to find him a police officer to get Antonio arrested. He instructs him to intimate Antonio two weeks in advance so that he can repay the loan. He also tells him that if he fails to do so in those two weeks, he would be glad to take a pound of his flesh and thus flourish in his business at Venice. Lastly, he tells Tubal to meet him at the synagogue later.

(v) Shylock is very obsessive of his wealth more than his daughter only expresses his sorrow and anger over his daughter's treachery by grieving about the lost diamonds and ducats. This gives us an impression that Shylock is materialistic and is least bothered about his daughter.

Q. 21. **Read the extract given below and answer the questions that follow :**

Portia : **Go, draw aside the curtains, and discover**
The several caskets to this noble prince.
(The curtains are drawn back)
Now make your choice.

Portia : **Some god direct my judgement !**
Let me see :
I will survey the inscriptions back again.

(i) **Where are Portia and Morocco at this time?**

(ii) **Which are 'the several caskets' ? What are the inscriptions that Morocco has just read on 'the several caskets' ?**

(iii) **Why does Morocco say : 'Some god direct my judgement !' ? What are the conditions Morocco had to abide by, before making his choice of the caskets ?**

(iv) **Morocco later says, 'As much as I deserve'. What does he deserve ?**

(v) **Which casket does Morocco finally choose ? What two reasons does he give for his choice ? What do these reasons reveal about his character ?**

(vi) **State clearly what you feel for Morocco at the end of this scene.** **[1999]**

Ans. **(i)** Portia and Morocco are in a room in Portia's house in Belmont.

(ii) There are three caskets made up of—gold, silver and dull lead. The inscription on the gold one reads 'who chooseth me shall gain what many men desire'.

The inscription on the silver one reads 'who chooseth me shall get as much as he deserves'.

The inscription on the casket made of lead reads, 'who chooseth me must give and hazard all he hath'.

(iii) Morocco is Portia's suitor and he wants to win her hand by choosing the right casket. He feels that making the right choice depends on good luck too. Therefore he prays that God may help him in making the correct choice.

The conditions Morocco has to abide by before making his choice of the caskets are :

(a) If he chooses the wrong casket, he can never speak to Portia again.

(b) He can never propose marriage to any woman thereafter.

(iv) Morocco reads the inscription on the gold casket and then repeats 'As much as I deserve'. According to him, he deserves the fair lady because of his noble birth, natural virtues, and education.

(v) Morocco finally chooses the golden casket. The reasons he gives for his choice are :

(a) Portia is like a gem and a gem of that value and beauty is always set in the precious metals of all—Gold.

(b) He says that in England a figure of an angel is engraved upon a gold coin. Similarly, Portia who too is an angel lies inside the golden casket.

These reasons tell us that Morocco is a man who believes only in superficiality. For him, everything that glitters is gold. He always take things at their face value and his judgement never run deep.

(vi) We feel that Morocco is a pompous fool who should never have chosen the golden casket in the first place. However, there is also a feeling of pity for Morocco who loves Portia dearly and wanted to win her.

Q. 22. Read the extract given below and answer the questions that follow :

Duke : With all my heart : some three or four of you

Go give him courteous conduct to this place. (Exeunt Officers)

Clerk
(reads): 'Your grace shall understand that at the receipt of your letter I am very sick, but in the instant that your messenger came, in loving visitation was with me a young doctor of Rome; his name is Balthazar. I acquainted him with the cause in controversy between the Jew and Antonio the Merchant ....'

(i) Who is referred to as 'him' in the second line of this extract ? Why has this person come to this place ?

(ii) What is meant by 'courteous conduct to this place' ?

(iii) Who is Dr. Bellario ? Why did the Duke send a messenger to him ? What request does Dr. Bellario make to the Duke regarding the 'young doctor of Rome' at the end of his letter ?

(iv) What is meant by 'controversy' ? How did the controversy arise ?

(v) What does the 'young doctor of Rome' say about the nature of the controversy a little later ? What request does the 'young doctor of Rome' make to Shylock regarding the 'controversy' ?

(vi) From what happens later in this scene, what is your opinion of the 'young doctor of Rome' ? Give a justification for your opinion. **[1999]**

Ans. **(i)** The learned doctor Balthazar who is actually Portia is referred to as 'him' in the second line of the extract. This person has come to defend Antonio in the trial scene against Shylock.

(ii) The Duke instructs the assistants to cordially bring Dr. Balthazar to court.

(iii) Dr. Bellario is a lawyer of good repute and is also Portia's cousin. The Duke has sent a letter to him to defend Antonio in court and put some sense into Shylock's head. At the end of the letter, Dr. Bellario requests the Duke to contest the trial and not let his young age be taken as a hindrance in his competence.

(iv) Controversy is an altercation between two or more parties on some major issue. This controversy is between Antonio and Shylock.

Antonio, a moneylender himself had borrowed three thousand ducats from Shylock. Shylock who hated Antonio cleverly manipulated the situation. He made Antonio sign a contract to the effect that if he failed to repay the borrowed money with interest during the stipulated period, Shylock would cut off a pound of flesh from Antonio's body in lieu of payment.

Since Antonio was unable to pay the debt within the stipulated period of time, Shylock wanted his pound of flesh. Naturally, everyone was against this inhuman act and thus it became a raging controversy.

(v) The 'young doctor of Rome' says that the controversy is of a rather strange nature. Dr. Balthazar requests Shylock to show some mercy and let him tear the bond.

(vi) The 'young doctor of Rome' Dr. Balthazar who is actually Portia in disguise is quite clever and intelligent. He turns the case to Antonio's advantage right under our noses. He manages to turn the tables on Shylock and in the end, it's Shylock who is begging for mercy since Portia charges him with an attempt to seek the life of a citizen and also gets his property confiscated by the court.

Poetry

A Collection of Poems

Q. 1. **Read the extract given below and answer the questions that fol low:**

> But a caged bird stands on the grave of dreams
> His shadow shouts on a nightmare scream
> His wings are clipped and his feet are tied
> So he opens his throat to sing.
> —*I Know Why the Caged Bird Sings,*
> **Maya Angelo**

(i) **In the context of the poem who is a 'free bird' and who is a 'caged bird'?**
What mood do the above lines convey?

(ii) **How does a free bird live his life?**
What are the things he thinks of and dreams about?

(iii) **What does the caged bird sing about?**
What are the restrictions that a caged bird has to deal with?

(iv) **What do you understand from the title of the poem?**
What do you like about the poem?

(v) **Explain what you understand by the following lines:**
  • **'.....a bird that stalks down his narrow cage'**
  • **'he names the sky his own'**   **[2020]**

🗒 Marking Scheme

(i) • Any person who is free to make life choices / white.
  • A person whose life is restricted by rules and laws imposed on them / black / African American
  • Desperation / frustration / defiance / sadness / horror / fear / suffering / pain / agony.
    (Any plausible answer)

(ii) • Free to do as he pleases / soars high / leaps / floats / dips wing / dares to claim the sky
  • Thinks of 'another breeze' / other places / good food 'fat worms' / enjoys trade winds soft / names the sky as his own.

(iii) Freedom / he craves / has never experienced / things unknown / still longs for them.
  • bars (of cage) / he can seldom see; restricted view
  • narrow cage / clipped wings / tied feet.

(iv) Title – Maya Angelou / autobiographical / Poet can empathise with a caged bird / feels the agony of black people / had suffered a traumatic childhood and therefore could identify and understand the condition of a bird in a cage. She understood what compels a bird in a cage to sing.
The caged bird represents those who are oppressed / indicates racial discrimination / discrimination based on gender / restrictions.
Personal Response: What do you like?
(Any plausible reason / aspect of the poem accepted)

(v) • . ... a bird that stalks down his narrow cage – paces / impatient / enraged by limitation of cage / bird represents people who are oppressed / African American not free / confined, helpless / can hardly move.
  • Names the sky his own – sense of freedom / without limit / claims the wide-open spaces / the sky belongs to him: he owns the sky / shows his courage and confidence.
    (Any other plausible response)

Ans. **(i)** The poem 'Why the caged bird sings' is a reflection on social disparity, and the ideals of freedom and justice. Angelou presents the inequality of justice seen in the society of her times which differentiated between the African-American community and its White American counterpart. Maya Angelou can be regarded as the caged bird in the poem, but she is also the representative of the 'blacks'.
The agony and cruelty of the oppression of marginalized communities and their anger expressed through the civil rights movement is the context of the poem.

(ii) The first stanza of the poem describes a free bird who is able to choose where he goes. When he rides the wind, enjoys the sun, and "dares to claim the sky", he is the ruler of his own destiny. He thinks about the big fat worms as he cuts through the breeze and trade winds. He spreads his wings as though he is the proprietor of the whole universe and sees the world and everything in it, as his own.

(iii) A caged bird sings of freedom which it cannot enjoy. The bird moves angrily and silently in a small cage and can barely see through either the cage bars or his own anger. His wings are cut so he cannot fly and his feet are tied together. He is restricted to enjoy the happiness of a free human. He cannot see the world outside, nor freely express his thoughts and feelings, nor have a say in matters that matter.

The oppression of the cage doesn't just keep the bird captive; the captivity changes the bird, and in doing so, robs the bird of its very self.

(iv) The title suggests the reason why the caged bird sings. It sings of its anguish at not being able to see beyond the cage. It is not only physical captivity but also mental agony as its mental sight is also limited by the anger it feels in the oppressing environment. This might be seen as the poet's message to raise our voice, to express ourselves even though the strong wants to suppress the weak and to never ever give up, no matter what situation we are in.

The contrast between freedom and oppression is expressed effectively in words that convey joy and misery. The juxtaposition brings out clearly the feelings of the poetess, who herself has been a victim of oppression. It subtly asserts that the anguish forced on black communities by white oppression must be acknowledged. It is the intense desire reflected through apt words that appeals to me the most.

(v) The caged bird struggles to be free but in vain. The cage is narrow and its confining bars fill it with rage. It is angry with its situation. Its wings are clipped, that is, its freedom is forcibly taken away. Wings that enable the bird to fly are associated with freedom. Its feet are tied. A bird tied to the ground represents an image completely opposite to its true nature, confirming the alienation from the actual world. But the most important thing is that despite being in this utterly despondent predicament, the caged bird 'opens his throat to sing.' That seems to be his only joy and achievement.

However, reflecting its freedom the free bird is the master of the sky. It dares to think of another breeze and the winds of change. It eagerly finds the "fat worms waiting on a dawn-bright lawn" even as he claims the sky is his own. This is exactly what the caged bird wants to do.

Q. 2. **Read the extract given below and answer the questions that follow:**
Abou Ben Adhem (may his tribe increase!)
Awoke one night from a deep dream of peace,
—*Abou Ben Adhem*, **Leigh Hunt**

(i) **What did Abou Ben Adhem see when he woke from a deep sleep one night?**

(ii) **What did Abou Ben Adhem ask the angel?**

What was the angel's response?

(iii) **What did Abou request the angel to do when he learnt that his name did not appear among the names of those who loved the lord?**

What does this reveal to us of Abou Ben Adhem's character?

(iv) **When and how did the angel appear to Abou Ben Adhem again?**

What did the angel show Abou this time?

(v) **What does the poet mean by 'May his tribe increase!'?**

Why do you think he says this? What is the central message of the poem? **[2020]**

📋 Marking Scheme -

(i) • room flooded with moonlight
• an angel
• writing in a golden book

(ii) • Abou Ben Adhem asked the angel what it was writing
• Angel replied: the **names** of those / **who love the Lord.**

(iii) • Abou asks angel to write his name as one who loves his fellow human beings
• Abou was a devout man – dedicated his life to the service of others.
• He served God by serving others / gentle/ kindness / saintly / noble / optimistic / humble / gentle / devout / pious / spiritual / humane / cheerful

(iv) • Next night
• In a blinding flash of **light** that awakened Abou.
• Abou's name at the top of the list of names of those / whom 'Love of God' had blest.

(v) • May there be more and more people like Abou Ben Adhem / more of his kind

> • The world needs more people who devote their lives to the service of others (**personal response**).
>
> Central message: The best way to show your love for God is to engage in service of your fellow human beings / love your neighbor / be kind / service to God will bless you.

Ans. **(i)** Abou woke up to see a room flooded with moonlight. An angel was writing in a book of gold.

(ii) "What writest thou?" asked Abou—The vision raised its head, and answered, "The names of those who love the Lord."

He asked whether his name is in the list and the angel said "Nay, not so".

Abou cheerily requested to write his name as "One that loves his fellow men".

(iii) He requested the angel to write him as one that loves his fellow men. It reveals that he is selfless in his approach; he loves his fellowmen more than himself. He sees God in them.

(iv) The next night the angel appeared again "With a great wakening light", He showed the names whom God has blessed, suprisingly, Abou found his name at the top of this list. "And lo! Ben Adhem's name led all the rest".

(v) The poet says there should be more lovers of fellow beings like Abou Ben Adhem. The world is full of egotistic and egocentric beings and there should be more humane characters. The central message of the poem is love and care for all. This endears to God more than selfish prayers and show of piety. The central idea of the poem "Abou Ben Adhem" is that God blesses and loves those who love and serve their fellowmen. If one wants to please God, one must serve one ' s brothers.

Q. 3. **Read the extract given below and answer the questions that follows:**

> There's nobody on the house-tops now......
> Just a palsied few at the windows set;
> For the best of the sight is, all allow,
> At the Shambles' Gate.......or, better yet,
> By the very scaffold's foot, I trow.
>
> —*The Patriot*, **Robert Browning**

(i) **Who is the speaker? Where is he being taken? Why?**

(ii) **Describe the scene when he had walked down the same street a year ago.**

(iii) **Where does the speaker think all the people had gathered that day?**

Why does he think so?

(iv) **Describe the speaker's physical condition.**

(v) **What is the centre message of the poem?**

Does the poem end on a note of hope or despair?

Give one reason for your answer. [2019]

Marking Scheme

(i) • The Patriot
   • to the gallows/Shambles' Gate/scaffold
   • to be hanged/he has lost favour/support of the people.

(ii) • Roses/myrtle/flowers strewn in his path/ Large crowds gathered on rooftops to catch a glimpse of him/it seemed as if the roof were heaving and swaying/ The church spires were ablaze with colourful flags/church bells were rung/ old walls rocked – signs of public adulation all round. (*Any three*)

(iii) • at the Shambles' Gate or at the foot of the gallows/scaffold
   • They would be assured of the best view – ringside view/to watch him being hanged publicly/the people were angry with him/No one on the rooftops, only palsied few at the windows (*Any two*)

(iv) He's drenched in the rain/His hands are tied behind his back/rope cuts into his wrist/blood trickles down his forehead/in pain caused by stones flung at him by people. (*Any three*)

(v) • Public adulation is short lived/people are fickle-minded.
   • Praise and glory are fleeting – do not last. (Either there must be *two separate points* or *one message + explanation*)
Personal Response:
   • Hope
   • the patriot believes that God will reward him according to his true merit or any other plausible reason.
          Or
   • Despair
   • Please accept any plausible reason – e.g. he is bitter and disillusioned – believes he did so much for the people, yet they did not appreciate all that he had done.

Ans. **(i)** The patriot is the speaker.

The patriot is being taken to the scaffold for his execution. He is being executed for his misdeeds. Nobody remembers what he had done for his countrymen now.

(ii) The patriot was given a grand welcome when he had walked down the street a year ago. Elaborate arrangements were made to welcome him as he returned from his grand victory in a war. His path was filled with roses and myrtles. The overcrowded house-roofs seemed to heave and sway in jubilation. The church towers blazed with victory flags. People went mad with frenzy.

(iii) A year ago, the people gathered in large numbers on their house-roofs to welcome the patriot and cheer him, but now he sees that no one is there for him except a few crippled watching him from their windows. Most of the people have gone to the "Shamble's Gate" or are near the scaffold to get a better view of his execution.

The patriot thinks that the people have forgotten what he did for them and are now full of contempt for him.

(iv) The present condition of the patriot is miserable. He is being taken to the scaffold for his execution. It's pouring heavily and he's completely drenched in the rain. A tight rope cuts his wrists behind. His forehead bleeds because of the stones hurled at him by the people. There is nobody on the house-tops now, just a few crippled watching him from their windows. All are at the Shambles' gate or by the very scaffold's foot to get a better view of his execution.

(v) The central idea of the poem revolves around the rise and fall of one's fortunes. The opinions of fickle-minded people change rapidly, without lending much thought to justice and truth. The patriot is initially worshipped and celebrated, the people go mad with frenzy to catch a glimpse of him but within a year he is taken down for execution. Justice is not meted out to him and he believes that real justice can only be delivered by God. The message of this poem also depicts a contrast between the fickleness of the public and the divine nature of God.

The poem ends on a note of hope and optimism because the patriot puts immense faith in the justice of God. He believes that God will give him his due rewards. He feels safer knowing that God knows he stood for what he thought was right and thus he will be safe in His hands.

Q. 4. **Read the extract given below and answer the questions that follows:**

All round the field spectators were gathered
Cheering on all the young women and men
Then the final event of the day was approaching
The last race about the begin.
—*Nine Gold Medals*, **David Roth**

(i) Where had the 'young women and men' come from?

What had brought them together?

He had they prepared themselves for the event?

(ii) What was the last event of the day?

How many athletes were participating in this event?

What signal were they waiting for?

(iii) What happened to the youngest athlete half way through the race?

How did he respond?

(iv) What 'strange' turn did the story take at this point?

(v) Why does the poet say that the banner—'Special Olympics' could not have been nearer the mark?

What human quality does the poem celebrate? **[2019]**

Marking Scheme ----------------

(i) • From many countries
• The desire to compete/prove themselves/win medals at the Special Olympics/participate in the Olympic games/to win glory for their country *(Any one)*
• Spent a long time/many weeks and months in training.

(ii) • The one hundred metres run
• Nine
• The sound of the gun/pistol

(iii) • Youngest athlete stumbled/staggered
• fell to the ground/on his knees
• Cried out in frustration and anguish/all his dreams and efforts had been 'dashed in the dirt.'

(iv) • The other eight athletes stopped in their tracks/one they turned round/came back helped him/lifted the lad to his feet/joined hands/walked to the finish line *(Any three)*

(iv) Poet uses Word play (pun)
• Special Olympics – races for people with special needs/specially abled athletes
• The actions of the athletes (*descriptions of the actions or a brief paraphrase of the poem*) made this event 'special' in a different sense – remarkable
• Their actions embodied the true spirit of sportsmanship and took it beyond the level of petty competition.
• Personal response – the human quality of cooperation/collaboration/compassion/caring etc.

Ans. **(i)** The young men and women had come from various countries to take part in the Special Olympics.

The event, Special Olympics, had brought them together. They had come to run for the gold, the silver, and the bronze.

The athletes had vigorously prepared for the event. They had spent many weeks and months in training, all building up to the games.

(ii) The last event of the day was the hundred metres race to be run by the athletes.

Nine athletes were participating in the event.

The participants were waiting for the sound of the gun. It was their signal to start the race.

(iii) The youngest among the athletes stumbled and staggered and fell on his knees to the ground.

He gave out a cry of frustration and anguish as all his dreams and efforts were dashed in the dirt.

(iv) When the youngest athlete fell down, the other eight athletes stopped in their track.

They turned around one by and one and came back to help him. They lifted the young lad to his feet. Then all the nine runners joined hands and continued. The one hundred metres race turned into a walk.

(v) The poet says that the banner- 'Special Olympics' could not have been nearer the mark because of the special incident that happened. All the eight runners came back to help the youngest athlete when he stumbled and staggered and fell on his knees to the ground. Without caring about the competition, all of them came back because of their human compassion and generosity. Hence, the event was 'special' in every way.

The poem celebrates the virtues of goodness and kindness. Their radiant display of warmth, affection, and companionship is what the poem celebrates. Their empathetic behaviour for their fellow athlete made them win everyone's applause and appreciation.

Prose

A Collection of Short Stories

Q. 1. Read the extract given below and answer the questions that follow :

So the little girl walked about the streets on her naked feet, which were red and blue with cold. In her old apron she carried a great many matches, and she had a packet of them in her hand as well.

  (i) Who was 'she'?

    What can you conclude about her condition from the above description?

 (ii) What time of the year was it? Why did she not want to go home?

(iii) What did she use the matches for? What happened when she lit the first match?

(iv) Whom did she love dearly? What did she say when this person appeared before her?

 (v) What happened to the little girl at the end of the story?

    Would you consider this a happy ending or a sad one? Give one reason for your answer. **[2020}**

📋 Marking Scheme

  (i) • The Little Match Girl / The Little girl
- No shoes – feet were naked, red and blue / old apron
- She came from a desperately poor home – no shoes at the peak of winter.
- Pathetic / miserable / cold / poor

 (ii) • Winter / New Year's Eve / 31st December / last evening of the year
- She had not sold any matches (or earned a single penny) – this would make her father very angry – he would beat her.
- Home was very cold too – wind whistled through the roof which was stuffed with rags and straw.

(iii) • For light and heat / warm herself / numb fingers.
- A great iron stove with polished brass knobs and ornaments appeared before her.
- A fire burned beautifully in it / gave out warmth / when she stretched her feet to warm them the stove vanished / simply an illusion.

(iv) • Her grandmother
- begged her grandmother to take her with her.

- Was afraid her grandmother would vanish / like all the other beautiful visions had that evening / the warm stove, the roast goose and the glorious Christmas Tree.

(iv) • she died
- Either Happy + reason: All her troubles ended and she joined her grandmother in heaven where she would not feel cold or hunger / needs.

OR

Sad + reason: A little life full of promise is put out. Indifference of society to her suffering. Irony that she died of cold and starvation at a time / season when all the world talks about giving to others.

Ans.   **(i)** The little girl in the story, 'The Little Match Girl' is referred to as 'she'. She was poor and walked bareheaded and barefooted. So, her feet were red and blue with cold. The packets of matches in her apron and hand suggest she sold matches for living. Her 'old' apron also showed that she came from a desperately poor home. She was shivering and hungry; a picture of misery!

 (ii) It was New Year's eve, the peak of winter. The little girl had not sold any match and did not have a penny. She was afraid that her father would beat her for the same if she went home. Besides, there was no protection from cold at home too, as the roof had many holes in it and wind whistled through them.

(iii) She lit the first match to warm herself but in the light, she saw a big iron oven with polished brass knobs ornaments. She felt its heat warming her feet. But as she stretched her feet, the flame went off and she found herself sitting with a burnt matchstick.

(iv) She loved her grandmother dearly who was no more. She was the only one who ever loved the little girl. She pleaded with her granny to take her along with her before she vanished like the stove, the roast goose and the Christmas tree.

 (v) She froze to death. The dawn saw her sitting huddled in the corner of two houses, with rosy cheeks and a smile on her face. She was holding a half burnt packet of matches. It is sad to think that a little girl died because she was poor and had no one to take care of her. The tragedy deepens because it happened on a New Year's Eve, when all were celebrating with plenty. But the smile on her blissful face makes the reader feel happy that she had escaped the misery of this uncaring world and escaped into a world of heavenly joy and gladness.

Q. 2. Answer the following questions with reference to Norah Burke's short story, "The Blue Bead".

(i) Describe Sibia's experience at the Bazaar.

What were the things that filled her with wonder?

(ii) Who were the Gujars? Give a brief description of their lifestyle.

(iii) Describe how Sibia rescued the Gujar woman from the crocodile.

What did Sibia regard as the highlight of that fateful day?

What does this tell us about Sibia?

[2020]

🗒 **Marking Scheme**

(i) • Amazed at the sweetmeats – brilliant honey confections – smelled wonderful – sweets were green and magenta
  • Cloth stall with rolls of new cotton cloth
  • Satin sewn with silver thread
  • Tin trays from Birmingham
  • Sari with bits of glass embroidered into it.
  • Dawn coloured silks sold by a Kashmiri travelling merchant.
  • The little locked chest with turquoises and opals belonging to the merchant
  • Best of all a box – when you pressed it a bell tinkled and a yellow chicken jumped out.
  • Milling people or crowds / dogs and monkeys full of flees / gossiping and bargaining people / bell of the sacred bull / spitting betel juice
    (Any four of the above)

(ii) • Nomadic graziers (nomads) / junglis / born and bred in the forest / man in pastoral wandering age
  • Lived in grass huts – temporary shelters / they got their living from the animals, grass and trees
  • Fetched water from the river
  • Counted wealth in large herds and silver jewellery/ wore large rings made with melted coins
  • Since the Gujars were nomads they moved on when plants and shrubs for grazing their animals were depleted.

• Other reasons were inability to sell butter and milk.
  • They would leave a place when a tiger was taking away their cattle.

(iii) • Gujar woman was attacked when she came to collect the water.
  • The woman screamed, dropped her pots and turned away but the crocodile's jaws closed on her leg.
  • She clung to a log jammed between rocks – crocodile pulled on her leg.
  • Sibia saw this – leapt over the rocks – reached the spot.
  • She aimed at the crocodile's eye – drove the hayfork at the eyes – one prong went right in.
  • Crocodile reared up in pain – tail and nose almost meeting as it convulsed – crashed back into the water and vanished.
  • Sibia helped the fainting woman – dragged her from the water – bound her wounds with a rag and helped her home to the Gujar camp. *(six in totality)*
  • **Finding the blue glass bead** for her necklace.
  • That she is at heart an **innocent** little girl no **different from other girls** her age despite all her bravery and her heart is gladdened by something she considers pretty / it speaks about her poverty / happy in all achievements/ overlooked a brave achievement.

Ans. (i) Sibia had visited the bazaar of the little town at the railhead. She had walked through milling people, the dogs and the monkeys full of fleas, and heard the bell of sacred bull. She was amazed at the display of green and magenta sweetmeats, 'the brilliant honey confections'. Then there was the cloth stall, satins and silks, tin trays and mirror work sari, a chest with gems and a box that had a chicken jumping out. All these filled her with wonder.

(ii) Gujars were the nomadic graziers who changed their habitats hen there was no grass to feed the cattle and they were not able to sell their white butter and milk. The Gujars were 'junglis' born and bred in forests. They get their living from animals, grass and trees. Theirs was a hard life, fetching water from faraway places, cutting grass with sickles, gathering firewood, and putting dung to dry. Their wealth was determined according to the number of cattle they possessed or the large silver rings that they wore, made from melted coins.

(iii) The crocodile attacked when the Gujar woman was filling water. Its jaws closed on her leg and she slipped on the bone breaking stone. She was hanging on to a log, when Sibia saw her. She sprang. She came "leaping like a rock goat", from boulder to boulder. In a moment, she was beside the shrieking woman. The crocodile slapped its tail and the water rose high. But this did not deter the brave girl. She aimed her hayfork into the eyes of the crocodile. One prong went right in. The huge animal rocked in convulsions, crashed back exploding the water and disappeared in 'bloody foam'. She got her arms around the fainting woman and dragged her from the water. She stopped her wounds with sand and bound them with a rag. Thus, she helped her to reach the encampment and some men carried her for treatment.

For Sibia, the highlight was accidentally procuring the blue bead with which she could make a necklace. The bead was beautiful 'with sunlight shuffling in it like gold dust'. It was even pierced ready for use. Her joy knew no bounds.

Sibia comes across as a brave girl who had the courage to fight a violent crocodile single-handedly. Danger was natural to a forest girl like her and she did not think twice about the brave deed she had done. In fact, she did not even think about how she endangered her life to save the Gujar woman. She charged like a rock goat and leapt over the slippery boulders to reach the victim in time. Focus, determination, sterling courage were the hallmarks of her personality. Completely matter of fact, she did everything to save the woman's life. She displayed immense common sense and equanimity of mind. Her courage was heroic. However, at heart was an innocent little girl, no different than any other girl of her age despite all her bravery, she was only thrilled about the bead she got. "I found a blue bead for my necklace, look!"

Q. 3. **Read the extract given below and answer the questions that follow:**

An angry athlete is an athelete who will make mistakes, as any coach will tell you I was no exception. On the first of my three qualifying jumps, I leaped from several inches beyond the take-off board for a foul.

(i) When and where is this story set?

What reason does the narrator Jesse Owens give for the heightened nationalistic feelings at this time?

(ii) In which event had Owens been confident of winning a gold medal? Why?

(iii) What had made Owens angry enough to make mistakes?

(iv) Name Owens' rival who approached him at this point.

What advice did this athlete give Owens?

(v) How did the two atheletes perform in the finals?

What does Jesse Owens consider his 'Greatest Olympic Prize'? Why? **[2019]**

📋 Marking Scheme

(i)
- Summer of 1936/Olympic Games
- Berlin/Germany
- Hitler's insistence that his athletes were members of a 'master/Aryan/superior race' led to heightened nationalistic feelings.

(ii)
- the running broad jump/ long jump
- A year ago, Jesse Owens had *set the world record* (26 feet 8-1/4 inches as a sophomore at the Ohio State University).
- Had trained for 6 years
- Everyone expected him to win the event with ease. *(Any two)*

(iii)
- Owens had been very *confident* of winning a gold medal in the running broad jump event.
- He was *shocked/surprised* to see/a tall German (Luz Long)/hitting the pit at over 26 feet in the trial jumps/Luz Long qualified easily/He was told that Hitler had kept him (Luz Long) a secret and wanted him to win the broad jump.
- Owens was a negro/ coloured man – he was angry at Hitler's superior attitude – if Luz Long won it would add to the Nazis Aryan-Supremacy theory/Owens was determined to prove Hitler wrong. *(Any three)*

(iv)
- Luz Long
- Long advised Owens to draw a line a few inches in back of the board/jump or take off from there.
- That would ensure he would not foul/ yet jump far enough to qualify/it wasn't important to be first in the trials/qualifying for the finals was more important. *(Any three)*

(v)
- Luz Long - broke his own personal record
- Owens - set Olympic record (of 26 feet 5-5/16 inches)/ won the Gold Medal
- The friendship that sprang up between himself and Luz Long.
- It proved that it was possible for two people to rise above petty barriers like race and colour – to compete with each other and yet remain the best of friends

(or any acceptable reason)

Ans. **(i)** The story is set in Berlin, Germany in 1936 during the Olympic Games. The two participants of this game were Jesse Owens and Luz Long.

The nationalistic feelings were at an all-time high because Hitler insisted that his performers were members of a 'master race'. Hence, feelings of nationalism were high in the other players, particularly Jesse Owens, the American Negro athlete.

(ii) Jesse Owens was confident of winning a gold medal in the running broad jump.

Owens was confident because he had trained, sweated, and disciplined himself for six years to take part in the Olympic Games. A year before, as a student at Ohio State University, he had set the world's record of 26 feet 8-1/4 inches. Everyone expected him to win that Olympic hands down.

(iii) Jesse Owens was angry at Hitler's theory because he believed that his performers were part of a 'master race' and were superior and better than all the others. Owens had been very confident of winning a gold medal in the running broad jump. During the trials, Jesse Owens was startled to see a tall German, named Luz Long. He was told that Hitler had kept him secret from the others, and was hoping to win the broad–jumping event with him. If Luz Long had won the medal, it would have supported the Aryan superiority theory. After all, Owens was a Negro and Luz Long was a German. This made him angry enough to make mistakes.

(iv) Luz Long, the tall German broad jumper with friendly blue eyes, approached Owens at this point.

Luz suggested that Jesse should draw a line a few inches in the back of the board, and aim at making his take off from there. He would definitely not foul, and would certainly jump far enough to qualify for the finals. Owens drew a line confidently, a full foot in back of the board and proceeded to jump from there. Consequently, he qualified with almost a foot to spare.

(v) Luz Long broke his own past record in the finals. In doing so, he pushed Jesse on to a peak performance. Jesse's final jump set the Olympic record of 26 feet 5-5/16 inches.

Jesse Owens considered his friendship with Luz Long to be his 'Greatest Olympic Prize.' He felt immense respect for Luz at that time when he was there congratulating Jesse Owens with a smile. He felt he had won the precious medal of friendship which was more valuable to him than the gold medal. One could melt down all the gold medals and cups he had but they would not even form plating on the 24-carat friendship that he felt for Luz Long at that moment.

Q. 4. **Answer the following questions with reference to Ray Douglas Bradbury's short story, 'All Summer in a Day'.**

(i) **Name the planet on which this story is set. Describe everyday life on this planet.**

(ii) **Why was there so much excitement in the school room that morning? What set Margot apart from the other children?**

(iii) **Describe how the planet was transformed when the sun came out and shone briefly over it. Why was Margot not able to witness this phenomenon? What emotion do you suppose the other children experienced when Margot emerged at the end of the story?** **[2019]**

📋 Marking Scheme

(i) • Venus
- Incessant rain/non-stop for 7 years/ thousands and thousands of days of rain.
- Deafening/drumming/gushing of water/ sweet fall of showers/concussions of storms/caused tidal waves to wash over the islands.
- A thousand forests grew rapidly/only to be crushed by the rain/grow again and be crushed once more.
- No sun for 7 years/ people used sun lamps/ lived in underground houses, tunnels

(Any three)

(ii) • The sun would shine that day for a brief 2 hours/happened only once in 7 years/they had waited for this day/The sun was to appear that day and the children (all 9-year olds) were excited because they had no personal memory of seeing/experiencing the sun /they had only heard of it and were eager to experience it for themselves. *(Any two)*

• Margot was different/ she would not play (*did not run when they tagged her*) with the other children/she refused to sing along with them/sang only if song was about sun or summer.

- Her biggest crime was that she had come to Venus only 5 years ago/so she remembered experiencing the warmth of the sun/the other children picked on her because she was different/they had been on Venus all their lives. (Any two)

(iii) *(Any 6 of the following **but not more than 2 points about the children's response**)*

- A sudden silence descended on the planet/ as if all loud thunderous **sound had been cut** off in a film about a tornado/avalanche/ hurricane, etc.
- It seemed a **beautiful tropical picture** had replaced the dreary landscape
- Everything was still – the **silence** was deafening
- The doors opened, and the children could **smell** the waiting world
- The sun came out – colour of flaming bronze – it **was huge**
- The sky was a **blazing blue** tile colour
- The jungle **burned with the sunlight**/the children rushed out into the springtime
- The children **ran, turned their faces to the sun**/took off their jackets/allowed the sun to burn their arms
- They **lay on the rapidly growing plants**/ and delighted in the feel of the warm sun/ they ran and played/laughed and fell/ **breathed** the fresh air and **listened** to the silence/didn't stop running for over an hour.

- Because Margot had been locked into the closet by the other children.
- Personal response (on the lines of) – they must have felt guilt/shame/regret/remorse/ awareness of wrongdoing/realization/ solemn/at having deprived Margot of this marvellous experience – something that she had been yearning for/could not meet each others' glance.

Ans. **(i)** Venus is the planet on which this story is set.

The 'rocket men and women' lived here with their families. It had been raining for seven years; 'thousands upon thousands of days compounded and filled from one end to the other with rain, with the drum and gush of water, with the sweet crystal fall of showers and the concussion of storms' were so heavy that they were like tidal waves over the islands. 'A thousand forests had been crushed under the rain and grown up a thousand times to be crushed again.' There was no sun for seven years. The people used to live in underground houses and tunnels and used sun lamps. This was the way, life was on the planet Venus.

(ii) There was so much excitement in the school room that morning because the scientists had predicted that the sun would appear, only for two hours. They were all nine year olds, and they had last seen the sun, seven years ago, when the sun came out for an hour and showed its face to the stunned world. But they have forgotten how it felt. All day, the day before, the children had read about the sun in class, about how like a lemon it was, and how hot. They had written small stories or essays or poems about it. Everyone was eagerly waiting for the sun to appear.

Margot was one of the children who lived on the planet Venus. She was nine years old, a very frail girl. She always stood separate, away from the other children and refrained from playing with them. When the class sang songs, her lips barely moved. She only sang when they sang about the sun and the summer. She longed for the warmth of the sun as she had come here only five years ago from Earth. She remembered the sun and the way the sun was and the sky was when she was four in Ohio, while the other children had been on Venus all their lives. They were only two years old when they last saw the sun and had long since forgotten the colour and heat of it and the way it really was. However, Margot remembered how the sun looked. All these facts set Margot apart from the other children.

(iii) The rain finally stopped. 'It seemed as if in the midst of a film concerning an avalanche, a tornado, a hurricane, or a volcanic eruption' something had gone wrong with the sound apparatus, cutting off all noise, all of the blasts and repercussions and thunders, and then, ripped the film from the projector and inserted in its place a beautiful tropical slide which did not tremble. The world ground to a standstill. The silence was immense and unbelievable.

The children put their hands to their ears. They stood apart. Finally, the sun came out. It was the colour of 'flaming bronze' and was huge in size. The sky around was 'a blazing blue tile colour'. The jungle burned with sunlight. The children were running and turning their faces up to the sky and feeling the sun on their cheeks like a warm iron; they were taking off their jackets and letting the sun burn their arms. They stopped running and stood in the great jungle that covered Venus. It was a nest of octopi, clustering up great arms of weed, wavering, flowering in that brief spring. It was the colour of rubber and ash', that jungle, from the many years without the sun. It was 'the colour of stones and white cheeses and ink, and it was 'the colour of the moon'. The children lay out, laughing, on the jungle mattress, and heard it sigh and squeak under them resilient and alive. The whole planet came alive.

Margot was unable to witness the phenomenon because the children had put her in the closet. They surged about her, caught her up and bore her back into 'a tunnel, a room, a closet, where they slammed and locked the door'.

When Margot emerged from the closet, the children could feel a pang of tremendous guilt and shame. They could not meet each other's glances and their faces were solemn and pale. The sun had played an important role in this. Lack of exposure to sunlight had made them pale and colourless. It had also taken away their compassion and kindness. Then they understood what they had been lacking in.

HINDI

Composition

Long Answer Type Questions

Q. 1. Write a short composition in Hindi of approximately 250 words on any one of the following topics :

निम्नलिखित विषयों में से किसी एक विषय पर हिंदी में लगभग 250 शब्दों में संक्षिप्त लेख लिखिए :   [2020]

(i) जीवन में खेलकूद मनोरंजन प्रदान करने के साथ-साथ सुख समृद्धि भी देते हैं। विद्यार्थी जीवन में इसकी उपयोगिता बहुत अधिक है। अपने किसी प्रिय खेल का वर्णन करें तथा यह खेल भविष्य में आपको कैसे लाभान्वित कर सकता है, एक निबन्ध में अपनी भविष्य की योजनाएँ भी बताइए।

(ii) सादा जीवन उच्च विचार ही मनुष्य के जीवन को अनुकरणीय और महान बनाते हैं। किसी महान व्यक्ति के अच्छे गुणों का वर्णन कीजिए जिन्हें आप अपने जीवन में सबसे अच्छा मानते हैं, वह आपके गुरु, माता-पिता, या कोई महान व्यक्ति हो सकता है।

(iii) 'स्वच्छता अभियान में सरकारी तंत्र की अपेक्षा नागरिकों की जागरूकता अधिक प्रभावपूर्ण मानी जाती है' जनता के सहयोग से ही देश स्वच्छ सुन्दर बन सकता है, आप इस कथन से कहाँ तक सहमत हैं? स्पष्ट करें।

Ans.

(i) जीवन में खेलों का महत्त्व

जीवन में खेलकूद मनोरंजन प्रदान करने के साथ-साथ सुख समृद्धि भी देते हैं। विद्यार्थी जीवन में इसकी उपयोगिता बहुत अधिक है। खेल हमारे जीवन में अत्यधिक महत्त्वपूर्ण हैं। मनोरंजन का उत्तम माध्यम है, खेलकूद। कुछ खेल शारीरिक क्षमता वाले होते हैं, तो कुछ मानसिक, लेकिन सभी खेलों से मनुष्य का भरपूर मनोरंजन होता है। खेलों से शरीर स्वस्थ व सुगठित बनता है।

विद्यार्थी जीवन में खेलकूद की उपयोगिता बहुत अधिक है। खेलकूद छात्रों के सर्वांगीण विकास के लिए, अति आवश्यक हैं। छात्र खेल के मैदान में अनुशासन, संगठन, आज्ञापालन, साहस, आत्मविश्वास, संगठन, आज्ञापालन, साहस, आत्मविश्वास तथा एकाग्रचित्तता जैसे गुणों का अभ्यास और विकास करते हैं। छात्र स्वस्थ रहते हैं और चुस्त व फुर्तीले होते हैं।

मेरा प्रिय खेल हॉकी है। मुझे हॉकी खेल बहुत पसंद है। हॉकी भारत का राष्ट्रीय खेल भी है। इसमें दो टीमें होती हैं। प्रत्येक टीम में ग्यारह खिलाडी होते हैं। हॉकी का एक मैच 60 मिनट का होता है जो कि 15.15 मिनट के 4 भागों में खेला जाता है। इस खेल को खेलने के लिए एक गेंद और लकड़ी की छड़ी का इस्तेमाल किया जाता है। हॉकी को पूरे विश्व में खेला जाता है।

मैं स्कूल की हॉकी टीम में भी हूँ। गतवर्ष हॉकी प्रतियोगिता जो क्षेत्रीय स्तर पर हुई थी, उसमें हमारी टीम जीती थी। मैं प्रतिदिन तीन घंटे का अभ्यास करता हूँ। मेरा सपना है कि मैं अपने देश के लिए खेलूँ।

भविष्य में हॉकी खेल से मैं नाम के साथ-साथ खूब पैसा भी कमा सकता हूँ। हॉकी खेल में सर्वश्रेष्ठ प्रदर्शन देकर देश का ही नहीं बल्कि विश्व का सर्वश्रेष्ठ व उत्तम खिलाड़ी बनना चाहता हूँ। इस खेल से मेरी ही नहीं बल्कि मेरे परिवार की आर्थिक स्थिति भी मजबूत व अच्छी होगी। मैं अपने माता-पिता का ख्याल अच्छे से रख पाऊँगा। उन्हें सारी सुख-सुविधाएँ प्रदान करूँगा।

भविष्य में, बच्चों को हॉकी का प्रशिक्षण देने के लिए एक अकादमी भी खोलूँगा। इस अकादमी का मकसद प्रतिभावान खिलाड़ियों को प्रशिक्षण देना और देश को उत्तम खिलाड़ी भेंट करना होगा। मैं विश्व-कप जीतकर पुन: एक बार देश का गौरव बढ़ाऊँ और विश्व-पटल पर देश की शान बढ़ाऊँ यह मेरा उद्देश्य रहेगा।

(ii) सादा जीवन उच्च विचार

'सादा जीवन उच्च विचार' ही मनुष्य के जीवन को अनुकरणीय व महान बनाते हैं। लाल बहादुर शास्त्री जी का कथन सादा जीवन उच्च विचार, हर समय, हर काल में महत्वपूर्ण है, क्योंकि यह कथन वास्तविकता में मनुष्य का जीवन सुख व शांतिपूर्ण बना देता है। सादगी भरा रहन-सहन, खान-पान और सरल विनम्र व्यवहार से मनुष्य सबका प्रिय, आदरणीय और महान बन जाता है। यह नीतिवचन मनुष्य को अपनी जरूरतों और इच्छाओं को सीमित करने की सलाह देते हैं।

आज का युग प्रदर्शन व कृत्रिमता का युग बनकर रह गया है। तड़क-भड़क और बाह्य आडम्बर को अधिक महत्व दिया जाने लगा है। स्वार्थ व महत्वकांक्षाओं की अंधी दौड़ में मनुष्य अपनी पहचान तक भुला चुका है। इसी का दुष्परिणाम पूरे समाज के नैतिक पतन, भ्रष्टाचार एवं आचारहीनता के रूप में हमारे सामने आ रहा है।

हमारे देश को अहिंसा व सत्याग्रह के बल पर आजाद करवाने वाले 'राष्ट्रपिता महात्मा गांधी' का जीवन सादगी से

परिपूर्ण था। एक लंगोटी और ऊपर से एक चादर वह भी अपने हाथों से काती गई खादी की। उनका आहार भी एकदम सादा था। वे मोटा खाते, मोटा पहनते और बकरी के दूध से संतोष अनुभव करते थे। उनके विचार भी उच्च कोटि के थे। उन्होंने सादा जीवन और उच्च विचारों के कारण ही देश की जनता को जागृत करके, उसे सुगठित बनाकर देश को अंग्रेजों की गुलामी से मुक्त करवाया।

मैं गांधीजी के महान व्यक्तित्व से प्रभावित हूँ। उनका जीवन हमारे लिए एक महान आदर्श है और अनुकरणीय है। कठोरता पर कोमलता से विजय प्राप्त की जा सकती है। इच्छाओं को सीमित कर संतुष्टि का फल प्राप्त किया जा सकता है। दूसरों के दु:ख को अपना दु:ख मानना व सबकी खुशियों को अपनी खुशी समझने वाला ही सच्चा मानव कहलाने का अधिकारी है। चाहे जो चुनौती आए, सत्य की राह पर चलना और परिस्थितियों से न घबराना ही मेरे जीवन का मूलमंत्र होगा।

मैं भी गांधीजी की तरह ही अपना जीवन सादगीपूर्ण बिताना चाहता हूँ। दिखावे व आडम्बर से दूर रहना चाहता हूँ और अपना जीवन मानव सेवा के लिए समर्पित करना चाहता हूँ।

(iii) स्वच्छता अभियान में जनता की भूमिका

स्वच्छ भारत अभियान भारत के प्रधानमंत्री श्री नरेंद्र मोदी जी ने महात्मा गांधी जी की जयंती पर 2 अक्टूबर 2014 को आरंभ किया था। साफ-सफाई को लेकर भारत की छवि को बदलने के लिए मोदी जी ने देश को एक मुहिम से जोड़ने के लिए जन आंदोलन बनाकर इसकी शुरुआत की। भारत के राष्ट्रपिता महात्मा गांधी का सपना था 'स्वच्छ-भारत'।

स्वच्छता ही अच्छे स्वास्थ्य का आधार है। स्वच्छता एक ऐसा कार्य नहीं है जो हम किसी के दबाव में आकर करें स्वच्छता तो हमारे जीवन का अभिन्न अंग है। इस अभियान की सफलता तभी संभव है जब हम दिखावे के लिए नहीं बल्कि बल्कि मन से इसमें भाग लें। पहल हमें अपने घर से करनी होगी। हम अगर अपने आस-पास की जगह, गली, सड़क को साफ रखेंगे, कूड़ा-कचरा यथास्थान पर डालेंगे, तो स्वत: ही हमारा गाँव, नगर, शहर और देश स्वच्छ और सुन्दर बन जाएगा।

इस अभियान में शौचालयों का निर्माण, गली मोहल्लों की सफाई और गाँवों की सफाई के प्रति जागरुकता बढ़ाना। इसके अतिरिक्त राजनेता, अभिनेता व उच्च पदाधिकारी भी इस अभियान से जुड़े हुए हैं। आज समाज के हर वर्ग का व्यक्ति इस अभियान में अपना महत्वपूर्ण योगदान दे रहा है। हर देशवासी अगर यह शपथ ले ले कि वह न तो गंदगी फैलाएगा और न दूसरों को फैलाने देगा, तो निश्चित ही 'स्वच्छ-भारत' 'स्वस्थ भारत' का सपना पूरा हो जाएगा।

आसपास में फैली हुई गंदगी के कारण ही कई जानलेवा बीमारियाँ फैलती है। जिनसे बचने का सबसे अच्छा और श्रेष्ठ तरीका है आस-पास सफाई बनाए रखना। भारत को स्वच्छ बनाने के साथ-साथ पूरी तरह से खुले में शौच मुक्त बनाना

है। हर घर में शौचालय का निर्माण होना चाहिए। इसके लिए हमें सरकार व नगर-निगम के अधिकारियों पर निर्भर नहीं होना चाहिए। इसके लिए प्रत्येक भारतीय को अपनी कर्मठता का परिचय देना होगा।

'स्वच्छता-अभियान' एक राष्ट्रव्यापी अभियान है। आइये सब मिलकर स्वच्छ भारत व स्वस्थ भारत का सपना पूरा करें। बच्चों से लेकर बूढ़ों तक स्वच्छता का पूरा-पूरा ध्यान रखेंगे और दूसरों को भी सफाई रखने की प्रेरणा देंगे।

Q. 2. **Write a short composition in *Hindi* of approximately 250 words on any *one* of the following topics:**

निम्नलिखित विषयों में से किसी एक विषय पर हिंदी में लगभग 250 शब्दों में संक्षिप्त लेख लिखिए:　　[2019]

(i) आपके विद्यालय में एक मेले का आयोजन किया गया था। यह किस अवसर पर, किस उद्देश्य से किया गया था? उसके लिए आपने क्या-क्या तैयारियाँ कीं? आपने और आपके मित्रों ने एवं शिक्षकों ने उसमें क्या सहयोग दिया था? इन बिन्दुओं को आधार बनाकर एक प्रस्ताव विस्तार से लिखिए।

(ii) यात्रा एक उत्तम रुचि है। यात्रा करने से ज्ञान तो बढ़ता ही है, स्थान विशेष की संस्कृति तथा परम्पराओं का परिचय भी मिलता है। अपनी किसी यात्रा के अनुभव तथा रोमांच का वर्णन करते हुए एक प्रस्ताव लिखिए।

(iii) 'वन है तो भविष्य है' आज हम उसी भविष्य को नष्ट कर रहे हैं, कैसे? कथन को स्पष्ट करते हुए जीवन में वनों के महत्व पर अपने विचार लिखिए।

🗒 Marking Scheme ------------

संक्षिप्त लेख–

(i) भूमिका– विद्यालय में मेले का आयोजन।
　मध्य भाग– अवसर मेले का उद्देश्य, तैयारियाँ, सहयोग।
　उपसंहार।

(ii) भूमिका– यात्रा किसे कहते हैं? यात्रा का वर्णन।
　मध्य भाग– यात्रा का लाभ– नई जानकारी एकत्रित करना, समय नियोजन, यात्रा का बजट और उसका पालन, सामाजिक, भौगोलिक, ऐतिहासिक एवम् धार्मिक महत्त्व, संस्कृति, परम्परा, खान-पान, वेश-भूषा, रीति-रिवाज, नृत्य-संगीत आदि का परिचय।
　उपसंहार।

(iii) कथन का स्पष्टीकरण
　वनों का महत्त्व
　उपसंहार

Ans. 　　**(i)** 　**विद्यालय में आयोजित मेले का वर्णन**

भारतीय संस्कृति में मेलों का विशेष महत्व है। मेला व्यापार का केन्द्र ही नहीं बल्कि मनोरंजन का भी उत्तम साधन है। ऐसे ही एक मेले का आयोजन हमारे विद्यालय में हुआ। विद्यालय का स्वर्ण जयन्ती वर्ष था तो इस दिन पर कुछ विशेष करने का

निश्चय किया गया और सभी अध्यापकों के सुझाव पर एक मेले का आयोजन करना सुनिश्चित किया गया।

मेले की रूपरेखा बनाने के लिए अध्यापकों व दसवीं कक्षा के कुछ छात्रों की एक समिति बनायी गई। उस छात्र मण्डल के सदस्यों में मैं और मेरे मित्र भी थे। हम सब में अति उत्साह और जोश था। समिति की बैठक तीन से चार घण्टे तक चली। मेले का आयोजन कब, कहाँ, कैसे और कितने दिनों तक होगा आदि विषयों पर गहन चिंतन-मनन हुआ। निर्णय यह किया गया कि मेले का आयोजन दो दिन (शनिवार व रविवार) को विद्यालय के खेल मैदान में किया जाएगा। यह भी निर्णय लिया गया कि मेले से होने वाले लाभ को अनाथ आश्रम के बच्चों की शिक्षा के लिये सहयोग राशि के रूप में दिया जायेगा।

मेले का प्रवेश शुल्क 20 रुपये तय किया गया था। योजनानुसार मेले की पूरी तैयारी जोर-शोर से चल रही थी। मैदान के एक कोने में सांस्कृतिक कार्यक्रम भी रखा गया। कपड़े, खिलौने, साज-सज्जा का सामान, रसोईघर का सामान आदि कई दुकानें लगायी गयीं। मेले में कुछ मनोरंजक खेल भी रखे गए, जिसका आयोजन कक्षा दसवीं के छात्रों ने किया। शिक्षकों को टिकट काउंटरों पर बिठाया गया।

मेले में हमने एक तरफ भारत के स्वतन्त्रता सेनानियों व दुनिया के सात अजूबों की प्रदर्शनी भी लगायी। इस प्रदर्शनी की पूरी जिम्मेदारी मुझ पर और मेरे दोस्त पर थी। भूगोल और इतिहास की अध्यापिका ने इसमें हमारा मार्गदर्शन किया और सहयोग भी दिया। मेले में आए हर व्यक्ति ने इस प्रदर्शनी की खूब तारीफ की। यह प्रदर्शनी ज्ञानवर्धक भी थी।

खाने-पीने की दुकानों में बहुत भीड़ थी। मेले में शाम को रंग-बिरंगी लाइट जला दी गई थी, जिसके कारण यह दृश्य बहुत ही मनोहर लग रहा था।

हम सब छात्रों व अध्यापकों द्वारा इस मेले का आयोजन सार्थक सिद्ध हुआ। करीब-करीब एक लाख चालीस हजार रुपये इकट्ठे हुए। हमारे प्रधानाचार्य के सुझावानुसार अनाथ आश्रम के बच्चों के नाम पूरी धनराशि दान कर दी गई।

इस तरह मेले के आयोजन से हमें एक अनोखी खुशी मिली। यह मेला मेरे लिए अविस्मरणीय था। मेले से मानवता की ओर उठे ये कदम कई दिलों में परोपकार की लौ जगा गए और नन्हें मासूम बच्चों के मन में कुछ बनने की आशा जगा गए।

(ii) एक अविस्मरणीय यात्रा का रोमांच तथा अनुभव

कौतूहल या जिज्ञासा मानव की एक मूल प्रवृत्ति है। नित नवीन स्थानों, लोगों को जानने देखने के लिए वह सदैव आतुर रहा है। इसी उत्सुकता की पूर्ति के लिए मनुष्य यात्रा करता है। यात्रा ज्ञान प्राप्त करने का उत्तम साधन है। यात्रा पर जाने से हम उस स्थान की नयी-नयी जानकारियाँ, खान-पान, पहनावा, वहाँ की संस्कृति के बारे में जान सकते हैं।

पिछले वर्ष मुझे भी ऐसी ही एक यात्रा करने का अवसर मिला, जिसमें मैंने बहुत कुछ सीखा और जाना। मैं और मेरे दो दोस्तों ने ऊटी जाने का निश्चय किया। दो दिनों के लिये

हमारा बजट 15 हजार बना जिसमें हमने आने जाने का खर्चा और रहना-खाना भी सम्मिलित करने का निश्चय किया। ऊटी नीलगिरि की राजधानी है, इसे उद्गमंडल के नाम से भी जाना जाता है। यह स्थान समुद्रतल से 2200 मीटर की ऊँचाई पर है। हमारी गाड़ी पर्वतों के घुमावदार रास्ते से आगे बढ़ रही थी। चारों ओर हरियाली थी। प्रकृति के सान्निध्य का आनन्द रोमांचक था। चाय बगानों को पहली बार देखा था।

शाम तक हम होटल पहुँच गये। फिर हम कुछ खा-पीकर बाहर निकले। हम दोदाबेट्टा पीक पर पहुँचे। यह स्थान ऊटी का सबसे ऊँचा स्थान है। हल्की-हल्की ठण्ड और तेज हवाएँ और प्रकृति की अनुपम सुन्दरता। ऐसा लग रहा था मानो धरती का स्वर्ग यहीं है।

अगले दिन हम मुदुमलाई अभयारण्य गए। यहाँ बहुत से पेड़-पौधे और जीव-जन्तुओं की दुर्लभ प्रजातियाँ हैं। हमें हाथी, बड़ी गिलहरियाँ, साँभर, चीतल, भौंकने वाले हिरण और जंगली बिल्लियाँ देखने को मिलीं। रंग-बिरंगे तोते, काले कठफोड़वे, गरुड़ आदि नाना प्रकार के पक्षियों को भी देखा।

हम नौका विहार के लिए ऊटी झील भी गये। नौका विहार का आनन्द अविस्मरणीय था। नीलगिरि की पर्वतमालाओं में एक विशिष्ट जनजाति रहती है–"टोडा"। हमने इन आदिवासियों के घर देखे। इनके घर बांस और नारियल के सूखे पत्तों से बने थे। कृषि इनके जीवन निर्वाह का प्रमुख साधन था। इस जनजाति की भाषा में तमिल भाषा के काफी शब्द पाये जाते हैं। इनके खान-पान में चावल और सब्जी प्रमुख है।

हमने ऊटी में घुड़सवारी भी की। ऊटी से हमने हाथ से बनी चॉकलेट, नीलगिरि तेल और इलायची वाली चाय पत्ती खरीदी। यह यात्रा मेरे लिए ज्ञानवर्धक और मनोरंजक साबित हुई। विभिन्न स्थानों की जानकारी और कुछ अच्छा समय व्यतीत करने के उद्देश्य से हम सबको वर्ष में एक बार ऐसे किसी स्थान का भ्रमण अवश्य करना चाहिये।

(iii) ''वन है तो भविष्य है''

"वन है तो भविष्य है।" वृक्षों के समूह को वन, जंगल या कानन कहते हैं। वन प्रकृति का अनुपम हिस्सा हैं। वृक्ष और वन हमारे लिए वरदान हैं। हमारी प्राणवायु का स्रोत भी वन ही हैं।

प्राकृतिक सौन्दर्य तथा पर्यावरण का आधार वन हैं। वन, वर्षा में सहायक होते हैं तथा वायु को शुद्ध करते हैं। भूमि कटाव को रोकने, भूमि को उर्वरक बनाने में भी इनका महत्वपूर्ण योगदान है।

सभ्यता के विकास के साथ-साथ वनों की अन्धाधुन्ध कटाई होती गई तथा भारत ही नहीं, पूरे विश्वभर में मानव ने प्रकृति को भरपूर क्षति पहुँचाई। जनसंख्या की उत्तरोत्तर वृद्धि भी वनों के ह्रास का कारण बनी। वनों की कटाई जारी रहने से धीरे-धीरे उपजाऊ भूमि बंजर होती गई। मौसम चक्र में बदलाव आने लगा। कहीं बाढ़ तो कहीं सूखा पड़ने लगा। औद्योगिक विकास के अन्तर्गत कारखानों की स्थापना के लिए

वनों को काटा गया। इस कारण वृक्षों की अनेक प्रजातियाँ भी लुप्त हो गयीं। प्रदूषण का प्रकोप भी बढ़ता जा रहा है।

मानव का जीवन आज भी वनों पर आश्रित है। वन हमारी आर्थिक सम्पदा के स्रोत हैं। देश में प्रयुक्त 80: ईंधन और फर्नीचर के लिए लकड़ी हमें वनों से ही प्राप्त होती है। हमारा वर्तमान और भविष्य वनों पर ही निर्भर है।

वनों के इस महत्व को आज विश्वभर में समझा जा रहा है। सन् 1952 में सरकार ने नई वन नीति की घोषणा करके वन महोत्सव की प्रेरणा दी। वनों की रक्षा तथा समतल व पर्वतीय प्रदेशों में वृक्षारोपण करने का निश्चय किया गया। सरकार ने वनों की कटाई पर भी रोक लगा दी।

आज अनेक सामाजिक संस्थाएँ भी वृक्षारोपण के लिए समय-समय पर 'वृक्ष लगाओ' अभियान चलाती हैं। यदि सचमुच हम चाहते हैं कि मानव-जाति और उसके अस्तित्व की आधार स्थली धरती, प्रकृति का सन्तुलन बना रहे, तो हमें काटे जा रहे पेड़ों के अनुपात से कहीं अधिक पेड़ उगाने होंगे। अनावश्यक वन कटाव को कठोरता से रोकना होगा। हमारे वर्तमान और भविष्य को सुनहरा बनाने के लिए हम सबका बराबर योगदान होना अनिवार्य है। तो आइए—

"पेड़ लगाएँ वन बचाएँ,

जीवन में खुशहाली लाएँ"

Q. 3. Write a short composition in *Hindi* of approximately *250* words on any *one* of the following topics:

निम्नलिखित विषयों में से किसी एक विषय पर हिंदी में लगभग 250 शब्दों में संक्षिप्त लेख लिखिए: [2018]

(i) 'परोपकार की भावना लोक-कल्याण से पूर्ण होती है।' हमें भी परोपकार से भरा जीवन ही जीना चाहिए। विषय को स्पष्ट करते हुए अपने विचार लिखिए।

(ii) "आजकल देश में आवासीय विद्यालयों (Boarding Schools) की बाढ़ सी आ गई है। आवासीय विद्यालयों की छात्रों के जीवन में क्या उपयोगिता हो सकती है?"—इस प्रकार के विद्यालयों की अच्छाइयों और बुराइयों के बारे में बताते हुए वर्तमान में इनकी आवश्यकता पर अपने विचार लिखिए।

(iii) संयुक्त परिवार के किसी ऐसे उत्सव के आनंद का विस्तार से वर्णन कीजिए, जहाँ आपके परिवार के बच्चे-बुजुर्ग सभी उपस्थित थे।

📋 **Marking Scheme** ------------------------

(i) संक्षिप्त लेख परोपकार की भावना का लोक कल्याण के कार्यों का वर्णन। (भूमिका)
जीवन में परोपकार का महत्त्व
उपसंहार

(ii) आवासीय विद्यालयों की छात्रों के जीवन में उपयोगिताओं का वर्णन। (भूमिका)
इस प्रकार के विद्यालयों की अच्छाइयों एवं बुराइयों का वर्णन।

वर्तमान में इनकी आवश्यकताओं के बारे में जानकारी दिया जाना।
उपसंहार

(iii) परिवार किसे कहते हैं ? परिवार के विषय में वर्णन (भूमिका)
संयुक्त परिवार के उत्सव का वर्णन।
उपसंहार

Ans. (i) **"परोपकार की भावना लोक-कल्याण से पूर्ण होती है"**

मनुष्य एक सामाजिक प्राणी है। समाज में वह मिल-जुलकर रहता है। एक-दूसरे के सुख-दु:ख में भागीदार होता है। मानव समाज के सुसंचालन के लिए मानव हृदय में परोपकार की भावना का होना नितांत आवश्यक है। मनुष्य तो स्वभाव से ही परोपकारी जीव है। दूसरों के कष्टों को देखकर हम प्रभावित होते हैं और उन्हें दूर करने का जो भाव हमारे दिल में उत्पन्न होता है तब यहीं परोपकार की भावना का जन्म होता है।

परोपकार शब्द 'पर'. 'उपकार' दो शब्दों से मिलकर बना है। जिसका अर्थ है दूसरों की भलाई करना।

परहित सरिस धर्म नहीं भाई।

पर पीड़ा सम नहिं अधमाई।।

अनंत जलराशि का भार ढोने वाली नदियाँ अपने जीवन में सुबह से शाम तक लगातार सिर्फ दूसरों के कल्याण के लिए ही बहती हैं। वृक्ष भी आँधी-तूफान सहते हुए चुपचाप खड़े रहते हैं ताकि थके, भूखे लोगों को अपनी छाया तथा फल प्रदान करके उनकी भूख और थकावट दूर कर सकें।

मानवता का उद्देश्य तथा मानव जीवन तभी सार्थक हो सकता है जब वह अपने कल्याण के साथ-साथ दूसरों के कल्याण के विषय में भी सोचें। यदि हमारे पास धन है तो निर्धनों की मदद करें, यदि विद्या है तो अशिक्षित को शिक्षा प्रदान करें, अत: परहित साधना ही सच्ची मानवता है।

हमारे देश में अनेक परोपकारी महान पुरुषों ने जन्म लिया है, जिन्होंने परोपकारी अमरबेल को सींचा है। जैसे—रंतिदेव ने भूख से व्याकुल होने पर भी अपना भोजन से भरा थाल एक भूखे व्यक्ति को दे दिया। महाराज शिवि ने एक कबूतर की प्राण रक्षा की खातिर अपने शरीर का मांस तक दान कर दिया। महाकवि निराला जी का पूरा जीवन ही परमार्थ में बीता।

परोपकार की शिक्षा किसी भी विद्यालय में नहीं सिखाई जाती है। परोपकार करने की शिक्षा अपने घर-परिवार से ही प्राप्त होती है। परोपकार की भावना से मनुष्य का हृदय बिना पानी और बिना साबुन के ही निर्मल बन जाता है। देश के उत्थान के लिए सदैव ही परोपकारी व्यक्तियों की आवश्यकता होती है।

आज आवश्यकता इस बात की है कि मानव अपने स्वार्थ की भावना को त्याग करके, मानवता के कल्याण के लिए प्रयत्न करे। वास्तव में परोपकार से बड़ा न कोई पुण्य है न कोई धर्म।

(ii) आवासीय विद्यालयों के लाभ एवं हानियाँ

प्रारंभिक वर्षों में शिक्षा के लिए घर और स्कूल दोनों में पढ़ाई करने की आवश्यकता होती है। अधिकांश घरों में छोटे परिवार होते हैं, और अधिकांश मामलों में माता-पिता दोनों जीविका चलाने के लिए कार्य करते हैं, उस समय वे बच्चों की पढ़ाई और पालन-पोषण को अधिक समय नहीं दे पाते।

ऐसे परिदृश्य में अपने बच्चे को एक बोर्डिंग स्कूल में स्थानांतरित करना हमेशा बेहतर होता है। इसके लिए सबसे अच्छी आयु सात वर्ष की होती है।

बोर्डिंग स्कूल के कई लाभ हैं, सबसे पहले सभी बच्चों को समान स्तर मिलता है, सभी एक ही लाभ प्राप्त करते हैं। बोर्डिंग स्कूल हर एक छात्र के समग्र विकास पर अधिक ध्यान देते हैं और दैनिक दिनचर्या और नियमों का पालन करने के लिए अनुशासन पैदा करते हैं। बोर्डिंग स्कूल में पढ़ने वाले युवाओं के व्यवहार में सकारात्मक परिवर्तन दिखाई देते हैं।

सभी छात्रों को खेल और अन्य सह पाठ्यक्रम से जुड़ी गतिविधियों के साथ-साथ अच्छी तरह संतुलित दिनचर्या के माध्यम से पर्याप्त रूप से अध्ययन कराया जाता है।

इसका फायदा यह भी है कि छात्रों की छोटी संख्या और शिक्षकों के साथ पूर्ण समय बिताने के कारण शिक्षकों और छात्रों के बीच घनिष्ठ संबंध विकसित हो जाता है। वे भावनात्मक, शारीरिक और शैक्षणिक सभी पहलुओं में छात्र के विकास में शामिल होते हैं और उनके भविष्य में आने वाली हर परिस्थितियों का सामना अच्छे से कर सकें; इसके लिए तैयार करते हैं।

बोर्डिंग स्कूल का सबसे बड़ा नुकसान यह है कि कई विद्यालयों में बच्चों से अनावश्यक सख्ती बरती जाती है। परिवार से दूर रहकर वे भावनात्मक रूप से कमजोर महसूस करते हैं। वे अपना बचपन जी नहीं पाते। माता-पिता तथा भाई-बहनों के साथ भावनात्मक रूप से जुड़ नहीं पाते हैं। छात्र के लिए बोर्डिंग स्कूल में रहना कठिन होता है क्योंकि वहाँ नये लोगों को अपना दोस्त बनाने में समय लगता है, परिवार के साथ समय नहीं बिता पाते हैं। बोर्डिंग स्कूल के नियम और कानून बहुत सख्त होते हैं; जिन्हें निभाना कठिन होता है। लेकिन वर्तमान में अभिभावकों के पास समय की कमी के कारण वे अपने बच्चों को बोर्डिंग स्कूल में डालना पसंद करते हैं। जैसे कि हम जानते ही हैं कि हर चीज के फायदे-नुकसान दोनों ही होते हैं अत: बोर्डिंग स्कूल छात्र जीवन के लिये उपयोगी होते हैं। यहाँ उनका चरित्र निखरता है, हाँ माता-पिता से अपेक्षित है कि बच्चे को बिल्कुल अकेला ना छोड़ें। समय-समय पर मिलते रहें और वहाँ हो रही गतिविधियों के बारे में जानकारी प्राप्त करते रहें।

(iii) संयुक्त परिवार में विवाह एक उत्सव का वर्णन

परिवार, पति-पत्नी और बच्चों के समूह को कहते हैं किंतु दुनिया के अधिकांश भागों में वह सम्मिलित वास वाले रक्त संबंधियों का समूह है जिसमें विवाह और दत्रक प्रथा स्वीकृत व्यक्ति भी सम्मिलित हैं।

मैं एक संयुक्त परिवार में रहता हूँ। दादा-दादी, चाचा-चाची सभी साथ रहते हैं और समय-समय पर अन्य रिश्तेदार भी मिलते रहते हैं।

पिछले साल गर्मियों की छुट्टियों में मुझे एक विवाह में जाने का अवसर मिला। मुझे मेरे मामा के बेटे की शादी में शामिल होने का निमंत्रण मिला। शादी जून की दस तारीख को थी। मेरे मामाजी का घर एक गाँव में है।

हम एक दिन पहले सपरिवार उनके गाँव पहुँच गये। घर में बहुत रौनक थी। मेरे मामाजी ने हम सबका स्वागत किया। मेरे नानाजी व नानीजी मुझे देखकर बहुत प्रसन्न हुए। चाय नाश्ते के बाद सभी बातें करने लगे। एक तरफ गाँव की स्त्रियाँ ढोलक पर गीत गा रही थीं। दूसरी तरफ हलवाई मिठाइयाँ बना रहे थे। मेरे मामाजी का घर बहुत बड़ा था। बाहर घर के बुजुर्ग आपस में शादी की तैयारियों के बारे में चर्चा कर रहे थे।

अगले दिन दोपहर में हम सभी बाराती गाड़ियों द्वारा गाजियाबाद स्टेशन को रवाना हो गये। क्योंकि हमें वहाँ से ट्रेन द्वारा मुरादाबाद जाना था। बारात में बड़े-बुजुर्ग और बच्चे कुल मिलाकर सौ लोग थे। ट्रेन के आते ही हम सब डिब्बे में चढ़ गये। मामाजी ने पहले ही सबके लिए सीटों का आरक्षण करा लिया था, जिससे किसी को किसी भी प्रकार की कोई परेशानी नहीं हुई। ट्रेन में सभी अपने-अपने हमउम्र लोगों के साथ हंसी-मजाक कर रहे थे। बच्चे ट्रेन में दौड़ रहे थे। बड़े लोगों ने उन्हें डाँटकर बिठा दिया। रास्ते में मामाजी ने सभी को नाश्ता दिया जो कि उन्होंने बारात के चलते समय ही रखवा लिया था। इसी तरह हँसते-गाते और मस्ती करते हुए हम सभी शाम को करीब चार बजे मुरादाबाद पहुँच गये। स्टेशन पर उतरकर मेरे मामाजी ने सभी को इकट्ठा करके गिनती की। स्टेशन पर कन्या पक्ष के लोग हमारा स्वागत करने के लिए आये थे। वहाँ से वे हमें कारों द्वारा धर्मशाला ले गये। जहाँ बारात के ठहरने का बड़ा सुंदर इंतजाम किया गया था।

धर्मशाला के कमरों में हमने अपना-अपना सामान रखा। मामाजी ने मुझे वर के साथ ही ठहरने को कहा। धर्मशाला में हम सभी नहा-धोकर तैयार हुए, वहाँ हमें नाश्ता कराया गया जो कि बहुत स्वादिष्ट था।

शाम सात बजे बारात के चलने की तैयारी शुरू हो गई। मैंने अपने मामा के लड़के को तैयार किया। वह बहुत ही सुंदर लग रहा था। उसे एक सुंदर सी सजी हुई घोड़ी पर बैठाया गया। हम लोग रास्ते भर नाचते-गाते हुए कन्या पक्ष के घर पहुँचे।

घर पहुँचते ही द्वार पर फूलों की माला पहनाकर हम सभी का स्वागत किया गया। हमें शीतल पेय पीने को दिया गया। दूल्हे को घोड़ी से उतारकर स्टेज पर ले जाया गया; जहाँ दुल्हन के आने पर एक-दूसरे को वरमाला पहनाई गई।

तत्पश्चात शादी की कुछ रस्में पूरी की गईं। फिर हम सभी को भोजन के लिए बुलाया गया। खाना बहुत स्वादिष्ट था। तरह-तरह के पकवान थे। हम सभी ने पेट भरकर खाया। भोजन समाप्त करने के बाद फेरों की तैयारियाँ शुरू हो गईं।

घर वालों को छोड़कर बाकी सभी बाराती धर्मशाला में आराम करने चले गये। प्रात: विदाई की तैयारियाँ शुरू हो गईं।

सभी बारातियों को सुबह का नाश्ता कराया गया और बारात विदा हो गई। हम सभी फिर से ट्रेन द्वारा वापस गाज़ियाबाद आ गये।

विवाह एक ऐसा आनंद का उत्सव है जिसमें पूरा परिवार आनंदित होता है हर उम्र के लोग आनंद प्राप्त करते हैं।

Q. 4. Write a short composition in *Hindi* of approximately *250* words on any *one* of the following topics:

निम्नलिखित विषयों में से किसी एक विषय पर हिंदी में लगभग 250 शब्दों में संक्षिप्त लेख लिखिए: **[2017]**

(i) पुस्तकें ज्ञान का भण्डार होती हैं तथा हमारी सच्ची मित्र एवं गुरु भी होती हैं। हाल ही में पढ़ी गई अपनी किसी पुस्तक के विषय में बताते हुए लिखिए कि वह आपको पसंद क्यों आई और आपने उससे क्या सीखा?

(ii) 'पर्यावरण है तो मानव है' विषय को आधार बनाकर पर्यावरण सुरक्षा को लेकर आप क्या-क्या प्रयास कर रहे हैं? विस्तार से लिखिए।

(iii) कम्प्यूटर तथा मोबाइल मनोरंजन के साथ-साथ हमारी जरूरत का साधन अधिक बन गए हैं। हर क्षेत्र में इनसे मिलने वाले लाभों तथा हानियों का वर्णन करते हुए, अपने विचार लिखिए।

Ans. **(i) पुस्तकें ज्ञान का भण्डार होती हैं**

सृष्टि के आरंभिक काल में आदिमानव को भाषा ज्ञान नहीं था, वह संकेतों से अपने भावों की अभिव्यक्ति करता था। शनैः-शनैः भाषा का आविष्कार हुआ और लोग अपनी इच्छाओं व भावनाओं को समझने व समझाने में समर्थ हो सके। इस विकास के पश्चात् लेखन क्रिया का भी विकास हुआ और पुस्तकें लिखी जाने लगीं। पुस्तकें ज्ञान का भण्डार होती हैं तथा पुस्तकों द्वारा ही हमारा बौद्धिक व मानसिक विकास संभव है। समाज के परिष्कार, व्यावहारिक ज्ञान में वृद्धि एवं कार्यकुशलता व कार्यक्षमता के पोषण में भी पुस्तकों की महत्वपूर्ण भूमिका होती है।

पुस्तकों के क्षेत्र में हमारा देश भारतवर्ष तो विश्व गुरु के नाम से जाना जाता है। सर्वप्रथम वेद, पुराण तथा उपनिषद् जैसे कितने ही अनगिनत धर्म ग्रंथ हमारे देश की अमूल्य संपत्ति हैं। आज की पीढ़ी पुस्तकों के अभाव में कैसे जान सकती थी कि रामकृष्ण, स्वामी विवेकानंद, ऋषि वशिष्ठ जैसे असंख्य महापुरुष इस देश में उत्पन्न हुए। कौन जानता कि महर्षि दधीचि ने देवताओं की प्राण रक्षा के लिए सजीव अपने प्राण त्यागकर अपनी अस्थियाँ दान कर दीं। आज देश विकास की ऊँचाइयों को छू रहा है उसका श्रेय उन महान वैज्ञानिकों को है जो इतिहास के पन्नों में अपना नाम अमर कर गये हैं। कौन जानता कि सोने की चिड़िया कहे जाने वाले भारत को मुगलों और अंग्रेजों ने किस प्रकार लूटकर भारतीयों पर असंख्य अत्याचार किये। खगोल, भूगोल, अध्यात्म, विज्ञान कोई भी क्षेत्र क्यों न हों पुस्तकों के अतिरिक्त कोई विकल्प नहीं है।

जब मन उदास हो श्रीमद्भागवद्गीता उठाकर पढ़ लीजिए। मन के सारे विषाद मिट जाएँगे। श्रीभागवद् पुराण, श्रीरामचरितमानस पढ़ लीजिए मन बाग-बाग हो जाएगा। स्वामी विवेकानंद, दयानंद, रामकृष्ण परमहंस जैसे महापुरुषों को पढ़ लीजिए, ऐसा अनुभव होने लगेगा कि मनुष्य राम, रहीम, अल्लाह-खुदा के भेदभाव में क्यों फँसा है—भगवान ने तो इंसान बनाया है जाति व धर्म तो हमारी देन है।

मैंने श्री डोंगरा जी महाराज का श्रीमद्भागवद् महापुराण पढ़ा व सुना है। इसकी कथा मनुष्य को मृत्यु के भय से छुटकारा दिलाने वाली है। यह एक अमर कथा है, जिसमें भगवान श्रीकृष्ण की लीलाओं का वर्णन है, जो अमृत से भी उत्कृष्ट है। इस कथा में महाभारत के पाँच पाँडवों में से एक अर्जुन के पुत्र अभिमन्यु के पुत्र परीक्षित की कथा है। कलियुग के प्रभाव में आकर परीक्षित ने प्यास से पीड़ित होने के कारण तप में लीन शमीक ऋषि के गले में मरा हुआ सर्प डाल दिया। इस घटना से क्रोधित होकर ऋषि पुत्र शृंगी ने परीक्षित को शाप दे दिया कि आज से सातवें दिन तक्षक नाम का सर्प आकर परीक्षित को काटेगा और उसकी मृत्यु हो जाएगी।

परीक्षित ने इस शाप से मुक्ति का उपाय ढूँढ़ा। उन्होंने सात दिन तक एक ही आसन पर बैठकर श्रीमद्भागवत महापुराण की कथा मुनि शुकदेव जी से सुनी और मृत्यु के भय से मुक्त हो गये। उन्हें ऐसा प्रतीत हुआ कि मरता शरीर है तथा आत्मा अमर है। अत: तक्षक का भय उन्हें नहीं रहा।

यह कथा बड़ी रसमयी है। भगवान श्रीकृष्ण का रूप मनोरंजक है। श्रोता इस कथा को सुनकर अति आनंदित होते हैं तथा मन पूर्णरूप से आह्लादित हो जाता है।

"पुस्तकें ज्ञान का भण्डार होती हैं" यह बात शत-प्रतिशत सही है। दूसरे शब्दों में हम यह कह सकते हैं कि पुस्तकें हमारे ज्ञान की धरोहर हैं जो एक पीढ़ी नहीं अपितु पीढ़ी दर पीढ़ी अतीत काल के ज्ञान का आवंटन करती हुई, इस परंपरा को सजीव बनाए रखती हैं। यह हमारी सच्ची गुरु व सच्ची मित्र होती हैं।

(ii) पर्यावरण है तो मानव है

''जीवन का आधार बनाओ, विश्व में हरियाली लाओ।
क्या बिना पेड़ों के जी पाओगे, पशु-पक्षियों को भी रुलाओगे।
देख लेना एक दिन मानव रोता रह जायेगा
जब जमीन पर पेड़ पौधे नहीं होंगे
हर आँख में आँसू बहते होंगे
साँस लेने के लिए भी मानव तरस जायेगा।''

उपर्युक्त कविता का एक-एक शब्द खतरे की घंटी के समान है। कवि चीख-चीखकर समझाना चाहता है। अब भी समझ जाओ नहीं तो साँस की घुटन मौत बन जायेगी। पानी नहीं मिलेगा, प्यासे मर जाओगे। जानवर चारे व पानी के अभाव में दम तोड़ देंगे।

प्रकृति स्वयं को असंख्य रूपों में अभिव्यक्त करती है। इसकी शुद्धता, सात्विकता, सुंदरता, विशालता, असीमता तथा तेजस्विता मानव मन में नाना प्रकार की भावना उत्पन्न करती है। प्रकृति का दूसरा नाम ही पर्यावरण है। हमारा पर्यावरण शुद्ध रहे तभी हम जीवित रह सकते हैं। निरोगी रह सकते हैं।

पर्यावरण सुरक्षा को लेकर आजकल प्रत्येक नागरिक प्रयासरत है। मैं भी इस दिशा में प्रयासरत हूँ। मैंने अपने मित्रों के साथ मिलकर 'पर्यावरण मित्र' नाम से एक टोली बनाई है जो जगह-जगह पर जाकर स्वच्छता अभियान चलाती है तथा झुग्गी-झोंपड़ियों में जाकर उन्हें स्वच्छता रखने की प्रेरणा देती है। हमारी टोली को लोगों द्वारा बहुत पसंद किया जा रहा है तथा हमारे प्रयास से पर्यावरण को स्वच्छ रखने में सहायता मिली है। कुछ समाजसेवी संस्थाओं की ओर से हमें ऐसे डस्टबिन नि:शुल्क दिए गए हैं जिन्हें हमने अपने नगर के विभिन्न स्थानों पर रखा है, जिससे कि लोग बेकार की चीजें, कागज के टुकड़े, फलों के छिलके आदि इसमें डालें।

हमारा यह प्रयास बहुत सफल रहा है तथा हमारी टोली 'पर्यावरण मित्र' के साथ बहुत से लोग जुड़ते जा रहे हैं। हम 'नुक्कड़ नाटकों' के द्वारा भी लोगों में स्वच्छता के प्रति जागरुकता लाने का प्रयास कर रहे हैं। सप्ताह में एक दिन हमारी टोली विभिन्न क्षेत्रों में जाकर श्रमदान करके स्वच्छता अभियान चलाती है। हमारे प्रयास को देखकर उन क्षेत्रों के निवासी भी स्वच्छता अभियान में संलग्न हो जाते हैं। हमारी टोली द्वारा पर्यावरण को स्वच्छ रखने के लिए एक और विशेष प्रयास किया गया है—वह है वृक्षारोपण। वृक्षारोपण पर्यावरण प्रदूषण को रोकने के लिए सर्वोच्च उपाय माना गया है क्योंकि वृक्ष ही हमसे अशुद्ध वायु लेकर हमें शुद्ध वायु प्रदान करते हैं और पर्यावरण को स्वच्छ रखते हैं। हमने अपने अध्यापकों की सहायता से नगर निगम के उद्यान विभाग की ओर से अनेक पौधे प्राप्त कर लिए हैं, जिन्हें हम अपने अध्यापकों के मार्गदर्शन में ही शहर में जगह-जगह पर लगाते हैं तथा वहाँ के लोगों को भी वृक्षारोपण के लिए प्रेरित करते हैं। हमारे इस प्रयास की बहुत सराहना की गई है।

पर्यावरण शुद्धि के लिए सरकार के भी प्रयास प्रबल हैं। सरकार ने पुरानी गाड़ियों को नगर से बहिष्कृत किया है। फैक्ट्रियाँ नगर से बाहर सुदूर क्षेत्रों में लगायी गयी हैं। उत्तर प्रदेश के मुख्यमंत्री जी ने नदियों को शुद्ध करने के कड़े निर्देश दिये हैं। इस क्षेत्र में हम सब मिलकर प्रयास करेंगे तभी मनुष्य जीवित रहेगा।

(iii) कम्प्यूटर एवं मोबाइल की लाभ और हानियाँ

आज का युग वैज्ञानिक युग है। वैज्ञानिक युग का अभिप्राय है कि इस युग में अनेकानेक चमत्कारी आविष्कार हुए, जिनसे जनमानस का जीवन जटिलताओं से सरलता की ओर मुड़ने लगा। उसमें जीवन के प्रति आकर्षण उत्पन्न हुआ। कम्प्यूटर एक ऐसा ही अनोखा बल्कि मानव जीवन में अत्यंत अपरिहार्य यंत्र है जिसके बिना एक कदम भी आगे नहीं बढ़ा जा सकता। इसी के छोटे भाई के रूप में मोबाइल के आविष्कार ने तो लोगों की दिनचर्या ही बदल दी। आधुनिक समय में एक रिक्शे वाला भी अपना कॉलर उतना ही ऊँचा करके चलता है जितना एक मँहगी कार में बैठा अरबपति। वह अपने छोटे से मोबाइल से फोन तो करता ही है परंतु इसके अतिरिक्त क्रिकेट मैच की कमेंट्री, नेताजी का भाषण आदि के साथ-साथ गानों का भी भरपूर आनंद लेता है। उसे मोबाइल के उपयोग के सारे तरीके इसलिए आते हैं क्योंकि वह उन्हें सीखना चाहता है।

कम्प्यूटर एक तरह का यांत्रिक मस्तिष्क है। इसकी काम करने की गति बहुत तेज है। आज के युग में कोई क्षेत्र कम्प्यूटर से अछूता नहीं है। रेलवे, हवाई जहाज, बैंक, व्यापार, रीयल स्टेट, विद्यालय, विश्वविद्यालय आदि सभी क्षेत्रों में कम्प्यूटर का प्रयोग होता है। इस प्रकार हम कह सकते हैं कि जीवन में आने वाली हर आवश्यकता की पूर्ति कम्प्यूटर है। जरा-सा सर्वर डाउन हुआ नहीं कि लोग निकम्मे से हो जाते हैं। कम्प्यूटर के द्वारा इंटरनेट की सहायता से कई सोशल नेटवर्किंग साइट्स उपयोग की जा सकती हैं। संगीत सुनना, फिल्में देखना आदि भी कम्प्यूटर पर संभव है, कम्प्यूटर आवश्यकता के साथ-साथ मनोरंजन का भी साधन है। दूसरी ओर मोबाइल तो कम्प्यूटर से भी बढ़कर चमत्कारी है। छोटा-सा यंत्र वो करिश्मे दिखाता है कि लोग दंग रह जाते हैं। ट्विटर से तो सभी परिचित हैं। एक शिकायत ट्विटर पर प्रधानमंत्री जी को भेज दो, पुलिस तुरंत ही चली आयेगी। नोटबंदी के बाद मोबाइल फोन का कार्य अति प्रशंसनीय रहा है। कैशलैस बैंकिंग इसका अनूठा उपयोग है। इंटरनेट बैंकिंग, पेटीएम आदि ऐप्स के द्वारा घर बैठे यात्रा टिकट कराना, विभिन्न प्रकार के बिलों की अदायगी आदि सारे काम मोबाइल से घर बैठे हो सकते हैं। वीडियो कॉलिंग से अपने प्रियजनों से फेस टू फेस बातें करना, अपने प्रियजनों के शुभ-अशुभ समाचार प्राप्त करना सब कुछ मोबाइल पर संभव है। दूसरे शब्दों में हम कह सकते हैं कि मोबाइल एक चलता फिरता कम्प्यूटर है।

हर वस्तु के दो पहलू होते हैं—अच्छा व बुरा। उपर्युक्त वर्णन कम्प्यूटर व मोबाइल के लाभों की कहानी थी। इसके नुकसान भी बड़े खतरनाक होते हैं। लोग अपने मोबाइल को एक सुरक्षित यंत्र समझकर अपने सभी गोपनीय दस्तावेज उसमें दाखिल कर देते हैं, लेकिन अगर दुर्भाग्यवश मोबाइल खो गया तो बैंक अकाउण्ट से पैसे उड़ जाते हैं, पासवर्ड के माध्यम से लोगों को बहुत अहम जानकारियाँ मिल जाती हैं जो बहुत भयानक सिद्ध होती हैं। लड़कियों की अश्लील फोटो, ब्लू फिल्म अथवा बच्चों को अगवा करके उन्हें उत्पीड़ित करना भी सभी मोबाइल फोन और कम्प्यूटर के ही नुकसान हैं।

अत: यह कहना भी अति आवश्यक है कि जो दवा रोग दूर करने में सहायक होती है उसी का दुरुपयोग जीवन के लिए खतरा भी बन सकता है।

Q. 5. Write a short composition in *Hindi* of approximately *250* words on any *one* of the following topics:

निम्नलिखित विषयों में से किसी एक विषय पर हिन्दी में लगभग 250 शब्दों में संक्षिप्त लेख लिखिए: **[2016]**

(i) पश्चिमी सभ्यता के प्रभाव से फैशन एवं प्रदर्शन की प्रवृत्ति बढ़ती जा रही है, जिसके कारण अनेक प्रकार की समस्याओं का जन्म हो रहा है तथा नैतिक मूल्यों का ह्रास हो रहा है। अपने विचारों द्वारा स्पष्ट कीजिये।

(ii) "सादगी भी लोगों के दिलों में अमिट छाप छोड़ सकती है" कथन को ध्यान में रखते हुए अपने देश के किसी ऐसे व्यक्तित्व के विषय में लिखिये जिन्होंने 'सादा जीवन उच्च विचार' को आधार मानकर अपना जीवन बिताया, आपके ऊपर उस व्यक्ति का प्रभाव किस प्रकार का रहा यह भी स्पष्ट कीजिये।

(iii) योग के माध्यम से हम शरीर तथा मन दोनों को स्वस्थ कर सकते हैं, जीवन में योग की अनिवार्यता तथा उससे मिलने वाले लाभों का वर्णन करते हुए अपने विचार लिखिए।

Ans. **(i) पश्चिमी सभ्यता से प्रभावित युवा वर्ग की मानसिकता**

पश्चिमी सभ्यता के प्रभाव से फैशन और प्रदर्शन की प्रवृत्ति बढ़ती जा रही है। इस कथन में लेशमात्र भी मिथ्या नहीं है। पाश्चात्य सभ्यता इतनी प्रभावशाली हो गई है कि लोगों की विवेकबुद्धि कुंठित हो गई है। क्या सही है, क्या गलत है, यह उन्होंने सोचना ही बन्द कर दिया है। कभी-कभी तो यह फैशन इतना हास्यास्पद प्रतीत होता है कि लोगों की बुद्धि पर दया आती है। फैशन में भी तो एक सन्तुलन होना चाहिए। फैशन के नाम पर भारतीय संस्कृति को तिलांजलि देकर पाश्चात्य संस्कृति को अपनाना अपनी ही जड़ों पर कुठाराघात किये जाने के समान है। नवीनता लाना या परिवर्तन लाना बुरी बात नहीं है, लेकिन उसमें शालीनता भी होनी चाहिए। फैशन के नाम पर नग्नता, अश्लीलता, मर्यादाहीनता आदि सराहनीय नहीं है। इससे समाज में विकृति उत्पन्न होती है। ऐसा प्रतीत होता है कि पश्चिमी देशों की नकल करके हम लोग फूहड़ और लज्जाहीन हो गये हैं। पाश्चात्य संस्कृति को आत्मसात करके हम अपने रीति-रिवाजों और श्रेष्ठ परम्पराओं को नष्ट करते जा रहे हैं। फलस्वरूप समाज में अपराध, अशिष्टता, अश्लीलता, पारिवारिक विघटन उत्पन्न हो रहे हैं। आज लोगों को वेलेन्टाइन डे, अप्रैल फूल, रोज डे, मदर्स डे, फादर्स डे आदि तो याद रहते हैं। परन्तु माता-पिता, गुरु आदि के प्रति आदर भाव याद नहीं रहता है। पाश्चात्य सभ्यता का ही परिणाम है कि शादी के बाद बहुत शीघ्र सम्बन्ध विच्छेद हो रहे हैं।

हमारे पूर्वजों ने एक लम्बे और गहन अध्ययन के बाद मनुष्य के लिए एक सभ्य समाज की संरचना हेतु हर क्षेत्र में कुछ आदर्श, कुछ मूल्य, कुछ सीमाएँ निर्धारित की थीं। जिनके अनुपालन से भारतीय संस्कृति विश्व में पूजनीय बनी। परन्तु आज उन्हीं आदर्शों की अवहेलना से हमारे नैतिक मूल्यों का निरन्तर पतन हो रहा है। यह पाश्चात्य संस्कृति का ही प्रभाव है कि पति-पत्नी के सम्बन्धों के बीच तीसरे की उपस्थिति न्यायोचित ठहराई जा रही है। शर्म की बात तो यह है कि भारतीय नारी जिसकी सुन्दरता तथा शृंगार उसकी लज्जा हुआ करती थी। आज वह पूर्णतया लज्जारहित हो गयी है। युवक-युवतियों पर माता-पिता का कोई अंकुश नहीं रहा। 'गर्लफ्रेंड', 'बॉयफ्रेंड' आधुनिक फैशन है। देर रात तक घर से बाहर रहना, क्लब में पार्टी, ड्रिंक व डांस करना यह सब पाश्चात्य संस्कृति का ही प्रभाव है। 'प्रेम विवाह' इसी संस्कृति की देन है। पाश्चात्य सभ्यता ने माँ को 'मॉम' व पिता को 'डैड' कर दिया है। गुरु-शिष्य तथा भाई-बहन आदि के अतिरिक्त समाज के अहम व महत्त्वपूर्ण सम्बन्ध भी इतने दूषित हो गये हैं जिन्हें सुनकर लोग शर्मसार हो जाते हैं।

इतिहास साक्षी है कि जब कभी भी किसी देश, समाज, धर्म या समुदाय को हानि पहुँची है तो उसका कारण उसकी सभ्यता व संस्कृति तथा उसके आदर्शों पर कुठाराघात है। मार्क्स ने कहा था कि इस पाश्चात्य संस्कृति का भारत पर हावी होने का कारण अर्थ अथवा पूँजी है। यह पूँजी ही आधुनिक परिवेश में समाज के लिए स्वादिष्ट विष परोस रही है जो सम्पूर्ण मानव जाति को पतन की ओर ले जा रहा है।

(ii) 'सादा जीवन उच्च विचार'

'सादा जीवन उच्च विचार' बड़ी सारगर्भित उक्ति है। भले ही आज के आकर्षण-युक्त परिवेश में इस उक्ति का महत्व न रहा हो परन्तु युगों-युगों से यह कथन महत्वपूर्ण रहा है क्योंकि अनेक महापुरुषों ने इसके महत्त्व को द्विगुणित किया है। कौन नहीं जानता महान विभूति, लाल बहादुर शास्त्री को, जो गुदड़ी के लाल कहे जाते थे। वह सादगी में पले बढ़े तथा जीवन में संघर्षों से निरन्तर लड़ते रहे।

ऐसी ही एक महान विभूति ईश्वरचन्द्र विद्यासागर जो सादगी की प्रतिमूर्ति थे। ऐसे ही लोगों में मेरी प्रेरणा का स्रोत रहे पूर्व राष्ट्रपति स्व. डॉ. ए. पी. जे. अब्दुल कलाम। जिन्होंने 'सादा जीवन उच्च विचार' को अपने जीवन में अपनाया।

हमारे देश को विकसित राष्ट्रों की पंक्ति में पहुंचाने का स्वप्न देखने वाले डॉ. ए. पी. जे. अब्दुल कलाम हमारे राष्ट्र के बारहवें राष्ट्रपति रहे। इन्होंने अपने जीवन में कर्मठता को अपनाया। उन्होंने किसी राजनीतिक दल से सम्बन्ध नहीं रखे। साथ ही ये राष्ट्रपति के पद को शोभायमान करने वाले देश के पहले वैज्ञानिक थे। 15 अक्टूबर 1931 को तमिलनाडु राज्य में रामेश्वरम के पास एक मछुआरे परिवार में जन्मे डॉ. कलाम एक मध्यवर्गीय परिवार से सम्बन्धित थे। इनका पूरा नाम अब्दुल पाकिर जैनुलब्दीन अब्दुल कलाम था।

बचपन से ही इनमें आत्मनिर्भरता का जज्बा था। जिस उम्र में बच्चों को खेलकूद में रुचि होती है, उस आयु में अखबार बेचकर परिवार के सहयोगी बन गए थे। शिक्षा प्राप्ति के बाद प्रशिक्षु के रूप में बैंगलौर के हिन्दुस्तान एरोनॉटिक्स लिमिटेड जा पहुँचे। वहीं उन्हें पुस्तकीय ज्ञान का व्यावहारिक रूप सीखने का अवसर मिला था। अब्दुल कलाम ने सदैव निराशा के समय भी इस गुरुमन्त्र को आधार बनाया था कि जिस प्रकार रोज सूर्योदय अवश्य होता है, प्रतिवर्ष बसन्त अवश्य आता है, उसी प्रकार हमें भी आशा नहीं खोनी चाहिए। ये सभी बातें मुझे भी प्रेरित करती हैं।

ऐसे प्रतिभावान व्यक्तित्व की सादगी व विचारों की श्रेष्ठता मुझे सदैव प्रोत्साहित करती रही है। अपने जीवन में डॉ. कलाम ने 20 साल रक्षा अनुसंधान एवं विकास प्रयोगशाला में बिताये। उनकी लगन व स्वप्न हमेशा उनकी प्रेरणा रही। ऐसे होनहार, ईमानदार, सादगी पसन्द कर्मठ, सचरित्र अनुशासन प्रिय देशभक्त डॉ. कलाम सदा ही मेरे जीवन की प्रेरणा रहेंगे।

अनेकानेक उपाधियों व उपलब्धियों से झोली भरी होने पर भी उनका व्यक्तित्व बहुत विनम्र था। वह कभी किसी धर्म व समुदाय के पक्षधर नहीं रहे। मुझे ही नहीं देश के प्रत्येक नागरिक को उनकी मानवतावादी विचारधारा प्रेरणा से भरती रहेगी। मैं भी उनके जीवन के समान अगर देश व मानवता की सेवा में अपना जीवन अर्पित कर सकूँ तो श्रेष्ठ बन सकूँगा। उन्होंने धन के प्रति उदासीनता, मानव मूल्यों के सम्वाहक बन सादगी से जीवन बिताते हुए अन्त समय तक कर्मनिष्ठता का आदर्श प्रस्तुत किया। मेरा जीवन ऐसे ही कर्मनिष्ठता व सादगी से भरा रहे, ये प्रेरणा जीवनपर्यन्त मेरे मन में समाहित रहेगी।

(iii) योग साधना का महत्व

योग शब्द 'युज' धातु से बना है। संस्कृत व्याकरण में दो युज धातुओं का उल्लेख है। एक का अर्थ है जोड़ना, दूसरे का मन की स्थिरता। हमारे जीवन में योग का महत्वपूर्ण स्थान है। यह अक्षरश: सत्य है कि योग के माध्यम से हम अपने मन व शरीर को पूर्णरूपेण स्वस्थ बना सकते हैं। यदि वास्तव में हम अपने जीवन को सुखी व समृद्ध बनाना चाहते हैं तथा दु:खों से छुटकारा पाना चाहते हैं तो हमें नियमित रूप से योग करना चाहिए। यूँ तो जीवन में सुख-दु:ख आते रहते हैं, लेकिन मन को स्वस्थ रखने के लिए हमें शरीर को पुस्त-दुरुस्त रखना अति आवश्यक है।

कर्म साधना के लिए शरीर का स्वस्थ होना आवश्यक है, लेकिन मन की स्वस्थता ही कर्म करने की प्रेरणा देती है। अत: नियमित योग के माध्यम से ही तन व मन दोनों स्वस्थ रह सकते हैं। नियमित योगासनों को करने से शरीर में शक्ति तो आती ही है साथ ही रूप में लावण्य आता है। खुली हवा में योग करना फेफड़ों में ऑक्सीजन की वृद्धि करता है। शरीर का अंग-प्रत्यंग क्रियाशील होता है तथा शरीर में लचीलापन आता है। योग के द्वारा अनेक रोगों से भी रक्षा होती है तथा यह रक्त को शुद्ध करता है। हृदय को शुद्ध रक्त प्राप्त होता है। शरीर का आलस्य दूर होता है तथा क्रियाशीलता बढ़ती है।

योग करने का सबसे श्रेष्ठ समय प्रात:काल होता है। सूर्य नमस्कार करने से भयंकर से भयंकर रोगों से निवृत्ति मिल जाती है। योग करने से खूब भूख लगती है तथा पाचन शक्ति दुरुस्त रहती है। आत्मविश्वास, एकाग्रता एवं मस्तिष्क में बल वृद्धि होती है। शरीर से पसीना निकलता है जिससे शरीर की गन्दगी दूर होती है।

योग न करने से शरीर आलसी, रोगी व अनमना-सा रहता है। काम करने में मन नहीं लगता। भोजन में आसक्ति नहीं रहती। हमेशा प्रतीत होता है कि जैसे हम बीमार हैं। चिकित्सक के पास जाकर भी सन्तुष्टि नहीं होती। योग बिना पैसे का उपचार है। यह सब योग का ही चमत्कार है कि हमारे ऋषि-मुनियों ने योग के बल पर निराहार रहकर वर्षों तक एक पैर पर खड़े होकर तपस्याएँ कीं हैं। यही कारण है आज भी ऋषि-मुनियों ने व्यायाम और योगासन पर बहुत बल दिया है। बाबा रामदेव का योग आज के युग में योग का स्पष्ट उदाहरण है। उन्होंने योग के क्षेत्र में क्रांति ला दी है। उन्होंने योग के माध्यम से लोगों के लाइलाज रोगों को भी दूर किया है। उन्होंने प्राणायाम और योग के अनेक आसन बताये हैं। इन योगासनों का ज्ञान बाबा रामदेव मौखिक और लिखित रूप में टेलीविजन के आस्था और संस्कार चैनलों पर नियमित देते हैं।

योग का सबसे बड़ा लाभ तो यह है कि योगी व्यक्ति को बहुत जल्दी बुढ़ापा नहीं आता। उसके शरीर का हर अंग नियमित व्यायाम व योग से क्रियाशील बना रहता है। आज के समय में बी. पी., डाइबिटीज, आर्थराइटिस, थायरॉइड जैसे अनेक रोग लगे हुए हैं, परन्तु इसमें सन्देह नहीं है कि जिन्होंने बचपन से योग व व्यायाम को अपनी नियमित दिनचर्या बनाया है, उसे कोई बीमारी छू नहीं सकती।

हमारे देश के प्रधानमन्त्री श्री नरेन्द्र मोदी जी तो व्यायाम व योग के प्रबल समर्थक हैं। उन्होंने प्रत्येक व्यक्ति के लिए योग की आवश्यकता पर जोर दिया है। इसके महत्व को दर्शाने के लिए उन्होंने 21 जून को ''योग दिवस'' का भी आयोजन किया था। वह स्वयं योग करते हैं। कहने का अभिप्राय यह है कि योग करने वाले की कार्यक्षमता एवं मस्तिष्क क्षमता में अत्यधिक वृद्धि होती है। इसलिए मन, बुद्धि एवं शरीर को स्वस्थ रखने के लिए योग करना चाहिए।

Q. 6. Write a short composition in *Hindi* of approximately *250* words on any *one* of the following topics:

निम्नलिखित विषयों में से किसी एक विषय पर हिन्दी में लगभग 250 शब्दों में संक्षिप्त लेख लिखिए: {2015}

(i) **'विश्वासपात्र मित्र जीवन की एक औषध है।' कथन के आधार पर बताइए कि मानव के जीवन में मित्रों का क्या महत्व है? वे किस प्रकार व्यक्ति के जीवन को प्रभावित करते हैं? आप अपने मित्र का चुनाव करते समय उसमें किन गुणों का होना आवश्यक समझेंगे? अपने विचार स्पष्टत: लिखिए।**

(ii) भारतीय संस्कृति में 'अतिथि को देवता के समान माना जाता है।' वर्तमान परिस्थितियों में यह मान्यता कहाँ तक सत्य के रूप में दिखाई दे रही है? अतिथि कब बोझ बन जाता है और किस प्रकार? विचारों द्वारा समझाइए।

(iii) स्वच्छता हम सभी के लिए लाभदायक है, यदि आपको स्वच्छ भारत अभियान में सहयोग देने के लिए कोई तीन कार्य करने के लिए कहा जाए तो आप किन कार्यों को करना पसन्द करेंगे तथा क्यों? अपने विचारों द्वारा स्पष्ट कीजिए।

Ans. **(i)** **विश्वासपात्र मित्र जीवन की एक औषध है।**

मनुष्य एक सामाजिक प्राणी है। अत: सामाजिक प्राणी होने के नाते मनुष्य सभी के साथ मिल-जुलकर समूह में रहना पसन्द करता है। ये व्यक्ति एक-दूसरे के रिश्तेदार या सम्बन्धी ही नहीं होते हैं। इन सम्बन्धों को मित्रता की संज्ञा दी गयी है। अच्छी मित्रता के अभाव में जीवन नीरस हो जाता है। इसलिए मानव जीवन में मित्रता की बहुत उपयोगिता है। जिस प्रकार धर्म और विवेक मनुष्य को पाप से बचाते हैं, उसी प्रकार एक विश्वासपात्र मित्र अपने मित्र को संकट के समय बचाता है। एक सच्चा मित्र अपने मित्र को कुमार्ग से हटाकर सन्मार्ग की तरफ ले जाता है। जब-जब मनुष्य को निराशा घेरती है और वह कर्तव्य विमुख होने लगता है तब-तब एक आदर्श मित्र उसे कल्याणकारी उपदेश देता है। यहाँ पर हम महाभारत के उस प्रसंग को याद कर सकते हैं जब रणक्षेत्र में अर्जुन मोहग्रस्त होकर कर्तव्य विमुख हो रहे थे, तब श्रीकृष्ण ने अर्जुन को कर्मयोग का उपदेश दिया था। हमें यह ज्ञात है कि श्रीकृष्ण और अर्जुन अभिन्न मित्र थे।

मित्रता जीवन निर्माण का एक बहुत ही महत्वपूर्ण अंग होता है अत: मित्र बनाते समय हमें अपने विवेक और बुद्धि से काम लेना चाहिए। जो लोग ऊपरी व्यक्तित्व से प्रभावित होकर बिना सोच-विचार किये मित्र बनाते हैं, वे जीवन में लाभ के बजाय हानि उठाते हैं।

इस प्रकार हमें भी सच्चा मित्र बनना चाहिए तथा मित्र की आँख में धूल नहीं झोंकनी चाहिए।

सर्वप्रथम एक अच्छे मित्र में मित्रवत् व्यवहार का गुण होना चाहिए। एक अच्छे मित्र को धैर्यवान होना चाहिए। उसे एक अच्छा श्रोता तथा अच्छा वक्ता होना चाहिए ताकि वह अपने मित्र की समस्याओं को धैर्य से सुने और उनका समाधान कर सके। एक अच्छे मित्र में जीवंतता होनी चाहिए और उसमें हास्यप्रियता का गुण होना चाहिए। इसके अतिरिक्त उसे सत्यवादी, ईमानदार और नि:स्वार्थी होना चाहिए।

एक आदर्श मित्र विपत्ति और संकट में अपने मित्र की सहायता करने को सदैव तत्पर रहता है। जिस प्रकार श्रीकृष्ण ने सुदामा की संकट में सहायता की थी, वैसी आदर्श मित्रता का उदाहरण किसी अन्य देश में नहीं मिलता है।

आज व्यक्ति का मुख्य ध्येय धनोपार्जन करना और भौतिक विलास के साधन जुटाना मात्र रह गया है, तो ऐसे युग में जिस व्यक्ति का एक ही सच्चा मित्र है, वह व्यक्ति सही अर्थों में भाग्यशाली है। हमारी प्रतिष्ठा इस बात में नहीं है कि हमारे कितने मित्र हैं अथवा हमारे मित्रों की संख्या कितनी अधिक है, बल्कि इस बात में है कि हमारे जो भी मित्र हैं, वे किस आचरण के हैं और आदर्श मित्र की कसौटी पर खरे उतरते हैं या नहीं। अत: इस प्रकार हम कह सकते हैं कि एक सच्चा और विश्वासपात्र मित्र जीवन की औषधि के समान होता है।

(ii) **भारतीय संस्कृति में अतिथि का स्वरूप**

भारत एक ऐसा देश है जिसमें एक नहीं अनेक विशेषताएँ हैं। फिर चाहे वे अपनत्व की भावना हो, या रिश्तों का मान-सम्मान हो, सब कुछ अपने आप में विशाल है। इन सबके अलावा एक और परम्परा जो हमारे देश में युगों-युगों से चली आ रही है और आज भी चल रही है। वह परम्परा है "अतिथि देवो भव" की। भारतीय संस्कृति में अतिथि को देवता के समान माना जाता है। 'अतिथि' का शाब्दिक अर्थ है, जिसके आने की कोई निश्चत तिथि न हो। कालान्तर में 'अतिथि' शब्द हमारे घर आने वाले मेहमान के अर्थ में रूढ़ हो गया। हमारे घर जब भी कोई मेहमान आता है तो हम उसकी सेवा में कोई कमी नहीं रखते। गृहस्वामी उसको जल, आसन, भोजन आदि प्रदान कर उसका सम्मान करते हैं। उनके लिए घर में अच्छे-अच्छे व्यंजन तैयार करते हैं, उन्हें अपने साथ दर्शनीय स्थलों का भ्रमण कराते हैं।

समयानुसार, आज परिस्थितियाँ कुछ बदल चुकी हैं। आज लोगों के पास समय का अभाव है, इसलिए आने वाले व्यक्ति को भी आने से पहले दूरभाष द्वारा अपने आने की सूचना देनी चाहिए। जिससे मेज़बान स्वयं को मानसिक रूप से तैयार कर ले। यदि वह नौकरी करता है, तो उस दिन के लिए अवकाश स्वीकृत करा लेगा। जहाँ पति-पत्नी दोनों ही नौकरी करते हैं वहाँ तो यह अत्यन्त आवश्यक है कि आने वाला उनकी परेशानी का कारण न बने। दूसरे, आज की परिस्थितियों को देखते हुए मेहमान को अधिक समय तक नहीं ठहरना चाहिए क्योंकि जिनके घर वह आया हुआ है, हो सकता है उसके कारण उन पर कार्य का भार अधिक बढ़ जाय, जिसके कारण वे परेशानी महसूस करें।

अतिथि यदि स्वयं विवेक और सहयोग से कार्य ले, तो वह कभी बोझ नहीं बन सकता, इसमें कोई सन्देह नहीं है। यदि गृहस्वामी आर्थिक रूप से कमज़ोर है तो मेहमान के आने पर उसके घर का बजट गड़बड़ा जाता है। ऐसे समय पर मेहमान स्वयं ही यदि फल, सब्जियाँ आदि उपहार के रूप में लाये तो गृहस्वामी अतिरिक्त भार से बच सकते हैं। यदि पति-पत्नी दोनों नौकरी करते हैं और मेहमान को रुकना आवश्यक है तो वह उन्हें अवकाश लेने के लिए विवश न करे अपितु गृहकार्य में उनका सहयोग करे तो इससे उन्हें खुशी होगी। साथ ही मेहमान को चाहिए कि वह उनसे अनावश्यक खर्च न कराये तथा सामान्य पारिवारिक सदस्य की तरह ही रहे।

अन्त में हम कह सकते हैं कि हमारे देश में 'अतिथि देवो भव:' की भावना अभी भी वैसी ही है जैसी प्राचीनकाल में थी, किन्तु अतिथि भी यदि मेजबान के घर की परिस्थितियों को समझकर अपनेपन की भावना रखे तो मेज़बान यह कभी नहीं सोचेगा, "अतिथि तुम कब जाओगे ?" बल्कि द्वार पर उन्हें विदा करते समय यही पूछेगा 'अतिथि, फिर तुम कब आओगे ? हम तुम्हारी प्रतीक्षा करेंगे।'

(iii) स्वच्छता की आवश्यकता

स्वच्छता से मनुष्य का तन मन स्वस्थ रहता है और वातावरण अच्छा और स्वास्थ्यप्रद। स्वच्छता को प्राचीनकाल से ही बहुत अधिक महत्त्व प्रदान किया गया है। शौच अर्थात् स्वच्छता। स्वच्छता आन्तरिक और बाह्य दो प्रकार की होती है—आन्तरिक स्वच्छता अर्थात् अपने मन को ईर्ष्या, द्वेष, क्रोध, मोह आदि विकारों से मुक्त रखना और बाह्य स्वच्छता है अपने शरीर को स्वच्छ रखना तथा अपने आसपास के वातावरण को स्वच्छ और शुद्ध रखना। मन को स्वच्छ करके हम अच्छा आचरण अपनाते हैं और अपने शरीर तथा वातावरण को स्वच्छ करके हम अच्छा स्वास्थ्य प्राप्त कर सकते हैं।

अभी विगत् 2 अक्टूबर गाँधी जयन्ती को वर्तमान प्रधानमन्त्री श्री नरेन्द्र मोदी ने 'स्वच्छ भारत अभियान' के रूप में मनाने की घोषणा की। स्वास्थ्यप्रद शुरुआत के सन्दर्भ में नदियों की सफाई का अभियान भी चलाया गया। हम सभी का कर्तव्य है कि हम सब 'स्वच्छ भारत अभियान' का हिस्सा बनें और संकल्प करें कि हम अपने देश को साफ-सुथरा रखेंगे। जब प्रत्येक व्यक्ति स्वच्छता के लिए एकजुट हो जायेगा तो स्वच्छ भारत का स्वप्न साकार हो जायेगा। स्वच्छता अभियान में सहयोग देने के लिए मैंने अपने सहपाठियों से बात की और हमने तीन कार्यों को करने का संकल्प लिया। जो इस प्रकार हैं—

1. **स्वच्छता की शुरुआत अपने घर से**—उठते ही अपना बिस्तर ठीक करना, कमरा साफ करना, अपने सभी सामान को तरीके से लगाना और अपने घर में किसी को भी गन्दगी फैलाने से रोकना, पॉलीथिन का प्रयोग न करना और न करने देना, कूड़ा कूड़ेदान में डालना आदि।

2. **कक्षा-कक्ष में**—हम कभी भी कक्षा-कक्ष को गन्दा नहीं करेंगे। कागज़, पेन्सिल की छीलन, रैपर आदि सब कूड़ेदान में डालेंगे। कक्षा-कक्ष के एक कोने में कूड़ेदान रखा रहेगा। कोई भी छात्र कक्षा को गन्दा न करे, इस बात का हम सब मिलकर ध्यान रखेंगे।

3. **अपने आस-पड़ोस की स्वच्छता**—प्राय: देखा जाता है, लोग कूड़ा सड़कों पर डाल देते हैं जिसे कुत्ते या अन्य जानवर फैलाकर और गन्दगी फैलाते रहते हैं। इसके लिए हम ध्यान रखेंगे कि कोई भी पड़ोसी अपने घर का कूड़ा बाहर न डाले, कोई सड़क पर थूके नहीं और अपने घर के पास पेड़-पौधे आदि लगाकर पर्यावरण शुद्ध रखे।

इसके साथ ही लोगों को हम स्वच्छता के प्रति जागरूक करना चाहेंगे।

वास्तविकता यह है कि लोग स्वच्छता के महत्व को जानते हैं, किन्तु आलस्यवश इसको नजरअन्दाज करते हैं। जिसका परिणाम होता है; गन्दगी, बीमारियाँ, प्रदूषण आदि। अत: हमें स्वच्छता के महत्व को समझते हुए स्वच्छता के प्रति जागरूक रहना चाहिए तथा अपने घर, विद्यालय और देश को स्वच्छ रखने का संकल्प लेना चाहिए।

Story Writing

Long Answer Type Questions

Q. 1. Write a short composition in *Hindi* of approximately 250 words of the following topic: [2020]

निम्नलिखित विषय पर हिंदी में लगभग 250 शब्दों में संक्षिप्त लेख लिखिए:

एक ऐसी मौलिक कहानी लिखो, जिसके अंत में आपके विचार से यह स्पष्ट हो कि बिना विचार जो करे सो पाछे पछताए।'

Ans. **"बिना विचारे जो करे"**

ईश्वर ने मनुष्य को विलक्षण बुद्धि वाला अद्भुत मस्तिष्क दिया है। अत: उसे अपनी बुद्धि से विचार करके ही कार्य करना चाहिए। कुछ लोग जल्दबाजी में काम को बिगाड़ देते हैं। कितना ही मनुष्य चालाक क्यों न हों कहीं न कहीं गलती हो ही जाती है। बिना सोचे-विचारे कोई कार्य नहीं करना चाहिए, ऐसा करने से काम बिगड़ता है और मन में भी दु:ख होता है। ईश्वर ने हमें बुद्धि इसीलिए दी है कि हम हर कार्य को अपनी बुद्धि से सोच समझकर करें।

एक समय की बात है एक गाँव में एक शिकारी रहता था। उसके घर में एक छोटा बच्चा था और एक कुत्ता था जो शिकारी की अनुपस्थिति में उस बच्चे की रक्षा करता था। शाम को शिकारी आकर उस कुत्ते को बहुत प्यार करता था और अपने हाथ से उसे खाना देता था। एक दिन शिकारी अपने बच्चे को कुत्ते की देख-देख में छोड़कर शिकार खेलने के लिए वन में चला गया। इसी बीच एक भेड़िया घर में घुस आया और उस बच्चे को खाने के लिए पालने में से उठा लिया। इतने में कुत्ते ने झपट कर बच्चे को उसके मुँह से छुड़ा लिया। बच्चा रोता हुआ सरक-सरक कर अन्दर के कमरे में चला गया और कुछ देर बाद वहीं सो गया। इधर कुत्ते और भेड़िये की खूब लड़ाई हुई, लेकिन कुत्ते ने उसे मार गिराया। कुत्ता बाहर बैठकर अपने स्वामी की राह देखने लगा। शाम को जैसे ही शिकारी आया तो कुत्ते ने उसका रोज की तरह स्वागत किया लेकिन शिकारी को कुत्ते के मुँह में खून देखकर अचम्भा हुआ। जब उसने पालने को खाली पाया तो उसका पारा चढ़ गया कि आज तो उसके कुत्ते ने उसके बच्चे को खा लिया। उसने आव देखा न ताव बन्दूक उठाकर अपने कुत्ते को गोली मार दी। एक चीत्कार के साथ कुत्ता वहीं ढेर हो गया। घबराहट और क्रोध भरी मुद्रा में वह भीतर के कमरे में घुसा तो मालूम हुआ कि कोने में उसका बच्चा सो रहा है और वहीं थोड़ी दूर पर एक भेड़िया मरा पड़ा है।

अब तो उसे समझने में देर न लगी कि उसके वफादार कुत्ते ने बच्चे की रक्षा करते हुए उस भेड़िए को मार डाला है। उसने बच्चे को गोद में उठाया और अपनी गलती पर रोने लगा। बच्चे को सुरक्षित देखकर उसे अपनी गलती और जल्दबाजी का ज्ञान हुआ। वह कुत्ते के पास पहुँच कर सिर धुन-धुन कर अपनी भूल और जल्दबाजी पर पश्चाताप करने लगा। सच ही कहा गया है

''बिना विचारे जो करे, सो पाछे पछताए।
काम बिगाड़े आपनो, जग में होत हँसाय।।''

Q. 2. Write a short composition in *Hindi* of approximately 250 words of the following topic: [2019]

निम्नलिखित विषय पर हिंदी में लगभग 250 शब्दों में संक्षिप्त लेख लिखिए:

एक मौलिक कहानी लिखिए जिसका अन्त प्रस्तुत वाक्य से किया गया हो—और मैंने राहत की साँस लेते हुए सोचा कि आज मेरा मानव जीवन सफल हो गया।

Marking Scheme

भूमिका

कहानी का विस्तार– मौलिकता, उद्देश्य, कथानक। (मानवता के गुणों से सम्बन्धित)

उपसंहार– दी गई अंतिम पंक्ति से अन्त करते हुए।

Ans. **"मेरा मानव जीवन सफल हुआ"**

मानव जीवन दुर्लभ है। मानव जीवन की सार्थकता कुछ कर गुजरने में है। दूसरों के कष्टों को देखकर हम प्रभावित होते हैं और उन्हें दूर करने या कुछ कम करने के भाव हृदय में अवश्य उत्पन्न होते हैं। मुझमें इस भावना का बीज मेरे पिताजी ने बोया था। मेरे पिताजी सरकारी स्कूल में इतिहास पढ़ाते हैं। मैं भी उसी स्कूल में आठवीं कक्षा का छात्र हूँ। हमारा गाँव छोटा-सा था। हमारा यह सरकारी स्कूल भी कुछ बड़ा न था। पूरे स्कूल में मात्र दो अध्यापक ही थे। एक मेरे पिताजी और दूसरे मास्टर राजाराम।

गाँवों में अधिकांश लोग अनपढ़ थे और खेती करते थे। गाँव के 8–10 घरों में दूरदर्शन था। जहाँ स्कूल की छुट्टी के बाद हम सब जमा हो जाते और कार्टून देखते थे। कार्टून के बीच में आने वाले विज्ञापनों को भी हम बड़े शौक से देखते थे।

एक दिन मेरी नजर और सोच एक विज्ञापन पर टिक गई, वह विज्ञापन शौचालय के बारे में था। "शौचालय" एक नया

विचार, एक नयी सोच थी मेरे लिए। हमारे गाँव में शौचालय नहीं था। शौचालय न होने के कारण लघु शंका अथवा नित्यकर्म के लिए घर से बाहर ही जाना पड़ता था।

मोदी जी ने शौचालय और उसकी स्वच्छता व महत्ता के बारे में "मन की बात" में बताया। इस बारे में मैंने पिताजी से बात की, तो उन्होंने छोटा बच्चा समझकर बात को टाल दिया।

मैंने मन ही मन यह संकल्प कर लिया कि गाँव में शौचालय जरूर बनवायेंगे और खुले में शौच नहीं जायेंगे। मैंने गाँव के पंचों से भी बात की। पर फिर वही हुआ। काका ने कहा, ''अभी तेरे खेलने की उम्र है। इन सब बातों में मत पड़।'' मन फिर भी न माना।

जिलाधीश को गाँव और शौचालय निर्माण का निवेदन करते हुए एक पत्र लिखा। पत्र का कोई जवाब नहीं आया। पता नहीं चल रहा था कि मुझे आगे क्या करना चाहिए। पिताजी से पुन: इस बारे में बात की। इस बार उन्होंने बात की गम्भीरता को समझा और आशा की लौ जगायी। उन्होंने कहा,

"अपना हाथ जगन्नाथ"

तो फिर दूसरों के भरोसे क्यों बैठे रहें। पिताजी और मैंने गाँव के लोगों को इकट्ठा किया। शौचालय के बारे में बताया तो रघु दादा और बहुत से लोग भड़क उठे। उन्होंने कहा कि वे अपने घरों में गन्दगी नहीं करेंगे। ऐसा करने से घर अपवित्र हो जायेंगे और वे पूजा-पाठ नहीं कर पायेंगे। हमारी पहल बेकार गई। मैंने फिर भी हिम्मत न हारी। हमने लोगों में जागरूकता लाने के लिए कई पोस्टर बनाकर गाँव में लगाए। लेकिन हर प्रयास असफल रहा।

पिताजी से बात की। उनसे घर में एक शौचालय बनवाने को कहा। अनुमति मिलने पर मैं और मेरे दोस्त ईंट, मिट्टी, सीमेंट सब लेकर आए। गाँव के मिस्त्री को बुलाया। उसे एक छोटा-सा शौचालय बनाने को कहा। पिताजी की मदद से शहर जाकर कमोड लेकर आए और उसे वहीं लगवा दिया। संयोग की बात है कि एक दिन रघु दादा को दस्तों की शिकायत हो गई। बार-बार बाहर जाने में तकलीफ होने लगी। तब पिताजी उन्हें घर लेकर आये। शौचालय का प्रयोग करवाया। पूरा गाँव शौचालय देखने आया। सबने अपने घरों में शौचालय बनाने की ठान ली और मैंने राहत की साँस लेते हुए सोचा कि आज मेरा मानव जीवन सफल हो गया।

Q. 3. **Write a short composition in *Hindi* of approximately 250 words of the following topic:** [2018]

निम्नलिखित विषय पर हिंदी में लगभग 250 शब्दों में संक्षिप्त लेख लिखिए:

एक ऐसी मौलिक कहानी लिखिए जिसके अंत में यह वाक्य लिखा गया हो—'अंतत: मैं अपनी योजना में सफल हो सका/हो सकी।'

📋 **Marking Scheme** - - - - - - - - - - - - - - - - - -

मौलिक कहानी (भूमिका)
कहानी जिसमें योजना का वर्णन विस्तार से किया गया हो।
सीख (उपसंहार)

Ans.

"अपनी योजना में सफल हो सका"

रीता मेरी बचपन की मित्र थी। कक्षा 1 से हम एक ही विद्यालय में पढ़ते आ रहे हैं। उसके परिवार में उसकी एक छोटी बहन गीता, एक छोटा भाई राजू तथा माता-पिता थे। उसके पिता एक सरकारी दफ्तर में काम करते थे। वह एक मध्यमवर्गीय परिवार था।

रीता पढ़ाई-लिखाई में बहुत ही होशियार थी। हमेशा कक्षा में प्रथम आती थी। पढ़ने के साथ-साथ वह खेलने, गाने-नाचने में भी होशियार थी। विद्यालय का कोई भी सांस्कृतिक या खेल का कार्यक्रम हो, रीता के बिना नहीं होता था। घर के कामों में भी वह अपनी माँ का हाथ बँटाया करती थी। सभी उसको बहुत पसंद करते थे। दसवीं कक्षा में भी उसने प्रथम स्थान प्राप्त किया। वह बहुत खुश थी। फिर उसने ग्यारहवीं कक्षा में प्रवेश लिया। उसी की कक्षा में एक नई लड़की ने प्रवेश लिया जिसका नाम मीरा था। वह एक बड़े व्यवसायी की इकलौती पुत्री थी, जिसको अपने पैसे का घमण्ड था। रीता भी उसकी सहेली बन गई थी। अब उसने मेरे साथ बात करना और रहना बिल्कुल छोड़ दिया था। वह अब हर समय मीरा के साथ ही रहती थी। मीरा एक बिगड़ी हुई लड़की थी। फैशन करना, पिक्चरें देखना, पार्टियाँ करना उसके यही शौक थे। रीता भी धीरे-धीरे उसके रंग में रंगने लगी थी। अब उसका मन पढ़ाई में भी नहीं लगता था। उस पर भी फैशन करने का भूत सवार हो गया था। सीधी सादी रीता को अब पार्टियों में मजा आने लगा था।

अब वह घर से भी गायब रहती थी तथा अपने माता-पिता से नाजायज़ माँगें करती थी, महँगी ड्रेस या पिक्चर के लिए पैसे माँगती थी। उसके माता-पिता जब उसकी माँगें पूरी नहीं करते थे तो उनसे झगड़ा करती थी। कभी-कभी वह चोरी भी करने लगी थी। उसकी इन आदतों से उसके घर वाले और स्कूल के लोग भी परेशान थे।

मैं भी अपनी मित्र को इस तरह गलत रास्ते पर जाते देख परेशान थी।

मैंने इस बारे में प्रधानाचार्य जी से बात की। एक दिन स्कूल की प्रधानाचार्या ने उसके माता-पिता को बुलाया और रीता के बारे में बताया। उसकी माँ ने प्रधानाचार्या से मिलकर एक योजना बनाई। अगले दिन जब वह सोकर उठी और स्कूल के लिए तैयार होने लगी तो घर में किसी ने उससे बातचीत नहीं की। उसने अपनी छोटी बहन और भाई से भी बात करनी चाही पर कोई नहीं बोला। सभी अपने-अपने काम में लगे रहे। उसके बहन-भाई भी उसके साथ स्कूल नहीं गये। उसे अकेले ही जाना पड़ा। स्कूल में भी कक्षा में किसी ने भी उससे बात नहीं की न उसके साथ कोई बैठा। उसको बड़ा अजीब सा लगा, लेकिन उसने कोई ध्यान नहीं दिया और वह मीरा के साथ घूमने लगी तथा स्कूल के बाद पिक्चर देखने चली गई। रात को देर से घर आने पर भी उसको डाँट नहीं पड़ी। कई दिन तक ऐसा ही चलता रहा अब उसे कुछ भी अच्छा नहीं लग रहा था। वह रात को सो नहीं सकी। सारी रात वह अपने पिछले

दिनों किये गये बर्ताव के बारे में सोचती रही और उसे अब पश्चाताप होने लगा, वह सारी रात रोती रही।

सुबह उठते ही वह अपनी माँ के पास गई और अपने किये गये व्यवहार के लिए क्षमा माँगी और भविष्य में इस तरह का काम न करने की कसम खाई। माँ, पिताजी व भाई बहनों ने उसे माफ कर दिया। विद्यालय में भी उसने सभी अध्यापिकाओं और प्रधानाचार्या जी से माफी माँगी। तभी उसके माता-पिता भी वहाँ आये और उन्होंने रीता को बताया कि तुमको सुधारने के लिए हमने प्रधानाचार्या से मिलकर यह योजना बनाई थी। इस प्रकार अतत: मैं अपनी योजना में सफल हो सकी।

Q. 4. Write a short composition in *Hindi* of approximately 250 words of the following topic: [2017]

निम्नलिखित विषय पर हिंदी में लगभग 250 शब्दों में संक्षिप्त लेख लिखिए:

अरे मित्र! "तुमने तो सिद्ध कर दिया कि तुम ही मेरे सच्चे मित्र हो।" इस पंक्ति से आरंभ करते हुए कोई कहानी लिखिए।

Ans. **सच्चे मित्र पर आधारित कहानी**

"अरे मित्र! तुमने तो सिद्ध कर दिया कि तुम्हीं मेरे सच्चे मित्र हो।" अपने मित्र राहुल से यह बात कहते हुये मेरी आँखें आँसुओं से भर आईं।

बात उस समय की है जब पाकिस्तानियों ने हमारे देश के पाक अधिकृत क्षेत्र की एक बहुत ऊँची इमारत की रखवाली करने वाले अठारह जवानों की प्रात: छ: बजे उस समय हत्या कर दी जब वे रातभर सीमा पर अपनी ड्यूटी पूरी करके सो रहे थे। उस समय देश में इस घटना से अफरा-तफरी मची हुई थी। पूरे विश्व में पाकिस्तान की इस काली करतूत की निंदा हो रही थी।

हमारे प्रधानमंत्री माननीय श्री नरेन्द्र मोदी जी के दिल में बड़ा दर्द था। हमारी सेना के अफसरों की नींद उड़ी हुई थी। सबके दिमाग में एक ही बात थी कि पाकिस्तान को इसका सबक कैसे सिखाया जाये? मेरे दोस्त ! उसी समय मेरी माताजी का मेरे पास फोन आया—बेटा ! पिताजी को डॉक्टर ने कैंसर की पहली स्टेज बताई है। मैं सुनकर काँप गया और मुझे लगा अब शायद मेरे पिताजी जीवित ना रहेंगे। मेरे सामने एक तरफ मेरे देश की सुरक्षा का कर्तव्य और दूसरी ओर मेरे पिता के जीवन का प्रश्न। मेरे लिए दोनों ही कर्तव्य महत्वपूर्ण थे।

मुझे उस समय वह दिन याद आया जब मैंने जेओसी (जूनियर ऑफिसर कमाण्ड) की शपथ ली थी तब हमें कहा गया था कि आज से आपके लिए देश पहले, परिवार बाद में है। फिर क्या था मुझे भारत माता की देहलीज (सीमा) याद आयी और पिता को भूल गया।

इसी बीच हमारे देश के माननीय प्रधानमंत्री व सेना के अफसरों ने पाकिस्तान पर सर्जिकल स्ट्राइक की योजना बना डाली, उसमें मैं भी एक सिपाही था। हम लोगों ने रातों-रात उनके अनगिनत ठिकानों पर बम बरसाये और लगभग 150

आतंकवादियों को मार गिराया। उन्होंने 18–20 मारे, हमने उनके कई गुने ज्यादा मारे।

जब सर्जिकल स्ट्राइक से मैं वापस आया तो मैंने अपने साहब से पिताजी के विषय में चर्चा करके बात करने की इच्छ व्यक्त की तो उन्होंने मुझे एक हफ्ते की छुट्टी देकर गाँव जाने के लिए कहा। मैं जब गाँव आया तो मुझे पता चला कि मेरी अनुपस्थिति में मेरे मित्र राहुल ने मेरा परिचय देकर पास के मिलिट्री अस्पताल में मेरे पिताजी का सफल इलाज कराया जिससे उनके कैंसर का खतरा समाप्त हो गया और वह धीरे-धीरे स्वास्थ्य लाभ कर रहे थे।

''दुनिया में मित्र तो बहुत होते हैं परंतु तुम्हारे जैसा मित्र किसी सौभाग्यशाली को ही मिलता है। अत: मैं बड़े गर्व से कह सकता हूँ कि तुमने वास्तव में सिद्ध कर दिया कि तुम ही मेरे सच्चे मित्र हो।''

Q. 5. Write a short composition in *Hindi* of approximately *250* words of the following topic:

निम्नलिखित विषय पर हिन्दी में लगभग 250 शब्दों में संक्षिप्त लेख लिखिए: [2016]

एक कहानी लिखिए जिसका आधार निम्नलिखित उक्ति हो:—

"मज़हब नहीं सिखाता आपस में बैर रखना"

Ans. "मज़हब नहीं सिखाता आपस में बैर रखना।"

इस वाक्य का भाव है कि मजहब अर्थात् कोई धर्म परस्पर दुश्मनी करने की शिक्षा नहीं देता। हम अपने प्राचीन इतिहास को उठाकर देखें तो पता चलता है कि भिन्न-भिन्न धर्मों और सम्प्रदायों के धर्म-गुरुओं ने आपस में प्रेम, बन्धुत्व और सद्भाव का ही पाठ पढ़ाया है। मिल-जुलकर सभी समस्याओं का समाधान सम्भव है। किन्तु धर्म व सम्प्रदायों का आश्रय लेकर उनसे जुड़ी मानसिक संकीर्णताओं में फंसकर लड़ना-झगड़ना केवल वैमनस्य और अराजकता को ही जन्म देता है।

जब तक हम एक-दूसरे की भावनाओं को नहीं समझेंगे, परस्पर एक-दूसरे का आदर नहीं करेंगे, एक-दूसरे के हित का चिन्तन नहीं करेंगे तब तक आपसी सद्भाव का अभाव ही रहेगा। हमें अपने आपको, अपनी जबान को और अपनी आने वाली पीढ़ी को झूठी शानो-शौकत और श्रेष्ठता की चकाचौंध से बचाना होगा। हमारे मन्दिरों, मस्जिदों, गिरजाघरों और गुरुद्वारों के उत्थान में हमारी संस्कृति और सभ्यता के दर्शन होते हैं। इनमें हमारे पूर्वजों के परिश्रम व प्यार की मिसालें हैं हमें उनका आदर करना चाहिए। हम सब एक ही परमात्मा की सन्तानें हैं। हिन्दू, मुस्लिम, सिक्ख, ईसाई से भी बढ़कर एक धर्म है और वह है मानव धर्म। हमें उसकी अवहेलना नहीं करनी चाहिए। यदि इस भाव को हम हृदय में धारण करें तो बहुत सहज है कि हम एक-दूसरे से भाईचारा बढ़ा सकेंगे, फिर बैर कहाँ होगा ?

हमारे धर्मों के पैगम्बर और गुरुओं ने लोगों को हमेशा समानता की शिक्षा दी। जैन गुरु महावीर स्वामी के समीपस्थ

वातावरण में तो हिंसक जंगली पशु भी हिंसा त्यागकर प्रेम से रहते थे। बौद्ध धर्म के प्रवर्तक महात्मा बुद्ध का कहना था कि "लोगों के दिलों में मोहब्बत के फूल खिलाना हजारों तीर्थों से बेहतर है।" भगवान श्रीकृष्ण ने प्रेम के वशीभूत होकर अपने मित्र सुदामा के कंटक भरे चरणों को अपने अश्रुजल से ही धो डाला था। महान् बलिदानी प्रभु ईसा मसीह मानव जाति की भलाई के लिए सूली पर चढ़ गये थे। ममतामयी माँ मदर टेरेसा ने बिना किसी धर्म व सम्प्रदाय का विचार किये हर पीड़ित, निराश्रित व दुःखी को हृदय से लगाया। हम यदि इतने बड़े कार्य न भी करें तो क्या मज़हब को बीच में न लाकर प्यार से नहीं रह सकते? यह तो बहुत छोटी-सी बात है जो हर प्राणी को प्रसन्नता दे सकती है। इसी सन्दर्भ में मुझे एक कहानी याद आ गई।

राम और रहीम दो मित्र थे। दोनों में बड़ी घनिष्ठता थी। राम के घर में कोई उत्सव होता या कोई परेशानी होती तो रहीम जी जान से राम के उस कार्य में शरीक होता। रहीम के घर में ईद की सिंवइयों का भरपूर आनन्द राम का पूरा परिवार लेता था। एक बार हिन्दू मुसलमानों में झगड़ा छिड़ गया। राम का घर रहीम की बस्ती में था। सारे मुसलमानों ने राम के घर पर धावा बोल दिया। रहीम को इस बात का अंदेशा था। वह अपनी कटार लेकर राम के दरवाजे पर बैठ गया। उसने चेतावनी दी कि मेरा कत्ल करने के बाद ही कोई राम के घर में घुसेगा। लोग दो दिन तक सिर पीटते रहे। कोई परिणाम न निकला। वह केवल एक पंक्ति गुनगुनाता रहा "ईश्वर अल्लाह तेरो नाम सबको सन्मति दे भगवान।" अन्त में लोगों को इस बात का ज्ञान हुआ कि परमात्मा ही ईश्वर है, वही अल्लाह है, वही ईसा मसीह और वही वाहे गुरु है और हम सभी उसी एक की सन्तानें हैं। आपस में भाई-बहन हैं। फिर एक-दूसरे के दुश्मन कैसे हो सकते हैं? यह बात सबको समझ आ गई। सभी ने रहीम से माफी माँगी और राम को गले लगाया। सब आपस में मित्र बन गये। बात सद्भाव की है अगर मन में सभी प्राणियों के प्रति सद्भाव होगा तो बैर अपने आप समाप्त हो जायेगा।

Q. 6. **Write a short composition in *Hindi* of approximately *250* words of the following topic:**

निम्नलिखित विषय पर हिन्दी में लगभग 250 शब्दों में संक्षिप्त लेख लिखिए: {2015}

एक कहानी लिखिए जिसका आधार निम्नलिखित उक्ति हो:
'मन के हारे हार है, मन के जीते जीत।'

Ans.

'मन के हारे हार है, मन के जीते जीत।'

मोहन अपनी कक्षा में सभी विषयों में ठीक था, किन्तु हिन्दी में वह हमेशा से ही पिछड़ा हुआ था। हिन्दी भाषा में उसके अंक सबसे कम रहते थे। इस कारण वह कक्षा में प्रथम नहीं आ पाता था। परीक्षा परिणाम आने के बाद सब उससे यही कहते थे कि यदि हिन्दी में भी तेरे अच्छे अंक आ जायें तो तू कक्षा में प्रथम आ जायेगा। सहपाठी भी उसका मज़ाक बनाने लगे थे। जिससे वह बहुत निराश हो गया था। कुछ दिन बाद वह इस बार की वार्षिक परीक्षा में भी हिन्दी विषय में कम अंक आने के कारण प्रथम नहीं आ सका। अब मोहन ने मन ही मन यह स्वीकार कर लिया था कि वह हिन्दी नहीं सीख सकता।

मोहन की नई हिन्दी शिक्षिका, बीना शर्मा भी इस बात को समझ चुकी थीं। एक दिन उन्होंने मोहन को अपने पास बुलाया और पूछा—'मोहन, तुम्हें हिन्दी में क्या परेशानी है? तुम मात्राओं का प्रयोग क्यों नहीं समझ पाते हो?'

'मैम, मैंने हिन्दी सीखने की बहुत कोशिश की पर नहीं सीख पाया।' कहते-कहते मोहन की आँखों में आँसू आ गये। शिक्षिका उसकी ओर देखकर बोलीं—तुम सीख सकते हो मोहन, दुनिया में ऐसा कोई काम नहीं है, जो नहीं किया जा सकता हो। हिन्दी सीखना भी असम्भव नहीं है। तुम अभी से अपने मन से यह बात निकाल दो कि तुम हिन्दी नहीं सीख सकते हो।'

मोहन केवल उन्हें देखे जा रहा था। शिक्षिका ने अपनी बात आगे बढ़ाते हुए कहा—'तुम्हें पता है कि तुम्हारे ठीक तरह से हिन्दी न सीख पाने का क्या कारण है? किसी भी भाषा को समझने के लिए हमें उसे ध्यानपूर्वक सुनना पड़ता है और शिक्षक जिस प्रकार उच्चारण करते हैं वैसा ही उच्चारण करने का अभ्यास करना चाहिए।

दूसरी बात, जब हम पढ़ें तो पुस्तक में शब्दों और मात्राओं को ध्यानपूर्वक देखना चाहिए और उनका प्रयोग समझना चाहिए और जब लिखें तो ध्यानपूर्वक लिखो और फिर उसे पढ़ो ताकि यह जान सको कि वह मात्राएँ सही हैं या नहीं। तुम आज से ही इस कार्य को प्रारम्भ कर दो। मुझे पूरा विश्वास है कि तुम बहुत जल्दी ही मात्राओं का सही प्रयोग सीख जाओगे।' शिक्षिका के मार्गदर्शन से, मन से हारे हुए मोहन में आत्मविश्वास जाग उठा। कुछ समय बाद जब परीक्षा हुई तो मोहन को हिन्दी में सबसे अधिक अंक मिले। अत: सच ही कहा गया है—'मन के हारे हार है, और मन के जीते जीत।'

Picture Composition

Long Answer Type Questions

Q. 1. Write a short composition in *Hindi* of approximately 250 words of the following topic:

निम्नलिखित विषय पर हिंदी में लगभग 250 शब्दों में संक्षिप्त लेख लिखिए: **[2020]**

नीचे दिए गए चित्र को ध्यान से देखिए और चित्र को आधार बनाकर उसका परिचय देते हुए कोई लेख, घटना अथवा कहानी लिखिए, जिसका सीधा व स्पष्ट संबंध, चित्र से होना चाहिए।

Ans. चित्र प्रस्ताव

दिए गए चित्र का सीधा संबंध बाढ़ से है। चित्र में चारों ओर पानी ही पानी दिखाई दे रहा है। एक कार पानी में डूबी हुई है। पेड़-पौधे भी गिरे हुए हैं। बिजली का खंभा भी टूट चुका है। बाढ़ से लोगों को बचाने के लिए सहायक दल पहुँच चुका है। नाव में एक महिला और एक बच्चा बैठा है। बचाव टीम के कुछ सदस्य और अन्य व्यक्ति भी नाव को पकड़कर चल रहे हैं। उनके पीछे कुछ लोग चल रहे हैं। घुटनों से भी ऊपर तक पानी है। बाढ़ का यह दृश्य अत्यंत विनाशकारी लग रहा है और मन को भयभीत कर रहा है तथा प्रभावित लोगों के प्रति करुणा उत्पन्न कर रहा है।

प्रकृति का कल्याणकारी रूप मानव के लिए समृद्धि तथा आनंद का कारण है, तो इसका विनाशकारी रूप अहितकर। कभी-कभी प्रकृति कुपित होकर अपना विनाशकारी रूप भी दिखाती है। वर्षा-ऋतु जीवनदायिनी तो है, पर अतिवृष्टि भयंकर बाढ़ों का कारण भी बन जाती है। बाढ़ का दृश्य अत्यंत विनाशकारी होता है। हमारा घर यमुना नदी से थोड़ी ही दूरी पर है। पिछले दिनों भयंकर वर्षा हुई तथा दो-तीन दिन तक लगातार होती रही जिसके कारण यमुना का जलस्तर बढ़ गया और देखते-ही-देखते उसका पानी खेतों में भर गया। पता चला कि यमुना से निकलने वाली एक नहर, जो सिंचाई के लिए बनाई गई थी उसका बहुत बड़ा भाग टूट गया है तथा उसका जल तेजी से शहर में भर रहा है।

रेडियो तथा टी.वी. पर स्थानीय प्रशासन द्वारा अब लोगों को सुरक्षित स्थानों पर चले जाने संबंधी सूचना प्रसारित की जा रही थी। भयभीत लोग अपना कुछ सामान उठाए, अपने बाल-बच्चों को साथ लिए सुरक्षित स्थानों की ओर दौड़े जा रहे थे। देखते-ही-देखते जलस्तर बहुत बढ़ गया। गरीब लोगों की झोंपड़ियाँ जलमग्न हो गईं। उनका सामान जल में तैरने लगा। उन लोगों के बर्तन, कपड़े आदि पानी पर तैरते दिखायी दे रहे थे।

कुछ लोग जान बचाने के लिए ऊँचे-ऊँचे वृक्षों पर चढ़ गए थे। विद्युत और संचार व्यवस्था भी ठप्प होती जा रही थी। हमारे आस-पास के लोग छतों पर शरण लिए हुए थे। जलस्तर बढ़ता ही जा रहा था। शहर का आधा भाग जलमग्न हो चुका था। तभी सेना की नौकाएँ आती दिखाई दीं। वे अपने साथ खाने-पीने का सामान तथा अन्य जरूरी चीजें लेकर आए थे। बाढ़ की विनाशलीला देर रात्रि तक चलती रही। तब तक अनेक मकान, पेड़-पौधे ढह चुके थे तथा जान-माल की भारी क्षति हो चुकी थी। प्रातःकाल होते-होते बाढ़ का प्रकोप कम होने लगा, पानी का स्तर घटने लगा। तब लोगों ने राहत की साँस ली।

हमारे देश के अनेक राज्यों में हर साल बाढ़ आती है जिससे, जन-धन की भारी क्षति होती है। इस कारण ये राज्य प्रगति की दौड़ में पिछड़े हुए हैं। बाढ़ के कारण किसानों की फसलें खराब हो जाती हैं तथा पशु, धन एवं व्यापार की भी भारी हानि होती है। बाढ़ अपने साथ महामारियाँ ही नहीं, गरीबी और भूख भी साथ लाती है। सरकार को चाहिए कि इन क्षेत्रों में बाढ़ पर नियंत्रण लगाने के लिए ठोस उपाय करे और प्रकृति के कहर से देशवासियों को बचाये।

Q. 2. Write a short composition in *Hindi* of approximately 250 words of the following topic:

निम्नलिखित विषय पर हिंदी में लगभग 250 शब्दों में संक्षिप्त लेख लिखिए: **[2019]**

नीचे दिए गए चित्र को ध्यान से देखिए और चित्र को आधार बनाकर उसका परिचय देते हुए कोई लेख, घटना अथवा कहानी लिखिए, जिसका सीधा व स्पष्ट संबंध, चित्र से होना चाहिए।

Marking Scheme -------------------------------

भूमिका- चित्र परिचय- स्वच्छता, बालश्रम, काल्पनिक विचारों को आधार बनाकर उत्तर लिखना।

लेख अथवा कहानी का विस्तार।

उपसंहार।

Ans.

चित्र प्रस्ताव

प्रस्तुत चित्र का सम्बन्ध बाल मजदूरी से है। चित्र में बच्चे ईंट भट्टे पर ईंट निर्माण का काम कर रहे हैं। एक बच्चा फावड़े से मिट्टी को उठा रहा है। चित्र में लड़के के पीछे ईंटें लगी हुई हैं। पीछे और दो बच्चे दिखाई दे रहे हैं, जो इसी काम में व्यस्त हैं।

बाल मजदूरी दुनिया का सबसे बड़ा अभिशाप है। चित्र में काम करते हुए बच्चों को देखकर मन दुखी और विवश हो जाता है कि देशहित के लिए कानून बनाने मात्र से कुछ नहीं होने वाला। इन कानूनों को प्रयोगात्मक रूप से अपनाना होगा।

भारतीय संविधान में बहुत पहले से ही यह कानून बनाया जा चुका है कि चौदह वर्ष से कम उम्र के बच्चों से काम करवाना कानूनी अपराध है, फिर भी छोटे-छोटे बच्चे काम करते हुये आसानी से देखे जा सकते हैं।

सरकार ने गरीब बच्चों के लिए शिक्षा नि:शुल्क रखी है, फिर भी निर्धन बच्चों के माता-पिता उन्हें स्कूल नहीं भेजते और किसी न किसी काम पर लगा देते हैं। घरेलू काम जैसे बरतन धोना, कपड़े धोना, घर की सफाई करना, होटलों में जूठी प्लेटें उठाना, टेबलों की सफाई, करना, सुबह-सवेरे अखबार वितरित करना, फैक्ट्रियों व कारखानों में काम करना आदि।

इन बच्चों के माता-पिता अशिक्षित और गरीब होने के कारण बालश्रम को गलत नहीं समझते। उन्हें लगता है कि बच्चों के कमाने से परिवार चलाने में उन्हें सहायता मिलती है।

खेलने-कूदने और पढ़ने की उम्र में इन मासूम कन्धों पर जब काम का बोझ लाद दिया जाता है, तो मन बड़ा द्रवित हो जाता है। बचपन जीवन का स्वर्णिम काल होता है और खुशी तथा उत्साह से जीने का अधिकार हर बच्चे को है।

इस अभिशाप को जड़ से उखाड़ने के लिए हमें एक बड़े स्तर पर अभियान चलाना होगा। निर्धन वर्ग के लिए रोजगार के अवसर प्रदान करने होंगे। धनी और सभ्य लोगों को यह कसम लेनी होगी कि वे चौदह वर्ष से कम उम्र के बच्चों से काम नहीं करवाएँगे। लोगों को स्वार्थ को परे रखना होगा। परमार्थ और परोपकार की भावना का विकास करना होगा।

सरकार ही नहीं बल्कि जनता को भी एकजुट होकर काम करना होगा। तभी देश का हर बच्चा शिक्षित होगा, बचपन का आनन्द ले पाएगा। बाल मजदूरी करवाने वालों पर सरकार को कठोर कदम उठाने होंगे और उन्हें कड़ी-से-कड़ी सजा देनी होगी।

"बाल मजदूरी एक अभिशाप है"
बच्चों से काम करवाना पाप है।
इन्हें इनका बचपन लौटाएँ
भविष्य इनका सुनहरा बनाएँ।"

Q. 3. Write a short composition in *Hindi* of approximately *250* words of the following topic:

निम्नलिखित विषय पर हिंदी में लगभग 250 शब्दों में संक्षिप्त लेख लिखिए: [2018]

नीचे दिए गए चित्र को ध्यान से देखिए और चित्र को आधार बनाकर उसका परिचय देते हुए कोई लेख, घटना अथवा कहानी लिखिए, जिसका सीधा व स्पष्ट संबंध चित्र से होना चाहिए।

Marking Scheme -------------------------------

चित्र को आधार बनाकर उसका परिचय देते हुए कोई कहानी, घटना अथवा लेख लिखना।

Ans.

चित्र प्रस्ताव

प्रस्तुत चित्र में एक गाँव दिखाया गया है जिसमें किसी विद्यालय के बच्चे दिखाये गये हैं। इस चित्र में चार लड़कियाँ और तीन लड़के दिखाई दे रहे हैं। सभी बच्चों के हाथ में लैपटॉप दिखाई दे रहे हैं। जो इनको विद्यालय की तरफ से बाँटे गये हैं, जिससे बच्चे नई तकनीकी से शिक्षा प्राप्त कर सकें। आजकल शहरों में ही नहीं गाँवों में भी कम्प्यूटर पहुँच गये हैं।

शिक्षा के क्षेत्र को कम्प्यूटर ने बहुत अधिक प्रभावित किया है इसलिए सभी शिक्षण संस्थानों में इसकी शिक्षा अनिवार्य होती जा रही है। इसके द्वारा विश्वभर का ज्ञान पल भर में पी. सी. के स्क्रीन पर देखा जा सकता है। इसकी शिक्षा के बाद भारी भरकम पुस्तकों को रखने, सँभालने और उन्हें उलटने-पलटने की आवश्यकता समाप्त हो जायेगी। पुस्तकों से भरी बड़ी-बड़ी लाइब्रेरियों की जगह सी.डी. ले रही हैं। जिनमें हजारों पृष्ठ की सामग्री एक छोटी-सी डिबिया में सुरक्षित रखी जा सकती है। शिक्षा के डिजिटलीकरण के द्वारा सारा विश्व एक पाठशाला में बदल गया है।

कम्प्यूटर मशीनी मानव की तरह दिखता है। कम्प्यूटर के कार्य का क्षेत्र बड़ा होने के कारण उससे जुड़ी हर जानकारी बहुत जरूरी है इसीलिए विद्यालयों में भी बच्चों को इसकी शिक्षा पर बल दिया गया है। इसकी सहायता से बच्चे अपने विषय से संबंधित जानकारी प्राप्त कर सकते हैं तथा उस विषय को अच्छे से समझ सकते हैं।

वस्तुत: आज का समय कम्प्यूटर का ही समय है। कम्प्यूटर की सहायता से बहुत से कार्य सरल हो गये हैं। इनसे पढ़ाई–लिखाई आसान हो गई है जिससे विद्यार्थियों को नई शिक्षा और नई गति प्राप्त हुई है।

Q. 4. Write a short composition in *Hindi* of approximately *250* words of the following topic:

निम्नलिखित विषय पर हिंदी में लगभग 250 शब्दों में संक्षिप्त लेख लिखिए: **[2017]**

प्रस्तुत चित्र को ध्यान से देखिए और चित्र को आधार बनाकर उसका परिचय देते हुए कोई लेख, कहानी अथवा घटना लिखिए जिसका सीधा व स्पष्ट संबंध चित्र से होना चाहिए।

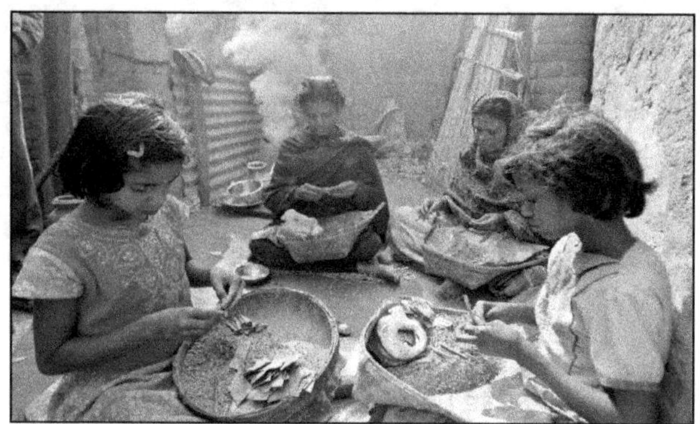

Ans. चित्र प्रस्ताव

यह चित्र गरीब महिलाओं व दो लड़कियों से संबंधित है। यह एक खुली जगह है। यहाँ दो महिलाएँ और दो लड़कियाँ बैठी हुई हैं। एक तरफ लोहे की चद्दर खड़ी हुई है। एक छोटा–सा घड़ा, एक प्लेट व एक कटोरा रखा है। दो महिलाओं व एक लड़की के सामने सूप रखे हैं तथा एक अन्य लड़की के सामने लोहे का तसला रखा है। स्त्रियों के पीछे टूटे–फूटे दरवाजे और कुछ बीड़ी बनाने के पत्तों की ढेरियाँ रखी हुई हैं। वस्तुत: ये चारों लोग बीड़ियाँ बना रही हैं क्योंकि इनके सामने कुछ बीड़ियाँ बनी रखी हैं। बीड़ी में भरने वाला तंबाकू भी रखा हुआ है। ये सब बीड़ियाँ इसलिए बना रही हैं ताकि अपनी जीविका चला सकें। सभी लोग बड़ी तन्मयता से इस काम को कर रही हैं। ताकि अपनी जीविका चला सकें।

भारतवर्ष आदिकाल से ही बड़ा कर्मठ और बहुउद्योगीय देश रहा है। यहाँ के लोग बहुत परिश्रमी होते थे। नैतिक मूल्यों से इनका विकास होता था। मेहनत की रोटी कमाना और संतोषपूर्वक सादा जीवन व्यतीत करना ही इनके जीवन का उद्देश्य था।

धीरे–धीरे मशीनी युग आया। लोगों के काम–धंधे छिन गये और काम–धंधों के लिए तरस गये। इसीलिए गाँवों से शहर की ओर पलायन हुआ क्योंकि शहर में ही कोई काम मिले। बड़े–बड़े दुकानदार अपनी दुकान के छोटे–छोटे काम गरीब औरतों व लड़कियों को दे देते हैं जैसे बीड़ी बनाना, मोमबत्ती बनाना, साड़ियों में फॉल लगाना आदि काम जो स्त्रियाँ पढ़ी–लिखी नहीं होती हैं, वे अपना घरेलू काम समाप्त

करके ऐसे काम ले आती हैं। ये काम करके वे अपना हाथ खर्च निकाल लेती हैं। ये छोटे कुटीर–धंधे हैं जिनमें लोग स्वयं को व्यस्त रखना चाहते हैं परन्तु छोटी बालिकाओं या बालकों को इस कार्य में लगाना कानूनी रूप से गलत है। यद्यपि गरीब परिवारों को अपनी जीविका के लिये बच्चों से काम कराना पड़ता है परन्तु इसके बावजूद भी वे शोषण का ही शिकार रहते हैं। उन्हें गंदे वातावरण में 10 से 12 घण्टे तक काम करना पड़ता है और वेतन के नाम पर इन्हें चंद रुपये ही दिये जाते हैं। इसके साथ–साथ बीड़ी में उपयोग होने वाला तम्बाकू अप्रत्यक्ष रूप से बच्चों के स्वास्थ्य को भी हानि पहुँचाता है। नशे से आंतरिक अंग शिथिल हो जाते हैं तथा श्वास में विकार पैदा करते हैं। फलस्वरूप ये बालक खतरनाक बीमारियों के शिकार हो जाते हैं। अत: आवश्यकता इस बात की है कि हम पूरी दृढ़ता से इस तथ्य को स्वीकारें कि हम नशीली वस्तुओं और बालश्रम का अपने जीवन से बहिष्कार करें और शुद्ध प्रकृति के वातावरण में जीवन बिताएँ।''

Q. 5. Write a short composition in *Hindi* of approximately *250* words of the following topic:

निम्नलिखित विषय पर हिंदी में लगभग 250 शब्दों में संक्षिप्त लेख लिखिए:

नीचे दिये गये चित्र को ध्यान से देखिए और चित्र को आधार बनाकर उसका परिचय देते हुए कहानी अथवा लेख लिखिए, जिसका सीधा सम्बन्ध चित्र से होना चाहिए।

[2016]

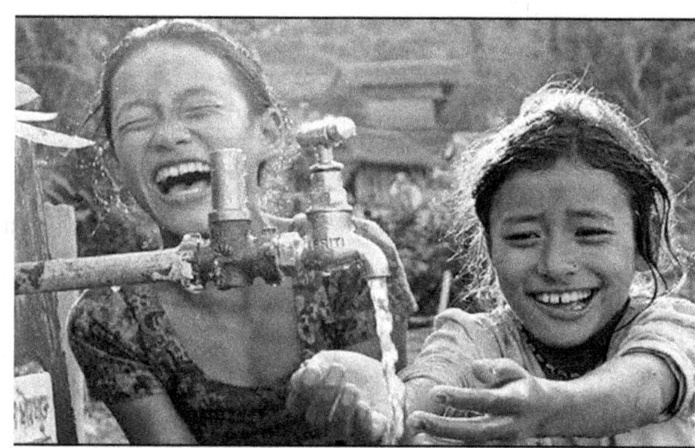

Ans. चित्र प्रस्ताव

प्रस्तुत चित्र में दो 12–13 वर्ष की बालिकाएँ दर्शायी गई हैं। वह दोनों एक नल के पास बैठी हुई हैं। नल में बहुत तेज़ पानी आ रहा है जिसे देखकर वे दोनों अप्रत्याशित रूप से प्रसन्न हो रही हैं। ऐसा प्रतीत हो रहा है जैसे बहुत दिनों के बाद उन्हें नल में पानी की प्राप्ति हुई हो। उनकी हँसी ऐसी है जैसे बहुत समय के पश्चात् जब बादल बरसते हैं तो लोग खुशी से झूम उठते हैं।

जल ही जीवन है। जल के बिना जीवन का अस्तित्व नहीं है। कवि रहीम ने जल के महत्व को दर्शाति हुए लिखा है—

"रहिमन पानी राखिये बिन पानी सब सून।
पानी गये न ऊबरे मोती मानुष चून''।।

प्राणिमात्र के जीवन का आधार जल है। जल के बिना जीवन की सम्भावना कदाचित् असम्भव है। हमारे देश में इस समय जल संकट बहुत अधिक है। आपने अक्सर नलों पर प्रातःकाल से ही बर्तनों की भीड़ देखी होगी। पानी प्राप्त करने के लिए लोगों को झगड़ते भी देखा होगा। हमारी सरकार प्रकृति प्रदत्त जल सबको प्राप्त कराने में सर्वथा अशक्त है। इस चित्र के माध्यम से इसी भाव की अभिव्यक्ति हो रही है।

यह एक कस्बे का चित्र है जहाँ पर वहाँ के निवासियों ने बहुत दिनों से जल संस्थान अधिकारियों से कस्बे में जल की व्यवस्था के लिए अनेक प्रार्थना-पत्र दिये। बड़े समूह में एकत्रित होकर बार-बार जल संकट की शिकायत की। उन्होंने यह भी बताया कि कुएँ सूख गये हैं व नलकूप व्यर्थ हो गये हैं। यहाँ के निवासी प्यास से व्याकुल हैं तथा पशुओं के लिए भी पानी की व्यवस्था नहीं है। बार-बार प्रार्थना किए जाने पर शायद अधिकारियों को दया आ गई, और उन्होंने उस क्षेत्र में पाइप लाइन बिछवा दी। अब पाइप लाइन तो बिछ गई परन्तु पाइप में पानी नहीं था। पुनः सभी क्षेत्रवासियों ने प्रदेश की सरकार से अपनी कठिनाई बताई। उसमें भी एक-दो महीने लग गये। कई बार तो जल संस्थान से पानी का टैंकर भेजकर लोगों की कठिनाई को दूर किया गया, लेकिन यह स्थायी समाधान नहीं था। पुनः कुछ लोग सीधे मुख्य मन्त्री के पास पहुँचे और अपनी दीन-दशा का वर्णन किया। मन्त्री जी ने लोगों के कष्ट को समझा और तुरन्त अपने अधीनस्थ अधिकारियों को कड़े आदेश देकर तुरन्त कार्यवाही करने के लिए कहा। परिणामस्वरूप वहाँ के निवासियों की मेहनत रंग लाई और आज नलों में पानी आने लगा जिसे देखकर यह दोनों बालिकाएँ अत्यन्त प्रसन्न हैं तथा सम्पूर्ण कस्बे के निवासियों की समस्या का भी समाधान हो गया।

यह कहानी बताती है कि सही दिशा में परिश्रम करने से सफलता अवश्य मिलती है।

Q. 6. **Write a short composition in *Hindi* of approximately *250* words of the following topic:**

निम्नलिखित विषय पर हिन्दी में लगभग 250 शब्दों में संक्षिप्त लेख लिखिए:

नीचे दिये गये चित्र को ध्यान से देखिए और चित्र को आधार बनाकर वर्णन कीजिए अथवा कहानी लिखिए, जिसका सीधा व स्पष्ट सम्बन्ध चित्र से होना चाहिए।

[2015]

Ans. **चित्र प्रस्ताव**

प्रस्तुत चित्र में कुछ छात्र-छात्राएँ प्रधानमन्त्री श्री नरेन्द्र मोदी के 'स्वच्छता अभियान' को साकार रूप प्रदान कर रही हैं। इस बार 2 अक्टूबर, गाँधी जयन्ती को 'स्वच्छता दिवस' के रूप में मनाया गया। इस दिन स्कूल के छात्र-छात्राओं ने 'स्वच्छ भारत' का सपना साकार करने के लिए अपने हाथों में झाड़ू ली। वे सड़क पर आए और अपनी-अपनी झाड़ू से सड़क की सफाई करने लगे। सभी छात्र-छात्राओं ने सिर पर टोपी पहनी हुई थी। उनमें से कोई झाड़ू लगा रहा था तो कोई कचरे को उठाकर बोरी में भर रहा था। सभी में एक अपूर्व जोश था। स्वयं सफाई करने में उन्हें आत्मसन्तोष का अनुभव हो रहा था।

वस्तुतः अपने आस-पास सफाई रखना बहुत अच्छी बात है। हमें प्रारम्भ से ही सफाई की आदत डालनी चाहिए। इसकी शुरुआत तभी से हो सकती है जब बच्चा नर्सरी कक्षा में पढ़ता है। उसे अपनी पुस्तक, पेंसिल, स्कूल बैग आदि उचित स्थान पर रखने के लिए सीख दी जानी चाहिए। फर्श पर इधर-उधर कूड़ा बिखेरने से रोकना चाहिए, इसलिए कमरे के एक कोने में कूड़ेदान रख दिया जाना चाहिए। इसी प्रकार से अपनी कक्षा में भी स्वच्छता का ध्यान रखना बहुत आवश्यक है। अपने शरीर की स्वच्छता के प्रति हमें लापरवाह नहीं होना चाहिए इसलिए प्रातः स्नान करना तथा स्वच्छ और धुले हुए कपड़े पहनना आवश्यक है। बाल उचित तरह से काढ़े हुए होने चाहिए तथा नाखून भी समय-समय पर काटते रहना चाहिए। अपने शरीर की और अपने आस-पास की स्वच्छता रखने से हम स्वस्थ रहते हैं तथा रोग के कीटाणुओं को पनपने का अवसर नहीं मिलता।

जब हम सभी मिलकर स्वच्छता का ध्यान देंगे तो स्वस्थ भारत का सपना साकार होने में देर नहीं लगेगी। इसलिए हम सबको स्वच्छता रखने का संकल्प लेना चाहिए।

 **Long Answer Type Questions**

Q. 1. **Write a letter in *Hindi* in approximately *120* words on any *one* of the topics given below:**

निम्नलिखित में से किसी एक विषय पर हिंदी में लगभग 120 शब्दों में पत्र लिखिए:

(i) ''आप अपने परिवार के साथ किसी सुन्दर शहर की यात्रा करके आए हैं आपने वहाँ क्या-क्या देखा? वह शहर इतना प्रसिद्ध क्यों है? अपने मित्र को पत्र लिखकर वर्णन करें।''

(ii) आपके क्षेत्र में मलेरिया तथा डेंगू का प्रकोप बढ़ गया है। इसकी रोकथाम के लिए नगर-निगम के अध्यक्ष को एक पत्र लिखिए। **[2020]**

Ans. **(i)** परीक्षा भवन

आगरा।

दिनांक : 6.12.20XX

प्रिय मित्र विजय,

सप्रेम नमस्कार।

मैं यहाँ पर कुशलपूर्वक हूँ। आशा करता हूँ कि तुम भी वहाँ कुशलपूर्वक होंगे। जैसा कि तुम जानते हो कि इस बार की छुट्टियों में मैं अपने परिवार के साथ बेंगलौर गया था।

बेंगलौर बड़ा ही सुन्दर शहर है। यहाँ चारों ओर हरियाली ही हरियाली है। कर्नाटक की राजधानी है। इस शहर को 'गार्डन सिटी ऑफ इंडिया' के रूप में जाना जाता है। सबसे पहले हम 'विधान सौध' देखने गए। यह भवन सचिवालय और राज्य की विधान सभा का कार्य स्थल होने के साथ-साथ ईंट और पत्थर से बना एक उत्कृष्ट निर्माण है। उसके बाद हम बेंगलौर-पैलेस और उल्सूर झील देखने गए। मौसम सुहावना था। उल्सूर झील का नजारा बड़ा ही अनुपम था। इसके अलावा हमने लाल बाग की सैर की, बुल टेंपल गए। हम प्रसिद्ध गवीपुरम गुफा मंदिर भी देखने गए। यह शहर रेशम की साड़ियों व चंदन से बनी चीजों के लिए बहुत प्रसिद्ध हैं। यहाँ के सुविख्यात होटल एम.टी.आर. में हमने गरम-गरम इडली और डोसा भी खाए। रात को हम यूबी सिटी भी देखने गए। यह गगनचुंबी इमारत अद्वितीय है।

यह यात्रा मेरे लिए अविस्मरणीय यात्रा थी। खूब मजा आया। तुमने छुट्टियाँ कैसे बितायी, यह जरूर बताना।

तुम्हारा मित्र,

भरत।

(ii) प्रेषक

भरत

03, राजगली

आगरा।

दिनांक : 6.12.20XX

सेवा में,

अध्यक्ष महोदय

आगरा नगर निगम, आगरा।

विषय : मलेरिया व डेंगू के रोकथाम हेतु पत्र।

महोदय,

इस पत्र के माध्यम से आपका ध्यान शहर के उपनगर गांधीनगर में फैल रहे मलेरिया व डेंगू के बढ़ते प्रकोप और रोकथाम हेतु उपाय करने की ओर आकर्षित करना चाहता हूँ।

मलेरिया व डेंगू संक्रामक रोग हैं, जो बड़ी तेजी से फैलते हैं। बरसात का पानी कई स्थानों पर रूका हुआ है, और इसी कारण मच्छर बहुत अधिक उत्पन्न हो रहे हैं। हमारे क्षेत्र में कई लोग बीमार पड़ चुके हैं। कई लोगों की स्थिति अधिक खराब हो जाने पर उन्हें अस्पताल में भी भर्ती करवाना पड़ा है।

मेरा आपसे सविनय निवेदन है कि आप इन संक्रामक रोगों की रोकथाम के लिए पूरे क्षेत्र में मच्छर मारने की दवा छिड़कवाएँ। दूरदर्शन पर इन बीमारियों के फैलने के कारण, लक्षण व बचने के उपाय आदि की विस्तृत जानकारी बताकर, सबको जागरूक करें।

आशा है, आप इन रोगों को फैलने से रोकने के लिए तुरंत उचित कार्यवाही करेंगे।

धन्यवाद।

भवदीय

भरत

Q. 2. **Write a letter in *Hindi* in approximately *120* words on any *one* of the topics given below:**

निम्नलिखित में से किसी एक विषय पर हिंदी में लगभग 120 शब्दों में पत्र लिखिए:

(i) आप अपने परिवार के साथ किसी एक प्रदर्शनी (Exhibition) को देखने गए थे। वहाँ पर आपने क्या-क्या देखा? वहाँ कौन-कौन सी चीजों ने आकर्षित किया? जीवन में उनकी क्या उपयोगिता है? अपना अनुभव बताते हुए अपने प्रिय मित्र को पत्र लिखिये।

(ii) दिन-प्रतिदिन बढ़ते हुए जल संकट की ओर ध्यान आकर्षित करते हुए नगर-पालिका के अध्यक्ष को एक पत्र लिखिए। जिसमें वर्षा के जल का संचयन (rain-water harvesting) करने के लिए व्यापक स्तर पर परियोजना चलाने का सुझाव दिया गया हो।

[2019]

 Marking Scheme

(i) परिवार के साथ प्रदर्शनी जाना, क्या-क्या देखा ? जीवन में उसकी उपयोगिता का वर्णन और अनुभव।

(ii) प्रारूप
विषय– जल संकट की समस्या क्यों, वर्षा के जल का संचयन करने की सुझाव प्रक्रिया।

Ans. **(i)** राजगली

राज नगर,

आगरा।

दिनांक : 26.04.20XX

प्रिय मित्र,

हम सब यहाँ कुशल हैं तुम भी कुशल होंगे, ऐसी ईश्वर से मेरी प्रार्थना है। यह पत्र मैं तुम्हें अपनी खुशियों के पलों में शामिल करने के लिए लिख रहा हूँ। कुछ दिनों पहले मैं अपने परिवार के साथ एक वैज्ञानिक प्रदर्शनी को देखने गया था। प्रदर्शनी मान्यता टेक्नो पार्क में लगी थी।

विज्ञान की तरक्की देखकर आँखें खुली की खुली रह गईं। यह प्रदर्शनी वैज्ञानिकों ने लगाई थी। इस प्रदर्शनी का मुख्य उद्देश्य छात्रों में विज्ञान एवं प्रौद्योगिकी में अभिरुचि पैदा करने एवं अपनी प्रतिभा को पहचानने का अवसर प्रदान करना था। प्रदर्शनी में चंद्रग्रहण, सूर्यग्रहण, ध्वनि तरंगों का संचरण, सौरमण्डल, सैटेलाइट, रॉकेट का निर्माण, सौर ऊर्जा आदि के बारे में विस्तृत जानकारी मिली। रोबोट और उसके कार्यकलापों को देखकर मन रोमांचित हो उठा। पर्यावरण की सुरक्षा व प्रदूषण की रोकथाम के लिए विविध वैज्ञानिक उपकरणों के आविष्कार सराहनीय थे, क्योंकि मनुष्य के जीवन का आधार प्रकृति व पर्यावरण ही है। बहुत ही ज्ञानवर्धक और प्रेरक प्रदर्शनी थी। आशा है अगली बार ऐसे किसी अवसर पर भी तुम भी साथ रहो।

अब मैं अपनी लेखनी को यहीं विराम देता हूँ। चाचा-चाची को मेरा प्रणाम।

तुम्हारा विश्वसनीय,
क.ख.ग.

(ii) प्रेषक
क. ख. ग.

04, राजाजीनगर

आगरा–4 ।

दिनांक : 26.02.20XX

सेवा में,

नगर निगम अधिकारी/अध्यक्ष

राजाजीनगर नगरपालिका

आगरा–4 ।

विषय—वर्षाजल संचयन परियोजना हेतु।

महोदय,

मैं क.ख.ग. राजाजीनगर का निवासी हूँ। मैं इस पत्र के माध्यम से आपका ध्यान दिन-प्रतिदिन बढ़ते हुए जल संकट की ओर आकर्षित करना चाहता हूँ।

पर्याप्त वर्षा के बावजूद लोग पानी की एक-एक बूँद के लिये तरसते हैं तथा कई जगह संघर्ष की स्थिति भी पैदा हो जाती है। इसका प्रमुख कारण यह है कि हमने अनमोल वर्षा जल का संचय नहीं किया और वह व्यर्थ में बहकर दूषित जल बन गया। अतः हमारा दायित्व है कि हम वर्षाजल का संरक्षण करें तथा प्राकृतिक जलस्रोतों को प्रदूषण से बचाएँ।

जलसंकट से उबरने के लिये वर्षा जल का संचयन आवश्यक है। अतः आपसे निवेदन है कि आप वर्षा के जल का संचयन करने के लिए व्यापक स्तर पर एक परियोजना तैयार करें और जल्द-से-जल्द उसे लागू कराएँ।

धन्यवाद।

भवदीय
क.ख.ग

Q. 3. Write a letter in *Hindi* in approximately *120* words on any *one* of the topics given below:

निम्नलिखित में से किसी एक विषय पर हिंदी में लगभग 120 शब्दों में पत्र लिखिए:

(i) आप अपने विद्यालय के 'सफाई अभियान दल' के नेता हैं। एक योजना के अंतर्गत आप छात्रों के एक दल को किसी इलाके में सफाई के प्रति जागरूक करने हेतु ले जाना चाहते हैं। अपने विद्यालय के प्रधानाचार्य/प्रधानाचार्या जी को इसके लिए स्वीकृति हेतु पत्र लिखिए।

(ii) पिछले महीने कुछ प्रयासों द्वारा आपके विद्यालय के छात्रों ने कुछ धनराशि एकत्रित करके मूक-बधिर (deaf and dumb) विद्यालय के विद्यार्थियों की सहायता की थी। इसका वर्णन करते हुए अपने मित्र को एक पत्र लिखिए और बताइए कि हमें समाज के विकलांग लोगों के प्रति कैसा व्यवहार रखना चाहिए व उनकी सहायता के लिए किस प्रकार के प्रयास करने चाहिए।

[2018]

 **Marking Scheme**

  (i) विद्यार्थी का परिचय (कक्षा, पद इत्यादि) स्पष्ट होना।
- योजना का स्पष्ट होना।
- इलाके का स्पष्ट होना।
- प्रार्थना करना भी स्पष्ट होना।

  (ii) मित्र को पत्र में अपने विद्यालय के छात्रों के द्वारा मूक-बधिर विद्यालय के छात्रों की सहायता का वर्णन। समाज के विकलाँग लोगों के प्रति किए जाने वाले व्यवहार तथा सहायता का वर्णन।

Ans.   (i) सेवा में,

प्रधानाचार्य जी,

दिल्ली पब्लिक स्कूल,

नई दिल्ली।

विषय—लोगों को सफाई के प्रति जागरूक करने के लिए अपने विद्यालय के सफाई दल को ले जाने के लिए स्वीकृति हेतु पत्र।

महोदय,

सविनय निवेदन है कि आप जानते ही हैं कि आजकल देश में स्वच्छ भारत की एक मुहिम छेड़ी जा रही है। देशभर में लोगों में इसके लिए अच्छा-खासा उत्साह है।

देश के बड़े-बड़े लोग, चाहे वे खिलाड़ी हों, व्यवसायी हों, नेता हों या अभिनेता हों, सभी सफाई के प्रति लोगों को जागरूक कर रहे हैं। मैं भी अपने विद्यालय के सफाई दल का नेता हूँ। इसलिए मैं भी अपने दल के साथ पास की एक झुग्गी-झोंपड़ी बस्ती में रहने वालों को सफाई के प्रति जागरूक करने के लिए जाना चाहता हूँ। उन लोगों को सफाई के लाभ बताना चाहता हूँ। अत: आपसे निवेदन है कि आप हमारे दल को वहाँ ले जाने की स्वीकृति प्रदान करें। आपकी अति कृपा होगी।

धन्यवाद !

आपका आज्ञाकारी शिष्य

राजेश कुमार

कक्षा: 10 अ

दिनांक: 10.10.20XX

  (ii) 15/13, राजपुर रोड,

दिल्ली।

प्रिय मित्र रमेश,

सप्रेम नमस्ते,

आशा करता हूँ कि वहाँ पर सब कुशल मंगल होंगे। यहाँ पर सभी ठीक प्रकार से हैं। तुम्हारी पढ़ाई कैसी चल रही है ? मेरी परीक्षाएँ शुरू हो गई हैं। आशा है तुम्हारी परीक्षाएँ भी अच्छी होंगी।

मैं तुम्हें एक बात बताना चाहता हूँ। पिछले कुछ महीनों से हमारे विद्यालय की टीम ने एक अभियान चलाया था जिसमें हमने मूक-बधिर छात्रों की सहायता के लिए धनराशि एकत्रित की थी और उन लोगों की पढ़ाई, खाने-पीने, रहने और कपड़े आदि में मदद की थी। इसके लिए सभी ने हमारी सराहना की थी। तुम भी इस प्रकार अपने विद्यालय के छात्रों की एक टीम बनाकर मदद कर सकते हो। तुम कोई भी सहयोग राशि एकत्र करके मूक-बधिर विद्यालय में दान कर सकते हो। ये विद्यालय विशेष रूप से इन्हीं की शिक्षा के लिये बनाये जाते हैं जहाँ ये बेसिक शिक्षा अपने लिये अनुकूल वातावरण में प्राप्त कर सकें। मैं तुम्हें बताना चाहता हूँ कि किस प्रकार और कैसा व्यवहार करना चाहिए कि इनकी जिंदगी में रोशनी की एक किरण बनकर सपनों को साकार कर सकते हैं।

हमें विकलांगों के प्रति सकारात्मक रहना चाहिए। किसी भी विकलांग जैसे नेत्रहीन, शारीरिक असमर्थता से ग्रसित हो तो उनको सड़क पार करवाने, बस में बैठाने-उतारने में मदद करनी चाहिए। विकलांग छात्रों को सरकारी योजनाओं से लाभ प्राप्त करने में मदद कर सकते हैं, किसी विकलांग छात्र के स्कूल की फीस या दवा का खर्च उठा सकते हैं। इस प्रकार छोटी-छोटी मदद करके हम उनकी सहायता कर सकते हैं। शेष फिर बताना कि क्या तुमने ऐसा करने की कोशिश की ? घर पर अपने सभी बड़ों को चरणस्पर्श तथा छोटों को प्यार देना। पत्रोत्तर की प्रतीक्षा में।

तुम्हारा मित्र,

सुरेश

Q. 4. Write a letter in *Hindi* in approximately *120* words on any *one* of the topics given below:

निम्नलिखित में से किसी एक विषय पर हिंदी में लगभग 120 शब्दों में पत्र लिखिए:

  (i) आपके क्षेत्र में एक ही साधारण सा सरकारी अस्पताल है, जिसके कारण आम जनता को बहुत अधिक परेशानियों का सामना करना पड़ रहा है। उन परेशानियों का उल्लेख करते हुए एक और सुविधायुक्त सरकारी अस्पताल खुलवाने का अनुरोध करते हुए स्वास्थ्य अधिकारी को पत्र लिखिए।

  (ii) ओलंपिक में अपने देश के बढ़ते कदम देखकर आपको बहुत ही प्रसन्नता हो रही है। इस वर्ष के ओलंपिक की उपलब्धियों को बताते हुए अपने मित्र को पत्र लिखिए। **[2017]**

Ans.   (i) सेवा में,

श्रीमान् स्वास्थ्य अधिकारी,

जिला, आगरा।

विषय—सुविधायुक्त सरकारी अस्पताल खुलवाने की संस्तुति हेतु।

महोदय,

इस पत्र के माध्यम से मैं आपको अवगत कराना चाहती हूँ कि मेरे क्षेत्र में जो आगरा के समीप ही एक कस्बे में साधारण-सा अस्पताल बना हुआ है। उसमें न तो कोई योग्य चिकित्सक है और न ही कोई कम्पाउण्डर और न ही वहाँ से कोई भी दवाइयाँ प्राप्त की जा सकती हैं। जितने दिन या समय तक चिकित्सक उपलब्ध होते हैं वे भी सभी मरीजों का इलाज करने के लिये पर्याप्त नहीं हैं। समीप ही कोई अच्छे सरकारी अस्पताल के अभाव में मरीज अपनी जान से हाथ धो बैठते हैं क्योंकि उन्हें समय पर उचित उपचार नहीं मिलता। इस क्षेत्र के लोग अधिक सम्पन्न नहीं हैं कि वे प्राइवेट अस्पतालों का खर्चा नहीं उठा सकते। मरीजों के लिए अस्पताल में बैड भी नहीं हैं। शौचालयों की दशा इतनी खराब है कि संक्रमण लगने का डर रहता है। पानी की भी सुविधा नहीं है। फलस्वरूप मरीज यहाँ आकर और बीमार हो जाता है और उचित इलाज के अभाव में जान से हाथ धो बैठता है।

अतः आपसे विनम्र निवेदन है कि सरकार की सहायता से इस क्षेत्र में एक अच्छा सरकारी अस्पताल बनवाने की व्याख्या कीजिए। उसमें कम से कम दो योग्य चिकित्सक एवं कम से कम आठ अन्य कर्मचारी होने चाहिए। अस्पताल में स्वच्छता का विशेष ध्यान रखना चाहिए। साथ ही बिजली व पानी की सही व्यवस्था की जानी चाहिए। ऐसा होने पर यहाँ के लोग अपने जीवन की रक्षा भी कर सकेंगे साथ ही सरकार का दायित्व जनता के प्रति निभाया जा सकेगा।

मुझे आशा ही नहीं वरन् पूर्ण विश्वास है कि आप हमारे क्षेत्र में एक ऐसे चिकित्सालय के निर्माण की आज्ञा देंगे जो यहाँ के निवासियों के लिए वरदान साबित होगा और आप उदारता के पात्र होंगे। आपकी इस कृपा के हम आभारी रहेंगे।

सधन्यवाद !

भवदीय

रजनी अरोरा

कुकथला, बिचपुरी रोड

रुनकता, आगरा।

दिनांक 05.11.20XX

(ii) 17, कमला नगर

आगरा

दिनांक 07.11.20XX

प्रिय मित्र,

सप्रेम नमस्ते,

कुशलपूर्वक रहकर तुम्हारी कुशलता की सदैव कामना करता हूँ। आज मैं इस बात से बेहद प्रसन्न हूँ कि भारत ने ओलंपिक खेलों में उत्कृष्ट प्रदर्शन किया। रियो ओलंपिक 2016 में भारत की ओर से 124 खिलाड़ियों का दल भेजा गया। पूर्व स्वर्ण पदक विजेता अभिनव बिन्द्रा भारतीय दल के ध्वजवाहक बने और समापन पर साक्षी मलिक ने यह उत्तरदायित्व निभाया। दीपा कर्माकर ने ओलम्पिक में पहली बार भारतीय जिमनास्ट के रूप में पदार्पण किया और चौथे स्थान पर रहीं। ओलंपिक खेलों में महिलाओं ने देश का नाम रोशन किया। बैडमिन्टन में पी. वी. सिन्धु ने रजत पदक तथा साक्षी मलिक ने कुश्ती प्रतियोगिता में कांस्य पदक जीता।

मित्र! यह सच है कि हमारे खिलाड़ियों में जज्बा तो है, परंतु उनके लिए अवसरों की कमी है। उनके पास उन पर्याप्त साधनों की कमी है जो विदेशों में खिलाड़ियों को प्राप्त होते हैं। मैं उन भारतीय खिलाड़ियों को उनकी सफलता पर बधाई देता हूँ तथा समस्त भारतवासियों को भी बधाई देता हूँ।

आपके माता-पिता को मेरा चरण स्पर्श कहना। छोटे भाई को आशीर्वाद देना।

पत्रोत्तर की प्रतीक्षा में

तुम्हारा मित्र,

वरुण

Q. 5. **Write a letter in *Hindi* in approximately *120* words on any *one* of the topics given below:**
निम्नलिखित में से किसी एक विषय पर हिंदी में लगभग 120 शब्दों में पत्र लिखिए:

(i) आपके टेलीविजन द्वारा विभिन्न चैनलों पर अन्धविश्वास तथा तन्त्र-मन्त्र से सम्बन्धित कार्यक्रम दिखाकर जनता को भ्रमित किया जा रहा है। भारत सरकार के सूचना एवं प्रसारण मन्त्री को इसकी जानकारी देते हुए ऐसे कार्यक्रमों पर रोक लगाने का अनुरोध कीजिए।

(ii) आपकी चचेरी बहन जो गाँव में रहती है, उसकी दसवीं के बाद शिक्षा रोक दी गई है अतः उसकी आगे की शिक्षा जारी रखने का निवेदन करते हुए अपने चाचाजी को पत्र लिखिये जिसमें नारी शिक्षा की आवश्यकता और उसके लाभों की भी चर्चा कीजिए। **[2016]**

Ans. **(i)** प्रतिष्ठा में,

माननीय सूचना एवं प्रसारण मन्त्री,

भारत सरकार,

दिल्ली।

विषय—टेलीविजन पर प्रसारित अन्धविश्वास एवं तन्त्र-मन्त्र से सम्बन्धित कार्यक्रमों पर प्रतिबन्ध लगाने हेतु।

माननीय महोदय,

आज के इस वैज्ञानिक युग में टेलीविजन के चैनलों पर अनेक प्रकार के अन्धविश्वासों एवं तन्त्र-मन्त्र मिश्रित कार्यक्रमों की भरमार है। आश्चर्य की बात तो यह है कि इनके प्रभाव से कमिश्नर, कलेक्टर, वकील जैसे प्रबुद्ध लोग भी अछूते नहीं रह सके हैं।

सुख व दु:ख मानव जीवन के दो अंग हैं। कभी सुख तो कभी दु:ख आते ही रहते हैं। इसी प्रकार से मानव शरीर मानसिक व शारीरिक रोग से ग्रसित होता रहता है। उसका उपाय ओझा, ज्योतिषी या फिर झाड़-फूंक करने वाले तान्त्रिक नहीं कर सकते हैं। उसका उपचार तो चिकित्सकों व वैद्यों के पास होता है, न कि अन्धविश्वासी धन ऐंठने वाले या भ्रमित करने वाले पाखण्डी पण्डितों या तान्त्रिकों के पास है।

महोदय, कभी गणेशजी की पत्थर की मूर्ति को दूध पिला रहे हैं। कभी भूत-प्रेत का बहाना कर एक निर्दोष पुरुष या स्त्री को कोड़ों से मार रहे हैं। दूध उफन गया तो अपशकुन हो गया। बिल्ली रास्ता काट गई तो अशुभ है। लम्बी बीमारी हो गई तो ग्रह शान्ति के लिए यज्ञ, दान आदि करना—ये सारे कृत्य भोले-भाले लोगों को पथभ्रष्ट करके धन अर्जित करने के साधन हैं।

टेलीविजन का कोई भी चैनल खोलकर देखिये हर चैनल पर एक नया ज्योतिषी दिखाई देगा। जिसका कार्य ऐसे कृत्य कर भोली-भाली जनता से धन ऐंठना है। सच तो यह है कि मनुष्य पुरुषार्थ करना भूल गया है। यही पर्याप्त नहीं है, कई पुरोहित तो लड़कियों के इलाज के बहाने व्यभिचार करते हैं।

महोदय मेरा आपसे विनम्र निवेदन है कि जनता की ईश्वर में आस्था बनी रहने देने के लिए और लोगों की सोच सकारात्मक बनाने के लिए अतिशीघ्र इन ढोंगी व पाखण्डियों के कार्यक्रमों पर प्रतिबन्ध लगाने का कष्ट करें ताकि व्यक्ति, समाज एवं देश का उद्धार हो सके। आशा है आप मेरे इस प्रस्ताव पर गम्भीरता से विचार करेंगे।

सधन्यवाद।

प्रार्थी,
रवि शुक्ला
लखनऊ।
दिनांक 05.03.20XX

(ii) 15/25 कमला नगर,
नई दिल्ली।
दिनांक 16.3.20XX

आदरणीय चाचाजी,
सादर चरण स्पर्श।

कुशलपूर्वक रहकर आपकी सपरिवार कुशलता की कामना करता हूँ। कल ही मुझे निशा का पत्र मिला और ज्ञात हुआ कि आपने उसकी कक्षा दस की परीक्षा उत्तीर्ण करने के पश्चात् उसे आगे अध्ययन करने की अनुमति नहीं दी है। यह जानकर बहुत कष्ट हुआ। चाचाची आप एक अध्यापक हैं। लड़कियों की शिक्षा कितनी महत्त्वपूर्ण है, इस विषय में आपसे अधिक कौन जान सकता है? शिक्षा लड़कियों का वह शस्त्र है जिसके

सहारे वे अपने जीवन को मजबूत आधार दे सकती हैं। क्या आप जानते नहीं कि समाज में कितना नारी उत्पीड़न हो रहा है? जीवन में कभी यदि कोई विषमता आ जाये तो शिक्षित नारी अपने जीवन की समस्याओं का समाधान करने योग्य तो होती है। आज के इस विकसित परिप्रेक्ष्य में भी आप मेरी बहन को केवल चूल्हे चाकी तक ही सिमटा देना चाहते हैं। आप नहीं चाहते कि वह भी अच्छी पढ़ाई करके अपने पैरों पर खड़ी हो जाये और खुशहाल जिन्दगी जी सके।

चाचाजी मेरी आपसे प्रार्थना है कि आप निशा की आगे की पढ़ाई आरम्भ कराइये तथा वह जो सपने हृदय में संजोये है, उन्हें पूरे करने में उसकी सहायता कीजिए।

आशा है आप मेरे इस सुझाव का आदर करते हुए निशा के बेहतर भविष्य के बारे में सोचेंगे। चाचाजी को सादर प्रणाम। घर में सबको यथा योग्य।

पत्रोत्तर की प्रतीक्षा में।

आपका भतीजा
सुशील

Q. 6. Write a letter in *Hindi* in approximately *120* words on any *one* of the topics given below:

निम्नलिखित विषयों में से किसी एक विषय पर हिन्दी में लगभग 120 शब्दों में पत्र लिखिए:

(i) आपकी कॉलोनी में कुछ असामाजिक तत्व (Antisocial elements) आकर बस गये हैं। उनकी गुंडागर्दी बढ़ने के कारण नागरिकों का जीवन कठिन हो गया है। अपने शहर के 'पुलिस कमिश्नर' को पत्र लिखकर उनकी शिकायत कीजिए तथा सुव्यवस्था के लिए शीघ्र कदम उठाए जाने की प्रार्थना कीजिए।

(ii) आपका छोटा भाई किसी दूसरे शहर में पढ़ने गया है, जहाँ वह खेलने के लिए समय नहीं निकाल पा रहा है। खेलों का महत्त्व समझाते हुए उसे पत्र लिखिए।

[2015]

Ans. **(i)** सेवा में,
पुलिस आयुक्त महोदय,
आगरा महानगर,
आगरा।

महोदय,
मैं आपके संज्ञान हेतु निवेदन कर रहा हूँ कि कुछ दिनों पूर्व हमारी कॉलोनी के एक मकान में कुछ लड़के किराए पर आकर रहने लगे हैं। देखने में वे किसी कॉलेज में पढ़ने वाले छात्र मालूम पड़ते हैं, किन्तु यहाँ उनकी असामाजिक गतिविधियाँ काफी बढ़ गई हैं। उनकी वजह से कॉलोनी की लड़कियों का स्कूल और कॉलेज जाना मुश्किल हो गया है। प्रात: जैसे ही लड़कियाँ कॉलेज के लिए घर से निकलती हैं, वैसे ही वे सब अपने कमरे की

बालकनी से फिकरेबाज़ी शुरू कर देते हैं। प्रतिदिन अति तेज ध्वनि में पाश्चात्य संगीत चलाते हैं जिससे छात्रों की पढ़ाई में व्यवधान आता है। इस विषय में उनसे बात की गई तो इस पर वे साफ मुकर गये और अपने आपको निर्दोष बताने लगे।

आपसे प्रार्थना है कि कृपया छात्र-छात्राओं की सुरक्षा के लिए और कॉलोनी में शान्ति व्यवस्था बनाये रखने के लिए तुरन्त कार्यवाही करने की कृपा करें। कृपया सम्बन्धित पुलिस अधिकारियों को निर्देशित करने का कष्ट करें कि हमारे द्वारा बताए हुए उक्त मकान में रहने वाले लड़कों की पूरी छानबीन की जाए और छात्र-छात्राओं की सुरक्षा का पूर्ण प्रबन्ध किया जाए।

सधन्यवाद।

प्रार्थी,
अनिल कुमार
संजय प्लेस, आगरा।
दिनांक 8.9.20XX

(ii) 18, सुहागनगर
अलीगढ़
दिनांक 20.8.20XX

प्रिय अनुज,
तुम्हारा पत्र मिला, पढ़कर हाल-चाल मालूम हुए। तुमने लिखा है कि वहाँ जाकर तुम्हारे ऊपर पढ़ाई-लिखाई का इतना भार हो गया है कि तुम खेलने के लिए समय नहीं निकाल पा रहे हो। पढ़ाई में व्यस्त रहना वैसे तो अच्छी बात है, किन्तु खेल से विमुख हो जाना भी ठीक नहीं है। अच्छा स्वास्थ्य बनाए रखने के लिए खेल बहुत आवश्यक हैं। खेल से मनुष्य का शारीरिक स्वास्थ्य तो अच्छा होता ही है, उसका मन भी प्रफुल्लित रहता है। जब मन खुश रहता है तो तन भी स्वस्थ होता है और जब तन स्वस्थ होता है तो हम बहुत से काम उत्साहित होकर कर पाते हैं जिससे उनका परिणाम अच्छा निकलता है।

लगातार पढ़ाई करते रहने से तथा एक जैसी दिनचर्या से मानसिक थकान होने लगती है। इससे हमारी कार्य करने की क्षमता प्रभावित होती है और इससे हमारी स्मरण शक्ति पर भी प्रभाव पड़ता है।

इसलिए इस बात का ध्यान रखो कि जितना आवश्यक पढ़ाई करना है, उतना ही आवश्यक खेल-खेलना भी है। खेल हमारी दिनचर्या का एक अंग होना चाहिए। अत: तुम अपनी दिनचर्या इस प्रकार बनाओ कि उसमें एक या दो घण्टे खेल के लिए भी निकाल सको। इसके लिए अपने समय के विभाजन का एक चार्ट बनाओ और उसी प्रकार से सारे कार्य करो। जब हम अपने सारे कार्य सही समय पर और व्यवस्थित तरीके से करते हैं तो हमें समय का अभाव नहीं होता। खेलने से तुम्हारे मन में उत्साह बढ़ेगा और तुम अपनी पढ़ाई पर पहले से अधिक ध्यान दे सकोगे। मुझे आशा है कि अब तुम खेल और पढ़ाई दोनों में संतुलन बनाओगे। शेष सब कुशल है।

तुम्हारा बड़ा भाई
राजन

Chapter

5

Comprehension

Short-Long Answer Type Questions

Q. 1. **Read the passage given below and answer in *Hindi* the questions that follow, using your own words as far as possible:**

निम्नलिखित गद्यांश को ध्यान से पढ़िए तथा उसके नीचे लिखे गए प्रश्नों के उत्तर हिंदी में लिखिए। उत्तर यथासंभव आपके अपने शब्दों में होने चाहिए:

जापान के विरुद्ध दूसरे महायुद्ध में अमेरिका ने अणुबम का प्रयोग किया। सन् 1945 की गर्मियों में जापान खंडहरों का देश बन गया। लाखों आदमी मर गए थे। चालीस प्रतिशत नगर नष्ट हो गए थे। शहर की आबादी आधी रह गई थी। भूखा जापान-चिथड़ों में लिपटी जनता दीन-हीन, स्तब्ध, हैरान और क्षत-विक्षत हो गई थी। जापान में न कोयला होता है, न लोहा, न तेल और न ही यूरेनियम। बस थोड़ी सी कृषि योग्य भूमि। इस पराजय, दुःख और विनाश के बावजूद भी जापान फिर खड़ा हो गया। यह दुनिया का सबसे ज्यादा विकसित और औद्योगिक राष्ट्र बन गया। यह चमत्कार कैसे हुआ ? जापान की समृद्धि और प्रगति के लिए संभवत: राष्ट्रीय गुणों को टटोलना होगा, जो कि वहाँ की जनता की स्वभाविक खूबियों और चरित्र से मिलता है।

जापान और पराजय के पश्चात् एक अमेरिकी व्यापारिक संस्था ने अपनी शाखा जापान में खोली। उसने शाखा में सभी कर्मचारी जापानी रखे। अमेरिकी नियम के अनुसार जापान में सप्ताह में पाँच दिन काम करने का निश्चय किया गया। दो दिन शनिवार और रविवार की छुट्टी रखी गई। उसने सोचा था कि उसकी उदारता का जापानी कर्मचारी और कारीगर स्वागत करेंगे लेकिन यह देखकर संस्था के व्यवस्थापक को आश्चर्य हुआ कि जापानी कर्मचारी इस व्यवस्था का सामूहिक विरोध कर रहे थे। उसने कर्मचारियों को बुलाया और उसका कारण पूछा।

जापानी कर्मचारी एक आवाज में बोले,—''हमें कष्ट है। हम दो दिन खाली नहीं रहना चाहते। हमारे लिए सप्ताह में सिर्फ एक दिन का ही अवकाश काफी है। ज्यादा आराम से हम प्रसन्न नहीं होंगे। इससे हम आलसी बन जाएँगे, मेहनत के काम में हमारा दिल नहीं लगेगा, हमारा स्वास्थ्य गिरेगा। हमारा राष्ट्रीय चरित्र गिरेगा। अवकाश की वजह से हम व्यर्थ ही घूमेंगे-फिरेंगे, हम फिजूलखर्च बनेंगे। जो छुट्टी हमारी सेहत बिगाड़े तथा आदत खराब करें, आर्थिक स्थिति खराब करें, हमें ऐसा अवकाश नहीं चाहिए।''

अमेरिकी व्यवस्थापक ने अपनी टोपी सिर से नीचे उतारी। उसने जापानी कारीगरों का अभिवादन करते हुए कहा —''आप

जापानी भाइयों की समृद्धि और सफलता का रहस्य आपका परिश्रम और लगन है। आप कभी भी बीमार तथा गरीब नहीं रह सकते।

(i) जापान में विनाशकारी दुर्घटना कब और कैसे हुई? उसका क्या परिणाम हुआ?

(ii) उस देश के पास अपने प्राकृतिक संसाधन क्या हैं? वह पुन: विकसित और समृद्ध राष्ट्र कैसे बना?

(iii) व्यापार की दृष्टि से जापान में कौन आया? उसके आश्चर्य-चकित होने का क्या कारण था?

(iv) जापानी कर्मचारी उस व्यापारिक संस्था का विरोध क्यों कर रहे थे? उन्होंने व्यवस्थापक से क्या कहा?

(v) व्यवस्थापक पर कर्मचारियों की बात का क्या प्रभाव पड़ा? उसने उनसे क्या कहा? [2020]

Ans. **(i)** जापान में विनाशकारी दुर्घटना दूसरे विश्वयुद्ध के समय सन् 1945 में हुई। इस विश्वयुद्ध में जापान के विरुद्ध अमेरिका ने अणुबम का प्रयोग किया। जापान खंडहरों का देश बन गया। लाखों आदमी मर गए थे। चालीस प्रतिशत नगर नष्ट हो गए थे। देश की आबादी आधी रह गई थी। भूखा जापान चिथड़ों में लिपटी जनता दीन-हीन, स्तब्ध, हैरान और क्षत-विक्षत हो गई थी।

(ii) उस देश के पास अपने प्राकृतिक संसाधन के नाम पर थोड़ी सी कृषि योग्य भूमि है। वह पुन: विकसित और समृद्ध राष्ट्र उसकी जनता की कर्मठता व परिश्रम करने के चारित्रिक विशेषताओं के कारण बना।

(iii) व्यापार की दृष्टि से जापान में एक अमेरिकी व्यापारिक संस्था ने अपनी शाखा खोली। इस व्यापारिक संस्था ने अपनी शाखा में सभी कर्मचारी जापानी रखे। कम्पनी ने दो दिन शनिवार और रविवार की छुट्टी रखने का निश्चय किया। यह देखकर संस्था के व्यवस्थापक को आश्चर्य हुआ कि जापानी कर्मचारी इस व्यवस्था का सामूहिक विरोध कर रहे थे। वे दो दिन का साप्ताहिक अवकाश नहीं चाहते थे।

(iv) जापानी कर्मचारी शनिवार और रविवार को दी जाने वाली छुट्टी के कारण व्यापारिक संस्था का विरोध कर रहे थे। उन्होंने व्यवस्थापक से कहा कि वे दो दिन खाली नहीं रहना चाहते। उनके लिए सप्ताह में सिर्फ एक दिन का ही अवकाश काफी था। ज्यादा आराम करने से वे आलसी बन जाएँगे। उनका स्वास्थ्य गिरेगा। उनका राष्ट्रीय चरित्र गिरेगा। अवकाश की वजह से वे व्यर्थ ही घूमेंगे-फिरेंगे और फिजूलखर्ची करेंगे।

(v) व्यवस्थापक पर कर्मचारियों की बात का गहरा प्रभाव पड़ा। उन्होंने अपनी टोपी सिर से नीचे उतारी और कर्मचारियों का अभिवादन करते हुए कहा कि जापानी भाइयों की समृद्धि और सफलता का रहस्य उनका परिश्रम और लगन है। वे कभी भी बीमार तथा गरीब नहीं रह सकते।

Q. 2. **Read the passage given below and answer in *Hindi* the questions that follow, using your own words as far as possible:**

निम्नलिखित गद्यांश को ध्यान से पढ़िए तथा उसके नीचे लिखे गए प्रश्नों के उत्तर हिंदी में लिखिए। उत्तर यथासंभव आपके अपने शब्दों में होने चाहिए:

एक रियासत थी। उसका नाम था कंचनगढ़। वहाँ बहुत गरीबी थी। लोग कमजोर थे और धरती में कुछ उगता न था। चारों ओर भुखमरी थी। एक दिन राजा कंचनदेव राज्य की दशा से चिंतित हो उठे। अचानक उनके पास एक साधु आए। राजा ने उन्हें प्रणाम किया। राजा ने साधु को अपने राज्य के बारे में बताया कुछ उपाय करने की प्रार्थना की। साधु मुस्कराकर बोले—"कंचनगढ़ के नीचे सोने की खान है।" इतना कहकर साधु चले गए।

राजा ने खुदाई करवाई। वहाँ सोने की खान निकली। राजा का खजाना सोने से भर गया। राजा ने अपने राज्य में जगह-जगह मुफ्त भोजनालय बनवाए, दवाखाने खुलवाए, चारागाह बनवाए तथा अन्य सुख-सुविधा के साधन उपलब्ध करा दिए। अब वहाँ कोई दुखी नहीं था। सब लोग खुश थे। धीरे-धीरे लोग आलसी हो गए। कोई काम नहीं करता था। भोजन तक मुफ्त में मिलने लगा था। मन्त्री ने राजा को बहुत समझाया और कहा—"महाराज, लोग आलसी होते जा रहे हैं। उनको काम दिया जाए।" परन्तु राजा ने मन्त्री की बात को टाल दिया।

कंचनगढ़ की समृद्धि को देखकर पड़ोसी रियासत के राजा को ईर्ष्या हुई। उसने अचानक कंचनगढ़ पर चढ़ाई कर दी और माँग की — "सोना दो या लड़ो।" कंचनगढ़ के आलसी लोगों ने राजा से कहा—"हमारे पास बहुत सोना है, कुछ दे दें। बेकार खून क्यों बहाया जाए?" राजा ने लोगों की बात मान ली और सोना दे दिया। कुछ दिनों बाद उसी पड़ोसी राजा ने कंचनगढ़ पर फिर चढ़ाई कर दी। इस बार उसका लालच और बढ़ गया था। इसी प्रकार उसने कई बार चढ़ाई कर-करके कंचनगढ़ से सोना ले लिया। यह सब देखकर राजा का मन्त्री बहुत परेशान हो गया। वह राजा को समझाना चाहता था, किन्तु राजा के सम्मुख कुछ बोलने की हिम्मत नहीं हो पा रही थी। अंत में उसने युक्ति से काम लिया।

एक दिन मन्त्री कंचनदेव को घुमाने के लिए नगर के पूर्व की ओर बने गुलाब के बाग की ओर ले गया। राजा कंचनदेव ने देखा कि बाग में दाने बिखरे पड़े हैं। कबूतर दाना चुग रहे हैं। थोड़ी दूर कुछ कबूतर मरे पड़े हैं। कुछ भी समझ में न आने पर राजा ने मरे हुए कबूतरों के बारे में मन्त्री से पूछा।

मन्त्री ने बताया — "महाराज, इन्हें शिकारी पक्षियों ने मारा है।" राजा ने पूछा — "तो कबूतर भागते क्यों नहीं?" "भागते हैं

लेकिन लालच में फिर से आ जाते हैं, क्योंकि उनके लिए यहाँ आपकी आज्ञा से दाना डाला जाता है।" — मंत्री ने बताया। राजा ने कहा — "दाना डलवाना बंद कर दो।" मंत्री ने वैसा ही किया।

राजा अगले दिन फिर घूमने निकले। उन्होंने देखा कि दाना तो नहीं है, किन्तु कबूतर आ-जा रहे हैं। राजा ने मंत्री से इसका कारण पूछा। मंत्री ने बताया — "महाराज, इन्हें बिना प्रयास के ही दाना मिल रहा था। यह अब दाने-चारे की तलाश की आदत भूल चुके हैं, आलसी हो गए हैं। शिकारी पक्षी इस बात को जानते हैं कि कबूतर तो यहीं आएँगे अत: वे इन्हें आसानी से मार डालते हैं।" राजा चिंता में पड़ गए। उन्होंने शाम को मंत्री को बुलाकर कहा — "नगर के सारे मुफ्त भोजनालय बन्द करवा दो। जो मेहनत करे, वही खाए। लोग निकम्मे और आलसी होते जा रहे हैं। और हाँ, एक बात और। मैं अब शत्रु को सोना नहीं दूँगा, बल्कि उससे लड़ाई करूँगा। जाओ, सेना को मजबूत करो।" मंत्री राजा की बात सुनकर बहुत खुश हो गया।

(i) राजा कंचनदेव की चिन्ता का क्या कारण था? उन्होंने साधु से क्या प्रार्थना की?

(ii) साधु ने राजा को क्या बताया? उसके बाद राजा ने राज्य के लिए क्या-क्या कार्य किये?

(iii) पड़ोसी राजा के आक्रमण करने पर कंचनगढ़ का राजा क्या करता था और क्यों?

(iv) कबूतरों की दशा कैसी थी? उस दशा को देखकर राजा ने क्या सीखा?

(v) राजा ने मंत्री को क्या आदेश दिए? आदेश सुनकर मंत्री की क्या स्थिति हुई? [2019]

📋 Marking Scheme

अपठित गद्यांश

(i) राजा कंचनदेव के राज्य में बहुत गरीबी थी। लोग कमज़ोर थे और धरती में कुछ उगता न था। चारों ओर भुखमरी थी। एक दिन राजा कंचनदेव राज्य की दशा से चिंतित हो उठे।

(ii) राजा कंचनदेव अपने राज्य की दुर्दशा से चिन्तित थे। उन्होंने एक साधु को कुछ उपाय करने की प्रार्थना की। साधु ने राजा को बताया कि कंचनगढ़ के नीचे सचमुच सोने की खान है। इतना कहकर साधु चले गए।

राजा ने खुदाई करवाई। वहाँ सोने की खान निकली। राजा का खजाना सोने से भर गया। राजा ने अपने राज्य में जगह-जगह मुफ्त भोजनालय बनवाए, दवाखाने खुलवाए, चारागाह बनवाए तथा अन्य सुख-सुविधा के साधन उपलब्ध करा किए।

(iii) कंचनगढ़ की समृद्धि देखकर पड़ोसी रियासत के राजा को ईर्ष्या हुई। उसने अचानक कंचनगढ़ पर चढ़ाई कर दी। उसने राजा से माँग कर दी कि सोना दो या मुझसे लड़ाई करो। कंचनगढ़ के आलसी लोगों के कहने पर राजा ने उसे सोना दे दिया। कुछ दिनों बाद उसी पड़ोसी राजा ने कंचनगढ़ पर फिर चढ़ाई कर दी। इस बार उसका लालच और बढ़ गया था। इस प्रकार उसने कई बार चढ़ाई कर-करके कंचनगढ़ से सोना ले लिया। राजा हर बार अपने आलसी लोगों की सलाह मानकर पड़ोसी राजा को अपना सोना दे देता था क्योंकि वह राजा अपने विवेक का इस्तेमाल नहीं करता था। वह बहुत आलसी तथा लापरवाह भी हो गया था।

(iv) राज्य को लुटते देख मंत्री परेशान हो गया। वह राजा को कुछ कह नहीं पा रहा था। एक दिन वह उन्हें एक बाग में ले गया जहाँ कबूतर दाना चुग रहे थे। मंत्री ने राजा को दिखाया कि उनके आदेश पर कबूतरों को बिना प्रयास के ही दाना मिल रहा था। वे अब दाने-चारे की तलाश की आदत भूल चुके थे और आलसी तथा लालची हो गए थे। शिकारी पक्षी इस बात को जानते थे कि कबूतर तो यही आएँगे अत: जब कबूतर वहाँ आते तो वे उन्हें आसानी से मार डालते। यह दशा को देखकर राजा समझ गए कि यही हालत उनके राज्य के लोगों की है। वे काम करना ही भूल गए हैं। हर समय आलस में पड़े रहते हैं। लोगों की इसी कमजोरी का पड़ोसी राजा फायदा उठा रहा था। यदि इसी तरह वे सोना देते रहे तो वह दिन दूर नहीं जब राज्य के लोगों को भूखा मरना पड़ेगा।

(v) मंत्री ने राजा की आँखें खोल दी थीं। अत: शाम को राजा ने मंत्री को बुलाकर कहा कि नगर के सारे मुफ्त भोजनालय बंद करवा दो। जो मेहनत करेगा, वही खाएगा। लोग निकम्मे और आलसी होते जा रहे हैं। अब मैं शत्रु को सोना नहीं दूँगा, बल्कि उससे लड़ाई करूँगा। जाओ, सेना को मज़बूत करो। आदेश सुन कर मंत्री की चिंता दूर हो गई वह बहुत खुश हो गया।

Ans. (i) राजा कंचनदेव की चिंता का कारण उनके राज्य कंचनगढ़ की गरीबी थी। वहाँ की प्रजा कमजोर थी। धरती भी बंजर थी। राज्य में चारों ओर भुखमरी थी। राजा ने साधु को अपने राज्य के बारे में बताया और कुछ उपाय करने की प्रार्थना की।

(ii) साधु ने राजा को बताया कि कंचनगढ़ के नीचे सोने की खान है। साधु की बात सुनकर राजा ने खुदाई करवाई। वहाँ सोने की खान निकली। उस सोने से राजा ने अपने राज्य में जगह-जगह मुफ्त भोजनालय बनवाए, दवाखाने खुलवाए, चारागाह बनवाए तथा अन्य सुख-सुविधा के साधन भी उपलब्ध करवाए।

(iii) पड़ोसी राजा के आक्रमण करने पर कंचनगढ़ का राजा अपनी प्रजा की बात मान कर उसे सोना दे देता था। सारी सुविधाएँ मिलने के कारण लोग आलसी हो गए थे। इसलिए वे राजा को यह सुझाव देते थे कि थोड़ा-सा सोना पड़ोसी राजा को दे दिया जाए। युद्ध में खून बहाना बेकार है। राजा हर बार अपनी आलसी हो चुकी प्रजा का कहना मान लेता था, अपने विवेक का इस्तेमाल नहीं करता था।

(iv) बिना प्रयास के दाना मिलने के कारण कबूतर आलसी हो गए थे। जब राजा ने दाना डलवाना बन्द कर दिया, तब भी वे कबूतर उसी जगह पर दाने के लिए आते और शिकारी पक्षी द्वारा आसानी से मारे जाते। कबूतरों की ऐसी दशा को देखकर राजा समझ गये कि यही दशा उनके राज्य के लोगों की है, मुफ्त में अन्न और सुख-सुविधायें उपलब्ध होने की वजह से वे आलसी हो गये हैं। इसी कमजोरी का फायदा पड़ोसी राजा उठा रहा है।

(v) राजा ने मन्त्री को आदेश दिया कि नगर के सारे मुफ्त भोजनालय बन्द करवा दिए जाएँ। मेहनत करने वाले को ही खाना मिलेगा। राजा ने यह भी कहा कि अब वे पड़ोसी राजा को सोना नहीं देंगे। बल्कि उनसे लड़ाई करेंगे। वे मंत्री को सेना को मज़बूत करने का आदेश देते हैं। आदेश सुनकर मन्त्री बहुत खुश हुआ।

Q. 3. **Read the passage given below and answer in *Hindi* the questions that follow, using your own words as far as possible:**

निम्नलिखित गद्यांश को ध्यान से पढ़िए तथा उसके नीचे लिखे गए प्रश्नों के उत्तर हिंदी में लिखिए। उत्तर यथासंभव आपके अपने शब्दों में होने चाहिए:

सूर्य अस्त हो रहा था। पक्षी चहचहाते हुए अपने नीड़ की ओर जा रहे थे। गाँव की कुछ स्त्रियाँ अपने घड़े लेकर कुएँ पर जा पहुँचीं। पानी भरकर कुछ स्त्रियाँ तो अपने घरों को लौट गईं, परंतु चार स्त्रियाँ कुएँ की पक्की जगत पर ही बैठकर आपस में बातचीत करने लगीं। तरह-तरह की बातचीत करते-करते बात बेटों पर जा पहुँची। उनमें से एक की उम्र सबसे बड़ी लग रही थी। वह कहने लगी—"भगवान सबको मेरे जैसा ही बेटा दे। वह लाखों में एक है। उसका कंठ बहुत मधुर है। उसके गीत को सुनकर कोयल और मैना भी चुप हो जाती हैं। सच में मेरा बेटा तो अनमोल हीरा है।"

उसकी बात सुनकर दूसरी अपने बेटे की प्रशंसा करते हुए बोली—"बहन मैं तो समझती हूँ कि मेरे बेटे की बराबरी कोई नहीं कर सकता। वह बहुत ही शक्तिशाली और बहादुर है। वह बड़े-बड़े पहलवानों को भी पछाड़ देता है। वह आधुनिक युग का भीम है। मैं तो भगवान से कहती हूँ कि वह मेरे जैसा बेटा सबको दे।"

दोनों स्त्रियों की बात सुनकर तीसरी भला क्यों चुप रहती? वह भी अपने को रोक न सकी। वह बोल उठी—"मेरा बेटा साक्षात् बृहस्पति का अवतार है। वह जो कुछ पढ़ता है, एकदम याद कर लेता है। ऐसा लगता है बहन, मानो उसके कंठ में सरस्वती का वास हो।"

तीनों की बात सुनकर चौथी स्त्री चुपचाप बैठी रही। उसका भी एक बेटा था, परंतु उसने अपने बेटे के बारे में कुछ नहीं कहा।

जब पहली स्त्री ने उसे टोकते हुए पूछा कि उसके बेटे में क्या गुण है, तब चौथी स्त्री ने सहज भाव से कहा—"मेरा बेटा न गंधर्व-सा गायक है, न भीम-सा पहलवान और न ही बृहस्पति-सा बुद्धिमान।" यह कहकर वह शांत बैठ गई। कुछ देर बाद जब वे घड़े सिर पर रखकर लौटने लगीं, तभी किसी के गीत का मधुर स्वर सुनाई पड़ा, गीत सुनकर सभी स्त्रियाँ ठिठक गईं। पहली स्त्री शीघ्र ही बोल उठी—"मेरा हीरा गा रहा है। तुम लोगों ने सुना, उसका कंठ कितना मधुर है।" तीनों स्त्रियाँ बड़े ध्यान से उसे देखने लगीं। वह गीत गाता हुआ उसी रास्ते से निकल गया। उसने अपनी माँ की तरफ ध्यान नहीं दिया।

थोड़ी देर बाद दूसरी का बेटा दिखाई दिया। दूसरी स्त्री ने बड़े गर्व से कहा, "देखो मेरा बलवान बेटा आ रहा है। वह बातें कर ही रही थीं कि उसका बेटा भी उसकी ओर ध्यान दिए बगैर निकल गया।"

तभी तीसरी स्त्री का बेटा उधर से संस्कृत के श्लोकों का पाठ करता हुआ निकला। तीसरी ने बड़े गद्गद् स्वर में कहा, "देखो, मेरे बेटे के कंठ में सरस्वती का वास है।" वह भी माँ की ओर देखे बिना आगे बढ़ गया।

वह अभी थोड़ी दूर गया होगा कि चौथी स्त्री का बेटा भी अचानक उधर से आ निकला। वह देखने में बहुत सीधा-सादा और सरल प्रकृति का लग रहा था। उसे देखकर चौथी स्त्री ने कहा, "बहन, यही मेरा बेटा है।" तभी उसका बेटा पास आ पहुँचा। अपनी माँ को देखकर रुक गया और बोला, "माँ लाओ मैं तुम्हारा घड़ा पहुँचा दूँ। माँ ने मना किया, फिर भी उसने माँ के सिर से पानी का घड़ा उतारकर अपने सिर पर रख लिया और घर की ओर चल पड़ा।

तीनों स्त्रियाँ बड़े ही आश्चर्य से देखती रहीं। एक वृद्ध महिला बहुत देर से उनकी बातें सुन रही थी। वह उनके पास आकर बोली, "देखती क्या हो? यही सच्चा हीरा है।"

(i) पहली तथा दूसरी स्त्री ने अपने-अपने बेटे के विषय में क्या कहा?

(ii) तीसरी स्त्री ने अपने बेटे को 'बृहस्पति का अवतार' क्यों कहा?

(iii) पहली स्त्री द्वारा पूछे जाने पर चौथी स्त्री ने क्या कहा?

(iv) चौथी स्त्री के बेटे ने अपनी माँ के साथ कैसा व्यवहार किया, यह देखकर तीनों स्त्रियों को कैसा लगा?

(v) बच्चों को अपने माता-पिता के साथ कैसा व्यवहार करना चाहिए? समझाइए। [2018]

📋 Marking Scheme

(i) पहली स्त्री ने अपने बेटे के गुणों की प्रशंसा करते हुए कहा कि भगवान मेरे जैसा बेटा सब को दे, वह तो लाखों में एक है, वह तो कोयल की तरह मीठा गाता है, उसके गीत को सुनकर कोयल और मैना भी चुप हो जाती हैं, शरमा जाती हैं, वह तो हीरा है।

दूसरी स्त्री ने कहा, कि बहन मैं तो समझती हूँ कि मेरे बेटे जैसा बेटा दुनिया में नहीं है वह बहुत ही शक्तिशाली, बहादुर है, बड़े से बड़े पहलवानों को हरा देता है।

(ii) तीसरी स्त्री भी अपने बेटे को सर्वगुणी गानती थी। उसने उसकी प्रशंसा करते हुए कहा कि उसका बेटा बहुत ही विद्वान है, वह जो पढ़ता है उसे कंठस्थ हो जाता है, वह एक पाठी है, बृहस्पति का अवतार है, ज्ञान में उसकी बराबरी कोई नहीं कर सकता है।

(iii) पहली स्त्री ने देखा कि चौथी स्त्री बड़ी चुपचाप बैठी है तब उसने उससे पूछा कि तुम्हारे बेटे के क्या गुण हैं– तो उसने कहा कि वह ना गंधर्व है ना गायक। न भीम जैसा बलवान ना बृहस्पति जैसा बुद्धिमान।

(iv) चौथी स्त्री के बेटे ने जब देखा कि उसकी माँ पानी का घड़ा सिर पर रखकर जा रही है तो उसने तुरंत माँ की मदद करते हुए उसका घड़ा लिया और वह घर की ओर चल पड़ा। यह देखकर सभी स्त्रियों को आश्चर्य हुआ।

(v) बच्चों को अपने माता-पिता का सम्मान करना चाहिए, हर पल उनकी मदद करनी चाहिए। अंहकारी बनकर जीने के बदले श्रवण बनकर माता-पिता की सहायता करनी चाहिए।

Ans.

(i) पहली स्त्री ने कहा "भगवान सबको मेरे जैसा ही बेटा दे, उसका कंठ बहुत मधुर है। उसके गीत को सुनकर कोयल और मैना भी चुप हो जाती हैं। मेरा बेटा अनमोल हीरा है।"

दूसरी स्त्री ने कहा, "मेरा बेटा बहुत ही शक्तिशाली और बहादुर है। बड़े-बड़े पहलवानों को पछाड़ देता है। वह आधुनिक युग का भीम है।"

(ii) तीसरी स्त्री ने अपने बेटे को बृहस्पति का अवतार इसलिए कहा क्योंकि वह जो कुछ पढ़ता था, एकदम याद कर लेता था। ऐसा लगता है मानो उसके कंठ में सरस्वती का वास हो। अर्थात् वह एक पाठी है, ज्ञान में उसकी बराबरी कोई नहीं कर सकता है।

(iii) पहली स्त्री द्वारा पूछे जाने पर चौथी स्त्री ने कहा कि उसका बेटा न गंधर्व सा गायक है और न भीम सा बलवान और न ही बृहस्पति सा बुद्धिमान।

(iv) चौथी स्त्री के बेटे ने जब अपनी माँ को पानी का घड़ा लेकर आते हुए देखा तो अपनी माँ के पास पहुँचकर बोला "माँ, लाओ मैं तुम्हारा घड़ा पहुँचा दूँ।" माँ के मना करने पर भी उसने घड़ा अपने सिर पर रख लिया और घर की ओर चल दिया। यह देखकर तीनों स्त्रियाँ आश्चर्यचकित रह गईं।

(v) हम जीवन में चाहें कितनी भी उन्नति क्यों न करें, लेकिन हमें अपने माता-पिता के साथ सम्मानजनक व्यवहार करना चाहिए एवं उनकी आज्ञा को सर्वोपरि समझना चाहिये। क्योंकि हमारी उन्नति के पीछे उनका त्याग, बलिदान व प्रेरणा होती है। इसलिए जहाँ तक हो सके उनकी मदद करें और उन्हें खुशियाँ प्रदान करें।

Q. 4. Read the passage given below and answer in *Hindi* the questions that follow, using your own words as far as possible:

निम्नलिखित गद्यांश को ध्यान से पढ़िए तथा उसके नीचे लिखे गए प्रश्नों के उत्तर हिंदी में लिखिए। उत्तर यथासंभव आपके अपने शब्दों में होने चाहिए:

पंजाब में उस वर्ष भयंकर अकाल पड़ा था। उन दिनों वहाँ महाराजा रणजीत सिंह का राज था। उन्होंने यह घोषणा करवा दी, "महाराज के आदेश से शाही भण्डार-गृह हर जरूरतमंद के लिए खुला है। प्रत्येक जरूरतमंद एक बार में जितना उठा सके, ले जाये।" यह घोषणा सुनते ही गाँवों व शहरों से जरूरतमंदों की भीड़ राजमहल में उमड़ पड़ी।

उन दिनों लाहौर में एक सद्गृहस्थ बूढ़े सज्जन रहते थे। वे कट्टर सनातनी विचारों के थे। उन्होंने जीवन में कभी भी किसी के आगे अपना हाथ नहीं फैलाया था। अँधेरा होने पर वह शाही भण्डार के दरवाजे पर पहुँचे। द्वार खुला था, किसी तरह की कोई जाँच-पड़ताल नहीं हुई। उन्होंने बड़े संकोच से

अपनी चादर को फैलाया, उसके कोने में थोड़ा-सा अनाज बाँध लिया। ज्यादा अनाज उठाना उनके लिए मुश्किल था। इतने में पगड़ी बाँधे एक व्यक्ति वहाँ आया। उसने कहा, "भ्राताजी आपने तो काफी कम अनाज लिया है।" बूढ़े सज्जन ने कहा, "असल में मैं बूढ़ा लाचार हूँ। इस अकाल में तो थोड़ा अनाज लेना ही सही है, जिससे सब जरूरतमंदों को मिल जाये।"

उस व्यक्ति ने बूढ़े की गठरी खोल दी। उसमें भरपूर अनाज भर दिया। बूढ़े सज्जन ने कहा, "मैं इतना अनाज नहीं उठा सकता और न ही इसकी मजदूरी का पैसा दे सकता हूँ।" इतने में उस अजनबी ने बूढ़े की गठरी अपने कंधों पर ले ली और बूढ़े के पीछे-पीछे चल पड़ा। जब वे बूढ़े के घर के द्वार पर पहुँचे तो वहाँ दो बच्चे उनकी प्रतीक्षा कर रहे थे। उन्हें देखते ही वे बोले—"बाबा, कहाँ चले गये थे?" बूढ़ा खामोश रहा। अजनबी ने कहा, "घर में कोई बड़ा लड़का नहीं है?" बूढ़ा बोला, "लड़का था लेकिन काबुल की लड़ाई में शहीद हो गया। अब बहू है तथा मेरे ये पोते हैं।" वह अजनबी बोला, "भाई जी धन्य हैं आप, जिनका बेटा देश के लिए शहीद हो गया।"

रोशनी में बूढ़े ने उस अजनबी को पहचान लिया। वे खुद महाराज रणजीत सिंह थे। बूढ़े ने पोतों से कहा, "इनके सामने दण्डवत प्रणाम करो।" और स्वयं भी प्रणाम करने लगे और थोड़ी देर बाद बोले, "आज मुझसे बड़ा पाप हो गया। आपसे बोझा उठवाया।" नहीं, यह पाप नहीं, मेरा सौभाग्य था कि मैं शहीद के परिवार की सेवा कर सका। आप सबकी सेवा करना मेरा फर्ज है। अब आप जीवन भर हमारे साथ रहिए और हमें कृतार्थ कीजिए।"

(i) राज्य को किस विपत्ति का सामना करना पड़ा था? उन दिनों वहाँ के राजा कौन थे और उन्होंने उस समस्या का क्या समाधान निकाला?

(ii) राजा ने राज्य में क्या घोषणा करवाई और क्यों?

(iii) बूढ़े आदमी के बारे में आप क्या जानते हैं? उनका पूर्ण परिचय दीजिए।

(iv) बूढ़े आदमी ने थोड़ा-सा अनाज ही क्यों लिया था? कारण स्पष्ट करते हुए बताइए कि उस अजनबी व्यक्ति ने उस बूढ़े की कैसे सहायता की?

(v) इस गद्यांश से मिलने वाली शिक्षाओं पर प्रकाश डालिए।   [2017]

Ans.   **(i)** प्रांत में दुर्भिक्ष (अकाल) की स्थिति उत्पन्न हो गयी थी। लोग भूखे मरने लगे। उस समय वहाँ के राजा, महाराजा रणजीत सिंह थे। उन्होंने इस समस्या से छुटकारा पाने के लिए अपने शाही भण्डार गृह का द्वार हर जरूरतमंद के लिए खोल दिया।

(ii) महाराजा ने यह घोषणा करवाई कि शाही भण्डार-गृह हर जरूरतमंद के लिए खुला है। जिसको जितना अनाज चाहिए वह उसमें से उठाकर ले जाये। इसे सुनकर पीड़ितों को राहत मिली। ऐसा उन्होंने इसलिए किया क्योंकि वह अपनी प्रजा से बहुत प्यार करते थे और उन्हें भूखा मरते नहीं देखना चाहते थे।

(iii) वह सात्त्विक वृत्ति वाले सज्जन व्यक्ति थे। सनातन धर्म में उनका अगाध विश्वास था तथा वह बहुत स्वाभिमानी प्रवृत्ति के थे। किसी के सामने याचना करना उनके स्वभाव में नहीं था। उनका बेटा काबुल की लड़ाई में शहीद हो गया था और अब बहू तथा दो पोतों की जिम्मेदारी उन पर ही थी।

(iv) बूढ़े सज्जन ने कम अनाज लिया क्योंकि वे शरीर से कमजोर थे, अधिक अनाज लेकर चल नहीं सकते थे। इसके साथ ही उनका मानना था कि संकट की इस स्थिति में कम अनाज लेना ही उचित है ताकि सबको अनाज मिल सके।

अजनबी ने उनकी सहायता करने के लिये उनकी गठरी खोलकर उसमें अधिक अनाज भर दिया और स्वयं कंधे पर लादकर उनके घर तक छोड़ कर आये।

(v) यह एक शिक्षाप्रद कहानी है जिसमें राजा रणजीत सिंह की प्रजावत्सलता को दिखाया गया है। वे बहुत दयालु थे और दीन-दुखियों की खूब सेवा करते थे। वे बूढ़ों को बहुत आदर देते थे। वे देशभक्तों व शहीदों का सम्मान करते थे और उनके परिवार के पालन-पोषण की जिम्मेदारी अपने ऊपर लेकर अपने कर्तव्य का पालन करते थे। इस कहानी में यह भी दिखाया गया है कि इंसान को लोभी व स्वार्थी नहीं होना चाहिए। उसे दूसरों की भलाई के बारे में भी सोचना चाहिए।

Q. 5. Read the passage given below and answer in *Hindi* the questions that follow, using your own words as far as possible:

निम्नलिखित गद्यांश को ध्यान से पढ़िए तथा उसके नीचे लिखे प्रश्नों के उत्तर हिन्दी में लिखिए। उत्तर यथासम्भव आपके अपने शब्दों में होने चाहिए:

बहुत समय पहले एक गाँव में हरिहर नाम का एक दयालु और सीधा-सच्चा किसान रहता था। वह खेती-बाड़ी का काम करता था। वह पूरा दिन अपने खेत में जी-तोड़ मेहनत करता था और शाम का समय ईश्वर की प्रार्थना में बिताता था। जीवन में उसकी मात्र एक इच्छा थी। वह उडुपि के मन्दिर में भगवान श्रीकृष्ण के दर्शन करना चाहता था। उडुपि दक्षिण कर्नाटक का प्रमुख तीर्थस्थान है। वह अपनी गरीबी के कारण तीर्थयात्रा की इच्छा पूरी नहीं कर पाता था। इसी तरह कुछ वर्ष बीत गए। समय के साथ-साथ हरिहर की आर्थिक स्थिति भी सुधरती गई। अब उसने तीर्थयात्रा की योजना बनाई। उसकी पत्नी ने उसके लिए पर्याप्त भोजन बाँध दिया।

हरिहर तीर्थयात्रियों के एक दल के साथ उडुपि की ओर चल दिया। मार्ग में उसे एक स्थान पर एक बूढ़ा आदमी मिला। उसकी दशा बहुत ही दयनीय थी। वह कई दिनों से भूखा-प्यासा था और पीड़ा के कारण कराह रहा था। जैसे ही हरिहर की नजर उस पर पड़ी, उसका हृदय करुणा से भर गया। उसने बूढ़े के पास जाकर पूछा, "बाबा, क्या तुम भी तीर्थयात्रा

करने उडुपि जा रहे हो ?" बूढ़े आदमी ने उत्तर दिया, "मेरा एक बेटा बीमार है और दूसरे बेटे ने भी तीन दिनों से कुछ नहीं खाया। फिर मैं तीर्थयात्रा कैसे करूँ।"

हरिहर समझता था कि दीन-दुखियों की सेवा ही ईश्वर की सबसे बड़ी सेवा है इसलिए उसने उडुपि जाने से पहले उस बूढ़े के घर पहले जाने का निश्चय किया। उसके साथियों ने उसे बहुत समझाया "बहुत मुश्किल से तुमने धन एकत्र किया है, अगर यह नष्ट हो गया तो फिर तुम कभी तीर्थयात्रा नहीं कर पाओगे।" हरिहर पर उनकी बातों का कोई प्रभाव नहीं पड़ा। वह बूढ़े के घर जा पहुँचा। उसने सबसे पहले घर के सभी व्यक्तियों को भरपेट भोजन कराया। फिर वह बीमार बच्चे के लिए दवा ले आया। उसने बूढ़े आदमी को खेत में बोने के लिए बीज भी ला दिये। वह कुछ दिन वहाँ रुका। उसने बूढ़े आदमी के बेटे की सेवा की, जिससे वह कुछ दिनों में स्वस्थ हो गया लेकिन इन सारे कार्यों में उसके सारे पैसे खर्च हो गये।

अब उसने अपनी तीर्थयात्रा बीच में ही छोड़कर वापस घर लौटने का निश्चय किया। उसे उडुपि न जा पाने का बिल्कुल भी दुःख न था। क्योंकि वह जानता था कि उसने अपना सारा धन दीन-दुखियों की सेवा में खर्च किया था। घर पहुँचकर उसने अपनी पत्नी को सारी बातें बता दीं। पत्नी भी इस पर प्रसन्न हुई क्योंकि वह भी धार्मिक स्वभाव की महिला थी। उस रात हरिहर ने सपने में भगवान श्रीकृष्ण को देखा, जो उससे कह रहे थे, "हरिहर, तुम मेरे सच्चे भक्त हो। तुमने उस बूढ़े आदमी की सहायता की और अपनी इच्छा का बलिदान कर दिया। वह बूढ़ा आदमी कोई और नहीं मैं ही था। तुम्हारी परीक्षा के लिए ही मैं उस बूढ़े आदमी का वेश धारण कर वहाँ आया था। तुम मेरे सच्चे सेवक हो।" इस तरह हरिहर बगैर तीर्थयात्रा पर गए पुण्य का भागीदार बना।

 (i) हरिहर क्या काम करता था? उसकी एकमात्र इच्छा क्या थी?

 (ii) हरिहर को तीर्थयात्रा के मार्ग में कौन मिला? उसकी क्या स्थिति थी?

 (iii) हरिहर ने बूढ़े व्यक्ति की कैसे सहायता की?

 (iv) हरिहर ने घर लौटने का निश्चय क्यों किया? वहाँ लौटने पर हरिहर ने क्या स्वप्न देखा?

 (v) इस गद्यांश से आपको क्या शिक्षा मिलती है?

[2016]

Ans. **(i)** सीधे-सादे स्वभाव का व्यक्ति हरिहर एक कृषक था। वह पूरे दिन अपने खेत में जी-तोड़ मेहनत करता था। सन्ध्या समय वह अपने प्रभु श्रीकृष्ण की आराधना में व्यतीत करता था।

दक्षिण कर्नाटक में उडुपि नाम का एक प्रमुख तीर्थस्थान है। उसमें उसकी घनिष्ठ आस्था थी। उसके दर्शन करने की उसकी प्रबल तथा एकमात्र अभिलाषा थी। परन्तु द्रारिद्रता के कारण इच्छा पूरी नहीं कर पाता था।

 (ii) हरिहर ने कड़ी मेहनत करके कुछ धन एकत्रित किया और वह तीर्थयात्रियों के एक समूह के साथ उडुपि नामक तीर्थस्थान की ओर चल दिया। अभी वह थोड़ी ही दूर चला, तभी मार्ग में उसे एक वृद्ध व्यक्ति मिला जिसकी दशा अत्यन्त दयनीय थी। वह कई दिनों से भूख-प्यास से पीड़ित और दर्द से कराह रहा था। उसकी दयनीय अवस्था से हरिहर दयाद्रवित हो गया। उस बूढ़े से बातचीत करके हरिहर को ज्ञात हुआ कि उसका एक पुत्र बीमार है, दूसरा तीन दिन से भूखा है। हरिहर समझ रहा था कि शायद इस भीड़ में मिलने वाला वह बूढ़ा भी तीर्थयात्री है, परन्तु जब उसे उसका सच पता चला तो उसका हृदय करुणा से भर गया।

 (iii) हरिहर दीन-दु:खियों की सेवा को परमात्मा की सच्ची भक्ति समझता था। उसने उडुपि जाने का निश्चय त्याग दिया। उसके साथियों के बार-बार समझाने के उपरान्त भी उसने दीन-दु:खियों की सेवा को ही अपना प्रथम कर्तव्य समझा। हरिहर की पत्नी ने तीर्थयात्रा पर चलते समय बहुत-सा भोजन रखा था। सर्वप्रथम हरिहर ने बूढ़े के घर जाकर उस भोजन से उसके घर के भूखे व्यक्तियों को भरपेट भोजन करवाकर उन्हें तृप्त किया। तत्पश्चात् वह बीमार बच्चे के लिए दवा लेकर आया। यही नहीं उसने बूढ़े के खेत में अनाज बोने के लिए बीज लाकर दिये। वह कुछ दिन वहाँ ठहरा। उसने उसके बीमार बच्चे की सेवा-सुश्रूषा की जिससे वह स्वस्थ हो गया। उसने अपने पैसे परमार्थ के कार्यों में खर्च किये।

 (iv) उस बूढ़े व्यक्ति के परिवार की सेवा व सहायता करते हुए उसके कई दिन व्यतीत हो गये साथ ही उडुपि नामक तीर्थस्थान के दर्शन हेतु जो उसने धन एकत्रित किया था, वह भी वहाँ समाप्त हो गया। उसने अपने इस कर्म को हरि इच्छा समझा और प्रसन्न मन से अपने घर के लिए लौट पड़ा।

उसी रात हरिहर ने स्वप्न में भगवान श्रीकृष्ण के दर्शन किये जो कह रहे थे "हरिहर, तुम मेरे सच्चे भक्त हो, वह बूढ़ा कोई और नहीं, मैं ही था, मैं तो तुम्हारी परीक्षा ले रहा था। तुम परीक्षा में सफल हुए और तुम्हें तीर्थ का पुण्य भी प्राप्त हुआ।"

 (v) इस गद्यांश से हमें यह शिक्षा मिलती है कि जो सुख व सन्तुष्टि दीन-दु:खी की सेवा और पीड़ा दूर करने में है, वह तीर्थ आदि के दर्शन करने में नहीं है। तीर्थ में स्थित परमात्मा हर मनुष्य के हृदय में स्थित है। मनुष्य की सेवा करने से उसके अन्दर विद्यमान परमात्मा प्रसन्न होता है। इसलिए पीड़ितों की सेवा परमात्मा की सच्ची सेवा है।

Q. 6. **Read the passage given below and answer in *Hindi* the questions that follow, using your own words as far as possible:**

निम्नलिखित गद्यांश को ध्यान से पढ़िए तथा उसके नीचे लिखे प्रश्नों के उत्तर हिन्दी में लिखिए। उत्तर यथासम्भव आपके अपने शब्दों में होने चाहिए।

कौशल देश के वृद्ध राजा के चार पुत्र थे। उन्हें यह चिन्ता सताने लगी कि राज्य का उत्तराधिकारी किसे बनाया जाए? सोच-विचार के बाद अपने चारों पुत्रों को बुलाकर राजा ने कहा–"तुम चारों में से जो सबसे बड़े धर्मात्मा को मेरे पास लेकर आएगा, वही राज्य का स्वामी बनेगा।" तत्पश्चात् चारों राजकुमार अपने-अपने घोड़ों पर सवार होकर चल पड़े।

कुछ दिनों बाद बड़ा पुत्र अपने साथ एक महाजन को लेकर आया और राजा से बोला–"ये महाजन लाखों रुपयों का दान कर चुके हैं, अनेक मन्दिर व धर्मशालाएँ बनवा चुके हैं तथा साधु-सन्तों और ब्राह्मणों को भोजन कराने के उपरान्त ही ये भोजन करते हैं। इनसे बड़ा धर्मात्मा कौन होगा?"

"हाँ, वास्तव में ये धर्मात्मा हैं।" राजा ने कहा था तथा सत्कारपूर्वक विदा किया।

इसके बाद दूसरा पुत्र एक कृशकाय ब्राह्मण को लेकर आया और राजा से बोला–"ये ब्राह्मण देवता चारों धामों की यात्रा कर आए हैं, कोई तामसी वृत्ति इन्हें छू नहीं गई है। इनसे बढ़कर कोई धर्मात्मा नहीं है।"

राजा ब्राह्मण के समक्ष नतमस्तक हुए और दान-दक्षिणा देकर बोले–"इसमें कोई सन्देह नहीं कि ये एक श्रेष्ठ धर्मात्मा हैं।"

तभी तीसरा पुत्र साधु को लेकर पहुँचा और बोला–"ये साधु महाराज सप्ताह में केवल एक बार दूध पीकर रहते हैं। भयंकर सर्दी में जल में खड़े रहते हैं और गर्मी में पंचाग्नि तापते हैं। ये सबसे बड़े धर्मात्मा हैं।"

राजा ने साधु को प्रणाम किया और कहा–"निश्चय ही ये एक उत्तम साधु हैं।" साधु महाराज राजा को आशीर्वाद देकर विदा हुए।

अन्त में सबसे छोटा पुत्र एक निर्धन किसान के साथ आया। किसान दूर से ही भय के मारे हाथ जोड़ता चला आ रहा था। तीनों भाई छोटे भाई की मूर्खता पर ठहाका लगाकर हँस पड़े। छोटा पुत्र बोला–"एक कुत्ते के शरीर पर लगे घाव को यह आदमी धो रहा था। पता नहीं कि यह धर्मात्मा है या नहीं। अब आप ही इससे पूछ लीजिए।"

राजा ने पूछा–"तुम क्या धर्म-कर्म करते हो?" किसान डरते-डरते बोला "मैं अनपढ़ हूँ, धर्म किसे कहते हैं, यह मैं नहीं जानता। कोई बीमार होता है तो सेवा कर देता हूँ। कोई माँगता है तो मुट्ठी भर अन्न अवश्य दे देता हूँ।"

राजा ने कहा–"यह किसान ही सबसे बड़ा धर्मात्मा है।" राजा की बात सुनकर तीनों बड़े लड़के एक दूसरे का मुँह ताकने लगे। राजा ने पुनः कहा–"तीर्थयात्रा करना, भगवत आराधना में लीन रहना, दान-पुण्य करना और जप-तप करना

भी धर्म है, किन्तु बिना किसी स्वार्थ के किसी दीन-दुःखी और कष्ट में पड़े हुए प्राणी की सेवा करना सबसे बड़ा धर्म है। जो परोपकार करता है, वही सबसे बड़ा धर्मात्मा है।"

(i) राजा को क्या चिन्ता थी? उसने अपने पुत्रों को बुलाकर क्या कहा?

(ii) बड़े पुत्र की दृष्टि में सबसे बड़ा धर्मात्मा कौन था और उसका क्या कारण था?

(iii) साधु किसके साथ आया था? उसका परिचय किस प्रकार दिया गया?

(iv) किसान को राजा के सामने कौन लाया था और क्यों? राजा ने किसान को ही सबसे बड़ा धर्मात्मा क्यों कहा?

(v) प्रस्तुत गद्यांश से क्या शिक्षा मिलती है? [2015]

Ans.

(i) कौशल देश के राजा वृद्ध हो चुके थे इसलिए उन्हें यह चिन्ता थी कि वे अपने राज्य का उत्तराधिकारी अपने चारों पुत्र में से किसको बनाएँ। कुछ सोच-विचार करने के बाद उन्होंने अपने चारों पुत्रों को बुलाया और कहा कि तुम चारों में से जो भी सबसे बड़े धर्मात्मा को मेरे पास लेकर आएगा, राज्य का उत्तराधिकारी उसी को बनाया जायेगा।

(ii) बड़े पुत्र की दृष्टि में एक महाजन सबसे बड़े धर्मात्मा थे। उसका कारण था कि वह लाखों रुपए का दान कर चुके थे, बहुत से मन्दिर और धर्मशालाएँ बनवा चुके थे और भोजन भी वह तभी करते थे जब पहले बहुत से साधु-सन्तों और ब्राह्मणों को भोजन करवा देते थे।

(iii) साधु तीसरे पुत्र के साथ आया था। उसने उसका परिचय इस प्रकार दिया कि ये साधु महाराज सप्ताह में केवल एक बार दूध पीकर ही रहते हैं और भयानक सर्दी में भी ये जल में खड़े रहते हैं तथा गर्मियों में पंचाग्नि जलाकर तप करते हैं अतः यही सबसे बड़े धर्मात्मा हैं।

(iv) किसान को राजा के सामने उसका सबसे छोटा पुत्र लेकर आया था क्योंकि उसने उसे एक कुत्ते के घावों को साफ करते हुए देखा था। राजा ने उस किसान को ही सबसे बड़ा धर्मात्मा घोषित किया क्योंकि उनके अनुसार बिना किसी स्वार्थ के दीन-दुःखियों की और कष्ट में पड़े हुए प्राणियों की सेवा करना सबसे बड़ा धर्म है। अतः यह किसान ही सबसे बड़ा धर्मात्मा है।

(v) प्रस्तुत गद्यांश से हमें यह शिक्षा मिलती है कि जब हम पुण्य लाभ के लिए जप-तप, दान-धर्म आदि करते हैं तो उसमें हमारा स्वार्थ होता है, किन्तु बिना किसी स्वार्थ के निर्बल, दीन दुःखियों की सहायता करना ही सबसे बड़ा धर्म है अतः हमें निःस्वार्थ भाव से उनकी सहायता करनी चाहिए।

Short Answer Type Questions

Q. 1. Answer the following according to the instructions given:

निम्नलिखित प्रश्नों के उत्तर निर्देशानुसार लिखिए:

(i) निम्नलिखित शब्दों में से किन्ही दो शब्दों के विलोम लिखिए—

सेवक, बुद्धिमान, न्याय, स्वदेश।

(ii) निम्नलिखित शब्दों में से किसी एक शब्द के दो पर्यायवाची शब्द लिखिए—

कपड़ा, भाग्य, सुगन्ध।

(iii) निम्नलिखित शब्दों में किन्हीं दो शब्दों से विशेषण बनाइए—

भारत, आदर, पीड़ा, डर।

(iv) निम्नलिखित शब्दों में से किन्हीं दो शब्दों के शुद्ध रूप लिखिए—

राछस, क्योकी, आदरनिय, कार्यकर्म।

(v) निम्नलिखित मुहावरों में से किसी एक की सहायता से वाक्य बनाइए—

दाँत पीसना, घुटने टेकना, जमीन ताकना।

(vi) कोष्ठक में दिए गए वाक्यों में निर्देशानुसार परिवर्तन कीजिए—

(a) रमेश ईश्वर में बहुत विश्वास रखता है।

(रेखांकित शब्दों के लिए एक शब्द का प्रयोग करके वाक्य पुनः लिखिए।)

(b) जज ने अपराधी को सजा सुनाई।

('द्वारा' शब्द का प्रयोग करके वाक्य पुनः लिखिए।)

(c) छात्र यात्रा पर जा रहे हैं।

(भविष्यकाल में बदलिए) **[2020]**

Ans. (i) **सेवक** – स्वामी

बुद्धिमान – बुद्धिहीन

न्याय – अन्याय

स्वदेश – विदेश

(ii) **कपड़ा** – वस्त्र, चीर, वसन, परिधान, अंबर, पट।

भाग्य – किस्मत, विधि, नियति, होनी।

सुगन्ध – महक, खुशबू, सुरभि, सौरभ, सुवास।

(iii) **भारत** – भारतीय   **आदर** – आदरणीय

पीड़ा – पीड़ित   **डर** – डरावना

(iv) **राछस** – राक्षस   **क्योकी** – क्योंकि

आदरनिय – आदरणीय   **कार्यकर्म** – कार्यक्रम

(v) **दाँत पीसना (बहुत क्रोध आना)**—परिवार के सामने अपनी बेइज्जती होने के कारण राजेश दाँत पीसकर रह गया।

घुटने टेकना (हार मानना)—भारतीय सेना के आगे शत्रुओं को घुटने टेकने पड़े।

ज़मीन ताकना (लज्जित होना)—चोरी पकड़ी जाने पर अमीना ज़मीन ताक रही थी।

(vi) (a) रमेश आस्तिक है।

(b) जज द्वारा अपराधी को सजा सुनाई गई।

(c) छात्र यात्रा पर जाएँगे।

Q. 2. Answer the following according to the instructions given:

निम्नलिखित प्रश्नों के उत्तर निर्देशानुसार लिखिए:

(i) निम्नलिखित शब्दों में से किन्हीं दो शब्दों के विलोम लिखिए—

अपना, देव, नवीन, सम्मानित।

(ii) निम्नलिखित शब्दों में से किसी एक शब्द के दो पर्यायवाची शब्द लिखिए—

इच्छा, आदेश, शिक्षक।

(iii) निम्नलिखित शब्दों में किन्हीं दो शब्दों से भाववाचक संज्ञा बनाइए—

सफेद, युवा, हिंसक, जागना

(iv) निम्नलिखित शब्दों में से किन्हीं दो शब्दों के शुद्ध रूप लिखिए—

कवित्री, अशीरवाद, कृतग्य, विदूषी।

(v) निम्नलिखित मुहावरों में से किसी एक की सहायता से वाक्य बनाइए—

चंपत होना, डींग हाँकना।

(vi) कोष्ठक में दिए गए वाक्यों में निर्देशानुसार परिवर्तन कीजिए—

(a) प्राचीन काल में लोग पत्तों की बुनी कुटिया में रहते थे।

(रेखांकित का एक शब्द लिखते हुए वाक्य पुनः लिखिए।)

(b) बीमार होने के कारण सुमन समारोह में नहीं आ सकी।

('इसलिए' का प्रयोग कर वाक्य पुनः लिखिए)

(c) बच्चे आम तोड़ने के लिए वृक्षों पर चढ़ गए थे।

(वचन बदलिए) **[2019]**

📋 Marking Scheme

(i) अपना – पराया

देव – दानव, दैत्य, राक्षस, असुर, निशाचर, रजनीचर

नवीन – प्राचीन, पुराना, पुरातन

सम्मानित – अपमानित, तिरस्कृत

(ii) इच्छा – अभिलाषा, लालसा, आशा, चाह, कामना, मनोरथ, स्पृहा, आकांक्षा, वांछा, उत्कंठा

आदेश – आज्ञा, हुक्म, निर्देश, अनुमति, निदेश, फरमान, मनोकामना, मनोवांछा, तमन्ना, अरमान, ईप्सा

शिक्षक – गुरू, आचार्य, अध्यापक, ज्ञानदाता, पथप्रदर्शक, मास्टर, उस्ताद, मार्गदर्शक

(iii) सफेद – सफेदी

युवा – यौवन, युवावस्था

हिंसक – हिंसा

जगना – जागरण, जागृति

(iv) कवित्री – कवयित्री

आशीरवाद – आशीर्वाद

कृतग्य – कृतज्ञ

विदेशी – विदुषी

(v) चंपत होना – भाग जाना

चोर दुकान से लाखों के गहने चुराकर चम्पत हो गए।

डींग हाँकना – बड़ी-बड़ी बातें करना।

कर्मशील व्यक्ति कभी डींग नहीं हाँकते, वह तो कर्म करते हैं।

(vi) (a) प्राचीन काल में पर्णकुटी में रहते थे। झोपड़ी/पर्णशाला

(b) सुमन बीमार थी इसीलिए समारोह में नहीं आ सकी।

(c) बच्चा आमों को (आम को) तोड़ने के लिए वृक्ष पर चढ़ जाता है। चढ़ा/चढ़ता या/चढ़ गया था।

"आम या आमों" दोनों ठीक हैं।

Ans. (i) **अपना** – पराया **देव** – दानव

नवीन – प्राचीन **सम्मानित** – अपमानित

(ii) **इच्छा** – आकांक्षा, चाह, आशा

आदेश – निर्देश, आज्ञा, हुक्म

शिक्षक – अध्यापक, गुरु, आचार्य

(iii) **सफेद** – सफेदी **युवा** – यौवन

हिंसक – हिंसा **जागना** – जागरण

(iv) **कवित्री** – कवयित्री **आशीरवाद** – आशीर्वाद

कृतग्य – कृतज्ञ **विदुषी** – विदुषी

(v) **चंपत होना (भाग जाना)**—चोर चोरी करके चंपत हो गया।

डींग हाँकना (बड़ी-बड़ी बातें करना)—डींगें हाँकना सरल था पर काम करना मुश्किल।

(vi) (a) प्राचीन काल में लोग पर्णकुटी में रहते थे।

(b) सुमन बीमार थी इसलिए समारोह में नहीं आ सकी।

(c) बच्चा आमों को तोड़ने के लिए वृक्ष पर चढ़ गया था।

Q. 3. Answer the following according to the instructions given:

निम्नलिखित प्रश्नों के उत्तर निर्देशानुसार लिखिए:

(i) निम्नलिखित शब्दों में से दो शब्दों के विलोम लिखिए—

कीर्ति, निर्मल, विजय, निर्दोष।

(ii) निम्नलिखित शब्दों में से किसी एक शब्द के दो पर्यायवाची शब्द लिखिए—

धनवान, किनारा, दूध।

(iii) निम्नलिखित शब्दों से विशेषण बनाइए—

अपेक्षा, गुण

(iv) निम्नलिखित शब्दों में से किन्हीं दो शब्दों के शुद्ध रूप लिखिए—

प्रदर्षनी, लच्छमी, अपरीचीत।

(iv) निम्नलिखित मुहावरों में से किसी एक की सहायता से वाक्य बनाइए—

आसमान से बातें करना, उड़ती चिड़िया पहचानना।

(vi) कोष्ठक में दिए गए वाक्यों में निर्देशानुसार परिवर्तन कीजिए—

(a) मोहन और रमेश सच्चे मित्र थे।

('मित्रता' शब्द का प्रयोग कीजिए।)

(b) मुझसे कोई भी बात कहने में संकोच न करें।

(रेखांकित के लिए एक शब्द का प्रयोग करते हुए वाक्य को पुनः लिखिए।)

(c) शिक्षक ने अपने शिष्य को आदेश दिया।

(वचन बदलिए) [2018]

📋 Marking Scheme

(i) विलोम:–

कीर्ति – अपकीर्ति, निर्मल – मलिन

विजय – पराजय, निर्दोष – सदोष

(पूछे गए शब्दों के वैकल्पिक सही विलोम शब्द स्वीकार्य।)

(ii) पर्यायवाची:–

धनवान – धनी, अमीर, संपन्न, धनाढ्य, समृद्ध, धनिक, दौलतमंद, रईस

किनारा – कूल, कगार, तट, तीर

दूध – क्षीर, पय, दुग्ध, गोरस, स्तन्य

(iii) विशेषण:–

अपेक्षा–अपेक्षित, गुण–गुणी, गुणवान, गुणवती, गुणहीन

(iv) शब्द शुद्धि:–

प्रदर्शनी, लक्ष्मी, अपरिचित।

(v) मुहावरे:–

आजकल छोटे घर लुप्त होते जा रहे हैं, सारी इमारतें आसमान से बातें कर रही हैं।

राम शहर जाकर इतना होशियार बन गया है कि वह उड़ती चिड़ियाँ पहचानने में माहिर हो गया है।

(vi) निर्देशानुसार वाक्य में परिवर्तन:–

(a) मोहन और रमेश के बीच सच्ची मित्रता थी।

(b) मुझसे कोई भी बात निःसंकोच कहे।

(c) शिक्षकों ने अपने शिष्यों को आदेश दिए।

Ans. (i) **कीर्ति** – अपकीर्ति **विजय** – पराजय
 निर्मल – मलिन **निर्दोष** – दोषी

(ii) **धनवान** – धनी, धनाढ्य **किनारा** – तट, कगार
 दूध – पय, दुग्ध

(iii) **अपेक्षा** – अपेक्षित **गुण** – गुणी

(iv) **प्रदर्षनी** – प्रदर्शनी **लच्छमी** – लक्ष्मी
 अपरीचीत – अपरिचित

(v) **आसमान से बातें करना (बहुत ऊँचा होना)**
 —आजकल की इमारतें आसमान से बातें करती हैं।

 उड़ती चिड़िया पहचानना (दूर से ही मन की बात जान लेना)—रामू के दादा जी इतने अनुभवी हैं कि उड़ती चिड़िया पहचानने में देर नहीं लगाते।

(vi) (a) मोहन और रमेश में सच्ची **मित्रता** थी।

 (b) मुझसे कोई भी बात **निःसंकोच** कहें।

 (c) **शिक्षकों** ने अपने **शिष्यों** को आदेश दिये।

Q. 4. **Answer the following according to the instructions given:**

निम्नलिखित प्रश्नों के उत्तर निर्देशानुसार लिखिए:

(i) निम्नलिखित शब्दों में से किसी एक शब्द के दो पर्यायवाची शब्द लिखिए—
 आनंद, पुत्र, राक्षस।

(ii) निम्नलिखित शब्दों में से किन्हीं दो शब्दों के विलोम लिखिए—
 आलस्य, सदाचार, सामिष, कृत्रिम।

(iii) निम्नलिखित शब्दों में से किन्हीं दो शब्दों को शुद्ध कीजिए—
 प्रतीष्ठा, गृन्थ, परीस्थती।

(iv) निम्नलिखित में से किसी एक मुहावरे की सहायता से वाक्य बनाइये—
 अपना उल्लू सीधा करना, हाथ मलना।

(v) कोष्ठक में दिए गए निर्देशानुसार वाक्यों में परिवर्तन कीजिए—

 (a) विद्यार्थी को जानने की इच्छा रखने वाला होना चाहिए।
 (रेखांकित शब्दों के स्थान पर एक शब्द का प्रयोग कीजिए।)

 (b) इतनी आयु होने पर भी वह विवाहित नहीं है।
 ('नहीं' हटाइए परंतु वाक्य का अर्थ न बदले।)

 (c) रात में सर्दी बढ़ जायेगी।
 (अपूर्ण वर्तमानकाल में बदलिए)

 (d) अन्याय का सब विरोध करते हैं।
 (रेखांकित का विशेषण लिखते हुए वाक्य पुनः लिखिए) **[2017]**

Ans. (i) **आनंद** – प्रसन्नता, हर्ष, उल्लास, आह्लाद

 पुत्र – सुत, आत्मज

 राक्षस – निशाचर, दानव

(ii) **आलस्य** – स्फूर्ति **सदाचार** – दुराचार
 सामिष – निरामिष **कृत्रिम** – प्राकृत

(iii) **प्रतिष्ठा** - प्रतिष्ठा **गृन्थ** – ग्रन्थ
 परिस्थती - परिस्थिति।

(iv) **अपना उल्लू सीधा करना (अपना मतलब निकालना)**
 —राजनेता चुनाव के समय भोली-भाली जनता को झूठे वादों में फँसा, वोट लेकर **अपना उल्लू सीधा कर** लेते हैं।

 हाथ मलना (पछताना)—कुछ लोग समय रहते अपना कार्य पूरा नहीं करते, लेकिन जब समय निकल जाता है तो **हाथ मलते** रह जाते हैं।

(v) (a) विद्यार्थी को **जिज्ञासु** होना चाहिए।

 (b) इतनी आयु होने पर भी वह **अविवाहित** है।

 (c) रात में सर्दी **बढ़ रही** है।

 (d) अन्याय के सब **विरोधी** होते हैं।

Q. 5. **Answer the following according to the instructions given:**

निम्नलिखित प्रश्नों के उत्तर निर्देशानुसार लिखिए:

(i) निम्न शब्दों के विशेषण बनाइए—
 लोभ, इतिहास।

(ii) निम्न शब्दों में से किसी एक शब्द के दो पर्यायवाची शब्द लिखिए—
 बादल, स्वतन्त्र।

(iii) निम्नलिखित शब्दों में से किन्हीं दो शब्दों के विपरीतार्थक शब्द लिखिए—
 उपकार, कोमल, नूतन, स्वामी।

(iv) निम्नलिखित मुहावरों में से किसी एक की सहायता से वाक्य बनाइए—
 अपने पैर पर आप कुल्हाड़ी मारना, बाल-बाल बचना।

(v) भाववाचक संज्ञा बनाइए—
 अधिक, भक्त।

(vi) कोष्ठक में दिए गए निर्देशानुसार वाक्यों में परिवर्तन कीजिए—

 (a) महाराणा प्रताप के साहस की तुलना नहीं की जा सकती है।
 (रेखांकित शब्दों के स्थान पर एक शब्द का प्रयोग कीजिये)

 (b) मेरे घर में जो नौकर काम करता है वह भाग गया है।
 (सरल वाक्य बनाइये)

 (c) राजा का सेवक बहुत बुद्धिमान था।
 (लिंग बदलकर वाक्य दोबारा बनाइये) **[2016]**

Ans. (i) **लोभ** – लोभी, **इतिहास** – ऐतिहासिक

(ii) **बादल** – मेघ, वारिद,
 स्वतन्त्र – स्वच्छन्द, स्वेच्छाचारी।

(iii) **उपकार** – अपकार **कोमल** – कठोर
 नूतन – पुरातन **स्वामी** – सेवक।

(iv) अपने पैर पर आप कुल्हाड़ी मारना (अपना नुकसान स्वयं करना)—रमेश ने अपराधी को जेल से भगाने में सहायता करके अपने पैरों पर स्वयं कुल्हाड़ी मारी है।

बाल बाल बचना (बहुत कम अंतर से बचना)— ट्रक और कार की टक्कर में पास में ही खड़ा बालक बाल–बाल बच गया।

(v) **अधिक**–अधिकता, भक्त–भक्ति।

(vi) (a) महाराणा प्रताप का साहस **अतुलनीय** है।

(b) मेरे घर में काम करने वाला नौकर भाग गया है।

(c) रानी की **सेविका** बहुत **बुद्धिमती** थी।

Q. 6. **Answer the following questions according to the instructions given :**

निम्नलिखित प्रश्नों के उत्तर निर्देशानुसार लिखिए:

(i) निम्नलिखित शब्दों के विशेषण बनाइए: पूजा, धर्म।

(ii) निम्नलिखित शब्दों में से किसी एक शब्द के दो-दो पर्यायवाची शब्द लिखिए: राजा, जलाशय।

(iii) निम्नलिखित शब्दों में से किन्हीं दो शब्दों के विपरीतार्थक शब्द लिखिए: निर्माण, क्रोध, देहाती, मूर्खता।

(iv) भाववाचक संज्ञा बनाइए: साधु, तपस्वी।

(v) निम्नलिखित मुहावरों में से किसी एक की सहायता से वाक्य बनाइए: कान का कच्चा, श्रीगणेश करना।

(vi) कोष्ठक में दिये गये वाक्यों में निर्देशानुसार परिवर्तन कीजिए:

(a) कश्मीर में अनेक दर्शनीय पर्यटक स्थल देखने योग्य हैं। (वाक्य को शुद्ध कीजिए)

(b) मैं कलम से लिखूँगा। (वाक्य को भूतकाल में बदलिए)

(c) आप <u>परिवार के साथ</u> हमारे घर आइएगा। (रेखांकित के स्थान पर एक शब्द का प्रयोग कीजिए) [2015]

Ans. **(i)** **पूजा** – पूज्य, पूजनीय

धर्म – धार्मिक।

(ii) **राजा** – नृप, नरेश।

जलाशय – तालाब, सरोवर।

(iii) **निर्माण** – विनाश

देहाती – शहरी

क्रोध – शान्ति

मूर्खता – बुद्धिमानी

(iv) **साधु** – साधुता, साधुत्व

तपस्वी – तपस्या, तप।

(v) **कान का कच्चा (सुनी-सुनाई बात पर विश्वास करना)**—स्वयं परिस्थिति को देख-समझकर निर्णय लिया करो। कान का कच्चा होना अच्छी बात नहीं है।

श्रीगणेश करना (शुरुआत करना)—दो महीने बाद मेरी परीक्षाएँ हैं। अभी तक मैंने पढ़ाई का श्रीगणेश नहीं किया है।

(vi) (a) कश्मीर में अनेक दर्शनीय पर्यटन स्थल हैं।

या

कश्मीर में अनेक पर्यटन स्थल देखने योग्य हैं।

(b) मैंने कलम से लिखा था।

(c) आप सपरिवार हमारे घर आइएगा।

Long Answer Type Questions

Chapter 1. बात अठन्नी की (Baat Athanni Ki)

—सुदर्शन (Sudarshan)

Q. 1. **Read the extract given below and answer in *Hindi* the questions that follow:**

निम्नलिखित गद्यांश को पढ़िए और उसके नीचे लिखे प्रश्नों के उत्तर हिंदी में लिखिए:

रमजान ने ठंडी साँस भरी। उसने रसीला को ठहरने का संकेत किया और आप कोठरी में चला गया। थोड़ी देर बाद उसने कुछ रूपये रसीला की हथेली पर रख दिए। रसीला के मुँह से एक शब्द भी न निकला। सोचने लगा ''बाबू साहब की मैंने इतनी सेवा की पर दुख में उन्होंने साथ न दिया। रमजान को देखो गरीब है, परंतु आदमी नहीं देवता है। ईश्वर उसका भला करें।''

(i) रमजान कौन है? उसका परिचय दीजिए। [2]

(ii) रसीला और रमजान किस-किस के यहाँ काम करते थे? उन दोनों में क्या समानता थी? [2]

(iii) रसीला ने रमजान को देवता क्यों कहा है? समझाकर लिखिए। [3]

(iv) कहानी के शीर्षक की सार्थकता पर प्रकाश डालिए। [2020] [3]

Ans. **(i)** रमजान शेख सलीमुद्दीन का चौकीदार व रसीला का परम मित्र था। जब रसीला को पैसों की जरूरत थी, तब रमजान ने ही पैसे देकर रसीला की मदद की। रसीला ईमानदार, कर्त्तव्यनिष्ठ व दयालु व्यक्ति था।

(ii) रसीला इंजीनियर बाबू जगतसिंह के यहाँ काम करता था।

रमजान ज़िला मजिस्ट्रेट शेख सलीमुद्दीन के यहाँ काम करता था। दोनों एक-दूसरे के गहरे मित्र थे दोनों गरीब थे व एक दूसरे का दुख दर्द समझते थे। दोनों अपने-अपने मालिक के प्रति ईमानदार थे।

(iii) रसीला का परिवार गाँव में रहता था। घर से खत आता है कि उसके बच्चे बीमार हैं। वह मालिक जगतसिंह से पैसे देने की प्रार्थना करता है पर कठोर जगतसिंह साफ मना कर देता है। तब रमजान रुपए देकर रसीला की मदद करता है। समय पर मदद करने पर रसीला रमजान से कहता है कि वह आदमी नहीं देवता है। ईश्वर उसका भला करे।

(iv) कहानी 'बात अठन्नी की' का शीर्षक सार्थक व उपयुक्त है। सुदर्शन जी द्वारा लिखित 'बात अठन्नी की' एक व्यंग्यात्मक कहानी है। इंजीनियर बाबू जगतसिंह के नौकर रसीला ने मात्र आठ आने की हेरा-फेरी की थी। इस हेरा-फेरी के लिए जगतसिंह उसे मारते हैं और रिश्वत देकर पुलिस के हवाले कर देते हैं। माफी माँगने पर भी उसे माफी नहीं मिलती और मजिस्ट्रेट साहब उसे छ: महीने की सजा सुना देते हैं। फैसला सुनकर रमज़ान को बहुत गुस्सा आता है। रिश्वत लेकर अमीर लोग सम्मानित जीवन जीते हैं, और एक निर्धन व्यक्ति को केवल अठन्नी की हेरा-फेरी के लिए सजा दी जाती है। अत: यह स्पष्ट हो जाता है कि कहानी का शीर्षक सार्थक है।

Q. 2. **Read the extract given below and answer in *Hindi* the questions that follow:**

निम्नलिखित गद्यांश को पढ़िए और उसके नीचे लिखे प्रश्नों के उत्तर हिंदी में लिखिए:

"उसने कोई बहाना न बनाया। चाहता तो कह सकता कि यह साजिश है। मैं नौकरी नहीं करना चाहता इसीलिए हलवाई से मिलकर मुझे फँसा रहे हैं, पर एक और अपराध करने का साहस वह न जुटा पाया। उसकी आँखें खुल गई थीं।"

(i) किसे कौन फँसा रहा था? उसने क्या अपराध किया था? [2]

(ii) रसीला कौन है? उसका परिचय दीजिए। [2]

(iii) हमें अपने नौकरों से कैसा व्यवहार करना चाहिए? कहानी के आधार पर उदाहरण देकर समझाइए। [3]

(iv) इस कहानी में लेखक ने समाज की कौन-सी बुराई को प्रकट करने का प्रयास किया है? क्या वे अपने प्रयास में सफल हुए? समझाकर लिखिए। [3]

[2017]

Ans. **(i)** कहानीकार सुदर्शनजी के द्वारा रचित कहानी "बात अठन्नी की" में कहानी के प्रधान पात्र इंजीनियर बाबू जगतसिंह अपने नौकर रसीला को फँसा रहे थे।

उसका यह अपराध था कि इंजीनियर बाबू जगतसिंह ने नौकर रसीला से 5 रुपये की मिठाई मँगवाई थी। रसीला ने थोड़ी बेईमानी कर ली और वह 5 रुपये की जगह साढ़े चार रुपये की मिठाई लाया। अठन्नी उसने

अपने मित्र रमजान को दे दी क्योंकि उसके ऊपर रमजान की अठन्नी उधार थी।

(ii) रसीला, इंजीनियर बाबू जगतसिंह के यहाँ नौकरी करता है। उसे वहाँ काम करने का 10 रुपये वेतन मिलता है। गाँव में उसके बूढ़े पिता, पत्नी, एक लड़की और दो लड़के रहते हैं। वह परिवार के प्रति अपने उत्तरदायित्व को समझता है। वह अपनी नौकरी भी ईमानदारी से करता है। मित्र की सहायता पाने पर वह मित्र के प्रति भी कृतज्ञ है। अपनी चोरी पकड़े जाने पर वह गलती स्वीकार कर क्षमा भी माँग लेता है। रसीला एक परिश्रमी, ईमानदार, स्वामिभक्त, सीधा-सादा और ईश्वर से डरने वाला व्यक्ति है।

(iii) हमें अपने नौकरों के साथ सद्व्यवहार करना चाहिए। हमें उन्हें अपने समान ही समझना चाहिए। वे हमारी दिन-रात सेवा करते हैं। हमें भी उनके सुख-दु:ख में भागीदार होकर उनके प्रति सहानुभूति बरतनी चाहिए। मान लो यदि एक बार उसने विवशता में आकर गलती की तो उसके माफी माँगने पर उसे क्षमा कर देना

चाहिए। जिस प्रकार इंजीनियर बाबू ने रसीला की मदद नहीं की वह गलत था। उन्हें रसीला की परिस्थिति समझ उसे क्षमा कर देना चाहिये।

(iv) इस कहानी में लेखक श्री सुदर्शन जी ने धनवान मालिकों के क्रूर चरित्र का पर्दाफाश किया है। स्वयं रिश्वत लेकर अट्टालिकाओं में सुख-सुविधाओं के साथ रहते हैं लेकिन गरीब नौकरों के साथ अत्याचार करते हुए उनका दिल नहीं काँपता। इन्हें यह नहीं पता कि नौकरों की मेहनत पर ही इनकी सुखद जिंदगी चल रही है।

इस कहानी के माध्यम से लेखक ने अमीरज़ादों की रिश्वतखोरी का खुलासा किया है। जो कि खुद बड़े चोर हैं लेकिन छोटे मजबूर नौकर को जेल में डलवाकर शराफत का चोगा पहनकर घूमते हैं। हाँ, लेखक ने इस बात को स्पष्ट किया है कि एक रिश्वतखोर न्यायाधीश न्याय का चोगा पहनकर गरीब मजदूर को छ: महीने के लिए हवालात में डाल देता है। इस प्रकार लेखक ने गरीबों के प्रति होने वाले अत्याचार तथा समाज में व्याप्त रिश्वतखोरी व भ्रष्टाचार को उजागर किया है।

Chapter 2. काकी (Kaki)

—सियारामशरण गुप्त (Siyaramsharan Gupt)

Q. 1. Read the extract given below and answer in *Hindi* the questions that follow:

निम्नलिखित गद्यांश को पढ़िए और उसके नीचे लिखे प्रश्नों के उत्तर हिंदी में लिखिए:

उसके अन्तस्तल में वह शोक जाकर बस गया था। वह प्राय: अकेला बैठा-बैठा शून्य मन से आकाश की ओर ताका करता। एक दिन उसने ऊपर आसमान में पतंग उड़ती देखी। न जाने क्या सोचकर उसका हृदय एकदम खिल उठा। विश्वेश्वर के पास जाकर बोला, "काका! मुझे एक पतंग मँगा दो।"

(i) 'उसके' शब्द का प्रयोग किसके लिए किया गया है? उसके दुखी होने का क्या कारण था? [2]

(ii) क्या देखकर उसका हृदय खिल उठा था? उसने अपने पिता से क्या माँगा? [2]

(iii) उसने उस चीज का प्रबन्ध कैसे किया? क्या उसके इस कार्य को अपराध कहना उचित होगा? समझाइए। [3]

(iv) विश्वेश्वर ने बालक के साथ कैसा व्यवहार किया? संक्षेप में समझाते हुए उनके इस तरह के व्यवहार का कारण तथा सच्चाई जानने के बाद की स्थिति का भी वर्णन कीजिए। [3]

[2019]

Marking Scheme

(i) 'उसके' शब्द का प्रयोग अबोध बालक श्यामू के लिए किया गया है। वह विश्वेश्वर तथा उमा का पुत्र था।

उसके दु:ख का कारण यह था कि उसकी माँ की मृत्यु हो गई थी। वह अपनी माँ से बहुत प्यार करता था और उसे 'काकी'

कहकर पुकारता था। वह उसका वियोग सहन नहीं कर सका। वह इस कठोर सत्य को स्वीकार नहीं कर पाया था। उसका कोमल बाल मन अपनी माँ को भगवान के घर से वापस बुलाने के लिए हर समय सोच-विचार में डूबा रहता।

(ii) श्यामू एक नादान तथा मासूम बालक था, जिसकी माँ की असमय मृत्यु हो गई थी। वह शोक-सागर में डूब गया था। वह हर समय अपनी माँ को भगवान के घर से वापस बुलाने के लिए शून्य मन से आकाश की ओर ताका करता। एक दिन उसने आसमान में पतंग उड़ती देखी। उसे देखकर उसके मन में एक विचार आया और उसका हृदय खिल उठा। उसने अपने पिता से पतंग मँगवाने को कहा। वह पतंग के माध्यम से काकी को अपना संदेश भेजना चाहता था और उन्हें वापस नीचे बुलाना चाहता था।

(iii) बालक श्यामू पतंग पाने के लिए बहुत उत्कंठित था। उसने अपने पिता को पतंग मँगवाने को कहा परन्तु पिता ने उसकी माँग की ओर ध्यान नहीं दिया। वह अपनी इच्छा को किसी भी तरह रोक नहीं सका। एक जगह खूँटी पर पिता का कोट टंगा था। उसने उसमें से चवन्नी निकाल ली और भोला से पतंग मँगवा ली। भोला सुखिया दासी का पुत्र था और श्यामू का हमउम्र था। श्यामू ने भोला को अपनी सारी योजना बता दी थी अत: भोला ने पतंग के लिए पतली डोरी की जगह मोटी रस्सियाँ मंगवाने का सुझाव दिया। उसने कहा कि पतली डोरी से यदि काकी नीचे उतरती तो उसके टूट जाने की सम्भावना थी। अब रस्सियाँ मंगवाने के लिए श्यामू को पुन: पैसों की आवश्यकता पड़ी। उसने दूसरे दिन भी पहले की तरकीब से पिता के कोट से एक रुपया निकाल लिया। यद्यपि श्यामू ने पैसों का प्रबंध करने के लिए चोरी की थी परन्तु इसे चोरी कहना उचित नहीं होगा क्योंकि वह एक अबोध बालक था,

जो अपनी माँ का वियोग सहन नहीं कर पा रहा था। उसके पिता उसके दु:ख और मनोभावों को समझ नहीं पा रहे थे। इस प्रकार यह उसका बाल-अपराध था, जो कि क्षमा किया जा सकता है।

(iv) विश्वेश्वर श्यामू के पिता थे। जब उन्हें अपने कोट की जेब में रखे पैसे कम मिले तो वे श्यामू को खोजते हुए सीधे अँधेरी कोठरी में पहुँच गए जहाँ श्यामू और भोला पतंग में मोटी रस्सी बाँध रहे थे और उसे काकी के पास भेजने की तैयारी कर रहे थे। विश्वेश्वर ने पुत्र से सच्चाई जाननी चाही। तभी भोला डर गया और उसने विश्वेश्वर को सच बता दिया कि श्यामू ने पतंग मँगवाने के लिए पैसे निकाले थे। यह सुनते ही विश्वेश्वर को क्रोध आया उसने श्यामू के मुँह पर दो तमाचे जड़ दिए। उसके कान मले और उसे खूब डांटा। पास में रखी उसकी पतंग भी फाड़ दी। विश्वेश्वर एक आदर्शवादी व्यक्ति थे। वे पुत्र की चोरी करने की सहन नहीं कर सके। जब भोला ने उन्हें बताया कि श्यामू भैया पतंग तानकर काकी को राम के यहाँ से नीचे उतारेंगे। यह सच्चाई जानने के बाद तो वे हतबुद्धि रह गए। उन्हें दु:ख हुआ और अपने किए पर पछतावा भी हुआ। वह सोचने लगे कि वह अपने ही दु:ख को बड़ा समझ रहे थे उस बालक के विषय में सोचा ही नहीं जिस की माँ की मृत्यु हुई है।

Ans. (i) उसके शब्द का प्रयोग 'श्यामू' के लिए किया गया है। उसकी माँ की मृत्यु के कारण वह दुखी था। वह यह कठोर सत्य स्वीकार नहीं कर पा रहा था कि उसकी माँ अब इस दुनिया में नहीं हैं। उसका अबोध बाल मन अपनी माँ को भगवान के घर से वापस बुलाने के लिये हर समय सोच विचार में डूबा रहता और वह दुखी रहता।

(ii) आसमान में उड़ती हुई पतंग को देखकर श्यामू का हृदय खिल उठा था। उसने सोचा कि पतंग के सहारे वह अपनी काकी को रामजी के यहाँ से नीचे उतार सकता है। उसने अपने पिता से एक पतंग मँगाने का कहा।

(iii) पिता से कहने पर भी श्याम को पतंग नहीं मिलती है। पतंग का प्रबन्ध करने के लिए श्यामू अपने पिता विश्वेश्वर के कोट से चवन्नी निकाल लेता है।

उसके इस कार्य को अपराध कहना उचित नहीं होगा, क्योंकि श्यामू एक अबोध बालक है। वह अपनी माँ से बहुत प्यार करता है। रामजी के यहाँ से अपनी काकी को नीचे उतारने के उद्देश्य से वह चोरी करता है। श्यामू को चोरी, अपराध जैसी बातों का अर्थ ही नहीं पता था। अत: श्यामू की चोरी को अपराध कहना अनुचित है।

(iv) पत्नी की मृत्यु के बाद विश्वेश्वर अन्यमनस्क रहा करते थे। जब उन्हें पता चलता है कि उनके बेटे श्यामू ने उनके कोट की जेब से पैसे चुराए हैं और चोरी के पैसों से पतंग और डोर मँगवायी है, तो वे अपने क्रोध पर काबू नहीं कर पाते हैं। गुस्से में आकर वे श्यामू के मुँह पर दो तमाचे भी जड़ देते हैं और पतंग को फाड़ देते हैं। कोठरी में पड़ी रस्सी के बारे में जब भोला यह बताता है कि इस रस्सी को पतंग से जोड़कर वे काकी को रामजी के यहाँ से नीचे उतारेंगे, तब विश्वेश्वर हतबुद्धि होकर वहीं खड़े रह जाते हैं। फटी हुई पतंग को उठाकर देखते हैं। पतंग पर चिपके हुए कागज पर 'काकी' लिखा देखकर, वे अपनी भूल पर पश्चाताप करते हैं। सच्चाई जानने के बाद उनका गुस्सा शांत हो जाता है, और उनका मन ग्लानि से भर जाता है।

Chapter 3. महायज्ञ का पुरस्कार (Mahayagya Ka Puraskar)

—यशपाल (Yashpal)

Q. 1. **Read the extract given below and answer in *Hindi* the questions that follow:**

निम्नलिखित गद्यांश को पढ़िए और उसके नीचे लिखे प्रश्नों के उत्तर हिंदी में लिखिए:

"पर, 'सब दिन होत न एक समान' अकस्मात् दिन फिरे और सेठ को गरीबी का मुँह देखना पड़ा। संगी-साथियों ने भी मुँह फेर लिया और नौबत यहाँ तक आ गई कि सेठ व सेठानी भूखे मरने लगे।"

(i) **अकस्मात् बुरा समय किसका आ गया था तथा बुरा समय आने से पहले उसकी दशा कैसी थी?** [2]

(ii) **अपना बुरा समय दूर करने के लिए सेठ ने क्या उपाय सोचा? इस उपाय के लिए उन्हें किसके पास जाना पड़ा?** [2]

(iii) **सेठ ने मार्ग में कौन-सा महायज्ञ किया था? क्या वह वास्तव में महायज्ञ था? समझाकर लिखिए।** [3]

(iv) **कहानी का उद्देश्य लिखिए।** [3]
[2018]

📋 **Marking Scheme**

(i) एक धनी सेठ के जीवन में परिवर्तन आ गया तथा उन्हें बुरे समय का सामना करना पड़ गया। बुरा समय आने से पहले वे बहुत अमीर थे, साथ ही विनम्र, धर्म परायण और दयालु थे। उनका भण्डार सभी के लिए हमेशा खुला रहता था। दीन-दुखियों की सेवा करते थे और समय-समय पर यज्ञ भी करते थे। दान में न जाने कितना धन दीन-दुखियों में बाँट दिया था। कोई भी साधु-संत उनके द्वार से निराश नहीं लौटता था।

(ii) अपना बुरा समय दूर करने के लिए पत्नी के कहने पर यज्ञ बेचने का उपाय सोचा, जिससे गरीबी की स्थिति में उन्हें कुछ धन प्राप्त हो सके ताकि वे कुछ दिन भुखमरी से बच सकें। यज्ञ बेचने के उपाय के लिए सेठ को कुन्दनपुर नामक नगर के धन्ना सेठ के घर जाना पड़ा। लोग उन्हें 'धन्ना सेठ' कहते थे। यह अफवाह थी कि उनकी सेठानी को कोई दैवी शक्ति प्राप्त है, जिससे वह तीनों लोकों की बात जान लेती हैं।

(iii) यज्ञ बेचने के लिए सेठ जब कुन्दनपुर जा रहे थे। भूख लगने पर भोजन करने के लिए मार्ग में रुके तब उन्होंने देखा कि सामने एक कुत्ता भूख के कारण छटपटा रहा है। सेठ ने अपनी चार रोटियों में से पहले एक रोटी उसे दी, खाने के बाद कुत्ते में थोड़ी ताकत आई देखकर सेठ ने एक-एक करके चारों रोटियाँ उस कुत्ते को खिला दीं और स्वयं पानी पीकर अपनी भूख को शान्त किया। इस प्रकार सेठ ने निःस्वार्थ भाव का महायज्ञ किया। नहीं वह महायज्ञ नहीं था वह तो सेठ के विचारों के अनुसार केवल मानवोचित कर्तव्य था। हाँ, मानवोचित कार्य महायज्ञ से भी बड़ा होता है।

(iv) प्रस्तुत कहानी द्वारा लेखक पाठकों को यह बताना चाहता है कि प्राणी-मात्र की सेवा ही सच्ची सेवा है। साथ ही यह भी बताया गया है कि किया हुआ शुभ-कार्य कभी खाली नहीं जाता है। अच्छे कार्य का फल हमें सदैव कभी न कभी किसी न किसी रूप में अवश्य मिलता है। अतः मनुष्य को सदैव सत्कार्य करने चाहिए। मनुष्य को निःस्वार्थ भाव से सबकी सेवा करनी चाहिए। हर परिस्थिति में धर्मपूर्ण आचरण करना चाहिए। जैसा कि कहानी में सेठ ने किया। वह उस समय विपत्ति में थे, इसलिए यज्ञ बेचने गए थे। रास्ते में भूख लगने पर भी उन्होंने अपनी चारों रोटियाँ कुत्ते को खिला दी। अर्थात् विषम परिस्थिति में भी उन्होंने अपना सत्कार्य नहीं छोड़ा, जिसका फल उन्हें खजाने के रूप में प्राप्त हुआ।

Ans. (i) अकस्मात् बुरा समय एक धनी सेठ का आ गया था। बुरा समय आने से पहले वे बहुत उदार थे। इतने धर्मपरायण थे कि कोई भी साधु-संत या याचक उनके दरवाजे से खाली हाथ नहीं जाता था। सभी को भरपेट भोजन मिलता था। कितने ही दीन-दुःखियों को धन दान दिया करते थे।

(ii) अपना बुरा समय दूर करने के लिए सेठ ने अपने अच्छे समय में किए गए यज्ञ को बेचने का निश्चय किया। इसके लिए उन्हें दस-बारह कोस की दूरी पर कुंदनपुर नगर में एक धन्ना सेठ के पास उनकी सेठानी को यज्ञ बेचने के लिए जाना पड़ा।

(iii) सेठ ने मार्ग में भूख से व्याकुल एक छटपटाते कुत्ते को अपनी सारी रोटियाँ खिला दी थीं। सेठ के अनुसार, यह महायज्ञ नहीं था क्योंकि किसी भूखे को भोजन कराना कोई यज्ञ नहीं बल्कि निःस्वार्थ भाव से किया गया मानवोचित कार्य था। भूखे को अन्न देना सभी का कर्तव्य है। हाँ, मानवोचित कार्य महायज्ञ से भी बड़ा होता है।

(iv) प्रस्तुत कहानी 'महायज्ञ का पुरस्कार' यशपाल जी द्वारा लिखी गई कहानी है। इस कहानी में लेखक ने बताया है कि मानव सेवा ही ईश्वर सेवा होती है तथा जीवों के दुःख दूर करने से हम ईश्वर को प्रसन्न कर सकते हैं। जैसे सेठजी ने अपने भोजन को स्वयं न खाकर एक भूखे, निर्बल, मरियल कुत्ते को खिला दिया था। ऐसा केवल निःस्वार्थ भाव से उन्होंने किया था। लेखक ने बताया है भूखे को भोजन देना सभी का कर्तव्य है। इससे ईश्वर प्रसन्न होते हैं। यज्ञ, हवन आदि धार्मिक कार्यों से भी ऊपर प्राणी मात्र की सेवा करना है।

Chapter 4. नेता जी का चश्मा (Netaji Ka Chashma)

—स्वयं प्रकाश (Swayam Prakash)

Q. 1. Read the extract given below and answer in *Hindi* the questions that follow:

निम्नलिखित गद्यांश को पढ़िए और उसके नीचे लिखे प्रश्नों के उत्तर हिंदी में लिखिए:

"नेताजी सुंदर लग रहे थे। कुछ-कुछ मासूम और कमसिन। फौजी वर्दी में। मूर्ति को देखते ही 'दिल्ली चलो' और 'तुम मुझे खून दो……' वगैरह याद आने लगते थे। इस दृष्टि में यह सफल और सराहनीय प्रयास था। केवल एक चीज़ की कसर थी जो देखते ही खटकती थी।"

(i) मूर्ति किसकी थी और वह कहाँ लगाई गई थी? **[2]**

(ii) यह मूर्ति किसने बनाई और इसकी क्या विशेषताएँ थीं? **[2]**

(iii) मूर्ति में क्या कमी थी? उस कमी को कौन पूरा करता था और कैसे? **[3]**

(iv) नेताजी का परिचय देते हुए बताइए कि चौराहे पर उनकी मूर्ति लगाने का क्या उद्देश्य रहा होगा? क्या उस उद्देश्य में सफलता प्राप्त हुई? स्पष्ट कीजिए। **[3]**

[2017]

Ans. (i) मूर्ति नेताजी सुभाषचन्द्र बोस की थी और वह किसी उत्साही बोर्ड या प्रशासनिक अधिकारी ने शहर के मुख्य बाज़ार के मुख्य चौराहे पर लगवा दी थी। वे चाहते थे कि आने वाली पीढ़ी नेताजी के बारे में जान सके।

(ii) कस्बे के इकलौते हाईस्कूल ड्राइंग मास्टर मोतीलाल जी ने नेताजी सुभाषचन्द्र बोस की संगमरमर की नई मूर्ति बनाई थी। इस प्रकार मूर्ति आकर्षण का केंद्र थी। इसकी विशेषताएँ यह थीं कि टोपी की नोक से कोट के दूसरे बटन तक कोई दो फुट ऊँची मूर्ति थी जिसमें नेताजी सुन्दर लग रहे थे। कुछ-कुछ मासूम और कमसिन।

(iii) उस मूर्ति में एक कमी थी और वह थी कि नेताजी की आँखों पर चश्मा नहीं था अर्थात् चश्मा संगमरमर का नहीं था।

उस कमी को एक कैप्टन चश्मेवाला पूरा किया करता था। वह मूर्ति को अपने पास उपलब्ध चश्मे के फ्रेमों में से कोई चश्मा पहना देता था। कभी गोल, कभी चौकोर, कभी काला, कभी लाल, वह चश्मा बदल-बदल कर नेताजी को पहनाता था। इसी प्रकार से कैप्टन नेताजी के चश्मों को रोज बदलता रहता था।

(iv) नेताजी सुभाषचंद्र बोस एक महान नेता और क्रान्तिकारी थे। नगरपालिका द्वारा कस्बे के बीच चौराहे पर नेताजी की मूर्ति लगवाना उनके प्रति श्रद्धा भावना को दर्शाता है तथा आने वाली पीढ़ियों में देशभक्ति की भावना उत्पन्न करता है।

यह उद्देश्य सफल भी रहा है, कैप्टन चश्मेवाले की मृत्यु के बाद बच्चों का सरकण्डे का चश्मा बनाकर मूर्ति को पहनाना इस बात की ओर संकेत करता है कि आने वाली पीढ़ी भी नेताजी के प्रति सम्मान की भावना रखती है।

Chapter 6. बड़े घर की बेटी (Bade Ghar ki Beti)

—प्रेमचंद (Premchand)

Q. 1. **Read the extract given below and answer in *Hindi* the questions that follow:**

निम्नलिखित गद्यांश को पढ़िए और उसके नीचे लिखे प्रश्नों के उत्तर हिंदी में लिखिए:

आनंदी की त्यौरी चढ़ गई। झुँझलाहट के मारे बदन में ज्वाला-सी दहक उठी। बोली, "जिसने तुमसे यह आग लगाई है, उसे पाऊँ तो मुँह झुलस दूँ।

(i) आनंदी की त्यौरी क्यों चढ़ी हुई थी? वह किसका इंतजार कर रही थी? **[2]**

(ii) श्रीकंठ सिंह ने आनंदी से क्या जानना चाहा? **[2]**

(iii) इससे पहले लालबिहारी और बेनीमाधव सिंह श्री कंठ सिंह से क्या कह चुके थे? **[3]**

(iv) आनंदी से घटना का हाल जानकर श्रीकंठ सिंह को कैसा लगा? उन्होंने अपने पिता से क्या कहा? **[3]**

[2018]

दिन अनर्थ हो जाएगा। वे बड़े घर की बेटी हैं तो वह लोग भी कोई कुर्मी-कहार नहीं हैं। बेनी माधव सिंह ने भी कहा कि बहू-बेटियों को मर्दों के मुँह नहीं लगना चाहिए।

(iv) आनन्दी से पूरी घटना की जानकारी लेने के बाद श्रीकंठ सिंह को क्रोध आया। वे बोले कि उस छोकरे का साहस यहाँ तक हो गया। आनन्दी के आँसू ने क्रोधाग्नि में घी डालने का काम किया। रातभर वे नहीं सोए। प्रात:काल उन्होंने पिताजी से कहा कि अब इस घर में उनका निर्वाह नहीं होगा। मैं लाल बिहारी का मुँह नहीं देखना चाहता। मेरी पत्नी के प्रति ऐसा अत्याचार असहनीय है। मैं पत्नी के मान-सम्मान के लिए ईश्वर के दरबार में उत्तरदाता हूँ। अत: अब इस घर में लाल बिहारी रहेगा या मैं।

Ans. **(i)** आनंदी की त्यौरियाँ इसलिए चढ़ गई थीं क्योंकि उसके देवर लाल बिहारी ने खाने में घी न डालने पर उसके साथ बुरा बर्ताव किया था भोजन की थाली फेंक दी थी तथा खड़ाऊ फेंककर मारी थी। इसलिए आनंदी झुँझलाहट भरे मन से अपने पति श्रीकंठ सिंह का इंतजार कर रही थी।

(ii) श्रीकंठ सिंह ने आनंदी से लड़ाई का कारण जानना चाहा कि असली बात क्या है ? लड़ाई किस बात पर हुई थी ? जब आनंदी ने उसे जब पूरी बात बतायी तब उसे दुख हुआ और क्रोध भी आया।

(iii) इससे पहले लालबिहारी श्रीकंठ से कह चुके थे कि भैया आप जरा भाभी को समझा दीजिएगा कि मुँह सँभालकर बातचीत किया करे नहीं तो एक दिन अनर्थ हो जाएगा। बेनी माधव ने कहा कि बहू-बेटियों का यह स्वभाव अच्छा नहीं कि मर्दों के मुँह लगें। अपने मैके के सामने हमें कुछ समझती ही नहीं।

(iv) आनंदी से घटना का हाल जानकर श्रीकंठ सिंह की आँखें लाल हो गईं, वे रात-भर नहीं सोये और बोले यहाँ तक हो गया छोकरे का साहस। उन्होंने अपने पिता से कहा दादा अब इस घर में मेरा निर्वाह न होगा। उन्होंने कहा मैं लाल बिहारी का मुँह नहीं देखना चाहता। अत: इस घर में लाल बिहारी रहेगा या मैं।

📋 **Marking Scheme**

(i) जब श्रीकंठ के कमरे में आते ही आनंदी ने पूछा कि चित्त तो प्रसन्न है? श्रीकंठ ने उत्तर दिया कि बहुत प्रसन्न है। इसके पश्चात् उन्होंने कहा कि तुमने आजकल घर में यह क्या उपद्रव मचा रखा है? उसपर आनंदी की त्यौरी चढ़ गई।

आनंदी की त्यौरी इसलिए भी चढ़ी हुई थी कि एक दिन खाना खाते समय दाल में घी न होने के कारण लाल बिहारी क्रोध से भन्ना गया और भोजन की थाली फेंक दी और एक खड़ाऊँ उठाकर आनंदी की तरफ फेंकी। आनंदी ने हाथ से उसे न रोक लिया होता तो उसका सिर फूटता। हाथ में जरूर चोट लगी। तभी से वह श्रीकंठ सिंह का झुँझलाहट भरे मन से इंतजार कर रही थी जोकि नौकरी से शनिवार को लौटते थे।

(ii) श्रीकंठ सिंह ने आनंदी से कारण जानना चाहा कि आखिर ऐसा क्या हुआ कि आनन्दी क्रोधित हुई थी। आनंदी ने उसे जब पूरी जानकारी दी तब उसे दुख हुआ और उसे क्रोध भी आ गया।

(iii) इससे पहले लाल बिहारी ने कहा था कि भाभी उससे यों ही उलझ पड़ी। मैके के सामने उन लोगों को कुछ समझती ही नहीं। वो जरा मुँह संभाल कर बात किया करे, नही ‌तो एक

Chapter 9.   भेड़ें और भेड़िए (Bheden Aur Bhediye)

— हरिशंकर परसाई (Harishankar Parsai)

Q. 1. **Read the extract given below and answer in** *Hindi* **the questions that follow:**

निम्नलिखित गद्यांश को पढ़िए और उसके नीचे लिखे प्रश्नों के उत्तर हिन्दी में लिखिए:

उनका 'हृदय' परिवर्तन हो गया है। वे आज सात दिनों से घास खा रहे हैं। रात-दिन भगवान के भजन और परोपकार में लगे रहते हैं। उन्होंने अपना जीवन जीव-मात्र की सेवा में अर्पित कर दिया है। अब वे किसी का दिल नहीं दुखाते। किसी का रोम तक नहीं छूते।

(i) प्रस्तुत कथन किसने, किससे और क्यों कहा? स्पष्ट कीजिए। [2]

(ii) वक्ता ने किसके 'हृदय परिवर्तन' की बात कही? उसने उसके बारे में क्या-क्या कहा? [2]

(iii) वक्ता का चरित्र-चित्रण कीजिए। वह चुनावी सभा में किसे जिताना चाहता था और कैसे? [3]

(iv) चुनाव का क्या परिणाम हुआ? इस कहानी के माध्यम से लेखक क्या स्पष्ट करना चाहते हैं? चुनाव जीतने वाले ने सबसे पहला क्या नियम बनाया और इस नियम से किसका अधिक लाभ हुआ? [3]
[2020]

Ans. (i) प्रस्तुत कथन बूढ़े सियार ने संत के दर्शन करने को इकट्ठी हुईं, सैकड़ों भेड़ों से कहा। भेड़ों ने जब संत के रूप में भेड़िए को देखा तो सभी भेड़ें डर गईं। अपनी जान की रक्षा के लिए भेड़ें इधर-उधर भागने लगीं। भागती हुई भेड़ों को रोकने के लिए और उन्हें विश्वास दिलाने के लिए बूढ़ा सियार कहता है कि भेड़िया राजा संत हो गया है।

(ii) बूढ़े सियार ने 'भेड़िए' के 'हृदय परिवर्तन' की बात कही। बूढ़े सियार ने कहा कि भेड़िया राजा संत हो गए हैं। उन्होंने हिंसा बिल्कुल छोड़ दी है। भेड़िए का हृदय परिवर्तन हो गया है। वे आज सात दिनों से घास खा रहे हैं। रात-दिन भगवान के भजन और परोपकार में लगे रहते हैं। उन्होंने अपना जीवन जीव-मात्र की सेवा में अर्पित कर दिया है। अब वे किसी का दिल नहीं दुखाते। भेड़ों से उन्हें विशेष प्रेम है।

(iii) वक्ता बूढ़ा सियार चापलूसों का प्रतीक है। वह चालाक, मौकापरस्त, स्वार्थी व धूर्त है। ऐसे चापलूस लोग भ्रष्ट नेताओं की चापलूसी करते हैं, अपना स्वार्थ पूरा करते हैं और भोली-भाली जनता को बहला-फुसलाकर भ्रष्ट नेताओं को वोट दिलवाते हैं।

वह चुनावी सभा में भेड़िए को जिताना चाहता था। भेड़िए को जितवाने के लिए वह योजना बनाता है। भेड़िए का रूप बदल देता है। उसके मस्तक पर तिलक लगाकर, गले में कंठी पहनाकर और मुँह में

घास के तिनके खोंसकर उसे संत बना देता है। जंगल में भेड़िए के प्रचार-प्रसार के लिए तीन सियारों को रंग देता है—'पीला सियार' विद्वान, विचारक, कवि व लेखक का प्रतीक था। 'नीला-सियार' नेता और पत्रकार और 'हरा-सियार' धर्मगुरु का प्रतीक था। रंगे सियार भेड़ों को संबोधित करते हुए अपने भाषण में भेड़िए का खूब प्रचार करते हैं। भेड़ों को विश्वास दिलाते हैं कि भेड़िया ही उनका सच्चा और अच्छा नेता है।

(iv) पंचायत के चुनाव में भेड़ों के हितों की रक्षा के लिए भेड़िए प्रतिनिधि बनकर गए। भेड़िए चुनाव जीत गए। इस कहानी के माध्यम से लेखक ने धोखेबाज, झूठे, ढोंगी व चालाक राजनेताओं की पोल खोली है। राजनेता अपना स्वार्थ सिद्ध करते हैं तथा भोली-भाली जनता का शोषण करते हैं।

चुनाव जीतने वाले भेड़ियों ने सब से पहले यह नियम बनाया कि हर भेड़िये को सवेरे नाश्ते के लिए भेड़ का एक मुलायम बच्चा दिया जाए, दोपहर के भोजन में एक पूरी भेड़ तथा शाम को स्वास्थ्य के ख्याल से कम खाना चाहिए, इसलिए आधी भेड़ दी जाए। इस नियम से सबसे अधिक लाभ भेड़ियों को हुआ।

Q. 2. **Read the extract given below and answer in** *Hindi* **the questions that follow:**

निम्नलिखित गद्यांश को पढ़िए और उसके नीचे लिखे प्रश्नों के उत्तर हिन्दी में लिखिए:

"बड़े भोले हैं आप सरकार! अरे मालिक, रूप-रंग बदल देने से तो सुना है आदमी तक बदल जाते हैं। फिर ये तो सियार हैं।"

(i) उपर्युक्त कथन कौन, किससे क्यों कह रहा है? [2]

(ii) बूढ़े सियार ने भेड़िए का रूप किस प्रकार बदला? [2]

(iii) यह कैसी कहानी है, बूढ़े सियार ने किन बातों का ख्याल रखने के लिए कहा? क्यों कहा? [3]

(iv) सियारों को किन-किन रंगों में रंगा गया? वे किसके प्रतीक थे? इस कहानी से आपको क्या शिक्षा मिलती है? [3]
[2017]

Ans. (i) "बड़े भोले हैं आप सरकार··············" यह कथन बूढ़े सियार ने भेड़िये का हाथ चूमकर इसलिए कहा था क्योंकि वन में प्रजातन्त्र के लिए चुनाव होने वाले थे। यहाँ भेड़ों की संख्या अधिक थी तथा भेड़िये कम थे। उन्हें डर था कि यदि शासन भेड़ों का हो गया तो भेड़िये भूखे मर जायेंगे, लेकिन बूढ़ा सियार उसे समझाने की चेष्टा करते हुए कहता है कि रूप बदल देने से आदमी

बदल जाता है और वे इसी प्रकार की नीति अपनाने वाले थे इसीलिए वह भेड़िए को निश्चिन्त करने का प्रयास कर रहा है।

(ii) बूढ़े सियार ने भेड़िए का रूप परिवर्तित करने के लिए उसके माथे पर तिलक लगाया, गले में कंठी पहनाई तथा मुँह में घास के तिनके ठूँस दिये।

(iii) "भेड़ें और भेड़िये" हरिशंकर परसाई की बहुचर्चित व्यंग्यात्मक कहानी है जिसका संकेत सीधे राजनेताओं के प्रति है कि किस तरह राजनेता अपना उल्लू सीधा करने के लिए जनता को बेवकूफ बनाते हैं फिर उनका उत्पीड़न व उन पर अत्याचार करते हैं। इस तथ्य को प्रकाश में लाना ही लेखक का उद्देश्य रहा है। कहानीकार ने सामाजिक और राजनैतिक जीवन में व्याप्त भ्रष्टाचार व शोषण पर करारा व्यंग्य किया है। बूढ़े सियार ने जब भेड़िये का रूप परिवर्तन किया तो तीन बातें कहीं—(1) अपनी हिंसक आँखों को ऊपर न उठाना, (2) हमेशा जमीन की तरफ देखते रहना, कुछ बोलना मत नहीं तो पोल खुल जायेगी, (3) वहाँ बहुत

सी भेड़ें आयेंगी—सुन्दर तथा मुलायम तो कहीं किसी को तोड़कर मत खा जाना।

(iv) बूढ़ा सियार बहुत चतुर था। भेड़ों पर शासन करने के लिए उसने बड़ी कठोर कूटनीति अपनाई। वह तीन सियारों को लेकर आया। उसमें से एक को पीला, दूसरे को नीला और तीसरे को हरे रंग से रंग दिया। पीले रंग का सियार विद्वता का प्रतीक है तथा बड़ा विचारक और कवि के रूप में जाना जायेगा। नीला सियार नेता व पत्रकार के रूप में होगा और हरे रंग में रंगा सियार धर्मगुरु होगा। ये तीनों सियार भेड़िये के सीधेपन का प्रचार करेंगे।

इस कहानी के माध्यम से लेखक हरिशंकर परसाई यह शिक्षा देना चाहते हैं कि प्रजातन्त्र के नाम पर स्वार्थी, ढोंगी और चालाक राजनेता सीधे-सादे लोगों का शोषण करते हैं। इसके लिए वह कवि, विद्वान और धर्मगुरु जैसे लोगों का सहारा लेते हैं। कहानी समझाती है कि हम लोगों को ऐसे लोगों के झाँसे में नहीं आना चाहिए।

Chapter 10.   दो कलाकार (Do Kalakar)
—मन्नू भंडारी (Mannu Bhandari)

Q. 1. **Read the extract given below and answer in *Hindi* the questions that follow:**

निम्नलिखित गद्यांश को पढ़िए और उसके नीचे लिखे प्रश्नों के उत्तर हिंदी में लिखिए:

विदेशों में उसके चित्रों की धूम मच गयी। भिखारिन और दो अनाथ बच्चों के उस चित्र की प्रशंसा में तो अखबारों के कॉलम के कॉलम भर गए। शोहरत से ऊँचे कगार पर बैठ चित्रा जैसे अपना सब कुछ भूल गयी।

(i) 'उसके चित्रों' से क्या तात्पर्य है? समझाइए। **[2]**

(ii) चित्रा कौन थी? उसके चरित्र की मुख्य विशेषता को बताइए। **[2]**

(iii) अरुणा कौन थी जब उसे भिखारिन वाली घटना का पता चला तो उस पर क्या प्रभाव पड़ा और उसने क्या किया? **[3]**

(iv) चित्रकारिता और समाज सेवा में आप किसे उपयोगी मानते हैं और क्यों? कहानी के माध्यम से समझाइए। **[3]**
[2019]

📋 **Marking Scheme**

(i) 'उसके चित्रों' से तात्पर्य उस भिखारिन वाले चित्र से है, तथा अन्य चित्रों से भी है जिन्हें चित्रा ने बनाया था। चित्रा जिस दिन होस्टल से अपने घर जा रही थी, उस दिन वह अपने गुरुजी से मिलने गई थी। लौटते समय उसने गर्ग स्टोर के सामने पेड़ के नीचे भिखारिन को मरी पड़ी देखा। उसके दोनों बच्चे उसके सूखे शरीर के साथ चिपककर बुरी तरह से रो रहे थे। उस दृश्य को देखकर वह स्वयं को रोक न सकी। उसने कच्चा सा रेखाचित्र बना डाला। कालान्तर में उसी विषय पर

उसने एक चित्र बना डाला जिसका शीर्षक 'अनाथ' रखा। विदेश में अनेक प्रतियोगिताओं में उसे इसी चित्र पर प्रथम पुरस्कार मिला। जाने क्या था उस चित्र में, जो देखता चकित रह जाता। विदेश में अखबारों में भी उसे खूब ख्याति मिली। इसी के साथ-साथ चित्रा ने जो अन्य चित्र बनाए थे जैसे बाढ़, कन्फ्यूजन आदि का, उन्हें भी लोगों ने पसन्द किया था।

(ii) चित्रा एक धनी पिता की इकलौती संतान थी। वह अरुणा की घनिष्ठ सहेली थी। वे दोनों एक ही कमरे में रहती थीं। चित्रा एक चित्रकार थी, जो तूलिकाओं व रंगों की दुनिया में निमग्न रहती थी। वह अपनी कला को ऊँचे आयाम देना चाहती थी। उसके लिए किसी भी घटना का तब तक कोई महत्त्व नहीं रहता जब तक उसमें चित्रकारिता के लिए कोई स्थान न हो। चित्रा एक महत्त्वाकांक्षी युवती थी। वह विदेश में जाकर खूब धन तथा ख्याति अर्जित करना चाहती थी। उसमें स्वार्थपरता भी दृष्टिगोचर होती है। उसने उस भिखारिन को मरी हुई देखकर उसके बिलखते हुए बच्चों का कच्चा रेखाचित्र बना लिया लेकिन उन बच्चों की करुण चीखों से भी उसका हृदय नहीं पसीजा। उसमें भाव-शून्यता और संवेदनहीनता भी दिखाई देती थी जब वह अरुणा को उन गरीब बच्चों को पढ़ाते हुए देखती थी तो उन्हें बन्दर कहकर संबोधित करती थी। निष्कर्षस्वरूप हम कह सकते हैं कि चित्रा एक दृढ़-निश्चयी तथा कर्मठ नारी थी जिसने अपनी मेहनत तथा लगन से खूब ख्याति प्राप्त की थी।

(iii) अरुणा, चित्रा की सहेली थी। वह होस्टल में रहकर पढ़ाई कर रही थी। वह एक सच्ची समाज-सेविका थी। समाज के निर्धन, असहाय तथा शोषित वर्ग के लिए उसके हृदय में दया, उदारता तथा सहानुभूति की भावना थी। वह बस्ती के चौकीदारों, चपरासियों तथा नौकरों के बच्चों को समय निकालकर पढ़ा देती थी ताकि उनका भविष्य सँवर सके। समाज-सेवा उसके जीवन का मुख्य लक्ष्य था।

(iv) जैसे ही अरुणा को चित्रा से उस भिखारिन की असमय मृत्यु के बारे में पता चला तो उसे अत्यधिक दु:ख हुआ। उसके हृदय में उन अनाथ बच्चों के लिए दया, करुणा तथा प्रेम के भाव उत्पन्न हुए। वह तुरंत उनकी सहायता करने के लिए चली गई। अरुणा ने उन अनाथ बच्चों को अपना लिया। मनोज से विवाह कर उसने उन दोनों बच्चों को गोद ले लिया और उन पर अपनी ममता न्योछावर कर दी। उन बेसहारा बच्चों को माता-पिता का प्यार और सुन्दर घर-संसार मिल गया। इस प्रकार अरुणा ने समाज में एक मिसाल कायम की।

(v) चित्रकला और समाज-सेवा दो भिन्न-भिन्न कलाएँ हैं। दोनों की कोई तुलना नहीं की जा सकती। चित्रकला एक अभिरुचि है, जिससे मन-बहलाव होता है। इससे धन, प्रतिष्ठा और ख्याति भी प्राप्त होती है। इसमें भावनाओं का कोई स्थान नहीं होता। चित्रकार आत्मकेंद्रित हो जाता है और दूसरों के बारे में नहीं सोचता।

इसके विपरीत समाज-सेवा परोपकार का कार्य है इसमें व्यक्ति समाज के गरीब, बेसहारा तथा शोषित लोगों के उत्थान के लिए कार्य करता है। इससे समाज का भला होता है। 'बहुजन हिताय, बहुजन सुखाय'।

प्रस्तुत कहानी में चित्रा अपनी चित्रकारिता के क्षेत्र में खूब उन्नति करती है। वह विदेश जाकर खूब पैसा, नाम और शौहरत कमाती है। दूसरी ओर, अरुणा गरीब बच्चों को पढ़ाकर उनका भविष्य सँवारती है। बाढ़-पीड़ितों की सेवा कर उनके आँसू पोंछती है। अंत में गरीब भिखारिन के अनाथ बच्चों को अपनाकर उन्हें जीवन की सारी खुशियाँ दे देती है। इस प्रकार अरुणा की कला एक बड़े परिप्रेक्ष्य में उपयोगी साबित होती है।

Ans. (i) 'उसके चित्रों' से तात्पर्य चित्रा द्वारा गर्ग स्टोर के सामने पेड़ के नीचे मृत पड़ी भिखारिन और उसके अनाथ बच्चों का बना चित्र तथा अन्य चित्रों से भी है, भिखारिन के चित्र ने देश-विदेश में बहुत नाम कमाया है। यह चित्र अभी दिल्ली में उसके चित्रों की प्रदर्शनी में लगा हुआ है। जिसका शीर्षक 'अनाथ' रखा है।

(ii) चित्रा एक धनी पिता की इकलौती बेटी थी। वह अरुणा की पक्की सहेली थी। वे दोनों हॉस्टल में एक ही कमरे में रहती थीं। चित्रा एक महान चित्रकार बनना चाहती है। इसी उद्देश्य से वह विदेश भी जाती है और सफल भी होती है। चित्रा भौतिकवादी व संवेदनहीन है। वह अपने लक्ष्य के प्रति दृढ़ है और कर्मठता से उसे पाने में सफल भी होती है।

(iii) अरुणा चित्रा की सहेली तथा सहपाठिन है। वह भावुक और संवेदनशील है। समाज सेवा उसके जीवन का लक्ष्य है। जब उसे पता चलता है कि गर्ग स्टोर के सामने पेड़ के नीचे मृत भिखारिन के सूखे शरीर से चिपककर उसके दोनों बच्चे रो रहे हैं, तो वह अत्यन्त भावुक और दुखी हो जाती है। वह तुरंत उन बच्चों को घर लेकर आ जाती है। वह उन दोनों बच्चों को अपना लेती है और उनका पालन-पोषण करती है।

(iv) चित्रकारिता और समाज सेवा में, मैं समाज सेवा को उपयोगी मानता हूँ। अरुणा यथार्थवाद का परिचय देती है। मानवता मनुष्य का सबसे बड़ा धर्म होता है। अरुणा इस धर्म का पालन करती है और दोनों अनाथ बच्चों को अपने संरक्षण में रखकर माँ की तरह पालन-पोषण करती है। लोगों के दुख दर्द में सहभागी बनना और उनकी मदद करना ही मनुष्य के जीवन का लक्ष्य होना चाहिए। कुछ बनने की इच्छा रखना गलत नहीं है, क्योंकि व्यक्ति की महत्वाकांक्षा ही उसे सफल और प्रसिद्ध बनाती है। चित्रा महान चित्रकार तो बन जाती है पर उसके हृदय में मानवता व परोपकार को भावनाएँ नहीं हैं।

Poems

Long Answer Type Questions

Chapter 1. साखी (Sakhi)

—कबीर दास (Kabir Das)

Q. 1. Read the extract given below and answer in *Hindi* the questions that follow:

निम्नलिखित पद्यांश को पढ़िए और उसके नीचे लिखे प्रश्नों के उत्तर हिन्दी में लिखिए:

पाहन पूजे हरि मिले, तो मैं पूजूँ पहार।
ताते ये चाकी भली, पीस खाय संसार।।
सात समंद की मसि करौं, लेखनि सब बनराय।
सब धरती कागद करौं, हरि गुन लिखा न जाय।।

(i) कबीरदास जी ने पहाड़ पूजने की बात क्यों कही है? इस दोहे के माध्यम से वे हमें क्या सन्देश देना चाहते हैं? मूर्ति पूजा के बारे में उनके क्या विचार थे? **[2]**

(ii) उन्होंने चक्की की तुलना किससे की है? वे उसे अच्छा क्यों मानते हैं? **[2]**

(iii) उन्होंने 'स्याही' और 'लेखनी' किसे बनाने की बात कही है? वे किस पर हरि कथा लिखना चाहते हैं? **[3]**

(iv) 'हरि गुन लिखा न जाए' —इस कथन से उनका क्या आशय है? समझाकर लिखिए। संत कबीर की भक्ति भावना की विशेषताएँ बताइए और वह कैसे भगवान की पूजा करना चाहते थे? **[2020] [3]**

Ans. **(i)** कबीरदास जी कहते हैं कि अगर पत्थर पूजने से भगवान की प्राप्ति हो जाती है तो वे पहाड़ को ही पूजते। इस दोहे में कबीरदास जी ने हिंदुओं की मूर्ति-पूजा पर व्यंग्य किया है। इस दोहे से ने यह संदेश देना चाहते हैं कि बाहरी आडम्बर व दिखावे से भगवान नहीं मिलते। वे मूर्ति पूजा का विरोध करते हैं। वे इसे अंधविश्वास मानते हैं।

(ii) कबीरदास ने चक्की की तुलना ईश्वर के साकार रूप (पत्थर की मूर्ति) से की है। वे चक्की के पत्थर को मूर्ति के पत्थर से अधिक अच्छा मानते हैं क्योंकि उससे पिसे आटे से संसार की भूक शान्त होती है।

(iii) उन्होंने सातों समुद्रों के जल को स्याही और सारे जंगल की लकड़ी को लेखनी बनाने की बात कही है। सम्पूर्ण धरती को कागज बनाकर, उस कागज पर हरि कथा लिखना चाहते हैं।

(iv) कवि कहते हैं कि यदि सातों समुद्रों के जल को स्याही बना लिया जाय ओर सारे जंगल की लकड़ी को लेखनी बनाकर, सारी धरती को कागज बना दिया जाए तब भी ईश्वर का गुणगान करना असंभव है। ईश्वर शब्दातीत है।

संत कबीर निर्गुण भक्ति शाखा के ज्ञानाश्रयी कवियों में सर्वोपरि हैं। कबीर निर्गुण ब्रह्म के उपासक थे। इसलिए इन्होंने मूर्ति पूजा, कर्मकाण्ड तथा बाहरी आडंबरों का खुलकर विरोध किया। वे राम रहीम की एकता में विश्वास रखते थे।

Q. 2. Read the extract given below and answer in *Hindi* the questions that follow:

निम्नलिखित पद्यांश को पढ़िए और उसके नीचे लिखे प्रश्नों के उत्तर हिन्दी में लिखिए:

गुरु गोविन्द दोऊ खड़े काके लागूँ पायँ।
बलिहारी गुरु आपनो जिन गोविंद दियौ बताय।।
जब मैं था तब हरि नहीं, अब हरि है मैं नाहि।
प्रेम गली अति साँकरी, तामे दो न समाहि।।

(i) कवि किसके बारे में क्या सोच रहे हैं? **[2]**

(ii) कवि किसके ऊपर न्योछावर (समर्पण) हो जाना चाहते हैं तथा क्यों? **[2]**

(iii) ईश्वर का वास कहाँ नहीं होता है? कवि हमें क्या त्यागने की प्रेरणा दे रहे हैं? कवि का संक्षिप्त परिचय देते हुए बताइए। **[3]**

(iv) 'साँकरी' शब्द का क्या अर्थ है? प्रेम गली से कवि का क्या तात्पर्य है? उसमें कौन दो एक साथ नहीं रह सकते हैं समझाइए। **[3]**

[2017]

Ans. **(i)** प्रस्तुत दोहे भक्तिकालीन कवि कबीरदास द्वारा रचित हैं। प्रथम दोहे में कवि गुरु एवं गोविन्द अर्थात् परमेश्वर दोनों के विषय में विचार कर रहे हैं। वह अपने हृदय में सोच रहे हैं कि मेरे समक्ष मेरे सद्गुरु और प्रभु दोनों ही खड़े हैं, परन्तु मुझे किसके प्रथम चरण स्पर्श करना चाहिए।

(ii) कबीरदास जी पूर्ण समर्पण भाव से अपने सद्गुरु पर न्यौछावर होना चाहते हैं क्योंकि, गुरु ही वह माध्यम है जिसके द्वारा परमात्मा को प्राप्त किया जा सकता है। अत: वह बताना चाहते हैं कि प्रभु से भी अधिक गुरु महत्वपूर्ण हैं क्योंकि गुरु के बिना भगवान के दर्शन असम्भव है।

(iii) प्रस्तुत दोहे में कबीरदास जी यह बताना चाहते हैं कि जब मनुष्य में अहं (मैं) अहंकार का भाव रहेगा तब तक उसके हृदय में भगवान का वास नहीं होगा। कवि कहते हैं कि यदि तुम्हें हृदय में हरि अर्थात् प्रभु को बसाना है तो 'मैं हूँ' इस भाव का त्याग कर दो।

कबीर का व्यक्तित्व न केवल हिन्दी सन्त कवियों में अपितु पूरे हिन्दी साहित्य में बेजोड़ है। कबीरदास जब साहित्य के क्षेत्र में आये वह समय कुरीतियों और अन्धविश्वासों से भरा था। वह हिन्दुओं के लिए अवतार एवं मुसलमानों के लिए पीर थे। उन्होंने खुले दिल से हिन्दू व मुसलमानों की बुराइयों का विरोध किया।

हिन्दुओं के लिए "माला फेरत जुग गया, गया न मन का फेर" लिखा तो मुसलमानों के लिए "कांकड़ पाथर जोरि कै, मस्जिद लई बनाय, ता चढ़ि मुल्ला बांग दे क्या बहरा हुआ खुदाय।" इस प्रकार की बातों से दोनों ही धर्मों की कुरीतियों व अंधविश्वासों पर कवि ने चोट पहुँचाई है।

(iv) 'साँकरी' शब्द का अर्थ संकुचित अर्थात् पतली है। परमात्मा से प्रेम करने वाले भाव से कवि का तात्पर्य है कि प्रभु से प्रेम करने वाला रास्ता बहुत ही तंग है। उसमें दो चीजें एक साथ नहीं समा सकतीं। एक तो अहंकार और दूसरे प्रभु। इसलिए अपने प्रभु को निवासित करना हो तो अहंकार का त्याग करना पड़ेगा। तभी हरि से प्रेम हो सकता है।

Chapter 2.   कुंडलियाँ (Kundaliya)

—गिरिधर कविराय (Giridhar Kavi Rai)

Q. 1.   Read the extract given below and answer in *Hindi* the questions that follow:

निम्नलिखित पद्यांश को पढ़िए और उसके नीचे लिखे प्रश्नों के उत्तर हिंदी में लिखिए:

लाठी में हैं गुण बहुत, सदा रखिये संग।
गहरि नदी, नाली जहाँ, तहाँ बचावै अंग।।
तहाँ बचावै अंग, झपटि कुत्ता कहँ मारे।
दुश्मन दावागीर होय, तिनहूँ को झारे।।
कह 'गिरिधर कविराय' सुनो हे दूर के बाठी।।
सब हथियार न छाँड़ि, हाथ महँ लीजै लाठी।।

(i) इस कुंडली में किसकी उपयोगिता बताई गई है? कवि ने किस समय मनुष्य को लाठी रखने का परामर्श दिया है? **[2]**

(ii) लाठी हमारे शरीर की सुरक्षा किस प्रकार करती है? **[2]**

(iii) लाठी किन तीनों से निपटने में सहायक होती है और किस प्रकार? **[3]**

(iv) कवि सब हथियार छोड़कर लाठी लेने की बात क्यों कर रहे हैं? अपने विचार व्यक्त करते हुए कुंडलियाँ लेखन का उद्देश्य स्पष्ट कीजिए। **[3]**

[2018]

📋 Marking Scheme

(i) इस कुंडली में लाठी की उपयोगिता बताई गई है। कवि ने यात्रा करते समय मनुष्य को लाठी रखने का परामर्श दिया है।

(ii) कहीं पर गड्ढा आने पर हमारे शरीर का संतुलन बनाने में, रास्ते में नदी पड़ जाने पर पानी की गहराई का अनुमान लगाने में, नाली आने पर लाठी पर शरीर का भार डालकर आसानी से पार किया जा सकता है, इस तरह वह हमारे शरीर की सुरक्षा करती है।

(iii) कुत्ता मार्ग में बाधा बने तो लाठी से मारकर भगाया जा सकता है, दुश्मन मिल जाए तो अपनी रक्षा लाठी से की जा सकती है। लुटेरा मिल जाए तो लाठी से सामना किया जा सकता है। कुत्ता, दुश्मन एवं लुटेरा तीनों से निपटने में सहायक है।

(iv) कवि के अनुसार अन्य हथियारों से लाठी लाभकारी है। तत्कालीन हथियार तलवार, चाकू आदि तो लड़ाई में काम आ सकते हैं, परन्तु लाठी तो सभी व्यवधानों को दूर करने में सहायक होती है। क्योंकि लाठी हमारी आत्मरक्षा के साथ-साथ कई और तरीकों से उपयोग में आती है। कवि सुरक्षा के लिए यात्रा करते समय लाठी सदा अपने पास रखने को कहते हैं क्योंकि यही बुद्धिमानी का काम है।

Ans.   **(i)** इस कुंडली में लाठी की उपयोगिता बताई गई है। कवि ने लाठी रखने का परामर्श यात्रा के समय दिया है।

(ii) लाठी हमारे शरीर की दुश्मनों से रक्षा करती है। नदी नाले को पार कराने में मदद करती है तथा जानवरों से रक्षा करती है।

(iii) पहला, रास्ते में यदि कोई नदी या नाला आ जाता है तो लाठी के सहारे से उसे पार कर सकते हैं।

दूसरा, दुश्मन से हमारी रक्षा करती है लाठी के द्वारा उससे लड़कर उस पर विजय प्राप्त कर सकते हैं।

तीसरा, जंगली जानवरों से लाठी हमारी रक्षा करती है, यदि कोई कुत्ता या जानवर आ जाये तो ये उसे भगा सकती है।

(iv) कवि सब हथियार छोड़कर लाठी लेने की बात इसलिए कर रहा है क्योंकि साधारण वस्तु भी जीवन में उपयोगी होती है। अन्य हथियार तो केवल लड़ाई में ही काम आते हैं परन्तु एक ही लाठी कई प्रकार से उपयोग में लाई जा सकती है और सभी तरह हमारी रक्षा कर सकती है।

इस कुण्डलियाँ लेखन का मुख्य उद्देश्य लोक व्यवहार की बातों से परिचित कराना है।

Chapter 3. स्वर्ग बना सकते हैं (Swarg Bana Sakte Hai)

—रामधारी सिंह 'दिनकर' (Ramdhari Singh 'Dinkar')

Q. 1. Read the extract given below and answer in Hindi the questions that follow:

निम्नलिखित पद्यांश को पढ़िए और उसके नीचे लिखे प्रश्नों के उत्तर हिंदी में लिखिए:

"न्यायोचित सुख सुलभ नहीं
जब तक मानव-मानव को
चैन कहाँ धरती पर तब तक
शांति कहाँ इस भव को ?
जब तक मनुज-मनुज का यह
सुख भाग नहीं सम होगा
शमित न होगा कोलाहल
संघर्ष नहीं कम होगा।"

(i) 'भव' शब्द का क्या अर्थ है? कवि के अनुसार इस भव में शान्ति क्यों नहीं है? **[2]**

(ii) शब्दों के अर्थ लिखिए—न्यायोचित, सम, सुलभ कोलाहल। **[2]**

(iii) 'शमित न होगा कोलाहल संघर्ष नहीं कम होगा' पंक्ति का भावार्थ लिखिए। **[3]**

(iv) उपरोक्त पंक्तियाँ 'दिनकर जी' की किस प्रसिद्ध रचना से ली गई हैं? कविता का केन्द्रीय भाव लिखते हुए बताइए। **[3]**

[2019]

Marking Scheme

(i) 'भव' शब्द का अर्थ 'संसार' (धरती) होता है। कवि धरती पर स्वर्ग बनाना चाहते हैं। वे कहते हैं कि जब तक धरती पर रहने वाले प्रत्येक मनुष्य को न्यायपूर्ण सुख प्राप्त नहीं होता तब तक इस संसार में अमन, चैन और शांति स्थापित नहीं हो सकती। कवि के कहने का तात्पर्य यह है कि ईश्वर ने इस संसार के सभी मनुष्यों के लिए एक समान रूप से सुख-साधन उपलब्ध किए है परन्तु मानव स्वार्थ में अंधा होकर दूसरों के सुख-साधन छीन लेता है। इस प्रकार मानवता का हनन होता है। ऐसे में धरती पर सुख-चैन स्थापित नहीं हो सकता। सम्पूर्ण संसार का विकास तभी संभव हो पाएगा जब सभी मनुष्यों के साथ न्याय और समानता का व्यवहार होगा और उन्हें विकास के समान अवसर प्राप्त होंगे। कोई किसी का अधिकार छीनने का प्रयास नहीं करेगा।

(ii) न्यायोचित – न्याय के अनुसार उचित (ठीक), न्यायसंगत नियम के अनुसार

सम – बराबर, समता, समान

सुलभ – आसानी से मिलने वाला, आसानी से उपलब्ध/आसानी से प्राप्त होने वाला।

कोलाहल – शोरगुल, शोरशराबा।

(iii) जब तक प्रत्येक मनुष्य को अपने भाग का सुख नहीं मिलेगा और सबका भाग एक जैसा नहीं होगा तब तक यह शोर यह लड़ाई झगड़ा समाप्त नहीं होगा। मनुष्यों में आपसी विषमता के कारण यह अशांति बनी ही रहेगी। 'सर्वे सन्तु सुखिनः, सर्वे सन्तु निरामया:' कवि मानव-कल्याण की भावना

से अभिभूत हैं और धरती पर रहने वाले सभी मनुष्यों के सुख-कल्याण की कामना करते हैं। उनका मानना है कि धरती पर अमन-शान्ति तभी स्थापित हो सकती है जब सभी मनुष्यों को जीने के लिए समान अधिकार मिलेंगे और उनमें आपसी विद्वेष की भावना मिट जाएगी। लोगों में मानवीय मूल्यों का विकास करना होगा। उन्हें निजी स्वार्थ, अंहकार, लालच तथा संचय की भावना से ऊपर उठना होगा। ऊँच-नीच, जात-पात, धर्म-सम्प्रदाय आदि के नाम पर किए जाने वाले भेदभाव दूर करने होंगे। सभी के हृदय में प्रेम, दया, सहानुभूति, त्याग, भाईचारा, सहनशीलता आदि सद्भावनाएँ उत्पन्न करनी होंगी। जब सभी मनुष्य 'जियो और जीने दो' के सिद्धांत का अनुसरण करेंगे तो संसार में शांति स्थापित हो सकेगी।

(iv) उपरोक्त पंक्तियाँ 'दिनकर जी' की प्रसिद्ध रचना 'कुरुक्षेत्र' से ली गई हैं। ये पंक्तियाँ भीष्म पितामह और युधिष्ठिर को आत्मग्लानि तथा अपराधबोध होने के कारण समझाते हुए कह रहे हैं। कवि धरती पर स्वर्ग बनाना चाहते हैं। उनका मानना है कि ईश्वर ने सभी मनुष्यों को एक समान बनाया है। उनके जीने के लिए धरती पर प्रचुर मात्रा में प्राकृतिक सम्पदा उत्पन्न की है। अत: हमें उसका समान रूप से वितरण करना चाहिए। सभी व्यक्तियों के साथ हमें न्यायपूर्ण व्यवहार करना चाहिए तथा उन्हें उन्नति के समान अवसर प्रदान करने चाहिए। हमें अपने भीतर प्रेम, दया, सहानुभूति, नि:स्वार्थ सेवा आदि मानवीय गुणों का विकास करना चाहिए। किसी भी मनुष्य को तुच्छ या छोटा समझने की भूल नहीं करनी चाहिए। हमें अपने भीतर से स्वार्थ, लोभ, अहंकार, ईर्ष्या, असंतोष, हिंसा, बैर आदि दुर्भावनाओं को दूर करना चाहिए। हमें आपसी मनमुटाव तथा लड़ाई-झगड़े दूर कर प्रेम तथा भाईचारे के साथ रहना चाहिए। हमें सत्य और अहिंसा का मार्ग अपनाते हुए अपने आसपास खुशहाली का वातावरण बनाना चाहिए। इस प्रकार हम 'वसुधैव कुटुम्बकम' की भावना को चरितार्थ कर धरती पर स्वर्ग बना सकते हैं।

Ans. **(i)** 'भव' शब्द का अर्थ है 'संसार'। कवि के अनुसार जब तक प्रत्येक मनुष्य को न्यायपूर्ण सुख नहीं मिलेगा तब तक इस संसार में शांति नहीं मिलेगी। धरती पर सुख-चैन तभी स्थापित होगा जब ईश्वर प्रदत्त सुख-सुविधायें सभी मनुष्यों को समान रूप से प्राप्त होंगी। कोई किसी का अधिकार छीनने का प्रयास नहीं करेगा।

(ii) शब्दों का अर्थ—

न्यायोचित — न्याय संगत नियम के अनुसार, न्याय के अनुसार उचित

सम — समान, बराबर

सुलभ — सरल, आसान

कोलाहल — शोरगुल, अशांति

(iii) "शमित न होगा कोलाहल संघर्ष नहीं कम होगा।" पंक्ति का भावार्थ है कि जब तक मनुष्य के जीवन में समता का सुख नहीं होगा, जब तक मनुष्य के मन में असन्तोष

होगा और अशांति होगी। जब तक समानता की दृष्टि से सबको नहीं देखा जाएगा, तब तक शांति और समता के लिए संघर्ष जारी रहेगा। कवि ने स्वार्थरहित समतापूर्ण समाज की कल्पना की है।

(iv) उपर्युक्त पंक्तियाँ दिनकर जी की प्रसिद्ध रचना 'कुरुक्षेत्र' से ली गई हैं। ये पंक्तियाँ भीष्म पितामह युधिष्ठिर को आत्मग्लानि तथा अपराधबोध होने के कारण समझाते हुए कह रहे हैं। कवि की यह कल्पना है कि उसका देश, उसकी मातृभूमि स्वर्ग के समान सुन्दर हो जाए। यह तभी होगा जब हमारे देश से भाषा, धर्म, रंग, जाति आदि के नाम पर कोई भेदभाव नहीं होगा। सभी देशवासियों को न्यायोचित सुख मिले। कवि को यह विश्वास है कि समता और प्रेम के आधार पर इस धरती को स्वर्ग बनाया जा सकता है।

Chapter 4.   वह जन्मभूमि मेरी (Wah Janmabhumi Meri)

—सोहनलाल द्विवेदी (Sohanlal Dwivedi)

Q. 1. **Read the extract given below and answer in** *Hindi* **the questions that follow:**

निम्नलिखित पद्यांश को पढ़िए और उसके नीचे लिखे प्रश्नों के उत्तर हिंदी में लिखिए:

जन्मे जहाँ थे रघुपति जन्मी जहाँ थी सीता।
श्री कृष्ण ने सुनाई, वंशी पुनीत गीता।।
गौतम ने जन्म लेकर जिसका सुयश बढ़ाया।
जग को दया दिखाई, जग को दिया दिखाया।।
वह युद्धभूमि मेरी, वह बुद्धभूमि मेरी।
वह जन्मभूमि मेरी, वह मातृभूमि मेरी।।

(i) प्रस्तुत कविता किस प्रकार की है? इस कविता में किसका गुणगान किया गया है? **[2]**

(ii) कवि ने भारत को युद्धभूमि और बुद्धभूमि क्यों कहा है? समझाकर लिखिए। **[2]**

(iii) प्रस्तुत कविता में जन्मभूमि की किन-किन प्राकृतिक विशेषताओं का उल्लेख किया गया है? स्पष्ट कीजिए। **[3]**

(iv) प्रस्तुत पद्यांश में कवि ने भारत को किन-किन महापुरुषों की भूमि कहा है? कविता का केन्द्रीय भाव लिखते हुए स्पष्ट कीजिए। **[3]**

[2019]

📋 Marking Scheme

(i) यह देशभक्ति से परिपूर्ण कविता है।

'जननी जन्मभूमिश्च स्वर्गादपि गरीयसी' अर्थात जननी और जन्मभूमि का स्थान स्वर्ग से भी श्रेष्ठ और महान होता है। इसी भावना से ओतप्रोत कवि ने भारत भूमि का गुणगान किया है। उनके हृदय में मातृभूमि के प्रति प्रेम तथा श्रद्धा भावना है क्योंकि उनका मानना है कि इसकी रज में लोट-लोटकर हम बड़े हुए हैं। इसने हमें पौष्टिक आहार दिए और हमारा पालन-पोषण किया। इसका ऋण हम कभी भी नहीं चुका सकते। कवि ने भारत की विभिन्न विशेषताओं का उल्लेख कर उसकी महानता की ओर हमारा ध्यान केन्द्रित किया है। कवि ने भारत की प्राकृतिक सुषमा का आलौकिक वर्णन किया है। देश में जन्म लेने वाले महापुरुषों का उल्लेख कर कवि ने हमारे भीतर अपनी मातृभूमि के प्रति अनूठा अनुराग उत्पन्न किया है। कवि भारत का उत्थान चाहते हैं इसलिए भारतवासियों के हृदय में राष्ट्रीयता की भावना जगाने का प्रयास कर रहे हैं।

(ii) कवि ने भारत भूमि को युद्धभूमि कहा है क्योंकि यहाँ पर सत्य की रक्षा के लिए अनेक युद्ध हुए। कवि महाभारत की भीषण लड़ाई का उल्लेख करते हुए कहते हैं कि यह युद्ध असत्य पर सत्य की विजय दिखाता है। इस युद्ध में श्रीकृष्ण अर्जुन के सारथी बने थे। उन्होंने युद्ध स्थल पर अर्जुन को गीता का परम ज्ञान दिया था– 'कर्मण्येवाधिकारस्ते मा फलेषु कदाचन'। इस उपदेश ने अर्जुन के ज्ञान-चक्षु खोले थे, जिससे वे युद्ध के लिए तैयार हो गए थे और विजय हुए थे।

कवि ने भारत को बुद्धभूमि इसलिए कहा है क्योंकि यहाँ परम ज्ञानी महात्मा गौतम बुद्ध उत्पन्न हुए थे जिन्होंने दुनिया को सत्य और अहिंसा का पाठ पढ़ाया। जीव-मात्र के प्रति प्रेम और दया भावना सिखाई। उन्होंने सम्राट अशोक का हृदय-परिवर्तन किया था और उन्हें मानवता का पाठ पढ़ाया था। 'बुद्धं शरणं गच्छामि' की गूँज सारे विश्व में सुनाई दे रही है।

(iii) प्रस्तुत कविता में कवि ने भारत के प्राकृतिक सौन्दर्य का अनुपम वर्णन किया है। कवि कहते हैं कि भारत एक ऐसा देश है जिसके मस्तक पर सबसे ऊँचा हिमालय पर्वत मुकुट के सामान सुशोभित है। उसके चरणों में सागर बहते हैं। ऐसा लगता है मानो सागर भारत माता के चरण धो रहे हों। हमारे देश में गंगा, यमुना और सरस्वती जैसी पावन नदियाँ बहती हैं और धरा को सरसाती हैं। यहाँ घने जंगल हैं तथा ऊँचे-ऊँचे पहाड़ हैं। पहाड़ों से अनेक झरने बहते हैं। झाड़ियों में से चिड़ियों के चहचहाने का मधुर स्वर सुनाई देता है। आम के पेड़ों पर कोयल मधुर आवाज़ में कूकती है। मलय पर्वत से आने वाली शीतल हवा वातावरण को मनमोहक बनाती है। इस प्रकार भारत भूमि पर 'सुजलाम सुफलाम, मलयज शीतलाम' का सौन्दर्यपूर्ण प्रत्यक्ष नज़ारा दिखाई देता है।

(iv) कवि ने भारत भूमि को महापुरुषों की भूमि कहा है क्योंकि इसी पुण्य भूमि पर बड़े-बड़े महापुरुषों ने जन्म लिया था और अपने चरित्र, ज्ञान और उपदेशों के माध्यम से देशवासियों का मार्गदर्शन किया था। हमारी मातृभूमि पर रघुवंशी मर्यादा पुरुषोत्तम श्रीराम ने जन्म लिया था। इसी पुनीत धरा पर आदर्श नारी सीता भी प्रकट हुई थीं। यही पर श्रीकृष्ण जी ने अपनी मधुर बाँसुरी की धुन बजाई थी और देशवासियों को मंत्र-मुग्ध किया था। महाभारत के युद्धस्थल पर श्रीकृष्ण ने भटके हुए अर्जुन को पावन गीता का उपदेश दिया था और उसे सत्य की राह दिखाई थी। इसी भूमि पर महात्मा बुद्ध का भी जन्म हुआ था। जिन्होंने सारी दुनिया को अहिंसा और मानवता का पाठ पढ़ाया और निष्काम कर्म करने की प्रेरणा दी थी। इस प्रकार भारत में अनेक महापुरुष हुए हैं

जिन्होंने अपने महान कार्यों से भारत के यश-ख्याति में वृद्धि की। प्रस्तुत कविता लेखन का मुख्य भाव देशभक्ति को जागृत करना तथा बढ़ावा देना है। भारत के प्राकृतिक सौन्दर्य तथा गौरवशाली अतीत के दर्शन कराना है। कवि यह भी चाहते है कि आज की युवापीढ़ी पूर्वजों द्वारा किए गए सत्कर्मों से परिचित हो, देशवासी कृष्ण तथा गौतम बुद्ध द्वारा दिखाए गए मार्ग पर चलें।

Ans. (i) 'वह जन्मभूमि मेरी' कविता देश-प्रेम की भावना का परिचय कराती है। इस कविता में मातृभूमि की विशेषताओं का गुणगान किया गया है। भारत की भूमि, वह पवित्र भूमि है, जहाँ राम, कृष्ण, बुद्ध जैसे महापुरुषों ने जन्म लिया है।

(ii) महाभारत के युद्ध के समय अर्जुन मोहवश युद्ध नहीं करना चाहते थे। कुरुक्षेत्र के मैदान में श्रीकृष्ण ने अर्जुन को उपदेश दिया कि कर्मठता मनुष्य का कर्त्तव्य होना चाहिए। निष्काम कर्म करना चाहिए, फल की अपेक्षा नहीं करनी चाहिए। युद्धभूमि में दिया गया यह उपदेश भगवत्गीता में संकलित है और युगों-युगों तक सबका मार्गदर्शन करता रहेगा। इसलिए कवि ने भारत को युद्धभूमि कहा। इसे बुद्धभूमि कहा क्योंकि भगवान् बुद्ध ने यहाँ जन्म लिया और संसार को दया और प्रेम का सन्देश दिया और अहिंसा का मार्ग दिखाया। बुद्धं शरणं गच्छामि की गूँज सारे विश्व को सुनाई दे रही है।

(iii) अपने देश के भौगोलिक परिवेश का वर्णन करते हुए कवि का कहना है कि भारत की उत्तरी सीमा में खड़ा हिमालय पर्वत आसमान को चूमता है। भारतभूमि की पहाड़ियों से अनेक सुन्दर झरने झरते हैं। गंगा, यमुना जैसी पवित्र नदियाँ मातृभूमि की सुन्दरता को बढ़ाती हैं। भारत की दक्षिणी सीमा में समुद्र इसकी शोभा बढ़ाता है। घाटियों की हरियाली मनमोहक है। यहाँ पर सुगन्धित पवन बहती है, जो तन-मन को प्रसन्नता से भर देती है। जन्मभूमि की प्राकृतिक विशेषतायें अत्यन्त ही आकर्षक और मनमोहक हैं। इस प्रकार भारत भूमि पर 'सुजलाम सुफलाम, मलयज शीतलाम' का सौन्दर्य पूर्ण नज़ारा दिखाई देता है।

(iv) प्रस्तुत पद्यांश में कवि ने भारत को राम-सीता, कृष्ण और गौतम बुद्ध आदि महापुरुषों की जन्मभूमि कहा है। कवि ने अपने देश के भौगोलिक, प्राकृतिक एवम् आध्यात्मिक रूपों का वर्णन किया है। यह कविता देश प्रेम की भावना को दर्शाती है। कवि अपने देश के गौरव का गान करते हुए हिमालय, सागर, नदियाँ, झरने तथा अमराइयों की प्रशंसा करते हैं। अपनी मातृभूमि का गौरवगान करते हुए कवि ने इसे पुण्यभूमि, स्वर्णभूमि, धर्मभूमि, कर्मभूमि, युद्धभूमि और बुद्धभूमि जैसे विशेषणों से सम्बोधित किया है। प्रस्तुत कविता लेखन का मुख्य भाव देश भक्ति को जागृत करना तथा बढ़ावा देना है। भारत के प्राकृतिक सौन्दर्य तथा गौरवशाली अतीत के दर्शन कराना है। कवि यह भी चाहते हैं कि आज की युवा पीढ़ी पूर्वजों द्वारा किए गए सत्कर्मों से परिचित हो, देशवासी कृष्ण तथा गौतम बुद्ध द्वारा दिखाए गए मार्ग पर चलें।

Chapter 5. मेघ आए (Megh Aaye)

—सर्वेश्वर दयाल सक्सेना (Sarveshwar Dayal Saxena)

Q. 1. Read the extract given below and answer in *Hindi* the questions that follow:

निम्नलिखित पद्यांश को पढ़िए और उसके नीचे लिखे प्रश्नों के उत्तर हिन्दी में लिखिए:

"मेघ आए बड़े बन-ठन के, सँवर के
आगे-आगे नाचती-गाती बयार चली,
दरवाजे-खिड़कियाँ खुलने लगीं गली-गली,
पाहुन ज्यों आये हों, गाँव में शहर के !
मेघ आए बड़े बन -ठन के, सँवर के !"

(i) मेघ कहाँ आए हुए हैं? कवि को मेघ देखकर क्या प्रतीत हो रहा है? [2]

(ii) 'बयार' शब्द से आप क्या समझते हैं? कवि इसके बारे में क्या बताना चाहता है? [2]

(iii) दरवाजे-खिड़कियाँ क्यों खुलने लगी हैं? किसका स्वागत कहाँ पर किस प्रकार किया जाने लगा है? कवि के भाव स्पष्ट कीजिए। [3]

(iv) कविता का केन्द्रीय भाव लिखिए। [3]

[2017]

Ans. (i) आकाश में मेघों के छाने का मानवीकरण करते हुए कवि सर्वेश्वर दयाल सक्सेना कहते हैं कि वर्षाकाल में पानी से भरे हुए मेघ आकाश में आने लगे तब ऐसा प्रतीत होने लगा कि ये मेघ शहर से सजे-सँवरे मेहमानों की भाँति गाँव में आये हैं।

(ii) 'बयार' शब्द का अभिप्राय 'हवा' होता है। कवि इसके विषय में यह बताना चाहता है कि जब आकाश में घने-घने बादल छाते हैं तो हवा उमंगित हो उठती है। वह उल्लास में भरकर सब जगह नाचती इठलाती हुई घूमती फिरती है अर्थात् जब आकाश में बादल छाते हैं तो बड़ी ठण्डी-ठण्डी हवा बहती है और उसके लिये दरवाजे खिड़कियाँ खुलने लगते हैं।

(iii) जब बादल छाते हैं तो शीतल हवाएँ चलने लगती हैं। जब तेज हवाएँ चलती हैं तो दरवाजे, खिड़कियाँ, स्वत: ही खुलने लगते हैं। कवि यहाँ पर इस भाव को अभिव्यक्त करना चाहते हैं कि जिस प्रकार से हमारे घर कोई मेहमान आता है तो उसकी अगवानी में हम खिड़की, दरवाजे खोल देते हैं। उसी प्रकार आज मेघ हमारे अतिथि के

रूप में गाँव में आये हैं, इसीलिये हमारे घर के द्वार व खिड़कियाँ उनके स्वागत में खुल गये हैं।

(iv) कवि कहते हैं कि आकाश में जब पानी से भरे बादल छा गये तो प्रतीत हुआ जैसे शहर के मेहमान सज सँवरकर गाँव में आ गये हो और उनके आने पर सर्वत्र खुशी की लहर दौड़ गयी। हवा सब जगह खुशी से नाचती फिर रही है। अतिथि के स्वागत में दरवाजे खिड़कियाँ खुल गये हैं। पुराने पीपल के वृक्ष ने बढ़कर बादलों का अभिवादन किया। नदी ने घूँघट हटाकर बादलों के सुन्दर दृश्य का नजारा देखा। लता ने दरवाजे के पीछे से छिपकर कहा पूरे एक साल बाद तुम्हें याद आयी है। जल से भरे बादलों को देखकर तालाब बहुत प्रसन्न हैं ऐसा लग रहा है कि मानो परात में पानी भरकर वह अतिथि के चरण-प्रक्षालन करना चाहते हैं । काले घने बादलों से सर्वत्र अँधेरा छा गया है और बीच-बीच में बिजली चमकने लगी है। वह इस बात का संकेत दे रही है कि अब इसमें कोई सन्देह नहीं कि पानी नहीं बरसेगा। अर्थात् अब तो पानी अवश्य ही बरसेगा। इस कविता के माध्यम से कवि ने उस स्वागत-सत्कार और उल्लास का वर्णन किया है जो ग्रामीण संस्कृति में बादलों के आने पर होता है।

Chapter 6.   सूर के पद (Sur Ke Pad)

—सूरदास (Surdas)

Q. 1. Read the extract given below and answer in *Hindi* the questions that follow:

निम्नलिखित पद्यांश को पढ़िए और उसके नीचे लिखे प्रश्नों के उत्तर हिंदी में लिखिए:

"मैया मेरी, चंद्र खिलौना लेहौं।
धौरी को पय पान न करिहौं, बेनी सिर न गुथैहौं।
मोतिन माल न धरिहौं उर पर झुंगली कंठ न लैहौं।
जैहौं लोट अबहिं धरनी पर, तेरी गोद न ऐहौं।।
लाल कहिहौं नंद बाबा को, तेरो सुत न कहैहौं।।"

(i) प्रस्तुत पद्य में कौन अपनी माता से जिद कर रहे हैं? वे क्या प्राप्त करना चाहते हैं? [2]

(ii) उनकी माता कौन हैं? वे अपने पुत्र को देखकर कैसा अनुभव कर रही हैं? स्पष्ट कीजिए। [2]

(iii) खिलौना न मिलने की स्थिति में बाल कृष्ण अपनी माँ को क्या-क्या धमकियाँ दे रहे हैं? स्पष्ट कीजिए। [3]

(iv) रूठे हुए बालक को बहलाने के लिए माँ क्या कहती है? बालक पर उसका क्या प्रभाव पड़ता है? सूरदास जी की भक्ति भावना का परिचय देते हुए समझाइए। [3]

[2019]

📋 Marking Scheme

(i) प्रस्तुत पद्य में श्रीकृष्ण अपनी माता यशोदा से ज़िद कर रहे हैं। वे चाँद को खिलौना समझ रहे हैं और उसे पाने का हठ कर रहे हैं। वे चन्द्रमा के सौन्दर्य पर मुग्ध हो गए हैं और उसे पाने के लिए माँ को तरह-तरह की धमकियाँ भी दे रहे हैं। प्रस्तुत पद्य वात्सल्य रस से परिपूर्ण है। इसमें श्रीकृष्ण की बाललीला का बड़ा ही सुन्दर वर्णन किया गया है। इसमें दिखाया गया है कि अबोध बालक किसी भी वस्तु को पाने का हठ कर बैठते हैं। ऐसे में माँ उन्हें बहला-फुसलाकर मना ही लेती है।

(ii) श्रीकृष्ण की माता यशोदा हैं। वे अपने पुत्र के क्रियाकलाप देखकर अत्यधिक हर्षित हो रही हैं। उनके हृदय में वात्सल्य भाव है अत: उन्हें अपने पुत्र का रूठना, मनुहार करना तथा ज़िद करना बहुत प्रिय लग रहा है। वे उन्हें बड़े प्यार से पालने में झुलाती हैं। उनसे खूब लाड़-दुलार करती हैं तथा उन्हें पुचकारती जाती हैं। जब श्रीकृष्ण आँखों में नींद भरी होने के कारण चिड़चिड़ाने लगते हैं तो वे मधुर गीत सुनाकर उन्हें सुलाने का प्रयास करती हैं। उनके मुख पर शान्ति का भाव देखकर माता यशोदा आत्मिक संतोष का अनुभव करती हैं।

(iii) बच्चे बड़े ही हठी स्वभाव के होते हैं। वे अपनी हर बात मनवाना चाहते हैं। यदि माँ बच्चे की माँग पर ध्यान नहीं देती तो वे उसे धमकियाँ देने लगते हैं। ऐसे ही बाल श्रीकृष्ण चाँद को खिलौना समझ उसे पाने का हठ कर बैठते हैं। जब यशोदा माँ उनकी माँग पर ध्यान नहीं देतीं तो वे उन्हें धमकी देते हुए कहते हैं कि यदि तुम मुझे चाँद रूपी खिलौना नहीं दोगी तो मैं तुम्हारी कोई बात नहीं मानूँगा। मैं सफ़ेद गाय का दूध भी नहीं पीऊँगा। अपने बालों की चोटी भी नहीं गुथवाऊँगा। अपने हृदय पर मोतियों की माला भी नहीं धारण करूँगा। गले में वस्त्र भी नहीं डालने दूँगा। अभी ज़मीन पर लोट जाऊँगा और तेरी गोद में भी नहीं आऊँगा। सिर्फ नंद बाबा का लाल कहलाऊँगा। तेरा सुत कभी भी नहीं बनूँगा। इस प्रकार जब कृष्ण माँ को धमकियाँ देते हैं तो वे उन्हें बहलाने लगती हैं।

(iv) बाल कृष्ण की धमकी सुनकर यशोदा माँ उन्हें बहलाने लगती हैं। वे चुपके से उनके कान में कहती हैं ताकि बलराम न सुन लें। वे कहती हैं कि तेरे लिए चाँद से भी सुन्दर नयी-नवेली दुल्हन लाऊँगी और तेरे साथ उसका ब्याह रचाऊँगी। माँ की बात सुनकर बालक श्रीकृष्ण अत्यधिक प्रसन्न हो जाते हैं। वे उनके बहकावे में आ जाते हैं। वे ब्याह के लिए इतने अधिक उत्साहित हो जाते हैं कि अपनी माँ से कहते हैं कि माँ मुझे तेरी सौगंध है, मैं अभी ब्याह करने जाऊँगा। मेरे सारे सखा बाराती बन जाएँगे और वे मंगल गीत गाएँगे। इस प्रकार अबोध श्रीकृष्ण अपनी दुल्हन को चाँद रूपी खिलौना समझकर उसे शीघ्र ही पाना चाहते हैं और उसके लिए अधीर हो उठते हैं। सूरदास जी सगुण धारा के श्रेष्ठ कवि थे, उनकी भक्ति सखा भाव दास्य भाव की थी, वे वात्सल्य रस के सम्राट थे। वह ईश्वर के समक्ष अनेक प्रकार की विनय भावना रखते थे।

Ans. **(i)** प्रस्तुत पद्य में बाल कृष्ण अपनी माता से जिद कर रहे हैं। वे चाँद को खिलौना समझ उसे प्राप्त करना चाहते हैं। वे अपनी माता से चन्द्रमा रूपी खिलौना ला देने का कहते हैं।

(ii) बाल कृष्ण की माता यशोदा हैं। श्रीकृष्ण के बाल हठ में वह बहुत प्रसन्न हैं। बालक की अबोधता व मासूमियत का आनन्द ले रही हैं। वह अपने पुत्र के बालपन, हठ और दर्शन का सुख प्राप्त कर रही हैं। वह उस सुख को निरन्तर प्राप्त करना चाहती हैं। उनका हृदय आनंदित व प्रफुल्लित है।

(iii) चाँद रूपी खिलौना न मिलने की स्थिति में बाल कृष्ण ने अपनी माँ को यह धमकियाँ दीं कि वे अपनी चोटी नहीं गुंथवाएँगे, दूध नहीं पियेंगे। वे यह भी कहते हैं कि वे मोतियों की माला नहीं पहनेंगे और कंठ का आभूषण भी नहीं पहनेंगे। वे धरती पर लोट जाएँगे और यशोदा की गोद में भी नहीं आयेंगे। वे नन्द बाबा के बेटे कहलाएँगे, यशोदा माँ के नहीं। इस प्रकार जब कृष्ण माँ को धमकियाँ देते है तो वे उन्हें बहलाने लगती हैं।

(iv) रूठे हुए कृष्ण को बहलाने के लिए यशोदा उनके कान में धीरे से कहती हैं कि यह बात दाऊ से मत कहना कि मैं तेरे लिए चाँद से भी अधिक सुन्दर दुल्हनियाँ ब्याह कर लाऊँगी। यह बात सुनकर कृष्ण प्रसन्न हो जाते हैं और कहते हैं कि वे तुरन्त विवाह करने जायेंगे उनके सभी सखा बराती होंगे और नये मंगल गीत गाये जायेंगे। सूरदास श्रीकृष्ण के अनन्य भक्त थे। श्री कृष्ण के प्रति अपनी भक्ति वे कृष्ण की बाल लीलाओं के वर्णन द्वारा करते हैं।

Chapter 7. विनय के पद (Vinay Ke Pad)

—*तुलसीदास (Tulsidas)*

Q. 1. **Read the extract given below and answer in** *Hindi* **the questions that follow:**

निम्नलिखित पद्यांश को पढ़िए और उसके नीचे लिखे प्रश्नों के उत्तर हिंदी में लिखिए:

जाके प्रिय न राम वैदेही।

तजिए ताहि कोटि बैरी सम जदपि परम सनेही।।

तज्यो पिता प्रहलाद, विभीषण बन्धु, भरत महतारी।

बलि गुरु तज्यो, कन्त ब्रज बनितिहिन, भए मुद मंगलकारी।।

नाते नेम राम के मनियत, सुहृद, सुसेव्य जहाँ लौं।

अंजन कहा आँख जेहि फूटै, बहु तक कहौं कहाँ लौं।।

(i) 'तजिए ताहि कोटि बैरी सम' से कवि क्या कहना चाहता है? स्पष्ट कीजिए। [2]

(ii) राम की भक्ति में किन-किन लोगों ने किनका त्याग किया है? [2]

(iii) 'अंजन कहा आँख जेहि फूटै, बहु तक कहौं कहाँ लौं।' पंक्ति की व्याख्या कीजिए। [3]

(iv) कवि तुलसी के इष्टप्रभु का नाम बताइए। उनकी भाषा और भक्तिभावना का परिचय दीजिए। [3]

[2020]

Ans. **(i)** कवि तुलसीदास कहते हैं कि जिसे राम-जानकी प्यारे न हों उसे करोड़ों शत्रुओं के समान त्याग देना चाहिए, चाहे वह अपना अत्यंत स्नेही और प्रिय क्यों न हो? इस प्रकार कवि तुलसी ने अपनी अनन्य भक्ति व श्रद्धा प्रभु राम और माँ जानकी (सीता) के प्रति प्रकट की है।

(ii) राम की भक्ति में प्रहलाद ने अपने पिता हिरण्यकश्यप को, विभीषण ने अपने भाई रावण को, भरत ने अपनी माता कैकेयी को, राजा बलि ने अपने गुरु शुक्राचार्य को तथा ब्रज में गोपियों ने अपने-अपने पतियों को त्याग दिया था। इसी को तो भक्ति की पराकाष्ठा कहते हैं कि जो भक्ति के मार्ग में अवरोध पैदा करता है, उसे त्याग देना ही भक्त के हित में है।

(iii) प्रस्तुत पंक्ति के द्वारा कवि तुलसीदास ने अपने आराध्य प्रभु राम के प्रति अपनी अनन्य भक्ति को दर्शाया है। इसी संदर्भ में वे आगे कहते हैं कि जिस अंजन (काजल) को लगाने से आँखें फूट जाएँ, वह अंजन ही किस काम का? कवि कहते हैं कि जिसे प्रभु राम के चरणों में प्रेम भाव हो, वही सब प्रकार से अपना परम हितैषी, पूजनीय और प्राणों से भी अधिक प्रिय है तथा इसके विपरीत जो राम के प्रति स्नेह व भक्ति न रखता हो, वह सदा के लिए अप्रिय और त्याज्य है।

(iv) कवि तुलसी के इष्टप्रभु का नाम 'राम' है। उनकी भाषा ब्रज और अवधी थी।

भक्तिभावना—भगवान राम के अनन्य भक्त हैं राम भक्ति शाखा के प्रमुख कवि हैं। इनकी भक्ति में दास्य-भावना है। इन्होंने रामचरितमानस में राम के चरित्र का विस्तृत व आदर्श वर्णन कर उन्हें मर्यादा पुरुषोत्तम बना दिया है।

Chapter 9.   चलना हमारा काम है (Chalna Hamara Kaam Hai)
—शिवमंगल सिंह 'सुमन' (Shivmangal Singh 'Suman')

Q. 1. **Read the extract given below and answer in *Hindi* the questions that follow:**

निम्नलिखित पद्यांश को पढ़िए और उसके नीचे लिखे प्रश्नों के उत्तर हिंदी में लिखिए:

"मैं पूर्णता की खोज में
दर-दर भटकता ही रहा
प्रत्येक पग पर कुछ-न-कुछ
रोड़ा अटकता ही रहा
पर हो निराशा क्यों मुझे ?
जीवन इसी का नाम है।
चलना हमारा काम है।"

(i) कवि ने मनुष्य के जीवन के बारे में क्या कहा है तथा क्यों ?   [2]

(ii) कवि के अनुसार जीवन का महत्व किसमें है? स्पष्ट कीजिए।   [2]

(iii) जीवन में सुख-दुःख और आशा-निराशा के प्रति हमारा क्या दृष्टिकोण होना चाहिए? अपने दुःखों और निराशा के लिए हमें किसको दोष देना उचित नहीं है तथा क्यों? समझाकर लिखिए।   [3]

(iv) प्रस्तुत कविता के माध्यम से कवि ने पाठकों को क्या संदेश दिया है?   [3]

[2018]

📋 Marking Scheme

(i) कवि ने मनुष्य के जीवन के बारे में यह कहा है कि मनुष्य का जीवन सुख-दुख और आशा-निराशा का नाम है। सुख और दुख जीवन का एक भाग है जो सभी के जीवन में आता-जाता रहता है। दुख आने पर निराश नहीं होना चाहिए क्योंकि जीवन की यही परिभाषा है कि जीवन में सुखों और दुखों को सहन करते हुए निरन्तर आगे की ओर बढ़ते रहना चाहिए क्योंकि जीवन इसी का नाम है। किसी को भी जीवन में पूर्णता प्राप्त नहीं होती।

(ii) कवि के अनुसार जीवन का महत्व गतिशीलता में ही है। यदि हम चलते रहते हैं तभी हम जीवित हैं। जीवन की गतिशीलता ही जीवन के महत्व को प्रस्तुत करती है। किसी भी सुख-दुख और आशा-निराशा के कारण जीवन रुकता नहीं है बल्कि निरन्तर गतिशील रहता है। इस प्रकार जीवन में गतिमान रहना और चलते रहना ही हमारा काम है अर्थात जीवन के हर पहलू को सहजता से स्वीकार करने में है।

(iii) जीवन में सुख-दुख और आशा-निराशा के प्रति हमारा यह दृष्टिकोण होना चाहिए कि शान्त और समान भाव से सुख और दुख के क्षणों को जीते हुए यह समझना चाहिए कि इस संसार में वह अकेला ऐसा प्राणी नहीं है जिसे दुख सहन करना पड़ रहा है। अपने दुखों और निराशा के लिए हमें ईश्वर या भाग्य को दोष देना उचित नही है

क्योंकि सुख-दुख तो जीवन का एक भाग है जो सभी के जीवन में आता-जाता है। इससे दुखी नहीं होना चाहिए। लगातार कर्म करना और चलते रहना ही हमारी नियति (भाग्य) है। गति जीवन का शाश्वत सत्य है। इस बात को हमें कभी भूलना नहीं चाहिए।

(iv) प्रस्तुत कविता के माध्यम से कवि ने पाठकों को यह सन्देश दिया है कि गति ही हमारे जीवन का शाश्वत सत्य है। चलना जिन्दगी का दूसरा नाम है और रुकना मृत्यु का सूचक है। हँस-बोलकर जिन्दगी जीना सरल होता है जबकि अपनी अपूर्णता या दुख को देखकर निराशा में डूब जाना मूर्खता है। अपने दुखों और निराशा के लिए ईश्वर को दोष देना अनुचित है। जो व्यक्ति गिरकर सँभल जाए, निराशा में आशा की किरण खोज ले, अमृत मिश्रित ज़हर को हँसकर पी जाए और जिन्दगी से कोई शिकायत न करे उसी का जीवन सच्चा जीवन है। अतः चलना हमारा काम है और हमें अपने जीवन-पथ पर निरन्तर चलते रहना चाहिए।

Ans. **(i)** कवि ने मनुष्य के जीवन के बारे में कहा कि जीवन से सफलता के साथ असफलता, सुख के साथ दुःख और सरलता के साथ बाधाएँ लगी रहती हैं। इसलिए बाधाओं को देखकर निराश नहीं होना चाहिए। जीवन इसी का नाम है। किसी को भी जीवन में पूर्णता प्राप्त नही होती है।

(ii) कवि के अनुसार जीवन का महत्व निरंतर चलते रहने में है। जो लोग अपने जीवन की गति को निरंतर कायम रखते हैं वे ही जीवन में सफल होते हैं।

(iii) जीवन में सुख-दुःख और आशा-निराशा आने पर भी हमें उनसे निराश नहीं होना चाहिए। इसके लिए हमें ईश्वर और भाग्य को दोष नहीं देना चाहिए कि मेरा भाग्य मेरे विपरीत चल रहा है या ईश्वर मेरा साथ नहीं दे रहा है। बल्कि अपने कर्म को निडरता और दृढ़तापूर्वक करते हुए आगे बढ़ना चाहिए और अपना भाग्य स्वयं बनाना चाहिए। क्योंकि गति जीवन का सत्य है।

(iv) कवि पाठकों को संदेश देता है कि जीवन में विकास की ओर हमेशा अग्रसर रहना चाहिए। कवि कहना चाहता है कि हमारे जीवन में सुख-दुःख, आशा-निराशा आते-जाते रहते हैं कभी-कभी अपने भी हमारा साथ छोड़ जाते हैं, लेकिन हार न मानते हुए अपने लक्ष्य की ओर बढ़ते रहना चाहिए क्योंकि चलना हमारा काम है।

Novel: Naya Raasta

Long Answer Type Questions

Q. 1. Read the extract given below and answer in *Hindi* the questions that follow:

निम्नलिखित गद्यांश को पढ़िए और उसके नीचे लिखे प्रश्नों के उत्तर हिंदी में लिखिए:

मेहमानों का शानदार स्वागत किया गया। मीनू को देखने के लिए अमित, उसके पिता मायारामजी, माताजी व छोटी बहन मधु आये थे। उनके आतिथ्य में किसी प्रकार की कमी नहीं छोड़ी गयी थी। परिवार के हर सदस्य के हृदय में नया जोश व उमंग था, मानो उनके घर कोई देवता आ गये हो।

(i) मेहमान कौन हैं? वे कहाँ और क्यों आए हैं? [2]

(ii) किसके, हृदय में जोश और उमंग था? क्यों? [2]

(iii) मेहमानों के स्वागत के लिए क्या-क्या तैयारियाँ की गई? [3]

(iv) अमित और मीनू के बीच हुई बातचीत को संक्षेप में लिखिए। [2020] [3]

Ans. **(i)** मेहमान के रूप में मायाराम, उनकी पत्नी, बेटा अमित व छोटी बेटी मधु आए हैं। वे सभी दयाराम के घर उनकी बड़ी बेटी मीनू के विवाह के सिलसिले में उसे देखने आए हैं।

(ii) दयाराम के परिवार के हर सदस्य के हृदय में जोश और उमंग था। दयाराम की बड़ी बेटी मीनू को देखने मायाराम व उनका परिवार आया हुआ था। बेटी के विवाह के सिलसिले में कई जगह असफल होने के बाद इस बार उन्हें व उनके परिवार को इस बात का विश्वास है कि उनकी बेटी मीनू का रिश्ता मायाराम जी के बेटे अमित के साथ पक्का हो जाएगा। इसलिए दयाराम का परिवार काफी उमंग व जोश में था।

(iii) मेहमानों के स्वागत के लिए विभिन्न प्रकार की तैयारियाँ कीं गई थीं। घर की सारी चीजें झाड़-पोंछकर यथास्थान लगा दी गई थीं। बैठक को विशेष रूप से सुसज्जित किया गया था। घर में विभिन्न प्रकार के व्यंजन बनाए गए थे। अनेक प्रकार की मिठाइयाँ बाजार से मँगाई गई थीं। इस तरह मेहमानों के स्वागत के लिए शानदार तैयारियाँ की गई थीं।

(iv) अमित ने मीनू से उसके एम.ए. के परिणाम के बारे में पूछा तो मीनू उसे बताती है कि वह प्रथम श्रेणी में पास हुई है। इस पर अमित ने प्रसन्नता के साथ मीनू की प्रशंसा की। अमित ने मीनू से उसके घरेलू कार्यों की रूचि के संदर्भ में प्रश्न किया। मीनू ने उत्तर दिया कि वह घर के सभी कामों, जैसे सिलाई, बुनाई, कटाई, खाना बनाना, पेंटिंग आदि करने में कुशल है। 'अमित'

मीनू से पूछता है कि क्या वह संयुक्त परिवार में उसके माता-पिता व बहन के साथ रहना पसंद करेगी? मीनू इस प्रश्न पर अपनी सहमति प्रदान करती है।

Q. 2. Read the extract given below and answer in *Hindi* the questions that follow:

निम्नलिखित गद्यांश को पढ़िए और उसके नीचे लिखे प्रश्नों के उत्तर हिंदी में लिखिए:

धनीमल जी व मायाराम जी ने आपस में कुछ बातें की और सब वहाँ से उठकर चल दिए। अमित व सरिता को एकांत में बात करने का अवसर दिया गया। अमित ने सरिता से कुछ प्रश्न किए।

(i) धनीमल जी और मायाराम जी का परिचय देते हुए बताइए कि उनमें किस विषय पर बातचीत हो रही थी? [2]

(ii) सरिता को देखकर अमित के मन में क्या विचार आए थे? स्पष्ट कीजिए। [2]

(iii) अमित के माता-पिता उसका रिश्ता सरिता के साथ क्यों करना चाहते थे? इस सम्बन्ध में उन्होंने क्या तर्क दिये? [3]

(iv) अमित के चरित्र पर प्रकाश डालिए। [2020] [3]

Ans. **(i)** धनीमल जी मेरठ के रहने वाले धनी व्यक्तियों में से एक हैं। मायाराम अमित के पिता थे। मायाराम जी धनीमल जी के घर पर उनकी बेटी सरिता को देखने आए हैं। दोनों के बीच सरिता और अमित के विवाह के दहेज के विषय पर बातचीत हो रही थी।

(ii) सरिता को देखते ही अमित के पैरों तले जमीन खिसक गई। उसने मन ही मन अनुभव किया कि नाक-नक्शे में सरिता से कहीं ज्यादा मीनू ही अच्छी है। नाक-नक्शे में सिर्फ उसकी आँखें ही बड़ी थीं। रंग तो मीनू के सामने कहीं ज्यादा दबा हुआ था।

(iii) अमित के माता-पिता उसका रिश्ता सरिता के साथ करना चाहते थे क्योंकि वह अमीर घर से थी और दहेज में पाँच लाख रुपये लाने वाली थी। अमित की माँ यह तर्क देती है कि सरिता में कोई बुराई नहीं है। देखने में वह उन्हें अच्छी लगी। भले ही सरिता का रंग थोड़ा-सा दबा हुआ है, पर वह भी शादी के बाद निखर आएगा। रंग से क्या लेना-देना, दुनिया में गोरा-काला दो ही रंग होते हैं, पर शादी तो सबकी होती है।

(iv) 'अमित' मायाराम जी का पुत्र है। वह संस्कारी, जिम्मेदार, आज्ञाकारी पुत्र था। वह दहेज विरोधी था।

मीनू पसंद होने पर भी वह सरिता से शादी करने के लिए तैयार हो जाता है। वह माता-पिता का विरोध नहीं करता। दुर्घटनाग्रस्त होकर अस्पताल में भर्ती होने पर वह मीनू से क्षमा माँगता है। अपने किए पर शर्मिन्दा होता है। अंत में अमित व मीनू का विवाह हो जाता है।

Q. 3. Read the extract given below and answer in *Hindi* the questions that follow:

निम्नलिखित गद्यांश को पढ़िए और उसके नीचे लिखे प्रश्नों के उत्तर हिंदी में लिखिए:

मीनू आज दुल्हन के रूप में कितनी सुन्दर लग रही थी, मीनू दुल्हन बनी, उसकी डोली सजी और अपने पिया संग ससुराल को चल दी।

(i) मीनू ने पहले शादी से क्यों मना कर दिया था? [2]

(ii) मीनू अब शादी करने के लिए क्यों तैयार हो गई? [2]

(iii) तब की मीनू और अब की मीनू में क्या अंतर है? [3]

(iv) हमारे समाज में फैली 'दहेज की कुप्रथा' पर एक टिप्पणी लिखिए। [2020] [3]

Ans. **(i)** मीनू ने पहले शादी से मना कर दिया था क्योंकि रंग साँवला होने के कारण उसे बार-बार लड़के वाले अस्वीकार कर देते हैं। मीनू समाज की कठोरता को समझती है। लड़के वाले लड़की के गुणों को अनदेखा कर बाहरी सुंदरता और धन को प्रमुख समझते हैं।

(ii) अब मीनू एक प्रतिष्ठित वकील बन गई थी। उसने आत्मविश्वास व लगन से विशेष ख्याति प्राप्त कर ली थी। आज वह समाज में सिर उठाकर जीने के काबिल बन चुकी थी। उसने अपने बचपन के सपने को पूरा कर लिया था। इसलिए मीनू अब शादी करने के लिए तैयार हो गई थी।

(iii) उपन्यास के आरंभ में मीनू मानसिक व भावनात्मक स्तर पर कमजोर युवती थी। वह अपने आपको दुर्भाग्यशाली मानती है। वह जीवन से निराश हो जाती है। साँवले रंग-रूप तथा कद-काठी को लेकर कई बार लड़के वाले उससे शादी करने से इन्कार कर देते हैं। वह हीनभावना से ग्रस्त रहती है। तब की मीनू का मन दु:ख, निराशा व उदासी से भरा था। उसे आत्मग्लानि होने लगी थी।

तब की मीनू और अब की मीनू में जमीन-आसमान का अंतर था। अब वह प्रतिष्ठित वकील बन चुकी थी। अपने आत्मविश्वास व रोबदार व्यक्तित्व के कारण बहुत प्रसिद्ध हो चुकी थी। अब वह आत्मनिर्भर थी। स्वाभिमानी व उदार चरित्र की बेटी को पाकर उसके माँ-बाप भी अपने आप को धन्य महसूस कर रहे थे।

(iv) दहेज प्रथा एक सामाजिक अभिशाप है। प्राचीन काल में माता-पिता सामान व धन देते थे। किन्तु धीरे-धीरे इस कुप्रथा ने उग्र रूप धारण कर लिया। अब दहेज लड़की के माता-पिता को अपनी इच्छानुसार नहीं वरन् वर पक्ष की इच्छानुसार देना पड़ता है। दहेज के अभाव

में युवा पुत्री को कुंआरी बैठी देखकर घर का वातावरण तनावपूर्ण हो उठता है। ऐसे वातावरण में जब युवती अपना मानसिक सन्तुलन खो बैठती है तभी वह आत्महत्या के लिए विवश हो उठती है।

उपन्यास 'नया रास्ता' की मुख्य पात्रा मीनू भी इसका शिकार होती है। गुणवती होने पर भी उसे रूप और दहेज की कमी होने के कारण लड़के वाले अस्वीकार कर देते हैं।

Q. 4. Read the extract given below and answer in *Hindi* the questions that follow:

निम्नलिखित गद्यांश को पढ़िए और उसके नीचे लिखे प्रश्नों के उत्तर हिंदी में लिखिए:

"मीनू......अरे मीनू कैसे कर सकती है? यह रस्म तो शादीशुदा बहन ही कर सकती है। मीनू की तो अभी शादी भी नहीं हुई।"

(i) उपर्युक्त कथन की वक्ता कौन है उसका परिचय दीजिए। [2]

(ii) वक्ता ने क्यों कहा कि मीनू यह रस्म नहीं कर सकती? यहाँ किस रस्म की बात हो रही है? [2]

(iii) वक्ता की बात सुनकर मीनू तथा मीनू की माँ की स्थिति का वर्णन करते हुए बताइए कि क्या उसके द्वारा वह रस्म पूरी की गई थी? स्पष्ट कीजिए। [3]

(iv) "एक अविवाहित स्त्री को समाज में उचित सम्मान नहीं मिलता।" उपन्यास के आधार पर अपने विचार लिखिए। [3]
[2019]

📋 Marking Scheme

(i) उपर्युक्त कथन की वक्ता बुआजी है जो मीनू के पिता की बहन है वह स्पष्टवक्ता, कटुभाषी महिला हैं।

(ii) वक्ता ने यह कथन इसलिए कहा क्योंकि वह रस्म सिर्फ शादीशुदा बहन ही कर सकती है और मीनू अविवाहित थी। मीनू की छोटी बहन का विवाह हो रहा है। यहाँ विवाह की रस्म जिसमें बड़ी बहन को आरती उतारनी होती है, उसी रस्म की बात हो रही है।

(iii) वक्ता की बात सुनकर मीनू का चेहरा मुरझा गया। मीनू के मुरझाये चेहरे को देखकर माँ उसकी मन:स्थिति समझ गई और वक्ता से बोली कि ''आजकल कौन मानता है इन सब बातों को? मीनू ही करेगी सारी रस्में।'' उन्होंने पूजा का थाल सजा कर मीनू को दे दिया। आस-पड़ोस की सभी महिलाओं की कटाक्षपूर्ण निगाहें मीनू को बेचैन कर रहीं थी किंतु फिर भी मीनू के द्वारा ही वह रस्म पूरी की गई।

(iv) ''एक अविवाहित स्त्री को समाज में उचित सम्मान नहीं मिलता।'' यह कथन उपन्यास के आधार पर बिलकुल उपयुक्त है। उपन्यास की नायिका मीनू पढ़ाई के साथ-साथ घर के सभी कार्यों में कुशल है। सामाजिक कारणों के कारण वह विवाह न करने का निर्णय लेती है। उसकी छोटी बहन के विवाह के समय अड़ोस-पड़ोस की महिलाएँ उसके अविवाहित होने पर कटाक्ष करती है तथा उसकी बुआ आरती की रस्म करने के लिए इसलिए मना करती है कि वह अविवाहित है। अत: इससे पता चलता है कि अविवाहित स्त्री को आज भी समाज में उपेक्षा की दृष्टि से देखा जाता है तथा लोगों के ताने सुनने पड़ते हैं।

Ans. **(i)** उपर्युक्त कथन की वक्ता दयाराम जी की बहन और मीनू की बुआ है। बुआजी पुराने विचारों की थीं। वह लड़कियों की शिक्षा में विश्वास नहीं रखती थीं। उनके अनुसार लड़कियों का विवाह कर उन्हें ससुराल भेजना ही उचित था। वह स्पष्ट वक्ता और कटु भाषी महिला थीं।

(ii) वक्ता ने कहा कि मीनू यह रस्म नहीं कर सकती, क्योंकि मीनू शादीशुदा नहीं थी। छोटी बहन की शादी में, एक रस्म के अनुसार बड़ी बहन को आरती उतारनी होती है। आशा की आरती, अविवाहित होने के कारण मीनू नहीं कर सकती थी।

(iii) बुआजी की बात सुनकर मीनू और उसकी माँ का चेहरा मुरझा जाता है। वह उदास हो जाती हैं। मीनू के मुरझाये चेहरे को देखकर माँ उसकी मन:स्थिति समझ जाती है और बुआजी से कहती है कि आजकल इन सब बातों को कोई नहीं मानता। बड़ी बहन होने के नाते मीनू सारी रस्में करेगी। ऐसा कहते हुए माँ पूजा का थाल सजाकर मीनू को देती है और उससे आरती उतारने की रस्म पूरी करवाती है।

(iv) हाँ यह सत्य है कि एक अविवाहित स्त्री को समाज में उचित सम्मान नहीं मिलता। उपन्यास में यह प्रमाण प्रत्यक्ष है। आशा की शादी की रस्में करने के लिए मीनू को मना किया जाता है, क्योंकि वह अविवाहित थी। आशा के विवाह में आई महिलाएँ भी मीनू के अविवाहित होने पर तीखे कटाक्ष करती हैं कि आजकल की लड़कियों के बड़े नखरे होते हैं, पढ़ाई के चक्कर में कौन जवान बेटियों को घर में रखता है? आज भी समाज में लड़कियों की शिक्षा को नहीं बल्कि उनके विवाह को अधिक महत्व दिया जाता है।

Q. 5. **Read the extract given below and answer in *Hindi* the questions that follow:**

निम्नलिखित गद्यांश को पढ़िए और उसके नीचे लिखे प्रश्नों के उत्तर हिंदी में लिखिए:

आखिर सरिता को देखने का दिन आ ही गया। अमित के घर में विशेष चहल-पहल थी। अमित की माताजी में विशेष उत्साह नज़र आ रहा था। माताजी के कहने में आकर उसके पिता भी इस रिश्ते में रुचि लेने लगे थे। अमित की बहन मधु भी अपनी होने वाली भाभी को देखने के लिए उत्सुक थी।

(i) अमित कौन है? उसका संक्षिप्त परिचय दीजिये। **[2]**

(ii) विशेष चहल-पहल का क्या कारण था? इस अवसर पर अमित की स्थिति स्पष्ट कीजिए। **[2]**

(iii) मायारामजी को स्वर्ग की अनुभूति कहाँ और कैसे होती है और क्यों होती है? **[3]**

(iv) अमित और सरिता के बीच हुई बातचीत को संक्षेप में लिखिये। **[3]**

[2019]

(i) उपन्यास का प्रमुख पात्र 'अमित' मायाराम जी का पुत्र है। वह दूसरों का सम्मान करना जानता है। वह दहेज विरोधी व संस्कारी है। अमित मीनू के रंग-रूप, व्यवहार तथा सादगी से प्रभावित है। अंत में अमित और मीनू का विवाह हो जाता है।

(ii) विशेष चहल-पहल अमित के घर में थी। अमित का रिश्ता सरिता से तय होने जा रहा था। उसके माता-पिता पूरी रुचि दिखलाते हुए सरिता को देखने के लिए तैयार थे। इसलिए घर के सभी सदस्य उत्साहित नज़र आ रहे थे। इस अवसर पर अमित के चेहरे पर उदासी थी वह सोच रहा था कि उसके माता-पिता उसे एक धनी घर की लड़की के हाथों बेच रहे हैं।

(iii) मायाराम जी अपने परिवार के साथ अपने बेटे अमित के लिए धनीमल जी के घर उनकी बेटी सरिता के देखने के लिए आए थे क्योंकि सरिता के साथ अमित का रिश्ता तय हो रहा था। धनीमल जी ने मायाराम जी के लिए कार भेजी थी। जब मायाराम जी, उनकी पत्नी, अमित व उसकी बहन मधु कार में बैठकर धनीमल जी के घर पहुँचे और कार में से उतर कर सब ने घर के अंदर प्रवेश किया तो उन्हें लगा मानो वे स्वर्ग में आ गए हों क्योंकि धनीमल जी की कोठी के बाहर लॉन में घास मखमल के सामान बिछी थी। लॉन में बेंत की सुंदर रंग-बिरंगी कुर्सियाँ पड़ी थीं। रंग-बिरंगे फूलों के गमले कोठी की शोभा में चार-चाँद लगा रहे थे। पूरा वातावरण तथा वहाँ की सुख समृद्धि देखकर स्वर्ग के समान आनंद की अनुभूति करा रहा था।

(iv) अमित और सरिता को जब बातचीत का अवसर प्राप्त हुआ तो अमित ने सरिता से उसकी पसंद, उसकी रुचि, कार्य-व्यवहार के बारे में तरह-तरह के प्रश्न किए। जैसे उसकी किस चीज में रूचि है– अपनी रूचि के अलावा वह घर के काम-काज कर लेती होगी, शादी के बाद यदि घर का काम करना पड़ा तो किस प्रकार करेगी। उसकी पढ़ाई-लिखाई (एजुकेशन) क्या है? अमित के इन सभी सवालों का सरिता ने भी बड़ी बेबाकी से जवाब दिया। उसने बताया कि उसकी विशेष रूचि पेंटिंग और कार ड्राइविंग में है। घर के काम उसे करने नहीं आते उसकी जरूरत भी उसे नहीं पड़ती है क्योंकि सारा काम नौकर-चाकर करते हैं। शादी के बाद भी पिताजी एक नौकर की व्यवस्था कर देंगे, वही सारा काम कर देगा। एजुकेशन के बारे में बताते हुए उसने कहा कि उसने सेकंड डिवीज़न से बी.ए. पास किया है। आदि सारी व्यवहारिक बातें उन दोनों में हुई।

Ans. **(i)** उपन्यास का प्रमुख पात्र 'अमित' मायाराम जी का पुत्र है। वह दूसरों का सम्मान करना जानता है। वह दहेज विरोधी व संस्कारी है। अमित मीनू के रंग-रूप, व्यवहार तथा सादगी से प्रभावित है। अंत में अमित और मीनू का विवाह हो जाता है।

(ii) अमित के घर में विशेष चहल-पहल होने का कारण यह था कि अमित, उसके माता-पिता व उसकी बहन मधु, अमित के लिए लड़की देखने धनीमल जी के घर जा रहे थे। इस अवसर पर अमित के चेहरे पर उदासी थी। इस कल्पना मात्र से ही वह उदास था कि उसके माता-पिता उसे एक धनी घर की लड़की के हाथों बेचना चाहते थे।

(iii) मायाराम जी को स्वर्ग की अनुभूति धनीमल जी के घर पर होती है। धनीमल जी के घर जाने के लिए कार भी वे ही भेजते हैं। कार जैसे ही धनीमल जी की कोठी के बाहर रुकती है और ड्राइवर कार का दरवाजा खोलता है, तो मायाराम जी को लगता है जैसे वे कोई बड़े अफसर बन गए हों। आलीशान कोठी के अन्दर जाते ही उन्हें लगा मानो स्वर्ग में आ गए हो। कोठी के बाहर लॉन में घास मखमल के समान बिछी थीं। लॉन में बेंत की सुन्दर रंग-बिरंगी कुर्सियाँ पड़ी थी। धनीमल जी के घर पर उनका विशेष स्वागत हुआ। घर के सभी नौकर खाकी वर्दी में थे। अनेक प्रकार के मिष्ठान, फल व मेवा उनके सामने रखे गए। मायारामजी को मध्यम वर्गीय परिवार के होने के कारण धनीमल जी की आलीशान कोठी में स्वर्ग की अनुभूति होती है।

(iv) अमित व सरिता का वार्तालाप एकांत में शुरू हुआ। अमित ने सरिता से उसकी रुचि, शिक्षा, घरेलू काम-काज आदि के बारे में पूछा। सरिता ने अमित के प्रश्नों के उत्तर में कहा कि उसकी रुचि पेंटिंग व कार ड्राइविंग में विशेष है। उसने यह भी बताया कि वह बी.ए. द्वितीय श्रेणी में पास है। घरेलू काम-काज उसे नहीं आता है। घर का सारा काम नौकर-चाकर ही करते हैं। शादी के बाद भी वह सारा काम नौकर द्वारा ही कराएगी। सरिता की बातों को सुनकर अमित चकित रह जाता है।

Q. 6. Read the extract given below and answer in *Hindi* the questions that follow:

निम्नलिखित गद्यांश को पढ़िए और उसके नीचे लिखे प्रश्नों के उत्तर हिंदी में लिखिए:

मीनू के हृदय में बचपन से ही अपंगों के लिए दया की भावना थी, परन्तु मनोहर को तो वैसे वह बचपन से जानती थी। इसीलिए उसकी यह हालत उससे देखी नहीं जा रही थी। मीनू ने मन ही मन निश्चय किया कि वह किसी न किसी रूप में मनोहर की सहायता अवश्य करेगी। विवाह के फालतू खर्च में से कुछ रुपये बचाकर अपाहिज मनोहर की सहायता करने का उसने संकल्प लिया।

(i) मनोहर कौन था? वह मीनू के पास क्यों आया था?　　　　**[2]**

(ii) उसकी यह दशा कैसे हो गयी थी? संक्षेप में समझाइए।　　　　**[2]**

(iii) मीनू ने मन ही मन क्या निश्चय किया और मनोहर की सहायता कैसे की?　　　　**[3]**

(iv) मीनू के इस कार्य से आपको क्या प्रेरणा मिलती है? क्या आपने भी कभी किसी की इस प्रकार से सहायता की है, समझाइए।　　　　**[3]**

[2019]

(i) मनोहर राजो का चचेरा भाई था। राजो, मीनू के यहाँ काम करती थी और उसके साथ मेरठ भी गई थी। मनोहर बचपन में अक्सर राजो के साथ उसके घर आता था। अब वह अपंग हो गया था। उसके पास रोजी-रोटी का कोई साधन नहीं था। वह मीनू के घर काम की तलाश में आया था। उसने सोचा कि विवाह वाला घर है तो उसके योग्य कोई न कोई काम निकल ही आएगा।

(ii) मनोहर एक स्वस्थ युवक था परन्तु एक दुर्घटना में वह अपंग हो गया था। वह छोटी उम्र में ही काम करने लग गया था। वह एक फैक्ट्री में नौकरी करता था। एक दिन काम करते-करते उसका एक पैर मशीन में आ गया और कट गया। पैर के साथ उसकी सीधे हाथ की दो अंगुलियाँ भी कट गई थीं। इस प्रकार वह अपंग हो गया था।

(iii) मनोहर के साथ हुई दुर्घटना के बारे में जानकर मीनू बहुत उदास हो गई थी। नियति पर किसी का कोई जोर नहीं। इस घटना ने मनोहर की ज़िंदगी में एक तूफ़ान ला खड़ा किया था। मनोहर के ये शब्द कि कौन मुझ अपाहिज को नौकरी देगा, मीनू का हृदय द्रवित हो उठा था। उसने मन ही मन निश्चय कर लिया कि वह किसी न किसी रूप में मनोहर की सहायता अवश्य करेगी। उसने विवाह के फालतू खर्च में से कुछ रुपये बचाकर अपाहिज मनोहर की सहायता करने का संकल्प ले लिया।

मीनू भावुक तथा संवेदनशील युवती थी। बचपन से ही उसके हृदय में अपंगों के लिए दया भावना थी। मनोहर को वैसे ही वह बचपन से जानती थी अतः उसकी यह हालत उससे देखी नहीं जा रही थी। वह बहुत समझदार थी। उसका मानना था कि यदि हर संपन्न व्यक्ति अपनी ज़िंदगी में किसी एक अपंग व्यक्ति की सहायता कर उसे कोई छोटा सा काम करा दे तो हमारे देश से इन अपंगों की बेरोजगारी की समस्या दूर हो जाएगी।

(iv) मीनू ने अपने विवाह के फ़िज़ूल के खर्चों में से पाँच हज़ार रुपये निकालकर मनोहर को पान की एक दुकान खुलवा दी। एक पैर न होने के कारण वह चल-फिर नहीं सकता था फिर उसकी सीधे हाथ की दो अंगुलियाँ भी नहीं थीं। ऐसे में वह एक स्थान पर बैठकर अपनी बाकी तीन अंगुलियों के सहारे पान तो लगा ही सकता था। इस प्रकार मीनू ने अपाहिज मनोहर की सहायता कर मानवता का धर्म निभाया।

'परहित सरिस धर्म नहीं भाई'– अर्थात परोपकार से बड़ा कोई धर्म नहीं है। मीनू के इस परोपकार भरे कार्य को देखकर हमें अपंगों की सहायता करने की प्रेरणा मिलती है। यदि प्रत्येक संपन्न व्यक्ति अपनी ज़िंदगी में किसी एक अपंग व्यक्ति की सहायता कर उसे छोटा सा काम करा दे तो हमारे देश में इन अपंगों की बेरोजगारी की समस्या नहीं रहेगी। इस प्रसंग से हमें यह भी प्रेरणा मिलती है कि विवाह में फिजूलखर्ची से बचना चाहिए। हाँ मैंने भी एक बार एक अपंग व्यक्ति की सहायता की थी जिस से उसका जीवन ही बदल गया था। आज भी मैं उसे अपने घर के सदस्य की भाँति मानती हूँ।

Ans. **(i)** मनोहर राजो का चचेरा भाई था। राजो, मीनू के यहाँ काम करती थी और उसके साथ मेरठ भी गई थी। मनो. हर बचपन में अक्सर राजो के साथ उसके घर आता था। अब वह अपंग हो गया था। उसके पास रोजी-रोटी का कोई साधन भी नहीं था। वह मीनू के घर काम की

तलाश में आया था। उसने सोचा कि विवाह वाला घर है तो उसके योग्य कोई-न-कोई काम निकल ही आएगा।

(ii) मनोहर को छोटी उम्र में ही फैक्ट्री में नौकरी करनी पड़ी थी। एक दिन काम करते-करते उसका पैर मशीन में आ जाता है। पैर के साथ उसके सीधे हाथ की दो अंगुलियाँ भी कट जाती हैं। इस प्रकार वह अपंग हो गया था।

(iii) मीनू ने मन ही मन यह निश्चय किया कि वह मनोहर की सहायता अवश्य करेगी। विवाह के फालतू खर्च व पंडाल की सजावट से कुछ रुपये बचाकर वह मनोहर की सहायता करने का संकल्प लेती है। पाँच हजार रुपये बचाकर वह मनोहर को उसके घर के सामने ही पान की दुकान खुलवा देती है। इस तरह मीनू की दया भावना से अपंग मनोहर की ज़िन्दगी सुधर जाती है।

(iv) मीनू के इस कार्य से हमें यह प्रेरणा मिलती है कि हमें शादी-ब्याह, जन्मदिन आदि उत्सवों में फिजूलखर्च न करके, उन पैसों से किसी अपंग या जरुरतमंद की सहायता करनी चाहिए। यदि प्रत्येक सम्पन्न व्यक्ति अपनी ज़िन्दगी में किसी एक अपंग की सहायता कर उसे कोई रोजगार करा दे तो हमारे देश में अपंगों की बेरोजगारी की समस्या दूर हो जायेगी।

हाँ, मैंने भी अपनी पॉकेट मनी से पैसे बचाकर एक गरीब बच्चे को पढ़ने के लिए किताबें लाकर दीं। ऐसा करके मुझे बहुत अच्छा लगा। मीनू का हर गुण हमें अपने जीवन में अपनाना चाहिए।

Q. 7. **Read the extract given below and answer in** *Hindi* **the questions that follow:**

निम्नलिखित अवतरण को पढ़िए और उसके नीचे लिखे प्रश्नों के उत्तर हिंदी में लिखिए:

अमित मेज़ पर बैठा खाना खाने लगा। माँ भी उसके पास बैठ गई। बैठे-बैठे वह न जाने किन विचारों में खो गई और एकटक अमित की ओर ही देखती रही।

(i) माँ अमित की तरफ देखते हुए क्या सोच रही थी? [2]

(ii) दीपक कौन है? उन्हें किस बात का कार्ड मिला? [2]

(iii) मधु के बारे में माँ ने अमित से क्या कहा? [3]

(iv) माँ को घर में बहू की कमी क्यों अखरती थी? [3]

[2018]

📋 Marking Scheme

(i) अमित जब खाना खा रहा था तो माँ उसके पास बैठकर उसको एकटक देख रही थी तो अमित ने पूछा कि माँ क्यों विकल हो? माँ कहती है कि धनीमल की बेटी से सम्बन्ध टूटने के बाद वह शादी के लिए तैयार ही नहीं है। दीपक उम्र में कम है पर उसकी शादी हो रही है परन्तु तुम..... उससे बड़े होते हुए भी तुम्हारी शादी नहीं हो पायी है। –और सोच रही थी कि उसको कितना अरमान था बहू लाने का। वह सपने सँजोए बैठी थी कि जब अमित की बहू घर में आएगी तो रौनक बढ़ जाएगी। बेटी का अधिकतर समय तो कॉलेज और पढ़ाई में लग जाता था। मायाराम जी व अमित फैक्ट्री चले जाते थे।

(ii) दीपक अमित की माँ के भाई का लड़का है। माँ को दीपक की शादी का कार्ड मिला। जिसमें शनिवार की शादी थी तथा रविवार को प्रीतिभोज था। वह बहुत प्रसन्न है। बहुत दिनों से वह भाई के यहाँ कानपुर नहीं गई है। अब शादी के बहाने जाकर कुछ दिनों तक वहाँ रहेगी।

(iii) अमित की बहन मधु के बारे में माँ ने अमित से कहा कि मधु भी शादी के योग्य हो गई है। वह उसकी शादी करना चाहती है। परन्तु उससे पहले अमित की शादी हो जाती तो अच्छा था क्योंकि वह मधु से सात साल बड़ा है। घर में पहले बहू आएगी तो मधु की शादी में हाथ बँटाएगी। बहू घर के काम में भी मदद करेगी।

(iv) घर में बहू होगी तो उसका अकेलापन दूर होगा। घर के कामों में उसे मदद मिलेगी। मधु की शादी में भी वह उसका हाथ बँटाएगी। मायारामजी और अमित के काम पर जाने के बाद उसे अकेलेपन में बहू की कमी विशेष रूप से अखरती है। अमित हर बार शादी की बात टाल जाता है।

Ans. **(i)** माँ अमित की तरफ देखकर सोच रही थी कि दीपक अमित से दो वर्ष छोटा है और उसका विवाह हो रहा है और सोच रही थी कि उसको कितना अरमान था बहू लाने का। वह सपने सँजोए बैठी थी कि जब अमित की बहू घर में आएगी तो रौनक बढ़ जाएगी। बेटी का अधिकतर समय तो कॉलेज और पढ़ाई में लग जाता था। मायाराम जी व अमित फैक्ट्री चले जाते थे।

(ii) दीपक अमित के मामा का लड़का है। अमित की माँ का भतीजा है और उन्हें दीपक की शादी का कार्ड मिला है।

(iii) अमित की बहन मधु के बारे में माँ ने अमित से कहा कि मधु भी शादी के योग्य हो गई है। वह उसकी शादी करना चाहती है। परन्तु उससे पहले अमित की शादी हो जाती तो अच्छा था क्योंकि वह मधु से सात साल बड़ा है। घर में पहले बहू आएगी तो मधु की शादी में हाथ बँटाएगी। बहू घर के काम में भी मदद करेगी।

(iv) अमित की माँ को घर में बहू की कमी अखरती थी क्योंकि अमित और उसके पिताजी फैक्ट्री चले जाते थे और मधु अपने कॉलेज चली जाती थी। इसलिए अकेले होने पर उन्हें बहू की कमी अखरती थी। वे सोचती थीं कि बहू घर में होती तो उन्हें अकेले न रहना पड़ता। घर में रौनक रहती और रागय का पता ही नहीं चलता।

Q. 8. **Read the extract given below and answer in** *Hindi* **the questions that follow:**

निम्नलिखित अवतरण को पढ़िए और उसके नीचे लिखे प्रश्नों के उत्तर हिंदी में लिखिए:

"दूसरे ही क्षण मीनू उसके सामने आ गई और खुशी से उसके हाथ चूम लिए। अरे मीनू! आज तो बहुत प्रसन्न दिखाई दे रही हो। क्या बात है? नीलिमा ने पूछा।"

(i) मीनू कौन है? उसकी प्रसन्नता का कारण क्या है? [2]

(ii) 'उसके' सर्वनाम का प्रयोग किसके लिए किया गया है? उसका संक्षिप्त परिचय दीजिए। [2]

(iii) मीनू के चेहरे पर किस बात को सोचकर उदासी छा जाती है? मीनू की उदासी कब और किस प्रकार दूर होती है? समझाकर लिखिए। [3]

(iv) प्रस्तुत उपन्यास का उद्देश्य स्पष्ट कीजिए। [3]

[2018]

📋 Marking Scheme

(i) मीनू दयाराम जी की सबसे बड़ी पुत्री है। वह विवाह योग्य हो गई है। उसके पिता ने मीनू के रिश्ते के लिए उसका फोटो मेरठ भेजा था। उसका फोटो मेरठ वालों को पसंद आ गया है। कल मीनू को देखने के लिए अमित, उसके पिता मायाराम जी, माता जी और छोटी बहन मधु मेरठ से आ रहे हैं। उसकी प्रसन्नता का यही कारण है।

(ii) उसके सर्वनाम का प्रयोग नीलिमा के लिए किया गया है। नीलिमा मीनू की सहेली है। वह नयन-नक्श और रूप-रंग में बहुत सुन्दर है। उसने भी मीनू के साथ एम.ए. की परीक्षा दी है। नीलिमा एक संवेदनशील युवती है। मीनू के दिल में छिपी पीड़ा का उसे आभास हो जाता है। वह उसकी पीड़ा से ध्यान हटाने का सार्थक प्रयास करती है।

(iii) मीनू को अपनी जिन्दगी के बीते क्षण याद आ गये। पहले भी उसे कई लड़कों ने देखा है। किसी ने कद की छोटी तो किसी ने साँवली बताकर उससे शादी करने से इन्कार कर दिया। मेरठ वालों को उसका फोटो पसंद तो आ गया है, छोटा कद और साँवले रंग के कारण कहीं वे भी नापसंद कर दें तो एक बार फिर वह इस परीक्षा में असफल हो जाएगी, यही सोचकर मीनू उदास हो जाती है। नीलिमा ने मीनू का मन बहलाने के लिए उसे अपनी कई तस्वीरें दिखाई। मीनू व नीलिमा ने एम.ए. की परीक्षा दी थी। मीनू का भाई रोहित जब परीक्षा के परिणाम का अखबार लेकर आया तो दोनों अखबार पर झपट पड़ती हैं। मीनू प्रथम श्रेणी में तथा नीलिमा द्वितीय श्रेणी में पास हुई थी। प्रथम श्रेणी में पास होने पर मीनू खुशी से फूली न समायी। इसी कारण मीनू की उदासी दूर हो जाती है।

(iv) 'नया रास्ता' उपन्यास एक सामाजिक उपन्यास है जिसका उद्देश्य यह बताना है कि स्त्री 'अबला नहीं बल्कि सबला है।' मीनू देखने में अत्यधिक सुन्दर नहीं। उसकी शादी इसी कारण नहीं हो पाती रिश्ता आता है और वापस चला जाता है। तभी मीनू विवाह न करने का फैसला कर लेती है और मेरठ में रहकर वकालत की पढ़ाई शुरू करती है। तीन साल की वकालत प्रथम श्रेणी में पास करने के बाद वह वकील बन जाती है।

वकील बनकर मीनू यह सिद्ध कर देती है कि नारी अबला नहीं सबला है। वह भी पढ़-लिखकर अपने पैरों पर खड़ी हो सकती है। लड़की का केवल रंग-रूप ही उसका जीवन निर्धारित नहीं करता बल्कि उसकी प्रतिभा, योग्यता अधिक महत्व रखती है। मीनू की शादी अन्त में अमित के साथ हो जाती है।

इस प्रकार उपन्यास का उद्देश्य यही स्पष्ट करना है कि स्त्री कमजोर नहीं है उसमें भी प्रतिभा है और योग्यता है। उसका रंग-रूप देखकर शादी तय करना उचित बात नहीं है। किसी के रंग-रूप के आधार पर उसका तिरस्कार बहुत ही अनुचित बात है। मीनू इसी अयोग्यता को योग्यता में बदलकर अपनी मंजिल तक पहुँचती है।

Ans. (i) मीनू 'नया रास्ता' नामक उपन्यास की नायिका है। वह दयाराम जी की सबसे बड़ी पुत्री है। उसकी खुशी का कारण था कि उसे देखने लड़के वाले आ रहे थे। वे मेरठ में रहते थे। उन्हें मीनू का फोटो पसंद आ गया था। इसी खुशी को अपनी सहेली नीलिमा को बताने आई थी।

(ii) 'उसके' सर्वनाम का प्रयोग नीलिमा के लिए किया गया है। नीलिमा मीनू की पक्की सहेली थी। वह बहुत सुंदर थी। वह अपने पति सुरेन्द्र के साथ एक सुखी जीवन बिता रही थी। मीनू के दिल में छिपी पीड़ा का उसे आभास हो जाता है। वह उसकी पीड़ा हटाने का सार्थक प्रयास करती है।

(iii) मीनू के चेहरे पर उदासी इसलिए छा जाती है कि उसकी फोटो तो सबको पसंद आ जाती थी, लेकिन रंग तथा कद के कारण लड़के वाले उसे नापसंद कर जाते थे। मीनू व नीलिमा ने एम.ए. की परीक्षा दी थी। मीनू का भाई रोहित जब परीक्षा के परिणाम का अखबार लेकर आता है तो दोनों अखबार पर झपट पड़ती है। मीनू प्रथम श्रेणी में तथा नीलिमा द्वितीय श्रेणी में पास हुई थी। प्रथम श्रेणी में पास होने पर मीनू खुशी से फूली न समायी। इसी कारण मीनू की उदासी दूर हो जाती है।

(iv) 'नया रास्ता' उपन्यास एक सामाजिक उपन्यास है जिसका उद्देश्य यह बताना है कि स्त्री 'अबला नहीं बल्कि सबला है।' मीनू देखने में अत्यधिक सुन्दर नहीं है। उसकी शादी इसी कारण नहीं हो पाती रिश्ता आता है और वापस चला जाता है तभी मीनू विवाह न करने का फैसला कर लेती है और मेरठ में रहकर वकालत की पढ़ाई शुरू करती है। तीन साल की वकालत प्रथम श्रेणी में पास करने के बाद वह वकील बन जाती है।

वकील बनकर मीनू यह सिद्ध कर देती है कि नारी अबला नहीं सबला है। वह भी पढ़-लिखकर अपने पैरों पर खड़ी हो सकती है। लड़की का केवल रंग-रूप ही उसका जीवन निर्धारित नहीं करता बल्कि उसकी प्रतिभा, योग्यता अधिक महत्व रखती है। मीनू की शादी अन्त में अमित के साथ हो जाती है।

इस प्रकार उपन्यास का उद्देश्य यही स्पष्ट करना है कि स्त्री कमजोर नहीं है उसमें भी प्रतिभा और योग्यता है। उसका रंग-रूप देखकर शादी तय करना उचित बात नहीं है किसी के रंग-रूप के आधार पर उसका तिरस्कार बहुत ही अनुचित बात है। मीनू इसी अयोग्यता को योग्यता में बदलकर अपनी मंजिल तक पहुँचती है।

Q. 9. Read the extract given below and answer in *Hindi* the questions that follow:

निम्नलिखित अवतरण को पढ़िए और उसके नीचे लिखे प्रश्नों के उत्तर हिंदी में लिखिए:

"परंतु तुम ये तो सोचो कि आजकल शादी के बाद ही दावत दी जाती है। यदि हम प्रीतिभोज नहीं देंगे तो दुनिया वाले क्या कहेंगे और फिर बड़े घर की लड़की आ रही है। दावत नहीं देंगे तो सब लोग बात बनाएँगे।"

(i) उपर्युक्त कथन किसने, किस अवसर पर कहा था? [2]

(ii) 'बड़े घर की लड़की' किसको कहा गया है? उसका संक्षिप्त परिचय दीजिए। [2]

(iii) उपर्युक्त कथन के विषय में अमित के क्या विचार हैं? वह इस शादी से सहमत क्यों नहीं है? धनीमल जी ने शादी के प्रस्ताव के साथ क्या लालच दिया था? [3]

(iv) आजकल के मध्यमवर्गीय परिवारों में विवाह आदि रीति-रिवाजों के अवसर पर होने वाले फिजूलखर्ची पर अपने विचार लिखिए। **[3]**

[2018]

📋 Marking Scheme --------

(i) उपर्युक्त कथन मायाराम जी ने अपनी पत्नी से तब कहा जब उनके लड़के अमित की शादी धनीमल जी की लड़की सरिता के साथ होने में केवल एक महीना रह गया था। उनके विवाह की तैयारियाँ धूमधाम से की जा रही थी। उसी प्रसंग में मायाराम जी तथा उनकी पत्नी के बीच वार्तालाप हो रहा है कि शादी के बाद प्रीतिभोज किया जाए या पहले ही मढ़े पर सब बिरादरी वालों और जान-पहचान वालों को खाना खिला दिया जाए।

(ii) 'बड़े घर की लड़की' धनीमल जी की लड़की सरिता को कहा गया है। सरिता के पिता बहुत धनवान हैं, इसीलिए उसे बड़े घर की लड़की कहा गया है। सरिता अपने पिता धनीमल की सबसे छोटी बेटी है। उसे बाल कटवाने का शौक है। उसके नयन-नक्श मीनू से ज्यादा अच्छे नहीं हैं। वह पेंटिंग और कार ड्राइविंग में विशेष रुचि रखती है। उसको घर के काम में कोई रुचि नहीं है। उसने बी.ए. की परीक्षा द्वितीय श्रेणी में उत्तीर्ण की है। वह अपने पिता की लाडली पुत्री है।

(iii) उपर्युक्त कथन के विषय में अमित कोई विचार प्रकट नहीं करता है। वह अपने माता-पिता से कहता है कि वे जैसा उचित समझें कर लें। अमित इस शादी से सहमत नहीं है क्योंकि उसके विचार में दयाराम जी की लड़की मीनू, सरिता की अपेक्षा अधिक गुणी तथा उसके घर के वातावरण के अनुकूल है। अमित के अनुसार धनी पिता की संतान होने के कारण सरिता घर के काम-काज नहीं कर पाएगी। धनीमल जी ने अमित की शादी अपनी बेटी सरिता के साथ करने के लिए यह लालच दिया था कि वे शादी में पाँच लाख रुपये खर्च करेंगे। उन्होंने साथ ही यह भी कहा कि मेरी तो बस तीन बेटियाँ है। मरने के बाद सब कुछ इन्हीं का है। उन्होंने मायाराम जी को धन का लालच दिया था।

(iv) आजकल के मध्यमवर्गीय परिवारों में विवाह आदि के अवसरों पर अत्यधिक फिजुलखर्च करने की प्रवृत्ति दिखाई पड़ती है। वे लोग उच्च वर्ग का अनुसरण करते हुए अधिक से अधिक दिखावा करके समाज में अपनी धाक जमाना चाहते हैं भले ही उन्हें इसके लिए ऋण ही क्यों न लेना पड़े। विवाह आदि रीति-रिवाजों के अवसर पर लोग अपनी हैसियत से अधिक खर्च कभी-कभी लड़के वालों के जोर देने पर भी करते हैं क्योंकि उन्हें समाज तथा बिरादरी वालों के सामने अपनी प्रशंसा सुनने का शौक रहता है। बे इस बात को भूल जाते हैं कि लड़की वालों को इस तरह के खर्च करने में कितनी कठिनाइयों का सामना करना पड़ता है।

Ans. (i) उपर्युक्त कथन अमित के पिताजी मायाराम ने अपनी पत्नी से कहा था जब उनके घर में अमित की शादी की तैयारियाँ चल रही थीं।

(ii) बड़े घर की लड़की सरिता को कहा गया है जो धनीमल जी की सबसे छोटी पुत्री है जिसका विवाह अमित के साथ तय हुआ है। वह अधिक सुंदर नहीं है, पढ़ाई में भी अच्छी नहीं है तथा उसे फैशन में रहने की आदत है। उसे पेंटिंग और ड्राइविंग का शौक है। वह अपने पिता की लाडली पुत्री है।

(iii) अमित अपनी शादी में कोई रुचि नहीं ले रहा था। पूछने पर कह देता था कि जैसा आप उचित समझें। वह इसलिए सहमत नहीं था क्योंकि उसे लगता था कि बड़े घर की बेटी माता-पिता की सेवा नहीं कर पायेगी। धनीमल जी ने शादी के प्रस्ताव के साथ-साथ यह लालच दिया कि वह अपनी बेटी को पाँच लाख रुपए देंगे तथा यह भी कहा कि मरने के बाद सब कुछ मेरी तीन लड़कियों का है। उन्होंने मायाराम जी को धन का लालच दिया।

(iv) आजकल विवाह के रीति रिवाजों में आडंबर दिखावा और नये-नये खर्चे जुड़ते जा रहे हैं। बड़े-बड़े पार्टी हॉल, विभिन्न प्रकार के खाद्य व्यंजन, सौन्दर्य प्रसाधन आदि पर मध्यमवर्गीय परिवार भी दिखावा करने लगा है। एक मध्यमवर्गीय परिवार में जहाँ पहले तीन चार सौ लोग आमंत्रित होते थे आज उनकी संख्या हजार के करीब पहुँच चुकी है।

Q. 10. Read the extract given below and answer in *Hindi* the questions that follow:

निम्नलिखित अवतरण को पढ़िए और उसके नीचे लिखे प्रश्नों के उत्तर हिन्दी में लिखिए:

माँ को लगा, शायद अमित सरिता के रिश्ते को तैयार नहीं है। इसलिए वह बोली, "बेटे, व्यवहार का तो किसी को भी पता नहीं है। न, सरिता के बारे में ही कुछ कहा जा सकता है न ही मीनू के बारे में व्यवहार का तो साथ रहने पर ही पता चलता है।"

(i) माँ को कैसे पता चलता है कि अमित सरिता के रिश्ते के लिए तैयार नहीं है? **[2]**

(ii) अमित के पिता मायाराम जी सरिता के रिश्ते को क्यों नहीं करना चाहते हैं? **[2]**

(iii) अमित और सरिता का रिश्ता तय होने के लिए माँ किसको और क्यों उकसाती है? माँ की ऐसी धारणा से उनके स्वभाव के बारे में क्या पता चलता है? समझाकर लिखिए। **[3]**

(iv) शादी के विषय में समाज की क्या परम्परा है? आप इससे कहाँ तक सहमत हैं? स्पष्ट कीजिए। **[3]**

[2017]

Ans. (i) मीनू को देखने के पश्चात् धनाढ्य परिवार की लड़की सरिता जिसके पिता पाँच लाख दहेज में देने वाले थे, को अमित देखने गया, धन के मद में खोई हुई सरिता अमित को पसन्द नहीं आई थी क्योंकि उसके रिश्ते व फोटो आदि में अमित ने रुचि नहीं ली। वह माँ से कहता है, "क्या बड़े घर की बेटी तुम्हारे साथ रह सकेगी? क्या वह हमारे घर के वातावरण में घुल-मिल सकेगी?" उसके इसी व्यवहार को देखकर माँ को लगा कि अमित को सरिता पसन्द नहीं है।

(ii) अमित के पिता मायाराम दहेज विरोधी थे। जब सरिता के पिता धनीमल जी ने विवाह में 5 लाख (दहेज) देने की बात कही तब उन्होंने स्पष्ट शब्दों में कहा इसकी जरूरत नहीं है। हम एक लड़की देख के आये हैं।

सबको पसन्द है। उनका कहना था कि बड़े घर की लड़की लेकर वह अपने बेटे को बेचना नहीं चाहते। उसके पाँवों में वे बेड़ियाँ नहीं डालना चाहते हैं। बड़े घर की बेटी दहेज तो लायेगी लेकिन परिवार वालों के साथ मिलकर नहीं रह सकेगी।

(iii) अमित और सरिता का रिश्ता तय होने के लिए माँ अमित के पिता को उकसाने का कार्य करती है। माँ की इस धारणा से उनके लालची स्वभाव के बारे में पता चलता है। वह एक स्वार्थी और दहेज लोभी महिला हैं। उनके लिये धन से अधिक कुछ भी महत्वपूर्ण नहीं है।

(iv) शादी के विषय में हमारे समाज में यह परम्परा विद्यमान है कि लड़की वालों को हमेशा शादी विवाह के समय छोटा समझा जाता है। लड़के वाले अपने को बहुत उच्च समझते हैं। दहेज के लिये लड़की को प्रताड़ित किया जाता है।

मैं इस सामाजिक कुरीति का विरोध करता हूँ। आज के आधुनिक युग में लड़के व लड़की में कोई भेदभाव नहीं होना चाहिये।

Q. 11. **Read the extract given below and answer in** *Hindi* **the questions that follow:**

निम्नलिखित अवतरण को पढ़िए और उसके नीचे लिखे प्रश्नों के उत्तर हिन्दी में लिखिए:

"मीनू ने अमित के कमरे में प्रवेश किया, तो देखा कि अमित अपने पलंग पर लेटा हुआ है। मीनू को देखकर उन्होंने उसे प्रेमपूर्वक बैठाया। उसे देखकर अमित के मुरझाये चेहरे पर भी खुशी की लहर दौड़ गई।"

  (i) मीनू अमित को देखने कहाँ गई थी? जाते समय वह मन में क्या सोच रही थी? **[2]**

  (ii) कमरे में प्रवेश करते ही उसने क्या देखा? अमित की माँ ने मीनू से क्या पूछा? उसने क्या उत्तर दिया? **[2]**

  (iii) मीनू के वकालत पास करने पर अमित की माँ को विशेष खुशी क्यों हो रही थी? क्या उन्हें अपनी गलती का अहसास हो गया था? तर्कपूर्ण उत्तर दीजिए। **[3]**

  (iv) मीनू के हृदय में बचपन से ही किसके प्रति दया की भावना थी? वह उनकी किस प्रकार सहायता करने का निश्चय कर रही है? **[3]**

    [2017]

Ans. **(i)** मीनू उसे देखने अस्पताल गयी थी वहाँ उसकी माताजी भी बैठी हुई थीं। मीनू को अमित व उसकी माँ ने बैठने के लिए कहा। अस्पताल जाते समय उसके दिल में अन्तर्द्वन्द्व था कि वह अस्पताल जाये या नहीं। अन्त में उसे लगा कि उसे अस्पताल जाना चाहिए।

  (ii) कमरे में प्रवेश करते ही मीनू ने देखा कि अमित एक पलंग पर लेटा हुआ है और माँ से बात कर रहा है। तभी अमित की माँ ने मीनू से पूछा—"तुम्हारी वकालत तो पूरी हो गई है न?" उसने उत्तर दिया, "हाँ आण्टी! मैंने प्रथम श्रेणी में वकालत पास कर ली है और यहाँ मेरठ में ही प्रैक्टिस भी शुरू कर दी है।"

(iii) मीनू के वकालत पास करने पर अमित की माँ को विशेष प्रसन्नता हो रही थी कि वह अपने पैरों पर खड़ी हो गई है। आत्मनिर्भर हो गई है। उनका लड़का अमित एक्सीडेंट के कारण बिस्तर पर है। उनका पुत्र मीनू को ही प्यार करता है। अब मीनू से विवाह होने पर वह अमित का सहारा बन जाएगी। उसके बेटे के साथ कंधे से कंधा मिलाकर चलेगी। उनके बुढ़ापे का भी सहारा बन जायेगी। इसलिए अमित की माँ मीनू के वकील बन जाने पर बहुत प्रसन्न हैं। उसे अपनी गलती का अहसास हो गया था क्योंकि मीनू ने अमित को उस समय अपनाया जब वह अस्पताल में असहाय पड़ा हुआ था। जिस अमीर लड़की से उन्होंने अमित की शादी तय कराई थी वह रिश्ता तोड़कर चली गयी थी। उसके अमीर पिता ने अमित को छोड़कर अपनी पुत्री का दूसरे लड़के से विवाह करने का निश्चय कर लिया था। मीनू ने अमित को उसी असहाय अवस्था में स्वीकार कर लिया था क्योंकि वह अमित से सच्चा प्यार करती थी। अमित की माँ की आँखें खुल गई थी। उसे आत्मनिर्भर मीनू पर गर्व एवं प्रसन्नता हो रही थी।

(iv) मीनू के हृदय में बचपन से ही गरीब-बेसहारा, अपाहिज लोगों के लिए दया की भावना थी। उसके विवाह में सजावट पर उसके पिता दस हजार रुपये खर्च करना चाहते हैं। तभी वह अपने पिता को इस बात के लिए रोकती है और कहती है पिताजी कुछ घण्टों की रौनक के लिए आप दस हजार रुपये बर्बाद कर रहे हैं इनमें से पाँच हजार रुपये गरीब बेसहारा लोगों को दे दीजिए जिससे वे कुछ कार्य शुरू कर सकें। तभी उसे राजो का चचेरा भाई मनोहर दिखाई दिया वह अपंग था। उसने उसी क्षण उसकी सहायता करने का निश्चय कर लिया।

Q. 12. **Read the extract given below and answer in** *Hindi* **the questions that follow:**

निम्नलिखित अवतरण को पढ़िए और उसके नीचे लिखे प्रश्नों के उत्तर हिन्दी में लिखिए:

अमित का नाम सुनते ही दरवाजे की ओर पीठ किए बैठी मीनू ने मुड़कर देखा तो वह आश्चर्यचकित रह गई। मीनू जब भी अमित को देखती, उसके मन में अजीब सी घृणा उत्पन्न हो जाती। अमित व उसके सभी मित्र वहाँ आ चुके थे, परन्तु मीनू अभी भी सोच में डूबी हुई थी।

  (i) मीनू इस समय कहाँ थी? वहाँ अमित से उसकी कैसे मुलाकात हो गई? **[2]**

  (ii) मीनू और अमित के बीच क्या सम्बन्ध था? वह उससे घृणा क्यों करती थी? **[2]**

  (iii) उसे वहाँ किस सच्चाई का पता चला? उन बातों का उस पर क्या प्रभाव पड़ा? **[3]**

  (iv) "मीनू परिस्थितियों से हार मानने वाली कोई साधारण नारी नहीं थी" — स्पष्ट कीजिए कि उसने अपने जीवन को कैसे नई दिशा दी? **[3]**

    [2017]

Ans. **(i)** मीनू इस समय अपनी सहेली नीलिमा के घर पर थी। नीलिमा के घर उसके पुत्र का नामकरण संस्कार था। इस उत्सव के उपलक्ष्य में नीलिमा के पति सुरेन्द्र के अनेक मित्र एकत्रित हुए थे। अमित सुरेन्द्र का घनिष्ठ मित्र था। अमित भी उस उत्सव में आया था। वहीं पर मीनू की अमित से मुलाकात हुई।

(ii) मीनू मीरापुर के दयाराम की बड़ी पुत्री थी। एक बार शादी के लिए अमित, उसके पिता मायाराम, उनकी पत्नी एवं उसकी छोटी बहन मीनू को देखने आये। अमित को मीनू पसन्द थी। उसका आचार-व्यवहार अमित को पसन्द आया। वह उससे विवाह करना चाहता था, परन्तु बात पक्की करने से पहले मायाराम के पास धनीमल नाम का एक धनी व्यक्ति अपनी पुत्री सरिता का रिश्ता लेकर आया और उसने पाँच लाख दहेज में देने की बात कही। माँ को दहेज का लालच आ गया। उसने मीनू से मुँह फेर लिया, लेकिन अमित को सरिता नहीं मीनू पसंद थी। माता-पिता के द्वारा मीनू को कोई जबाव न देने के कारण बात अधूरी रह गयी। उन दोनों के बीच कोई रिश्ता नहीं था, परन्तु उपरोक्त घटना के कारण वे दोनों एक दूसरे को जानते थे।

वह अमित से घृणा इसलिए करती थी क्योंकि दहेज के लालच में आकर उसने व उसके परिवार ने उसके पिता को धोखा दिया था।

(iii) जब मीनू नीलिमा के पुत्र के नामकरण संस्कार में शामिल होने के लिए उसके घर गई तो वहाँ उसे नीलिमा से पता चला कि अमित, नीलिमा के पति सुरेन्द्र का मित्र था। उसका मेरठ के किसी घराने में रिश्ता तय होकर टूट गया था। विवाह से एक माह पूर्व लड़की वालों ने अपनी पुत्री को दहेज़ में एक फ्लैट देने की बात कही थी। यह बात अमित व उसके माता-पिता को पसंद नहीं आई। अमित अपने माता-पिता से अलग होकर अपनी गृहस्थी नहीं बसाना चाहता था। अत: उनका रिश्ता टूट गया।

नीलिमा ने यह भी बताया कि अमित ने मीरापुर में एक लड़की देखी थी जो उन्हें पसंद भी आई थी परन्तु उस समय उनके माता-पिता की गलती से वह रिश्ता नहीं हो सका। अमित आज भी वे यह चाहते हैं कि यदि उस लड़की की शादी न हुई हो तो वे उसी से शादी करें। उस लड़की ने अपनी पहली मुलाकात में ही न जाने उन पर क्या जादू कर दिया था। नीलिमा को यह ज्ञात नहीं था कि वह लड़की मीनू ही थी। ये सारी बातें सुनकर मीनू के हृदय से अमित के प्रति घृणा के भाव दूर हो गए।

(iv) मीनू की शादी के लिए अनेक रिश्ते आये, किन्तु उसके कद और साँवले रंग के कारण सभी लोग वापस चले गये, किन्तु मीनू ने हार नहीं मानी, वह एक प्रतिभाशाली और उच्च आत्मविश्वास वाली लड़की थी। कई बार उसमें हीन भावना आई, परन्तु उसने अपना मनोबल गिरने नहीं दिया। अन्त में उसने निश्चय कर लिया कि वह शादी नहीं करेगी। वह वकालत पढ़ेगी। वह सदैव कक्षा में प्रथम स्थान पाती थी। वकालत की परीक्षा भी उसने प्रथम श्रेणी में उत्तीर्ण की। वकालत पास करके मेरठ में ही उसने अपनी प्रैक्टिस शुरू कर दी।

उपन्यास में बताया गया है कि यदि इरादे नेक हों तथा आत्मबल मजबूत हो तो मनुष्य को सफलता मिलती है जैसा मीनू के जीवन में घटित हुआ।

10 Ekanki Sanchay

 Long Answer Type Questions

Chapter 1. संस्कार और भावना (Sanskar Aur Bhavna)

—विष्णु प्रभाकर (Vishnu Prabhakar)

Q. 1. Read the extract given below and answer in *Hindi* the questions that follow:

निम्नलिखित अवतरण को पढ़िए और उसके नीचे लिखे प्रश्नों के उत्तर हिंदी में लिखिए:

''मिसरानी कह रही थी'' बहू कैसी भी हो, पर अपने प्राण देकर उसने पति को बचा लिया है, अकेली थी, पर किसी के आगे हाथ पसारने नहीं गई।

(i) 'बहू अकेली थी' ऐसा क्यों कहा गया है? [2]

(ii) 'बहू की किन विशेषताओं ने सास को कुछ सोचने पर विवश कर दिया? [2]

(iii) माँ का चरित्र-चित्रण कीजिए। [3]

(iv) समाज के लिए जातिवाद किस प्रकार अहितकर है? [2020] [3]

Ans. (i) माँ ने मिसरानी द्वारा कही गई बात उमा को बतायी। माँ अपने बड़े बेटे अविनाश की विजातीय बहू को स्वीकार नहीं करती, जिससे अविनाश उससे अलग रहता है। अविनाश के बीमार पड़ने पर बहू अकेली उसकी सेवा करती थी। 'बहू अकेली थी' इसलिए कहा गया है।

(ii) **बहू की विशेषताएँ :** बहू अविनाश की सेवा करती है। हैजा होने पर अविनाश की तन-मन से सेवा करती है। अकेली होने पर भी ससुराल वालों से मदद नहीं माँगती। वह स्वयं दवा लाती, घर का काम भी करती और अविनाश की देखभाल भी करती है।

(iii) **माँ का चरित्र-चित्रण :** एकांकी में माँ संक्रांति काल की एक हिंदू नारी है जो रूढ़िवादी है और प्राचीन काल के संस्कारों के जाल में फँसी हुई है। इसी कारण वह अविनाश की विजातीय बहू को स्वीकार नहीं करती है। वह जातिवाद को मानती है। इसी कारण बीमार बेटे से मिलने नहीं जाती। जब माँ को विजातीय बहू के मरणासन्न होने की खबर मिलती है, तब उसकी ममतामयी भावना जाग उठती है। उसे पता है कि बहू को कुछ हो गया तो उसका बेटा भी जिंदा नहीं रह पायेगा। माँ का हृदय परिवर्तित हो जाता है और अंत में वह अपनी बहू को अपनाने के लिए तैयार हो जाती है। फिर वह संस्कारों की दासता से मुक्त हो जाती है।

(iv) समाज के लिए जातिवाद अहितकर है। जातिवाद के कारण समाज अनगिनत वर्गों में बँट चुका है। लोग अपनी जाति को ऊँचा तथा अन्य जातियों को हीन समझकर उनका तिरस्कार करते हैं। इस कारण समाज में वैमनस्य बढ़ता है तथा सद्भावना एवं एकता खंडित होती है।

एकांकी में माँ अविनाश के अंतर्जातीय विवाह को स्वीकार नहीं करती। वह जातिवाद की बेड़ियों में जकड़ी होने के कारण अपने बेटे से दूर हो जाती है।

Q. 2. Read the extract given below and answer in *Hindi* the questions that follow:

निम्नलिखित अवतरण को पढ़िए और उसके नीचे लिखे प्रश्नों के उत्तर हिंदी में लिखिए:

"काश कि मैं निर्मम हो सकती, काश कि मैं संस्कारों की दासता से मुक्त हो सकती! हो पाती तो कुल धर्म और जाति का भूत मुझे तंग न करता और मैं अपने बेटे से न बिछुड़ती।"

(i) वक्ता कौन है? यह वाक्य वह किसे कह रही है? [2]

(ii) 'संस्कारों की दासता सबसे भयंकर शत्रु है' यह कथन एकांकी में किसका है? उसने ऐसा क्यों कहा? [2]

(iii) संस्कारों की दासता के कारण वक्ता को किन-किन कठिनाइयों का सामना करना पड़ा? [3]

(iv) प्रस्तुत एकांकी द्वारा एकांकीकार ने क्या संदेश दिया है? [3]

[2018]

Marking Scheme

(i) वक्ता माँ है। यह वाक्य माँ अतुल की पत्नी उमा से कह रही है। जो उनके छोटे बेटे की वधु/बहू है। जो संस्कारों के बन्धन में जकड़ी एक हिन्दू नारी है। अविनाश तथा अतुल की माँ है।

(ii) यह कथन अविनाश यानि माँ के बड़े बेटे का है। अविनाश अपनी माँ के संस्कारों की जकड़न के कारण अलग रहने को मजबूर हो गया। विजातीय लड़की से विवाह करना, जातिवाद की समर्थक माँ बहू को अपना नहीं पाती है।

(iii) संस्कारों की दासता के कारण माँ को अपने बड़े बेटे और बहू से अलग रहना पड़ा, साथ रह रहे बहू बेटे की निकटता भी प्राप्त न हो सकी। कुल, जाति, धर्म के प्रति कट्टरता माँ की सोच को पंगु बना देती है, नवीन बातें अपनाने में असमर्थता के कारण अपने बेटों के प्रेम से वंचित रही। संस्कार दीवार बनकर बेटे के प्रेम में खड़े है। वह सामाजिक बुराइयों का शिकार बनता है। यदि बेटा खोने का भय न होता माँ आजीवन संस्कारों की दासता से बँधी रहती। अन्त में माँ संस्कार की दासता से मुक्त होती है और बहू को अपनाने का विचार कर उसके पास जाती है।

(iv) प्रस्तुत एकांकी के द्वारा एकांकीकार ने यह संदेश दिया है कि आपसी रिश्तों एवं सम्बन्धों में प्रेम एवं स्नेह से बढ़कर कुछ नहीं होता। अपने जीवन में आदर्शों एवं सिद्धांतों को लेकर चलना एक अच्छी बात है।

– संस्कारों के बंधन तोड़कर हमें बदलाव लाना है।

– जात-पात व ऊँच-नीच के बंधन समाज व राष्ट्र की उन्नति में बाधक।

– संस्कारों का मोह छोड़ने में समझदारी।

पर उन सिद्धांतों एवं आदर्शों को जिद की तरह ढोना कभी-कभी अत्यंत भयावह हो जाता है। हर मनुष्य में अच्छे संस्कारों का होना जरूरी है। पर हमारे संस्कार जब हमारी भावनाओं को ठेस पहुँचाते हैं, तब उन संस्कारों का कोई महत्व नहीं रह जाता।

अत: 'संस्कार और भावना' एकांकी के माध्यम से एकांकीकार ने यह स्पष्ट करने का प्रयास किया है कि यदि रिश्तों को बनाए रखने हेतु हमें अपने संस्कारों व परम्पराओं से समझौता करना पड़े तो अवश्य करना चाहिए। भावनाएँ सदैव संस्कारों से अधिक महत्वपूर्ण होती हैं।

(ii) यह कथन अविनाश यानि माँ के बड़े बेटे का है। अविनाश अपनी माँ के संस्कारों की जकड़न के कारण अलग रहने को मजबूर हो गया। विजातीय लड़की से विवाह करना, जातिवाद की समर्थक माँ अपना नहीं पाती है। अत: संस्कारों के गुलाम बन जाना सबसे बड़ा शत्रु है।

(iii) वह अपने मनमुताबिक जीवन नहीं जी सकी और अपने पुत्र से अलग होकर दु:खी जीवन जी रही थी। वह नवीन बातों को अपना नहीं पाई। कुल, धर्म, जातिवाद जैसी बातों की कट्टर समर्थक बनी रही। साथ में रह रहे दूसरे बहू बेटे की निकटता भी प्राप्त नहीं कर सकी।

(iv) एकांकी द्वारा उन्होंने बताया है कि कई बार हमारे संस्कार हमारी बेड़ियाँ बन जाते हैं। उनके दास बन हम अपनी भावनाओं का गला घोंट देते हैं। इसलिए आज के बदलते आधुनिक समाज में सही जीवन व्यतीत करने के लिए जात-पात और रूढ़िवादिता से अलग होकर नये परिवेश में जीना चाहिए। अत: संस्कार और भावना एकांकी के माध्यम से एकांकीकार ने यह स्पष्ट करने का प्रयास किया है कि यदि रिश्तों को बनाए रखने हेतु हमें अपने संस्कारों व परम्पराओं से समझौता करना पड़े तो अवश्य करना चाहिए। भावनाएँ सदैव संस्कारों से अधिक महत्वपूर्ण होती है।

Ans. **(i)** वक्ता माँ है। यह वाक्य वह अपनी बहू और अतुल की पत्नी से कह रही है। जो संस्कारों के बन्धन में जकड़ी एक हिन्दू नारी है।

Chapter 2. बहू की विदा (Bahu ki Vida)

—विनोद रस्तोगी (Vinod Rastogi)

Q. 1. **Read the extract given below and answer in *Hindi* the questions that follow:**

निम्नलिखित गद्यांश को पढ़िए और उसके नीचे लिखे प्रश्नों के उत्तर हिंदी में लिखिए:

अब भी आँखें नहीं खुलीं ? जो व्यवहार अपनी बेटी के लिए दूसरों से चाहते हो वही दूसरे की बेटी को भी दो। जब तक तुम बहू और बेटी को एक-सा नहीं समझोगे, न तुम्हें सुख मिलेगा न शांति।

(i) वक्ता का परिचय देते हुए कथन का सन्दर्भ लिखिए। **[2]**

(ii) "अब भी आँखें नहीं खुलीं?" कहने से वक्ता का क्या अभिप्राय है? पाठ के सन्दर्भ में समझाइए। **[2]**

(iii) एकांकी के अन्त में श्रोता क्या फैसला लेता है क्यों? समझाइए। **[3]**

(iv) इस एकांकी से आपको क्या शिक्षा मिलती है? एकांकी के उदाहरण सहित स्पष्ट कीजिए। **[3]**

[2019]

📋 **Marking Scheme**

(i) यहाँ वक्ता राजेश्वरी है।

प्रस्तुत कथन राजेश्वरी ने जीवनलाल से कहा जब पहले सावन के मौके पर उनकी पुत्री गौरी को लेने गया उसका भाई रमेश खाली हाथ लौटा। गौरी के ससुराल वालों ने उसको विदा नहीं किया था क्योंकि उनका कहना था कि विवाह में दहेज़ पूरा नहीं दिया गया। इस बात को सुनकर जीवनलाल अत्यंत क्रोधित हुए

और गौरी के ससुराल वालों को लोभी कहने लगे। इधर वे स्वयं अपनी बहू कमला को पहले सावन के मौके पर विदा नहीं कर रहे थे। उसका भाई प्रमोद भी उसे लेने नहीं आया था। उन्होंने प्रमोद को खूब खरी-खोटी सुनाई थी और कहा था कि विवाह में दहेज़ कम दिया गया। अत: जब तक प्रमोद दहेज़ के पाँच हज़ार रुपये नहीं चुका देता बहू की विदा नहीं होगी। अब जब अपनी बेटी के साथ भी यही बात हुई तो राजेश्वरी चुप नहीं रह सकी।

(ii) 'अब भी आँखें नहीं खुलीं' कहने से वक्ता राजेश्वरी का यह अभिप्राय है कि क्या उन्हें अभी भी सच्चाई का ज्ञान नहीं हुआ ? राजेश्वरी जीवनलाल को यह कहती है कि बहू के दहेज़ में कोई कमी नहीं थी। उसके लिए उसे पहले सावन के मौके पर मायके न भेजना अन्यायपूर्ण है। कमला की माँ भी अपनी बेटी का उसी उत्साह के साथ इंतजार कर रहीं होगी जिस तरह वे अपनी बेटी गौरी का इंतजार कर रहे थे। वह अपने पति को यह समझाना चाहती है कि जो व्यवहार तुम अपनी बेटी के लिए दूसरों से चाहते हो, वही दूसरे की बेटी को भी दो। जब तक बहू और बेटी को एक-सा नहीं समझोगे तब तक तुम्हें न सुख मिलेगा न शान्ति।

(iii) एकांकी के अंत में जीवनलाल अपनी बहू कमला को बिना दहेज के ही विदा करने को तैयार हो जाते है। जीवनलाल अपनी बहू के परिवार वालों द्वारा दहेज की पूरी रकम न दे पाने के कारण उसे सावन में उसके घर नहीं जाने देते किंतु जब उन्हें पता चलता है कि उनकी बेटी को भी उसे ससुराल वालों ने कम दहेज के कारण उसे विदा नहीं किया। अपनी बेटी के ससुराल वालों का ऐसा व्यवहार देख उनकी आँखें खुल जाती हैं और उनके व्यवहार

में अंतर आ जाता है। अत: अंत में वह अपनी बहू को विदा करने का फैसला लेते हैं। क्योंकि अब उन्हें अपनी भूल का अहसास हो चुका होता है, उनके दिमाग से बेटी तथा बहू का अन्तर मिट जाता है। अब वह अपनी भूल सुधारना चाहते हैं।

(iv) प्रस्तुत एकांकी दहेज की समस्या पर आधारित है, जिसका उद्देश्य समाज से इस कुप्रथा को जड़ से निकाल फेंकना है। दहेज रूपी दानव धीरे-धीरे समाज की जड़ों को खोखला करता जा रहा है। प्रतिवर्ष न जाने कितनी कन्याएँ दहेज़ की बलिवेदी पर चढ़ा दी जाती हैं। कितनी बिन ब्याही रह जाती हैं। दहेज़ देने के डर से कितनी कन्याओं की भ्रूण-हत्या कर दी जाती है। दहेज़ के लोलुप व्यक्ति कभी भी संतुष्ट नहीं होते। वे बहुओं पर अत्याचार करते हैं। इस प्रकार दहेज़ नारी जाति पर अत्याचार है। इससे समाज में पुरुष की तुलना में स्त्री दर घटती जा रही है। यह एक चिंताजनक विषय है जो समाज में भ्रष्टाचार को जन्म देता है। इस कुप्रथा को दूर करना परिवार, समाज और राष्ट्र की उन्नति के लिए आवश्यक है। एकांकी में यह भी समझाया गया है कि बहू और बेटी में अंतर नहीं करना चाहिए। बहू के प्रति प्रेम, दया तथा सहानुभूति रखनी चाहिए और उसके साथ न्यायपूर्ण व्यवहार करना चाहिए। 'जैसा बोएंगें वैसा काटेंगें' यदि हम आज किसी की बेटी को सताएँगें तो कल हमारी बेटी भी दुखी रहेगी।

Ans. **(i)** वक्ता जीवनलाल की पत्नी राजेश्वरी और श्रोता जीवनलाल है। जीवनलाल की बेटी को दहेज पूरा नहीं देने के कारण ससुराल वाले विदा नहीं करते हैं। जीवनलाल बहुत अपमानित महसूस करते हैं। तब राजेश्वरी कहती है कि तुम भी तो अपनी बहू को दहेज कम देने के कारण उसे मायके नहीं भेज रहे हो। अब वैसा ही व्यवहार तुम्हारी बेटी के ससुराल वाले तुम्हारे साथ कर रहे हैं। अब तो तुम्हारी आँखें खुल जानी चाहिए।

(ii) "अब भी आँखें नहीं खुली" से वक्ता राजेश्वरी का यह अभिप्राय है कि जीवनलाल ने जैसा व्यवहार उसकी बहू के साथ किया, ठीक उसी तरह का व्यवहार बेटी के ससुराल वालों ने उसके साथ किया है। क्या अब भी उसे गलती का अहसास नहीं हुआ है? दहेज का लालच न करके उसे बेटी और बहू दोनों को समान समझना चाहिए और दोनों के साथ समान व्यवहार करना चाहिए।

(iii) एकांकी के अंत में श्रोता जीवनलाल का हृदय परिवर्तन हो जाता है। पहले वह उसकी बहू के मायके वालों से दहेज की माँग करता है, पर बेटी के ससुराल वालों द्वारा दहेज माँगने व बेटी को विदा न करने पर उसकी आँखें खुल जाती हैं। वह आत्मचिंतन करने को मजबूर हो जाता है। उसके मन से बहू और बेटी में अन्तर मानने की भावना समाप्त हो जाती है और वह बिना कुछ लिए ही खुशी-खुशी अपनी बहू को मायके भेजने का फैसला लेता है।

(iv) इस एकांकी से हमें यह शिक्षा मिलती है कि हमें बहू और बेटी में कोई फर्क नहीं करना चाहिए। बहू की भावनाओं का भी सम्मान करना चाहिए। इस एकांकी में दहेजरूपी सामाजिक कुप्रथा पर चोट की गई है और यह बताया

गया है कि हमें दहेज न देना चाहिए और न लेना चाहिए। जब प्रमोद अपनी बहन कमला की विदा के लिए आता है, तो जीवनलाल उसे अपमानित करते हैं और कहते हैं कि उन्हें दहेज के रूप में जब तक पाँच हजार रुपये नहीं मिलेंगे तब तक उसकी बहन विदा नहीं होगी, किन्तु जब उन्हीं की बेटी गौरी के साथ उसके ससुराल वालों द्वारा इसी तरह का व्यवहार किया जाता है, तब जीवनलाल का हृदय परिवर्तन होता है और वे अपनी बहू कमला की विदाई सहर्ष करते हैं। एकांकी में यह भी समझाया गया है कि बहू और बेटी में अंतर नहीं करना चाहिए। बहू के प्रति प्रेम, दया तथा सहानुभूति रखनी चाहिए और उसके साथ न्यायपूर्ण व्यवहार करना चाहिए। जैसा बोएंगे, वैसा काटेंगे। यदि हम आज किसी की बेटी को सताएँगे तो कल हमारी बेटी भी दुखी रहेगी।

Q. 2. **Read the extract given below and answer in *Hindi* the questions that follow:**

निम्नलिखित अवतरण को पढ़िए और उसके नीचे लिखे प्रश्नों के उत्तर हिन्दी में लिखिए:

"दहेज देना तो दूर, बारात की खातिर भी ठीक से नहीं की गई। मेरे नाम पर जो धब्बा लगा, मेरी शान में जो ठेस पहुँची, भरी बिरादरी में जो हँसी हुई, उस करारी चोट का घाव आज भी हरा है। जाओ, कह देना अपनी माँ से कि अगर बेटी को विदा कराना चाहती है तो पहले उस घाव के लिए मरहम भेजे।"

(i) प्रस्तुत कथन किसने, किससे कहा? सन्दर्भ सहित उत्तर लिखिए। **[2]**

(ii) 'मरहम' का क्या अर्थ है? यहाँ मरहम से क्या तात्पर्य है? स्पष्ट कीजिए। **[2]**

(iii) वक्ता के चरित्र की विशेषताएँ लिखिए। **[3]**

(iv) प्रस्तुत एकांकी में किस समस्या को उठाया गया है? उस समस्या को दूर करने के लिए क्या-क्या कदम उठाये जा रहे हैं? अपने विचार दीजिए। **[3]**

[2017]

Ans. **(i)** प्रस्तुत कथन लेखक विनोद रस्तोगी द्वारा रचित एकांकी 'बहू की विदा' में दहेज लोभी प्रधान पात्र जीवनलाल द्वारा बहू के भाई प्रमोद से तब कहा गया था जब वह अपनी बहन की शादी के बाद पहले सावन के त्योहार पर उसे घर ले जाने आया था उसने प्रमोद को अपनी बहू के समक्ष बारात की खातिर और दहेज कम देने को लेकर बहुत ताने सुनाये और कहा कि इससे उसके मान-सम्मान को ठेस पहुँची हैं। उनके हृदय पर गहरे घाव हुए हैं। उसके लिए उन्हें मरहम चाहिए और उस मरहम की कीमत है पाँच हज़ार रुपए। जब वे पाँच हज़ार की रकम दे देंगे, तभी कमला विदा होगी।

(ii) 'मरहम' का अभिप्राय ऐसी दवाई है जिसे घाव पर लगाने से घाव ठीक हो जाता है। यहाँ मरहम का प्रयोग जीवनलाल ने दहेज के पाँच हजार की कमी को पूरा करने के लिए किया है। साथ ही बारात की

खातिरदारी में जो कमी रह गई थी, जीवनलाल बहू के भाई से उसे पूरा करके घावों पर मरहम लगाने की बात कह रहे हैं।

(iii) जीवनलाल इस एकांकी के प्रमुख पात्र हैं। उनकी चारित्रिक विशेषतायें निम्न हैं—

लालची: वह एक धनी व्यापारी है और अपनी बहू कमला के मायके से इच्छनुसार दहेज न मिलने के कारण वह उसको मायके के लिए विदा नहीं करता। इससे यह कहा जा सकता है कि वह एक लालची किस्म के व्यक्ति हैं व दहेज लोभी हैं।

अभिमानी: जीवनलाल बहू के भाई प्रमोद से कहते है कि बारात की उचित खातिरदारी न करके उन लोगों ने उनको गहरी चोट पहुँचाई है और अगर उस चोट पर मरहम लगानी और बहन विदा करानी है तो पाँच हज़ार रूपयों का प्रबंध करना होगा।

कठोर: कम दहेज मिलने के कारण वह अपनी बहू को पहले सावन के मौके पर मायके नहीं जाने देते। इतनी ही नहीं, वे उसके भाई प्रमोद को खूब खरी-खोटी सुनाकर अपमानित भी करते हैं। वे बेटी और बहू में अंतर मानते हैं। उनकी तुलना में अपने घराने को प्रतिष्ठित बताते हैं।

सद्हृदय: उन्हें अपनी गलती का अहसास तब होता है जब उनकी खुद की बेटी को कम दहेज देने के कारण विदा नहीं करा पाते। वह उस वक्त भौचक्के रह जाते हैं, उन्हें बुरा-भला कहते हैं परंतु इसके साथ ही उनका हृदय परिवर्तित हो जाता है। वे एकदम पिघल जाते हैं। उसके बाद अपनी बहू को विदा कर भूल सुधार लेते हैं।

(iv) इस एकांकी में लेखक ने समाज में व्याप्त दहेज प्रथा की अभिशाप समान बुराई को उठाया है। इस बुराई के लिए दहेज विरोधी कानून बनाया गया है, किन्तु आज के युग में भी दहेज के समर्थक माता-पिता ही नहीं बल्कि स्वयं लड़के भी इसमें पीछे नहीं हैं। यद्यपि आज के पढ़े-लिखे नवयुवक प्रेम विवाहों के माध्यम से इस प्रथा को समाप्त करने में सहायक हैं तथापि जहाँ बात माता-पिता के द्वारा आयोजित विवाह की आती है, वहाँ तो दहेज चलता ही है। इसके अतिरिक्त समाज के धनकुबेर भी दहेज को बढ़ावा देते हैं। इस स्थिति में जिनके पास पर्याप्त धन नहीं है उनकी गुणवती बेटियाँ भी अविवाहित बैठी रहती हैं। सरकार दहेज के लोभियों को कड़ी सजा देती है। आज अगर लड़कियाँ शिक्षित है तो अपने ऊपर होने वाले अत्याचारों का सामना कर सकती हैं।

Chapter 3. मातृभूमि का मान (Matribhoomi Ka Man)
—हरिकृष्ण 'प्रेमी' (Harikrishna 'Premi')

Q. 1. Read the extract given below and answer in *Hindi* the questions that follow:

निम्नलिखित गद्यांश को पढ़िए और उसके नीचे लिखे प्रश्नों के उत्तर हिंदी में लिखिए:

आपके विवेक पर सबको विश्वास है। मैं आपसे निवेदन करने आई हूँ कि यद्यपि समय के फेर से आज हाड़ा, शक्ति और साधनों में मेवाड़ के उन्नत राज्य से छोटे हैं, फिर भी वे वीर हैं। मेवाड़ को विपत्ति के दिनों में सहायता देते रहे हैं। यदि उनसे कोई धृष्टता बन पड़ी हो, तो महाराणा उसे भूल जाएँ और राजपूत शक्तियों में स्नेह का सम्बन्ध बना रहने दें।

(i) प्रस्तुत कथन, किसने, किससे कहा है? स्पष्ट कीजिए। [2]

(ii) मेवाड़ को विपत्ति के दिनों में किसने सहायता दी है? चारणी यह बात क्यों याद दिलाती है? स्पष्ट कीजिए। [2]

(iii) चारणी ने महाराणा को अपनी प्रतिज्ञा पूरी करने का क्या उपाय बताया? यह कितना उचित था, इस सन्दर्भ में अपने विचार दीजिए। [3]

(iv) 'मातृभूमि का मान' कैसी एकांकी है? शीर्षक की सार्थकता सिद्ध करते हुए बताइए। [3]

[2019]

📋 Marking Scheme

(i) प्रस्तुत कथन चारणी ने मेवाड़ के महाराणा लाखा से कहा है। चारणी महाराणा लाखा के दरबार में राजपूतों की वीरता के गीत गाने वाली एक गायिका थी। वह एक बुद्धिमान नारी थी। उसे पता चला था कि महाराणा लाखा ने बूँदी के राव हेमू से पराजित होने के बाद अपने अपमान का बदला लेने के लिए यह प्रतिज्ञा ले ली थी कि जब तक मैं बूँदी के किले में ससैन्य प्रवेश नहीं करूँगा तब तक अन्न-जल ग्रहण नहीं करूँगा। वह राजपूतों में आपसी स्वाधीनता के लिए कुछ काम करने का सन्देश दे रही थी। यह गीत सुनकर महाराणा लाखा को आत्मबोध होता है और वे चारणी से कहते हैं कि मैं स्वयं इस श्रृंखला को तोड़ने जा रहा हूँ और दो जातियों में जानी दुश्मनी पैदा करने जा रहा हूँ। इसके प्रत्युत्तर में चारणी उन्हें कहती है कि महाराणा विवेकशील हैं और राबको ठन गर विश्वास है कि ने राजपूत शक्तियों में आपसी दुश्मनी पैदा नहीं होने देंगे।

(ii) मेवाड़ को विपत्ति के दिनों में बूँदी के हाड़ाओं ने सहायता दी थी। चारणी महाराणा को यह बात इसलिए याद दिलाती है क्योंकि वह राजपूतों में दुश्मनी पैदा नहीं होने देना चाहती। उसका मानना है कि राजस्थान के सभी राजपूतों को एकजुट होकर विदेशी शक्ति का सामना करना चाहिए।

चारणी एक समझदार महिला थी। वह गीतों के माध्यम से राजपूतों में वीरता का संचार करती थी। वह राजस्थान की सभी रियासतों में एकता और अंखडता स्थापित करना चाहती थी। उसमें तर्कशीलता भी थी। वह अपनी विवेकशीलता से महाराणा का पथ प्रदर्शन करना चाहती थी।

(iii) चारणी ने महाराणा को अपनी प्रतिज्ञा को पूरी करने का यह उपाय बताया कि मेवाड़ में बूँदी का एक नकली दुर्ग बनाएँ और महाराणा उसे विध्वंस करके अपनी शपथ पूरी करें।

मेरी दृष्टि में चारणी ने महाराणा को उनकी शपथ पूरी करने को जो उपाय बताया, वह उचित था। इसका कारण यह है कि महाराणा के व्यर्थ के दंभ में यदि युद्ध होता तो राजपूत भाइयों में शत्रुता और कटुता की भावना बढ़ जाती। युद्ध में अनेक वीर राजपूत सैनिक मारे जाते। उनकी सैन्य शक्ति कमज़ोर पड़ जाती और वे विदेशी शक्ति का सामना न कर पाते। इसके विपरीत यदि युद्ध रुक जाता तो राजपूतों के संबंधों में प्रगाढ़ता आती, जो सारे राज्य के लिए हितकारी होती।

(iv) यह देश भक्ति से परिपूर्ण ऐतिहासिक एकांकी है। प्रस्तुत एकांकी का शीर्षक मातृभूमि का मान रोचक तथा शिक्षाप्रद है। इसमें राजपूतों का अपनी मातृभूमि के लिए प्रेम तथा भक्ति भाव दर्शाया गया है। वे उसकी रक्षा के लिए अपना तन-मन-धन, सब कुछ न्यौछावर कर देते थे। प्रस्तुत एकांकी में बूँदी के सैनिक वीर सिंह का अपनी मातृभूमि के प्रति प्रेम उल्लेखनीय है, जिसने बूँदी के नकली दुर्ग की रक्षा के लिए अपने प्राणों की आहुति दे दी थी।

महाराणा लाखा अपनी मातृभूमि का मान रखने के लिए बूँदी को हराकर अपने अधीन करना चाहते थे ताकि अपने मस्तक पर लगे हार के कलंक को धो डालें।

बूँदी के राव हेमू भी अपनी मातृभूमि से बहुत प्रेम करते थे इसलिए उन्होंने महाराणा लाखा का प्रस्ताव ठुकरा दिया था। वे विदेशी अथवा देशी किसी भी शक्ति की अधीनता स्वीकार नहीं करते। उनका मानना था कि बूँदी एक स्वतन्त्र राज्य है। वह स्वतन्त्र रहकर महाराणाओं का आदर कर सकता है। इस प्रकार इस एकांकी का शीर्षक अपने उद्देश्य की पूर्ति करता है तथा उपयुक्त प्रतीत होता है।

Ans. (i) प्रस्तुत कथन चारणी ने मेवाड़ के शासक महाराणा लाखा से कहा। वह गीत गाते-गाते प्रवेश करती है। वह सम्पूर्ण राजस्थान को एकता के सूत्र में बाँधने की प्रार्थना करती है। वह महाराज से हाड़ा वीरों के द्वारा की गई गलती को भूल जाने का निवेदन करती है और आपस में स्नेह का सम्बन्ध बनाए रखने को कहती है।

(ii) मेवाड़ को विपत्ति के दिनों में बूँदी के शासक व उसके वीरों ने सहायता दी है। चारणी देश की स्वाधीनता को महत्व देती है और कहती है कि इस वक्त सम्पूर्ण राजस्थान को एकता के सूत्र में बाँधने की आवश्यकता है। वह महाराणा लाखा को याद दिलाती है क्योंकि वह राजपूतों में दुश्मनी पैदा नहीं होने देना चाहती। वह कहती है कि महाराज लाखा के विवेक पर सबको भरोसा है। वे हाड़ाओं द्वारा की गई धृष्टता को भूल जाएँ।

(iii) बूँदी के राव हेमू द्वारा मेवाड़ के साथ हाथ मिलाने के प्रस्ताव को इंकार करना और धोखे से युद्ध में महाराणा लाखा को परास्त कर दिया गया था। एक सच्चे राजपूत होने के कारण महाराणा लाखा गुस्से में आकर यह प्रतिज्ञा लेते हैं कि जब तक वे बूँदी के किले पर मेवाड़ का झंडा नहीं फहराएँगे, तब तक अन्न-जल ग्रहण नहीं करेंगे। तब

उनकी भीषण प्रतिज्ञा की पूर्ति हेतु चारणी बूँदी का नकली दुर्ग बनाकर, उसे महाराणा स्वयं ध्वस्त कर अपने अपमान का बदला लेकर प्रण पूरा करने का सुझाव देती है। उसका यह सुझाव उचित है क्योंकि ऐसा करने से बूँदी का असली दुर्ग सुरक्षित रहेगा। किसी के प्राणों की हानि नहीं होगी और दोनों राज्यों में प्रेम और सौहार्द भी बना रहेगा।

(iv) 'मातृभूमि का मान' देश भक्ति से परिपूर्ण एतिहासिक एकांकी है। प्रस्तुत एकांकी का शीर्षक मातृभूमि का मान रोचक तथा शिक्षाप्रद है। इसमें राजपूतों का अपनी मातृभूमि के लिए प्रेम तथा भक्ति भाव दर्शाया गया है। वे रउसकी रक्षा के लिए अपना तन-मन-धन, सब कुछ न्यौछावर कर देते थे।

महाराणा लाखा अपनी मातृभूमि का मान रखने के लिए बूँदी को हराकर अपने आधीन करना चाहते थे ताकि अपने मस्तक पर लगे हार के कलंक को धो डालें।

बूँदी के राव हेमू भी अपनी मातृभूमि से बहुत प्रेम करते थे इसलिए उन्होंने महाराणा लाखा का प्रस्ताव ठुकरा दिया था। वे विदेशी अथवा देशी किसी भी शक्ति की अधीनता स्वीकार नहीं करते। उनका मानना था कि बूँदी एक स्वतन्त्र राज्य है। वह स्वतन्त्र रहकर महाराणाओं का आदर कर सकता है। इस प्रकार इस एकांकी का शीर्षक अपने उद्देश्य की पूर्ति करता है तथा उपयुक्त प्रतीत होता है।

Q. 2. **Read the extract given below and answer in** *Hindi* **the questions that follow:**
निम्नलिखित अवतरण को पढ़िए और उसके नीचे लिखे प्रश्नों के उत्तर हिन्दी में लिखिए:

'प्राण जायें पर वचन न जायें' —यह हमारे जीवन का मूलमन्त्र है। जो तीर तरकश से निकलकर कमान से छूट गया, उसे बीच में लौटाया नहीं जा सकता। मेरी प्रतिज्ञा कठिनाई से पूरी होगी, यह मैं जानता हूँ और इस बात की हाल के युद्ध में पुष्टि भी हो चुकी है कि हाड़ा जाति वीरता में हम लोगों से किसी प्रकार हीन नहीं है।"

(i) उपर्युक्त कथन के वक्ता और श्रोता का संक्षिप्त परिचय दीजिए। [2]

(ii) वक्ता ने क्या प्रतिज्ञा ली थी? कारण सहित लिखिए। [2]

(iii) हाड़ा वंश के राजा कौन थे? हाड़ा लोगों की क्या विशेषताएँ थीं? उन पर प्रकाश डालिए। [3]

(iv) 'प्राण जायें पर वचन न जाये' —इस कहावत का क्या अर्थ है? एकांकी के सन्दर्भ में समझाइए। [3]
[2017]

Ans. (i) उपर्युक्त कथन के वक्ता महाराणा लाखा सिसौदिया वंश के राजपूत और मेवाड़ के शासक थे। वह राजपूतों में एकता की भावना सुदृढ़ बनाने के लिए असंगठित राजपूतों को एकजुट बनाने की भावना से बूँदी राज्य को अपने राज्य में मिलाना चाहते थे। उन्हें बाप्पा रावल और वीरवर हम्मीर की वीरता तथा शौर्य पर गर्व था।

इस कथन का श्रोता अभयसिंह है। वह मेवाड़ का सेनापति एवं महाराणा लाखा का विश्वासपात्र मेवाड़ सैनिक है। राजपूतों में एकता के भाव की वृद्धि के लिए बूँदी लेकर राज्य में मिला लेने का सन्देश वही राव हेमू के पास गया। उनसे अत्यन्त मधुरता से बात करता है। इससे प्रतीत होता है वह सबको समान रूप से सम्मान देने वाला विनम्र, बुद्धिमान, मृदुभाषी सैनिक है।

(ii) कथन के वक्ता महाराणा लाखा जो चित्तौड़ का सिसौदिया वंशी शासक था, एक बार युद्ध में बूँदी के राजपूतों द्वारा धोखे से हराये जाने के कारण उसका खून खौलता रहता है इसलिए उन्होंने प्रतिज्ञा कर ली कि जब तक वह बूँदी में ससैन्य प्रवेश कर उसे पराजित नहीं कर देंगे तब तक अन्न ग्रहण नहीं करेंगे।

(iii) हाड़ा वंश का राजा राव हेमू है। राव हेमू हाड़ा जाति के राजपूतों में से है। वह महाराणा लाखा और सिसौदिया वंश के अन्य राजपूतों के साथ प्रेम का सम्बन्ध रखना चाहते हैं। वे सबके प्रति सुख व दु:ख में सहायक हैं, किन्तु किसी प्रकार की अधीनता वह किसी की स्वीकार नहीं करना चाहते। वह अनुशासन में विश्वास करते हैं। महाराणा लाखा ने राव हेमू के द्वारा अधीनता स्वीकार न करने के कारण नकली बूँदी का किला बनवाकर

ससैन्य प्रवेश कर उसे पराजित करने का प्रयास किया, लेकिन उस समय भी हाड़ा वीरों व उनके एक वीर सेनानी वीरसिंह ने डटकर सामना किया और मातृभूमि पर अपना बलिदान दे दिया। हाड़ा राजपूत अत्यन्त वीर होते हैं। वे अपनी मातृभूमि की रक्षा में प्राणों की परवाह नहीं करते।

(iv) 'प्राण जाये पर वचन न जाये' यह कथन मेवाड़ के शासक महाराणा लाखा के द्वारा कहा गया है। जब उन्होंने प्रतिज्ञा की थी कि जब तक बूँदी को पराजित नहीं कर दूँगा अन्न ग्रहण नहीं करूँगा। ऐसी प्रतिज्ञा पर चारणी ने महाराणा को प्रतिज्ञा न करने की बात कही तब महाराणा लाखा कहते हैं कि राजपूतों की तो यह पहचान है कि वे प्राण त्याग देंगे, परन्तु वचन को नहीं त्यागेंगे।

इस कथन का अभिप्राय यही है कि प्राण भले ही चले जायें, परन्तु वचन को अवश्य पूरा किया जायेगा। महाराजा दशरथ ने वचन निभाने के लिए प्राण त्याग दिये थे। यह राजपूतों की शान व मान है। एकांकी के सन्दर्भ में भी यह उक्ति सटीक है। महाराणा लाखा ने भी बूँदी से बदला लेने के लिए अपने वचन को बनाये रखा दूसरी तरफ यदि हम देखें तो हाड़ा राजपूतों की सेना का सैनिक वीरसिंह इसका जीता जागता उदाहरण है।

Chapter 4.   सूखी डाली (Sukhi Dali)

—उपेन्द्रनाथ 'अश्क' (Upendranath 'Ashka')

Q. 1. **Read the extract given below and answer in** *Hindi* **the questions that follow:**

निम्नलिखित गद्यांश को पढ़िए और उसके नीचे लिखे प्रश्नों के उत्तर हिंदी में लिखिए:

बेटा, बड़प्पन बाहर की वस्तु नहीं — बड़प्पन तो मन का होना चाहिए। और फिर बेटा घृणा को घृणा से नहीं मिटाया जा सकता। बहू तभी पृथक होना चाहेगी जब उसे घृणा के बदले घृणा दी जाएगी। लेकिन यदि उसे घृणा के बदले स्नेह मिले तो उसकी समस्त घृणा धुँधली पड़कर लुप्त हो जाएगी।

(i) प्रस्तुत कथन का वक्ता कौन है? उसका संक्षिप्त परिचय दीजिए। **[2]**

(ii) श्रोता ने वक्ता को छोटी बहू के सम्बन्ध में क्या बताया था? **[2]**

(iii) वक्ता ने परिवार में एकता बनाये रखने का क्या उपाय निकाला? क्या वे इसमें सफल हुए? स्पष्ट कीजिए। **[3]**

(iv) प्रस्तुत एकांकी किस प्रकार की एकांकी है? इस एकांकी लेखन का क्या उद्देश्य है? **[3]**

[2019]

📋 **Marking Scheme**

(i) प्रस्तुत कथन के वक्ता दादाजी मूलराज हैं। वे एक धनी तथा प्रतिष्ठित व्यक्ति हैं। उनके पास ज़मीन-जायदाद है, फार्म, डेयरी तथा चीनी के कारखाने हैं जिनकी देखभाल उनके दो बेटे तथा पोते करते हैं। वे एक बड़े से परिवार के मुखिया हैं। उनकी उम्र 72 (बहत्तर) वर्ष है। वे शरीर से स्वस्थ तथा हृष्ट-पुष्ट हैं।

(ii) श्रोता कर्मचंद ने दादाजी को यह बताया कि छोटी बहू परिवार में खुश नहीं है। शायद परेश और वो अलग होना चाहते हैं। दादाजी के पूछने पर कर्मचंद ने कहा कि जहाँ तक मेरा विचार है छोटी बहू के मन में दर्प की मात्रा ज़रूरत से कुछ ज़्यादा है। मैंने वह मलमल के थान और रज़ाई के अबरे लाकर दिए थे। सबने तो रख लिए पर छोटी बहू को वे पसंद नहीं आए। वह अपने मायके के घराने को शायद इस घराने से बड़ा समझती है और इस घर को घृणा की दृष्टि से देखती है।

(iii) दादाजी बहुत अनुभवी, समझदार तथा दूरदर्शी व्यक्ति थे। वे परिवार में एकता और अखंडता बनाये रखने में विश्वास रखते थे। जब उन्हें कर्मचंद से पता चला कि छोटी बहू परिवार में खुश नहीं है तो उन्होंने उसे छोड़कर परिवार के सभी सदस्यों को अपने पास बुलाया और उनसे कहा कि मुझे यह जानकर बहुत दु:ख हुआ कि छोटी बहू का यहाँ मन नहीं लगा। इसमें दोष उसका नहीं, हमारा दोष है। वह एक बड़े घर की बेटी है। अत्यधिक

पढ़ी-लिखी है। सबसे आदर पाती और राज करती आई है। यहाँ उसे हर एक का आदर करना पड़ता है। छोटी बहू अपनी बुद्धि और योग्यता में निश्चय ही हमसे बड़ी है। हमें उसे आदर देना चाहिए तथा उसके गुणों से लाभ उठाना चाहिए। मेरी यह इच्छा है कि सब उसका कहना मानें, उससे परामर्श लें और उसका काम भी आपस में बाँट लें। उसे पढ़ने-लिखने का अधिक अवसर दें। जी हाँ, दादाजी का यह उपाय पूर्णतया सफल हुआ। छोटी बहू को मान-सम्मान तथा प्रेम मिला। वह भी परिवार के साथ मिलकर रहना और काम करना सीख गई। इस प्रकार परिवार बिखरने से बच गया।

(iv) प्रस्तुत एकांकी संयुक्त परिवार प्रणाली पर आधारित परिवारिक तथा सामाजिक एवम एक शिक्षाप्रद एकांकी है, जिसमें संयुक्त परिवार की समस्याओं को दर्शाया गया है। बड़े परिवार में भिन्न-भिन्न स्वभाव के लोग होते हैं। उनमें वैचारिक मतभेद भी हो जाते हैं जो आपसी कलह तथा ईर्ष्या-द्वेष का कारण बनते हैं। परिवार में प्रेम, अनुशासन तथा आपसी सूझ-बूझ से एकता और अखंडता बनाए रखी जा सकती है। परिवार के मुखिया को समझदार, दूरदर्शी तथा निष्पक्ष स्वभाव का होना चाहिए ताकि वह परिवार के सदस्यों में ताल-मेल बैठा सके। जैसे कि दादाजी ने छोटी बहू और परिवार के सदस्यों के बीच ताल-मेल बैठाया। परिवार में नयी आई बहू भिन्न परिवेश की होने के कारण समायोजन करना सीख नहीं पाती। उसे प्रेम तथा आदर देकर परिवार के माहौल में ढालना चाहिए। बहू को भी बात-बात पर मायके से तुलना नहीं करना चाहिए तथा व्यंग्यात्मक बातों से बचना चाहिए। इस प्रकार एकांकीकार अपने उद्देश्य की पूर्ति करने में सफल हुए हैं।

Ans. (i) प्रस्तुत कथन के वक्ता दादा मूलराज हैं और श्रोता कर्मचन्द हैं। दादाजी कहानी के मूल पात्र हैं। वे एक धनी तथा प्रतिष्ठित व्यक्ति हैं। उनकी आयु 72 वर्ष है तथा वे शरीर से हष्ट-पुष्ट तथा स्वस्थ हैं। वे संयुक्त परिवार के समर्थक हैं। दादाजी समझदार और अनुशासित हैं। उनके कुशल नेतृत्व के कारण ही उनका परिवार प्रगति पथ पर निरन्तर बढ़ता गया और प्यार और एकता के सूत्र में बँधा हुआ था।

(ii) श्रोता कर्मचन्द दादाजी को बताता है कि छोटी बहू परिवार में खुश नहीं है, वह और परेश शायद अलग होना चाहते हैं। घमण्ड के कारण छोटी बहू मायके के घराने को बड़ा समझती है और इस घर को घृणा की दृष्टि से देखती है। छोटी बहू बेला को मलमल का थान और रजाई भी पसन्द नहीं आयी।

(iii) वक्ता दादाजी मूलराज अनुभवी, होशियार और समझदार व्यक्ति थे। जब उन्हें छोटी बहू बेला के बारे में पता चलता है तो वे उसके मन की घृणा को मिटाने के लिए स्नेह देना चाहते थे। उनका विचार था कि यदि घृणा के बदले में स्नेह दिया जाए, तो घृणा अपने आप समाप्त हो जायेगी। दादा मूलराज बेला के अतिरिक्त घर के सभी सदस्यों को बुलाकर कहते हैं कि बेला बड़े घर की बेटी है। यहाँ उसका व्यक्तित्व दबकर रह गया है। व्यक्ति उम्र और दर्जे से नहीं बल्कि बुद्धि और योग्यता से बड़ा होता है। वे सभी सदस्यों को कहते हैं

कि सभी बेला का आदर सत्कार करें, उसका कहना मानें, उससे परामर्श लें और घर का काम न करवाकर पढ़ने-लिखने का अवसर दें। कोई उसका मजाक न उड़ाए। सभी सदस्यों ने दादाजी के कहे अनुसार ही बेला के साथ व्यवहार किया। दादाजी अपनी इस योजना में सफल हुए। अन्त में बेला को अपनी भूल का अहसास होता है और वह ससुराल वालों के साथ घुल-मिल जाती है।

(iv) प्रस्तुत एकांकी "सूखी डाली" संयुक्त परिवार की महत्ता को बताने वाली एकांकी है। उस संयुक्त परिवार की एकता को बनाए रखने और सभी के साथ प्रेम एवं आदर का व्यवहार करने की महत्ता को बताना ही एकांकी का मुख्य उद्देश्य है। एकांकीकार ने मूलराज के परिवार का उदाहरण देकर यह बताया है कि साथ रहने में सुख है और घर के बड़े नहीं चाहते कि घर के सदस्य अलग हो जाएं। दादाजी अपनी समझदारी से बेला को परिवार का हिस्सा बनाने में कामयाब हो जाते हैं तथा परिवार की एकता को छिन्न-भिन्न हो जाने से बचा लेते हैं।

Q. 2. **Read the extract given below and answer in** *Hindi* **the questions that follow:**

निम्नलिखित अवतरण को पढ़िए और उसके नीचे लिखे प्रश्नों के उत्तर हिन्दी में लिखिए:

"मेरी आकांक्षा है कि सब डालियाँ साथ-साथ फलें-फूलें, जीवन की सुखद, शीतल वायु के स्पर्श से झूमें और सरसराएँ। विटप से अलग होने वाली डाली की कल्पना ही मुझे सिहरा देती है।"

(i) उपर्युक्त कथन कौन, किससे, किस सन्दर्भ में कह रहा है? [2]

(ii) सब डालियाँ साथ-साथ फलने-फूलने से क्या आशय है? 'डालियाँ' शब्द किसके लिए प्रयुक्त हुआ है? [2]

(iii) किसकी आकांक्षा है कि सब खुशहाल रहें और क्यों? इस एकांकी से आपको क्या शिक्षा मिलती है? [3]

(iv) प्रस्तुत कथन से वक्ता की किस चारित्रिक विशेषता का पता चलता है? अपने विचार भी प्रस्तुत कीजिए। [3]

[2017]

Ans. (i) उपर्युक्त कथन श्री उपेन्द्रनाथ 'अश्क' के द्वारा रचित एकांकी 'सूखी डाली' के महत्वपूर्ण पात्र मूलराज छोटी बहू के अतिरिक्त परिवार के सभी सदस्यों से कह रहे हैं। यह बात इस सन्दर्भ में कही गई है कि दादा मूलराज का परिवार एक संयुक्त परिवार है। इन्दु व परेश की बहू बेला में अक्सर नोंक-झोंक इस बात पर होती है क्योंकि वह एक सम्पन्न परिवार की सुशिक्षित लड़की है। इधर इन्दु को लगता है कि बेला अपने सामने सबको मूर्ख, गँवार व असभ्य समझती है। चूँकि दादाजी ने सम्पूर्ण परिवार को एक बड़े वटवृक्ष की फलती-फूलती डालियों के रूप में देखा है। वह उसे उसी रूप में

फलता-फूलता देखना चाहते हैं। इसीलिए वह अपनी पोती ही नहीं अपितु घर के सभी सदस्यों को नई बहू बेला के साथ तालमेल बैठाते हुए उसको प्यार व सम्मान देने की बात कहते हैं।

(ii) सब डालियाँ साथ-साथ फलने-फूलने से अभिप्राय यह है कि परिवार का हर सदस्य खुश व सुखी रहे। उनमें आपस में किसी भी प्रकार की हीनभावना या वैमनस्य नहीं होना चाहिए। ''डालियाँ'' शब्द का प्रयोग दादा मूलराज ने परिवार के सदस्यों के लिये किया है, दादाजी एक वट वृक्ष हैं। उनके पुत्र, वधुएँ, पोते सभी वट वृक्ष की डालियों की भाँति डालियाँ हैं। उन्होंने कहा है कि सब एकता के सूत्र में बँधकर एक-दूसरे को समझकर कार्य करें।

(iii) 'सूखी डाली' एकांकी के मुख्य पात्र दादा मूलराज जो 72 वर्षीय परिवार के मुखिया हैं उनकी इच्छा है कि उनके परिवार के सभी सदस्य खुशी से भरपूर और प्रसन्नमुख रहें। इसका कारण यह है कि दादाजी स्वयं उनमें से किसी को कोई कष्ट नहीं होने देना चाहते हैं। उनके पास ऐसे समाधान हैं जिनसे वे उन सबको परस्पर घृणा, ईर्ष्या, अपमान या किसी को छोटा या गँवार समझने की बुराई

को दूर करने में सक्षम हैं। उनके इसी गुण के कारण परिवार का हर सदस्य उनके सामने नतमस्तक है।

यह एकांकी सुखद स्वस्थ एवं खुशहाल संयुक्त परिवार की नींव डालने पर बल देती है। दादाजी इसके मेरु हैं जिसने पूरे परिवार को एक स्वस्थ व्यवस्था प्रदान की है। वे सभी परिवारियों के साथ समान प्यार, सहानुभूति एवं सद्भावनापूर्ण व्यवहार करते हैं। वह दार्शनिक और मनोवैज्ञानिक हैं। हम लोगों को भी ऐसे ही संयुक्त परिवार की रचना करनी चाहिए जिसमें परस्पर प्रेम, दूसरों की भावनाओं का आदर, सहनशक्ति एवं तालमेल का गुण होना अति आवश्यक है।

(iv) प्रस्तुत कथन से वक्ता दादा मूलराज की चरित्र की दार्शनिक, मनोवैज्ञानिक व सूझ-बूझ वाली विशेषता का पता चलता है कि वे अपने संगठित परिवार को फलते-फूलते देखना चाहते हैं। जिस प्रकार वट वृक्ष की वृद्धि या विकास अथवा उसकी शक्ति उसकी डालियाँ हैं उसी प्रकार एक संगठित संयुक्त हँसता, खेलता तथा मुस्कराता परिवार ही अच्छे परिवार की पहचान है। संयुक्त परिवार को बनाये रखने में दादाजी ने कोमल स्वभाव द्वारा कठोरता को जीतने की बात सिद्ध कर दी है।

Chapter 6. दीपदान (Deepdan)

—डॉ. रामकुमार वर्मा (Dr. Ram Kumar Verma)

Q. 1. **Read the extract given below and answer in *Hindi* the questions that follow:**

निम्नलिखित अवतरण को पढ़िए और उसके नीचे लिखे प्रश्नों के उत्तर हिंदी में लिखिए:

मैं ही क्या, सारे नगर-निवासी यह त्योहार मना रहे हैं, नहीं मना रही हो तो तुम! धाय माँ तुम! पहाड़ बनने से क्या होगा? राजमहल पर बोझ बनकर जाओगी, बोझ! और नदी बनो तो तुम्हारा बहता हुआ बोझ पत्थर भी अपने सिर पर धारण करेंगे, पत्थर भी!

(i) वक्ता का संक्षिप्त परिचय दीजिए। **[2]**

(ii) 'पहाड़' और 'नदी' से वक्ता का क्या तात्पर्य है? वह श्रोता को क्या सुझाव देती है? **[2]**

(iii) वक्ता के सुझाव पर श्रोता की क्या प्रतिक्रिया होती है? समझाकर उत्तर लिखिए। **[3]**

(iv) श्रोता का चरित्र किस प्रकार प्रेरणादायक है? एकांकी के आधार पर समझाइए। **[3]**
[2020]

Ans. (i) वक्ता: सोना-रावल सरूपसिंह की अत्यंत सलोनी एवं रूपवती पुत्री थी। सोलह वर्षीय सोना कुँवर उदय सिंह के बचपन की मित्र है। वह नृत्यकला में पारंगत है। बनवीर द्वारा दिए गए प्रलोभनों की ओर आकर्षित होती है। स्वभाव से नटखट भी है। कुँवर के साथ खेलती है। वह वाक्पटु भी है।

(ii) वक्ता सोना श्रोता पन्ना धाय को राजमहल पर पहाड़ जैसा बोझ बनकर रहने से अच्छा नदी की तरह बहते रहने का सुझाव देती है। वह कहती है कि अगर तुम नदी बनकर रहोगी तो तुम्हारे जीवन में आनंद और मंगल का प्रवाह सदा बना रहेगा। सोना कहती है कि पन्ना बनवीर पर संदेह न करे और दीपदान के उत्सव में भाग लें।

(iii) श्रोता 'पन्ना-धाय' अनुभवी है। वह अच्छी तरह समझती है कि ऐसे उत्सवों के पीछे एक षड्यंत्र रचा गया है। इन्हीं उत्सवों के बहाने सत्ता परिवर्तन तथा किसी विशेष व्यक्ति की हत्या अवश्य होती है। इसलिए वह उस उत्सव में न तो स्वयं जाती है न ही उदयसिंह को भेजती है। वह सोना को भी समझाती है। वह यह भी कहती है कि 'चित्तौड़' राग-रंग की भूमि नहीं है, जौहर की भूमि है।

(iv) श्रोता 'पन्ना-धाय' का चरित्र सबके लिए प्रेरणादायक है। वह देश-प्रेम की भावना हर पाठक के दिल में जगाती है। 'पन्ना-धाय' महाराणा सांगा के छोटे पुत्र उदयसिंह की संरक्षिका है। बनवीर से कुँवर की रक्षा हेतु अपने पुत्र चंदन का बलिदान कर देती है। उसकी कर्त्तव्यनिष्ठा सबके लिए प्रेरणादाई है। अपनी स्वामिभक्ति व राष्ट्रीयता के गुणों के कारण वह आदर्श भारतीय नारी का अनुपम उदाहरण पेश करती है। वह एक सच्ची भारतीय वीरांगना व अमर पात्रा है।

Q. 2. **Read the extract given below and answer in** *Hindi* **the questions that follow:**

निम्नलिखित अवतरण को पढ़िए और उसके नीचे लिखे प्रश्नों के उत्तर हिंदी में लिखिए:

"आज कुसमय नाच-रंग की बात सुनकर मेरे मन में शंका हुई थी। इसलिए मैंने कुँवर को वहाँ जाने से रोक दिया था। संभव था कि कुँवर वहाँ जाते और बनवीर अपने सहायकों से कोई काण्ड रच देता।"

(i) उपर्युक्त कथन का वक्ता कौन है? उसका संक्षिप्त परिचय दीजिए। **[2]**

(ii) नाच-रंग का आयोजन किसने और किस उद्देश्य से किया था? **[2]**

(iii) बनवीर कौन है? उसका परिचय देते हुए उसका चरित्र-चित्रण कीजिए। **[3]**

(iv) 'दीपदान' एकांकी के शीर्षक की सार्थकता बताइए तथा एकांकी के माध्यम से एकांकीकार ने क्या शिक्षा दी है? **[3]**

[2018]

📋 **Marking Scheme**

(i) उपर्युक्त कथन की वक्ता पन्ना है। पन्ना 'खीचो' जाति की एक राजपूत महिला है। पन्ना चित्तौड़ के महाराणा साँगा के छोटे पुत्र उदय सिंह की धाय एवं संरक्षिका है। पन्ना एक अत्यंत कर्त्तव्यनिष्ठ एवं ममतामयी धाय-माँ है जिसके बिना उदयसिंह पलभर भी नहीं रह पाते। वह बहुत समझदार और सहनशील स्त्री है जिसे बनवीर के षडयंत्र तथा चित्तौड़ पर आने वाली मुसीबत का पहले से अंदाज़ा हो जाता है।

(ii) नाच-रंग का आयोजन महाराणा संग्रामसिंह के छोटे भाई पृथ्वीसिंह के दासी-पुत्र बनवीर ने किया था। महाराणा संग्राम सिंह की मृत्यु के बाद बनवीर चित्तौड़ का शासक बनना चाहता था। अपनी इस महत्वाकांक्षा की पूर्ति के लिए पहले वह सोते हुए विक्रमादित्य की हत्या कर देता है फिर कुँवर उदयसिंह की हत्या करने के लिए मयूर-पक्ष कुण्ड में असमय ही दीपदान का आयोजन करता है। उदय सिंह राणा साँगा का पुत्र है जो चित्तौड़ राज्य का सच्चा उत्तराधिकारी है।

(iii) बनवीर महाराणा साँगा के भाई पृथ्वीसिंह का दासी पुत्र थां। महाराणा की मृत्यु के बाद उसे कुँवर उदयसिंह का संरक्षक और उनके वयस्क होने तक राज्य का संचालक बना दिया गया था।

(iv) किसी भी रचना का शीर्षक संक्षिप्त, उद्देश्यपूर्ण कहानी के कलेवर को घेरे हुए एवं जिज्ञासापूर्ण होना चाहिए। इस दृष्टि से 'दीपदान' शीर्षक पूर्णतः उपयुक्त है। इसमें एकांकी का समस्त कथासार समाहित है। अपने पथ को निष्कंटक बनाने के लिए मयूर-पक्ष नामक कुण्ड में तुलजा भवानी की पूजास्वरूप दीपदान का उत्सव आयोजित कर बनवीर पन्ना धाय के पुत्र चंदन को उदयसिंह समझकर, यमराज को दीपदान करता है। पन्ना धाय भी चित्तौड़ के कुलदीपक की रक्षा हेतु अपने कुल के दीपक (चन्दन) का दान कर देती है। इसके साथ ही शीर्षक कौतूहल पूर्ण, आकर्षक एवं संक्षिप्त भी है। 'दीपदान' शीर्षक

पढ़ते ही मन में जिज्ञासा उत्पन्न होने लगती है कि किसका व कैसा और कौन सा दीपदान है। एकांकी को पढ़ने की इच्छा जागृत हो जाती है। प्रस्तुत एकांकी के 'प्राणदान', 'पुत्र का बलिदान', 'चन्दन की हत्या', 'हत्यारा बनवीर', 'पन्ना का त्याग', 'उदयसिंह की रक्षा' आदि और भी अनेक शीर्षक हो सकते हैं पर 'दीपदान' ही श्रेष्ठ व उपयुक्त शीर्षक है क्योंकि इसमें एक अच्छे शीर्षक के सभी गुण विद्यमान हैं।

'दीपदान' एकांकी द्वारा एकांकीकार ने पन्ना के माध्यम से यह शिक्षा दी है कि राष्ट्र-प्रेम, पुत्र प्रेम से बड़ा और महान है। हमें कभी भी अपना विवेक खोकर अन्यायपूर्ण आचरण नहीं करना चाहिए। इसके अतिरिक्त एकांकीकार ने यह शिक्षा भी दी है कि हमें अपने निजी स्वार्थ से ऊपर उठकर अपने कर्त्तव्य का पालन करना तथा समाज में आदर्श एवं मूल्यों की स्थापना करनी चाहिए।

Ans. **(i)** उपर्युक्त कथन की वक्ता पन्ना धाय है। वह चित्तौड़ के महाराणा सांगा के पुत्र कुँवर उदय सिंह की संरक्षिका है। वह सच्ची एवं कर्त्तव्यनिष्ठ सेविका है। राजभक्त है, ममतामयी है, बलिदानी और त्यागी, बुद्धिमान एवं दूरदर्शी है।

(ii) नाच-रंग का आयोजन महाराणा संग्राम सिंह के छोटे भाई पृथ्वीसिंह के दासी पुत्र बनवीर ने करवाया था। उसका उद्देश्य था कि नगर के लोग नाच-रंग में डूबे रहेंगे और वह उदय सिंह को मार सकेगा, क्योंकि उसके रहते बनवीर कभी राजा नहीं बन सकता था। अपनी इस महत्वाकांक्षा की पूर्ति के लिए वह सोते हुए विक्रमादित्य की हत्या कर देता है फिर कुंवर उदयसिंह की हत्या करने के लिए मयूर-पक्ष कुण्ड में असमय ही दीपदान का आयोजन करता है।

(iii) बनवीर महाराणा के भाई पृथ्वीसिंह का दासी पुत्र है। वह अत्यंत क्रूर, विलासी और धूर्त किस्म का व्यक्ति है जो राज्य के लालच में पहले विक्रमादित्य की हत्या करता है फिर कुँवर उदय सिंह को मारना चाहता है जिससे बिना किसी बाधा के राज्य कर सके।

(iv) इस एकांकी के लिए दीपदान शीर्षक सर्वथा उपयुक्त एवं सार्थक है। क्योंकि, किसी भी रचना का शीर्षक उसकी कथा के मूल के निकट उद्देश्यपूर्ण, संक्षिप्त एवं रोचक होना चाहिए। इस शीर्षक में पूरी कथा का सार निहित है क्योंकि बनवीर उदयसिंह को मारने के लिए मयूरपंख नामक कुंड में तुलजा भवानी की पूजास्वरूप दीपदान का उत्सव आयोजित करता है तथा नाच-रंग का कार्यक्रम आयोजित करता है। उसकी आड़ में वह उदयसिंह को मारने का प्रयास करता है, लेकिन पन्ना धाय के कारण उसका षड्यंत्र पूरा नहीं हो पाता है। पन्ना अपने पुत्र चंदन का बलिदान कर देती है। चित्तौड़ के दीपक को बचाने के लिए अपने कुल के दीपक (चंदन) को दान कर देती है, इसलिए शीर्षक सार्थक है। इस एकांकी के माध्यम से नागरिक के कर्त्तव्य (राष्ट्र की सुरक्षा) को सफलता से दिखाया गया है। देश प्रेम की भावना की शिक्षा दी है। इस एकांकी में एकांकीकार ने शिक्षा दी है; कि राष्ट्रप्रेम पुत्र प्रेम से बड़ा और महान है।

HISTORY
&
CIVICS

Chapter 1

The Union Parliament

Very-Short Answer Type Questions

Q. 1. Name the two Houses of the Indian Parliament. [2020, 2015]

Ans. The two Houses of the Indian Parliament are Lok Sabha and Rajya Sabha.

Q. 2. What is meant by the term 'Session'? [2020]

Ans. Sessions are formal sitting of both the Houses of the Parliament to conduct its transactions and business of the Houses. Normally, there are three sessions (i) Budget Session, (ii) Winter Session, (iii) Monsoon Session.

Q. 3. How is the Speaker of the Lok Sabha elected? [2020]

Ans. The speaker of Lok Sabha is elected by the members of the House.

Q. 4. What is the term of office of a Rajya Sabha member? [2020]

Ans. The term of office of a Rajya Sabha member is 6 years.

Q. 5. What is the normal term of office of the Lok Sabha? [2019, 2016]

Ans. Five years

Q. 6. State the meaning of the term, 'Question Hour'. [2019]

Ans. The first hour of sitting in both the Houses of Parliament is allotted for asking and answering of questions, unless otherwise decided by the Speaker. This hour (which usually starts at 11 a.m.) is known as the Question Hour.

Q. 7. Name the Presiding Officer of the Lok Sabha. [2019]

Ans. The Speaker

Q. 8. State any one condition when the Parliament can legislate on subjects in the State List. [2019]

Ans. During the Proclamation of a National Emergency.

Q. 9. What happens when a motion of 'No-Confidence' is passed against a Minister? [2019, 2015]

Ans. If a motion of No-Confidence is passed against a minister. The entire Ministry resigns en bloc (the Government has to resign.)

Q. 10. Name the bill that cannot originate in the Rajya Sabha. [2018]

Ans. Money bills cannot originate in the Rajya Sabha.

Q. 11. What is meant by the term, 'quorum'? [2018]

Ans. Quorum means the prescribed minimum number of members to be present to hold the meeting of a collective body or any House of the Parliament, such as the Lok Sabha or the Rajya Sabha. The Quorum to constitute a meeting of the House is one-tenth of the total strength of the House.

Q. 12. What is the maximum gap allowed between the two Parliamentary sessions? [2018]

Ans. The maximum gap allowed between the two Parliamentary sessions is six months.

Q. 13. State any one federal feature of the Indian Constitution. [2017]

Ans. They are :
1. A written constitution.
2. Bicameral legislature.
3. An independent judiciary/(Supreme Court is the Final Interpreter of the Constitution).
4. Division of powers/(between the Union and the States)

Q. 14. How are the Rajya Sabha members elected? [2017]

Ans. The representatives of each state in the Rajya Sabha are elected indirectly by the elected members of the Legislative Assembly of each state in accordance with the system of proportional representation by means of a single transferable vote.

Q. 15. Who presides over the Joint Session of the two Houses of Parliament? [2017]

Ans. The Speaker of the Lok Sabha presides over the joint session of the two Houses of Parliament.

Q. 16. When can the Speaker of the Lok Sabha cast his vote? **[2017]**

Ans. The Speaker of the Lok Sabha puts the issues to vote and announces the results. The Speaker does not vote in the House, except when there are equal votes on both sides, *i.e.*, the Treasury Benches and the Opposition.

Q. 17. How long can the Rajya Sabha retain the money bill sent by the Lok Sabha? **[2017]**

Ans. Money bills can only be introduced in the Lok Sabha, and upon being passed, are sent to the Rajya Sabha, where it can be deliberated on for upto 14 days.

Q. 18. What is meant by Residuary Powers of the Parliament? **[2016]**

Ans. The Parliament possesses Residuary Powers. It means that, it can make laws with respect to all those matters which are not mentioned in any of the three Lists — The Union List, the State List and the Concurrent List.

Q. 19. State any one subject wherein the Lok Sabha and the Rajya Sabha enjoy co-equal powers in the legislation of laws. **[2016]**

Ans. The Constitution puts the Rajya Sabha on an equal footing with the Lok Sabha in matters such as:

1. The election of the President
2. Impeachment of the President
3. Removal of the Judges
4. Proclamation of Emergency
5. Promulgation of Ordinances
6. Constitutional Amendments and Ordinary Bills.

Q. 20. How many members are nominated by the President to the Lok Sabha? Which community do they represent? **[2015]**

Ans. Two members of the Anglo-Indian Community may be nominated by the President to the Lok Sabha, in case he feels that this community is not adequately represented.

Q. 21. What is the required quorum to hold the meetings of the Lok Sabha? **[2015]**

Ans. The required quorum of the Lok Sabha is one-tenth of the total membership of the House. This means that, the House cannot conduct its proceedings or pass bills and resolutions without the presence of at least one-tenth of its total membership.

Q. 22. Mention one provision of the Constitution which clearly establishes the supremacy of the Lok Sabha with regard to money bills. **[2015]**

Ans. In case of money bills, the Rajya Sabha has virtually no powers. It can neither reject a money bill nor amend it by virtue of its own powers. It must, within the stipulated period of 14 days, return the bill to the Lok Sabha, which may thereupon either accept or reject all or any of the recommendations of the Rajya Sabha.

Q. 23. Why is the Rajya Sabha called a 'Permanent House'? **[2014]**

Ans. The term of the members elected to the Rajya Sabha is six years. However, every second year, one-third of the members retire and there are new entrants. The Rajya Sabha cannot be dissolved by the President of India. Thus, this House is never empty and therefore, it is called a 'Permanent House'.

Q. 24. State the minimum number of times the Lok Sabha must meet in a year. **[2014]**

Ans. According to the Constitution, the Lok Sabha must meet at least twice a year with not more than six months break between the two sessions.

Q. 25. Name the two types of authority in a federal set up in India. **[2013]**

Ans. Two types of authority in a federal set up in India are the Central Government and the State Government.

Q. 26. How is the Speaker of the Lok Sabha elected? **[2013]**

Ans. The Speaker of the Lok Sabha is elected from among its own members by the majority vote.

Q. 27. When can the Vice-President cast a vote in the Rajya Sabha? **[2013]**

Ans. The Vice-President can cast a vote in the Rajya Sabha in case of a deadlock, *i.e.*, an equality of votes.

Q. 28. Name the law making body of the Union Government. **[2012]**

Ans. The Legislature is the law making body of the Union Government.

Q. 29. What is the difference in the term of office between the Lok Sabha and the Rajya Sabha? **[2012]**

Ans. The term of office of the Lok Sabha is five years whereas, the Rajya Sabha is the permanent House, but one-third of its members retire after every second year. Thereafter, fresh elections are announced for the seats vacated at the beginning of the third year. Every member enjoys a six-year term and is eligible for re-election.

Q. 30. Name the bill which cannot originate in the Rajya Sabha. [2012]

Ans. Money bills cannot originate in the Rajya Sabha.

Q. 31. Mr. Ajayveer Singh is a member of the Lok Sabha. Can he be appointed as a Governor of a State? If so, under what criterion? [2012]

Ans. Yes, he can be appointed as a Governor of the state but, he has to resign from the membership of the Lok Sabha.

Q. 32. Name the main constituents of the Indian Parliament. [2011]

Ans. The main constituents of the Indian Parliament are:

1. The President of the Union

2. The Rajya Sabha (*i.e.,* the Upper House) or the Council of States.

3. The Lok Sabha (*i.e.,* the Lower House) or the House of the People.

Q. 33. Elections in India are held by secret ballot. Give a reason for the same. [2011]

Ans. Elections in India are held by the secret ballot so that a voter may indicate his choice in favour of any of the candidates without any fear.

Q. 34. Mention any one circumstance when the Parliament can make laws on a state subject. [2011]

Ans. The Parliament can make laws on a state subject during the proclamation of emergency.

Q. 35. Mention any one situation when both the Houses of Parliament meet for a joint session. [2010]

Ans. When there is a deadlock between the two Houses of Parliament, while passing an ordinary bill, the President calls for the joint session of both the Houses.

Q. 36. Mr. Gurudev was nominated by the President to the Rajya Sabha. Mention any one criterion on which the President would have nominated him.

How many such members can the President nominate to the Rajya Sabha? [2010]

Ans. Mr. Gurudev might be having special knowledge or practical experience or expertise in matters, such as literature, science, art and social service. So, the President of India might have nominated him.

The President can nominate 12 such members to the Rajya Sabha.

Q. 37. What happens to the ruling government when a vote of No-Confidence is passed against it? [2010]

Ans. When a vote of No-Confidence is passed against the ruling government, then it has to resign.

Long Answer Type Questions

Q. 1. With reference to the Union Legislature, answer the following questions :

(a) Explain any three Legislative powers of the Union Parliament.

(b) State any three exclusive powers of t h e Lok Sabha that is not enjoyed by the other House. [2020]

📋 Marking Scheme

(a) Legislative powers of the union parliament:
 – To make laws in the union list /97 subjects
 – Matters in the concurrent list/47 subjects
 – Residuary powers/matters not mentioned in 3 lists
 – Matters in the state list
 – during an emergency

 – approved by 2/3 majority by the Rajya Sabha
 – when two or more states ask
 – President's Rule
 – Ordinances must be approved
 – Powers during emergency/67 subjects in state list.
 (Any three points)

(b) – Motions of No-Confidence against the government can only be introduced and passed in the Lok Sabha/ answerable to the Lok Sabha only/ enjoy power only until they enjoy the trust of the house
 – Money bills can be introduced only in the Lok Sabha and the Rajya Sabha cannot reject or amend it. /budget is passed/controls the national purse/has complete control over finance
 – In case of a deadlock between the two houses, the will of the Lok Sabha prevails due to its higher numerical strength.
 – Can pass an Adjournment Motion. *(Any three points)*

Ans. **(a)** **The three Legislative powers of the Union Parliament are given below:**

1. The Parliament is a law-making body and it is considered as the centre of all democratic political process. It has exclusive powers to make laws on all subjects listed in Union List and Concurrent List.

2. The Parliament has power of financial control through budget discussion. For example : Fiscal Policy.

3. It acts as an arbitrary power of other organs—Judiciary and Executive.

4. During a National Emergency, the union system of the government becomes a unitary one by granting Parliament the power to make laws on the 66 subjects of the State List. Also, all state money bills are referred to the Parliament for its approval.

(b) **Exclusive powers of Lok Sabha :**

1. Motion of No Confidence against the government can only be introduced and passed in the Lok Sabha.

2. Money bills can only be introduced in Lok Sabha.

3. In case of deadlock between the two houses over non financial ordinary bill, the Lok Sabha normally prevails as a strength which includes more than twice as many members as the Rajya Sabha.

Q. 2. **The Parliament is the body of people's representative that has the Supreme power in a democracy. With reference to the Union Legislature, answer the following:**

(a) **How are the members of the Rajya Sabha elected?**

(b) **Why is it called a Permanent House?**

(c) **State any two Financial and any two Legislative powers of the Indian Parliament.** **[2019]**

📋 Marking Scheme ----------------------------------

(a) Elected by the members of elected Legislative Assemblies.
Indirectly elected on the basis of proportional representation with a single transferable vote.

(b) 1/3 of its members retire every two years
The house is never dissolved as a whole

(c) Financial Powers
– Passes the Budget of the Union Parliament,
– Determines the Salaries & Allowances of the members of Parliament,

–No taxes can be imposed unless approved by the Parliament,
– Passes the Supplementary grants
– Vote on account,
– Passes the Money Bill. *(Any two points)*
Legislative Powers
– Makes laws on subjects in the Union List
– Makes laws on subjects in the State List (under certain conditions)
– Makes laws on subjects in the Concurrent list
– Possesses Residuary power.
– Approves Ordinances.
– Power during an Emergency.
– Makes amendments to the Constitution.
(Any two points)

Ans. **(a)** The representatives of each State in the Rajya Sabha are elected by the elected members of the Legislative Assembly in accordance with the system of proportional representation by means of a 'single transferable vote'.

(b) The term of the members elected to the Rajya Sabha is six years. However, every second year, one-third of the members retire and there are new entrants. The Rajya Sabha cannot be dissolved by the President of India. Thus, this House is never empty and therefore, it is called a 'Permanent House'.

(c) **Legislative Powers of the Parliament:**

1. The Parliament has exclusive powers to make laws with respect to matters mentioned in the Union List. The Parliament and the State Legislatures, both have the right to make laws on the subjects mentioned in the Concurrent List, but in the case of a conflict, the laws made by the Parliament shall prevail.

2. The Parliament possesses residuary powers, meaning that it can make laws with respect to all those matters that are not mentioned in any of the three lists.

Financial Powers of the Parliament:

1. The Parliament passes the Union Budget containing estimates of receipts and expenditure of the Government for a financial year.

2. The salaries and allowances of the Members of Parliament or MPs, Ministers and Judges of the Supreme Court and the High Courts are determined by the Parliament.

Q. 3. **With reference to the Union Parliament, answer the following questions:**

(a) How many members may be nominated to the Lok Sabha and the Rajya Sabha? Give one reason, as to why they may be nominated to the Lok Sabha.

(b) Mention any three qualifications required for a member to be elected to the Lok Sabha.

(c) What is meant by the term, 'Session'? Name the three Sessions of the Union Parliament. **[2018]**

Ans. **(a)** The President of India can nominate two members in the Lok Sabha and twelve members in the Rajya Sabha of those having special knowledge and practical experience in fields of literature, art, science or social service.

He nominates two members in the Lok Sabha from the Anglo-Indian community, if he feels that this community has not been adequately represented in the House.

(b) Three qualifications needed for a member to be elected to the Lok Sabha are:

1. He/She should be a citizen of India.
2. He/She should not be less than 25 years of age.
3. He/She should not be a proclaimed criminal, that is, he or she should not be a convict, a confirmed debtor or otherwise disqualified by law.

(c) 'Session' means a period during which a House meets to conduct its business. The session of each House of Parliament are summoned by the President.

The three sessions of the Union Parliament are: (a) The Budget Session (February – May) (b) The Monsoon Session (July – August) and (c) The Winter Session (November – December).

Q. 4. The Powers and Functions of the Indian Parliament are wide-ranging. In this context, answer the following:

(a) Explain three ways by which the Legislature exercises control over the Executive.

(b) Mention any three Special powers of the Rajya Sabha that are usually not enjoyed by the other House. **[2017]**

Ans. **(a) Three ways by which the Legislature exercises control over the Executive are:**

1. **Interpellation:** The Question Hour, Calling Attention Notices and Half-an-Hour discussions are some of the devices to seek information from the government about its policies and performance. Of these, the most important is the Question Hour. The first hour of a sitting in both the Houses is allotted for asking and answering of questions. The questions are asked to obtain information on a matter of public importance, or to highlight a grievance.

2. **Vote of No-Confidence:** If a Government acts against the Constitutional provisions, it can be voted out of office by passing a vote of 'No-Confidence'.

3. **Adjournment Motion:** The motion for adjournment is aimed, at censuring the acts of omission and commission of the ministers. The following are some of the occasions on which the adjournment motions have been allowed in the past: (a) death of several persons due to the consumption of unlicensed liquor; (b) killing of a senior IPS Officer in a place of worship, etc.

(b) Three special powers of the Rajya Sabha that are usually not enjoyed by the other House are:

1. The Rajya Sabha has some exclusive powers. Though the Parliament cannot, in normal times, make laws on a subject in the State List, the Constitution states that under Article 249, the Rajya Sabha, may by a resolution adopted by two-third majority, empower the Parliament to make laws with respect to a matter in the State List. The Lok Sabha has no authority to assert itself in such matters.

2. The other special power enjoyed by the Rajya Sabha is that, it may declare that the creation of new All India Services be made in the national interest. Thereupon, Parliament may create new services.

3. If the Lok Sabha is dissolved before or after the declaration of a national emergency, the Rajya Sabha becomes the sole *de facto* and *de jure* Parliament, *i.e.*, it takes over the functions of the Parliament. It cannot be dissolved. This is a limitation on the Lok Sabha.

Q. 5. **With reference to the Union Legislature, answer the following questions:**

(a) **How is the Speaker of the Lok Sabha elected? State two Disciplinary Functions of the Speaker.**

(b) **Explain two conditions under which a member of Parliament can be disqualified under the Anti-Defection Law.**

(c) **Give reasons to justify why the Lok Sabha is considered to be more powerful than the Rajya Sabha.** **[2016]**

Ans. **(a)** The Speaker of the Lok Sabha is elected from among its own members soon after the newly elected House meets for the first time. When the House is dissolved, the Speaker does not vacate his office, until a new Speaker is elected by the new Lok Sabha in its first meeting. The Speaker is elected for a term of five years.

Two Disciplinary Functions of the Speaker are :

1. The Speaker maintains order in the House. When members become unruly, he may also order them to withdraw. He may suspend a member, if he/she disregards the authority of the Chair. In case of grave disorder, he can adjourn the House.

2. The Speaker decides whether there is a case for a matter relating to a breach of privilege or contempt of the House.

(b) **Two conditions under which a Member of Parliament can be disqualified under the Anti-Defection Law are:**

1. An elected Member of Parliament (MP) or a State Legislature, who has been elected as a candidate set up by a political party, would be disqualified on the ground of defection, if he voluntarily relinquishes his membership of such political party or votes or abstains from voting in the House, contrary to any direction of such party.

2. A nominated Member of Parliament or a State Legislature, who is a member of a political party at the time he takes his seat would be disqualified on the ground of defection, if he voluntarily gives up his membership of the party or votes or abstains from voting in the House, contrary to the directions of the party.

(c) **The special powers which make the Lok Sabha more powerful than the Rajya Sabha are:**

1. Motions of No-Confidence against the government can only be introduced and passed in the Lok Sabha. If passed by a majority vote, the Prime Minister and the Council of Ministers resign collectively. The Rajya Sabha has no power over such a motion, and hence, no real power over the Executive.

2. Money bills can only be introduced in the Lok Sabha and upon being passed, they are sent to the Rajya Sabha, where it can be deliberated on for upto 14 days.

3. In case of a deadlock between the two Houses over a non-financial (ordinary) bill, the will of the Lok Sabha normally prevails, as its strength is more than that of the Rajya Sabha.

4. The Lok Sabha has a greater say in the elections of the President and the Vice-President of India, impeachment of the President, judges of the high courts and the Supreme Court because of its numerical strength.

Q. 6. **The Rajya Sabha is the second chamber of the Indian Parliament and represents the interest of the States. In this context, explain the following:**

(a) **Its composition.**

(b) **Qualifications for membership.**

(c) **Term of the House and any two of its Legislative Powers.** **[2015]**

Ans. The Rajya Sabha is the second chamber of the Indian Parliament and represents the interest of the states. In this context, explanations of the following points are:

(a) **Its Composition:** The maximum strength of the Rajya Sabha can be 250 members. The members fall into two categories, *i.e.* nominated and elected.

1. **Nominated members:** The nominated members are 12 in number. They are nominated by the President from among people having special knowledge or practical experience in matters, such as literature, science, art and social service.

2. **Elected members:** About 238 members are elected by the states in the Union. The allocation of seats among the states is not equal, as this would be undemocratic. Seats are allocated to the States and the Union Territories on the basis of their population.

(b) Qualification for membership: Qualifications for membership of the Rajya Sabha are the same as those for the membership of the Lok Sabha except, that of the age criteria. The minimum age for contesting election for the Rajya Sabha is 30 years. The qualifications for membership of the Rajya Sabha are given below:

1. He should be an Indian citizen.
2. He should be at least 30 years of age.
3. He should have his name in the electoral rolls in some part of the country.
4. He should not be an insolvent, *i.e.,* he should not be in debt and should have the ability to meet his financial commitments.
5. He should not hold any office of profit under the government.
6. He should not be a proclaimed criminal.
7. He should not be of unsound mind.

(c) Term of the House and any two of its Legislative Powers: The Rajya Sabha is a Permanent House. It cannot be dissolved like the Lok Sabha. Each member of the Rajya Sabha is elected for a period of six years. One-third of the total members of the House retire after every two years. Members can be re-elected, if they desire so and if their electors support them.

Legislative Powers:

1. The Rajya Sabha has special powers of declaring any subject in the State List as a subject of national interest and empowering the Parliament to pass the legislature on it.
2. All bills, other than the money bills, can originate in any House of the Parliament. No bill can become a law unless agreed upon by both the Houses. If there is disagreement, the President may summon both the Houses of Parliament in a joint meeting. At the joint meeting, issues are decided by a majority of the members of both the Houses present and voting.

Q. 7. **With reference to the Indian Parliament, explain the following:**

(a) The tenure of the members of the Lok Sabha and the Rajya Sabha.

(b) The composition of the Lok Sabha and the Rajya Sabha.

(c) Its powers to make laws on subjects mentioned in the

(i) Union List

(ii) Concurrent List **[2014]**

Ans. **(a)** The term of the members of the Lok Sabha is five years unless, it is dissolved. In cases of emergency, the term can be extended by the President for about a year. The tenure of the members of the Rajya Sabha is six years and is not subject to dissolution.

(b) Rajya Sabha: The Rajya Sabha is composed of 238 members representing the States and the Union Territories. The President nominates 12 members, who have special knowledge or expertise in the fields of Science, Literature, Social Service and Art.

Lok Sabha: The maximum strength of the Lok Sabha is 552, out of which 530 members represent the States, 20 members represent the Union Territories and 2 members are nominated by the President from the Anglo-Indian Community. The members representing the States and Union Territories are directly elected by the people through adult franchise. The strength of the Lok Sabha is not fixed, as members may resign or may be suspended.

(c) Both the Houses of the Indian Parliament together have got executive powers to make laws on:

1. Subjects mentioned in the Union List, such as Foreign Policy, Currency, Defence, Atomic Energy, Banking, State trade and Commerce, etc. There are altogether 97 subjects in the Union List.
2. The Concurrent List consists of subjects like education, labour welfare, books and printing press, criminal and civil law, marriage and divorce, etc. The Parliament can make laws on the 47 subjects mentioned in the Concurrent List.

Q. 8. **With reference to the Union Parliament, answer the following questions:**

(a) What is the maximum strength of the Lok Sabha provided by the Constitution?

How many members does the President nominate to the Lok Sabha?

How are members to the Lok Sabha elected?

(b) The two Houses of the Parliament enjoy co-equal powers in many spheres — explain it by giving any three examples.

(c) **Explain any four of the Rajya Sabha's powers in India's federal set up.** [2012]

Ans (a) The maximum strength of the Lok Sabha provided by the Constitution is 552 members. The President nominates two members of the Anglo-Indian community to the Lok Sabha.

The members of the Lok Sabha are directly elected by the people. The principle of Universal Adult Franchise has been adopted which means that all the citizens of the age of 18 and above have the right to vote, if not otherwise disqualified under the law.

(b) **The two Houses of the Parliament enjoy co-equal powers in many spheres because:**
1. Either House can frame charges and impeach the President for violation of the Constitution.
2. An ordinary bill can originate in either House of the Parliament and must be passed by both the Houses of Parliament.
3. Both the Houses have equal rights of asking questions or bringing in various kinds of motions against the government.

(c) **The following are the four powers of the Rajya Sabha:**
1. Only Rajya Sabha has the power to declare that a subject of the State List has assumed national importance and should be included in the Union List.
2. If the Lok Sabha is dissolved due to internal disturbances or a civil war, then the Rajya Sabha shoulders all the responsibilities of the Union Legislature.
3. The Rajya Sabha can decide by 2/3rd majority to set up a new All India Service.
4. The Rajya Sabha has the exclusive right to initiate a resolution for the removal of the Vice President.

Q. 9. Keeping in view the powers of the Union Parliament, answer the following questions:
(a) Mention three of its Legislative Powers.
(b) Mention three of its Financial Powers.
(c) Mention four of its Administrative or Executive Powers. [2011]

Ans (a) Refer to Long Answer Type Questions, Answer 1(a).

(b) **Three Financial Powers of Parliament are :**
1. **The Budget:** The Parliament passes the annual Union Budget containing the estimates of receipts and expenditures of the government for a financial year. The budget is presented in two parts, namely, the Railway Budget and the General Budget.
2. **Supplementary Grants:** If the amount authorised for the current financial year is not sufficient, the government may make a fresh demand known as the 'Supplementary Grant'. It is also passed in the same manner as the annual budget is passed.
3. **Votes on Account:** If the Union Budget is not passed before the beginning of the new financial year, *i.e.* April 1, there would be no money for the government to spend. There is, therefore, a device known as 'Vote on Account' which authorises the government to draw funds from the Consolidated Fund of India until the Budget is passed by the Parliament.
4. **Fixation of Salaries:** The salaries and allowances of MPs and Ministers are determined by the Parliament.
5. **Permission for Taxes:** No tax can be imposed or money spent by the government, without the approval of the Parliament. **(any three)**

(c) **The four Administrative or Executive Powers of the Union Parliament are:**
1. **Monetary Control:** The Parliament can move a cut motion when the Union Budget is under consideration. The Parliamentary Committee ensures that the public money is spent in accordance with Parliament's decision.
2. **Censures Motion and the No Confidence Motion:** If the Parliament disapproves of some action or policy of the Union Council or any of its members, they can move a censure motion which would result in the resignation of the government. They can also carry out a 'No Confidence Motion'.

3. **Adjournment Motion:** The routine business of the Parliament can be postponed by this and the House can discuss about the government for its acts of omission or commission.

4. **Question Hour:** Through this, the Parliament seeks information from the government about its policies and performances. The first hour in both the Houses is allotted for this.

Q. 10. **The Legislative Council in the States and the Rajya Sabha are Permanent Houses. With reference to the two Houses, answer the following questions:**

(a) **Mention two ways in which the Rajya Sabha and the Legislative Council can control the Executive. Explain one of its limitations in this regard.**

(b) **How many members constitute the Rajya Sabha? How many members does the Governor nominate to the Vidhan Parishad?**

How are the members elected to the Rajya Sabha?

(c) **Mention four special powers of the Rajya Sabha.** [2010]

Ans (a) **Two ways in which the Rajya Sabha and the Legislative Council can control the Executive are:**

1. It can reject an Ordinary Bill passed by the Lower House which would then be resolved by a joint session.

2. Though a Money Bill originates in the Lower House, it can be sent back by the Upper House with recommendations.

One limitation in this regard is that, the Lower House is not bound to follow the recommendations of the Rajya Sabha and the Legislative Council.

(b) According to the Constitution, the Rajya Sabha shall be composed of not more than 250 members out of whom, 238 shall be representatives of the States and Union Territories and 12 shall be nominated by the President.

The strength of the Vidhan Parishad should not be more than one-third of the members of the Legislative Assembly but not less than 40. Out of this, one-sixth are nominated by the Governor to the Vidhan Parishad.

The members in the Rajya Sabha are elected by the State Legislative Assemblies in accordance with a single transferable vote.

(c) **Four Special Powers of the Rajya Sabha are:**

1. The proclamation of emergency by the President is passed by the Rajya Sabha, if the Lok Sabha is not in session or has been dissolved.

2. The Rajya Sabha enjoys equal powers with the Lok Sabha in matters like amendments of the Constitution, elections and impeachment of the President, Vice President and judges of the Supreme Court and High Courts.

3. No laws on any subject of the State list can be made by the Lok Sabha without a two-third majority of the Rajya Sabha.

4. The approval of the Rajya Sabha is necessary in case of creating one or more All India Services common to the Union as well as the States.

Chapter 2

The Executive (President and Vice-President)

Very Short Answer Type Questions

Q. 1. Who is the Supreme Commander of the Armed forces of India ? [2020]

Ans. The Supreme Commander of the armed forces of India is the President.

Q. 2. What is the normal term of office of the Vice President of India ? [2020]

Ans. The normal term of office of the Vice President of India is 5 years.

Q. 3. Who appoints the Prime Minister of India ? [2020]

Ans. The President appoints the Prime Minister of India.

Q. 4. Write any one circumstance when the President can declare a National Emergency. [2019]

Ans. The President can declare a National Emergency, when there is a danger of foreign aggression or threat to the peace and security of the country because of a Civil War, due to the failure of the Constitutional machinery in the states, or if there is a threat to the financial stability of the country.

Q. 5. Who administers the Oath of Office to the Council of Ministers? [2018]

Ans. The President administers the Oath of Office to the Council of Ministers.

Q. 6. What is an Ordinance? [2018]

Ans. An Ordinance is a temporary law that is enforced by the President when the Parliament is not in session.

Q. 7. State any one reason why the President is elected indirectly. [2018, 2013]

Ans. The President is the nominal head. His indirect election makes him the elected representative of the whole nation. The real power lies in the hands of the Prime Minister and the Parliament. Hence, it would be an anomaly if the President is elected directly and not given any power.

Q. 8. Who presides over the meeting of the Rajya Sabha in the absence of the Vice President of India? [2016]

Ans. The Deputy Chairman presides over the meeting of the Rajya Sabha in the absence of the Vice President of India. In the absence of the Chairman, he performs all the functions and duties of the Chairman.

Q. 9. Name the official procedure by which the President can be removed. [2016]

Ans. The President may be removed for the violation of the Constitution, from the office by the process of impeachment.

Q. 10. Mention any one important occasion when the President addresses a Joint Session of Parliament. [2016]

Ans. The President addresses a Joint Session of Parliament at the commencement of the first session after each General Election, each year.

Q. 11. Who has the power to promulgate an Ordinance at the Centre? When can it be promulgated? [2015]

Ans. The President is empowered to promulgate an ordinance at a time, when the Parliament is not in a session. It has the same effect as an act. All ordinances must be put up before both the Houses for their approval.

Q. 12. Mention any one discretionary power of the President. [2015]

Ans. A discretionary power of President is the appointment of a Prime Minister in case of sudden death (for example, by assassination as in the case of Mrs. Indira Gandhi) of the incumbent, where the ruling legislature party is unable to meet immediately to elect a leader.

Q. 13. State any one qualification necessary for the election of the President of India. [2015]

Ans. One of the qualifications necessary for the election of the President of India is that:
He/she should be a citizen of India.

Q. 14. Who is the Chairman of the Rajya Sabha? [2015]

Ans. The Vice President of the Indian Union acts as the ex-officio Chairman of the Rajya Sabha.

Q. 15. State the composition of the Electoral College in the election of the President of India. [2014]

Ans. The Electoral College, in the election of the President of India, is composed of—
1. The elected members of both the Houses of the Parliament.

2. The elected members of the Legislative Assemblies of the States including the Union Territories possessing assemblies.

Q. 16. What is an 'Ordinance'? When can it be passed? [2014]

Ans. An 'ordinance' is a temporary law that is enforced when the Parliament is not in session. The power to pass an ordinance is accorded to the President of India and is passed in cases of emergency.

Q. 17. Who is the Executive Head of a State? [2013]

Ans. There is a Governor for each state, who is appointed by the President. He is the Executive Head of the State.

Q. 18. Who settles disputes arising in connection with the election of the President of India? [2012]

Ans. According to the 29th and 44th Constitutional Amendment Act, the Supreme Court decides any disputes regarding the election of the President.

Q. 19. Mention one difference between the election of the President and the Vice President of India. [2010]

Ans. The President is elected indirectly by an Electoral College composed of elected members of the Parliament and the State Legislative Assemblies, including the Councils whereas, the Vice President is indirectly elected by the members of both the Houses of Parliament, at a joint meeting.

 Long Answer Type Questions

Q. 1. The Executive Power of the Indian Union is vested in the President. In this context, answer the following :

 (a) How is the President of India elected ? State the composition of the electoral College that elects him.

 (b) Explain any three Discretionary Powers of the President.

 (c) Mention any four Executive Powers of the President. [2020]

 Marking Scheme

(a) 1. President is elected indirectly by the members of an electoral college. /single transferable vote/ proportional representation.

  2. Composition of Electoral college:
   – Elected members of both houses [LS and RS] of parliament
   – Elected members of the legislative assemblies of the states including the national capital territory of Delhi and the union territory of Puducherry.
   – OR MPs and MLAs

(b) **The discretionary powers:**
   – Where he uses his wisdom and judgement.
   – Dissolution of Lok Sabha during constitutional crisis
   – Explore possibilities of alternative government at the centre
   – Dismissal of ministers when the government collapses due to No confidence.
   – Appointment of the PM where no single party commands
   – Appointment of PM in case of death
   – May withhold assent to an ordinary bill or send it back for reconsideration
   – No time limit within which he is to declare his assent/refusal of bill. (Any three points)

(c) **The Executive powers:**
   – Head of the Union administration/administration of the country runs in his house/All orders are issued in his name
   – Appointment of officials of the state
   - Appoints the
    • Attorney General
    • Auditor General
    • Ambassador
    • Members of UPSC
    • Judges of High Court and Supreme Court
    • Members of the Planning Commission
    • Election Commissioner
    • Governors of State
    • PM and the Council of Ministers.
   – Control over state governments during emergency
   – And Union territories and border areas/exercises power through an administrator appointed by the President. *(Any four points)*

Ans **(a)** The President is elected indirectly by the members of Electoral College consisting of the elected members of both the Houses of Parliament and the elected members of legislative Assembly and the states including the National Capital Territory of Delhi and Union Territory of Pondicherry (Official name : Puducherry)The election of the President is held in accordance with the system of proportional representation by means of single transferable vote and such election is done by secret ballot.

 (b) **Discretionary powers of the President are :**

1. He also appoints incumbent Prime Minister in case of sudden death, where the ruling legislative party is unable to meet immediately to elect a leader.

2. When the ruling party would lose majority support in Lok Sabha or when a vote of no confidence may have been passed against, it requires a President to dissolve the Lok Sabha. Then, it is at discretion of the President to whether dissolve the House or ask another party to prove majority on the floor of the House.

3. The President can dismiss ministers in case the Council of Ministers loses the confidence of the House but refuses to resign.

(c) Four Executive Powers of the President are:

1. Being the Head of the Union administration, executive orders are issued in the name of the President.

2. The President makes appointments to run the government administration.

3. For example, appointment of the Prime Minister and Council of Ministers, appointment of Chief Justice and other judges of the Supreme Court, appointment of the Governors of the State, appointment of the Attorney General of India.

4. The administration of the Union Territories and the border areas is the responsibility of the President.

Q. 2. The President and the Vice-President are part of the Union Executive.

In this context, answer the following questions:

(a) State any three qualifications required for a candidate to be elected as the Vice President of India.

(c) Explain briefly any two Legislative and any two Executive Powers of the President. **[2018]**

Ans (a) Three qualifications needed for a candidate to be elected as the Vice President of India are:

1. Must be a citizen of India.

2. Must have completed 35 years of age.

3. Must be eligible to be a member of the Rajya Sabha.

(c) (i) Legislative Powers: The President of India is an integral part of the Union Parliament. The legislative powers of the President may be discussed under the following heads:

1. **Power to summon and prorogue the Parliament and dissolve the Lok Sabha:** The President has the power to summon and prorogue the Houses of Parliament and to dissolve the Lok Sabha. The power to summon Parliament is subject to the condition, that six months shall not intervene between the last sitting in one session and first sitting in the next session. The President has the power to dissolve the Lok Sabha. The Rajya Sabha is a permanent body, not subject to dissolution.

2. **Nominating members to the Houses:** The President nominates twelve members to the Rajya Sabha from among persons having special knowledge or practical experience in these matters-literature, science, art and social service.

The President may nominate two members of the Anglo-Indian Community to the Lok Sabha, in case that Community is not adequately represented in the House.

(ii) Executive Powers: The Constitution says that the "Executive power of the Union shall be vested in the President." The executive power embraces the following activities of the Union:

1. **Head of the Union Executive:** All executive orders are issued in the name of the President.

2. **Formation of the Council of Ministers:** The Constitution lays down that the Prime Minister is to be appointed by the President and the other Ministers are appointed by the President on the advice of the Prime Minister. It is the duty of the Prime Minister to communicate to the President all decisions of the Council of Ministers.

Q. 3. The President of India is the Constitutional Head of the Indian Republic. In this context, answer the following questions:

(a) How is the President elected?

(b) Mention three types of emergencies that the President is empowered to proclaim.

(c) **Explain briefly any four 'Executive Powers' of the President.** **[2016]**

Ans. (a) Refer to Long Answer Type Questions, Answer 1(a).

(b) **The three types of emergencies that the President is empowered to proclaim are:**

1. **National or General Emergency:** If the President is satisfied that a grave emergency exists whereby, the security of India or any part of its territory is threatened, either by war or by external aggression or armed rebellion, he may proclaim an Emergency. The President cannot issue such a proclamation unless he has the approval in writing of the Union Cabinet.

2. **Breakdown of Constitutional Machinery:** If the President, on receipt of a report from the Governor or otherwise, is satisfied that the governance of a state cannot be carried on in accordance with the provisions of the Constitution; he may declare an Emergency in the state. This is called President's Rule, because the President may assume to himself all or any of the functions of the government of the state.

3. **Financial Emergency:** If the President is satisfied that a situation has arisen whereby, the financial stability or credit of the nation is threatened, he can declare a Financial Emergency. Such a proclamation has to be laid before both Houses of Parliament and is valid for two months unless it is approved by resolutions of both Houses of Parliament.

(c) Refer to Long Answer Type Questions, Answer 1. (c).

Q. 4. **The President of India is the Head of the Indian Republic while the Governor is the Head of the State Government. In this context, answer the following questions:**

(a) **Enumerate three similar features in the legislative powers of the President and the Governor.** **[2012]**

(b) **Under what circumstances can the President of India declare an emergency in the country?** **[2012, 2010]**

Ans. (a) **Three similar Legislative Powers of the President and the Governor are:**

1. The first session of the Parliament is addressed by the President, similarly at the State level, it is the Governor who addresses the first session of the Legislative Assembly.

2. Both exercise similar powers to summon or prorogue the session of the Parliament and the State Assembly, respectively.

3. The President may appoint two members of the Anglo-Indian Community to the Lok Sabha. The Governor may exercise similar power if he feels that the community is not adequately represented in the Vidhan Sabha.

(b) **The President can declare an Emergency under the following circumstances:**

1. There is a danger of foreign aggression or danger to the peace and security of the country because of a civil war, insurgency or any other such case.

2. A setback to the financial stability or credit feasibility of the country is likely to occur or has occurred.

3. The constitutional machinery in a state has broken down or there is a deadlock because of political uncertainties or otherwise.

Q. 5. **The President of India is a nominal and constitutional head of the nation. In this context, answer the following questions:**

(a) **Why is the President of India referred to as a nominal head of the State? State two examples of his legislative powers that suggest his nominal status.**

(b) **Explain two discretionary powers of the President.** **[2010]**

Ans. (a) The President of India is referred to as the nominal head of the State because India follows a parliamentary system of government. The President is the chief executive of the state, but he does not exercise real executive power. The administration of the Union is carried on in his name. The real power is exercised by the Prime Minister and Council of Ministers.

Two Legislative Powers of the President that suggest his nominal status are:

1. According to the Constitution, the President is required to exercise his powers on the aid and advice of his Council of Ministers.

2. All proclamations of emergency made by the President have to be approved by the Parliament within one month. If it's not approved, then it ceases to exist.

(b) Refer to Long Answer Type Questions, Answer 1 (b)

The Prime Minister and The Council of Ministers

Very Short Answer Type Questions

Q. 1. State the body that decides the major policies of the government. [2020]

Ans. The Cabinet formulates the major policies of the government.

Q. 2. On whose advice can the President appoint the Council of Ministers? [2019]

Ans. The Prime Minister.

Q. 3. Under what condition can a non-member of Parliament be made a Minister? [2017]

Ans. Normally, only the members of Parliament are appointed as Ministers. In case, a non-member is appointed as a Minister, he must be elected or nominated to the Parliament within six months from the date of his appointment as per the desire of the Prime Minister. Failing this, he will have to resign from the post of a Minister.

Q. 4. When can the President use his Discretionary Power to appoint the Prime Minister? [2017]

Ans. If no political party has a clear majority and a coalition of parties form the government; in such a situation, the President can use his discretion and appoint the Prime Minister, who in his view can form a stable government.

Q. 5. What is meant by 'Collective Responsibility' of the Cabinet? [2017]

Ans. The Cabinet is collectively responsible to the Parliament and has to resign if it loses the confidence of the Lok Sabha. It means that all ministers swim and sink together.

Q. 6. By whom and on whose advice are the Council of Ministers appointed? [2016]

Ans. The Council of Ministers are appointed by the President on the advice of the Prime Minister.

Q. 7. Who administers the Oath of Office to the Council of Ministers? [2014]

Ans. The President of India administers the Oath of Office to the Council of Ministers.

Q. 8. Mention one way by which the authority of the Prime Minister can be checked? [2014]

Ans. If the Prime Minister fails to carry out obligations or makes detrimental choices, then the members of the House can pass a motion of No-Confidence. This deems him 'not fit' to hold the position, anymore. Thus, the authority of the Prime Minister can be checked.

Q. 9. What is understood by the term, 'Individual Responsibility' in a Parliamentary Democracy? [2014]

Ans. 'Individual Responsibility' in a Parliamentary Democracy means that a member of the Parliament is accountable for his or her actions and decisions. If the member fails to discharge his or her responsibilities, then he or she alone is expected to take the blame and resign.

Q. 10. Mention the different categories of ministers in the Union Council of Ministers. [2013]

Ans. The ministers in the Union Council are of three categories: Cabinet Ministers, Ministers of State and Deputy Ministers.

Q. 11. Explain the term, 'Collective Responsibility'. [2013]

Ans. 'Collective Responsibility', means that ministers are collectively responsible to the Legislature. It signifies that if 'No Confidence Motion' is passed against a single minister, the entire Council of Ministers shall resign.

Q. 12. Mention one circumstance when the President can appoint the Prime Minister using his discretionary power. [2011]

Ans. The President can appoint the Prime Minister using his discretionary power in the case of no single party getting a clear majority and if a coalition of parties stakes its claim to form the government, the President has to use his individual judgment and invite such a leader to head the government as Prime Minister who can provide a stable government to the country.

Q. 13. State one point of difference between the Cabinet and the Council of Ministers with reference to their responsibilities in the Government. [2010

Ans. **Cabinet:** The Cabinet enforces collective responsibility of the Council to the Lower Chamber.

Council of Ministers: The Council of Ministers are collectively responsible to the Lower House of the Parliament.

 # Long Answer Type Questions

Q. 1. The Council of Ministers headed by the Prime Minister, is the most Powerful Institution in the Indian Polity. In this context, answer the following:

(a) State briefly the position of the Prime Minister in the Parliamentary system of Government. State any two powers the Prime Minister has as a leader of the Nation.

(b) Distinguish between the Council of Ministers and the Cabinet. **[2019]**

Marking Scheme ----------------------------

(a) Position: The Prime Minister is the de facto or the real leader of the nation.

- He is the Leader of the Lok Sabha.
- He is the chief spokesperson of the Government.
- He is the defender of Government policies.
- He intervenes in case of controversial issues.
- Addresses nation during emergency or on important occasions.
- Represents and visits countries – for economic and social issues of the nation.
- Chairman of Niti Aayog and Atomic Energy Commission
- Decides what kind of relations India would have with other countries.
- Keeps President informed of the decision of the Cabinet. **(Any three points)**

(b)

S.No.	Council of Ministers	Cabinet
1.	Consists of all the three categories of ministers.	Is a group of senior ministers holding important portfolios
2.	The PM may or may not consult them	The PM always consults them.
3.	Rarely meets as a whole	Meets as frequently as possible
4.	Does not advise the President	Advises the President through the PM
5.	Larger Group	Smaller Group
6.	May or may not hold important portfolios	Hold important portfolios

(Any three points)

Ans. (a) 1. The Prime Minister heads the Council of Ministers and aids and advises the President.
2. He is the real executive of the Indian Union.
3. The Prime Minister is the chief spokesperson and defender of the Government in the Parliament.
4. The Prime Minister exercises vast authority both in legislation and finance.

Prime Minister as a Leader of the Nation:
1. The Prime Minister represents the nation, when he speaks, the whole nation is supposed to be speaking through him.
2. During the national crisis like war, even the opposition parties support the Prime Minister.

(b)

Council of Ministers	Cabinet
1. The Council of Ministers consists of all categories of Ministers – Cabinet Ministers, Ministers of State and Deputy Ministers.	The Cabinet is a smaller group consisting of some 25 senior Ministers holding important portfolios, such as Defence, Finance, Home, etc.
2. The Prime Minister may or may not consult the other Ministers, below the rank of Cabinet Ministers.	They are the most trusted colleagues of the Prime Minister. The Prime Minister always consults them. The decisions of the Cabinet are binding on all the members.
3. In the day-to-day working of the Government, the Council of Ministers, as a whole, rarely meets.	The Cabinet is a small cohesive group of senior Ministers who determine the policies and programmes of the Government; so they meet as frequently as possible.

Q. 2. The Union Executive which consists of the President, Prime Minister and the Council of Ministers is a powerful body in a Parliamentary Democracy. In this context, answer the following questions:

(a) State the position of the Prime Minister and state any two of his powers in relation to the President.

(b) Mention the three categories of Ministers in order of their rank and status. **[2017]**

Ans. (a) (i) **The Position of the Prime Minister:** While the President is the nominal head of the State, with the backing of a majority in the Lok Sabha, the Prime Minister is the real head of the nation. But in a Parliamentary democracy, his deeds are closely judged not only by the opposition but also by the members of his own party. If he tries to assume dictatorial tendencies, he cannot escape the loss of confidence of the Parliament during his tenure as well as that of the electorate in the following general elections. Thus, he is the head of the Government and is answerable to the people of the country.

(ii) Prime Minister's two powers in relation to the President:

1. All authority vested on the President is exercised by the Prime Minister. He is the principal advisor of the President. Thus, the President is the nominal head and the Prime Minister is the real executive of the Indian Union.

2. It is on the advice of the Prime Minister that the President summons and prorogues the Parliament and dissolves the Lok Sabha.

(b) Three categories of Ministers in order of their rank and status:

1. **Cabinet ministers:** They are the most important and senior members of the Council of Ministers. They hold important portfolio like Home, Defence, Finance, External Affairs, Railways, etc. Only Cabinet Ministers have a right to attend the meetings of the Cabinet. They together determine the policies and programmes of the Government.

2. **Ministers of State:** They are the second category of ministers. They may or may not hold an independent charge of any portfolio. The Prime Minister may or may not consult them. They do not participate in the Cabinet meetings. But they may be invited to attend meetings when matters concerning their departments are being considered.

3. **Deputy Ministers:** They are the third category of ministers, who assist the Cabinet Ministers and the Council of Ministers. They are junior ministers and are placed under senior ministers, whom they have to assist. They take no part in Cabinet deliberations.

Q. 3. The makers of our Constitution adopted the Parliamentary and the Cabinet form of Government. With reference to this, answer the following questions:

(a) (i) Who is the Constitutional Head of the Union Government?

(ii) What is meant by the Collective and Individual Responsibility of the members of the Cabinet?

(b) Explain briefly the position and powers of the Prime Minister in relation to the Cabinet.

(c) Distinguish between the Cabinet and the Council of Ministers. **[2015]**

Ans. **(a) (i)** While the President is the nominal head of state, with the backing of a majority in the Lok Sabha, the Prime Minister is the real or the Constitutional head of the Union Government.

(ii) Collective Responsibility: Under Article 75(3) of the Constitution, 'the Council of Ministers shall be collectively responsible to the House of the People.' The principles of collective responsibility implies that:

1. The decisions taken in the meetings of the cabinet are equally applicable to all the ministers even though they may differ among themselves on a particular policy.

2. All ministers jointly share the responsibility for the government's policies and performance. The ministers must function as a team in supporting and defending government policies inside as well as outside the Parliament.

Individual Responsibility: The ministers are individually responsible to the President, *i.e.,* they hold office during the pleasure of the President and may be dismissed by him, on the advice of the Prime Minister even when they may have the confidence of the Legislature.

Each Minister is answerable to the Parliament for the department under his control. It is obligatory for him to answer all the questions asked by the MPs, regarding the functioning of his department.

(b) The Prime Minister is the head of the Cabinet. No provision is made in the Constitution for the appointment of different categories of ministers such as Ministers of the Cabinet rank, Ministers of State and Deputy Ministers. The Prime Minister has the liberty to decide on these matters.

Position and powers of the Prime Minister in relation to the Cabinet are as follows:

1. **Power to allocate portfolios and to reshuffle the Council of Ministers:** It is the Prime Minister who allocates departments or portfolios to the Ministers. He can reshuffle his Council of Ministers whenever he pleases.

2. **Power to select and dismiss ministers:** The Prime Minister chooses the Ministers and has the power to dismiss them too. He can ask an erring minister to resign.

3. **Power to direct and coordinate policy:** The Prime Minister coordinates the working of various departments so that administration is carried on smoothly. In critical matters such as foreign, defense, economic and technological affairs, he coordinates the policy of the government.

4. **Resignation of the Prime Minister:** The Prime Minister's resignation implies the resignation of the whole cabinet.

(c) Refer to Long Answer Type Questions, Answer 1 (b).

Q. 4. The Cabinet holds a pivotal position in the working of the Indian Parliamentary Government. In this context discuss the following:

The formation of the Cabinet.

Ans.
1. The Cabinet holds an important pivotal position in the working of the Government. The Cabinet is a body consisting of important senior leaders of the party.

2. They hold important portfolios like Defence, Railways and decide major policies of the Government.

Chapter 4

The Union Judiciary (The Supreme Court)

Very Short Answer Type Questions

Q. 1. Name the courts that are empowered to issue Writs for the enforcement of Fundamental Rights. **[2020]**

Ans. The Supreme Court and High Courts are empowered to issue Writs for the enforcement of Fundamental Rights of the citizens of India.

Q. 2. What is meant by Appellate Jurisdiction of the Supreme Court? **[2019]**

Ans. The Supreme Court is the final court of Appeal. Appellate Jurisdiction of the Supreme Court means an appeal lies to the Supreme Court from any judgement or final order of a High Court or a Lower Court in the country.

Q. 3. On what grounds can a Supreme Court Judge be removed from office? **[2019]**

Ans. A Supreme Court Judge can be removed by the President only if proved of misbehaviour or incapacity.

Q. 4. Name any two writs issued by the Supreme Court. **[2018]**

Ans. Two writs issued by the Supreme Court are:

　　1. Writ of Habeas Corpus

　　2. Writ of Mandamus

Q. 5. What is meant by a 'Single Integrated Judicial System' as provided in the Indian Constitution? **[2014]**

Ans. In a 'Single Integrated Judicial System' provided in the Indian Constitution, the Supreme Court of India is the apex court of India and administers both the Union and the State laws. Below the Supreme Court are the High Courts in each state or group of states followed by Subordinate Courts.

Q. 6. Name the courts that are empowered to issue writs for the enforcement of Fundamental Rights. **[2013]**

Ans. The Supreme Court and the High Courts are empowered to issue writs for the enforcement of Fundamental Rights.

Q. 7. What is the tenure of a judge of the Supreme Court? **[2012]**

Ans. A judge of the Supreme Court works till he attains the age of 65 years.

Q. 8. Who can increase the number of Judges of the Supreme Court? **[2011]**

Ans. The number of judges of the Supreme Court can be increased by the Parliament of India.

Q. 9. What is meant by the term Judicial Review? **[2010]**

Ans. Judicial review is a process through which the judiciary examines, whether a law enacted by a legislature or an action of the executive is in accordance with the Constitution or not. A law may be declared 'Ultra vires' or null and void, if it is against the letter and spirit of the Constitution or infringes any provision of the Constitution. A minimum of 5 judges are required to hear and decide a case involving the Constitution.

Q. 10. Why is the Supreme Court said to be the guardian of the Constitution? **[2010]**

Ans. Supreme Court is said to be the guardian of the constitution as it can issue writs for the enforcement of Fundamental Rights.

Long Answer Type Questions

Q. 1. With reference to the Supreme Court as the Apex Court in our Indian Judiciary, explain the following :

(a) Any three cases that come under the Original Jurisdiction of the Supreme Court.

(b) **Power of Judicial Review.**

(c) **'Supreme Court as a Court of Record.**
[2020]

📋 Marking Scheme

(a) Original Jurisdiction
- Centre state
- interstate disputes
- Union and state on one side and other states on other side
- Protection of Fundamental rights
- Transfer of cases from lower courts
- Interpretation of constitution (Any three points)

(b) **Power of Judicial Review:**
- The Supreme Court is the interpreter of the Constitution
- It has the power to review laws passed by the union or state legislatures or executive.
- The Supreme Court can declare a law ultra vires or null and void, if it is against the letter and spirit of the Constitution or contravenes any provision of the constitution.

(c) **The court of record has two implications:**
- Its judgement and orders are preserved as a record.
- This can be produced in any court as precedents.
- future references
- testimony
- If a person commits a contempt of court, the court has the authority to punish contempt.
- The Supreme Court acts as the Guardian of the constitution. (*Any two points*)

Ans. **(a)** **Three cases that come under the Original Jurisdiction of the Supreme Court of India are :**

1. Disputes between Government of India and any state, or between two or more states.
2. The original jurisdiction also extends to cases of violation of Fundamental Rights of individuals and the court can issue several writs for the enforcement of these rights.
3. All cases in which the interpretation of the Constitution is required, can be directly filed in the Supreme Court. The Supreme Court has a power of exclusive jurisdiction in regard to questions asked on constitutional validity of Central laws.

(b) **Power of Judicial Review :**

1. Supreme Court is an interpreter of the Constitution and its decision is final. It holds a power to review law passed by the union or state legislature.

2. The Supreme Court can strike down a law that goes against Fundamental Rights; this implicitly gives Supreme Court the power of judicial review.
3. The Supreme Court or High Courts can examine the constitutionality of any law. If the court arrives at the conclusion that a law is inconsistent with the provisions of the Constitution, such a law is declared as unconstitutional and inapplicable.

(c) **Supreme Court as a Court of Record :**

1. A court of record is a court, whose acts and proceedings are enrolled for perpetual memory and testimony. The judgements are in nature of the precedent *i.e.,* the High Court and other courts are bound to give same decisions in similar cases.
2. Article 129 provides that the Supreme Court shall be a court of record and shall have all the powers of such a court including the power to punish for contempt of itself.
3. Article 215 contains similar provision in respect of the High Court. Both the Supreme Court as well as the High Courts are courts of record having powers to punish for contempt including the power to punish for contempt of itself.

Q. 2. **Our Judicial system has a Supreme Court as its Apex, followed by the High Court and other Subordinate Courts. In the light of this statement, explain the following:**

(a) **Any three types of cases in which the Supreme Court exercises its Original Jurisdiction.**

(c) **'Advisory' and 'Revisory' Jurisdiction of the Supreme Court.** **[2018]**

Ans. **(a)** Refer to Long Answer Type Questions, Answer 1 (a).

(c) 1. **Advisory Jurisdiction:** Under Article 143 of the Constitution, President can seek advisory opinion of the Supreme Court when it appeals to him that a question of law or fact has arisen, or is likely to arise, which is of such a nature and of such public importance that it is expedient to obtain the opinion of the Supreme Court upon it. The President is not bound to accept the opinion of the Supreme Court. The Supreme Court is not bound to give its advice.

2. Revisory Jurisdiction: Under Article 137, the Supreme Court can revise its own judgement, order or direction Besides, Article 138 and Article 139 provides that the Parliament by law can extend the jurisdiction of the Supreme Court.

Q. 3. The Supreme Court has an extensive jurisdiction. In the light of this statement, answer the following questions:
(a) What are the qualifications of the Judges of the Supreme Court?
(b) (i) Explain the composition of the Supreme Court.
(ii) How are the Judges of the Supreme Court appointed?
(c) Explain the cases in which the Supreme Court enjoys Original Jurisdiction. [2016]

Ans. **(a)** A Judge of the Supreme Court must be a citizen of India, and:

1. must have been for at least five years a Judge of a High Court or of two or more such courts in succession; or

2. has been for at least ten years an advocate of a High Court or of two or more such courts in succession; or

3. must be, in the opinion of the President, a distinguished jurist.

(b) **1. Composition of the Supreme Court:** The Supreme Court of India consists of a Chief Justice of India and not more than thirty other judges, until the Parliament by law prescribes a large number of judges.

2. Appointments of Judges of the Supreme Court: Every judge of the Supreme Court is appointed by the President of India in consultation with the judges of the Supreme Court and High Courts, besides the Cabinet In case of appointment of a judge other than that of the Chief Justice, the Chief Justice of India shall be consulted. Consultation would generally mean concurrence. In case of the Chief Justice, usually the senior most judge of the Supreme Court is appointed.

(c) Refer to Long Answer Type Questions, Answer 1(a).

Q. 4. With reference to the Supreme Court, explain its functions stated below:
(a) Original Jurisdiction.
(b) Advisory Function.

(c) As a Guardian of Fundamental Rights.
[2014]

Ans. **(a)** Refer to Long Answer Type Questions, Answer 1(a).

(b) Refer to Long Answer Type Questions, Answer 2 (c) (i).

(c) Guardian of Fundamental Rights:
1. The Constitution guarantees the citizen the right to move the court for the enforcement of Fundamental Rights.

2. It can issue orders or writs like Habeas Corpus for the enforcement of Fundamental Rights.

3. Any law passed by the Parliament which abridges or takes away the Fundamental Rights will be declared null and void by the Supreme Court.

Q. 5. The country's Judicial System has a Supreme Court at its apex. In this context discuss the following:
(a) Manner of appointment of judges.
(b) Term of office and removal of judges.
(c) Its power of 'Judicial Review'. [2013]

Ans. **(a)** Refer to Long Answer Type Questions, Answer 3(b) (ii).

(b) Term of office and removal of Judges: A judge of the Supreme Court continues in office until he attains the age of 65. However, Article 124 (2) provides that a judge may resign by writing letter addressed to the President.

A judge of the Supreme Court may be removed from office on the grounds of proved misbehaviour and incapacity, by the President, by an order issued after an address has been presented to him by the Parliament. Such an address must be supported by a majority of not less than two-thirds of the members present and voting in each House of Parliament.

(c) Refer to Long Answer Type Questions, Answer 1(b).

Q. 6. The Supreme Court is the apex court of our country. In this context, explain the following:
The composition of the Supreme Court of India.

Ans. Refer to Long Answer Type Questions, Answer 3(b) (i).

Q. 7. The Supreme Court is the apex court in the entire judicial set up in India. In this context answer the following questions:
(a) What is meant by the term single-integrated judicial system?

(b) Explain the impeachment procedure for the removal of judges.

(c) In the extensive jurisdiction of the Supreme Court state the difference between the original jurisdiction and the appellate jurisdiction. Mention two functions that come under original jurisdiction. **[2010]**

Ans. **(a)** This means that the Supreme Court is at the apex of this hierarchical body with high courts, District Courts and Subordinate Courts at different levels. The Constitution clearly states that the interpretation of the laws of the country by the Supreme Court shall be binding on all courts within the territory of India. All cases can be taken from Lower to High Court and then to the Supreme Court. This is what is meant by single-integrated judicial system.

(b) A judge can be impeached on grounds of proven misbehaviour or incapacity. The process involves a motion being passed by a special majority of each House of Parliament.

1. A motion addressed to the President, which has been signed by at least 100 members of the Lok Sabha or 50 of the Rajya Sabha is given to the Chairman or Speaker.

2. It is then investigated by a committee of 2 Supreme Court judges and a distinguished jurist.

3. If the motion is found acceptable, then it is given to the initiating House for consideration.

4. It is prospected to the President after it has been passed by two-third majority of each House.

5. The judge will be removed after the President gives the order for his removal.

(c) Original jurisdiction means the cases brought before the court for the first time, whereas Appellate jurisdiction means the court's power to hear appeals. In most cases, it requires a certificate from the High Court about whether it is fit for consideration by the Supreme Court or not.

Two functions that come under original jurisdiction are:

1. Disputes between government of India and States or between States in any combination.

2. Suits involving fundamental rights brought by individuals before the court.

Chapter 5

The State Judiciary (The High Court)

 ## Very Short Answer Type Questions

Q. 1. State one other qualification required to become a Judge of the High Court, apart from Indian citizenship. **[2017]**

Ans. He should not be over 62 years and he should have held a Judicial office in the territory of India for at least ten years.

Q. 2. Who administers the Oath of Office to the High Court Judges? **[2011]**

Ans. The Oath of Office is administered to the High Court Judges by the State Governor.

 ## Long Answer Type Questions

Q. 1. India has a single integrated judicial system that is Independent and Supreme. With reference to the Judiciary, answer the following:

(i) Who appoints the Judges of the High Court?

(ii) State any two qualifications required for a person to be appointed as a High Court Judge.

 **Marking Scheme**

(i) President

(ii)

1. One should be a citizen of India.
2. One should have held a judicial office in India for at least 10 years.
3. One should have been advocate of a High Court for at least 10 years.
4. He should not be over 62 years of age.

(Any three points)

Ans. (i) The Chief Justice of a High Court is appointed by the President of India in consultation with the Chief Justice of the Supreme Court and the Governor of the concerned State. The other Judges of the High Court are also to be appointed in the same manner except that in their case the Chief Justice of the High Court shall also be consulted.

(ii) Qualifications for appointment as a High Court Judge:

1. One should be a citizen of India.
2. One should have held a judicial office in India for at least ten years.
3. One should have been an advocate of a High Court for at least ten years.

Chapter 6

The State Judiciary (The Subordinate Courts)

Very Short Answer Type Questions

Q. 1. Mention any one advantage of the Lok Adalat. [2020]

OR

State one advantage of a Lok Adalat. [2015]

Ans. Lok Adalat plays an important role in the settlement of family feuds, disputes between the neighbours and minor cases of assault and injury by settling the disputes by compromise.

Q. 2. State one point of distinction between a District Judge and a Sessions Judge.

[2019, 2014]

Ans. The District Judge decides civil cases related to land, property, money transactions, arbitration, guardianship, marriage, divorce and will.

The Sessions Judge decides criminal cases like murders, theft, dacoity, pick-pocketing, etc. Sessions Judge has no administrative power but District Judge has.

Q. 3. Name the highest criminal court in a district. [2018]

OR

Which is the highest criminal court in a district? [2013]

Ans. The Sessions Court is the highest criminal court in a district.

Q. 4. What is meant by Lok Adalats? [2018, 2016]

Ans. Lok Adalats mean 'People's Courts'. On the recommendation of Justice P.N. Bhagwati, Lok Adalats were set up by Legal Services Authorities' Act, 1987 as a legal forum to provide legal aid and quick justice to those who are not in a position to engage lawyers or bear the expenses of legal proceedings.

Q. 5. Mention one reason to state that the Lok Adalat has its own advantage. [2017]

Ans. It is generally referred as the 'Court of the common people'. It solves cases through friendly compromise among the disputed parties.

Advantages:

1. They are quick and inexpensive.
2. Work with a spirit of compromise and not to prolong litigation.
3. Their judgements are final and not for appeal.
4. Reduce the load of work on other courts.

Q. 6. Name the highest Civil Court in a District. [2016]

Ans. The Court of the District Judge is the principal or the highest Civil Court of the district.

Q. 7. Mention one reason why the system of Lok Adalat has become popular. [2011]

Ans. Lok Adalat has become popular because it works in the spirit of compromise and delivers speedy and inexpensive justice.

Q. 8. Mention the three types of courts that a district usually has. [2010]

Ans. The three types of courts that a district usually has are Civil Courts, Criminal Courts and Revenue Courts.

Long Answer Type Questions

Q. 1. The High Court is the apex of the judiciary in the state. In this context, answer the following questions:

(a) **State the composition of the High Court. State the qualifications required to become a High Court Judge.**

(b) **Why is the High Court also known as a Court of Record?**

(c) (i) **What is the meaning of Lok Adalat?**

(ii) **State any three advantages of the Lok Adalat.** [2012]

Ans. (a) The Constitution provides for a High Court for each state. Parliament may, however, establish a common High Court for two or more States/Union Territories.

Composition: Each High Court consists of a Chief Justice and such other judges as the President of India may appoint from time to time.

Besides, the President has the power to appoint:

1. Additional judges for a temporary period not exceeding two years, for the clearance of arrears of work in a High Court.
2. An acting judge when a permanent judge (other than the Chief Justice) is temporarily absent or unable to perform his duties or is appointed to act temporarily as Chief Justice. The acting judge holds office until the permanent judge resumes his office.

Qualifications: According to the Constitution, a person shall be qualified for appointment as a judge of a High Court under the following conditions:

1. He should be a citizen of India.
2. He should have held a judicial office in any court in India for not less than ten years.

OR

He has for at least ten years been an advocate of a High Court or of two or more courts in succession.

(b) The High Court is a 'Court of Record' like the Supreme Court. It means its judgements and orders are preserved as a record to be referred to by its courts in future cases. They can be produced as precedents. The law laid down by the High Court is binding on all subordinate courts in the concerned State. But it does not bind the other High Courts, although it is of great significance and can be produced in support of an argument. The High Court can punish anyone who commits a contempt of its orders.

(c) (i) Lok Adalats mean 'People's Courts'. On the recommendation of Justice P.N. Bhagwati, Lok Adalats were set up by Legal Services Authorities' Act, 1987 as a legal forum to provide legal aid and quick justice to those who are not in a position to engage lawyers or bear the expenses of legal proceedings.

(ii) It is generally referred as the 'Court of the common people'. It solves cases through friendly compromise among the disputed parties.

Advantages:

1. They are quick and inexpensive.
2. Work with a spirit of compromise and not to prolong litigation.
3. Their judgments are final and not for appeal.
4. Reduce the load of work on other court

Chapter 7

First War of Independence: 1857

Short Answer Type Questions

Q. 1. What was the General Service Enlistment Act? **[2019, 2013]**

Ans. According to traditional belief, it was considered a taboo for a Brahmin to cross the seas. The British Parliament passed the General Service Enlistment Act in 1856. As per this Act, Indian soldiers could be sent overseas on duty. The Act did not take into account the religious sentiments of the Indian soldiers. The Brahmin soldiers saw in this a danger to their caste which led to a feeling of resentment, against the Britishers among them.

Q. 2. What impact did the uprising of 1857 have on the Mughal Rule ? **[2016]**

Ans. After the 1857 rebellion, Bahadur Shah Zafar was deported to Rangoon and the Mughal dynasty came to an end along with the end of their titles.

Q. 3. State any two political causes responsible for the First War of Independence. **[2014]**

Ans. Two important political causes responsible for the First War of Independence were :

1. The British policy of annexation of kingdoms under the pretext of inefficient administration of the rulers.

   E.g. : Awadh was annexed by Lord Dalhousie on the pretext of alleged misrule.

2. The Doctrine of Lapse introduced by Lord Dalhousie that imposed unsentimental law of 'no adoption policy' for zamindars and landowners and the lapse of kingdom into the hands of the British in the absence of natural heir.

Q. 4. What was Nana Saheb's grievance against the British? **[2012]**

Ans. The British refused to accept Nana Saheb, the adopted son of the last Peshwa, Baji Rao II, as the ruler of the Marathas.

Q. 5. Why did the 'Doctrine of Lapse' become a political cause for the revolt of 1857? **[2010]**

Ans. According to the 'Doctrine of Lapse', if a king died without an heir to the throne, his adopted son could not succeed him and it would be taken over by the British Government. This caused a lot of discontent amongst the Indian kings.

Long Answer Type Questions

Q. 1. By 1857, conditions were ripe for a mass uprising in the form of the Great Revolt of 1857. In this context, explain the following :
   (a) Any three Economic causes for the revolt of 1857.
   (b) Any three Military causes.
   (c) Any three Political causes of the revolt. **[2020]**

OR

Explain the causes of the Great Revolt of 1857, with reference to the following : **[2016]**

   (a) Any three Political Causes.
   (b) Any three Military Causes.
   (c) Any four Economic Causes.

OR

The First War of Independence of 1857 was a culmination of people's dissatisfaction with the British rule. In this context enumerate the following causes: **[2011]**
   (a) Military causes
   (b) Economic causes
   (c) Political causes.

📋 **Marking Scheme**

(a) – Exploitation of economic resources
  – Drain of wealth
  – Decay of cottage industries and handicrafts
  – Economic decline of peasantry
  – Growing unemployment
  – Inhuman treatment of indigo cultivators
  – Poverty and famines
  – Decline of landed aristocracy
  – Heavy duties on Indian goods like silk and cotton
  – British imports with no nominal duty
  – Impoverishment of peasants/different revenue system
  – India was reduced to an agricultural colony
  – Annexation of rent-free lands and estates/Inam Commission
  – Drain of wealth to England
  – Spinning and weaving became extinct
  – Loss of livelihood. (Any three points)

(b) – Ill treatment of Indian soldiers/treated as servants/ social distance between officers and Indian soldiers
  – General service enlistment act
  – Large proportion of Indians in the British army
  – Bleak prospects of promotions
  – Deprivation of allowances
  – Faulty distribution of troops
  – Poor performance of British troops.
  – Lower salaries
  – Introduction of Enfield Rifles
  – Loss of prestige in Afghan War
  – Disbanding of troops [Awadh]. (Any three points)

(c) – Policy of expansion
  – Subsidiary Alliance
  – By outright wars / Sind / Punjab / Buxar / Anglo Maratha/Anglo Mysore/Anglo Sikh
  – By using the doctrine of lapse/Explanation of the policy/States affected like Satara/Jhansi
  – On the pretext of alleged misrule [Awadh]
  – Disrespect shown to Bahadur Shah
  – Absentee sovereignty of the British/India was governed from foreign land.
  – Treatment given to Nana Sahib and Rani Lakshmi Bai. (Any four points)

Ans. **(a)** Three economic causes for the revolt of 1857 were:

1. **Exploitation of economic resources :** India was forced to export raw materials like cotton textiles and raw silk at cheaper rates that the British industries needed urgently. India was made to accept readymade British goods which were duty-free or at nominal duty rates while Indian products were subjected to high import duties.

2. **Drain of wealth:** The British purchased raw materials for their industries in England from the surplus revenues of Bengalis and profits from duty-free inland trade. The drain of wealth also included the salaries, income and savings of Englishmen, British expenditure in India on the purchase of military groups, office establishment, interest on debts, necessary expenditure on the army, etc.

3. **Growing unemployment :** The traditional rulers had given financial support to scholars, preachers and men of fine arts. The arrival of the British led to the decline of such rulers and gradually the patronage came to an end. And all those who had depended on the patronage were impoverished.

(b) Three military causes were :

1. **Ill treatment of Indian soldiers and lower salaries:** The Indian soldiers were poorly paid, they were ill fed and badly housed. British military authorities forbade the sepoys from wearing caste or sectarian marks.

2. **General Service Enlistment Act:** According to the General Service Enlistment Act, Indian soldiers could be sent overseas on duty but it was a taboo for a Brahmin to cross the sea. So, the British did not take into account the sentiments of the Indian soldiers.

3. **Less chances of promotions:** All higher posts were reserved for the British. The Indian soldiers couldn't go above the post of Subedar. Thus, the future of Indian soldiers was bleak.

4. **Faulty distribution of troops:** Places of strategic importance like Delhi and Allahabad had no British armies and were wholly held by the Indian soldiers.

5. **Performance of the British troops :** The British army suffered major reverse in the first Afghan War and the Crimean War broke the myth that the Britishers were invincible. It further was revealed to the Indian soldiers that the British army could be defeated by determined Indian army.

(c) Political causes of the revolt of 1857 were :

1. **British policy of expansion:** The British tried to expand their political power in India by four ways that were by out right wars, the system of Subsidiary Alliance, by adopting the Doctrine of Lapse and on the pretext of alleged misrule.

2. **Disrespect shown to Bahadur Shah:** In 1856, Lord Canning announced that after the death of Bahadur Shah his successors would not be allowed to use the imperial titles with their names and would not be known as the real princes.

3. **Treatment given to Nana Sahib :** Nana Sahib was the adopted son of Bajirao II, the last Peshwa. The British refused to grant Nana Saheb the pension they were paying to Bajirao II. This was widely resented in Maratha state.

4. **Absentee sovereignty of the British:** Since India was being ruled by the British government from England at a distance of thousand miles this was resented by the Indians. The Indians felt that they were being ruled from England and India's wealth was being drained to England and not utilized for their welfare.

Q. 2. Numerous causes gave rise to the First War of Independence and its consequences led to several changes in the British Government in India. In this context, answer the following:
 (a) **Explain any three political causes of the Revolt of 1857.**
 (b) **Briefly explain the immediate cause of the Great Revolt.**

Ans. (a) Refer to Long Answer Type Questions Answer 1 (c).

(b) 1. The immediate cause of the War of Independence was the introduction of Enfield Rifles in place of the old iron made Brown Bess Guns. The cartridges to be used for the Enfield Rifles were greased with the fat of cows and pigs. The cow, as we know, is sacred for the Hindus and the Muslims consider pig as unclean. The information about the greased cartridges spread like wildfire. The whole Bengal Army was seized with panic as it went against their religious sentiments.

2. On 24th April, 1857, some soldiers stationed at Meerut also refused to use the cartridges. On 9th May, 1857, they were severely punished for this. This incident sparked off a general mutiny among the sepoys of Meerut. On 10th May, 1857, these rebel soldiers killed their British officers, released their imprisoned comrades and hoisted the flag of revolt. This was the official beginning of the 'Great Revolt'.

Rise of Nationalism and Establishment of the Indian National Congress

 **Short Answer Type Questions**

Q. 1. Name each of the organisations founded by Jyotiba Phule and Raja Rammohan Roy. **[2019]**

Ans. Jyotiba Phule – Satya Shodhak Samaj

Raja Rammohan Roy – Brahmo Samaj

Q. 2. Name the two Presidents under whom the first two sessions of the Indian National Congress were held. **[2018]**

OR

Name the Presidents who presided over the first two sessions of the Indian National Congress. **[2016]**

Ans. Womesh Chunder Bonnerjee and Dadabhai Naoroji were the two Presidents under whom the first two sessions of the Indian National Congress were held.

Q. 3. Mention any two contributions of Jyotiba Phule in preparing the ground for the National Movement. **[2015]**

Ans. Jyotiba Phule was an urban educated member of low caste. His education and personal experience had made him critical of Hindu religion and customs.

The contributions of Jyotiba Phule in preparing the ground for National Movement are as follows :

1. In 1854, he established a school for the untouchables.
2. He started a private orphanage for the widows. He wanted to liberate the depressed classes and make them aware of their rights by educating them.
3. He founded the Satya Shodhak Samaj in 1873 with the aim of securing social justice for weaker sections of society. He pioneered the widow remarriage movement in Maharashtra and worked for the education of women.

Q. 4. What was the role of the press in promoting nationalistic sentiments amongst the Indians? **[2014]**

Ans. The press gained prominence in the later half of the 19th century. As newspapers were published in both English and Vernacular languages, the press was successful in voicing out people's opinions, crusading political movements and creating an impact on the public. Thus, promoting nationalistic sentiments amongst Indians.

Q. 5. What was the influence of Western education on the minds of the educated Indians in the 19th Century ? **[2013]**

Ans. **The influence of western education :** The introduction of western education by the British in India provided opportunities for assimilation of modern western ideas of democracy and nationalism. This in turn gave a new direction to Indian political thinking and to national awakening. The English system of education opened, to the newly educated Indians the floodgates of liberal European thought. Through the study of European history, political thought and economic ideas; educated Indians had an access to the ideals of liberty, nationality, equality, rule of law and self-government.

The spread of English language in all parts of India gave the educated Indians a common language, in which they could communicate with one another. In the absence of such a common language it would have been very difficult for the Indians to speak different regional languages to come on a common platform and to organise a movement of an all India character.

Q. 6. There were various factors that promoted the growth of Nationalism in India in the 19th century. Give the meaning of 'Nationalism' in this context. **[2011]**

Ans. 'Nationalism' means patriotism. A person who is patriotic loves his country and feels loyal towards it. The Nationalist Movement started as a revolt against racial discrimination and repressive policies of Lord Lytton and Ilbert Bill controversy etc.

Q. 7. **Mention two objectives of the Congress as enumerated by W.C. Bonnerjee.** **[2011]**

Ans. Two objectives of the Congress as enumerated by W.C. Bonnerjee are :

1. To enable national workers from all parts of India to become personally known to each other.

2. To end all racial, religious and provincial prejudices and to promote a feeling of national unity among all lovers of the country.

 Long Answer Type Questions

Q. 1. **With reference to the rise of 'National Consciousness' in India, explain the following :**

    (a) **The influence of Western Education.**

    (b) **Any three contributions of Raja Rammohan Roy.** **[2017]**

Ans. **(a)** The influence of western education : The introduction of western education by the British in India provided opportunities for assimilation of modern western ideas of democracy and nationalism. This in turn gave a new direction to Indian political thinking and to national awakening. The English system of education opened, to the newly educated Indians the floodgates of liberal European thought. Through the study of European history, political thought and economic ideas; educated Indians had an access to the ideals of liberty, nationality, equality, rule of law and self-government.

The spread of English language in all parts of India gave the educated Indians a common language, in which they could communicate with one another. In the absence of such a common language it would have been very difficult for the Indians to speak different regional languages to come on a common platform and to organise a movement of an all India character.

(b) **Three contributions of Raja Rammohan Roy :**

1. In 1828, he founded the Brahmo Sabha, which was later renamed, Brahmo Samaj. The Brahmo Samaj believed in Monotheism or worship of one God. It condemned idol worship and laid emphasis on prayer, meditation, charity, morality and strengthening the bonds of unity between men of all religions and creeds.

2. He was against the rigidity of the caste system. He started a campaign for the abolition of Sati and Purdah system, condemned polygamy, discouraged child marriages and advocated the right of widows to remarry.

3. It was because of the efforts made by Raja Rammohan Roy that William Bentinck, the Governor General of India, passed a law in 1821 making the practice of Sati illegal and punishable by law. He also protested against restrictions on the freedom of press.

Chapter 9

First Phase of the Indian National Movement (1885-1907)

Short Answer Type Questions

Q. 1. State any two methods adopted by the Early Nationalists in the National Movement. [2020]

Ans. Methods adopted by the Early Nationalists in the National Movement were :
1. The first set of method was to educate people in India in modern politics to arose national political consciousness and to create united public opinion.
2. They held meetings where speeches of resolutions for the popular demands were passed.
3. They made use of press to criticise government policies.
4. They sent memorandums and petitions to government officials and British Parliament.
5. They made use of three P's—petitions, prayers and protest. They sent petitions, request and letters of protest to the British government and forced them to look into the problems of the Indians.*(Any two)*

Q. 2. Name the two books that Dadabhai Naoroji authored explaining the 'Drain of India's Wealth'. [2019]

Ans. Poverty and Un-British Rule in India

Q. 3. Who is regarded as the political guru of Mahatma Gandhi ? Give a reason for him being considered as the Mahatma's Guru. [2015]

Ans. Gopal Krishna Gokhale, because he went to South Africa where he helped Gandhiji in his fight against racial discrimination. The credit of persuading Gandhiji to return to India and join Indian public life also goes to him.

Q. 4. Who exposed the economic exploitation of India through his book 'Poverty and Un-British Rule in India' ? [2013]

Ans. Dadabhai Naoroji exposed the economic exploitation of India through his book 'Poverty and Un-British rule in India'.

Q. 5. Mention two reasons for the Moderate's faith in the British sense of justice. [2012]

Ans. The Moderates had faith in the British sense of justice because they relied on the solemn pledges given by the British government from time to time. They also considered their association with England a boon as the British had done a lot of good to India by removing various defects from Indian society.

Q. 6. Mention any two achievements of the Moderates. [2011]

Ans. Two achievements of the moderates were :
1. They infused national consciousness among various sections of public life.
2. They promoted the ideas of democracy, fraternity, civil liberties and representative institutions.

Q. 7. Mention the regional association that each nationalist was associated with: [2010]

(i) **Surendranath Banerjee**

(ii) **Dadabhai Naoroji**

Ans. (i) Surendranath Banerjee—Indian Association in 1876.

(ii) Dadabhai Naoroji—East India Association in 1866.

Long Answer Type Questions

Q. 6. The establishment of the Indian National Congress led to the development of the National Movement in India. In this context answer the following :

(a) When was the Indian National Congress established ? Who presided over its first session ?

(b) What were the four aims of the Congress?

(c) Mention four basic beliefs of the Early Nationalists. [2014]

Ans. (a) The Indian National Congress was established on 28th December, 1885. Womesh Chandra Bonnerjee presided over the first session of the Indian National Congress in Bombay.

(b) The immediate objectives of the Indian National Congress: In the Presidential address of the first session of the Indian National Congress held at Mumbai in December, 1885, W.C. Bonnerjee declared the following as the objectives of the Indian National Congress:

1. To promote friendly relations between nationalist political workers from different parts of the country.
2. To develop and consolidate the feelings of national unity irrespective of caste, religion or province.
3. To formulate popular demands and present them before the government.
4. To train and organise public opinion in the country.

The Congress held its sessions every year in December to chalk out programmes to achieve its aims. Changes were made in the above mentioned aims of the Congress from time to time according to the changed circumstances.

(c) The basic beliefs of the early nationalists were :

1. They had faith in the sense of justice, fair play, honesty and integrity of the British.
2. It was their hope that the British would grant 'Home Rule' to them and relied on the solemn pledges made by the British Government.
3. They believed that the British rule had many benefits e.g.: It helped in removing social evils, like sati, child marriage, untouchability etc.
4. They thought that the British would help Indians to govern themselves according to western standards.

10 Second Phase of the Indian National Movement (1905-1916)

Short Answer Type Questions

Q. 1. Mention any two contributions of Bipin Chandra Pal in promoting Nationalism. **[2020]**

Ans. Two contributions of Bipin Chandra Pal were:

1. As a journalist he worked for Bengal Public Opinion, The Tribune and New India to propagate his brand of nationalism.

2. He opposed the caste system and other rigid rules concerning inter-dining and intermixing.

3. Advocated widow remarriage.

4. He preached the use of Swadeshi and boycott of foreign goods to eradicate poverty and unemployment.

5. He demanded 48 hours of work in a week and increase in the wages. *(Any two)*

Q. 2. Write any two contributions of Lala Lajpat Rai to the National Movement. **[2019]**

OR

Mention two important contributions of Lala Lajpat Rai.

Ans. Contributions by Lala Lajpat Rai :

1. He transformed the freedom struggle into the agitation of the millions and the common masses. Through his speeches and writings, he accelerated its pace and widened its base. He presided over historic session of the Congress in 1920. It was here that the resolution of "Non-Cooperation" was adopted by the Congress.

2. He led the demonstration against the Simon Commission. He was assaulted by a British Sergeant in the ensuing lathi charge and could not recover from it. He sacrificed his life so that India could win its freedom before his death, he said, "Lathi blows inflicted on me would prove one day as nails in the coffin of the British Empire."

Q. 3. Name the nationalist who said, 'Swaraj is my birthright and I shall have it'. State any one of his contributions to the National Movement. **[2018]**

Ans. Bal Gangadhar Tilak made the statement, 'Swaraj is my birthright and I shall have it'. In 1893, he started the celebration of the Ganapati festival and the Shivaji festival in 1895. The object was to instil in the masses a spirit of discipline and patriotism.

Q. 4. Give the names of two leaders who led the Home Rule Movement in India. **[2017]**

Ans. Two leaders who led the Home Rule Movement in India were Bal Gangadhar Tilak and Annie Besant.

Q. 5. Who founded the Home Rule Leagues in India ? What was its objective ? **[2015]**

Ans. Bal Gangadhar Tilak founded the Indian Home Rule Leagues in April 1916 and Annie Besant founded the Home Rule League in September 1916.

The main objectives of the Home Rule Movement was to attain self-government within the British Empire by constitutional means. That is to say, the country should have a government by Councils, whose members would be elected by the people. The Council would pass the Country's budget and the ministers should be made responsible to the legislature. The Home Rule League raised the slogan of Swadeshi, National Education and Home Rule for India.

Q. 6. Mention any two causes for the rise of Assertive Nationalism. **[2015]**

Ans. Two causes for the rise of Assertive Nationalism were :

1. Famine and plague of 1896 affected crores of people and caused death. The British government provided slow relief.

2. Economic exploitation: Prolonged drought and famine increased the misery of the peasants/Indian traders and manufacturers lost confidence in the

British Government/India's gold reserves were transferred to London/India was starved of its own resources.

Q. 7. **What were the two methods adopted by the Radical nationalists in the freedom struggle?** **[2010]**

Ans. Two achievements of the Radical Nationalists were:

1. They infused a new confidence and spirit among the people. They popularised the use of Swadeshi goods.
2. They broadened the social base of the movement by extending it to the masses — the workers, peasants, women and the youth.

 # Long Answer Type Questions

Q. 1. **The Second half of the 19th century witnessed the growth of a strong feeling of Nationalism. With reference to the statement, answer the following :**

(b) **State any three ways in which the Press played an important role in developing nationalism amongst Indians.**

(c) **Explain briefly any three differences in the methods adopted between the Early Nationalists and Radicals, in the National Movement.** **[2019]**

 **Marking Scheme**

(b) The press:
(i) Spread the message of patriotism
(ii) Spread the ideals of liberty, freedom and equality
(iii) Popularised the ideas of Home Rule and Independence
(iv) Carried on daily criticism of the British policies
(v) Exposed the true nature of British rule in India
(vi) Helped in the exchange of views among people from different parts of the country
(vii) Made the Indians aware of what was happening in the world.
(viii) Aroused public opinion in the country (Any two points)

(c) Early Nationalists (Any two points)
(i) They believed in the policy of constitutional agitation within the legal framework, and slow orderly political progress.
(ii) They held meetings where speeches were made and resolutions for popular demands were passed.
(iii) They made use of the press to criticise government policies,
(iv) They sent memorandums and petitions.
(v) They made use of three P's – Petitions, Prayers and Protests.
(vi) A British Committee of the Indian National Congress was set up in London in 1889, which published a weekly journal, India, to present India's case before the British public.
(vii) Deputations of Indian leaders were sent to Britain. These political leaders carried on active propaganda in Britain.

Radicals: Methods: (Any two points)
(i) Swadeshi
(ii) Boycott
(iii) National Education
(iv) Passive Resistance
(v) Revivalism
(vi) Personal Sacrifices
(vii) Mass movement
(viii) Aggressive or assertive method

Ans. (b) **Role of Press in developing nationalism amongst Indians:**

1. It was through the Press that the message of patriotism and modern liberal ideas of liberty, freedom, equality, home rule and independence, spread among the people.
2. The Press carried on daily criticism of the unjust policies of the British Government in India and exposed the true nature of British rule in India.
3. It made possible the exchange of views among different social groups from different parts of the country.

(c)

	Early Nationalists	Radicals
1.	The Early Nationalists wanted to achieve self-government and they strove for autonomy within the Empire and not for absolute independence.	The Radicals aimed for nothing less than Swaraj as it existed in the United Kingdom.
2.	They believed in constitutional methods and worked within the framework of the law.	They were assertive in their approach.

3.	They held good positions under the British government.	They denounced British rule and defied it.
4.	They had faith in the British sense of justice and fair play.	They rejected British rule and held it responsible for the prevailing poverty of the Indian people.

Q. 2. **The conflict between the two sections of the Congress came to surface in its Session in 1906 at Calcutta. In this context explain the following :**

With reference to the picture given below, answer the following :

(i) What were the three personalities popularly known as ?

(ii) Which section of the Congress did they represent?

(iii) Mention two of their popular Beliefs.

(c) State any four methods that they advocated for the achievement of their aims. [2017]

Ans. **(i)** Lal-Bal-Pal trio.

(ii) Assertive Nationalists.

(iii) Two popular beliefs were :

1. These 'angry young men' stood for complete Swaraj to be achieved by more self-reliant methods. They also wanted to have a mass-base for their movement.

2. They had a different outlook that advocated active resistance to the British imperialism. They condemned the British rule in India and held it responsible for the country's downfall. They called upon the people of India to make sacrifices for the sake of their country.

(c) Four methods advocated by the Assertive Nationalists for the achievement of their aims were :

1. **Swadeshi :** It means producing necessary items in one's own country and using them for one's use without being dependent on imported goods. This idea was popularized by occasional bonfires of foreign cloth, salt and sugar.

2. **Boycott :** Swadeshi and boycott are the two sides of the same coin. Tilak said, "When you accept Swadeshi, you must boycott foreign goods". Economic boycott of British goods and use of Swadeshi was designed to encourage Indian industries and provide the people with more opportunities for employment.

3. **National education:** A National scheme of education was planned which was to replace Government controlled universities and colleges. The Assertive Nationalists tried to enlist the students in their service. When the British government threatened to take disciplinary action against the students, the national leaders advocated national universities that were free from government control. A large number of national schools were established in East Bengal, and Bengal National College was set up at Kolkata and Pachaiyappa National College at Chennai.

4. **Passive resistance:** The Assertive leaders believed in adopting the policy of non-violent resistance and vigorous political action to achieve their aims. They believed that political rights could not be won by an organisation which could not "distinguish between begging rights and claiming them". They, therefore, asked the people to refuse to cooperate with the government and to boycott government service, courts, schools and colleges.

Q. 3. With reference to the growth of National Consciousness in India, explain each of the following :

    (a) The immediate objectives of the Indian National Congress.

    (b) Two contributions of Dadabhai Naoroji.

    (c) The impact of the Swadeshi and the Boycott Movement.   **[2015]**

Ans. **(a)** **The immediate objectives of the Indian National Congress :** In the Presidential address of the first session of the Indian National Congress held at Mumbai in December, 1885, W.C. Bonnerjee declared the following as the objectives of the Indian National Congress :

1. To promote friendly relations between nationalist political workers from different parts of the country.

2. To develop and consolidate the feelings of national unity irrespective of caste, religion or province.

3. To formulate popular demands and present them before the government.

4. To train and organise public opinion in the country.

The Congress held its sessions every year in December to chalk out programmes to achieve its aims. Changes were made in the above mentioned aims of the Congress from time to time according to the changed circumstances.

(b) **Two contributions of Dadabhai Naoroji:**

1. **Role in the Congress :** Dadabhai's role in the Congress was praiseworthy. He took an active part in the foundation of the Indian Nationalist Congress and was elected as its President thrice in 1886, 1893 and 1906. Four resolutions on Self-government, Boycott, Swadeshi and National Education were passed by the Congress under his Presidentship.

The credit for demanding Swaraj from the Congress platform for the first time (1906) goes to him. In his Presidential address, he said that Congress wanted self-government or Swaraj like that of the United Kingdom or the Colonies.

2. **Exposed the economic ills in India :** As an economic thinker, he came to the conclusion that the root cause for the economic ills of India was the exploitation in India by the British. Dadabhai's views on Indian economy are given in his work entitled 'Poverty and Un-British Rule in India'. His famous 'Drain Theory' explained how India's wealth was being 'drained' to England through various ways.

Dadabhai passed away in 1917 leaving behind a lesson of selfless service to the nation. C.Y. Chintamani had rightly said, "The public life of India had been adorned by a galaxy of brilliant intellects and selfless patriots, but there has been in our time none comparable with Dadabhai Naoroji."

(c) The Swadeshi Movement failed to destabilise the government. It did not bring about immediate union of the two Bengals – but instilled courage and fearlessness, and also taught people to openly flout the rules and regulations of the government.

Impact of Swadeshi and Boycott Movements as part of the Anti-Partition Movement :

1. **Participation of diverse social sections:** The Swadeshi Movement drew a large section of society into active participation in freedom movement for the first time. Many zamindars who had been loyal to the British joined the movement. Active participation of women as well as students was a remarkable achievement. Despite the efforts of the British to keep Muslims away from the movement, some Muslim leaders like Abdul Rashul, a barrister; Ghuznavi, a businessman; and Liaquat Hussain, a popular leader joined the movement.

2. Encouragement to indigenous industries: The Swadeshi and Boycott Movements laid emphasis on self-reliance which meant assertion of self-confidence. It aimed at the promotion of indigenous industries for strengthening the country. In the economic field, self-reliance gave a stimulus to cottage industries and also to large-scale enterprises. Many textile mills, soap and match factories, handloom weaving concerns were opened. This increased demand for swadeshi goods and led to the increase in production of indigenous goods.

3. Reduction in the import of foreign goods: The Boycott Movement was an eye-opener for the Indians as it made them realise that the import of British goods was one of the primary reasons for the economic distress.

Q. 4. The early Congressmen were liberal in their views and programmes. This led to the rise of Assertive Nationalists who demanded more forceful action against the British. In this context discuss the following :

(a) Reasons why the early Congressmen were called Moderates.

(b) How did Moderates differ from the Assertive Nationalists in realizing their objectives ?

(c) How did Tilak bring a new wave in Indian politics that was distinct from the early Congressmen ?   **[2013]**

Ans. **(a)** The earlier leaders of the Congress were called the 'Moderates' as they were not extreme in their thinking and activities. In other words, the demands raised by the earlier leaders of the Congress were of moderate nature. Moreover, they used constitutional and peaceful methods like filing petitions, appeals, resolutions, etc. Therefore, the period from 1885 to 1905 is generally described as being the moderate phase. The Congress was controlled by the moderate leaders such as Dadabhai Naoroji, Pherozeshah Mehta, Gopal Krishna Gokhale, W. C. Bonnerjee, Surendranath Bannerjee and Madan Mohan Malaviya.

(b) Difference between Moderates and Assertive Nationalists:

	Basis	Moderates	Assertive Nationalists
1.	**Basic beliefs**	The Moderates looked to England for inspiration and guidance. Gokhale, Ranade, Naoroji and other moderate leaders had almost unlimited faith in the British goodness. They readily conceded the benefits of British rule to India.	They had a great dislike for the British. Tilak, Lajpat Rai, Bipin Chandra Pal and others had no faith in the goodness of the British. They cursed the British rule that brought misery to the people of India.
2.	**Their ultimate**	In 1906, the Moderates t talked of Swaraj as the goal of India. It meant the system of government as found in the self-governing British colonies.	They did not aim at mere economic or administrative reforms. Their ideal was 'Absolute Swaraj'.
3.	**Their programmes and methods of struggle**	The Moderates carried on their work by means of petitions, appeals, resolutions, meetings and deputations.	The Extremists described t these methods as "Political Mendicancy" because they believed in direct action.
4.	**Approach to boycott**	The Moderates' boycott was launched only to the British goods.	The Nationalists' boycott also included boycott of government services, titles and honours.

5.	Inclusion of masses in freedom struggle	The Moderates believed in constitutional methods, as such the efforts bore the mark of individuality and were isolated from the masses.	The Aggressive Nationalists believed in the strength of masses. They promoted the freedom movement into a mass struggle.

(c) The new wave in Indian politics was the result of efforts put in by **Bal Gangadhar Tilak**. The distinct features of his movement to attain Swaraj were :

1. **His role in the Anti-Partition Movement:** The partition of Bengal gave him a big opportunity to expose evil design of the government. Leaders like Tilak, Bipin Chandra and Lajpat Rai transformed the anti-partition movement into a movement of Swaraj.

2. **Bitter attacks on government :** Year after year, the Congress passed nearly the same resolutions, without much effect on the government. Therefore, Tilak came to the conclusion that "reforms would be secured not by talk, but by action".

3. **Home Rule Movement :** The year 1916 saw the establishment of the Home Rule Leagues in Madras (Chennai) and Maharashtra. The two leagues were led by Annie Besant and Tilak.

4. **Tilak's political beliefs – "Swaraj is my birth Right and I shall have it" :** Tilak talked of 'Swaraj' in as early as 1896-97. Swaraj and Swadeshi had become the battle cry of him.

Q. 5. From 1905 to 1918, there emerged a new and a younger group of leaders within the Congress who did not agree with the old leadership. In this context, answer the following questions: **[2010]**

(a) Differentiate between the Moderates and the Radical nationalists in their objectives and achievements, stating one objective and two achievements of each wing of the Congress.

(b) Name the radical leader known as the foreruner of Gandhiji ?

(c) Explain how the represive policies of Lord Curzon and influence of international events led of radical nationalism.

Ans. **(a)** **Objective:** The objective of the Moderates was to attain 'Swaraj' within the framework of the British rule.

The Radicals demanded nothing less than 'absolute' Swaraj or complete independence as the goald for India.

The achievements of the Modeates were:

1. The Moderates became instrumental in spreading information regarding democracy, civil liberties, public welfare and nationalism.

2. The Moderates were also successful in exposing the true nature of British rule. Dadabhai Naoroji, through his 'drain theory', raised questions concerning the systematic plunder of the country's wealth by the British rulers.

The achievements of the Radicals were:

1. They broadened the social base of the National Movement to include women students, zamindars and to some extent the peasantry. This participation made the movement a 'mass' one.

2. They made the common people realise that India would settle for nothing less than complete independence. They made 'Swaraj' the clarion call of the National Movement.

(b) Bal Gangadhar Tilak has been regarded as the forerunner of Gandhiji as the methods he adopted were later followed by Gandhiji. For example, Swadeshi and Boycott were practiced by Gandhiji also. Gandhiji's concept of complete independence was same as Tilak's ideal of

Swaraj. Therefore, Tilak was undoubtedly the predecessor of Gandhiji.

(c) Lord Curzon followed policies of repression just as Lord Lytton. He did not want to grant any kind of freedom to the Indians. His one point agenda was to crush the growing demand of self-rule by Indians. Some of the Acts were:

1. The Culcutta Corporation Act (1899)— Reduced elected members to half.

2. The Indian Universities Act (1904)— Reduced authonomy of the universities and imposed strict control.

3. The official Secrets Act (1904)—Sought to curtail the freedom of the press.

At the same time, events in other parts of the world also pupularised radical action. The defeat of Russia by Japan and that of Italy by Ethiopia showed that the Europeans were not invincible. In South Africa, the Boers fought against the British for 3 years. Revolutionary Movements in Turkey, China, Iran and Egypt convinced the Indians that they could also defeat the Britishers.

Chapter 11

The Partition of Bengal

Short Answer Type Questions

Q. 1. Why is October 16, 1905 regarded as an important day in the history of the Indian National Movement ? **[2020]**

Ans. October 16, 1905 is regarded as an important day in the history of Indian National Movement because the scheme of partition of Bengal was implemented on this day, which meant to foster the division of Bengal on the basis of religion. East Bengal to be predominantly a Muslim majority state and West Bengal would be a Hindu majority state.

Q. 2. State two reasons given by Lord Curzon to justify the Partition of Bengal. **[2016]**

OR

How did Lord Curzon justify the Partition of Bengal ? **[2010]**

Ans. Two reasons given by Lord Curzon to justify the Partition of Bengal are :

1. The province of Bengal was too big to be efficiently administered by a single provincial government. It was a mere readjustment of administrative boundaries to protect pockets of minorities both in West Bengal as well as East Bengal.

2. To fetch more revenue through trade outlets.

Q. 3. State any two repressive policies of Lord Curzon. **[2012]**

Ans. Two repressive policies of Lord Curzon were the Indian Universities Act of 1904 and the Sedition Act, and the Official secrets Act, which curtailed the liberties of all sections of society.

Q. 4. When was Bengal partitioned ? Name the Viceroy responsible for it. **[2011]**

Ans. The partition of Bengal happened in 1905 and Lord Curzon, the Governor General was responsible for it.

Long Answer Type Questions

Q. 1. One of Lord Curzon's administrative measures that resulted in a strong resentment from the masses was the Partition of Bengal in 1905. In this context, answer the following questions :

(a) What was Lord Curzon's argument in favour of the Partition of Bengal ?

How did the nationalists interpret Lord Curzon's motives ?

(b) How did the people react to the Partition of Bengal ?

(c) What was the impact of the Swadeshi Movement on Indian Industries ? [2012]

Ans. **(a)** Lord Curzon's argument in favour of the partition of Bengal was an 'administrative necessity'. According to him, Bengal was a very big province to be administered efficiently by a single provincial government. So, it was to be divided for better administration of the province.

The Indian Nationalists interpreted this as follows :

1. Bengal was the nerve centre of Indian Nationalism at that time. So, the British hoped to stop the rising tide of nationalism by partitioning Bengal.

2. The partition of Bengal intended to curb Bengali influence by not only placing Bengalis under two administrations but by reducing them to a minority in Bengal itself.

3. The partition was meant to foster division on the basis of religion. East Bengal would be predominantly a Muslim majority state and West Bengal a Hindu majority state.

4. It was considered as a price for the Muslim league's loyalty towards the British.

(b) When the proposal was published, then there was a great hue and cry from all quarters. When the partition came into effect the people started a strong movement against it known as the 'Anti-partition' movement. The people, under the leadership of great nationalist leaders, understood the real motive of the partition which was to flare up the confrontation between the Hindus and the Muslims. The people felt humiliated, insulted and tricked. They were ready to sacrifice their lives and face death fearlessly.

(c) The Swadeshi movement had a positive impact on the Indian industries. It gave new life to Indian industries, especially cottage industry as the use of India made goods replaced the foreign goods in Indian homes. It led to the increased demand of Swadeshi goods like handlooms and handicrafts, match boxes, soaps and textiles. It gave employment to the unemployed craftsmen and gave an impetus to the cottage industries.

Formation and Objectives of the Muslim League

 ## Short Answer Type Questions

Q. 1. State any two objectives of the Muslim League. **[2018]**

Ans. Two objectives of the Muslim League were :

1. Protecting the political and other rights of the Muslims so that they could extend the needs and sentiments of the Indian Muslims before the British government.

2. Propagating the sentiment of loyalty for the British government amongst the Muslims and removing misunderstanding about the Muslims.

Q. 2. When was the Muslim League formally founded ? Who presided over its session at Dhaka ? **[2012]**

Ans. The Muslim League was formed in 1906. Waqar-ul-Mulk presided over its session at Dhaka.

Long Answer Type Questions

Q. 1. **The Partition of Bengal and the Formation of the Muslim League were two important events that had its impact on the National Struggle for Independence. In this context, explain the following :**

(a) **Impact of Swadeshi and Boycott movements as part of the Anti-Partition Movement.**

(c) **Objectives of the Muslim League. [2016]**

Ans. (a) The Swadeshi Movement failed to destabilise the government. It did not bring about immediate union of the two Bengals – but instilled courage and fearlessness, and also taught people to openly flout the rules and regulations of the government.

Impact of Swadeshi and Boycott Movements as part of the Anti-Partition Movement :

1. **Participation of diverse social sections:** The Swadeshi Movement drew a large section of society into active participation in freedom movement for the first time. Many zamindars who had been loyal to the British joined the movement. Active participation of women as well as students was a remarkable achievement. Despite the efforts of the British to keep Muslims away from the movement, some Muslim leaders like Abdul Rashul, a barrister; Ghuznavi, a businessman; and Liaquat Hussain, a popular leader joined the movement.

2. **Encouragement to indigenous industries:** The Swadeshi and Boycott Movements laid emphasis on self-reliance which meant assertion of self-confidence. It aimed at the promotion of indigenous industries for strengthening the country. In the economic field, self-reliance gave a stimulus to cottage industries and also to large-scale enterprises. Many textile mills, soap and match factories, handloom weaving concerns were opened. This increased demand for swadeshi goods and led to the increase in production of indigenous goods.

3. **Reduction in the import of foreign goods:** The Boycott Movement was an eye-opener for the Indians as it made them realise that the import of British goods was one of the primary reasons for the economic distress.

(c) **The Objectives of the Muslim League were laid down as follows :**

1. To promote, among the Muslims of India, support for the British government and to remove any misconceptions regarding the intention of the government in relation to Indian Muslims.
2. To protect and advance the political rights and interests of the Muslims.
3. To present the needs and aspirations of the Muslims to the government.
4. To prevent the feelings of hostility between the Muslims of India and other communities.

Q. 2. **The reasons for the formation of the Muslim League were many. In this context explain :**

(b) **Any three demands made by the Muslim Deputation in 1906 to the Viceroy Lord Minto.**

(c) **What were the aims and objectives of the Muslim League ?** **[2013]**

Ans. **(b)** **The three demands made by the Muslim Deputation in 1906 to the Viceroy Lord Minto were :**
1. **Separate electorates:** The Muslims should be given the right of sending their representatives to the Provincial Councils and Imperial Legislative Council through separate communal electorates.
2. **Separate representation in the municipal and University bodies:** There should be some scheme for giving adequate representation to the Muslims in municipal and District Boards and the senates and syndicate of Indian Universities.

3. **Greater representation in civil, military and Judicial services:** There should be greater representation of the Muslims in all services–civil and military. Further, there should be Muslim judges in every High Court.

(c) Refer to Long Answer Type questions Answer 1 (c).

Q. 3. **With reference to Nationalism and the birth of the Indian National Congress, explain each of the following :**

State any four immediate objectives of the Indian National Congress. **[2012]**

Ans. **The immediate objectives of the Indian National Congress :** In the Presidential address of the first session of the Indian National Congress held at Mumbai in December, 1885, W.C. Bonnerjee declared the following as the objectives of the Indian National Congress :
1. To promote friendly relations between nationalist political workers from different parts of the country.
2. To develop and consolidate the feelings of national unity irrespective of caste, religion or province.
3. To formulate popular demands and present them before the government.
4. To train and organise public opinion in the country.

The Congress held its sessions every year in December to chalk out programmes to achieve its aims. Changes were made in the above mentioned aims of the Congress from time to time according to the changed circumstances.

Chapter 13

Mahatma Gandhi and Popular National Movements

 Short Answer Type Questions

Q. 1. Name any two leaders of the Khilafat Movement. **[2020]**

Ans. Two leaders of Khilafat Movement were :

1. Muhammad Ali 2. Shaukat Ali.

Q. 2. State any two causes for the Non-Cooperation Movement. **[2020]**

Ans. Two causes for the Non-Cooperation Movement were :

1. Rowlatt Act was passed in March 1919 which gave extraordinary powers to the British to imprison any person without trial. There was a terrible massacre at Jallianwala Bagh, Amritsar on April 13, 1919 which led to the Non-Cooperation movement.

2. Khilafat Movement was started by Ali Brothers in August 1920 for the preservation of the Khalifa, the religious head of the Muslims. Gandhiji combined the Khilafat Movement with the Non-Cooperation Movement as he saw this as an opportunity to unite Hindus and Muslims.

Q. 3. State any two causes that led to the Civil Disobedience Movement in 1930. **[2018]**

Ans. The causes that led to the launch of Civil Disobedience Movement in 1930 were :

1. The British government appointed an all white commission consisting of 7 members known as the Simon Commission, hurting Indian sentiments.

2. Declaration of Poorna Swaraj at Lahore session (1929).

Q. 4. What was the Khilafat Movement ? **[2017]**

Ans. The Sultan was deprived of real authority over his territories and this angered the Muslims in India. The Muslim population in India started a powerful agitation known as the Khilafat Movement, under the leadership of the Ali Brothers (Mohammad Ali and Shaukat Ali), Maulana Azad, Hakim Ajmal Khan and Hasrat Mohani.

Q. 5. State any two provisions of the Rowlatt Act passed by the Government in 1919. **[2017]**

Ans. The Rowlatt Act implied :

1. Arrest and deportation of any person without warrant.

2. Trial of all political cases by tribunals to be set up for the purpose.

3. Possession of seditions pamphlets was declared to be a punishable offence.

The Act came like a sudden blow to the Indians who were expecting self-governance.

Q. 6. Why did Mahatma Gandhi start his historic march to Dandi ? **[2017]**

Ans. The government did not reply to Gandhiji's eleven-point ultimatum. He selected to attack the salt laws because the salt tax affected all sections of society, especially the poor. By breaking the salt laws it marked the beginning of the Civil Disobedience Movement.

Q. 7. Why was the Congress session held at Lahore in 1929 significant to the National Movement ? **[2016]**

Ans. Jawaharlal Nehru was appointed as the President of the Congress at the historic Lahore session of 1929. It passed a resolution declaring Poorna Swaraj (complete independence) to be objective of the Congress and took steps to launch the Civil Disobedience.

On the midnight of December 31, 1929, Jawaharlal Nehru led a procession to the banks of the river Ravi at Lahore and hoisted the tricolor flag. He proclaimed that it was a crime against man and God to surrender any longer to British rule.

That's why the Congress session that was held at Lahore in 1929 became significant to the National Movement.

Q. 8. **Why was the Simon Commission rejected by the Congress ?** **[2015]**

Ans. In November 1927, the British government appointed the Indian Statutory Commission, popularly known as the Simon Commission, to investigate the need for further constitutional reforms. The Commission was composed of seven British members of Parliament. It had no Indian member. This was seen as a violation of the principle of self-determination and a deliberate insult to the self-respect of the Indians. At its Madras session in 1927, presided over by Dr. Ansari, the National Congress decided to boycott the commission 'at every stage and in every form'.

Q. 9. **Mention any one provision each of the Gandhi-Irwin Pact signed in 1931.** **[2014]**

Ans. An 'ordinance' is a temporary law that is enforced when the Parliament is not in session. The power to pass an ordinance is accorded to the President of India and is passed in cases of emergency.

Q. 10. **Name the leaders of the Khilafat Movement that was launched in India to champion the cause of the Caliph of Turkey.** **[2013]**

Ans. Mohammad Ali and Shaukat Ali (The Ali brothers) were the leaders of the Khilafat Movement that was launched in India to champion the cause of the Caliph of Turkey.

Q. 11. **Why was the Simon Commission boycotted by the Indians ?** **[2013]**

Ans. All the political parties including the Congress and Muslim League decided to boycott the commission because it was an all-white commission with no Indian associated with it. It was completely unrepresentative of Indians and was received with black flags, mass demonstrations, hartals and slogans of 'Simon Go back' all over the country.

 ## Long Answer Type Questions

Q. 1. **With reference to the picture given below, answer the following questions :** **[2019]**

    (a) **(i) Identify the Memorial built for those who were killed in this incident.**

    (ii) Where did this incident take place ?

    (iii) Name the movement launched by Gandhi in 1920 as a consequence.

    (b) **Explain briefly the reason for the suspension of this particular movement by Gandhi in 1922.**

    (c) **State any four impacts of the movement.**

Marking Scheme

(a) – Jallianwala Bagh Memorial
   – Jallianwala Bagh in Amritsar
   – Non-Cooperation Movement.

(b) – The tragedy at Chauri Chaura, a village in Gorakhpur district in Uttar Pradesh.
   – A procession of about 3,000 peasants marched to the police station to protest against the police officer.
   – Police fired at the peasants.
   – Peasants reacted and set the police station on fire.
   – 22 policemen were killed.
   – Gandhiji, who believed in Ahimsa was greatly shocked and withdrew the movement on February 12, 1922.
   – A police officer had beaten some farmers picketing a liquor shop.

(*Narration of Incident with any of the three points cited in the answer*)

(c) Impact of Non-Cooperation Movement:
   – The National Movement became a Mass Movement (Gave a national base to the Congress Party)
   – Instilled Confidence, Patriotism among people.
   – Congress became a revolutionary party
   – Undermined the power and prestige of British government
   – Fostered Hindu-Muslim unity.
   – Promoted Social reforms (like removal of untouchability/promotion of khadi/setting up of national schools)
   – Promoted the cult of Swaraj.

   – Showed the true nature of the British.
   –Spread Nationalism to every part of the country
   – Affected British trade
   – Showed power of passive resistance

(*Any four points*)

Ans. **(a)** **(i)** Jallianwala Bagh Memorial.

(ii) Jallianwala Bagh in Amritsar, Punjab.

(iii) Non-Cooperation Movement.

(b) The tragedy at Chauri-Chaura, a village in Gorakhpur district in Uttar Pradesh, occurred on February 5, 1922. A procession of about 3,000 peasants marched to the nearby police station to protest against the police officer who had beaten some volunteers picketing a liquor shop. The police fired at the peasants. The infuriated demonstrators set the police station on fire, killing 22 policemen who were inside the police station. There were also a few violent incidents in other parts of the country. Gandhiji, a firm believer in 'Ahimsa' was greatly shocked at these incidents and he withdrew the Non-Cooperation Movement on February 12, 1922.

(c) 1. **The National Movement became a Mass Movement:** The Indian national movement, for the first time in history, acquired a real mass base with the participation of different sections of Indian society such as peasants, workers, students, teachers and women.

2. **Instilled Confidence among the people:** The movement undermined the power and prestige of the British Government. It generated a desire for freedom and inspired people to challenge the colonial rule.

3. **The Congress became an organised fighting force:** The weapons of Satyagraha and Non-Cooperation changed the character of the Congress overnight. It transformed the Indian National Congress from a deliberative assembly into an organised fighting force, pledged to revolution.

4. **Fostered Hindu-Muslim Unity:** It fostered Hindu-Muslim unity which could be seen in the merger of the Khilafat issue with this movement.

Q. 2. **In 1930 Mahatma Gandhi's demands were rejected by the British, as a result of which he launched the Civil Disobedience Movement. In this context explain the following : [2015]**

(a) **Name the famous march undertaken by Gandhiji. Where did he begin this march ? State two of its features.**

(b) **The Gandhi-Irwin Pact as a consequence of this Movement.**

(c) **Significance of the Second Round Table Conference.**

Ans. **(a)** On 12th March, Mahatma Gandhi began a historic march from Sabarmati Ashram to Dandi and a number of people followed him. On the morning of 6th April, Gandhiji violated the Salt Law at Dandi by picking up some salt left by the sea-waves.

The government had the monopoly to manu-facture and sell the salt. He had selected to attack the Salt Law because the salt tax affected all sections of society, especially the poor. Gandhiji's breaking of the Salt Law marked the beginning of Civil Disobedience Movement.

(b) **Provisions of the Gandhi-Irwin Pact as a result of the Civil Disobedience Movement :** Since the satyagraha could not be suppressed, the Government, through Tej Bahadur Sapru and Jayakar, started negotiations with Gandhiji in jail. This resulted in the signing of a pact by Gandhiji and Lord Irwin, the Viceroy, in March 1931. This is known as the Gandhi-Irwin Pact. The government agreed to :

1. Allow people living near seashore to manufacture salt.

2. Release all political prisoners, except those guilty of violence.

3. Permit peaceful picketing of liquor and foreign cloth shops.

4. Restore the confiscated properties of the Congressmen.

The Congress, in its turn, consented to the following :

1. To suspend the Civil Disobedience Movement.

2. To participate in the second session of the Round Table Conference.

3. Not to press for investigation into police assesses.

(c) Significance of the Second Round Table Conference : It was attended by Gandhiji as a sole representative of the Congress, according to the terms of the Gandhi-Irwin Pact of 1931. The conference was soon deadlocked on the minorities issue, with separate electorates being demanded not only by Muslims but also by the Depressed Classes, Sikhs, Indian Christians and Anglo-Indians.

The question of Independence or setting up of a responsible Government receded into the background. The British government refused to concede the immediate grant of dominion status, Gandhiji returned to India disappointed.

Q. 3. **In the Nagpur session, 1920, the Congress ratified the resolution to launch the Non-Cooperation Movement under the leadership of Gandhiji. In this context :**

(a) What do you understand by the term Non-Cooperation?

(b) What were the objectives which the movement sought to achieve ?

(c) Explain the impact of the Non-Cooperation Movement in India's struggle for freedom [2014]

Ans. **(a)** Non-cooperation is a way of protesting in which one does not cooperate with the evil doer. Gandhiji asked the people not to assist the foreign government to rule over them.

(b) **The objectives of the Non-Cooperation Move-ment were :**

1. To attain self-government within the British empire or attaining Swaraj.

2. Annulment of the Rowlatt Act and punishing those guilty of atrocities in Punjab i.e., the British Government should express its regret on the happenings in Punjab.

3. The British should adopt a lenient attitude towards Turkey, and restore the old status of the Sultan of Turkey.

(c) 1. **The National Movement became a Mass Movement :** The Indian national movement, for the first time in history, acquired a real mass base with the participation of different sections of Indian society such as peasants, workers, students, teachers and women.

2. **Instilled Confidence among the people:** The movement undermined the power and prestige of the British Government. It generated a desire for freedom and inspired people to challenge the colonial rule.

3. **The Congress became an organised fighting force:** The weapons of Satyagraha and Non-Cooperation changed the character of the Congress overnight. It transformed the Indian National Congress from a deliberative assembly into an organised fighting force, pledged to revolution.

4. **Fostered Hindu-Muslim Unity:** It fostered Hindu-Muslim unity which could be seen in the merger of the Khilafat issue with this movement.

Q. 4. **Gandhiji introduced new ideas in politics and adopted new methods to give a new direction to the political movement. In this context, answer the following questions :**

(a) Gandhiji's doctrine of Satyagraha.

(b) Gandhiji's Social Ideals.

(c) Which mass struggle was launched by him on non-violent lines in 1920 ?

Explain in brief the programmes of such a campaign. [2012]

Ans. **(a)** Gandhiji's philosophy was based on non-violence. Satyagraha was one of his great weapons. Satyagraha means to 'disobey the law without resorting to violence'. According to him, passive resistance was the weapon of the weak while, Satyagraha was the weapon of the strong. He believed that a Satyagrahi must be morally and spiritually strong so that, he could fight injustice with non violence. He laid stress upon peaceful talks, non-cooperation, picketing, strike, social boycott, hunger strike, civil disobedience etc. to realize his aim of Satyagraha.

(b) Gandhiji was a great social reformer. He was against the caste system and considered untouchability a curse on the Hindu society. He called the untouchables 'Harijans' and requested people to respect them like human beings. In fact, he lived with them in their colonies. Under his guidance, the Congress adopted the programme for their upliftment.

He even advocated for equal rights and status for women and inspired them to play an important role in the national movement.

He also introduced a new system of basic education, wherein, the children learnt some art so that they could earn while learning. He attached great importance to character building and acquiring skills and stressed upon simple and moralistic life.

(c) In 1920, Gandhiji launched the Non-Cooperation Movement. Non-Cooperation means withdrawal of all support and cooperation. The target of this programme was the British government. It had only one objective and that was to cripple the government and to create such problems to the administration that would make it difficult to function without the willing cooperation of the Indian people. Another objective was to make it known to the British that they could not run the administration of India even for a day unless the Indians cooperated with them. The people returned all titles, honours, awards, degrees given by the government. They boycotted government functions, lawyers gave up their practice, students left schools and colleges, teachers resigned from their posts. People started boycotting assembly and provincial elections and gave up their seats. People observed strikes and refused to pay taxes. Khadi became the symbol of freedom.

Q. 5. **The Civil Disobedience Movement was significant in the history of the National Movement. In this context write briefly on the following points:**

(a) **The circumstances leading to the Civil Disobedience Movement**

(b) **The Second Round Table Conference**

(c) **The Gandhi-Irwin Pact.** **[2011]**

Ans. **(a)** **The circumstances leading to the Civil Disobedience Movement were as follows :**

1. In May, 1929, the British Government declared that it would consider dominion status for India. It also decided to hold Round Table Conference in London to examine the Simon Commission's report on India. But the Government did not keep its promise.

2. In the meantime, the Indian National Congress held a historic session at Lahore in December 1929, where resolution of Complete Independence- "Poorna Swaraj" was passed.

3. Gandhiji wrote a letter to Viceroy Irwin as an ultimatum, that, if his eleven points were not implemented by the government then he would start a massive non-violent Civil Disobedience Movement. The Viceroy did not respond positively, so Gandhiji was forced by circumstances to launch the Civil Disobedience Movement by undertaking Dandi March on 12th March, 1930.

(b) **Significance of the Second Round Table Conference :**

It was attended by Gandhiji as a sole representative of the Congress, according to the terms of the Gandhi-Irwin Pact of 1931. The conference was soon deadlocked on the minorities issue, with separate electorates being demanded not only by Muslims but also by the Depressed Classes, Sikhs, Indian Christians and Anglo-Indians.

The question of Independence or setting up of a responsible Government receded into the background. The British government refused to concede the immediate grant of dominion status, Gandhiji returned to India disappointed.

(c) **Provisions of the Gandhi-Irwin Pact as a result of the Civil Disobedience Movement :** Since the satyagraha could not be suppressed, the Government, through Tej Bahadur Sapru and Jayakar, started negotiations with Gandhiji in jail. This resulted in the signing of a pact by Gandhiji and Lord Irwin, the Viceroy, in March 1931. This is known as the Gandhi-Irwin Pact. The government agreed to :

1. Allow people living near seashore to manufacture salt.
2. Release all political prisoners, except those guilty of violence.
3. Permit peaceful picketing of liquor and foreign cloth shops.
4. Restore the confiscated properties of the Congressmen.

The Congress, in its turn, consented to the following :

1. To suspend the Civil Disobedience Movement.
2. To participate in the second session of the Round Table Conference.
3. Not to press for investigation into police assesses.

Q. 6. **The Simon Commission was appointed in November 1927 by the British Government. Subsequently the Civil Disobedience Movement began. In this context answer the following questions:**

(a) **Why was the Simon Commission appointed by the British Government? Why did the Congress boycott the Commission ?**

(b) **The Civil Disobedience Movement was launched by Gandhiji with his famous Dandi March on 12th March 1930. Mention the significance of this historic event.**

(c) **Why did Gandhiji call off the Civil Disobedience Movement and later renew it?** **[2010]**

Ans. **(a)** The Simon commission was appointed by the government to look into the working of the government of India Act, 1919 and suggest further reforms.

The congress decided to boycott it because:

(i) It was an 'all white' commission. No Indian was included in it.

(ii) It refused to accept the demand for swaraj.

(b) On 12th March 1930, Mahatma Gandhi undertook Dandi March to break the Salt Law to symbolize refusal of Indian people to obey British Laws.

The manufacture of salt was a government monopoly and no individual was allowed to make it. Gandhiji violated the law by picking up a handful of salt. It signified a challenge to the authority of the government.

The civil disobedience Movement also brought about a change in the women of the country. Gandhiji appealed to the women to take up spinning and picketing. The emancipation of Indian women, which was necessary for a successful movement, began with this movement.

(c) The civil disobedience movement was suspended in March 1931 so that Gandhiji could attend the second round table Conference in London. A pact was signed between Gandhiji and viceroy Irwin. The civil disobedience movement was suspended so that the plan for the constitutional government of India can be discussed at the next round table conference.

Gandhiji was refused to meet with Viceroy Willington, instead, he was arrested along with Sardar Patel. Thus, civil disobedience movement was renewed with non-payment of taxes, picketing of shops, manufacture and collection of salt and boycott of all British goods.

Chapter 14

Events Leading to the Quit India Movement (1935-1943)

 Long Answer Type Questions

Q. 1. With reference to the Mass Phase of the National Movement under the leadership of Gandhi, answer the following :
 (a) Briefly explain the Dandi March of 1930.
 (b) State any three reasons for the launching of the Quit India Movement.
 (c) Explain any four significant effects of the Quit India Movement. **[2020]**

Marking Scheme

(a) – On 2nd March 1930, Gandhi wrote a letter to the Viceroy
 – communicating his decision to start the Civil Disobedience Movement.
 – On 12th March began Mahatma Gandhi's historic march from Sabarmati Ashram to Dandi, a village on the Gujarat seacoast
 – 78 persons followed him.
 – He reached Dandi on 5th April.
 – On the morning of 6th of April, Gandhi violated the salt-laws by picking up some salt left by the sea-waves.
 – Gandhi's signal to disobey the government law. *(Any three points)*

(b) **Reasons for launching the Quit India Movement:**
 – Failure of the Cripps Mission
 – Worsening of Communal Problem
 – Japan posed a serious threat to India.
 (Any two points)

(c) **Significant consequences of the Quit India Movement**
 – Important landmark – It saw disturbances practically all over India.
 – It warned the British that they were not wanted in India/days were limited/collapse of authority
 – Demand from Indians that they could have nothing short of Independence
 – Quit India Movement strengthened the Congress Socialist Party.
 – In the Quit India Movement, the Indian Revolution reached its climax.
 – Led to political awakening
 – Indian problem attracted the attention of the world especially USA
 – Symbolic of new confidence among Indians
 – Demonstrated nationalistic feelings

 – Mass movement/last mass movement
 – United young and old and people of different religions and regions
 – No political activity till after the war ended in 1945. *(Any four points)*

Ans. **(a)** On 12th March, Mahatma Gandhi began a historic march from Sabarmati Ashram to Dandi and a number of people followed him. On the morning of 6th April, Gandhiji violated the Salt Law at Dandi by picking up some salt left by the sea-waves.

The government had the monopoly to manufacture and sell the salt. He had selected to attack the Salt Law because the salt tax affected all sections of society, especially the poor. Gandhiji's breaking of the Salt Law marked the beginning of Civil Disobedience Movement.

(b) **The three reasons for the launching of the Quit India Movement are given below:**

1. **Failure of the Cripps Mission:** The Cripps Mission proposed India's dominion status. It did not propose any immediate transfer of power. It was rejected as it did not bring with it the promise of Independence in the near future. It was felt among the Indians that the provisions of this mission could divide India into hundreds of independent provinces.

2. **The threat of the Japanese:** In 1942, the Japanese Army attacked Myanmar and marched towards India. British presence in India was an invitation to the Japanese Army to invade India. Gandhiji asked the British to quit India, i.e., immediate withdrawal of the British.

3. **Disagreement between the Congress and the Muslim League:** In the Lahore Session in 1940, the Muslim League put forward the

demand for Pakistan. The leaders declared that Muslims in India would not get justice from the Congress. The Congress felt that if the British withdraw from India, people would settle their differences peacefully.

(c) Four significant effects of the Quit India Movement:

1. Demonstrated the depth of nationalistic feelings in India and the capacity of Indians for struggle and sacrifice.

2. It made it clear to the British that they could no longer find it possible to rule India against the wishes of its people.

3. People of all sections of society participated in this movement, the Hindus, Muslims, Christians and Parsis and even people from the princely states participated.

4. The Quit India Movement strengthened the Congress Socialist Party because of its heroic role in the movement.

Q. 2. Through various National Movements, Gandhiji mobilised public support to win freedom for India. In this context, state the following :

(a) Any three causes for Gandhi to launch the Non-Cooperation Movement.

(b) The name given to the uprising of 1942. Two reasons for launching this mass uprising.

(c) The impact of the Non-Cooperation Movement in India's freedom struggle.
[2016]

Ans. **(a) Three causes for Gandhi to launch the Non-Cooperation Movement :**

1. **Khilafat Movement:** The Muslim population in India started a powerful agitation known as the Khilafat Movement, under the leadership of the Ali Brothers - Mohammad Ali and Shaukat Ali because the Sultan Of Turkey felt that any weakening of the Caliph's position would adversely affect the position of the Muslims. In the First World War, the British fought against Turkey. Gandhiji saw the Khilafat Movement as an opportunity for uniting the Hindus and the Muslims. He was elected as the President of the All India Khilafat Conference in November 1919. He advised the Khilafat Committee to adopt a policy of non-cooperation with the government.

2. **Rowlatt Act:** On receiving a report from the Sedition Committee headed by Justice Rowlatt, two bills were introduced in the Central Legislature in February, 1919. The purpose of the bills was to curb the growing upsurge in the country. In spite of opposition from the Indians, the Rowlatt Act was passed in March, 1919. This Act authorised the Government to imprison any person without trial and convict him in a court. The Act came like a sudden blow to the Indians who were expecting self-governance. Gandhiji appealed to the Viceroy to withhold his consent to such measures. However, his appeal was ignored. He started 'Satyagraha' as a challenge to the Government.

3. **Jallianwala Bagh Tragedy:** A large but peaceful crowd gathered at the Jallianwala Bagh in Amritsar on April 13, 1919, to protest against the arrest of leaders. General Dyer, the Military Commander of Amritsar surrounded the Bagh with his soldiers. After closing the exit gate with his troops, he ordered them to shoot at the crowd. About one thousand innocent demonstrators were killed and many more wounded. After the massacre, the British Government made a half-hearted attempt at constitutional reform. But, it also made it clear that it had no intention of parting with political power or sharing it with Indians.

(b) Refer to Long Answer Type Questions Answer 1 (b).

(c) 1. The National Movement became a Mass Movement : The Indian national movement, for the first time in history, acquired a real mass base with the participation of different sections of Indian society such as peasants, workers, students, teachers and women.

2. **Instilled Confidence among the people :** The movement undermined the power and prestige of the British Government. It generated a desire for freedom and inspired people to challenge the colonial rule.

3. **The Congress became an organised fighting force:** The weapons of Satyagraha and Non-Cooperation changed the character of the Congress overnight. It transformed the Indian National Congress from a deliberative assembly into an organised fighting force, pledged to revolution.

4. **Fostered Hindu-Muslim Unity:** It fostered Hindu-Muslim unity which could be seen in the merger of the Khilafat issue with this movement.

Q. 3. **The Congress working committee passed the famous 'Quit India' resolution at Wardha in July 1942. With reference to this, answer the following questions :**

(a) **What were the reasons for the passing of this resolution ?**

(b) **What was the British Government's reaction to the 'Quit India' Movement ?[3]**

(c) **What was the impact and significance of this movement ?** **[2013]**

Ans. (a) Refer to Long Answer Type Questions Answer 1 (b).

(b) The British government's reaction to the 'Quit India Movement' was rather harsh.

The oppressive measures included :

1. The British government reacted quickly and used all types of means to suppress this movement. It used lathi charges, mass arrest and firing in many parts of the country.

2. The government imposed restrictions on the press. These years were a period of terrible sufferings for the Indians.

3. All the important Indian leaders including Gandhiji and Nehru were arrested and taken to unknown destinations and the Congress was once again declared illegal.

4. The British government succeeded in crushing the movement. New ordinances were promulgated to frighten the people. Heavy fines were imposed on the people. Many villages were searched and burnt.

5. The government imposed martial law to terrorize the people. By the end of 1942, more than 60,000 people were arrested and sent to jails without any trial.

   They were treated badly and the prisoners had to live in inhuman conditions. The oppressive measures used by the government killed nearly ten thousand people and wounded many more.

(c) Refer to Long Answer Type Questions Answer 1 (c).

Chapter 15: Subhash Chandra Bose and the Indian National Army (INA)

 ## Short Answer Type Questions

Q. 1. Mention any two objectives of the Forward Bloc. [2020]

Ans. Immediate objective of Forward Bloc was liberation of India with the support of workers, peasants and other organisations. **Two general objectives of the Forward Bloc were:**

1. Re-organisation of agriculture and industry on socialist lines.

2. Abolition of zamindari system and introduction of new monetary and credit system.

Q. 2. Mention any two objectives of the Indian National Army. [2017]

Ans. The main objectives of the Indian National Army (INA) were :

1. To establish an armed revolution and to fight the British army with modern arms.

2. To organise a provisional government of free India.

3. To prepare the Indians inside and outside India for "an armed struggle". Subhash said, "Since the enemy fights with the sword, we too should fight with the sword." Only then we can win the race and get the reward of freedom.

Q. 3. Mention any two contributions of the INA to the National Movement. [2016]

OR

Mention two contributions of INA (Indian National Army) to the Indian freedom movement.

Ans. **Two contributions of the INA to the National Movement were :**

1. The INA along with Japanese army overran many territories in South-East Asia. In May 1944, INA captured Mowdok, an outpost situated south-east of Chittagong. In 1944, they advanced up to the frontier of India. The INA gave a tough fight to the British forces in the Assam hills and succeeded in capturing Ukhral and Kohima. They raised the Tricolor Flag for the first time on the liberated Indian soil on March 19, 1944.

2. The Indian Naval ratings in Mumbai rose up in revolt in February, 1946. The heroic deeds and sacrifices of the soldiers of INA led to political consciousness among the Indian forces. The British now realised that they could not rely on the Indian forces to continue their rule in India.

Q. 4. Who founded the Forward Bloc ? Mention any one of its objectives. [2015]

Ans. Subhash Chandra Bose felt the urgent need for an organised left-wing party in the Congress. After resigning from the Presidentship of the Congress in 1939, he laid the foundation of a new party within the Congress to bring the entire left-wing under one banner. This party, known as Forward Bloc, was formed on May 3, 1939.

Forward Bloc's immediate objective was liberation of India with the support of workers, peasants, youths and other organisations.

Q. 5. State two important objectives of the Indian National Army. [2014]

Ans. If the Prime Minister fails to carry out obligations or makes detrimental choices, then the members of the house can pass a motion of No-Confidence. This deems him 'not fit' to hold the position, anymore. Thus, the authority of the Prime Minister can be checked.

Q. 6. Name the party formed by Subhash Chandra Bose. What was its immediate objective ? [2012]

Ans. According to the 29th and 44th constitution Amendment Act, the Supreme Court decides any disputes regarding the election of the President.

Q. 7. Mention two contributions of Subhash Chandra Bose to India's freedom struggle. [2011]

Ans. Two contributions of Subhash Chandra Bose to India's freedom struggle were :

1. He formed the Indian National Army (INA) which incited the armed forces to revolt against the British Raj.
2. He gave the call to his countrymen "You give me blood and I will give you freedom". He gave the clarion call to INA soldiers 'Delhi Chalo' as their ultimate destination.

Long Answer Type Questions

Q. 1. **Study the picture given below and answer the following questions :**

(a) (i) **Identify the leader given in the picture.**

(ii) **Name the Political party and Military Organisation that he formed.**

(b) **State any three objectives of the Political party that he founded.**

(c) **Mention any four objectives of the Military Organisation that he formed.**
[2018]

Ans. **(a)** **(i)** This is the picture of Netaji Subhash Chandra Bose.

(ii) The political party that Netaji formed was the 'Forward Bloc' and the military organization developed by Netaji was 'Indian National Army' or INA.

(b) Three objectives of the political party 'Forward Bloc' are as follows :

1. Abolition of the Zamindari system.
2. Introduction of a new monetary and credit system.
3. Liberation of India.

(c) **Four objectives of the military organisation or 'Indian National Army' or 'INA' are as follows :**

1. To organise an armed revolution to fight the British army with modern arms.
2. To form a provisional government of free India.
3. The motto of the INA was 'unity, faith, sacrifice'.
4. To train people for armed struggle inside and outside the country.

Chapter 16 — Towards Independence and Partion of India (1944-1947)

 Short Answer Type Questions

Q. 1. State any two provisions of the Indian Independence Act of 1947 that was to decide the fate of the Princely States. [2019]

Ans. According to the Indian Independence Act of 1947, the Princely States would become independent and all the powers exercised by the British authority were to be terminated. All treaties and agreements made by the British with reference to States would lapse from August 15, 1947. They would be free to associate themselves with either of the two Dominions or remain independent.

Q. 2. Write any two reasons for the acceptance of the Mountbatten Plan by the Congress. [2019]

Ans. Reasons for the acceptance of the Mountbatten Plan by the Congress were:

1. The large-scale communal riots that engulfed the whole country convinced all that the only solution to the communal problem lay in the Partition of India.

2. The League had joined the Interim Government to obstruct and not to cooperate. Experience of working with the League had convinced the Congress that it could not have a joint administration with the League.

Q. 3. Name the last Viceroy of India. State any one of the provisions of the Indian Independence Act, 1947. [2018]

Ans. Lord Mountbatten was the last Viceroy of India.

Two provisions of the Indian Independence Act, 1947 :

1. On 15th August 1947, after the Partition of India, two independent dominions, India and Pakistan would be established.

2. There would be a Governor-General for each of the dominions.

Q. 4. Why was Mountbatten's Plan finally accepted by the Congress ? [2016]

Ans. Mountbatten's Plan was finally accepted by the Congress because :

1. The large-scale communal riots that engulfed the whole country convinced all that the only solution to the communal problem lay in the partition of India.

   The leaders felt that further delay in the transfer of power could find India in the midst of civil war.

2. A smaller India would be more viable with a strong central authority than with a weak centre.

Q. 5. What were the two proposals related to the Princely States in the Mountbatten Plan ? [2013]

Ans. The ministers in the Union Council are of three categories : Cabinet Ministers, Ministers of State and Deputy Ministers.

 Long Answer Type Questions

Q. 1. With reference to the Partition Plan, answer the following :

(a) (i) Name the last Viceroy of India.

    (ii) State any two reasons for him to come to India.

(b) Mention any three proposals under his plan.

(c) State any four reasons for the Congress to finally accept the Plan. [2020]

 Marking Scheme

(a) (i) Lord Mountbatten
    (ii) He came to India for the purpose of taking necessary steps for the transfer of power to the Indians. /To restore peace among the two sections of Congress and the League. /To present a plan for the partition.

(b) **Three proposals under his Plan:**
  – Partition –into two dominions

> - Relations between the two new Dominions -to decide what relation to have between each other and the commonwealth
> - A Boundary Commission-to settle the boundaries
> - Princely States-treaties would end, and they could decide to join either of the dominions or remain independent
> - Bengal & Punjab-legislative assemblies to decide
> - Sindh-legislative assembly to decide
> - N.W. Frontier Province-to decide by a referendum
> - District of Sylhet-to decide by a referendum
> - Constituent Assembly-separate Constituent assembly for both the parties
> - Transfer of Power-would take place before 1948.
>
> *(Any four points)*
>
> **(c) Acceptance of Plan:**
> - Large scale communal riots
> - League joined Interim government to obstruct and not to cooperate.
> - Only alternative to Partition was a Federation with a weak centre.
> - Any further continuation of British rule would mean a greater calamity for India. /People and leaders were fed up with their rule in India/ wanted to get rid of the British rule by paying any price.
> - Further delay could find India in a Civil War.
> - Leaders felt that partition would aid the Constitutions of separate electorates. /and other undemocratic procedures.
>
> *(Any three points)*

Ans. **(a) (i)** Lord Mountbatten was the last Viceroy of India.

(ii) Lord Mountbatten came to India mainly for two reasons :

1. **To restore the peace among the two warring sections:** The Congress and the Muslim League.

2. Mountbatten realised that the Cabinet Mission Plan was unworkable and partition of India was inevitable. Therefore, he sought to effect the transfer of power without any delay.

(b) Three proposals under Mountbatten Plan were :

1. The country would be divided into two Dominions : India and Pakistan.

2. The partition of Bengal and Punjab was provided the legislative assemblies of the two provinces decided in favour of the partition.

3. The existing Constituent Assembly would continue to work but the Constitution framed by it would not apply to Pakistan.

(c) All India Congress Committee accepted the Mountbatten Plan because according to Maulana Azad, the Congress had no other alternative. The reason for finally accepting the Mountbatten Plan may be summarised as follows :

1. The large scale communal riots that engulfed the whole country and convinced that the only solution to the communal problem is in Partition of India.

2. The League joined the Interim Government to obstruct or not to cooperate. The experience of working with the League had convinced the Congress that it could not have a joint administration with the League.

3. The only alternative to Partition was a federation with a weak centre. A smaller India with strong Central authority was better than a big state with a weak centre.

4. Any further contribution of British rule in India would mean a great calamity for India. The leaders felt that delay in the transfer of power could find India in the midst of a civil war.

Q. 2. **With reference to the National Movement from 1930 to 1947, answer the following :**

(a) State any three features of the Programme of the Civil Disobedience Movement launched in 1930.

(b) What was the significance of the Second Round Table Conference held in 1931 ?

[2019]

 **Marking Scheme**

(a) Gandhi reached Dandi on 5th April,1930 and next morning Gandhi violated the salt-laws by picking up some salt left by the sea waves. Gandhi's campaign against the salt-laws was a signal to disobey – civil laws.

Civil Disobedience campaign involved:

- Defiance of salt laws.
- Boycott of liquor/schools and colleges/ Government jobs.
- Boycott of foreign cloth and British goods of all kinds.
- It also involved non-payment of taxes and land-revenue and violation of laws of different kinds, including forest laws.
- Spread to NWFP where Khan Abdul Gaffar Khan took the campaign against the government and he was called as Frontier Gandhi.
- Paralysed the British Government.

(Any three points)

(b) **Gandhi was chosen as the sole representative of the Congress for the Second Round Table Conference.**

- The Second Round Conference devoted most of its time to the communal question and the representation of minorities-the Muslims, Sikhs, the Christians and Anglo-Indians-in legislatures both at the Centre and in the Provinces.
- Gandhi was disgusted to find that most leaders were concerned only about seats in the legislatures for their respective communities.
- The question of Independence or of setting up a Responsible Government receded into background.
- Gandhi returned 'empty handed' as he could not persuade the British government to grant Freedom or even the Dominion Status to India.

(Any three points)

Ans. **(a)** Gandhiji reached Dandi on 5th April, 1930 and next morning Gandhiji violated the Salt Laws by picking up some salt left by the sea waves. Gandhiji's campaign against the Salt Laws was a signal to disobey civil laws.

Features of the Programme of the Civil Disobedience Movement:

1. Defiance of Salt Laws.
2. Boycott of liquor.
3. Boycott of foreign cloth and British goods of all kinds.
4. Non-payment of taxes and revenues.

(b) **Significance of the Second Round Table Conference:**

It was attended by Gandhiji as a sole representative of the Congress, according to the terms of the Gandhi-Irwin Pact of 1931. The conference was soon deadlocked on the minorities issue, with separate electorates being demanded not only by Muslims but also by the Depressed Classes, Sikhs, Indian Christians and Anglo-Indians.

The question of Independence or setting up of a responsible Government receded into the background. The British government refused to concede the immediate grant of dominion status, Gandhiji returned to India disappointed.

Q. 3. **The Quit India Resolution in 1942 was one of the final calls given by Gandhi for the Britishers to leave India. Moving towards Independence, Lord Mountbatten's Plan was significant. In this context, answer the following :**

(a) **State two reasons for the launching of the Quit India Movement.**

(b) **Give any three effects of the Quit India Movement launched by Gandhi in 1942 that was significant to the last phase of the National Movement of India.**

(c) **Give any four clauses of the Mountbatten Plan of 1947?** **[2018]**

Ans. **(a)** **The three reasons for the launching of the Quit India Movement are given below :**

1. **Failure of the Cripps Mission:** The Cripps Mission proposed India's dominion status. It did not propose any immediate transfer of power. It was rejected as it did not bring with it the promise of Independence in the near future. It was felt among the Indians that the provisions of this mission could divide India into hundreds of independent provinces.

2. **The threat of the Japanese:** In 1942, the Japanese Army attacked Myanmar and marched towards India. British presence in India was an invitation to the Japanese Army to invade India. Gandhiji asked the British to quit India, i.e., immediate withdrawal of the British.

3. **Disagreement between the Congress and the Muslim League :** In the Lahore Session in 1940, the Muslim League put forward the demand for Pakistan. The leaders declared that

Muslims in India would not get justice from the Congress. The Congress felt that if the British withdraw from India, people would settle their differences peacefully.

(b) Four significant effects of the Quit India Movement:

1. Demonstrated the depth of nationalistic feelings in India and the capacity of Indians for struggle and sacrifice.

2. It made it clear to the British that they could no longer find it possible to rule India against the wishes of its people.

3. People of all sections of society participated in this movement, the Hindus, Muslims, Christians and Parsis and even people from the princely states participated.

4. The Quit India Movement strengthened the Congress Socialist Party because of its heroic role in the movement.

(c) Refer to Long Answer Type Questions Answer 1 (b).

Q. 4. **The period between 1920 to 1947 was marked with major events and reforms that finally led us to our Independence. In this context, answer the following questions :**

State three provisions of the Gandhi-Irwin Pact as a result of the Civil Disobedience Movement.

Ans. **Provisions of the Gandhi-Irwin Pact as a result of the Civil Disobedience Movement:** Since the satyagraha could not be suppressed, the Government, through Tej Bahadur Sapru and Jayakar, started negotiations with Gandhiji in jail. This resulted in the signing of a pact by Gandhiji and Lord Irwin, the Viceroy, in March 1931. This is known as the Gandhi-Irwin Pact. The government agreed to :

1. Allow people living near seashore to manufacture salt.

2. Release all political prisoners, except those guilty of violence.

3. Permit peaceful picketing of liquor and foreign cloth shops.

4. Restore the confiscated properties of the Congressmen.

The Congress, in its turn, consented to the following :

1. To suspend the Civil Disobedience Movement.

2. To participate in the second session of the Round Table Conference.

3. Not to press for investigation into police assesses.

Q. 5. **With reference to the transfer of power to India, answer the following :**

(b) **Mention any two clauses of the Indian Independence Act 1947.**

(c) **Why did the Congress accept the Mountbatten Plan ?** **[2015]**

Ans. **(b)** **Two Clauses of the Indian Independence Act, 1947:**

1. **Two new dominions :** India would be partitioned and two independent dominions India and Pakistan would be created from August 15, 1947. The Act provided legislative supremacy of both the dominions. The territories of the two dominions were divided in such terms that Pakistan would comprise Sindh, British Baluchistan, North West Frontier Province, the West Punjab and East Bengal. India was to comprise all the remaining territories included in the British India. The exact boundaries of the dominions would be determined by a Boundary Commission.

2. **Provisions of partition:** (1) Both Bengal and Punjab would be divided. The Provincial Assemblies of the two parts would meet separately, reprinting the Hindu majority districts and the Muslim majority district and would decide through a majority vote whether they wanted the division of the province or not.

   (2) A plebiscite would be held in North West Frontier Province (NWFP) as well as in Sylhet district (Muslim majority area) in East Bengal to determine whether they would like to join Pakistan or India. (Both these provinces joined West and East Pakistan, respectively).

(c) Refer to Long Answer Type Questions Answer 1 (c).

Q. 6.

With reference to the picture given above answer the following :

(a) Identify the Viceroy in the picture.

(b) Why was he sent to India ?

(c) How did he plan to solve the communal problem existing in India ?

(d) Why did the Congress accept the Plan? State three reasons to justify its acceptance. **[2014]**

Ans. **(a)** The Viceroy in the picture is Lord Mountbatten, a member of the British royal family.

(b) Lord Clement Atlee sent Lord Mountbatten as the Viceroy of India :

   1. To take steps for the transfer of power to the Indians.

   2. To restore peace amongst the Congress and the League.

(c) Lord Mountbatten came to a conclusion that partition of the India was the only solution to the existing communal problem in India. Therefore in his plan, he proposed :

   1. That the country would be divided into two dominions, that is, India and Pakistan.

   2. The Princely States could either choose between the two countries or resolve to remain independent.

   3. A plebiscite would be held in the North-West Frontier Province to ascertain their choice between the two dominions.

   4. The provinces of Assam, Bengal and Punjab would be divided and the boundaries would be delineated.

(d) Refer to Long Answer Type Questions Answer 1 (c).

Q. 7.

(a) Identify the event in the above picture. Name the Lady seen in the given picture. Mention the year when the event took place.

(b) What were the main provisions of the Indian Independence Act ?

(c) Mention the reasons that made the Congress accept the Partition Proposals.

[2011]

Ans. **(a)** The event in the given picture is the swearing ceremony of Jawaharlal Nehru as the Prime Minister of Independent India. The lady seen in the picture is Lady Mountbatten, the wife of the first Governor-General of India, Lord Mountbatten and the year is 1947.

(b) The main provisions of the Indian Independence Act were :

   1. Two new dominions to be known as India and Pakistan came into existence. Pakistan was to include East Bengal, West Punjab, Sindh, Baluchistan, North West Frontier Province and district of Sylhet in Assam and India included the remaining territories of British India.

   2. Each dominion to have a Governor-General who would act as a Constitutional Head.

3. Division of the Indian Army and sharing of assets between the two dominions.

4. Princely states would become independent.

5. Constituent Assemblies would serve as Central Legislatures and make the constitution.

6. Safeguarding the interests of existing officers.

(c) Refer to Long Answer Type Questions Answer 1 (c).

Q. 8.

In the above historic photograph, Pandit Jawaharlal Nehru, is seen giving his famous speech in the Constituent Assembly on August 14, 1947. In this context, answer the following:

(a) Mention the Provisions of the Indian Independence Act of 1947 regarding the Constituent Assemblies.

(c) Mention four important reasons for the All-India Congress Committee accepting the Mountbatten Plan. **[2010]**

Ans. **(a) The provisions of the constituent assemblies in the Indian Independence Act were :**

(i) The constituent assemblies would draft the constitutions of the two dominions separately and decide whether to stay with the Commonwealth or not.

(ii) The constituent assembly of each dominion is to exercise the power of central legislatures and to make laws for that dominion.

(c) Four important reasons why the All India congress committee accepted the mountbatten plan were :

(i) Any delay in the extension of the British rule was considered harmful to India.

(ii) The congress was assured that it was not possible to run the administration of the country jointly.

(iii) It was believed that a smaller India with a strong centre would be more powerful than a larger India with a weak federation and a weak centre.

(iv) The congress had realised that it would be an impossible task to work with the Muslim League, because of its increasing rigidity and the growing communal problem. The choice the country had to make was "partition or constant battles."

Chapter 17

World War-I and Treaty of Versailles

 ## Short Answer Type Questions

Q. 1. **What was meant by the term 'Imperialism', as a cause for World War I ?** **[2020]**

Ans. Imperialism refers to the state policy or practice by which a powerful nation establishes its control over another country, either by direct territorial acquisition or by gathering political and economic control.

Q. 2. **State any two objections imposed by the Treaty of Versailles on the German military power.** **[2019]**

Ans. 1. The German Army was restricted to a force of 1,00,000 soldiers and the Navy was limited to 15,000 men and 36 ships.

2. The Air Force and submarines of German Army were banned.

Q. 3. **Name the Signatory Countries of the Triple Alliance.** **[2019]**

Ans. Germany, Austria-Hungary and Italy were the signatory countries of the Triple Alliance.

Q. 4. **Name the two rival blocs formed in Europe before World War I.** **[2015]**

Ans. There were two kinds of rival blocs formed in Europe before World War I or in the early 20th century i.e. Triple Alliance and Triple Entente.

Q. 5. **Mention any two terms of the Treaty of Versailles signed on June 28, 1919.** **[2014]**

Ans. In a 'Single Integrated Judicial System' provided in the Indian Constitution, the Supreme Court of India is the apex court of India and administers both the Union and the State laws. Below the Supreme Court are the High Courts in each state or group of states followed by Subordinate Courts.

Q. 6. **What was the immediate cause of the First World War ?** **[2013]**

Ans. The assassination of Austrian Prince Archduke Franz Ferdinand in Sarajevo on June 28, 1914 was the immediate cause of the First World War.

Q. 7. **Name the signatory countries of the Triple Alliance (1882). State the rival bloc that was formed.** **[2012]**

Ans. The Triple Alliance, also known as the Triplice, was a secret agreement between Germany, Austria, Hungry and Italy formed on 20 May, 1882 and renewed periodically, until World War I.

In 1882, Serbia joined the alliance, in effect, through a treaty with Austria-Hungry.

Romania joined the group in 1883 and a powerful Central European bloc was created.

Q. 8. **How much did Germany have to pay as war reparation charges according to the Treaty of Versailles ?** **[2010]**

Ans. Germany paid 33 billion dollars as war reparation charges according to the treaty of Versailles.

Long Answer Type Questions

Q. 1. **The War that broke out in 1914 was different from the previous wars in many ways. In this context discuss the following points briefly :**

(a) Militant Nationalism as a cause of the War.

(b) How did the Treaty of Versailles seek to cripple Germany's military strength ?

Ans. **(a)** An important cause of the war was competitive patriotism or extreme nationalism/William Kaiser went about proclaiming that Germany was going to be the leader of the world/In the Franco-Prussian war, Germany had seized the province of Alsace and parts of Lorraine which were rich in minerals and industrial products. The French wanted to recover their lost provinces/Italians looked discontented/There was unsatisfied national spirit of Balkan states/The political leaders and rulers succeeded in fanning hatred and passion under the cover of nationalism.

(b) Treaty of Versailles and Germany: As a result of the discussions at the Paris Conference, on June 28, 1919, The Treaty of Versailles was signed. It ended the war. The basis of the treaty's negotiations was the American President Wilson's Fourteen Points. The treaty was designed to prevent Germany from going to war again.

Terms of the Treaty:

1. The treaty declared Germany guilty of aggression.

2. Germany was required to pay for the losses and damages suffered by the Allies during the war. The amount of reparations was fixed at 33 billion dollars. Germany had to cede her merchant ships to the Allies as compensation, and had to supply huge quantities of coal to France, Italy and Belgium for ten years.

3. German colonies in the Pacific and the areas under her control in China were given to Japan. China was aligned with the Allies during the war but her areas under German control were given away to Japan.

4. The German Army was restricted to a force of 1,00,000 soldiers and the Navy was limited to 15,000 men and 36 ships. The Air Force and submarines were banned.

Defeat in the First World War and the conditions imposed by the Treaty of Versailles made the Germans feel humiliated and helpless. Germans looked down upon the Wiemer Republic which had signed such a disgraceful treaty. The terms of this treaty were greatly resented by the Germans who eagerly looked for an opportunity to avenge the same. These sentiments were exploited by Hitler. He openly encouraged the Germans to consign the Treaty of Versailles into the waste-paper basket, to rebuild the empire of Germany, and to recapture the lost colonies.

Q. 2. With reference to the First World War answer the following questions :

(a) Explain any three causes of the First World War.

(b) Mention three points under the Treaty of Versailles, which affected Germany.

Ans. (a) Three causes of the First World War were :

1. **Aggressive Nationalism:** The unlimited spirit of Nationalism was another cause for the Great War. Love for one's own country led to intense hatred for the other. There existed strong feelings of hatred between France and Germany, between Germany and England and between Russia and the Balkans. After the expulsion of Turks from Europe, there were widespread revolts. Each nation wanted "National Honour" and the idea of mutual give and take did not exist among the European nations. This narrow nationalism of competitive patriotism led to bitterness and suspicion amongst nations.

2. **Economic Imperialism:** There was a race for colonial expansion among the European countries. The rapid growth of industrialization brought great demand from the colonies for raw materials and to find new markets for their finished goods. This resulted in colonial conflicts and national rivalries. Each country wanted to fight for its commerce and trade. The entry of Germany in the race for colonies complicated matters further.

3. **Armament Race:** Germany defeated France in the Franco Prussian War and took away the provinces of Alsace and Lorraine. The French never recovered from the sheck of this defeat. They waited to take revenge and recover their lost territories. The Italians and Balkan states of Poland, Austria-Hungary, Serbia and Bulgaria were also dissatisfied. By 1914, all European countries were armed and ever ready to fight at the smallest provocation.

The intense nationalism and distrust triggered armament race among

European nations. Each country began preparing for war by arming itself to the teeth by stockpiling of arms and ammunition. Germany too began to increase its naval force and started large scale production of arms and ammunitions.

(b) Four terms of the Treaty of Versailles which affected Germany after World War I:

1. The treaty declared Germany guilty of aggression. Germany was required to pay for the loss and damages suffered by the Allies during the war. The amount of reparations was fixed at 33 billion dollars. Germany had to cede her merchant ships to the Allies as compensation and had to supply huge quantities of coal to France, Italy and Belgium for ten years.

2. The area of the Rhine Valley was to be demilitarised and the German territory west of Rhine was to be occupied by the Allied troops for 15 years.

3. Germany lost Alsace-Lorraine to France, Eupen-et-Malmedy to Belgium, and Schleswig to Denmark. Danzig became a free port in the Polish territory.

4. Germany ceded parts of her pre-war territory to Denmark, Belgium, Poland, Czechoslovakia and France. The coal mines in the German area called Saar were ceded to France for 15 years and the area was to be governed by the League of Nations.

Chapter 18

Rise of Dictatorships (Rise of Fascism and Nazism)

Short Answer Type Questions

Q. 1. Give any two similarities between the ideologies of Nazism and Fascism. **[2018]**

Ans. Two similarities between Nazism and Fascism were :

1. Both propagated totalitarian ideologies that regulated all aspects of private and public spheres.

2. Both wanted to prevent the spread of communism in their respective countries.

Q. 2. What is the meaning of 'Fascism' ? **[2015]**

Ans. The Vice-President of the Indian Union acts as the ex-officio Chairman of the Rajya Sabha.

Q. 3. Give two similarities in the foreign policies of Mussolini and Hitler. **[2012]**

Ans. Two similarities in the foreign policies of Mussolini and Hitler were :

1. To do away with the evil effects of the humiliating Treaty of Versailles.

2. To increase the prestige and glory of their respective countries in international spheres.

Q. 4. State two underlying Principles of Fascism. **[2011]**

Ans. Two underlying principles of Fascism are:

1. The Fascists believed in having a powerful dictatorship by controlling all aspects of life of the citizens.

2. For a Fascist, everything is the state; nothing else exists outside the state.

Q. 5. Mention two underlying similarities between Fascism and Nazism. **[2010]**

Ans. Two underlying similarities between fascism and Nazism were:

1. Both Mussolini and Hitler aimed at restoring the status and dignity of their respective nations by making them strong powers.

2. Both aimed at providing strong, stable and efficient governments.

Long Answer Type Questions

Q. 1. With reference to the Rise of Dictatorships and the Second World War, answer the following :
Name the two rival blocs that fought against each other during World War II and state its signatory countries. **[2019]**

Marking Scheme

Axis – Germany Italy & Japan
Allies – Britain, France, USSR and later USA joined the Allies. (Any three countries)

Ans. The two rival blocs that fought against each other during the World War II were:

1. Allied Powers.
2. Axis Powers.

Signatory Countries:

1. **Allied Powers:** The Allied Powers included countries of Britain, France, (except during the German occupation, 1940-44), the Soviet Union, China and the United States of America.

2. **Axis Powers :** Axis Powers included Germany, Italy and Japan. These countries came together as a result of the resentment due to the unjust treatment meted out to them after the World War I.

Q. 2.

(a) Identify the leader in the picture. Give two examples to state that the leader followed an expansionist policy.

(c) **State four similarities between the ideologies of Nazism and Fascism.**

[2016]

Ans. **(a)** The leader in the picture is Benito Mussolini. Under Benito Mussolini's leadership, militarism and nationalism grew to a large extent. The foreign policy introduced was both nationalistic and imperialistic. The two examples to state that this leader followed an expansionist policy were :

1. In 1924, the free state of Fiume was partitioned between Italy and Yugoslavia.

2. The agreements with Albania in 1926 and 1927 made Albania an Italian protectorate and in 1939, Mussolini annexed Albania. Also in 1936, Ethiopia became a part of the Italian empire.

(c) **Similarities between the ideologies of Nazism and Fascism were:**

1. To hold that the state is supreme and it could suppress the fundamental rights and freedoms of individuals.

2. To believe in aggressive nationalism and imperialism.

3. To regard war as an instrument for furthering national interests.

4. To uphold intensely nationalistic, anti-communist and anti-democratic rule.

Q. 3.

Study the picture given above and answer the questions that follow:

(a) Identify the leader in the picture.

(c) Why did he invade Poland? State two similarities between Fascism and Nazism.

[2013]

Ans. **(a)** The above picture is of 'Adolf Hitler' who joined German army as a member of NSDAP. Hitler began his political career

at Munich and rose to the position of undisputed dictator of the third Reich.

(c) **The main reason, why Hitler invaded Poland may be listed as follows :**

1. To negate any military alliance between Poland and other European nations against Germany.

2. To gain a foothold in the territory surrounding Russia.

3. To make the world know his aversion to the Treaty of Versailles.

4. Hitler despised Chamberlain's guarantee to support Poland in case of an attack by Germany. He attacked Poland to teach Chamberlain a lesson.

5. Hitler entered into a pact with Stalin which included a secret clause to divide Poland between them. It was disagreement also which worked as a shield and prompted him to attack Poland.

The two similarities between Fascism and Nazism were :

1. Negation of democracy and belief in one-party or one-man rule. Both Fascists and Nazis did not allow the rule of any other party.

2. Aggressive Nationalism and Imperialistic policies were followed by both the Nazis and the Fascists. They glorified the nation. They followed an aggressive foreign policy. For example, Italy annexed Abyssinia in 1936 and Hitler occupied Austria and called it the Aunschluss or union with Austria.

Q. 4. **There were several far reaching consequences as a result of the First World War. In this context, answer the following :**

(a) Explain how World War I brought about a changed political scenario of the world.

(b) What did France gain from the Treaty of Versailles ?

Ans. **(a)** War transformed the political map of the world, particularly of Europe. Three ruling dynasties were destroyed- the Romanov in Russia during the war itself, the Hohenzollern in Germany and the Hapsburg in Austria-Hungary. Austria and Hungary became separate independent states. Czechoslovakia and Yugoslavia emerged as independent states. The war gave a blow to the autocratic monarchial system and led to the development of democracy in Europe. Empires having different cultures were dissolved and independent states having distinct cultures emerged after the war.

(b) France gained a lot from the Treaty of Versailles. Alsace and Lorraine were returned by Germany to them. France was compensated for the destruction of its coal mines by Germany in 1918. Therefore, she was given full control over the rich coal mines in Saar basin, but the area was to be controlled by the League of Nations. France shared the colonies of Togo and Cameroon with Britain. France was supposed to get 10 years of supply of coal from Germany, along with Belgium and Italy.

Chapter 19 — The Second World War

Short Answer Type Questions

Q. 1. **Name the countries that formed the Axis Bloc during the World War II.** **[2018]**

Ans. During the World War II, the Axis Bloc included countries such as Italy, Japan and Germany.

Q. 2. **Give the reason as to why Japan invaded China.** **[2017]**

Ans. Japan invaded China due to the following reasons:

1. Japan's policy of expansion. (Policy of Imperialism)

2. Japan was determined to dominate the Far East.

3. Japan's ambitions for more conquests and for more wealth increased after the First World War, Japan was not satisfied with only Manchuria.

Long Answer Type Questions

Q. 1. **With reference to the Two Major World Wars in the 20th century, answer the following questions :**
   (a) Explain briefly the causes of World War I with reference to Nationalism and Imperialism.
   (c) State any four causes that led to the Second World War. **[2018]**

Ans. **(a) As far as the Nationalism and Imperialism contexts are concerned, the causes of World War I are as follows:**

1. Aggressive nationalism meant love for one's own country and hatred for the other countries. Each nation thought about its own national interests and did not care for the interests of the other nations. These countries developed expansionist policies in the name of nationalism. Every country began to increase her military power. The assassination of Archduke Ferdinand also hurt the nationalistic feelings of the people of Austria. They were backed by various other countries which ultimately led to the outbreak of the war. The unsatisfied nation spirit of Balkans, discontentment among Italians also helped fuel the war.

2. Imperialism is when a country takes over new lands or countries and makes them subject to its rule. By 1900, the British Empire extended over five continents and France had to control large areas of Africa. With the rise of industrialism, new markets were needed.

3. The amount of lands 'owned' by Britain and France increased the rivalry with Germany who had entered the scramble to acquire colonies late and only had small areas of Africa.

(c) Four causes that spearheaded the Second World War are as follows :

1. Italian Fascism of the 1920 and Nazi spirit in Germany.
2. Japanese militarism and aggression on China.
3. Hitler's invasion of Poland.
4. Failure of League of Nations.

Q. 2. **The 1914 and 1939 Wars that engulfed almost the entire world, were known as the World Wars due to its unprecedented impact and damage. In this context, answer the following:**
   (a) Explain the immediate cause of the First World War.
   (c) Mention any four terms of the Treaty of Versailles which affected Germany after World War I. **[2017]**

Ans. **(a)** Immediate cause : Archduke Francis Ferdinand, the heir to the throne of Austria-Hungary, was assassinated at Sarajevo, capital of Bosnia on June 28,

1914. The assassination was organised by a secret society called 'Black Hand' or 'Union of Death' formed by extremist Serbian nationalists whose aim was to unite all Serbians into a single Serbian State. Austria declared an ultimatum on Serbia on July 23 making eleven demands. Serbia accepted most of the demands except those that would have led to the loss of her sovereignty.

Austria declared war on Serbia on July 28, 1914. This was the beginning of the First World War.

(c) Four terms of the Treaty of Versailles which affected Germany after World War I:

1. The treaty declared Germany guilty of aggression. Germany was required to pay for the loss and damages suffered by the Allies during the war. The amount of reparations was fixed at 33 billion dollars. Germany had to cede her merchant ships to the Allies as compensation and had to supply huge quantities of coal to France, Italy and Belgium for ten years.

2. The area of the Rhine Valley was to be demilitarised and the German territory west of Rhine was to be occupied by the Allied troops for 15 years.

3. Germany lost Alsace-Lorraine to France, Eupen-et-Malmedy to Belgium, and Schleswig to Denmark. Danzig became a free port in the Polish territory.

4. Germany ceded parts of her pre-war territory to Denmark, Belgium, Poland, Czechoslovakia and France. The coal mines in the German area called Saar were ceded to France for 15 years and the area was to be governed by the League of Nations.

Q. 3. With reference to the causes of the Second World War answer the following :

(i) Explain how the ideologies of Fascism and Nazism led to the Second World War.

(ii) How did the Japanese invasion of China create conditions for the outbreak of the war ?

Ans. (i) The rise of Fascism and Nazism as a cause to the Second World War :

1. Italy wanted to revive the glory of the old empire.

2. She joined the Anti-Comintern Pact in 1937 and formed a ten year alliance with Germany to strengthen her position.

3. Italy demonstrated her imperialistic designs by attacking Abyssinia.

In Germany :

1. Hitler wanted to re-establish the German empire in the International field.

2. He flouted the military causes in the Treaty of Versailles and declared rearmament.

3. In 1938, he annexed Austria and dismembered Czechoslovakia.

(ii) 1. Japan was determined to dominate the Far-East.

2. It intervened in Manchuria and occupied it and set up a government in spite of League's opposition.

3. Japan also started an undeclared war against China in 1931. China appealed to the League to declare sanctions against Japan.

4. Japan joined the Berlin-Rome Axis to form the Rome-Berlin-Tokyo Axis to further its policy of expansion and conquest.

5. In 1933, Japan left the League and started occupying the British and American properties in China.

6. Britain and France followed the policy of appeasement, thinking that Japanese could be used to weaken China.

Q. 4. State how each of the following factors were the causes of the Second World War :

The Aggressive Nationalism of Germany.

Ans. The Aggressive Nationalism of Germany: There was an economic crisis in various nations of the world after the First World War and there was large scale food shortage, inflation and unemployment. The democratic governments of Europe were not able to face it effectively and people suffered a lot of hardships. The dictators took advantage of this and offered a programme of aggressive nationalism to build up support for their respective parties.

20 The United Nations (Origin and Purpose)

 **Short Answer Type Questions**

Q. 1. What is meant by the term 'Veto' power ? **[2019]**

OR

What is meant by the term 'Veto Power' which is enjoyed by the permanent members of the Security Council ? **[2011]**

Ans. Each member of the UN Security Council has one vote. Decisions on procedural matters are made by an affirmative vote of nine members, including the concurring votes of all five permanent members. The negative vote of a permanent member is called a veto. The Council is powerless to act if any of the five permanent members uses the Veto power.

Q. 2. Mention two functions of the General Assembly. **[2014]**

Ans. 1. The General Assembly promotes international peace and security through disarmament.

2. To make recommendations for peaceful settlement of disputes.

Q. 3. Who appoints the Secretary General of the United Nations ? **[2012]**

Ans. The Secretary General of the united nations is appointed by the General Assembly on the recommendation of the Security Council.

 **Long Answer Type Questions**

Q. 1. Study the picture given below and answer the questions that follow :

(a) Identify the organisation associated with the above emblem.
Mention any three principles of this organisation.
(b) Where is the headquarters of this organisation located ?
Who can become its member ?
(c) Name the principal judicial organ of this organisation and explain its composition. **[2012]**

Ans. (a) The organisation associated with the emblem is the United Nations organisation. Its three principles are:

1. It is based on the sovereign equality of all its members.

2. The U.N.O. will not intervene in the internal affairs of a country.

3. Member nations will not use the threat of violence in their international relations.

(b) The headquarters of this organisation is located in New York city. Its European office is in Geneva.

Its membership is open to all peace-loving nations, which agree with the objectives of the U.N. and are ready to abide by its principles. The admission, suspension and expulsion of members are decided by the General Assembly on the recommendation of the Security Council by a 2/3rd majority of votes. Almost all countries of the world are its members now.

(c) The principal judicial organ of UNO is the International Court of Justice.

Its composition: The court is composed of 15 judges elected to 9-year term of office by the United Nations General Assembly and Security Council sitting independently of each other. It may not include more than one judge from any nationality. Elections are held every 3 years. One-third of the seats and retiring judges may be re-elected.

The United Nations (Major Agencies and Their Functions)

 **Short Answer Type Questions**

Q. 1. **Give the full form of UNICEF and WHO.** **[2020]**

Ans. **Full form of UNICEF:** United Nations International Children's Emergency Fund.

Full form of WHO: World Health Organisation.

Q. 2. **Give the full form of UNESCO.** **[2018]**

Ans. The full form of UNESCO is United Nations Educational, Scientific and Cultural Organisation.

Q. 3. **Mention any two functions of UNESCO in the field of Education.** **[2017]**

Ans. **Functions of UNESCO in the field of Education :**

1. Removal of illiteracy by encouraging adult education, distance education and the open school system.

2. Provision of grants and fellowships to teachers and scholars, organisation of library.

3. Financial assistance for the education of disabled children.

4. Organisation of book fairs and festivals at international and national levels.

Q. 4. **State the full forms of the following agencies of the United Nations :**

UNICEF and UNESCO. **[2016]**

Ans. **Full forms of the following agencies of the United Nations are:**

1. **UNICEF :** United Nations International Children's Emergency Fund.

2. **UNESCO :** United Nations Educational, Scientific and Cultural Organisation.

 **Long Answer Type Questions**

Q. 1.

(a) **Name the organization associated with the above Emblem. Mention any two of its objectives.**
(b) **Mention any three functions of WHO, as its agency.**
(c) **Name the Principal Judicial Organ of this organization and explain its composition.** **[2020]**

Marking Scheme

(a) United Nations
Objectives:
– Maintain international peace and security.
– To develop friendly relations among nations.
– To achieve international cooperation among nations
– Solving problems of economic, social, cultural& humanitarian character.

– To be a centre for harmonizing the actions of nations.
– To disarm
– Decolonize
– And develop
– Create faith in human rights.
– Establish conditions to maintain International law and international treaties.
– Save from scourge of war.   *(Any three points)*

(b) **Functions of WHO:**
– Direct and coordinate health work on an international scale.
– Works in fields of communicable diseases
– Maintains child health
– Mental heath
– Cancer
– Diabetes
– Eradicate scale /smallpox was eradicated by global campaign by WHO.
– Promote the provision of good health and living conditions of the people.
– To set international standards with regard to food and medicines.
– To provide safe drinking water.

– Vaccination/immunization against six major diseases like, measles, diphtheria, tetanus, TB, polio & whooping cough/diarrheal deaths have reduced
– Promote research, to cure and prevent diseases.
– Organizes conferences, research, seminars, etc.
– Publishes health journals/ bulletins/magazines
– Set international standards for biological products and pharmaceutical products such as rugs, medicines, vaccines
– Bring about improvement in nutrition
– Housing
– Sanitation
– Work conditions
– Hygiene
– Built medical sciences library in Geneva
– Infant mortality rate has dropped
– Organised malaria and polio eradication programmes globally.

(Any three points)

(c) The International Court of Justice
Composition:
– Consists of 15 judges.
– Elected for a period of 9 years.
– Elected by the General Assembly and the Security Council.
– Each judge is from different country.
– Elects its President and Vice President for a period of 3 years.
– Appoints a registrar.
– Retiring judge may be elected.

(Any three points)

Ans. **(a) Organization associated with the above emblem is United Nations Organisation or UNO. Two objectives are :**

1. To maintain international peace and security and to take collective measures for the prevention and removal of threat to peace, to suppress acts of aggression or other breaches of peace.

2. To develop friendly relation among nations based on respect for the principle of equal rights and self-determination of people.

3. To achieve international cooperation in solving international economic, social, cultural, humanitarian problems and increasing respect for human rights and fundamental freedoms.

4. To be a centre for harmonizing the actions of nations in the attainment of these common ends.(Any two)

(b) **Three functions of WHO are:**

1. It helps countries to improve their health system by building of infrastructure especially manpower, institution and services for the individual and community.

2. The WHO launched a programme to immunize children against six major diseases like, Measles, Diphtheria, Tetanus, Tuberculosis, Polio and Whooping cough.

3. It promotes research to cure and prevent diseases. It arranged for investigation of cancer and heart diseases in laboratories in many countries to identify diseases to improve vaccines and train research workers.

4. It works towards providing safe drinking water and adequate waste disposal. It organizes conferences, seminars and training for healthcare personnel from different countries.

5. It aims at fighting diseases and preventing them from spreading.

6. Defines standard for the strength and purity of medicine including biological products.

7. It publishes health journals like the Bulletin of the World Health Organization to create health consciousness among people.

(Any three)

(c) The principal judicial organ of UNO is the International Court of Justice.

Its composition—The court is composed of 15 judges elected to 9-year term of office by the United Nations General Assembly and Security Council sitting independently of each other. It may not include more than one judge from any nationality. Elections are held every 3 years. One- third of the seats and retiring judges may be re-elected.

Q. 2. **The necessity to maintain International peace led to the establishment of the United Nations Organisation. With reference to the statement, answer the following :**

(a) Write any three functions of UNESCO that preserves our 'Cultural Heritage'.

(b) State the Composition of the Security Council.

(c) Write any four functions of the General Assembly. **[2019]**

Marking Scheme

(a) Preservation of Cultural Heritage:
- UNESCO provides technical advice and assistance, equipment and funds for the preservation of monuments and other works of art. It has prepared a World Heritage List to identify the monuments and sites which are to be protected.
- It aims to protect the world inheritance of books, works of art and rare manuscripts.
- It gives encouragement to artistic creations in literature and fine arts.
- It pays attention towards the cultural development through the medium of films.
- It sends cultural missions to different countries so that there would be development of contacts which may promote peace and prosperity.
- It helps the member states in the preservation of their cultural heritage.
- It encourages translation of rare manuscripts.
- It plays a vital role in distributing knowledge about Human Rights.

(Any three points)

(b) Composition:
- The Council consists of 15 members.
- It has five permanent members – China, France, Russia, Britain and the United States of America.
- The regional representation of the ten non-permanent members is:
  (i) Afro-Asian Countries - 5
  (ii) Latin American Countries – 2
  (iii) West European and other Countries – 2
  (iv) East European Countries - 1
- The ten non-permanent members are elected by the General Assembly by a two-third majority for a term of two years.
- A retiring member is not eligible for immediate re-election.
- The Presidency of the Council rotates monthly, according to the English alphabetical listing of its member states.

(Any three points)

(c) Functions of General Assembly:
- To make recommendations for the peaceful settlement of disputes
- To promote political, social and economic cooperation
- To receive and consider reports from the Security Council and other organs of UN.
- To consider and approve the budget of the UN.
- To regulate the working of other organs and agencies of UN.
- To elect the non-permanent members of the Security Council.
- To elect judges of the ICJ.
- To appoint Secretary General on the recommendation of Security Council.
- To amend the UN Charter.

- Functions under 'Uniting for Peace Resolution' 1950.
- New members are admitted by the General Assembly on the recommendation of Security Council.

(Any four points)

Ans.

(a) 1. It helps the member states in the preservation of their cultural heritage and encourages translation of rare manuscripts. It adopted a Convention to ensure that member states take measures to protect monuments of artistic or historic interest.

2. It encourages cultural interchange. UNESCO provides travel grants to writers and artists under a project named Mutual Appreciation of Eastern and Western Cultural Values.

3. It gives every possible encouragement to artistic creations in the field of literature and fine arts.

4. It plays a vital role in distribution of knowledge about the human rights.

(b) Composition of the Security Council :
1. The Council consists of 15 members. It has five permanent members – China, France, Russia, Britain and the USA.

2. **The regional representation of the ten non-permanent members is :**
Afro-Asian countries (5)
Latin American countries (2)
West European and other countries (2)
East European countries (1)

3. The ten non-permanent members are elected by the General Assembly by a two-third majority for the term of two years. A retiring member is not eligible for immediate re-election.

4. The Presidency of the Council rotates monthly, according to the English alphabetical listing of its member states.

(c) Functions of the General Assembly:
1. To discuss any question relating to international peace and security.

2. The General Assembly regulates the working of other organs and agencies of the United Nations.

3. The General Assembly considers and approves the budget of the United Nations.

4. The Assembly elects the non-permanent members of the Security Council and the members of the Economic and Social Council.

Q. 3. With reference to the United Nations and its Specialised Agencies, answer the following :
(a) Mention any three functions of the International Court of Justice.
(b) State the composition of the General Assembly.
(c) State any two functions of the UNICEF and any two functions of WHO.   [2018]

Ans. **(a)** Three functions of the International Court of Justice are as follows:

1. To settle disputes between member states.
2. To give advisory opinions on legal matters referred to it by authorized UN organs and specialised agencies, when the court is authorised by the General Assembly.
3. The ICJ is a judicial institution that decides cases on the basis of international law as it exists on the date of the decision. It cannot formally create law as it is not a legislative organ.

(b) The General Assembly shall consist of all the members of the United Nations. Each member state shall have not more than five representatives in the General Assembly. Each state has only one vote. It is a kind of Parliament. At the starting of each session the Assembly elects a new President and 21 Vice-Presidents. The Presidency rotes each year among five group of state.

(c) Two functions of the UNICEF are as follows:

1. To render assistance in providing protective food like milk, meat, fish and fat to the children throughout the world. It also takes care of interests of women and pregnant mothers.
2. To provide funds for training of health and sanitation workers, nutritionists and creche workers.

Two functions of WHO are as follows:

1. It helps the countries to build-up infrastructure in health.
2. It promotes research for developing new technologies in health, nutrition, maternal and child care, etc.

Q. 4. With reference to the United Nations and its related agencies, answer the following questions :
(a) Explain any three functions of the WHO.
(b) State the composition of the International Court of Justice.

(c) State any four functions of the General Assembly.   [2016]

Ans. **(a)** Refer to Long Answer Type Questions Answer 1 (b).
(b) Refer to Long Answer Type Questions Answer 1 (c).
(c) Refer to Long Answer Type Questions Answer 2 (c).

Q. 5. The United Nations was established to be an effective peace keeping international organization. In this context explain the following :
(a) Its objectives and purposes.
(c) Name the agency that the UN set up to deliver relief to children and mothers after World War II. State any three of its functions.   [2015]

Ans. The United Nations was established to be an effective peace keeping International Organisation.

(a) Objectives and purposes of the un: The purposes of the United Nations, defined in Article 1 of the Charter, are as follows :

1. To maintain international peace and security; to take collective measures for the prevention and removal of threats to peace, to suppress acts of aggression or other breaches of peace.
2. To develop friendly relations among nations based on respect for the principle of equal rights and self-determination of people.
3. To achieve international cooperation in solving international economic, social, cultural, or humanitarian problems and encouraging respect for human rights and for fundamental freedoms.
4. To be the centre for harmonising the actions of nations in the attainment of these common ends.

Objectives of UN : Disarm, decolonise and develop are the three new objectives set by the UN.

(c) United Nations International Children's Emergency Fund (UNICEF) is the agency that the UN set up to deliver relief to children and mothers after World War II.

Functions of UNICEF: UNICEF provides services in primary healthcare nutrition, basic education, sanitation and women's development in developing countries.

The main functions of UNICEF are broadly divided into the following categories :

1. UNICEF works for the protection of children in respect of their survival, health, and well-being. This is done in cooperation with individuals, civic groups, governments and the private sector.

2. It provides funds for training the personnel, including health and sanitation workers, teachers and nutritionists. Universal child immunisation against preventable diseases was one of the leading goals of UNICEF.

3. It assists Governments to plan, develop and extend community-based services in the fields of maternal and child health, nutrition, clean water and sanitation.

4. It provides help to children and mothers in emergencies arising from natural calamities, civil strifes and epidemics.

5. UNICEF performs various other functions. As the sole agency for children, it speaks on behalf of children and upholds the convention on the rights of the child and works for its implementation.

Q. 6. **The United Nations Organization was established to maintain peace and 'promote social progress and better standards of life in larger freedom'. With reference to this, explain the following :**

    (a) **The composition of the Security Council.**

    (b) **The functions of the Security Council related to maintaining World Peace.**

    (c) **The role of UNESCO in the development of Science and Technology.** **[2013]**

Ans. **(a)** Refer to Long Answer Type Questions Answer 2 (b).

    (b) **The functions of the Security Council are :**

       1. To maintain international peace and security in accordance with the principles and purposes of the United Nations.

       2. To investigate any dispute or situation which might lead to international friction and to take military action against an aggressor.

       3. To recommend methods of adjusting such disputes or the terms of settlement and to formulate plans for the establishment of a system to regulate armaments.

    (c) **The role of UNESCO in the development of Science and Technology are :**

       1. **Promotes basic research :** UNESCO pro-motes basic research in the fields like geology, mathematics, physics and oceanography. Engineering and Technology schemes in a number of developing countries are being financed by UNESCO.

       2. **Organizes conferences :** It organizes regional and world conferences to bring together scientists, technicians and technologists who have a common interest.

       3. **Providing information :** It brings the benefits of science to all countries by providing information through bulletins, journals and exhibitions. 'Courier' is the official monthly magazine of UNESCO.

       4. **Encouraging studies :** It encourages the study of social sciences, especially to ensure that attention is paid to the topics like factors causing violence or conflicts and violation of human rights.

Q. 7. **The United Nations apart from its main organs also work through its allied agencies. In this context, answer the following questions :**

    (a) **Write the expanded form of UNESCO. Mention two of its functions in the field of education.**

    (b) **Explain three vital roles that the WHO plays in combating diseases.**

    (c) **Mention four functions of the Security Council in maintaining peace.** **[2010]**

Ans. **(a)** The expanded form of unesco in United Nations Educational, scientific and cultural organization.

    Two functions performed by it in the educational field are :

       1. To promote education among children and adults and to work for universal primary education.

       2. To give financial assistance for the education of the disabled children, the girl child and women.

    (b) Refer to Long Answer Type Questions Answer 4 (a).

    (c) Refer to Long Answer Type Questions Answer 6 (b).

 22 The Non-Aligned Movement

 ## Short Answer Type Questions

Q. 1. What is meant by the term 'Non-Aligned Movement'? **[2015]**

Ans. The concept of 'non-alignment' emerged during the Cold War. Non-alignment is the international policy of a sovereign state according to which it does not align itself with any of the power blocs and at the same time actively participates in the world affairs to promote international peace, harmony and cooperation.

Q. 2. Name the two architects of NAM. **[2013]**

Ans. The two architects of the NAM were:
1. Jawaharlal Nehru of India
2. Joseph Broz Tito of Yugoslavia

 ## Long Answer Type Questions

Q. 1. With reference to the Second World War and the Non-Aligned Movement, answer the following:
   (a) Explain briefly three reasons for the Dissatisfaction with the Treaty of Versailles.
   (c) Mention any four chief architects of the Non-Aligned Movement. **[2020]**

Marking Scheme

(a) – Demanded annexation of German territories and creation of many states.
   – Germans felt humiliated and helpless.
   – Sowed the seeds of bitterness and conflict.
   – All the German colonies were forcibly taken away and was divided into two parts for the benefit of Poland.
   – Burdened with huge war indemnity which could never be paid.
   – This humiliation gave rise to the spirit of revenge and Germany started looking for an opportunity to do away with the Treaty.
   – This was not possible without aggressive policy and armaments. War became inevitable.
   – Germany had to pay 33 billion dollars.
   – It had to cede large territories to France, Belgium, Poland, and Denmark.
   – Italians felt they won the war but lost the peace.
   – Allies deserted her and she received no valuable addition to her territories.
   – Germany was crippled.
   – Danzig was internationalized. (Any three points)

(c) The four architects of NAM are:
   – Jawaharlal Nehru of India,
   – Joseph B. Tito of Yugoslavia
   – Nasser of Egypt
   – Sukarno of Indonesia

Ans. **(a) Dissatisfaction with the Treaty of Versailles were:**

   1. The treaty demanded annexation of German territories and creation of many states.

   2. German colonies were forcibly taken away and Germany was divided into two parts for the benefit of Poland. Germany was burdened with huge war indemnity which she could never be paid.

   3. Germany's military power was reduced. This humiliation gave rise to the spirit of revenge and Germany started looking for opportunity to do away with the harsh treaty.

(c) Chief architects of the Non-Aligned Movement:

   1. Prime Minister Pandit Jawaharlal Nehru of India.

   2. President Josip Broz Tito of Yugoslavia.

   3. President Gamal Abdel Nasser of Egypt.

   4. President Sukarno of Indonesia.

Q. 2. The horrors of the two World Wars, led to the formation of the United Nations Organization, while the formation of the Non-Aligned Movement followed later. In this context, answer the following:
   (a) Mention any three aims and objectives of the United Nations Organization.

(b) Explain any three functions of the Security Council.

(c) Explain any four factors that led to the formation of the Non-Aligned Movement. **[2017]**

Ans. **(a)** Organization associated with the above emblem is United Nations Organisation or UNO.

Two objectives are :

1. To maintain international peace and security and to take collective measures for the prevention and removal of threat to peace, to suppress acts of aggression or other breaches of peace.

2. To develop friendly relation among nations based on respect for the principle of equal rights and self-determination of people.

3. To achieve international cooperation in solving international economic, social, cultural, humanitarian problems and increasing respect for human rights and fundamental freedoms.

4. To be a centre for harmonizing the actions of nations in the attainment of these common ends. (Any two)

(b) **Three functions of the Security Council are :**

1. To maintain international peace and security in accordance with the principles and purposes of the United Nations.

2. To investigate any dispute or situation which might lead to international friction and to take military action against an aggressor.

3. To recommend methods of adjusting such disputes or the terms of settlement and to formulate plans for the establishment of a system to regulate armaments.

(c) **Four factors that led to the formation of the Non-Aligned Movement were:**

1. **Global tension caused by Cold War:** Most of the newly independent countries of Asia and Africa realised that the division of the world into two power blocs was not in their large interest; and this might endanger world peace. These nations felt that by maintaining distance from both the superpowers they would put off the danger of war or a nuclear holocaust.

2. **Struggle against imperialism and neo-colonisation:** The newly independent nations opted for non-alignment because of some emotional and psychological constraints. They wanted to enjoy their newly acquired freedom and the power that had come with it without any pressure from other bigger nations.

3. **Right of independent judgement:** The newly independent nations were able to keep their own identity by not aligning with any of the power blocs. They wanted to solve their problems themselves without any outside interference or influence.

4. **Use of moderation in relations to all big powers:** The newly independent nations wanted to promote goodwill and cooperation among the nations of Asia and Africa, and to explore and advance their mutual interests by establishing friendly relations with all the nations.

Q. 3. With reference to the Non-Aligned Movement, explain the following :

(a) 'Non-Alignment'.

(b) Two factors responsible for its formation.

Ans. **(a)** 'Non-Alignment' is the international policy of a sovereign state meant to settle international disputes through non-violence and international cooperation by refusing India's alignment with any power bloc or alliance. (The United States or the Soviet Union, in particular.) This policy aimed at being neutral.

(b) Refer to Long Answer Type Questions Answer 2 (c).

Q. 4. With reference to the Cold War and the Non-Aligned Movement, explain the following : Mention four major objectives of the Non-Aligned Movement.

Ans. The four objectives of the non-Aligned Movement are :

1. **Maintenance of international peace:** Non-aligned nations work for the maintenance of international peace and security. They feel that the course adopted by them is best designed to minimize the threat to peace.

2. **Disarmament:** NAM favours disarmament and in particular opposes the possession and use of nuclear weapons.

3. **Creation of a new international economic order:** Since 1970s, developing states are looking for a new international economic order based on equality and justice. They are demanding reforms in International financial institutions like world bank and IMF, favourable terms for foreign trade, technology transfer and foreign investment to boost their economies.

4. **Enforcement of human rights:** Enforcement of human rights has been a major objective of the non-aligned movement.

GEOGRAPHY

Physical Features and The Climate of India

 **Short Answer Type Questions-I**

Q. 1. (a) (i) Name one state in the north western part of India that receives rainfall during winter.
(ii) What is the source of this rainfall?
(b) Give a reason for each of the following:
(i) Rainy season in India is after the summer season.
(ii) Tamil Nadu has more rainy months than Kerala, yet, Kerala receives more rainfall than Tamil Nadu.

Ans. (a) (i) Punjab
(ii) Westerly depressions or temperate cyclones is the reason for rainfall.
(b) (i) It is so because the mainland of India experiences extremely high temperature that leads to development of low-pressure trough.
(ii) Because Kerala experiences burst of monsoon and 85% of rain received in Kerala is contributed by monsoon winds.

Q. 2. (a) (i) What type of wind is 'Monsoon'? What is its direction during summer?
(ii) Mention two characteristics of the Indian monsoon.
(b) With reference to the summer season in India, answer the following questions:
(i) Mention the duration of the summer season in India.
(ii) What is the atmospheric pressure condition during summer season over the central part of India? **[2019]**

Ans. (a) (i) Monsoon wind is a periodic wind. It's direction during summer is south-west to north-east.
(ii) The characteristics of Indian monsoon are:
1. South-West monsoon is erratic in nature.
2. Distribution of rainfall is uneven.
3. It is largely controlled by orography *i.e.* the effects caused due to the presence of Himalayas and the Western Ghats on the amount of rainfall.

(b) (i) The summer season or hot dry season in India commences in March and continues till the end of May.
(ii) During the summer season as the whole country swelters, the low pressure conditions over the central part of India become more severe and a low pressure trough develops between the Thar Desert and the Chotanagpur Plateau.

Q. 3. (a) How is the winter rainfall of the *northwest part* of India different from the winter rainfall of the *southeast part* of India?
(b) (i) Name a state that is *first* to experience the onset of the monsoon.
(ii) How does the "Mango shower" influence the state of Karnataka?
[2018]

Ans. (a) The winter rainfall of the north-west part of India is different from the winter rainfall of the south-east part of India as the north-west part of India gets winter rain due to the temperate cyclones, whereas the south-east part of India recieves rain due to winter monsoon or retreating monsoon.

(b) (i) Kerala
(ii) Mango showers are the name of the local winds that blow in South India, majorly in Karnataka during the month of April or May. These winds bring a little rainfall and are good for the growth and early ripening of the mangoes. Thus, influencing the trade of mangoes as well as of tea and coffee in the state of Karnataka.

Q. 4. (a) Mention the four seasons that prevail in India stating the months for each.
(b) State the agricultural benefits derived from:
(i) The Westerly Depressions in Punjab.
(ii) The Kalbaisakhi in Assam. **[2017]**

Ans. (a) Four seasons in India are:
1. The hot/Summer season (March–May).
2. The rainy season or the season of south-west monsoon (June–September).

3. The season of the retreating south-west monsoon (October–November).
4. The cold/winter season (December–February)

(b) **(i)** Wheat and Barley in Punjab
(ii) Tea in Assam

Q. 5. **(a)** **What is the name given to the climate of India? Mention any two factors responsible for such a type of climate.**
(b) **Name the following:**
(i) **The winds that bring heavy rain to Cherrapunji.**
(ii) **The local wind that brings light rainfall to South India and is good for tea and coffee crops.**
[2016, 2012]

Ans. **(a)** Tropical Monsoon type of Climate.
The factors responsible for such type of climate in India:
1. Effect of Himalayas
2. Latitudinal extent
(b) **(i)** Cherrapunji receives rains from the Bay of Bengal branch of South-West Monsoon winds.
(ii) Mango showers/Cherry blossoms.

Q. 6. **(a)** **Explain two factors that affect the climate of India giving a suitable example for each.**
(b) **State two differences between the rainfalls that occur from June to September and that from December to February in North India.** **[2015]**

Ans. **(a)** The factors that affect the climate of India are as follows:
(i) **Altitude:** Temperature decreases at the rate of 1°C for every 166 m rise in height. Thus, the mountains are always cooler than the plains. For example, Darjeeling is cooler than Kolkata in summer.
(ii) **Distance from the sea:** The areas in the interior of the country have an extreme type of climate while the coastal areas have a moderate climate. This is mainly due to the influence of land and sea breezes caused by differential heating and cooling of land and sea. For example, Delhi experiences an extreme type of climate while Mumbai experiences an equable type of climate.
(b) The rainfall that occurs during June-September is orographic, heavy, torrential and causes destruction. The rainfall that takes place during December to February is cyclonic, light and beneficial.

Q. 7. **(a)** **Mention the different sources of rain in Punjab and Tamil Nadu during the winter season.**
(b) **State the benefits that are derived from the local winds that blow in summer in the following states:**
(i) **Kerala**
(ii) **West Bengal** **[2014]**

Ans. **(a)** Punjab receives rainfall due to the western disturbances that originate over the Eastern Mediterranean Sea during the winter season.
Tamil Nadu receives rainfall from the North-East Monsoon winds during the winter season.
(b) **(i)** **Kerala:** The local wind is called Mango showers. They bring little rain in April and May, which is helpful in the early ripening of mangoes, tea and coffee plants.
(ii) **West Bengal:** The local wind is called Nor'westers or Kalbaisakhi. The rain is useful for rice and jute in West Bengal.

Q. 8. **(a)** **Name two types of cyclonic systems that affect India and two areas that receive rainfall from these systems.**
(b) **Give two important characteristics of the South-West Monsoon rainfall.** **[2013]**

Ans. **(a)** Two cyclonic systems that affect India are:
(i) Temperate cyclones – North-west of India (Punjab, Haryana)
(ii) Tropical cyclones – Eastern coast of India (Andhra Pradesh, Tamil Nadu, West Bengal).
(b) Characteristics of South - West monsoon rainfall are:
(i) Orographic in nature.
(ii) Uncertain in amount and time.

Q. 9. **What is the direction of the summer monsoon? Why?** **[2012]**

Ans. South-west, because the intense heat that prevails over India develops low pressure over the northern plains. It attracts moisture bearing South-East Trade winds from the southern hemisphere. After crossing the equator, they are deflected towards the right and blow over India as South-West monsoon winds.

Q. 10. **(a)** **Give two important characteristics of the summer monsoon rainfall in India.**
(b) **'Rainfall in India is Orographic in nature.' Give an example with reference to the distribution of rainfall and the effect of relief on its distribution.** **[2011]**

Ans. **(a)** Two important characteristics of the summer monsoon rainfall in India are as follows:

(i) The monsoon rainfall in India is unevenly spread and sporadic. Thus, places like the Western Ghats receive heavy rainfall of more than 200 cm, whereas, the desert regions of Rajasthan receive scanty rainfall of less than 50 cm a year.

(ii) Monsoon rainfall in India is orographic in nature. Thus, the windward slopes of the Western Ghats receive more rain than the leeward slopes.

(b) Relief plays a very important role in the distribution of rainfall in India. The windward slopes of the Western Ghats obstruct the moist winds from the sea and cause heavy rainfall while the leeward slopes remain dry.

Q. 11. (a) Mention two differences in the climatic conditions which prevail over Kerala and Uttar Pradesh in the month of June.

(b) Name:

(i) The source of the winter rain to Tamil Nadu. **[2010]**

Ans. **(a)** Kerala faces the South-West monsoon which starts by the end of May and brings heavy rain. The climate is cool. Uttar Pradesh, on the other hand, lies to the north, in the interior. It recieves rain from the Bay of Bengal branch of the South-West monsoon which reaches there by the end of June or by the beginning of July. This rain also is much less as the winds continue dropping their moisture on the way. The plains are very hot in the month of June.

(b) **(i)** The North-East Monsoon.

Short Answer Type Questions-II

Q. 1. **(a)** **(i)** **What do you understand by the term "Burst of Monsoon"? Name the state that experiences the "Burst of Monsson".**

(ii) **Even though India gets abundant rainfall during the rainy season, yet, some places experience drought. Explain giving suitable examples.**

(iii) **Why is Shimla colder than Delhi during summer?**

(b) **Study the climatic data given below and answer the questions that follow:**

Month	JAN.	FEB.	MAR.	APR.	MAY	JUNE	JULY	AUG.	SEPT.	OCT.	NOV.	DEC.
Temp. °C	8.4	11.5	21.6	28.3	35.1	38.5	41.0	38.0	30.0	29.2	15.6	10.2
Rainfall cm	1.5	0.9	0.5	–	–	12.5	17.8	18.5	12.5	12.5	6.2	2.1

(i) **Calculate the annual range of temperature.**

(ii) **State whether the station is located in the coastal area or in the continental interior.**

(iii) **Name the wind that brings most of the rainfall to this area.**

Ans. **(a)** **(i)** "Burst of Monsoon" is when the intensity of rain suddenly increases at the arrival of monsoon and it continues for several days.

The state that experiences such situation is Kerala.

(ii) This condition happens because monsoon winds are highly unpredictable. It also varies direction and moisture for example average annual rainfall received in Jaipur is 30 cm and in Bhopal is 140 cm.

(iii) The key factor behind this phenomenon is higher altitude. We know as the height increases, temperature decreases.

(d) **(i)** Annual range of temperature (max. temperature – min. temperature) 41 – 8.4 = 32.6°C.

(ii) The station is located in continental interior.

(iii) South West monsoon.

Q. 2. **(a)** **Give a reason for each of the following:**

(i) Goa receives heavier rainfall than Puducherry.

(ii) Mawsynram receives the highest average annual rainfall.

(iii) Mangaluru is cooler than Delhi in summer season.

(b) **Study the data of distribution of temperature and rain for Station X and answer the questions that follow:**

Month	JAN	FEB	MAR	APR	MAY	JUN	JUL	AUG	SEP	OCT	NOV	DEC
Temp. °C	10	11	23	35	39	42	40	33	30	25	13	11
Rainfall cm	2	1	0	5	15	62	71	81	59	12	10	3

(i) Is station X in the coastal area *or* in the interior of the country?

(ii) Calculate the total annual rainfall for station X.

(iii) Name the wind that brings *most* of the rainfall to Station X. **[2019]**

📋 Marking Scheme

(a) (i) Goa is located on the windward side of Western Ghats so Arabian Sea Branch of south west monsoon brings heavier rainfall and Puducherry is located on the eastern coast and receives lighter rainfall from North East Monsoon.

(ii) Mawsynram experiences Orographic rainfall as it is located on windward side of Garo hill. Bay of Bengal branch of South West Monsoon brings heavy rain to this area/ funnel shape of Garo, Khasi, Jaintia hill lead to trapping of clouds leading to more rains.

(iii) Mangalore has a coastal location, but Delhi lies in the interior. Due to distance from the sea, Mangalore is cooler than Delhi in summer.

(b) (i) It is in the interior.

(ii) 321 cm.

(iii) South-west Monsoon

Ans. **(a)** **(i)** Goa is located on the windward side of the Western Ghats so the Arabian Sea branch of South-West monsoon brings heavier rainfall while Puducherry is located on the eastern coast and gets lighter rainfall from North-East monsoon.

(ii) Mawsynram is situated along the edge of the Meghalaya Plateau and stands at the end of a funnel-shaped valley, on the windward side of the Khasi hills which acts as a trap for the rain-bearing Bay of Bengal branch of the South-West monsoon forcing them to shed huge amounts of moisture.

(iii) Mangaluru is situated on the western coast, and thus enjoys the influence of the sea and stays relatively cooler. On the other hand, Delhi lies in the interior and experiences continental type of climate. So, summers in Delhi are very hot.

(b) **(i)** Station X is situated in the interior parts of the country.

(ii) 321 cm.

(iii) South-West monsoon winds.

Q. 3. **(a)** Give a reason for each of the following:

(i) Kanyakumari experiences equable climate.

(ii) Central Maharashtra gets less rainfall than the coastal area of Maharashtra.

(iii) Jaipur has a higher annual range of temperature than Mumbai.

(b) Write three differences between summer monsoon season and retreating monsoon season. **[2018]**

📋 Marking Scheme

(a) (i) Kanyakumari is near the sea and is also near the equator and so has equable climate.

(ii) Central Maharashtra lies in the rain shadow area whereas coastal Maharashtra is on the windward side of Western Ghats.

(iii) Jaipur lies in continental interior whereas Mumbai lies close to the sea. Thus, Jaipur has extremes of temperature, but Mumbai has equable climate.

(b)

Summer Monsoon Season	Retreating Monsoon Season
– Wind is onshore from South-West direction.	– Wind direction is North-east./ withdrawal of monsoon.
– Heavy rain, high humidity, high temperature.	– Clear sky, high temperature, low humidity.
– There is rain in almost whole country.	– There is no rain in most parts of India but when wind pick up moisture from Bay of Bengal it brings rain to coromandel coast.

Ans. **(a)** **(i)** Kanyakumari experiences equable climate as it lies in the coastal region of the subcontinent of India and experiences moderating influence of the sea and land breezes.

(ii) Central Maharashtra gets less rainfall than the coastal area of Maharashtra as it lies in the rain shadow area of the south-west monsoon. Whereas coastal Maharashtra is located on the windward side of Western Ghats.

(iii) Jaipur has a higher annual range of temperature than Mumbai because it is an inland city which is situated away from the coastal area. Thus, it is far from the moderating impact of the ocean.

(b)

Summer Monsoon	Retreating Monsoon
(i) Low pressure is over the land.	(i) Low pressure is over the sea.
(ii) Winds blow from the sea towards the land.	(ii) Winds blow from the land towards the sea.

Month	JAN.	FEB.	MAR.	APR.	MAY	JUNE	JULY.	AUG.	SEP.	OCT.	NOV.	DEC.
Temp. °C	12.0	25.5	26.3	27.1	30.0	36.2	36.0	35.9	30.3	28.4	21.0	16.6
Rainfall cm	1.5	0.1	0.0	1.4	1.1	21.0	25.3	27.2	24.0	9.4	1.5	0.4

(i) What is the annual range temperature of the station?

(ii) What is the total annual rainfall experienced by the station?

(iii) Why would it be correct to presume that the station lies in the interior and not on the coast? **[2017]**

Ans. **(a)** **(i)** The Bay of Bengal branch of South-West monsoon is deflected towards the west along the Himalayas. The rainfall goes on decreasing as it proceeds through the Ganga valley and on its way, it gives more rainfall to Kolkata in West Bengal. By the time it reaches Lucknow in Uttar Pradesh, it has already shed its moisture and hence gives less rainfall.

(ii) A high pressure gradient builds up between the hot North India with intense low pressure and cooler water bodies surrounding it with high pressure. The low pressure area attracts the South-East trade winds blowing in the Southern hemisphere. After crossing the equator, these winds are deflected towards their right to the Indian subcontinent and blow towards West coast from South-West coast over the Arabian Sea.

(iii) The Arabian Sea branch of South-West monsoon blows parallel to the Aravalli range that do not intercept the winds. Therefore the Thar desert, located in the east, does not recieve any rain. Less than 25 cm of rainfall occurs in winter due to the westerly depressions. The Bay of Bengal branch of South-West monsoon is exhausted by the time it reaches the windward slopes of the Aravallis. These winds shed no rain on the leeward side where the Thar desert lies. Humidity is very low in summer. The moisture evaporates before it could rain. The moisture laden winds blowing over Rajasthan do not saturate as the heat of the Thar region increases the capacity to hold moisture, so there is no rainfall.

(b) **(i)** $36 \cdot 2°C - 12 \cdot 0°C = 24 \cdot 2°C$.

(ii) $112 \cdot 9$ cm.

(iii) It is in the interior because its annual range of temperature is high, and rainfall is low, which is expected to be pretty heavy on the coastal areas.

Q. 4. **(a)** Give a reason for each of the following:

(i) Kolkata receives heavier rain than Lucknow.

(ii) The Summer Monsoon winds blow over the Arabian sea from the South-west.

(iii) Thar is a desert.

(b) Study the climatic data given below and answer the questions that follow:

Q. 5. **(a)** Give a geographical reason for each of the following:

(i) Kanpur has extreme temperature conditions.

(ii) Kochi is warmer than Mumbai even though both lie on the western coast of India.

(iii) The Ganga Plain gets the monsoon rain much later than the west coast of India.

(b) Study the climatic data of station x given below and answer the questions that follow:

Month	JAN.	FEB.	MAR.	APR.	MAY	JUNE	JULY.	AUG.	SEP.	OCT.	NOV.	DEC.
Temp. °C	24.5	25.7	27.7	28.4	30.0	32.5	31.0	30.2	29.8	28.0	25.9	24.7
Rainfall cm	4.3	1.6	1.7	2.4	2.8	4.6	8.6	11.4	11.8	30.6	35.0	13.9

    (i) **Calculate the total annual rainfall experienced by the station.**

    (ii) **What is the annual range of temperature?**

    (iii) **On which coast of India does the station lie? Give a reason for your answer.** [2016]

Ans. (a) (i) Kanpur is situated in the interior part of the country and is away from the influence of the sea. So, it is very cold in winter and very hot in summer.

    (ii) Kochi is located closer to the equator than Mumbai. So, Kochi experiences vertical rays of the sun.

    (iii) Ganga plain lies in North India and the South-West monsoon, first strikes the west coast of India before North India.

(b) (i) 128.7 cm

    (ii) $32.5°C - 24.5°C = 8°C$

    (iii) The station lies on the east coast. As the station receives the bulk of its rainfall in the months of October and November which is due to the retreating monsoon and north-east monsoon.

Q. 6. (a) **Give a geographic reason for each of the following:**

    (i) **Kerala has the longest rainy season.**

    (ii) **The Konkan coast experiences orographic rainfall.**

    (iii) **The city of Kanpur in Uttar Pradesh has a higher range of temperature than that of Chennai in Tamil Nadu.**

(b) **Study the climatic data given below and answer the questions that follow:**

Month	JAN.	FEB.	MAR.	APR.	MAY	JUNE	JULY.	AUG.	SEP.	OCT.	NOV.	DEC.
Temp. °C	21·0	21·9	24·3	27·2	28·0	26·4	26·1	25·4	25·0	26·0	23·8	21·2
Rainfall cm	5·1	2·8	1·2	1·7	3·9	4·6	8·4	11·4	11·9	31·6	34·5	14·8

    (i) **Identify the hottest month.**

    (ii) **Calculate the annual rainfall.**

    (iii) **Name the winds that bring the maximum rainfall to this city.** [2015]

Ans. (a) (i) Kerala lies on the Malabar coast and on the windward side of the South-West monsoon winds. As the Western Ghats obstruct the monsoon winds, it causes very heavy monsoon rainfall for a long duration along this coast.

    (ii) Orographic rainfall is mainly caused by the presence of a relief barrier. The Konkan coast comprises a part of the Western Ghats which obstructs the onshore Arabian sea branch of the South-West monsoon winds. This causes heavy rainfall on the western slopes of the Western Ghats which comprises the windward side of the Konkan coast, while the eastern slopes receive less rainfall resulting in a rain shadow area. Hence, the Konkan coast receives orographic rainfall due to the influence of the Western Ghats.

    (iii) Kanpur has an interior location while Chennai has a coastal location. The areas in the interior of the country have an extreme type of climate resulting in high annual range of temperature while the coastal areas have a moderate climate. This is mainly due to the influence of land and sea breezes caused by differential heating and cooling of land and sea. Therefore, Kanpur has a higher range of temperature than Chennai.

(b) (i) Hottest month is May.

    (ii) Total annual rainfall is 131.9 cm.

    (iii) Retreating monsoon

Q. 7. (a) **Mention a geographical reason for each of the following:**

    (i) **Patna receives heavier rain than Delhi.**

    (ii) **Western Rajasthan receives no rain from the Arabian sea branch of the South-West monsoon winds.**

    (iii) **Mangalore is not cold even in the month of December.**

(b) **Study the climatic data given below and answer the questions that follow:**

Month	JAN.	FEB.	MAR.	APR.	MAY	JUNE	JULY.	AUG.	SEP.	OCT.	NOV.	DEC.
Temp. °C	25·0	25·5	26·3	27·1	30·0	36·2	36·0	35·9	30·3	28·4	27·0	24·6
Rainfall cm	24·5	23·1	15·0	2·4	0·1	11·0	9·3	7·2	4·0	9·4	14·5	20·4

    (i) **Calculate the annual temperature range.**

    (ii) **What is the total annual rainfall?**

    (iii) **Presuming that the station is located in India, give a reason for its location being on the east coast or the west coast of India.** [2014]

Ans. **(a)** **(i)** Patna receives heavier rain than Delhi because the Bay of Bengal branch of South-West monsoon sheds its moisture goes up the Ganga plain. As it proceeds up the Ganga valley, the amount of rainfall keeps decreasing east to west. Since Patna is located to the east of Delhi, it receives 102 cm of rainfall while Delhi gets 50 cm of rainfall, annually.

(ii) The Arabian Sea branch of South-West monsoon strikes the Saurashtra peninsula and passes over the Western Rajasthan, parallel to the Aravalli range. It hardly causes any rain in the Western Rajasthan because it undergoes thermal heating on blowing over the hot sands and gets unsaturated. As the area lies on the leeward side of the Aravalli range, no rain takes place.

(iii) Mangalore is located at the south of Tropic of Cancer along the Western Coast of India and enjoys the moderating influence of land and sea breezes throughout the year. The climate over there being equable or maritime type, the place does not experience any winter.

(b) **(i)** Annual range of temperature = 36·2°C – 24·6°C = 11·6°C.

(ii) Total annual rainfall = 24.5 + 23.1 + 15.0 + 2.4 + 0.1 + 11.0 + 9.3+ 7.2 + 4.0 + 9.4 + 14.5 + 20.4 = 140.9 cm

(iii) The station is located on the east coast of India because heavy rainfall is observed in winter season.

Q. 8. **(a)** **Give reasons for the following:**
(i) When the Malabar coast is receiving heavy rainfall in July, the Tamil Nadu coast is comparatively dry.
(ii) The Northern Plains of India have a continental type of climate.
(iii) Central Maharashtra receives little rainfall.

(b) Study the climatic data given below and answer the questions that follow:

Month	JAN.	FEB.	MAR	APR.	MAY	JUNE	JULY.	AUG.	SEP	OCT.	NOV.	DEC.
Temp. °C	23·1	24·8	26·5	29·3	32	32·8	33·1	32·1	30·5	29·3	28·7	26·1
Rainfall cm	15·3	10·1	0·3	0·1	1·3	4·5	6·1	10·2	10·5	20·1	16·8	19·0

(i) Calculate the annual rainfall experienced by the station.
(ii) Suggest a name of this station, giving a reason for your answer.
(iii) Name the season during which the rainfall is heaviest. [2013]

Ans. **(a)** **(i)** When the Malabar coast is receiving heavy rainfall in July, the Tamil Nadu coast is dry because it lies in rain shadow region of Arabian Sea branch and Bay of Bengal is parallel to the coast.

(ii) Northern Plains experience continental type of climate because they are away from the moderating influence of the sea.

(iii) Central Maharashtra receives little rainfall because it lies in the rain shadow region of the Western Ghats when Arabian Sea branch strikes it.

(b) **(i)** Annual rainfall is 114·3 cm.
(ii) Suggested name is Chennai because the station is receiving most of its rainfall in October and November.
(iii) Retreating monsoon season.

Q. 9. **(a)** **Give geographical reasons for the following:**
(i) Even in summer, Shimla is cooler than Delhi.
(ii) The northern plains of India do not freeze in winter.
(iii) Kochi has a lesser annual range of temperature than Agra.

(b) Study the climatic data given below and answer the questions that follow:

Month	JAN.	FEB.	MAR	APR.	MAY	JUNE	JULY.	AUG.	SEP	OCT.	NOV.	DEC.
Temp. °C	23·8	25·0	27·7	28·3	30·2	30·3	30·4	33·3	30·0	30·3	25·5	24·2
Rainfall cm	0	0	1·1	1·5	2·1	45·3	46·5	45·4	43·3	20·1	3·0	0·1

(i) Calculate the mean annual temperature.
(ii) What is the total rainfall during the monsoon season?
(iii) Does the station have a maritime or a continental climate?

Give a reason for your answer. [2012]

Ans. **(a)** **(i)** Shimla is cooler than Delhi in summer as it is located at a higher altitude than Delhi. Thus due to Normal Lapse Rate, Shimla enjoys a cooler climate than Delhi.

(ii) The Himalayas prevent the bitterly cold winds of the north from entering into India and help to keep the temperature of the northern plains at a moderate level.

(iii) Kochi has a coastal location while Agra has a continental location. Due to the influence of the moist winds from the sea, it experiences moderate climatic conditions throughout the year. Whereas, Agra has extreme temperature conditions resulting in high annual range of temperature.

(b) **(i)** 28°C   **(ii)** 180·5 cm.

Month	JAN.	FEB.	MAR	APR.	MAY	JUNE	JULY.	AUG.	SEP	OCT.	NOV.	DEC.
Temp. °C	24·5	25·7	27·7	20·4	30·0	32·5	31·0	30·2	29·8	28·0	25·9	24·7
Rainfall cm	4·6	1·8	1·3	1·8	3·8	4·5	8·7	11·3	11·9	30·6	35·0	13·9

(i) Name the driest month.

(ii) Calculate the annual rainfall experienced by the station.

(iii)What is the annual range of temperature?   **[2011]**

Ans. **(a)** **(i)** The coastal areas of India do not experience a significant variation in temperature between summer and winter months due to the effect of land and sea breezes caused by differential rate of heating and cooling of the land and sea which results in an equable and moderate climatic conditions.

(ii) The Arabian Sea branch of the South West monsoon which blows towards the Gujarat coast goes of unhindered towards the Himalayas. The Aravalli hills lie parallel to the winds and offer no obstacle to the winds. Rajasthan, therefore, remains dry. The Bay of Bengal branch which blows from the east, sheds its rain on the way and gets dry by the time it reaches the west. Rajasthan also lies in the rain shadow of the Aravalli range. Hence Rajasthan gets little rain, overall about 25 cm.

(iii) The Coromandel coast remains dry during the summer monsoon season because it is located parallel to the Bay of Bengal branch and lies in the leeward side of the Arabian sea branch. However, during the retreating monsoon season, a low pressure condition prevails in the centre of Bay of Bengal and is marked by cyclonic depressions.

(iii) The station has a maritime climate as the range of temperature is very low *i.e.* 6·6°C.

Q. 10. (a) **Give a reason to explain why:**

(i) The coastal areas of India do not experience a significant variation in temperature between summer and winter months.

(ii) The annual rainfall in Rajasthan is less than 25 cm.

(iii)The Coromandel coast gets most of its rain during the winter season.

(b) **Study the climatic data given below and answer the questions that follow:**

These cyclonic depressions move from the north-east to the south-west and results in heavy rainfall.

(b) **(i)** The driest month is March (1.3 cm).

(ii) The annual rainfall experienced by the station is 129.2 cm.

(iii) The annual range of temperature is 12.1°C.

Q. 11. (a) **Give geographical reasons for:**

(i) The rivers of South India are easier to tap for power than the rivers of North India.

(ii) Roads and railways are easier to lay down in the Northern plains than in Peninsular India.   **[2010]**

Ans. **(a)** **(i)** The rivers of South India arise from the Western Ghats. They are not so high as the Himalayas, and hence, it is easier to construct dams to store water and use it for generating electricity.

(ii) The northern plains are one of the most vast level and extensive plains in the world. Peninsular India in the deccan region is rugged. Hence, it is easy to construct roads and railways in the northern plains.

Q. 12. (a) **Name the following:**

(i) The river which is known as the Ganga of the South.

(ii) The plateau in India which is rich in minerals.

(iii) The highest peak in South India.   **[2010]**

Ans. **(a)** **(i)** Godavari

(ii) Deccan Plateau

(iii) Annaimudi

Q. 13. **(a)** Give reasons for the following:

(i) The North-East Monsoons bring almost no rain to most of India.

(ii) The mango showers are beneficial local winds.

(iii) The latitudinal extent of India is responsible for the variation in the climatic conditions which prevail in the country.

(b) Study the climatic data provided below and answer the questions that follow:

Month	Jan.	Feb.	Mar.	Apr.	May	Jun.	Jul.	Aug.	Sep.	Oct.	Nov.	Dec.
Station A												
Temp °C	21.0	22.6	26.3	29.2	29.7	27.5	25.1	24.5	24.8	25.5	22.5	20.5
Rain cm	0.1	0.1	0.5	1.5	2.7	11.4	16.7	9.0	13.4	9.0	2.7	0.3
Station B												
Temp °C	24.4	24.4	26.7	28.3	30.0	28.9	27.2	27.2	27.2	28.3	27.2	25.0
Rain cm	0.2	0.3	0.3	1.7	1.9	50.2	61.0	37.0	27.0	4.8	1.4	0.3

(i) Calculate the annual range of temperature of Station B.

(ii) Calculate annual rainfall of Station A.

(iii) Presuming that both the stations are located in West India, state giving a reason as to which of the two lies on the windward side of the Western Ghats. **[2010]**

Ans. **(a)** **(i)** The North-East Monsoon is a dry wind blowing from the Asian landmass. It collects moisture from the Bay of Bengal. It brings less rain to East India, except the Chennai coast.

(ii) Mango showers are local winds which bring rain to Kerala in the month of May. It is favourable for the growth of mangoes.

(iii) The northern plains lie to north of the Tropic of Cancer in the temperate zone. The winters are much colder. South India lies below the Tropic of Cancer, in the tropics and recieves the direct rays of the Sun. Hence, it is hot most of the year. And the winters are not so cold.

(b) **(i)** $30°C - 24.4°C = 5.6°C$

(ii) 67.4 cm

(iii) Station B lies on the windward side of the Western Ghats as it gets more rainfall in the months of June, July and August.

Soils in India and Natural Vegetation of India

Short Answer Type Questions-I

Q. 1. **(a)** **(i)** Name the parent rock that contributes to the formation of red soil.

      (ii) How does this soil get its 'red' colour?

   (b) Name the following :

      (i) a soil that occurs in situ and is good for cotton crop.

      (ii) Soil that is formed due to high temperature and heavy rainfall.

Ans. **(a)** **(i)** Acid granites and gneisses.

      (ii) Because this soil is composed of high iron content. Gradually, this iron gets oxidized giving red colour.

   (b) **(i)** Black soil.

      (ii) Laterite soil.

Q. 2. **(a)** **(i)** State two ways by which forests help in protecting the environment.

   (b) With reference to Tropical Deciduous forests answer the following questions:

      (i) Name two states where it is found.

      (ii) Name two important trees found in this forest.

Ans. **(a)** **(i)** The two ways are:
- Forests prevent soil erosion.
- They provide habitat to a variety of flora and fauna.

   (b) **(i)** Tropical Deciduous forests are found in Madhya Pradesh and Odisha.

      (ii) Sal and teak.

Q. 3. **(a)** **(i)** Name the Indian soil which is formed due to the weathering of basic igneous rocks.

      (ii) Name two states of India where this type of soil is found.

   (b) Name the following:

      (i) An important transported soil of India.

      (ii) Soil that is rich in iron oxide. [2019]

Ans. **(a)** **(i)** Black soil.

      (ii) Maharashtra and Gujarat.

   (b) **(i)** Alluvial soil.

      (ii) Red soil.

Q. 4. **(a)** Give *two reasons* to explain as to why we need to conserve our forest resource.

   (b) **(i)** Mention two conditions required for the growth of Littoral Forest.

      (ii) State *one characteristic* feature of the forest found in the Nilgiri Hills. [2019]

Ans. **(a)** The conservation of forest resources is essential for the survival of human beings, wildlife and other species, as forests play an important role in the development of soil and enriching its fertility, conserving water in the subsoil, absorbing insolation, causing rain, maintaining ecological balance, preventing floods and soil erosion.

   (b) **(i)** Conditions required for the growth of littoral forests are:

      1. Delta regions or creeks and estuaries which are prone to tidal influence.

      2. Temperature 26°C to 29°C.

      3. Rainfall over 200 cm.

      (ii) Mountain forests consist of mixed deciduous and coniferous trees in transition zone. The main tree is Eucalyptus. The forests are characterized by giant, multilayered species with luxuriant vegetation. The height of the trees goes up to 150 feet and may be supported by buttresses.

Q. 5. **(a)** **(i)** Why does alluvial soil differ in texture?

      (ii) State two cash crops that grow well in alluvial soil.

   (b) With reference to *black soil* answer the following:

      (i) Name one important crop which grows in this soil.

      (ii) Give one chemical property of this soil. [2018]

Ans. **(a)** **(i)** Alluvial soil differs in texture as it is formed by the deposition of rivers and it is composed of pure substances like silica, clay and chalk. Coarse material is deposited in higher altitude areas and fine material is brought to lower plain.

    (ii) Sugarcane, Jute.
  (b)   **(i)** Cotton.
    (ii) It contains high quantity of lime, iron, alumina, potash, calcium and magnesium carbonate, but lacks in phosphorus and nitrogen.

Q. 6. **(a)** **(i)** Name an area in India where Tropical Monsoon forest is found.
    (ii) How is this forest of great commercial value to India?
  (b) With reference to Littoral forest, answer the following questions:
    (i) Why do the trees in this forest grow aerial roots?
    (ii) Name one area in India where this forest is found.   **[2018]**

Ans. **(a)** **(i)** Tropical monsoon forests are found in the foothills of Himalayas, eastern slopes of Western Ghats, Shiwalik range and the northeastern part of the Deccan plateau.
    (ii) The tropical monsoon forests provide valuable timber from teak, sal and shisham trees thereby increasing its commercial value to India.
  (b) **(i)** Trees in the littoral forest grow aerial roots as these trees grow in swampy areas. Thus these roots help the plant to survive in the shifting mud of the coastal region which is affected by tides by acting like respiratory organs.
    (ii) Sunderbans in West Bengal.

Q. 7. **(a)** Mention two differences between Alluvial Soil and Black Cotton Soil.
  (b) Name an area in India in which each of the following processes take place:
    (i) Sheet erosion
    (ii) Gully erosion   **[2017]**

Ans.

(a)

Alluvial Soil	Black Cotton Soil
1. It is transported soil which is brought down by the agents of erosion.	**1.** It is residual soil which is formed by denudation of lava rocks.
2. It is pale brown in colour, sandy in texture.	**2.** It varies in colour from deep black to chestnut brown, clayey in texture.
3. It is replenished by floods during rainy season.	**3.** This soil is formed in situ.
4. It is found in the flood plains and delta regions.	**4.** It is found in the Deccan Trap region.

  (b) **(i)** The flood plains of Kosi, Damodar, Nilgiris.
    (ii) Chambal valley.

Q. 8. **(a)** How do trees in the Tropical Desert forests adapt themselves to the dry climate?
  (b) Name the tree as per its characteristics given below:
    (i) The wood is hard and suitable for shipbuilding.
    (ii) The stilt roots are underwater during high tide.   **[2017]**

Ans. **(a)** **1.** The tropical desert forests are xerophyte in nature. They have very thin leaves or no leaves.
    2. Their stems and leaves are often covered by sharp spines and thorns.
    3. They have long roots to draw water as the rainfall is scarce and also have thick fleshy stems to store water during drought.
  (b) **(i)** Teak.
    (ii) Sundari.

Q. 9. **(a)** What is soil erosion? Mention two steps that could be taken to prevent soil erosion.
  (b) Mention two similarities between red soil and laterite soil.   **[2016]**

Ans. **(a)** Soil erosion is the removal of top soil by different agents of weathering like running water, wind, overgrazing, etc.

The two steps to prevent soil erosion are:
1. Afforestation
2. Terrace farming

  (b) Both the soils are of red colour due to the presence of iron oxide. They are also not moisture-retentive.

Q. 10. **(a)** **(i)** Name the forest which is commercially most important in India.
    (ii) Name two trees which grow in this forest.
  (b) **(i)** Name the forests which grow on the windward slope of the Western Ghats.
    (ii) Why do such forests grow in this region?   **[2016]**

Ans. **(a)** **(i)** Tropical deciduous forests.
    (ii) Teak, Sal, and Sandalwood **(Any two)**
  (b) **(i)** Tropical Evergreen forests/Tropical rainforests grow on the windward slopes of Western Ghats.
    (ii) Tropical Evergreen forests are found in regions receiving more than 200 cm of rainfall and where the annual temperature is 25°C to 27°C. The windward slopes of the Western

Ghats experience the same climatic conditions, making it suitable for the growth of these forests.

Q. 11. (a) State the characteristic of each of the soils named below that makes them most suitable for crop cultivation:

(i) Black soil

(ii) Red soil

(b) State the geographic term for each of the following processes:

(i) The process by which soluble minerals dissolve in rainwater and percolate to the bottom, leaving the top soil infertile.

(ii) The process by which rainwater, flowing in definite paths, removes the top soil, thus causing deep cuts to the surface of the land. **[2015]**

Ans. **(a)** **(i)** Black soil is suitable for crop cultivation as it is clayey in nature and has high water holding capacity. Moreover, it is rich in lime, iron, magnesium, etc.

(ii) Red soil is suitable for crop cultivation as it is rich in potash and iron. Red soil responds well to irrigation and fertilizers, and thus stands suitable for crop cultivation.

(b) **(i)** Leaching

(ii) Gully erosion

Q. 12. (a) State two characteristics of Tropical Deciduous forests.

(b) State two reasons why Tropical Evergreen forests are difficult to exploit. **[2015, 2012]**

Ans. **(a)** Two characteristics of Tropical Deciduous forests are:

(i) The trees shed their leaves for 6-8 weeks in the hot weather season.

(ii) The trees occur in pure stands.

(b) Tropical Evergreen forests are difficult to exploit due to the following two reasons:

(i) The forests are dark and dense multi-layered and the forest floor is covered with shrubs and undergrowths. This makes the exploitation difficult.

(ii) Moreover, the trees do not occur in pure stands and are hard woods, making it difficult to carry.

Q. 13. (a) State any two methods of controlling soil erosion.

(b) Mention two differences between alluvial soil and red soil. **[2014]**

Ans. **(a)** **(i)** Terrace farming.

(ii) Planting shelter belts to check the speed of wind in the dry areas.

(b)

Alluvial Soil	Red Soil
(i) Alluvial soil is transported soil.	Red soil is residual (in situ) soil.
(ii) Alluvial soil is highly moisture-retentive and fertile.	Red soil is not highly moisture-retentive and infertile.

Q. 14. (a) Write two reasons why monsoon deciduous forests are commercially more valuable than other types of forests.

(b) How do forests:

(i) have a favourable effect on the climate of the region?

(ii) act as a flood control measure? **[2014]**

Ans. **(a)** The monsoon deciduous forests are commercially more valuable because:

(i) They are found in pure stands.

(ii) They are not as dense as the tropical evergreen forests.

(iii) They yield valuable timber.

(b) **(i)** Forests transmit moisture into the air by the means of transpiration which induces precipitation. Forests turn carbon dioxide into oxygen, and thus help to purify the air we breathe.

(ii) The roots of plants and trees hold the soil, and thus forests check or prevent soil erosion, especially in hilly areas. Hence, they also help in checking floods.

Q. 15. (a) State two differences between Bhangar and Khadar.

(b) Name the process by which Laterite soil is formed. Mention one disadvantage of this soil. **[2013]**

Ans. **(a)**

Khadar	Bhangar
(i) Clayey	Siliceous.
(ii) Replenished by floods therefore more fertile.	Not replenished hence less fertile.

(b) Laterite soil is formed by leaching in the region of alternate wet and dry spells. Disadvantage: It is acidic in nature and cannot retain moisture.

Q. 16. (a) Mention two main characteristics of Tropical Rainforests.

(b) Briefly explain two reasons for forests being an important natural resource. **[2013]**

Ans. **(a)** 1. Trees are dense and evergreen.

2. The thick ground cover of forests is characterized by climbers and epiphytes.

(b) Forests are an important natural resource because:
   (i) They provide timber, medicinal plants, etc.
   (ii) They help in purifying air and bringing rain.

Q. 17. (a) State two methods of controlling the erosion of soil caused by running water.
(b) Mention two differences in the alluvial soil of the northern plains and the alluvial soil on the coastal plains of India. [2012]

Ans. **(a)** **(i)** Soil erosion can be prevented by growing more trees and grass to bind the soil.
   (ii) Plugging of gullies and ravines.

(b)

Alluvial Soil of Northern Plains	Alluvial Soil on the Coastal Plains
(1) Light in colour	Dark in colour
(2) Sandy	Clayey
(3) Porous	Non-porous
(4) Coarse in texture	Fine in texture

Q. 18. Give two characteristics of Tidal forests. [2012]

Ans. Two characteristics of Tidal forests are:
   (i) They thrive in saline conditions.
   (ii) They possess breathing roots or pneumatophores.

Q. 19. (a) Name two states in India where Regur soil is found. In what way does Regur soil help in agriculture?
(b) Mention two main characteristics of Laterite soil. [2011]

Ans. **(a)** Two states in India where Regur soil is found are Maharashtra and Gujarat.
Regur soil has high quantities of lime, iron and magnesium. Moreover, it is clayey in nature which makes it highly retentive of moisture. These characteristics make the soil suitable for different types of crops like cotton, jowar, wheat, sugarcane, linseed and grass.

(b) **(i)** Coarse, porous leached soil.
   (ii) Poor in lime, nitrogen, magnesium, low moisture retentive and infertile.

Q. 20. (a) What are 'Tidal forests'? Name two typical trees found there.
(b) Write two main characteristics of the Deciduous Monsoon forests. [2011]

Ans. **(a)** Tidal forests are found in wet marshy areas, river deltas, saline or swampy areas along the sea coast. These forests consist of evergreen species with stilt roots which are submerged under water.
Two typical trees found there are Sundari and Casuarina.

(b) Two characteristics of Deciduous Monsoon forests are:
   (i) The trees of these forests shed their leaves for six to eight weeks during spring and early summer.
   (ii) The trees occur in pure stands which makes it suitable for commercial exploitation.

Q. 21. (a) Name the soil which:
   (i) covers the summits of the Eastern Ghats.
   (ii) makes up the delta of the River Ganga.
   (iii) is the most suitable for the cultivation of cotton.
   (iv) is sticky when wet and cracks when dry.
(b) What is soil conservation? How does reafforestation help in soil conservation? [2010]

Ans. **(a)** **(i)** Laterite soil
   (ii) Alluvial soil
   (iii) Black soil
   (iv) Black soil

(b) Soil conservation refers to the methods of protecting the soil from erosion.
Roots of the trees protect the soil by holding it in place against agents like wind and water. Reafforestation means replanting trees which have been cut down. For every tree that is cut, two or more trees are grown. And in this way, forest cover increases.

Short Answer Type Questions-II

Q. 1. **(a) With reference to Alluvial Soil answer the following:**
   (i) What are the two types of Alluvial Soil?
   (ii) Name an area where Alluvial soil is found.
   (iii) Name two crops that grow well in this soil.

(b) **(i) Define the term 'Residual' soil.**
   (ii) Name two crops that are grown on laterite soil.

(iii) Name two important agents of soil erosion.

Ans. **(a)** **(i)** The two types of Alluvial soil are young khadar soil and old bhangar soil.

(ii) Alluvial soil is found mainly in riverine plains of North India and deltaic coastal strip of eastern coastal plains.

(iii) Alluvial soil is ideal for the production of wheat and sugarcane.

(b) **(i)** Residual soil means those which are formed due to insitu weathering of the parent rock.

(ii) Laterite soil is suitable for plantation crops like rubber and coffee.

(iii) Two important agents of soil erosion are wind and running water.

Q. 2. **(a)** Briefly explain the following:

(i) Why are Tropical Evergreen forests called "Evergreen"?

(ii) Why is afforestation essential in the cities that have Iron and Steel industries?

(iii) How do forests act as a source of income for the people.

(b) Give a reason for each of the following:

(i) The Tropical Deciduous forests is commercially the most important forest belt in India.

(ii) Tropical Evergreen forests occur on the windward side of Western Ghats.

(iii) It is very difficult to move through tidal forests.

Ans. **(a)** **(i)** Because they do not shed their leaves at the same time and thus appear green always.

(ii) Because trees provide clean environment as they take carbon dioxide and provide the surroundings with oxygen.

(iii) Forests provide useful timber, medicinal plants and many other products which have very high market value.

(d) **(i)** Tropical Deciduous forests yield valuable timber and other products. Species like teak, sal, sandalwood, eucalyptus have very high commercial value.

(ii) It is so because windward side of Western Ghats receives very high amount of rainfall (more than 400 cms).

(iii) It is so because tidal forests are very dense, having deep roots and are found in marshy areas.

Q. 3. **(a)** Give a geographical reason for each of the following:

(i) Terrace farming is an ideal soil conservation method for hilly regions.

(ii) Dry farming is preferred in areas with red soil.

(iii) Wind is a common agent of soil erosion in arid regions.

(b) Briefly answer the following:

(i) Mention one way in which man is responsible for soil erosion.

(ii) How can deepening of the river beds help in preventing soil erosion?

(iii) Mention a physical characteristic of Laterite soil. [2019]

📑 Marking Scheme

(a) **(i)** Terraces check the speed of running water and thus reduce the chance for erosion.

(ii) Red soil is ideal for dry farming because it is porous and does not retain moisture.

(iii) Soil erosion by wind is common in arid regions because arid areas do not support vegetation and since there are no roots to hold the soil together, the wind can carry away the loose soil easily/wind speed is high due to absence of obstruction.

(b) **(i)** Man is responsible for soil erosion because of large scale deforestation done for agriculture/industrialisation/urbanisation/ he allows his livestock to overgraze land/faulty farming practices/mining/ construction/quarrying, excessive usage of chemical fertiliser, pesticide or insecticide/ shifting agriculture. *(Any one)*

(ii) Deepening the river bed increases the capacity of the river to hold water which then will not overflow to cause soil erosion.

(iii) It is red in colour/dry/porous/hardens when dry/coarse/does not retain moisture/soft and friable/colour varies from red to brown to yellow. *(Any one)*

Ans. **(a)** **(i)** Terrace farming checks erosion as it controls the direct flow of water down the slopes.

(ii) Regions that receive less than 75 cm of rainfall are suitable for dry farming. Crops like millets, pulses, oil seeds need less rainfall and grow well in red soil. So, dry farming is preferred in areas of red soil.

(iii) Arid regions are extensive flat lands with no or few vegetation cover. So, when dry winds blow over these regions, the upper soil surface becomes loose due to lack of moisture.

(b) **(i)** Man's activities like construction work, ploughing, cutting down trees, quarrying, mining causes soil erosion.

(ii) Much of the soil erosion caused by floods can be checked by deepening of the river beds. Deepening the river beds increases the capacity of the river to hold water and thus reduces the speed of the overflowing water. This greatly helps in preventing large scale soil erosion.

(iii) Laterite soil is reddish brown in colour due to the presence of iron oxide. It is coarse and porous in nature.

Q. 4. **(a)** **(i) Give *two reasons* to explain as to why the Tropical Evergreen Forests are difficult to exploit for commercial purpose.**

(ii) Name any *two trees* found in Tropical Evergreen forests.

(b) Briefly explain each of the following:

(i) The trees in the Tropical Desert Forest have stunted growth.

(ii) There is a gradual increase in the forest cover in India in recent times.

(iii) The trees in Monsoon Deciduous forests, shed their leaves for about 6-8 weeks during March and April.

[2019]

📋 Marking Scheme ------------------------------------

(a) (i) – Thick under growth / inaccessible
– Trees are not in pure stand/mixed stand.
– Heavy rainfall.
– Lack of transportation.
– Hard wood difficult to cut.
– Dark and dense/marshy area/ very tall trees/water logging. *(Any two points)*

(ii) Rosewood, Ironwood, Ebony, Cinchona, Mahogany, bamboo. *(Any one)*

(b) (i) This is due to non-availability of enough water for growth of trees.

(ii) This is due to check on deforestation/ banning shifting agriculture/government initiative such as agroforestry, farm forestry, social forestry, Van Mahotsav, afforestation and re-afforestation.

(iii) Lack of sufficient moisture for leaves to withstand dry weather conditions/to conserve moisture/to reduce loss of water through transpiration, to have less surface area/subsoil water is not enough for trees to retain leaf cover/to survive heat and drought condition during autumn, spring and early summer.

Ans. **(a)** **(i)** Tropical Evergreen Forests are difficult to exploit due to:
1. Dense undergrowth.
2. Lack of transport facilities.
3. Absence of trees found in pure stands.
4. Logs are heavy so, they do not float in the river. Thus adding to transportation expense.

(ii) Rosewood, Ebony, Mahogany, Shisham.

(b) **(i)** The trees in the tropical desert forest have stunted growth due to constant wind and scarce water supply.

(ii) 1. There is gradual increase in the forest cover due to programmes like 'Van Mahotsava' under which all government employees plant trees.

2. Due to Afforestation scheme in which trees are planted in Rajasthan, West Uttar Pradesh and Kutch region.

3. Due to Reafforestation scheme in which 2 saplings, are planted for every tree that is cut.

(iii) Trees of monsoon deciduous forests shed their leaves for about 6-8 weeks during March and April. To prevent transpiration and to preserve water for survival in dry months.

Q. 5. **(a) Give one geographical reason for each of the following:**

(i) Red soil requires irrigation.

(ii) Afforestation prevents soil from getting eroded.

(iii) Laterite soil is red in colour.

(b) **(i) What is soil erosion?**

(ii) Mention two causes of soil erosion in India. **[2018]**

📋 Marking Scheme ------------------------------------

(a) (i) Red soil need irrigation as it does not retain moisture since it is highly porous.

(ii) The roots of the trees hold the soil together.

(iii) Rich in iron oxide

(b) (i) Removal and destruction of soil is called soil erosion.

(ii) Causes – deforestation/poor farming techniques/overgrazing/wind/heavy rainfall/human activities/running water shifting cultivation.

Ans. **(a)** **(i)** Red soil requires irrigation as it is coarse, porous and crumbly; and its water retaining capacity is less.

(ii) Afforestation prevents soil from getting eroded as the roots of the trees bind the soil, thus preventing soil erosion.

  (iii) Laterite soil is red in colour due to the presence of iron oxide.

(b) **(i)** The removal of the top layer of soil by water, wind and human activities is known as soil erosion.

  (ii) Two causes of soil erosion in India are:

    1. Running water.

    2. Overgrazing.

Q. 6. **(a)** **(i)** Name a state in India where thorn and scrub forest is found.

  (ii) Give two ways by which the trees that are found here have adapted to the climate.

(b) **(i)** Give two ways in which forests are important.

  (ii) Mention one forest conservation method followed in India. **[2018]**

📋 Marking Scheme

(a) **(i)** S.W. Punjab, U.P., Central & eastern Rajasthan, M.P., Gujarat.

  (ii) Trees have adapted by developing long roots, leaves turning to spines, thick fleshy stems to store water drought resistant/ xerophytic.

(b) **(i)** Forests are moderators of climate, play important role in carbon cycle, control soil erosion, help water percolation, add humus to soil and are habitat for animals and birds. Maintain ecological balance.

  (ii) Afforestation/re-afforestation/Van Mahotsav/ social forestry/farm forestry, agroforestry/ silviculture/joint forest management.

Ans. **(a)** **(i)** South-West Punjab

  (ii) Two ways by which the trees in Rajasthan have adapted to the climate are:

    1. Trees have long tapering roots.

    2. They have thorny branches with small fleshy leaves turning to spines.

(b) **(i)** Two ways in which forests are important:

    1. Forests prevent soil erosion and help in minimising pollution and water percolation.

    2. Forests are the moderators of climate, they control humidity, temperature and precipitation.

  (ii) Afforestation around industrial units is one of the forest conservation methods followed in India.

Q. 7. **(a)** **What is soil conservation? State a method of soil conservation in the:**

  (i) **Arid and Semi-arid region**

  (ii) **River valleys prone to flood**

(b) **Name the soil which:**

  (i) **is good for cultivation of sugarcane**

  (ii) **is acidic in nature**

  (iii) **occurs ex situ.** **[2017]**

Ans. **(a)** Soil conservation is a method of preventing soil erosion to retain the fertility of the soil.

  (i) **Arid and Semi-arid region:** Belts of trees, and shrubs should be planted to check the velocity of wind, and thus to prevent soil erosion.

  (ii) **River valleys prone to flood:** Dams and barrages should be constructed so that they check the speed of water and prevent soil from eroding. Afforestation is another method to prevent soil erosion.

(b) **(i)** Alluvial soil/Black soil.

  (ii) Laterite soil.

  (iii) Alluvial soil.

Q. 8. **(a)** **Explain why the forest cover in India is shrinking?**

(b) **Name the natural vegetation found in the following regions:**

  (i) **The western slopes of the Western Ghats.**

  (ii) **The Nilgiris.**

  (iii) **Western Rajasthan.** **[2017]**

Ans. **(a)** Forest cover in India is shrinking for the following reasons:

  1. Increasing urbanisation and industrialisation is an important cause of degradation of forest areas.

  2. Construction of hydroelectric projects have caused submergence of forest area, faulty agricultural practices like Jhumming.

  3. Human activities like mining, quarrying and building have resulted in deforestation on a large scale.

  4. Growing demand for agricultural land with growing population and demand for food products has caused considerable shrinkage of forest areas.

(b) **(i)** Tropical evergreen forests.

  (ii) Mountain forests

  (iii) Desert or semi-desert vegetation.

Q. 9. **(a)** **Give a geographical reason for each of the following:**

  (i) **Alluvial soil differs in texture.**

  (ii) **Black soil does not get leached.**

  (iii) **Khadar is more fertile than bhangar.**

(b) **Define the following:**

  (i) **Sheet erosion**

(ii) Soil conservation

(iii) In situ soil [2016]

Ans. **(a)** **(i)** Alluvial soil is coarse in the upper valley of the rivers because the eroded matter is carried away by the fast flowing river but in the lower course, the river reduces its speed and the soil particles become finer due to attrition or because the load itself gets eroded.

(ii) Black soil does not get leached because it is clayey and sticky and moisture retentive and therefore the rain connot wash out the silicates.

(iii) Khadar is the newer alluvium which keeps setting replenished by the river bringing down more eroded material.

(b) **(i)** **Sheet erosion:** It is the slow removal of a thin layer of soil by rainwater washing it away.

(ii) **Soil conservation:** Soil conservation refers to the steps taken to protect the soil from erosion to retain the fertility of the soil.

(iii) **In situ soil:** In situ means to develop in one area without any movement. In situ soil has not been transported from its original place of deposition. For example, black soil.

Q. 10. **(a)** **To which type of forest do the following trees belong?**

(i) Hintal and Sundari

(ii) Rosewood and Ebony

(iii) Deodar and Chir Pine

(b) **Give three reasons for rapid depletion of forest resources in India in the past.** [2016]

Ans. **(a)** **(i)** Littoral or tidal or mangrove forests

(ii) Tropical evergreen forest/Tropical rainforest

(iii) Mountain forest

(b) **(i)** **Shifting cultivation:** Jhumming or shifting agriculture by tribals in the hilly areas of North-east India caused extensive damage.

(ii) **Growing demand for agricultural land:** With growing population, demand for food products and agricultural raw materials increased significantly. This had caused considerable shrinkage in forest area.

(iii) **Growing human activity:** Human activities like mining, quarrying, urbanisation, industrialisation and construction of hydroelectric projects like Narmada Project have caused submergence or degradation of forests.

Q. 11. **(a)** **Define the following:**

(i) Pedogenesis **(ii) Humus**

(iii) Bhangar.

(b) **Give a geographic reason for each of the following:**

(i) Alluvial soil is extremely fertile.

(ii) Need for soil conservation.

(iii) Reafforestation should be practised extensively. [2015]

Ans. **(a)** **(i)** Pedogenesis refers to the process of soil formation. Soils are derived by the weathering of parent rock materials which combine with decomposed vegetable and animal remains adding to the fertility of the soil.

(ii) Humus refers to the organic matter present in the soil. It mainly comprises dead and decomposed plant and animal remains.

(iii) Bhangar refers to the old alluvial soil found about 30 m above sea level in river terraces. It is light grey in colour and consists of calcareous clay.

(b) **(i)** Alluvial soil is extremely fertile because it is rich in various minerals such as potash, humus and lime. Moreover, it is clayey in nature and has high water holding capacity. This makes it suitable for the cultivation of various types of crops.

(ii) Soil conservation is necessary as the removal of the topsoil results in loss of fertility, decreases soil moisture, and increase the frequency of floods and droughts.

(iii) Reafforestation should be practised extensively in order to compensate for the large scale deforestation occurring because of industrialisation and other factors, which result in land degradation.

Q. 12. **(a)** **Identify the tree as per its characteristics mentioned below:**

(i) It yields wood that is hard and scented and is usually found in high altitudes.

(ii) It is generally found in deltaic regions and is used to make boats.

(iii) The furniture made from the wood of this tree is generally the most expensive.

(b) Differentiate between afforestation and deforestation. State a disadvantage of deforestation. [2015]

Ans. **(a)** **(i)** Deodar

(ii) Sundari

(iii) Mahogany

(b)

Afforestation	Deforestation
It is the planting of trees in abandoned areas, or any other suitable place, in order to improve the environment.	It is the process of cutting down trees for various purposes like, industrialisation, colonisation, etc.

Disadvantage of deforestation:

1. Loss of flora and fauna.
2. Loosening of soil particles, which eventually results in soil erosion and surface water run off.
3. Increase in temperatures / floods.
4. An imbalance is generated amongst the soil minerals, and the soil loses its fertility and mineral content.

(Any one)

Q. 13. (a) Give a geographical reason for:

(i) different regions in India having different kinds of soil.

(ii) black soil being suitable for growth of cotton.

(iii) the conservation of soil as a natural resource.

(b) Name the soil which:

(i) is good for the cultivation of cashew nuts.

(ii) covers almost all of West Bengal.

(iii) is a result of leaching. [2014]

Ans. **(a)** **(i)** Factors affecting soil formation are climate, vegetation, parent rock, relief and slope of the land. India has varied relief features, landforms, climatic realms and vegetation types. These have led to the development of a variety of soils in the country.

(ii) Black soil contains lime, alumina, iron, potash, magnesium and calcium, and also retains moisture which helps the growth of cotton plants.

(iii) As the soil helps us to get most of our food and clothing directly or indirectly and also ensures agricultural prosperity of a country, availability of soil is most critical. Retaining of this valuable resource by way of soil conservation is important and essential.

(b) **(i)** Laterite soil

(ii) Alluvial soil

(iii) Laterite soil

Q. 14. (a) Give one important use of each of the following types of trees:

(i) Sundari **(ii) Sandalwood**

(iii) Rosewood

(b) Name the natural vegetation largely found in the following regions:

(i) The delta of the Ganga river.

(ii) The windward side of the Western Ghats.

(iii) The Deccan Plateau. [2014]

Ans. **(a)** **(i)** Sundari trees are ideal for building boats as they are hardwood, light-weighted and durable.

(ii) Sandalwood is a fragrant wood which is used to make incense sticks, decorative articles and oil. The oil is added to cosmetics, bathing soaps, etc.

(iii) Rosewood is termite resistant, and is used for making expensive furniture and carvings.

(b) **(i)** Mangrove or littoral forests

(ii) Tropical evergreen forests.

(iii) Monsoon deciduous forests.

Q. 15. (a) Differentiate between Transported soil and In Situ soil, quoting a suitable example for each.

(b) With reference to Red soil in India, answer the following questions:

(i) Name two states where it is found.

(ii) State two advantages of this type of soil.

(iii) Mention two important crops grown in this soil. [2013]

Ans. **(a)** Transported Soil: If a soil is carried elsewhere by the agents of gradation from the place of its origin, it is called transported soil *e.g.*—Alluvial soil.

In Situ Soil: If the soil remains at the place of its origin, it is called in situ *e.g.* Black soil.

(b) With reference to Red Soil:

(i) Tamil Nadu and Karnataka.

(ii) Advantages:

(1) It has high iron oxide content and potash.

(2) It becomes productive with proper use of fertilizers.

(iii) Important crops are rice, millets and sugarcane.

Q. 16. (a) Name the tree, the timber of which could be used for the following:

(i) A soft and white timber used for making toys and match boxes.

     (ii) **A hard durable timber used for ship building and furniture making.**

     (iii) **A sweet smelling timber which yields an oil, used for making handicrafts.**

  (b) (i) **Name one region in India for each of the following:**

     (1) Tidal forests.

     (2) Thorn and Shrubs.

    (ii) **Explain why thorns and shrubs forests are found in the above-mentioned region.** **[2013]**

Ans. (a) (i) Semal   (ii) Teak

    (iii) Sandalwood.

  (b) (i) 1. **Tidal forests:** Deltas of Ganga, Mahanadi, Godavari, Krishna and Kaveri.

    2. **Thorn and shrubs forests:** Rajasthan and Gujarat.

    (ii) Thorn and Shrubs forests found in regions of Rajasthan and Gujarat because these areas experience less than 25 cm of rainfall and average temperature of 25°C to 27°C.

Q. 17. (a) **Mention any three characteristics of black soil which makes the soil fertile.**

  (b) **Give geographical reasons for the following:**

    (i) **Laterite soil is not suitable for cultivation.**

    (ii) **Red soil is red in colour.**

    (iii) **Khadar soils are preferred to Bhangar soils.** **[2012]**

Ans. (a) (i) Rich in iron, potash, lime, calcium and humus.

    (ii) It is clayey in nature so has high water holding capacity.

    (iii) It develops cracks when dry and hence has self-ploughing characteristics.

  (b) (i) Laterite soil is acidic in nature and has low water retaining capacity. It is poor in nitrogen and lime.

    (ii) Red soil has high percentage of iron oxides which makes it red in colour.

    (iii) Khadar soils are preferred to Bhangar soils as they are replenished every year by floods.

Q. 18. (a) **Mention three reasons why forests must be conserved.**

  (b) **Name any three trees found in monsoon deciduous forests and state one use of each of these trees.** **[2012]**

Ans. (a) Three reasons to conserve forests are:

    (i) Forest conservation is needed to prevent soil erosion.

    (ii) Forest conservation helps to save the habitat of the wild animals.

    (iii) It also prevents desertification and floods.

  (b) Three trees found in monsoon deciduous forests and their uses are:

    (i) **Sal:** Used for furniture making, railway sleepers.

    (ii) **Sandalwood:** Used for extracting sandalwood oil, handicrafts and perfumes.

    (iii) **Mulberry:** Used for rearing silkworms.

Q. 19. (a) **State the difference between Alluvial soils found in the lower courses and the upper courses of rivers.**

  (b) **Name two important agents of erosion. For each, state one method of controlling the erosion caused.** **[2011]**

Ans. (a) Difference between alluvial soils in the upper and lower courses of the rivers:

Upper course	Lower course
(i) It is coarser, *i.e.* particles are bigger in size.	It is finer and finest in the lowest section.
(ii) It is dry and less compact.	It is moist and more compact.

  (b) The two important agents of erosion are:

    (i) Water   (ii) Wind.

  Methods of controlling erosion:

    (i) **Erosion by water:** During heavy downpours deep 'gullies' are made on account of water run off. Gully erosion can be stopped by plugging it with stones and pebbles or quick growing grasses can be grown in gullies to stop its expansion.

    (ii) **Erosion by wind:** Wind erosion reduces the productive capacity of the soil by removing the loose particles of soil with the high velocity wind. The nutrients required by the plants are taken away by the wind. Therefore, more and more trees should be planted along the edges of the fields, waste land and also on the steep slopes. If it is difficult to grow trees, grass should be grown but no land should be left devoid of plants.

Q. 20. (a) **Name the type of forests found in the western part of the Western Ghats.**

  Give two reasons why these forests are so named.

(b) Mention three methods for the conservation and development of forests in India. **[2011]**

Ans. **(a)** The Tropical Evergreen forests are found in the western part of the Western Ghats. The trees of Tropical Evergreen forests are so called because the trees in these forests do not have a fixed time to shed their leaves. Thus they appear evergreen throughout the year. Moreover, these forests receive very heavy rainfall. The high humidity in these forests does not necessitate the trees to shed their leaves during a particular part of the year, to check the loss of moisture through evaporation of water via transpiration. Thus the forests appear evergreen, as they do not shed their leaves during a particular time of the year.

(b) Three methods for the conservation and development of forests in India are:

(i) Increasing the practise of afforestation.

(ii) Some forest regions are being declared 'Reserved Sanctuaries' to preserve the ecosystem and protect animals.

(iii) Afforestation and Reafforestation: Afforestation is the planting of more trees and Reafforestation is to plant trees in place of those which are cut down. The policy of the Government is to plant two trees in place of every one tree that is cut.

Q. 21. **(a)** Name the process by which laterite soil is formed. What climatic conditions are responsible for its formation?

(b) Give reasons for:

(i) Black soil is largely found in the Deccan Trap region.

(ii) Khadar is more fertile than Bhangar.

(iii) Soil erosion by wind is common in arid regions. **[2010]**

Ans. **(a)** Laterite soil is the result of intensive leaching brought on by heavy rains. It is found in regions having high temperature and heavy rainfall with alternating wet and dry periods which is typical of monsoon lands.

(b) **(i)** Black soil is formed as a result of the denudation of the lava flow brought on by the volcanic activity in the Deccan Plateau in the past.

(ii) Khadar alluvium is more fertile than Bhangar alluvium as it is replenished by floods every year. It is free from kankar (lime nodules). Bhangar alluvium is found on river terraces. It is free from floods. It contains kankar which make it less fertile.

(iii) Arid regions have no vegetation cover. The wind blows away fine particles of sand depositing them in other areas rendering both areas unproductive.

Short Answer Type Questions-I

Q. 1. (a) Mention any two methods of recharging ground water aquifers.

(b) (i) Name the most common means of irrigation used in India.

(ii) Give one reason for the popularity of this means of irrigation in our country.

Ans. (a) Groundwater aquifers can be recharged through flooding and check dam method.

(b) (i) Canal irrigation

(ii) Canal irrigation is cheaper in long run.

Q. 2. (a) "The modern means of irrigation are gaining popularity."
Give *two reasons* to justify this statement.

(b) Mention *two factors* that favour the development of tube well irrigation in Punjab. **[2019]**

Ans. (a) The modern means of irrigation like sprinkler or drip irrigation are by far the best methods for conserving water as:
1. There is no wastage of water due to seepage or evaporation.
2. High application efficiency.
3. Labour cost is less.
4. Prevents water pollution.

(b) Two reasons for development of tube well irrigation in Punjab are:
1. Soft alluvial soil facilitate digging as deep as required.
2. Cheap HEP is available to draw water through the tube well.
3. High water table with perennial water supply.

Q. 3. (a) There is plenty of rain in India during the rainy season, yet we need irrigation. Give two reasons to support this statement.

(b) (i) Name three traditional means of irrigation.

(ii) Give a reason why traditional means of irrigation are still important in most parts of India. **[2018]**

Ans. (a) Rainfall in India is uneven, seasonal and unequal. Monsoons cause rainfall only for 3 to 4 months in a year, but for crops to grow, water is required all round the year. Thus, irrigation is needed although India receives plenty of rain during the rainy season.

(b) (i) Wells, tanks and canals.

(ii) Traditional means of irrigation are still important in most parts of India as they involve low initial cost burden, easy to operate and easily accessible to farmers.

Q. 4. (a) Give a reason for the significance of irrigation in:
(i) Punjab (ii) Rajasthan

(b) Name a state where:
(i) Tube wells are common.
(ii) Tank irrigation is popular. **[2017]**

Ans. (a) (i) **Punjab:** South-West monsoon brings rain only during the period from end of July to middle of September. Otherwise monsoon is sporadic, erratic, uncertain and unevenly distributed. To meet the demand for water in dry season, irrigation is needed.

Some crops like rice, sugarcane needs more water. Punjab receives rainfall of about 50 cm annually. So, there is a need for irrigation to grow crops throughout the year.

(ii) **Rajasthan:** Rajasthan receives 25 cm-50 cm of rainfall from South-west monsoon. To meet the growing demand of food for the growing population, irrigation is required with the right amount of water at the right time, *e.g.* cotton.

(b) (i) Uttar Pradesh/Bihar/Punjab/Haryana.
(ii) Andhra Pradesh / Telangana / Tamil Nadu.

Q. 5. (a) "Without irrigation, development of agriculture is difficult in India." Clarify the statement by giving two reasons.

(b) Mention two factors which are essential for the development of tube well irrigation. **[2016]**

Ans. **(a)** The rainfall in India is restricted from June to September except in Tamil Nadu.

 1. Only 30% of the cultivated area receives rainfall above 100 cm, while about 40% of the cultivated area receives less than 75 cm of annual rainfall. In these areas crops cannot be grown without irrigation.

 2. Some crops like rice, sugarcane, jute, cotton, etc., need more water. Hence, need to be irrigated to cater to increasing demand of food and cash crops, there is a need to grow crops all the year round.

(b) **(i)** High underground water level or fertile agricultural land

 (ii) Cheap supply of electricity.

Q. 6. **(a)** State two reasons why irrigation is important to a country like India.

 (b) Name two modern methods of irrigation. State one important reason for their growing popularity. **[2015]**

Ans. **(a)** Irrigation is important in India due to the following reasons:

 (i) Monsoon rainfall is uncertain and unevenly distributed in India. Thus, irrigation becomes necessary in areas of low and scanty rainfall.

 (ii) Different types of crops are grown in India which have varying water requirements. Crops like rice, wheat, sugarcane and jute need more water than other crops. This makes irrigation necessary.

(b) Two modern methods of irrigation are drip irrigation and sprinkler irrigation.

 In the conventional methods of irrigation, a large quantity of water is wasted due to water logging and often results in gradual salinity of the soil. This has made the modern methods of irrigation more popular.

Q. 7. **(a)** State two reasons why tank irrigation is popular in South India.

 (b) Mention two advantages that surface wells have over inundation canals.**[2014]**

Ans. **(a)** The reasons for the popularity of tank irrigation in South India are as follows:

 (i) There is little percolation of rain-water due to hard rock structure of Deccan Plateau and groundwater is not available in large quantity.

 (ii) Most of the rivers of this region are seasonal and dry up in summer season. Therefore, they cannot supply water to canals throughout the year.

(b) Surface wells are an independent source of irrigation. They may be used when the necessity arises.

 Two advantages that surface wells have over inundation canals are:

 (i) They are simplest and cheapest source of irrigation, can be dug at any convenient place. While inundation canals are dug at places close to water bodies.

 (ii) Inundation canals are 'floodwater' canals and have water in them only when the river is flooded during the rainy season. While surface wells are a perennial source of water.

Q. 8. **(a)** Name two states in which tube wells are extensively used. Give a reason to explain its importance as a source of irrigation.

 (b) Give two main reasons why water scarcity occurs in India. **[2013]**

Ans. **(a)** Tube wells are extensively used in Punjab and Haryana because the land is soft to bore and availability of electric power.

 (b) Water scarcity occurs because of:

 (i) Seasonal rainfall

 (ii) More demand due to increase in population and polluted water.

Q. 9. Why are inundation canals being converted to perennial canals? Give two reasons.

 [2012]

Ans. Inundation canals are converted to perennial canals because:

 (i) Depend on flood water and dry up during summers, while perennial canals can provide water throughout the year.

 (ii) Perennial canals irrigate a vast area, since they are lined to dams and barrages to provide water all round the year.

Q. 10. **(a)** Name two states in which well irrigation is widely used. OR Mention one advantage of well irrigation in India.

 (b) Mention two disadvantages of tank irrigation. **[2011]**

Ans. **(a)** Two states in which well irrigation is widely used are Uttar Pradesh and Rajasthan.

 One advantage of well irrigation is that it is the simplest and the cheapest source of irrigation and it can be dug at any convenient place.

(b) Two disadvantages of tank irrigation are:

 (i) Tanks occupy large surface area, which could otherwise have been used for cultivation.

 (ii) Many tanks dry up during the dry season and fail to provide water for irrigation.

 ## Short Answer Type Questions-II

Q. 1. **(a) (i)** Name two states of India where Canal irrigation is extensively used.

(ii) Name the types of canals used in India.

(iii) Mention one point of difference between the types of canals mentioned by you.

(b) (i) What geographical conditions make irrigation necessary in the country?

(ii) How has irrigation changed the cropping pattern in India?

(iii) Why is there a scarcity of surface water in our country.

Ans. **(a) (i)** Punjab and Haryana.

(ii) There are two types of canals used in India: Inundation and Perennial Canals.

(iii) Inundation canals are taken out from the rivers when they are in floods. But perennial canals are useful throughout the year as they are taken out from the perennial rivers.

(b) (i) The uneven and uncertain distribution of rainfall in India makes irrigation necessary because farmers cannot survive on rainwater.

(ii) Many farmers because of the increased availability of water have switched over to the cultivation of water intensive commercial crops such as jute, cotton and sugarcane, rather than food grains such as bajra, wheat and ragi.

(iii) Surface water gets lost through the process of evaporation, plant transpiration and water seepage.

Q. 2. **(a)** Give a reason for each of the following:

(i) Most of the South Indian states are *not suitable* for development of canal irrigation.

(ii) There is an urgent need for water conservation in India.

(iii) Development of irrigation is essential for the growth of the agriculture sector of India.

(b) Briefly explain the following terms:

(i) Inundation canal.

(ii) Rooftop rainwater harvesting.

(iii) Surface water. **[2019]**

Marking Scheme

(a) (i) South Indian states have uneven terrain hence they are not suitable for constructing canals/rivers are seasonal/hard rocks make it difficult to construct canals.

(Any one point)

(ii) – To meet the increasing demand of growing population.
– To provide water for irrigation and industrial use/increase crop production.
– To reduce the water scarcity/pollution of water/depleting ground water/wastage of water/rain is seasonal and unreliable.

(Any one point)

(iii) Rainfall in India is seasonal/uncertain/ unevenly distributed/annual crops need water all through the year/to maximize the agricultural production.
– To attain self sufficiency
– Certain crops need more water
– For success of green revolution

(Any one point)

(b) (i) The canals that are taken out from the rivers without any regulating system like weirs, etc at their head / the canal that are filled with water only during floods.

(ii) Rainwater can be collected over rooftop and collected water channelized through small PVC pipes into the underground pits, wells, etc.

(iii) Water found on the surface of the earth in the form of rivers, lakes, ponds, etc. is called surface water.

Ans. **(a) (i)** Most of the rivers in South India are non-perennial. Deccan Plateau consisting of hard igneous and metamorphic rocks makes it difficult to dig. So, states in South India are not suitable for canal irrigation.

(ii) As freshwater resources such as rivers, lakes and ponds are drying up due to excessive use and climate change. Industrial development is leading to the pollution of freshwater bodies like lakes, river and ponds. Thus, with rising water scarcity and growing population there is an urgent need to conserve water in India for the future generations.

(iii) Only 30% of the cultivated area receives sufficient annual rainfall while 40% receives less than 75 cm of annual rainfall.

1. Rabi crops need irrigation as most parts of India receives no rain during winter.

2. Some crops like rice, jute, sugarcane need more water. So, India needs enhanced irrigation facilities to get maximum yield from the same land.

(b) **(i)** Inundation canals are taken out from perennial rivers without any regulating systems like weirs and barrages to regulate the flow of river. The supply of water comes only when the river is flooded in the lower level regions only. This type of irrigation is cheap and can also be useful in controlling floods.

(ii) Rooftop rainwater harvesting is a technique through which rainwater is captured from the roof catchments and stored in reservoirs. This harvested rainwater can be stored in subsurface groundwater reservoirs by adopting artificial recharge techniques to meet the household needs through storage tanks.

(iii) Surface water is available on the surface of the earth in the form of rivers, lakes, ponds and canals. Rivers are the most important source of surface water. Most of the Himalayan rivers are perennial while the rivers of the Peninsular India are seasonal.

Q. 3. **(a)** **(i) Differentiate between Surface water and Groundwater.**

(ii) Mention two reasons to explain as to why we are facing water scarcity in recent times.

(b) **(i) What is rainwater harvesting?**

(ii) What are the advantages of rain-water harvesting?

(iii) Name two water harvesting systems practised in India. [2018, 2016, 2012]

Marking Scheme

(a) (i) Surface water – Water available in lakes, ponds, river and streams/polluted, ground-water – water available below land in aquifer/pure/improve quality of ground water

(ii) We face water scarcity as a lot of water is either wasted or polluted. Demand of pure potable water is therefore, more than its supply.

(b) Rainwater harvesting:

(i) It is the procedure of augmenting the natural filtration of rainwater to recharge groundwater and storing it in underground reservoirs, borewells, dug wells etc.

(ii) To increase the ground water table, to meet the demands of increased population and agricultural activities.

(iii) 1. Rain water Harvesting
2. Roof top harvesting system
3. Ground water recharge. *(Any two)*

Ans. **(a)** **(i)**

Surface water	Groundwater
Water on land is the result of precipitation or seepage from underground which forms rivers and streams is known as surface water.	Water which gets collected under the surface of the land or groundwater which remains in the soil, subsoil or bedrock is known as groundwater.

(ii) We are facing water scarcity in recent times due to:

1. Usage has increased tremendously because of increase in population.

2. Increase in industries and factories, the process of their waste management (dumping it in rivers) has also rendered available water useless, thus causing scarcity. Demand for pure water is therefore more than its supply.

(b) **(i)** Collecting, filtering and storing rain-water for further use; either directly or by recharging it into the ground to improve groundwater storage in the aquifer is known as rainwater harvesting.

(ii) Rainwater harvesting has many advantages like it helps to increase the availability of water during dry season and also to increase the groundwater levels of dried bore-well and surface wells.

(iii) Two water harvesting systems practised in India are:

1. Tanks, kunds or keres.
2. Groundwater recharge

Q. 4. **(a)** Give one geographical reason for each of the following:

    (i) Sprinkler irrigation is practised in arid and semi-arid regions.

    (ii) A tube well should be installed in a fertile and productive region.

    (iii) Canal irrigation is more suitable in the Northern Plains.

(b) Study the diagram below and answer the questions that follow:

    (i) Name the activity shown in the diagram.

    (ii) Give two objectives of the activity named in (b) (i). [2017, 2013]

Ans. **(a)** **(i)** In areas with limited supply of water, sprinkler irrigation is practiced. Sprinkler does not interfere with cultivation and results in less wastage of water with higher application efficiency.

    (ii) Since the cost of installation of a tube well is high, the farmer needs to grow HYV seeds all round the year to earn more which is only possible in the fertile regions like North Indian plains.

    (iii) Perennial rivers, soft and flat land and fertile soil have encouraged canal irrigation in Northern Plains.

(b) **(i)** Technique of rainwater harvesting known as recharging of groundwater through handpumps.

    (ii) 1. The recharging of the shallow or deep aquifers by handpumps may increase the level of underground water.

    2. Improves the quality of groundwater which can be used till the next rainfall.

3. To reduce surface run off.
4. To reduce soil erosion.

Q. 5. **(a)** Give one reason for each of the following:

    (i) The Northern Plain of India is found suitable for canal irrigation.

    (ii) Tank irrigation is an important method of irrigation in Karnataka.

    (iii) Although expensive, yet, sprinkler irrigation is gaining popularity in recent times.

(b) **Mention two objectives of rainwater harvesting.** [2016]

Ans. **(a)** **(i)** Perennial source of water i.e. snow-fed rivers and low relief with deep fertile soil are responsible for the development of canal irrigation in Northern India.

    (ii) Karnataka, in Deccan region, consists of underlying hard rocks which are impervious. It does not allow the water to seep through. The region has large number of natural depressions where tanks can be built. It is also difficult and expensive to built canals or wells as a form of irrigation.

    (iii) Sprinkler irrigation does not involve any loss of water by seepage or evaporation as the water is supplied by pipes. It is not exposed to the sun. It is the best method for conserving water.

(b) Two objectives are:

1. Recharging the groundwater and raising its level to meet the demand of water requirement in the dry season.
2. Checking the rainwater from flowing far away so as to prevent soil erosion and flooding of the surrounding areas.

Q. 6. **(a)** **(i) Why is well irrigation still a popular means of irrigation? Give two reasons to support your answer.**

    (ii) State the significance of rainwater harvesting.

(b) **(i) Why is the world in danger of facing a severe water shortage in the coming future? Give two reasons to support your answer.**

    (ii) State one measure the Government should adopt to handle the present water crisis. [2015]

Ans. **(a)** **(i)** Well irrigation is a popular method of irrigation due to the following reasons:

    1. Wells can be dug very easily in areas of soft soil.

2. By the use of pumps and tubewells, water can be lifted even from great depths.

(ii) The significance of rainwater harvesting is as follows:

1. This method helps to raise the groundwater table by recharging of groundwater reserves.

2. It helps to reduce surface run-off and avoid flooding.

(b) (i) The world is in danger of facing an acute water crisis due to the following reasons:

1. The rapid increase in the world population has resulted in over exploitation of underground water in order to meet the increased demand for freshwater supply.

2. Irrigation utilizes more than 90% of total freshwater supply. Besides, the increased industrial demand further adds to the water scarcity problem.

(ii) The Government should undertake proper water harvesting methods that promote reuse and recycling of water to reduce water scarcity problem.

Q. 7. (a) Give one geographical reason for each of the following statements:

(i) Irrigation is necessary despite the monsoon.

(ii) The drip method of irrigation is the best among all modern methods of irrigation.

(iii) Canal irrigation leads to the ground around it becoming unproductive.

(b) Give three reasons for conservation of water resources. **[2014]**

Ans. (a) (i) Indian monsoons are the most uncertain. Late arrival or early withdrawal of the monsoon affects crop production severely. Only irrigation can provide security to agriculture from such irregularity.

(ii) The drip method of irrigation does not involve any loss of water by seepages because water is supplied through pipes. No water is lost by evaporation because water is supplied directly onto the roots of the plants.

(iii) Excessive flow of water in the fields raises the groundwater level. Capillary action brings alkaline salts to the surface and makes the areas close to the canals unfit for agriculture.

(b) Conservation of water resources is essential because:

(i) The increase in population with the progress of time, results in water scarcity.

(ii) Our water resources like the rivers, lakes etc., are polluted and their water can hardly be used without adequate treatment.

(iii) The water demand for industrial use is increasing day by day.

Q. 8. (a) (i) Name two states where perennial canals are widely used.

(ii) Briefly explain two reasons for perennial canals being a popular form of irrigation in the named states.

(b) Name two methods of water harvesting in India. **[2013]**

Ans. (a) (i) Two states are Punjab and Haryana.

(ii) Perennial canals are popular there because:

(a) Rivers here are perennial.

(b) Land is soft and fertile.

(b) Two methods of water harvesting in India are:

(1) Collecting rainwater on the rooftops and directing it to tanks.

(2) Watershed is defined as a geographic area through which water flows across the land and drains into common body of water such as stream, river, lake, ocean, etc.

Q. 9. (a) Give two advantages and one disadvantage that tube wells have over surface wells.

(b) Where are tanks most widely used in India? Why? **[2012]**

Ans. (a) **Advantages:**

(i) Tube wells do not result in evaporation of water like surface wells.

(ii) It irrigates larger areas (400 hectares as compared to surface wells.

Disadvantage: However, tube wells are only possible in areas where the groundwater level is not too low, power is needed to drain water.

(b) Tanks are mostly used in Peninsular India. This is because:

    (i) Peninsular India consists of hard impervious rocks which favour the storage of water.

    (ii) Depressions in the plateau region act as natural tanks.

Q. 10. (a) Give three reasons to justify the need to conserve water.

(b) Mention any three water harvesting systems practised in India. **[2011]**

Ans. **(a)** The need to conserve water can be stated as follows:

    (i) The over exploitation of underground water often results in the lowering of the water table.

    (ii) Water resources like the rivers, lakes and underground water are polluted and their water can be hardly used without adequate treatment.

    (iii) The increase in population with the progress of time results in water scarcity.

(b) **(i)** The simplest rainwater harvesting technique is the check dam. It is a small barrier built across streams. Dams store water during the monsoons which can then be used for irrigation purposes.

    (ii) Another water harvesting technique is the storage tank kept underground and connected to the pipe coming down from the roof. The rainwater enters the tank through a filter which removes leaves and other debris. The system contains a pump which pushes or sucks the rainwater back into the house which is then delivered to the garden, washing clothes, etc.

(iii) Another rainwater collection system is the garden watersaver diverter. It is a downspout rainwater diverter which simplifies the collection of rain water. It has advantages over other rainwater collection systems and it can be installed in minutes and deactivated in seconds during winter, when the stored water isn't much needed.

Chapter 4

Minerals and Energy Resources

 **Short Answer Type Questions-I**

Q. 1. **(a)** **(i)** Why is iron ore called the back bone of our modern industry?

(ii) Mention two uses of iron ore.

(b) Mention one agricultural and one industrial problem solved by the Bhakra Nangal Dam.

Ans. **(a)** **(i)** It is so because it provides raw material to run many other industries.

(ii) Iron ore is used in making pig iron, sponge iron and steel.

(b) Bhakra Nangal Dam solved the agricultural problem of flooding and soil erosion. By providing regular electricity supply, it solved the power crisis for industries.

Q. 2. **(a)** Give *two advantages* of using biogas as a source of power.

(b) Name the following:

(i) *A metallic mineral* for which the Balaghat district of Madhya Pradesh is famous.

(ii) The multi-purpose project based on the River Sutlej. **[2019]**

Ans. **(a)** Biogas energy uses organic material and waste like agricultural waste and household waste for its production. So, it is a sustainable source of energy. Its usage as a source of power has many advantages such as:

1. The process emits far less greenhouse gases into the air than in fossil fuels.
2. It is cost-effective.
3. It saves about 70 lakh tons of fuel wood and reduces dependence on fossil fuels.

(b) **(i)** Copper.
(ii) Bhakra Nangal Project.

Q. 3. **(a)** Give two advantages that non-conventional energy sources have over conventional energy sources.

(b) **(i)** Mention one advantage of the use of natural gas over coal or petroleum.

(ii) Name one of shore oilfield of India.

[2018]

Ans. **(a)** Two advantages of non-conventional energy sources over conventional energy sources are:

(i) Non-conventional energy is renewable and pollution-free whereas, conventional energy sources are non-renewable and cause pollution.

(ii) Non-conventional energy sources are generally inexhaustible whereas, conventional energy sources are usually exhaustible.

(b) **(i)** One advantage of using natural gas over coal or petroleum is that it causes less damage to environment. It is made up of methane and results in less carbon emission than fossil fuels.

(ii) Mumbai High.

Q. 4. **(a)** Give the names of four important types of iron ore found in India.

(b) Name the following:

(i) An offshore oilfield in the Gulf of Cambay.

(ii) An oil refinery in Bihar. **[2017]**

Ans. **(a)** **(i)** Magnetite **(ii)** Hematite
(iii) Limonite **(iv)** Siderite

(b) **(i)** Aliabet island close to Bhavnagar in Gulf of Cambay.

(ii) Barauni.

Q. 5. **(a)** **(i)** Name any three types of coal found in India.

(ii) Which type of coal is mostly used in iron and steel industries?

(b) Name the following:

(i) An offshore oilfield of India.

(ii) An iron ore mine of Karnataka.

[2016]

Ans. **(a)** **(i)** Anthracite, Bituminous and Lignite are the three types of coal found in India.

(ii) Bituminous

(b) **(i)** Mumbai High

(ii) Iron ore mines in Karnataka are Simoga / Bellary / Hospate / Chitradurga/Kemmangundi

(Any one)

Q. 6. State the most important use of the following:
(i) Iron ore **[2015]**

Ans. (i) Iron ore is mainly used to make steel. Raw iron is alloyed with other elements to make good quality steel which is used for construction, automobiles, other forms of transportation, etc.

Q. 7. (a) **Mention any two uses of manganese.**
(b) **Which of the different varieties of coal is used for domestic purposes and why?**
[2014]

Ans. (a) (i) Manganese is used to increase the strength of steel in iron and steel industry.
(ii) It is also used as raw material for manufacturing paints, glassware, insecticides, bleaching powder and dry cell batteries.
(b) Bituminous coal is used for domestic purposes as its carbon content is high and emits less smoke.

Q. 8. (a) (i) Name two leading states producing Manganese.
(ii) Name one use of the mineral.
(b) (i) Name two varieties of iron ore used in industry.
(ii) How is the low grade iron ore utilized? **[2012]**

Ans. (a) (i) Jharkhand and Odisha.
(ii) It is widely used in iron and steel industry for hardening steel.
(b) (i) Hematite and Magnetite.
(ii) The inferior variety is often used in manufacturing sponge iron and converted into pellets and then exported.

Q. 9. (a) **What grade of iron ore is mostly mined in India?**
Name two leading iron ore producing states.
(b) **What is lignite? Name the two areas where lignite is found in India.** **[2011]**

Ans. (a) Hematite variety of iron ore is mostly mined in India. Chhattisgarh and Jharkhand are two leading iron ore producing states of India.
(b) Lignite refers to inferior variety coal which contains about 40% of carbon and a good amount of moisture and less of combustible matter.
Two states where lignite is found are Tamil Nadu and Gujarat.

Q. 10. (a) **Name one centre in each of the following states where iron is mined:**
(i) **Odisha**
(ii) **Jharkhand**
(b) **Which variety of coal is popular for domestic use?**
Give a reason for your answer. **[2010]**

Ans. (a) (i) Keonjhar
(ii) Singhbhum
(b) Bituminous coal is popular for domestic use because of its high calorific value.

Q. 11. **Name the gas that is generated in biogas plants and then harnessed for power. Mention one advantage of biogas plants over the other sources of power.** **[2010]**

Ans. Methane gas is generated in biogas plants. The advantage of biogas is that it is a non-conventional source of energy with higher thermal efficiency and is pollution free.

Short Answer Type Questions-II

Q. 1. (a) (i) **Name the state that is the leading producer of Manganese.**
(ii) **Name the mineral of oil fields of India which is the largest producer of Petroleum.**
(b) (i) **Mention one disadvantage of using natural gas as a source of power.**
(ii) **How is the residue from a Biogas plant put to use?**
(iii) **Why is the use of alternative sources of energy becoming essential in modern time?**

Ans. (a) (i) Odisha
(ii) Bombay High
(b) (i) Natural gas as a source of energy cannot be used at a large scale.
(ii) The residue from a Bio gas plant can be used as manure or fertilizer for plants.
(iii) Alternative sources of energy are needed because the ever-growing demand for energy cannot be meet by conventional sources of energy.

Q. 2. (a) **Give a reason for each of the following:**
(i) *Odisha* **has benefited greatly from the** *Hirakud project.*
(ii) **Copper is used to make** *electric wires.*
(iii) **India's location is advantageous for the generation of** *solar power.*
(b) **Briefly answer the following:**
(i) **Name a mineral used to generate nuclear power.**

(ii) Why is petroleum often referred to as *"liquid gold"*?

(iii) State *one disadvantage* of using coal as a source of power. **[2019]**

Marking Scheme

(a) (i) The Hirakud project generates power/provides water for irrigation for both the *kharif* and *rabi* crops/controls floods on the River Mahanadi/soil conservation/fish culture/industrial growth/water supply/inland waterways. *(Any one)*

(ii) Copper is a good conductor of electricity / is ductile and malleable and so is used to make electric wires. *(Any one)*

(iii) India lies between 8°N and 37°N with the Tropic of Cancer running through it and so receives a lot of sunlight with 300 clear days in a year. This is advantageous for the generation of solar power.

(b) (i) Uranium / Thorium / Beryllium/Plutonium/Zirconium *(Any one)*

(ii) Petroleum is a versatile mineral. It generates power/used as a fuel for vehicles and in factories/used as a raw material for products like plastics, tarpaulin, wax etc./by-products like kerosene are very useful/Not even the smallest part of the crude oil goes waste or remains unused and is therefore called liquid gold /because of high economic value.

(iii) It leads to pollution/it is exhaustible/it is non-renewable/heavy transport cost/problem of disposal of residue/health hazard.

Ans. **(a)** **(i)** Odisha has benefited greatly from the Hirakud project as the canals originating from the dam help irrigate vast areas of agricultural land. The project also provides navigation facilities for the transportation of goods. The project also has two power houses; Chiplima power house and Hirakud power house which supply power to a number of industries, thus making a valuable contribution to the industrial development of Odisha as it has rich reserves of mineral resources like iron, bauxite, manganese, etc.

(ii) Copper is a good electrical conductor. So, it is used in the electrical industry mainly to make copper wires.

(iii) The sun offers 'direct' and inexhaustible source of energy, especially in a tropical country like India, with over 300 days of clear sky, that can be utilised to generate electrical energy. Thus, India's location is advantageous for the generation of solar power.

(b) **(i)** Uranium/ Plutonium/ Beryllium/ Thorium.

(ii) Petroleum, can be extracted easily at a low cost, sold at a cheaper cost compared to other sources of energy. It can generate up to 10,000 kilo calories of energy and can be easily transported. So, it is known as liquid gold.

(iii) Using coal as a source of power requires burning it. Burning coal emits harmful waste like carbon dioxide, sulphuric acid, arsenic, ash, nitrogen oxide and sulphur dioxide, increasing greenhouse gases into the atmosphere. It may also cause acid rain.

Q. 3. **(a)** Answer the following:

(i) State one industrial use of copper.

(ii) Mention one advantage of generating power from biogas.

(iii) Name the mineral that toughens steel and makes it rust-proof.

(b) **(ii)** Which multi-purpose project provides power to both Punjab and Himachal Pradesh? **[2018]**

Marking Scheme

(a) (i) Copper is used for making wire and for alloys.

(ii) Non-polluting/waste put to good use/residue used as manure/inexhaustible/reduces dependence on fossil fuels/cleans environment.

(iii) Manganese is used to make steel tough and rust proof.

(b) (ii) Bhakra Nangal.

Ans. **(a)** **(i)** Used for making electrical machinery.

(ii) It is clean, non-polluting and cheap.

(iii) Manganese.

(b) **(ii)** Bhakra Nangal Dam.

Q. 4. State an important industrial use of:

(i) Manganese **(ii)** Coal **[2017]**

Ans. **(i)** Manganese: It is the most important mineral for making iron and steel.

(ii) Coal: Coal is used in the generation of electric power/used in the iron and steel industry as well as in cement industry.

Q. 5. **(a)** Name the following:

(i) Largest coolfield of India.

(ii) Oldest oilfield of India.

(iii) Best variety of iron ore.

Ans. **(a)** **(i)** Jharia/Raniganj

(ii) Digboi

(iii) Magnetite

Q. 6. **(a)** Name the:
    (i) Largest oil refinery in the public sector.
    (ii) State that is the largest producer of coal.
    (iii) Best variety of iron ore.
  (b) Give a geographic reason for each of the following:
    (i) Many port cities have their own oil refineries.
    (ii) Petroleum is called a 'fossil fuel'.
    (iii) Coal is called a versatile mineral.
                          [2015]

Ans. **(a)** **(i)** Mathura
       (ii) Jharkhand
       (iii) Magnetite
  (b) **(i)** Many port cities have their own oil refineries as the location of the oil refineries near the coast minimizes the cost of transport and also reduces the risk of transporting the oil inside the country due to its inflammable nature.
    (ii) Petroleum is formed by the accumulation of vegetative matter. This vegetative matter when subjected to heat and pressure results in physical and chemical changes due to the increasing weight of the overlying layers of sediments and earth movements. Moreover, petroleum is the basic source of energy. Thus, it is known as a fossil fuel.
    (iii) Coal is known as a versatile mineral due to its varied uses:
    1. It is used as a source of power for running machines, trains, ships, etc.
    2. It is used in manufacturing steel.
    3. Various by-products of coal such as ammonia, benzol, etc., are manufactured from coal.

Q. 7. Which state is the leading producer of the following minerals?
    (i) Coal   **(ii)** Oil
    (iii) Manganese   **[2014]**

Ans. **(i)** Coal: Jharkhand
  (ii) Oil: Maharashtra.
  (iii) Manganese: Orissa (Odisha).

Q. 8. **(a)** **(i)** Name two industries that use a high quantity of coal.
    (ii) Name one important area that has large coal deposits in the states of Jharkhand and West Bengal.
  (b) **(i)** Which state is the largest producer of mineral oil?
    (ii) Name two coastal and two inland oil refineries in India.   **[2013]**

Ans. **(a)** Two industries that use high quantity of coal are:
    (i) Iron and Steel Industry, Sugar Industry.
    (ii) Jharkhand – Jharia, in West Bengal – Raniganj.
  (b) **(i)** Largest producer of mineral oil is Assam.
    (ii) Two coastal oil refineries are Kochi and Chennai.
    Two inland oil refineries are Barauni and Mathura.

Q. 9. **(a)** Give geographical reasons why:
    (i) Anthracite is used for domestic purposes.
    (ii) Oil refineries are located close to oil fields or near ports.
    (iii) The location of coal fields is an important factor in industrial development.
  (b) Name the mineral:
  The largest deposits of which are found in Balaghat in Madhya Pradesh.   **[2012]**

Ans. **(a)** **(i)** Anthracite is used for domestic purposes as it has a very high carbon content and emits very less smoke.
    (ii) Oil refineries located near the oil fields help to transport crude oil through pipelines and hence reduce the transportation cost. Moreover, if located near the port it helps to import the crude oil.
    (iii) Coal is a bulky and heavy raw material. Industries located away from coal fields incur huge transport costs and affects the cost of production on a large scale.
  (b) Manganese

Q. 10. Name the leading producer of Manganese in India.
Name two important industrial uses of Manganese.   **[2011]**

Ans. Odisha is the leading producer of manganese in India.

Two important industrial uses of manganese are:
  (i) It is an important raw material for iron and steel industry which is used to make steel tough and resistant to rusting.
  (ii) Manganese is used in the manufacturing of black enamel in chemical industries for the manufacturing of bleaching powder, electrical and glass industries.

Q. 11. **(a)** **Name a region which has natural gas deposits. Mention two uses of natural gas.**

(b) **Why is an oil refinery located either close to an oil field or in a coastal city? Name one oil refinery in the private sector.** **[2010]**

Ans. **(a)** Almost 70% of India's natural gas reserves are found in the Bombay High Basin and Gujarat. Offshore gas reserves are also located in Krishna-Godavari Basin and Cauvery Basin. Onshore reserves are located in Gujarat and northeastern states (Assam and Tripura). Natural gas is used as a source of energy for heating, cooking and as fuel for vehicles.

(b) India has vast oil bearing areas both onshore and offshore. Since crude petroleum has to be refined, its availability near the refinery reduces cost of transportation. Also, since the products of the refinery are also to be exported and crude oil is also to be imported, so location of the refinery near major ports reduces transportation cost.

One oil refinery in the private sector is Numaligarh in Assam.

Q. 12. **Mention three advantages that hydroelectric power has over thermal power.** **[2010]**

Ans. Hydroelectric power is produced from falling water and is renewable, and is the cheapest source of power which is also pollution free. On the other hand, thermal power is generated by burning fossil fuels like coal, petroleum, natural gas, etc. which is non-renewable, expensive and causes a lot of pollution.

Agriculture in India

 **Short Answer Type Questions-I**

Q. 1. **Explain briefly the following terms:**

(i) Ginning

(ii) Ratooning.

Ans. (i) The process of removal of unwanted debris and seeds of the cotton plant is known as Ginning.

(ii) It is a process in which the lower part of the stem is left intact in soil, which later on begins to grow again. This is called as ratooning.

Q. 2. **Mention *two steps* taken by the government to boost agricultural production in India.**
[2019]

Ans. Two steps are:

1. Use of HYV seeds.
2. Rural electrification.
3. Supply of agricultural credit.
4. Land reforms law.
5. Irrigation facilities.
6. Opening of agricultural universities.

Q. 3. **(a)** **With reference to the cultivation of tea answer the following:**
 (i) Why is tea grown on hill slopes?
 (ii) Why tea bushes have to be pruned at regular intervals?
 (b) **With reference to rice cultivation answer the following:**
 (i) Why does the cultivation of rice require a lot of manual labour?
 (ii) Mention two geographical conditions which suit the cultivation of rice. **[2018]**

Ans. **(a)** (i) Tea is grown on hill slopes as the roots of tea bushes cannot tolerate stagnant water and the hill slopes drain away the water helping the tea bushes to grow properly.

(ii) Tea bushes have to be pruned at regular intervals to encourage the growth of new leaves and to keep the height of the bushes low for the women who do the plucking of the tea leaves.

(b) (i) Rice cultivation requires many activities to be done manually like sowing seeds, transplanting seedlings in puddled fields, spraying insecticides etc. Therefore, it requires a lot of manual labour.

(ii) Temperature: about 24°C with a range of 16°C to 32°C.
Rainfall: 150-200 cm and flooded fields.
Soil: Alluvial with a subsoil of clay.

Q. 4. **Give the geographical requirements for the cultivation of sugarcane.** **[2017]**

Ans. Temperature: 20°C–30°C.

Rainfall: 100 cm–200 cm rainfall.

Soil: Alluvial or black soil.

Q. 5. **(a)** **Mention any two reasons for the importance of agriculture in India.**
 (b) **With reference to rice cultivation answer the following:**
 (i) Why does rice grow well in a soil with a clay like subsoil?
 (ii) What is the advantage of growing rice in nurseries before it is transplanted? **[2016, 2012]**

Ans. **(a)** 1. Agriculture not only provides food and fodder to human beings for their livestock but it is also the source of raw material for many industries like sugar, textile and edible oil. It provides employment to millions of people as it acts as a consumer of many industrial products.

2. Agriculture also helps us to earn foreign exchange by exporting tea, coffee, jute, etc.

(b) (i) Rice needs ankle-deep standing water during the period of growth. Clay soil does not allow the water to seep through it, so it is an ideal soil for the growth of rice.

(ii) There is less wastage of seeds through broadcasting method and during the process of transplantation, the weeds can be easily removed.

Q. 6. **(a)** **Differentiate between a Rabi crop and a Kharif crop.**

(b) State an important difference between the climatic requirements for growing cotton and jute. [2015]

Ans. **(a)**

	Rabi crops	Kharif crops
(i)	They are sown in October-November and are harvested in March-April.	They are sown in June-July and are harvested in October-November.
(ii)	The crops mainly include wheat, barley, gram, mustard, etc.	It includes crops like rice, jowar, bajra, sugarcane, etc.

(b)

	Basis	Cotton	Jute
(i)	Climatic condition	Bright sunny weather condition.	Hot and humid condition.
(ii)	Temperature	20 °C-32 °C	21 °C-35 °C
(iii)	Rainfall	Moderate rainfall from 50 cm-120 cm.	The annual rainfall should be more than 150 cm.

Q. 7. How has poverty and fragmentation of land become problems of agricultural India?

Ans. Inheritance laws in the country have led to a continuous fragmentation of land over the years reducing the size of the land holdings. Farm fragmentation reduces the size of farm on which it is not possible to use harvesters or other farm machinery. This results in the large scale wastage of fertile land and labour, and they become uneconomic for any useful agricultural activity.

Q. 8. With reference to rice cultivation, answer the following:
    (i) Name two leading states in the production of rice.
    (ii) Give two advantages of growing rice in nurseries. [2013]

Ans. With reference to rice:
    (i) Tamil Nadu and West Bengal.
    (ii) Two advantages of growing rice in nurseries are:
      (1) It increases the yield by 45%.
      (2) Uses water economically.

Q. 9. Name a state which produces short staple cotton. Which climatic and soil conditions favour the cultivation of cotton in the state mentioned? [2012]

Ans. Maharashtra

Temperature: 21°C–32°C. Rainfall: 50 cm-120 cm and at least 200 frost free days. Sunny weather during ripening and harvesting.

Soil: Black cotton soil or alluvial soil rich in lime, potash, calcium and magnesium.

Q. 10. (a) Mention any two problems of agriculture in India.
    (b) State two geographical requirements for the growth of wheat in India. [2011]

Ans. **(a)** Two problems of agriculture in India are:
    (i) Soil erosion is a major cause for decreasing soil fertility and also loss of valuable crop land.
    (ii) Agriculture in India is dependent on monsoon rainfall. Over 60% of the net cropped area lacks irrigation facilities.

  (b) The geographical requirements for the growth of wheat in India are as follows:
    Temperature: Ideal temperature between 10°C – 15°C is suitable for sowing and 20°C – 25°C during harvest.
    Rainfall: About 80 cm of annual rainfall is ideal for wheat cultivation.
    Soil: Wheat grows best in well-drained clayey black soil.

Q. 11.

(a) Study the picture given above and answer the following questions:
    (i) Name the crop which is being planted. Give one benefit of this method of planting this crop.
    (ii) Mention the climatic conditions which favour the cultivation of the crop being planted.

(b) Name the state in India which leads cotton cultivation. Mention two climatic factors which affect the cotton cultivation adversely. [2010]

Ans. **(a)** **(i)** Rice transplantation. It increases yields by 30% to 40%.
    (ii) Rice requires mean temperatures from 25°C to 32°C and abundant

rainfall from 150 to 200 cm. It thrives best where there is 5 to 10 cm of standing water in the fields.

(b) Maharashtra is the state leading in cotton cultivation. Two climatic factors affecting cotton cultivation are:

1. Frost is very injurious to the cotton plant.

2. There should be at least 200 frost-free days. Warm days and cool nights are good for the development of the bolls and fibre.

3. Rain during this time will render the fibres moulded and discoloured.

Short Answer Type Questions-II

Q. 1. (a) With reference to the wheat crop answer the following questions:

(i) Name the state which is the leading producer of this crop in India.

(ii) Mention the climatic conditions found suitable for the cultivation of this crop.

(d) Give a geographical reason for each of the following :

(i) Cultivation of rice requires flat level land.

(ii) Pulses are important rotation crops.

Ans. (a) (i) Punjab

(ii) Wheat is a rabi crop which requires a temperature between 10°C to 15°C degree at the time of sowing.

(d) (i) It is so because rice plant needs a lot of moisture *i.e.*, wet land. The flat land does not allow the water to flow away, thus retaining the moisture content.

(ii) Since pulses are leguminous crops, fixing the atmospheric nitrogen and enhancing the fertility of the soil.

Q. 2. (a) Study the picture given below and answer the questions that follow:

(i) Mention the climatic condition that is suitable for the cultivation of this crop.

(ii) Name the state that produces the largest amount of this crop.

(iii) In which cropping season is this crop grown in India?

(b) Give a geographical reason for each of the following:

(i) Cultivation of wheat is confined to the northern part of India.

(iii) Ratoon cropping is gaining popularity among sugarcane cultivators. [2019]

Marking Scheme

(a) (i) Temperature: 18 °C to 32 °C.
Rainfall: 50 cm to 80 cm / 200 frost free days/ bright sunshine during harvest.
(ii) Maharashtra/Gujarat
(iii) Kharif

(b) (i) Ideal temperature of 10 °C to 20 °C that is suitable growth of wheat is available in north India/In north India winter rain occurs which is found suitable for its growth/50 cm - 100 cm rain in north-west India. Wheat is a temperate crop. India is a warm country so cool climate is found in north during winter. *(Any one)*

(iii) Mature faster/ saves time and money/ less labour required/cost effective. *(Any one)*

Ans. (a) (i) The temperature should be in between 21°C to 27°C and should not be less than 20°C. The rainfall should be between 50-80 cm and should be well distributed as stagnant water and excessive rain can be harmful to the plant.

The cotton crop needs 200 frost-free days during the period of growth.

(ii) Punjab.

(iii) In North India, it is a Rabi crop but in South India, it is Kharif crop.

(b) (i) Wheat grows well in a cool climate with 50 cm to 100 cm of rainfall during the growing season. It needs an average temperature of 10°-15°C at the time of sowing and 20°-25°C during the harvesting period. North India enjoys this type of climate, whereas South India does not. So, wheat cultivation is confined to North India only.

(iii) Ratoon cropping does not involve any extra expenditure for replanting the crop. It involves shorter maturation period. So, it is gaining popularity among sugarcane cultivators.

Q. 3. **(a)** Give a geographical reason for each of the following:
   (i) Cotton is a labour intensive crop.
   (iii) The growing of pulses is important in India.
   (b) **(i)** Why is agriculture important in India?
   (ii) Name the two main agricultural seasons of India. **[2018]**

Marking Scheme ·······························

   (a) **(i)** Cotton is propagated by sowing seeds on the farm/Cotton has to be protected against weevils and other insects, therefore, pesticides have to be sprayed/Cotton is a soil exhausting crop, therefore, fertilizers have to be used/Mechanized harvesting of cotton is not possible, has to be done manually which goes on for three months. *(Any one)*
   (iii) Pulses are a source of proteins, particularly for the vegetarians/good as a rotation crop/leguminous, therefore has nitrogen fixing quality in the soil/used as cattle feed. *(Any one)*
   (b) **(i)** It is important as it provides employment, raw material for industries and export surplus/provides food and fodder.
   (ii) Rabi/Kharif

Ans. **(a)** **(i)** Cotton is a labour intensive crop because harvesting is done by hand and cannot be mechanised. The crop has to be protected against weevils and other insects.

   (iii) Growing of pulses is important in India as they are leguminous plants and help in crop rotation. They can be grown under a diverse climate. They are highly nutritious and vegetarian population is largely dependent on it.

   (b) **(i)** **1.** Agriculture is important in India as it provides food for our ever-expanding population and fodder for our livestock.
      2. It provides employment to millions of people.
   (ii) Rabi and Kharif seasons are the two main agricultural seasons of India.

Q. 4. **(a)** Explain the following terms and name the crop with which each is associated:
   (ii) Ratooning   **(iii)** Ginning

(b) Give geographical reasons for the following:
   (i) Regular pruning is essential for tea bushes. **[2017]**

Ans. **(a)** **(ii)** **Ratooning:** It is associated with sugarcane. After the first crop, the sugarcane is cut leaving the root intact in the soil. The lower part of the stem which is left in the soil is well fertilised and the stem begins to grow again.
   (iii) **Ginning:** It is associated with cotton. The cotton fibre is separated from the raw materials or the seeds.

(b) **(i)** Pruning is essential for tea bushes because the removal of the central stem encourages the quick development of lateral branches. Pruning also helps in growing new shoots bearing soft leaves in plenty.

Q. 5. **(a)** Study the picture given below and answer the questions that follow:

   (i) Name one state where this crop grows well.
   (ii) Why are mostly women employed to harvest it?
   (iii) Mention two geographical conditions suitable for the cultivation of this crop.
   (b) Explain briefly the following terms:
   (ii) Oil cake **[2016]**

Ans. **(a)** **(i)** Brahmaputra Valley and Surma Valley of Assam.
   (ii) The women are mostly employed in the tea plantations as they are the source of cheap and skilled labour to facilitate plucking of tea leaves.
   (iii) **Temperature Range:** 24°C–30°C.
      Rainfall: 150 to 350 cm annually, well distributed throughout the year is needed for the tea crop.
      Soil: Well drained, deep friable soil.
   (b) **(ii)** **Oil cake:** After extraction of oil from the oil seeds, the leftover residue is known as oil cake which can be

used as an important cattle feed and organic manure.

Q. 6. **(a)** **Give the geographic term for each of the following:**
   (i) Cultivation of sugarcane from the root stock of the cane which has been cut.
   (ii) The residue left behind after the crushing of oilseeds.
(b) **Give a geographical reason for each of the following:**
   (i) Tea is cultivated on hill slopes.
   (ii) The yield per hectare of sugarcane is higher in the Southern states.
   (iii) Pulses are important food crops.
   [2015]

Ans. **(a)** **(i)** Ratooning **(ii)** Oil cake
(b) **(i)** Tea plants require well drained soils. The hill slopes are ideal for tea plantations as the rolling hill slopes prevent water logging.
   (ii) The yield per hectare of sugarcane is higher in the Southern states due to the availability of better quality of the crop, presence of maritime climate free from the effect of summer loo and winter frost, sufficient irrigation and newer farming techniques.
   (iii) Pulses are important food crops as they consist of many crops which are leguminous and rich in protein. Thus, they are considered an important part of vegetarian diet.

Q. 7. **(a)** **Mention three differences in the geographical conditions and cultivation of rice and wheat.**
(b) **Give a geographical reason for each of the following:**
   (i) Cotton grows widely in Maharashtra.
   (ii) Clonal planting is the best method for tea propagation.
   (iii) Oil seeds are an important commercial crop grown in India.
   [2014]

Ans.

(a) Rice	Wheat
(i) It is a Kharif crop sown in June and harvested in October.	It is a Rabi crop sown in October-November and harvested in March-April.
(ii) During ripening stage the temperature should be 18°C-32°C. Mean temperature should be 24°C. Rice needs more than 150 cm of annual rainfall.	Wheat needs a temperature of about 10°C-15°C during the period of growth and 20°C-25°C during harvest. About 50 – 100 cm annual rainfall is ideal.
(iii) Harvested by hand.	Harvesters are used.

(b) **(i)** Cotton plant needs 21°C to 30°C of temperature, at least 200 frost free days and 50–80 cm of rainfall, well distributed during the period of growth. Abundant sunshine and no rain is required during ripening and picking period. Since, Maharashtra has black soil and all the required climatic conditions as stated above, so cotton grows well in Maharashtra.
   (ii) Cuttings are taken from a tea plant called the 'mother plant', known for its better yield, special flavour and quality. They are grown so as to produce tea shrubs yielding the same superior quality of tea. Thus, clonal planting is the best method for the tea propagation.
   (iii) Oil is extracted in mills or in village ghanis which provide employment to 10 million people both in rural and urban areas. India exports oil. 20% vegetable oil is consumed by the industry to make paints, varnishes, lubricants and seasoning wood. Oil is exported to earn foreign exchange.

Q. 8. **(a)** **(ii)** **What conditions of soil and climate are favourable for the cultivation of coffee?**
(b) **Explain in brief the following:**
   (ii) Ginning
   (iii) Broadcasting **[2013]**

Ans. **(a)** **(ii)** Conditions required for coffee cultivation are:
   Soil: Red and Laterite soils well drained with humus.
   Climate: It requires temperature ranging between 18°C to 28°C and rainfall between 125 cm to 200 cm. well distributed throughout the year.
(b) **(ii)** **Ginning:** Removal of cotton seed from cotton fibre is called ginning.

(iii) Broadcasting: Scattering of seeds by hand, over the soil is the broadcasting method of sowing seeds.

Q. 9. **(a)** Give geographical reasons for the following:

(ii) Tea is grown on hill slopes.

(b) Explain the following:

(i) The propagation of sugarcane by ratooning.

(ii) The propagation of paddy by transplantation. **[2012]**

Ans. **(a)** **(ii)** Tea is grown on the hill slopes as it requires a moderate temperature of 18°C-28°C. Moreover, the hill slopes do not allow the stagnation of water which is essential for tea plants as they cannot tolerate waterlogged conditions.

(b) **(i)** Ratooning involves the cutting of the cane close to the ground where the sugar content is maximum. After the crop has been cut, the stem begins to grow again and produces second crop called the ratoon.

(ii) Transplantation involves the sowing of rice seeds in nurseries at the beginning of monsoons. When the plants are about 15-20 cm tall, they are uprooted and replanted in parallel rows at regular intervals in flooded fields and left to grow till they mature.

Q. 10. **(b)** Explain the following terms:

(i) Withering

(iii) Drilling **[2011]**

Ans. **(b)** **(i) Withering:** The tea leaves are spread over shelves called withering racks and hot air is blown over the leaves to reduce their moisture content and to make them soft and flexible.

(iii) Drilling: It refers to the dropping of rice seeds in a straight line at regular intervals through a bamboo shaft attached to the plough which makes furrows.

Q. 11. **(a)** Answer the following questions with reference to sugarcane:

(i) Mention two different ways in which it is propagated.

(ii) Why is a lot of labour required for its cultivation?

(iii) Why must the sugar mills be near the sugar fields?

(b) Give geographical reasons for the following:

(i) Tea bushes are pruned at regular intervals.

(ii) Oil cake is a useful residue. **[2010]**

Ans. **(a)** **(i)** Two methods of propagating sugarcane plant:

1. The sugarcane is cut into pieces from stalk cuttings of two or three joints, known as setts. These setts are taken from the healthy plants of cane and casted by hand in the furrows made by the plough. The distance of 30 cm between the furrows should be kept so that there is no hindrance when they develop into cane.

2. The second method is known as ratooning. At the time of harvesting, the lower portion of the plant and the roots are left as they are in the fields. The stem begins to grow from the same roots and gains maturity in due course. This method is desirable for two years at the most.

(ii) Sugarcane is a long duration crop occupying the field for 12 months or more. The field has to be prepared by ploughing twice or thrice. It is a soil exhausting crop requiring lot of manure. Hence, lot of labour is required.

(iii) The raw material of sugarcane is bulky, hence difficult and expensive to transport. Also, if it is transported from one place to another, its sucrose content will reduce.

(b) **(i)** Pruning encourages the growth of new shoots with softer leaves.

(ii) Oil cake is an excellent cattle feed and it can also used as fertilizer.

Industries in India and Waste Generation and Management

 **Short Answer Type Questions-I**

Q. 1. (a) Give two reasons as to why Mumbai has developed into an important cotton textile centre.

(b) (i) What are Basic Industries?

(ii) Give one example of a Basic Industry in India.

Ans. (a) (1) Mumbai's location as an international port helps in import and export.

(2) Humid climate of Mumbai is ideal for this industry.

(b) (i) Basic industries are those industries which supply their products(semi-finished) to manufacture other goods.

(ii) Iron and steel Industry

Q. 2. (a) (i) What do you mean by segregation of waste?

(ii) Why is segregation of waste essential before its disposal?

(b) Why should sewage be treated before disposal?

Ans. (a) (i) Segregation of waste means waste from residential or commercial sources must be divided into biodegradable and non-biodegradable waste.

(ii) It is very important otherwise the unsegregated waste will be the part of landfills and the whole process of waste management will fail.

(b) The sewage should be treated before disposal because of the following reasons:

1. Untreated sewage causes many water related illness like diarrhoea.

2. The process of eutrophication takes place due to introduction of nutrients and chemicals through discharge of sewage.

Q. 3. (a) (i) Name the private sector iron and steel plant of India.

(ii) From where does it get its supply of:
1. Iron ore   2. Manganese
3. Coal

(b) Mention any two problems faced by the cotton textile industry of India.   **[2018]**

Ans. (a) (i) Tata Iron and Steel Company (TISCO).

(ii) 1. Iron ore—Gorumahisani in Mayurbhanj district of Odisha, Noamundi in Singhbhum, Jharkhand.

2. Manganese—Joda in Keonjhar district.

3. Coal—Jharia and Bokaro.

(b) Problems faced by the cotton textile industry of India:
1. Shortage of raw material.
2. Competition from other countries like Egypt.

Q. 4. (a) Give two reasons as to why there is a need for safe waste disposal.

(b) How can waste be reused? Explain with the help of an example.   **[2018]**

Ans. (a) Reasons for the need of safe waste disposal are:

(i) Accumulation of waste looks ugly, smells foul, attracts insects and spreads diseases.

(ii) It also causes pollution.

(b) Waste can be reused by recycling it and making new product out of it; e.g., shoes from old tyres, water bags from leather, etc.

Q. 5. (a) Differentiate between mineral-based industry and agro-based industry giving one example for each.

(b) 'Though Uttar Pradesh has the largest number of sugar mills yet Maharashtra is the largest producer of sugar.' Give any two reasons to justify the statement.   **[2017]**

Ans. (a) (i) Mineral-based industry depends on the minerals for their raw material, *e.g.*, iron and steel industry.

(ii) Agro-based industry depends on the agricultural products for their raw material, *e.g.*, jute industry/sugar industry.

(b) (i) Tropical climate, black soil, high temperature throughout the year, good rainfall, irrigation, and frost free growing season are best suited geographical conditions which gave high yield per unit in Maharashtra as compared to North India (Uttar Pradesh).

(ii) The sucrose content is higher in the tropical variety of sugarcane in Maharashtra as compared to that in Uttar Pradesh.

(iii) The cooperative sugar mills are better managed in Maharashtra, than in Uttar Pradesh.

(iv) Most of the mills are new in Maharashtra with modern machinery as compared to Uttar Pradesh.

(Any two)

Q. 6. **(a)** 'The Iron and Steel industry constitutes the backbone of modern industrial economy.' Give two reasons to justify the statement.

(b) **(i)** Name an Iron and Steel Industry set up in Orissa with the help of a famous German firm.

(ii) From where does the industry named in (b) (i) get its iron ore and manganese? **[2017]**

Ans. **(a)** **(i)** Iron and Steel industry is the key element in the heavy industrial structure of a nation. Most of the important industries such as automobile, locomotives, railway tracks, ship-building, machine and tools, and defence equipments depend on iron and steel industry.

(ii) The production and consumption of iron and steel is one of the most significant measures of the level of industrialisation and economic growth of a country.

(b) **(i)** Rourkela Steel Plant.

(ii) 1. Iron ore comes from Sundargarh and Keonjhar districts, these sources are located 77 km from its location.

2. Manganese comes from Noamundi or Keonjhar.

Q. 7. Mention two problems of the Cotton Textile industry in India. **[2016]**

Ans. Problems of cotton textile industry are:

1. **Obsolete machinaries:** Most of the mills have obsolete machinaries being thirty years old. This has resulted in low productivity and inferior quality.

2. **Inadequate power supply:** With increasing population, the problem of power supply is becoming acute and the industry suffers from the shortage of power.

3. **Low productivity of the labour:** Labour productivity is extremely low in India as compared to that of advanced countries.

4. **Stiff competition:** Indian cotton textile industry has to face stiff competition from the power loom and the synthetic fiber products. **(Any two)**

Q. 8. **(a)** Mention two advantages that a mini steel plant has over an integrated iron and steel plant.

(b) **(i)** Name an iron and steel plant which was established with British collaboration.

(ii) From where does it get its supply of:
1. iron ore   2. manganese
3. coal   **[2016, 2012]**

Ans. **(a)** 1. A mini steel plant uses scrap iron which is easily available and it does not require heavy capital investment.

2. These plants can be set up at any convenient place as they do not need huge infrastructure. Also they do not cause pollution as they use electric arc furnaces.

3. Since they are located in industrial towns so transport cost is reduced.

(Any two)

(b) **(i)** Durgapur Steel Plant

(ii) 1. It gets its iron ore from Keonjhar in Odisha and Singhbhum in Jharkhand.

2. Manganese comes from Keonjhar in Odisha.

3. Coking coal comes from Raniganj and Jharia.

Q. 9. **(a)** **(i)** Mention any two sources of waste.
(ii) What are biodegradable wastes? **[2016]**

Ans. **(a)** **(i)** Various sources of waste are :
1. Domestic waste
2. Industrial waste
3. Agricultural waste
4. Municipal waste   **(Any two)**

(ii) It is a waste which decomposes through the actions of bacteria, fungi and other living organisms.

Q. 10. Why is the cotton textile industry called an agro-based industry? **[2015]**

Ans. Cotton textile industry is considered as an agro based industry, as the industry depends on the raw material produced by the agricultural sector.

Q. 11. **(a)** **(i)** Why is the iron and steel industry called a basic industry?

(ii) Define a mini steel plant.

(b) With which large scale industry would you identify the following manufacturing centres?
(i) Kanpur   (ii) Rourkela
(iii) Pune   (iv) Mangalore   [2015]

Ans. **(a)** **(i)** Iron and steel industry is known as the basic industry as it forms the backbone of the modern industries. It is used to manufacture industrial machinery, railway tracks, dams, etc., which helps in industrialization and economic development of the country.

(ii) Mini steel plants usually have smaller operational units as compared to the integrated steel plants. They use cheaply available scrap iron in electric furnaces, which cater the local market, and hence produce fewer items like stainless steel, alloy steel, etc.

(b) **(i)** Kanpur–Sugar industry
(ii) Rourkela–Iron and steel plant
(iii) Pune–Cotton textile industry
(iv) Mangalore–Oil refining

Q. 12. (a) **(i) What is understood by biodegradable waste?**
(ii) State one source of gaseous waste.
[2015]

Ans. **(a)** **(i)** Biodegradable wastes are easily broken down by natural processes of decomposition. For example, leaves, plant remains, etc.

(ii) Gaseous waste exhausts from vehicles/burning of fossil fuels in factories and thermal power plants/ burning of wheat or rice straw/ methane from cattle sheds.

(Any one)

Q. 13. Give two reasons for each of the following:
(i) Kolkata is an important cotton manufacturing centre even though West Bengal is not a leading producer of cotton.   [2014]

Ans. **(i)** The hot and humid climate of Kolkata facilitates the spinning of yarn of finer cotton. It recieves soft water from river Ganga for bleaching and dying, sufficient power supply, cheap labour and excellent means of transportation.

Q. 14. (a) Name one integrated iron and steel plant in the private sector. Where does it obtain its iron and coal from?
(b) Name two raw materials used in the petrochemical industry and state two advantages of petrochemical products.
[2014]

Ans. **(a)** Tata Iron and Steel Company.
It obtains iron ore from Singhbhum in Jharkhand and Mayurbhanj, and Bonai in Odisha. Coal is secured from Jharia in Jharkhand.

(b) Naphtha, Propylene, Ethylene and Benzene are the raw materials used in the petrochemical industry.
Advantages:
(i) They are durable and cheaper.
(ii) They are not dependent on agricultural raw materials. Hence, there is no fluctuation in production due to climatic factors.

Q. 15. (a) Name any two large sugar producing states, one each in north and south India.
(b) Name an agro-based industry based in the following industrial centres:
(i) Ahmedabad   (ii) Mysore   [2013]

Ans. **(a)** Two large sugar producing states are:
In North India—Uttar Pradesh
In South India—Maharashtra

(b) **(i)** An agro-based industry in Ahmedabad—Cotton textile industry.
(ii) Mysore—Silk textile industry.

Q. 16. (a) **(i) What is the significance of the Electronics Industry in recent times?**
(ii) Name two cities that have leading Software Companies.
(b) Name the steel plants that were set up with Russian collaboration.   [2013]

Ans. **(a)** **(i)** Significance of electronic industry: It covers a wide range of products including television, transistor, cellular telecom, computers, defence, railways, meteorological equipments, space research as well as medical equipments. It has revolutionised the lifestyle of the Indian masses in the recent past.

(ii) Two cities are Bengaluru and Pune.

(b) Two steel plants are:
(i) Bokaro   **(ii)** Bhilai

Q. 17. (a) **(i) State the main objective of the treatment of gaseous waste.**
(ii) Name two common diseases caused as a result of gaseous pollution.
[2013]

Ans. **(a)** **(i)** The objectives of the treatment of gaseous waste is to drain the harmful particles and allow clean air to escape through chimneys.

(ii) Two diseases are lung cancer and asthma.

Q. 18. (a) What are petrochemicals?
   Name any two products made from petrochemicals.
   (b) Why has the electronics industry grown in importance? **[2012]**

Ans. **(a)** Petrochemicals are chemicals derived from petroleum, LPG and coal products. Products—Synthetics, fibres, plastics.
   (Any two)
   (b) The electronic products like telephone and internet services have made communication easy and fast, so the demand for such commodities is high. Industrial and technological development has also increased the demand for electronic products. It does wonders in the field of entertainment, defence equipments and medical diagnosis.

Q. 19. Name and define two important by-products of the sugar industry. **[2011]**

Ans. **(i) Bagasse:** The left over cane, after crushing is used for producing steam which is used as a source of power. It is also used for making card boards and paper.
   (ii) Molasses: It is used in alcohol industry for distillation of liquor. It is also used for making synthetic rubber.

Q. 20. (a) Which iron and steel industry of India is located away from the main coal areas? What is the main source of energy in the absence of coal?
   (b) Give two geographical reasons for the growth of IT industries in Bengaluru. **[2011]**

Ans. **(a)** Visveswaraya Iron and Steel Plant is located away from the main coal producing areas.
   Forests on the Western Ghats supply charcoal which is the main source of energy.
   (b) The growth of IT industries in Bengaluru is due to:
   (i) Readily available world class IT infrastructure.
   (ii) High concentration of IT companies and quality research and development institutions.

Q. 21. Classify industries on the basis of the nature of products. Give one example of each. **[2010]**

Ans. **(i)** Basic—Iron and steel
   (ii) Secondary—Paper, dyes
   (iii) Tertiary—Railways, road ways.

Q. 22. (a) Mention two reasons for the development of the petrochemical industry in India.
   (b) What is the difference between a public sector industry and one which is in the private sector? Give an example of an industry in each of the two sectors. **[2010]**

Ans. **(a)** The raw materials for the petrochemicals industry are cheaper. They are easily available and not dependent on the traditional raw materials like, metal, wood or agricultural products.
   (b) Public sector industries are owned and controlled by the central or state governments; for example, iron and steel, aircraft, petroleum refineries.
   Private sector industries are owned and managed by private industrialists as joint stock companies or proprietary concerns, for example, cement, paper, textiles.

Short Answer Type Questions-II

Q. 1. (a) (ii) Mention the most important factor for location of Sugar industries.

   (b) Briefly answer the following:
   (i) From where does the Rourkela Steel Plant obtain its supply of coal?
   (ii) From where does the Tata Iron and Steel Plant obtain its supply of iron ore?
   (iii) Name two cities that are important for the production of Electronics.

Ans. **(a) (ii)** Most deciding factor for location of sugar industry is its main raw material *i.e.* sugarcane. Sugarcane is a heavy and perishable material and has to be crushed within 24 hours.
   (d) (i) Rourkela Steel Plant obtains its coal from Jharia (Jharkhand), Talcher (Odisha) and Korba (Chhattisgarh) Coalfields.
   (ii) Tata Iron and Steel Plant obtains its iron ore from Singhbhum (Jharkhand) and Mayurbhanj (Odisha).
   (iii) Bengaluru and Hyderabad are important for the production of Electronics.

Q. 2. **(a)** Briefly answer each of the following:

(iii) What is the benefit of Composting?

(b) **(i)** How can recycling of waste help in reducing waste? Explain with suitable examples.

(ii) Mention one initiative taken by the Government to manage waste.

(iii) How can you as an individual contribute towards waste management?

Ans. **(a)** **(iii)** The benefits of composting are:

1. Conversion of organic waste into valuable fertilizers.

2. Reduction of the quantity of waste.

(b) **(i)** Recycling of waste turns the waste into raw material usable in other useful materials.

For example recycled paper can be used as in making new paper and box board and bagasse (residue of sugarcane) is used for manufacturing paper.

(ii) The Government of India initiated "Swachh Bharat Mission" on 2nd Oct, 2014.

(iii) As an individual we must follow the rule of three R's, *i.e.*, Reduce, reuse and recycle of waste.

Q. 3. **(a)** With reference to *sugar industries* answer the following questions:

(i) Why should these industries be located close to the sugarcane growing areas?

(ii) Name *two* by-products of the sugar industry.

(iii) Mention *one* leading sugar producing state in North India and *one* in South India.

(b) Give a reason for each of the following:

(i) *Ahmedabad* is an important cotton textile producing centre in India.

(ii) Cottage industries are significant for our economy.

(iii) Petrochemical industries are usually located close to the oil refineries.

[2019]

📋 **Marking Scheme** -

(a) **(i)** Sugarcane starts losing its sucrose after it is cut/to reduce the transportation cost/must be crushed within 48 hours/sugarcane is perishable.

(ii) Molasses/bagasse/press mud. *(Any two)*

(iii) North India – Uttar Pradesh/Bihar/Haryana /Punjab *(Any one)*
South India – Maharashtra/Karnataka/Tamil Nadu/Andhra Pradesh/Telangana *(Any one)*

(b) **(i)** Humid climate/availability of raw material/ availability of skilled and unskilled labours/ availability of cheap hydroelectricity/good transport network/port nearby/market/ capital or credit facility available/soft water available/government support. *(Any one)*

(ii) – Provides employment
– Brings in foreign exchange
– Need less built up area
– Can be started with less capital investment
– Uses local raw material
– Keeps the traditions alive from one generation to another
Fulfil local need/ low cost of transport *(Any one)*

(iii) Raw materials used in petrochemical industries are mainly derived from petroleum hence these industries are located close to oil refineries.

Ans. **(a)** **(i)** Sugarcane needs to be crushed within 24 to 48 hrs, otherwise, the sucrose content is reduced. So, the sugar industry should be located close to the sugarcane growing areas.

(ii) Molasses, Bagasses, Press mud.

(iii) North India — UP/Punjab/Bihar/ Haryana.
South India — Maharashtra/ Karnataka/ Tamil Nadu.

(b) **(i)** Ahmedabad is located right in the centre of the cotton producing area. It enjoys humid climate which is ideal for cotton thread. It provides a huge ready market for cheaper cloth among the poor masses of India. It also has an advantange of both Kandla (free trade zone) and Mumbai port for export and import. So, Ahmedabad is an important cotton textile centre.

(ii) Cottage industries are significant for our economy in the following ways:

1. Cottage industries provide employment to a large number of people in India.

2. It also helps India to earn considerable amount of foreign exchange.

3. It also stops rural to urban migration.

(iii) Petrochemical industry gets its raw materials from the oil refineries. So, they are located close to the oil refineries.

Q. 4. **(a)** **(i)** **What can an individual do to reduce waste at home?**

(ii) **Why must segregation of waste be done before disposal?**

(iii) **How has composting proven to be great help in managing waste?**

(b) **Give a reason for each of the following:**

(i) **Trees must be planted in the industrial areas.**

(ii) **Chemical fertilizers must be replaced by organic manure.**

(iii) **Plastic and polythene products must be banned.** **[2019]**

Ans. **(a)** **(i)** 1. Instead of discarding household items, one can reuse the items after repairing and polishing them.

2. Household waste like vegetable peels, garden waste etc. can be reduced by making compost.

3. Use products which do not generate too much waste, are eco-friendly and biodegradable.

(ii) Waste from residential areas, hotels, offices and commercial areas must be segregated into different categories of biodegradable and non-biodegradable wastes for treating, recycling and disposing appropriately.

(iii) Composting has proven to be of great help in managing waste as it has lead to:

1. Conversion of organic waste into valuable fertilizers.

2. Reduction of the quantity of waste to be disposed off by the householder.

3. It is a normal waste disposal system and help nutrients get back into the soil.

(b) **(i)** Trees must be planted in and around the industrial areas as trees can arrest the pollutants and avoid health hazards of the human and animal population living in and around the industries.

(ii) Chemical fertilizers remain in the soil for a long time contaminating the

top soil and ground water while the organic manure improves the texture of the soil, aids plant growth and increase the water holding capacity of the soil. Thus, chemical fertilizers must be replaced by organic manure.

(iii) Disposal of plastics and its effects on human health are a matter of great concern. Coloured plastics are harmful as their pigment contains heavy metals that are highly toxic other toxic contents like chromium, cobalt, lead and copper in plastics cause great harm to both humans and animals.

Q. 5. **(a)** **Give the geographical reason for each of the following:**

(ii) **Petrochemical products are gaining popularity in modern times.**

(iii) **The electronics industry is proving to be an asset for our country in the field of education.**

(b) **Name the following:**

(i) **A city most famous for electronics and hence called "The Electronics Capital of India."**

(ii) **The location of an iron and steel industry set up with German collaboration.**

(iii) **A by-product of sugar industry which is used in the manufacture of wax and shoe polish.** **[2018]**

📋 Marking Scheme ------------------------------

(a) **(ii)** Petrochemicals are cost effective, durable, cheaper, and available in plenty/generation of employment/not dependent on agriculture.

(iii) Computer, IWB, Multimedia presentation, laptop, palmtop, eBooks, e-content etc. is helpful in education field.

(b) **(i)** Bengaluru

(ii) It is in Sundergarh district of Odisha at the confluence of Sankha and Koel in Rourkela.

(iii) Press mud.

Ans. **(a)** **(ii)** Petrochemical products are gaining popularity in modern times as they are economically stable and cheaper as they are produced at mass scale. Raw material is easily available.

(iii) The electronics industry is proving to be an asset for our country in the field of education as all the electronic gadgets *i.e.,* mobile, computers, IWB, Laptops, e-Books, etc. are the sources of knowledge for the modern world.

(b) (i) Bengaluru.

(ii) Rourkela Steel Plant.

(iii) Press mud.

Q. 6. **What do you mean by the following terms?**
(i) **Segregation.** (ii) **Composting.**
(iii) **Dumping.** [2018]

 Marking Scheme ----------------------

(i) Segregation: It means dividing the waste separately by sorting degradable from nondegradable substances.

(ii) Composting: It is an aerobic method of decomposing of organic waste.

(iii) Dumping: In this method waste is dumped in open low-lying areas far from the city.

Ans. (i) **Segregation:** Separating the waste into biodegradable and non-biodegradable.

(ii) **Composting:** It is an aerobic (in the presence of air) method of decomposing solid wastes. The process involves decomposition of organic waste into humus known as compost which is a good fertilizer for plants.

(iii) **Dumping:** In this method, waste materials are dumped in open low lands away from the city.

Q. 7. **(a)** **Give the geographic term for each of the following:**
(ii) **Rejected cane after crushing.**

(b) **With reference to the cotton textile industry answer the following questions:**
(i) **Give two reasons why Mumbai is an important cotton textile industry.**
(ii) **Mention two more important centres of cotton textile industry in India.** [2017]

Ans. **(a)** (ii) Bagasse.

(b) (i) 1. Easy availability of raw cotton in and around Mumbai.

2. Humid climate of shore-based Mumbai is ideal for this industry as the thread does not break so easily.

3. Cheap hydroelectric power is available from Tata HEP grid from Western Ghats.

4. Mumbai's location as an important international port, helps in import of long-staple cotton and machinery, and export of finished goods.

(ii) 1. Ahmedabad in Gujarat.

2. Coimbatore in Tamil Nadu.

Q. 8. **(a)** **Name a manufacturing centre for each of the following industries:**
(i) **Aircraft** (ii) **HMT**
(iii) **Railway coaches**

(b) **Name two products of each of the following industries:**
(i) **Petrochemical industry**
(ii) **Heavy engineering industry**
(iii) **Electronic industry** [2017]

Ans. **(a)** (i) Aircraft—Bengaluru.

(ii) HMT—Hyderabad.

(iii) Railway coaches—Kapurthala in Punjab.

(b) (i) **Petrochemical industry:** Polythene, PVC of plastic group, nylon, dacron, synthetic rubber.

(ii) **Heavy engineering:** Engine, generator, pumps, machines, railway wheels, railway tracks.

(iii) **Electronic industry:** Components like capacitor, resistor, printed circuit board, computers, monitors, television sets, defence equipments.

Q. 9. **(a)** **What do you mean by the following:**
(iii) **Recycling**

Ans. **(a)** (iii) **Recycling:** It is a process in which the waste is converted into raw material that is usable in other useful manufacturing process. This helps to reduce the waste generation by reversing or recycling it.

Q. 10. **(a)** **Give a reason for each of the following:**
(i) **Products made from petrochemicals are growing in popularity.**
(ii) **The electronics industry contributes to the development of the country.**

(b) **Name the industrial product for which the following centres are well known:**
(ii) **Chittaranjan**
(iii) **Koraput** [2016]

Ans. **(a)** (i) They are cost effective as produced at mass scale, and because of their durability and washability they are growing very popular.

(ii) The electronic industry contributes to the development of the country as it has diversified its production range to meet the needs of the post and telegraph department, railways, defense, overseas communication services and electricity board.

It has contributed to the space technology and various electronic and space research programmes.

(b) (ii) Chittaranjan Locomotive Works – For the production of electric railway engines.

(iii) Koraput – The engines for MIG Aircrafts are manufactured.

Q. 11. (a) Explain briefly the meaning of the following terms:
(i) Composting
(iii) Segregation [2016]

Ans. **(a) (i) Composting:** Composting is biodegradable organic waste like tree leaves, vegetable peel and discarded food items (converted into useful manure).

(iii) Segregation: The waste from residential areas, hotels, restaurants, office complexes and commercial areas must be segregated at source into different categories of bio-degradable, non-biodegradable, bio-medical, toxic and non-toxic waste.

Q. 12. (a) (i) State two major problems faced by the sugar industry.
(ii) Name two by-products of the sugar industry.
(b) (ii) Why are synthetic fibres popular? [2015]

Ans. **(a) (i)** Two problems faced by the sugar industry are as follows:
1. The sugarcane cultivated in India is of poor quality and have low sucrose content.
2. The cost of production is quite high because of the inefficient and uneconomic nature of production.
(ii) Two by-products of sugar industry are molasses and bagasse.
(b) (ii) Synthetic fibres are cheaper and more durable, thus, they are more popular.

Q. 13. (a) (i) State two reasons for the growing importance in the status of petrochemical industries.
(ii) Name two products of the petroleum industry.
(b) (i) State two conditions necessary for the setting up of a heavy engineering industry.
(ii) Name a shipbuilding yard on the east coast and a centre for making electric locomotives. [2015]

Ans. **(a) (i)** The reasons for the growing importance of the petrochemical industry are as follows:
1. The petrochemical products do not depend on agricultural raw materials, hence, there is no fluctuation in production due to climatic factors.
2. The petrochemical products like plastics, PVC pipes, synthetic fibres are cheaper and more durable.
(ii) Two products are plastics and PVC pipes.
(b) (i) Two conditions required for setting up of heavy engineering industry are as follows:
1. Availability of heavy and bulky raw materials like iron ore.
2. Large capital investment.
(ii) Ship-building yard on East coast of India–Vishakhapatnam.
Electric locomotives centre-Chittaranjan.

Q. 14. (a) (i) "Waste segregation is important". Give a reason to support your answer.
(iii) Explain briefly how as a student, you can help in the reduction of waste generation. [2015]

Ans. **(a) (i)** Segregation of wastes according to the methods of treatment is necessary for proper waste management. Thus, wastes are separately collected in different bins for biodegradable and non-biodegradable products.
(iii) Generation of wastes can be reduced by reducing, recycling and reusing of wastes known as 3Rs.

Q. 15. Mention three factors that have helped the sugar industry flourish in the peninsular region rather than in the northern regions of India. [2014]

Ans. The geographical conditions are more suitable in the peninsular region than in North India for the cultivation of sugarcane because of the following factors:
(i) The crushing season is longer and mills are near the plantations in the peninsular region and so there is no loss of sucrose. In North India, it is seasonal in character as sugarcane is available only at the time of harvest and the crushing season is short. So, there is increase in cost of production.
(ii) The sugar industry is better organized in the peninsular region as the mills are better managed in the cooperative sector, factories are closer to the centre of large consumption. This lowers the transport costs and overall prices. In North India, there are great distances between the

factories and the fields which causes increase in the cost of production.

(iii) The outmoded and worn-out machinery of North Indian mills leads to low milling efficiency and wastage. The mills in peninsular India are new, efficient and very large.

Q. 16. (a) Give a reason for each of the following:
    (i) Vishakhapatnam is a leading centre for shipbuilding.
    (ii) Mini steel plants cause less pollution than integrated steel plants.
    (iii) The electronic industry has made an impact on both entertainment and education.
(b) Name a manufacturing centre for each of the following industries:
    (i) Engines for MIG aircraft
    (ii) Diesel locomotives
    (iii) Software   **[2014]**

Ans. **(a) (i)** Hindustan Shipyard at Vishakhapatnam is a leading ship-building centre of deep navigable water off the coast, with an excellent transport network, technical know-how, availability of steel and demand for the ships, gets its iron and steel from VISL, power from Nagarjuna Sagar Dam, labour from Andhra Pradesh and Odisha.

(ii) Mini steel plants work through electric furnaces causing less pollution, whereas the integrated steel plants use blast furnaces where coking coal are fed continuously to melt the iron ore, causing huge pollution.

(iii) Electronic industry with mass scale integration process has produced computers, servers, displays, TVs and cameras, telephone exchanges, etc., to enable capture and broadcast news, advertisements, cinema, educational programs, etc., to large section of the population over the country and overseas, thus, revolutionizing the lifestyle of the Indian masses.

(b) (i) Engines for MIG aircraft—Koraput in Odisha.

(ii) Diesel locomotives—Chittaranjan in West Bengal/Varanasi in Uttar Pradesh.

(iii) Software—Bengaluru in Karnataka.

Q. 17. Give geographical reasons for the following:

It is necessary to crush sugarcane within 24 hours of harvesting.   **[2013]**

Ans. Geographical reasons are:

It is necessary to crush sugarcane within 24 hours of harvesting because the sugar content decreases as it dries up.

Q. 18. (a) Explain three reasons as to why there is a large concentration of iron and steel plants in the Chota Nagpur Region.
(b) What industrial products are the following centres noted for?
    (i) Gurgaon
    (ii) Perambur
    (iii) Chittaranjan.   **[2013]**

Ans. **(a)** Three reasons for large concentration of iron and steel plants in Chhota Nagpur region are:
    (i) Availability of iron ore
    (ii) Availability of coal for power
    (iii) Availability of cheap labour

(b) Industrial products are:
    (i) Gurgaon—Maruti cars.
    (ii) Perambur—Railway coaches.
    (iii) Chittaranjan—Locomotives.

Q. 19. (a) Mention three problems of the sugar industry in India.
(b) In what way does the cotton industry contribute to the economy of India? Mention any three relevant factors.   **[2012]**

Ans. **(a)** Problems of the sugar industry are:
    1. The industry is seasonal in character, so there is an overall increase in the cost of production due to short crushing season.
    2. There are great distances between the factories and the fields. The increased transportation cost increases the cost of production.
    3. The low sugar content is due to poor quality cane which tends to dry if not crushed within 24 hours.

(b) **1.** The cotton industry is a major foreign exchange earner for India.
    2. It provides employment to a large section of the population.
    3. Supports a large number of industries like chemical, packaging material, etc.

Q. 20. (a) Name:
    (i) A city on the east coast of India which has a shipbuilding yard.
    (ii) The iron and steel plant set up with German collaboration.
    (iii) A city which has a plant manufacturing Maruti cars.   **[2012]**

Ans. **(a)** **(i)** Vishakhapatnam
  (ii) Rourkela Steel Plant
  (iii) Gurgaon

Q. 21. With reference to the cotton textile industry:
  (i) Which is the country's most important manufacturing centre?
  (ii) State two geographical reasons for its importance. [2011]

Ans. **(i)** Mumbai.
  (ii) (1) The hinterland of Mumbai has Black Regur soil so plenty of raw material is easily available.
  (2) The humid climate of Mumbai favours the production of yarns of finer quality.

Q. 22. (a) With reference to the Bokaro Steel Plant, from where does it get its
  (i) coal
  (ii) iron ore
  (iii) water supply
  (b) Name one important centre each for the production of the following:
  (i) Electronic goods
  (ii) Petrochemicals. [2011]

Ans. **(a)** **(i)** Coal from Bokaro and Jharia.
  (ii) Iron ore from Bonaigarh and Noamundi.
  (iii) Water supply from Damodar river.
  (b) **(ii)** Electronic goods—Bengaluru
  (iii) Petrochemicals—Haldia.

Q. 23. (a) (i) Mention two reasons for the importance of the cotton textile industry.
  (ii) Mention one reason responsible for its poor performance.
  (b) Give geographical reasons for the following:
  (i) Kolkata has many cotton mills though cotton is not grown in West Bengal.
  (iii) India produces very little sugarcane though it is one of the largest producers of sugarcane in the world. [2010]

Ans. **(a)** **(i)** There is great demand for cotton, especially, in the south which is a region of warm and equable climate.
  The climatic conditions too are suitable *e.g.* humid and warm climate and the black soil. The alluvial soil in the north is also suitable.
  (ii) India's production of finer varieties of cotton is inadequate for its needs. Being an agricultural product, in years of drought there are fluctuations in quantity and price.

(b) **(i)** Kolkata has a humid climate, and soft water received from the river, Hooghly. It has sufficient power supply because it is near the Jharia and Raniganj coalfields. It has abundant capital and cheap labour.
  (iii) The areas producing sugarcane are far away from the factories. This implies transport which increases the cost. Besides, the sucrose content decreases rapidly after 24 to 48 hours. This lowers the quality of sugarcane.

Q. 24. (a) (i) How is it advantageous for a mini steel plant:
  (1) to use electric furnaces?
  (2) not to be located close to the location of the raw material?
  (ii) From where does the integrated steel plant at Bhilai get its requirement of iron and coal?
  (b) Name the following:
  (i) A city in India where MIG aircrafts are manufactured.
  (ii) A centre where railway coaches are manufactured.
  (iii) The foreign collaborator of the iron and steel plant at Durgapur. [2010]

Ans. **(a)** **(i) (1)** Mini steel plants are small size steel plants having less production capacity of one lakh metric tonnes or less. They are also meant to produce liquid steel used for ingots, billets. They therefore, do not require big furnaces as the blast furnace.
  (2) They use scrap iron (iron that is left after the steel is manufactured). There is no need for them to be located near the location of the raw material. The government is going in for more such plants in various parts of the country which would help in meeting the steel requirements and bring about a more balanced growth.
  (ii) The Bhilai steel plant gets iron ore from the Dalli-Rajhara mines in Durg district. The Korba coalfields in Madhya Pradesh supply coal. Better quality coal is obtained from Raniganj and Jharia coalfields.
  (b) **(i)** Nasik
  (ii) Perambur
  (iii) British Company

Chapter 7

Transport

 Short Answer Type Questions-I

Q. 1. **(a)** **With reference to Waterways answer the following questions:**

(i) **Mention two advantages of inland water transport.**

(ii) **Why is inland water transport not well developed in India?**

(b) **Even though all means of transport are well developed in India, yet, road transport remains the most popular means of transport. Justify this statement.**

Ans. **(a)** **(i)** Two advantages of inland water transport are:

1. Inland water transport is considered as cheapest mean of transport for both passenger and cargo traffic.

2. Inland water transport consumes very less energy as compared to other means of transport.

(ii) Because the seasonal variation in the volume of water, due to monsoon rain, affects the navigability of rivers.

(b) Undoubtedly, the road transportation is very common in India because:

1. Roadways feed other modes of transportation.

2. Roads provide door to door facilities.

3. Even the remote areas of deserts or mountains can be accessible through road network.

Q. 2. **(a)** **"Roadways are an important means of transport in India." Give *two reasons* to justify the statement.**

(b) **(i)** **Why are South Indian rivers *not ideal* for the inland water transport?**

(ii) **Mention one advantage of coastal shipping.** **[2019]**

Ans. **(a)** Roadways are an important means of transport in India because:

1. Road construction can be undertaken in remote areas, difficult terrains, high altitudes and steep slopes.

2. Road transport provides door to door service. So, the cost of transport is reduced.

3. It provides a link between the railways and the ports.

4. For perishable commodities like fruits and vegetables, road transport is the best means.

(b) **(i)** Rivers in South India flow in rocky areas and have an irregular terrain with a number of waterfalls and sharp bends. So, the rivers are not suitable for inland water transport.

(ii) Coastal shipping is the most economical and environment friendly mode of transport as compared to railways and airways as it saves fuel, reduces the burden on rail and road transport systems and provides employment to thousands of people.

Q. 3. **(a)** **Give two reasons for the "means of transport" being called the lifelines of a nation's economy.**

(b) **Give two ways in which rail transport is useful for the people of India.** **[2018]**

Ans. **(a)** Two reasons why "means of transport" are called the lifelines of a nation's economy, are:

(i) It aids in the process of industrialisation and urbanisation.

(ii) It helps in better utilisation of the resources of backward areas by linking them with the more advanced areas.

(b) Two ways in which rail transport is useful for the people of India are:

(i) Helps in easy movement of heavy goods and perishable commodities to distant places.

(ii) Being cheaper and safer than other forms of transport, it greatly helps during natural calamities.

Q. 4. **(a)** **Mention two reasons why more people use railways rather than airways?**

(b) **Why is inland waterways declining in its importance? Give two reasons for your answer.** **[2017, 2012]**

Ans. **(a)** 1. Air transport is very expensive so most people cannot afford it.
2. Not all places are connected by airways.
(b) 1. It is slower means of transport.
2. Water transport provides access to limited areas.
3. Diversion of water from the river for the purpose of irrigation and silting of the river beds have reduced the importance of inland water transport.

Q. 5. **Roadways are always considered more important than any other means of transportation. Give two reasons in support of the statement.** **[2016]**

Ans. Roadways are considered more important because roads can be constructed in remote areas, difficult terrain, high altitudes and steep slopes where no other means of transport can reach. Roads provide door to door service. They are quicker and safer means of transport; thus the cost of transportation is reduced considerably.

Q. 6. **(a)** **(i) Why is the Railways an important means of transport as compared to Airways?**
(ii) State one economic benefit of the Golden Quadrilateral Project. **[2015]**

Ans. **(a)** **(i)** Railways are an important means of transport as compared to air transport because railways can carry large number of people and transport heavy and bulky goods over a long distance.
(ii) The Golden Quadrilateral Project helps in the transport of agricultural products from hinterlands to major cities and ports. This promotes agricultural as well as industrial growth.

Q. 7. **(a)** **Why is road transport in India considered more useful than rail transport? State two reasons in support of your answer.**

(b) **Mention one advantage and one disadvantage each of inland waterways.** **[2014]**

Ans. **(a)** **(i)** Road transport is more flexible than rail as buses, trucks and cars may be stopped anywhere and at any time for passengers and goods, whereas trains stop at stations only.
(ii) Road transport provides door to door facility. Roads can negotiate high gradients and sharp turns to reach at almost all areas, whereas trains cannot do the same. Roads can be constructed in hilly areas also.

(b) **Advantage:** Inland waterways are the cheapest means of transport and suitable for carrying heavy and bulky materials.
Disadvantage: Water transport is limited to the areas where rivers are navigable and oceanic routes exist.

Q. 8. **Give one disadvantage of air transport. Why is it still a popular means of transportation in India?** **[2013]**

Ans. Air transport has limited carrying capacity. Still it is popular because it is free of physical barriers such as mountain ranges, valleys, etc.

Q. 9. **Name two areas where helicopter services may be used?** **[2012]**

Ans. 1. Mountain and hilly areas.
2. Flooded areas.

Q. 10. **(a)** **Why is road transport favoured in the northern plains of India?**
(b) **Give reasons to explain the lack of rail transport in Northern India.** **[2011]**

Ans. **(a)** Road transport is favoured in the Northern plains due to its fertile soils and the high density of population.
(b) Northern India has rugged relief and large number of rivers, existence the Himalayas and steep valleys, which makes construction of railways expensive.

Short Answer Type Questions-II

Q. 1. **(a)** **Give a reason for each of the following :**
(i) **Roadways is not well developed in North East India.**
(ii) **Railways are under the public sector.**
(iii) **A good network of transport is of great help for the development of the economy.**

(d) **(i)** **Give two disadvantages of airways traffic in recent years?**
(ii) **Why is there an increase of airway traffic in recent years?**

Ans. **(a)** **(i)** Because north-eastern part of India has geographically unfavourable conditions to support road network. This region mainly consists of hilly terrain, huge rainfall and thick forest cover.

(ii) Railways help in administration of our country. It helps in easy movement of heavy defense equipments, troops, police and military within the country.

(iii) A good transport network helps in boosting the agriculture and industrial sector. A good transport network is the basis to develop national and international trade.

(b) (i) Two disadvantages of airways are:

1. Airways are among the mode source of transportation.

2. Aircrafts cannot carry bulky equipments and goods.

(ii) Despite its exorbitant price, air travel has been gaining popularity in recent years as airways are fast, comfortable and time saving.

Q. 2. (a) Give a reason for each of the following:

(i) Nearly seventy percent of Indians do not use air transport.

(ii) A well-developed transport network is important for industrial growth.

(iii) Water transport is not as popular as land transport in India.

(b) (i) "The railways is an important means of transport as compared to airways." State two reasons to support the statement.

(ii) Mention one disadvantage of rail transport. **[2019]**

📋 **Marking Scheme** -

(a) (i) Air transport is very expensive hence it is not used by many people/carry less luggage/ not comfortable for long journey/no airport in small town.

(ii) Transportation helps in easy movement of raw materials and finished goods/ connect backward areas/mobility of skilled and unskilled labour/decentralised growth.

(iii) Water transport is limited to areas which have navigable water source. It is slow and not well connected.

(a) (i) – It carries bulky raw materials and heavy goods.
– It is cheaper than airways.
– Caters to more number of passengers at one time.
– Can carry more amount of goods.
– Comfortable for long journey

(Any two points)

(ii) – The flow of goods and passengers are hampered in India as the railways' operation is on three gauges.
– Shifting from one gauge to another is time consuming and expensive.

– Perishable items cannot stand the delay.
– The tracks are not able to carry increased goods and accidents are becoming frequent.
– Poor maintenance of tracks.
– Outdated engines and compartments.
– It causes pollution.
– Overcrowded
– Delays

(Any one point)

Ans. **(a) (i)** Air transport is very expensive. It tends to serve only a particular sector who can afford the exorbitant fares. These fares are normally beyond the reach of the common man. Thus, seventy percent of Indians cannot afford it.

(ii) Transport links consumption to production and hinterland to the production centres. It also links the country with rest of the world. Thus, a well-developed transport network is important for the overall industrial growth of the country.

(iii) Water transport is a very slow means of transport as compared to land transport. In India, there is always a chance of failure of monsoon which may result into a fall of water level in the rivers making navigation difficult whereas, land transport does not face any such seasonal difficulties. Water transport is more risky as compared to land transport because there is always a danger of sinking of ships or boats. Thus it is not as popular as land transport in India.

(b) (i) Rail transport is the cheapest mode of transport for bulky products like food grain, minerals, heavy defence equipments, etc., whereas, air transport is expensive for both passenger and freight. Rail transport helps to link the rural India with the urban cities, on the other hand air transport links only the major cities of the country to one another. Thus, railways is an important means of transport as compared to airways.

(ii) Railways is unsafe due to poor maintenance, frequent accidents, terror attacks and faulty repairs. Poor management, poor catering and lack of amenities at railway stations have resulted in an inefficient image of the railways in the eyes of the public.

Q. 3. **(a)** **(i)** State one advantage of inland waterways.

(ii) State one advantage of roadways.

(iii) State one disadvantage of water transport.

(b) Give three reasons as to why airways are becoming a popular means of transport in modern India. **[2018]**

📋 Marking Scheme

(a) (i) It is cheaper, eco-friendly/low maintenance.
(ii) Cheaper/door to door service/safer movement of goods/links other means of transport.
(iii) It is time consuming/depends on whether/ can cause sea sickness.
(b) Airways are faster.
Comfortable
Can cross natural barriers with ease.
Provide quick help in natural calamities.

Ans. **(a)** **(i)** It is suitable for carrying heavy and bulky material within a particular country or continent.

(ii) It provides door to door service so that every village and hamlet can be reached.

(iii) It is majorly affected by weather conditions.

(b) Reasons as to why airways are becoming a popular means of transport in modern India are:

(i) Airways is the fastest and most comfortable mode of transport.

(ii) It is helpful during natural calamities.

(iii) The speed and ease with which aeroplanes cross mountains, sandy desert, water bodies and forests make the air transport indispensable.

Q. 4. Mention two advantages and one disadvantage of waterways. **[2016]**

Ans. The two advantages of water transport are:

1. It is suitable for carrying heavy and bulky goods.

2. It is fuel efficient and an environment friendly mode of transport.

Disadvantages: The seasonal rivers of peninsular India are not navigable. It is the slow means of transport.

Due to silting of river beds and diversion of water for irrigation canals the river beds have become shallow so navigation is not possible in all rivers.

Q. 5. **(a)** **(i)** State one important difference between an expressway and a highway.

(ii) Name the first expressway constructed in the country.

(iii) State a reason why the Northern rivers are more suitable for navigation than the Deccan rivers. **[2015]**

Ans. **(a)** **(i)** One of the major differences between a highway and an expressway is that a highway is a high speed road connecting two or more cities, while an expressway is a very high speed highway that has limited or controlled access for two wheelers and three wheelers, but has features like lane dividers and access ramps to provide a pleasing motoring experience at high speed to motorists.

(ii) Ahemdabad-Vadodara Expressway is the first expressway of India.

(iii) The Northern rivers are more suitable for navigation than the Deccan rivers as the former has a perennial flow while the latter has seasonal flow of water. Moreover, the presence of waterfalls, sharp bends, etc., also hamper the navigation in case of the Deccan rivers.

Q. 6. **(a)** **(i)** Give two reasons why peninsular rivers are not ideal for navigation.

(ii) Name a port on the east coast which is often hit by cyclones during the months of October and November. **[2013]**

Ans. **(a)** Peninsular rivers are not ideal for navigation because:

(i) **(1)** Rivers are seasonal in nature
(2) Rivers flow through undulating rocky plateau region.

(ii) Vishakhapatnam port is often hit by cyclones during October and November.

Q. 7. **(a)** Mention any three problems being faced by the Indian Railways.

(b) What is the Golden Quadrilateral? Mention any two ways in which it will help in the economic development of the country? **[2012]**

Ans. **(a)**
1. Railways are difficult to construct in the hilly and mountainous parts of India.
2. The huge size of the country makes it difficult to connect the remote parts of the country.
3. Obsolete trains, tracks and equipments make railways unsafe.

(b) The Golden Quadrilateral is a highway network connecting India's four largest metropolises: Delhi, Mumbai, Chennai and Kolkata. The project will help industrial development by easing the process of supply of raw materials. It will also help to connect many remote areas with the main cities.

Q. 8. **(a) Name the following:**
(i) An important inland waterway of north-east India.
(ii) One expressway with its terminal cities.
(iii) A major port which is not located on the sea coast and is at a distance of 128 km from the coast along the banks of a river.

(b) Mention two advantages and one disadvantage of air transport. **[2011]**

Ans. **(a)**
(i) The National Waterway No. 2— The river Brahmaputra connecting Dhubri—Guwahati—Dibrugarh.
(ii) The Sher Shah Suri Marg connecting Delhi and Amritsar.
(iii) Kolkata port.

(b) Two advantages of air transport are:
(i) It is the fastest and the most comfortable mode of transport. It connects the remote areas of the country.
(ii) Air transport can move across mountain barriers, sandy deserts, large expanses of water and forests.

One disadvantage of air transport: It depends on weather conditions. Flights are often delayed due to bad weather.

8 Topographical Maps

Short Answer Type Questions-I

Q. 1. Study the extract of the Survey of India Map sheet No. 45D/10 and answer the following questions :

(a) (ii) Give a four figure grid reference for open scrub South of Dhad Talao.

(b) (i) What is the meaning of the term 'Contour interval'?

(ii) What is the contour interval of the sheet provided to you?

(c) What is the area in kilometre square of the region between 06 and 09 Eastings and 22 and 27 Northings?

(d) What is the significance of the following colours used on the survey map?

(i) Yellow colour

(ii) Green colour

(e) What is the compass direction of?

(i) Idarla (0825) from Bhamra (0420).

(ii) Dhana (0623) from Amarapura (0124).

(f) (i) Name the settlement pattern seen in the grid square 0819.

(ii) Name the drainage pattern seen in the grid square 0827.

(g) (i) Name two man made features seen in the grid square 0723.

(ii) Name two natural features seen in the grid square 0218.

(h) (i) What is the black horizontal line drawn between 18 and 19 Northings?

(ii) Name the most important settlement of the region shown on the map extract.

(j) (i) Give one evidence to prove that the regions shown on the map extract receive scanty rainfall.

Ans. (a) (ii) 0721

(b) (i) Contour Interval is the interval of difference between two successive contours. It is also known as vertical interval.

(ii) Contour Interval is 20

(c) 15 km²

(d) (i) Yellow colour represents agricultural land.

(ii) Green colour signifies dense mixed jungles

(e) (i) North East

(ii) North West

(f) (i) Jolpur

(ii) Dendritic drainage pattern

(g) (i) Two man made features seen in grid square 0723 are Huts and well.

(ii) Two natural features seen in grid square 0218 are Sukhi Nadi and dry river bed.

(h) (i) The black horizontal line drawn between 18 and 19 northings is fire line.

(ii) The most important settlement of the region shown on the map extract is ABU.

(j) (i) The region shown on the map extract receives scanty rainfall as this region have abundance of open scrubs.

Q. 2. Study the extract of the *Survey of India* Map Sheet No. *45D/10* and answer the following questions:

(a) (ii) Give the *four-figure* grid reference for a settlement where people of the region meet socially and for trade at least once in a year.

(b) (i) What is the pattern of drainage seen in the grid square *2118*?

(ii) What is the pattern of settlement seen in the grid square *1923?*

(c) What do each of the two numbers (281 printed in black colour and 20 printed in red colour) in the grid square *1818* indicate?

(d) (i) Name any *two* man-made features in grid square *2419*.

(ii) Name any *two* natural features in grid square *2118*.

(e) What is the significance of the following?

(i) *Fire line* in grid square 2417.

(ii) Water body found in grid square *2221*.

(f) Calculate the *area* of the region between *16* and *19* Eastings and *18* and *22* Northings. Give your answer in *kilometre square*.

(g) Give a reason for each of the following:
  (i) The water in some of the wells in the north-west quarter of the map is *not* fit for drinking.
  (ii) The region near Anadra and Gulabganj has many causeways.
(h) **(i)** What is the main means of irrigation used by people living in the area shown on the map?
  (ii) What is the main occupation of the people of the region shown on the map?
(i) Which according to you is the most important settlement? Give a reason to support your answer.
(j) Name any two means of transport used by the people living in the area shown on the map extract. **[2019]**

🗒 Marking Scheme ------------------

(a) (ii) 1622 / 1520 / 1519 / 1620
(b) (i) 2118 – Radial pattern.
  (ii) 1923 – Nucleated / Compact / Clustered.
          (Any one term)
(c) 281 – Spot height/altitude of 281 m above mean sea level
  20 – Distance stone along the metalled road/ milestone
(d) **Man-made features :** Cart track / lined perennial well / permanent hut / unlined perennial well / cultivated land/footpath
  Natural features : Hill / seasonal stream / rocky slope / forest area / valley / spur   (Any two)
(e) (i) Fire line is made to protect the forest from spread of forest fire.
  (ii) It is a reservoir where river water is stored by constructing a dam / embankment. This water is used for irrigation through canal/ for providing water for nearby areas.
(f) 12 km^2
(g) (i) The water in some of the wells is brackish/ salty/saline
  (ii) There are many streams/seasonal streams in the region and causeways have to be built when metalled roads are constructed to enable it to cross the stream.
(h) (i) Lined perennial well/lined well
  (ii) Cultivation/agriculture/farming.
(i) **Anadra :** it has a metalled road passing near it /Dispensary/Dak-Bungalow/Post and Telegraph office / Police Chowki.
(j) Metalled road / Cart track / Pack track / Foot path.

Ans. **(a)** **(ii)** Village Pamera 1622 or Village Malgaon 1520.
  (b) **(i)** Radial
    (ii) Nucleated or clustered.
  (c) 281 in Black $\longrightarrow$ Spot height
    20 in Red $\longrightarrow$ Milestone

(d) **(i)** Cart track, lined perennial well, permanent hut.
  (ii) Seasonal streams, Bhuni Magri hill.
(e) **(i)** Fire line $\longrightarrow$ A clearing made in the forest to prevent the spread of fire.
  (ii) It is the Tokra reservoir/Talao which provides the supply of water for domestic as well as agricultural use.
(f) Distance on the map between eastings 16 to 19 = 6 cm.
  Distance on the map between northings 18 to 22 = 8 cm.
  As per the scale, 2 cm on the map is equal to 1 km on the ground.
  6 cm on the map is equal to 1 km on the ground $\frac{1}{2} \times 6 = 3$ km
  8 cm on the map is equal to 1 km on the ground $\frac{1}{2} \times 8 = 4$ km
$$\text{Area} = 3 \text{ km} \times 4 \text{ km}$$
$$= 12 \text{ sq km.}$$
(g) **(i)** The water in the wells in the north-west quarter of the map is brackish. Meaning that the water in these wells is salty. Thus, it is not suitable for drinking.
  (ii) Area between Gulabganj and Anadra is a region of scanty rainfall with a number of seasonal streams. So, elevated roads across minor streams are possible—leading to the region having many causeways.
  Natural–River, dry stream.
(h) **(i)** Canal and lined perennial well.
  (ii) Agriculture.
(i) Anadra is the most important settlement as it has a post and telegraph office, Dak-Bungalow, police chowki and dispensary
(j) Metalled roads and cart tracks.

Q. 3. Study the extract of the *Survey of India* Map Sheet No. *45D/7* and answer the following questions:
(b) Name the following:
  (i) The drainage pattern seen in 9185.
  (ii) The pattern of settlement seen in 9787.
(c) What do the following symbols mean?
  (ii) 200 in 9383.
(d) Name two types of vegetation found in the region east of easting 93.
(e) Give two evidences which suggest that the rainfall received in the region shown on the map extract is seasonal.

(f) Calculate the area of the region between 85 – 90 northing and 90 – 95 easting. Give your answer in kilometer.

(g) Mention any *two* manmade features and *two* natural features in grid square 9080.

(h) What is the direct distance in kilometers between the *surveyed* tree west of Rampura (9580) to the *Chhatri* in Juvol (9282)?

(i) Mention:

   (i) The most commonly used means of transport in the area shown on the map extract.

   (ii) The main occupation of the people of the region in the southeastern part of the map extract.

(j) **(i)** What is the compass direction of Rampura (9580) from Karja (9781)?

   (ii) Identify the landform marked by contours in 9782.   **[2018]**

📋 Marking Scheme --------------------------------

  (b) (i) 9185 – Radial
     (ii) 9787 – Scattered/Dispersed
  (c) (ii) 200 in 9383 – the value of the contour line is 200 m above mean sea level.
  (d) Dense mixed jungle, open scrub.
  (e) Seasonal streams/seasonal tanks/dry tank/ broken ground.   *(Any two)*
     Seasonal river with water channel/ dry stream.
  (f) There are 25 grid squares in this boundary limit. Scale of map is 2 cm = 1 km.
     Area of 1 grid square is 1 km² ∴ Area of 25 squares is 25 km².
  (g) Manmade features – cart track/cultivated land/ permanent hut/Temple/Ranawas settlement/ lined perennial well.   *(Any two)*
     Natural features – seasonal stream/plain/broken ground/disappearing stream/barren land/dry river/intermittent stream.   *(Any two)*
  (h) 6.7 cm
     Scale is 2 cm = 1 km
     ∴ 6.7 cm = 6.7 ÷ 2 = 3.35 km ~ (3-4 km)
     (accepted range 3.25 – 3.45 km) i.e. 6.5 – 6.9 cm
  (i) (i) Cart track/pack track
     (ii) Cultivation/Agriculture/Farming.
  (j) (i) South-west
     (ii) Conical hill/valley/spur/water shed/ escarpment/steep slope.

Ans. **(b)** **(i)** Radial   **(ii)** Dispersed or Scattered

    (c) **(ii)** Height of contour line.

    (d) Dense mixed jungle, open scrub, dense jungle, deciduous trees, open mixed jungle.

    (e) Presence of broken ground, dry stream, dry tank, seasonal streams.

    (f) 25 km²

(g) Manmade: settlement, cart track, perennial lined well.
    Natural: river, dry stream.

(h) 3.5 km.

(i) **(i)** Cart track.

   (ii) Agriculture, trade, lumbering or forestry, sheep and goat rearing.

(j) **(i)** South-west   **(ii)** Escarpment.

Q. 4. Study the extract of the *Survey of India* Map Sheet No. *45D/10* and answer the following questions:

(b) On which bank of Sukli Nadi lies:

   (i) Butri

   (ii) Padrugarh

(c) Differentiate between the drainage pattern shown in grid square:

   (i) 0704   **(ii)** 0705

(d) The region in this map extract receives seasonal rainfall. Give two reasons for your answer.

(e) Calculate the distance in km between settlement Bhatana and Makawal along the cart track.

(f) State the compass direction of the following:

   (i) Dattani from Marol

   (ii) Dhavli from Makawal.

(g) **(i)** Mention a social activity of the people living in Marol.

   (ii) What is the main occupation of the people living in this region?

(h) What do you understand by:

   (i) The black broken line in 0807

   (ii) The vertical black line close to Easting 10

(i) What is the main source of water supply to Bhatana? Give a reason for your answer.

(j) **(i)** Name one natural feature in the grid square 0905.

   (ii) Identify one man made feature in the grid square 1003.   **[2017]**

Ans. **(b)** **(i)** Butri - Left bank

     (ii) Padrugarh - Right bank

    (c) **(i)** Trellised   **(ii)** Radial

    (d) Open scrub, seasonal streams, dry river beds, broken ground, causeway. (any two)

    (e) Distance on the map between Bhatana and Makawal along the cart track is 9.8 cm.

As per scale 2 cm on the map is equal to 1 km on the ground.

So, 9.8 cm on the map is equal to $\frac{1}{2}$ × 9.8 – 4.9 km = 5 km

(f) **(i)** SW   **(ii)** NE

(g) **(i)** Monthly fair at Marol

(ii) Agriculture/Farming

(h) **(i)** 0807–Disappearing drainage pattern

(ii) 72°35′ East longitude

(i) Perennial lined wells because seasonal streams and dry tanks cannot provide water to the settlement of Bhatana.

(j) **(i)** 0905–Broken ground

(ii) 1003–Huts/Cart track

Q. 5. Study the extract of the *Survey of India* **Map Sheet No.** *45D/7* **and answer the following questions:**

(b) **What is the direction of flow of Banas river? Give one evidence for your answer.**

(c) **What do you understand by:**

(ii) **180 in the grid square 9182.**

(d) **Calculate the area in kilometer of the region between 93 and 99 eastings and 76 and 81 northings.**

(e) **(i)** **What is the compass direction of settlement Juvol from settlement Arnivada?**

(ii) **Give the difference in altitude between the highest point on the map to the altitude of Moti Bhatamal.**

(f) **Name the feature depicted by:**

(i) **Blue line in Balaram nadi**

(ii) **Brown patch in 9678**

(g) **Name the drainage pattern found in:**

(i) **9782**   **(ii)** **9478**

(h) **What do you infer about the climate of the region by the information provided on the map? Give an evidence in support of your answer.**

(i) **Name two manmade and two natural features in 9580.**

(j) **What do the following denote:**

(i) **Black vertical line running along with 93 eastings**

(ii) **RS near Chitrasani settlement.**

[2016]

Ans. **(b)** North-east to west

Spot heights are decreasing towards west

(c) **(ii)** It is a contour line showing 180 meters above mean sea level.

(d) Area: Length – 76 to 81 Northing = 10 cm > 5 km, Breadth – 93 to 99 Easting = 12 cm > 6 km.

As per scale 2 cm to 1 km. So the area = 5 km × 6 km = 30 sq km.

(e) **(i)** North-west

(ii) Highest point on the map is 542 meter, Moti Bhatamal 198 meter. So the difference in altitude is 542 m – 198 m = 344 m

(f) **(i)** Blue line in Balaram nadi indicates perennial flow of water

(ii) Sand dunes

(g) **(i)** Radial drainage pattern

(ii) Disappearing drainage pattern

(h) The region receives seasonal scanty rainfall.

Open scrub – broken ground – large number of seasonal streams – large number of perennial wells, indicate the region receives seasonal scanty rainfall.

(i) Manmade features are permanent huts and cart track. Natural features are Banas river, broken ground, etc.

(j) **(i)** Line of Longitude

(ii) Railway station

Q. 6. **Study the extract of the Survey of India Map Sheet No.** *45D/10* **and answer the following questions:**

(a) **Give the four figure grid reference for a figure similar to the one given below. Identify the figure:**

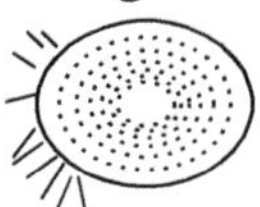

(b) **How is the drainage pattern in grid square 1606 different from that in grid square 1608?**

(d) **Name the most prominent settlement other than ABU. Give two reasons to support your answer.**

(e) **(i)** **What is the general slope of the land in the north-west corner of the map extract?**

(ii) **What is the compass direction of Chandela (1803) from Hanumanji ka Mandir (2208)?**

(f) **What do you understand by the following terms as used on the map extract:**

(i) **Causeway (1702)**

(ii) **Falls 25m (2307).**

(g) **(i)** If you were to cycle at 10 km an hour, how much time would it take to cover the north-south distance depicted on this map extract?

(ii) Calculate the area enclosed by Eastings 19 to 22 and Northings 04 to 09.

(h) **(i)** Identify one natural feature in grid square 1610.

(ii) Identify one man-made feature in grid square 1903.

(i) Give two probable reasons, other than dry water features, to indicate that the region depicted on the map extract receives seasonal rainfall.

(j) Calculate, in meters, the difference in height between the highest point on the map extract and the contour height given in grid square 2402. **[2015]**

Ans. **(a)** Dry tank with an embankment -1511/1811

(b) Drainage pattern in 1606 is radial pattern and in 1608 is trellised pattern

(d) Vajna (1503) as it has a police chowki and metalled road.

(e) **(i)** Towards the west/south-west

(ii) South-west

(f) **(i)** Causeway: It is a raised metalled road over a non-perennial stream or a marshy area.

(ii) Falls 25 m indicate that the waterfall is located at a height of 25 m.

(g) **(i)** 1 hour

(ii) Total number of grids = 15
Area of 1 grid = 1 sq km.
Thus, area of 15 grids =15 sq km.

(h) **(i)** 1610: broken ground/seasonal stream/dry stream.

(ii) 1903: permanent settlement/ embankment.

(i) Presence of broken ground/causeways/ road motorable in dry season.

(j) Highest point 1409 metres – contour height to 280 metres = 1129 metres.

Q. 7. **Study the extract of the Survey of India Map Sheet No. *45D/10* and answer the following questions:**

(a) **(i)** Give the four figure grid reference of the settlement of Hamirpura.

(b) **(i)** What does the blue coloured circle in the grid square 0619 represent?

(ii) What is the compass direction of Dantrai from Jolpur?

(c) What is the difference between :

(i) The pattern of settlements in 0725 and the settlement of Idarla?

(ii) The drainage pattern of the streams in 0624 and those in 0824?

(d) What is the value of the contour line in square 0226? What is the contour interval in the map?

(e) Mention any two factors which provide evidence that the region in the map extract is a rural region.

(f) **(i)** How does the feature, indicated by the black curves in 0721? Show that rainfall in this region is seasonal.

(ii) Mention one man-made feature in the map which also provides evidence that the rainfall is seasonal.

(g) **(i)** Name two natural features in 0527.

(ii) Name two manmade features in 0325.

(h) Name two features which make Dantrai a more important settlement than the other settlements in the map extract.

(i) Calculate the area of the region which lies to the south of northing 21 in square kilometers.

(j) What are the following?

(i) The black vertical line between eastings 09 and 10.

(ii) 302 in grid square 0425. **[2014]**

Ans. **(a)** **(i)** 0123

(b) **(i)** Perennial lined well (though the circle is not given in the map)

(ii) Towards north-west

(c) **(i)** Settlement in 0725—Dispersed.
Settlement Idarla—Nucleated.

(ii) Drainage of 0624—Trellised.
Drainage of 0824—Dendritic.

(d) 300 meters above mean sea level. Contour interval - 20 meters.

(e) No large settlement, no metalled road.

(f) **(i)** The black curves line in 0721 is broken ground. Broken ground is formed due to alternating dry and wet periods along with the banks of seasonal river where the soil is soft.

(ii) Large number of lined perennial wells.

(g) **(i)** At 0527, the natural features are seasonal stream, trees and barren land.

(ii) Cart track and permanent settlement.

(h) The settlement Dantrai has a police chowki and post office. Other settlements do not have them.

(i) Length—19.5 cm → 9.75 km
Breadth—6 cm → 3 km
(as per Scale 2 cm to 1 km)
Area = 9.75 × 3 = 29.25 sq km

(j) (i) Line of Longitude
(ii) 302 in grid square 0425 is a spot height.

Q. 8. Study the extract of the Survey of India Map Sheet No. 45D/7 and answer the following questions:

(b) (i) Name the left bank tributary of the main river.
(ii) State the direction in which this left bank tributary is flowing.

(c) (i) Mention a special feature associated with the streams in grid square 9879.
(ii) Name the types of drainage pattern found in grid square 9382.

(d) Give the four grid reference of each of the following:
(i) Open scrub
(ii) Bantawada.

(e) Name two relief features that can be seen in grid square 9782 and 9574.

(f) Why do you find limited cultivation in the map extract?
Give two reasons for your answer.

(g) What is the compass direction of Atroli (9576) and Chekhla (9281) from Sangla?

(h) What type of rainfall is experienced in the region shown in the map extract? Justify your answer by giving one reason.

(i) Calculate the distance in kilometres along the cart track between Chitrasani (999747) and Pirojpura (978753).

(j) (i) What is the geographical name that you would give to the general pattern of settlements in the region shown on the map?

Ans. **(b)** (i) Left bank tributary is Balaram Nadi.
(ii) It is flowing from SE to NW.

(c) (i) Feature associated with streams is broken ground.
(ii) Dendritic pattern.

(d) Four figure grid reference :
(i) Open scrub – 9573
(ii) Bantawada – 9978

(e) Two relief features are:
9782 – Conical hill
9574 – Steep slope

(f) There is limited cultivation in the map because of :
(i) Scarce rainfall.
(ii) Sandy or desert area.

(g) Sangla to Atroli – North-East.
Sangla to Chekhla – North.

(h) The region experiences seasonal rainfall. The different evidences are dry tanks, dry rivers, sand features, broken ground.

(i) Distance in cm = 5·2
Distance in km = (scale 2 cm to 1 km)
Distance in km = 2·6.
Ans. 2·6 km.

(j) (i) General pattern of settlement is Nucleated.

Q. 9. Study the extract of the Survey of India Map Sheet No. 45D/10 and answer the following questions :

(a) Name and give the four figure grid reference of a settlement where the people of the region meet at least once a year.

(b) What does the conventional symbol at grid reference 145132 mean ?

(c) If a man were to walk from Gulabganj (1820) to Harmatiya (1916) :
(i) In which direction would he be walking ?
(ii) Which are the two different kinds of roads that he would be using ?

(d) What do the following numbers in grid square 1718 and 1818 mean ?
(i) 280   (ii) 281

(e) What are the two differences between the settlement Bamba in 1914 and those in 1813 ?

(f) Name four facilities that Anadra has which makes it an important settlement.

(g) What is the quickest means of communication for the people of Dabani (1313) ?

(h) What do the following mean :
(i) brackish in 1915
(ii) causeway in 1715

(i) Mention two factors which support the following :
(i) The Sipu river is in its middle course.

    (ii) The rainfall in the region shown in the map extract is seasonal.

(j) What is the distance in kilometres between the distance stone 20 in 1818 and the causeway in 1715 along the metalled road ? **[2012]**

Ans. **(a)** Malgaon 1520 or Pamera 1622

    (b) A temple

    (c) **(i)** South-East

        (ii) Metalled road and cart track

    (d) **(i)** Contour height—280 m above sea level.

        (ii) Spot height—281 m above sea level.

    (e) In Bamba, settlements are nucleated and temporary and in square 1813, the settlements are dispersed and permanent.

    (f) Facilities in Anadra are PTO (Post and Telegraph Office), police chowki, DB (Dak Bungalow), and dispensary.

    (g) Telephone.

    (h) **(i)** Brackish : Water has high salt content and is not fit for drinking but may be used for irrigation.

        (ii) Causeway : A raised road over a stream.

    (i) **(i)** The Sipu Nadi is in its middle course because there are meanders and the land is level which shows that the river is slow.

        (ii) The rainfall in the region is seasonal :

            1. The rivers and tanks are seasonal in nature.

            2. There are many causeways in the map.

    (j) The distance is 2.8 km to 3 km.

    5·6 cm on map (as per scale 2 cm equals to 1 km)

$$\text{so } 5{\cdot}6 \rightarrow \frac{5.6}{2} = 2{\cdot}8 \text{ km on ground.}$$

Q. 10. Study the extract of the Survey of India Map Sheet No. *45D/10* and answer the following questions:

    (b) What is the difference in the pattern of drainage in grid square 0916 and in 0712?

    (c) Give the four figure grid reference of each of the following:

        (i) Stony waste

        (ii) Open shrubs

    (d) Calculate the distance in kilometers along the metalled road between the causeways in grid square 0512 and 0808.

(e) **(i)** What do the tiny curved black lines in grid square 0315 indicate?

    (ii) What is the main cause for this feature?

(f) **(i)** What is the geographical name that you would give to the general pattern of settlements in the region shown on the map?

    (ii) Give a reason for your answer.

(g) What is the general direction of flow of the Sipu Nadi, given in the map extract? Give a reason to support your answer.

(h) Name two probable occupations of the people in the settlement of Revdar in grid square 0313 and 0413.

(i) What kind of roads connect (i) Marol with Mitan and (ii) Revdar with Karaunti respectively?

(j) Give two reasons to show that the area depicted in the map experiences seasonal rainfall. **[2011]**

Ans. **(b)** 0916 Radial, 0712 Trellis

    (c) **(i)** 1014   **(ii)** 0816, 0916

    (d) 5.7 km

    (e) **(i)** Broken ground

        (ii) Flooding, hot and dry weather or spell.

    (f) **(i)** Nucleated

        (ii) Settlements close together.

    (g) North-east to south-west because spot heights are receding from NE to SW, e.g., 261, 257 and 249.

    (h) Agriculture and services.

    (i) **(i)** Marol to Mitan cart track.

        (ii) Revdar to Karaunti metalled road

    (j) **(i)** Dry tank

        (ii) Dry streams.

Q. 11. Study the extract of the Survey of India Map sheet No. *45D/7* and answer the following questions:

    (b) Give the four figure grid reference of each of the following:

        (i) The confluence of the Sipu River and the Mahadeviyo Nala.

        (ii) Sheet rock.

    (c) Measure the shortest distance in kilometres between the temple in grid square 8192, and the perennial lined well at Bhakodar 8188.

(d) What do the following represent?

    (i) Black curved lines in 7788.

    (ii) The blue line in the bed of the Sipu River.

(e) **(i)** What is the general pattern of settlements in the region shown on the map?

    (ii) Give a reason for your answer.

(f) Which is the chief form of irrigation shown in the map extract? Why is it necessary?

(g) **(i)** What is the main form of transport in this region?

    (ii) Give the map evidence for your answer.

(h) **(i)** What is the compass direction of Dantiwada, 8582, from Bhadli Kotha, 7886?

    (ii) What is the general direction of flow of the Arado. N?

(i) **(i)** Name the type of drainage pattern found in grid square 8584.

(j) **(i)** What is meant by 'R.F.'?

    (ii) What is the R.F. shown on this map extract? [2010]

Ans. **(b)** **(i)** 8189   **(ii)** 8088 or 8188

(c) 4·4 kms.

(d) **(i)** Broken ground **(ii)** Water channel

(e) **(i)** Nucleated or clustered

    (ii) Settlements are grouped.

(f) Lined perennial wells because the rivers are seasonal.

(g) **(i)** Cart tracks

    (ii) Single red lines shown on the map (Settlements are mostly connected by way of cart tracks)

(h) **(i)** South-east

    (ii) South or south-west

(i) **(i)** Dendritic

(j) **(i)** Representative fraction: it is the ratio of the horizontal distance between two points on the map to the distance of the corresponding points on the ground.

    (ii) 1: 50000

Map Skills

Very Short Answer Type Questions

Q. 1. On the outline map of India provided :

(a) Mark and name Nilgiris.

(c) Mark and name the Karakoram Pass.

(d) Mark and name $82^{1/2}°$E Longitude.

(e) Shade and name the Coromandel Coastal Plain.

(f) Mark and name the River Brahmapurta.

(g) Mark and name the Gulf of Kutch.

(h) Mark and name the Satpura.

(i) Mark using arrows, the direction of the South West Monsoon wind during summer over the Arabian Sea and label it.

(j) Shade and label a sparsely populated region in India.

Ans.

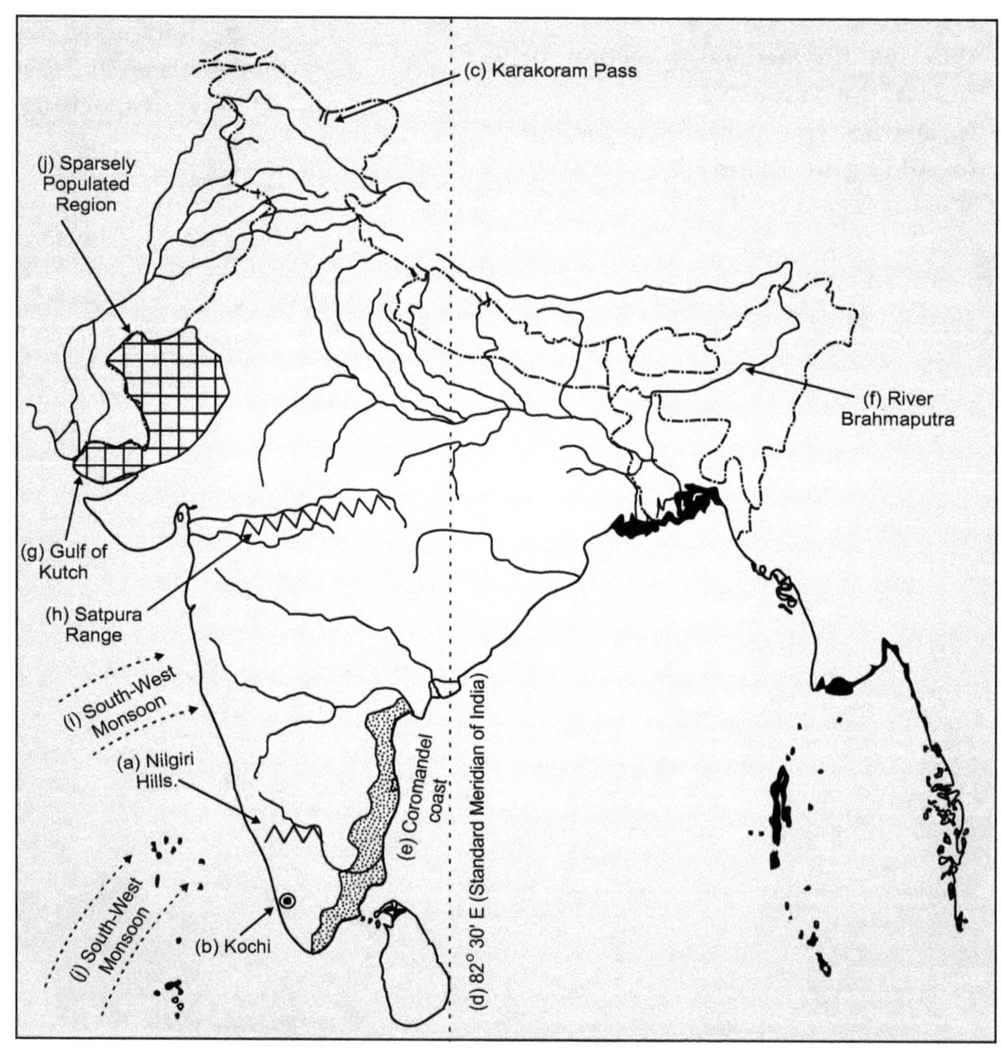

Q. 2. On the outline map of India provided:

   (a) Shade and label the Gangetic Plain.

   (c) Mark and label the Karakoram Mountains.

   (e) Shade and label the river Cauveri.

   (f) Mark and name Mumbai.

   (i) Shade and name the Deccan Plateau.

   (j) Shade and label the river Jhelum.

                                [2019]

📋 **Marking Scheme**

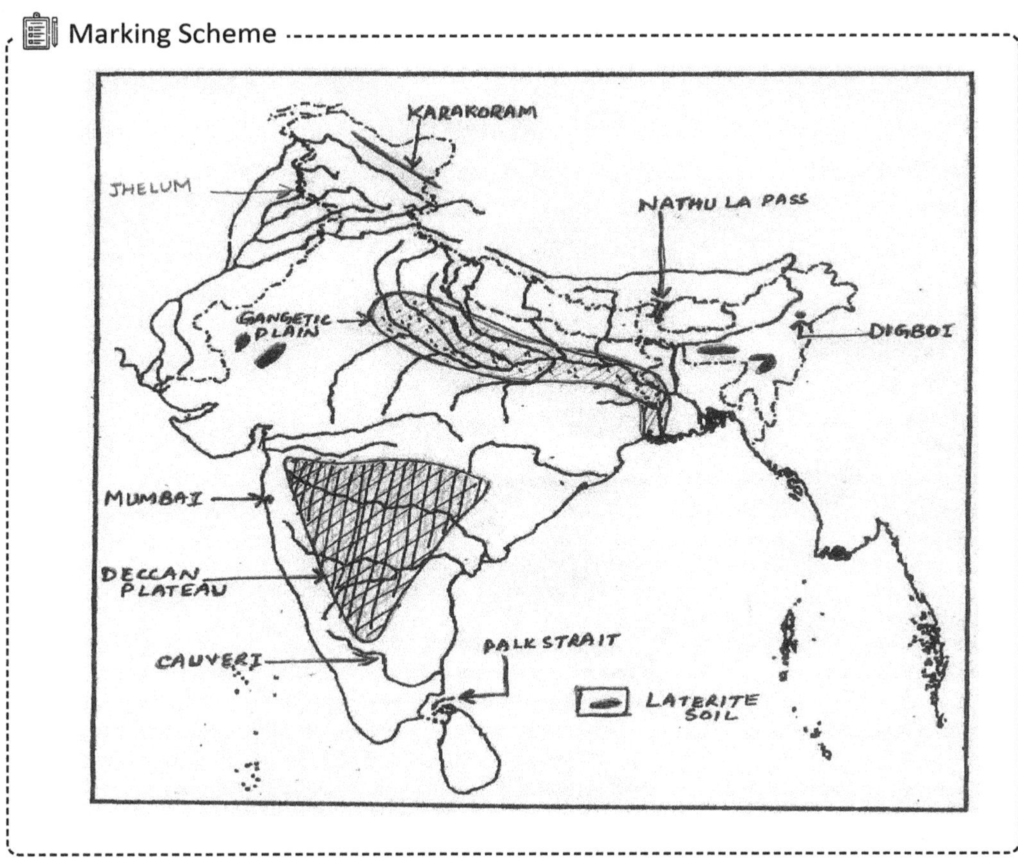

Ans.

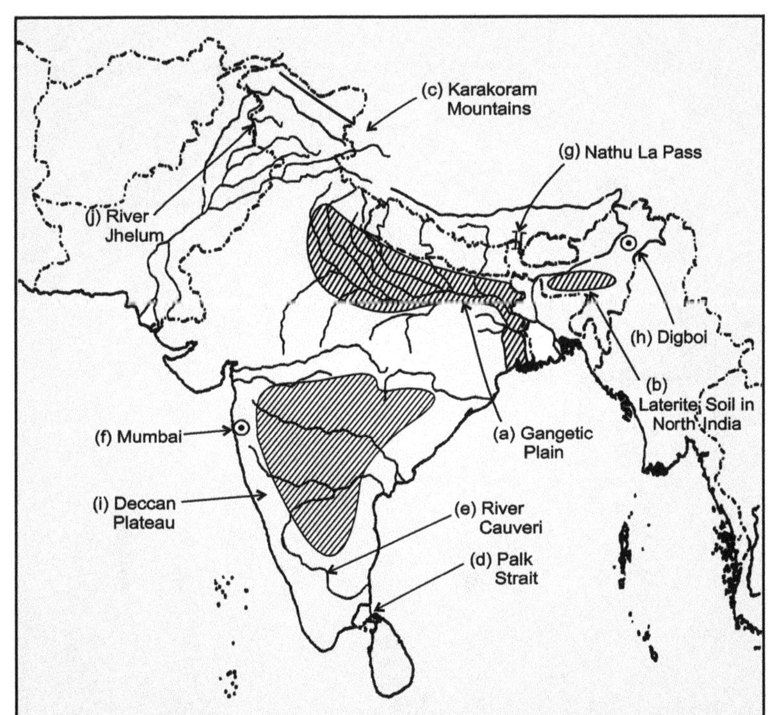

Q. 3. On the outline map of India provided:
  (a) Shade and label Thar desert.
  (b) Label the river Narmada.
  (e) Mark and name Mount Kanchenjunga.
  (f) Shade and label a densely-populated region in India.
  (h) Mark with a dot and name Chennai.
  (i) Mark and label the Arabian Sea branch of S.W. Monsoon. **[2018]**

📋 Marking Scheme --------

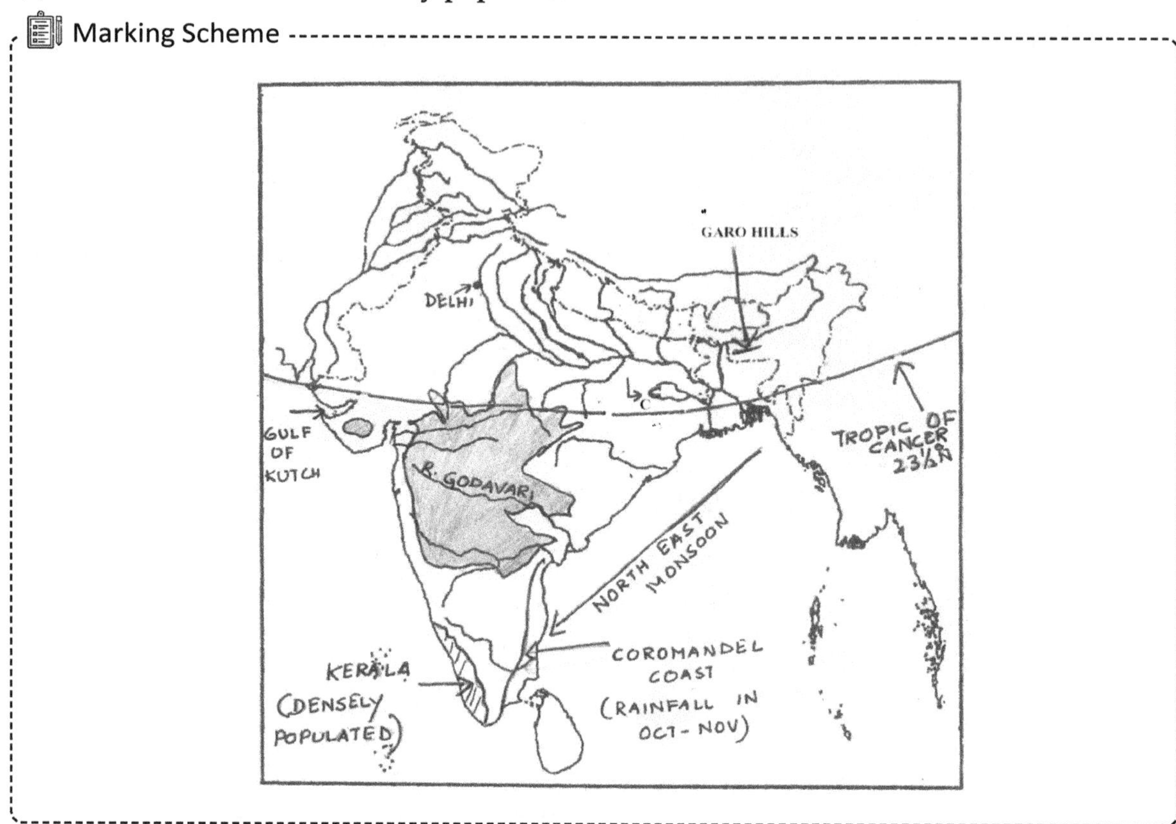

Ans.

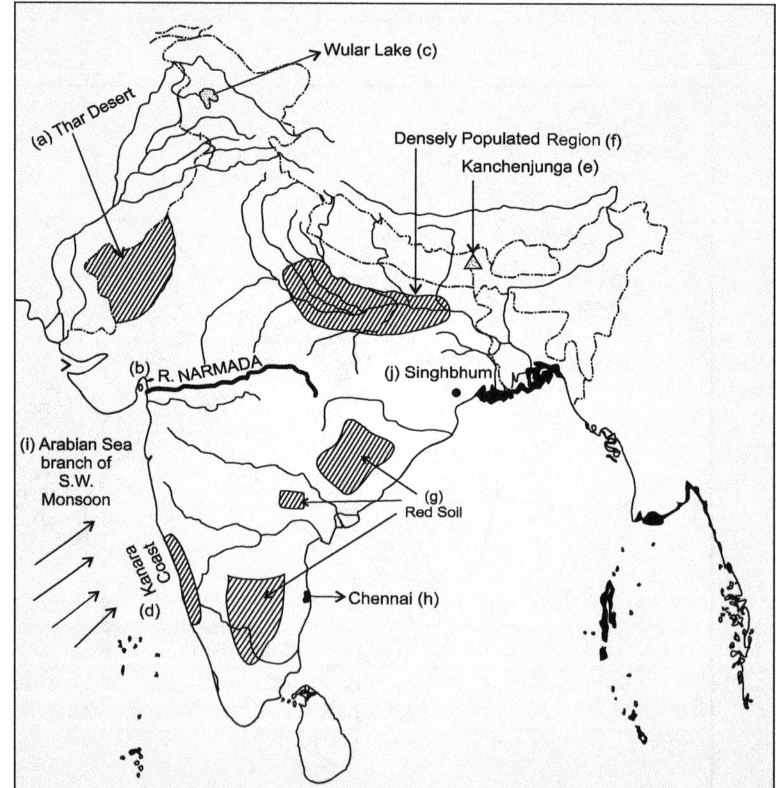

Q. 4. On the outline map of India provided:

(b) Label the river Godavari.

(d) Mark C on the coal fields in Jharia.

(e) Mark with an arrow and name the NE monsoon over the Bay of Bengal.

(f) Shade and name the Gulf of Kutch.

(g) Shade and name the coastal plain that receives rainfall in October-November.

(h) Mark with a dot and name Delhi.

(i) Shade a region with Black Cotton soil.

(j) Use an arrow to point at a densely populated state in South India.   [2017]

Ans.

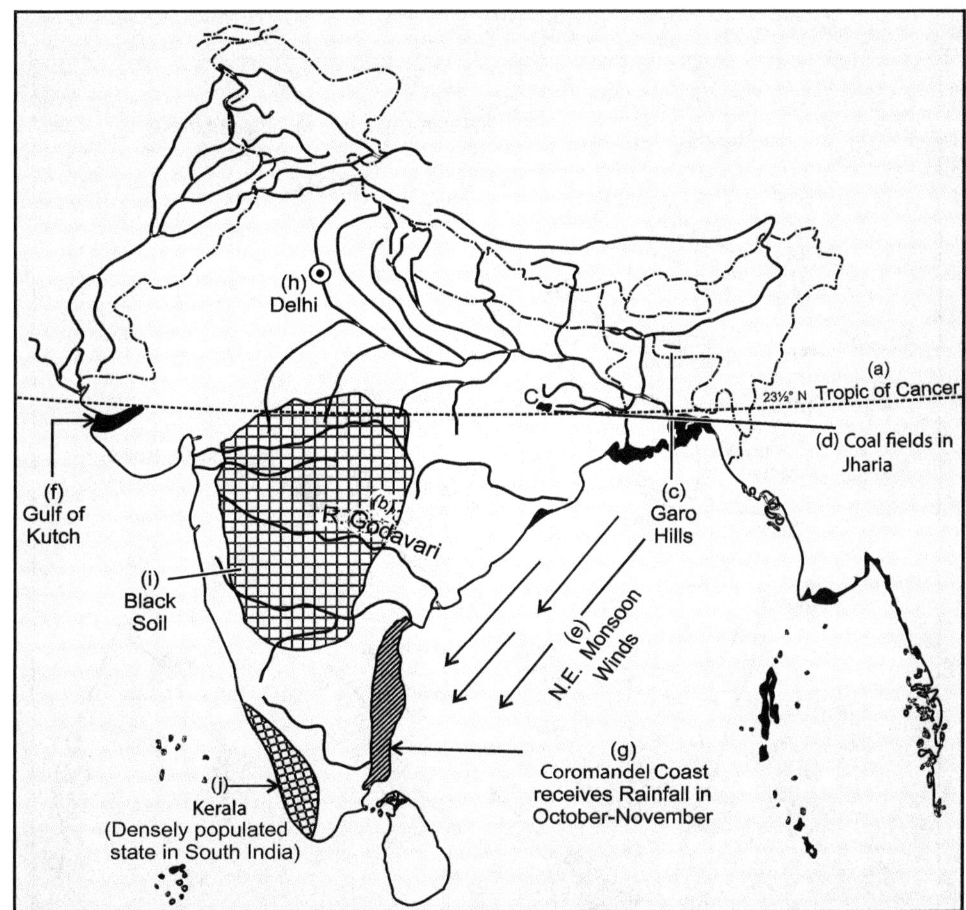

Q. 5. On the outline map of India provided:

(a) Draw and number the Standard Meridian of India.

(b) Label the river Mahanadi.

(c) Mark and name Lake Chilka.

(e) Mark and name the Vindhya Mountains.

(f) Shade and name a sparsely populated region in western India.

(g) Shade a region with alluvial soil in South India.

(h) Mark and name Kolkata.

(i) Mark with arrows and name South-West Monsoon winds over the Bay of Bengal.

(j) Mark and name Mumbai High. [2016]

Ans.

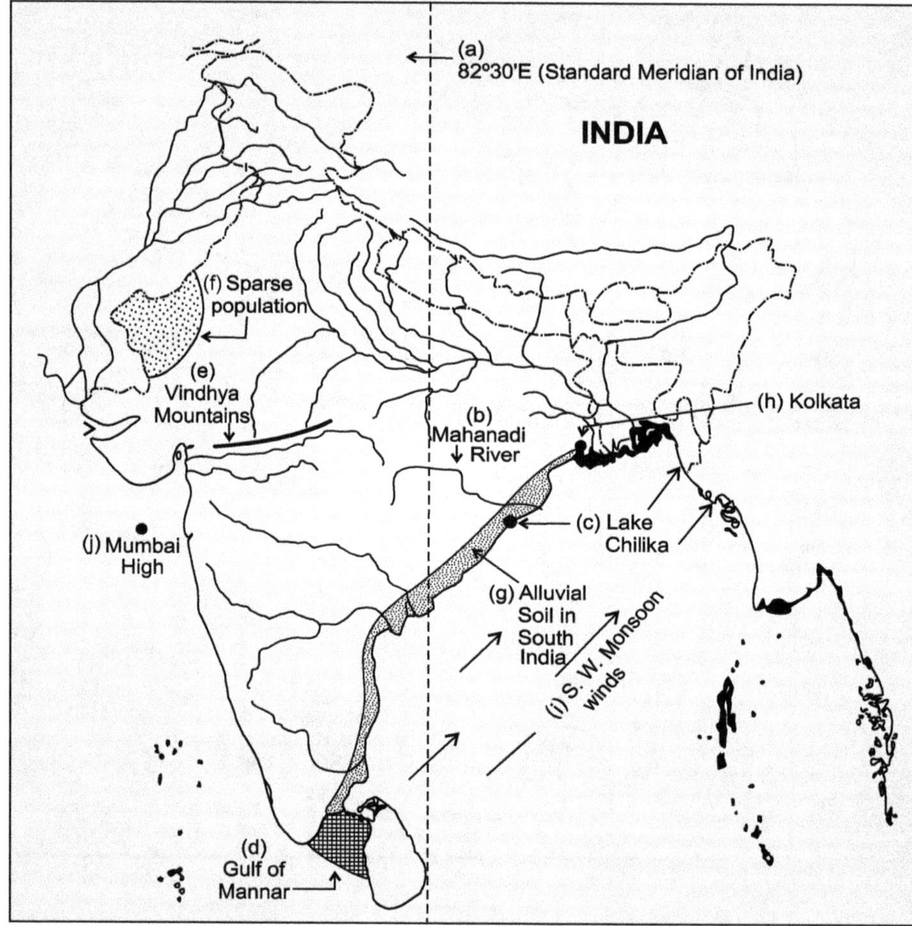

Q. 6. On the outline map of India provided:

(a) Mark and name the Nilgiris.

(c) Shade and label the Malabar Coastal Plains.

(e) Shade and name the Andaman Sea.

(f) Mark and name Allahabad.

(g) Mark with a single arrow and name the winds that bring winter rain to the North-west India.

(j) Mark and name the Karakoram pass. [2015]

Ans.

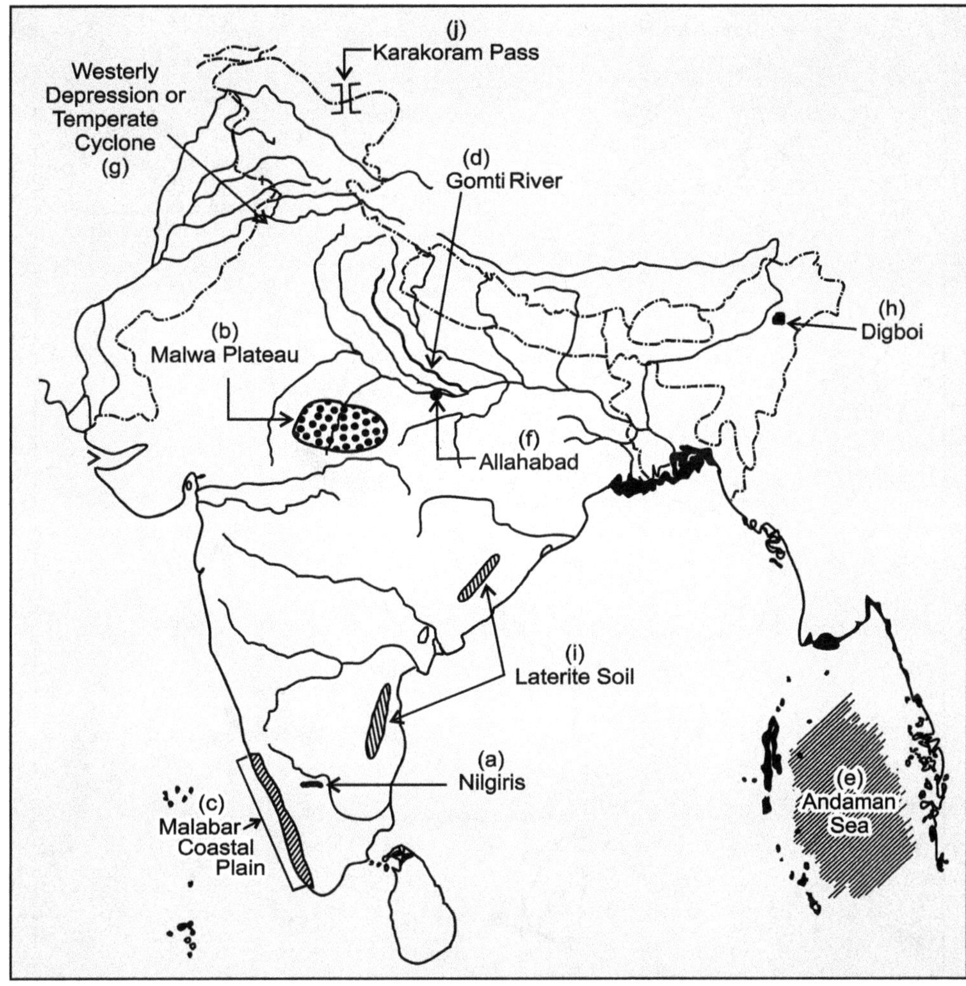

Q. 7. On the outline map of India provided:

    (a) Draw, name and number the Standard Meridian.

    (b) Label the river Yamuna.

    (c) Shade and name the Gulf of Khambhat.

    (e) Mark and name the Karakoram Range.

    (f) Shade and name a sparsely populated State in North-east India.

    (i) Mark and name the winds that bring rain to West Bengal in summer.   **[2014]**

Ans.

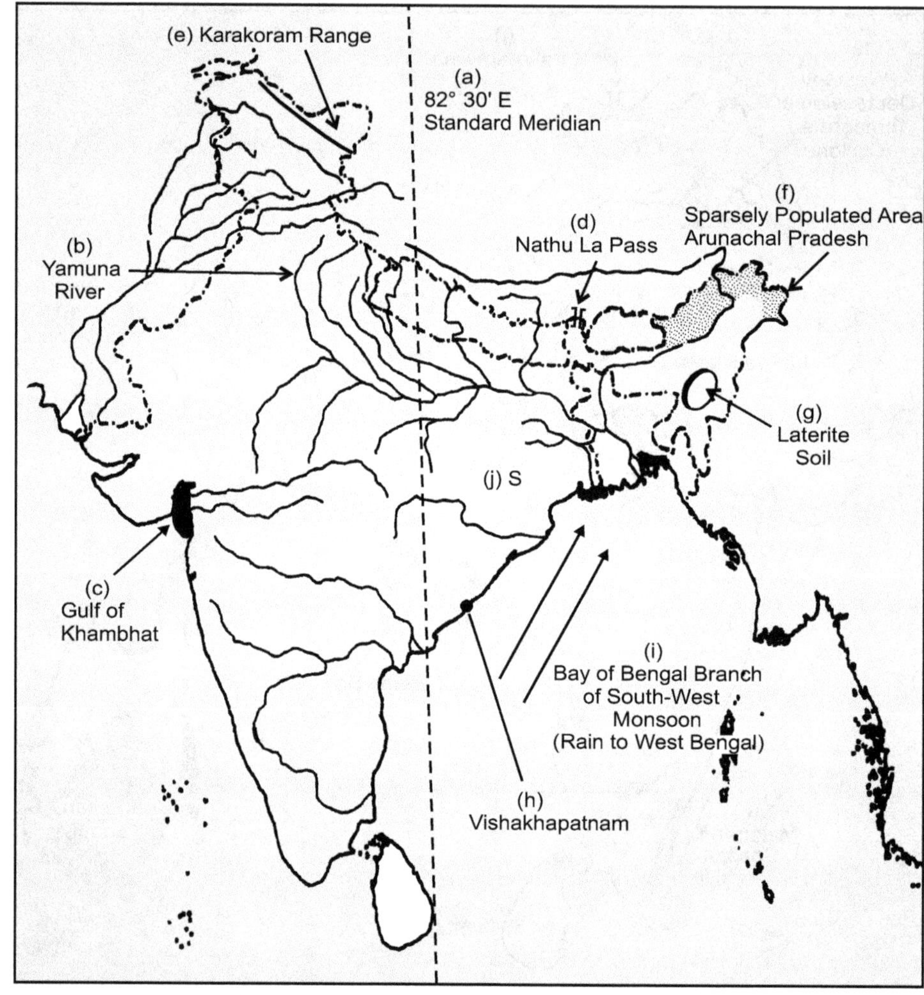

Q. 8. On the outline map of India provided:

(a) Mark and name Chennai

(b) Label the river Godavari

(c) Shade and label the Chota Nagpur Plateau

(d) Shade and name the Gulf of Kachchh

(e) Mark and name the Indo-Gangetic Plains

(g) Mark and name the winds which bring rain to Mumbai in July and August

(h) Mark and name the Satpura Range

(i) Mark and name the Jharia Coalfield

Ans.

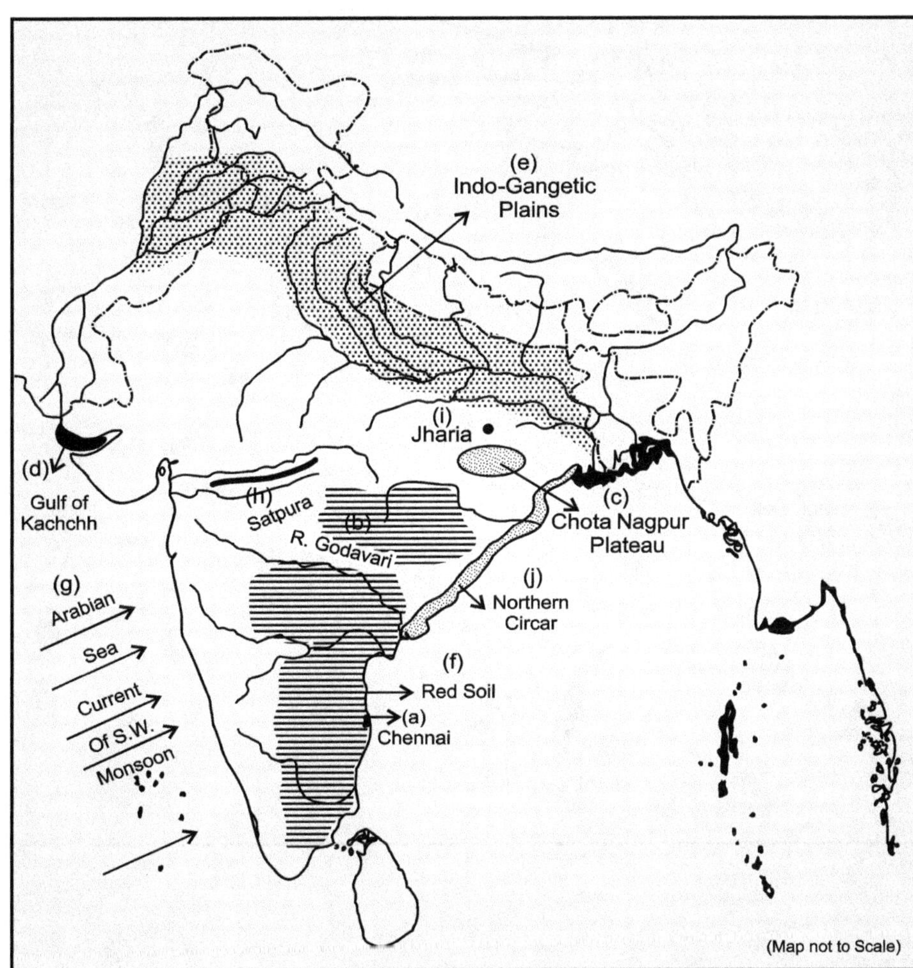

Q. 9. On the outline map of India provided:

   (b) Label the river Narmada

   (c) Shade and name Lake Chilka

   (d) Mark and name the Aravali Mountains

   (e) Mark and name the Karakoram Pass

   (f) Shade and name a densely populated state in South India

   (g) Shade and name a region with black soil

   (i) Mark and name the winds which bring rain in winter to the Coromandel Coast

Ans.

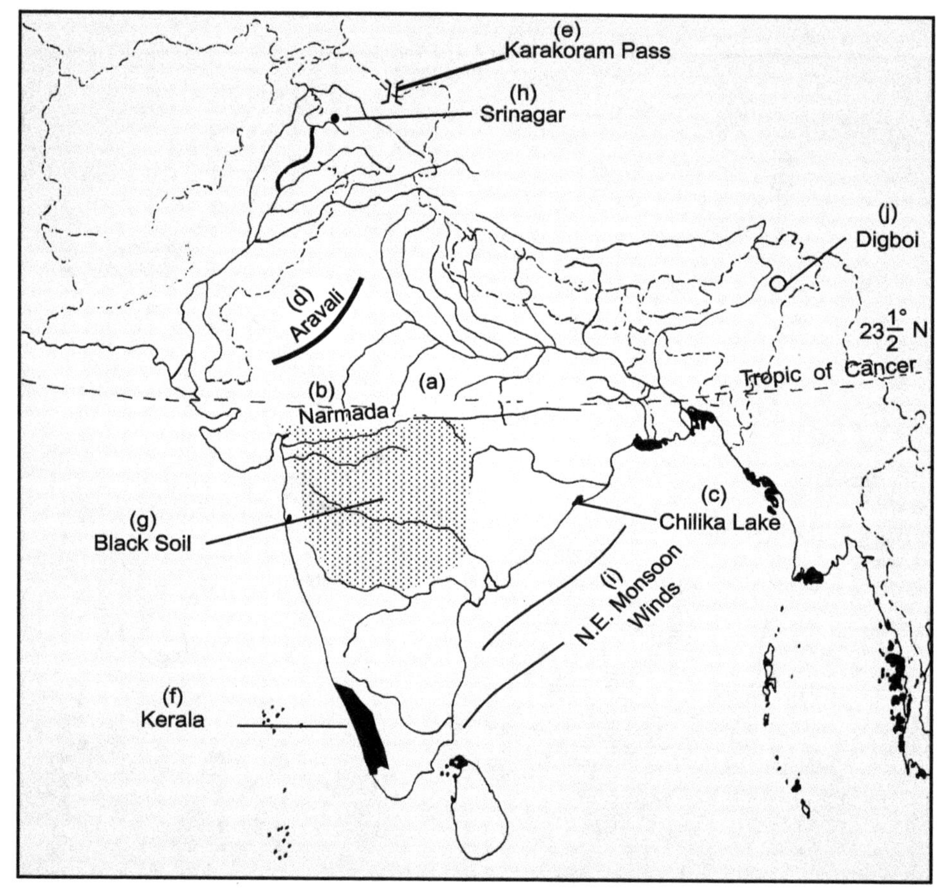

Q. 10. On the outline map of India provided:

(b) Label the river Krishna.

(d) Mark and label the Konkan coast.

(f) Shade and label an alluvial soil area in Peninsular India.

(g) Mark with arrows the direction of the Arabian Sea branch of South-West Monsoon Winds.

(h) Shade and label the Western Ghats.

(i) Mark the Jharia coal field.

(j) Shade and name a densely populated area. [2011]

Ans.

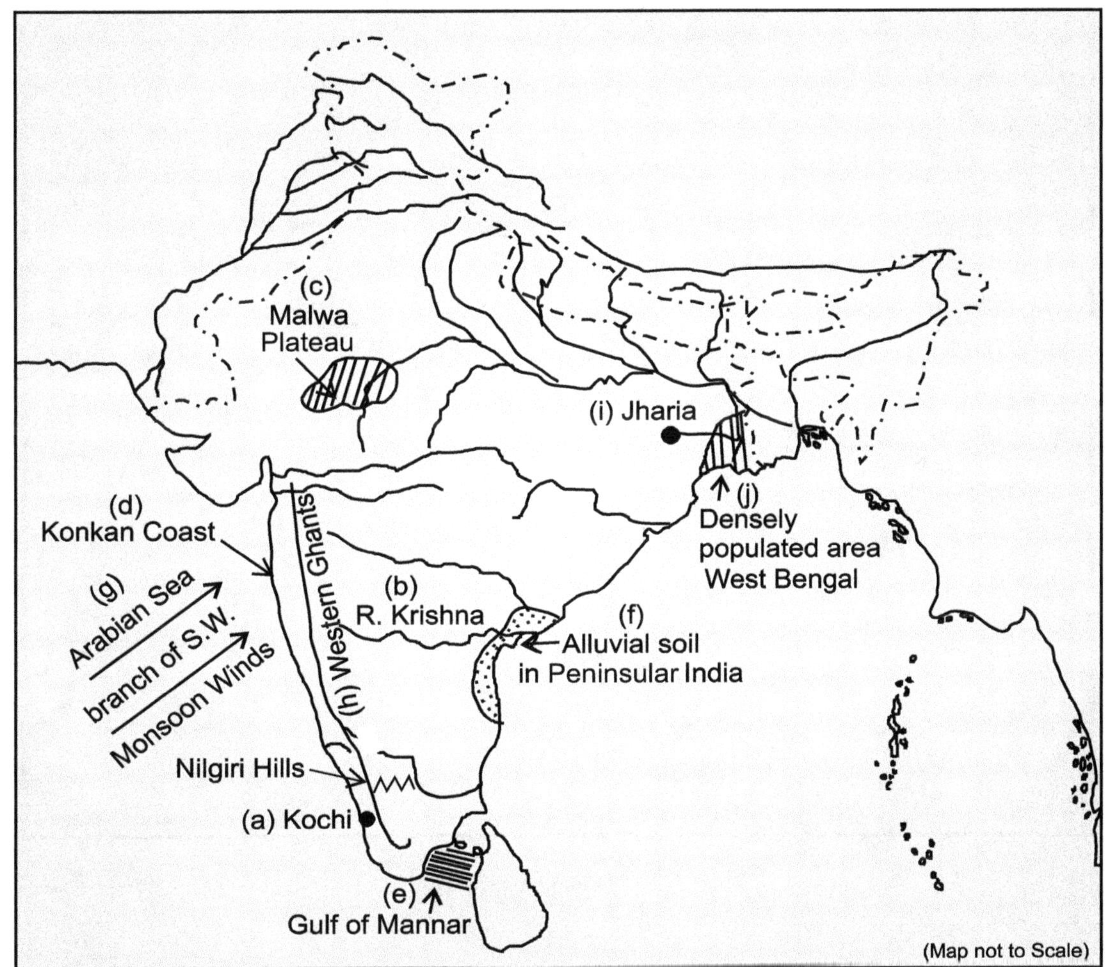

Q. 11. On the outline map provided:-

   (b) Label the river Chambal.

   (c) Shade and label the Nilgiri Hills.

   (d) Mark and label the Eastern Ghats.

   (h) Mark and name the winds which bring rain to Mumbai in July and August. [2010]

Ans.

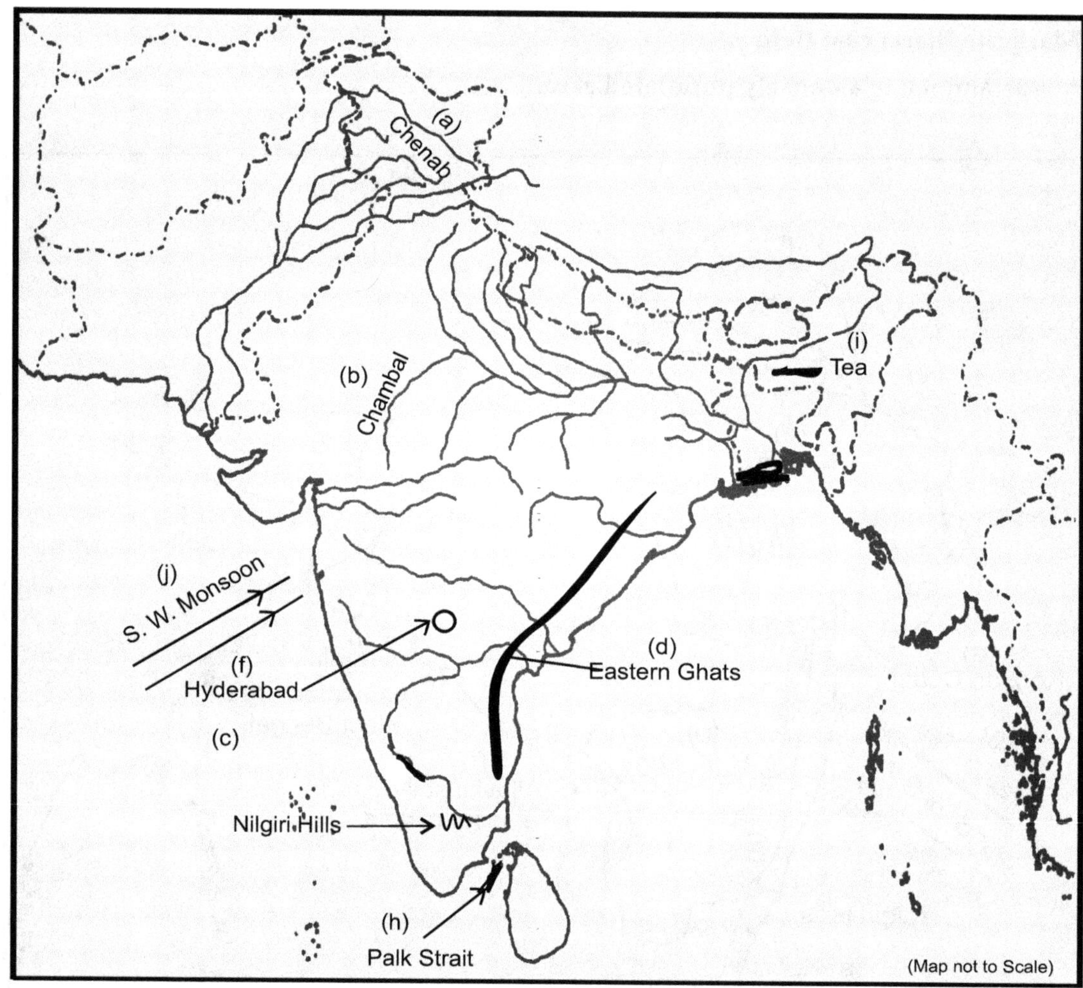

MATHEMATICS

Goods and Services Tax (GST)

Long Answer Type Questions

Q. 1. Mr. Bedi visits the market and buys the following articles : **[2020]**

Medicines costing ₹ 950, GST @ 5%

A pair of shoes costing ₹ 3000, GST @ 18%

A laptop bag costing ₹ 1000 with a discount of 30%, GST @ 18%.

(i) Calculate the total amount of GST paid.

(ii) The total bill amount including GST paid by Mr. Bedi.

 **Marking Scheme**

Medicine: GST $= \dfrac{5}{100} \times 950 = ₹ 47.50$

Shoes: GST $= \dfrac{18}{100} \times 3000 = ₹ 540$

Laptop Bag: Discounted price

$= 1000 - \dfrac{30}{100} \times 1000 = ₹ 700$

$\therefore$ GST $= \dfrac{18}{100} \times 700 = ₹ 126$

$\therefore$ Total GST = ₹ 47.50 + ₹ 540 + ₹ 126 = ₹ 713.50

$\therefore$ Total Bill = 950 + 3000 + 700 + 713.50 = ₹ 5363.50

Ans. **(i)**

$$\text{Cost of medicines} = ₹ 950$$
$$\text{GST on medicines} = 5\% \text{ of } 950$$
$$= \dfrac{5}{100} \times 950$$
$$= ₹ 47.50$$

$$\text{Cost of a pair of shoes} = ₹ 3000$$
$$\text{GST on shoes} = 18\% \text{ of } ₹ 3000$$
$$= \dfrac{18}{100} \times 3000$$
$$= ₹ 540$$
$$\text{Cost of laptop bag} = ₹ 1000$$
$$\text{Discount on bag} = 30\% \text{ of } 1000$$
$$= \dfrac{30}{100} \times 1000$$
$$= ₹ 300$$

$\therefore$ Cost of laptop bag after discount
$$= ₹ (1000 - 300)$$
$$= ₹ 700$$
$$\text{GST on laptop bag} = 18\% \text{ of } ₹ 700$$
$$= \dfrac{18}{100} \times 700$$
$$= ₹ 126$$

$\therefore$ Total GST on all items
$$= ₹ (47.50 + 540 + 126)$$
$$= ₹ 713.50$$

(ii) Total bill including GST = cost of (medicines + shoes + laptop bag) + Total GST on all items.

$$= ₹ (950 + 3000 + 700) + ₹ 713.50$$
$$= ₹ (4650 + 713.50)$$
$$= ₹ 5363.50$$

 **Short Answer Type Questions**

Q. 1. Mr. Sonu has a recurring deposit account and deposits ₹ 750 per month for 2 years. If he gets ₹ 19125 at the time of maturity, find the rate of interest. **[2020]**

Marking Scheme

$$I = \frac{750 \times 24 \times 25 \times r \times 1}{2 \times 100 \times 12}$$

$$= \frac{375}{2}r$$

Amount deposit = 750 × 24 = ₹ 18000
Maturity value = ₹ 19125
Interest = ₹ 19125 - 18000 = ₹ 1125

$$1125 = \frac{375\,r}{2}$$

$$r = 6\,\%$$

Ans. Here, P = ₹ 750, n = 2 years = 24 months and M.V. = ₹ 19125

We know, $\quad$ M.V. $= P \times n + \dfrac{P \times n(n+1)}{2 \times 12} \times \dfrac{r}{100}$

$$\Rightarrow \quad 19125 = 750 \times 24$$
$$+ \frac{750 \times 24(24+1)}{2 \times 12} \times \frac{r}{100}$$

$$\Rightarrow \quad 19125 = 18000 + 750 \times 25 \times \frac{r}{100}$$

$$\Rightarrow \quad 19125 - 18000 = \frac{750 \times r}{4}$$

$$\Rightarrow \quad 1125 = \frac{750 \times r}{4}$$

$$\Rightarrow \quad r = \frac{1125 \times 4}{750} = 6$$

Hence, the rate of interest is 6% p.a.

Q. 2. Rekha opened a recurring deposit account for 20 months. The rate of interest is 9% per annum and Rekha receives ₹ 441 as interest at the time of maturity.

Find the amount Rekha deposited each month. **[2019]**

Marking Scheme

Let monthly deposit be x

$$\text{Interest} = \frac{P \times n(n+1) \times r}{100 \times 2 \times 12}$$

$$441 = \frac{x \times 20(20+1) \times 9}{100 \times 2 \times 12}$$

$$\frac{63x}{40} = 441 \text{ Equating interest to 441}$$

$$\therefore \ x = ₹\ 280$$

Ans. Given, number of months (n) = 20
Rate of interest (r) = 9% p.a.
Interest received (I) = ₹441
Let the monthly deposit be ₹P.

$$\therefore \qquad I = P \times \frac{n(n+1)}{2 \times 12} \times \frac{r}{100}$$

$$\Rightarrow \qquad 441 = P \times \frac{20(20+1)}{2 \times 12} \times \frac{9}{100}$$

$$\Rightarrow \qquad P = \frac{441 \times 2 \times 12 \times 100}{20 \times 21 \times 9} = ₹\,280$$

∴ The required monthly deposit is ₹280.

Q. 3. Sonia had recurring deposit account in a bank and deposited ₹600 per month for $2\frac{1}{2}$ years. If the rate of interest was 10% p.a., find the maturity value of this account. **[2018]**

Ans. Here, P = ₹600, $n = 2\frac{1}{2}$ years = 30 months, r = 10%

$$\therefore \qquad \text{Interest, I} = P \times \frac{n(n+1)}{2 \times 12} \times \frac{r}{100}$$

$$= 600 \times \frac{30 \times 31}{2 \times 12} \times \frac{10}{100}$$

$$= ₹\,2325$$

∴ Maturity value,
$$\text{M.V.} = Pn + I$$
$$= 600 \times 30 + 2325$$
$$= ₹\,20325.$$

Q. 4. Priyanka has a recurring deposit account of ₹1000 per month at 10% per annum. If she gets ₹5550 as interest at the time of maturity, find the total time for which the account was held. **[2018]**

Ans. Given, $P = ₹1,000$, $r = 10\%$, $I = ₹5,550$, $n = ?$

$$\therefore \quad I = P \times \frac{n(n+1)}{2 \times 12} \times \frac{r}{100}$$

$$\Rightarrow \quad 5550 = 1000 \times \frac{n^2 + n}{24} \times \frac{10}{100}$$

$$\Rightarrow \quad 555 = \frac{5}{12}(n^2 + n)$$

$$\Rightarrow \quad 5n^2 + 5n = 6660$$

$$\Rightarrow \quad 5(n^2 + n) = 6660$$

$$\Rightarrow \quad n^2 + n = 1332$$

$$\Rightarrow \quad n^2 + n - 1332 = 0$$

$$\Rightarrow \quad n^2 + 37n - 36n - 1332 = 0$$

$$\Rightarrow \quad n(n+37) - 36(n+37) = 0$$

$$\Rightarrow \quad (n+37)(n-36) = 0$$

$$\Rightarrow \quad n + 37 = 0 \text{ or } n - 36 = 0$$

$$\Rightarrow \quad n = -37 \text{ or } n = 36$$

$$\therefore \quad n = 36$$

$$(\because n \text{ cannot be negative})$$

Hence, total time for which amount was held is 36 months or 3 years.

Q. 5. **Mr. Richard has a recurring deposit account in a bank for 3 years at 7.5% p.a. simple interest. If he gets ₹ 8325 as interest at the time of maturity, find:**
(i) The monthly deposit
(ii) The maturity value. **[2017]**

Ans. No. of months $(n) = 3 \times 12 = 36$, $R = 7.5\%$, Interest $= ₹ 8325$

(i) Let monthly deposit be $₹ x$

$$\therefore \quad I = P \times \frac{n(n+1)}{2 \times 12} \times \frac{r}{100}$$

$$8325 = x \times \frac{36 \times 37}{2 \times 12} \times \frac{7.5}{100}$$

$$x = \frac{8325 \times 2 \times 100}{3 \times 37 \times 7.5}$$

$$\therefore \quad = 2000$$

$\therefore$ Monthly deposit is $₹ 2,000$.

(ii) Total deposits $= ₹ 2,000 \times 36 = ₹ 72,000$

$\therefore$ Maturity value $= ₹ (72,000 + 8,325)$

$$= ₹ 80,325$$

Q. 6. **Mohan has a recurring deposit account in a bank for 2 years at 6% p.a. simple interest. If he gets ₹1200 as interest at the time of maturity, find:** **[2016]**
(i) the monthly instalment
(ii) the amount of maturity.

Ans. **(i)** Given, number of months $(n) = 24$ and rate of interest $(r) = 6\%$ and Interest $= ₹1,200$

$$I = P \times \frac{n(n+1)}{2 \times 12} \times \frac{r}{100}$$

$$1200 = P \times \frac{24(24+1)}{2 \times 12} \times \frac{6}{100}$$

$$P = \frac{1,200 \times 24 \times 100}{6 \times 24 \times 25}$$

$$= ₹800$$

$\therefore$ Monthly instalment $= ₹800$

(ii) Sum deposited $= ₹800 \times 24$

$$= ₹19,200$$

Amount of maturity $= ₹19,200 + ₹1,200$

$$= ₹20,400$$

Q. 7. **Katrina opened a recurring deposit account with a Nationalised Bank for a period of 2 years. If the bank pays interest at the rate of 6% per annum and the monthly instalment is ₹1,000, find the:**
(i) interest earned in 2 years.
(ii) maturity value. **[2015]**

Ans. Since, money deposited $= ₹1,000$ per month
i.e., $P = ₹1,000$

and number of months $= 2 \times 12 = 24$ *i.e.*, $n = 24$

and $r = 6\%$

(i) Interest earned in 2 years

$$= P \times \frac{n(n+1)}{2 \times 12} \times \frac{r}{100}$$

$$= 1,000 \times \frac{24(24+1)}{2 \times 12} \times \frac{6}{100}$$

$$= ₹1,500.$$

(ii) Maturity value $=$ Sum deposited $+$ Interest

$$= ₹(1,000 \times 24) + ₹1,500$$

$$= ₹25,500$$

Q. 8. **Shahrukh opened a Recurring Deposit Account in a bank and deposited ₹800 per month for $1\frac{1}{2}$ years. If he received ₹15,084 at the time of maturity, find the rate of interest per annum.** **[2014]**

Ans. Given, $P = ₹800$ per month,

$$n = 1\frac{1}{2} \text{ years} = 18 \text{ month}.$$

Maturity value $= ₹15,084$

As we know,

$$I = \frac{Pn(n+1)r}{2 \times 12 \times 100}$$

$$M.V. = P \times n + I$$

Maturity value $= P \times n + \frac{Pn(n+1)r}{2 \times 12 \times 100}$

$$15,084 = 800 \times 18 + \frac{800 \times 18 \times 19 \times r}{2,400}$$

$$15{,}084 - 14{,}400 = 6 \times 19r$$

$$\frac{684}{6 \times 19} = r$$

$$\therefore \qquad r = 6\% \text{ p.a.}$$

Q. 9. Mr. Britto deposits a certain sum of money each month in a Recurring Deposit Account of a bank. If the rate of interest is of 8% per annum and Mr. Britto gets ₹8,088 from the bank after 3 years, find the value of his monthly instalment. **[2013]**

Ans. Let the monthly instalment be ₹x.

Here, $n = 36$, M.V. = ₹8,088, $r = 8\%$ p.a.,

$$\therefore \qquad I = P \frac{n(n+1)}{2 \times 12} \times \frac{r}{100}$$

$$M.V. = P \times n + I$$

$$8{,}088 = x \times 36 + \left[\frac{x \times 36 \times 37}{2 \times 12} \times \frac{8}{100} \right]$$

$$8{,}088 = 36x + \frac{111x}{25}$$

$$8{,}088 = \frac{900x + 111x}{25}$$

$$8{,}088 \times 25 = 1011x$$

$$\therefore \qquad x = \frac{8088 \times 25}{1011} = 200.$$

$\therefore$ Monthly instalment is ₹200.

Q. 10. Kiran deposited ₹200 per month for 36 months in a bank's recurring deposit account. If the bank pays interest at the rate of 11% per annum, find the amount she gets on maturity. **[2012]**

Ans. Given, P = ₹200, $n = 36$ months, R = 11%

$$\text{Interest} = \frac{P \times n(n+1) \times R}{2 \times 12 \times 100}$$

$$= \frac{200 \times 36 \times 37 \times 11}{2{,}400}$$

$$= 3 \times 37 \times 11 = ₹1{,}221$$

Sum deposited = $n \times P$

$$= 36 \times 200 = ₹7{,}200$$

$$\Rightarrow \qquad \text{Amount} = nP + I$$

$$= 7{,}200 + 1{,}221$$

$$= ₹8{,}421$$

$\therefore$ Total amount she will get is ₹8,421.

Q. 11. Ahmed has a recurring deposit account in a bank. He deposits ₹2,500 per month for 2 years. If he gets ₹66,250 at the time of maturity, find:

(i) The interest paid by the bank

(ii) The rate of interest. **[2011]**

Ans. (i) P = ₹2500, $n = 2$ years, *i.e*, 24 months

$$\text{Total deposited amount} = ₹2500 \times 24$$

$$= ₹60{,}000$$

$$\text{Maturity amount} = ₹66{,}250$$

$\therefore$ The interest paid by the bank

$$= ₹(66{,}250 - 60{,}000)$$

$$= ₹6{,}250$$

(ii) $$I = \frac{P \times n(n+1)}{2 \times 12} \times \frac{r}{100}$$

$$6250 = \frac{2500 \times 24 \times 25}{2 \times 12} \times \frac{r}{100}$$

$$r = \frac{6250}{25 \times 25} = 10\% \text{ p.a.}$$

$\therefore$ Rate of interest is 10% p.a.

Q. 12. Mrs. Goswami deposits ₹1000 every month in a recurring deposit account for 3 years at 8% interest per annum. Find the matured value. **[2009]**

Ans. Given, Monthly Instalment = ₹1000, R = 8%, Time = 3 years,

i.e., $n = 3 \times 12 = 36$

$$P = \frac{36(36+1)}{2} \times 1000$$

$$\text{Interest} = \frac{36 \times 37 \times 1000 \times 8}{2 \times 12 \times 100}$$

$$= 12 \times 37 \times 10 = ₹4440$$

Matured value $= 36000 + 4440$

$$= ₹40440$$

Q. 13. David opened a Recurring Deposit Account in a bank and deposited ₹300 per month for two years. If he received ₹7725 at the time of maturity, find the rate of interest per annum. **[2008]**

Ans. Given, Amount deposited per month = ₹300

Total number of months in 2 years = 24

$\therefore$ Principal for interest

$$= \frac{24 \times 25}{2} \times 300 = 12 \times 7500$$

$$= ₹90000$$

$\therefore$ Maturity value $= 24 \times 300 + \dfrac{90000 \times R \times 1}{12 \times 100}$

$$7725 = 7200 + 75 \times R$$

$$75R = 7725 - 7200$$

$$\Rightarrow \qquad 75\,R = 525$$

$$\Rightarrow \qquad R = \frac{525}{75} = 7\% \text{ p.a.}$$

Hence, the required rate of interest is 7% p.a.

Q. 14. Saloni deposited ₹150 per month in her bank for eight months under the Recurring Deposit Scheme. What will be the maturity value of her deposit, if the rate of interest is 8% per annum and the interest is calculated at the end of every month? **[2007]**

Ans. Saloni deposits ₹150 per month for 8 months.

$$\therefore \quad \text{Sum deposited} = 150 \times 8 = ₹1200$$

$$\text{Number of months of interest} = \frac{8(8+1)}{2} = 36$$

$$\therefore \text{Interest} = \frac{150 \times 36 \times 8 \times 1}{100 \times 12} = ₹36$$

$\therefore$ At the maturity she will get

$$= 1200 + 36 = ₹1236.$$

Q. 15. Mohan deposits ₹80 per month in a cumulative deposit account for six years. Find the amount payable to him on maturity, if the rate of interest is 6% per annum. **[2006]**

Ans. Here, $\quad$ P = ₹80 (Per month)

$$\text{Time } (n) = 6 \text{ years} = 6 \times 12 = 72 \text{ months}$$

$$\text{Rate} = 6\%$$

Equivalent principal for 72 months

$$= P \times \frac{n(n+1)}{2} = \frac{80 \times 72 \times 73}{2}$$

$\therefore \quad$ S.I. $= \dfrac{\text{PRT}}{100}$, we get

$$= 80 \times \frac{72 \times 73}{2 \times 12} \times \frac{6}{100} = ₹1,051.20$$

Total money deposited by Mohan

$$= 80 \times 72 = ₹5,760$$

$\therefore$ Maturity Amount

$$= \text{Money deposited} + \text{Interest}$$
$$= ₹5,760 + ₹1,051.20$$
$$= ₹6,811.20$$

 ## Long Answer Type Questions

Q. 1. Mr. Gupta opened a recurring deposit account in a bank. He deposited ₹2,500 per month for two years. At the time of maturity he got ₹67,500. Find:

(i) the total interest earned by Mr. Gupta.

(ii) the rate of interest per annum. **[2010]**

Ans. (i) Given, $n = 2 \times 12 = 24$, P = ₹2,500,

$$\text{Total amount deposited} = 24 \times 2,500$$
$$= ₹60,000$$
$$\text{Maturity} = ₹67,500$$

$\therefore$ Interest on his deposit

$$= ₹(67,500 - 60,000)$$
$$= ₹7,500$$

(ii) $\quad$ Interest $= \dfrac{n(n+1)}{2} \times \dfrac{\text{Instalment} \times \text{Rate}}{100 \times 12}$

$$\Rightarrow \quad 7,500 = \frac{24 \times 25}{2} \times \frac{2,500 \times \text{Rate}}{100 \times 12}$$

$$\Rightarrow \quad \text{Rate} = \frac{7,500 \times 100 \times 24}{24 \times 25 \times 2,500}$$

$$= 12\% \text{ p.a.}$$

$\therefore$ Rate of interest is 12% p.a.

Linear Inequations in One Variable

 **Short Answer Type Questions**

Q. 1. Solve the following inequation and represent the solution set on the number line. **[2020]**

$$\frac{3x}{5} + 2 < x + 4 \le \frac{x}{2} + 5, \, x \in R$$

Marking Scheme

$$\frac{3x}{5} - x < 4 - 2 \qquad x - \frac{x}{2} \le 5 - 4$$

(Any one transformation of x terms on one side)

$$\frac{3x - 5x}{5} < 2 \qquad \frac{2x - x}{2} \le 5 - 4$$

$$-2x < 10 \qquad \frac{x}{2} \le 1$$

$$\therefore 2x > -10 \qquad x \le 2$$
$$x > -5$$

Solution : $\{x : -5 < x \le 2, x \, \varepsilon \, R\}$

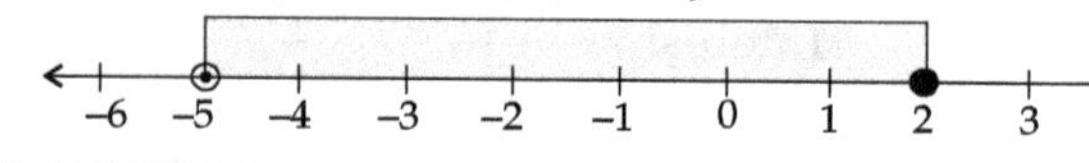

Ans. Given : $\quad \dfrac{3x}{5} + 2 < x + 4 \le \dfrac{x}{2} + 5$

Now, $\quad \dfrac{3x}{5} + 2 < x + 4$

$\Rightarrow \quad \dfrac{3x}{5} - x < 4 - 2$

$\Rightarrow \quad \dfrac{3x - 5x}{5} < 2$

$\Rightarrow \quad -2x < 10$

$\Rightarrow \quad x > -\dfrac{10}{2}$

$\Rightarrow \quad x > -5$

And, $\quad x + 4 \le \dfrac{x}{2} + 5$

$\Rightarrow \quad x - \dfrac{x}{2} \le 5 - 4$

$\Rightarrow \quad \dfrac{x}{2} \le 1$

$\Rightarrow \quad x \le 2$

Hence, $\quad -5 < x \le 2$

Q. 2. Solve the following inequation and write down the solution set:

$$11x - 4 < 15x + 4 \le 13x + 14, \, x \in W$$

Represent the solution on a real number line. **[2019]**

Marking Scheme

$11x - 4 < 15x + 4 \le 13x + 14, \, x\varepsilon W$

$11x - 4 < 15x + 4 \qquad 15x + 4 \le 13x + 14$ (Transforming

$11x - 15x < 4 + 4 \qquad 15x - 13x \le 14 - 4 \quad x$ terms on one

$-4x < 8 \qquad\qquad 2x \le 10 \qquad$ side and constants on

$+ 4x > -8 \qquad\qquad x \le 5 \qquad\qquad$ the other side)

$x > -2$

Solution : $\{-1, 0, 1, 2, 3, 4, 5\}$

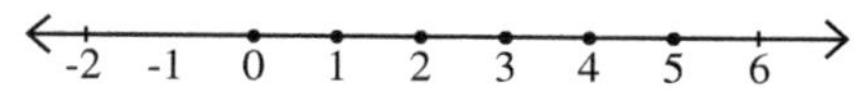

Ans. Given, $11x - 4 < 15x + 4 \le 13x + 14, \, x \in W.$

$\therefore \quad 11x - 4 < 15x + 4$ and $15x + 4 \le 13x + 14$

$\Rightarrow \quad 11x - 15x < 4 + 4$ and $15x - 13x \le 14 - 4$

$\Rightarrow \qquad\qquad -4x < 8$ and $2x \le 10$

$\Rightarrow \qquad \dfrac{-4x}{-4} > \dfrac{8}{-4}$ and $\dfrac{2x}{2} \le \dfrac{10}{2}$

$\Rightarrow \qquad\qquad x > -2$ and $x \le 5$

$\therefore \qquad\qquad -2 < x \le 5$

$\therefore$ Solution set $(w) = \{0, 1, 2, 3, 4, 5\}$

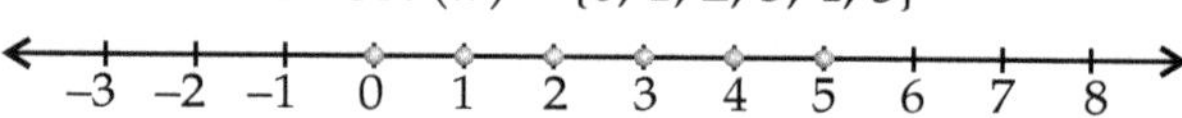

Q. 3. Solve the following inequation, write down the solution set and represent it on the real number line:

$$-2 + 10x \le 13x + 10 < 24 + 10x, \, x \in Z \quad \textbf{[2018]}$$

Ans. Given inequation is,

$$-2 + 10x \le 13x + 10 < 24 + 10x, \, x \in Z$$

$\Rightarrow \qquad -2 + 10x \le 13x + 10;$

$\Rightarrow \qquad 10x - 13x \le 10 + 2;$

$\Rightarrow \qquad\quad -3x \le 12;$

$\Rightarrow \qquad\qquad -x \le 4;$

$\Rightarrow \qquad\qquad x \ge -4;$

$$13x + 10 < 24 + 10x$$
$$13x - 10x < 24 - 10$$
$$3x < 14$$
$$x < \dfrac{14}{3}$$

$\therefore \qquad -4 \le x < 4\dfrac{2}{3}$

$\therefore$ Solution set $= \{-4, -3, -2, -1, 0, 1, 2, 3, 4\}$

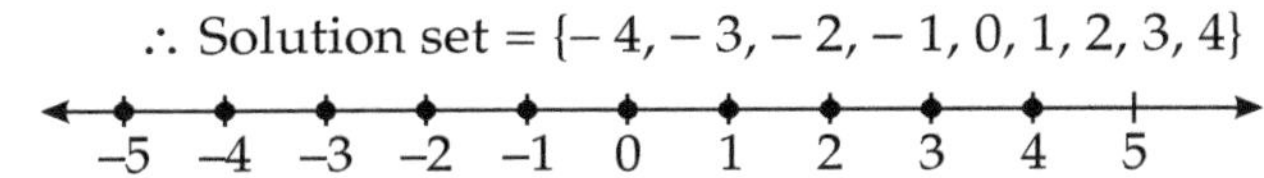

Q. 4. Solve the following inequation and represent the solution set on a number line.

$$-8\frac{1}{2} < -\frac{1}{2} - 4x \leq 7\frac{1}{2}, \, x \in I \qquad [2017]$$

Ans. Given inequation is,

$$-8\frac{1}{2} < -\frac{1}{2} - 4x \leq 7\frac{1}{2}, \, x \in I$$

$$\Rightarrow \quad -\frac{17}{2} < \frac{-1-8x}{2} \leq \frac{15}{2}$$

$$\Rightarrow \quad -\frac{17}{2} \times 2 < \frac{-1-8x}{2} \times 2 \leq \frac{15}{2} \times 2$$

[Multiplying with 2 in complete inequation]

$$\Rightarrow \quad -17 < -1 - 8x \leq 15$$

$$\Rightarrow \quad -17 + 1 < -1 + 1 - 8x \leq 15 + 1$$

[Adding 1 in complete inequation]

$$\Rightarrow \quad -16 < -8x \leq 16$$

$$\Rightarrow \quad \frac{-16}{-8} > \frac{-8x}{-8} \geq \frac{16}{-8}$$

[Dividing by -8 in the inequation]

$$\Rightarrow \quad 2 > x \geq -2$$

$$\Rightarrow \quad -2 \leq x < 2$$

$\therefore$ Solution set $= \{-2, -1, 0, 1\}$

Q. 5. Solve the following inequation, write the solution set and represent it on the number line.

$$-3(x-7) \geq 15 - 7x > \frac{x+1}{3}, \, x \in R$$

where R is a set of real numbers. [2016]

Ans. Given, $-3(x-7) \geq 15 - 7x > \dfrac{x+1}{3}$

$\Rightarrow -3(x-7) \geq 15 - 7x$ and $\Rightarrow 15 - 7x > \dfrac{x+1}{3}$

$\Rightarrow -3x + 21 \geq 15 - 7x$ and $\Rightarrow 45 - 21x > x + 1$

$\Rightarrow 7x - 3x \geq 15 - 21$ and $\Rightarrow -21x - x > 1 - 45$

$\Rightarrow \quad 4x \geq -6$ and $\Rightarrow -22x > -44$

$\Rightarrow \quad x \geq -\dfrac{3}{2}$ and $\Rightarrow \quad x < 2$

On simplifying, the given inequation reduces to $-\dfrac{3}{2} \leq x < 2$ and the required number line is

Solution set is : $\left\{x : -\dfrac{3}{2} \leq x < 2, \, x \in R\right\}$

Q. 6. Solve the following inequation and write the solution set:

$$13x - 5 < 15x + 4 < 7x + 12, \, x \in R$$

Represent the solution on a real number line. [2015]

Ans. Given, $13x - 5 < 15x + 4 < 7x + 12$

$\Rightarrow \quad 13x - 5 < 15x + 4$ and $15x + 4 < 7x + 12$

$\Rightarrow \quad 13x - 15x < 4 + 5$ and $15x - 7x < 12 - 4$

$\qquad -2x < 9$ and $\qquad 8x < 8$

$\qquad -x < \dfrac{9}{2}$ and $\qquad x < 1$

$\qquad x > -4.5$

$\therefore \quad$ Solution set $= \{x : -4.5 < x < 1$ and $x \in R\}$

Required number line,

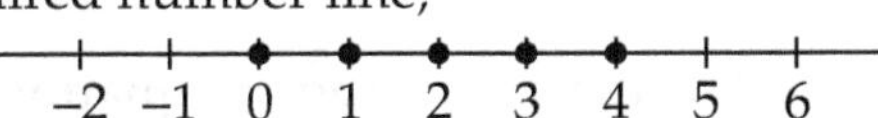

Q. 7. Find the values of x, which satisfy the inequation $-2\dfrac{5}{6} < \dfrac{1}{2} - \dfrac{2x}{3} \leq 2, \, x \in W$. Show or represent the solution set on the number line, where W is the set of whole numbers. [2014]

Ans. $-2\dfrac{5}{6} < \dfrac{1}{2} - \dfrac{2x}{3} \leq 2$

Taking, $\qquad -2\dfrac{5}{6} < \dfrac{1}{2} - \dfrac{2x}{3}$

$$-\frac{17}{6} < \frac{1}{2} - \frac{2x}{3}$$

$$-\frac{17}{6} - \frac{1}{2} < -\frac{2x}{3}$$

$$\frac{-17-3}{6} < -\frac{2x}{3}$$

$$-\frac{20}{6} < -\frac{2x}{3} \Rightarrow \frac{10}{3} > \frac{2x}{3}$$

$$5 > x \Rightarrow x < 5 \qquad \ldots(i)$$

Now, taking $\qquad \dfrac{1}{2} - \dfrac{2x}{3} \leq 2$

$$-\frac{2x}{3} \leq 2 - \frac{1}{2}$$

$$-\frac{2x}{3} \leq \frac{3}{2}$$

$$-x \leq \frac{9}{4} \Rightarrow x \geq -\frac{9}{4} \qquad \ldots(ii)$$

From (i) and (ii), we get

$$-\frac{9}{4} \leq x < 5 \Rightarrow -2\frac{1}{4} \leq x < 5, \, x \in W$$

But as $x \in W$ the solution set is, $\{0, 1, 2, 3, 4\}$.

Required number line,

Q. 8. Solve the following inequation, write the solution set and represent it on the number line:

$$-\frac{x}{3} \leq \frac{x}{2} - 1\frac{1}{3} < \frac{1}{6}, \, x \in R,$$

Where R is a set of real numbers. [2013]

Ans. $-\dfrac{x}{3} \le \dfrac{x}{2} - 1\dfrac{1}{3} < \dfrac{1}{6},\, x \in \mathrm{R},$

$-\dfrac{x}{3} \le \dfrac{x}{2} - 1\dfrac{1}{3}$ $\Big|$ $\dfrac{x}{2} - \dfrac{4}{3} < \dfrac{1}{6}$

$-\dfrac{x}{3} \le \dfrac{x}{2} - \dfrac{4}{3}$ $\Big|$ $\dfrac{x}{2} < \dfrac{1}{6} + \dfrac{4}{3}$

$\dfrac{4}{3} \le \dfrac{x}{2} + \dfrac{x}{3}$ $\Big|$ $\dfrac{x}{2} < \dfrac{1+8}{6}$

$\dfrac{4}{3} \le \dfrac{5x}{6}$ $\Big|$ $x < \dfrac{9 \times 2}{6}$

$\dfrac{6}{5} \times \dfrac{4}{3} \le x$ $\Big|$ $x < 3$ …(ii)

$\dfrac{8}{5} \le x$ …(i)

From equations (i) and (ii), we get

$$\dfrac{8}{5} \le x < 3$$

or $1.6 \le x < 3$

∴ Solution set $\{x : 1.6 \le x < 3, x \in \mathrm{R}\}$

Required number line is,

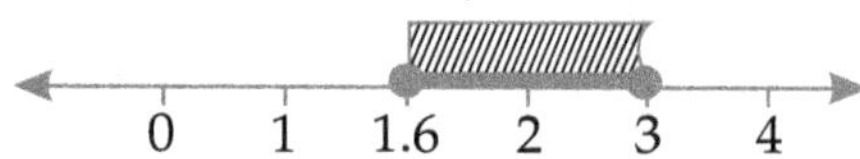

Q. 9. Solve the following inequation and represent the solution set on the number line:

$$4x - 19 < \dfrac{3x}{5} - 2 \le \dfrac{-2}{5} + x,\ x \in \mathrm{R},$$

Where R is a set of real numbers. [2012]

Ans. $4x - 19 < \dfrac{3x}{5} - 2 \le \dfrac{-2}{5},\ x \in \mathrm{R}$

$\Rightarrow$ $4x - 19 < \dfrac{3x}{5} - 2$ $\Big|$ $\dfrac{3x}{5} - 2 \le \dfrac{-2}{5} + x$

$4x - \dfrac{3x}{5} < -2 + 19$ $\Big|$ $\dfrac{3x}{5} - x \le \dfrac{-2}{5} + 2$

$\Rightarrow$ $\dfrac{17x}{5} < 17$ $\Big|$ $-2x \le 8$

$\Rightarrow$ $x < 5$ $\Big|$ $2x \ge -8$

$\Rightarrow$ $-4 \le x < 5$ $\Big|$ $x \ge -4$

Solution Set : $\{x : -4 \le x < 5, x \in \mathrm{R}\}$

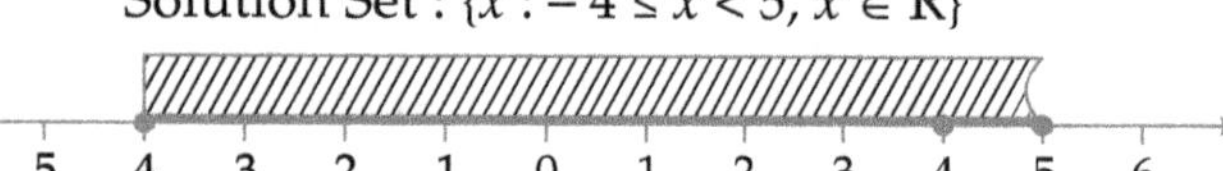

Q. 10. Solve the following inequation and represent the solution set on the number line $2x - 5 \le 5x + 4 < 11$, where $x \in \mathrm{I}$, I is a set of integers. [2011]

Ans. $2x - 5 \le 5x + 4 < 11, x \in \mathrm{I}$

$2x - 5 \le 5x + 4$ $\Big|$ $5x + 4 < 11$

$2x - 5x \le 4 + 5$ $\Big|$ $5x < 11 - 4$

$-3x \le 9$ $\Big|$ $5x < 7$

$3x \ge -9$ $\Big|$ $x < \dfrac{7}{5}$

$x \ge -3$

$-3 \le x$ …(i) $\Big|$ $x < 1\dfrac{2}{5}$ …(ii)

From (i) and (ii), $-3 \le x < 1\dfrac{2}{5}, x \in \mathrm{I}$

∴ Solution set $= \{-3, -2, -1, 0, 1\}$

Q. 11. Solve the following inequation and represent the solution set on the number line.

$$-3 < -\dfrac{1}{2} - \dfrac{2x}{3} \le \dfrac{5}{6},\, x \in \mathbf{R}.$$ [2010]

Ans. Given, $-3 < -\dfrac{1}{2} - \dfrac{2x}{3} \le \dfrac{5}{6}$

$-3 < -\dfrac{1}{2} - \dfrac{2x}{3}$ $\Big|$ $-\dfrac{1}{2} - \dfrac{2x}{3} \le \dfrac{5}{6}$

$-3 < \dfrac{-3 - 4x}{6}$ $\Big|$ $\dfrac{-3 - 4x}{6} \le \dfrac{5}{6}$

$-18 + 3 < -4x$ $\Big|$ $-4x \le 8$

$-15 < -4x$ $\Big|$ $-x \le 2$

or $15 > 4x$ $\Big|$ $x \ge -2$ …(ii)

or $4x < 15$

or $x < \dfrac{15}{4}$ …(i)

From equations (i) and (ii)

$$-2 \le x < \dfrac{15}{4}$$

∴ Solution set is $\{-2 \le x < \dfrac{15}{4}, x \in \mathrm{R}\}$

Q. 12. Solve the inequation and represent the solution set on the number line.

$$-3 + x \le \dfrac{8x}{3} + 2 \le \dfrac{14}{3} + 2x, \text{ where } x \in \mathrm{I}$$ [2009]

Ans. Given, $-3 + x \le \dfrac{8x}{3} + 2 \le \dfrac{14}{3} + 2x, x \in \mathrm{I}$

$\Rightarrow$ $-3 + x \le \dfrac{8x}{3} + 2$ …(i)

and $\dfrac{8x}{3} + 2 \le \dfrac{14}{3} + 2x$ …(ii)

$\Rightarrow$ $-5 \le \dfrac{5x}{3}$ and $\dfrac{2x}{3} \le \dfrac{8}{3}$

$\Rightarrow$ $x \ge -3$ and $x \le 4$

∴ $-3 \le x \le 4$

Solution set $= \{-3, -2, -1, 0, 1, 2, 3, 4\}$

Number line

Q. 13. Solve the given inequation and graph the solution on the number line.

$$2y - 3 < y + 1 \le 4y + 7;\, y \in \mathrm{R}.$$ [2008]

Ans. Given inequation is,

$$2y - 3 < y + 1 \le 4y + 7, y \in R$$
$$\Rightarrow \quad y - 3 < 1 \le 3y + 7$$
$$\Rightarrow \quad y - 3 < 1 \quad \text{and} \quad 1 \le 3y + 7$$
$$\Rightarrow \quad y < 4 \quad \text{and} \quad 3y \ge -6$$
$$\quad\quad\quad\quad\quad\quad\quad\quad\quad\quad y \ge -2$$
$$\Rightarrow \quad -2 \le y < 4$$

Q. 14. Solve the following inequation and graph the solution on the number line.

$$-2\frac{2}{3} \le x + \frac{1}{3} < 3\frac{1}{3}; x \in \mathbf{R}.$$ [2007]

Ans. The given inequation has two parts:

$$-2\frac{2}{3} \le x + \frac{1}{3} \quad \text{and} \quad x + \frac{1}{3} < 3\frac{1}{3}$$
$$-\frac{8}{3} \le x + \frac{1}{3} \quad \text{and} \quad x + \frac{1}{3} < \frac{10}{3}$$
$$-\frac{8}{3} - \frac{1}{3} \le x \quad \text{and} \quad x < \frac{10}{3} - \frac{1}{3}$$

$$-\frac{9}{3} \le x \quad \text{and} \quad x < \frac{9}{3}$$
$$-3 \le x \quad \text{and} \quad x < 3$$
$$\therefore \quad\quad -3 \le x < 3$$

The required number line is:

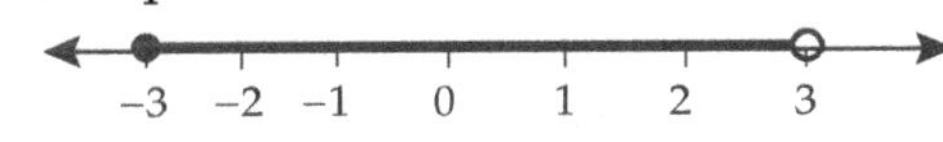

Q. 15. Given that $x \in \mathbf{R}$, solve the following inequality and graph the solution on the number line:

$$-1 \le 3 + 4x \le 23$$ [2006]

Ans. $-1 \le 3 + 4x \le 23$

$$-1 - 3 \le 4x \quad\quad \text{or} \quad\quad 4x \le 23 - 3$$
$$-4 \le 4x \quad\quad \text{or} \quad\quad 4x \le 20$$
$$-1 \le x \quad\quad \text{or} \quad\quad x \le 5$$

Solution Set $= \{x : -1 \le x \le 5, x \in R\}$

Chapter 5

Quadratic Equations in One Variable

 **Short Answer Type Questions**

Q. 1. Solve the following quadratic equation :
$$x^2 - 7x + 3 = 0$$
Give your answer correct to two decimal places. **[2020]**

Marking Scheme

$x^2 - 7x + 3 = 0$

$\therefore a = 1, b = -7, c = 3$

$$x = \frac{-b + \sqrt{b^2 - 4ac}}{2a}$$

$$x = \frac{-(-7) \pm \sqrt{(-7)^2 - 4 \times 1 \times 3}}{2 \times 1}$$

$$x = \frac{7 \pm \sqrt{49 - 12}}{2}$$

$$= \frac{7 \pm \sqrt{37}}{2}$$

$$= \frac{7 \pm 6.083}{2}$$

$$x = \frac{7 + 6.083}{2}, \frac{7 - 6.083}{2}$$

$$= \frac{13.083}{2}, \frac{0.917}{2}$$

$\therefore x = 6.541, 0.458$

$x = 6.54, 0.46$

(All solutions correct to two decimal places)

Ans. **Given :** $x^2 - 7x + 3 = 0$

Here, $a = 1, b = -7$ and $c = 3$

$$\therefore \quad x = \frac{-b \pm \sqrt{b^2 - 4ac}}{2a}$$

$$= \frac{-(-7) \pm \sqrt{(-7)^2 - 4 \times 1 \times 3}}{2 \times 1}$$

$$= \frac{7 \pm \sqrt{49 - 12}}{2}$$

$$= \frac{7 \pm \sqrt{37}}{2} - \frac{7 \pm 6.08}{2}$$

Taking positive sign,
$$x = \frac{7 + 6.08}{2} = 6.54$$

Taking negative sign,
$$x = \frac{7 - 6.08}{2} = 0.46$$

Hence, $x = 6.54$ and 0.46

Q. 2. The difference of two natural numbers is 7 and their product is 450. Find the numbers. **[2020]**

Marking Scheme

Let the numbers be x and $(x + 7)$

$x(x + 7) = 450$

$x^2 + 7x - 450 = 0$

$(x + 25)(x - 18) = 0$

$x = -25$ or 18

The numbers are 18 and 25.

(Any other correct method)

Ans. Let the two natural numbers be x and y such that $x > y$.

Then, $x - y = 7$

$\Rightarrow \qquad x = 7 + y$ ...(i)

and $xy = 450$

$\Rightarrow \qquad (7 + y)y = 450$ [Using (i)]

$\Rightarrow \qquad y^2 + 7y - 450 = 0$

$\Rightarrow \quad y^2 + 25y - 18y - 450 = 0$

$\Rightarrow \quad y(y + 25) - 18(y + 25) = 0$

$\Rightarrow \qquad (y + 25)(y - 18) = 0$

$\Rightarrow \qquad y = -25$ [Neglected]

or $\qquad y = 18$

$\therefore \qquad y = 18$

$\therefore \qquad x = 7 + 18 = 25$

Hence, the numbers are 25 and 18.

Q. 3. Solve for x the quadratic equation $x^2 - 4x - 8 = 0$.
Give your answer correct to three significant figures. **[2019]**

Marking Scheme

$x^2 - 4x - 8 = 0$

$$x = \frac{-(-4) \pm \sqrt{(-4)^2 - 4.1.(-8)}}{2 \times 1}$$

$$= \frac{4 \pm \sqrt{16 + 32}}{2}$$

$$= \frac{4 \pm \sqrt{48}}{2}$$

$$= \frac{4 \pm 4\sqrt{3}}{2}$$

$$= 2 \pm 2\sqrt{3} = 2 \pm 2 \times 1.732$$

$x = 2 \pm 3.464$

$\therefore x = 5.464$ or -1.464

$x = 5.46, -1.46$ (Correct to three significant figures)

Ans. Given quadratic equation is $x^2 - 4x - 8 = 0$.
Comparing it with $ax^2 + bx + c = 0$, we get
$$a = 1, \ b = -4 \text{ and } c = -8$$

$$\therefore \quad x = \frac{-b \pm \sqrt{b^2 - 4ac}}{2a}$$

$$= \frac{(-4) \pm \sqrt{(-4)^2 - 4 \times 1 \times (-8)}}{2 \times 1}$$

$$= \frac{4 \pm \sqrt{16 + 32}}{2} = \frac{4 \pm \sqrt{48}}{2} = \frac{4 \pm 6.928}{2}$$

$$= \frac{4 + 6.928}{2} \ \text{or} \ \frac{4 - 6.928}{2}$$

$$= \frac{10.928}{2} \ \text{or} \ \frac{-2.928}{2}$$

$$= 5.464 \ \text{or} \ -1.464$$

$\therefore \ x = 5.464$ or -1.464 (correct to 3 significant figures).

Q. 4. **The product of two consecutive natural numbers which are multiples of 3 is equal to 810. Find the two numbers.** **[2019]**

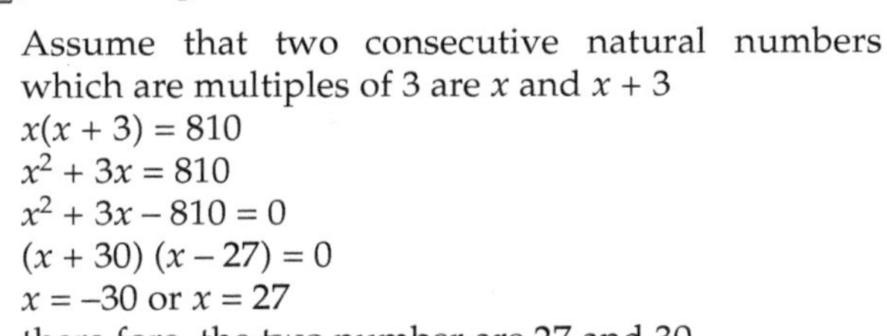

📋 Marking Scheme

Assume that two consecutive natural numbers which are multiples of 3 are x and $x + 3$
$x(x + 3) = 810$
$x^2 + 3x = 810$
$x^2 + 3x - 810 = 0$
$(x + 30)(x - 27) = 0$
$x = -30$ or $x = 27$
there fore, the two number are 27 and 30.

Ans. Let the two consecutive natural numbers which are multiples of 3 be x and $x + 3$.
According to the question,
$$x(x + 3) = 810$$
$$\Rightarrow \quad x^2 + 3x = 810$$
$$\Rightarrow \quad x^2 + 3x - 810 = 0$$
$$\Rightarrow \quad x^2 + 30x - 27x - 810 = 0$$
$$\Rightarrow \quad x(x + 30) - 27(x + 30) = 0$$
$$\Rightarrow \quad (x + 30)(x - 27) = 0$$
$$\Rightarrow \quad x + 30 = 0 \text{ or } x - 27 = 0$$
$$\Rightarrow \quad x = -30 \quad \text{or } x = 27$$
$$\therefore \quad x = 27$$
$$(\because -30 \text{ is not a natural number})$$
$$\therefore \quad x + 3 = 27 + 3 = 30$$
Hence, the two numbers are 27 and 30.

Q. 5. **Find the value of k for which the following equation has equal roots:**
$$x^2 + 4kx + (k^2 - k + 2) = 0 \quad \text{[2018]}$$

Ans. Given equation is, $x^2 + 4kx + (k^2 - k + 2) = 0$
Comparing it with $ax^2 + bx + c = 0$, we have,
$$a = 1, b = 4k, c = k^2 - k + 2.$$
$$\therefore \quad D = b^2 - 4ac = (4k)^2 - 4 \times 1 \times (k^2 - k + 2)$$
$$= 16k^2 - 4k^2 + 4k - 8$$
$$= 12k^2 + 4k - 8$$

$\because$ The roots of given equation are equal, so
$$D = 0$$
$$\Rightarrow \quad 12k^2 + 4k - 8 = 0$$
$$\Rightarrow \quad 3k^2 + k - 2 = 0$$
$$\Rightarrow \quad 3k^2 + 3k - 2k - 2 = 0$$
$$\Rightarrow \quad 3k(k + 1) - 2(k + 1) = 0$$
$$\Rightarrow \quad (k + 1)(3k - 2) = 0$$
$$\Rightarrow \quad k + 1 = 0 \quad \text{or} \quad 3k - 2 = 0$$
$$\Rightarrow \quad k = -1 \quad \text{or} \quad k = \frac{2}{3}$$
$\therefore$ The value of k is -1 or $\frac{2}{3}$.

Q. 6. **₹7500 were divided equally among a certain number of children. Had there been 20 less children, each would have received ₹100 more. Find the original number of children.** **[2018]**

Ans. Let the original number of children be x.
Total amount to be distributed = ₹7,500
$$\therefore \quad \text{Each will receive} = \frac{7,500}{x}$$
If the number of children are $x - 20$,
Then, Each will receive $= \dfrac{7,500}{x - 20}$

According to question,
$$\frac{7,500}{x - 20} - \frac{7,500}{x} = 100$$
$$\Rightarrow \quad 7,500\left(\frac{1}{x - 20} - \frac{1}{x}\right) = 100$$
$$\Rightarrow \quad \frac{x - x + 20}{x(x - 20)} = \frac{100}{7,500}$$
$$\Rightarrow \quad \frac{20}{x^2 - 20x} = \frac{1}{75}$$
$$\Rightarrow \quad x^2 - 20x = 1,500$$
$$\Rightarrow \quad x^2 - 20x - 1,500 = 0$$
$$\Rightarrow \quad x^2 - (50 - 30)x - 1,500 = 0$$
$$\Rightarrow \quad x^2 - 50x + 30x - 1,500 = 0$$
$$\Rightarrow \quad x(x - 50) + 30(x - 50) = 0$$
$$\rightarrow \quad (x - 50)(x + 30) = 0$$
$$\Rightarrow \quad x - 50 = 0 \text{ or } x + 30 = 0$$
$$\Rightarrow \quad x = 50 \text{ or } x = -30$$
$$\therefore \quad x = 50$$
$$(\because x \text{ cannot be negative})$$
$\therefore$ The original number of children = 50.

Q. 7. **Solve the quadratic equation $x^2 - 3(x + 3) = 0$; Give your answer correct to two significant figures.** **[2016]**

Ans. Given, $x^2 - 3(x + 3) = 0$
$$x^2 - 3x - 9 = 0$$

Since, middle term cannot be splitted.

So compare it with $ax^2 + bx + c = 0$, we get

$$a = 1, b = -3 \text{ and } c = -9$$

$\therefore \qquad D = b^2 - 4ac = (-3)^2 - 4 \times 1 \times (-9)$

$$= 9 + 36 = 45$$

$\therefore \qquad x = \dfrac{3 \pm \sqrt{45}}{2 \times 1} \qquad \left[\because x = \dfrac{-b \pm \sqrt{b^2 - 4ac}}{2a} \right]$

$\Rightarrow \qquad x = \dfrac{3 \pm 6.708}{2}$

$\Rightarrow \qquad x = \dfrac{3 + 6.708}{2} \text{ and } \dfrac{3 - 6.708}{2}$

$\Rightarrow \qquad x = 4.854 \text{ and } -1.854$

The roots of given equation are 4.85 and −1.85.

Q. 8. **A bus covers a distance of 240 km at a uniform speed. Due to heavy rain its speed gets reduced by 10 km/h and as such it takes two hrs longer to cover the total distance. Assuming the uniform speed to be 'x' km/h, form an equation and solve it to evaluate 'x'.** **[2016]**

Ans. Let the uniform speed of bus be x km/h.

$\therefore$ Time taken by it to cover 240 km $= \dfrac{240}{x}$ hrs.

$$\left[\because T = \dfrac{D}{S} \right]$$

Reduced speed of bus $= (x - 10)$ km/hr

$\therefore$ So, time taken by the bus to cover 240 km

$$= \dfrac{240}{x - 10} \text{ hrs.}$$

Now, according to the given condition

$\therefore \qquad \dfrac{240}{x - 10} - \dfrac{240}{x} = 2$

$\Rightarrow \qquad 240\left(\dfrac{1}{x - 10} - \dfrac{1}{x} \right) = 2$

$\Rightarrow \qquad 120\left(\dfrac{x - (x - 10)}{x(x - 10)} \right) = 1$

$\Rightarrow \qquad 120\left(\dfrac{10}{x(x - 10)} \right) = 1$

$\Rightarrow \qquad x^2 - 10x - 1200 = 0$

On splitting the middle term

$\Rightarrow \qquad x^2 - 40x + 30x - 1200 = 0$

$\Rightarrow \qquad x(x - 40) + 30(x - 40) = 0$

$\Rightarrow \qquad (x - 40)(x + 30) = 0$

$\Rightarrow \qquad x = 40$

or $\qquad x = -30$

Since, speed cannot be negative.

Hence, the value of $x = 40$.

i.e., the uniform speed of bus is 40 km/hr.

Q. 9. **Find the value of 'K' for which $x = 3$ is a solution of the quadratic equation,**

$$(K + 2)\, x^2 - Kx + 6 = 0.$$

Thus, find the other root of the equation. **[2015]**

Ans. Since $x = 3$ is the solution of the given equation $(K + 2)x^2 - Kx + 6 = 0$ ...(i)

we get,

$$(K + 2)(3)^2 - K(3) + 6 = 0$$

$\Rightarrow \qquad 9K + 18 - 3K + 6 = 0$

$\Rightarrow \qquad 6K = -24$

$\Rightarrow \qquad K = -4$

Now, putting $K = -4$ in equation (i), we get

$\Rightarrow \qquad (-4 + 2)\, x^2 - (-4)\, x + 6 = 0$

$\Rightarrow \qquad -2x^2 + 4x + 6 = 0$

$\Rightarrow \qquad x^2 - 2x - 3 = 0$

$\Rightarrow \qquad x^2 - 3x + x - 3 = 0$

$\Rightarrow \qquad x(x - 3) + 1(x - 3) = 0$

$\Rightarrow \qquad (x - 3)(x + 1) = 0$

$\Rightarrow \qquad x = 3 \text{ or } x = -1$

$\therefore \qquad$ The other root is −1.

Q. 10. **Sum of two natural numbers is 8 and the difference of their reciprocal is $\dfrac{2}{15}$. Find the numbers.** **[2015]**

Ans. Let, the two natural numbers be x and $8 - x$.

Given, $\qquad \dfrac{1}{x} - \dfrac{1}{8 - x} = \dfrac{2}{15}$

$\Rightarrow \qquad \dfrac{8 - x - x}{x(8 - x)} = \dfrac{2}{15}$

$$(8 - 2x)15 = 16x - 2x^2$$

$$120 - 30x = 16x - 2x^2$$

$$2x^2 - 46x + 120 = 0$$

$$x^2 - 23x + 60 = 0$$

On splitting the middle term, we get

$$x^2 - 20x - 3x + 60 = 0$$

$$x(x - 20) - 3(x - 20) = 0$$

$$(x - 3)(x - 20) = 0$$

$$x = 3 \text{ or } x = 20 \text{ (neglect it)}$$

$$(\because \text{ Sum of two natural numbers is 8})$$

Thus, one number = 3 and other number

$$= 8 - 3 = 5$$

$\therefore \qquad$ The natural numbers are 3 and 5.

Q. 11. **Solve for x using the quadratic formula. Write your answer correct to two significant figures.**

$$(x - 1)^2 - 3x + 4 = 0.$$ **[2014]**

Ans. $\qquad (x - 1)^2 - 3x + 4 = 0$

$$x^2 + 1 - 2x - 3x + 4 = 0$$

$$x^2 - 5x + 5 = 0$$

Since, middle term cannot be splitted, so we will compare it with $ax^2 + bx + c = 0$, we get

$$a = 1, b = -5, c = 5$$

By using the formula,

$$x = \frac{-b \pm \sqrt{b^2 - 4ac}}{2a}$$

$$= \frac{5 \pm \sqrt{25 - 20}}{2}$$

$$= \frac{5 \pm \sqrt{5}}{2}$$

$$x = \frac{5 \pm 2.24}{2}$$

Taking +ve sign | Taking –ve sign

$$x = \frac{5 + 2.24}{2} \qquad x = \frac{5 - 2.25}{2} = \frac{2.75}{2} = 1.38$$

$$\Rightarrow \quad x = 3.62$$

Thus, required values are 3.62 and 1.38.

Q. 12. **Solve the following equation and calculate the answer correct to two decimal places:**

$$x^2 - 5x - 10 = 0. \qquad \text{[2013]}$$

Ans. Given equation is, $x^2 - 5x - 10 = 0$

We know,

$$x = \frac{-b \pm \sqrt{b^2 - 4ac}}{2a}$$

(As, $a = 1$, $b = -5$ and $c = -10$)

$$\Rightarrow \quad x = \frac{5 \pm \sqrt{25 - 4 \times 1 \times (-10)}}{2}$$

$$= \frac{5 \pm \sqrt{65}}{2}$$

$$= \frac{5 \pm 8.062}{2}$$

$$x_1 = \frac{5 + 8.062}{2}$$

$$= \frac{13.062}{2}$$

$$= 6.531$$

$$= 6.53$$

and, $\quad x_2 = \dfrac{5 - 8.062}{2}$

$$= \frac{-3.062}{2} = 1.531$$

$$= -1.53$$

Q. 13. **Solve the following equation and give your answer correct to 3 significant figures:**

$$5x^2 - 3x - 4 = 0 \qquad \text{[2012]}$$

Ans. Given equation is, $5x^2 - 3x - 4 = 0$

On comparing with $ax^2 + bx + c = 0$, we get

$$a = 5, \ b = -3, \ c = -4$$

$$x = \frac{-b \pm \sqrt{b^2 - 4ac}}{2a}$$

$$\Rightarrow \quad x = \frac{3 \pm \sqrt{9 - 4 \times 5 (-4)}}{2 \times 5}$$

$$\Rightarrow \quad x = \frac{3 \pm \sqrt{9 + 80}}{10} = \frac{3 \pm \sqrt{89}}{10}$$

$$x = \frac{3 \pm 9.434}{10}$$

$$\Rightarrow \quad x = \frac{3 + 9.434}{10}$$

or $\quad x = \dfrac{3 - 9.434}{10}$

$$x = \frac{12.434}{10}$$

or $\quad x = \dfrac{-6.434}{10}$

$$x = 1.243$$

or $\quad x = -0.643$

Q. 14. **Solve the following equation:**

$$x - \frac{18}{x} = 6. \textbf{ Give your answer correct to two significant figures.} \qquad \text{[2011]}$$

Ans.

$$x - \frac{18}{x} = 6$$

$$\Rightarrow \quad \frac{x^2 - 18}{x} = 6$$

$$\Rightarrow \quad x^2 - 18 = 6x$$

or $\quad x^2 - 6x - 18 = 0$

Since middle term cannot be splitted. So compare with $ax^2 + bx + c = 0$

$$a = 1, b = -6, c = -18$$

$$x = \frac{-b \pm \sqrt{b^2 - 4ac}}{2a}$$

$$= \frac{-(-6) \pm \sqrt{(-6)^2 - 4(1)(-18)}}{2 \times 1}$$

$$= \frac{6 \pm \sqrt{36 + 72}}{2} = \frac{6 + \sqrt{108}}{2}$$

$$= \frac{6 \pm \sqrt{6 \times 6 \times 3}}{2}$$

$$= \frac{6 \pm 6\sqrt{3}}{2} = 3 \pm 3\sqrt{3} = 3 \pm 3(1.732)$$

$$= 3 \pm 5.196$$

$$x = 3 + 5.196 \qquad \text{or} \quad x = 3 - 5.196$$

$$x = 8.196 \qquad\qquad\qquad x = -2.196$$

$$x = 8.2 \text{ (2 sig. fig.)} \quad \text{or} \quad x = -2.2 \text{ (2 sig. fig.)}$$

Q. 15. **₹480 is divided equally among 'x' children. If the number of children were 20 more than each would have got ₹12 less. Find 'x'. [2011]**

Ans. Let, number of children be x

$$\text{Share of each child} = ₹\frac{480}{x}$$

Now, number of children $= x + 20$

$\because$ Share of each child $= ₹\dfrac{480}{x+20}$

Now, according to the question

$$\frac{480}{x} - \frac{480}{x+20} = 12$$

$\Rightarrow \quad \dfrac{480x + 9600 - 480x}{x(x+20)} = 12$

$\Rightarrow \quad 9600 = 12x\,(x+20)$

$\Rightarrow \quad 800 = x^2 + 20x$

$\Rightarrow \quad x^2 + 20x - 800 = 0$

$\Rightarrow \quad x^2 + 40x - 20x - 800 = 0$

$\Rightarrow \quad x(x+40) - 20(x+40) = 0$

$\Rightarrow \quad (x-20)(x+40) = 0$

Either $\qquad\qquad\qquad x = 20$

or $\qquad\qquad\qquad x = -40$ (not possible)

$\therefore$ Number of children is 20.

Q. 16. Without solving the following quadratic equation, find the value of 'p' for which the roots are equal.

$$px^2 - 4x + 3. \qquad\qquad \text{[2010]}$$

Ans. Given equation is,

$$px^2 - 4x + 3 = 0$$

Comparing with $\quad ax^2 + bx + c = 0$

We get, $a = p$, $b = -4$, $c = 3$

Since roots are equal.

$\therefore \qquad\qquad\qquad\qquad D = 0$

$\Rightarrow \qquad\qquad\qquad b^2 - 4ac = 0$

$\Rightarrow \qquad\qquad\qquad 16 - 4p(3) = 0$

$\Rightarrow \qquad\qquad\qquad 12p = 16$

$\therefore \qquad\qquad\qquad\qquad p = \dfrac{4}{3}.$

Q. 17. Solve the following quadratic equation and give the answer correct to two significant figures.

$$4x^2 - 7x + 2 = 0 \qquad\qquad \text{[2009]}$$

Ans. Given quadratic equation is

$$4x^2 - 7x + 2 = 0$$

Here, $a = 4$, $b = -7$, $c = 2$ (comparing with $ax^2 + bx + c = 0$)

$$x = \frac{7 \pm \sqrt{49 - 32}}{8} = \frac{7 \pm \sqrt{17}}{8}$$

$$x = \frac{7 \pm 4.12}{8}$$

Taking (+ve) sign $\qquad x = \dfrac{11.12}{8} = 1.4$

Taking (–ve) sign $\qquad x = \dfrac{2.88}{8} = 0.36$

Q. 18. Solve the following quadratic equation for x and give your answer correct to two decimal places:

$$5x(x+2) = 3 \qquad\qquad \text{[2008]}$$

Ans. Given equation is, $\qquad 5x\,(x+2) = 3$

$\Rightarrow \qquad\qquad\qquad 5x^2 + 10x - 3 = 0$

$\Rightarrow \quad a = 5$, $b = 10$, $c = -3$

$\qquad$ (comparing with $ax^2 + bx + c = 0$)

$\therefore \quad x = \dfrac{-b \pm \sqrt{b^2 - 4ac}}{2a} = \dfrac{-10 \pm \sqrt{100 + 60}}{10}$

$\qquad = \dfrac{-10 \pm \sqrt{160}}{10} = \dfrac{-10 \pm 12.649}{10}$

$\therefore \quad x = \dfrac{-10 + 12.649}{10} = \dfrac{2.649}{10} = 0.26$

or $\quad x = \dfrac{-10 - 12.649}{10} = \dfrac{-22.649}{10} = -2.26$

Q. 19. Solve the following quadratic equation for x and give your answer correct to two decimal places: $x^2 - 3x - 9 = 0$. $\qquad$ **[2007]**

Ans. Given: $\qquad\qquad x^2 - 3x - 9 = 0$

Comparing with $ax^2 + bx + c = 0$

$$a = 1, \ b = -3, \ c = -9$$

By quadratic equation

$$x = \frac{-b \pm \sqrt{b^2 - 4ac}}{2a}$$

$$x = \frac{-(-3) \pm \sqrt{(-3)^2 - 4(1)(-9)}}{2 \times 1}$$

$$= \frac{3 \pm \sqrt{9 + 36}}{2} = \frac{3 \pm \sqrt{45}}{2} = \frac{3 \pm 3\sqrt{5}}{2}$$

Taking (+) sign	Taking (−) sign
$\therefore \ x = \dfrac{3 + 3\sqrt{5}}{2}$	$\therefore \ x = \dfrac{3 - 3\sqrt{5}}{2}$
$= \dfrac{3 + 3 \times 2.236}{2}$	$= \dfrac{3 - 3 \times 2.236}{2}$
$= \dfrac{3 + 6.708}{2}$	$= \dfrac{3 - 6.708}{2}$
$= \dfrac{9.708}{2}$	$= \dfrac{-3.708}{2}$
$= 4.85$	$= -1.85$

Q. 20. Solve the equation $2x - \dfrac{1}{x} = 7$. Write your answer correct to two decimal places. $\quad$ **[2006]**

Ans.
$$2x - \frac{1}{x} = 7$$
$$2x^2 - 1 = 7x$$
$$2x^2 - 7x - 1 = 0$$
For quadratic equation $ax^2 + bx + c = 0$

$$x = \frac{-b \pm \sqrt{b^2 - 4ac}}{2a}$$

Here, $a = 2$, $b = -7$, $c = -1$

 ## Long Answer Type Questions

Q. 1. Solve $x^2 + 7x = 7$ and give your answer correct to two decimal places. **[2018]**

Ans. We have, $x^2 + 7x = 7$
$\Rightarrow \qquad x^2 + 7x - 7 = 0$

Comparing it with $ax^2 + bx + c = 0$, we have
$$a = 1, \quad b = 7, \quad c = -7$$

$$\therefore \qquad x = \frac{-b \pm \sqrt{b^2 - 4ac}}{2a}$$

$$= \frac{-7 \pm \sqrt{7^2 - 4 \times 1 \times (-7)}}{2 \times 1}$$

$$= \frac{-7 \pm \sqrt{49 + 28}}{2}$$

$$= \frac{-7 \pm \sqrt{77}}{2}$$

$$= \frac{-7 \pm 8.775}{2}$$

$$= \frac{-7 + 8.775}{2} \quad \text{or} \quad \frac{-7 - 8.775}{2}$$

$$= \frac{1.775}{2} \quad \text{or} \quad \frac{-15.775}{2}$$

$$= 0.8875 \text{ or } -7.8875$$

$$= 0.89 \text{ or } -7.89$$

(correct to 2 decimal places)

Q. 2. Solve the equation $4x^2 - 5x - 3 = 0$ and give your answer correct to two decimal places. **[2017]**

Ans. Given equation is, $4x^2 - 5x - 3 = 0$.
Comparing it with $ax^2 + bx + c = 0$, we have
$$a = 4, b = -5, c = -3$$
$$x = \frac{-b \pm \sqrt{b^2 - 4ac}}{2a}$$

$$= \frac{-(-5) \pm \sqrt{(-5)^2 - 4 \times 4 \times (-3)}}{2 \times 4}$$

$$= \frac{5 \pm \sqrt{25 + 48}}{8} = \frac{5 \pm \sqrt{73}}{8}$$

$$= \frac{5 \pm 8.544}{8}$$

$$= \frac{5 + 8.544}{8} \quad \text{or} \quad \frac{5 - 8.544}{8}$$

$$= \frac{13.544}{8} \quad \text{or} \quad \frac{-3.544}{8}$$

$$= 1.693 \text{ or } -0.443$$

$$= 1.69 \text{ or } -0.44$$

(correct to 2 decimal places)

Q. 3. The sum of the ages of Vivek and his younger brother Amit is 47 years. The product of their ages in years is 550. Find their ages. **[2017]**

Ans. Let Vivek's present age be x years.
$\therefore$ His brother's present age $= (47 - x)$ years.
According to question,
$$x(47 - x) = 550$$
$$\Rightarrow \qquad 47x - x^2 = 550$$
$$\Rightarrow \qquad x^2 - 47x + 550 = 0$$
$$\Rightarrow \quad x^2 - 25x - 22x + 550 = 0$$
$$\Rightarrow \quad x(x - 25) - 22(x - 25) = 0$$
$$\Rightarrow \qquad (x - 25)(x - 22) = 0$$
$$\Rightarrow \qquad x - 25 = 0 \text{ or } x - 22 = 0$$
$$\Rightarrow \qquad x = 25 \text{ or } x = 22$$

When $x = 25$, $47 - x = 47 - 25 = 22$
When $x = 22$, $47 - x = 47 - 22 = 25$

(does not satisfy the given condition)
$\therefore$ Vivek's age $= x = 25$ years.
His younger brother's age $= 22$ years.

Q. 4. A two digit positive number is such that the product of its digits is 6. If 9 is added to the number, the digits interchange their places. Find the number. **[2014]**

Ans. Let, the unit digit be x and tens digit will be $\frac{6}{x}$.
As two digit number is $(10a + b)$. Then, two digit number is $10 \times \frac{6}{x} + x = \frac{60}{x} + x$.

No. formed by interchanging digits $= \left(10x + \frac{6}{x}\right)$

From question,
$$\frac{60}{x} + x + 9 = 10x + \frac{6}{x}$$
$$\Rightarrow \qquad \frac{60 + x^2 + 9x}{x} = \frac{10x^2 + 6}{x}$$
$$\Rightarrow \qquad 60 + x^2 + 9x = 10x^2 + 6$$
$$\Rightarrow \qquad 9x^2 - 9x - 54 = 0$$
$$\Rightarrow \qquad 9(x^2 - x - 6) = 0$$
$$\Rightarrow \qquad x^2 - x - 6 = 0$$
$$\Rightarrow \qquad x^2 - 3x + 2x - 6 = 0$$

$$\Rightarrow \quad x(x-3)+2(x-3)=0$$
$$\Rightarrow \quad (x-3)(x+2)=0$$
$$\Rightarrow \quad x=-2 \text{ or } 3$$

As x can't be negative.

So, required two digit number.

$$=\frac{60}{x}+x=\frac{60}{3}+3=23.$$

Q. 5. **Without solving the following quadratic equation, find the value of 'p' for which the given equation has real and equal roots:**
$$x^2+(p-3)x+p=0 \qquad \textbf{[2013]}$$

Ans. Given quadratic equation is,
$$x^2+(p-3)x+p=0$$
Here $a=1, b=p-3, c=p$
For real and equal roots
$$D=b^2-4ac=0$$
$$\Rightarrow \quad (p-3)^2-4\times1\times p=0$$
$$\Rightarrow \quad p^2-6p+9-4p=0$$
$$\Rightarrow \quad p^2-10p+9=0$$
$$\Rightarrow \quad p^2-p-9p+9=0$$
$$\Rightarrow \quad p(p-1)-9(p-1)=0$$
$$\Rightarrow \quad (p-1)(p-9)=0$$
$$\Rightarrow \quad p=1 \text{ or } p=9$$
The value of p is 1 or 9.

Q. 6. **A shopkeeper purchase a certain number of books for ₹960. If the cost per book was ₹8 less, the number of books that could be purchased for ₹960 would be 4 more. Write an equation, taking the original cost of each book to be ₹x, and solve it to find the original cost of the books.** **[2013]**

Ans. Let , the original cost of each book be ₹x.

$\therefore$ Number of books purchased for ₹960 $=\dfrac{960}{x}$

Now, if cost of each book $=$ ₹$(x-8)$

$\therefore$ Number of books purchased for ₹960
$$=\frac{960}{x-8}$$
According to the question
$$\frac{960}{x}+4=\frac{960}{x-8}$$
$$\Rightarrow \quad \frac{960}{(x-8)}-\frac{960}{x}=4$$
$$\Rightarrow \quad \frac{960x-960x+7680}{x(x-8)}=4$$
$$\Rightarrow \quad 7680=4x^2-32x$$
$$\Rightarrow \quad x^2-8x-1920=0$$
$$\Rightarrow \quad x^2+40x-48x-1920=0$$
$$\Rightarrow \quad x(x+40)-48(x+40)=0$$
$$\Rightarrow \quad (x+40)(x-48)=0$$

$$\Rightarrow \quad x=-40, 48$$
As cost can't be negative
$$\therefore \quad x=₹48.$$
$\therefore$ Cost of each book is ₹48.

Q. 7. **Without solving the following quadratic equation, find the value of 'm' for which the given equation has real and equal roots.**
$$x^2+2(m-1)x+(m+5)=0 \qquad \textbf{[2012]}$$

Ans. Given quadratic equation
$$x^2+2(m-1)x+(m+5)=0$$
On comparing with $ax^2+bx+c=0$
$$a=1, b=2(m-1), c=(m+5)$$
Since equation has real and equal roots
$$\therefore \qquad\qquad D=0$$
$$\Rightarrow \qquad\qquad b^2-4ac=0$$
$$\Rightarrow \quad [2(m-1)]^2-4\times1\times(m+5)=0$$
$$\Rightarrow \quad 4(m-1)^2-4(m+5)=0$$
$$\Rightarrow \quad 4[(m-1)^2-(m+5)]=0$$
$$\Rightarrow \quad 4[m^2-2m+1-m-5]=0$$
$$\Rightarrow \qquad\qquad m^2-3m-4=0$$
$$\Rightarrow \qquad\qquad m^2-4m+m-4=0$$
$$\Rightarrow \qquad m(m-4)+1(m-4)=0$$
$$\Rightarrow \qquad\qquad (m+1)(m-4)=0$$

$$\begin{array}{c|c} m+1=0 & m-4=0 \\ m=-1 & \Rightarrow \quad m=4 \end{array}$$
$$\therefore \qquad m=-1, 4$$

Q. 8. **A car covers a distance of 400 km at a certain speed. Had the speed been 12 km/h more, the time taken for the journey would have been 1 hour 40 minutes less. Find the original speed of the car.** **[2012]**

Ans. Let the original speed of the car be x km/h,

So, time taken by car $=\dfrac{400}{x}$ hrs

When, $\qquad$ Speed $=(x+12)$ km/h

$\qquad$ Time taken by car $=\dfrac{400}{x+12}$ hrs

According to the question,
$$\frac{400}{x}-\frac{400}{x+12}=1 \text{ hour}+40 \text{ minutes}$$
$$\left[\left(1+\frac{40}{60}\right)\text{hour}\right]$$
$$400\left[\frac{(x+12-x)}{x(x+12)}\right]=1+\frac{2}{3}$$
$$\Rightarrow \qquad \frac{4800}{x^2+12x}=\frac{5}{3}$$
$$\Rightarrow \qquad 5(x^2+12x)=14,400$$
$$\Rightarrow \qquad x^2+12x-2880=0$$

$\Rightarrow \qquad x^2 + 60x - 48x - 2880 = 0$

$\Rightarrow \qquad x + (x + 60) - 48(x + 60) = 0$

$\Rightarrow \qquad (x + 60)(x - 48) = 0$

Either, $\qquad x + 60 = 0$

$\qquad\qquad x = -60$

(Neglect, speed can't be negative)

or $\qquad x - 48 = 0$

$\qquad\qquad x = 48$

Hence, original speed of the car = 48 km/h

Q. 9. **A positive number is divided into two parts such that the sum of the squares of the two parts is 208. The square of the larger part is 18 times the smaller part. Taking x as the smaller part of the two parts, find the number.** **[2010]**

Ans. Let the smaller part be x and larger part be y.

$\therefore \qquad x^2 + y^2 = 208 \qquad \ldots(i)$

Also $\qquad y^2 = 18x \qquad \ldots(ii)$

Put the value of y^2 from equation (ii) in equation (i)

$\qquad x^2 + 18x - 208 = 0$

or $\quad x^2 + 26x - 8x - 208 = 0$

$\qquad x(x + 26) - 8(x + 26) = 0$

$\qquad (x - 8)(x + 26) = 0$

$\qquad\qquad x = 8 \text{ or } x = -26$

Since the number is positive, therefore, we reject $x = -26$

$\therefore \qquad x = 8 \text{ (Smaller part)}$

From (ii), $\qquad y^2 = 18x = 18 \times 8 = 144$

$\therefore \qquad y = \sqrt{144} = 12 \text{ (Larger part)}$

$\therefore$ The number = $x + y = 8 + 12 = 20$

Q. 10. **The speed of an express train is x km/h and the speed of an ordinary train is 12 km/h less than that of the express train. If the ordinary train takes one hour longer than the express train to cover a distance of 240 km, find the speed of the express train.** **[2009]**

Ans. Let speed of the express train be x km/h

$\therefore$ Speed of the ordinary train = $(x - 12)$ km/h

Now, according to question

$$\frac{240}{x - 12} - \frac{240}{x} = 1$$

$$240\left[\frac{x - x + 12}{x(x - 12)}\right] = 1$$

$\Rightarrow \qquad 2880 = x^2 - 12x$

$\Rightarrow \quad x^2 - 12x - 2880 = 0$

$$x = \frac{12 \pm \sqrt{144 + 11520}}{2} = \frac{12 \pm 108}{2}$$

Taking (+) sign $\quad x = \dfrac{12 + 108}{2} = \dfrac{120}{2} = 60$

Taking (−) sign $\quad x = \dfrac{12 - 108}{2} = -\dfrac{96}{2} = -48$

(Impossible as speed can't be −ve)

Hence, the speed of the express train = 60 km/h

Q. 11. **Some students planned a picnic. The budget for the food was ₹480. As eight of them failed to join the party, the cost of the food for each member increased by ₹10. Find how many students went for the picnic.** **[2008]**

Ans. Let the total number of students be x.

Cost of food for each student = $\dfrac{480}{x}$

When 8 students failed to join, then cost of food for each student

$$= \frac{480}{x - 8}$$

$\therefore \qquad \dfrac{480}{x - 8} - \dfrac{480}{x} = 10$

$\Rightarrow \qquad 480\left[\dfrac{x - x + 8}{x(x - 8)}\right] = 10$

$\qquad\qquad 48 \times 8 = x(x - 8)$

$\qquad x^2 - 8x - 384 = 0$

$\qquad x^2 - 24x + 16x - 384 = 0$

$\qquad x(x - 24) + 16(x - 24) = 0$

$\Rightarrow \qquad (x - 24)(x + 16) = 0$

$\Rightarrow \qquad\qquad x = 24$

$\qquad (\because x = -16 \text{ not possible})$

$\therefore$ The number of students who went for picnic = $24 - 8 = 16$.

Q. 12. **Five years ago, a woman's age was the square of her son's age. Ten years later her age will be twice that of her son's age. Find:**

(i) The age of the son five years ago.

(ii) The present age of the woman. **[2007]**

Ans. Let five years ago the age of son be x years.

$\therefore$ Five years ago mother's age be x^2 years.

Present age of the son = $(x + 5)$ years

Present age of the woman = $(x^2 + 5)$ years

Ten years hence, age of the son = $[(x + 5) + 10]$

$= (x + 15)$ years

Ten years hence, age of the woman

$= [(x^2 + 5) + 10] = (x^2 + 15)$ years

$\therefore$ According to the problem

$\qquad x^2 + 15 = 2(x + 15)$

$\Rightarrow \qquad x^2 + 15 - 2x - 30 = 0$

$\Rightarrow \qquad x^2 - 2x - 15 = 0$

$\Rightarrow \qquad x^2 - 5x + 3x - 15 = 0$

$\Rightarrow \qquad x(x - 5) + 3(x - 5) = 0$

$\Rightarrow \qquad (x - 5)(x + 3) = 0$

$\Rightarrow$ Either $\qquad x - 5 = 0 \quad$ or $\quad x + 3 = 0$

$\Rightarrow \qquad\qquad x = 5 \quad$ or $\qquad x = -3$.

Age cannot be negative, so $x = -3$ is rejected.

$\therefore \qquad x = 5$

(i) The age of the son five years ago $= 5$ years.

(ii) The present age of the woman

$$= (x^2 + 5) \text{ years}$$
$$= (5^2 + 5) \text{ years}$$
$$= (25 + 5) \text{ years}$$
$$= 30 \text{ years}$$

Q. 13. A shopkeeper buys a certain number of books for ₹720. If the cost per book was ₹5 less, the number of books that could be bought for ₹720 would be 2 more. Taking the original cost of each book to be ₹x, write an equation in x and solve it. **[2006]**

Ans. Let original cost of each book be ₹x then number of books for ₹720 are $= \dfrac{720}{x}$

When cost decreases by 5 the number of books $= \dfrac{720}{x-5}$

From question

$$\frac{720}{x-5} - \frac{720}{x} = 2$$

$$\frac{720x - 720\,(x-5)}{(x-5)x} = 2$$

$$720x - 720x + 3600 = 2(x^2 - 5x)$$

$$2x^2 - 10x - 3600 = 0$$

$$x^2 - 5x - 1800 = 0$$

$$x^2 + 40x - 45x - 1800 = 0$$

$$x(x + 40) - 45(x + 40) = 0$$

$$(x + 40)(x - 45) = 0$$

$$x = 45 \text{ or}$$

$$x = -40 \text{ (not possible)}$$

Hence, cost of each book $= 45$.

Ratio and Proportion

 **Short Answer Type Questions**

Q. 1. Using properties of proportion find $x : y$, given : **[2020]**

$$\frac{x^2 + 2x}{2x + 4} = \frac{y^2 + 3y}{3y + 9}$$

 **Marking Scheme**

$$\frac{x^2 + 2x + 2x + 4}{x^2 + 2x - 2x - 4} = \frac{y^2 + 3y + 3y + 9}{y^2 + 3y - 3y - 9}$$

(using componendo and dividendo)

$$\frac{x^2 + 4x + 4}{x^2 - 4} = \frac{y^2 + 6y + 9}{y^2 - 9}$$

$$\frac{(x + 2)^2}{(x + 2)(x - 2)} = \frac{(y + 3)^2}{(y + 3)(y - 3)}$$

$$\frac{(x + 2)}{(x - 2)} = \frac{(y + 3)}{(y - 3)}$$

$$\frac{x + 2 + x - 2}{x + 2 - x + 2} = \frac{y + 3 + y - 3}{y + 3 - y + 3}$$

$$\frac{2x}{4} = \frac{2y}{6}$$

$$x : y = 2 : 3$$

Ans. Given : $\dfrac{x^2 + 2x}{2x + 4} = \dfrac{y^2 + 3y}{3y + 9}$

Using componendo and dividendo,

$$\frac{x^2 + 2x + 2x + 4}{x^2 + 2x - 2x - 4} = \frac{y^2 + 3y + 3y + 9}{y^2 + 3y - 3y - 9}$$

$$\Rightarrow \quad \frac{x^2 + 4x + 4}{x^2 - 4} = \frac{y^2 + 6y + 9}{y^2 - 9}$$

$$\Rightarrow \quad \frac{(x + 2)^2}{(x - 2)(x + 2)} = \frac{(y + 3)^2}{(y - 3)(y + 3)}$$

$$\Rightarrow \quad \frac{x + 2}{x - 2} = \frac{y + 2}{y - 2}$$

Again, using componendo and dividendo

$$\frac{x + 2 + x - 2}{x + 2 - x + 2} = \frac{y + 3 + y - 3}{y + 3 - y + 3}$$

$$\Rightarrow \quad \frac{2x}{4} = \frac{2y}{6}$$

$$\Rightarrow \quad \frac{x}{y} = \frac{4}{6} = \frac{2}{3}$$

Hence, $x : y = 2 : 3$

Q. 2. The following numbers, $K + 3$, $K + 2$, $3K - 7$ and $2K - 3$ are in proportion. Find K. **[2019]**

Marking Scheme

$K + 3$, $K + 2$, $3K - 7$ and $2K - 3$ are in proportion

$$\therefore \quad \frac{K + 3}{K + 2} = \frac{3K - 7}{2K - 3}$$

Or $(K + 3)(2K - 3) = (3K - 7)(K + 2)$
$2K^2 + 6K - 3K - 9 = 3K^2 - 7K + 6K - 14$
$K^2 - 4K - 5 = 0$
$(K - 5)(K + 1) = 2$
$\therefore \ K = 5, -1$

Ans. Given, $K + 3$, $K + 2$, $3K - 7$ and $2K - 3$ are in proportion.

$$\therefore \quad \frac{K + 3}{K + 2} = \frac{3K - 7}{2K - 3}$$

$$\Rightarrow \quad (K + 2)(3K - 7) = (K + 3)(2K - 3)$$

$$\Rightarrow \quad 3K^2 - 7K + 6K - 14 = 2K^2 - 3K + 6K - 9$$

$$\Rightarrow \quad 3K^2 - 2K^2 - K - 3K - 14 + 9 = 0$$

$$\Rightarrow \quad K^2 - 4K - 5 = 0$$

$$\Rightarrow \quad K^2 - 5K + K - 5 = 0$$

$$\Rightarrow \quad K(K - 5) + 1(K - 5) = 0$$

$$\Rightarrow \quad (K - 5)(K + 1) = 0$$

$$\Rightarrow \quad K - 5 = 0 \text{ or } K + 1 = 0$$

$$\therefore \quad K = 5 \text{ or } -1.$$

Q. 3. Using properties of proportion solve for x, given

$$\frac{\sqrt{5x} + \sqrt{2x - 6}}{\sqrt{5x} - \sqrt{2x - 6}} = 4 \qquad \textbf{[2019]}$$

 **Marking Scheme**

$$\frac{\sqrt{5x} + \sqrt{2x - 6}}{\sqrt{5x} - \sqrt{2x - 6}} = 4$$

$$\frac{\sqrt{5x} + \sqrt{2x - 6} + \sqrt{5x} - \sqrt{2x - 6}}{\sqrt{5x} - \sqrt{2x - 6} - \sqrt{5x} + \sqrt{2x - 6}} = \frac{4 + 1}{4 - 1}$$

Applying componendo and dividendo

$$\frac{2\sqrt{5x}}{2\sqrt{2x - 6}} = \frac{5}{3}$$

Squaring both sides
$$\frac{5x}{2x-6} = \frac{25}{9}$$
$45x = 50x - 150$
$5x = 150$
$\therefore\ x = 30$

Ans. Given, $\dfrac{\sqrt{5x} + \sqrt{2x-6}}{\sqrt{5x} - \sqrt{2x-6}} = \dfrac{4}{1}$

Applying componendo and dividendo,

$$\frac{(\sqrt{5x} + \sqrt{2x-6}) + (\sqrt{5x} - \sqrt{2x-6})}{(\sqrt{5x} + \sqrt{2x-6}) - (\sqrt{5x} - \sqrt{2x-6})} = \frac{4+1}{4-1}$$

$$\Rightarrow \frac{\sqrt{5x} + \sqrt{2x-6} + \sqrt{5x} - \sqrt{2x-6}}{\sqrt{5x} + \sqrt{2x-6} - \sqrt{5x} + \sqrt{2x-6}} = \frac{5}{3}$$

$$\Rightarrow \frac{2\sqrt{5x}}{2\sqrt{2x-6}} = \frac{5}{3}$$

$$\Rightarrow \frac{\sqrt{5x}}{\sqrt{2x-6}} = \frac{5}{3}$$

Squaring both sides, we get

$$\frac{5x}{2x-6} = \frac{25}{9}$$

$\Rightarrow\quad 25(2x-6) = 9 \times 5x$

$\Rightarrow\quad 50x - 150 = 45x$

$\Rightarrow\quad 50x - 45x = 150$

$\Rightarrow\quad 5x = 150$

$\Rightarrow\quad x = 30$

Q. 4. **Using properties of proportion, solve for x.**
Given that x is positive: [2018]

$$\frac{2x + \sqrt{4x^2 - 1}}{2x - \sqrt{4x^2 - 1}} = 4$$

Ans. Given, $\dfrac{2x + \sqrt{4x^2 - 1}}{2x - \sqrt{4x^2 - 1}} = \dfrac{4}{1}$

$$\Rightarrow \frac{2x + \sqrt{4x^2-1} + 2x - \sqrt{4x^2-1}}{2x + \sqrt{4x^2-1} - 2x + \sqrt{4x^2-1}} = \frac{4+1}{4-1}$$

(using componendo and dividendo)

$$\Rightarrow \frac{4x}{2\sqrt{4x^2-1}} = \frac{5}{3}$$

$$\Rightarrow 10\sqrt{4x^2-1} = 12x$$

$$\Rightarrow 100(4x^2-1) = 144x^2$$

(squaring both sides)

$\Rightarrow\quad 400x^2 - 100 = 144x^2$

$\Rightarrow\quad 400x^2 - 144x^2 = 100$

$\Rightarrow\quad 256x^2 = 100$

$$\Rightarrow\quad x^2 = \frac{100}{256}$$

$$\Rightarrow\quad x^2 = \left(\frac{10}{16}\right)^2$$

$$\Rightarrow\quad x = \pm\frac{10}{16} = \pm\frac{5}{8}$$

$$\therefore\quad x = \frac{5}{8} \qquad (\because x \text{ is positive})$$

Q. 5. **If b is the mean proportion between a and c,**
show that: [2017]

$$\frac{a^4 + a^2 b^2 + b^4}{b^4 + b^2 c^2 + c^4} = \frac{a^2}{c^2}$$

Ans. Given, b is mean proportion between a and c.

$$\therefore\qquad \frac{a}{b} = \frac{b}{c} = k \text{ (say)}$$

$$\Rightarrow\qquad b = kc;\ a = kb = k(kc) = k^2 c$$

$$\therefore\qquad \text{L.H.S.} = \frac{a^4 + a^2 b^2 + b^4}{b^4 + b^2 c^2 + c^4}$$

$$= \frac{(k^2 c)^4 + (k^2 c)^2 \cdot (kc)^2 + (kc)^4}{(kc)^4 + (kc)^2 c^2 + c^4}$$

$$= \frac{k^8 c^4 + k^6 c^4 + k^4 c^4}{k^4 c^4 + k^2 c^4 + c^4}$$

$$= \frac{k^4 c^4 (k^4 + k^2 + 1)}{c^4 (k^4 + k^2 + 1)} = k^4$$

and $\quad \text{R.H.S.} = \dfrac{a^2}{c^2} = \dfrac{(k^2 c)^2}{c^2} = \dfrac{k^4 c^2}{c^2} = k^4$

$\therefore\qquad$ L.H.S. = R.H.S. **Hence Proved.**

Q. 6. **If $\dfrac{7m + 2n}{7m - 2n} = \dfrac{5}{3}$ use properties of proportion**
to find [2017]
(i) $m:n$

(ii) $\dfrac{m^2 + n^2}{m^2 - n^2}$

Ans. **(i)** Given, $\dfrac{7m + 2n}{7m - 2n} = \dfrac{5}{3}$

Using componendo and dividendo,

$$\frac{(7m + 2n) + (7m - 2n)}{(7m + 2n) - (7m - 2n)} = \frac{5+3}{5-3}$$

$$\Rightarrow\qquad \frac{7m + 7m}{2n + 2n} = \frac{8}{2}$$

$$\Rightarrow\qquad \frac{14m}{4n} = \frac{4}{1}$$

$$\Rightarrow\qquad \frac{7m}{2n} = \frac{4}{1}$$

$$\Rightarrow\qquad \frac{m}{n} = \frac{4}{1} \times \frac{2}{7}$$

$$\Rightarrow\qquad m:n = 8:7$$

(ii) $\dfrac{m}{n} = \dfrac{8}{7} \Rightarrow \dfrac{m^2}{n^2} = \dfrac{64}{49}$

Using componendo and dividendo,

$$\dfrac{m^2 + n^2}{m^2 - n^2} = \dfrac{64 + 49}{64 - 49} = \dfrac{113}{15}$$

Q. 7. If $(3a + 2b) : (5a + 3b) = 18 : 29$. Find $a : b$.   [2016]

Ans.   Here, $\dfrac{3a + 2b}{5a + 3b} = \dfrac{18}{29}$

$$87a + 58b = 90a + 54b$$
$$-90a + 87a = -58b + 54b$$
$$-3a = -4b$$
$$\dfrac{a}{b} = \dfrac{4}{3}$$

i.e., $a : b = 4 : 3$

Q. 8. If $\dfrac{x}{a} = \dfrac{y}{b} = \dfrac{z}{c}$ show that $\dfrac{x^3}{a^3} + \dfrac{y^3}{b^3} + \dfrac{z^3}{c^3} = \dfrac{3xyz}{abc}$ [2016]

Ans.   Let $\dfrac{x}{a} = \dfrac{y}{b} = \dfrac{z}{c} = k$

then $x = ak$, $y = bk$ and $z = ck$.

Putting the values of x, y and z, in the given equation, we get

$$\text{L.H.S.} = \dfrac{x^3}{a^3} + \dfrac{y^3}{b^3} + \dfrac{z^3}{c^3}$$
$$= \dfrac{(ak)^3}{a^3} + \dfrac{(bk)^3}{b^3} + \dfrac{(ck)^3}{c^3}$$
$$= \dfrac{a^3 k^3}{a^3} + \dfrac{b^3 k^3}{b^3} + \dfrac{c^3 k^3}{c^3}$$
$$= k^3 + k^3 + k^3 = 3k^3$$
$$\text{R.H.S.} = \dfrac{3xyz}{abc}$$

(Put the value of x, y and z)
$$= \dfrac{3(ak)(bk)(ck)}{abc}$$
$$= 3k^3$$

$\therefore$ L.H.S. = R.H.S.   **Hence Proved.**

Q. 9. If a, b, c are in continued proportion, prove that
$(a + b + c)(a - b + c) = a^2 + b^2 + c^2$.   [2015]

Ans.   Given, a, b, c are in continued proportion.

$\therefore$ $a : b = b : c$

$\Rightarrow$ $\dfrac{a}{b} = \dfrac{b}{c}$

$\Rightarrow$ $b^2 = ac$

$$\text{L.H.S.} = (a + b + c)(a - b + c)$$
$$= a^2 - ab + ac + ab - b^2 + bc + ac - bc + c^2$$
$$= a^2 + 2ac - b^2 + c^2$$
$$= a^2 + 2b^2 - b^2 + c^2 \qquad (\because ac = b^2)$$
$$= a^2 + b^2 + c^2 = \text{R.H.S.}\qquad \textbf{Hence Proved}$$

Q. 10. Given $\dfrac{x^3 + 12x}{6x^2 + 8} = \dfrac{y^3 + 27y}{9y^2 + 27}$. Using componendo and dividendo find $x : y$.   [2015]

Ans.   Given, $\dfrac{x^3 + 12x}{6x^2 + 8} = \dfrac{y^3 + 27y}{9y^2 + 27}$

Applying componendo and dividendo, we get

$$\dfrac{x^3 + 12x + 6x^2 + 8}{x^3 + 12x - 6x^2 - 8} = \dfrac{y^3 + 27y + 9y^2 + 27}{y^3 + 27y - 9y^2 - 27}$$

$[\because (a + b)^3 = a^3 + 3a^2b + 3ab^2 + b^3$
$(a - b)^3 = a^3 + 3ab^2 - 3a^2b - b^3]$

$\Rightarrow$ $\dfrac{(x + 2)^3}{(x - 2)^3} = \dfrac{(y + 3)^3}{(y - 3)^3}$

Taking cube root on both the sides

$\Rightarrow$ $\dfrac{x + 2}{x - 2} = \dfrac{y + 3}{y - 3}$

Again using componendo and dividendo, we get

$$\dfrac{x + 2 + x - 2}{x + 2 - x + 2} = \dfrac{y + 3 + y - 3}{y + 3 - y + 3}$$
$$\dfrac{2x}{4} = \dfrac{2y}{6}$$
$$\dfrac{x}{y} = \dfrac{2}{3}$$

Hence, $x : y = 2 : 3$.

Q. 11. If, $\dfrac{x^2 + y^2}{x^2 - y^2} = \dfrac{17}{8}$, using the properties of proportion find the value of:

(i) $x : y$.   (ii) $\dfrac{x^3 + y^3}{x^3 - y^3}$.   [2014]

Ans.   (i) $\dfrac{x^2 + y^2}{x^2 - y^2} = \dfrac{17}{8}$

Applying componendo and dividendo rule,

$$\dfrac{x^2 + y^2 + x^2 - y^2}{x^2 + y^2 - x^2 + y^2} = \dfrac{17 + 8}{17 - 8}$$
$$\dfrac{2x^2}{2y^2} = \dfrac{25}{9}$$
$$\dfrac{x^2}{y^2} = \dfrac{25}{9}$$
$$\dfrac{x}{y} = \dfrac{5}{3}$$
$$x : y = 5 : 3$$

(ii)
$$\frac{x}{y} = \frac{5}{3}$$

Taking cube on both sides,
$$\frac{x^3}{y^3} = \frac{125}{27}$$

Applying componendo and dividendo rule,
$$\frac{x^3 + y^3}{x^3 - y^3} = \frac{125 + 27}{125 - 27}$$

$$\frac{x^3 + y^3}{x^3 - y^3} = \frac{152}{98} = \frac{76}{49}.$$

Q. 12. If $(x - 9) : (3x + 6)$ is the duplicate ratio of $4 : 9$, find the value of x using properties of proportion. **[2014]**

Ans. Given $(x - 9) : (3x + 6)$ is duplicate ratio of $4 : 9$.

$$\therefore \qquad \frac{x-9}{3x+6} = \left(\frac{4}{9}\right)^2$$

$$\Rightarrow \qquad \frac{x-9}{3x+6} = \frac{16}{81}$$

$$\Rightarrow \qquad 81\,(x - 9) = 16\,(3x + 6)$$

$$\Rightarrow \qquad 81x - 729 = 48x + 96$$

$$\Rightarrow \qquad 81x - 48x = 96 + 729$$

$$\Rightarrow \qquad 33x = 825$$

$$\Rightarrow \qquad x = \frac{825}{33} = 25$$

Thus, required value of x is 25.

Q. 13. Using the properties of proportion, solve for x, given

$$\frac{x^4 + 1}{2x^2} = \frac{17}{8}. \qquad \textbf{[2013]}$$

Ans. Given, $\dfrac{x^4 + 1}{2x^2} = \dfrac{17}{8}$

Using componendo and dividendo

$$\frac{x^4 + 1 + 2x^2}{x^4 + 1 - 2x^2} = \frac{17 + 8}{17 - 8}$$

$$\Rightarrow \qquad \frac{(x^2 + 1)^2}{(x^2 - 1)^2} = \frac{25}{9}$$

$$[\because (a + b)^2 = a^2 + 2ab + b^2$$
$$\text{and } (a - b)^2 = a^2 - 2ab - b^2]$$

$$\Rightarrow \qquad \frac{x^2 + 1}{x^2 - 1} = \frac{5}{3}$$

(Taking square root on both the sides)

Again applying componendo and dividendo

$$\frac{x^2 + 1 + x^2 - 1}{x^2 + 1 - x^2 + 1} = \frac{5 + 3}{5 - 3}$$

$$\Rightarrow \qquad \frac{2x^2}{2} = \frac{8}{2}$$

$$\Rightarrow \qquad x^2 = 4$$

$$\Rightarrow \qquad x = \pm 2$$

$\therefore$ Value of x is 2, –2.

Q. 14. The monthly pocket money of Ravi and Sanjeev are in the ratio 5 : 7. Their expenditures are in the ratio 3 : 5. If each saves ₹ 80 every month, find their monthly pocket money. **[2012]**

Ans. Let, the monthly pocket money of Ravi and Sanjeev be $5x$ and $7x$ respectively and their expenditures be $3y$ and $5y$.

So, $\qquad 5x - 3y = 80 \qquad \qquad …(i)$

And, $\qquad 7x - 5y = 80 \qquad \qquad …(ii)$

Multiplying equation (i) by 5 and equation (ii) by 3, we get

$$25x - 15y = 400 \qquad …(iii)$$
$$21x - 15y = 240 \qquad …(iv)$$

Sub. $\qquad - \qquad + \qquad -$

$$\overline{\qquad \qquad \qquad \qquad}$$

$$4x = 160$$
$$\Rightarrow \qquad x = 40$$

So monthly pocket money of Ravi

$$= ₹\, 5 \times 40 = ₹\, 200$$

And of Sanjeev $= ₹\, 7 \times 40 = ₹\, 280$

Q. 15. 6 is the mean proportion between two numbers x and y and 48 is the third proportional of x and y. Find the numbers. **[2011]**

Ans. Given, 6 is mean proportional between x and y.

$\Rightarrow x, 6, y$ are in continued proportion

$$\Rightarrow \qquad \frac{x}{6} = \frac{6}{y}$$

$$\Rightarrow \qquad xy = 36$$

$$\Rightarrow \qquad x = \frac{36}{y} \qquad …(i)$$

Also, 48 is third proportional of x and y (Given)

$\Rightarrow x, y, 48$ are in continued proportion.

$$\Rightarrow \qquad \frac{x}{y} = \frac{y}{48}$$

$$\Rightarrow \qquad y^2 = 48x \qquad …(2)$$

From (i) $\qquad y^2 = 48 \times \dfrac{36}{y}$

$$\Rightarrow \qquad y^3 = 48 \times 36$$

Taking cube root on both sides

$$\Rightarrow \qquad \sqrt[3]{y^3} = \sqrt[3]{12 \times 12 \times 12}$$

$$\Rightarrow \qquad y = 12$$

And $\qquad x = \dfrac{36}{y}$

$$= \dfrac{36}{12} = 3$$

∴ The numbers are 3 and 12.

Q. 16. Using componendo and dividendo, find the value of x $\dfrac{\sqrt{3x+4} + \sqrt{3x-5}}{\sqrt{3x+4} - \sqrt{3x-5}} = 9$. [2011]

Ans. Given, $\dfrac{\sqrt{3x+4} + \sqrt{3x-5}}{\sqrt{3x+4} - \sqrt{3x-5}} = \dfrac{9}{1}$

Using componendo and dividendo

$$\dfrac{\sqrt{3x+4} + \sqrt{3x-5} + \sqrt{3x+4} - \sqrt{3x-5}}{\sqrt{3x+4} - \sqrt{3x-5} - \sqrt{3x+4} + \sqrt{3x-5}}$$

$$= \dfrac{9+1}{9-1} = \dfrac{10}{8} = \dfrac{5}{4}$$

$$\dfrac{2\sqrt{3x+4}}{2\sqrt{3x-5}} = \dfrac{5}{4}$$

$$\Rightarrow \qquad \dfrac{3x+4}{3x-5} = \dfrac{25}{16}$$

(Squaring both sides)

$$\Rightarrow \qquad 48x + 64 = 75x - 125$$

$$\Rightarrow \qquad 75x - 48x = 125 + 64$$

$$27x = 189$$

$$\Rightarrow \qquad x = \dfrac{189}{27} = 7$$

Q. 17. If x, y, z are in continued proportion, prove that

$$\dfrac{(x+y)^2}{(y+z)^2} = \dfrac{x}{z}$$ [2010]

Ans. Since, x, y, z are in continued proportion,

$$\therefore \qquad \dfrac{x}{y} = \dfrac{y}{z} \Rightarrow y^2 = zx \qquad \ldots(i)$$

$$\dfrac{x+y}{y} = \dfrac{y+z}{z}$$

(By componendo)

$$\Rightarrow \qquad \dfrac{x+y}{y+z} = \dfrac{y}{z}$$

(By alternendo)

On squaring both sides

$$\Rightarrow \qquad \dfrac{(x+y)^2}{(y+z)^2} = \dfrac{y^2}{z^2}$$

$$\Rightarrow \qquad \dfrac{(x+y)^2}{(y+z)^2} = \dfrac{zx}{z^2}$$

[Using (i)]

$$\Rightarrow \qquad \dfrac{(x+y)^2}{(y+z)^2} = \dfrac{x}{z}$$

Hence Proved.

Q. 18. Given that $\dfrac{a^3 + 3ab^2}{b^3 + 3a^2b} = \dfrac{63}{62}$.

Using Componendo and Dividendo find $a : b$. [2009]

Ans. Given, $\dfrac{a^3 + 3ab^2}{b^3 + 3a^2b} = \dfrac{63}{62}$

By componendo and dividendo

$$\dfrac{a^3 + 3ab^2 + b^3 + 3a^2b}{a^3 + 3ab^2 - b^3 - 3a^2b} = \dfrac{63 + 62}{63 - 62}$$

$$\Rightarrow \qquad \dfrac{(a+b)^3}{(a-b)^3} = \left(\dfrac{5}{1}\right)^3$$

$$\Rightarrow \qquad \dfrac{a+b}{a-b} = 5$$

$$\Rightarrow \qquad a + b = 5a - 5b$$

$$\Rightarrow \qquad 4a - 6b = 0$$

$$\Rightarrow \qquad \dfrac{a}{b} = \dfrac{3}{2}$$

$$\therefore \qquad a : b = 3 : 2$$

Q. 19. If $\dfrac{8a-5b}{8c-5d} = \dfrac{8a+5b}{8c+5d}$, prove that $\dfrac{a}{b} = \dfrac{c}{d}$. [2008]

Ans. Given, $\dfrac{8a-5b}{8c-5d} = \dfrac{8a+5b}{8c+5d}$

by alternendo $\dfrac{8a-5b}{8a+5b} = \dfrac{8c-5d}{8c+5d}$

By componendo and Dividendo

$$\dfrac{8a-5b+8a+5b}{8a-5b-8a-5b} = \dfrac{8c-5d+8c+5d}{8c-5d-8c-5d}$$

$$\dfrac{16a}{-10b} = \dfrac{16c}{-10d}$$

$$\Rightarrow \qquad \dfrac{a}{b} = \dfrac{c}{d} \qquad \textbf{Hence Proved.}$$

Q. 20. If $\dfrac{3x+5y}{3x-5y} = \dfrac{7}{3}$, find $x : y$. [2006]

Ans. $\dfrac{3x+5y}{3x-5y} = \dfrac{7}{3}$

Apply componendo and dividendo,

$$\dfrac{3x+5y+3x-5y}{3x+5y-3x+5y} = \dfrac{7+3}{7-3}$$

$$\dfrac{6x}{10y} = \dfrac{10}{4}$$

$$\dfrac{x}{y} = \dfrac{10 \times 10}{4 \times 6}$$

$$\dfrac{x}{y} = \dfrac{25}{6}$$

$$\therefore \qquad x : y = 25 : 6$$

 ## Long Answer Type Questions

Q. 1. If $x = \dfrac{\sqrt{2a+1} + \sqrt{2a-1}}{\sqrt{2a+1} - \sqrt{2a-1}}$ prove that

$$x^2 - 4ax + 1 = 0 \qquad \text{[2020]}$$

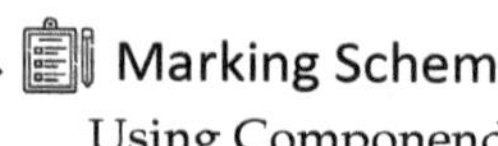 **Marking Scheme**

Using Componendo / Dividendo

$$\dfrac{\sqrt{2a+1} + \sqrt{2a-1} + \sqrt{2a+1} - \sqrt{2a-1}}{\sqrt{2a+1} + \sqrt{2a-1} - \sqrt{2a+1} + \sqrt{2a-1}} = \dfrac{x+1}{x-1}$$

$$\dfrac{2\sqrt{2a+1}}{2\sqrt{2a-1}} = \dfrac{x+1}{x-1} \text{ on squaring both sides}$$

$$\dfrac{\left(\sqrt{2a+1}\right)}{\left(\sqrt{2a+1}\right)} = \dfrac{(x+1)^2}{(x-1)^2} \Rightarrow \dfrac{2a+1}{2a-1} = \dfrac{x^2+2x+1}{x^2-2x+1}$$

$(2a+1)(x^2-2x+1) = (2a-1)(x^2+2x+1)$
$2ax^2 - 4ax + 2a + x^2 - 2x + 1 = 2ax^2 + 4ax + 2a - x^2 - 2x - 1$
$4ax + 4ax - x^2 - x^2 - 1 - 1 = 0$
$8ax - 2x^2 - 2 = 0 \Rightarrow 4ax - x^2 - 1 = 0$
$x^2 - 4ax - 1 = 0 \to$ proved

Ans. Given : $x = \dfrac{\sqrt{2a+1} + \sqrt{2a-1}}{\sqrt{2a+1} - \sqrt{2a-1}}$

Using componendo and dividendo,

$$\dfrac{x+1}{x-1} = \dfrac{\left\{\begin{array}{c}\sqrt{2a+1} + \sqrt{2a-1} \\ +\sqrt{2a+1} - \sqrt{2a-1}\end{array}\right\}}{\left\{\begin{array}{c}\sqrt{2a+1} + \sqrt{2a-1} \\ -\sqrt{2a+1} + \sqrt{2a-1}\end{array}\right\}}$$

$$\Rightarrow \qquad \dfrac{x+1}{x-1} = \dfrac{2\sqrt{2a+1}}{2\sqrt{2a-1}}$$

$$\Rightarrow \qquad \left(\dfrac{x+1}{x-1}\right)^2 = \left(\dfrac{\sqrt{2a+1}}{\sqrt{2a-1}}\right)^2$$

[Squaring both sides]

$$\Rightarrow \qquad \dfrac{x^2+1+2x}{x^2+1-2x} = \dfrac{2a+1}{2a-1}$$

Again, using componendo and dividendo,

$$\dfrac{x^2+1+2x+x^2+1-2x}{x^2+1+2x-x^2-1+2x} = \dfrac{2a+1+2a-1}{2a+1-2a+1}$$

$$\Rightarrow \qquad \dfrac{2(x^2+1)}{4x} = \dfrac{4a}{2}$$

$$\Rightarrow \qquad \dfrac{x^2+1}{2x} = 2a$$

$$\Rightarrow \qquad x^2 + 1 = 4ax$$

$$\Rightarrow \qquad x^2 - 4ax + 1 = 0 \qquad \textbf{Hence Proved.}$$

Q. 2. If $x = \dfrac{\sqrt{a+1} + \sqrt{a-1}}{\sqrt{a+1} - \sqrt{a-1}}$, using properties of proportion show that

$$x^2 - 2ax + 1 = 0 \qquad \text{[2012]}$$

Ans. Given, $\qquad x = \dfrac{\sqrt{a+1} + \sqrt{a-1}}{\sqrt{a+1} - \sqrt{a-1}}$

$$\Rightarrow \qquad \dfrac{x}{1} = \dfrac{\sqrt{a+1} + \sqrt{a-1}}{\sqrt{a+1} - \sqrt{a-1}}$$

Using componendo and dividendo

$$\Rightarrow \dfrac{x+1}{x-1} = \dfrac{\sqrt{a+1} + \sqrt{a-1} + \sqrt{a+1} - \sqrt{a-1}}{\sqrt{a+1} + \sqrt{a-1} - \sqrt{a+1} + \sqrt{a-1}}$$

$$\Rightarrow \qquad \dfrac{x+1}{x-1} = \dfrac{2\sqrt{a+1}}{2\sqrt{a-1}}$$

$$\Rightarrow \qquad \dfrac{(x+1)^2}{(x-1)^2} = \dfrac{a+1}{a-1}$$

(Squaring both side)

$$\Rightarrow \qquad \dfrac{x^2+2x+1}{x^2-2x+1} = \dfrac{a+1}{a-1}$$

Again using componendo and dividendo,

$$\dfrac{(x^2+2x+1)+(x^2-2x+1)}{(x^2+2x+1)-(x^2-2x+1)} = \dfrac{(a+1)+(a-1)}{(a+1)-(a-1)}$$

$$\Rightarrow \dfrac{x^2+2x+1+x^2-2x+1}{x^2+2x+1-x^2+2x-1} = \dfrac{a+1+a-1}{a+1-a+1}$$

$$\Rightarrow \qquad \dfrac{2x^2+2}{4x} = \dfrac{2a}{2}$$

$$\Rightarrow \qquad \dfrac{x^2+1}{2x} = \dfrac{a}{1}$$

$$\Rightarrow \qquad x^2 + 1 = 2ax$$

$$\Rightarrow \qquad x^2 - 2ax + 1 = 0.$$

Hence Proved.

Q. 3. Given: $x = \dfrac{\sqrt{a^2+b^2} + \sqrt{a^2-b^2}}{\sqrt{a^2+b^2} - \sqrt{a^2-b^2}}$

Use componendo and dividendo to prove that

$$b^2 = \dfrac{2a^2 x}{x^2+1}. \qquad \text{[2010]}$$

Ans. Given, $x = \dfrac{\sqrt{a^2+b^2} + \sqrt{a^2-b^2}}{\sqrt{a^2+b^2} - \sqrt{a^2-b^2}}$

Using componendo and dividendo,

$$\dfrac{x+1}{x-1} = \dfrac{\sqrt{a^2+b^2} + \sqrt{a^2-b^2} + \sqrt{a^2+b^2} - \sqrt{a^2-b^2}}{\sqrt{a^2+b^2} + \sqrt{a^2-b^2} - \sqrt{a^2+b^2} + \sqrt{a^2-b^2}}$$

$$\dfrac{x+1}{x-1}\dfrac{1}{3}\dfrac{1}{3} = \dfrac{2\sqrt{a^2+b^2}}{2\sqrt{a^2-b^2}}$$

Squaring both sides,

$$\frac{x^2 + 2x + 1}{x^2 - 2x + 1} = \frac{a^2 + b^2}{a^2 - b^2}$$

$$\left[\because \begin{array}{l} (a+b)^2 = a^2 + b^2 + 2ab \\ (a-b)^2 = a^2 + b^2 - 2ab \end{array}\right]$$

Again, using componendo and dividendo,

$$\frac{x^2 + 2x + 1 + x^2 - 2x + 1}{x^2 + 2x + 1 - (x^2 - 2x + 1)} = \frac{a^2 + b^2 + a^2 - b^2}{a^2 + b^2 - (a^2 - b^2)}$$

$$\Rightarrow \frac{(x^2 + 2x + 1 + x^2 - 2x + 1)}{x^2 + 2x + 1 - x^2 + 2x - 1} = \frac{a^2 + b^2 + a^2 - b^2}{a^2 + b^2 - a^2 + b^2}$$

$$\Rightarrow \frac{2(x^2 + 1)}{4x} = \frac{2a^2}{2b^2}$$

$$\Rightarrow \frac{x^2 + 1}{2x} = \frac{a^2}{b^2}$$

$$\Rightarrow b^2 = \frac{2a^2 x}{x^2 + 1}$$

Hence Proved.

Q. 4. If $x = \dfrac{\sqrt{a + 3b} + \sqrt{a - 3b}}{\sqrt{a + 3b} - \sqrt{a - 3b}}$, prove that $3bx^2 - 2ax + 3b = 0$. [2007]

Ans. Given, $\dfrac{x}{1} = \dfrac{\sqrt{a + 3b} + \sqrt{a - 3b}}{\sqrt{a + 3b} - \sqrt{a - 3b}}$

Apply componendo and dividendo

$$\frac{x + 1}{x - 1} = \frac{\sqrt{a + 3b} + \sqrt{a - 3b} + \sqrt{a + 3b} - \sqrt{a - 3b}}{\sqrt{a + 3b} + \sqrt{a - 3b} - \sqrt{a + 3b} + \sqrt{a - 3b}}$$

$$\frac{x + 1}{x - 1} = \frac{2\sqrt{a + 3b}}{2\sqrt{a - 3b}}$$

Squaring both sides, $\dfrac{x^2 + 2x + 1}{x^2 - 2x + 1} = \dfrac{a + 3b}{a - 3b}$

Again apply componendo and dividendo

$$\frac{x^2 + 2x + 1 + x^2 - 2x + 1}{x^2 + 2x + 1 - x^2 + 2x - 1} = \frac{a + 3b + a - 3b}{a + 3b - a + 3b}$$

$$\frac{2(x^2 + 1)}{2(2x)} = \frac{2(a)}{2(3b)}$$

$$3bx^2 + 3b = 2ax$$

$$\therefore \quad 3bx^2 - 2ax + 3b = 0. \qquad \textbf{Hence Proved.}$$

Factorization of Polynomials

  ## Short Answer Type Questions

Q. 1. Use factor theorem to factorise $6x^3 + 17x^2 + 4x - 12$ completely. **[2020]**

 **Marking Scheme**

$f(x) = 6x^3 + 17x^2 + 4x - 12$

$f(-2) = 6(-2)^3 + 17(-2)^2 + 4(-2) - 12$

$= 6 \times -8 + 17 \times 4 - 8 - 12$

$= -48 + 68 - 8 - 12$

$= -68 + 68 = 0$

$(x + 2)$ is factor

Correct substitution

$$\begin{array}{r} 6x^2 + 5x - 6 \\ x + 2) \overline{6x^3 + 17x^2 + 4x - 12} (\\ 6x^3 + 12x^2 \\ \hline - \quad - \\ \hline 5x^2 + 4x \\ 5x^2 + 10x \\ \hline - \quad - \\ \hline -6x - 12 \\ -6x - 12 \\ \hline + \quad + \\ \hline 0 \end{array}$$

$6x^2 + 5x - 6$

$6x^2 + 9x - 4x - 6$

$3x(2x + 3) - 2(2x + 3)$

$(3x - 2)(2x + 3)$

$\therefore$ Factors are $(x + 2)(3x - 2)(2x + 3)$

Ans. Let $p(x) = 6x^3 + 17x^2 + 4x - 12$

$\because \ p(-2) = 6 \times (-2)^3 + 17 \times (-2)^2 + 4(-2) - 12$

$= 6 \times (-8) + 17 \times 4 - 8 - 12$

$= -48 + 68 - 20$

$= -68 + 68 = 0$

$\therefore \ (x + 2)$ is a factor of $p(x)$

Dividing $p(x)$ by $(x + 2)$,

$$\begin{array}{r} x + 2) \overline{6x^3 + 17x^2 + 4x - 12} (6x^2 + 5x - 6 \\ 6x^3 + 12x^2 \\ \hline - \quad - \\ \hline 5x^2 + 4x \\ 5x^2 + 10x \\ \hline - \quad - \\ \hline -6x - 12 \\ -6x - 12 \\ \hline + \quad + \\ \hline 0 \end{array}$$

Now, in quotient

$\because \qquad 6x^2 + 5x - 6 = 6x^2 + 9x - 4x - 6$

$= 3x(2x + 3) - 2(2x + 3)$

$= (3x - 2)(2x + 3)$

Therefore,

$6x^3 + 17x^2 + 4x - 12 = (x + 2)(6x^2 + 5x - 6)$

$= (x + 2)(2x + 3)(3x - 2)$

Q. 2. What must be added to the polynomial $2x^3 - 3x^2 - 8x$, so that it leaves a remainder 10 when divided by $2x + 1$? **[2020]**

Marking Scheme

$f(x) = 2x^3 - 3x^2 - 8x$

Let k be added to $f(x)$

$\therefore f(x) = 2x^3 - 3x^2 - 8x + k$

Remainder $= f\left(-\dfrac{1}{2}\right) = 10$

$\Rightarrow 2\left(-\dfrac{1}{2}\right)^3 - 3\left(-\dfrac{1}{2}\right)^2 - 8\left(-\dfrac{1}{2}\right) + k = 10$

Putting $x = -\dfrac{1}{2}$

$\Rightarrow -\dfrac{1}{4} - \dfrac{3}{4} + 4 + k = 10$ \qquad Equating to 10

$\Rightarrow k + 3 = 10 \Rightarrow k = 7$ (or any other correct approach)

Ans. Let k be the required term to be added.

So, $p(x) = 2x^3 - 3x^2 - 8x + k$

$\because \ p(x)$ leaves remainder 10 when divided by $2x + 1$,

$\therefore \qquad p\left(-\dfrac{1}{2}\right) = 10$

$\Rightarrow \ 2 \times \left(-\dfrac{1}{2}\right)^3 - 3 \times \left(-\dfrac{1}{2}\right)^2 - 8 \times \left(-\dfrac{1}{2}\right) + k = 10$

$\Rightarrow 2 \times \left(-\dfrac{1}{8}\right) - 3 \times \dfrac{1}{4} + 4 + k = 10$

$\Rightarrow \qquad -\dfrac{1}{4} - \dfrac{3}{4} + 4 + k = 10$

$\Rightarrow \qquad k = 10 - 4 + \dfrac{1 + 3}{4}$

$\Rightarrow \qquad k = 6 + 1 = 7$

$\therefore \qquad k = 7$

Q. 3. Using the factor theorem, show that $(x - 2)$ is a factor of $x^3 + x^2 - 4x - 4$. Hence factorise the polynomial completely. **[2019]**

📋 Marking Scheme ------------------------------------

$f(x) = x^3 + x^2 - 4x - 4$

$f(2) = 2^3 + 2^2 - 4 \times 2 - 4$

$= 8 + 4 - 8 - 4$

$= 0$

$\therefore x - 2$ is a factor of $f(x)$

$x - 2\ |\ x^3 + x^2 - 4x - 4\ |\ x^2 + 3x + 2$

$\qquad \underline{x^3 - 2x^2}$

$\qquad\quad 3x^2 - 4x$

$\qquad\quad \underline{3x^2 - 6x}$

$\qquad\qquad\quad 2x - 4$

$\qquad\qquad\quad \underline{2x - 4}$

$\qquad\qquad\qquad\quad x$

$x^2 + 3x + 2 = (x + 1)(x + 2)$

$\therefore x^3 + x^2 - 4x - 4 = (x - 2)(x + 1)(x + 2)$

Ans. Let $\qquad f(x) = x^3 + x^2 - 4x - 4$

If $(x - 2)$ is a factor of $f(x)$, then

$$f(2) = 0$$

Now, $\qquad f(2) = 2^3 + 2^2 - 4 \times 2 - 4$

$$= 8 + 4 - 8 - 4$$

$$= 0$$

$\therefore (x - 2)$ is a factor of $f(x)$.

$$
\begin{array}{r}
x^3 + 3x + 2 \\
x - 2\overline{)\ x^3 + x^2 - 4x - 4} \\
x^3 - 2x^2 \\
-\quad + \\
\hline
3x^2 - 4x \\
3x^2 + 6x \\
-\quad + \\
\hline
2x - 4 \\
2x - 4 \\
-\quad + \\
\hline
\times
\end{array}
$$

Now, $\quad x^2 + 3x + 2 = x^2 + 2x + x + 2$

$$= x(x + 2) + 1(x + 2)$$

$$= (x + 2)(x + 1)$$

$\therefore \qquad f(x) = (x + 1)(x + 2)(x - 2)$

Q. 4. Using the Remainder Theorem, find the remainders obtained when $x^3 + (kx + 8)x + k$ is divided by $x + 1$ and $x - 2$.

Hence find k if the sum of the remainders is 1. **[2019]**

📋 Marking Scheme ------------------------------------

$x^3 + (kx + 8)x + k = x^3 + kx^2 + 8x + k$

When divided by $x + 1$

Remainder $= (-1)^3 + k(-1)^2 + 8(-1) + k$

$= -1 + k - 8 + k$

$= 2k - 9$

When divided by $x - 2$

Remainder $= (2)^3 + k(2)^2 + 8(2) + k$

$= 8 + 4k + 16 + k$

$= 5k + 24$

Hence $2k - 9 + 5k + 24 = 1$

$7k + 15 = 1$

$7k = -14$

$\therefore k = -2$

Ans. Let $\qquad f(x) = x^3 + (kx + 8)x + k$

when $f(x)$ is divided by $(x + 1)$ by Remainder theorem

Remainder, $f(-1) = (-1)^3 + \{k(-1) + 8\}(-1) + k$

$$= -1 + (-k + 8)(-1) + k$$

$$= -1 + k - 8 + k$$

$$= 2k - 9$$

when $f(x)$ is divided by $(x - 2)$,

Remainder, $f(2) = (2)^3 + (k.2 + 8)\,2 + k$

$$= 8 + 4k + 16 + k$$

$$= 5k + 24$$

Also, sum of remainders $= 1$

$$f(-1) + f(2) = 1$$

$\Rightarrow \qquad 2k - 9 + 5k + 24 = 1$

$\Rightarrow \qquad\qquad 7k + 15 = 1$

$\Rightarrow \qquad\qquad\quad 7k = 1 - 15$

$\Rightarrow \qquad\qquad\quad k = \dfrac{-14}{7} = -2$

Q. 5. If $(x + 2)$ and $(x + 3)$ are factors of $x^3 + ax + b$, find the values of 'a' and 'b'. **[2018]**

Ans. Let $\qquad f(x) = x^3 + ax + b$

$\because (x + 2)$ and $(x + 3)$ are factors of $f(x)$

$\therefore \qquad\qquad f(-2) = 0$

$\Rightarrow \qquad (-2)^3 + a(-2) + b = 0$

$\Rightarrow \qquad\quad -8 - 2a + b = 0$

$\Rightarrow \qquad\qquad -2a + b = 8$ $\qquad$ ...(i)

Also, $\qquad\qquad f(-3) = 0$

$\Rightarrow \qquad (-3)^3 + a(-3) + b = 0$

$\Rightarrow \qquad\quad -27 - 3a + b = 0$

$\Rightarrow \qquad\qquad -3a + b = 27$ $\qquad$ ...(ii)

Subtracting equation (ii) from equation (i), we have

$$-2a + b = 8$$

$$-3a + b = 8$$

$$\underline{+ \quad - \quad -}$$

$$a = -19$$

Putting the value of a in equation (i)

$-2 \times (-19) + b = 8$

$\Rightarrow \qquad b = 8 - 38 = -30$

$\therefore \qquad a = -19, b = -30.$

Q. 6. Use remainder theorem to factorize the following polynomial: **[2018]**

$$2x^3 + 3x^2 - 9x - 10.$$

Ans. Let $\quad f(x) = 2x^3 + 3x^2 - 9x - 10$

For $x = 2$,

$$f(2) = 2 \times 2^3 + 3 \times 2^2 - 9 \times 2 - 10$$
$$= 16 + 12 - 18 - 10$$
$$= 28 - 28 = 0.$$

$\therefore (x - 2)$ is a factor of $f(x)$

$$x - 2 \overline{)2x^3 + 3x^2 - 9x - 10}(2x^2 + 7x + 5$$
$$\underline{2x^3 - 4x^2}$$
$$-+$$
$$\overline{7x^2 - 9x}$$
$$7x^2 - 14x$$
$$-+$$
$$\overline{5x - 10}$$
$$5x - 10$$
$$-+$$
$$\overline{\times}$$

Now, $\quad 2x^2 + 7x + 5 = 2x^2 + 5x + 2x + 5$

$$= x(2x + 5) + 1(2x + 5)$$
$$= (2x + 5)(x + 1)$$

$\therefore \qquad f(x) = (x + 1)(x - 2)(2x + 5)$

Q. 7. What must be subtracted from $16x^3 - 8x^2 + 4x + 7$ so that the resulting expression has $2x + 1$ as a factor? **[2017]**

Ans. Let the required number be K.

Let $f(x) = 16x^3 - 8x^2 + 4x + 7 - K$

$\because \quad (2x + 1)$ is a factor of $f(x)$

$\therefore \qquad f\left(-\dfrac{1}{2}\right) = 0$

$\Rightarrow 16 \times \left(-\dfrac{1}{2}\right)^3 - 8 \times \left(-\dfrac{1}{2}\right)^2 + 4 \times \left(-\dfrac{1}{2}\right) + 7 - K = 0$

$\Rightarrow -16 \times \dfrac{1}{8} - 8 \times \dfrac{1}{4} - 4 \times \dfrac{1}{2} + 7 - K = 0$

$\Rightarrow \qquad -2 - 2 - 2 + 7 - K = 0$

$\Rightarrow \qquad -6 + 7 - K = 0$

$\Rightarrow \qquad 1 - K = 0$

$\Rightarrow \qquad K = 1$

$\therefore$ The required number to be subtracted is 1.

Q. 8. Using remainder theorem, find the value of k if on dividing $2x^3 + 3x^2 - kx + 5$ by $x - 2$ leaves a remainder 7. **[2016]**

Ans. Here, $\qquad f(x) = 2x^3 + 3x^2 - kx + 5 \qquad ...(i)$

and $\qquad x - 2 = 0 \Rightarrow x = 2$

Given, remainder is $7 \Rightarrow f(2) = 7$

Putting $x = 2$ in equation (i), we get

$$f(2) = 2(2)^3 + 3(2)^2 - k(2) + 5$$

$\Rightarrow \quad 16 + 12 - 2k + 5 = 7$

$\Rightarrow \qquad 2k = 26$

$\Rightarrow \qquad k = 13.$

Q. 9. Find 'a' if the two polynomials $ax^3 + 3x^2 - 9$ and $2x^3 + 4x + a$, leaves the same remainder when divided by $x + 3$. **[2015]**

Ans. Let $f(x) = ax^3 + 3x^2 - 9$ and $g(x) = 2x^3 + 4x + a$.

Since, the given polynomials leave the same remainder when divided by $x + 3$, so put $x + 3 = 0 \Rightarrow x = -3$ in $f(x)$ and $g(x)$.

By Remainder theorem,

$$f(-3) = g(-3)$$

$\Rightarrow \quad a(-3)^3 + 3(-3)^2 - 9 = 2(-3)^3 + 4(-3) + a$

$\Rightarrow \qquad -27a + 27 - 9 = -54 - 12 + a$

$\Rightarrow \qquad -27a - a = -66 - 18$

$\Rightarrow \qquad -28a = -84$

$\Rightarrow \qquad a = 3.$

Q. 10. Using the Remainder and Factor Theorem, factorise the following polynomial:

$$x^3 + 10x^2 - 37x + 26. \qquad \textbf{[2014]}$$

Ans. Given, $\quad f(x) = x^3 + 10x^2 - 37x + 26$

$$f(1) = 1 + 10 - 37 + 26 = 37 - 37 = 0$$

Thus, $(x - 1)$ is a factor of $f(x)$.

$$x - 1 \overline{)x^3 + 10x^2 - 37x + 26}(x^2 + 11x - 26$$
$$\underline{x^3 - x^2}$$
$$-+$$
$$\overline{11x^2 - 37x}$$
$$11x^2 - 11x$$
$$-+$$
$$\overline{-26x + 26}$$
$$-26x + 26$$
$$+-$$
$$\overline{0}$$

Thus, $\qquad f(x) = (x - 1)(x^2 + 11x - 26)$

$$= (x - 1)(x^2 + 13x - 2x - 26)$$
$$= (x - 1)[x(x + 13) - 2(x + 13)]$$
$$= (x - 1)(x - 2)(x + 13)$$

Thus, required factors are $(x - 1)$, $(x - 2)$ and $(x + 13)$.

Q. 11. If $(x - 2)$ is a factor of the expression $2x^3 + ax^2 + bx - 14$ and when the expression is divided by $(x - 3)$, it leaves a remainder 52, find the values of a and b. **[2013]**

Ans. Let, $\qquad f(x) = 2x^3 + ax^2 + bx - 14 \quad$ ...(i)

As $(x - 2)$ is a factor of equation (i)

$\therefore$ Putting $\quad x - 2 = 0$

$\Rightarrow \qquad x = 2$ in equation (i)

We get, $\qquad f(2) = 0$

and $\qquad f(2) = 2(2)^3 + a(2)^2 + b(2) - 14$

$\qquad\qquad 0 = 16 + 4a + 2b - 14$

$\therefore \qquad 4a + 2b = -2$

or $\qquad 2a + b = -1 \qquad$ ...(ii)

Again, when $f(x)$ is divided by $(x - 3)$, it leaves remainder 52.

Putting $\qquad x - 3 = 0$

$\Rightarrow \qquad x = 3$

We get, $\qquad f(3) = 52$

$\Rightarrow \qquad f(3) = 2(3)^3 + a(3)^2 + b(3) - 14$

and, $\qquad 52 = 54 + 9a + 3b - 14$

$\therefore \qquad 52 = 9a + 3b + 40$

$\Rightarrow \qquad 52 - 40 = 9a + 3b$

$\Rightarrow \qquad 12 = 9a + 3b$

or $\qquad 4 = 3a + b \qquad$ ...(iii)

Solving (ii) and (iii)

$$3a + b = 4$$
$$2a + b = -1$$

Subtracting $\underline{\quad - \quad - \quad\quad +\quad}$

$$a = 5$$

Substitute $a = 5$ in equation (iii),

$\Rightarrow \qquad 3 \times 5 + b = 4$

$\Rightarrow \qquad 15 + b = 4$

$\Rightarrow \qquad b = 4 - 15$

$\Rightarrow \qquad b = -11$

Q. 12. **Find the value of 'k' if $(x - 2)$ is a factor of:**

$$x^3 + 2x^2 - kx + 10$$

Hence, determine whether $(x + 5)$ is also a factor. **[2011]**

Ans. Let, $\qquad f(x) = x^3 + 2x^2 - kx + 10 \qquad$ ...(i)

As $(x - 2)$ is a factor of $f(x)$

Put $(x - 2) = 0 \Rightarrow x = 2$

$\therefore \qquad f(2) = (2)^3 + 2(2)^2 - k(2) + 10$

$\Rightarrow \qquad 0 = 8 + 8 - 2k + 10$

$\qquad$ [As $(x - 2)$ is a factor of $f(x) \Rightarrow f(2) = 0$]

$\Rightarrow \qquad 2k = 26$

$\Rightarrow \qquad k = \dfrac{22}{2} = 13$

$\therefore \qquad f(x) = x^3 + 2x^2 - 13x + 10 \qquad$ ...(ii)

To determine whether $(x + 5)$ is a factor of $f(x)$ or not

Put $\qquad x + 5 = 0 \quad i.e., \quad x = -5$ in (ii)

We get, $\quad f(-5) = (-5)^3 + 2(-5)^2 - 13(-5) + 10$

$\qquad\qquad\qquad [k = 13]$

$\qquad\qquad = -125 + 50 + 65 + 10 = 0$

$\Rightarrow (x + 5)$ is a factor of $f(x)$.

Q. 13. **When divided by $x - 3$ the polynomials $x^3 - px^2 + x + 6$ and $2x^3 - x^2 - (p+3)x - 6$ leave the same remainder. Find the value of 'p'.** **[2010]**

Ans. When $x^3 - px^2 + x + 6$ is divided by $(x - 3)$, then

Remainder$_1 = f(3) = (3)^3 - p(3)^2 + 3 + 6$

$\qquad\qquad = 27 - 9p + 9$

$\qquad\qquad = 36 - 9p \qquad$ ...(i)

When $2x^3 - x^2 - (p + 3)x - 6$ is divided by $(x - 3)$, then

Remainder$_2 = g(3) = 2(3)^3 - (3)^2 - (p + 3)(3) - 6$

$\qquad\qquad = 54 - 9 - 3p - 9 - 6$

$\qquad\qquad = 30 - 3p \qquad$ ...(ii)

Given, both remainders are equal, equating (i) and (ii)

$\therefore \qquad 36 - 9p = 30 - 3p$

$\Rightarrow \qquad -9p + 3p = 30 - 36$

$\Rightarrow \qquad -6p = -6$

$\Rightarrow \qquad p = 1$

Q. 14. **Use the Remainder Theorem to factorise the following expression:**

$$2x^3 + x^2 - 13x + 6 \qquad \textbf{[2010]}$$

Ans. Let $\qquad f(x) = 2x^3 + x^2 - 13x + 6$

Put $x = 2, \quad f(2) = 2(2)^3 + 2^2 - 13(2) + 6$

$\qquad\qquad = 0$, satisfied.

Hence $(x - 2)$ is a factor of $f(x)$ $x - 3$

$$\begin{array}{r} 2x^2 + 5x - 3 \\ x - 2 \overline{)\, 2x^3 + x^2 - 13x + 6} \\ \underline{2x^3 - 4x^2} \\ \underline{-\quad + \quad\quad\quad} \\ 5x^2 - 13x \\ 5x^2 - 10x \\ \underline{-\quad + \quad\quad} \\ -3x + 6 \\ -3x + 6 \\ \underline{+\quad - \quad} \\ 0 \end{array}$$

Thus, $\quad f(x) = (x - 2)(2x^2 + 5x - 3)$

$\qquad\qquad = (x - 2)(2x^2 + 6x - x - 3)$

$\qquad\qquad = (x - 2)[2x(x + 3) - 1(x + 3)]$

$\qquad\qquad = (x - 2)(x + 3)(2x - 1)$

Q. 15. **Show that $(x - 1)$ is a factor of $x^3 - 7x^2 + 14x - 8$. Hence, completely factorise the above expression.** **[2007]**

Ans. If $(x - 1)$ is a factor of $x^3 - 7x^2 + 14x - 8$

Then on putting $x - 1 = 0$

$$x = 1$$
$$f(1) = 0 = 1^3 - 7(1)^2 + 14(1) - 8$$
$$= 1 - 7 + 14 - 8 = 0$$

Hence $(x - 1)$ is one factor.

To find other factors:

$$x^3 - 7x^2 + 14x - 8 = x^2(x - 1) - 6x(x - 1) + 8(x - 1)$$
$$= (x - 1)(x^2 - 6x + 8)$$
$$= (x - 1)(x^2 - 4x - 2x + 8)$$
$$= (x - 1)\{x(x - 4) - 2(x - 4)\}$$
$$= (x - 1)(x - 2)(x - 4).$$

Q. 16. Show that $2x + 7$ is a factor of $2x^3 + 5x^2 - 11x - 14$. Hence factorise the given expression completely, using the factor theorem. **[2006]**

Ans. If $2x + 7$ in factor of $2x^3 + 5x^2 - 11x - 14$

then on putting $2x + 7 = 0$

$$x = -7/2$$

$$f(-7/2) = 2\left(-\frac{7}{2}\right)^3 + 5\left(-\frac{7}{2}\right)^2 - 11\left(-\frac{7}{2}\right) - 14$$

$$= \frac{-343}{4} + \frac{245}{4} + \frac{77}{2} - 14$$

$$= \frac{-399}{4} + \frac{245 + 154}{4} = \frac{-399 + 399}{4} = 0$$

Hence $(2x + 7)$ is one factor.

Now by dividing $2x^3 + 5x^2 - 11x - 14$ by $2x + 7$, we get

$$\begin{array}{r} x^2 - x - 2 \\ 2x + 7 \overline{)\ 2x^3 + 5x^2 - 11x - 14} \\ 2x^3 + 7x^2 \\ \hline \quad\ -2x^2 - 11x \\ -2x^2 - 7x \\ \hline \qquad\quad -4x - 14 \\ -4x - 14 \\ \hline \qquad\qquad\quad \times \end{array}$$

$$x^2 - x - 2 = x^2 - 2x + x - 2$$
$$= x(x - 2) + 1(x - 2) = (x + 1)(x - 2)$$

Here required factors of

$$2x^3 + 5x^2 - 11x - 14 = (2x + 7)(x + 1)(x - 2).$$

Long Answer Type Questions

Q. 1. Using the Remainder Theorem factorise completely the following polynomial.

$$3x^3 + 2x^2 - 19x + 6 \qquad \textbf{[2012]}$$

Ans. Let, $P(x) = 3x^3 + 2x^2 - 19x + 6$

Putting $x = 2$, $P(2) = 3 \times 2^3 + 2 \times 2^2 - 19 \times 2 + 6$

$$= 24 + 8 - 38 + 6$$
$$= 38 - 38 = 0$$

$\Rightarrow (x - 2)$ is a factor of $P(x)$

$$\begin{array}{r} 3x^2 + 8x - 3 \\ x - 2 \overline{)\ 3x^3 + 2x^2 - 19x + 6} \\ 3x^3 - 6x^2 \\ \hline \quad\ 8x^2 - 19x \\ 8x^2 - 16x \\ \hline \qquad\quad -3x + 6 \\ -3x + 6 \\ \hline \qquad\qquad\quad 0 \end{array}$$

$$\Rightarrow 3x^3 + 2x^2 - 19x + 6 = (x - 2) \cdot (3x^2 + 8x - 3)$$
$$= (x - 2)(3x^2 + 9x - x - 3)$$
$$= (x - 2)[3x(x + 3) - 1(x + 3)]$$
$$= (x - 2)(x + 3)(3x - 1)$$

Q. 2. Given that $x + 2$ and $x + 3$ are factors of $2x^3 + ax^2 + 7x - b$. Determine the values of a and b. **[2009]**

Ans. Given, $(x + 2)$ and $(x + 3)$ are factors of $2x^3 + ax^2 + 7x - b$.

$$\therefore \qquad\qquad x + 2 = 0$$
$$\Rightarrow \qquad\qquad x = -2$$
$$2(-2)^3 + a(-2)^2 + 7(-2) - b = 0$$
$$\Rightarrow \qquad\qquad 4a - b = 30 \qquad \text{...(i)}$$

Now, $\qquad\qquad x + 3 = 0$
$$\Rightarrow \qquad\qquad x = -3$$
$$2(-3)^3 + a(-3)^2 + 7(-3) - b = 0$$
$$\Rightarrow \qquad\qquad 9a - b = 75 \qquad \text{...(ii)}$$

Solving (i) and (ii) we get

$$4a - b = 30$$
$$9a - b = 75$$

on subtracting $\quad \dfrac{(-)\ \ (+)\ \ (-)}{-5a = -45}$

$$a = 9$$

From (i) $\qquad\qquad 4 \times 9 - b = 30$
$$b = 36 - 30$$
$$b = 6$$
$$\therefore \qquad\qquad a = 9, b = 6$$

Q. 3. If $(x - 2)$ is a factor of $2x^3 - x^2 - px - 2$.

(i) find the value of p.

(ii) with the value of p, factorize the above expression completely. **[2008]**

Ans. **(i)** If $(x - 2)$ is a factor of $2x^3 - x^2 - px - 2$, then value of expression will be zero at $x = 2$.

$\therefore \qquad 2(2)^3 - (2)^2 - p(2) - 2 = 0$

$\Rightarrow \qquad 16 - 4 - 2p - 2 = 0$

$\qquad\qquad\qquad 2p = 10$

$\qquad\qquad\qquad p = 5$

(ii) Now the given expression is $2x^3 - x^2 - 5x - 2$.

$(x - 2)$ is a factor of above expression.

$$\therefore \quad x - 2 \overline{)\,2x^3 - x^2 - 5x - 2\,}\big(2x^2 + 3x + 1$$

$$\underline{2x^3 - 4x^2 \qquad\qquad}$$
$$\underline{-\quad +\qquad\qquad\qquad}$$
$$3x^2 - 5x$$
$$3x^2 - 6x$$
$$\underline{-\quad +\qquad}$$
$$x - 2$$
$$x - 2$$
$$\underline{-\quad +\quad}$$
$$\times$$

$\therefore$ The expression can be written as $(2x^2 + 3x + 1)\,(x - 2)$

$\Rightarrow \quad (2x^2 + 2x + x + 1)(x - 2)$

$\Rightarrow \quad [2x(x + 1) + 1(x + 1)](x - 2)$

$\Rightarrow \quad (2x + 1)(x + 1)(x - 2)$.

? Short Answer Type Questions

Q. 1. Given $A = \begin{bmatrix} x & 3 \\ y & 3 \end{bmatrix}$

If $A^2 = 3I$, where I is the identity matrix of order 2, find x and y. **[2020]**

Marking Scheme

$A^2 = 3I$

$\begin{bmatrix} x & 3 \\ y & 3 \end{bmatrix}\begin{bmatrix} x & 3 \\ y & 3 \end{bmatrix} = 3\begin{bmatrix} 1 & 0 \\ 0 & 1 \end{bmatrix}$

$\begin{bmatrix} x^2 + 3y & 3x + 9 \\ xy + 3y & 3y + 9 \end{bmatrix} = 3\begin{bmatrix} 3 & 0 \\ 0 & 3 \end{bmatrix}$

$\therefore\ 3x + 9 = 0$ or $3y + 9 = 3$

$\therefore\ 3x = -9 \qquad 3y = -6$

$\therefore\ x = -3 \qquad y = -2$

$x = -3, \qquad y = -2$

Ans. Given : $A = \begin{bmatrix} x & 3 \\ y & 3 \end{bmatrix}$

Also, $A^2 = 3I$

$\Rightarrow \begin{bmatrix} x & 3 \\ y & 3 \end{bmatrix}\begin{bmatrix} x & 3 \\ y & 3 \end{bmatrix} = 3\begin{bmatrix} 1 & 0 \\ 0 & 1 \end{bmatrix}$

$\Rightarrow \begin{bmatrix} x^2 + 3y & 3x + 9 \\ xy + 3y & 3y + 9 \end{bmatrix} = \begin{bmatrix} 3 & 0 \\ 0 & 3 \end{bmatrix}$

Comparing both sides, we get

$3x + 9 = 0$

$\Rightarrow \qquad x = -\dfrac{9}{3} = -3$

and $\qquad 3y + 9 = 3$

$\Rightarrow \qquad 3y = 3 - 9 = -6$

$\Rightarrow \qquad y = -\dfrac{6}{3} = -2$

$\therefore \qquad x = -3$ and $y = -2$

Q. 2. If $A = \begin{bmatrix} 3 & 0 \\ 5 & 1 \end{bmatrix}$ and $B = \begin{bmatrix} -4 & 2 \\ 1 & 0 \end{bmatrix}$

Find $A^2 - 2AB + B^2$ **[2020]**

Marking Scheme

$A^2 - 2AB + B^2 = \begin{bmatrix} 3 & 0 \\ 5 & 1 \end{bmatrix}\begin{bmatrix} 3 & 0 \\ 5 & 1 \end{bmatrix} - 2\begin{bmatrix} 3 & 0 \\ 5 & 1 \end{bmatrix}\begin{bmatrix} -4 & 2 \\ 1 & 0 \end{bmatrix}$

$\qquad\qquad + \begin{bmatrix} -4 & 2 \\ 1 & 0 \end{bmatrix}\begin{bmatrix} -4 & 2 \\ 1 & 0 \end{bmatrix}$

$= \begin{bmatrix} 9 & 0 \\ 15+5 & 1 \end{bmatrix} - 2\begin{bmatrix} -12 & 6 \\ -20+1 & 10 \end{bmatrix} + \begin{bmatrix} 16+2 & -8 \\ -4 & 2 \end{bmatrix}$

$= \begin{bmatrix} 9 & 0 \\ 20 & 1 \end{bmatrix} - \begin{bmatrix} -24 & 12 \\ -38 & 20 \end{bmatrix} + \begin{bmatrix} 18 & -8 \\ -4 & 2 \end{bmatrix}$

$= \begin{bmatrix} 9 & 0 \\ 20 & 1 \end{bmatrix} + \begin{bmatrix} 24 & -12 \\ 38 & -20 \end{bmatrix} + \begin{bmatrix} 18 & -8 \\ -4 & 2 \end{bmatrix}$

$= \begin{bmatrix} 33 & -12 \\ 58 & -19 \end{bmatrix} + \begin{bmatrix} 18 & -8 \\ -4 & 2 \end{bmatrix} = \begin{bmatrix} 51 & -20 \\ 54 & -17 \end{bmatrix}$

Ans. Given : $A = \begin{bmatrix} 3 & 0 \\ 5 & 1 \end{bmatrix}$ and $B = \begin{bmatrix} -4 & 2 \\ 1 & 0 \end{bmatrix}$

Now, $A^2 - 2AB + B^2 = \begin{bmatrix} 3 & 0 \\ 5 & 1 \end{bmatrix}\begin{bmatrix} 3 & 0 \\ 5 & 1 \end{bmatrix}$

$\qquad - 2\begin{bmatrix} 3 & 0 \\ 5 & 1 \end{bmatrix}\begin{bmatrix} -4 & 2 \\ 1 & 0 \end{bmatrix} + \begin{bmatrix} -4 & 2 \\ 1 & 0 \end{bmatrix}\begin{bmatrix} -4 & 2 \\ 1 & 0 \end{bmatrix}$

$= \begin{bmatrix} 9+0 & 0+0 \\ 15+5 & 0+1 \end{bmatrix} - 2\begin{bmatrix} -12+0 & 6+0 \\ -20+1 & 10+0 \end{bmatrix}$

$\qquad\qquad + \begin{bmatrix} 16+2 & -8+0 \\ -4+0 & 2+0 \end{bmatrix}$

$= \begin{bmatrix} 9 & 0 \\ 20 & 1 \end{bmatrix} - 2\begin{bmatrix} -12 & 6 \\ -19 & 10 \end{bmatrix} + \begin{bmatrix} 18 & -8 \\ -4 & 2 \end{bmatrix}$

$= \begin{bmatrix} 9 & 0 \\ 20 & 1 \end{bmatrix} + \begin{bmatrix} 24 & -12 \\ 38 & -20 \end{bmatrix} + \begin{bmatrix} 18 & -8 \\ -4 & 2 \end{bmatrix}$

$= \begin{bmatrix} 9+24+18 & 0-12-8 \\ 20+38-4 & 1-20+2 \end{bmatrix}$

$= \begin{bmatrix} 51 & -20 \\ 54 & -17 \end{bmatrix}$

Q. 3. Simplify:

$\sin A \begin{bmatrix} \sin A & -\cos A \\ \cos A & \sin A \end{bmatrix} + \cos A \begin{bmatrix} \cos A & \sin A \\ -\sin A & \cos A \end{bmatrix}$

[2019]

📋 **Marking Scheme** -----------------------------

$$\sin A \begin{bmatrix} \sin A & -\cos A \\ \cos A & \sin A \end{bmatrix} + \cos A \begin{bmatrix} \cos A & \sin A \\ -\sin A & \cos A \end{bmatrix}$$

$$= \begin{bmatrix} \sin^2 A & -\sin A \cos A \\ \sin A \cos A & \sin^2 A \end{bmatrix} + \begin{bmatrix} \cos^2 A & \cos A \sin A \\ -\sin A \cos A & \cos^2 A \end{bmatrix}$$

$$= \begin{bmatrix} \sin^2 A + \cos^2 A & -\sin A \cos A + \cos A \sin A \\ \sin A \cos A - \sin A \cos A & \sin^2 A + \cos 2 A \end{bmatrix}$$

$$= \begin{bmatrix} 1 & 0 \\ 0 & 1 \end{bmatrix}$$

Ans.
$$\sin A \begin{bmatrix} \sin A & -\cos A \\ \cos A & \sin A \end{bmatrix} + \cos A \begin{bmatrix} \cos A & \sin A \\ -\sin A & \cos A \end{bmatrix}$$

$$= \begin{bmatrix} \sin^2 A & -\sin A \cos A \\ \sin A \cos A & \sin^2 A \end{bmatrix}$$

$$+ \begin{bmatrix} \cos^2 A & \sin A \cos A \\ -\sin A \cos A & \cos^2 A \end{bmatrix}$$

$$= \begin{bmatrix} \sin^2 A + \cos^2 A \\ \sin A \cos A - \sin A \cos A \end{bmatrix. \begin{matrix} -\sin A \cos A + \sin A \cos A \\ \sin^2 A + \cos^2 A \end{matrix}$$

$$= \begin{bmatrix} 1 & 0 \\ 0 & 1 \end{bmatrix} = I$$

$$[\because \sin^2 A + \cos^2 A = 1]$$

Q. 4. **Find the value of 'x' and 'y' if:**

$$2\begin{bmatrix} x & 7 \\ 9 & y-5 \end{bmatrix} + \begin{bmatrix} 6 & -7 \\ 4 & 5 \end{bmatrix} = \begin{bmatrix} 10 & 7 \\ 22 & 15 \end{bmatrix}$$ **[2018]**

Ans. We have,

$$2\begin{bmatrix} x & 7 \\ 9 & y-5 \end{bmatrix} + \begin{bmatrix} 6 & -7 \\ 4 & 5 \end{bmatrix} = \begin{bmatrix} 10 & 7 \\ 22 & 15 \end{bmatrix}$$

$$\Rightarrow \begin{bmatrix} 2x & 14 \\ 18 & 2y-10 \end{bmatrix} + \begin{bmatrix} 6 & -7 \\ 4 & 5 \end{bmatrix} = \begin{bmatrix} 10 & 7 \\ 22 & 15 \end{bmatrix}$$

$$\Rightarrow \begin{bmatrix} 2x+6 & 7 \\ 22 & 2y-5 \end{bmatrix} = \begin{bmatrix} 10 & 7 \\ 22 & 15 \end{bmatrix}$$

On comparing both sides, we get

$$\Rightarrow \quad 2x + 6 = 10, \qquad 2y - 5 = 15$$
$$\Rightarrow \quad 2x = 10 - 6, \qquad 2y = 15 + 5$$
$$\Rightarrow \quad 2x = 4, \qquad 2y = 20$$
$$\Rightarrow \quad x = \frac{4}{2}, \qquad y = \frac{20}{2}$$
$$\therefore \quad x = 2, y = 10.$$

Q. 5. **If** $A = \begin{bmatrix} 2 & 3 \\ 5 & 7 \end{bmatrix}$, $B = \begin{bmatrix} 0 & 4 \\ -1 & 7 \end{bmatrix}$ **and** $C = \begin{bmatrix} 1 & 0 \\ -1 & 4 \end{bmatrix}$, **find** $AC + B^2 - 10C$. **[2018]**

Ans. Given, $A = \begin{bmatrix} 2 & 3 \\ 5 & 7 \end{bmatrix}$, $B = \begin{bmatrix} 0 & 4 \\ -1 & 7 \end{bmatrix}$, $C = \begin{bmatrix} 1 & 0 \\ -1 & 4 \end{bmatrix}$

$$\therefore \quad AC + B^2 - 10C = \begin{bmatrix} 2 & 3 \\ 5 & 7 \end{bmatrix}\begin{bmatrix} 1 & 0 \\ -1 & 4 \end{bmatrix}$$

$$+ \begin{bmatrix} 0 & 4 \\ -1 & 7 \end{bmatrix}\begin{bmatrix} 0 & 4 \\ -1 & 7 \end{bmatrix} - 10\begin{bmatrix} 1 & 0 \\ -1 & 4 \end{bmatrix}$$

$$= \begin{bmatrix} 2-3 & 0+12 \\ 5-7 & 0+28 \end{bmatrix} + \begin{bmatrix} 0-4 & 0+28 \\ 0-7 & -4+49 \end{bmatrix}$$

$$- \begin{bmatrix} 10 & 0 \\ -10 & 40 \end{bmatrix}$$

$$= \begin{bmatrix} -1 & 12 \\ -2 & 28 \end{bmatrix} + \begin{bmatrix} -4 & 28 \\ -7 & 45 \end{bmatrix} - \begin{bmatrix} 10 & 0 \\ -10 & 40 \end{bmatrix}$$

$$= \begin{bmatrix} -5 & 40 \\ -9 & 73 \end{bmatrix} - \begin{bmatrix} 10 & 0 \\ -10 & 40 \end{bmatrix}$$

$$= \begin{bmatrix} -15 & 40 \\ 1 & 33 \end{bmatrix}$$

Q. 6. **Given** $A = \begin{bmatrix} 4\sin 30° & \cos 0° \\ \cos 0° & 4\sin 30° \end{bmatrix}$ **and** $B = \begin{bmatrix} 4 \\ 5 \end{bmatrix}$ **If** $AX = B$

(i) Write the order of matrix X.

(ii) Find the matrix 'X'. **[2016]**

Ans. **(i)** Given, $A = \begin{bmatrix} 4\sin 30° & \cos 0° \\ \cos 0° & 4\sin 30° \end{bmatrix}$ and $B = \begin{bmatrix} 4 \\ 5 \end{bmatrix}$

$$A = \begin{bmatrix} 4 \times \dfrac{1}{2} & 1 \\ 1 & 4 \times \dfrac{1}{2} \end{bmatrix}$$

$$A = \begin{bmatrix} 2 & 1 \\ 1 & 2 \end{bmatrix}$$

$\because$ The order of matrix A is 2×2
and the order of matrix B is 2×1
$\therefore$ The order of matrix X is 2×1.

(ii) Let $X = \begin{bmatrix} x \\ y \end{bmatrix}$

$$\therefore \quad \begin{bmatrix} 2 & 1 \\ 1 & 2 \end{bmatrix}\begin{bmatrix} x \\ y \end{bmatrix} = \begin{bmatrix} 4 \\ 5 \end{bmatrix}$$

$$\Rightarrow \quad \begin{bmatrix} 2x+y \\ x+2y \end{bmatrix} = \begin{bmatrix} 4 \\ 5 \end{bmatrix}$$

On comparing, we get
$$2x + y = 4 \qquad \qquad ...(i)$$
and $\quad x + 2y = 5 \qquad \qquad ...(ii)$

On multiplying equation (ii) by 2 and subtracting it from equation (i)

$$2x + y = 4$$
$$2x + 4y = 10$$
$$\underline{ - - -}$$
$$-3y = -6$$
$$y = 2$$

From equation (i)

$$2x + y = 4$$
$$2x + 2 = 4$$
$$x = 1$$

$\therefore$ The matrix $X = \begin{bmatrix} x \\ y \end{bmatrix} = \begin{bmatrix} 1 \\ 2 \end{bmatrix}$

Q. 7. If $A = \begin{bmatrix} 3 & x \\ 0 & 1 \end{bmatrix}$ and $B = \begin{bmatrix} 9 & 16 \\ 0 & -y \end{bmatrix}$, find x and y when $A^2 = B$. **[2015]**

Ans. Here, $A = \begin{bmatrix} 3 & x \\ 0 & 1 \end{bmatrix}$ and $B = \begin{bmatrix} 9 & 16 \\ 0 & -y \end{bmatrix}$

$A^2 = A \cdot A = \begin{bmatrix} 3 & x \\ 0 & 1 \end{bmatrix}\begin{bmatrix} 3 & x \\ 0 & 1 \end{bmatrix} = \begin{bmatrix} 9+0 & 3x+x \\ 0+0 & 0+1 \end{bmatrix}$

$= \begin{bmatrix} 9 & 4x \\ 0 & 1 \end{bmatrix}$

According to the given condition,

$$A^2 = B$$

$$\begin{bmatrix} 9 & 4x \\ 0 & 1 \end{bmatrix} = \begin{bmatrix} 9 & 16 \\ 0 & -y \end{bmatrix}$$

On comparing, we get,

$$4x = 16 \quad \text{and} \quad -y = 1$$
$$\therefore \qquad x = 4 \quad \text{and} \quad y = -1.$$

Q. 8. If $A = \begin{bmatrix} 3 & 7 \\ 2 & 4 \end{bmatrix}$ $B = \begin{bmatrix} 0 & 2 \\ 5 & 3 \end{bmatrix}$ and $C = \begin{bmatrix} 1 & -5 \\ -4 & 6 \end{bmatrix}$

Find AB – 5C. **[2015]**

Ans. Given, $A = \begin{bmatrix} 3 & 7 \\ 2 & 4 \end{bmatrix}, B = \begin{bmatrix} 0 & 2 \\ 5 & 3 \end{bmatrix}$

and $C = \begin{bmatrix} 1 & -5 \\ -4 & 6 \end{bmatrix}$

$\therefore \qquad AB = \begin{bmatrix} 3 & 7 \\ 2 & 4 \end{bmatrix}\begin{bmatrix} 0 & 2 \\ 5 & 3 \end{bmatrix}$

$= \begin{bmatrix} 0+35 & 6+21 \\ 0+20 & 4+12 \end{bmatrix} = \begin{bmatrix} 35 & 27 \\ 20 & 16 \end{bmatrix}$

and $\qquad 5C = \begin{bmatrix} 5 & -25 \\ -20 & 30 \end{bmatrix}$

$\therefore \qquad AB - 5C = \begin{bmatrix} 35 & 27 \\ 20 & 16 \end{bmatrix} - \begin{bmatrix} 5 & -25 \\ -20 & 30 \end{bmatrix}$

$= \begin{bmatrix} 35-5 & 27+25 \\ 20+20 & 16-30 \end{bmatrix}$

$= \begin{bmatrix} 30 & 52 \\ 40 & -14 \end{bmatrix}$

Q. 9. Find x, y if $\begin{bmatrix} -2 & 0 \\ 3 & 1 \end{bmatrix}\begin{bmatrix} -1 \\ 2x \end{bmatrix} + \begin{bmatrix} -2 \\ 1 \end{bmatrix} = 2\begin{bmatrix} y \\ 3 \end{bmatrix}$. **[2014]**

Ans. Given, $\begin{bmatrix} -2 & 0 \\ 3 & 1 \end{bmatrix}\begin{bmatrix} -1 \\ 2x \end{bmatrix} + 3\begin{bmatrix} -2 \\ 1 \end{bmatrix} = 2\begin{bmatrix} y \\ 3 \end{bmatrix}$

$\Rightarrow \begin{bmatrix} 2+0 \\ -3+2x \end{bmatrix} + \begin{bmatrix} -6 \\ 3 \end{bmatrix} = \begin{bmatrix} 2y \\ 6 \end{bmatrix}$

$\Rightarrow \begin{bmatrix} 2-6 \\ -3+2x+3 \end{bmatrix} = \begin{bmatrix} 2y \\ 6 \end{bmatrix}$

$\qquad \begin{bmatrix} -4 \\ 2x \end{bmatrix} = \begin{bmatrix} 2y \\ 6 \end{bmatrix}$

On comparing, we get

$\Rightarrow \qquad 2y = -4, \ 2x = 6$

$\Rightarrow \qquad y = -2, \quad x = 3$

Thus required values are $x = 3, y = -2$.

Q. 10. Given $A = \begin{bmatrix} 2 & -6 \\ 2 & 0 \end{bmatrix}, B = \begin{bmatrix} -3 & 2 \\ 4 & 0 \end{bmatrix} C = \begin{bmatrix} 4 & 0 \\ 0 & 2 \end{bmatrix}$

Find the matrix X such that A + 2X = 2B + C. **[2013]**

Ans. Given, $A = \begin{bmatrix} 2 & -6 \\ 2 & 0 \end{bmatrix} = B\begin{bmatrix} -3 & 2 \\ 4 & 0 \end{bmatrix} C = \begin{bmatrix} 4 & 0 \\ 0 & 2 \end{bmatrix}$

$$A + 2X = 2B + C$$

$\begin{bmatrix} 2 & -6 \\ 2 & 0 \end{bmatrix} + 2X = 2\begin{bmatrix} -3 & 2 \\ 4 & 0 \end{bmatrix} + \begin{bmatrix} 4 & 0 \\ 0 & 2 \end{bmatrix}$

$2X = \begin{bmatrix} -6 & 4 \\ 8 & 0 \end{bmatrix} + \begin{bmatrix} 4 & 0 \\ 0 & 2 \end{bmatrix} - \begin{bmatrix} 2 & -6 \\ 2 & 0 \end{bmatrix}$

$2X = \begin{bmatrix} -6+4-2 & 4+0+6 \\ 8+0-2 & 0+2-0 \end{bmatrix}$

$= \begin{bmatrix} -4 & 10 \\ 6 & 2 \end{bmatrix}$

$X = \dfrac{1}{2}\begin{bmatrix} -4 & 10 \\ 6 & 2 \end{bmatrix}$

$\therefore \qquad X = \begin{bmatrix} -2 & 5 \\ 3 & 1 \end{bmatrix}$

Q. 11. Find x and y if $\begin{bmatrix} x & 3x \\ y & 4y \end{bmatrix}\begin{bmatrix} 2 \\ 1 \end{bmatrix} = \begin{bmatrix} 5 \\ 12 \end{bmatrix}$. **[2013]**

Ans. Given, $\begin{bmatrix} x & 3x \\ y & 4y \end{bmatrix}\begin{bmatrix} 2 \\ 1 \end{bmatrix} = \begin{bmatrix} 5 \\ 12 \end{bmatrix}$

$\Rightarrow \begin{bmatrix} 2x+3x \\ 2y+4y \end{bmatrix} = \begin{bmatrix} 5 \\ 12 \end{bmatrix} \Rightarrow \begin{bmatrix} 5x \\ 6y \end{bmatrix} = \begin{bmatrix} 5 \\ 12 \end{bmatrix}$

On comparing, we get

$\Rightarrow \qquad 5x = 5$

$\Rightarrow \qquad x = 1$

and $\qquad 6y = 12$

$\Rightarrow \qquad y = 2$

Q. 12. Given $\begin{bmatrix} 2 & 1 \\ -3 & 4 \end{bmatrix} X = \begin{bmatrix} 7 \\ 6 \end{bmatrix}$. Write:

    (i) the order of the matrix X.

    (ii) the matrix X.   **[2012]**

Ans.   **(i)** $\begin{bmatrix} 2 & 1 \\ -3 & 4 \end{bmatrix}_{2\times 2} X = \begin{bmatrix} 7 \\ 6 \end{bmatrix}_{2\times 1}$

According to the given condition, the order of matrix X will be 2×1.

(ii) Let $\qquad X = \begin{bmatrix} a \\ b \end{bmatrix}$

so $\qquad \begin{bmatrix} 2 & 1 \\ -3 & 4 \end{bmatrix}\begin{bmatrix} a \\ b \end{bmatrix} = \begin{bmatrix} 7 \\ 6 \end{bmatrix}$

$\Rightarrow \qquad \begin{bmatrix} 2a + b \\ -3a + 4b \end{bmatrix} = \begin{bmatrix} 7 \\ 6 \end{bmatrix}$

$\Rightarrow \qquad\qquad 2a + b = 7 \qquad\qquad …(i)$

$\Rightarrow \qquad\qquad -3a + 4b = 6 \qquad\qquad …(ii)$

Multiplying by 4 in equation (i) and solving with equation (ii)

$$8a + 4b = 28$$
$$-\ 3a + 4b = 6$$
$$+ \quad - \qquad -$$
$$\overline{\qquad\qquad\qquad}$$
$$11a = 22$$

$\therefore \qquad\qquad a = 2$

Putting the value of a in equation (i), we get

$$2 \times 2 + b = 7$$

$\therefore \qquad\qquad b = 7 - 4 = 3$

$\Rightarrow \qquad\qquad X = \begin{bmatrix} 2 \\ 3 \end{bmatrix}$

Q. 13. If $A = \begin{bmatrix} 3 & 5 \\ 4 & -2 \end{bmatrix}$ and $B = \begin{bmatrix} 2 \\ 4 \end{bmatrix}$, is the product **AB possible? Give a reason. If yes, find AB.**

                           [2011]

Ans. $A = \begin{bmatrix} 3 & 5 \\ 4 & -2 \end{bmatrix}_{2\times 2}$ and $B = \begin{bmatrix} 2 \\ 4 \end{bmatrix}_{2\times 1}$

The order of matrix A is 2×2 and matrix B is 2×1.

The product AB is possible as the number of columns in A is equal to the number of rows in B.

Now, $\quad AB = \begin{bmatrix} 3 & 5 \\ 4 & -2 \end{bmatrix}\begin{bmatrix} 2 \\ 4 \end{bmatrix}$

$AB = \begin{bmatrix} 3\times 2 + 5\times 4 \\ 4\times 2 + (-2)\times 4 \end{bmatrix}$

$AB = \begin{bmatrix} 26 \\ 0 \end{bmatrix}$

Q. 14. If $A = \begin{bmatrix} 2 & 5 \\ 1 & 3 \end{bmatrix}$, $B = \begin{bmatrix} 4 & -2 \\ -1 & 3 \end{bmatrix}$ and **I is the identity matrix of the same order and A^t is the transpose of matrix A, find $A^t.B + BI$.**

                           [2011]

Ans. Given, $A = \begin{bmatrix} 2 & 5 \\ 1 & 3 \end{bmatrix}$, $B = \begin{bmatrix} 4 & -2 \\ -1 & 3 \end{bmatrix}$

and $\qquad I = \begin{bmatrix} 1 & 0 \\ 0 & 1 \end{bmatrix}$

$A^t = \begin{bmatrix} 2 & 1 \\ 5 & 3 \end{bmatrix}$

$A^t \cdot B = \begin{bmatrix} 2 & 1 \\ 5 & 3 \end{bmatrix}\begin{bmatrix} 4 & -2 \\ -1 & 3 \end{bmatrix}$

$A^t \cdot B = \begin{bmatrix} 8-1 & -4+3 \\ 20-3 & -10+9 \end{bmatrix}$

$A^t \cdot B = \begin{bmatrix} 7 & -1 \\ 17 & -1 \end{bmatrix} \qquad …(i)$

$BI = \begin{bmatrix} 4 & -2 \\ -1 & 3 \end{bmatrix}\begin{bmatrix} 1 & 0 \\ 0 & 1 \end{bmatrix}$

$BI = \begin{bmatrix} 4 & -2 \\ -1 & 3 \end{bmatrix} \qquad …(ii)$

From equation (i) and (ii)

$A^t \cdot B + BI = \begin{bmatrix} 7 & -1 \\ 17 & -1 \end{bmatrix} + \begin{bmatrix} 4 & -2 \\ -1 & 3 \end{bmatrix}$

$A^t \cdot B + BI = \begin{bmatrix} 7+4 & -1-2 \\ 17-1 & -1+3 \end{bmatrix}$

$= \begin{bmatrix} 11 & -3 \\ 16 & 2 \end{bmatrix}$

Q. 15. Given $A = \begin{bmatrix} 3 & -2 \\ -1 & 4 \end{bmatrix}$, $B = \begin{bmatrix} 6 \\ 1 \end{bmatrix}$, $C = \begin{bmatrix} -4 \\ 5 \end{bmatrix}$ and $D = \begin{bmatrix} 2 \\ 2 \end{bmatrix}$.

Find AB + 2C − 4D.   **[2010]**

Ans. $AB = \begin{bmatrix} 3 & -2 \\ -1 & 4 \end{bmatrix}\begin{bmatrix} 6 \\ 1 \end{bmatrix} = \begin{bmatrix} 18 & -2 \\ -6 & +4 \end{bmatrix}$

$= \begin{bmatrix} 16 \\ -2 \end{bmatrix}$

$\therefore \ AB + 2C - 4D = \begin{bmatrix} 16 \\ -2 \end{bmatrix} + 2\begin{bmatrix} -4 \\ 5 \end{bmatrix} - 4\begin{bmatrix} 2 \\ 2 \end{bmatrix}$

$= \begin{bmatrix} 16 \\ -2 \end{bmatrix} + \begin{bmatrix} -8 \\ 10 \end{bmatrix} - \begin{bmatrix} 8 \\ 8 \end{bmatrix}$

$= \begin{bmatrix} 16-8-8 \\ -2+10-8 \end{bmatrix} = \begin{bmatrix} 0 \\ 0 \end{bmatrix}$

Q. 16. Evaluate: $\begin{bmatrix} 4\sin 30° & 2\cos 60° \\ \sin 90° & 2\cos 0° \end{bmatrix}\begin{bmatrix} 4 & 5 \\ 5 & 4 \end{bmatrix}$ [2010]

Ans. $\begin{bmatrix} 4\sin 30° & 2\cos 60° \\ \sin 90° & 2\cos 0° \end{bmatrix}\begin{bmatrix} 4 & 5 \\ 5 & 4 \end{bmatrix}$

$$= \begin{bmatrix} 2 & 1 \\ 1 & 2 \end{bmatrix}_{2\times 2}\begin{bmatrix} 4 & 5 \\ 5 & 4 \end{bmatrix}_{2\times 2}$$

$$\begin{bmatrix} \because \sin 30° = \dfrac{1}{2} & \cos 60° = \dfrac{1}{2} \\ \sin 90° = 1 & \cos 0° = 1 \end{bmatrix}$$

$$= \begin{bmatrix} 8+5 & 10+4 \\ 4+10 & 5+8 \end{bmatrix}$$

$$= \begin{bmatrix} 13 & 14 \\ 14 & 13 \end{bmatrix}$$

Q. 17. Find x and y, if $\begin{bmatrix} 2x & x \\ y & 3y \end{bmatrix}\begin{bmatrix} 3 \\ 2 \end{bmatrix} = \begin{bmatrix} 16 \\ 9 \end{bmatrix}$. [2009]

Ans. Given, $\begin{bmatrix} 2x & x \\ y & 3y \end{bmatrix}\begin{bmatrix} 3 \\ 2 \end{bmatrix} = \begin{bmatrix} 16 \\ 9 \end{bmatrix}$

$$\begin{bmatrix} 6x+2x \\ 3y+6y \end{bmatrix} = \begin{bmatrix} 16 \\ 9 \end{bmatrix}$$

$$\therefore \qquad \begin{bmatrix} 8x \\ 9y \end{bmatrix} = \begin{bmatrix} 16 \\ 9 \end{bmatrix}$$

$\Rightarrow \qquad 8x = 16 \quad$ and $\quad 9y = 9$

$\Rightarrow \qquad x = 2 \quad$ and $\quad y = 1$

Q. 18. If $\begin{bmatrix} 1 & 4 \\ -2 & 3 \end{bmatrix} + 2M = 3\begin{bmatrix} 3 & 2 \\ 0 & -3 \end{bmatrix}$, **find the Matrix M.**

[2008]

Ans. Given:

$$\begin{bmatrix} 1 & 4 \\ -2 & 3 \end{bmatrix} + 2M = 3\begin{bmatrix} 3 & 2 \\ 0 & -3 \end{bmatrix}$$

$$\Rightarrow \quad 2M = \begin{bmatrix} 9 & 6 \\ 0 & -9 \end{bmatrix} - \begin{bmatrix} 1 & 4 \\ -2 & 3 \end{bmatrix} = \begin{bmatrix} 8 & 2 \\ 2 & -12 \end{bmatrix}$$

$$\Rightarrow \quad M = \begin{bmatrix} 4 & 1 \\ 1 & -6 \end{bmatrix}$$

Q. 19. Given $A = \begin{bmatrix} p & 0 \\ 0 & 2 \end{bmatrix}, B = \begin{bmatrix} 0 & -q \\ 1 & 0 \end{bmatrix}, C = \begin{bmatrix} 2 & -2 \\ 2 & 2 \end{bmatrix}$

and BA = C².

Find the values of p **and** q. [2008]

Ans. $A = \begin{bmatrix} p & 0 \\ 0 & 2 \end{bmatrix}, B = \begin{bmatrix} 0 & -q \\ 1 & 0 \end{bmatrix}, C = \begin{bmatrix} 2 & -2 \\ 2 & 2 \end{bmatrix}$

$$BA = \begin{bmatrix} 0 & -q \\ 1 & 0 \end{bmatrix}\begin{bmatrix} p & 0 \\ 0 & 2 \end{bmatrix} = \begin{bmatrix} 0 & -2q \\ p & 0 \end{bmatrix}$$

$$C^2 = \begin{bmatrix} 2 & -2 \\ 2 & 2 \end{bmatrix}\begin{bmatrix} 2 & -2 \\ 2 & 2 \end{bmatrix} = \begin{bmatrix} 0 & -8 \\ 8 & 0 \end{bmatrix}$$

$BA = C^2 \qquad \Rightarrow \qquad -2q = -8$

$$q = 4$$

$$p = 8$$

Q. 20. If $2\begin{bmatrix} 3 & 4 \\ 5 & x \end{bmatrix} + \begin{bmatrix} 1 & y \\ 0 & 1 \end{bmatrix} = \begin{bmatrix} 7 & 0 \\ 10 & 5 \end{bmatrix}$, **find the values of** x **and** y. [2007]

Ans. Given, $2\begin{bmatrix} 3 & 4 \\ 5 & x \end{bmatrix} + \begin{bmatrix} 1 & y \\ 0 & 1 \end{bmatrix} = \begin{bmatrix} 7 & 0 \\ 10 & 5 \end{bmatrix}$

$$\begin{bmatrix} 6 & 8 \\ 10 & 2x \end{bmatrix} + \begin{bmatrix} 1 & y \\ 0 & 1 \end{bmatrix} = \begin{bmatrix} 7 & 0 \\ 10 & 5 \end{bmatrix}$$

$$\begin{bmatrix} 7 & 8+y \\ 10 & 2x+1 \end{bmatrix} = \begin{bmatrix} 7 & 0 \\ 10 & 5 \end{bmatrix}$$

On comparing $\qquad 8 + y = 0$

$$y = -8$$

$$2x + 1 = 5$$

$$2x = 5 - 1$$

$$2x = 4$$

$$x = 2$$

$\therefore \qquad x = 2, y = -8.$

Q. 21. Let $A = \begin{bmatrix} 1 & 0 \\ 2 & 1 \end{bmatrix}, B = \begin{bmatrix} 2 & 3 \\ -1 & 0 \end{bmatrix}$. **Find** $A^2 + AB + B^2$. [2007]

Ans. Given,

$$A = \begin{bmatrix} 1 & 0 \\ 2 & 1 \end{bmatrix}, B = \begin{bmatrix} 2 & 3 \\ -1 & 0 \end{bmatrix}$$

$$A^2 = A \cdot A = \begin{bmatrix} 1 & 0 \\ 2 & 1 \end{bmatrix}\begin{bmatrix} 1 & 0 \\ 2 & 1 \end{bmatrix}$$

$$= \begin{bmatrix} 1\times 1+0\times 2 & 1\times 0+0\times 1 \\ 2\times 1+1\times 2 & 2\times 0+1\times 1 \end{bmatrix} = \begin{bmatrix} 1 & 0 \\ 4 & 1 \end{bmatrix}$$

$$AB = \begin{bmatrix} 1 & 0 \\ 2 & 1 \end{bmatrix}\begin{bmatrix} 2 & 3 \\ -1 & 0 \end{bmatrix}$$

$$= \begin{bmatrix} 1\times 2+0\times -1 & 1\times 3+0\times 0 \\ 2\times 2+1\times -1 & 2\times 3+1\times 0 \end{bmatrix} = \begin{bmatrix} 2 & 3 \\ 3 & 6 \end{bmatrix}$$

$$B^2 = B \cdot B = \begin{bmatrix} 2 & 3 \\ -1 & 0 \end{bmatrix}\begin{bmatrix} 2 & 3 \\ -1 & 0 \end{bmatrix}$$

$$= \begin{bmatrix} 2\times 2+3\times -1 & 2\times 3+3\times 0 \\ -1\times 2+0\times -1 & -1\times 3+0\times 0 \end{bmatrix} = \begin{bmatrix} 1 & 6 \\ -2 & -3 \end{bmatrix}$$

$\therefore \ A^2 + AB + B^2 =$

$$\begin{bmatrix} 1 & 0 \\ 4 & 1 \end{bmatrix} + \begin{bmatrix} 2 & 3 \\ 3 & 6 \end{bmatrix} + \begin{bmatrix} 1 & 6 \\ -2 & -3 \end{bmatrix} = \begin{bmatrix} 4 & 9 \\ 5 & 4 \end{bmatrix}.$$

 ## Long Answer Type Questions

Q. 1. Given $\begin{bmatrix} 4 & 2 \\ -1 & 1 \end{bmatrix} M = 6I$, where M is a matrix

and I is unit matrix of order 2×2.
  (i) State the order of matrix M.
  (ii) Find the matrix M. **[2019]**

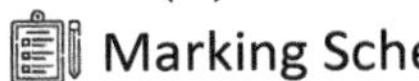 **Marking Scheme**

(i) $(2 \times 2)\,(m \times n) = (2 \times 2) \rightarrow$ order of matrix, M = (2×2)

(ii) $\begin{bmatrix} 4 & 2 \\ -1 & 1 \end{bmatrix} \times \begin{bmatrix} a & b \\ c & d \end{bmatrix} = 6\begin{bmatrix} 1 & 0 \\ 0 & 1 \end{bmatrix}$

$\begin{bmatrix} 4a + 2c & 4b + 2d \\ -a + c & -b + d \end{bmatrix} = \begin{bmatrix} 6 & 0 \\ 0 & 6 \end{bmatrix}$

$4a + 2c = 6$
$-a + c = 0$
$\therefore \quad a = 1$ and $c = 1$
$4b + 2d = 0$
$-b + d = 6$
$\therefore \quad b = -2$ and $d = 4$

$\therefore \quad M = \begin{bmatrix} 1 & -2 \\ 1 & 4 \end{bmatrix}$

Ans. Given, $\begin{bmatrix} 4 & 2 \\ -1 & 1 \end{bmatrix} M = 6I$

$\Rightarrow \quad \begin{bmatrix} 4 & 2 \\ -1 & 1 \end{bmatrix} M = 6\begin{bmatrix} 1 & 0 \\ 0 & 1 \end{bmatrix}$

$\Rightarrow \quad \begin{bmatrix} 4 & 2 \\ -1 & 1 \end{bmatrix} M = \begin{bmatrix} 6 & 0 \\ 0 & 6 \end{bmatrix}$ ...(i)

(i) $(2 \times 2)\,(m \times n) = (2 \times 2)$
$\Rightarrow$ Order of matrix, $M = 2 \times 2$.

(ii) Let, $M = \begin{bmatrix} a & b \\ c & d \end{bmatrix}$

$\therefore \quad \begin{bmatrix} 4 & 2 \\ -1 & 1 \end{bmatrix}\begin{bmatrix} a & b \\ c & d \end{bmatrix} = \begin{bmatrix} 6 & 0 \\ 0 & 6 \end{bmatrix}$ [using (i)]

$\Rightarrow \quad \begin{bmatrix} 4a + 2c & 4b + 2d \\ -a + c & -b + d \end{bmatrix} = \begin{bmatrix} 6 & 0 \\ 0 & 6 \end{bmatrix}$

$\therefore \qquad 4a + 2c = 6$ ...(ii)
$\qquad\qquad -a + c = 0$ ...(iii)$\times 4$

Solving equations (ii) and (iii),
$\qquad\qquad 4a + 2c = 6$
$\qquad\quad \underline{-4a + 4c = 0}$
$\qquad\qquad\qquad 6c = 6$

$\Rightarrow \qquad\qquad c = 1$
From equation (iii),
$\qquad\qquad -a + 1 = 0$

$\Rightarrow \qquad\qquad a = 1$
$\qquad\qquad 4b + 2d = 0$ ...(iv)
$\Rightarrow \qquad\qquad -b + d = 6$ ...(v)$\times 4$
Solving equations (iv) and (v),
$\qquad\qquad 4b + 2d = 0$
$\qquad\quad \underline{-4b + 4d = 24}$
$\qquad\qquad\qquad 6d = 24$
$\Rightarrow \qquad\qquad d = 4$
From equation (iv),
$\qquad\qquad -b + 4 = 6$
$\Rightarrow \qquad\qquad -b = 2$
$\Rightarrow \qquad\qquad b = 2$

$\therefore \qquad\qquad M = \begin{bmatrix} 1 & -2 \\ 1 & 4 \end{bmatrix}$

Q. 2. If $A = \begin{bmatrix} 1 & 3 \\ 3 & 4 \end{bmatrix}$ and $B = \begin{bmatrix} -2 & 1 \\ -3 & 2 \end{bmatrix}$ and $A^2 - 5B^2 = 5C$.

Find matrix C where C is a 2 by 2 matrix.
[2017]

Ans. Given, $A = \begin{bmatrix} 1 & 3 \\ 3 & 4 \end{bmatrix}$, $B = \begin{bmatrix} -2 & 1 \\ -3 & 2 \end{bmatrix}$

We have, $A^2 - 5B^2 = 5C$

$\Rightarrow \begin{bmatrix} 1 & 3 \\ 3 & 4 \end{bmatrix}\begin{bmatrix} 1 & 3 \\ 3 & 4 \end{bmatrix} - 5\begin{bmatrix} -2 & 1 \\ -3 & 2 \end{bmatrix}\begin{bmatrix} -2 & 1 \\ -3 & 2 \end{bmatrix} = 5C$

$\Rightarrow \quad 5C = \begin{bmatrix} 1+9 & 3+12 \\ 3+12 & 6+16 \end{bmatrix}$
$\qquad\qquad -5\begin{bmatrix} 4-3 & -2+2 \\ 6-6 & -3+4 \end{bmatrix}$

$\Rightarrow \quad 5C = \begin{bmatrix} 10 & 15 \\ 15 & 25 \end{bmatrix} - 5\begin{bmatrix} 1 & 0 \\ 0 & 1 \end{bmatrix}$

$\Rightarrow \quad 5C = \begin{bmatrix} 10 & 15 \\ 15 & 25 \end{bmatrix} - \begin{bmatrix} 5 & 0 \\ 0 & 5 \end{bmatrix}$

$\Rightarrow \quad 5C = \begin{bmatrix} 5 & 15 \\ 15 & 20 \end{bmatrix}$

$\Rightarrow \quad C = \frac{1}{5}\begin{bmatrix} 5 & 15 \\ 15 & 20 \end{bmatrix}$

$\Rightarrow \quad C = \begin{bmatrix} 1 & 3 \\ 3 & 4 \end{bmatrix}$

Q. 3. Given matrix $B = \begin{bmatrix} 1 & 1 \\ 8 & 3 \end{bmatrix}$. Find the matrix X if,

$X = B^2 - 4B.$

Hence, solve for a and b, given $X\begin{bmatrix} a \\ b \end{bmatrix} = \begin{bmatrix} 5 \\ 50 \end{bmatrix}$

[2017]

Ans. Given, $B = \begin{bmatrix} 1 & 1 \\ 8 & 3 \end{bmatrix}$

$\therefore \quad X = B^2 - 4B = \begin{bmatrix} 1 & 1 \\ 8 & 3 \end{bmatrix}\begin{bmatrix} 1 & 1 \\ 8 & 3 \end{bmatrix} - 4\begin{bmatrix} 1 & 1 \\ 8 & 3 \end{bmatrix}$

$= \begin{bmatrix} 1+8 & 1+3 \\ 8+24 & 8+9 \end{bmatrix} - \begin{bmatrix} 4 & 4 \\ 32 & 12 \end{bmatrix}$

$= \begin{bmatrix} 9 & 4 \\ 32 & 17 \end{bmatrix} - \begin{bmatrix} 4 & 4 \\ 32 & 12 \end{bmatrix}$

$= \begin{bmatrix} 5 & 0 \\ 0 & 5 \end{bmatrix}$

Now, $\qquad X\begin{bmatrix} a \\ b \end{bmatrix} = \begin{bmatrix} 5 \\ 50 \end{bmatrix}$

$\Rightarrow \quad \begin{bmatrix} 5 & 0 \\ 0 & 5 \end{bmatrix}\begin{bmatrix} a \\ b \end{bmatrix} = \begin{bmatrix} 5 \\ 50 \end{bmatrix}$

$\Rightarrow \quad \begin{bmatrix} 5a+0 \\ 0+5b \end{bmatrix} = \begin{bmatrix} 5 \\ 50 \end{bmatrix}$

$\Rightarrow \quad \begin{bmatrix} 5a \\ 5b \end{bmatrix} = \begin{bmatrix} 5 \\ 50 \end{bmatrix}$

On comparing the elements of matrices on both the sides, we get

$$5a = 5 \text{ and } 5b = 50$$

$\Rightarrow \qquad a = 1 \text{ and } b = 10$

Q. 4. Given $A = \begin{bmatrix} 2 & 0 \\ -1 & 7 \end{bmatrix}$ **and** $I = \begin{bmatrix} 1 & 0 \\ 0 & 1 \end{bmatrix}$ **and** $A^2 = 9A + mI$**. Find** m**.** [2016]

Ans. Here, $A = \begin{bmatrix} 2 & 0 \\ -1 & 7 \end{bmatrix}$

$\Rightarrow \quad A^2 = A \cdot A = \begin{bmatrix} 2 & 0 \\ -1 & 7 \end{bmatrix}\begin{bmatrix} 2 & 0 \\ -1 & 7 \end{bmatrix}$

$= \begin{bmatrix} 4+0 & 0+0 \\ -2-7 & 0+49 \end{bmatrix}$

$= \begin{bmatrix} 4 & 0 \\ -9 & 49 \end{bmatrix}$

Given, $A^2 = 9A + mI$

$\therefore \quad 9\begin{bmatrix} 2 & 0 \\ -1 & 7 \end{bmatrix} + m\begin{bmatrix} 1 & 0 \\ 0 & 1 \end{bmatrix} = \begin{bmatrix} 4 & 0 \\ -9 & 49 \end{bmatrix}$

$\Rightarrow \quad \begin{bmatrix} 18 & 0 \\ -9 & 63 \end{bmatrix} + \begin{bmatrix} m & 0 \\ 0 & m \end{bmatrix} = \begin{bmatrix} 4 & 0 \\ -9 & 49 \end{bmatrix}$

$\Rightarrow \quad \begin{bmatrix} 18+m & 0 \\ -9 & 63+m \end{bmatrix} = \begin{bmatrix} 4 & 0 \\ -9 & 49 \end{bmatrix}$

On comparing both sides, we get

$$18 + m = 4 \text{ and } 63 + m = 49$$

which gives $m = -14$.

Q. 5. Let $A = \begin{bmatrix} 2 & 1 \\ 0 & -2 \end{bmatrix}$**,** $B = \begin{bmatrix} 4 & 1 \\ -3 & -2 \end{bmatrix}$ **and** $C = \begin{bmatrix} -3 & 2 \\ -1 & 4 \end{bmatrix}$

Find $A^2 + AC - 5B$**.** [2014]

Ans. $A = \begin{bmatrix} 2 & 1 \\ 0 & -2 \end{bmatrix}$, $B = \begin{bmatrix} 4 & 1 \\ -3 & -2 \end{bmatrix}$, $C = \begin{bmatrix} -3 & 2 \\ -1 & 4 \end{bmatrix}$.

$A^2 = \begin{bmatrix} 2 & 1 \\ 0 & -2 \end{bmatrix}\begin{bmatrix} 2 & 1 \\ 0 & -2 \end{bmatrix}$

$= \begin{bmatrix} 4+0 & 2-2 \\ 0 & 0+4 \end{bmatrix} = \begin{bmatrix} 4 & 0 \\ 0 & 4 \end{bmatrix}$

$5B = 5\begin{bmatrix} 4 & 1 \\ -3 & -2 \end{bmatrix}$

$= \begin{bmatrix} 20 & 5 \\ -15 & -10 \end{bmatrix}$

$AC = \begin{bmatrix} 2 & 1 \\ 0 & -2 \end{bmatrix}\begin{bmatrix} -3 & 2 \\ -1 & 4 \end{bmatrix}$

$= \begin{bmatrix} -6-1 & 4+4 \\ 0+2 & 0-8 \end{bmatrix} = \begin{bmatrix} -7 & 8 \\ 2 & -8 \end{bmatrix}$

$\therefore \quad A^2 + AC - 5B = \begin{bmatrix} 4 & 0 \\ 0 & 4 \end{bmatrix} + \begin{bmatrix} -7 & 8 \\ 2 & -8 \end{bmatrix}$

$\qquad - \begin{bmatrix} 20 & 5 \\ -15 & -10 \end{bmatrix}$

$\Rightarrow \quad = \begin{bmatrix} 4-7-20 & 0+8-5 \\ 0+2+15 & 4-8+10 \end{bmatrix}$

$\Rightarrow A^2 + AC - 5B = \begin{bmatrix} -23 & 3 \\ 17 & 6 \end{bmatrix}$.

Q. 6. Let $A = \begin{bmatrix} 4 & -2 \\ 6 & -3 \end{bmatrix}$**,** $B = \begin{bmatrix} 0 & 2 \\ 1 & -1 \end{bmatrix}$ **and** $C = \begin{bmatrix} -2 & 3 \\ 1 & -1 \end{bmatrix}$**.**

Find $A^2 - A + BC$**.** [2006]

Ans. $A = \begin{bmatrix} 4 & -2 \\ 6 & -3 \end{bmatrix}$, $B = \begin{bmatrix} 0 & 2 \\ 1 & -1 \end{bmatrix}$ and $C = \begin{bmatrix} -2 & 3 \\ 1 & -1 \end{bmatrix}$

$\therefore \quad A^2 = \begin{bmatrix} 4 & -2 \\ 6 & -3 \end{bmatrix}\begin{bmatrix} 4 & -2 \\ 6 & -3 \end{bmatrix} = \begin{bmatrix} 16-12 & -8+6 \\ 24-18 & -12+9 \end{bmatrix}$

$= \begin{bmatrix} 4 & -2 \\ 6 & -3 \end{bmatrix}$

$BC = \begin{bmatrix} 0 & 2 \\ 1 & -1 \end{bmatrix}\begin{bmatrix} -2 & 3 \\ 1 & -1 \end{bmatrix} = \begin{bmatrix} 0+2 & 0-2 \\ -2-1 & 3+1 \end{bmatrix}$

$= \begin{bmatrix} 2 & -2 \\ -3 & 4 \end{bmatrix}$

Now $A^2 - A + BC = \begin{bmatrix} 4 & -2 \\ 6 & -3 \end{bmatrix} - \begin{bmatrix} 4 & -2 \\ 6 & -3 \end{bmatrix} + \begin{bmatrix} 2 & -2 \\ -3 & 4 \end{bmatrix}$

$\Rightarrow \quad = \begin{bmatrix} 0 & 0 \\ 0 & 0 \end{bmatrix} + \begin{bmatrix} 2 & -2 \\ -3 & 4 \end{bmatrix}$

$= \begin{bmatrix} 2 & -2 \\ -3 & 4 \end{bmatrix}$

 ## Short Answer Type Questions

Q. 1. If the 6th term of an A.P. is equal to four times its first term and the sum of first six terms is 75, find the first term and the common difference. **[2020]**

Marking Scheme

$t_6 = a + 5d = 4a \Rightarrow 3a = 5d \ldots \ldots .1$

$S_6 = \dfrac{6}{2} \{2a + 5d\} = 75 \Rightarrow 2a + 5d = 25 \ldots \ldots .2$

From 1 and 2
$2a + 3a = 25$
$\Rightarrow a = 5$
$d = 3$

Ans. Let the first term of an A.P. be a and the common difference be d.

$\because \qquad a_6 = 4a$ [Given]

$\Rightarrow \qquad a + 5d = 4a$

$\Rightarrow \qquad 5d = 3a$

$\therefore \qquad a = \dfrac{5d}{3}$ ...(i)

Also, $\qquad S_6 = 75$ [Given]

$\Rightarrow \dfrac{6}{2}[2a + (6-1)d] = 75$

$\Rightarrow 3\left[2 \times \dfrac{5d}{3} + 5d\right] = 75$ [Using (i)]

$\Rightarrow 3\left[\dfrac{10d + 15d}{3}\right] = 75$

$\Rightarrow \qquad 25d = 75$

$\therefore \qquad d = \dfrac{75}{25} = 3$

$\therefore \qquad a = \dfrac{5d}{3} = \dfrac{5 \times 3}{3} = 5$

Hence, $\qquad a = 5$ and $d = 3$

Q. 2. The sum of the first three terms of an Arithmetic Progression (A.P.) is 42 and the product of the first and third term is 52. Find the first term and the common difference. **[2019]**

Marking Scheme

Let the terms be $a - d, a, a + d$
$\therefore a - d + a + a - d = 42$
$3a = 42$
$\therefore a = 14$
$(a - d)(a + d) = 52$
$14^2 - d^2 = 52$
$d^2 = 196 - 52$
$d^2 = 144$
$\therefore d = \pm 12$
$d = 12,$ or -12

Ans. Let a and d be the first term and common difference.

By first condition,
$\qquad a_1 + a_2 + a_3 = 42$
$\Rightarrow \qquad a + a + d + a + 2d = 42$
$\Rightarrow \qquad 3a + 3d = 42$
$\Rightarrow \qquad 3(a + d) = 42$
$\Rightarrow \qquad a + d = \dfrac{42}{3} = 14$
$\Rightarrow \qquad d = 14 - a$ ...(i)

By second condition,
$\qquad a_1 \times a_3 = 52$
$\Rightarrow \qquad a \times (a + 2d) = 52$
$\Rightarrow \qquad a^2 + 2ad = 52$ ...(ii)

From equations (i) and (ii), we have
$\qquad a^2 + 2a(14 - a) = 52$
$\Rightarrow \qquad a^2 + 28a - 2a^2 = 52$
$\Rightarrow \qquad -a^2 + 28a = 52$
$\Rightarrow \qquad a^2 - 28a + 52 = 0$
$\Rightarrow \qquad a^2 - 26a - 2a + 52 = 0$
$\Rightarrow \qquad a(a - 26) - 2(a - 26) = 0$
$\Rightarrow \qquad (a - 26)(a - 2) = 0$
$\Rightarrow \qquad a - 26 = 0 \ \text{ or } a - 2 = 0$
$\Rightarrow \qquad a = 26 \text{ or } a = 2$
$\therefore \qquad a = 26 \text{ or } 2$

From equation (i),
when $a = 26$, $d = 14 - 26 = -12$
and when $a = 2$, $d = 14 - 2 = 12$

Q. 3. If $(k - 3)$, $(2k + 1)$ and $(4k + 3)$ are three consecutive terms of an A.P., find the value of k. **[2018]**

Ans. Given, $(k-3), (2k+1), (4k+3)$ are 3 consecutive terms of an A.P.

As the difference between the consecutive terms in A.P. are same, *i.e.*, $a_2 - a_1 = a_3 - a_2 = a_4 - a_3 = \ldots\ldots = d$.

$\therefore \qquad (2k+1) - (k-3) = (4k+3) - (2k+1)$

$\Rightarrow \qquad 2k+1-k+3 = 4k+3-2k-1$

$\Rightarrow \qquad k+4 = 2k+2$

$\Rightarrow \qquad k-2k = 2-4$

$\Rightarrow \qquad -k = -2$

$\Rightarrow \qquad k = 2$

 Long Answer Type Questions

Q. 1. In an Arithmetic Progression (A.P.) the fourth and sixth terms are 8 and 14 respectively. Find the:

    (i) first term

    (ii) common difference

    (iii) sum of the first 20 terms   **[2019]**

 Marking Scheme

Let a be the first term and d the common difference

$\therefore\ a + 3d = 8$ and $a + 5d = 14$

(i) Solving $a = -1$

(ii) $d = 3$

(iii) $S_n = \dfrac{n}{2}\{2 \times a + (n-1)d\}$

$S_{20} = \dfrac{20}{2}\{2 \times (-1) + (20-1)3\}$

$S_{20} = 10(-2 + 57)$

$S_{20} = 550$

Ans. Let a and d be the first term and common difference of the given A.P.

Then, $\quad a_4 = 8$ and $a_6 = 14$

$\Rightarrow \qquad a + 3d = 8 \qquad\qquad \ldots(i)$

and $\qquad a + 5d = 14 \qquad\qquad \ldots(ii)$

Subtracting equation (i) from (ii), we get

$\qquad\qquad 2d = 6$

$\Rightarrow \qquad\qquad d = 3$

Putting $d = 3$ in equation (i), we get

$\qquad\qquad a + 3 \times 3 = 8$

$\Rightarrow \qquad\qquad a = 8 - 9 = -1$

  (i) First term $(a) = -1$.

  (ii) Common difference $(d) = 3$.

  (iii) Sum of first 20 terms (S_{20})

$\because \qquad S_n = \dfrac{n}{2}[2a + (n-1)d]$

$\therefore \qquad S_{20} = \dfrac{20}{2}[2 \times (-1) + (20-1) \times 3]$

$\qquad\qquad = 10(-2 + 57)$

$\qquad\qquad = 550$

Q. 2. The 4th term of an A.P. is 22 and 15th term is 66. Find the first term and the common difference. Hence, find the sum of the series to 8 terms.   **[2018]**

Ans. Let a be the first term and d be the common difference of given A.P.

$\therefore \qquad T_4 = 22$ and $T_{15} = 66 \qquad$ (Given)

$\Rightarrow \qquad a + 3d = 22 \qquad\qquad \ldots(i)$

and $\qquad a + 14d = 66 \qquad\qquad \ldots(ii)$

Subtracting equation (i) from equation (ii), we get

$\qquad\qquad a + 14d = 66$

$\qquad\qquad a + 3d = 22$

$\qquad\qquad \underline{\quad-\quad-\quad-\quad}$

$\qquad\qquad\qquad 11d = 44$

$\Rightarrow \qquad\qquad d = 4$

From equation (i),

$\qquad\qquad a + 3 \times 4 = 22$

$\Rightarrow \qquad\qquad a = 22 - 12 = 10$

$\therefore \qquad\qquad a = 10, d = 4.$

Sum of series to 8 terms,

$\qquad S_8 = \dfrac{n}{2}[2a + (n-1)d]$

$\qquad\quad = \dfrac{8}{2}[2 \times 10 + (8-1)4]$

$\qquad\quad = 4(20 + 28)$

$\qquad\quad = 4 \times 48 = 192$

 ## Short Answer Type Questions

Q. 1. Find the value of 'p' if the lines, $5x - 3y + 2 = 0$ and $6x - py + 7 = 0$ are perpendicular to each other. Hence, find the equation of a line passing through $(-2, -1)$ and parallel to $6x - py + 7 = 0$. **[2020]**

 **Marking Scheme**

$5x - 3y + 2 = 0$ $\quad \therefore$ slope $= \dfrac{5}{3}$

$6x - py + 7 = 0$ $\quad \therefore$ slope $= \dfrac{6}{p}$

$\therefore$ they are right angles

$\therefore \dfrac{5}{3} \times \dfrac{6}{p} = -1$ $\qquad i.e.\ p = -10$

$6x - py + 7 = 0$

$6x + 10y + 7 = 0,$ $\qquad$ slope $= \dfrac{-6}{10} = \dfrac{-3}{5}$

Equation of line with slope $\dfrac{-3}{5}$ and passing through $(-2, -1)$ is

$y - (-1) = \dfrac{-3}{5}(x + 2)$

$5y + 5 = -3x - 6$

$3x + 5y + 11 = 0$

Ans. Given lines are,

$\qquad 5x - 3y + 2 = 0$

and $\quad 6x - py + 7 = 0$

Now, $5x - 3y + 2 = 0$

$\Rightarrow \qquad\qquad 3y = 5x + 2$

$\Rightarrow \qquad\qquad y = \dfrac{5}{3}x + \dfrac{2}{3}$

$\therefore \qquad$ Slope $(m_1) = \dfrac{5}{3}$

and $\quad 6x - py + 7 = 0$

$\Rightarrow \qquad\qquad py = 6x + 7$

$\Rightarrow \qquad\qquad y = \dfrac{6}{p}x + \dfrac{7}{p}$

$\therefore \qquad$ Slope $(m_2) = \dfrac{6}{p}$

Since, given lines are perpendicular to each other,

So, $\qquad m_1 \times m_2 = -1$

$\dfrac{5}{3} \times \dfrac{6}{p} = -1$

$\Rightarrow \qquad\qquad p = -10$

Now, slope $(m_2) = \dfrac{6}{p} = \dfrac{6}{-10} = -\dfrac{3}{5}$

$\because$ Slopes of parallel lines are equal.

So, slope of required line is $\left(-\dfrac{3}{5}\right)$.

Now, equation of required line is

$\dfrac{y - y_1}{x - x_1} = m$

$\Rightarrow \qquad \dfrac{y + 1}{x + 2} = -\dfrac{3}{5}$

$\Rightarrow \qquad 5y + 5 = -3x - 6$

$\Rightarrow 3x + 5y + 5 + 6 = 0$

$\Rightarrow \qquad 3x + 5y + 11 = 0$

Q. 2. M and N are two points on the X-axis and Y-axis respectively. $P(3, 2)$ divides the line segment MN in the ratio $2 : 3$.
Find:
(i) the coordinates of M and N
(ii) slope of the line MN. **[2019]**

Marking Scheme

Let M(x, 0) and N(0, 0) and N(0, y) be the two points on the X and Y axis respectively.

(i) P(3, 2) divides MN in the ratio 2 : 3

$\therefore\ 3 = \dfrac{2 \times 0 + 3 \times x}{2 + 3}$ $\qquad \therefore x = 5$

$2 = \dfrac{2 \times y + 3 \times 0}{2 + 3}$ $\qquad \therefore y = 5$

M(5, 0), N(0, 5)

(ii) Slope of MN : $\dfrac{5 - 0}{0 - 5} = -1$

Ans. Let $P(3, 2)$ divides the line segment joining $M(a, 0)$ and $N(0, b)$ in the ratio $2 : 3$.

Here, $\qquad x = 3,\ x_1 = a,\ x_2 = 0,\ m_1 = 2$

$\qquad\qquad y = 2,\ y_1 = 0,\ y_2 = b,\ m_2 = 3$

Now,
$$x = \frac{m_1 x_2 + m_2 x_1}{m_1 + m_2}$$

$$\Rightarrow \quad 3 = \frac{2 \times 0 + 3 \times a}{2 + 3}$$

$$\Rightarrow \quad 3 \times 5 = 0 + 3a$$

$$\Rightarrow \quad a = \frac{15}{3}$$

$$\Rightarrow \quad a = 5$$

and
$$y = \frac{m_1 y_2 + m_2 y_1}{m_1 + m_2}$$

$$\Rightarrow \quad 2 = \frac{2 \times b + 3 \times 0}{2 + 3}$$

$$\Rightarrow \quad 2 \times 5 = 2b + 0$$

$$\Rightarrow \quad b = \frac{10}{2}$$

$$\Rightarrow \quad b = 5$$

(i) The coordinates of $M = (a, 0) = (5, 0)$.

The coordinates of $N = (0, b) = (0, 5)$.

(ii) Slope of line $MN = \dfrac{y_2 - y_1}{x_2 - x_1} = \dfrac{5 - 0}{0 - 5} = -1$.

Q. 3. The vertices of a $\triangle ABC$ are $A\,(3, 8)$, $B\,(-1, 2)$ and $C(6, -6)$. Find:
(i) Slope of BC.
(ii) Equation of a line perpendicular to BC and passing through A. **[2019]**

 **Marking Scheme** ------------------------

$A(3, 8)$, $B(-1, 2)$ and $C(6, -6)$

(i) Slope of line BC $= \dfrac{-6 - 2}{6 + 1} = \dfrac{-8}{7}$

(ii) Slope of line perpendicular to BC is $\dfrac{7}{8}$; Line passing through $A(3, 8)$ Equation is :

$$y - 8 = \frac{7}{8}(x - 3)$$

$$8y - 64 = 7x - 21$$

$$7x - 8y + 43 = 0$$

Ans. Given, $A\,(3, 8)$, $B\,(-1, 2)$ and $C(6, -6)$

(i) Slope of BC $(m_1) = \dfrac{y_2 - y_1}{x_2 - x_1} = \dfrac{-6 - 2}{6 - (-1)}$

$$= \frac{-8}{7}$$

(ii) Slope of a line perpendicular to BC (m)

$$= -\frac{1}{m_1}$$

$$= -\frac{1}{-8/7} = \frac{7}{8}$$

Let the equation of the line perpendicular to BC and through A be

$$y - y_1 = m(x - x_1)$$

$$\Rightarrow \quad y - 8 = \frac{7}{8}(x - 3)$$

$$\Rightarrow \quad 8(y - 8) = 7(x - 3)$$

$$\Rightarrow \quad 8y - 64 = 7x - 21$$

$$\Rightarrow \quad 7x - 8y - 21 + 64 = 0$$

$$\Rightarrow \quad 7x - 8y + 43 = 0$$

which is the required equation.

Q. 4. If the straight lines $3x - 5y = 7$ and $4x + ay + 9 = 0$ are perpendicular to one another, find the value of a. **[2018]**

Ans. Given equation of lines are $3x - 5y = 7$ and $4x + ay + 9 = 0$

$$\Rightarrow \quad -5y = -3x + 7 \quad \text{and} \quad ay = -4x - 9$$

$$\Rightarrow \quad y = \frac{3}{5}x - \frac{7}{5} \quad \text{and} \quad y = -\frac{4}{a}x - \frac{9}{a}$$

Comparing both equations with $y = mx + c$, we get

$$m_1 = \frac{3}{5} \qquad m_2 = -\frac{4}{a}$$

The lines are perpendicular to each other,

$$\therefore \quad m_1 \times m_2 = -1$$

$$\Rightarrow \quad \frac{3}{5} \times \left(-\frac{4}{a}\right) = -1$$

$$\Rightarrow \quad -\frac{12}{5} = -a$$

$$\Rightarrow \quad a = 2\frac{2}{5}.$$

Q. 5. $A(-1, 3)$, $B(4, 2)$ and $C(3, -2)$ are the vertices of a triangle.
(i) Find the coordinates of the centroid G of the triangle.
(ii) Find the equation of the line through G and parallel to AC. **[2017]**

Ans. Given, $A(-1, 3)$, $B(4, 2)$, $C(3, -2)$.

(i) Coordinates of centroid

$$G = \left(\frac{x_1 + x_2 + x_3}{3}, \frac{y_1 + y_2 + y_3}{3}\right)$$

$$= \left(\frac{-1 + 4 + 3}{3}, \frac{3 + 2 - 2}{3}\right)$$

$$= \left(\frac{6}{3}, \frac{3}{3}\right) = (2, 1)$$

(ii) Slope of AC $= \dfrac{y_2 - y_1}{x_2 - x_1} = \dfrac{-2 - 3}{3 - (-1)} = \dfrac{-5}{4}$

Since, required line and the segment joining points A and C are parallel, so their slopes will be equal.

$\therefore$ Slope of the required line $(m) = \dfrac{-5}{4}$

Let the equation of the line through G, be

$$y - y_1 = m(x - x_1)$$

$$\Rightarrow \qquad y - 1 = -\dfrac{5}{4}(x - 2)$$

$$\Rightarrow \qquad 4y - 4 = -5x + 10$$

$$\Rightarrow \qquad 5x + 4y - 14 = 0$$

which is the required equation of line through G and parallel to AC.

Q. 6. The slope of a line joining **P (6, k)** and **Q (1– 3k, 3)** is $\dfrac{1}{2}$. Find:

(i) k

(ii) Midpoint of PQ, using the value of 'k' found in (i) **[2016]**

Ans. (i) Let P (6, k) be (x_1, y_1) and Q (1 – 3k, 3) be (x_2, y_2)

Given, slope of a line PQ is $\dfrac{1}{2}$

$$\dfrac{y_2 - y_1}{x_2 - x_1} = \dfrac{1}{2}$$

Here, $x_1 = 6$, $x_2 = 1 - 3k$, $y_1 = k$, $y_2 = 3$

$$\Rightarrow \qquad \dfrac{3 - k}{(1 - 3k) - 6} = \dfrac{1}{2}$$

$$\Rightarrow \qquad \dfrac{3 - k}{-5 - 3k} = \dfrac{1}{2}$$

$$\Rightarrow \qquad 2(3 - k) = -5 - 3k$$

$$\Rightarrow \qquad 6 - 2k = -5 - 3k$$

$$\Rightarrow \qquad k = -11$$

(ii) Coordinates P is (6, – 11) and Q is (34, 3)

Midpoint of P (6, – 11) and Q (34, 3).

$$\Rightarrow \qquad \left(\dfrac{6 + 34}{2}, \dfrac{-11 + 3}{2}\right) = (20, -4)$$

Q. 7. A line AB meets X-axis at A and Y-axis at B. P (4, –1) divides AB in the ratio 1 : 2.

(i) Find the coordinates of A and B.

(ii) Find the equation of the line through P and perpendicular to AB. **[2016]**

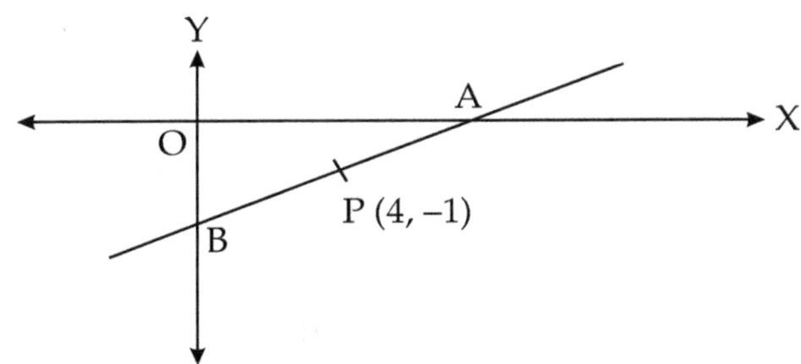

Ans. (i) Let the coordinates of A be $(x, 0)$ and B be $(0, y)$.

Given, P = (4, – 1) divides AB in the ratio 1 : 2.

Now, $\qquad x = \dfrac{m_1 x_2 + m_2 x_1}{m_1 + m_2}$

$$4 = \dfrac{1 \times 0 + 2 \times x}{1 + 2}$$

$$4 = \dfrac{2x}{3}$$

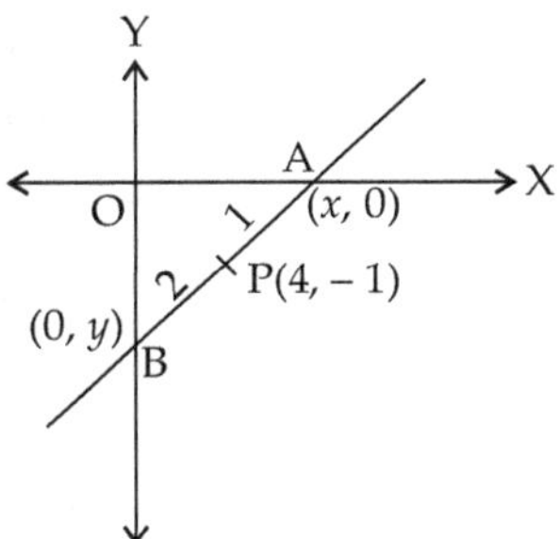

$\therefore \qquad\qquad x = 6$

and $\qquad y = \dfrac{m_1 y_2 + m_2 y_1}{m_1 + m_2}$

$$-1 = \dfrac{1 \times y + 2 \times 0}{1 + 2}$$

$$-1 = \dfrac{y}{3}$$

$\therefore \qquad\qquad y = -3$

$\therefore$ Coordinates of A are (6, 0) and coordinates of B are (0, – 3).

(ii) Slope of AB $= \dfrac{y_2 - y_1}{x_2 - x_1} = \dfrac{-3 - 0}{0 - 6} = \dfrac{-3}{-6} = \dfrac{1}{2}$

Now, slope of the line perpendicular to AB

$$= -\dfrac{1}{\text{slope of AB}}$$

$$= -\dfrac{1}{1/2} = -2$$

Equation of line, which passes through P (4, – 1) and $\perp$ to AB has slope –2 is

$$y - y_1 = m (x - x_1)$$

$$y - (-1) = -2 (x - 4)$$

$$y + 1 = -2x + 8$$

Hence, $\qquad 2x + y = 7$

Q. 8. Find the value of 'a' for which the following points A (a, 3), B (2, 1) and C (5, a) are collinear. Hence, find the equation of the line. **[2014]**

Ans. Equation of line passing through AC is

$$(y - y_1) = \dfrac{y_2 - y_1}{x_2 - x_1}(x - x_1)$$

Here, $x_2 = 0$, $y_1 = 3$, $x_2 = 5$, $y_2 = a$

$$\Rightarrow \quad (y-3)=\left(\frac{a-3}{5-a}\right)(x-a)$$

As if A, B and C are collinear then B will satisfy it, *i.e.*,

A (a, 3)   B (2, 1)   C (5, a)

$$(1-3)=\left(\frac{a-3}{5-a}\right)(2-a)$$

$$-2(5-a)=(a-3)(2-a)$$

$$-10+2a=2a-6-a^2+3a$$

$$a^2-3a-4=0$$

$$a^2-4a+a-4=0$$

$$a(a-4)+1(a-4)=0$$

$$(a-4)(a+1)=0$$

$$\Rightarrow \quad a=4 \text{ or } -1.$$

Thus, required equation of straight line is

When, $a=4$ | When, $a=-1$

$$(y-3)=\left(\frac{4-3}{5-4}\right)(x-4) \quad\Big|\quad (y-3)=\left(\frac{-1-3}{5+1}\right)(x+1)$$

$$y-3=\left(\frac{1}{1}\right)(x-4) \quad\Big|\quad (y-3)=\left(\frac{-4}{6}\right)(x+1)$$

$$x-y-1=0 \quad\Big|\quad y-3=\frac{-2}{3}(x+1)$$

$$\Big|\quad 3y-9=-2x-2$$

$$\Big|\quad 2x+3y-7=0$$

Q. 9. In $\triangle ABC$, A(3, 5), B(7, 8) and C(1, – 10). Find the equation of the median through A. **[2013]**

Ans. Given, A (3, 5), B (7, 8) and C (1, –10) are 3 co-ordinates of $\triangle$. Median is drawn from A at BC.

$$\text{Coordinates of } D=\left(\frac{7+1}{2},\frac{8-10}{2}\right)=(4,-1)$$

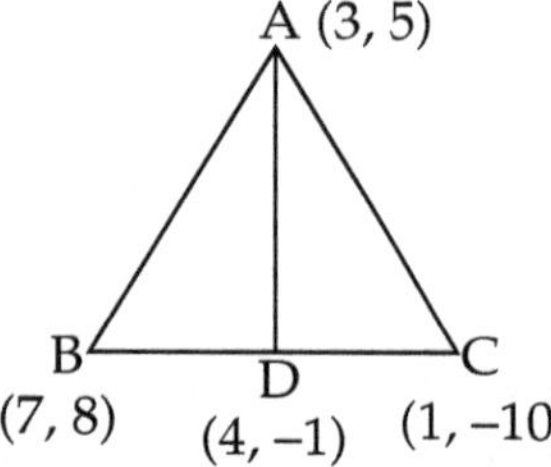

(Mid point formula)

Now, equation of AD {Median through A}

$$(y-y_1)=\frac{y_2-y_1}{x_2-x_1}(x-x_1)$$

$$x_1=3, \quad x_2=4$$

$$y_1=5, \quad y_2=-1$$

$$y-5=\frac{-1-5}{4-3}(x-3)$$

$$y-5=-6(x-3)$$

$$y-5=-6x+18$$

or $\quad 6x+y-23=0$

Q. 10. In the figure given below, the line segment AB meets X-axis at A and Y-axis at B. The point P (–3, 4) on AB divides it in the ratio 2 : 3. Find the coordinates of A and B. **[2013]**

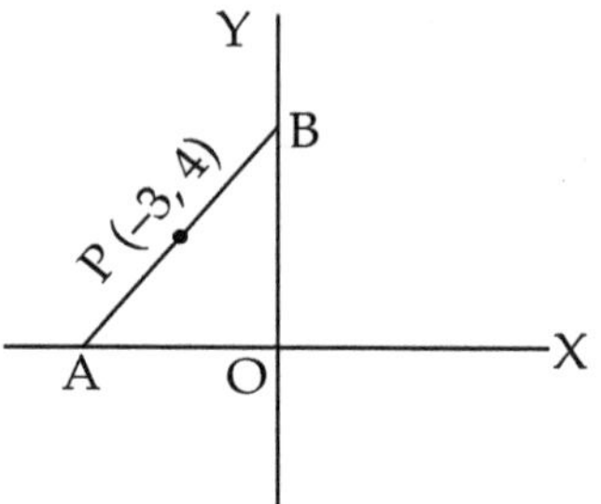

Ans. Given, AP : PB = 2 : 3

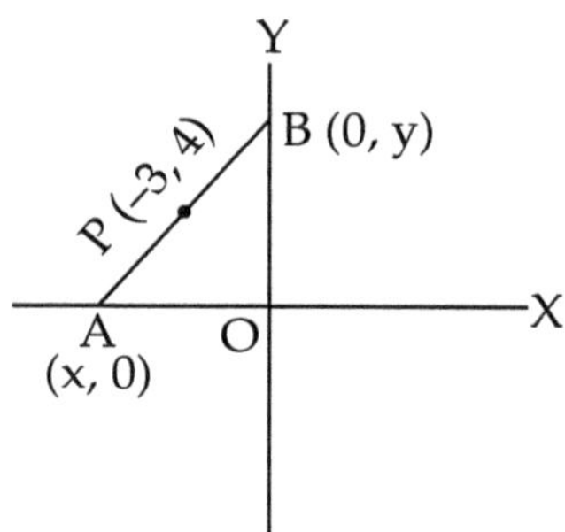

Let A $(x, 0)$ and B $(0, y)$

$\therefore$ By section formula,

$$\frac{m_1\times x_2+m_2 x_1}{m_1+m_2}=x$$

Here, $\quad m_1=2, m_2=3$

$$x_1=0, x_2=x$$

$$\Rightarrow \quad \frac{2\times 0+3\times x}{2+3}=-3$$

$$\Rightarrow \quad 3x=-15$$

$$x=-5$$

and $\quad y=\dfrac{m_1 y_2+m_2 y_1}{m_1+m_2}$

Here, $\quad m_1=2, m_2=3$

$$y_1=y, y_2=0$$

$$\Rightarrow \quad \frac{2\times y+3\times 0}{2+3}=4$$

$$\Rightarrow \quad 2y=20$$

$$\Rightarrow \quad y=10$$

$$A \; \underset{(x,\,0)}{\vdash} \overset{2}{\underline{\hspace{1.5cm}}} \underset{(-3,\,4)}{\overset{P}{|}} \overset{3}{\underline{\hspace{1.5cm}}} \underset{(0,\,y)}{\dashv} B$$

$\therefore$ Coordinates of

$$A \equiv (x, 0) \equiv (-5, 0)$$

and

$$B \equiv (0, y) \equiv (0, 10)$$

Q. 11. The line through A (–2, 3) and B (4, b) is perpendicular to the line $2x - 4y = 5$. Find the value of b. **[2012]**

Ans. Given, A (–2, 3), B (4, b)

$$\text{Slope of AB} = \frac{y_2 - y_1}{x_2 - x_1}$$

$$\Rightarrow \qquad m_1 = \frac{b - 3}{4 + 2}$$

$$\Rightarrow \qquad m_1 = \frac{b - 3}{6}$$

And $\qquad 2x - 4y = 5$

$$\Rightarrow \qquad 4y = 2x - 5$$

$$\Rightarrow \qquad y = \frac{1}{2}x - \frac{5}{4}$$

On comparing with $y = mx + c$

$$\text{Slope } (m_2) = \frac{1}{2}$$

Since both lines are perpendicular to each other

$$\therefore \qquad m_1 \times m_2 = -1$$

$$\frac{b - 3}{6} \times \frac{1}{2} = -1$$

$$b - 3 = -12$$

$$b = -9$$

Q. 12. The equation of a line is $3x + 4y - 7 = 0$. Find:
(i) the slope of the line.
(ii) the equation of a line perpendicular to the given line and passing through the intersection of the lines $x - y + 2 = 0$ and $3x + y - 10 = 0$. **[2010]**

Ans. Given, the equation of line is,

$$3x + 4y - 7 = 0 \qquad \qquad \text{...(i)}$$

$$\Rightarrow \qquad 4y = -3x + 7$$

$$\Rightarrow \qquad y = -\frac{3}{4}x + \frac{7}{4}$$

(i) Slope of the line, $m = -\dfrac{3}{\lambda}$

(ii) Equation of line perpendicular to the given line

The slope of the given line is $m_1 = \dfrac{-3}{4}$

$\because$ Two lines are perpendicular

$$m_1 \times m_2 = -1$$

$$-\frac{3}{4} \times m_2 = -1$$

$$m_2 = \frac{4}{3}$$

$\therefore$ Equation of line is

$$y = \frac{4}{3}x + \lambda \qquad \qquad \text{...(ii)}$$

Intersection of the lines $x - y + 2 = 0$ ...(iii)
and $\qquad 3x + y - 10 = 0 \qquad \qquad$ (iv)
Adding equation (iii) and (iv), we get

$$4x = 8$$

$$\Rightarrow \qquad x = 2$$

Put $x = 2$ in equation (iii), we get

$$2 - y + 2 = 0$$

$$\Rightarrow \qquad y = 4$$

$\therefore$ Point of intersection is (2, 4).

The line (ii) passes through points (2, 4)

$$\therefore \qquad 4 = \frac{4}{3} \times 2 + \lambda$$

$$\lambda = 4 - \frac{8}{3} = \frac{12 - 8}{3} = \frac{4}{3}$$

Hence, equation of line is

$$y = \frac{4}{3}x + \frac{4}{3}$$

$$\Rightarrow \qquad 3y = 4x + 4$$

$$\Rightarrow \qquad 4x - 3y + 4 = 0.$$

Q. 13. Find the value of p for which the lines $2x + 3y - 7 = 0$ and $4y - px - 12 = 0$ are perpendicular to each other. **[2009]**

Ans. Given lines are,

$$2x + 3y - 7 = 0 \quad \text{and} \quad 4y - px - 12 = 0$$

$$3y = -2x + 7 \qquad \qquad 4y = px + 12$$

$$y = -\frac{2}{3}x + \frac{7}{3} \qquad \qquad y = \frac{p}{4}x + 3$$

$\therefore$ slope of line $(m_1) = -\dfrac{2}{3}$

slope of line $(m_2) = \dfrac{p}{4}$

Lines are perpendicular,

$$\therefore \qquad \text{Product of slopes} = -1$$

$$\therefore \qquad -\frac{2}{3} \times \frac{p}{4} = -1$$

$$\Rightarrow \qquad p = 6$$

Q. 14. Find the equation of a line with x intercept = 5 and passing through the point (4, – 7). **[2009]**

Ans. Here, x - intercept $= 5$, $i.e., y = 0$

$\therefore$ Line passes through $(5, 0)$

Slope of the line passing through the points $(4, -7)$ and $(5, 0)$

$$= \frac{0-(-7)}{5-4} \qquad \left[m = \frac{y_2 - y_1}{x_2 - x_1} \right]$$

$$= 7$$

Equation of line passing through $(5, 0)$ and with slope 7 is

$$y - 0 = 7(x - 5) \qquad [y - y_1 = m(x - x_1)]$$
$$y = 7x - 35$$
$$7x - y - 35 = 0$$

Q. 15. The mid point of the line segment joining **(2a, 4) and (–2, 2b) is (1, 2a + 1). Find the value of a and b.** [2007]

Ans. Mid point of $(2a, 4)$ and $(-2, 2b)$ is $(1, 2a + 1)$

$$x = \frac{x_1 + x_2}{2} \qquad \bigg| \qquad y = \frac{y_1 + y_2}{2}$$

$$1 = \frac{2a - 2}{2} \qquad \bigg| \qquad 2a + 1 = \frac{4 + 2b}{2}$$

$$1 = a - 1 \qquad \bigg| \qquad 2 \times 2 + 1 = 2 + b$$

$$\therefore \quad a = 2 \qquad \bigg| \qquad 5 - 2 = b \qquad \therefore \quad b = 3$$

Hence, $a = 2, b = 3$.

Q. 16. Find the equation of the line parallel to the line **3x + 2y = 8 and passing through the point (0, 1).** [2007]

Ans. Given, Line $3x + 2y = 8$ and point $(0, 1)$.

For slope of line $\qquad 2y = -3x + 8$

or $\qquad\qquad\qquad y = -\frac{3}{2}x + \frac{8}{2}$

$\therefore \qquad\qquad\qquad \text{Slope} = -\frac{3}{2}$

Line is parallel to given straight line.

$\therefore \qquad$ Slope of this line $m = -\frac{3}{2}$

Equation of line through $(0, 1)$

$$y - y_1 = m(x - x_1)$$
$$y - 1 = -\frac{3}{2}(x - 0)$$
$$2y - 2 = -3x$$
$$3x + 2y = 2.$$

Q. 17. If the line joining the points A(4, – 5) and **B(4, 5) is divided by the point P such that** $\frac{AP}{AB} = \frac{2}{5}$**, find the co-ordinates of P.** [2007]

Ans. $A(4, -5), B(4, 5)$

Given $\qquad \dfrac{AP}{AB} = \dfrac{2}{5}$

$\therefore \qquad \dfrac{AP}{PB} = \dfrac{2}{3}$

Let coordinate of $P(x, y)$.

So $\qquad x = \dfrac{mx_2 + nx_1}{m + n}, \quad y = \dfrac{my_2 + ny_1}{m + n}$

$\qquad\qquad m = 2, n = 3$

$\qquad\qquad x_1 = 4, x_2 = 4$

$\qquad\qquad y_1 = -5, y_2 = 5$

$\therefore \qquad x = \dfrac{2 \times 4 + 3 \times 4}{2 + 3} = \dfrac{8 + 12}{5} = \dfrac{20}{5} = 4$

$\qquad y = \dfrac{2 \times 5 + 3 \times -5}{2 + 3} = \dfrac{10 - 15}{5} = \dfrac{-5}{5} = -1$

$\therefore$ Co-ordinates of P are $(4, -1)$.

Q. 18. If the lines $y = 3x + 7$ and $2y + px = 3$ are per- **pendicular to each other, find the value of p.** [2006]

Ans. $\qquad\qquad\qquad y = 3x + 7$

$\therefore \qquad$ Slope of line $m_1 = 3$

$\qquad\qquad\qquad 2y + px = 3$

$\qquad\qquad\qquad 2y = -px + 3$

$\qquad\qquad\qquad y = -\dfrac{p}{2}x + \dfrac{3}{2}$

$\therefore \qquad$ Slope of line $m_2 = \dfrac{-p}{2}$

Condition for perpendicular lines

$$m_1 \times m_2 = -1$$
$$3 \times -\frac{p}{2} = -1$$
$$\frac{-3p}{2} = -1$$
$$3p = 2 \Rightarrow p = \frac{2}{3}$$

Q. 19. Find the coordinates of the centroid of a **triangle whose vertices are:** **A (– 1, 3), B (1, – 1) and C (5, 1)** [2006]

Ans. If vertices $A(x_1, y_1), B(x_2, y_2)$ and $C(x_3, y_3)$ then centroid (x, y) is equal to

$$x = \frac{x_1 + x_2 + x_3}{3}$$
$$y = \frac{y_1 + y_2 + y_3}{3}$$

$\therefore \qquad x = \dfrac{-1 + 1 + 5}{3} = \dfrac{5}{3}$

$\qquad y = \dfrac{3 + (-1) + 1}{3} = 1$

$\therefore$ Centroid $\left(\dfrac{5}{3}, 1 \right)$

 **Long Answer Type Questions**

Q. 1. **In what ratio is the line joining P (5, 3) and Q (– 5, 3) divided by the y-axis ? Also find the coordinates of the point of intersection. [2020]**

Marking Scheme

Let P(0, y) divide the join of (5, 3) and (–5, 3) in the ratio $m : n$

$$x = \frac{mx_2 + nx_1}{m + n}$$

$$\Rightarrow 0 = \frac{m(-5) + n(5)}{m + n}$$

$$\Rightarrow -5m + 5n = 0 \Rightarrow 5m = 5n$$

$$\frac{m}{n} = 1$$

$$m : n = 1 : 1$$

$$\therefore y = \frac{3 + 3}{2} = 3$$

$$\therefore P(0, 3)$$

Ans. Given points are P(5, 3) and Q(– 5, 3)

Let the coordinates of the point where this line meets y-axis be A(0, y) and the ratio be $m : n$. Using section formula, we have

$$(x, y) = \left(\frac{mx_2 + nx_1}{m + n}, \frac{my_2 + ny_1}{m + n} \right)$$

$$\Rightarrow \qquad 0 = \frac{-5m + 5n}{m + n}$$

$$\Rightarrow \qquad 0 = -5m + 5n$$

$$\Rightarrow \qquad 5m = 5n$$

or $$m : n = 5 : 5 = 1 : 1$$

Now, $$y = \frac{m \times 3 + 3 \times n}{m + n}$$

$$= \frac{1 \times 3 + 1 \times 3}{1 + 1}$$

$$= \frac{3 + 3}{2}$$

$$= \frac{6}{2} = 3$$

Hence, the required ratio is 1 : 1 and the point of intersection is (0, 3).

Q. 2. **A(2, 5), B(–1, 2) and C(5, 8) are the vertices of a triangle ABC, 'M' is a point on AB such that AM : MB = 1 : 2. Find the coordinates of 'M'. Hence, find the equation of the line passing through the points C and M. [2018]**

Ans. Given, vertices of triangle are, A (2, 5), B (–1, 2), C (5, 8), AM : MB = 1 : 2.

$\because$ M is a point on AB.

Coordinates of M $= \left(\dfrac{m_1 x_2 + m_2 x_1}{m_1 + m_2}, \dfrac{m_1 y_2 + m_2 y_1}{m_1 + m_2} \right)$

Here, $m_1 : m_2 = 1 : 2, x_1 = 2, y_1 = 5, x_2 = -1, y_2 = 2$

$\therefore$ Coordinates of M

$$= \left(\frac{1 \times (-1) + 2 \times 2}{1 + 2}, \frac{1 \times 2 + 2 \times 5}{1 + 2} \right)$$

$$= \left(\frac{-1 + 4}{3}, \frac{12}{3} \right) = (1, 4)$$

The equation of line passing through C(5, 8) and M(1, 4) is

$$y - y_1 = \frac{y_2 - y_1}{x_2 - x_1}(x - x_1)$$

Here, $x_1 = 5, y_1 = 8, x_2 = 1, y_2 = 4$

$\therefore \qquad y - 8 = \dfrac{4 - 8}{1 - 5}(x - 5)$

$\Rightarrow \qquad y - 8 = \dfrac{-4}{-4}(x - 5)$

$\Rightarrow \qquad y - 8 = x - 5$

$\Rightarrow \qquad x - y + 3 = 0$

Q. 3. **P(1, –2) is a point on the line segment A(3, –6) and B(x, y) such that AP : PB is equal to 2 : 3. Find the coordinates of B. [2017]**

Ans. Given Co-ordinates are P (1, –2), A (3, –6), B (x, y), and AP : PB = 2 : 3

By section formula,

$$x = \frac{m_1 x_2 + m_2 x_1}{m_1 + m_2},$$

$$y = \frac{m_1 y_2 + m_2 y_1}{m_1 + m_2},$$

$\Rightarrow \quad 1 = \dfrac{2 \times x + 3 \times 3}{2 + 3},$ $\quad -2 = \dfrac{2 \times y + 3 \times (-6)}{2 + 3}$

$\Rightarrow \quad 5 = 2x + 9,$ $\qquad -10 = 2y - 18$

$\Rightarrow \quad 2x = 5 - 9,$ $\qquad 2y = -10 + 18$

$\Rightarrow \quad x = \dfrac{-4}{2},$ $\qquad y = \dfrac{8}{2}$

$\Rightarrow \quad x = -2,$ $\qquad y = 4$

The coordinates of B are (–2, 4)

Q. 4. Three vertices of a parallelogram ABCD taken in order are A (3, 6), B (5, 10) and C (3, 2) find:

(i) the coordinates of the fourth vertex D.

(iii) equation of side AB of the parallelogram ABCD. **[2015]**

Ans. (i) Let the coordinates of the fourth vertex of a parallelogram be D (x, y).

Since, diagonals of a parallelogram bisects each other

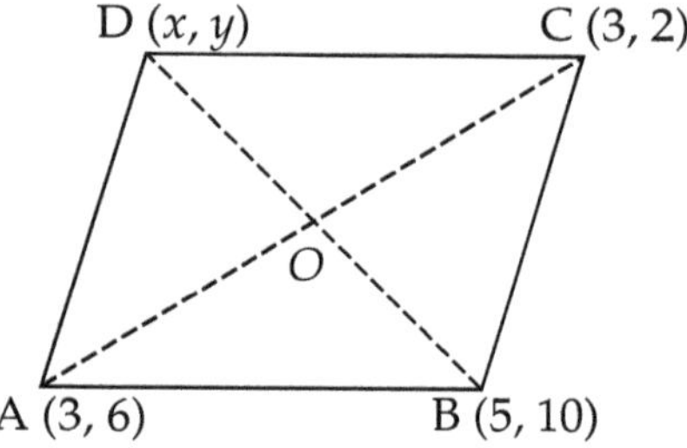

$\therefore$ Mid point of AC = Mid point of BD

$$\Rightarrow \left(\frac{3+3}{2}, \frac{6+2}{2}\right) = \left(\frac{5+x}{2}, \frac{10+y}{2}\right)$$

$$\Rightarrow (3,4) = \left(\frac{5+x}{2}, \frac{10+y}{2}\right)$$

$$\Rightarrow \frac{5+x}{2} = 3 \text{ and } \frac{10+y}{2} = 4$$

$$\Rightarrow 5+x = 6 \text{ and } 10+y = 8$$

$$\Rightarrow x = 1 \text{ and } y = -2$$

$\therefore$ The coordinates of the fourth vertex D is $(1, -2)$.

(iii) Here, A = (3, 6) and B (5, 10)

$$\text{i.e.,} \quad x_1 = 3, x_2 = 5$$
$$y_1 = 6, y_2 = 10,$$

$$\therefore \quad m = \frac{y_2 - y_1}{x_2 - x_1}$$
$$= \frac{10-6}{5-3} = 2$$

$\therefore$ Equation of side AB of the parallelogram ABCD is

$$y - y_1 = m (x - x_1)$$
$$\Rightarrow y - 6 = 2 (x - 3)$$
$$\Rightarrow y - 6 = 2x - 6$$
$$\Rightarrow y = 2x.$$

Q. 5. In the given figure ABC is a triangle and BC is parallel to the Y-axis. AB and AC intersects the y-axis at P and Q respectively.

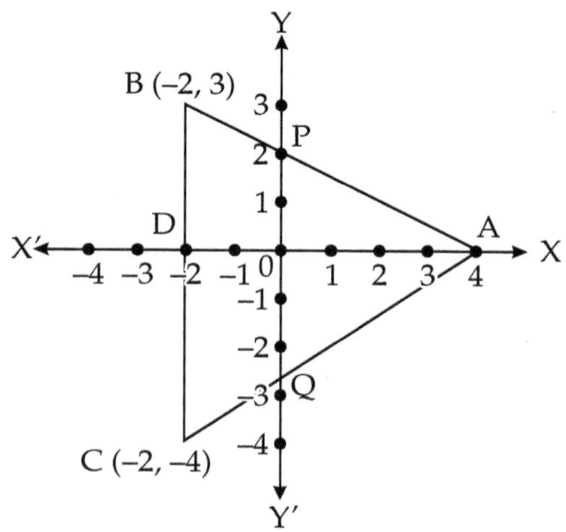

(i) Write the coordinates of A.

(ii) Find the ratio in which Q divides AC.

(iii) Find the equation of the line AC. **[2015]**

Ans. (i) Coordinates of A are (4, 0)

(ii) Let the required ratio be K : 1 and the point Q be $(0, y)$

We have, $$x = \frac{Kx_2 + x_1}{K+1}$$

$$\Rightarrow 0 = \frac{K(-2) + 4}{K+1}$$

$$\Rightarrow 0 = -2K + 4$$

$$\Rightarrow 2K = 4$$

$$\Rightarrow K = 2$$

$$\Rightarrow K:1 = 2:1$$

(iii) Equation of the line AC,

where, $$x_1 = 4, y_1 = 0$$
$$x_2 = -2, y_2 = -4$$

$$y - y_1 = \frac{y_2 - y_1}{x_2 - x_1}(x - x_1)$$

$$\Rightarrow y - 0 = \frac{-4-0}{-2-4}(x - 4)$$

$$\Rightarrow y = \frac{2}{3}(x - 4)$$

$$\Rightarrow 3y = 2x - 8$$

$$\Rightarrow 2x - 3y = 8$$

Q. 6. Calculate the ratio in which the line joining A (– 4, 2) and B (3, 6) is divided by point P $(x, 3)$. Also, find (i) x **[2014]**

Ans. Let the ratio in which P divides AB be $m_1 : m_2$.

$\therefore$

$$m_1 : m_2$$

A (– 4, 2)   P (x, 3)   B (3, 6)
(x_1, y_1) (x, y) (x_2, y_2)

y-coordinate of P

$$y = \frac{m_1 y_2 + m_2 y_1}{m_1 + m_2}$$

$$3 = \frac{6m_1 + 2m_2}{m_1 + m_2}$$

$$\Rightarrow \quad 3m_1 + 3m_2 = 6m_1 + 2m_2$$

$$\Rightarrow \quad 3m_1 - 6m_1 = 2m_2 - 3m_2$$

$$\Rightarrow \quad -3m_1 = -m_2$$

$$\Rightarrow \quad 3m_1 = m_2$$

$$\Rightarrow \quad \frac{m_1}{m_2} = \frac{1}{3}$$

$$\Rightarrow \quad m_1 : m_2 = 1 : 3$$

(i) Now,
$$x = \frac{m_1 x_2 + m_2 x_1}{m_1 + m_2}$$

$$x = \frac{1 \times 3 + 3(-4)}{1 + 3}$$

$$= \frac{3 - 12}{4} = -\frac{9}{4}$$

Q. 7. AB is a diameter of a circle with centre C = (– 2, 5). If A = (3, – 7). Find
(ii) the coordinates of B. [2013]

Ans. **(ii)** As 'C' is mid-point of AB

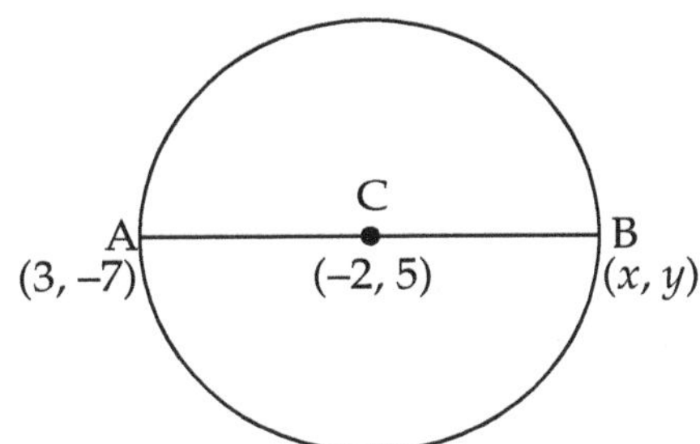

$$-2 = \frac{3 + x}{2} \quad \text{and} \quad 5 = \frac{-7 + y}{2}$$

[By mid-point formula]

or $-4 = 3 + x$ and $10 = -7 + y$

$$x = -7 \text{ and } y = 17$$

∴ Coordinates of B are (– 7, 17).

Q. 8. Given a line segment AB joining the points A (– 4, 6) and B (8, – 3). Find:
(i) the ratio in which AB is divided by the Y-axis.
(ii) find the coordinates of the point of intersection. [2012]

Ans.

$$\overset{k}{\underset{A\,(-4,\,6)}{\rule{3cm}{0.4pt}}} \overset{P}{\underset{P\,(x,\,y)}{\bullet}} \overset{1}{\underset{B\,(8,\,-3)}{\rule{3cm}{0.4pt}}}$$

Let the line segment AB is divided by Y-axis at point P in the ratio $k : 1$.

(i) Since P lies on Y-axis so $x = 0$, then coordinates of P are (0, y).

We have,
$$x = \frac{m_1 x_2 + m_2 x_1}{m_1 + m_2}$$

$$\Rightarrow \quad 0 = \frac{k \times 8 + 1 \times (-4)}{k + 1}$$

$$\Rightarrow \quad 8k - 4 = 0$$

$$\Rightarrow \quad 8k = 4$$

$$\Rightarrow \quad k = \frac{4}{8} = \frac{1}{2}$$

So, required ratio is 1 : 2

(ii) Now,
$$y = \frac{m_1 y_2 + m_2 y_1}{m_1 + m_2}$$

$$y = \frac{1 \times (-3) + 2 \times 6}{1 + 2}$$

$$= \frac{-3 + 12}{3} = 3$$

So, coordinates of point of intersection on Y axis are (0, 3).

Q. 9. The line through P (5, 3) intersects Y-axis at Q.

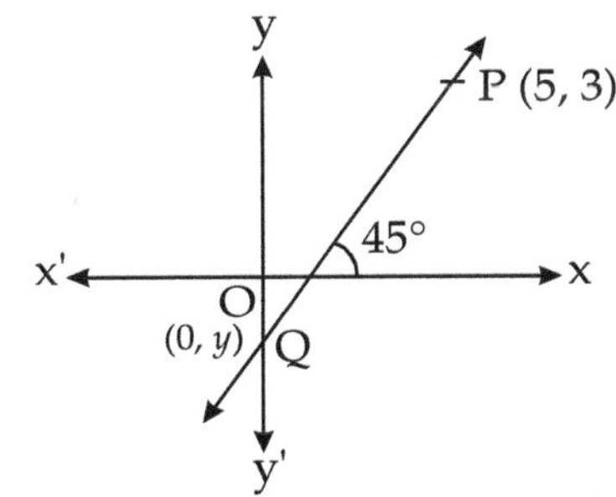

(i) Write the slope of the line.
(ii) Write the equation of the line.
(iii) Find the coordinates of Q. [2012]

Ans. **(i)** $m = \tan \theta = \tan 45°$

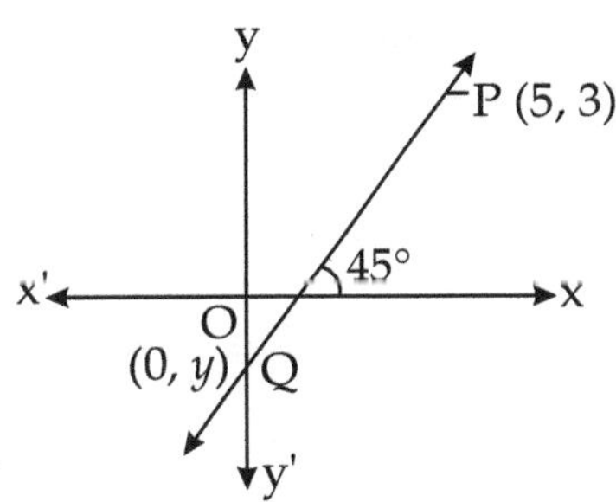

∴ Slope of the line
$$m = 1$$

(ii) Equation of line PQ,
where $x_1 = 5$, $y_1 = 3$ and $m = 1$

$$y - y_1 = m\,(x - x_1)$$

$$y - 3 = 1\,(x - 5)$$

$$y - 3 = x - 5$$

$$\Rightarrow \quad x - y - 2 = 0$$

(iii) Equation of line PQ is

$$x - y - 2 = 0$$

Put

$$x = 0$$

[Since, at Q coordinates are $(0, y)$]

$$-y - 2 = 0$$

$$\Rightarrow \qquad y = -2$$

So, coordinates of Q $(0, -2)$.

Q. 10. **ABCD is a parallelogram where A (x, y), B (5, 8), C (4, 7) and D (2, – 4). Find**
  (i) Coordinates of A
  (ii) Equation of diagonal BD. **[2011]**

Ans. Given, ABCD is a parallelogram, with A(x, y), B (5, 8), C (4, 7) and D (2, – 4)

(i) As diagonals of a parallelogram bisect each other.

∴ E is midpoint of BD as well as AC.

Coordinates of E are $= \left(\dfrac{x_1 + x_2}{2}, \dfrac{y_1 + y_2}{2} \right)$

$$= \left(\dfrac{5 + 2}{2}, \dfrac{8 - 4}{2} \right)$$

(Using coordinates of B and D)

$$= \left(\dfrac{7}{2}, 2 \right)$$

On comparing, $\dfrac{x + 4}{2} = \dfrac{7}{2}$ and $\dfrac{y + 7}{2} = 2$

(Using coordinates of A and C)

Coordinates of E are $= \left(\dfrac{x + 4}{2}, \dfrac{y + 7}{2} \right)$

$$\Rightarrow \qquad x = 3 \text{ and } y = -3$$

∴ Coordinates of A are $(3, -3)$.

(ii) Equation of diagonal BD,

$$y - y_1 = \dfrac{y_2 - y_1}{x_2 - x_1}(x - x_1)$$

$$\Rightarrow \qquad y - 8 = \dfrac{-4 - 8}{2 - 5}(x - 5)$$

$$\Rightarrow \qquad y - 8 = \dfrac{-12}{-3}(x - 5)$$

$$\Rightarrow \qquad y - 8 = 4(x - 5)$$

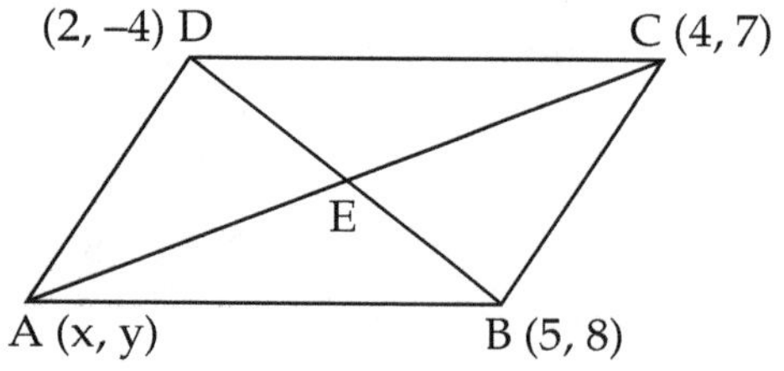

$$\Rightarrow \qquad y - 8 = 4x - 20$$

$$\Rightarrow \quad 4x - y - 12 = 0$$

Q. 11. **Given equation of line L_1 is $y = 4$.**
  (i) Write the slope of line L_2 if L_2 is the bisector of angle O.
  (ii) Write the coordinates of point P.
  (iii) Find the equation of L_2. **[2011]**

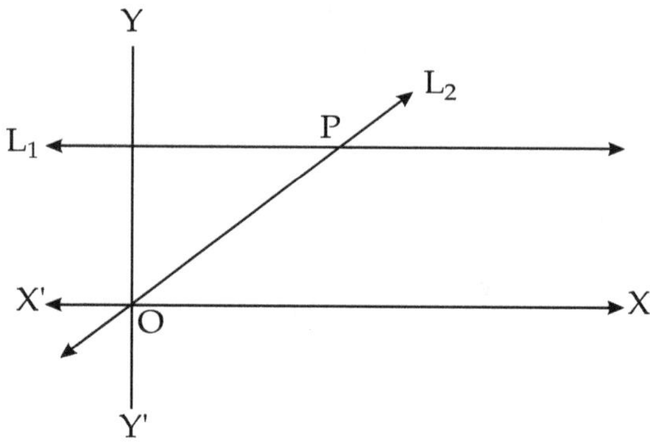

Ans. Equation of L_1 is $y = 4$ (given)
(i) As L_2 is bisector of $\angle$ O and $\angle$ O $= 90°$

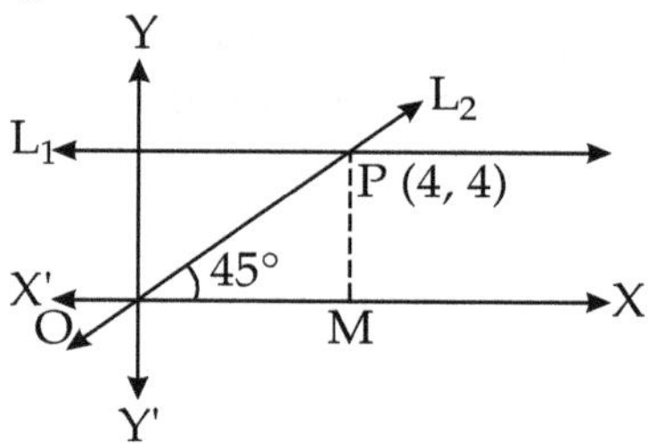

$\Rightarrow L_2$ is inclined at an angle of 45° with XX'
∴ Slope of $L_2 = m = \tan 45° = 1$

(ii) Slope of $L_2 = \dfrac{y_2 - y_1}{x_2 - x_1} = \dfrac{4 - 0}{x - 0}$

Where, $x_1 = 0, y_1 = 0$
$x_2 = x, y_2 = y$ (eq. of L_1 is $y = 4$)
Slope of $L_2 = 1$ (using (i))

$$\Rightarrow \qquad 1 = \dfrac{4}{x}$$

$$\Rightarrow \qquad x = 4$$

So, coordinates of P are (4, 4)
(iii) Equation of L_2

$$y - 4 = 1(x - 4)$$

$$\left(\begin{array}{l} L_2 \text{ pass through } (4, 4) \\ \text{and has slope } m = 1 \end{array} \right)$$

$$y - 4 = x - 4$$

or $\qquad x = y$

or $\qquad x - y = 0$

Q. 12. **ABC is a triangle and G (4, 3) is the centroid of the triangle. If A = (1, 3), B = (4, b) and C = (a, 1), find 'a' and 'b'.**
  Find the length of side BC.

Ans. Let A = $(1, 3) = (x_1, y_1)$, B = $(4, b) = (x_2, y_2)$,
C = $(a, 1) = (x_3, y_3)$ and G = $(4, 3) = (x, y)$

Coordinates of centroid

$$x = \frac{x_1 + x_2 + x_3}{3} \quad \text{and} \quad y = \frac{y_1 + y_2 + y_3}{3}$$

$$4 = \frac{1 + 4 + a}{3} \quad \text{and} \quad 3 = \frac{3 + b + 1}{3}$$

$$12 - 5 = a \quad \text{and} \quad 9 - 4 = b$$

$$a = 7 \quad \text{and} \quad b = 5 \qquad \textbf{Ans.}$$

Q. 13. A and B are two points on the X-axis and Y-axis, respectively. P (2, – 3) is the mid-point of AB. Find the:

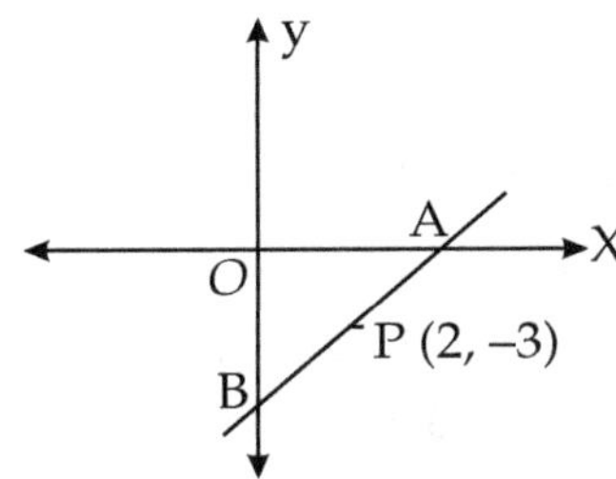

(i) Coordinates of A and B.
(ii) Slope of line AB.
(iii) Equation of line AB. [2010]

Ans. Let, the coordinates of A and B be $(x_1, 0)$ and $(0, y_2)$ where P $(2, - 3)$ is the mid-point of AB.

∴ By mid-point formula

$$a = \frac{x_1 + x_2}{2} \quad \text{and} \quad b = \frac{y_1 + y_2}{2}$$

$$\therefore \quad 2 = \frac{x_1 + 0}{2} \quad \text{and} \quad -3 = \frac{0 + y_2}{2}$$

$$\therefore \quad x_1 = 4 \quad \text{and} \quad y_2 = -6$$

(i) Coordinates of A are $(4, 0)$ and coordinates of B are $(0, -6)$

(ii) Let, slope of line AB be m

$$\text{Now,} \quad m = \frac{y_2 - y_1}{x_2 - x_1}$$

$$m = \frac{-6 - (-0)}{0 - 4}$$

$$= \frac{-6 + 0}{-4} = \frac{-6}{4}$$

$$m = \frac{3}{2}$$

(iii) Equation of line AB is

$$y - y_1 = m(x - x_1)$$

$$\Rightarrow \quad y - 0 = \frac{3}{2}(x - 4)$$

$$\Rightarrow \quad 2y = 3x - 12$$

Equation of line AB is
$$3x - 2y - 12 = 0$$

Q. 14. If A = (– 4, 3) and B = (8, – 6)
(i) Find the length of AB

(ii) In what ratio is the line joining AB, divided by the x-axis?

Ans. **(i)** A$(- 4, 3)$ and B$(8, - 6)$

$$AB = \sqrt{(x_2 - x_1)^2 + (y_2 - y_1)^2}$$

$$= \sqrt{(8 + 4)^2 + (-6 - 3)^2}$$

$$= \sqrt{144 + 81} = \sqrt{225} = 15 \text{ units}$$

(ii) The point on the x-axis has its y co-ordinate 0.

Let AB be divided by the point in the ratio $k : 1$.

$$\begin{array}{ccc} \text{A} & \xleftarrow{\quad k \quad} \quad \xrightarrow{\quad 1 \quad} & \text{B} \\ (-4, 3) & (x, 0) & (8, -6) \end{array}$$

$$\therefore \quad y = \frac{m_1 y_2 + m_2 y_1}{m_1 + m_2} = 0$$

$$\Rightarrow \quad \frac{k \times (-6) + 1(3)}{k + 1} = 0$$

$$-6k + 3 = 0$$

$$6k = 3$$

$$k = \frac{3}{6} = \frac{1}{2}$$

∴ Ratio is 1 : 2.

Q. 15. Points A and B have coordinates (7, –3) and (1, 9) respectively. Find
(i) the slope of AB.
(ii) the equation of the perpendicular bisector of the line segment AB.
(iii) the value of 'p' if (–2, p) lies on it. [2008]

Ans. **(i)** Here, given points are A $(7, -3)$ and B $(1, 9)$

$$\therefore \quad \text{slope of AB} = \frac{y_2 - y_1}{x_2 - x_1} = \frac{9 + 3}{1 - 7} = \frac{12}{-6} = -2$$

(ii) slope of ⊥ bisector $(m) = \frac{1}{2}$

$$\text{Mid point of AB} = \left(\frac{x_1 + x_2}{2}, \frac{y_1 + y_2}{2} \right)$$

$$= \left(\frac{7 + 1}{2}, \frac{-3 + 9}{2} \right) = (4, 3)$$

∴ Equation is
$$y - y_1 = m(x - x_1)$$

$$y - 3 = \frac{1}{2}(x - 4)$$

$$2y - 6 = x - 4$$

$$x - 2y + 2 = 0$$

(iii) $(- 2, p)$ lies on
∴
$\Rightarrow$

$$x - 2y + 2 = 0$$
$$-2 - 2p + 2 = 0$$
$$2p = 0$$
$$p = 0$$

Reflection

Long Answer Type Questions

Q. 1. Use graph paper for this question.

Take 1 cm = 1 unit on both x and y axes.

(i) Plot the following points on your graph sheets :

A (– 4, 0), B (–3, 2), C (0, 4), D (4, 1) and E (7, 3)

(ii) Reflect the points B, C, D and E on the x-axis and name them as B′, C′, D′ and E′ respectively.

(iii) Join the points A, B, C, D, E, E′, D′, C′, B′ and A in order.

(iv) Name the closed figure formed. **[2020]**

Marking Scheme

(i) Plotted the points A, B, C, D and E correctly.

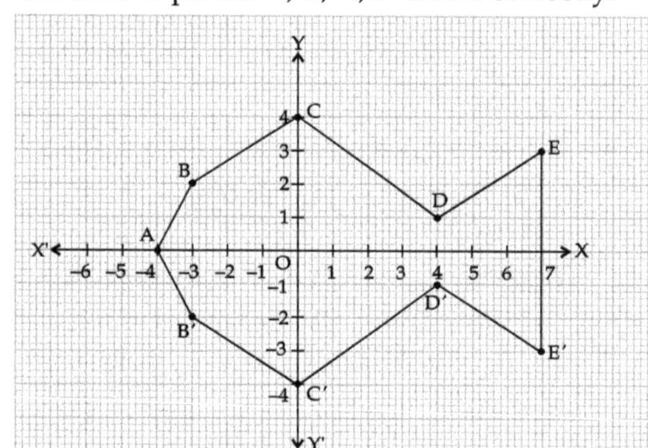

(ii) Reflected the points B, C, D and E on the x-axis and named them as B′, C′, D′ and E′ correctly.

(iii) Joined the points A, B, C, D, E, E′, D′, C′, B′ and A in order and completed the figure.

(iv) Nine-sided polygon or nonagon, polygon fish or kite.

Ans.

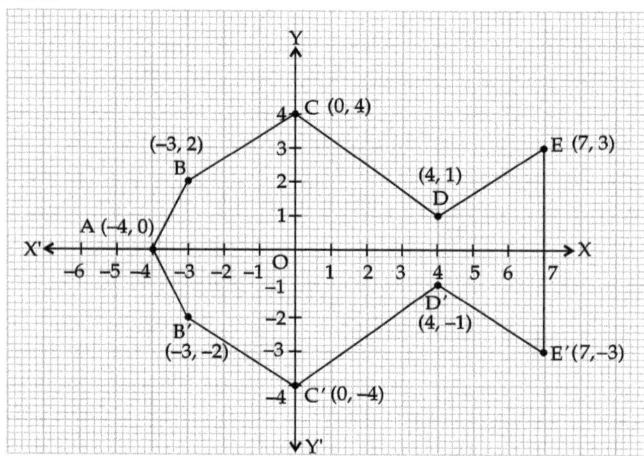

Note : Instead of 1 cm = 1 unit, we have used 0.5 cm = 1 unit on both axes.

(i), (ii) and **(iii)** see graph.

(iv) Nonagon (irregular), polygon fish

Q. 2. Use a graph sheet for this question

Take 1 cm = 1 unit along both X- and Y-axis.

(i) Plot the following points:

$A(0, 5)$, $B(3, 0)$, $C(1, 0)$ and $D(1, – 5)$

(ii) Reflect the points B, C and D on the Y axis and name them as $B′$, $C′$ and $D′$ respectively.

(iii) Write down the coordinates of $B′$, $C′$ and $D′$.

(iv) Join the points A, B, C, D, $D′$, $C′$, $B′$, A in order and give a name to the closed figure ABCDD′C′B′. **[2019]**

Marking Scheme

(i) The given points A(0, 5), B(3, 0), C(1, 0) and D(1, –5) are plotted on the graph Sheet

(ii) The points B, C and D are reflected on the y-axis as B′, C′ and D′ respectively.

(iii) $B(3, 0) \xrightarrow{y-axis} B'(-3, 0)$ Plotting A, B, C, D

$C(1, 0) \xrightarrow{y-axis} C'(1, 0)$ Reflected points B′, C′, D′

$D(1, – 5) \xrightarrow{y-axis} D'(-1, – 5)$

(iv) Arrow Head/Heptagon (or Septagon)

Ans. **(i)** The given points A (0, 5), B (3, 0), C (1, 0) and D (1, – 5) are plotted on the graph.

(ii) The points B, C and D are reflected on the Y-axis as B', C' and D' respectively.

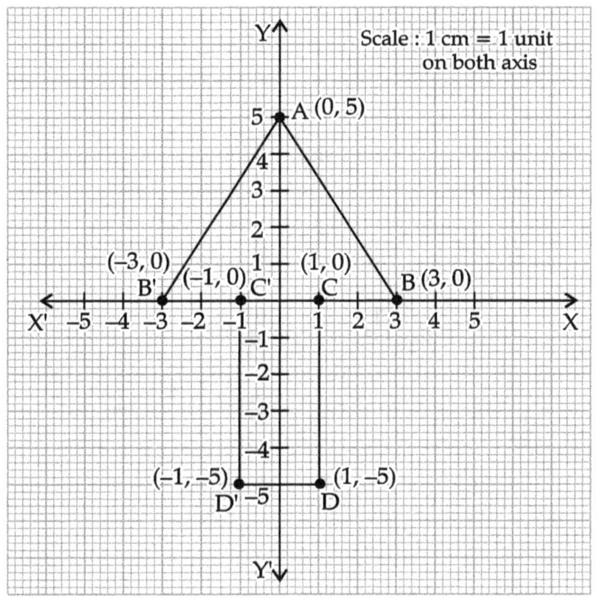

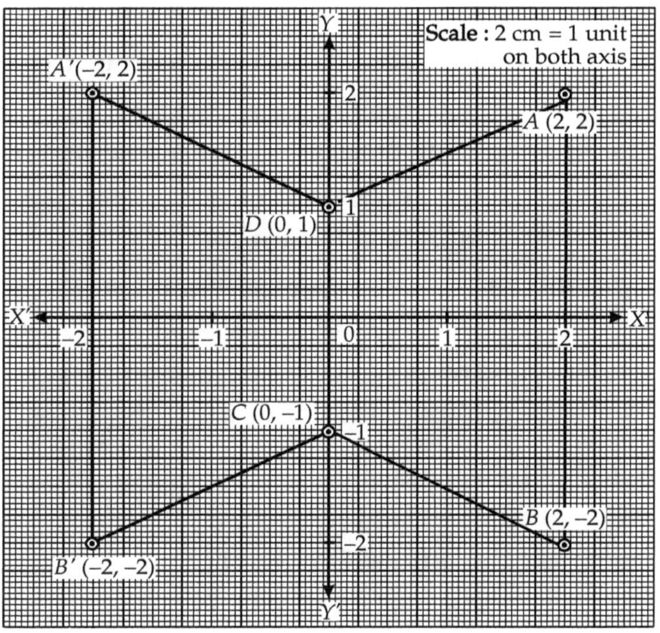

(iii) The coordinates of

$$B' = (-3, 0), \qquad C' = (-1, 0),$$

and $D' = (-1, -5)$

(iv) The name of the closed figure $ABCDD'C'B'$ is arrow head or heptagon.

Q. 3. Use graph paper for this question (Take 2 cm = 1 unit along both X and Y axis). ABCD is a quadrilateral whose vertices are A(2, 2), B (2, – 2), C(0, – 1) and D(0, 1).

(i) Reflect quadrilateral ABCD on the Y-axis and name it as A′B′CD.

(ii) Write down the coordinates of A′ and B′.

(iii) Name two points which are invariant under the above reflection.

(iv) Name the polygon A′B′CD. [2018]

Ans. **(i)** Reflected quadrilateral A′B′CD is shown in graph.

(ii) Coordinates of A′ = (– 2, 2)

Coordinates of B′ = (– 2, – 2)

(iii) Two invariant points are C(0, – 1) and D (0, 1)

(iv) A′B′CD is an isosceles trapezium.

Q. 4. Use graph paper for this question.

(Take 2 cm = 1 unit along both X and Y axis.)

Plot the points O(0, 0), A(–4, 4), B(–3, 0) and C(0, –3)

(i) Reflect points A and B on the Y-axis and name them A′ and B′ respectively. Write down their coordinates.

(ii) Name the figure OABCB′A′. [2016]

Ans. **(i)** Coordinates of A′ = (4, 4)

Coordinates of B′ = (3, 0)

(ii) Irregular Hexagon or Concave Irregon

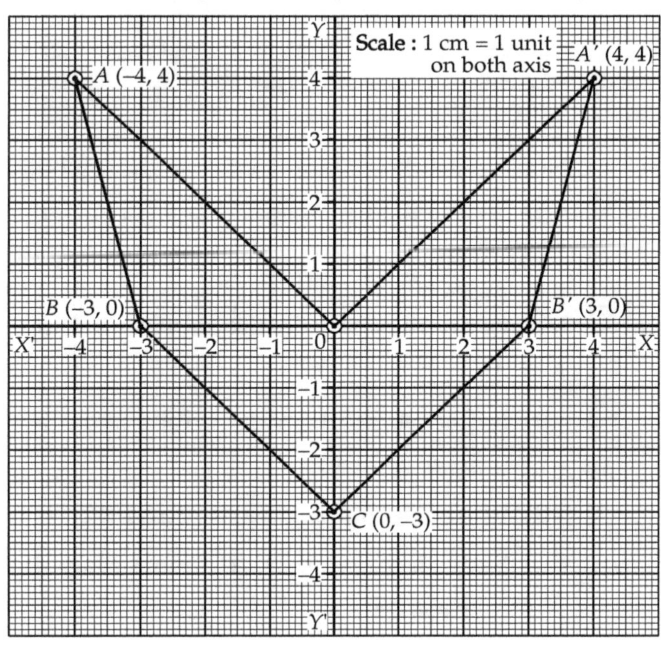

Q. 5. Use graph paper to answer the following questions. (Take 2 cm = 1 unit on both axis).

    (i) Plot the points A (–4, 2) and B (2, 4).

    (ii) A′ is the image of A when reflected in the Y-axis. Plot it on the graph paper and write the coordinates of A′.

    (iii) B′ is the image of B when reflected in the line AA′. Write the coordinates of B′.

    (iv) Write the geometric name of the figure ABA′B′. **[2014]**

Ans. (i) On the graph.

    (ii) Coordinates of A′ = (4, 2).

    (iii) Coordinates of B′ = (2, 0).

    (iv) Geometric name of figure ABA′B′ is Kite.

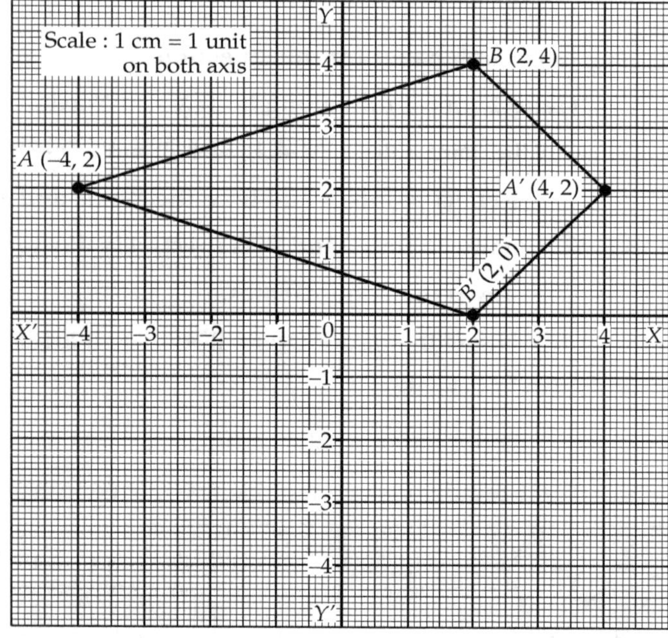

Note: Instead of taking 2 cm = 1 unit on both axis, we have taken 1 cm = 1 unit on both the axis.

Q. 6. Using a graph paper, plot the points A (6, 4) and B (0, 4).

    (i) Reflect A and B in the origin to get the images A′ and B′.

    (ii) Write the coordinates of A′ and B′.

    (iii) State the geometrical name for the figure ABA′B′.

    (iv) Find its perimeter. **[2013]**

Ans. (i)

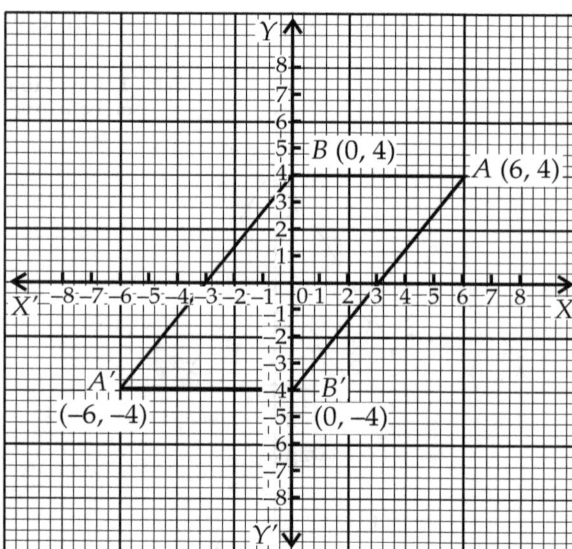

    (ii) Coordinates of A′ (–6, –4) and B′ (0, –4).

    (iii) ABA′B′ is a parallelogram.

    (iv) From the figure, AB = 6, BB′ = 8, A′B′ = 6.

In right angled $\triangle$ABB′,

$$(AB')^2 = (AB)^2 + (BB')^2$$

$$= 6^2 + 8^2 = 100$$

$\therefore$ AB′ = 10 = A′B

(ABA′B′ is a parallelogram)

$\therefore$ Perimeter of ABA′B′

$$= AB + BA' + A'B' + AB'$$

$$= 6 + 10 + 6 + 10$$

$$= 32 \text{ units}$$

Q. 7. Using graph paper and taking 1 cm = 1 unit along both X-axis and Y-axis.

    (i) Plot the points A (–4, 4) and B (2, 2).

    (ii) Reflect A and B in the origin to get the images A′ and B′ respectively.

    (iii) Write down the coordinates of A′ and B′.

    (iv) Give the geometrical name for the figure ABA′B′. **[2012]**

Ans. (i), (ii) on graph

    (iii) A′ (4, –4)

        B′ (–2, –2)

    (iv) Rhombus

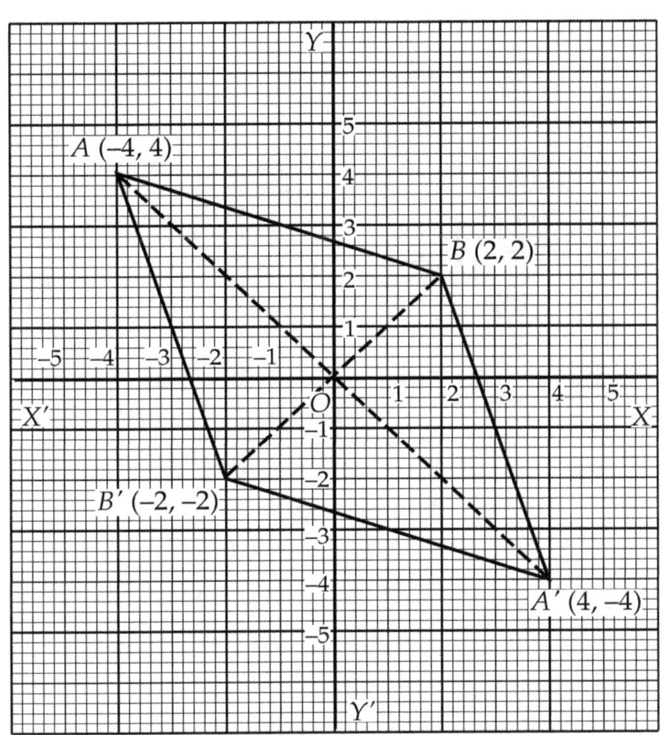

Q. 8. (Use graph paper for this question)

A(0, 3), B(3, –2) and O(0, 0) are the vertices of triangle ABO.

(i) Plot the triangle on a graph sheet taking 2 cm = 1 unit on both the axes.

(ii) Plot D the reflection of B in the Y–axis, and write its co-ordinates.

(iii) Give the geometrical name of the figure ABOD. [2010]

Ans. (i) Δ AOB is shown in the graph.

(ii) Coordinates of D are (–3, –2)

(iii) The geometrical name of the figure ABOD is Arrow Head.

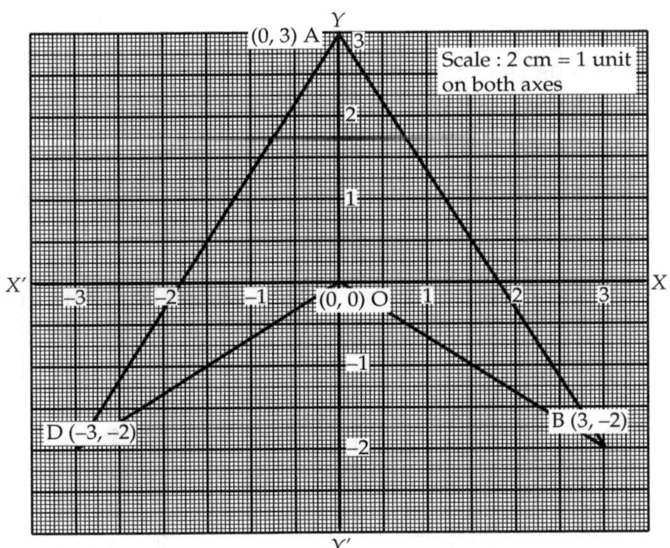

Q. 9. Use graph paper to answer this question:

(i) Plot the points A(4, 6) and B(1, 2).

(ii) A′ is the image of A when reflected in X-axis.

(iii) B′ is the image of B when B is reflected in the line AA′.

(iv) Give the geometrical name for the figure AB A′B′. [2009]

Ans. Take 1 cm = 1 unit on both axis

(i) Plot the point A(4, 6) and B(1, 2)

(ii) Plot A′(4, –6) as the image of A in the x-axis

(iii) Plot B′(7, 2) as the image of B in the line AA′.

(iv) Geometrical name for the figure ABA′B′ is Kite.

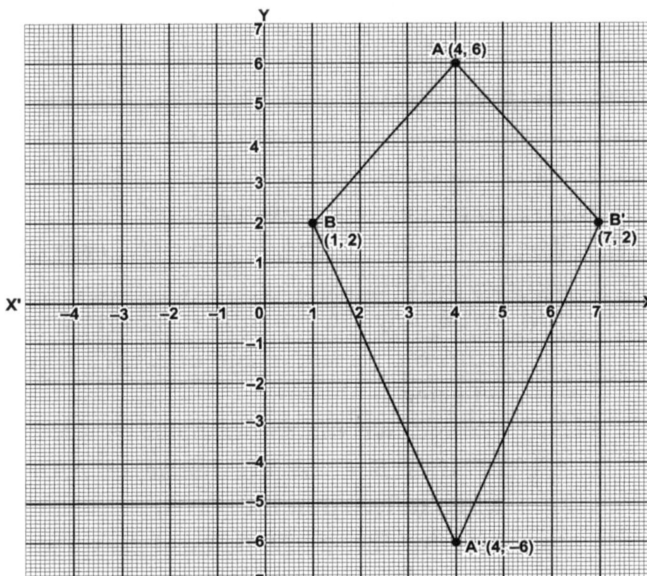

Q. 10. Use a graph paper for this question.

(i) The point $P(2, -4)$ is reflected about the line $x = 0$ to get the image Q. Find the co-ordinates of Q.

(ii) Point Q is reflected about the line $y = 0$ to get the image R. Find the co-ordinates of R.

(iii) Name the figure PQR.

(iv) Find the area of figure PQR. [2007]

Ans. (i) $P(2, -4)$ is reflected in ($x = 0$) y-axis to get Q-image.

$$P(2, -4) \xrightarrow{M_y} Q(-2, -4)$$

(ii) $Q(-2, -4)$ is reflected in ($y = 0$) x-axis and to get R-image

$$Q(-2, -4) \xrightarrow{M_x} R(-2, 4)$$

(iii) The figure PQR is right angle triangle as shown below:

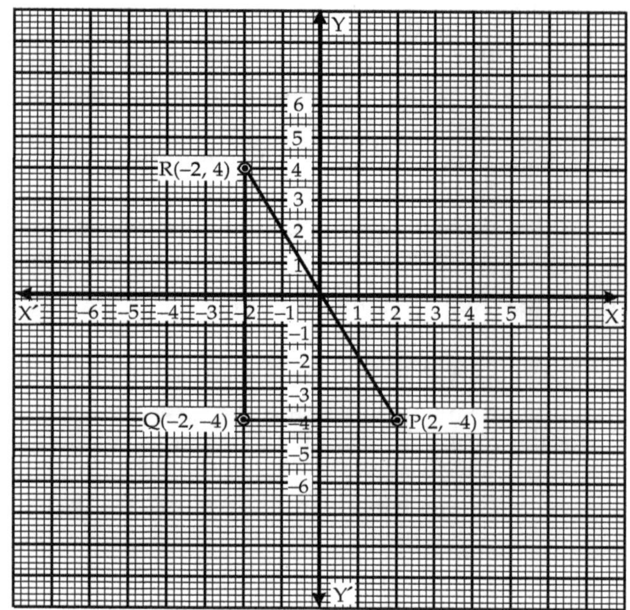

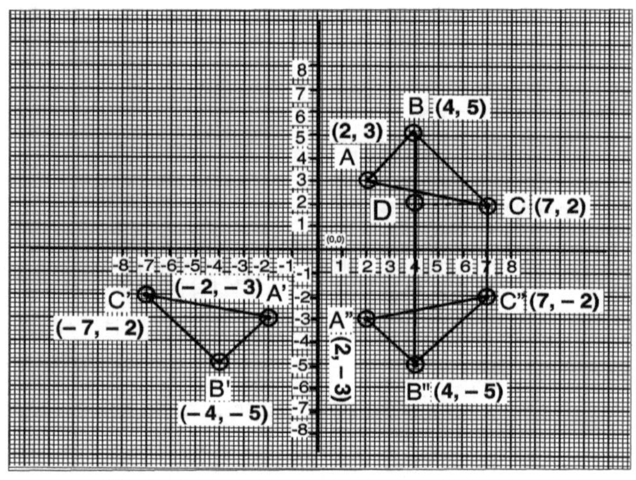

(i) Reflection in origin

$$(x,y)\xrightarrow{\text{M}_0} = (-x,-y)$$

$$\therefore \qquad A(2,3)\xrightarrow{\text{M}_0} = A'(-2,-3)$$

$$B(4,5)\xrightarrow{\text{M}_0} = B'(-4,-5)$$

$$C(7,2)\xrightarrow{\text{M}_0} = C'(-7,-2)$$

(ii) Now A, B, C is reflected in X axis.

Reflection in X axis

$$(x,y)\xrightarrow{\text{M}_x} = (x,-y)$$

$$\therefore \qquad A(2,3)\xrightarrow{\text{M}_x} = A''(2,-3)$$

$$B(4,5)\xrightarrow{\text{M}_x} = B''(4,-5)$$

$$C(7,2)\xrightarrow{\text{M}_x} = C''(7,-2)$$

(iii) $BCC''B''$ is an isosceles trapezium.

$$\text{Area of Trapezium} = \frac{1}{2}(CC''+BB'')\times CD$$

$$= \frac{1}{2}(4+10)\times 3$$

$$= \frac{1}{2}\times 14\times 3 = 21 \text{ sq. unit}$$

(iv) Area of $\Delta PQR = \dfrac{1}{2}\times PQ\times QR = \dfrac{1}{2}\times 4\times 8$

$$= 16 \text{ sq. unit.}$$

Q. 11. **Use graph paper for this question.**
The points $A(2, 3)$, $B(4, 5)$ **and** $C(7, 2)$ **are the vertices of** ΔABC**.**

    (i) Write down the coordinates of A', B', C' **if** $\Delta A'B'C'$ **is the image of** ΔABC, **when reflected in the origin.**

    (ii) Write down the co-ordinates of A'', B'', C'' **if** $A''B''C''$ **is the image of** ΔABC, **when reflected in the** *x***-axis.**

    (iii) Mention the special name of the quadrilateral $BCC''B''$ **and find its area.** [2006]

Ans. The point $A(2, 3)$, $B(4, 5)$ and $C(7, 2)$.

Long Answer Type Questions-I

Q. 1. **Use a graph paper for this question (Take 2 cm = 1 unit on both** *X* **and** *Y* **axis)**

    (i) Plot the following points :

        A(0, 4), B(2, 3), C(1, 1) and D(2, 0)

    (ii) Reflect points B, C, D on the Y-axis and write down their coordinates. Name the images as B′, C′, D′ respectively. [2017]

    (iii) Join the points A, B, C, D, D′, C′, B′ and A in order, so as to form a closed figure.

Ans. **(i)** On graph : A(0, 4), B(2, 3), C(1, 1), D(2, 0)

    (ii) B′(–2, 3), C′(–1, 1), D′(–2, 0)

(iii)

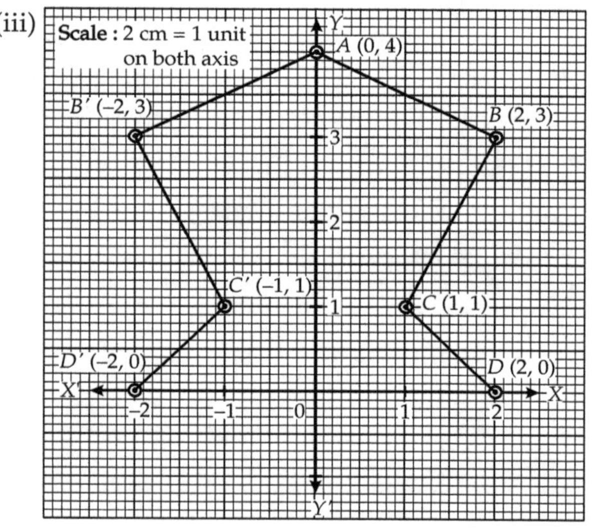

Q. 2. Use a graph paper for this question take 1 cm = 1 unit along both the X and Y axis:
  (i) **Plot the points A(0, 5), B(2, 5), C(5, 2), D(5, –2), E(2, –5) and F(0, –5).**
  (ii) **Reflect the points B, C, D and E on the Y-axis and name them respectively as B′, C′, D′ and E′.**
  (iii) **Write the coordinates of B′, C′, D′ and E′.**
  (iv) **Name the figure formed by BCDEE′D′C′B′.** [2015]

Ans. (i) Plot the given points on the graph as shown below:

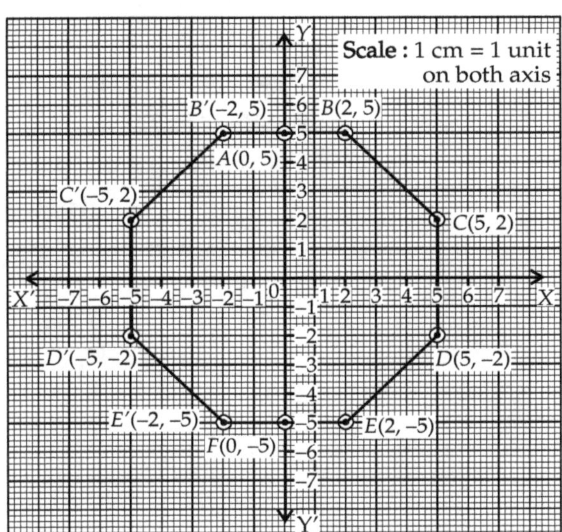

(ii) and (iii)

Reflection of B(2, 5) on the Y-axis = (–2 , 5) *i.e.,* B′

Reflection of C(5, 2) on the Y-axis = (–5 , 2) *i.e.,* C′

Reflection of D(5, –2) on the Y-axis = (–5, –2) *i.e.,* D′

Reflection of E(2, –5) on the Y-axis = (–2, –5) *i.e.,* E′

(iv) Figure formed by BCDEE′D′C′B′ is regular Octagon.

Q. 3. Use a graph paper to answer the following questions. (Take 1 cm = 1 unit on both axes):
  (i) **Plot A (4, 4), B (4, –6) and C (8, 0), the vertices of a triangle ABC.**
  (ii) **Reflect ABC on the Y-axis and name it as A′B′C′.**
  (iii) **Write the coordinates of the images A′, B′ and C′.**
  (iv) **Give a geometrical name for the figure AA′C′B′BC.** [2011]

Ans. (i) and, (ii) see the given graph.
(iii) A′ (–4, 4), B′ (–4, –6), C′ (–8, 0)
(iv) AA′ C′ B′ BC is a hexagon.

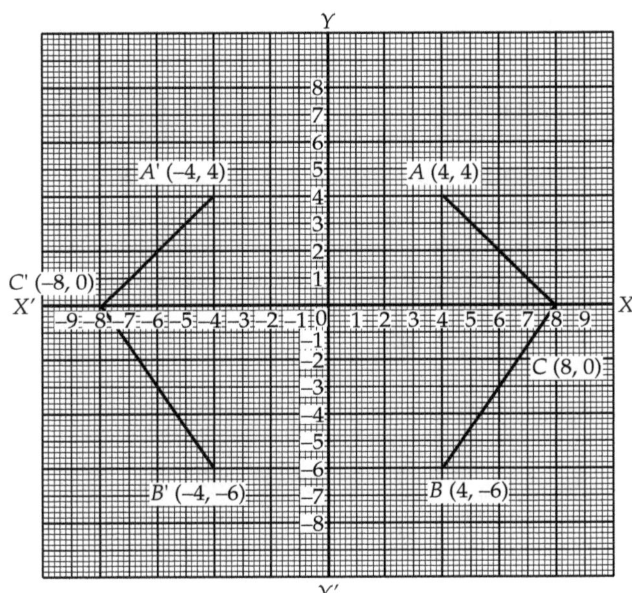

Q. 4. Use a graph paper for this question (Take 1 cm = 1 unit on both the axes).

Plot the points A (–2, 0), B (4, 0), C (1, 4) and D (–2, 4).

  (i) **Draw the line of symmetry of △ABC. Name it L₁.**
  (ii) **Point D is reflected about the Line L₁ to get the image E. Write the coordinates of E.**
  (iii) **Name the figure ABED.** [2008]

Ans. (i)

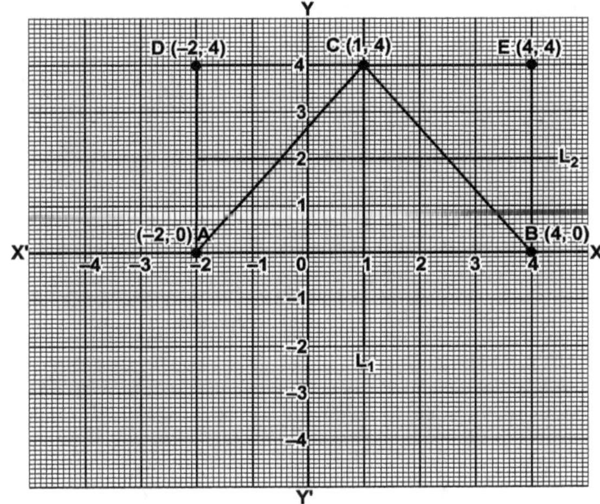

(ii) Co-ordinates of E (4, 4)
(iii) Rectangle

12   Similarity

Short Answer Type Questions

Q. 1. In the given figure AB = 9 cm, PA = 7.5 cm and PC = 5 cm. Chords AD and BC intersect at P.
(i) Prove that ΔPAB ~ ΔPCD
(ii) Find the length of CD.   **[2020]**

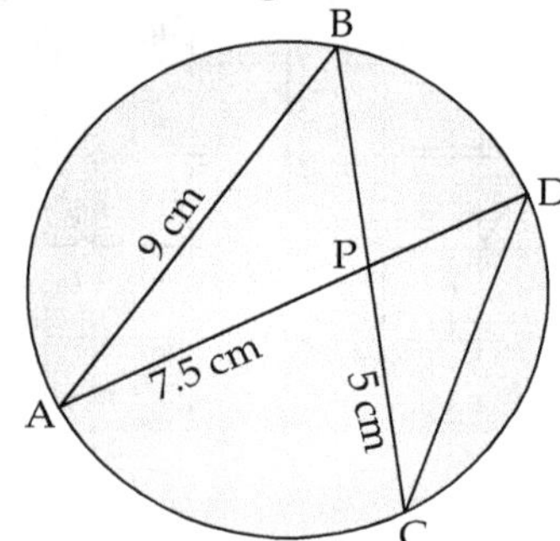

Marking Scheme

(i) In ΔPAB and ΔPCD

   $\angle$B = $\angle$D (angles in the same segment are equal)

   $\angle$APB = $\angle$CPD (vertically opposite angles)

   $\angle$PAB = $\angle$PCD (angles in the same segment are equal)

   $\therefore$ ΔPAB ~ ΔPCD (AAA)

(ii) Since the 2 triangles are ~

$\therefore \dfrac{AB}{CD} = \dfrac{PA}{PC} = \dfrac{PB}{PD}$

$\therefore \dfrac{9}{CD} = \dfrac{7.5}{5} = \dfrac{PB}{2.5}$

$\therefore CD = \dfrac{9 \times 5}{7.5}$

CD = 6 cm

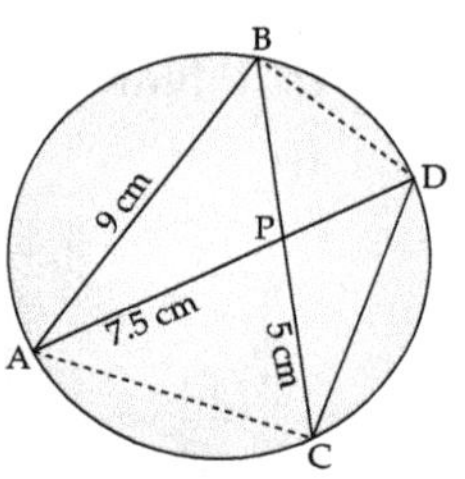

Ans. Given : AB = 9 cm, PA = 7.5 cm and PC = 5 cm

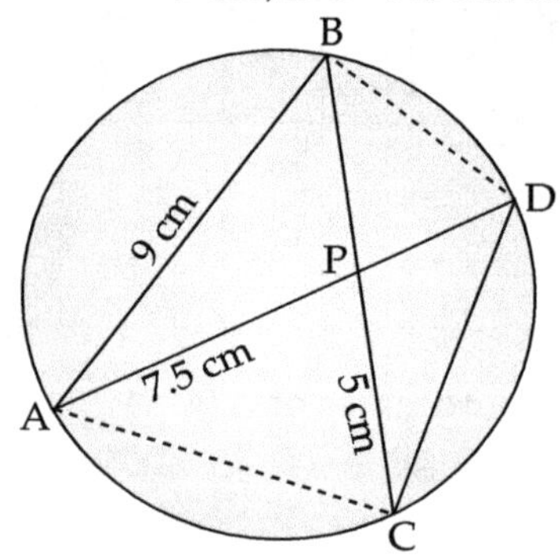

(i) In ΔPAB and ΔPCD,

    $\angle$ABC = $\angle$ADC

        [Angles made by same arc AC]

    $\angle$BAD = $\angle$BCD

        [Angles made by same arc BD]

  $\therefore$ ΔPAB ~ ΔPCD

        [By AA similarity axiom]

        Hence Proved.

(ii) $\because$ Ratio of corresponding sides of similar triangles is equal.

$\therefore \qquad \dfrac{AB}{CD} = \dfrac{PA}{PC} = \dfrac{PB}{PD}$

$\Rightarrow \qquad \dfrac{9}{CD} = \dfrac{7.5}{5}$

$\Rightarrow \qquad CD = \dfrac{9 \times 5}{7.5} = 6$ cm

Q. 2. In the given figure, $\angle PQR = \angle PST = 90°$, $PQ = 5$ cm and $PS = 2$ cm.
Prove that $\Delta PQR \sim \Delta PST$.   **[2019]**

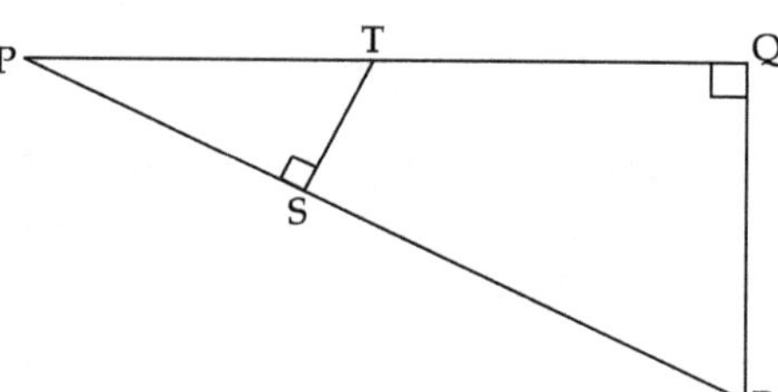

Marking Scheme

(i) In ΔPQR and ΔPST

   $\angle$PQR = $\angle$PST = 90° (given)

   $\angle$P is common to both triangles.

   $\therefore$ ΔPQR ~ ΔPST   (AAA)

Ans. Given, $\angle PQR = \angle PST = 90°$,
           $PQ = 5$ cm and $PS = 2$ cm

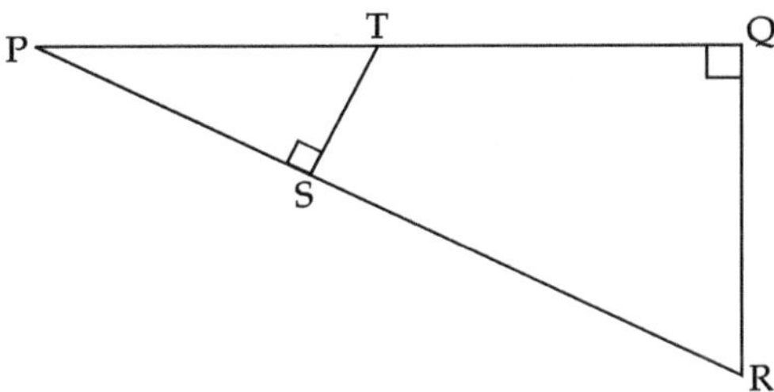

In ΔPQR and ΔPST,

$\quad\angle PQR = \angle PST = 90°$ (Given)

$\quad\angle QPR = \angle SPT$ (Common)

$\therefore\quad \Delta PQR \sim \Delta PST$ (By AA axiom)

Hence Proved.

Q. 3. **In ΔPQR, MN is parallel to QR and $\dfrac{PM}{MQ} = \dfrac{2}{3}$**

Prove that ΔOMN and ΔORQ are similar.

[2018]

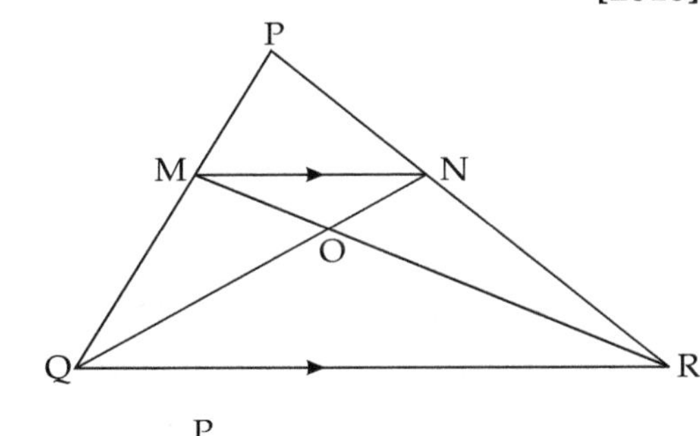

Ans.

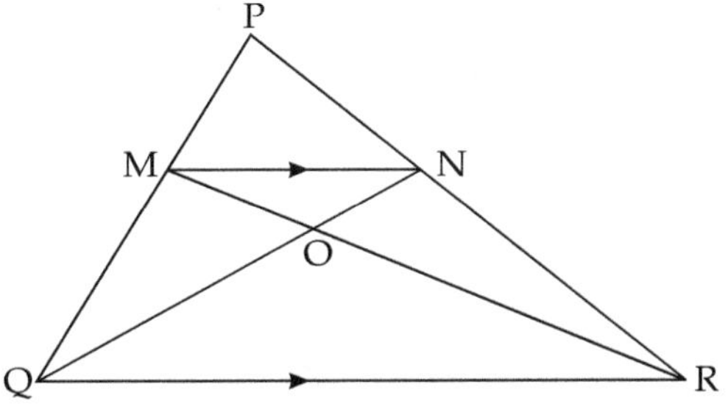

In ΔOMN and ΔORQ,

$\quad\angle MON = \angle QOR$

        (vertically opposite angles)

$\quad\angle OMN = \angle ORQ$

        (Alternate angles, MN ∥ QR)

$\therefore\quad \Delta OMN \sim \Delta ORQ$ (By AA axiom)

Q. 4. **PQR is a triangle. S is a point on the side QR of Δ PQR such that $\angle PSR = \angle QPR$. Given QP = 8 cm, PR = 6 cm and SR = 3 cm**

  (i) **Prove $\Delta PQR \sim \Delta SPR$**

  (ii) **Find the length of QR and PS**   **[2017]**

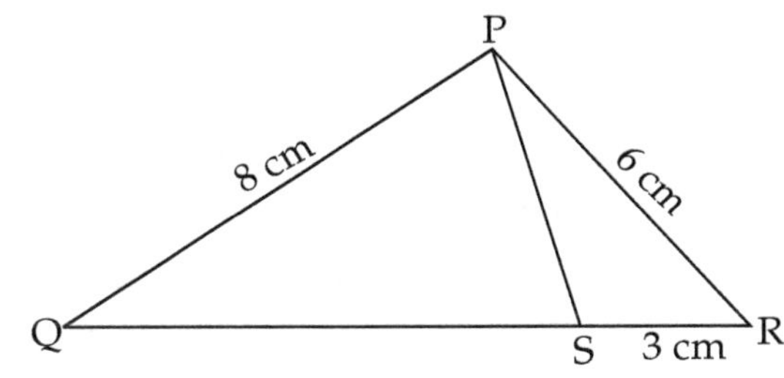

Ans. Given, $\angle PSR = \angle QPR$, QP = 8 cm, PR = 6 cm, SR = 3 cm.

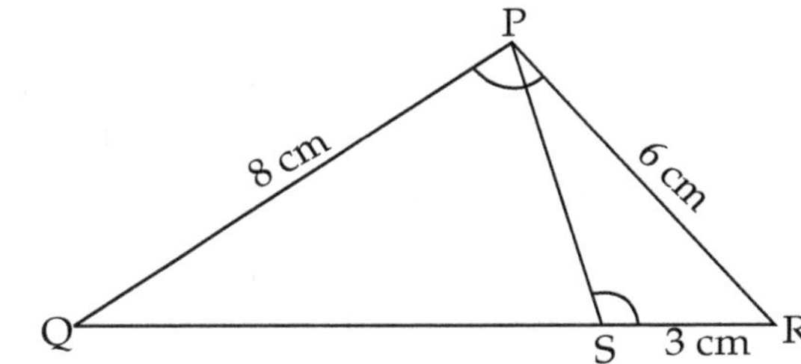

(i) In Δ PQR and Δ SPR

$\quad\quad\angle PSR = \angle QPR$ (Given)

$\quad\quad\angle R = \angle R$ (Common angle)

$\therefore\quad\quad \Delta PQR \sim \Delta SPR$ (AA axiom)

Hence Proved.

Since, corresponding sides of similar ΔS are Proportional.

(ii) $\dfrac{PQ}{PS} = \dfrac{QR}{PR} = \dfrac{PR}{SR}$ $(\because \Delta PQR \sim \Delta SPR)$

$\therefore\quad \dfrac{QR}{PR} = \dfrac{PR}{PS}$

$\Rightarrow\quad \dfrac{QR}{6} = \dfrac{6}{3}$

$\Rightarrow\quad QR = \dfrac{6 \times 6}{2} = 12$ cm

Also, $\quad \dfrac{PQ}{PS} = \dfrac{PR}{SR}$

$\Rightarrow\quad \dfrac{8}{PS} = \dfrac{6}{3}$

$\Rightarrow\quad PS = \dfrac{8 \times 3}{6}$

$\Rightarrow\quad PS = 4$ cm

Q. 5. **In the given figure, AB and DE are perpendicular to BC.**

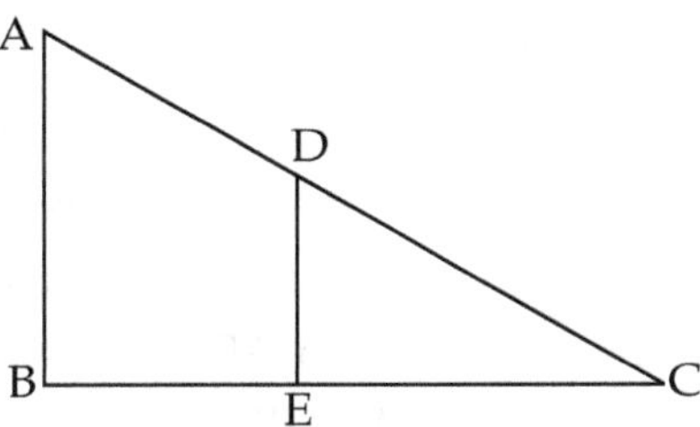

  (i) **Prove that $\Delta ABC \sim \Delta DEC$**

  (ii) **If AB = 6 cm; DE = 4 cm and AC = 15 cm. Calculate CD.**

Ans. **(i)** Given, in $\triangle ABC$,

$$AB \perp BC$$
$$DE \perp BC$$

To prove: $\triangle ABC \sim \triangle DEC$

Proof: In $\triangle ABC$ and $\triangle DEC$

$$\angle ABC = \angle DEC = 90° \quad \text{(Given)}$$
$$\angle C = \angle C \quad \text{(Common)}$$
$$\therefore \quad \triangle ABC \sim \triangle DEC \quad \text{(By AA criteria)}$$

Hence Proved.

(ii) $$AB = 6 \text{ cm}, DE = 4 \text{ cm}$$
$$AC = 15 \text{ cm}, CD = ?$$

Since $\triangle ABC \sim \triangle DEC$

$$\therefore \quad \frac{AB}{DE} = \frac{AC}{CD}$$

(Corresponding sides of similar triangles are proportional)

$$\Rightarrow \quad \frac{6}{4} = \frac{15}{CD}$$
$$\Rightarrow \quad CD = \frac{15 \times 4}{6} = 10 \text{ cm.}$$

Q. 6. **In the given figure $\triangle ABC$ and $\triangle AMP$ are right angled at B and M respectively.**

Given AC = 10 cm, AP = 15 cm and PM = 12 cm.
(i) Prove $\triangle ABC \sim \triangle AMP$.
(ii) Find AB and BC. **[2012]**

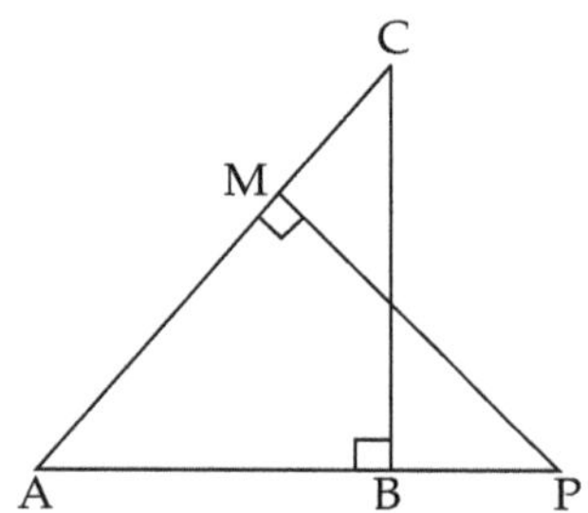

Ans. Given, $\triangle ABC$ and $\triangle AMP$, with right angle at B and M respectively. AC = 10 cm, AP = 15 cm, and PM = 12 cm.

(i) In $\triangle ABC$ and $\triangle AMP$

$$\angle ABC = \angle AMP \quad (90° \text{ each})$$
$$\angle A = \angle A \quad \text{(Common)}$$
$$\therefore \quad \triangle ABC \sim \triangle AMP \quad \text{(By AA similarity)}$$

Hence Proved.

(ii) Given, AC = 10 cm, AP = 15 cm, PM = 12 cm.

$$\because \quad \triangle ABC \sim \triangle AMP$$
$$\therefore \quad \frac{AB}{AM} = \frac{BC}{PM} = \frac{AC}{AP}$$

(corresponding sides of similar triangles are in proportion)

$$\Rightarrow \quad \frac{BC}{PM} = \frac{AC}{AP}$$
$$\Rightarrow \quad \frac{BC}{12} = \frac{10}{15}$$
$$\Rightarrow \quad BC = \frac{10}{15} \times 12$$
$$BC = 8 \text{ cm}$$

In $\triangle ABC$, right angled at B

$$\therefore \quad AC^2 = AB^2 + BC^2$$
$$\Rightarrow \quad AB^2 = AC^2 - BC^2$$
$$= 10^2 - 8^2 = 100 - 64 = 36$$

(Pythagoras theorem)

$$AB = 6 \text{ cm}$$

Q. 7. **In the given figure ABC is a triangle with $\angle EDB = \angle ACB$.**

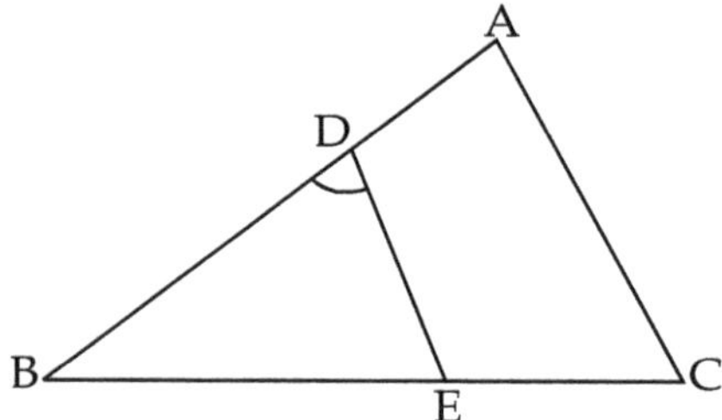

Prove that $\triangle ABC \sim \triangle EBD$.

If BE = 6 cm, EC = 4 cm, BD = 5 cm and area of $\triangle BED = 9 \text{ cm}^2$. Calculate the
(i) length of AB
(ii) area of $\triangle ABC$ **[2010]**

Ans. Given: A $\triangle ABC$ with $\angle BDE = \angle BCA$.

In $\triangle ABC$ and $\triangle EBD$,

$$\angle ACB = \angle EDB \quad \text{(Given)}$$
$$\angle ABC = \angle EBD \quad \text{(Common)}$$
$$\therefore \quad \triangle ABC \sim \triangle EBD \quad \text{(By AA axiom)}$$

Hence Proved.

(i) We have, $$\frac{AB}{BE} = \frac{BC}{BD}$$

(Corresponding sides of similar triangles are proportional)

$$\Rightarrow \quad AB = \frac{6 \times 10}{5} = 12 \text{ cm.}$$

(ii) $$\frac{\text{Area of } \triangle ABC}{\text{Area of } \triangle BED} = \left(\frac{AB}{BE}\right)^2$$

(Area Theorem of similar triangles)

$$\Rightarrow \quad \text{Area of } \triangle ABC = \left(\frac{12}{6}\right)^2 \times 9$$
$$= 4 \times 9 = 36 \text{ cm}^2$$

Q. 8. In the given figure, ABC and CEF are two triangles where BA is parallel to CE and AF : AC = 5 : 8.
   (i) Prove that $\triangle ADF \sim \triangle CEF$
   (ii) Find AD if CE = 6 cm.

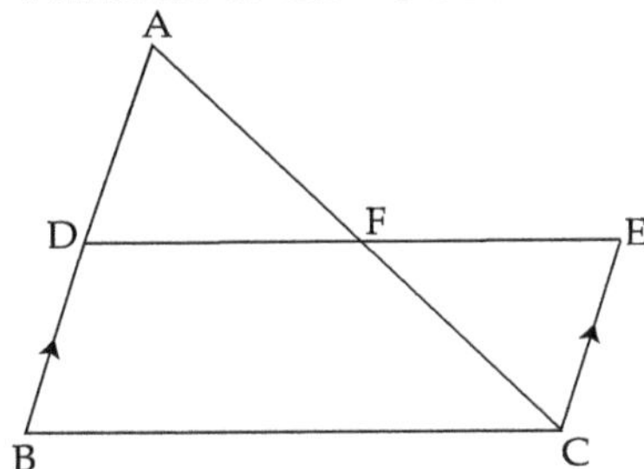

Ans.   (i) In $\triangle ADF$ and $\triangle CEF$
$$\angle DAF = \angle FCE \qquad \text{(alternate angles)}$$
$$\angle AFD = \angle CFE \qquad \text{(vertically opp. angles)}$$
$$\therefore \ \triangle ADF \sim \triangle CEF \qquad \text{(by A.A. axiom)}$$
Hence Proved

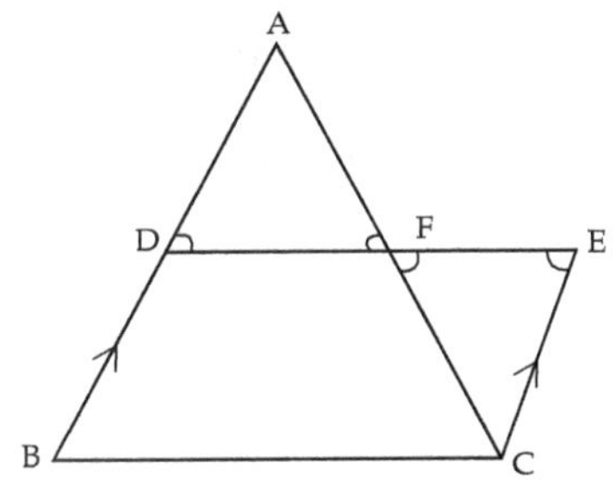

(ii) $\because \qquad \triangle ADF \sim \triangle CEF$

$$\therefore \qquad \frac{AD}{CE} = \frac{DF}{EF} = \frac{AF}{CQ}$$

$$\therefore \qquad \frac{AD}{CE} = \frac{AF}{FC}$$

Given, $\qquad \dfrac{AF}{AC} = \dfrac{5}{8}$

$$\frac{AF}{AF+FC} = \frac{5}{8}$$

$$\frac{AF+FC}{AF} = \frac{8}{5}$$

$$1 + \frac{FC}{AF} = \frac{8}{5}$$

$$\frac{FC}{AF} = \frac{3}{5}$$

$$\frac{AF}{FC} = \frac{5}{3}$$

From equation (1)

$$\frac{AD}{CE} = \frac{5}{3}$$

$$\frac{AD}{6} = \frac{5}{3}$$

$$AD = 10\,\text{cm.}$$

Q. 9. In the figure AB = 7 cm and BC = 9 cm.
   (i) Prove $\triangle ACD \sim \triangle DCB$.
   (ii) Find the length of CD.   **[2009]**

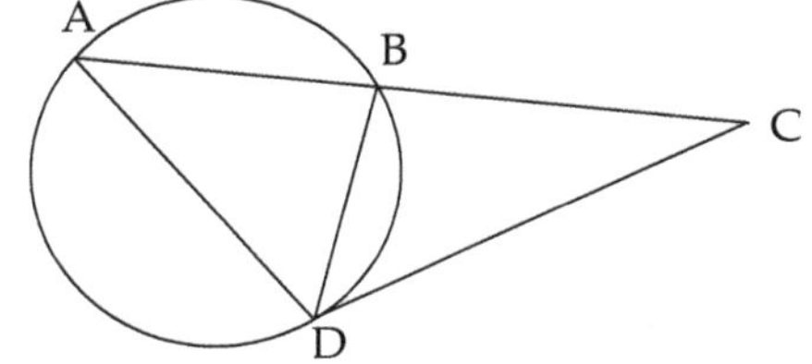

Ans.   In $\triangle ACD$ and $\triangle DCB$ $\angle C = \angle C$ (common)
$$\angle CAD = \angle CDB$$

[Angle between chord and tangent is equal to angle made by chord in alternate segment.]

$$\therefore \qquad \triangle ACD \sim \triangle DCB$$

$$\therefore \qquad \frac{AC}{DC} = \frac{DC}{BC}$$

$$\Rightarrow \qquad DC^2 = AC \times BC = 16 \times 9$$

$$\Rightarrow \qquad DC = 12\,\text{cm}$$

❓ Long Answer Type Questions

Q. 1. In the given figure PQRS is a cyclic quadrilateral PQ and SR produced meet at T.
   (i) Prove $\triangle TPS \sim \triangle TRQ$.
   (ii) Find SP if TP = 18 cm, RQ = 4 cm and TR = 6 cm.

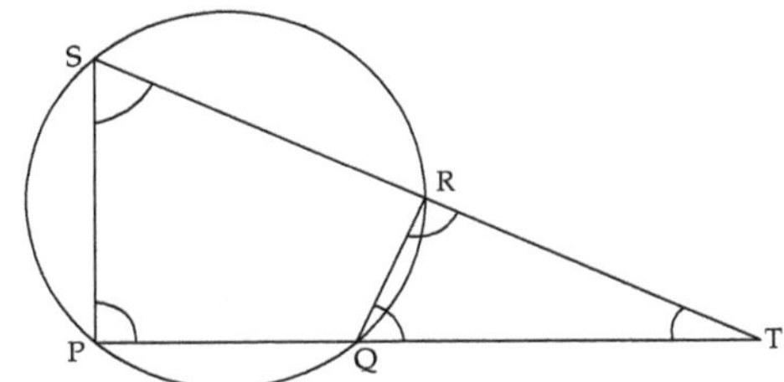

Ans.   (i) In $\triangle TPS$ and $\triangle TRQ$

$$\angle STP = \angle QTR \qquad \text{(common)}$$

$$\angle TPS = \angle TRQ$$

($\because$ Exterior angle of cyclic quadrilateral

= Interior opposite angle)

$$\therefore \ \triangle TPS \sim \triangle TRQ \qquad \text{[By AA similarity]}$$
Hence Proved.

(ii) Since $\triangle TPS \sim \triangle TRQ$

(Corresponding sides of similar as are proportional)

$$\therefore \quad \frac{TR}{TP} = \frac{RQ}{SP}$$

$$\frac{6}{18} = \frac{4}{SP}$$

$$SP = \frac{4 \times 18}{6} = 12 \, cm$$

Q. 2. ABC is a right angled triangle with $\angle ABC = 90°$, D is any point on AB and DE is perpendicular to AC. Prove that:

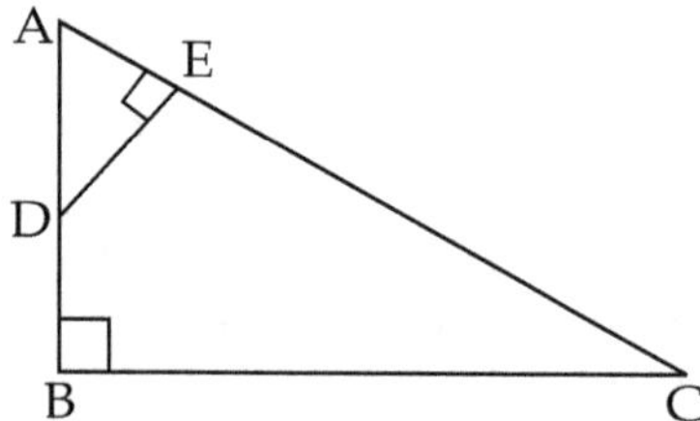

(i) $\triangle ADE \sim \triangle ACB$.

(ii) If AC = 13 cm, BC = 5 cm and AE = 4 cm. Find DE and AD.

Ans. **(i)** Given: $\triangle ABC$, right angled at B and DE perpendicular to AC.

To prove: $\triangle ADE \sim \triangle ACB$.

In $\triangle ADE$ and $\triangle ACB$,

$$\angle ABC = \angle AED = 90°$$

$$\angle A = \angle A \qquad \text{(Common)}$$

$\therefore$ By AA axiom, $\triangle ADE \sim \triangle ACB$.

(ii) Given: AC = 13 cm, BC = 5 cm and AE = 4 cm

In right angled triangle ABC

$$AB^2 + BC^2 = AC^2$$

(by applying Pythagoras Theorem)

$$AB^2 + (5)^2 = (13)^2$$

$$AB = \sqrt{169 - 25}$$

$$= 12 \, cm$$

Since, the $\triangle ADE$ and $\triangle ACB$ are similar, then their corresponding sides will be proportional.

$$\therefore \quad \frac{AC}{AD} = \frac{AB}{AE} \Rightarrow \frac{13}{AD} = \frac{12}{4}$$

$$\Rightarrow \quad AD = \frac{13 \times 4}{12} = 4.33 \, cm$$

$$\text{and} \quad \frac{BC}{DE} = \frac{AB}{AE} \Rightarrow \frac{5}{DE} = \frac{12}{4}$$

$$DE = \frac{5 \times 4}{12} = 1.67 \, cm.$$

Q. 3. In $\triangle ABC$, $\angle ABC = \angle DAC$, AB = 8 cm, AC = 4 cm, AD = 5 cm.

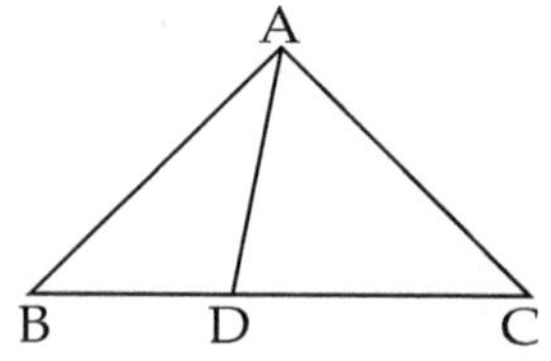

(i) Prove that $\triangle ACD \sim \triangle BCA$.

(ii) Find the length of BC and CD.

Ans. Given, $\angle ABC = \angle DAC$

$$AB = 8 \, cm,$$

$$AC = 4 \, cm, AD = 5 \, cm.$$

(i) In $\triangle ACD$ and $\triangle BCA$

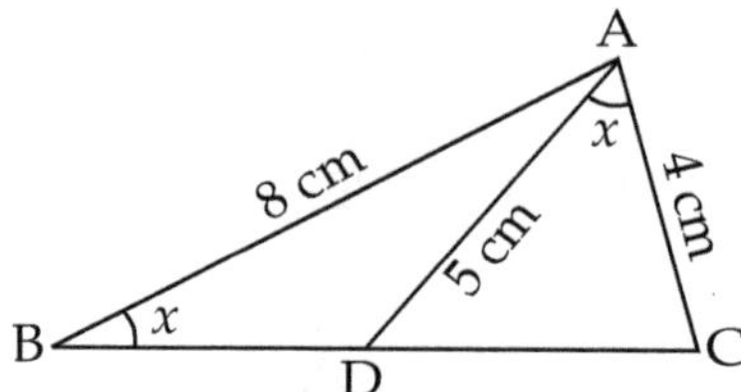

$$\angle ABC = \angle DAC \qquad \text{(Given)}$$
$$\angle ACD = \angle BCA \qquad \text{(Common)}$$
$$\Rightarrow \quad \triangle ACD \sim \triangle BCA \qquad \text{(By AA axiom).}$$

Hence, $\triangle ACD \sim \triangle BCA$ **Hence Proved.**

(ii) As we have,

Since $\triangle ACD \sim \triangle BCA$, then their corresponding sides will be proportional.

$$\frac{AC}{BC} = \frac{CD}{CA} = \frac{AD}{BA}$$

$$\Rightarrow \quad \frac{4}{BC} = \frac{CD}{4} = \frac{5}{8}$$

$$\Rightarrow \quad \frac{4}{BC} = \frac{5}{8}$$

$$\Rightarrow \quad BC = \frac{8 \times 4}{5} = \frac{32}{5} = 6.4 \, cm.$$

$$\text{and} \quad \frac{CD}{4} = \frac{5}{8} \Rightarrow CD = \frac{5 \times 4}{8}$$

$$\Rightarrow \quad CD = 2.5 \, cm.$$

Q. 4. In the following figure ABC is a right angled triangle with $\angle BAC = 90°$, and $AD \perp BC$.

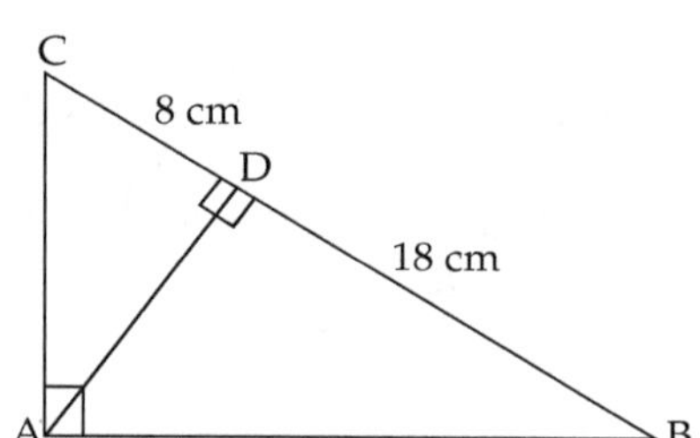

(i) Prove $\triangle ADB \sim \triangle CDA$.

(ii) If BD = 18 cm, CD = 8 cm find AD.

Ans. **(i)** Given, $\triangle ABC$ right angled at A, $AD \perp BC$, BD = 18 cm and CD = 8 cm.

Let $\angle ABD = x$

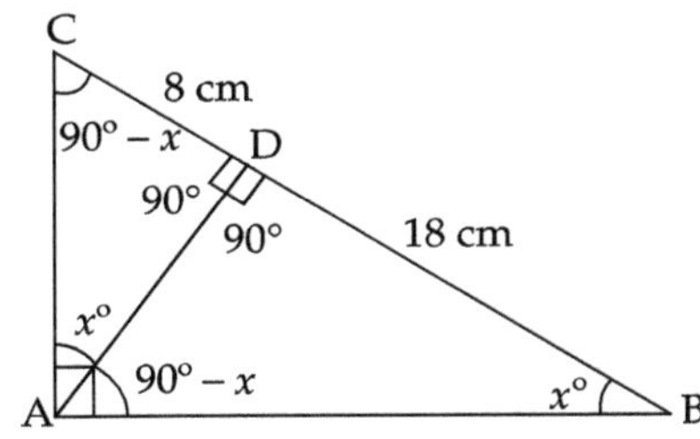

So, $\angle ACD = \angle ACB = 90 - x$ ...(i)
$(\because \angle BAC = 90°)$

Also $\angle BAD = 90 - x$ ...(ii)
$(\because \angle ADB = 90°)$

Now, in $\triangle ADB$ and $\triangle CDA$
$\angle ADB = \angle CDA$
$= 90°$ each (Given)

From (i) and (ii),
$\angle BAD = \angle ACD = 90 - x$

$\therefore$ $\triangle ADB \sim \triangle CDA$ (By AA axiom)
Hence Proved.

(ii) $\because$ $\triangle ADB \sim \triangle CDA$ [Proved in (i)]

$\therefore$ $\dfrac{AD}{BD} = \dfrac{CD}{AD}$

(Corresponding sides of similar triangles are proportional)

or $AD^2 = BD \times CD \Rightarrow AD^2 = 18 \times 8$
$(BD = 18, CD = 8, \text{given})$

$\Rightarrow$ $AD^2 = 144$

$AD = 12$ cm

Q. 5. **In the given figure, ABC is a triangle. DE is parallel to BC and $\dfrac{AD}{DB} = \dfrac{3}{2}$.**

(i) Determine the ratios $\dfrac{AD}{AB}, \dfrac{DE}{BC}$

(ii) Prove that $\triangle DEF$ is similar to $\triangle CBF$.

Hence, find $\dfrac{EF}{FB}$.

Ans.

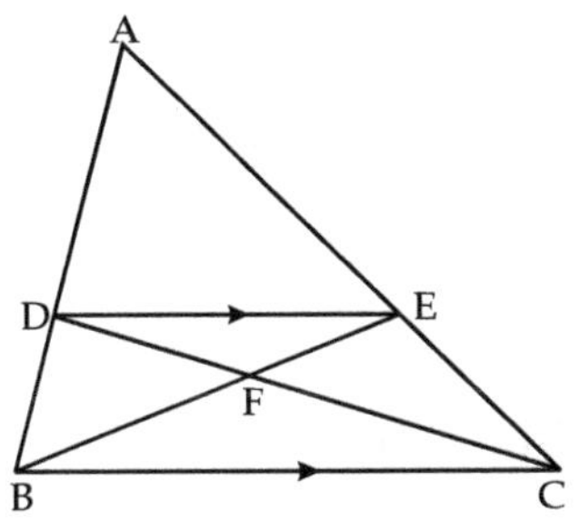

(i) Given: $DE \parallel BC$
and $\dfrac{AD}{DB} = \dfrac{3}{2}$

In $\triangle ADE$ and $\triangle ABC$, $\angle A = \angle A$,
(Common Angle)
$\angle D = \angle B$ (Corresponding Angles)

$\therefore$ $\triangle ADE \sim \triangle ABC$ (AA Axiom)

$\therefore$ $\dfrac{AD}{AB} = \dfrac{AE}{AC} = \dfrac{DE}{BC}$

Now $\dfrac{AD}{AB} = \dfrac{AD}{AD + DB} = \dfrac{3}{3+2} = \dfrac{3}{5}$

$\therefore$ $\dfrac{AD}{AB} = \dfrac{3}{5} = \dfrac{DE}{BC}$.

(ii) In $\triangle DEF$ and $\triangle CBF$, $\angle FDE = \angle FCB$
(Alternate Angle)
$\angle FED = \angle FBC$ (Alternate Angle)
$\angle DFE = \angle BFC$ (Vertically Opposite Angle)

$\therefore \triangle DEF \sim \triangle CBF$ (by AAA similarity rule)

$\dfrac{EF}{FB} = \dfrac{DE}{BC} = \dfrac{3}{5}$

$\therefore$ $\dfrac{EF}{FB} = \dfrac{3}{5}$.

14 Circles

 **Short Answer Type Questions**

Q. 1. In the figure given below, O is the centre of the circle and AB is a diameter.

If AC = BD and $\angle AOC = 72°$. Find :

(i) $\angle ABC$ (ii) $\angle BAD$

(iii) $\angle ABD$ **[2020]**

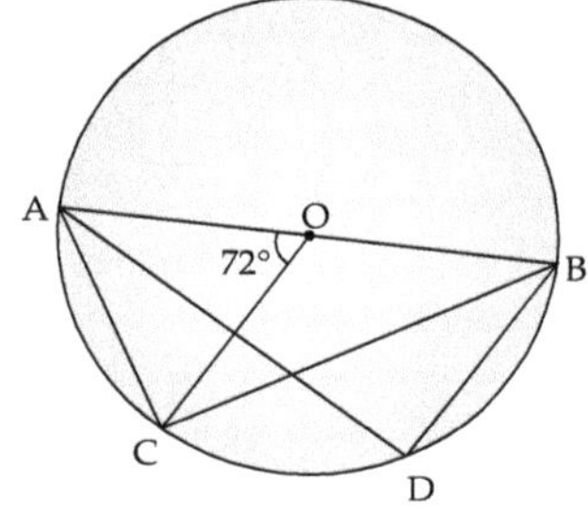

Marking Scheme

$\angle AOC = 72°$ (given)

(i) $\angle ABC = \dfrac{\angle AOC}{2} = \dfrac{72}{2}$ (Angle subtended at centre

$= 36°$ in double the angle made on circumference)

(ii) $\angle BAD = \angle ABC$ ($\because$ AC = BD, equal arcs subtend

$= 36°$ equal angles / or $\Delta BAD \cong \Delta ABC$)

(iii) $\angle ABD = 180° - (36 + 90)$

$= 180 - 126$

$= 54$ ($\angle D = 90°$ angle on a semi-circle and angles of a triangle adds upto 180°)

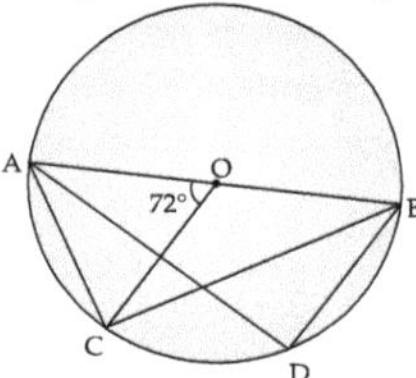

(OR any correct approach)

Ans. Given : AC = BD and $\angle AOC = 72°$

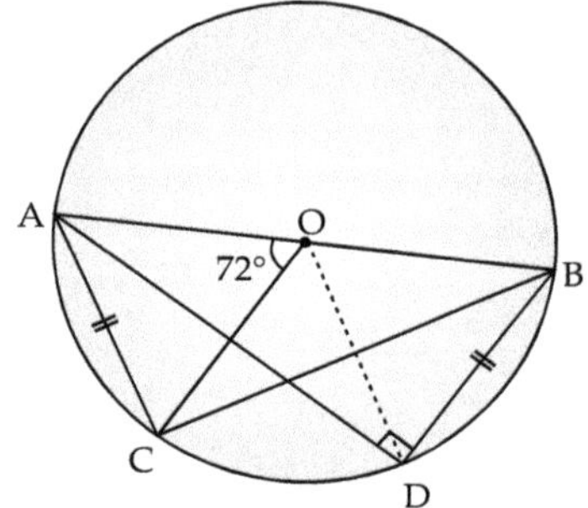

(i) $\because$ Angle subtended by an arc at the centre is twice the angle subtended by the same arc at any point on the remaining part of the circle.

$\therefore$ $\angle AOC = 2\angle ABC$

$\Rightarrow$ $\angle ABC = \dfrac{1}{2}\angle AOC$

$= \dfrac{1}{2} \times 72° = 36°$

(ii) Since $BD = AC$ and equal chords subtend equal angles at the centre.

So, $\angle BOD = \angle AOC = 72°$

and, $\angle BAD = \dfrac{1}{2}\angle BOD$

$= \dfrac{1}{2} \times 72° = 36°$

(iii) In ΔABD,

$\angle BAD + \angle ABD + \angle ADB = 180°$

$\Rightarrow$ $36° + \angle ABD + 90° = 180°$

$[\because \angle ADB$ is in semicircle$]$

$\Rightarrow$ $\angle ABD = 180° - 126°$

$= 54°$

Q. 2. In the given figure AC is a tangent to the circle with centre O.

If $\angle ADB = 55°$, find x and y. Give reasons for your answer. **[2019]**

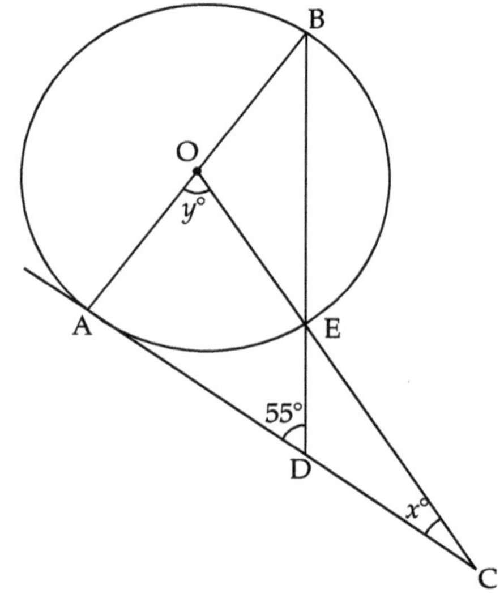

Marking Scheme

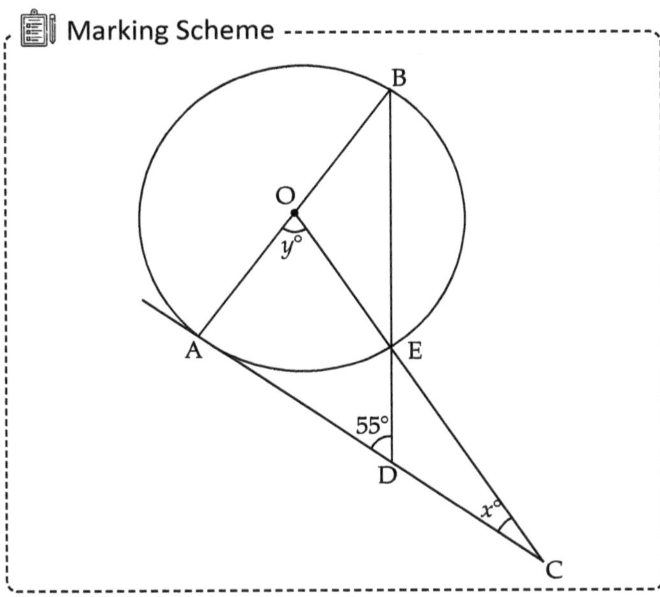

$$\Rightarrow \quad \angle ABD + 90° + 55° = 180°$$
$$\Rightarrow \quad \angle ABD = 180° - 145° = 35°$$
$$\therefore \quad \angle AOE = 2 \times \angle ABD$$

(Angle at centre is twice the angle at circumference)

$$\Rightarrow \quad y° = 2 \times 35°$$
$$\therefore \quad y° = 70°$$

In $\triangle AOC$,
$$\angle ACO + \angle OAC + \angle AOC = 180°$$

(Angle sum property)

$$\Rightarrow \quad x° + 90° + 70° = 180°$$
$$\Rightarrow \quad x° = 180° - 160° = 20°$$

Hence, $\quad x = 20°$ and $y = 70°$

Q. 3. In the figure given below 'O' is the centre of the circle. If QR = OP and $\angle ORP = 20°$. Find the value of 'x' giving reasons. **[2018]**

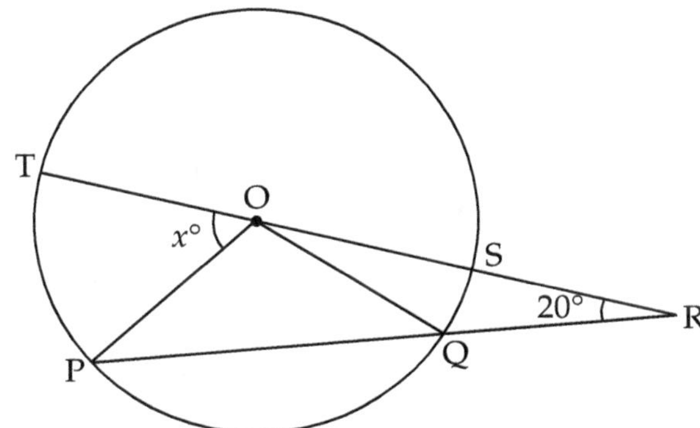

Ans. Given, QR = OP, $\angle ORP = 20°$

$$OP = OQ \quad \text{(radius of circle)}$$
$$\Rightarrow \quad OP = OQ = QR$$
$$\therefore \quad \angle QOS = \angle ORQ \quad (\because QR = OQ)$$
$$= 20°.$$
$$\therefore \quad \angle OQP = \angle QOR + \angle ORQ$$

(Exterior angle is equal to sum of interior opposite angles)

$$= 20° + 20° = 40°$$
$$\therefore \quad \angle OPQ = \angle OQP \quad (\because OP = OQ)$$
$$= 40°$$

AC is a tangent and OA is the radius.

$$\therefore \quad \angle BAC = 90°$$

In $\triangle ABD$
$$\angle BAD = 90°$$
$$\therefore \quad \angle B = 180° - (90° + 55°)$$
$$= 35° \quad \text{(angles of a triangle adds upto 180°)}$$
$$\angle y = 2\angle B$$
$$\therefore \quad y = 2 \times 35° = 70° \quad \text{(angle at the centre is double}$$
the angle in the remaining circumference)

In $\triangle AOC$
$$x = 180° - (90° + y)$$
$$= 180° - (90° + 70°)$$
$$= 20° \quad \text{(angles of a triangle adds upto 180°)}$$

Ans. Given, $\angle ADB = 55°$, AC is a tangent,
$\angle ACO = x°$, $\angle AOE = y°$

In $\triangle ABD$,
$$\therefore \quad \angle BAD = 90° \; (\because \text{Radius OA is}$$
perpendicular to tangent AC)
$$\therefore \quad \angle ABD + \angle BAD + \angle ADB = 180°$$

(Angle sum property)

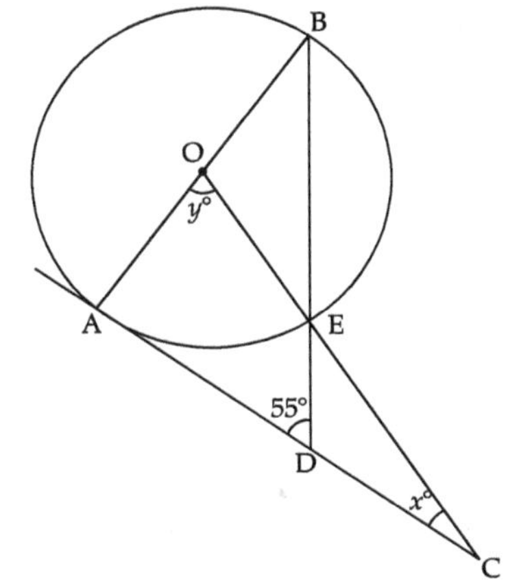

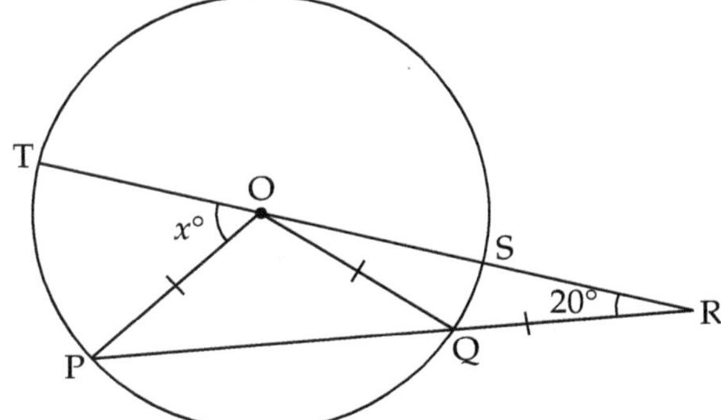

$$\therefore \quad \angle POQ + \angle OPQ + \angle OQP = 180°$$

(sum of angles in a triangle is 180°)

$\Rightarrow \qquad \angle POQ + 40° + 40° = 180°$

$\Rightarrow \qquad\qquad \angle POQ = 180° - 80° = 100°$

$\therefore \quad \angle POT + \angle POQ + \angle QOR = 180°$

(sum of angles on a straight line is 180°)

$\Rightarrow \quad x° + 100° + 20° = 180°$

$\Rightarrow \qquad\qquad x° = 180° - 120° = 60°.$

Q. 4. In the given figure PQ is a tangent to the circle at A. AB and AD are bisectors of $\angle CAQ$ and $\angle PAC$. If $\angle BAQ = 30°$, prove that:

(i) BD is a diameter of the circle.

(ii) ABC is an isosceles triangle. **[2017]**

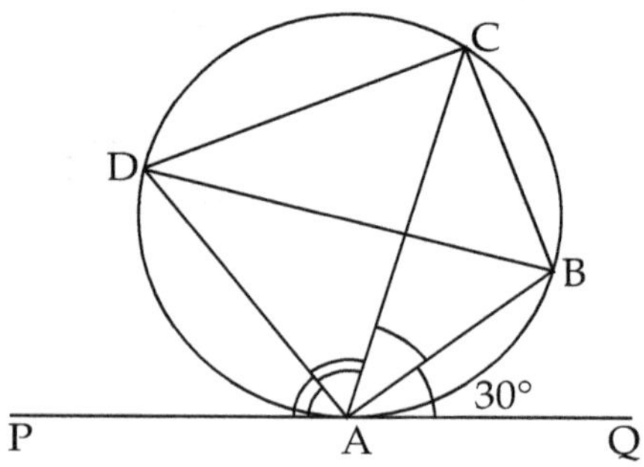

Ans. Given, $\angle BAQ = 30°$, AB and AD are bisectors of $\angle CAQ$ and $\angle PAC$.

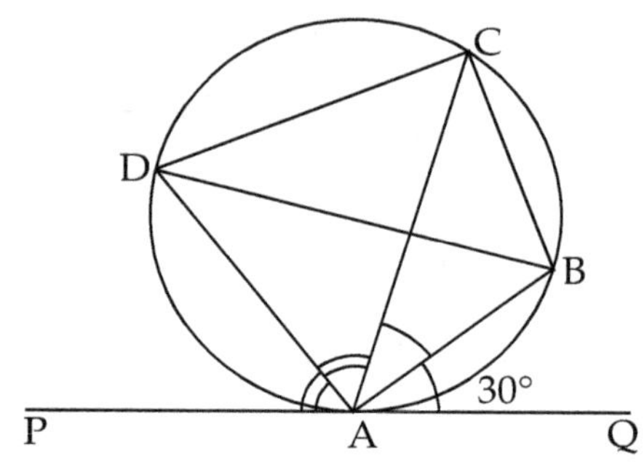

(i) $\qquad \angle BAC = \angle BAQ = 30°$

(AB bisects $\angle CAQ$)

$\angle CAQ = \angle BAC + \angle BAQ$

$\qquad = 30° + 30° = 60°$

$\angle PAC = 180° - \angle CAQ$

(Linear pair)

$\qquad = 180° - 60° = 120°$

$\angle CAD = \dfrac{1}{2} \angle PAC$

(AD bisects $\angle PAC$)

$\qquad = \dfrac{1}{2} \times 120° = 60°$

$\angle BAD = \angle BAC + \angle CAD$

$\qquad = 30° + 60° = 90°$

$\therefore$ BD is a diameter ($\angle BAD = 90°$ = angle in a semi-circle)

(ii) $\qquad \angle ADB = \angle BAQ = 30°$

(angles in an alternate segment are equal)

$\angle ACB = \angle ADB$

(angles in same segment are equal)

$\therefore \qquad \angle BAC = \angle ACB = 30°$

$\therefore \qquad\qquad AB = BC$

(sides opposite to equal angles are equal)

$\therefore \Delta ABC$ is an isosceles triangle.

Hence Proved.

Q. 5. AB and CD are two chords of a circle intersecting at P.

Prove that $AP \times PB = CP \times PD$ **[2015]**

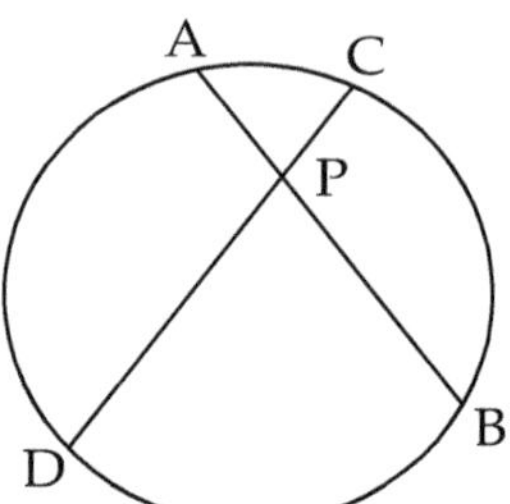

Ans. Given: Chord AB and CD of a circle intersect each other at point P inside the circle.

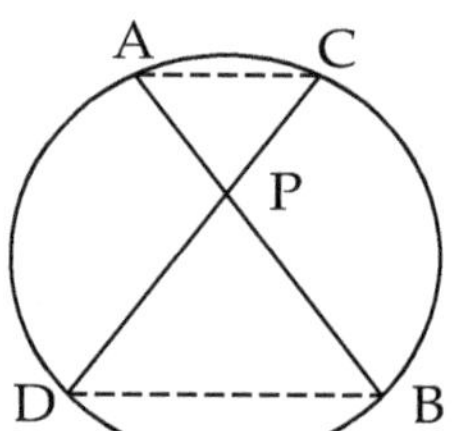

To prove: $AP \times PB = CP \times PD$

Construction: Join AC and BD

Proof: In Δ APC and Δ BPD

$\qquad \angle A = \angle D$

(Angles of same segment)

$\qquad \angle C = \angle B$

(Angles of same segment)

$\therefore \qquad \Delta APC \sim \Delta DPB$ (By AA axiom)

$\Rightarrow \qquad \dfrac{AP}{PD} = \dfrac{CP}{PB}$

(corresponding sides of similar triangles)

$\Rightarrow \qquad AP \times PB = CP \times PD.$ **Hence Proved.**

Q. 6. In the given figure, $\angle DBC = 58°$, BD is diameter of the circle. Calculate:

(i) $\angle BDC$

(ii) $\angle BEC$

(iii) $\angle BAC$ **[2014]**

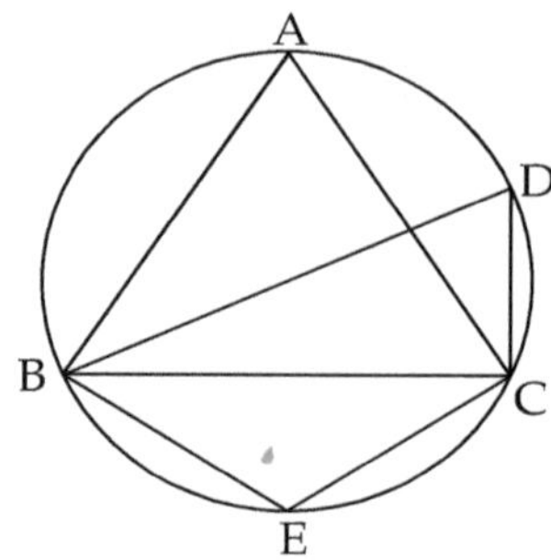

Ans. Given, $\angle DBC = 58°$, BD is the diameter.

∴ $\angle BCD = 90°$ (Angle in a semi-circle is right angle)

(i) Now, in ΔBDC

$\angle BDC + 90° + 58° = 180°$

(sum of the angles of a triangle)

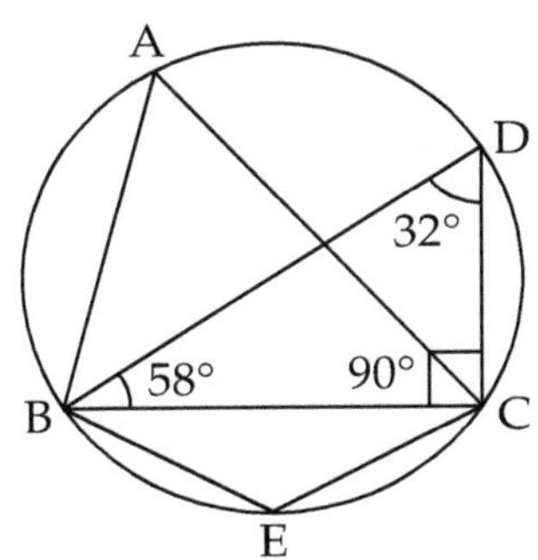

∴ $\angle BDC = 180° - (90° + 58°)$

$= 32°$

(ii) BECD is a cyclic quadrilateral.

∴ $\angle BEC + \angle BDC = 180°$

(Opp. angles of a cyclic quadrilateral)

∴ $\angle BEC = 180° - \angle BDC$

$= 180° - 32° = 148°$

(iii) $\angle BAC = \angle BDC$

$= 32°$

(Angles in the same segment of a circle)

Q. 7. **In the figure given below, diameter AB and chord CD of a circle meet at P. PT is a tangent to the circle at T. CD = 7.8 cm, PD = 5 cm, PB = 4 cm. Find:**

(i) **AB.**

(ii) **The length of tangent PT.** [2014]

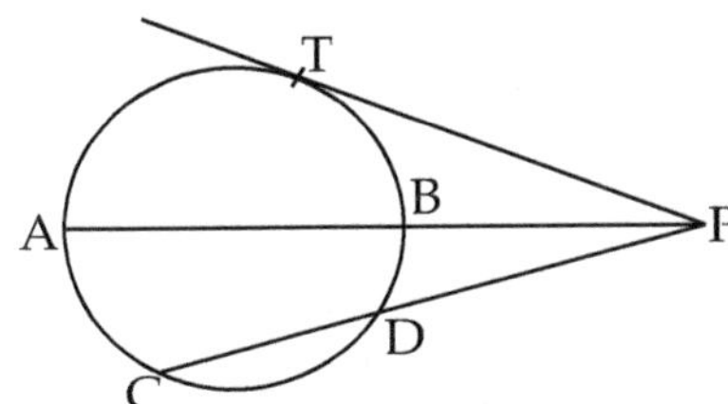

Ans. Given, CD = 7.8 cm, PD = 5 cm, PB = 4 cm and PT is a tangent.

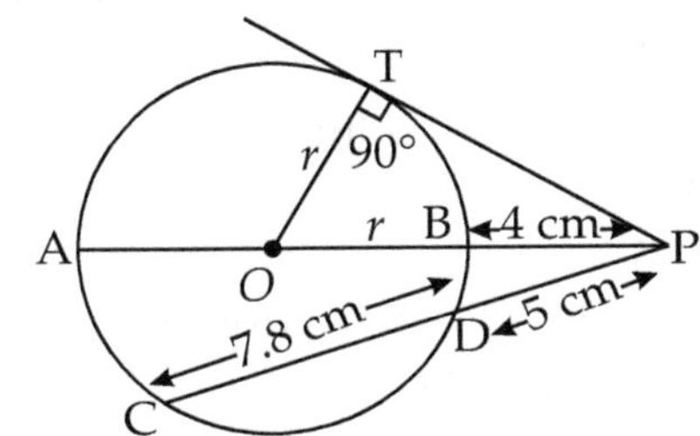

As we know,

∵ Square of the length of tangent is equal to the product of the length of segments of the chord from the point of contact to point of intersection.

$$PT^2 = PD \times PC$$

$\Rightarrow \quad PT^2 = PD \times (PD + CD)$

$= 5 \times (5 + 7.8)$

$\Rightarrow \quad PT^2 = 5 \times 12.8$

$\Rightarrow \quad PT^2 = 64$

$\Rightarrow \quad PT = 8$ cm

Now in ΔPOT

$$PO^2 = OT^2 + PT^2$$

(By Pythagoras Theorem)

$\Rightarrow \quad (r + 4)^2 = r^2 + 64$

$\Rightarrow \quad r^2 + 16 + 8r = r^2 + 64$

$\Rightarrow \quad 8r = 48$

$\Rightarrow \quad r = 6$

(i) Thus, $\quad AB = 2r = 12$ cm

(ii) Length of tangent PT = 8 cm.

Q. 8. **In the given figure, $\Rightarrow \angle BAD = 65°$ $\angle ABD = 70°$, $\angle BDC = 45°$.**

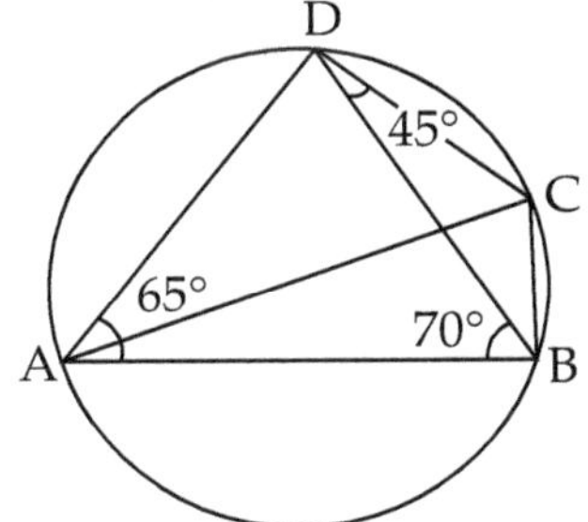

(i) **Prove that AC is a diameter of the circle.**

(ii) **Find $\angle ACB$** [2013]

Ans. Given: $\angle BAD = 65°$

$\angle ABD = 70°$

$\angle BDC = 45°$

(i) In ΔABD,

$\angle BAD + \angle ABD + \angle ADB = 180°$

(Sum of three angles of a Δ)

$65° + 70° + \angle ADB = 180°$

∴ $\angle ADB = 180° - (65° + 70°) = 45°$

∵ $\angle ADC = \angle ADB + \angle BDC$

$\Rightarrow \quad = 45° + 45° = 90°$

$\Rightarrow$ AC is the diameter of the circle. **Hence Proved.**

[Angle in a semi-circle is 90°]

(ii) $\angle ACB = \angle ADB = 45°$

(Angles in the same segment of a circle)

Q. 9. **In the given circle with centre O, $\angle ABC = 100°$, $\angle ACD = 40°$ and CT is a tangent to the circle at C. Find $\angle ADC$ and $\angle DCT$.** [2013]

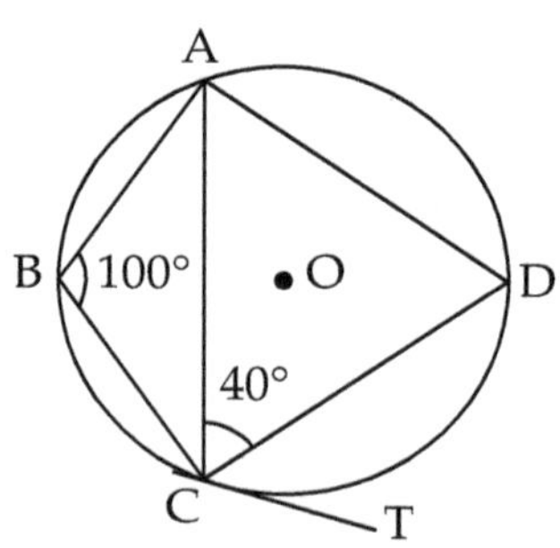

Ans. Given, $\angle ABC = 100°$, $\angle ACD = 40°$
and CT is a tangent at C.

$$\angle ABC + \angle ADC = 180°$$

    (Opposite angles of a cyclic quadrilateral)

$$100° + \angle ADC = 180°$$

$\therefore$ $\angle ADC = 180° - 100° = 80°$.

Now, in $\triangle$ ACD

$$\angle ACD + \angle ADC + \angle CAD = 180°$$

    (sum of angles of a $\triangle$)

$$40° + 80° + \angle CAD = 180°$$

$$\angle CAD = 180° - 120° = 60°$$

Now, $\angle DCT = \angle CAD = 60°$

    (Alternate segment theorem)

Q. 10. In the given figure O is the centre of the circle and AB is a tangent at B. If AB = 15 cm and AC = 7.5 cm. Calculate the radius of the circle. **[2012]**

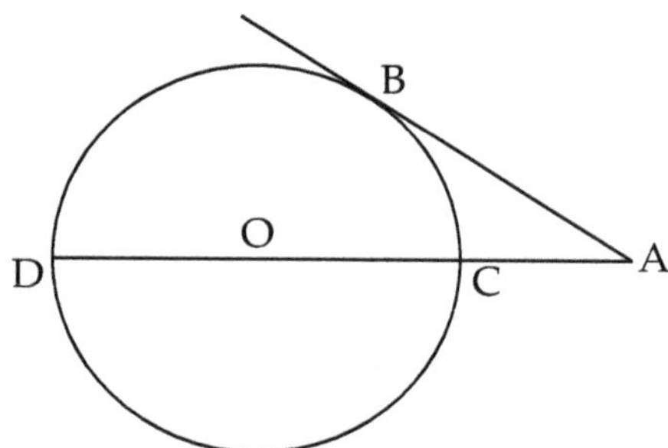

Ans. Given, AB = 15 cm, AC = 7.5 cm.

If a chord and a tangent intersect externally then product of segments of the chord is equal to square of the length of the tangent.

$$AB^2 = AC \times AD$$

$\Rightarrow$ $15^2 = 7.5 \times AD$

$\Rightarrow$ $AD = \dfrac{225}{7.5} = 30$

$\Rightarrow$ $CD = AD - AC$

$$= 30 - 7.5 = 22.5$$

$$\text{Radius} = \frac{1}{2} \times CD$$

$$\text{Radius} = \frac{1}{2} \times 22.5$$

$$\text{Radius} = 11.25 \text{ cm}.$$

Q. 11. In the given figure, AB is the diameter of a circle with centre O.

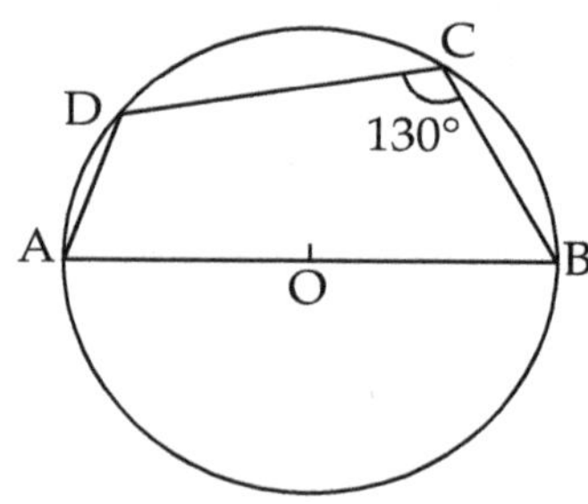

$\angle BCD = 130°$. **Find:**

(i) $\angle DAB$

(ii) $\angle DBA$ **[2012]**

Ans. **(i)** $\angle DAB + \angle BCD = 180°$

    (Opp. angles of a cyclic quadrilateral)

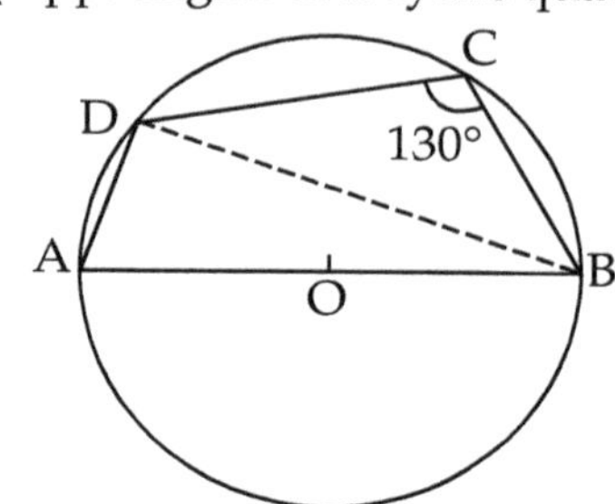

$\Rightarrow$ $\angle DAB + 130° = 180°$

      ($\angle BCD = 130°$ given)

$\Rightarrow$ $\angle DAB = 180° - 130°$

$\Rightarrow$ $\angle DAB = 50°$

(ii) $\angle ADB = 90°$

    (angle in semi-circle)

In $\triangle$ ADB,

$$\angle DAB + \angle ADB + \angle DBA = 180°$$

    (Angle sum property)

$\Rightarrow 50° + 90° + \angle DBA = 180°$

$\Rightarrow$ $\angle DBA = 180° - 140°$

$\Rightarrow$ $\angle DBA = 40°$

Q. 12. In triangle PQR, PQ = 24 cm, QR = 7 cm and $\angle PQR = 90°$. Find the radius of the inscribed circle. **[2012]**

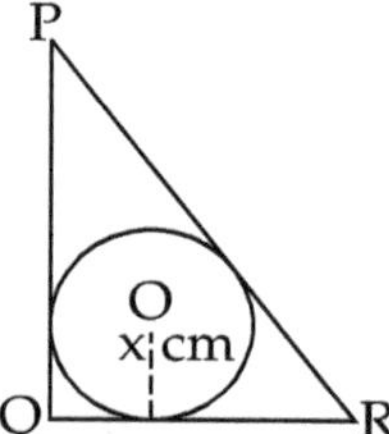

Ans. Given, PQ = 24 cm, QR = 7 cm, and $\angle PQR = 90°$.

Construction: Draw OM $\perp$ QR and ON $\perp$ PQ

In $\triangle PQR$, OM $\perp$ QR and ON $\perp$ PQ:

(Tangents and radius are perpendicular to each other)

OM = ON   (Radius)

QM = QN   (Tangents from an external point)

QMON is a square.

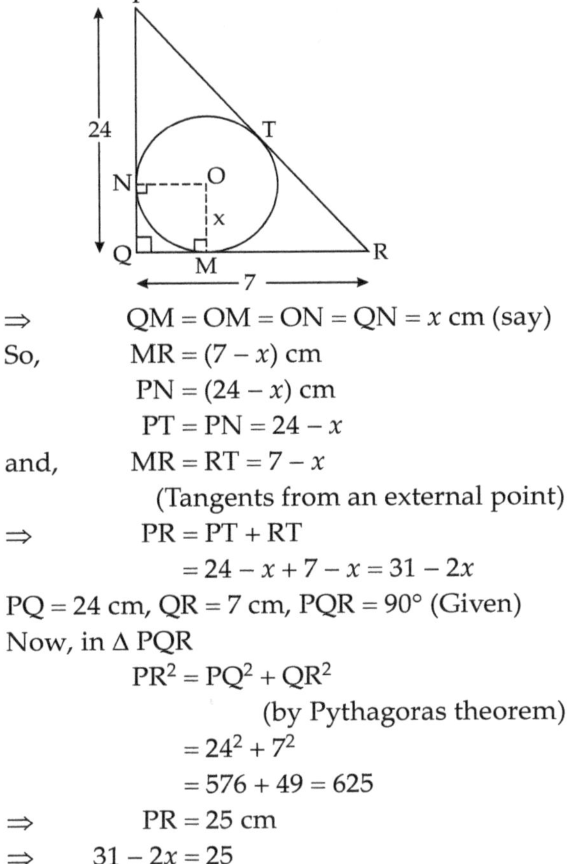

$\Rightarrow \qquad$ QM = OM = ON = QN = x cm (say)

So, $\qquad$ MR = $(7 - x)$ cm

$\qquad\qquad$ PN = $(24 - x)$ cm

$\qquad\qquad$ PT = PN = $24 - x$

and, $\qquad$ MR = RT = $7 - x$

$\qquad\qquad$ (Tangents from an external point)

$\Rightarrow \qquad$ PR = PT + RT

$\qquad\qquad$ = $24 - x + 7 - x = 31 - 2x$

PQ = 24 cm, QR = 7 cm, PQR = 90° (Given)

Now, in Δ PQR

$\qquad\qquad$ PR^2 = PQ^2 + QR^2

$\qquad\qquad\qquad$ (by Pythagoras theorem)

$\qquad\qquad$ = $24^2 + 7^2$

$\qquad\qquad$ = $576 + 49 = 625$

$\Rightarrow \qquad$ PR = 25 cm

$\Rightarrow \qquad 31 - 2x = 25$

$\Rightarrow \qquad 2x = 31 - 25$

$\Rightarrow \qquad 2x = 6$

$\Rightarrow \qquad x = 3$ cm

$\therefore$ Radius of the inscribed circle is 3 cm.

Q. 13. ABC is a triangle with AB = 10 cm, BC = 8 cm and AC = 6 cm (not drawn to scale). Three circles are drawn touching each other with the vertices as their centres. Find the radii of the three circles. [2011]

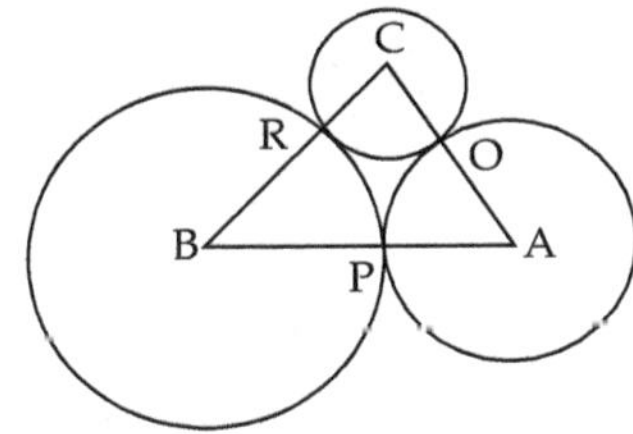

Ans. Given, AB = 10 cm, BC, = 8 cm, AC = 6 cm

Let the radii of three circles be r_1, r_2 and r_3 (shown in fig.)

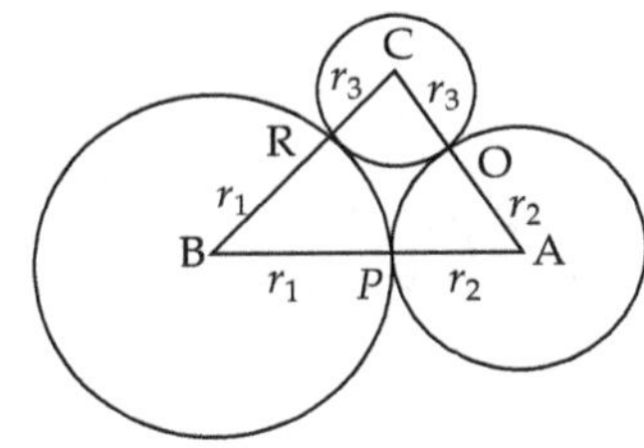

Now, $\qquad$ AB = $r_1 + r_2 = 10$ $\qquad$ ...(i)

$\qquad\qquad$ AC = $r_2 + r_3 = 6$ $\qquad$ ...(ii)

$\qquad\qquad$ BC = $r_3 + r_1 = 8$ $\qquad$ ...(iii)

Adding equations (i), (ii) and (iii)

$\qquad$ 2 $(r_1 + r_2 + r_3) = 10 + 6 + 8 = 24$

$\qquad\qquad r_1 + r_2 + r_3 = 12$ $\qquad$ ...(iv)

Subtract (i) from (iv)

$\Rightarrow \qquad\qquad r_2 = 12 - 10 = 2$ cm

Subtract (ii) from (iv)

$\Rightarrow \qquad\qquad r_1 = 12 - 6 = 6$ cm

Subtract (iii) from (iv)

$\Rightarrow \qquad\qquad r_2 = 12 - 8 = 4$ cm

Therefore, the radius of 3 circles are 2 cm, 6 cm and 4 cm.

Q. 14. In the figure given below AB and CD are two parallel chords and O is the centre. If the radius of the circle is 15 cm, find the distance MN between the two chords of length 24 cm and 18 cm respectively. [2010]

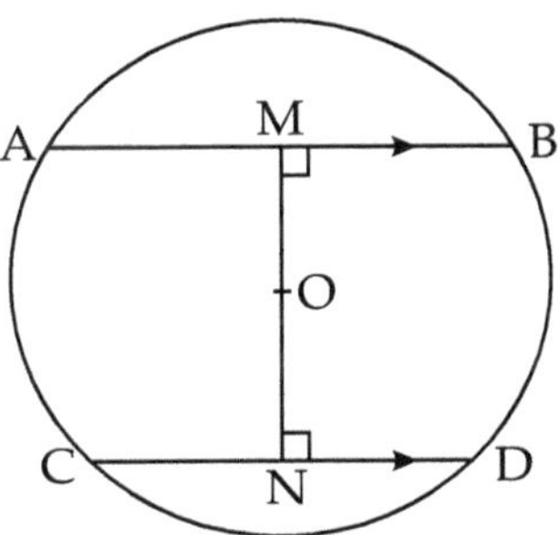

Ans. Given: OA = OC = 15 cm, AB = 24 cm, CD = 18 cm since, perpendicular drawn from the centre to the chord bisects the chord.

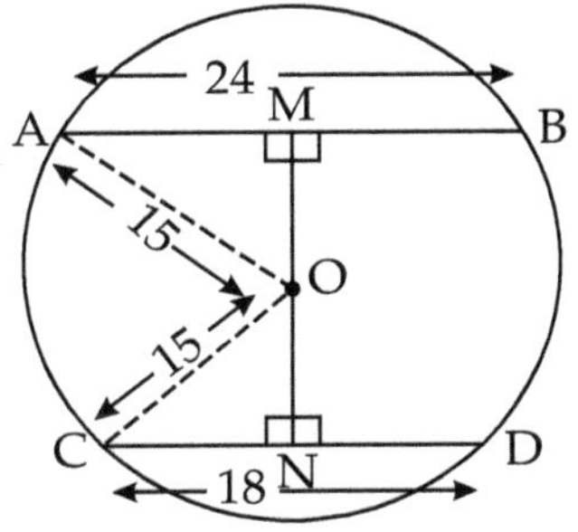

$\Rightarrow \qquad$ AM = MB = 12 cm,

$\Rightarrow \qquad$ CN = ND = 9 cm.

In ΔOMA, $\quad$ OM = $\sqrt{\text{OA}^2 - \text{AM}^2}$

$\qquad\qquad\qquad$ = $\sqrt{15^2 - 12^2}$ = 9 cm

In ΔONA, $\quad$ ON = $\sqrt{\text{OC}^2 - \text{CN}^2}$

$\qquad\qquad\qquad$ = $\sqrt{15^2 - 9^2}$ = 12 cm

$\therefore \qquad\qquad$ MN = OM + ON

$\qquad\qquad\qquad$ = 9 + 12 = 21 cm

Q. 15. In the following figure O is the centre of the circle and AB is a tangent to it at point B. $\angle$BDC = 65°. Find $\angle$BAO. [2010]

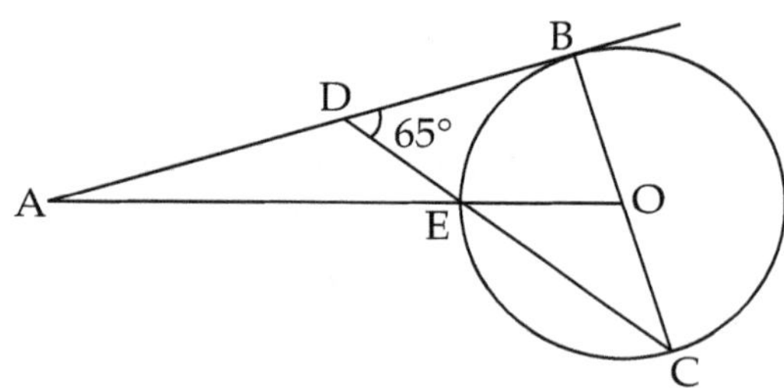

Ans. As AB is a tangent to the circle at B and OB is radius,

$\therefore \quad OB \perp AB \Rightarrow \angle CBD = 90°$

In $\triangle BCD$,

$\angle BCD + \angle CBD + \angle BDC = 180°$

(Angle sum property)

$\Rightarrow \quad \angle BCD + 90° + 65° = 180°$

$\Rightarrow \quad \angle BCD + 155° = 180°$

$\Rightarrow \quad \angle BCD = 180° - 155°$

$\Rightarrow \quad \angle BCD = 25°$

$\Rightarrow \quad \angle BOE = 2\,\angle BCE$

(Angle at centre is double the angle at the circumference of circle)

$\Rightarrow \quad \angle BOE = 2 \times 25° = 50°$

$\Rightarrow \quad \angle BOA = 50°$

In $\triangle BOA$,

$\angle BAO + \angle ABO + \angle BOA = 180°$

(Angle sum property)

$\Rightarrow \quad \angle BAO + 90° + 50° = 180°$

$\Rightarrow \quad \angle BAO + 140° = 180°$

$\Rightarrow \quad \angle BAO = 180° - 140°$

$\Rightarrow \quad \angle BAO = 40°$

Q. 16. In the given figure, AB is parallel to DC, $\angle BCE = 80°$ and $\angle BAC = 25°$. Find:

(i) $\angle CAD$ (ii) $\angle CBD$ (iii) $\angle ADC$

[2008]

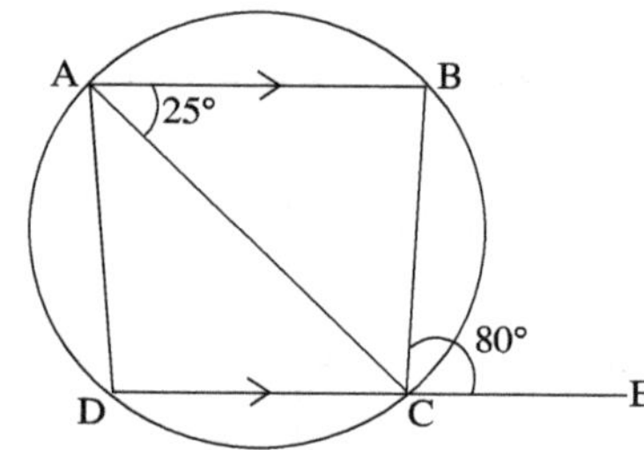

Ans. (i) $\angle CAD = \angle BCE - \angle BAC = 80° - 25°$

$= 55°$

$\because$ External of cyclic quadrilateral is equal to opposite internal

(ii) $\angle CBD = \angle CAD$ [Angles in the same segment]

$= 55°$

(iii) $\angle ADC = 180° - \angle DAB = 180° - 80° = 100°$

Q. 17. In the figure given below PQ = QR, $\angle RQP = 68°$, PC and CQ are tangents to the circle with centre O. Calculate the values of:

(i) $\angle QOP$ (ii) $\angle QCP$ [2008]

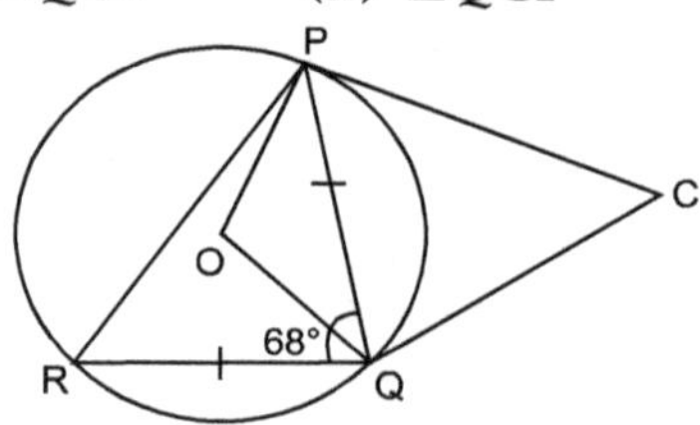

Ans. (i) $\angle QOP = 2\angle QRP$

[$\because$ angle at the centre is twice the angle at the circle]

$= \dfrac{2(180 - 68)}{2} = 112°$

(ii) $\angle CPQ = \angle CQP$

[$\because$ CP = CQ tangents are equal]

and $\angle CPQ = \angle CQP = \angle PRQ$

$\therefore \quad \angle CPQ = \angle CQP = 56°$

$\therefore \quad \angle QCP = 180 - (\angle CPQ + \angle CQP)$

$= 180 - 112° = 68°$

Q. 18. In the given figure, AE and BC intersect each other at point D. If $\angle CDE = 90°$, AB = 5 cm, BD = 4 cm and CD = 9 cm, find DE. [2008]

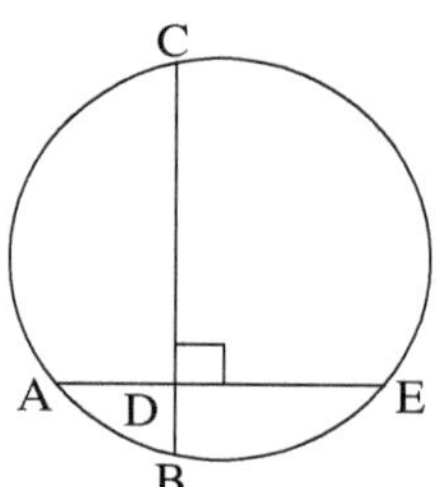

Ans.

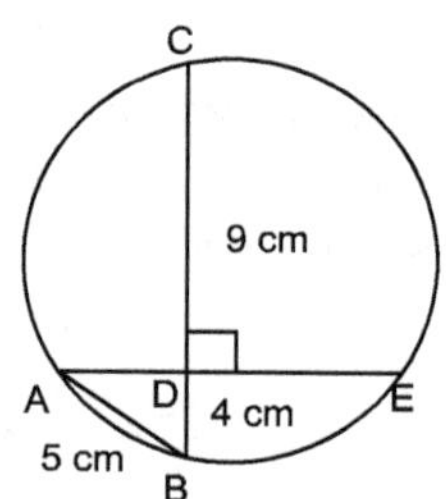

In $\triangle ADB$, $\angle D = 90°$

$AB^2 = AD^2 + BD^2$

(By Pythagoras Theorem)

$\therefore \quad AD = \sqrt{AB^2 - BD^2}$

$= \sqrt{25 - 16} = \sqrt{9} = 3$ cm.

Now, $AD \times DE = CD \times DB$

$3 \times DE = 9 \times 4$

$DE = 12$ cm.

Q. 19. In the given figure, O is the centre of the circle and $\angle PBA = 45°$. Calculate the value of $\angle PQB$. [2007]

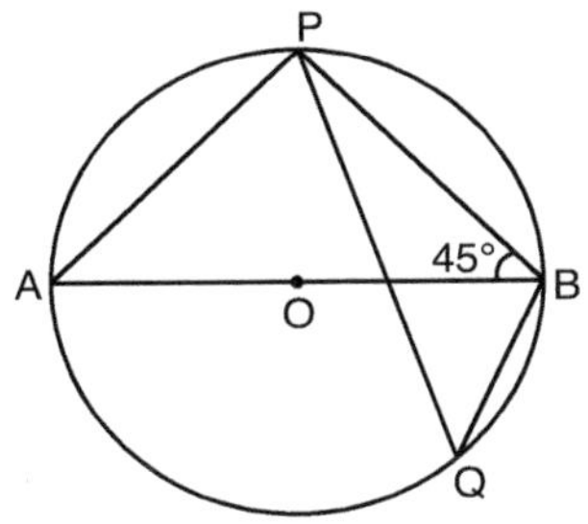

Ans. Given $\angle PBA = 45°$

AOB is diameter of circle.

$\therefore \qquad \angle APB = 90°$ (Angle in semi circle)

So in $\triangle$ APB, $\angle PAB = 180° - (90° + 45°) = 45°$

$\qquad\qquad \angle PQB = \angle PAB$ (Angle in same segment)

$\therefore \qquad \angle PQB = 45°.$

Q. 20. In the figure given below, PT is a tangent to the circle. Find PT if AT = 16 cm and AB = 12 cm. **[2007]**

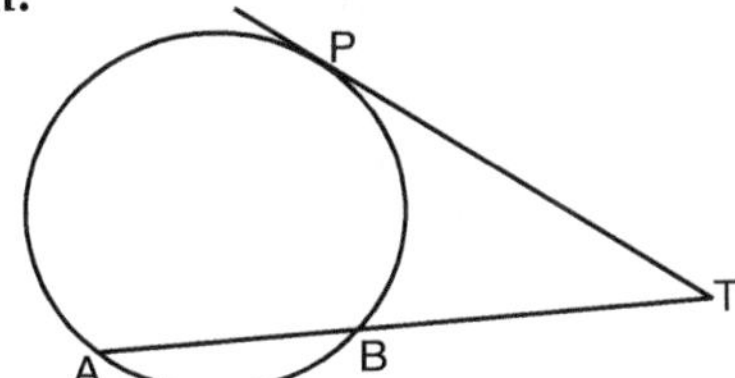

Ans. Given: AT = 16 cm, AB = 12 cm. PT is tangent. Hence by theorem,

$$PT^2 = AT \times BT$$
$$= 16 \times (AT - AB)$$
$$= 16 \times (16 - 12) = 16 \times 4 = 64$$
$$\therefore \qquad PT = 8 \text{ cm}.$$

Q. 21. In the given figure, AB is a diameter. The tangent at C meets AB produced at Q. If $\angle CAB = 34°$, find:

(i) $\angle CBA$, **(ii)** $\angle CQA$. **[2006]**

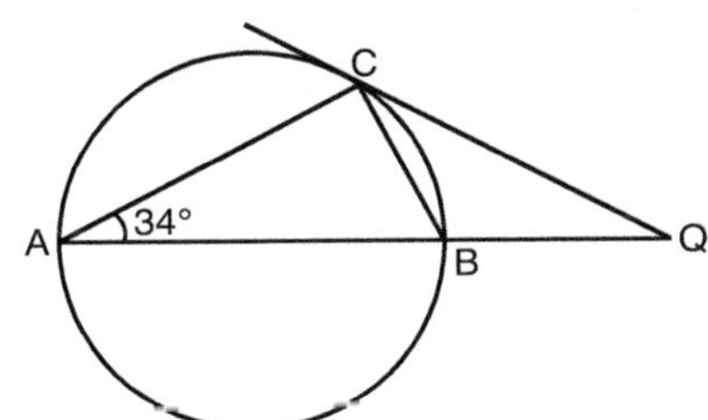

Ans. **(i)** AB is diameter.

$\therefore \qquad\qquad \angle ACB = 90°$

$\therefore$ In $\triangle ACB$,

$$\angle A + \angle C + \angle B = 180°$$
$$34 + 90 + \angle B = 180°$$
$$\angle B = 180° - (90° + 34°)$$
$$= 180° - 124°$$
$$\therefore \qquad \angle CBA = 56°$$

(ii) Now CQ is tangent

$\therefore \qquad \angle QCB = \angle CAB$ (Alternate segment angle)

$$= 34°$$

and $\quad \angle CBQ = 180° - \angle CBA$
$$= 180° - 56° = 124°$$

$\therefore \qquad \angle CQA = 180° - (\angle QCB + \angle CBQ)$
$$= 180° - (34° + 124°)$$
$$= 180° - 158° = 22°$$

Q. 22. In the given figure, PT touches a circle with centre O at R. Diameter SQ when produced meets PT at P. If $\angle SPR = x°$ and $\angle QRP = y°$. show that $x° + 2y° = 90°$. **[2006]**

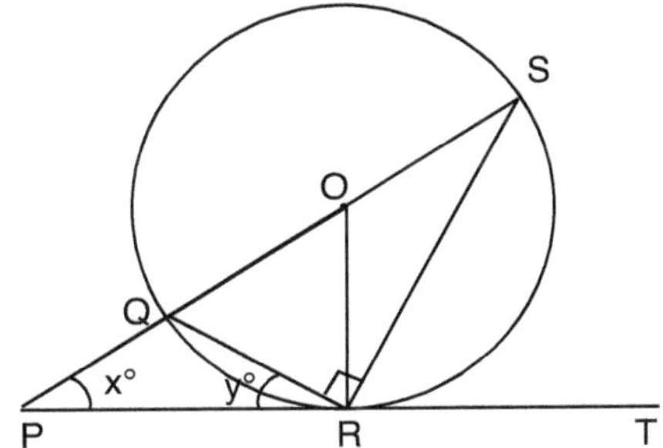

Ans. PRT is tangent at R and QR is chord.

$\therefore \qquad \angle QRP = \angle QSR = y°$

(Angle in alternate segment)

and $\qquad \angle QRS = 90°$

($\because$ QS is diameter and angle in semicircle is right angle)

Now in $\triangle PRS,$

$$\angle SPR + \angle PRS + \angle RSP = 180°$$
$$x° + y° + 90 + y° = 180°$$
$$x° + 2y° = 180° - 90°$$
$$x° + 2y° = 90°$$

Long Answer Type Questions

Q. 1. In the given figure TP and TQ are two tangents to the circle with centre O, touching at A and C respectively. If $\angle BCQ = 55^\circ$ and $\angle BAP = 60^\circ$, find :

(i) $\angle OBA$ and $\angle OBC$

(ii) $\angle AOC$

(iii) $\angle ATC$ **[2020]**

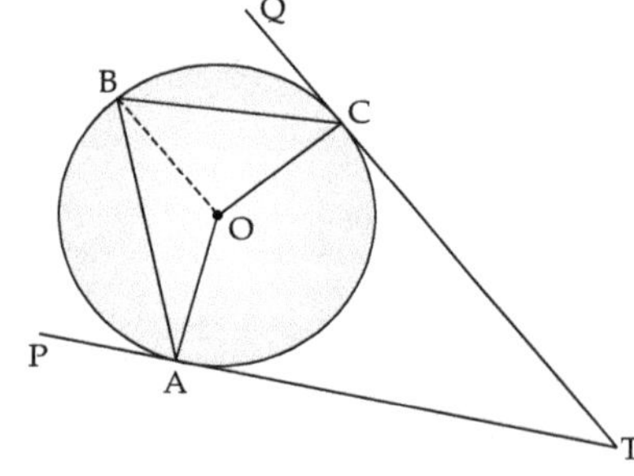

Marking Scheme

(i) $\angle BCQ = 55^\circ$ \ $\angle OCB = 90^\circ - 55^\circ = 35^\circ$

      (radius & tangent makes $\angle = 90^\circ$)

  \ $\angle OBC = \angle OCB = 35^\circ$ ($\because$ OB = OC)

  $\angle OBA = \angle OAB = 90^\circ - 60^\circ = 30^\circ$

      ($\because$ OA = OB & $\angle OAP = 90^\circ$)

  $\angle OBA = 30^\circ$

(ii) $\angle ABC = \angle OBA + \angle OBC = 30^\circ + 35^\circ = 65^\circ$

  \ $\angle AOC = 2\angle ABC = 2 \times 65^\circ = 130^\circ$

     (Angle at the centre is double angle at the

      $\angle AOC = 130^\circ$ remaining circumference)

(iii) $\angle ATC = 360^\circ - (90 + 90 + \angle AOC)$

     ($\because$ angles of quadrilateral adds upto 180°)

  $\angle ATC = 360^\circ - (180^\circ + 130^\circ)$

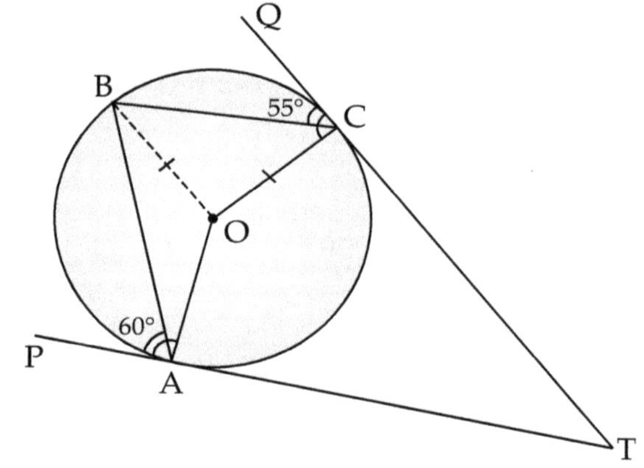

  $= 360^\circ - 310^\circ$

  $= 50^\circ$

Ans. Given : $\angle BCQ = 55^\circ$ and $\angle BAP = 60^\circ$

(i) $\angle OAP = 90^\circ$

           [$\because$ Tangent $\perp$ radius]

$\Rightarrow$ $\angle OAB + \angle PAB = 90^\circ$

$\Rightarrow$ $\angle OAB + 60^\circ = 90^\circ$

$\Rightarrow$ $\angle OAB = 90^\circ - 60^\circ = 30^\circ$

Now, in $\triangle AOB$

        $OA = OB$

          [Radii of same circle]

$\therefore$ $\angle OBA = \angle OAB = 30^\circ$

    [Equal angles opposite to equal sides]

Now, $\angle OCQ = 90^\circ$

          [$\because$ Tangent $\perp$ radius]

$\Rightarrow$ $\angle OCB + \angle BCQ = 90^\circ$

$\Rightarrow$ $\angle OCB + 55^\circ = 90^\circ$

$\Rightarrow$ $\angle OCB = 90^\circ - 55^\circ = 35^\circ$

In $\triangle BOC$,

        $OC = OB$

          [Radii of same circle]

$\Rightarrow$ $\angle OBC = \angle OCB = 35^\circ$

(ii) We know, angle subtended by an arc at the centre is double the angle subtended on the remaining part of the circle.

$\therefore$ $\angle AOC = 2\angle ABC$

         $= 2(\angle OBA + \angle OBC)$

         $= 2(30^\circ + 35^\circ)$

         $= 2 \times 65^\circ = 130^\circ$

(iii) In quad. $AOCT$,

  $\angle ATC + \angle OAT + \angle AOC + \angle OCT = 360^\circ$

$\Rightarrow$ $\angle ATC + 90^\circ + 130^\circ + 90^\circ = 360^\circ$

        [$\because \angle OAT = \angle OCT = 90^\circ$]

$\Rightarrow$ $\angle ATC = 360^\circ - 310^\circ = 50^\circ$

Q. 2. In the given figure, ABCDE is a pentagon inscribed in a circle such that AC is a diameter and side BC ‖ AE. If ∠BAC = 50°, find giving reasons: **[2019]**

(i) ∠ACB

(ii) ∠EDC

(iii) ∠BEC

Hence prove that BE is also a diameter.

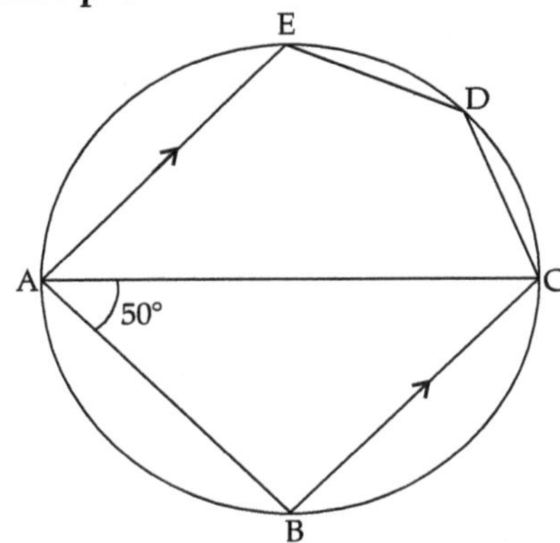

📋 Marking Scheme -

(i) In △ABC, ∠ABC = 90°   (Angle in a semi circle)
∠BAC = 50°   (given)
∴ ∠ACB = 40°

(ii) ∵ AE//BC
∴ ∠CAE = ∠ACB = 40°   (pair of alternate ∠s)
In cyclic quadrilateral ACDE

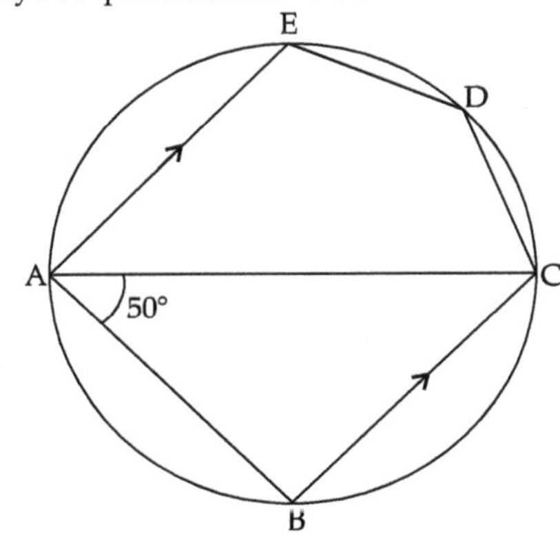

∠CAE + ∠EDC
= 180°   (opposite ∠s of cyclic quadrilateral are supplementary)

40° + ∠EDC = 180°
∠EDC = 140°

(iii) ∠BEC = ∠BAC = 50°   (angles in the same segment)

(iv) ∠AEB = 90 – 50 = 40°
∴ ∠EBC = 40°   (alternate angles)
∴ ∠ECB = 90°
∴ BE is a diameter.

Ans.   Given, AC is diameter, BC ‖ AE, and ∠BAC = 50°

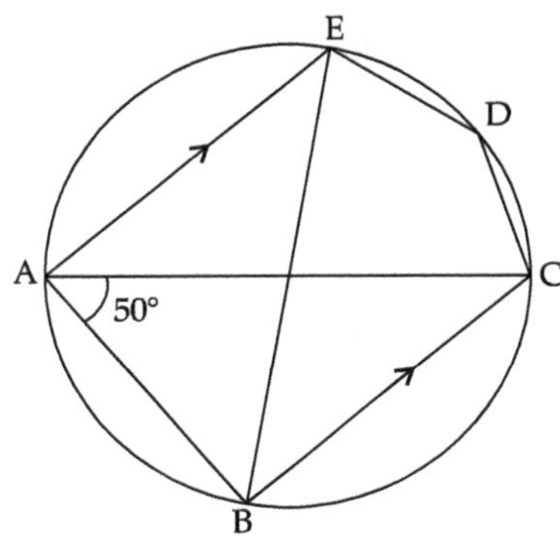

(i)   ∠ABC = 90°
(∵ AC is a diameter)

In △ABC,

∴ ∠ACB + ∠BAC + ∠ABC = 180°
(Angles sum property)

⇒   ∠ACB + 50° + 90° = 180°

⇒   ∠ACB = 180° – 140°

∠ACB = 40°

(ii)   ∠CAE = ∠ACB
(Alternate angles as BC ‖ AE)
= 40°

∴   ∠EDC + ∠CAE = 180°

(Sum of opposite angles of a cyclic quadrilateral is 180°)

⇒   ∠EDC + 40° = 180°

⇒   ∠EDC = 180° – 40°

∠EDC = 140°

(iii)   ∠BEC = ∠BAC

(Angles on same segment are equal)
= 50°

Now,   ∠BAE = ∠BAC + ∠CAE
= 50° + 40°
= 90°

We know that, if an angle of a triangle in a circle is 90°. Then, the hypotenuse must be the diameter of the circle.

Hence, BE is a diameter   (∵ ∠BAE = 90°)

Hence Proved.

Q. 3. PQRS is a cyclic quadrilateral. Given, ∠QPS = 73°, ∠PQS = 55° and ∠PSR = 82°, calculate:

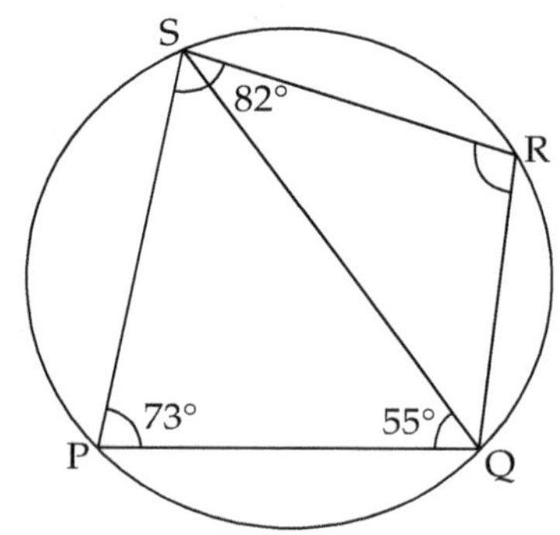

    (i) ∠**QRS**

    (ii) ∠**RQS**

    (iii) ∠**PRQ**   **[2018]**

Ans. Given, $\angle QPS = 73°$, $\angle PQS = 55°$, $\angle PSR = 82°$

  (i) $\angle QRS + \angle QPS = 180°$

        (sum of opposite angles of a cyclic quadrilateral are supplementary)

    $\Rightarrow$ $\angle QRS + 73° = 180°$

    $\Rightarrow$ $\angle QRS = 180° - 73° = 107°.$

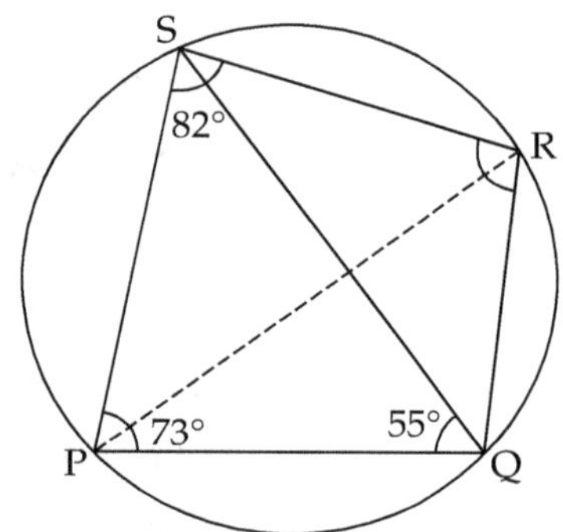

  (ii) $\angle PQR + \angle PSR = 180°$

        (Opposite angles of a cyclic quadrilateral are supplementary)

    $\Rightarrow$ $\angle PQR + 82° = 180°$

    $\Rightarrow$ $\angle PQR = 180° - 82°$

    $\Rightarrow$ $\angle PQR = 98°$

    $\Rightarrow$ $\angle RQS + \angle PQS = 98°$

    $\Rightarrow$ $\angle RQS + 55° = 98°$

    $\Rightarrow$ $\angle RQS = 98° - 55° = 43°.$

  (iii) $\angle PSQ + \angle QPS + \angle PQS = 180°$

        (sum of angles of a triangle is 180°)

    $\Rightarrow$ $\angle PSQ + 73° + 55° = 180°$

    $\Rightarrow$ $\angle PSQ = 180° - 128° = 52°$

    $\therefore$ $\angle PRQ = \angle PSQ$

        (angles on same segment are equal)

    $\Rightarrow$ $\angle PRQ = 52°.$

Q. 4. In the figure given, O is the centre of the circle. ∠**DAE = 70°**. Find, giving suitable reasons, the measure of:

  (i) ∠**BCD**   (ii) ∠**BOD**   (iii) ∠**OBD**

                           [2017]

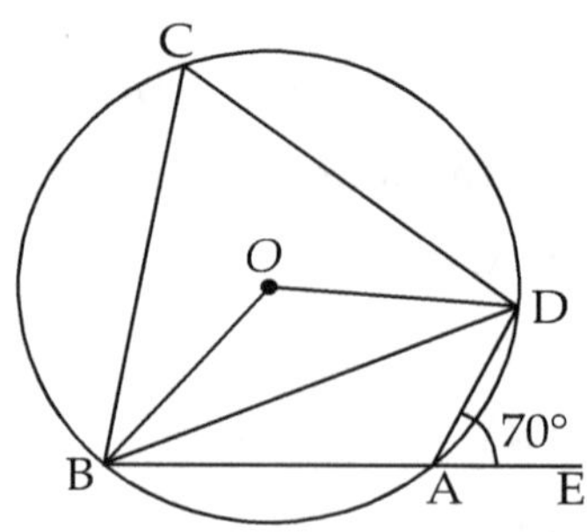

Ans. Given, $\angle DAE = 70°$

  (i) $\angle BAD + \angle DAE = 180°$ (Linear pair)

    $\Rightarrow$ $\angle BAD = 180° - 70° = 110°$

  Now, $\angle BCD + \angle BAD = 180°$.

        (Sum of opposite angles of cyclic quadrilateral is 180°)

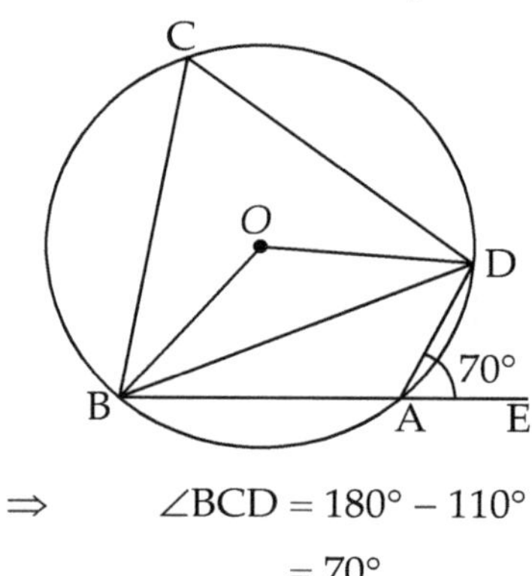

    $\Rightarrow$ $\angle BCD = 180° - 110°$

              $= 70°$

  (ii) $\angle BOD = 2\,\angle BCD$

    (Angle that an arc subtends at the centre is twice the angle at circumference of the circle)

              $= 2 \times 70°$

              $= 140°$

  (iii) $\angle OBD = \angle ODB$

             (OB = OD = radius)

    $\therefore$ $\angle OBD + \angle ODB + \angle BOD = 180°$

        (Sum of angles in a triangle is 180°)

    $\Rightarrow$ $\angle OBD + \angle OBD + 140° = 180°$

             ($\because \angle OBD = \angle ODB$)

    $\Rightarrow$ $2\,\angle OBD = 180° - 140°$

    $\Rightarrow$ $\angle OBD = \dfrac{40°}{2} = 20°$

Q. 5. In the figure given below, AD is a diameter. O is the centre of the circle. AD is parallel to BC and ∠**CBD = 32°**. Find:

  (i) ∠**OBD**   (ii) ∠**AOB**   (iii) ∠**BED**

                           [2016]

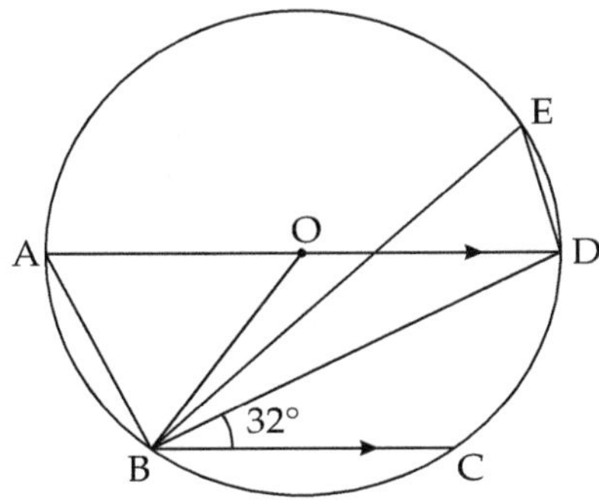

Ans. **(i)** Since, AD is parallel to BC and BD is a transversal.

$$\therefore \quad \angle ODB = \angle CBD$$

(Alternate interior angles)

Also, $\quad OB = OD \quad$ (Radii)

$$\therefore \quad \angle OBD = \angle ODB = 32°$$

(ii) $\quad \angle AOB = 2 \angle ADB$

(The angle that an arc of a circle subtends at the centre is double which it subtends at any point on the remaining part of the circle)

$$= 2 \times 32°$$
$$= 64°$$

(iii) In $\triangle AOB$ (OA = OB, radii of circle)

$$\therefore \angle OAB + \angle AOB + \angle OBA = 180°$$
$$\angle OAB + 64° + \angle OAB = 180°$$
$$2 \angle OAB = 180° - 64°$$
$$= 116°$$
$$\angle OAB = 58°$$
$$\angle OAB = \angle BED = 58°$$

(Angles in the same segment)

Q. 6. **In the figure given below, O is the centre of the circle and SP is a tangent. If $\angle SRT = 65°$, find the value of x, y and z.** **[2015]**

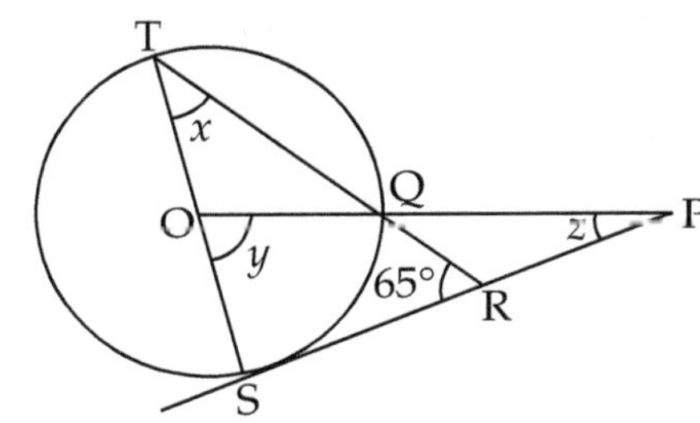

Ans. Given, $\quad \angle SRT = 65°$ and SP is a tangent

$$\therefore \quad \angle TSR = 90°$$

(angle between the radius and tangent)

In $\triangle STR$,

$$\angle TSR + \angle SRT + \angle STR = 180°$$

(Angle sum property of triangle)

$$\therefore \quad \angle STR = 180° - (65° + 90°)$$

$$x = 180° - 155°$$
$$x = 25°$$

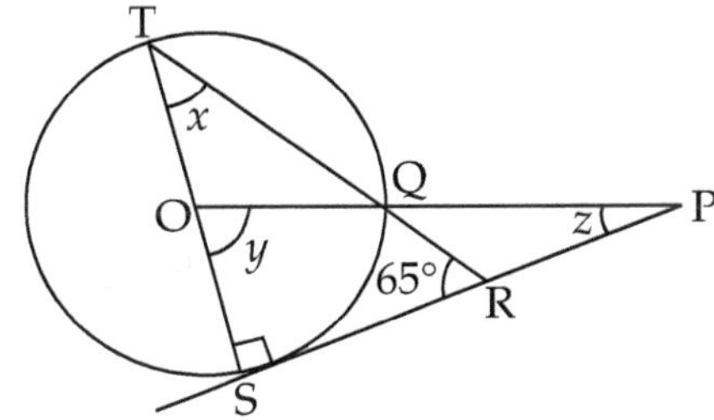

$$\angle y = 2 \angle x$$

(Angle subtended at the centre is double that of the angle subtended by the arc at same centre)

$$\therefore \quad y = 2 \times 25° = 50°$$

In $\triangle SPO$,

$$\angle SOP + \angle OSP + \angle SPO = 180°$$

(Angle sum property of triangle)

$$\therefore \quad \angle SPO = 180° - (90° + 50°)$$
$$z = 40°$$

Hence, $x = 25°$, $y = 50°$ and $z = 40°$

Q. 7. **In the given figure O is the centre of the circle. Tangents at A and B meet at C.**

If $\angle ACO = 30°$, find

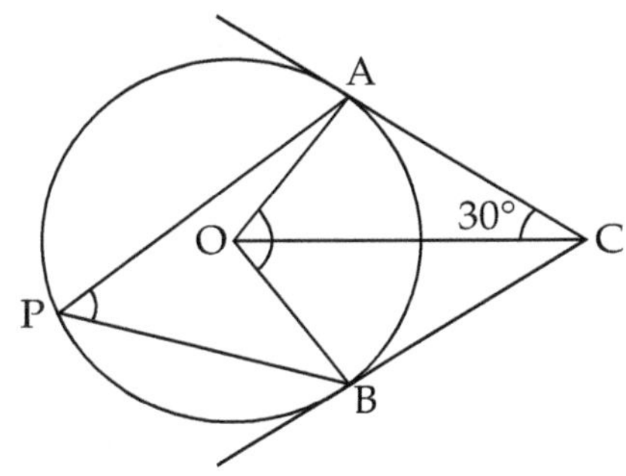

(i) $\angle BCO$

(ii) $\angle AOB$

(iii) $\angle APB$ **[2011]**

Ans. Given a circle with centre OCA and CB are tangent to it. $\angle OAC = \angle OBC = 90°$ and $\angle ACO = 30°$.

(i) Since, $\triangle ACO \cong \triangle OBC = 30°$ (By SSS)

(AC = BC, AO = OB and OC is common)

$$\because \angle ACO = \angle BCO = 30°$$

(ii) $\quad \angle OAC = \angle OBC = 90°$

$$\angle ACO = 30° \text{ (given)}$$

$$\angle AOC = \angle BOC \quad (\because \triangle ACO \cong \triangle BOC)$$

$$\therefore \quad \angle AOC = \angle BOC = 180° - (90° + 30°)$$

($\because$ sum of the 3 angles of a $\triangle$ is 180°)

$$\angle AOC = 180° - 120°$$
$$\angle AOC = 60°$$

$$\therefore \quad \angle AOB = \angle AOC + \angle BOC$$

$$= 60° + 60°$$
$$\angle AOB = 120°$$

(iii) $\quad \angle APB = \dfrac{1}{2}\angle AOB$

$$= \dfrac{120°}{2} = 60°$$

(∵ Angle subtended at the remaining part of the circle is half the angle subtended at the centre.)

Q. 8. **In the given figure O is the centre of the circle, $\angle BAD = 75°$ and chord BC = chord CD. Find:**

   (i) $\angle$**BOC**

   (ii) $\angle$**OBD**

   (iii) $\angle$**BCD.**   **[2009]**

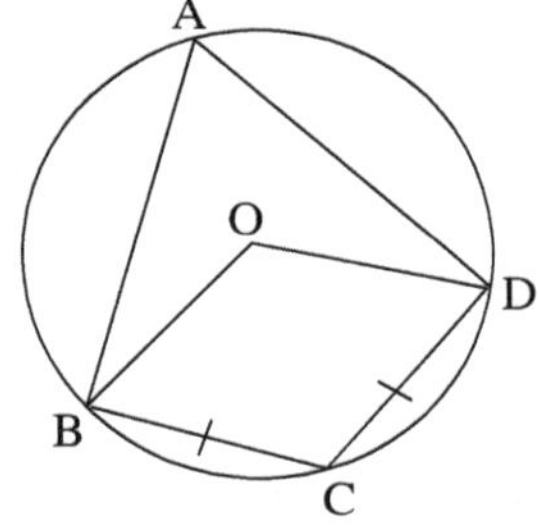

Ans. **(i)** Given, $\angle BAD = 75°$ and chord BC = chord CD

$$\angle BOD = 2 \cdot \angle BAD$$
$$= 2 \times 75° = 150°$$

$$\therefore\ \angle BOC = \dfrac{1}{2}\angle BOD = \dfrac{1}{2} \times 150° = 75°$$

(ii) $\quad \angle OBD = \dfrac{1}{2}(180° - \angle BOD)$

$$= \dfrac{1}{2}(180° - 150°) = 15°$$

(iii) $\quad \angle BCD = 180° - \angle BAD$

$$= 180° - 75° = 105°$$

Q. 9. **In the given figure, if $\angle ACE = 43°$ and $\angle CAF = 62°$? find the value of a, b and c.**   **[2007]**

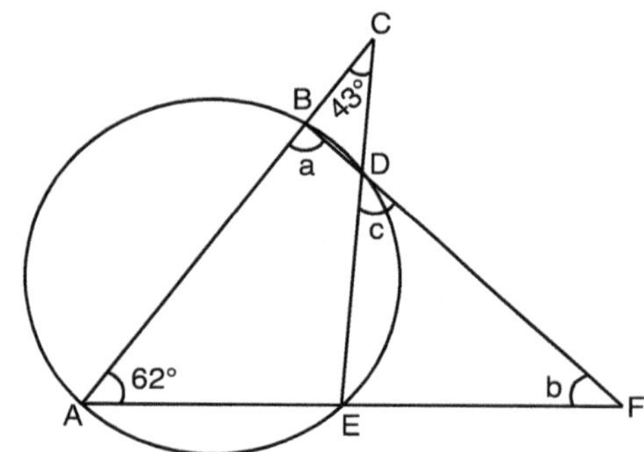

Ans. ABDE is cyclic quadrilateral.

$$\therefore\qquad \angle ABD + \angle AED = 180°$$

and $\qquad \angle EAB + \angle BDE = 180°$

Now in $\triangle ACE$,

$$\angle A + \angle C + \angle E = 180°$$
$$62° + 43° + \angle E = 180°$$
$$\angle E = 180° - 105° = 75°$$

so $\qquad \angle ABD + \angle AED = 180°$

$\therefore\qquad\qquad a + 75° = 180°$

$\therefore\qquad\qquad a = 105°$

$$\angle EDF = \angle BAE$$

(exterior angles of cyclic quadrilateral)

$$62° = c \qquad \therefore c = 62°$$

In $\triangle ABF$,

$$\angle ABF + \angle BAF + \angle BFA = 180°$$
$$105° + 62° + b = 180°$$
$$167° + b = 180°$$
$$b = 180° - 167° = 13°$$

$$a = 105°,\ b = 13°\ \text{and}\ c = 62°.$$

Q. 10. **In the given figure, $\angle BAD = 65°$, $\angle ABD = 70°$ and $\angle BDC = 45°$. Find:**

   (i) $\angle$**BCD,**

   (ii) $\angle$**ADB.**

Hence show that AC is a diameter.   **[2006]**

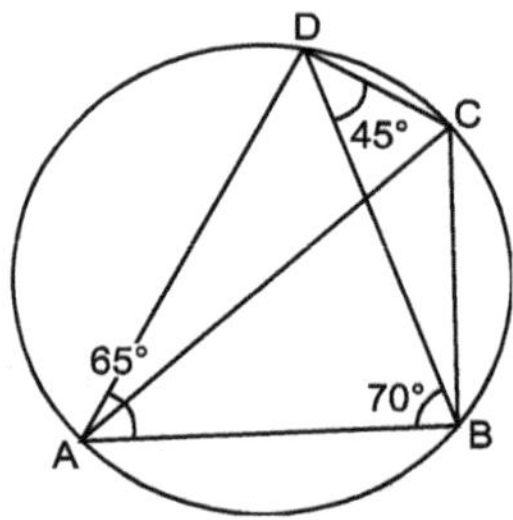

Ans. Given: $\angle BAD = 65°$, $\angle ABD = 70°$ and $\angle BDC = 45°$.

(i) Quadrilateral ABCD is cyclic quadrilateral.

$$\therefore\qquad \angle DAB + \angle BCD = 180°$$
$$65° + \angle BCD = 180°$$
$$\therefore\qquad \angle BCD = 180° - 65° = 115°$$

(ii) In $\triangle ADB$,

$$\angle \triangle AB + \angle ABD + \angle ADB = 180°$$
$$65° + 70° + \angle ADB = 180°$$
$$\angle ADB = 180° - 135°$$
$$\angle ADB = 45°$$

Now, $\qquad \angle BDC = 45°$ (given)

and $\qquad \angle ADB = 45°$ (Proved)

$\therefore\quad \angle BDC + \angle ADB = 45° + 45° = 90°$

$\therefore$ Hence AC is a diameter.

Volume and Surface Areas of Solids

Short Answer Type Questions

Q. 1. From a solid wooden cylinder of height 28 cm and diameter 6 cm, two conical cavities are hollowed out. The diameters of the cones are also of 6 cm and height 10.5 cm.

Taking $\pi = \dfrac{22}{7}$ find the volume of the remaining solid. **[2020]**

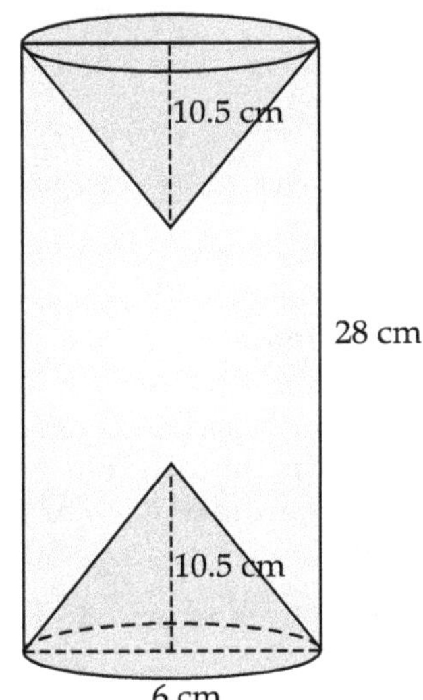

 **Marking Scheme**

Volume of Remaining Solid
= Volume of Cylinder − 2 × Volume of Cone

$$= \pi r^2 - 2 \times \frac{1}{3} \times \pi r^2 \times h$$

$$= \frac{22}{7} \times 3^2 \times 28 - 2 \times \frac{1}{3} \times \frac{22}{7} \times 3^2 \times 10.5$$

$$= \frac{22}{7} \times 3^2 \left[28 - \frac{2}{3} \times 10.5 \right]$$

$$= \frac{22}{7} \times 9 \times [28 - 7]$$

$$= \frac{22}{7} \times 9 \times 21$$

$$= 66 \times 9$$
$$= 594 \text{ cm}^3$$

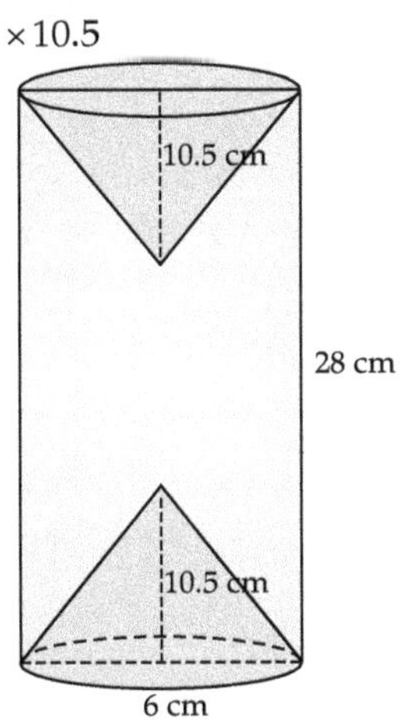

Ans. Given : Height of cylinder $(h) = 28$ cm

Diameter of cylinder = 6 cm

$\Rightarrow$ Radius of cylinder $(r) = \dfrac{6}{2} = 3$ cm

Also, height of cones (H) = 10.5 cm

And, diameter of cones = 6 cm

$\Rightarrow$ Radius of cones $(R) = \dfrac{6}{2} = 3$ cm

Now, volume of solid cylinder $= \pi r^2 h$

$$= \frac{22}{7} \times 3^2 \times 28$$

$$= \frac{22}{7} \times 9 \times 28$$

$$= 792 \text{ cm}^3$$

And, volume of two cones

$$= 2 \times \frac{1}{3} \pi R^2 H$$

$$= 2 \times \frac{1}{3} \times \frac{22}{7} \times 3^2 \times 10.5$$

$$= 198 \text{ cm}^3$$

So, volume of the remaining solid

$$= (792 - 198) \text{ cm}^3$$
$$= 594 \text{ cm}^3$$

Q. 2. The circumference of the base of a cylindrical vessel is 132 cm and its height is 25 cm. Find the
(i) radius of the cylinder
(ii) volume of cylinder.

$$\left(\text{use } \pi = \frac{22}{7} \right)$$ **[2018]**

Ans. Given, circumference of base of cylinder = 132 cm, height of cylinder, $h = 25$ cm.

(i) Let r be the radius of cylinder

$\therefore \qquad 2\pi r = 132$

$\Rightarrow \qquad 2 \times \dfrac{22}{7} \times r = 132$

$\Rightarrow \qquad r = \dfrac{132 \times 7}{2 \times 22} = 21$ cm

(ii) Volume of the cylinder

$$= \pi r^2 h$$

$$= \frac{22}{7} \times (21)^2 \times 25$$
$$= 34650 \text{ cm}^3.$$

Q. 3. A conical tent has to accommodate 77 persons. Each person must have 16 m³ of air to breathe. Given the radius of the tent as 7 m, find the height of the tent and also its curved surface area. **[2017]**

Ans. Given, number of persons = 77.

Volume of air required by each person = 16 m³

∴ Total volume of air required for 77 persons

$= 77 \times 16 \text{ m}^3 = 1232 \text{ m}^3.$

Radius $(r) = 7$ m

Let the height of tent be h m.

Then, Volume of tent $= \frac{1}{3}\pi r^2 h$

Long Answer Type Questions

Q. 1. The volume of a conical tent is 1232 m³ and the area of the base floor is 154 m². Calculate the:

(i) radius of the floor.

(ii) height of the tent.

(iii) length of the canvas required to cover this conical tent if its width is 2 m. **[2008]**

Ans. Given, Volume of cone = 1232 m³

(i) $\qquad$ Area of floor = 154 m²

$$\pi r^2 = 154$$
$$\frac{22}{7} \times r^2 = 154$$
$$r^2 = \frac{154 \times 7}{22} = 49$$
$$r = 7 \text{ m}.$$

(ii) $\qquad$ Volume of cone $= \frac{1}{3}\pi r^2 h$

$$1232 = \frac{1}{3} \times \frac{22}{7} \times 7 \times 7 \times h$$

$\Rightarrow \qquad h = \dfrac{1232 \times 3}{22 \times 7}$

$$= 24 \text{ m}$$

(iii) Curved surface area of cone

$$= \text{length of canvas} \times \text{width}$$
$$\pi r l = L \times 2$$

∴ $\qquad L = \dfrac{\pi r \sqrt{h^2 + r^2}}{2}$

$\Rightarrow \qquad 1232 = \dfrac{1}{3} \times \dfrac{22}{7} \times 7 \times 7 \times h$

$\Rightarrow \qquad h = \dfrac{1232 \times 2}{22 \times 7} = 24$ m

∴ $\qquad$ Required height = 24 m

Now, slant height $(l) = \sqrt{h^2 + r^2}$

$$= \sqrt{24^2 + 7^2} = \sqrt{576 + 49}$$
$$= \sqrt{625} = 25 \text{ m}$$

∴ The curved surface area

$$= \pi r l$$
$$= \frac{22}{7} \times 7 \times 25$$
$$= 550 \text{ m}^2$$

∴ $\qquad L = \dfrac{22 \times 7 \times \sqrt{24^2 + 7^2}}{7 \times 2}$

$$= 11 \times \sqrt{625}$$
$$= 11 \times 25 = 275 \text{ m}$$

Q. 2. A vessel in the form of an inverted cone is filled with water to the brim. Its height is 20 cm and diameter is 16·8 cm. Two equal solid cones are dropped in it so that they are fully submerged. As a result, one third of the water in the original cone overflows. What is the volume of each of the solid cones submerged? **[2006]**

Ans. height = 20 cm, diameter = 16.8 cm or

radius $= \dfrac{16.8}{2} = 8.4$ cm.

Volume of water in bigger cone $= \dfrac{1}{3}\pi r^2 h$

$$= \frac{1}{3} \times \frac{22}{7} \times 8.4 \times 8.4 \times 20$$
$$= 1478.4 \text{ cm}^3$$

Volume of water that overflows when two equal cones are submerged

$$= \frac{1}{3} \times 1478.4 = 492.8$$

∴ Volume of two equal cones = 492.8 cm³

So, Volume of each cone $= \dfrac{1}{2} \times 492.8 = 246.4$ cm³

17 Trigonometrical Identities

Short Answer Type Questions

Q. 1. Prove that :

$$\frac{\sin A}{1+\cot A} - \frac{\cos A}{1+\tan A} = \sin A - \cos A \qquad [2020]$$

Marking Scheme

$$\frac{\sin A}{1+\dfrac{\cos A}{\sin A}} - \frac{\cos A}{1+\dfrac{\sin A}{\cos A}}$$

$$\frac{\sin^2 A}{\sin A + \cos A} - \frac{\cos^2 A}{\cos A + \sin A} = \frac{\sin^2 A - \cos^2 A}{\sin A + \cos A}$$

$$\frac{(\sin A + \cos A)(\sin A - \cos A)}{(\sin A + \cos A)} = \sin A - \cos A$$

Ans. To prove :

$$\frac{\sin A}{1+\cot A} - \frac{\cos A}{1+\tan A} = \sin A - \cos A$$

$$\text{Taking, L.H.S.} = \frac{\sin A}{1+\cot A} - \frac{\cos A}{1+\tan A}$$

$$= \frac{\sin A \times \sin A}{\sin A + \cos A} - \frac{\cos A \times \cos A}{\cos A + \sin A}$$

$$= \frac{\sin^2 A - \cos^2 A}{\sin A - \cos A}$$

$$= \frac{(\sin A - \cos A)(\sin A + \cos A)}{(\sin A + \cos A)}$$

$$[\because a^2 - b^2 = (a-b)(a+b)]$$

$$= \sin A - \cos A = \text{R.H.S.}$$

Q. 2. Prove that:

$$(\operatorname{cosec} \theta - \sin \theta)(\sec \theta - \cos \theta)(\tan \theta + \cot \theta) = 1$$
$$[2019]$$

Marking Scheme

$$(\operatorname{cosec} \theta - \sin \theta)(\sec \theta - \cos \theta)(\tan \theta + \cot \theta) = 1$$

$$\text{LHS} - \left(\frac{1}{\sin \theta} - \sin \theta\right)\left(\frac{1}{\cos \theta} - \cos \theta\right)\left(\frac{\sin \theta}{\cos \theta} + \frac{\cos \theta}{\sin \theta}\right)$$

$$= \left(\frac{1 - \sin^2 \theta}{\sin \theta}\right) \times \left(\frac{1 - \cos^2 \theta}{\cos \theta}\right)\left(\frac{\sin^2 \theta + \cos^2 \theta}{\sin \theta \cos \theta}\right)$$

$$= \frac{\cos^2 \theta}{\sin \theta} \times \frac{\sin^2 \theta}{\cos \theta} \times \frac{1}{\sin \theta \cos \theta}$$

$$= 1 = \text{RHS}$$

Ans. To prove:

$$(\operatorname{cosec} \theta - \sin \theta)(\sec \theta - \cos \theta)(\tan \theta + \cot \theta) = 1$$
$$\text{L.H.S.} = (\operatorname{cosec} \theta - \sin \theta)(\sec \theta - \cos \theta)$$
$$(\tan \theta + \cot \theta)$$

$$= \left(\frac{1}{\sin \theta} - \sin \theta\right)\left(\frac{1}{\cos \theta} - \cos \theta\right)\left(\frac{\sin \theta}{\cos \theta} + \frac{\cos \theta}{\sin \theta}\right)$$

$$= \left(\frac{1 - \sin^2 \theta}{\sin \theta}\right)\left(\frac{1 - \cos^2 \theta}{\cos \theta}\right)\left(\frac{\sin^2 \theta + \cos^2 \theta}{\sin \theta \cos \theta}\right)$$

$$= \frac{\cos^2 \theta}{\sin \theta} \times \frac{\sin^2 \theta}{\cos \theta} \times \frac{1}{\sin \theta \cos \theta}$$

$$= \frac{\cos^2 \theta}{\cos^2 \theta} \times \frac{\sin^2 \theta}{\sin^2 \theta}$$

$$= 1 = \text{R.H.S.} \qquad \textbf{Hence Proved.}$$

Q. 3. Prove that $\sqrt{\sec^2 \theta + \operatorname{cosec}^2 \theta} = \tan \theta + \cot \theta$
$$[2018]$$

Ans. To prove, $\sqrt{\sec^2 \theta + \operatorname{cosec}^2 \theta} = \tan \theta + \cot \theta$

$$\therefore \qquad \text{L.H.S.} = \sqrt{\sec^2 \theta + \operatorname{cosec}^2 \theta}$$

$$= \sqrt{1 + \tan^2 \theta + 1 + \cot^2 \theta}$$

$$[\because 1 + \tan^2 \theta = \sec^2 \theta, \ 1 + \cot^2 \theta = \operatorname{cosec}^2 \theta]$$

$$= \sqrt{\tan^2 \theta + \cot^2 \theta + 2}$$

$$= \sqrt{\tan^2 \theta \cot^2 \theta + 2 \tan \theta \cdot \cot \theta}$$

$$[\because \tan \theta \cdot \cot \theta = 1]$$

$$= \sqrt{(\tan \theta + \cot \theta)^2}$$

$$[\because (a+b)^2 = a^2 + b^2 + 2ab]$$

$$= \tan \theta + \cot \theta$$

$$= \text{R.H.S.} \qquad \textbf{Hence Proved.}$$

Q. 4. Prove that $\dfrac{\sin \theta - 2 \sin^3 \theta}{2 \cos^3 \theta - \cos \theta} = \tan \theta$ $\qquad [2017]$

Ans. L.H.S. $= \dfrac{\sin \theta - 2 \sin^3 \theta}{2 \cos^3 \theta - \cos \theta}$

$$= \frac{\sin \theta(1 - 2 \sin^2 \theta)}{\cos \theta(2 \cos^2 \theta - 1)}$$

$$= \frac{\sin \theta\{1 - 2(1 - \cos^2 \theta)\}}{\cos \theta(2 \cos^2 \theta - 1)}$$

$$[\because \sin^2 \theta + \cos^2 \theta = 1 \Rightarrow \sin^2 \theta = 1 - \cos^2 \theta]$$

$$= \frac{\sin\theta(1 - 2 + 2\cos^2\theta)}{\cos\theta(2\cos^2\theta - 1)}$$

$$= \frac{\sin\theta(2\cos^2\theta - 1)}{\cos\theta(2\cos^2\theta - 1)}$$

$$= \frac{\sin\theta}{\cos\theta} = \tan\theta = \text{R.H.S.}$$

Hence Proved.

Q. 5. Prove that $\dfrac{\cos A}{1 + \sin A} + \tan A = \sec A.$ **[2016]**

Ans. L.H.S. $= \dfrac{\cos A}{1 + \sin A} + \tan A$

$$= \frac{\cos A}{1 + \sin A} + \frac{\sin A}{\cos A} \qquad \left[\because \tan\theta = \frac{\sin\theta}{\cos\theta}\right]$$

$$= \frac{\cos^2 A + \sin A + \sin^2 A}{(1 + \sin A)\cos A}$$

$$= \frac{1 + \sin A}{(1 + \sin A)\cos A} \quad [\because \cos^2\theta + \sin^2\theta = 1]$$

$$= \frac{1}{\cos A} = \sec A = \text{R.H.S.}$$

Hence Proved.

Q. 6. Prove the identity

$(\sin\theta + \cos\theta)(\tan\theta + \cot\theta) = \sec\theta + \csc\theta.$
   [2014]

Ans. L.H.S. $= (\sin\theta + \cos\theta)(\tan\theta + \cot\theta)$

$$= (\sin\theta + \cos\theta)\left(\frac{\sin\theta}{\cos\theta} + \frac{\cos\theta}{\sin\theta}\right)$$

$$\left[\because \tan A = \frac{\sin A}{\cos A}, \; \cot A = \frac{\cos A}{\sin A}\right]$$

$$= (\sin\theta + \cos\theta)\left(\frac{\sin^2\theta + \cos^2\theta}{\sin\theta\cos\theta}\right)$$

$$[\because \sin^2\theta + \cos^2\theta = 1]$$

$$= (\sin\theta + \cos\theta)\frac{1}{\sin\theta\cos\theta}$$

$$= \frac{\sin\theta}{\sin\theta\cos\theta} + \frac{\cos\theta}{\sin\theta\cos\theta}$$

$$= \frac{1}{\cos\theta} + \frac{1}{\sin\theta}$$

$$= \sec\theta + \csc\theta = \text{R.H.S.}$$

Hence Proved.

Q. 7. Show that, $\sqrt{\dfrac{1 - \cos A}{1 + \cos A}} = \dfrac{\sin A}{1 + \cos A}$ **[2013]**

Ans. To prove, $\sqrt{\dfrac{1 - \cos A}{1 + \cos A}} = \dfrac{\sin A}{1 + \cos A}$

L.H.S. $= \sqrt{\dfrac{1 - \cos A}{1 + \cos A}} = \sqrt{\dfrac{1 - \cos A}{1 + \cos A} \times \dfrac{1 + \cos A}{1 + \cos A}}$

$$= \sqrt{\frac{(1 - \cos^2 A)}{(1 + \cos A)^2}} = \sqrt{\frac{\sin^2 A}{(1 + \cos A)^2}}$$

$$= \sqrt{\left(\frac{\sin A}{1 + \cos A}\right)^2}$$

$$= \frac{\sin A}{1 + \cos A} = \text{R.H.S.} \qquad \textbf{Hence Proved.}$$

Q. 8. Prove that $\dfrac{\tan^2\theta}{(\sec\theta - 1)^2} = \dfrac{1 + \cos\theta}{1 - \cos\theta}$ **[2012]**

Ans. L.H.S. $= \dfrac{\tan^2\theta}{(\sec\theta - 1)^2}$

$$= \frac{\dfrac{\sin^2\theta}{\cos^2\theta}}{\left(\dfrac{1}{\cos\theta} - 1\right)^2}$$

$$\left(\because \tan\theta = \frac{\sin\theta}{\cos\theta}; \; \sec\theta = \frac{1}{\cos\theta}\right)$$

$$= \frac{\dfrac{\sin^2\theta}{\cos^2\theta}}{\dfrac{(1 - \cos\theta)^2}{\cos^2\theta}} = \frac{\sin^2\theta}{(1 - \cos\theta)^2}$$

$$= \frac{1 - \cos^2\theta}{(1 - \cos\theta)^2} \qquad (\because \sin^2\theta = 1 - \cos^2\theta)$$

$$= \frac{(1 - \cos\theta)(1 + \cos\theta)}{(1 - \cos\theta)^2}$$

$$= \frac{1 + \cos\theta}{1 - \cos\theta} = \text{R.H.S.} \qquad \textbf{Hence Proved.}$$

Q. 9. Prove the following identity :

$$\frac{\sin A}{1 + \cos A} + \frac{1 + \cos A}{\sin A} = 2\csc A \qquad \textbf{[2009]}$$

Ans. To prove, $\dfrac{\sin A}{1 + \cos A} + \dfrac{1 + \cos A}{\sin A} = 2\csc A$

L. H.S. $= \dfrac{\sin A}{1 + \cos A} + \dfrac{1 + \cos A}{\sin A}$

$$= \frac{\sin^2 A + 1 + \cos^2 A + 2\cos A}{(1 + \cos A)\sin A}$$

$$= \frac{2 + 2\cos A}{(1 + \cos A)\sin A}$$

$$= \frac{2(1 + \cos A)}{(1 + \cos A)\cdot\sin A} = \frac{2}{\sin A}$$

$$= 2\csc A = \text{R.H.S.} \qquad \textbf{Hence Proved.}$$

Q. 10. Prove the identity: $\dfrac{\sin A}{1 + \cos A} = \operatorname{cosec} A - \cot A.$ **[2008]**

Ans. L. H.S. $= \dfrac{\sin A}{1 + \cos A}$

$= \dfrac{\sin A(1 - \cos A)}{(1 + \cos A)(1 - \cos A)}$

[Multiplying by $(1 - \cos A)$ in Nr. & Deno.]

$= \dfrac{\sin A(1 - \cos A)}{1 - \cos^2 A} = \dfrac{\sin A(1 - \cos A)}{\sin^2 A}$

$= \dfrac{1 - \cos A}{\sin A} = \dfrac{1}{\sin A} - \dfrac{\cos A}{\sin A}$

$= \operatorname{cosec} A - \cot A = $ R.H.S.

Hence Proved.

Q. 11. Prove the identity: $\dfrac{\sec A - 1}{\sec A + 1} = \dfrac{1 - \cos A}{1 + \cos A}$ **[2007]**

Ans. L. H.S. $= \dfrac{\sec A - 1}{\sec A + 1} = \dfrac{\dfrac{1}{\cos A} - 1}{\dfrac{1}{\cos A} + 1} +$

$= \dfrac{\dfrac{1 - \cos A}{\cos A}}{\dfrac{1 + \cos A}{\cos A}} = \dfrac{1 - \cos A}{1 + \cos A} = $ R.H.S.

Hence Proved

Q. 12. Prove that $\dfrac{\sin\theta\ \tan\theta}{1 - \cos\theta} = 1 + \sec\theta.$ **[2006]**

Ans. L. H.S. $= \dfrac{\sin\theta\tan\theta}{1 - \cos\theta} = \dfrac{\sin\theta \cdot \dfrac{\sin\theta}{\cos\theta}}{1 - \cos\theta}$

$= \dfrac{\sin^2\theta}{\cos\theta(1 - \cos\theta)}$

$= \dfrac{1 - \cos^2\theta}{\cos\theta(1 - \cos\theta)}$

$= \dfrac{(1 - \cos\theta)(1 + \cos\theta)}{\cos\theta(1 - \cos\theta)}$

$= \dfrac{1 + \cos\theta}{\cos\theta} = \dfrac{1}{\cos\theta} + \dfrac{\cos\theta}{\cos\theta}$

$= \sec\theta + 1 = $ R.H.S.   **Hence Proved.**

💬 Long Answer Type Questions

Q. 1. Prove the identity

$$\left(\dfrac{1 - \tan\theta}{1 - \cot\theta}\right)^2 = \tan^2\theta$$ **[2020]**

📋 **Marking Scheme**

$$\left(\dfrac{1 - \tan\theta}{1 - \cot\theta}\right)^2 = \tan^2\theta$$

L.H.S. $\left(\dfrac{1 - \tan\theta}{1 - \cot\theta}\right)^2 = \dfrac{\left(\dfrac{1}{1} - \dfrac{\sin\theta}{\cos\theta}\right)^2}{\left(\dfrac{1}{1} - \dfrac{\cos\theta}{\sin\theta}\right)^2}$

$= \left(\dfrac{\dfrac{\cos\theta - \sin\theta}{\cos\theta}}{\dfrac{\sin\theta - \cos\theta}{\sin\theta}}\right)^2$

$= \left(\dfrac{\cos\theta - \sin\theta}{\cos\theta} \times \dfrac{\sin\theta}{-(\cos\theta - \sin\theta)}\right)^2$

$= \left(-\dfrac{\sin\theta}{\cos\theta}\right)^2 = (-\tan\theta)^2 = \tan^2\theta = $ R.H.S.

Alternative Method :

$\text{LHS} = \left(\dfrac{1 - \tan\theta}{1 - \dfrac{1}{\tan\theta}}\right)^2 = \left(\dfrac{1 - \tan\theta}{\tan\theta - 1}\right)^2 \times \tan^2\theta$

$\left(-\dfrac{1 - \tan\theta}{1 - \tan\theta}\right)^2 \tan^2\theta = \tan^2\theta = $ RHS

Ans. To prove :

$$\left(\dfrac{1 - \tan\theta}{1 - \cot\theta}\right)^2 = \tan^2\theta$$

Taking   L.H.S. $= \left(\dfrac{1 - \tan\theta}{1 - \cot\theta}\right)^2$

$= \left(\dfrac{1 - \tan\theta}{1 - \dfrac{1}{\tan\theta}}\right)^2$

$= \left(\dfrac{1 - \tan\theta}{\dfrac{\tan\theta - 1}{\tan\theta}}\right)^2$

$= \left(\dfrac{-\tan\theta(1 - \tan\theta)}{1 - \tan\theta}\right)^2$

$= (-\tan\theta)^2$

$= \tan^2\theta$

$= $ R.H.S.   **Hence Proved.**

Q. 2. Prove that $(1 + \cot\theta - \operatorname{cosec}\theta)(1 + \tan\theta + \sec\theta) = 2$ **[2018]**

Ans. To prove, $(1 + \cot\theta - \operatorname{cosec}\theta)(1 + \tan\theta + \sec\theta) = 2$

$\therefore$ L.H.S. $= (1 + \cot\theta - \operatorname{cosec}\theta)$

$(1 + \tan\theta + \sec\theta)$

$$= \left(1 + \frac{\cos\theta}{\sin\theta} - \frac{1}{\sin\theta}\right)\left(1 + \frac{\sin\theta}{\cos\theta} + \frac{1}{\cos\theta}\right)$$

$$= \left(\frac{\sin\theta + \cos\theta - 1}{\sin\theta}\right)\left(\frac{\cos\theta + \sin\theta + 1}{\cos\theta}\right)$$

$$= \frac{(\sin\theta + \cos\theta)^2 - (1)^2}{\sin\theta\cos\theta}$$

$$[\because (a+b)(a-b) = a^2 - b^2]$$

$$= \frac{\sin^2\theta + \cos^2\theta + 2\sin\theta\cos\theta - 1}{\sin\theta\cos\theta}$$

$$= \frac{1 + 2\sin\theta\cos\theta - 1}{\sin\theta\cos\theta}$$

$$[\because \sin^2\theta + \cos^2\theta = 1]$$

$$= \frac{2\sin\theta\cos\theta}{\sin\theta\cos\theta}$$

$$= 2 = \text{R.H.S.} \qquad \textbf{Hence Proved.}$$

Q. 3. Prove that $\dfrac{\sin\theta}{1 - \cot\theta} + \dfrac{\cos\theta}{1 - \tan\theta} = \cos\theta + \sin\theta$

[2015]

Ans. L.H.S. $= \dfrac{\sin\theta}{1 - \cot\theta} + \dfrac{\cos\theta}{1 - \tan\theta}$

$$= \frac{\sin\theta}{1 - \dfrac{\cos\theta}{\sin\theta}} + \frac{\cos\theta}{1 - \dfrac{\sin\theta}{\cos\theta}}$$

$$\left(\because \tan\theta = \frac{\sin\theta}{\cos\theta}, \ \cot\theta = \frac{\cos\theta}{\sin\theta}\right)$$

$$\Rightarrow \quad = \frac{\sin\theta}{\dfrac{\sin\theta - \cos\theta}{\sin\theta}} + \frac{\cos\theta}{\dfrac{\cos\theta - \sin\theta}{\cos\theta}}$$

$$= \frac{\sin^2\theta}{\sin\theta - \cos\theta} + \frac{\cos^2\theta}{\cos\theta - \sin\theta}$$

$$= \frac{\sin^2\theta}{\sin\theta - \cos\theta} - \frac{\cos^2\theta}{\sin\theta - \cos\theta}$$

$$= \frac{\sin^2\theta - \cos^2\theta}{\sin\theta - \cos\theta}$$

$$[\because a^2 - b^2 = (a-b)(a+b)]$$

$$= \frac{(\sin\theta + \cos\theta)(\sin\theta - \cos\theta)}{(\sin\theta - \cos\theta)}$$

$$= (\cos\theta + \sin\theta) = \text{R.H.S.}$$

$$\textbf{Hence Proved.}$$

Q. 4. Prove that

(cosec A – sin A) (sec A – cos A) sec² A = tan A.

[2011]

Ans. To prove, (cosec A – sin A) (sec A – cos A) · sec² A = tan A

L.H.S. = (cosec A – sin A) (sec A – cos A) · sec² A

$$= \left(\frac{1}{\sin A} - \sin A\right)\cdot\left(\frac{1}{\cos A} - \cos A\right)$$

$$\cdot\frac{1}{\cos^2 A}$$

$$\left[\sec A = \frac{1}{\cos A}, \ \operatorname{cosec} A = \frac{1}{\sin A}\right]$$

$$= \left(\frac{1 - \sin^2 A}{\sin A}\right) \times \left(\frac{1 - \cos^2 A}{\cos A}\right) \times \frac{1}{\cos^2 A}$$

$$= \frac{\cos^2 A}{\sin A} \times \frac{\sin^2 A}{\cos A} \times \frac{1}{\cos^2 A}$$

$$\left[\begin{array}{l} 1 - \sin^2 A = \cos^2 A \\ 1 - \cos^2 A = \sin^2 A \end{array}\right]$$

$$= \frac{\sin A}{\cos A} = \tan A$$

$$= \text{R.H.S.} \qquad \textbf{Hence Proved.}$$

18 Heights and Distances

Long Answer Type Questions

Q. 1. From the top of a cliff, the angle of depression of the top and bottom of a tower are observed to be 45° and 60° respectively. If the height of the tower is 20 m.

Find :
(i) the height of the cliff
(ii) the distance between the cliff and the tower. **[2020]**

 **Marking Scheme**

$\tan 45° = \dfrac{AB}{BE}, 1 = \dfrac{AB}{BE}$

$AB = BE$

$\tan 60° = \dfrac{AC}{CD}$

$\sqrt{3} = \dfrac{AB + 20}{BE}$

$\sqrt{3}\, BE = AB + 20$

$AB\sqrt{3} = AB + 20$

$AB(\sqrt{3} - 1) = 20$

$AB = \dfrac{20(\sqrt{3} + 1)}{2}$

$AB = 27.32$

(i) Height of cliff = 27.32 + 20 = 47.32 m
(ii) Distance between cliff and tower = 27.32 m
OR
47.3 m and 27.3 m

Ans. Let AB be the cliff and CD be the tower.

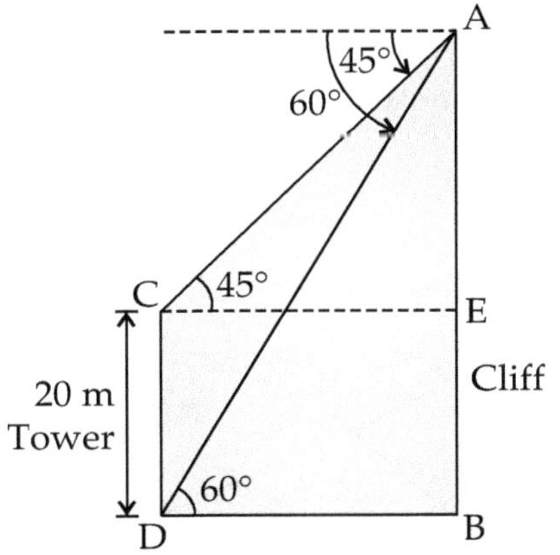

Also, let $DB = CE = x$ m and $AB = h$ m
(i) In $\triangle ABD$,

$\tan 60° = \dfrac{AB}{DB}$

$\sqrt{3} = \dfrac{h}{x}$

$h = x\sqrt{3}$ ...(i)

And, in $\triangle ACE$,

$\tan 45° = \dfrac{AE}{CE}$

$\Rightarrow \quad 1 = \dfrac{AB - BE}{x}$

$\Rightarrow \quad 1 = \dfrac{h - 20}{x}$

$x = h - 20$ ...(ii)

Putting the value of x in equation (i), we get

$h = (h - 20)\sqrt{3}$

$\Rightarrow \quad h = \sqrt{3}\, h - 20\sqrt{3}$

$\Rightarrow \quad \sqrt{3}\, h - h = 20\sqrt{3}$

$\Rightarrow \quad h(\sqrt{3} - 1) = 20\sqrt{3}$

$\Rightarrow \quad h = \dfrac{20\sqrt{3}}{\sqrt{3} - 1} \dfrac{\sqrt{3} + 1}{\sqrt{3} + 1}$

$\qquad = \dfrac{20\sqrt{3}\,(\sqrt{3} + 1)}{3 - 1}$

$\qquad = 10(3 + \sqrt{3}) = 10(3 + 1.732)$

$\qquad = 10 \times 4.732$

$\qquad = 47.32$ m

Hence, the height of cliff is 47.32 m.

(ii) Putting the value of h in equation (ii), we get

$x = h - 20 = 47.32 - 20$

$\qquad = 27.32$

Hence, the distance between the cliff and the tower is 27.32 m.

Q. 2. A man observes the angle of elevation of the top of the tower to be 45°. He walks towards it in a horizontal line through its base. On covering 20 m the angle of elevation changes to 60°. Find the height of the tower correct to 2 significant figures. **[2019]**

Marking Scheme

$$\tan 45° = \frac{y}{x+20} \qquad \{\tan 45° = 1\}$$

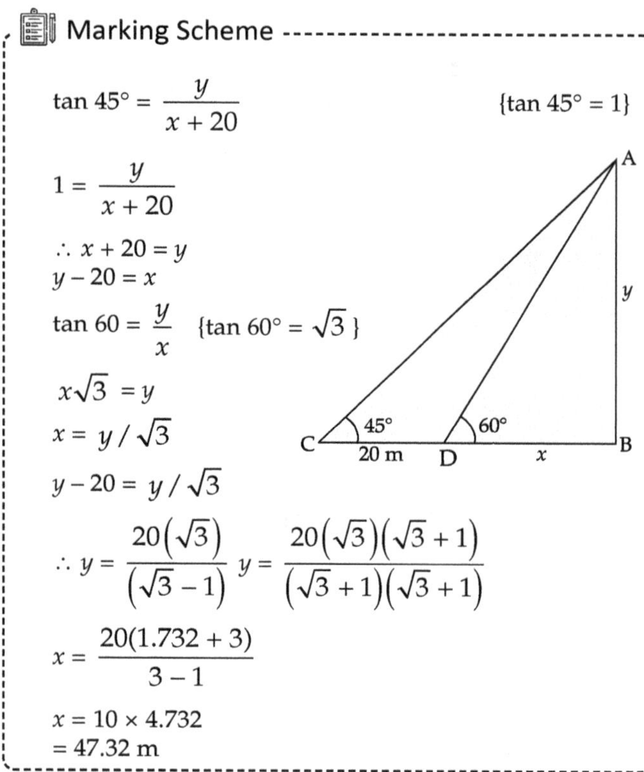

$$1 = \frac{y}{x+20}$$

$$\therefore x + 20 = y$$
$$y - 20 = x$$

$$\tan 60 = \frac{y}{x} \quad \{\tan 60° = \sqrt{3}\,\}$$

$$x\sqrt{3} = y$$

$$x = y/\sqrt{3}$$

$$y - 20 = y/\sqrt{3}$$

$$\therefore y = \frac{20\left(\sqrt{3}\right)}{\left(\sqrt{3}-1\right)} \quad y = \frac{20\left(\sqrt{3}\right)\left(\sqrt{3}+1\right)}{\left(\sqrt{3}+1\right)\left(\sqrt{3}+1\right)}$$

$$x = \frac{20(1.732+3)}{3-1}$$

$$x = 10 \times 4.732$$
$$= 47.32 \text{ m}$$

Ans. Let AB = x be the height of the tower and CD = 20 m be the distance he walked towards the tower

Let BD = y

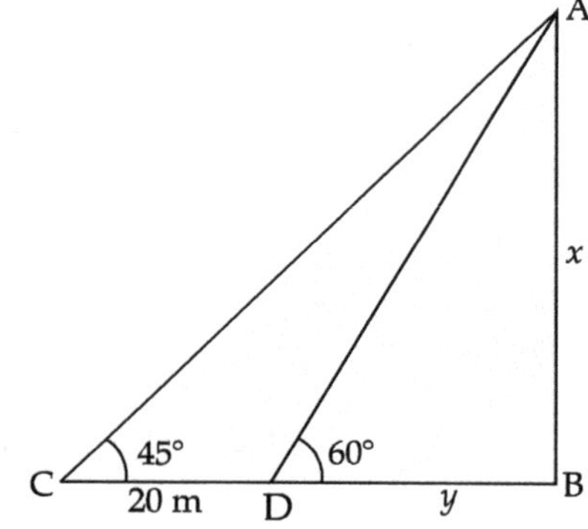

In $\triangle$ABD,

$$\tan 60° = \frac{x}{y}$$

$$\Rightarrow \qquad \sqrt{3} = \frac{x}{y}$$

$$\Rightarrow \qquad y = \frac{x}{\sqrt{3}} \qquad \qquad ...(i)$$

In $\triangle$ABC,

$$\tan 45° = \frac{x}{y+20}$$

$$\Rightarrow \qquad 1 = \frac{x}{y+20}$$

$$\Rightarrow \qquad x = y + 20 \qquad \qquad ...(ii)$$

From equations (i) and (ii), we get

$$x = \frac{x}{\sqrt{3}} + 20$$

$$\Rightarrow \qquad \sqrt{3}x = x + 20\sqrt{3}$$

$$\Rightarrow \qquad \sqrt{3}x - x = 20\sqrt{3}$$

$$\Rightarrow \qquad (\sqrt{3}-1)x = 20\sqrt{3}$$

$$\Rightarrow \qquad x = \frac{20\sqrt{3}}{\sqrt{3}-1}$$

$$\Rightarrow \qquad x = \frac{20\sqrt{3}(\sqrt{3}+1)}{(\sqrt{3}-1)(\sqrt{3}+1)}$$

$$\Rightarrow \qquad x = \frac{20\sqrt{3}(\sqrt{3}+1)}{(\sqrt{3})^2 - (1)^2}$$

$$= \frac{20\sqrt{3}(\sqrt{3}+1)}{3-1}$$

$$= \frac{20\sqrt{3}(\sqrt{3}+1)}{2}$$

$$= 10\sqrt{3}(\sqrt{3}+1)$$

$$= 10\sqrt{3} \times \sqrt{3} + 10\sqrt{3}$$

$$= 30 + 10 \times 1.732$$

$$= 30 + 17.32$$

$$= 47.32 \text{ m}$$

(Correct to 2 significant figures)

$\therefore$ Height of tower is 47.32 m.

Q. 3. The angle of elevation from a point P of the top of a tower QR, 50 m high is 60° and that of the tower PT from a point Q is 30°. Find the height of the tower PT, correct to the nearest metre. **[2018]**

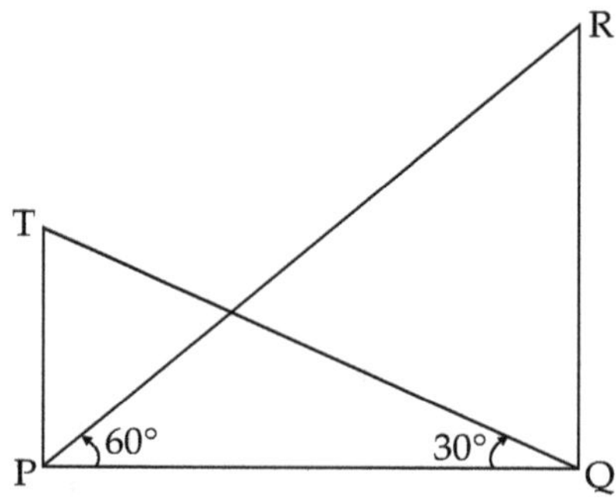

Ans. Given, QR = 50 m, $\angle$RPQ = 60°, $\angle$PQT = 30°.

Let PT = x m, PQ = y m

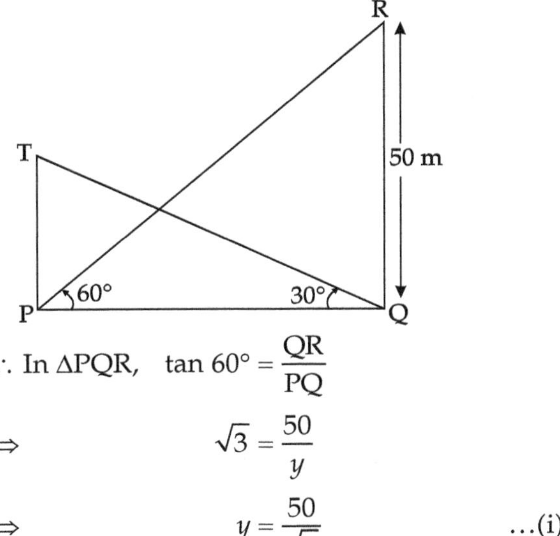

$\therefore$ In ΔPQR, $\quad \tan 60° = \dfrac{QR}{PQ}$

$\Rightarrow \qquad \sqrt{3} = \dfrac{50}{y}$

$\Rightarrow \qquad y = \dfrac{50}{\sqrt{3}}$ ...(i)

In ΔPQT, $\quad \tan 30° = \dfrac{PT}{PQ}$

$\Rightarrow \qquad \dfrac{1}{\sqrt{3}} = \dfrac{x}{y}$

$\Rightarrow \qquad x = \dfrac{y}{\sqrt{3}}$ ...(ii)

$\qquad = \dfrac{\frac{50}{\sqrt{3}}}{\sqrt{3}}$ [using eqn. (i)]

$\qquad = \dfrac{50}{\sqrt{3} \times \sqrt{3}} = \dfrac{50}{3}$

$\qquad = 16.67$

$\qquad = 17$ m

(correct to the nearest metre)

Q. 4. The angles of depression of two ships A and B as observed from the top of a light house 60 m high are 60° and 45° respectively. If the two ships are on the opposite sides of the light house, find the distance between the two ships. Give your answer correct to the nearest whole number. **[2017]**

Ans. Let CD be the light house

$\therefore$ CD = 60 m.

Let AD = x m, BD = y m.

In ΔACD,

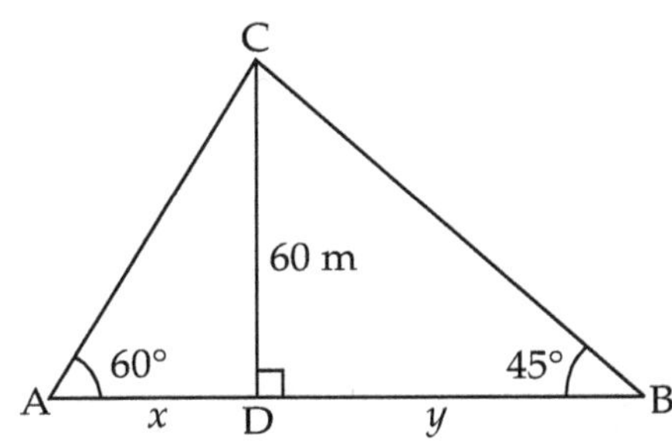

$\tan 60° = \dfrac{CD}{AD}$

$\Rightarrow \qquad \sqrt{3} = \dfrac{60}{x} \Rightarrow x = \dfrac{60}{\sqrt{3}}$

$\Rightarrow \qquad x = \dfrac{60}{\sqrt{3}} \times \dfrac{\sqrt{3}}{\sqrt{3}} = \dfrac{60\sqrt{3}}{3}$

$\qquad = 20 \times 1.732$

$\qquad = 34.64$ m

In ΔBCD,

$\tan 45° = \dfrac{CD}{BD}$

$\Rightarrow \qquad 1 = \dfrac{60}{y}$

$\Rightarrow \qquad y = 60$ m

$\therefore$ Distance between two ships

$\qquad = x + y = 34.64 + 60$

$\qquad = 94.64$ m

$\qquad = 95$ m (correct to nearest whole number)

Q. 5. An aeroplane at an altitude of **1500 metres** finds that two ships are sailing towards it in the same direction. The angles of depression as observed from the aeroplane are 45° and 30° respectively. Find the distance between the two ships. **[2016]**

Ans. Let AB be the altitude and C and D be the positions of two ships.

In right angled triangle ABC,

$\tan 45° = \dfrac{1500}{BC}$

$1 = \dfrac{1500}{BC}$

$BC = 1500$ m

In right angled triangle ABD,

$\tan 30° = \dfrac{1500}{BD}$

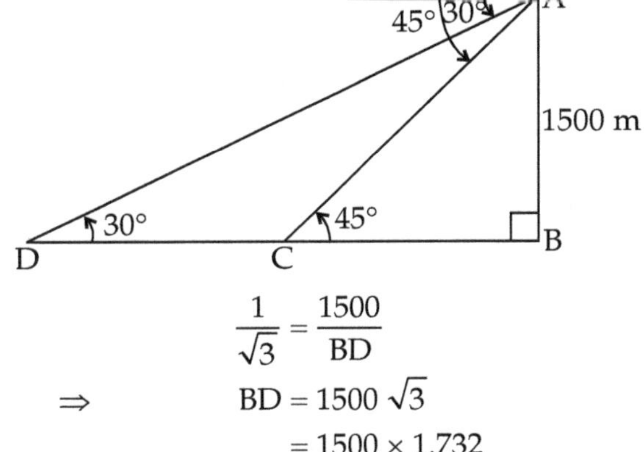

$\dfrac{1}{\sqrt{3}} = \dfrac{1500}{BD}$

$\Rightarrow \qquad BD = 1500\sqrt{3}$

$\qquad = 1500 \times 1.732$

$$= 2598 \text{ m}$$

$\therefore$ Distance between the two ships

$$= CD$$
$$= BD - BC$$
$$= 2598 - 1500$$
$$= 1098 \text{ m}$$

Q. 6. The horizontal distance between two towers is 120 m. The angle of elevation of the top and angle of depression of the bottom of the first tower as observed from the second tower is 30° and 24° respectively.

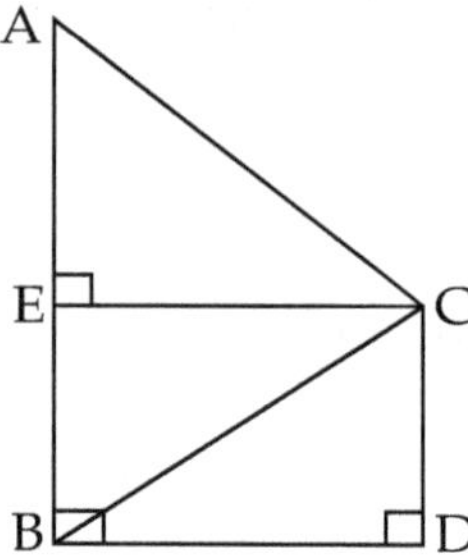

Find the height of the two towers. Give your answer correct to 3 significant figures. **[2015]**

Ans. Let, AB and CD be towers and BD = 120 m.
In right angled $\triangle$BDC

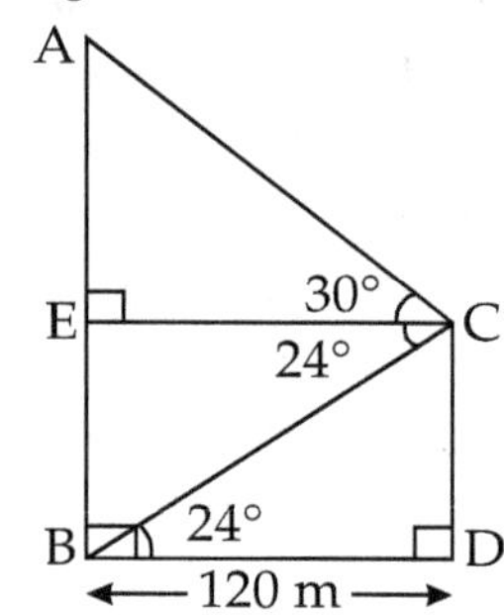

$$\tan 24° = \frac{CD}{BD}$$

$$0.4452 = \frac{CD}{120}$$

(using trigonometric table)

$$CD = 53.424 \text{ m}$$

In right angled $\triangle$AEC

$$\tan 30° = \frac{AE}{EC} = \frac{AE}{BD} \qquad (\because EC = BD)$$

$$\frac{1}{\sqrt{3}} = \frac{AE}{120}$$

$$AE = \frac{120}{\sqrt{3}}$$

$$AE = 69.284 \text{ m}$$

$\therefore \qquad AB = AE + EB \qquad (\because EB = CD)$

$$= 69.284 + 53.424$$
$$= 122.708 \text{ m}$$

Hence, the height of the towers are 53.424 m and 122.708 m.

Q. 7. An aeroplane at an altitude of 250 m observes the angle of depression of two boats on the opposite banks of a river to be 45° and 60° respectively. Find the width of the river. Write the answer correct to the nearest whole number. **[2014]**

Ans. Let aeroplane be at position A and BC be the river. Drop a perpendicular from A on BC let it intersect BC at D.

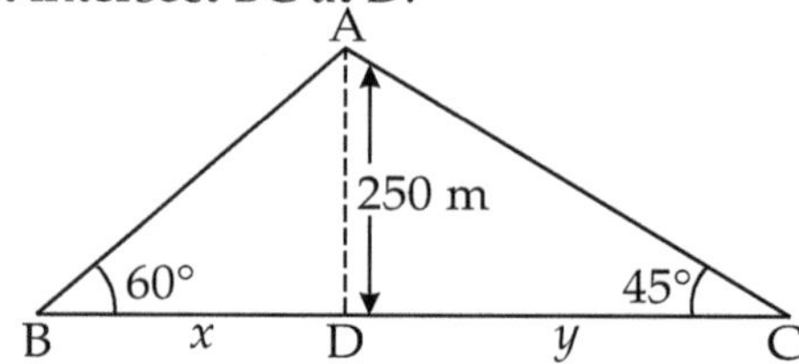

In $\triangle$ADB,

$$\tan 60° = \frac{AD}{BD}$$

$$\sqrt{3} = \frac{250}{x}$$

$$x = \frac{250}{\sqrt{3}} \text{ m} \qquad \qquad ...(i)$$

In $\triangle$ADC,

$$\tan 45° = \frac{AD}{DC}$$

$$1 = \frac{250}{y}$$

$$y = 250 \text{ m}$$

Thus, width of the river $= 250 + \dfrac{250}{\sqrt{3}} = 394$ m

Q. 8. In the figure given, from the top of a building AB = 60 m high, the angles of depression of the top and bottom of a vertical lamp post CD are observed to be 30° and 60° respectively. Find :

(i) the horizontal distance between AB and CD.

(ii) the height of the lamp post. **[2013]**

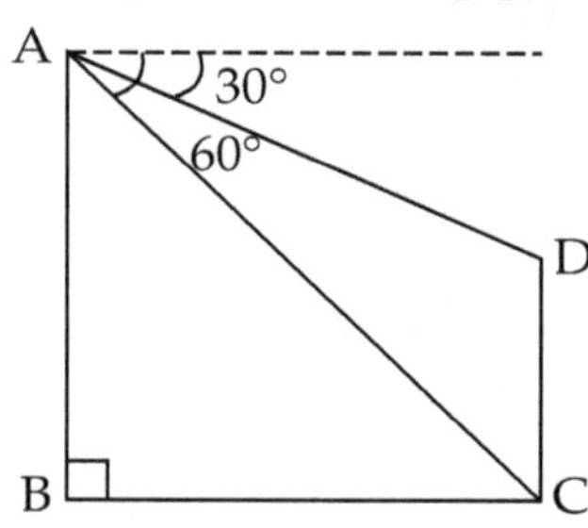

Ans. We draw DE $\perp$ AB

Let $\qquad BC = x = ED$

$$AB = 60 \text{ (given)}$$

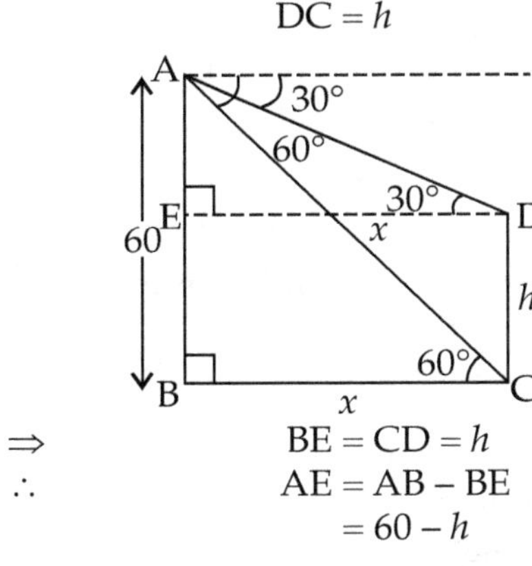

$$DC = h$$

$$\Rightarrow \qquad BE = CD = h$$
$$\therefore \qquad AE = AB - BE$$
$$= 60 - h$$

(i) In $\triangle ABC$, $\dfrac{AB}{BC} = \tan 60°$

$$\frac{60}{x} = \sqrt{3}$$

$$\Rightarrow \qquad x = \frac{60}{\sqrt{3}} \times \frac{\sqrt{3}}{\sqrt{3}} = \frac{60\sqrt{3}}{3}$$

$$= 20\sqrt{3} \text{ m}$$

Horizontal distance between lamp post and building is $20\sqrt{3}$ m.

(ii) In $\triangle AED$, $\dfrac{AE}{ED} = \tan 30°$

$$\frac{60 - h}{x} = \frac{1}{\sqrt{3}}$$

$$\Rightarrow \qquad \frac{60 - h}{20\sqrt{3}} = \frac{1}{\sqrt{3}}$$

$$\Rightarrow \qquad 60 - h = 20$$

$$\Rightarrow \qquad h = 60 - 20 = 40 \text{ m.}$$

$\therefore$ Height of lamp post is 40 m.

Q. 9. As observed from the top of a 80 m tall lighthouse, the angles of depression of two ships on the same side of the light house in horizontal line with its base are 30° and 40° respectively. Find the distance between the two ships. Give your answer correct to the nearest metre. **[2012]**

Ans. In fig. AB is 80 m tall light house, the two ships are at C and D.

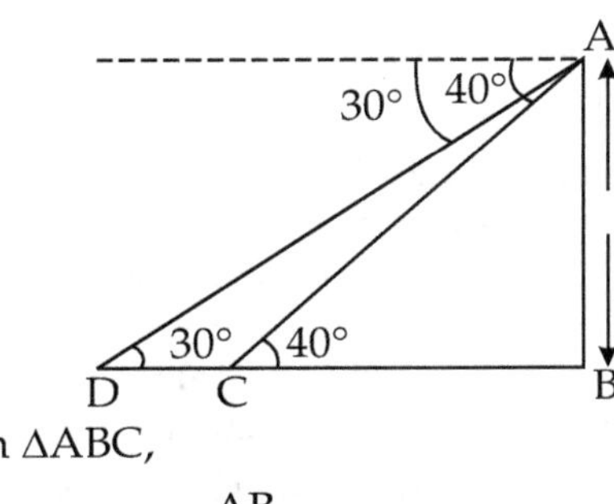

In $\triangle ABC$,

$$\tan 40° = \frac{AB}{BC}$$

$$\Rightarrow \qquad BC = \frac{AB}{\tan 40°}$$

$$BC = \frac{80}{0.8391}$$

(using trigonometric table)

$$= 95.34 \text{ m}$$

In $\triangle ABD$,

$$\tan 30° = \frac{AB}{BD}$$

$$\Rightarrow \qquad BD = \frac{AB}{\tan 30°} = \frac{80}{0.5774}$$

$$= 138.55 \text{ m}$$

Distance between two ships

$$DC = BD - BC$$

$$= 138.55 - 95.34$$

$$= 43.21 \text{ m} = 43 \text{ m (approx.)}$$

Q. 10. A man observes the angle of elevation of the top of a building to be 30°. He walks towards it in a horizontal line through its base. On covering 60 m the angle of elevation changes to 60°. Find the height of the building correct to the nearest metre. **[2011]**

Ans. Let, the height of the building be h

In $\triangle BCD$,

$$\frac{h}{x} = \tan 60°$$

$$\Rightarrow \qquad \frac{h}{x} = \sqrt{3}$$

$$\Rightarrow \qquad h = \sqrt{3}\,x \qquad \qquad \dots \text{(i)}$$

In $\triangle ACD$,

$$\frac{h}{x + 60} = \tan 30°$$

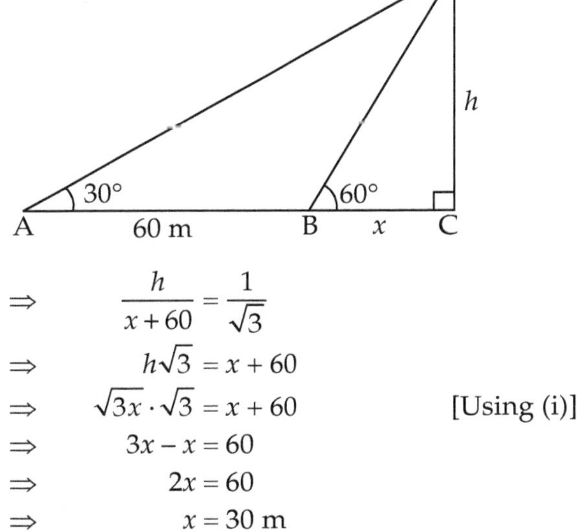

$$\Rightarrow \qquad \frac{h}{x + 60} = \frac{1}{\sqrt{3}}$$

$$\Rightarrow \qquad h\sqrt{3} = x + 60$$

$$\Rightarrow \qquad \sqrt{3}x \cdot \sqrt{3} = x + 60 \qquad \text{[Using (i)]}$$

$$\Rightarrow \qquad 3x - x = 60$$

$$\Rightarrow \qquad 2x = 60$$

$$\Rightarrow \qquad x = 30 \text{ m}$$

Now, from (i)

$$h = \sqrt{3}\ x$$
$$h = 30 \times \sqrt{3}$$
$$= 30 \times 1.732$$
$$\text{Height} = 51.96 \text{ m} = 52 \text{ m}$$

(rounded off)

The height of the building is 52 m.

Q. 11. **From the top of a light house 100 m high the angles of depression of two ships on opposite sides of it are 48° and 36° respectively. Find the distance between the two ships to the nearest metre.** **[2010]**

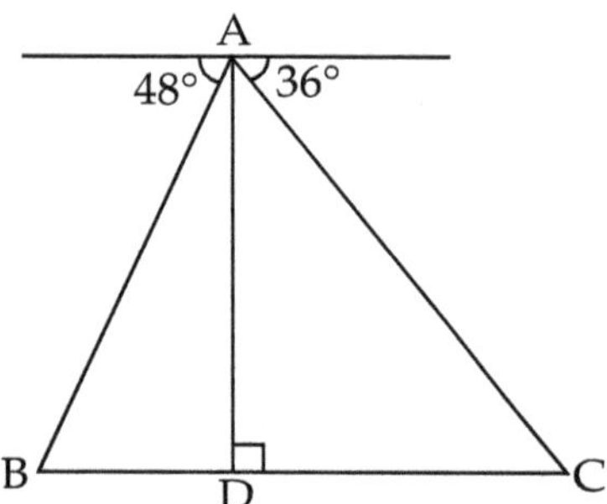

Ans. Let the distance of two ships from the light house be x and y respectively.

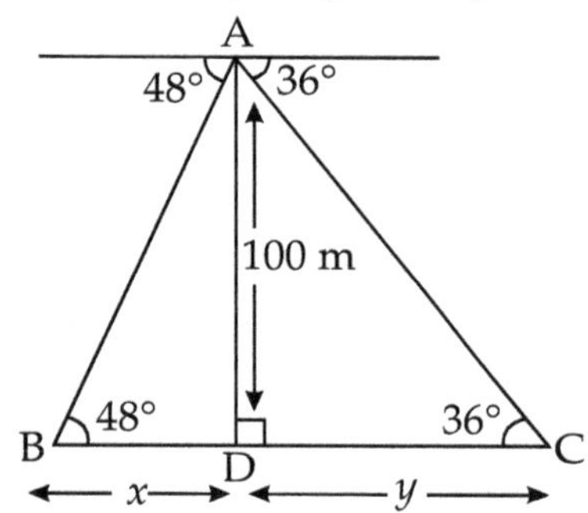

In right angled $\triangle ADC$,

$$\frac{AD}{CD} = \tan 36°$$

$$\Rightarrow \quad \frac{100}{y} = \tan 36°$$

$$\Rightarrow \quad y = \frac{100}{\tan 36°} \quad \text{(Using table)}$$

$$= \frac{100}{0.7265}$$

$$\Rightarrow \quad y = 137.46 \text{ m}$$

In right angled $\triangle ADB$,

$$\frac{AD}{BD} = \tan 48°$$

$$\Rightarrow \quad \frac{100}{x} = \tan 48°$$

$$\Rightarrow \quad x = \frac{100}{1.1106} \quad \text{(Using table)}$$

$$= 90.04 \text{ m}$$

$\therefore$ Distance between the ships

$$= x + y = 137.646 + 90.04$$
$$= 227.678 \text{ m}$$
$$= 228 \text{ m (approx.)}$$

Q. 12. **From two points A and B on the same side of a building, the angles of elevation of the top of the building are 30° and 60° respectively. If the height of the building is 10 m, find the distance between A and B correct to two decimal places.** **[2009]**

Ans. In right angled $\triangle DBC$,

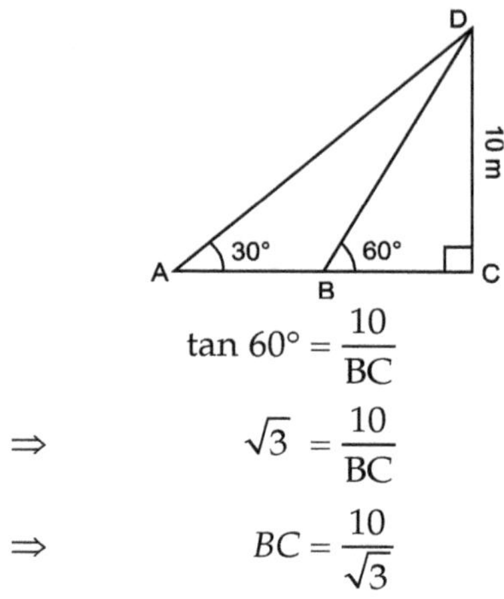

$$\tan 60° = \frac{10}{BC}$$

$$\Rightarrow \quad \sqrt{3} = \frac{10}{BC}$$

$$\Rightarrow \quad BC = \frac{10}{\sqrt{3}}$$

Again in right angled $\triangle DAC$,

$$\tan 30° = \frac{10}{BC + AB}$$

$$\Rightarrow \quad \frac{1}{\sqrt{3}} = \frac{10}{\dfrac{10}{\sqrt{3}} + AB}$$

$$\Rightarrow \quad \frac{1}{\sqrt{3}}\left(\frac{10}{\sqrt{3}} + AB\right) = 10$$

$$\Rightarrow \quad AB = 10\sqrt{3} - \frac{10}{\sqrt{3}}$$

$$= \frac{30 - 10}{\sqrt{3}} = \frac{20}{\sqrt{3}} = \frac{20\sqrt{3}}{3}$$

$$= \frac{20 \times 1.732}{3}$$

$$= 20 \times 0.577 = 11.54 \text{ m}$$

Hence the required distance between A and B is 11.54 m.

Q. 13. **A vertical pole and a vertical tower are on the same level ground. From the top of the pole the angle of elevation of the top of the tower is 60° and the angle of depression of the foot of the tower is 30°. Find the height of the tower if the height of the pole is 20 m.** **[2008]**

Ans. Let AB be the tower and CD be the pole. As given in the question BE = 20 m

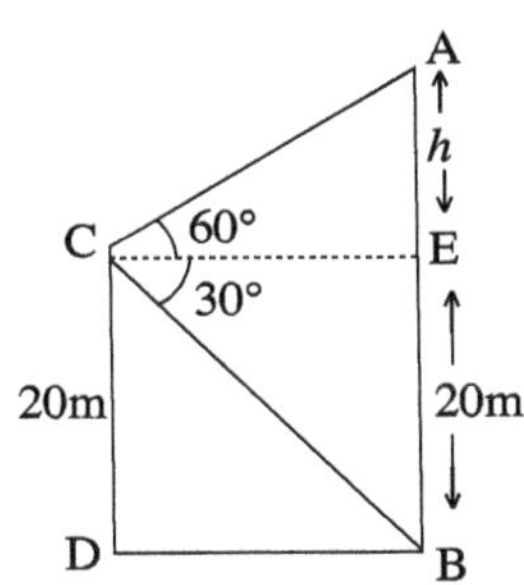

$\therefore$ In ΔBCE $\qquad \tan 30° = \dfrac{20}{CE}$

$\Rightarrow \qquad \dfrac{1}{\sqrt{3}} = \dfrac{20}{CE}$

$\Rightarrow \qquad CE = 20\sqrt{3}$

Now in ΔACE $\tan 60° = \dfrac{h}{CE}$

$\qquad \sqrt{3} = \dfrac{h}{20\sqrt{3}} \qquad \Rightarrow \quad h = 60$

$\therefore$ Height of tower $= 60 + 20 = 80$ m.

Q. 14. **From the top of a hill, the angles of depression of two consecutive kilometer stones, due east are found to be 30° and 45° respectively. Find the distance of the two stones from the foot of the hill.** **[2007]**

Ans. Let AB be hill of which B is foot and D, C are two consecutive km stones.

$\therefore \qquad DC = 1$ km $= 1000$ m

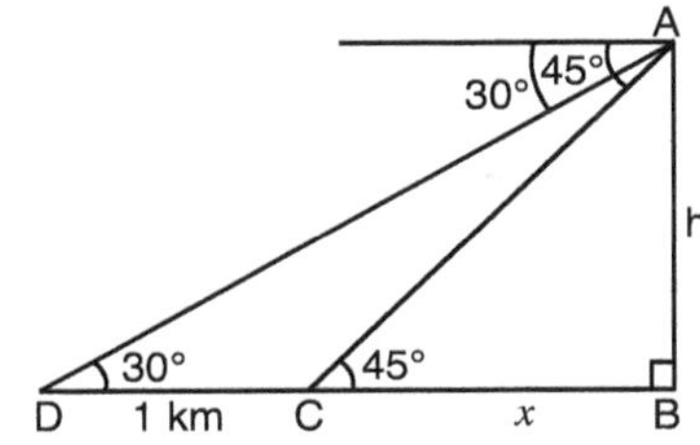

In right angled ΔABC,

$\qquad \tan 45° = \dfrac{AB}{BC}$

$\qquad 1 = \dfrac{h}{x}$

$\qquad x = h$ $\qquad\qquad ...(1)$

In right angled ΔABD,

$\qquad \tan 30° = \dfrac{AB}{BD}$

$\qquad \dfrac{1}{\sqrt{3}} = \dfrac{h}{x + 1000}$

$\qquad x + 1000 = h\sqrt{3}$ $\qquad ...(2)$

But from equation (1), $x = h$,

$\therefore \quad x + 1000 = x\sqrt{3}$

$x(\sqrt{3} - 1) = 1000$

$\qquad x = \dfrac{1000}{\sqrt{3} - 1} \times \dfrac{\sqrt{3} + 1}{\sqrt{3} + 1}$

$\qquad = \dfrac{1000(\sqrt{3} + 1)}{2}$

$\qquad = 500(\sqrt{3} + 1)$

$\qquad = 500 \times 2.732$

$\qquad = 1366$ metre $= 1.366$ km

$\therefore$ Ist km stone is 1.366 km and IInd km stone is 2.366 km from foot of hill.

Q. 14. **The shadow of a vertical tower on a level ground increases by 10 m when the altitude of the sun changes from 45° to 30° . Find the height of the tower, correct to two decimal places.** **[2006]**

Ans. Let the height of tower be h meter and length of shadow y meter initially.

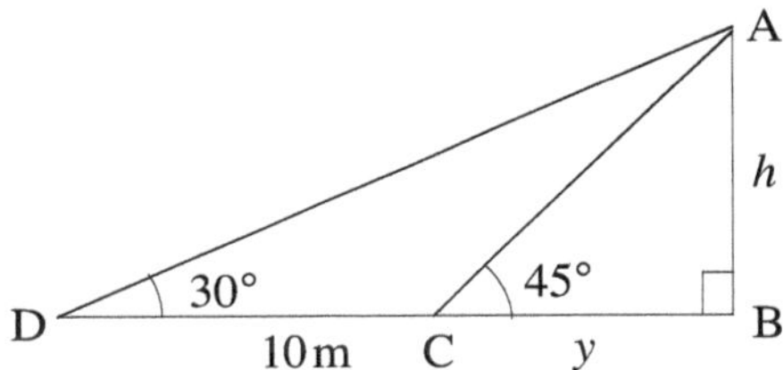

In ΔABC, $\tan 45° = \dfrac{AB}{BC}$

$\qquad 1 = \dfrac{h}{y}$

$\qquad y = h$ $\qquad\qquad ...(i)$

In ΔABD, $\tan 30° = \dfrac{AB}{DB}$

$\qquad \dfrac{1}{\sqrt{3}} = \dfrac{h}{y + 10}$

$\qquad y + 10 = h\sqrt{3}$ $\qquad ...(ii)$

Putting $y = h$ in eqn. (ii),

$\qquad h + 10 = h\sqrt{3}$

$\qquad h(\sqrt{3} - 1) = 10$

$\qquad h = \dfrac{10(\sqrt{3} + 1)}{(\sqrt{3} - 1)(\sqrt{3} + 1)}$

$\qquad = \dfrac{10}{(3 - 1)}(\sqrt{3} + 1)$

$\qquad = \dfrac{10}{2}(\sqrt{3} + 1) = 5(1.732 + 1)$

$\qquad = 5 \times 2.732 = 13.66$

Hence, the height of the tower is 13.66 metre.

Short Answer Type Questions

Q. 1. The mean of the following data is 16. Calculate the value of f. **[2020]**

Marks	5	10	15	20	25
No. of Students	3	7	f	9	6

Marking Scheme

Marks	No. of students	fx
5	3	15
10	7	70
15	f	$15f$
20	9	180
25	6	150

$fx = 415 + 15f$

$\Sigma f = f + 25$

$M = \dfrac{\Sigma fx}{\Sigma f} \quad \therefore \; 16 = \dfrac{15f + 415}{f + 25}$

$\Rightarrow f = 15$

Ans.

Marks x_i	No. of students f_i	$f_i x_i$
5	3	15
10	7	70
15	f	$15f$
20	9	180
25	6	150
	$\sum f_i = 25 + f$	$\sum f_i x_i = 415 + 15f$

We know, $\text{mean} = \dfrac{\sum f_i x_i}{\sum f_i}$

$\Rightarrow \quad 16 = \dfrac{415 + 15f}{25 + f}$

$\Rightarrow \quad 400 + 16f = 415 + 15f$

$\Rightarrow \quad 16f - 15f = 415 - 400$

$\Rightarrow \quad f = 15$

Q. 2. The data on the number of patients attending a hospital in a month are given below. Find the average (mean) number of patients attending the hospital in a month by using the shortcut method.

Take the assumed mean as 45. Give your answer correct to 2 decimal places. **[2019]**

Number of patients	10–20	20–30	30–40	40–50	50–60	60–70
Number of Days	5	2	7	9	2	5

Marking Scheme

C.I.	f	mid-value	d	fd
10 - 20	5	15	– 30	– 150
20 - 30	2	25	– 20	– 40
30 - 40	7	35	– 10	– 70
40 - 50	9	45	0	0
50 - 60	2	55	10	20
60 - 70	5	65	20	100
	30			– 140

Given assumed mean (A) = 45

$\text{Mean} = 45 + \left(\dfrac{-140}{30} \right)$

$= 45 - 4.67$

$= 40.33$

Ans. Given, Assumed mean (A) = 45.

Number of patients	Mid-value (x_i)	$d_i = x_i - A$	Number of days (f_i)	$f_i d_i$
10–20	15	–30	5	–150
20–30	25	–20	2	–40
30–40	35	–10	7	–70
40–50	45	0	9	0
50–60	55	10	2	20
60–70	65	20	5	100
			$\Sigma f_i = 30$	$\Sigma f_i d_i = -140$

$\text{Mean} = A + \dfrac{\sum f_i d_i}{\sum f_i}$

$$= 45 + \left(-\frac{140}{30}\right)$$

$$= 45 - 4.667$$

$$= 40.333$$

$$= 40.33$$

(Correct to 2 decimal places)

Q. 3. **If the mean of the following distribution is 24, find the value of 'a'.** **[2018]**

Marks	0–10	10–20	20–30	30–40	40–50
Number of students	7	a	8	10	5

Ans.

Marks	Mid values (x)	No. of students (f)	fx
0–10	5	7	35
10–20	15	a	15a
20–30	25	8	200
30–40	35	10	350
40–50	45	5	225
		$\Sigma f = 30 + a$	$\Sigma fx = 15a + 810$

$$\therefore \quad \text{Mean} = \frac{\Sigma fx}{\Sigma f}$$

$$\Rightarrow \quad 24 = \frac{15a + 810}{a + 30}$$

$$\Rightarrow \quad 24a + 720 = 15a + 810$$

$$\Rightarrow \quad 24a - 15a = 810 - 720$$

$$\Rightarrow \quad 9a = 90$$

$$\Rightarrow \quad a = 10.$$

Q. 4. **The marks obtained by 30 students in a class assessment of 5 subjects is given below:**

Marks	0	1	2	3	4	5
No. of Students	1	3	6	10	5	5

Calculate the mean, median and mode of the above distribution. **[2015]**

Ans.

Marks (x)	No. of students (f)	(f · x)	Cumulative frequency (c.f.)
0	1	0	1
1	3	3	4
2	6	12	10
3	10	30	20
4	5	20	25
5	5	25	30
	$\Sigma f = 30$	$\Sigma fx = 90$	

$$\therefore \quad \text{Mean} = \frac{\Sigma fx}{\Sigma f} = \frac{90}{30} = 3$$

$\therefore$ Mean marks is 3.

Here, $n = 30$, which is even

$$\therefore \quad \text{Median} = \frac{\left(\frac{n}{2}\right)^{th} \text{term} + \left(\frac{n}{2} + 1\right)^{th} \text{term}}{2}$$

$$= \frac{\left(\frac{30}{2}\right)^{th} \text{term} + \left(\frac{30}{2} + 1\right)^{th} \text{term}}{2}$$

$$= \frac{15^{th} \text{term} + 16^{th} \text{term}}{2}$$

$$= \frac{3 + 3}{2}$$

$\therefore$ Median marks = 3

Since, the number 3 has maximum frequency 10.

$\therefore$ Mode = 3

$\therefore$ Mean = 3, Median = 3 and Mode = 3.

Q. 5. **Calculate the mean of the following distribution:** **[2015]**

Class Interval	0–10	10–20	20–30	30–40	40–50	50–60
Frequency	8	5	12	35	24	16

Ans.

Class Interval	Freqency (f)	Mean value (x)	fx
0–10	8	5	40
10–20	5	15	75
20–30	12	25	300
30–40	35	35	1225
40–50	24	45	1080
50–60	16	55	880
	$\Sigma f = 100$		$\Sigma fx = 3600$

$$\therefore \quad \text{Mean} = \frac{\Sigma fx}{\Sigma f} = \frac{3600}{100} = 36$$

The mean of the given distribution is 36.

Q. 6. **Find the mode and median of the following frequency distribution:** **[2012]**

x	10	11	12	13	14	15
f	1	4	7	5	9	3

Ans.

x	f	cf
10	1	1

11	4	5
12	7	12
13	5	17
14	9	26
15	3	29

$\Rightarrow \qquad$ Mode = 14

(Since 9 is highest frequency)

Now, $\qquad$ N = 29 (odd)

$\therefore \qquad$ Median $= \left(\dfrac{n+1}{2}\right)^{th}$ value

$\qquad\qquad = \left(\dfrac{29+1}{2}\right)^{th}$ value

$\qquad\qquad$ = 15th value = 13

$\therefore \qquad$ Mode = 14 and Median = 13.

 **Long Answer Type Questions**

Q. 1. Draw a histogram for the given data, using a graph Paper : **[2020]**

Weekly Wages (in ₹)	No. of People
3000–4000	4
4000–5000	9
5000–6000	18
6000–7000	6
7000–8000	7
8000–9000	2
9000–10000	4

Estimate the mode from the graph.

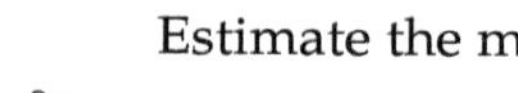 **Marking Scheme**

Correct axis, kink, Histogram drawn taking proper scales

Mode = 5400 ($\pm$ 100) with 3 lines drawn for locating mode

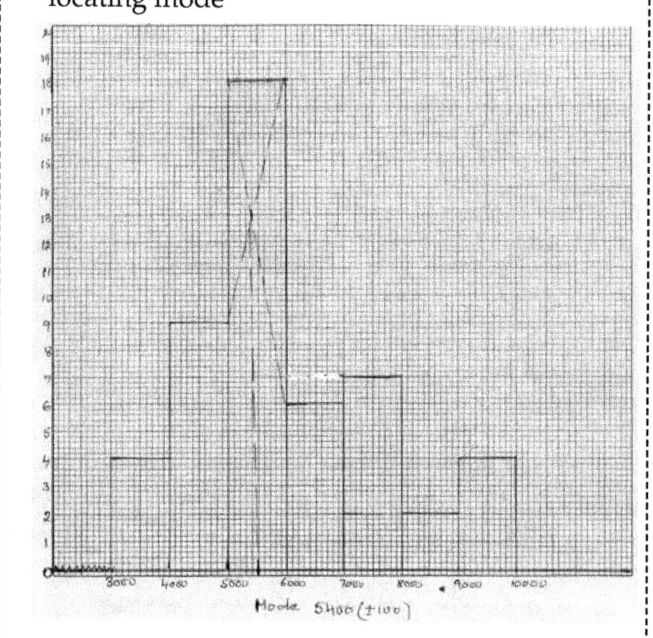

Ans.

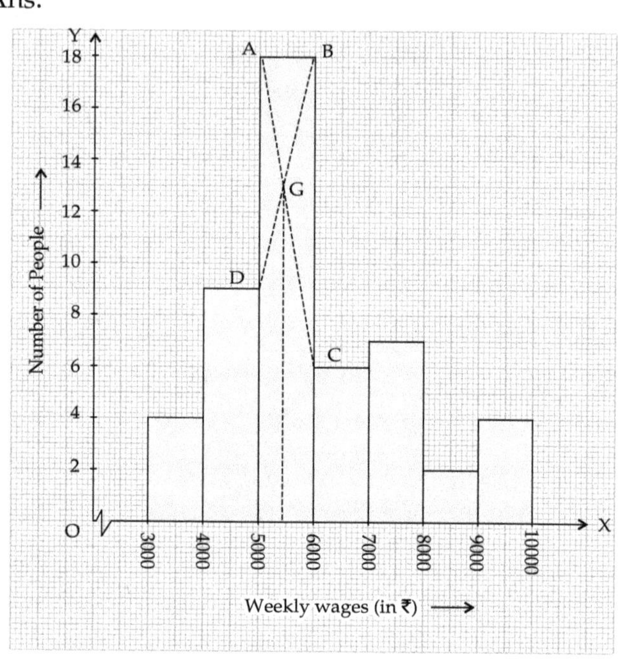

We have, maximum frequency = 18

$\therefore \qquad$ Modal class $= 5000 - 6000$

Join *AC* and *BD* and draw a perpendicular from point *G* to *X*-axis at 5450.

Hence, estimated mode is 5450.

Q. 2. In a class of 40 students, marks obtained by the students in a class test (out of 10) are given below: **[2019]**

Marks	1	2	3	4	5	6	7	8	9	10
Number of Students	1	2	3	3	6	10	5	4	3	3

Calculate the following for the given distribution:

(i) Median $\qquad$ (ii) Mode

Marking Scheme

Marks (x)	No. of Students (f)	cf
1	1	1
2	2	3
3	3	6
4	3	9
5	6	15
6	10	25
7	5	30
8	4	34
9	3	37
10	3	40
	$\Sigma = 40$	

(i) Median = 6   (ii) Mode = 6

Ans.

Marks	Number of Students	Cumulative Frequency
1	1	1
2	2	3

	3	6
	3	9
	6	15
	10	25
	5	30
	4	34
	3	37
	3	40
$n = 40$		

Here, $n = 40$ (even)

(i) Median

$$= \frac{\dfrac{n}{2}^{\text{th}} \text{ observation} + \left(\dfrac{n}{2}+1\right)^{\text{th}} \text{ observation}}{2}$$

$$= \frac{20^{\text{th}} \text{ observation} + 21^{\text{st}} \text{ observation}}{2}$$

$$= \frac{6+6}{2} = 6$$

(ii) $\because$ The highest frequency is 10.

$\therefore$ Mode = 6

Q. 3. Using a graph paper draw a histogram for the given distribution showing the number of runs scored by 50 batsmen. Estimate the mode of the data: [2018]

Runs scored	3000–4000	4000–5000	5000–6000	6000–7000	7000–8000	8000–9000	9000–10000
No. of batsmen	4	18	9	6	7	2	4

Ans.

Runs Scored	No. of batsmen
3000–4000	4
4000–5000	18
5000–6000	9
6000–7000	6
7000–8000	7
8000–9000	2
9000–10000	4

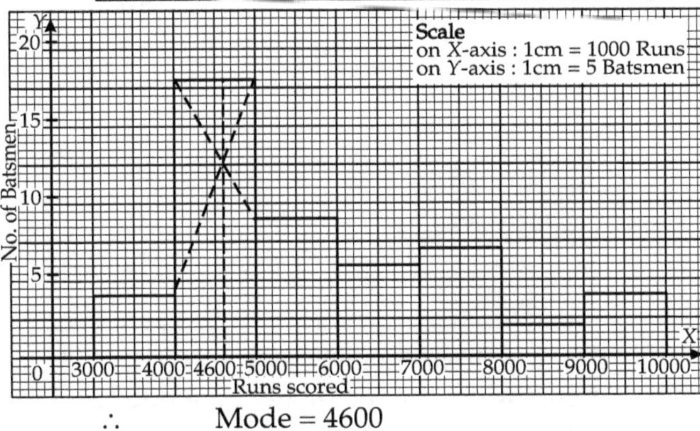

$\therefore$ Mode = 4600

Q. 4. Calculate the mean of the following distribution using step deviation method.   [2017]

Marks	0–10	10–20	20–30	30–40	40–50	50–60
Number of Students	10	9	25	30	16	10

Ans.

Marks	Mid values (x_i)	No. of students (f_i)	$d_i = x_i - A$	$t_i = \dfrac{d_i}{h}$	$f_i t_i$
0–10	5	10	−20	−2	−20
10–20	15	9	−10	−1	−9
20–30	25 = A	25	0	0	0
30–40	35	30	10	1	30
40–50	45	16	20	2	32
50–60	55	10	30	3	30
		$\Sigma f_i = 100$			$\Sigma f_i t_i = 63$

Let A = 25 and $h = 10$

$\therefore$ $$\text{Mean} = A + \frac{\Sigma f_i t_i}{\Sigma f_i} \times h$$

$$= 25 + \frac{63}{100} \times 10$$

$$= 25 + 6.3$$
$$= 31.3$$

Q. 5. The histogram below represents the scores obtained by 25 students in a mathematics mental test. Use the data to:

   (i) Frame a frequency distribution table.

   (ii) To calculate mean.

   (iii) To determine the modal class. **[2016]**

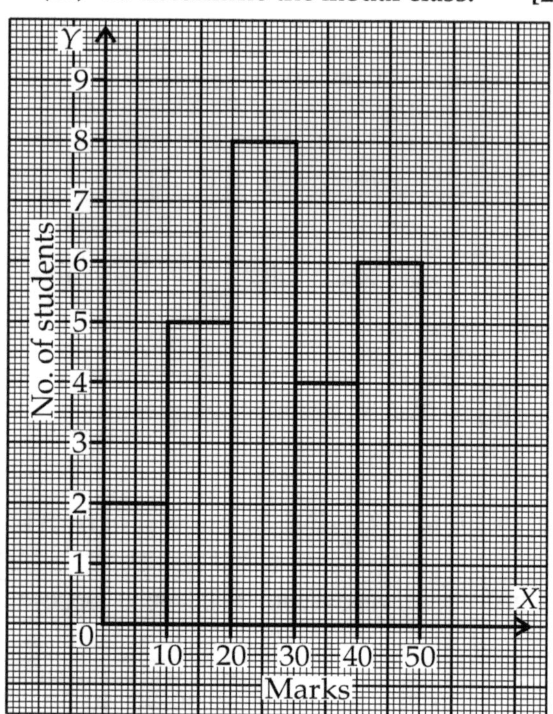

Ans.   **(i)** Using the given data, frequency distribution table is as given below:

Marks	No. of Students (f)	Class mark (x)	fx
0–10	2	5	10
10–20	5	15	75
20–30	8	25	200
30–40	4	35	140
40–50	6	45	270
	n = 25		Σf.x = 695

(ii) To calculate mean: Construct expanded table with class mark and *fx* as given above.

$$\therefore \quad n = \Sigma f = 25 \text{ and } \Sigma fx = 695$$

$$\text{Mean} = \frac{\Sigma fx}{n} = \frac{695}{25} = 27.8$$

(iii) 1. In the given histogram, inside the highest rectangle, which represents the maximum frequency (or modal class) draw two lines AC and BD diagonally from the upper corners to C and D of adjacent rectangles.

   2. Both the lines meet at a point K. Through the point K, draw KL perpendicular to the horizontal axis.

   3. The value of point L on the horizontal axis represents the value of mode.

$$\therefore \text{ Mode} = 24 \text{ and the modal class} = 20 - 30.$$

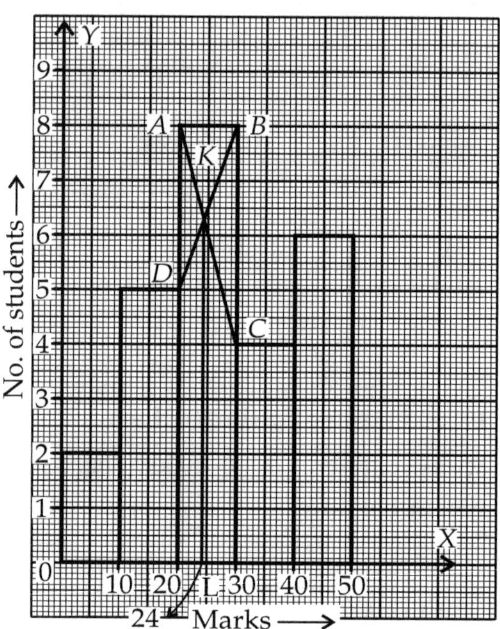

Q. 6. The daily pocket expenses of 200 students in a school are given below: (Use a graph paper for this question.)

Pocket expenses (in ₹)	Number of students (frequency)
0—5	10
5—10	14
10—15	28
15—20	42
20—25	50
25—30	30
30—35	14
35—40	12

Draw a histogram representing the above distribution and estimate the mode from the graph. **[2014]**

Ans. Histogram on the graph paper.

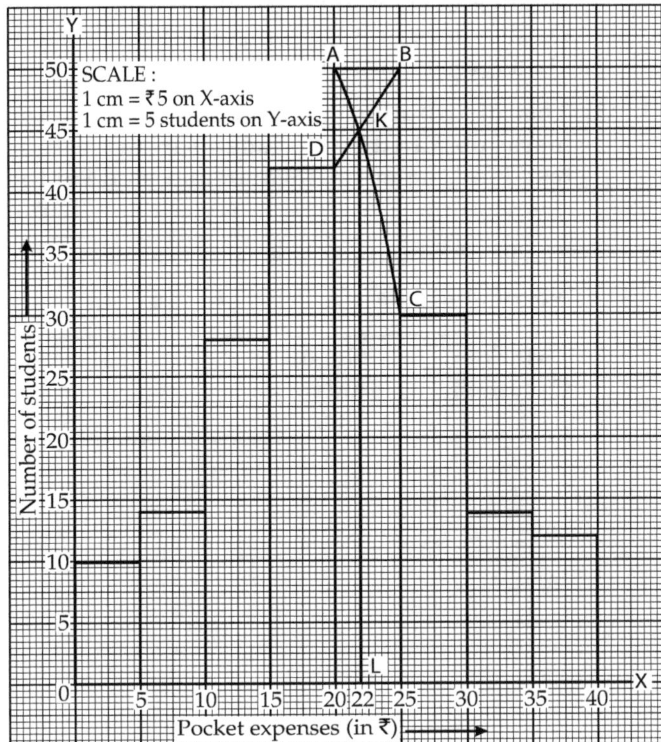

Join A to C and B to D. AC and BD meet at K. Drop a perpendicular from K to X-axis at L.

∴   Mode = 22.

Q. 7. Draw a histogram for the following frequency distribution and find the mode from the graph: [2013]

Class	0–5	5–10	10–15	15–20	20–25	25–30
Frequency	2	5	18	14	8	5

Ans.

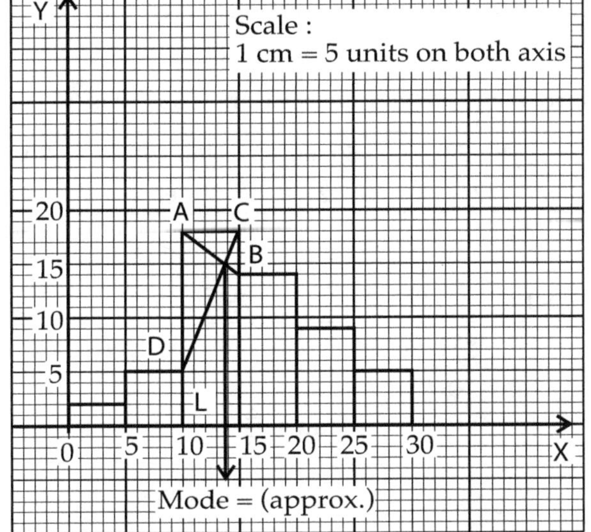

Using graph, in the biggest bar of class interval 10-15, we will join A to B and D to C. AB and CD meet at K. From K, drop a

perpendicular on X-axis at L. Therefore, mode is 14.

Q. 8. Find the mean of the following distribution by step deviation method: [2013]

Class interval	20–30	30–40	40–50	50–60	60–70	70–80
Frequency	10	6	8	12	5	9

Ans.

C.I.	f	$'x'$ mid values	$u = \dfrac{x - A}{h}$	$f.u$
20–30	10	25	–3	–30
30–40	6	35	–2	–12
40–50	8	45	–1	–8
50–60	12	55 = A	0	0
60–70	5	65	1	5
70–80	9	75	2	18
	$\Sigma f = 50$			$\Sigma fu = -27$

Here,   A = assumed mean = 55

      $h = 10$

$$\overline{X} = A + \frac{\Sigma fu}{\Sigma f} \times h$$

$$= 55 + \frac{(-27)}{50} \times 10$$

$$= 55 - 5.4 = 49.6$$

The mean of the distribution is 49.5.

Q. 9. Marks obtained by 40 students in a short assessment is given below, where a and b are two missing data.

Marks	5	6	7	8	9
No. of Students	6	a	16	13	b

If the mean of the distribution is 7.2, find a and b.   [2012]

Ans.

Marks (x)	No. of students (f)	$f \cdot x$
5	6	30
6	a	6a
7	16	112
8	13	104
9	b	9b
	$\Sigma f = 35 + a + b$	$\Sigma fx = 246 + 6a + 9b$

Now,

$$35 + a + b = 40$$
$$a + b = 5 \qquad \qquad \text{...(i)}$$

And, $$\overline{X} = \frac{\Sigma fx}{\Sigma f}$$

$$7.2 = \frac{246 + 6a + 9b}{40}$$

$$\Rightarrow \quad 6a + 9b + 246 = 288$$
$$\Rightarrow \quad 6a + 9b = 42$$
$$\Rightarrow \quad 2a + 3b = 14 \qquad \text{...(ii)}$$

Multiplying by 2 in equation (i) and solving with equation (ii)

$$2a + 2b = 10$$
$$2a + 3b = 14$$

On subtracting $\quad (-) \quad (-) \quad (-)$
$$\overline{\qquad - b = - 4 \qquad}$$
$$\Rightarrow \quad b = 4$$

Putting the value of b in equation (i) , we get

$$a + 4 = 5$$
$$\Rightarrow \quad a = 1$$
$$\therefore \quad a = 1, b = 4$$

Q. 10. A Mathematics aptitude test of 50 students was recorded as follows:

Marks	50–60	60–70	70–80	80–90	90–100
No. of Students	4	8	14	19	5

Draw a histogram for the above data using a graph paper and locate the mode. **[2011]**

Ans.

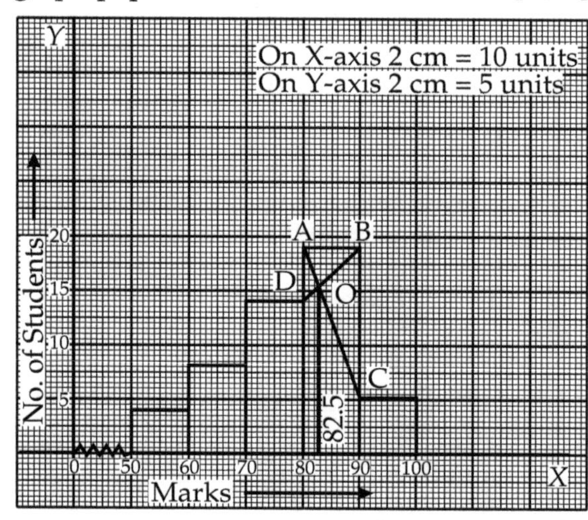

From the graph, the bar with the maximum height is of 80–90 interval. Join A to C and B to D. They meet at O. Drop perpendicular from O on X-axis. It meets at 82.5.

Q. 11. The distribution given below shows the marks obtained by 25 students in an aptitude test. Find the mean, median and mode of the distribution. **[2010]**

Marks obtained	5	6	7	8	9	10
No. of students	3	9	6	4	2	1

Ans.

Marks Obtained (x)	No. of Students (f)	$c\cdot f$	$f\cdot x$
5	3	3	15
6	9	12	54
7	6	18	42
8	4	22	32
9	2	24	18
10	1	25	10
	$\Sigma f = 25$		$\Sigma fx = 171$

$$\text{Mean } \bar{x} = \frac{\Sigma fx}{\Sigma f}$$
$$= \frac{171}{25}$$
$$= 6.84$$
$$n = \Sigma f = 25 \ (\text{odd})$$
$$\therefore \quad \text{Median} = \left(\frac{n+1}{2}\right)^{th} \text{term}$$
$$\text{Median} = \left(\frac{25+1}{2}\right)^{th} \text{term}$$
$$= 13^{th} \text{term} = 7$$

Since, the number 6 has maximum frequency 9
$$\therefore \quad \text{Mode} = 6$$

Q. 12. The mean of the following distribution is 52 and the frequency of class interval 30–40 is 'f'. Find 'f'.

Class Interval	10–20	20–30	30–40	40–50	50–60	60–70	70–80
Frequency	5	3	f	7	2	6	13

[2010]

Ans.

C.I.	Frequency (f)	Mid-value (x)	fx
10–20	5	15	75
20–30	3	25	75
30–40	f	35	35f
40–50	7	45	315
50–60	2	55	110
60–70	6	65	390
70–80	13	75	975
	$\Sigma f = 36 + f$		$\Sigma fx = 1940 + 35f$

$$\text{Mean} = \frac{\Sigma fx}{\Sigma f}$$
$$\Rightarrow \quad 52 = \frac{1940 + 35f}{36 + f},$$
$$\text{(Given, Mean = 52)}$$
$$\Rightarrow \quad 1872 + 52f = 1940 + 35f$$

$\Rightarrow \qquad 17f = 68$

$\therefore \qquad f = 4$

Q. 13. The following table gives the wages of workers in a factory:

Wages in ₹	No. of Workers
45–50	5
50–55	8
55–60	30
60–65	25
65–70	14
70–75	12
75–80	6

Calculate the mean by the short cut method.

[2009]

Ans.

Wages (₹)	No. of Workers (f)	Mid. mark x	$d = (x - A)$	$f \times d$
45–50	5	47.5	–15	–75
50–55	8	52.5	–10	–80
55–60	30	57.5	–5	–150
60–65	25	62.5 = A	0	0
65–70	14	67.5	5	70
70–75	12	72.5	10	120
75–80	6	77.5	15	90
	$\Sigma f = 100$			$\Sigma fd = -25$

$$\text{Mean} = A + \frac{\Sigma fd}{\Sigma f} = 62.5 + \frac{-25}{100}$$

$$= 62.5 - 0.25 = 62.25$$

Q. 14. Find the mean of the following distribution:

Class interval	0–10	10–20	20–30	30–40	40–50
Frequency	10	6	8	12	5

[2007]

Ans.

Class Interval	Frequency (f)	Mid value (x)	fx
0–10	10	5	50
10–20	6	15	90
20–30	8	25	200
30–40	12	35	420
40–50	5	45	225
	$\Sigma f = 41$		$\Sigma fx = 985$

$$\text{Mean} = \frac{\Sigma fx}{\Sigma f} = \frac{985}{41} = 24.02.$$

Q. 15. Find the mean of the following distribution:

Class interval	20–30	30–40	40–50	50–60	60–70	70–80
Frequency	10	6	8	12	5	9

[2006]

Ans.

Class Interval	Class Marks (x)	Frequency (f)	fx
20–30	25	10	250
30–40	35	6	210
40–50	45	8	360
50–60	55	12	660
60–70	65	5	325
70–80	75	9	675
		$\Sigma f = 50$	$\Sigma fx = 2,480$

$$\text{Mean} = \frac{\Sigma fx}{\Sigma f} = \frac{2,480}{50} = 49.6$$

Long Answer Type Questions-I

Q. 1. (i) Using step-deviation method, calculate the mean marks of the following distribution.

(ii) State the modal class. **[2011]**

Class interval	50–55	55–60	60–65	65–70	70–75	75–80	80–85	85–90
Frequency	5	20	10	10	9	6	12	8

Ans. (i)

C.I.	f	x	$u = \dfrac{x-A}{h}$ where $h = 5$	f·u
50–55	5	52.5	–3	–15
55–60	20	57.5	–2	–40
60–65	10	62.5	–1	–10
65–70	10	67.5 = A	0	0
70–75	9	72.5	1	9
75–80	6	77.5	2	12
80–85	12	82.5	3	36
85–90	8	87.5	4	32
	$\Sigma f = 80$			$\Sigma fu = 24$

$$\text{Mean } (\overline{X}) = A + \frac{\Sigma fu}{\Sigma f} \times h$$

$$(h = \text{length of C.I.} = 5)$$

$$= 67.5 + \frac{24}{80} \times 5 = 67.5 + 1.5$$

$$= 69$$

(ii) Modal class = 55–60

(Class with highest frequency)

Q. 2. Marks obtained by 200 students in an examination are given below:

Marks	0–10	10–20	20–30	30–40	40–50	50–60	60–70	70–80	80–90	90–100
Frequency	5	11	10	20	28	37	40	29	14	6

Draw an ogive for the given distribution taking 2 cm = 10 marks on one axis and 2 cm = 20 students on the other axis. Using the graph, determine:

(i) The median marks

(ii) The number of students who failed if minimum marks required to pass is 40.

(iii) If scoring 85 and more marks is considered as grade one, find the number of students who secured grade one in the examination. **[2011]**

Ans.

Marks	0–10	10–20	20–30	30–40	40–50	50–60	60–70	70–80	80–90	90–100
f	5	11	10	20	28	37	40	29	14	6
$c.f.$	5	16	26	46	74	111	151	180	194	200

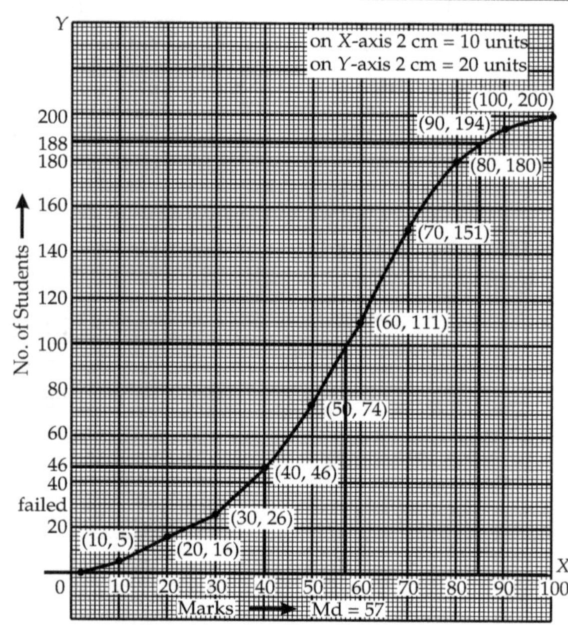

(i) From the graph:

$$\text{Median} = \left(\frac{n}{2}\right)^{th} \text{ observation}$$

$$= \left(\frac{200}{2}\right)^{th} \text{ observation}$$

$$= 100^{th} \text{ observation}$$

$$= 57$$

Using at graph: Draw a perpendicular from X-axis at 40 marks to the ogive. The point from where line touches ogive drop a perpendicular on the Y-axis. The point where it touches Y-axis is the answer.

(ii) No. of students who failed = 46

(iii) Same process as number of students who secured grade one = 200 – 188 = 12

Q. 3. The weights of 50 apples were recorded as given below. Calculate the mean weight, to the nearest gram, by the *Step Deviation Method.*

Weights in grams	No. of apples
80–85	5
85–90	8
90–95	10
95–100	12
100–105	8
105–110	4
110–115	3

[2008]

Ans.

weight in gms.	No. of apples	x	$x - A$	$u = \dfrac{x - A}{h}$	$f.u$
80–85	5	82.5	–15	–3	–15
85–90	8	87.5	–10	–2	–16
90–95	10	92.5	–5	–1	–10
95–100	12	(97.5) = A	0	0	0
100–105	8	102.5	5	1	8
105–110	4	107.5	10	2	8
110–115	3	112.5	15	3	9
	$\Sigma f = 50$				$\Sigma fu = -16$

Let the assumed mean be 97.5, $h = 5$

$$\therefore \quad \text{Mean} = A + \frac{\Sigma fu}{\Sigma f} \times h = 97.5 + \left(\frac{-16}{50}\right) \times 5$$

$$= 97.5 - 1.6 = 95.9 \cong 96 \text{ grams}$$

Q. 4. Using a graph paper, draw an ogive for the following distribution which shows the marks obtained in the General Knowledge paper by 100 students.

Marks	0–10	10–20	20–30	30–40	40–50	50–60	60–70	70–80
No. of Students	5	10	20	25	15	12	9	4

Use the ogive to estimate:
 (i) the median
(ii) the number of students who score marks above 65. [2008]

Ans.

Marks	No. of Students	c.f.	Points
0–10	5	5	(10, 5)
10–20	10	15	(20, 15)
20–30	20	35	(30, 35)
30–40	25	60	(40, 60)
40–50	15	75	(50, 75)
50–60	12	87	(60, 87)
60–70	9	96	(70, 96)
70–80	4	100	(80, 100)
	$n = 100$		

Total no. of students = $100 = n$

(i) Median = $\dfrac{n}{2}$th observation

$\qquad = \dfrac{100^{\text{th}}}{2}$ observation

$\qquad = 50^{\text{th}}$ observation

As shown in ogive; median = 36

(ii) Number of students who scored above $65 = 100 - 92 = 8$.

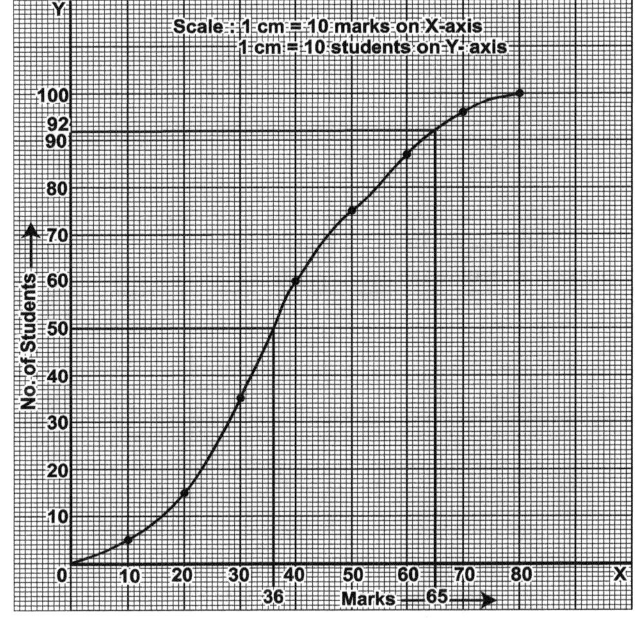

 Long Answer Type Questions-II

Q. 1. 40 students enter for a game of shot-put competition. The distance thrown (in metres) is recorded below : [2020]

Distance in m	Number of Students
12 – 13	3
13 – 14	9
14 – 15	12
15 – 16	9
16 – 17	4
17 – 18	2
18 – 19	1

Use a graph paper to draw an ogive for the above distribution.

Use a scale of 2 cm = 1 m on one axis and 2 cm = 5 students on the other axis.

Hence using your graph find :

(i) the median

(ii) Upper Quartile

(iii) Number of students who cover a distance which is above $16\frac{1}{2}$ m.

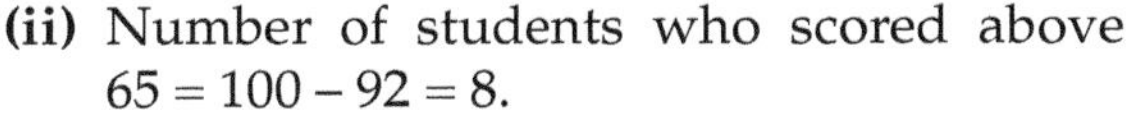 Marking Scheme

Distance in m	Number of students	Cumulative frequency (c.f.)
12 - 13	3	3
13 - 14	9	12
14 - 15	12	24
15 - 16	9	33
16 - 17	4	37
17 - 18	2	39
18 - 19	1	40

(i) Median = 14.7 m $\pm$ 0.2
(ii) Upper Quartile = 15.65 m $\pm$ 0.2
(iii) 40 − 35 = 5 students cover a distance above 16½ m.

Ogive : Scale 2 cm = 1 m along x-axis and
2 cm = 5 students along y-axis

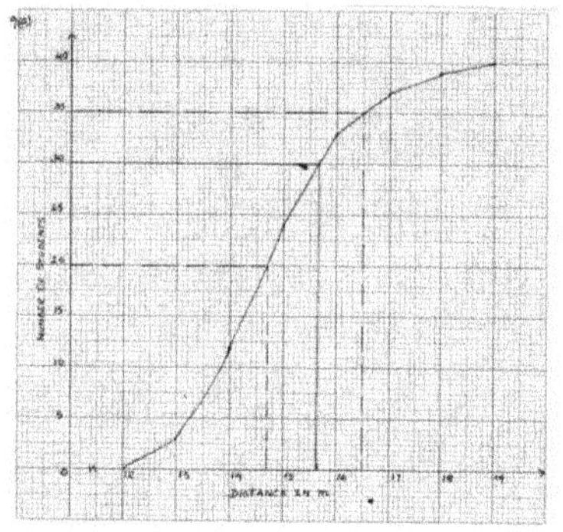

Ans.

Distance in m	Frequency (f)	$c.f.$
12 – 13	3	3
13 – 14	9	12
14 – 15	12	24
15 – 16	9	33
16 – 17	4	37
17 – 18	2	39
18 – 19	1	40

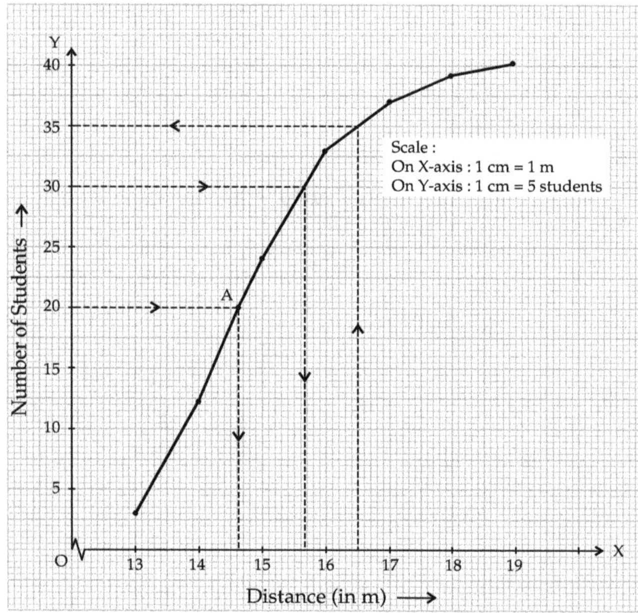

Note : Instead of 2 cm = 1 m and 2 cm = 5 students, we have used 1 cm = 1 m and 1 cm = 5 students on X and Y axes, respectively.

(i) Median = $\left(\dfrac{N}{2}\right)^{th}$ term

$\qquad\quad = \left(\dfrac{40}{2}\right)^{th}$ term

$\qquad\quad =$ 20th term

On the graph, through a point 20 on y-axis, draw a horizontal line which meets the ogive at point A. Through A, draw a vertical line which meets the x-axis at 14.7.

$\therefore \qquad$ Median = 14.7

(ii) Upper quartile (Q_3) = $\left(\dfrac{3N}{4}\right)^{th}$ term

$\qquad\qquad = \left(\dfrac{3 \times 40}{4}\right)^{th}$ term

$\qquad\qquad =$ 30th term

$\qquad\qquad =$ 15.7

(iii) Number of students who cover more than $16\dfrac{1}{2}$ m = 40 − 35 = 5

Q. 2. Use graph paper for this question.

The marks obtained by 120 students in an English test are given below: [2019]

Marks	Number of students
0–10	5
10–20	9
20–30	16
30–40	22
40–50	26
50–60	18
60–70	11
70–80	6
80–90	4
90–100	3

Draw the ogive and hence, estimate:

(i) the median marks.

(ii) the number of students who did not pass test if the pass percentage was 50.

(iii) the upper quartile marks.

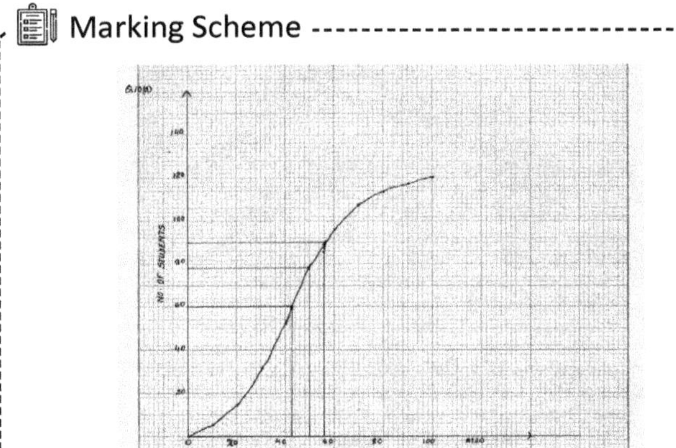

Marking Scheme

Scale : On X-axis, 1 cm = 20 marks

On Y-axis, 1 cm = 20 students

(i) Median = 43 marks

(ii) Number of students who did not pass the test 78

(iii) 56 marks ($\pm$ 1)

Ans.

Marks	Number of students	Cumulative frequency
0–10	5	5
10–20	9	14
20–30	16	30
30–40	22	52
40–50	26	78
50–60	18	96
60–70	11	107
70–80	6	113
80–90	4	117
90–100	3	120

$\therefore$ $N = 120$

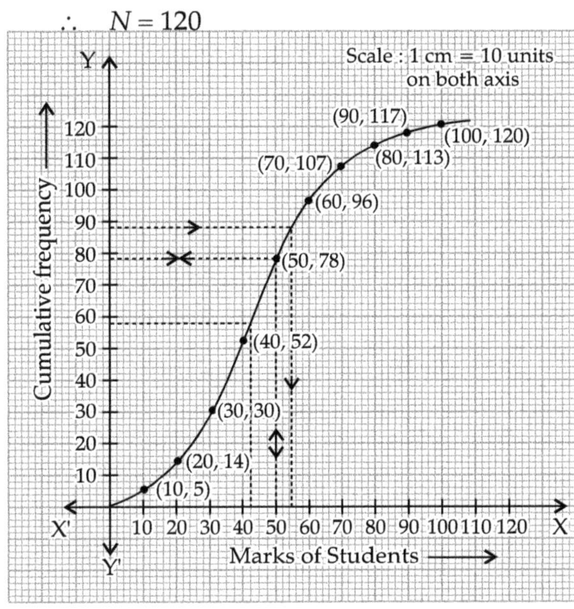

(i) Median marks = $\dfrac{N}{2}$th observation

$= \dfrac{120}{2}$th observation

$= 60$th observation

$= 43$ (from ogive)

(ii) Number of students who did not pass

$= 78$ (from ogive)

(iii) Upper quartile = $\dfrac{3N}{4}$th observation

$= \dfrac{3 \times 120}{4}$th observation

$= 90$th observation

$= 56$ (from ogive)

Q. 3. Use Graph paper for this question.

A survey regarding height (in cm) of 60 boys belonging to Class 10 of a school was conducted. The following data was recorded:

Height in cm	135–140	140–145	145–150	150–155	155–160	160–165	165–170
No. of boys	4	8	20	14	7	6	1

Taking 2 cm = height of 10 cm along one axis and 2 cm =10 boys along the other axis draw an ogive of the above distribution. Use the graph to estimate the following:

(i) the median

(ii) lower quartile

(iii) if above 158 cm is considered as the tall boys of the class. Find the number of boys in the class who are tall. **[2018]**

Ans.

Height in cm	No. of Boys	c.f.
135–140	4	4
140–145	8	12
145–150	20	32
150–155	14	46
155–160	7	53
160–165	6	59
165–170	1	60
	$n = 60$	

(i)
$$\text{Median} = \frac{n}{2}\text{th observation}$$

$$= \frac{60}{2}\text{th observation}$$

$$= 30\text{th observation}$$

$$= 150 \text{ cm} \qquad \text{(from ogive)}$$

(ii) Lower quartile $= \dfrac{n}{4}$th observation

$$= \frac{60}{4}\text{th observation}$$

$$= 15\text{th observation}$$

$$= 146 \text{ cm} \qquad \text{(from ogive)}$$

(iii) No. of boys whose height is less than 158 cm = 51. (from ogive)

∴ No. of tall boys = 60 – 51 = 9.

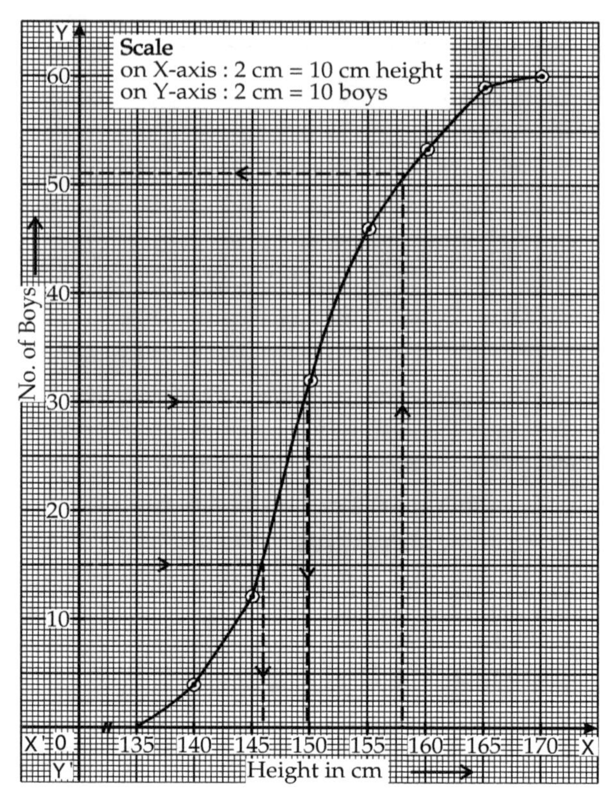

Q. 4. The daily wages of 80 workers in a project are given below.

Wages (in ₹)	400–450	450–500	500–550	550–600	600–650	650–700	700–750
No. of workers	2	6	12	18	24	13	5

Use a graph paper to draw an ogive for the above distribution. (Use a scale of 2 cm = ₹ 50 on X-axis and 2 cm = 10 workers on Y-axis). Use your ogive to estimate:

(i) the median wage of the workers.
(ii) the lower quartile wage of workers.
(iii) the number of workers who earn more than ₹ 625 daily. [2017]

Ans.

Wages (in ₹)	No. of Workers	Cumulative Frequency
400–450	2	2
450–500	6	8
500–550	12	20
550–600	18	38
600–650	24	62
650–700	13	75
700–750	5	80

∴ $n = 80$

(i) Median wage $= \dfrac{n}{2}$th value.

$$= \frac{80}{2}\text{th value}$$

$$= 40\text{th value}$$

$$= ₹\,605$$

(ii) Lower quartile $= \dfrac{n}{4}$ th value = 20th value

$$= ₹\,550$$

(iii) No. of workers earning more than ₹ 625 daily = 80 – 50 = 30

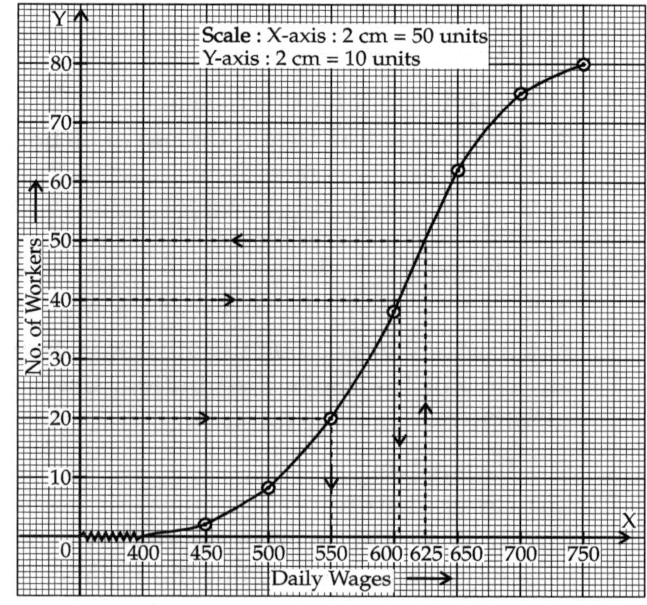

Q. 5. The table shows the distribution of the scores obtained by 160 shooters in a shooting competition. Use a graph sheet and draw an ogive for the distribution. (**Take 2 cm = 10 scores on the X-axis and 2 cm = 20 shooters on the Y-axis**) **[2016]**

Score	No. of Shooters
0–10	9
10–20	13
20–30	20
30–40	26
40–50	30
50–60	22
60–70	15
70–80	10
80–90	8
90–100	7

Use your graph to estimate the following:

(i) The median.
(ii) The interquartile range.
(iii) The number of shooters who obtained a score of more than 85%.

Ans.

Scores	No. of Shooters	Cumulative frequency (*c. f.*)
0—10	9	9
10—20	13	22
20—30	20	42
30—40	26	68
40—50	30	98
50—60	22	120
60—70	15	135
70—80	10	145
80—90	8	153
90—100	7	160

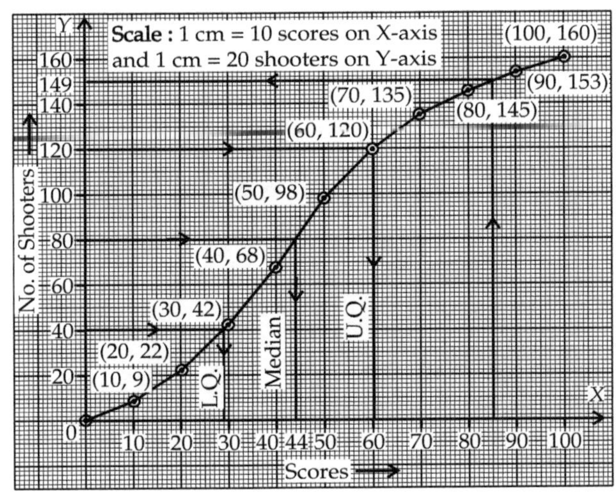

Using graph = 160

(i) Since, $n = 160$ (even)

$$\text{Median} = \left(\frac{n}{2}\right)^{th} \text{term}$$

$$= \left(\frac{160}{2}\right)^{th} \text{term}$$

$$= 80^{th} \text{term} = 44$$

(ii) Lower quartile

$$(Q_1) = \left(\frac{n}{4}\right)^{th} \text{term}$$

$$= \left(\frac{160}{4}\right)^{th} = 40^{th} \text{term}.$$

$$= 29$$

Upper quartile

$$(Q_3) = \left(\frac{3n}{4}\right)^{th} \text{term}$$

$$= \left(\frac{3 \times 160}{4}\right)^{th} \text{term}$$

$$= 120^{th} \text{term}.$$

$$= 60$$

Inter-quartile range

$$= Q_3 - Q_1$$

$$= 60 - 29 = 31$$

(iii) Since, 85% scores = 85% of 100 = 85.

Through mark for 85 on X-axis, draw a vertical line which meets the ogive at any point. Through that point, draw a horizontal line which meets the Y-axis at the mark of 149.

∴ The no. of shooters who obtained a score of more than 85%

$$= 160 - 149 = 11$$

Note: Instead of 2 cm = 1 unit, we have taken 1 cm = 1 unit both axis.

Q. 5. The weight of 50 workers is given below:

Weight in kg	50–60	60–70	70–80	80–90	90–100	100–110	110–120
No. of Workers	4	7	11	14	6	5	3

Draw an ogive of the given distribution using a graph sheet. Take 2 cm = 10 kg on one axis and 2 cm = 5 workers along the other axis. Use a graph to estimate the following:

(i) the upper and lower quartiles.

(ii) if weight 95 kg and above is considered overweight find the number of workers who are overweight. [2015]

Ans.

Weight (in kg)	No. of workers (f)	Cumulative frequency ($c.f.$)
50–60	4	4
60–70	7	11
70–80	11	22
80–90	14	36
90–100	6	42
100–110	5	47
110–120	3	50
	$N = \Sigma f = 50$	

Note: On Y-axis instead of 2 cm = 5 workers, we have taken 1 cm = 5 workers and on X-axis instead of 2 cm = 10 kg, we have taken 1 cm = 10 kg.

From graph,

(i) Upper quartile range

$$(Q_3) = \left(\frac{3N}{4}\right)^{th} \text{ term}$$

$$= \left(\frac{3 \times 50}{4}\right)^{th} \text{ term}$$

$$= 37.5^{th} \text{ term} = 92.5 \text{ kg}$$

Lower quartile range

$$(Q_1) = \left(\frac{N}{4}\right)^{th} \text{ term}$$

$$= \left(\frac{50}{4}\right)^{th} \text{ term}$$

$$= 12.5^{th} \text{ term}$$

$$= 71.5 \text{ kg.}$$

(ii) From the graph, No. of workers who are under-weight *i.e.*, less than 95 are 39.

No. of workers who are over-weight are

$(50 - 39) = 11.$

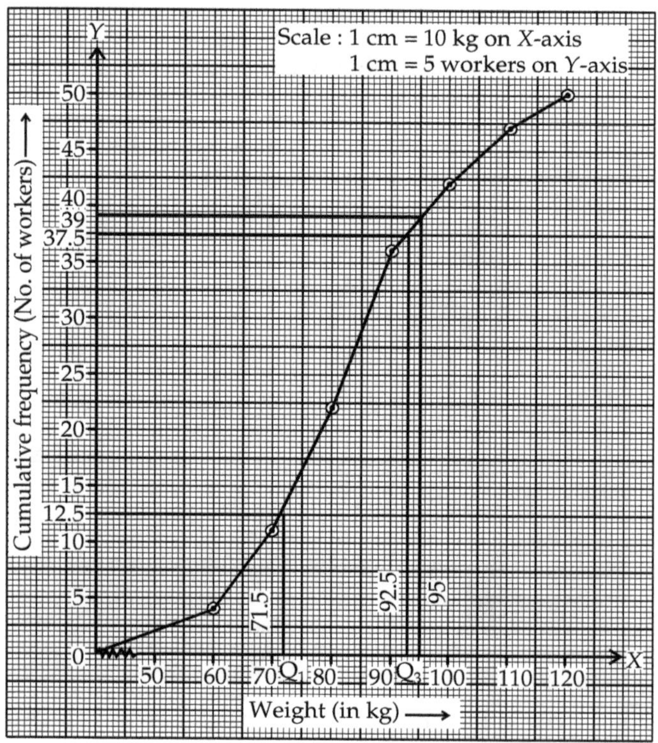

Q. 6. The marks obtained by 100 students in a Mathematics test are given below:

Marks	0–10	10–20	20–30	30–40	40–50	50–60	60–70	70–80	80–90	90–100
No. of Students	3	7	12	17	23	14	9	6	5	4

Draw an ogive for the given distribution on a graph sheet.

(Use a scale of 2 cm = 10 units on both axis).
Use the ogive to estimate the:
(i) median.
(ii) lower quartile.
(iii) number of students who obtained more than 85% marks in the test.
(iv) number of students who did not pass in the test if the pass percentage was 35.

[2014]

Ans.

Marks	c.f.	Points
Less than 10	3	(10, 3)
Less than 20	10	(20, 10)
Less than 30	22	(30, 22)
Less than 40	39	(40, 39)
Less than 50	62	(50, 62)
Less than 60	76	(60, 76)
Less than 70	85	(70, 85)
Less than 80	91	(80, 91)
Less than 90	96	(90, 96)
Less than 100	100	(100, 100)

Note: Instead of 2 cm = [0 units, we have taken 1 cm = 10 units on both axis].

Using graph,

(i) Median $= \left(\dfrac{N}{2}\right)^{th}$ observation

$= \left(\dfrac{100}{2}\right)^{th}$ observation

$= 50^{th}$ observation

$= 45$

(ii) Lower Quartile (Q_1)

$= \left(\dfrac{N}{4}\right)^{th}$ observation

$= \left(\dfrac{100}{4}\right)^{th}$ observation

$= 25^{th}$ observation $= 32$

(iii) Number of students who obtained more than 85% marks

$= (100 - 94) = 6.$　　Ans.

(iv) Number of students who did not pass if passing % of marks is 35

$= 30.$

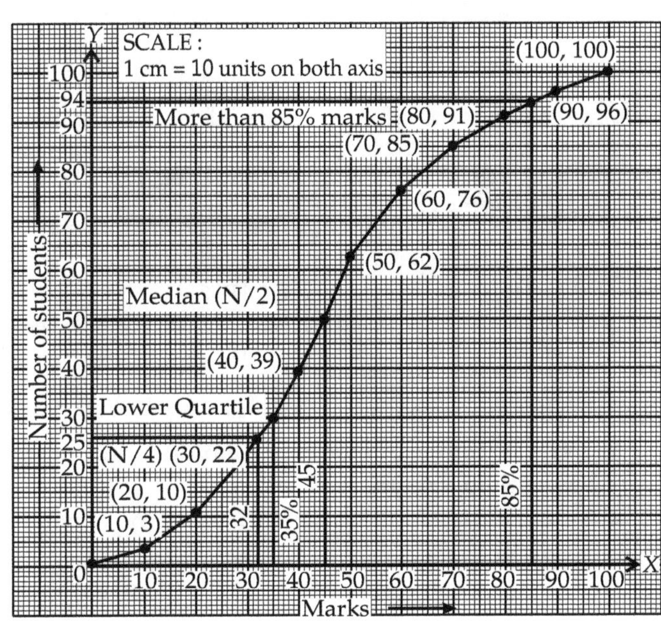

Q. 7. The marks obtained by 120 students in a test are given below:

Marks	0–10	10–20	20–30	30–40	40–50	50–60	60–70	70–80	80–90	90–100
No. of Students	5	9	16	22	26	18	11	6	4	3

Draw an ogive for the given distribution on a graph sheet.

Use suitable scale for ogive to estimate the following:

(i) The median.
(ii) The number of students who obtained more than 75% marks in the test.
(iii) The number of students who did not pass the test if minimum marks required to pass is 40.

[2013]

Ans.

Marks C.I.	No. of Students f	c.f.
0—10	5	5
10—20	9	14
20—30	16	30
30—40	22	52
40—50	26	78
50—60	18	96

60—70	11	107
70—80	6	113
80—90	4	117
90—100	3	120

(i) Using graph, $n = 120$ (even)

$$\therefore \quad \text{Median} = \left(\frac{120}{2}\right)^{th} \text{observation}$$

$$= 60^{th} \text{observation}$$

$$= 43 \text{ (approx.)}$$

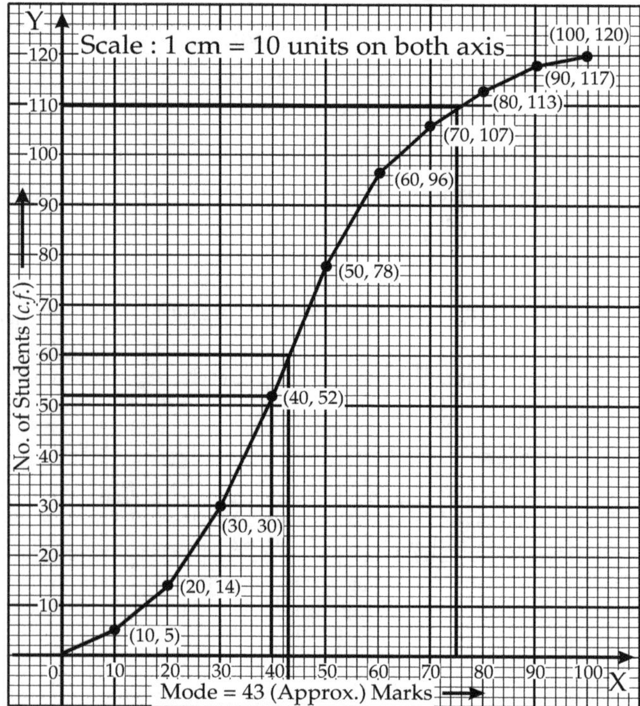

(ii) Number of students who obtained more than 75% marks in the test

$$= 120 - 110 = 10$$

(iii) Number of students who did not pass the test $= 52$

Q. 8. The following distribution represents the height of 160 students of a school.

Height (in cm)	No. of Students
140–145	12
145–150	20
150–155	30
155–160	38
160–165	24
165–170	16
170–175	12
175–180	8

Draw an ogive for the given distribution taking 2 cm = 5 cm of height on one axis and 2 cm = 20 students on the other axis. Using the graph, determine:

(i) The median height.

(ii) The interquartile range.

(iii) The number of students whose height is above 172 cm. **[2012]**

Ans.

Height (in cm)	No. of Students (f)	cf
140–145	12	12
145–150	20	32
150–155	30	62
155–160	38	100
160–165	24	124
165–170	16	140
170–175	12	152
175–180	8	160
	$\Sigma f = 160$	

We have to plot (145, 12), (150, 32), (155, 62), (160, 100), (165, 124), (170, 140), (175, 152) and (180, 160).

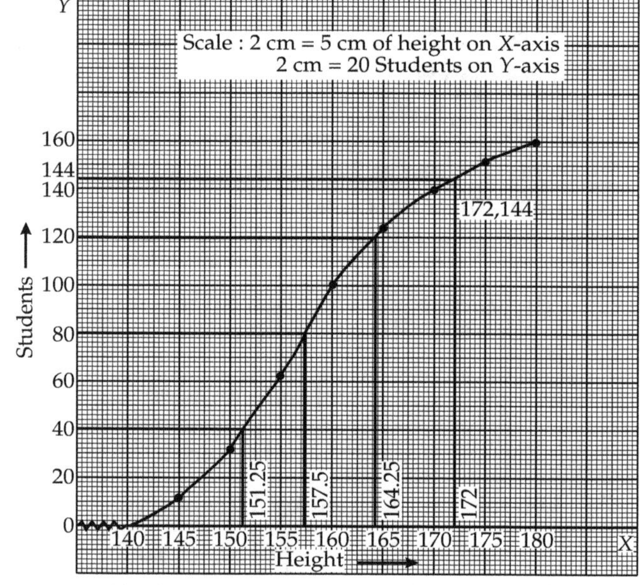

(i) Using graph,

$$N = 160 \text{ (even)}$$

$$\therefore \quad \text{Median} = \left(\frac{160}{2}\right)^{th} \text{term} = 80^{th} \text{term}$$

Now, we shall construct a horizontal line at cumulative frequency $= 80$:

Intersecting the ogive at (157.5, 80),

Hence, median height $= 157.5$ cm.

(ii) Lower quartile $(Q_1) = \left(\frac{N}{4}\right)^{th}$ term

$$= \left(\frac{160}{4}\right)^{th} \text{ term}$$

$$= 40^{th} \text{ term} = 151.25$$

$$\text{Upper quartile } (Q_3) = \left(\frac{3N}{4}\right)^{th} \text{ term}$$

$$= \left(\frac{3 \times 160}{4}\right)^{th} \text{ term}$$

$$= 120^{th} \text{ term} = 164.25$$

$$\therefore \quad \text{Interquartile range} = Q_3 - Q_1$$

$$= 164.25 - 151.25$$

$$= 13$$

(iii) The number of students whose height is above 172 cm

$$= 160 - 144 = 16$$

Q. 9. **The monthly income of a group of 320 employees in a company is given below:**

Monthly Income	No. of Employees
6000–7000	20
7000–8000	45
8000–9000	65
9000–10000	95
10000–11000	60
11000–12000	30
12000–13000	5

Draw an ogive of the given distribution on a graph sheet taking 2 cm = ₹ 1000 on one axis and 2 cm = 50 employees on the other axis. From the graph determine:

(i) the median wage

(ii) the number of employees whose income is below ₹ 8500.

(iii) If the salary of a senior employee is above ₹ 11,500, find the number of senior employees in the company.

(iv) the upper quartile. [2010]

Ans.

Monthly Income	No. of Employees	c.f.
6000—7000	20	20
7000—8000	45	65
8000—9000	65	130
9000—10000	95	225
10000—11000	60	285
11000—12000	30	315
12000—13000	5	320

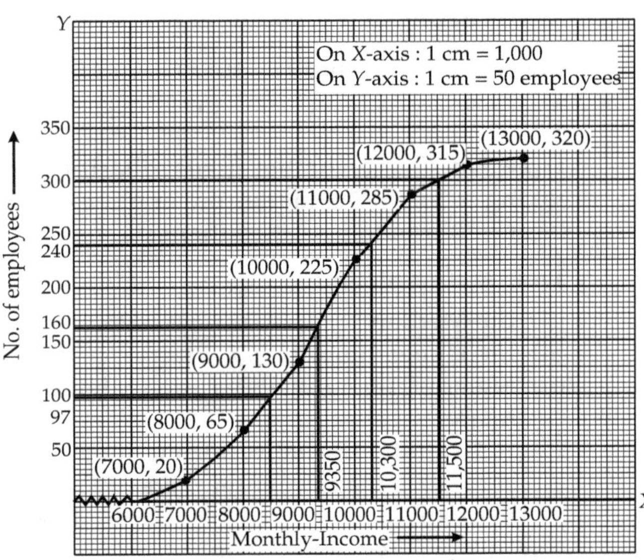

Note: On X-axis instead of 2 cm = ₹ 1000 we have taken 1 cm = ₹ 1000 and on Y-axis instead of 2 cm = ₹ 50 employees, we have taken 1 cm = 50 employees.

(i) $n = 320$ (even)

$$\text{Median} = \left(\frac{n}{2}\right)^{th} \text{ Observation}$$

$$= \left(\frac{320}{2}\right)^{th} \text{ Observation}$$

$$= 160^{th} \text{ Observation}$$

Draw a perpendicular from 160th observation on Y-axis at ogive and then drop a perpendicular on X-axis, which is the required median.

Required median = ₹ 9,350 (approx.)

(ii) To get this, in graph draw a perpendicular from ₹ 8,500 on X-axis at ogive. An then drop a perpendicular on Y-axis, which is the required no. of employees.

The number of employees whose income is below ₹ 8,500 = 97

(iii) The number of senior employees whose salary is above ₹ 11,500

The point on Y-axis is 300

$\therefore$ Required answer

$$= 320 - 300 = 20$$

(iv) Upper quartile $= \dfrac{3n}{4}$

$$= \frac{3 \times 320}{4}$$

$$= 3 \times 80 = 240^{th} \text{ observation}$$

i.e., Upper quartile = ₹ 10,300

Q. 10. Attempt this question on graph paper.

Marks obtained by 200 students in examination are given below:

Marks	0–10	10–20	20–30	30–40	40–50	50–60	60–70	70–80	80–90	90–100
No. of Students	5	10	14	21	25	34	36	27	16	12

Draw an Ogive for the given distribution taking 2 cm = 10 marks on one axis and 2 cm = 20 students on the other axis.

From the graph find:

(i) the Median

(ii) the Upper Quartile

(iii) Number of students scoring above 65 marks.

(iv) If 10 students qualify for merit scholarship, find the minimum marks required to qualify. **[2009]**

Ans. Cumulative Frequency table

Marks	No. of Students	c.f.	Points
0–10	5	5	(10, 5)
10–20	10	15	(20, 15)
20–30	14	29	(30, 29)
30–40	21	50	(40, 50)
40–50	25	75	(50, 75)
50–60	34	109	(60, 109)
60–70	36	145	(70, 145)
70–80	27	172	(80, 172)
80–90	16	188	(90, 188)
90–100	12	200	(100, 200)
	$n = 200$		

(i) Here, n (no. of students) = 200 (even)

$$\text{Median} = \left(\frac{n}{2}\right)^{th} \text{term}$$

$$= \left(\frac{200}{2}\right)^{th} \text{term}$$

$$= 100^{th} \text{term}$$

From the graph 100th term = 57.5

$$\text{Median} = 57.5$$

(ii) Upper quartile $= \left(\frac{3n}{2}\right)^{th}$ term;

$$= \frac{3 \times 200}{4}^{th} \text{term}$$

$$= \frac{600}{4}^{th} \text{term}$$

$$= 150^{th} \text{term}$$

From graph 150th term = 72

The upper quartile = 72

(iii) No. of students scoring above 65 marks
= Total No. of students – No. of students scoring less than or equal to 65 marks
= 200 – 126
= 74 (approx.)

(iv) From the above diagram, we observe the students from 191 to 200 qualify for merit scholarship.

∴ The student who qualifies for merit scholarship scores more than 91 marks.

∴ The minimum marks required to qualify for merit scholarship
= 92 (approx.)

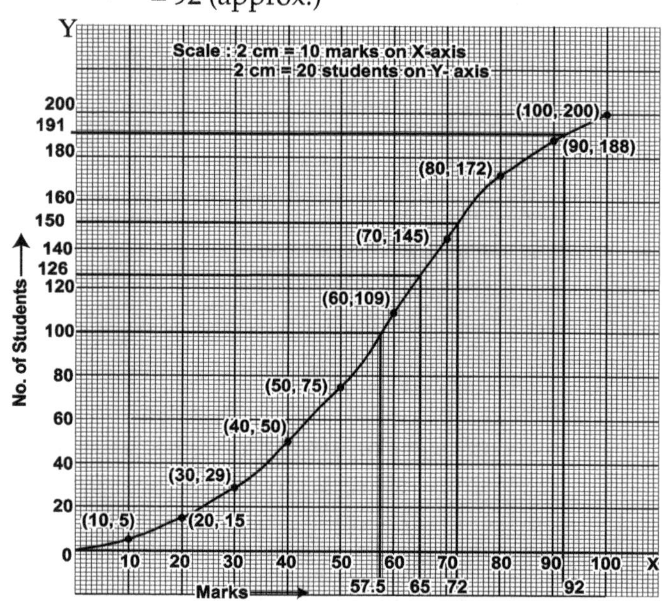

Q. 11. The table below shows the distribution of the scores obtained by 120 shooters in a shooting competition. Using a graph sheet, draw an ogive for the distribution.

Scores obtained	Number of shooters
0–10	5
10–20	9
20–30	16
30–40	22
40–50	26
50–60	18
60–70	11
70–80	6
80–90	4
90–100	3

Use your ogive to estimate:
(i) The Median
(ii) The inter quartile range
(iii) The number of shooters who obtained more than 75% scores. **[2007]**

Ans.

Class Interval	Frequency	Cumulative Frequency
0–10	5	5
10–20	9	14
20–30	16	30
30–40	22	52
40–50	26	78
50–60	18	96
60–70	11	107
70–80	6	113
80–90	4	117
90–100	3	120

As from graph paper:

(i) Median $= \dfrac{N}{2}$th term = 60th term = 43

(ii) Lower Quartile $Q_1 = \dfrac{n}{4}$th term

$\qquad\qquad\qquad\quad$ = 30th term = 30

Upper Quartile

$$Q_3 = \frac{3n}{4}\text{th term} = \text{90th term} = 57$$

Inter Quartile Range $= Q_3 - Q_1 = 57 - 30 = 27$

(iii) The number of shooter scores more than 75% = 120 − 110 = 10.

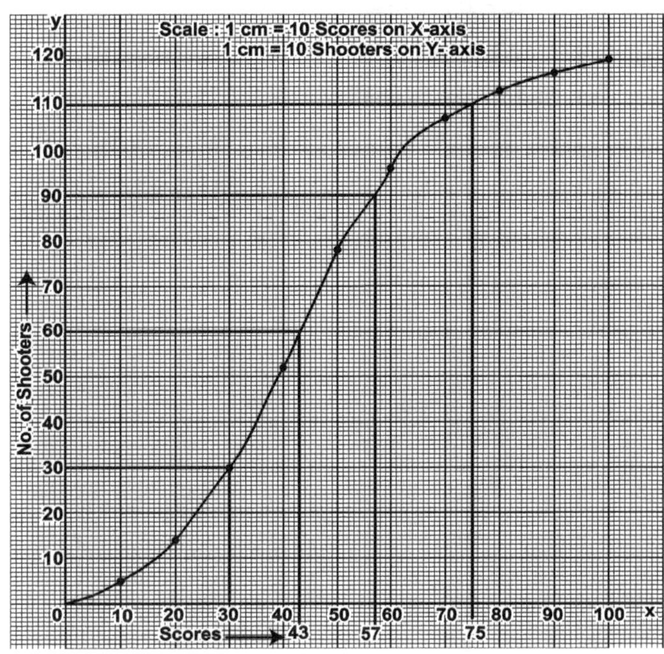

Q. 12. The daily wages of 160 workers in a building project are given below:

Wages in ₹	0–10	10–20	20–30	30–40	40–50	50–60	60–70	70–80
No. of Workers	12	20	30	38	24	16	12	8

Using a graph paper, draw an Ogive for the above distribution.

Use your Ogive to estimate:
(i) The median wage of the workers.
(ii) The upper quartile wage of the workers
(iii) The lower quartile wages of the workers
(iv) The percentage of workers who earn more than ₹ 45 a day. **[2006]**

Ans.

Wages (in ₹)	No. of Workers	Cumulative frequency
0–10	12	12
10–20	20	32
20–30	30	62
30–40	38	100
40–50	24	124
50–60	16	140
60–70	12	152
70–80	8	160

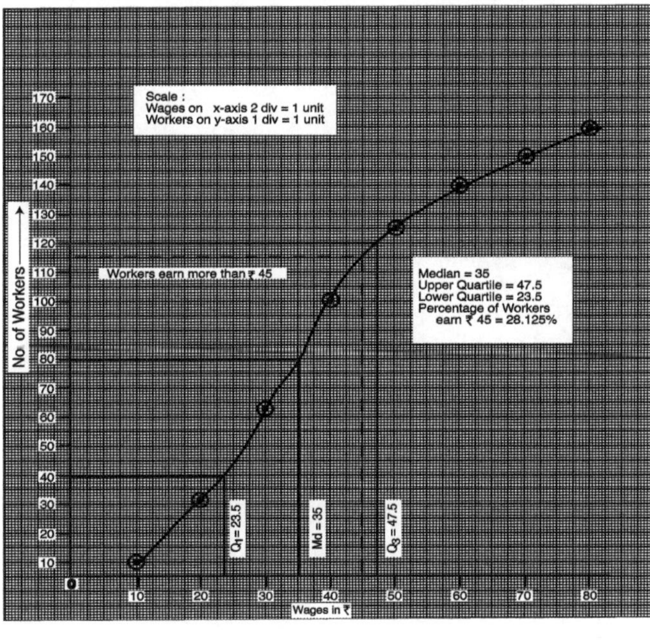

(i) Median $= \dfrac{160}{2} = 80^{\text{th}}$ term

Now the 80th position in the ogive diagram represents the median wage of workers by the graph = ₹ 35

(ii) Upper quartile $= \dfrac{3n}{4} = \dfrac{3 \times 160}{4} = 120^{th}$ term

Now, the 120th position in the ogive diagram represents wage of the workers

$(Q_3) = $ ₹ 47.5

(iii) Lower quartile $= \dfrac{n}{4} = \dfrac{160}{4} = 40^{th}$ term

The 40th position in the ogive diagram represents wage of the workers

$Q_1 = $ ₹ 23.5

(iv) The percentage of workers who earn more than ₹ 45

$$= \dfrac{160 - 115}{160} \times 100 = \dfrac{45 \times 10}{16}$$

$$= \dfrac{450}{16} = 28.125\%$$

Short Answer Type Questions

Q. 1. Each of the letters of the word 'AUTHORIZES' is written on identical circular discs and put in a bag. They are well shuffled. If a disc is drawn at random from the bag, what is the probability that the letter is :

(i) a vowel

(ii) one of the first 9 letters of the English alphabet which appears in the given word.

(iii) one of the last 9 letters of the English alphabet which appears in the given word ?   **[2020]**

 **Marking Scheme**

{A, U, T, H, O, R, I, Z, E, S} 10 letters

(i) Vowels are {A, E, I, O, U} 5 letters

$$\therefore \text{Prob. is} = \frac{5}{10} = \frac{1}{2}$$

(ii) {A, E, H, I}

$$\therefore \text{Prob. is} = \frac{4}{10} = \frac{2}{5}$$

(iii) {R, S, T, U, Z}

$$\therefore \text{Prob. is} = \frac{5}{10} = \frac{1}{2}$$

Ans. Letters are A, U, T, H, O, R, I, Z, E, S.

$\Rightarrow$ Total number of letters in the given word = 10.

(i) Here, vowels are A, U, O, I, E.

$\Rightarrow$ Number of vowels = 5

So, probability (a vowel) $= \dfrac{5}{10} = \dfrac{1}{2}$

(ii) Letters in the given word which are in first 9 letters of english alphabets are A, I, E and H.

$\Rightarrow$ Number of such letters = 4

$$\therefore \quad \text{Probability} = \frac{4}{10} = \frac{2}{5}$$

(iii) Letters in the given word which are in last 9 letters of english alphabets are U, T, R, Z and S.

$\Rightarrow$ Number of such letters = 5

$$\therefore \quad \text{Probability} = \frac{5}{10} = \frac{1}{2}$$

Q. 2. There are 25 discs numbered 1 to 25. They are put in a closed box and shaken thoroughly. A disc is drawn at random from the box.

Find the probability that the number on the disc is:

(i) an odd number

(ii) divisible by 2 and 3 both

(iii) a number less than 16.   **[2019]**

Marking Scheme

Total number of outcomes = 25

(i) favourable outcomes are {1, 3, 5, 7, 11, 13, 15, 17, 19, 21, 23, 25}

$$\therefore \text{ probability of being an odd number is} = \frac{12}{25}$$

(ii) favourable outcomes are {6, 12, 18, 24} i.e. 4

$\therefore$ probability of being divisible by both 2 and 3 is $= \dfrac{4}{25}$

(iii) favourable outcomes are

{1, 2, 3, 4, 5 ..... 15}, i.e. 15

$$\therefore \text{ probability} = \frac{15}{25} = \frac{3}{5}$$

Ans. Given, $n(S) = 25$

(i) Let A be the event of getting an odd number.

$\therefore \quad A = \{1, 3, 5, 7, 9, 11, 13, 15, 17, 19, 21, 23, 25\}$

$\therefore \quad n(A) = 13$

$$\therefore \quad P(A) = \frac{n(A)}{n(S)} = \frac{13}{25}$$

(ii) Let B be the event of getting a number divisible by 2 and 3 both.

$\therefore \quad B = \{6, 12, 18, 24\}$

$\therefore \quad n(B) = 4$

$$\therefore \quad P(B) = \frac{n(B)}{n(S)} = \frac{4}{25}$$

(iii) Let C be the event of getting a number less than 16.

$\therefore \quad C = \{1, 2, 3, 4, 5, 6, 7, 8, 9, 10, 11, 12, 13, 14, 15\}$

$\therefore \quad n(C) = 15$

$$\therefore \quad P(C) = \frac{n(C)}{n(S)} = \frac{15}{25} = \frac{3}{5}$$

Q. 3. Sixteen cards are labelled as a, b, c, ... m, n, o, p. They are put in a box and shuffled. A boy is asked to draw a card from the box. What is the probability that the card drawn is:

    (i) a vowel.

    (ii) a consonant.

    (iii) none of the letters of the word 'median'.

                                  [2017]

Ans. Here, sample space,

$(S) = \{a, b, c, d, e, f, g, h, i, j, k, l, m, n, o, p\}$

$\therefore \qquad n\,(S) = 16$

(i)   Vowels, $V = \{a, e, i, o\}$

$\therefore \qquad n\,(V) = 4$

$\therefore \qquad P\,(a\ vowel) = \dfrac{n(V)}{n(S)}$

$$= \dfrac{4}{16} = \dfrac{1}{4}$$

(ii) Consonants,

$C = \{b, c, d, f, g, h, j, k, l, m, n, p\}$

$\therefore \qquad n\,(C) = 12$

$\therefore \ P\,(a\ consonant) = \dfrac{n(C)}{n(S)}$

$$= \dfrac{12}{16} = \dfrac{3}{4}$$

(iii) None of the letters of the word 'median'

$(N) = \{b, c, f, g, h, j, k, l, o, p\}$

$\therefore \qquad n\,(N) = 10$

$\therefore \qquad P\,(N) = \dfrac{n(N)}{n(S)}$

$$= \dfrac{10}{16} = \dfrac{5}{8}$$

Q. 4. A game of numbers has cards marked with 11, 12, 13, ..., 40. A card is drawn at random. Find the probability that the number on the card drawn is:

    (i) A perfect square

    (ii) Divisible by 7   **[2016]**

Ans. The possible outcomes are 11, 12, 13 ......, 40. Total number of all possible outcomes *i.e.,* $n(S) = 30$

   (i) For getting a perfect square:

      The favourable outcomes are: $16, 25, 36$

      No. of favourable outcomes $n\,(A) = 3$

$$P(A) = \dfrac{n(A)}{n(S)} = \dfrac{3}{30} = \dfrac{1}{10}$$

   (ii) For getting a number divisible by 7: The favourable outcomes are: $14, 21, 28, 35$. No. of favourable outcomes, $n(B) = 4$

      Required probability

$$P(B) = \dfrac{n(B)}{n(S)} = \dfrac{4}{30} = \dfrac{2}{15}$$

Q. 5. A bag contains 5 white balls, 6 red balls and 9 green balls. A ball is drawn at random from the bag. Find the probability that the ball drawn is:

    (i) a green ball

    (ii) a white or red ball

    (iii) is neither a green ball nor a white ball.

                            [2015]

Ans. Given,

          Number of white balls $= 5$

          Number of red balls $= 6$

          Number of green balls $= 9$

$\therefore$ Total number of outcomes $= (5 + 6 + 9)$

$$= 20$$

(i)   P (getting a green ball) $= \dfrac{9}{20}$

(ii) P (getting a white or red ball) $= \dfrac{5}{20} + \dfrac{6}{20}$

$$= \dfrac{11}{20}$$

$$[\because P(A \cup B) = P(A) + P(B)]$$

(iii) P (getting neither a green ball nor a white ball) $= \dfrac{6}{20} = \dfrac{3}{10}$

Q. 6. A box contains some black balls and 30 white balls. If the probability of drawing a black ball is two-fifths of a white ball, find the number of black balls in the box. **[2013]**

Ans. Let the number of black balls $= x$

    White balls $= 30$

    Total balls $= x + 30$

$$P\,(Black\ ball) = \dfrac{x}{x + 30}$$

$$P\,(White\ ball) = \dfrac{30}{x + 30}$$

According to the question

$$P\,(Black\ ball) = \dfrac{2}{5}\,P\,(White\ ball)$$

$$\dfrac{x}{x + 30} = \dfrac{2}{5} \times \dfrac{30}{x + 30}$$

or $\qquad\qquad x = \dfrac{2}{5} \times 30$

$$x = 12$$

$\therefore$ Number of black balls $= 12$

Q. 7. Two coins are tossed once. Find the probability of getting:

    (i) 2 heads

    (ii) at least 1 tail.   **[2012]**

Ans. If two coins are tossed once, then total outcomes

$$S = \{HH, HT, TH, TT\}$$

$$\Rightarrow \qquad n(S) = 4$$

   (i) Let E be the event of getting two heads

$$E = \{HH\}$$

∴ Favourable outcomes
$$n(E) = 1$$
Required probability
$$P(E) = \frac{n(E)}{n(S)}$$
$$= \frac{1}{4}$$

(ii) Let F be the event of getting atleast one tail
$$(F) = \{HT, TH, TT\}$$
∴ Favourable outcomes
$$n(F) = 3$$
Required probability
$$P(F) = \frac{n(F)}{n(S)} = \frac{3}{4}$$

Q. 8. From a pack of 52 playing cards all cards whose numbers are multiples of 3 are removed. A card is now drawn at random.

What is the probability that the card drawn is:
(i) a face card (King, Jack or Queen)
(ii) an even numbered red card?   [2011]

Ans. The numbers which are multiple of 3 in 52 playing cards are 3, 6 and 9 *i.e.,* 3 cards of each denomination.
∴ All cards whose numbers are multiples of 3 are
$$= 4 \times 3 = 12 \text{ cards}$$
Remaining cards $= 52 - 12 = 40$
[Jack, Queen and King of each denomination]
(i) No. of face cards $= 12$
$$P \text{ (face card)} = \frac{12}{40} = \frac{3}{10}$$
(ii) Again, even numbered cards are 2, 4, 8 and 10 each of heart (red) and diamond (red).
∴ Total even numbered red cards $= 4 \times 2 = 8$
$$P \text{ (even numbered red card)} = \frac{8}{40} = \frac{1}{5}$$

Q. 9. Cards marked with numbers 1, 2, 3, 4, ... 20 are well shuffled and a card is drawn at ran-

dom. What is the probability that the number on the card is:
(i) a prime number   **(ii)** divisible by 3
(iii) a perfect square?   [2010]

Ans. **(i)** Total number of events $n(S) = 20$
Prime numbers from 1 to 20,
$$E = \{2, 3, 5, 7, 11, 13, 17, 19\}$$
$$\Rightarrow \quad n(E) = 8$$
Probability of a prime number,
$$P(E) = \frac{n(E)}{n(S)} = \frac{8}{20} = \frac{2}{5}$$

(ii) Numbers divisible by 3
$$E' = (3, 6, 9, 12, 15, 18)$$
i.e., $\quad n(E') = 6$
Probability of a number divisible by 3,
$$P(E') = \frac{6}{20} = \frac{3}{10}$$

(iii) Perfect squares $= \{1, 4, 9, 16\}$
i.e., $\quad n(E'') = 4$
Probability of a perfect square
$$P(E'') = \frac{4}{20} = \frac{1}{5}$$

Q. 10. A dice is thrown once. What is the probability that the
(i) number is even
(ii) number is greater than 2?   [2009]

Ans. Dice is thrown once.
Sample space $= \{1, 2, 3, 4, 5, 6\}$
i.e., $\quad n\,(S) = 6$
(i) Even number $= \{2, 4, 6\}$
No. of ways in favour $n(E) = 3$
∴
$$\text{Probability} = \frac{n(E)}{n(S)} = \frac{3}{6} = \frac{1}{2}$$
(ii) Numbers greater than 2 are $= \{3, 4, 5, 6\}$
i.e., No. of ways in favour $n(E) = 4$
∴
$$\text{Probability } n(p) = \frac{n(E)}{n(S)} = \frac{4}{6} = \frac{2}{3}$$

Long Answer Type Questions

Q. 1. Cards bearing numbers 2, 4, 6, 8, 10, 12, 14, 16, 18 and 20 are kept in a bag. A card is drawn at random from the bag. Find the probability of getting a card which is:
(i) a prime number.
(ii) a number divisible by 4.
(iii) a number that is a multiple of 6.
(iv) an odd number.   [2018]

Ans. Here, Sample Space,
$$S = \{2, 4, 6, 8, 10, 12, 14, 16, 18, 20\}$$
∴ $\quad n(S) = 10$
(i) Let A be the event of getting a prime number.
$$A = \{2\}$$
∴ $\quad n(A) = 1$
∴ $\quad P(A) = \frac{n(A)}{n(S)} = \frac{1}{10}$
(ii) Let B be the event of getting a number divisible by 4.

$\therefore \qquad\qquad B = \{4, 8, 12, 16, 20\}$

$\therefore \qquad\quad n(B) = 5$

$\therefore \qquad\quad P(B) = \dfrac{n(B)}{n(S)} = \dfrac{5}{10} = \dfrac{1}{2}$

(iii) Let C be the event of getting a number which is multiple of 6.

$\therefore \qquad\qquad C = \{6, 12, 18\}$

$\therefore \qquad\quad n(C) = 3$

$\therefore \qquad\quad P(C) = \dfrac{n(C)}{n(S)} = \dfrac{3}{10}$

(iv) Let D be the event of getting an odd number.

$\therefore \qquad\qquad D = \{\,\}$

$\therefore \qquad\quad n(D) = 0$

$\therefore \qquad\quad P(D) = \dfrac{n(D)}{n(S)} = \dfrac{0}{10} = 0$

Q. 2. A die has 6 faces marked by the given numbers as shown below:

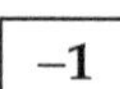

The die is thrown once. What is the probability of getting

(i) a positive integer.

(ii) an integer greater than –3.

(iii) the smallest integer. [2014]

Ans. 

Total number of outcomes = 6,

$$n(S) = 6$$

(i) A positive integer:
Favourable outcomes

$$n(P) = \{1, 2, 3\} = 3$$

$\therefore \qquad\quad Q(P) = \dfrac{n(P)}{n(S)} = \dfrac{3}{6} = \dfrac{1}{2}$

(ii) An integer greater than – 3,
Favourable outcomes $n(g)$

$$= \{1, 2, 3, -1, -2\} = 5$$

$\therefore \qquad\quad P(g) = \dfrac{n(g)}{n(S)} = \dfrac{5}{6}$

(iii) The smallest integer:
Favourable outcomes,

$$n(I) = \{-3\}$$

$\therefore \qquad\quad P(I) = \dfrac{n(I)}{n(S)} = \dfrac{1}{6}$

PHYSICS

1 Force

Short Answer Type Questions-I

Q. 1. (i) Define moment of force.
(ii) Write the relationship between the SI and CGS unit of moment of force. **[2020]**

Ans. (i) The turning effect of force on the body about an axis is due to the moment of force applied on the body and is equal to the product of the magnitude of the force and the perpendicular distance of the line of action of the force from the axis of rotation.
(ii) $1\ \text{Nm} = 10^7\ \text{dyn cm}$.

Q. 2. (i) Define couple.
(ii) State the S.I. unit of moment of couple. **[2019]**

Ans. (i) Two equal and opposite parallel forces, not acting along the same line forms a couple. A couple is always needed to produce rotation.
(ii) S.I. unit of moment of couple is Newton × metre (Nm).

Q. 3. (i) Why is the motion of a body moving with a constant speed around a circular path said to be accelerated?
(ii) Name the unit of physical quantity obtained by the formula $\dfrac{2K}{v^2}$.
where K: kinetic energy, v: linear velocity. **[2018]**

Ans. (i) The motion of a body moving with a constant speed around a circular path is accelerated due to the continuous change in its direction at each point of circular path. Hence the velocity of the body changes continuously.

(ii) $$\frac{2K}{v^2} = \frac{2 \times \frac{1}{2}mv^2}{v^2} = m$$

Hence, the physical quantity obtained is mass and its unit is kilogram (kg)/g/any unit of mass.

Q. 4. Why is a jack screw provided with a long arm? **[2017]**

Ans. A jack screw is provided with a long arm to increase the perpendicular distance of the point of application of force from the axis of rotation, so that we can apply a small force to rotate the jack to lift the heavy load.

Q. 5. (i) On what factor does the position of the centre of gravity of a body depend?
(ii) What is the S.I. unit of the moment of force? **[2015]**

Ans. (i) The position of the centre of gravity of a body depends on its shape, *i.e.*, the distribution of mass in it.
(ii) The S.I. unit of moment of force is newton metre (Nm).

Q. 6. Name the factors affecting the turning effect of a body. **[2015]**

Ans. The factors affecting the turning effects of a body are:
(i) the magnitude of force applied.
(ii) the perpendicular distance of the line of action of force from the axis of rotation.

Q. 7. (i) Define equilibrium.
(ii) In a beam balance when the beam is balanced in a horizontal position, it is in.........equilibrium. **[2015]**

Ans. (i) When a number of forces acting on a body produce no change in its state of rest or of motion, then the body is said to be in equilibrium.
(ii) Static

Q. 8. Explain the motion of a planet around the sun in a circular path. **[2015]**

Ans. The motion of a planet around the sun in a circular path is due to the centripetal force which is provided by the gravitational force of attraction on the planet by the sun.

Q. 9. What is the weight of a body placed at the centre of the earth? **[2014]**

Ans. The weight of a body placed at the centre of the earth is zero as
$$g = 0$$
$$\therefore \qquad W = mg = 0$$

Q. 10. Is it possible to have an accelerated motion with a constant speed? Explain. **[2014]**

Ans. Yes, it is possible to have accelerated motion with constant speed.

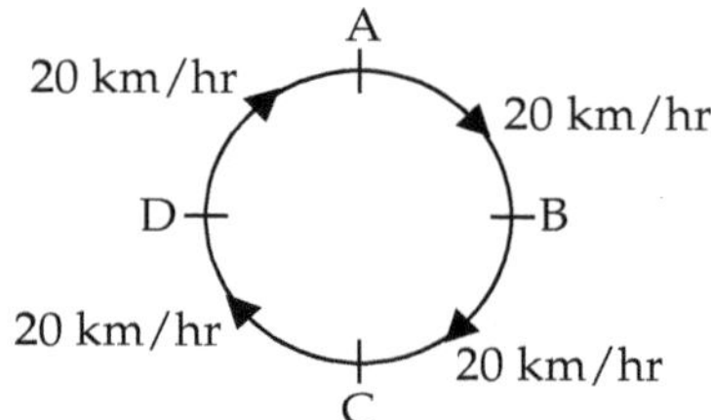

For example, in uniform circular motion, the magnitude of speed is constant but direction of motion changes so that acceleration is produced.

Q. 11. **(i) Where is the centre of gravity of a uniform ring situated?**

(ii) 'The position of the centre of gravity of a body remains unchanged even when the body is deformed.' State whether the statement is true or false. **[2013]**

Ans. **(i)** Centre of gravity of a uniform ring is at its centre.

(ii) False.

Q. 12. **A boy of mass 30 kg is sitting at a distance of 2 m from the middle of a see-saw. Where should a boy of mass 40 kg sit so as to balance the see-saw?** **[2012]**

Ans.

By principle of moments,
$$30 \times 2 = x \times 40$$

or
$$x = \frac{30 \times 2}{40} = 1.5 \text{ m}$$

So, the other boy should sit at a distance of 1.5 m from the mean position.

Q. 13. **(i) What is meant by the term 'moment of force'?**

(ii) If the moment of force is assigned a negative sign then will the turning tendency of the force be clockwise or anti-clockwise? **[2012]**

Ans. **(i) Moment of force:** It is equal to the product of the magnitude of the force and the perpendicular distance of the line of action of force from the axis of rotation.

(ii) If moment of force is assigned a negative value, it means turning tendency of force is in clockwise direction.

Q. 14. **Define one newton.** **[2011]**

Ans. One Newton: If a body of mass 1 kg moves with an acceleration of 1m/s^2 then force acting on the body is said to be one newton.

Q. 15. **Where does the position of centre of gravity lie for:**

(i) a circular lamina

(ii) a triangular lamina? **[2011]**

Ans. **(i)** Circular lamina – Centre of the lamina.

(ii) Triangular lamina – Point of intersection of medians.

Q. 16. **A man can open a nut by applying a force of 150 N by using a lever handle of length 0.4 m. What should be the length of the handle if he is able to open it by applying a force of 60 N?** **[2011]**

Ans. Given,
$$F_1 = 150 \text{ N}$$
$$l_1 = 0.4 \text{ m}$$
$$F_2 = 60 \text{ N}$$
$$l_2 = ?$$

$\because$ Force × Perpendicular distance
$$= \text{Constant}$$
$$F_1 \times l_1 = F_2 \times l_2$$

or
$$150 \times 0.4 = 60 \times l_2$$

$\therefore$
$$l_2 = 1 \text{ m}$$

Q. 17. **A uniform metre scale is kept in equilibrium when supported at the 60 cm mark and a mass M is suspended from the 90 cm mark as shown in the figure. State with reasons, whether the weight of the scale is greater than, less than or equal to the weight of mass M.** **[2006]**

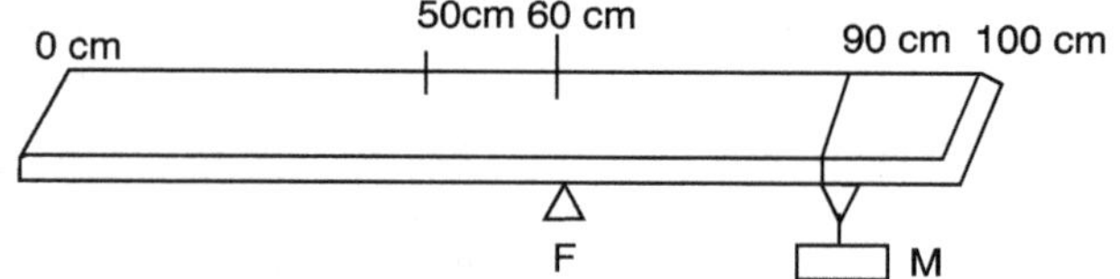

Ans. Let M be load.

$\therefore$ Load arm $= 90 - 60 = 30$ cm

Since weight of scale will act at centre of gravity of scale which is the midpoint of the scale.

$\therefore$ Effort arm $= 60 - 50 = 10$ cm

Let weight of scale be W

By principal of moments: $L \times d_L = E \times d_E$
$$M \times 30 = W \times 10$$
$$W = 3M$$

Since weight of scale is three times that of M,
$\therefore$ Weight of scale is greater than weight of M.

Short Answer Type Questions-II

Q. 1. **(i)** With reference to the direction of action, how does a centripetal force differ from a centrifugal during uniform circular motion ?

(ii) Is centrifugal force the force of reaction of centripetal force ?

(iii) Compare the magnitudes of centripetal and centrifugal force. **[2020, 2013]**

 Marking Scheme

> (i) Centripetal force acts radially inward and centrifugal force acts radially outward.
>
> (ii) No
>
> (iii) 1 : 1

Ans. **(i)** Centripetal force acts in a direction towards the centre of circular path whereas centrifugal force acts in a direction away from the centre of circular path.

(ii) No, centrifugal force is not the force of reaction of centripetal force because action and reaction do not act on the same body.

(iii) Magnitudes of centripetal and centrifugal forces are in the ratio 1 : 1.

Q. 2. A uniform meter scale is in equilibrium as shown in the diagram:

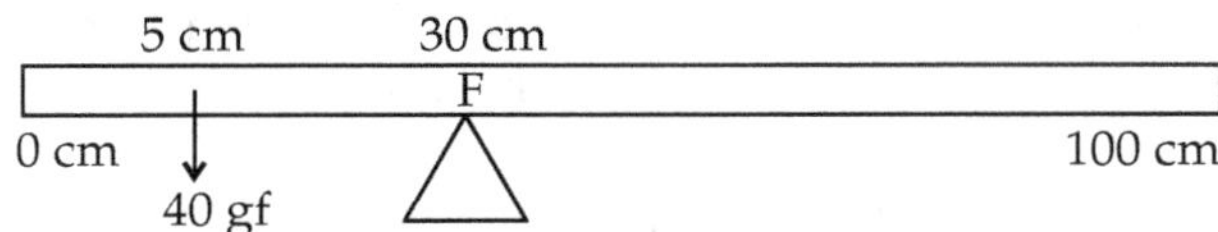

(i) Calculate the weight of the meter scale.

(ii) Which of the following options is correct to keep the ruler in equilibrium when 40 gf wt is shifted to 0 cm mark?

F is shifted towards 0 cm.

Or

F is shifted towards 100 cm. **[2019]**

 Marking Scheme

> (i) By pr.of moments
>
> $40 \times 25 = w \times 20$
>
> $\therefore w = \dfrac{40 \times 25}{20} = 50\, gf$
>
> (ii) F is shifted towards 0 cm

Ans. **(i)** Let the weight of the meter scale be x gf and it acts at the centre of gravity (*i.e.,* 50 cm mark)

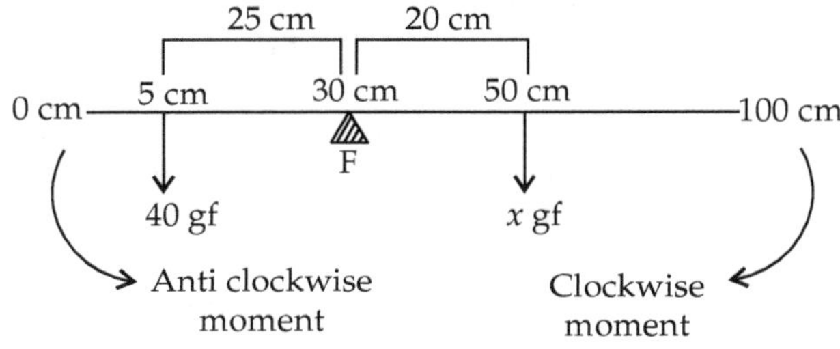

Anticlockwise moment = 40×25 gf cm

Clockwise moment = $x \times 20$ gf cm

when the meter scale is balanced,

Clockwise moment = Anticlockwise moment

$$\Rightarrow \qquad x \times 20 = 40 \times 25$$

$$\Rightarrow \qquad x = \dfrac{40 \times 25}{20}\, \text{gf} = 50\ \text{gf}$$

$\therefore$ Weight of meter scale is 50 gf.

(ii) F is shifted towards 0 cm.

Q. 3. A half metre rod is pivoted at the centre with two weights of 20 gf and 12 gf suspended at a perpendicular distance of 6 cm and 10 cm from the pivot respectively as shown below:

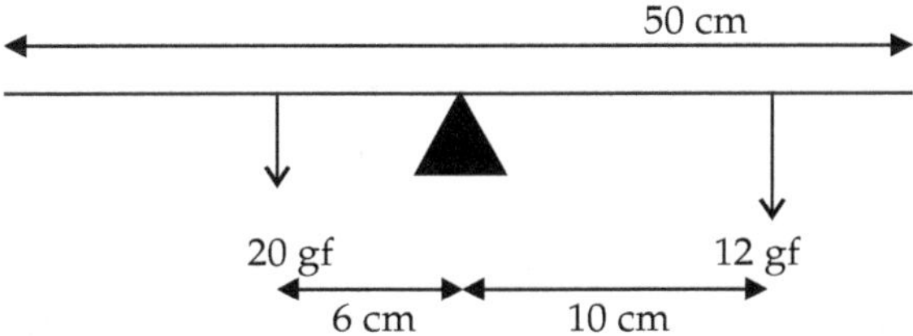

(i) Which of the two forces acting on the rigid rod causes clockwise moment?

(ii) Is the rod in equilibrium?

(iii) The direction of 20 kgf* force is reversed. What is the magnitude of the resultant moment of the forces on the rod?

* Mark is an error by the Council. We suggest you to use 'gf' instead of 'kgf'. **[2018]**

Ans. **(i)** The force of 12 gf causes a clockwise moment.

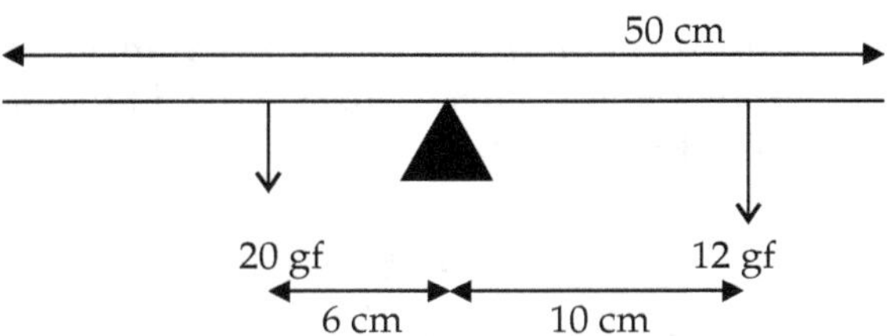

(ii) Clockwise moment

$= 12 \times 10$ gf cm $= 120$ gf cm

Anti-clockwise moment

$= 20 \times 6 = 120$ gf cm

$\because$ Clockwise moment

$=$ Anti-clockwise moment

$\therefore$ Yes, the rod is in equilibrium.

(iii) If the direction of 20 gf force is reversed, it will also create a clockwise moment.

$\therefore$ Resultant moment
$$= (120 + 120) \text{ gf cm (clockwise)}$$
$$= 240 \text{ gf cm}$$

Q. 4. A uniform half metre rule balances horizontally on a knife edge at 29 cm mark when a weight of 20 gf is suspended from one end.

(i) Draw a diagram of the arrangement.

(ii) What is the weight of the half metre rule? **[2017]**

Ans. **(i)** Let the weight of the half metre rule be x gf and it acts at the 25 cm mark (centre of gravity).

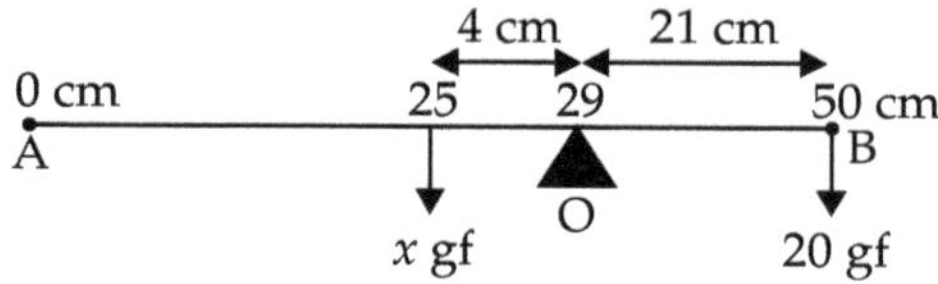

(ii) Anti-clockwise moment (ACWM)
$$= x \times 4 \text{ gf cm}$$
Clockwise moment (CWM)
$$= 20 \times 21 \text{ gf cm}$$
In equilibrium,
$$\text{ACWM} = \text{CWM}$$
or $\qquad x \times 4 = 20 \times 21$

$\therefore \qquad x = \dfrac{20 \times 21}{4} \text{ gf} = 105 \text{ gf}$

The weight of the half metre rule is 105 gf.

Q. 5. How does uniform circular motion differ from uniform linear motion? **[2017]**

Ans. In uniform linear motion, the speed and velocity are constant and acceleration is zero, whereas in a uniform circular motion, the velocity is variable (even though speed is uniform), so, it is an accelerated motion.

Q. 6. A stone of mass 'm' is rotated in a circular path with a uniform speed by tying a strong string with the help of your hand. Answer the following questions:

(i) Is the stone moving with a uniform or variable speed?

(ii) Is the stone moving with a uniform acceleration? In which direction does the acceleration act?

(iii) What kind of force acts on the hand and state its direction? **[2016]**

Ans. **(i)** The stone is moving with a uniform speed.

(ii) Yes, the stone is moving with a uniform acceleration, acting radially inward.

(iii) The force which acts on the hand is the centrifugal force. Its direction is opposite to the centripetal force *i.e.*, away from the centre.

Q. 7. **(i)** Which of the following remains constant in uniform circular motion. Speed or Velocity or both?

(ii) Name the force required for uniform circular motion. State its direction. **[2012]**

Ans. **(i)** In uniform circular motion, speed remains constant.

(ii) Force required for uniform circular motion is centripetal force. It is always directed along the radius of the circular path *i.e.*, towards the centre of the circle.

Q. 8. **(i)** Define the term momentum.

(ii) How is force related to the momentum of a body?

(iii) State the condition when the change in momentum of a body depends only on the change in its velocity. **[2010]**

Ans. **(i)** The momentum of a body is the product of the mass of the body and its velocity *i.e.*, $p = mv$.

(ii) Force is equal to the rate of change of momentum of the body.

(iii) If mass of the body m remains constant then the change in momentum of the body depends only on the change in its velocity.

Long Answer Type Questions-I

Q. 1. A uniform metre scale can be balanced at the 70.0 cm mark when a mass of 0.05 kg is hung from the 94.0 cm mark.

(i) Draw a diagram of the arrangement.

(ii) Find the mass of the metre scale. **[2011]**

Ans. **(i)** Diagram of the given arrangement is shown below:

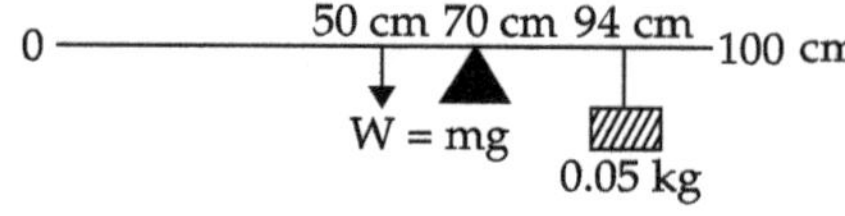

(ii) As the given meter scale is a uniform scale. So its centre of gravity lies at its centre, *i.e.*, 50 cm. Let mass of metre scale be m kg.

By principle of moments,
$$m_1 x_1 = x_2 x_2$$
or $\qquad m \times (70 - 50) = 0.05 \times (94 - 70)$

$\therefore \qquad m = \dfrac{0.05 \times 24}{20}$
$$= 0.06 \text{ kg} = 60 \text{ g}$$

Short Answer Type Questions-I

Q. 1. Define a kilowatt hour. How is it related to joule ? **[2020]**

Ans. One kilowatt hour (kWh) is the energy spent or work done by a source of power 1 kW in 1 hour.

$$1 \text{ kWh} = 3.6 \times 10^6 \text{ J or } 3.6 \text{ MJ}$$

Q. 2. A satellite revolves around a planet in a circular orbit. What is the work done by the satellite at any instant ? Give a reason. **[2020]**

Ans. The work done by the satellite at any instant is zero because the force required (centripetal force) to go around the planet is perpendicular to the displacement at any instant of its motion.

Q. 3. Give one example of each when :

(i) Chemical energy changes into electrical energy.

(ii) Electrical energy changes into sound energy. **[2020]**

Ans. (i) A dry cell in use.

(ii) Loud speaker.

Q. 4. A crane 'A' lifts a heavy load in 5 seconds, whereas another crane 'B' does the same work in 2 seconds. Compare the power of crane 'A' to that of crane 'B'. **[2020]**

Ans. Let the work done in both case be x joule.

Crane A	Crane B
$W_1 = x$ Joule	$W_2 = x$ Joule
$t_1 = 5$ s	$t_2 = 2$ s

$$P_A = \frac{W_1}{t_1} = \frac{x}{5} W \qquad P_B = \frac{W_2}{t_2} = \frac{x}{2} W$$

$$\therefore \ = \frac{P_A}{P_B} = \frac{x/5}{x/2} = \frac{x}{5} \times \frac{2}{x} = \frac{2}{5}$$

∴ Power of Crane A : Power of Crane B = 2 : 5

Q. 5. Two bodies A and B have masses in the ratio 5 : 1 and their kinetic energies are in the ratio 125 : 9. Find the ratio of their velocities. **[2019]**

Ans. Let mass, kinetic energy and velocity of bodies A and B be (m_A, m_B), (k_A, k_B) and (v_A, v_B) respectively.

Given: $\dfrac{m_A}{m_B} = \dfrac{5}{1}$

and $\dfrac{k_A}{k_B} = \dfrac{125}{9}$

$$\Rightarrow \frac{\frac{1}{2} m_A (v_A)^2}{\frac{1}{2} m_B (v_B)^2} = \frac{125}{9} \left[\because k = \frac{1}{2} mv^2 \right]$$

$$\Rightarrow \frac{m_A}{m_B} \times \left(\frac{v_A}{v_B} \right)^2 = \frac{125}{9}$$

$$\Rightarrow \frac{5}{1} \times \left(\frac{v_A}{v_B} \right)^2 = \frac{125}{9}$$

$$\Rightarrow \left(\frac{v_A}{v_B} \right)^2 = \frac{125}{9} \times \frac{1}{5} = \frac{25}{9}$$

$$\Rightarrow \frac{v_A}{v_B} = \sqrt{\frac{25}{9}} = \frac{5}{3}$$

$$\therefore \quad v_A : v_B = 5 : 3$$

Q. 6. (i) State and define the S.I. unit of power.

(ii) How is the unit horse power related to the S.I. unit of power? **[2018]**

Ans. (i) The S.I. unit of power is watt (W).

If 1 joule of work is done in 1 second, the power spent is said to be 1 watt.

(ii) 1 H.P. = 746 W

Q. 7. State the energy changes in the following cases while in use:

(i) An electric iron

(ii) A ceiling fan **[2018]**

Ans. (i) Electrical energy changes to heat energy.

(ii) Electrical energy changes to mechanical energy.

Q. 8. If the power of a motor be 100 kW, at what speed can it raise a load of 50,000 N? **[2017]**

Ans. Given: Power = 100 kW = 100×10^3 W = 10^5 W

Force (Weight) = 50,000 N = 5×10^4 N

Since, Power = Force × Average speed

$$\therefore \ \text{Average speed} = \frac{\text{Power}}{\text{Force}}$$

$$= \frac{10^5}{5 \times 10^4} \text{ ms}^{-1}$$

$$= \frac{10 \times 10^4}{5 \times 10^4} \text{ ms}^{-1} = 2 \text{ ms}^{-1}$$

Therefore, at a speed of 2 ms^{-1} the motor can raise a load of 50,000 N.

Q. 9. A boy weighing 40 kgf climbs up a stair of 30 steps each 20 cm high in 4 minutes and a girl weighing 30 kgf does the same in 3 minutes. Compare:

(i) The work done by them.

(ii) The power developed by them. **[2016]**

Ans. **(i)** Weight of a boy (F_1)

$$= 40 \text{ kgf}$$

Distance covered (d) $= 30 \times \dfrac{20}{100} = 6 \text{ m}$

Work done by boy (W_1) $= F_1 d$

$$= 40 \times 9.8 \times 6$$

$$(\because 1 \text{ kgf} = g = 9.8 \text{ N})$$

$$= 2352 \text{ J}$$

Weight of a girl (F_2)

$$= 30 \text{ kgf}$$

Work done by girl (W_2)

$$= F_2 d$$

$$= 30 \times 9.8 \times 6 = 1764 \text{ J}$$

On comparing work done by them, we get

$$\frac{W_1}{W_2} = \frac{2352 \text{ J}}{1764 \text{ J}} = \frac{4}{3}$$

(ii) Time taken by a boy (t_1)

$$= 4 \text{ min}$$

$$= 4 \times 60 = 240 \text{ sec}$$

Power developed by boy (P_1)

$$= \frac{W_1}{t_1} = \frac{2352}{240} = 9.8 \text{ W}$$

Time taken by a girl (t_2)

$$= 3 \text{ min}$$

$$= 3 \times 60 = 180 \text{ sec}$$

Power developed by girl (P_2)

$$= \frac{W_2}{t_2} = \frac{1764}{180} = 9.8 \text{ W}$$

On comparing power developed by them, we get

$$\frac{P_1}{P_2} = \frac{9.8 \text{ W}}{9.8 \text{ W}} = 1 : 1.$$

Q. 10. With reference to the terms Mechanical Advantage, Velocity Ratio and efficiency of a machine, name and define the term that will not change for a machine of a given design. **[2016]**

Ans. Velocity ratio will not change for a machine of a given design and it can be defined as the ratio of the displacement of the effort to the displacement of the load (in the same given time).

Q. 11. How is work done by a force measured when the force:

(i) is in the direction of displacement.

(ii) is at an angle to the direction of displacement. **[2015]**

Ans. **(i)** Work done is given by the product of the force (F) and the displacement (d) in the direction of the force.

i.e., Work done $= F \times d$

(ii) Work done is measured by the product of the force (F) and the component of displacement (d) in the direction of the force.

i.e., Work done $= F \times d \cos \theta$

where θ is the angle which the displacement makes with the direction of the force.

Q. 12. State the energy changes in the following while in use:

(i) Burning of a candle.

(ii) A steam engine. **[2015]**

Ans. **(i)** Chemical energy to the light and heat energy.

(ii) Chemical to heat energy to mechanical energy.

Q. 13. Rajan exerts a force of 150 N in pulling a cart at a constant speed of 10 m/s. Calculate the power exerted. **[2015]**

Ans. Power exerted $=$ Force $\times$ Average speed

$$= 150 \times 10$$

$$= 1500 \text{ W}$$

Q. 14. **(i)** When does a force do work?

(ii) What is the work done by the moon when it revolves around the earth? **[2014]**

Ans. **(i)** Work is said to be done when the applied force produces displacement in the direction of the force.

Work done $=$ Force $\times$ Displacement

(ii) Work done is zero by the moon, as there is no displacement since it is moving in a circular path.

Q. 15. What is the principle of an ideal machine? **[2014]**

Ans. An ideal machine works on the principle that work input = work output and has 100% efficiency as there is no energy loss.

OR

Work done by the machine = Work done on the machine.

Q. 16. The conversion of part of the energy into an undesirable form is called...... **[2014]**

Ans. Dissipation of energy.

Q. 17. Calculate the change in the Kinetic energy of a moving body if its velocity is reduced to 1/3rd of the initial velocity. **[2014]**

Ans. Let a body of mass 'm' kg is moving with velocity 'v' m/s. The initial kinetic energy is given by

$$\text{K.E}_i = \frac{1}{2}mv^2$$

Now, the velocity is reduced to $\frac{1}{3}$rd of the initial velocity. The final kinetic energy is given by

$$\text{K.E}_f = \frac{1}{2}m\left(\frac{v}{3}\right)^2$$
$$= \frac{1}{9}\left(\frac{1}{2}mv^2\right) = \frac{1}{9}\text{K.E}_i$$

So, K.E. becomes $\frac{1}{9}$th of its initial K.E.

Q. 18. State the energy changes in the following devices while in use:
 (i) A loud speaker
 (ii) A glowing electric bulb **[2014]**

Ans. (i) **Loud speaker:** Electrical energy to sound energy.
 (ii) **Glowing electric bulb:** Electrical energy to heat and light energy.

Q. 19. A force is applied on a body of mass 20 kg moving with a velocity of 40 ms⁻¹. The body attains a velocity of 50 ms⁻¹ in 2 second. Calculate the work done by the body. **[2013]**

Ans. Work done, $W = \frac{1}{2}m\,(v_2{}^2 - v_1{}^2)$
$$= \frac{1}{2} \times 20\,(50^2 - 40^2)$$
$$= 9000 \text{ J}$$

Q. 20. A type of single pulley is very often used as a machine even though it does not give any gain in mechanical advantage.
 (i) Name the type of pulley used.
 (ii) For what purpose is such a pulley used? **[2013]**

Ans. (i) Single fixed pulley.
 (ii) Single fixed pulley is used to change the direction of effort applied.

Q. 21. (i) In what way does an 'Ideal machine' differ from a 'Practical machine'?
 (ii) Can a simple machine act as a force multiplier and a speed multiplier at the same time? **[2013]**

Ans. (i) Ideal machine has 100% efficiency *i.e.,* work done on the machine is equal to the work done by the machine while a practical machine is not 100% efficient due to the energy loss in friction etc.
 (ii) No, it will either be acting as a speed multiplier or a force multiplier.

Q. 22. A girl of mass 35 kg climbs up from the first floor of a building at a height 4 m above the ground to the third floor at a height 12 m above the ground. What will be the increase in her gravitational potential energy? [g = 10 ms⁻²] **[2013]**

Ans. Increase in gravitational potential energy
$$= mg\,(h_2 - h_1)$$
$$= 35 \times 10\,(12 - 4)$$
$$= 350 \times 8 = 2800 \text{ J}$$

Q. 23. A ball is placed on a compressed spring. When the spring is released, the ball is observed to fly away.

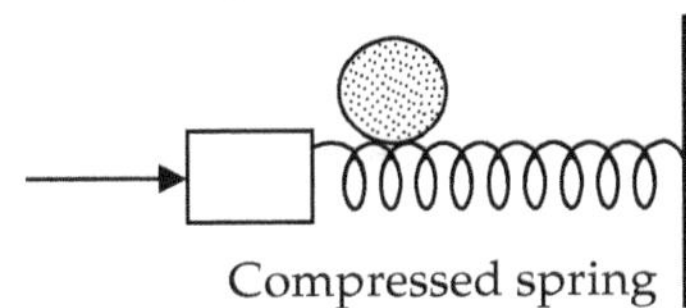
Compressed spring

 (i) What form of energy does the compressed spring possess?
 (ii) Why does the ball fly away? **[2012]**

Ans. (i) The Compressed spring possess potential energy.
 (ii) Potential energy of the spring is imparted to the ball in the form of kinetic energy.

Q. 24. A body of mass 0.2 kg falls from a height of 10 m to a height of 6 m above the ground. Find the loss in potential energy taking place in the body. [g = 10 ms⁻²] **[2012]**

Ans. Given, Mass = 0.2 kg
 Height, h = 10 m to 6 m
 Loss in Potential Energy
$$= mg\,(h_1 - h_2)$$
$$= 0.2 \times 10 \times (10 - 6) = 8 \text{ J}$$

Q. 25. Name a machine which can be used to:
 (i) multiply force
 (ii) change the direction of force applied. **[2011]**

Ans. (i) Nut cracker.
 (ii) Single fixed pulley.

Q. 26. A ball of mass 200 g falls from a height of 5 m. What will be its kinetic energy when it just reaches the ground? (g = 9.8 m s⁻²) **[2011]**

Ans. Given: $m = 200$ g, $h = 5$ m

When the ball reaches the ground, then

$$P.E. = K.E.$$

$$\therefore \quad K.E. = mgh = \frac{200}{1000} \times 9.8 \times 5$$

$$= 9.8 \text{ joule}$$

Q. 27. A body is acted upon by a force. State two conditions under which the work done could be zero. **[2010]**

Ans. Two conditions under which the work done is zero are:

(i) when displacement $= 0$

(ii) when displacement is normal to the direction of force applied.

Q. 28. A spring is kept compressed by a small trolley of mass 0.5 kg lying on a smooth horizontal surface as shown in the figure given below:

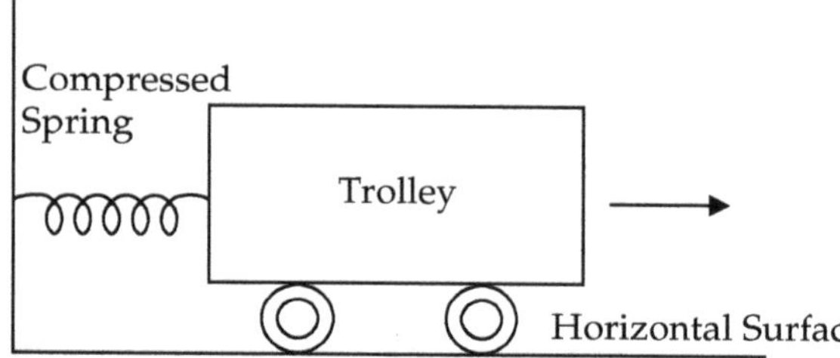

When the trolley is released, it is found to move at a speed of 2 ms⁻¹.

What potential energy did the spring possess when compressed? **[2010]**

Ans. Given: $m = 0.5$ kg, $v = 2$ ms^{-1}

By law of conservation of energy,

$$P.E. = K.E.$$

$$\therefore \quad U = \frac{1}{2} mv^2$$

$$= \frac{1}{2} \times 0.5 \times 2^2 = 1 \text{ J}$$

Q. 29. (i) Why is the mechanical advantage of a lever of the second order always greater than one?

(ii) Name the type of single pulley that has a mechanical advantage greater than one? **[2010]**

Ans. **(i)** The mechanical advantage of a lever of the second order is always greater than one because its effort arm is always longer than the load arm *i.e.,*

Effort arm > Load arm.

(ii) Single movable pulley has a mechanical advantage greater than one.

Q. 30. (i) With reference to the terms mechanical advantage, velocity ratio and efficiency of a machine, name the term that will not

change for a machine of a given design.

(ii) Define the term stated by you in part (i). **[2009]**

Ans. **(i)** Velocity ratio of a machine.

(ii) Velocity ratio is defined as the ratio of the displacement of the effort to the displacement of the load.

Q. 31. What is the SI unit of energy? How is the electron volt (eV) related to it? **[2009]**

Ans. The S.I. unit of energy is joule.

$$1 \text{ eV} = 1.6 \times 10^{-19} \text{ J}$$

Q. 32. State the energy changes that take place in the following when they are in use:
(i) a photovoltaic cell. **(ii) an electromagnet.** **[2009]**

Ans. **(i)** Light energy to electrical energy.

(ii) Electrical energy to magnetic energy.

Q. 33. A body of mass 5 kg is moving with a velocity of 10 m s⁻¹. What will be the ratio of its initial kinetic energy and final kinetic energy, if the mass of the body is doubled and its velocity is halved? **[2009]**

Ans. Given: $m_1 = 5$ kg, $v_1 = 10$ m/sec., $m_2 = 10$ kg, $v_2 = 5$ m/sec.

$$\frac{KE_1}{KE_2} = \frac{\frac{1}{2} m_1 v_1^2}{\frac{1}{2} m_2 v_2^2}$$

$$= \frac{5 \times 10^2}{10 \times 5^2} = \frac{2}{1}$$

Hence, the ratio of initial to final kinetic energy is 2 : 1.

Q. 34. When an arrow is shot from a bow, it has kinetic energy in it. Explain briefly from where does it get its kinetic energy? **[2008]**

Ans. Stretched string of the bow possesses potential energy on account of a change in its shape. When the arrow is released, the potential energy of the bow gets converted into the kinetic energy of the arrow.

Q. 35. What energy conversions take place in the following when they are working – (i) Electric toaster, (ii) Microphone? **[2008]**

Ans. Energy conversion taking place in:

(i) Electric toaster → Electrical energy to heat energy.

(ii) Microphone → Sound energy to electrical energy.

Q. 36. Copy the diagram of the forearm given below, indicate the positions of Load, Effort and Fulcrum. **[2008]**

Ans. Position of Load, Fulcrum and Effort are shown below.

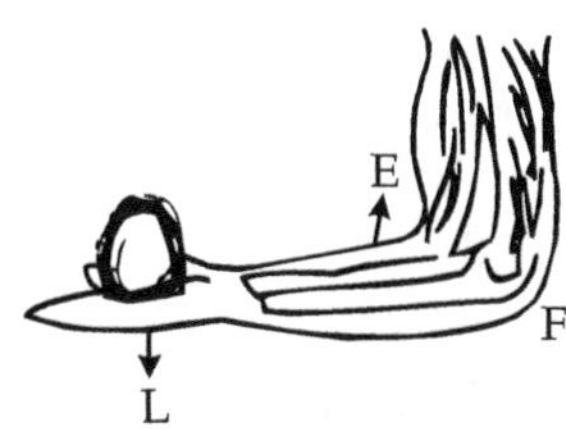

Q. 37. In what way will the temperature of water at the bottom of a waterfall be different from the temperature at the top? Give a reason for your answer. **[2008]**

Ans. When water falls from a height the potential energy stored changes into kinetic energy during the fall. On reaching the bottom, K.E. changes to heat energy.

So, water at the top will have slightly less temperature as compared to its bottom.

Q. 38. Two bodies, A and B of equal mass are kept at heights 20 m and 30 m respectively. Calculate the ratio of their potential energies. **[2007]**

Ans. Let the equal mass of two bodies A and B be m.

Given: height $h_1 = 20$ m and $h_2 = 30$ m

(P_1) Potential energy of body A $= mgh_1 = m \times g \times 20$

(P_2) Potential energy of body B $= mgh_2 = m \times g \times 30$

$$\therefore \quad \text{Ratio } \frac{P_1}{P_2} = \frac{m \times g \times 20}{m \times g \times 30} = \frac{2}{3}.$$

Q. 39. State the amount of work done by an object when it moves in a circular path for one complete rotation. Give a reason to justify your answer. **[2006]**

Ans. Amount of work done is equal to zero.

Work is said to be done only when there is displacement produced. In case of a body moving in a circular path, then body comes to its original place, therefore, net displacement is zero hence work done is zero.

Q. 40. Calculate the height through which a body of mass 0.5 kg should be lifted if the energy spent for doing so is 1.0 joule. ($g = 10$ ms^{-2}). **[2006]**

Ans. Given that: $m = 0.5$ kg, P.E. $= 1.0$ J, $g = 10$ m/s^2

We know that P.E. $= mgh$

or $$h = \frac{\text{P.E.}}{mg} = \frac{1}{.5 \times 10} = \frac{1}{5} = 0.2 \text{ m}$$

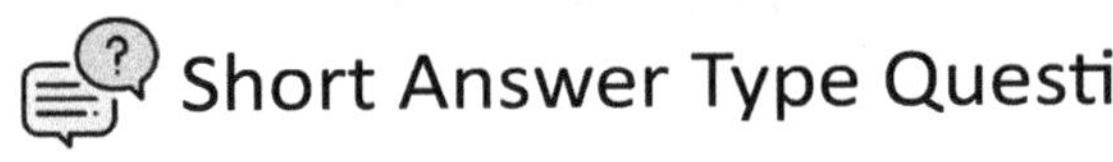

Short Answer Type Questions-II

Q. 1. The figure below shows a simple pendulum of mass 200 g. It is displaced from the mean position A to the extreme position B. The potential energy at the position A is zero. At the position B the pendulum bob is raised by 5 m.

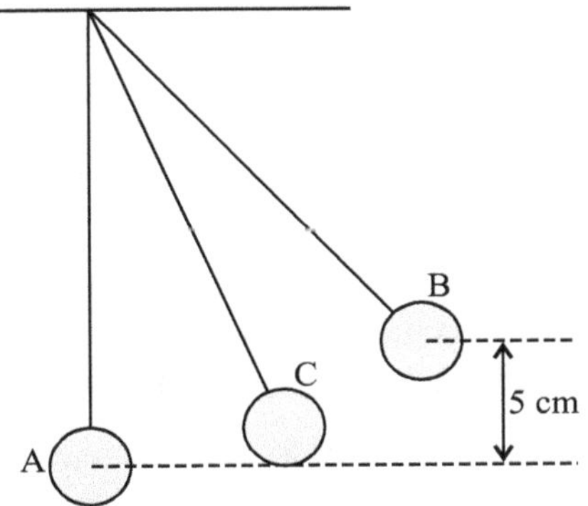

(i) What is the potential energy of the pendulum at the position B ?

(ii) What is the total mechanical energy at point C ?

(iii) What is the speed of the bob at the position A when released from B ?

(Take g = 10 ms^{-2} and there is no loss of energy.) **[2020]**

Marking Scheme

  (i)   PE $= mgh$
            $= 0.2 \times 10 \times 5 = 10$ J

  (ii) 10 J

  (iii) $v^2 = 2 \times E/m$ or $\frac{1}{2} mv^2 = mgh$

             $= \dfrac{2 \times 10}{0.2} = 100$ $\therefore$ $v = \sqrt{2}\,gh$

      $\therefore$ $v = 10$ m/s

Ans. **(i)** Given; $m = 200$ g $= 0.2$ kg, g $= 10$ ms^{-2},

$h = 5$ m

$\therefore$ Potential energy (U) $= mgh$

at position B $= 0.2 \times 10 \times 5 = 10$ J

(ii) 10 J   ($\because$ K + U = constant)

(iii) At position A, kinetic energy (K) $= 10$ J

$$\frac{1}{2} mv^2 = 10$$

$$\Rightarrow \quad \frac{1}{2} \times 0.2 \times v^2 = 10$$

$$\Rightarrow \qquad v^2 = \frac{10 \times 2}{0.2} = 100$$

$$\therefore \qquad v = \sqrt{100} = 10 \text{ ms}^{-1}$$

Q. 2. A body of mass 10 kg is kept at a height of 5 m. It is allowed to fall and reach the ground.
  (i) What is the total mechanical energy possessed by the body at the height of 2 m assuming it is a frictionless medium?
  (ii) What is the kinetic energy possessed by the body just before hitting the ground? (Take $g = 10$ m/s^2.) **[2019]**

Marking Scheme

  (i) Total mechanical energy possessed by the body at the height 2 m
    = P.E at the maximum height or pr. of conser vation of energy implied.
    = $10 \times 10 \times 5 = 500$ J
  (ii) K.E possessed by the body just befor hitting the ground
    = P.E at the maximum height = 500 J

Ans. Given: Mass $(m) = 10$ kg, height $(h) = 5$ m, $g = 10$ ms^{-2}, Potential energy (U) = mgh
    = $10 \times 10 \times 5$ J = 500 J

  (i) According to the law of conservation of energy, the sum of kinetic energy (k) and potential energy (U) remains constant when there are no frictional forces.

    $\therefore$ Total mechanical energy at height of 2 m
      = Initial potential energy
      = 500 J

  (ii) Similarly, according to the law of conservation of energy, the kinetic energy possessed by the body just before touching the ground = 500 J.

Q. 3. (i) Derive a relationship between S.I. and C.G.S. unit of work.
  (ii) A force acts on a body and displaces it by a distance S in a direction at an angle θ with the direction of force. What should be the value of θ to get the maximum positive work? **[2018]**

Ans. (i) The S.I. unit of work is joule (J) and C.G.S. unit is erg.

$$1 \text{ joule} = 1 \text{ newton} \times 1 \text{ metre}$$
$$= 10^5 \text{ dyne} \times 100 \text{ cm}$$
$$= 10^7 \text{ dyne cm}$$
$$(\because 1 \text{ dyne cm} = 1 \text{ erg})$$
$$= 10^7 \text{ erg}$$
$$\text{or} \qquad 1 \text{ J} = 10^7 \text{ erg}$$

  (ii) We know that,
$$W = FS \cos \theta$$

For maximum positive work, cos θ should be maximum.

    Maximum value of cos $\theta = 1$
$$\therefore \qquad \theta = 0°.$$

Q. 4. A boy uses a single fixed pulley to lift a load of 50 kgf to some height. Another boy uses a single movable pulley to lift the same load to the same height. Compare the effort applied by them. Give a reason to support your answer. **[2017]**

Ans. For single fixed pulley,
Load (L) = 50 kgf
Mechanical Advantage (M.A.) = 1

Since, $\text{M.A.} = \dfrac{\text{Load}}{\text{Effort}}$

$\therefore$ Effort (E_1) applied
$$= \frac{\text{Load}}{\text{M.A.}} = \frac{50}{1} = 50 \text{ kgf}$$

For a single movable pulley,
$$L = 50 \text{ kgf}$$
$$\text{M.A.} = 2$$

$\therefore$ Effort (E_2) applied
$$= \frac{\text{Load}}{\text{M.A.}} = \frac{50}{2} = 25 \text{ kgf}$$

Ratio of effort applied,
$$E_1 : E_2 = 50 : 25 = 2 : 1$$

Q. 5. From the diagram given below, answer the questions that follow:

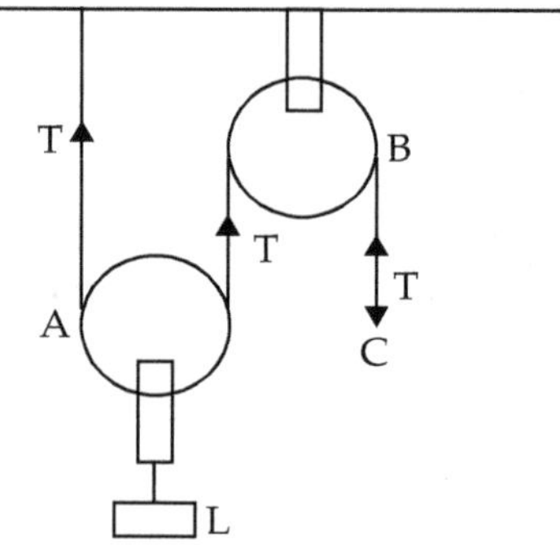

  (i) What kind of pulleys are A and B?
  (ii) State the purpose of pulley B.
  (iii) What effort has to be applied at C to just raise the load L = 20 kgf? **[2016]**
  (Neglect the weight of pulley A and friction)

Ans. (i) A is a single movable pulley.
    B is a single fixed pulley.

  (ii) It is quite difficult to apply effort in the upward direction, if no fixed pulley B is used. The fixed pulley changes the direction of effort from upwards to downwards, making the application of the effort more convenient and easier.

(iii) Given, $\quad$ L = 20 kgf

$\qquad$ Effort = ?

In equilibrium,

$\qquad$ L = 2T

At C, Effort (E) = T

$$\text{Effort needed} = \frac{L}{2} = \frac{20}{2} = 10 \text{ kgf.}$$

Q. 6. **(i)** **A body is thrown vertically upwards. Its velocity keeps on decreasing. What happens to its kinetic energy as its velocity becomes zero?**

(ii) **Draw a diagram to show how a single pulley can be used so as to have its ideal M.A. = 2.** **[2014]**

Ans. **(i)** K.E. completely changes to P.E. (K.E. becomes zero).

(ii) $\qquad$ Load, L = T + T = 2T

$\quad$ And $\quad$ Effort, E = T

Now, $\quad$ M.A. $= \dfrac{\text{Load}}{\text{Effort}}$

$\therefore \qquad$ M.A. $= \dfrac{2T}{T} = 2$

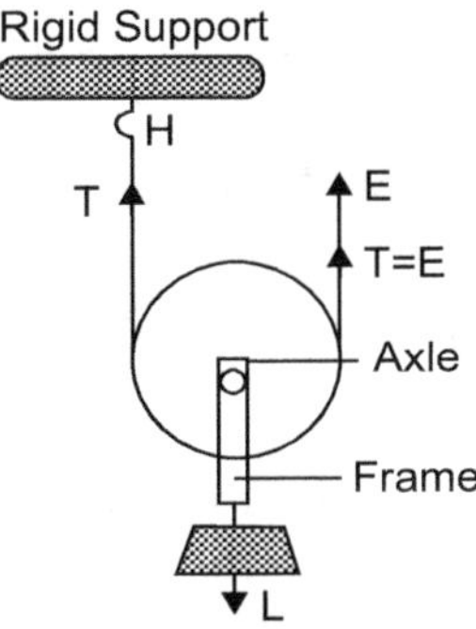

Q. 7. **Derive a relationship between mechanical advantage, velocity ratio and efficiency of a machine.** **[2014]**

Ans. $\qquad$ M.A. $= \dfrac{\text{Load}}{\text{Effort}}$

$\qquad$ V.R. $= \dfrac{\text{Displacement of the effort}}{\text{Displacement of the load}}$

$\quad$ Efficiency, $\eta = \dfrac{\text{Work output}}{\text{Work input}}$

$\qquad \eta = \dfrac{L \times d_{\text{load}}}{E \times d_{\text{effort}}}$

$\qquad \eta = \text{M.A.} \times \dfrac{1}{\text{V.R.}}$

$\qquad \eta = \dfrac{\text{M.A.}}{\text{V.R.}}$

Q. 8. **(i)** **State the principle of conservation of energy.** **[2013]**

(ii) **Name the form of energy which a body may possess even when it is not in motion.** **[2013]**

Ans. **(i)** **Principle of conservation of energy:** It states that energy can neither be created nor be destroyed but can be transformed from one form to another form. The total sum of energy in the universe always remains the same.

(ii) Potential energy.

Q. 9. **(i)** **What is meant by an ideal machine?**

(ii) **Write a relationship between the mechanical advantage (M. A.) and velocity ratio (V. R.) of an ideal machine.**

(iii) **A coolie carrying a load on his head and moving on a frictionless horizontal platform does no work. Explain the reason why.** **[2011]**

Ans. **(i)** **Ideal Machine:** It is a machine in which work done on the machine is equal to the work done by the machine.

(ii) We know

$\quad$ Efficiency (η)

$$= \frac{\text{Mechanical Advantage (M.A.)}}{\text{Velocity Ratio (V.R.)}}$$

$\quad$ And for an ideal machine

$$\eta = 1$$

So, $\quad$ M.A. = V.R.

(iii) We know, $W = F\,d \cos\theta$.

Since, force is normal to displacement, so $\theta = 90°$

Hence work done,

$$W = Fd \cos 90° = 0.$$

Q. 10. **Draw a diagram to show the energy changes in an oscillating simple pendulum. Indicate in your diagram how the total mechanical energy in it remains constant during the oscillation.** **[2011]**

Ans.

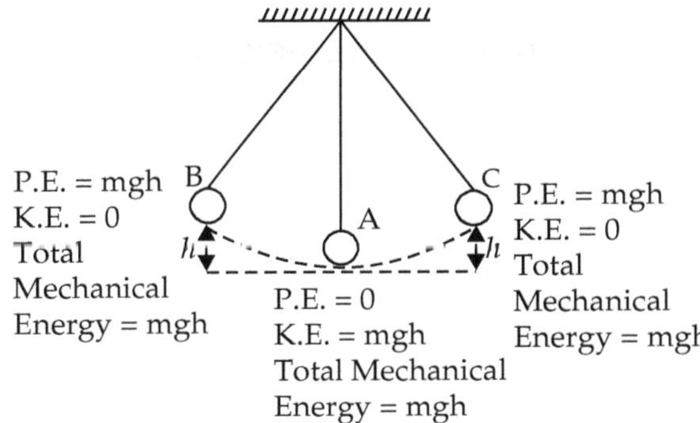

Q. 11. **A body of mass 50 kg has a momentum of 3000 kg ms⁻¹. Calculate:**

(i) **the kinetic energy of the body.**

(ii) **the velocity of the body.** **[2010]**

Ans. **(i)** Given: $m = 50$ kg, $p = 3000$ kg ms^{-1}

We know that,

$$p = mv$$

$$\therefore \qquad v = \frac{3000}{50} = 60 \text{ ms}^{-1}$$

Kinetic energy of the body

$$= \frac{1}{2} mv^2 = \frac{1}{2} \times 50 \times (60)^2$$
$$= 25 \times 3600 = 90000 \text{ J}$$

(ii) Velocity of the body,

$$v = 60 \text{ ms}^{-1}.$$

Q. 12. 6.4 kJ of energy causes a displacement of 64 m in a body in the direction of force in 2.5 seconds. Calculate (i) the force applied (ii) power in horse power (hp). (Take 1 hp = 746 W). **[2009]**

Ans. **(i)** We know, $\qquad$ W = F × d

$$\Rightarrow \qquad 6.4 \times 10^3 = \text{F} \times 64$$
$$\Rightarrow \qquad \text{F} = 100 \text{ N}$$

(ii) We have, $\qquad P = \dfrac{W}{t}$

$$\Rightarrow \qquad P = \frac{6 \cdot 4 \times 10^3}{2.5}$$
$$\Rightarrow \qquad P = 2560 \text{ watt.}$$

$$\because \qquad 746 \text{ watt} = 1 \text{ hp}$$
$$\Rightarrow \qquad 2560 \text{ watt} = \frac{1 \times 2560}{746}$$
$$P = 3.43 \text{ hp}$$

Q. 13. A pulley system comprises two pulleys, one fixed and the other movable.

(i) Draw a labelled diagram of the arrangement and show clearly the directions of all the forces acting on it.

(ii) What change can be made in the movable pulley of this system to increase the mechanical advantage of the system? **[2009]**

Ans. **(i)**

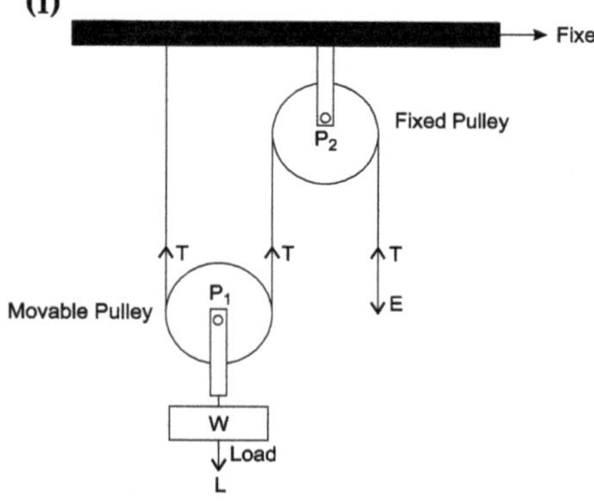

(ii) Mechanical advantage of the system can be increased by reducing the friction in the pulley bearings and reducing the weight of the pulley.

Q. 14. **(i)** A stone of mass 64.0 g is thrown vertically upward from the ground with an initial speed of 20.0 m/s. The gravitational potential energy at the ground level is considered to be zero. Apply the principle of conservation of energy and calculate the potential energy at the maximum height attained by the stone. (g = 10 ms⁻²).

(ii) Using the same principle, state what will be the total energy of the body at its half-way point? **[2008]**

Ans. **(i)** Given: $\qquad$ Mass of stone = 64.0 g.

$$\text{Initial speed} = 20.0 \text{ m/sec.}$$
$$\text{Initial K.E.} = \frac{1}{2} mv^2$$
$$= \frac{1}{2} \times \frac{64}{1000} \times 20^2$$
$$= 12.8 \text{ J.}$$

According to the principle of conservation of energy, initial K.E. = P.E. at maximum height.

So, P.E. at maximum height = 12.8 joule.

(ii) Total energy of the body at its half way will also be the same, because we know at every point of its path, total energy will be conserved.

So, Total energy = 12.8 joule.

Q. 15. Define 'Joule' , the SI unit of work and establish a relationship between the SI and CGS unit of work. **[2008]**

Ans. Joule: 1 joule of work is said to be done when a force of 1 N displaces a body through 1 meter in its own direction.

$$1 \text{ J} = 1 \text{ N} \times 1 \text{ m.}$$
$$= 10^5 \text{ dyne} \times 100 \text{ cm.}$$
$$= 10^7 \text{ dyne} \times \text{cm.}$$
$$1 \text{ J} = 10^7 \text{ erg.}$$

Q. 16. **(i)** Define a kilowatt hour. How is it related to the joule?

(ii) How can the work done be measured when force is applied at an angle to the direction of displacement? **[2007]**

Ans. **(i)** One kilowatt-hour is the electrical energy consumed by an electrical appliance of power 1 kilowatt when it is used for one hour.

$$1 \text{ kWh} = 3.6 \times 10^6 \text{ joule}$$

(ii) $$\text{Work} = \text{F} \times d \cos \theta$$

where θ is angle between force and the displacement.

Q. 17. **(i)** What is the main energy transformation that occurs in:

(1) Photosynthesis in green leaves;

(2) Charging of a battery.

(ii) Write an expression to show the relationship between mechanical advantage, velocity ratio and efficiency for a simple machine. **[2007]**

Ans. (i) (1) Light energy to chemical energy.

(2) Electric energy to chemical energy.

(ii) $\text{Efficiency} = \dfrac{\text{Mechanical advantage}}{\text{Velocity ratio}} \times 100$

Q. 18. Name the type of single pulley that can act as a force multiplier. Draw a labelled diagram of the above named pulley. **[2006]**

Ans. Single Movable Pulley

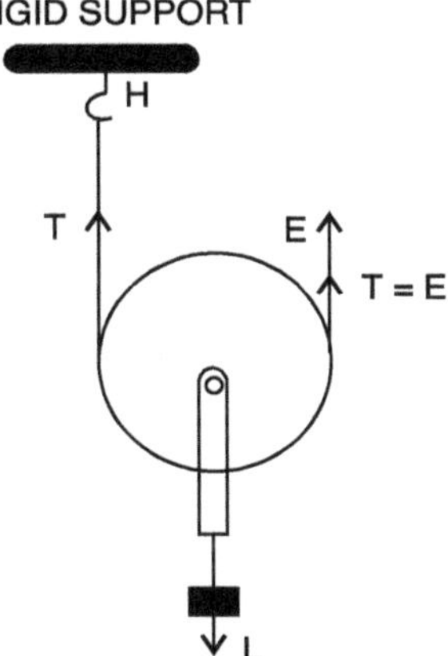

Q. 19. A pulley system has a velocity ratio of 4 and an efficiency of 90%. Calculate:

(i) The mechanical advantage of the system.

(ii) The effort required to raise a load of 300 N by the system. **[2006]**

Ans.

$$\text{V.R.} = 4, \ \eta = 90\%$$

(i) $$\text{M.A.} = \text{V.R.} \times \eta\%$$

$$= \frac{4 \times 90}{100} = 3.6$$

(ii) Since $$\text{M.A.} = \frac{\text{Load}}{\text{Effort}}$$

$$\therefore \quad \text{Effort} = \frac{\text{Load}}{\text{MA}}$$

$$= \frac{300}{3.6}$$

$$= 83.33 \ \text{N}$$

 **Long Answer Type Questions-I**

Q. 1. A block and tackle system of pulleys has velocity ratio 4.

(i) Draw a neat, labelled diagram of the system indicating clearly the points of application and direction of load and effort.

(ii) What will be its V. R. if the weight of the movable block is doubled ? **[2020]**

📋 Marking Scheme

(i)

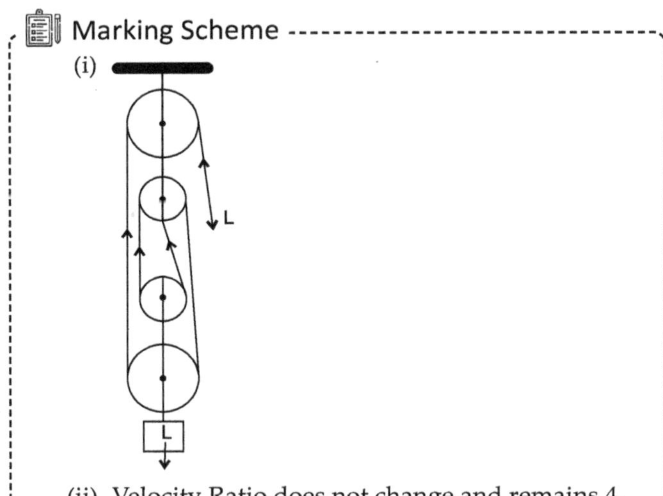

(ii) Velocity Ratio does not change and remains 4.

Ans. (i) Diagram of a block and tackle system having velocity ratio = 4

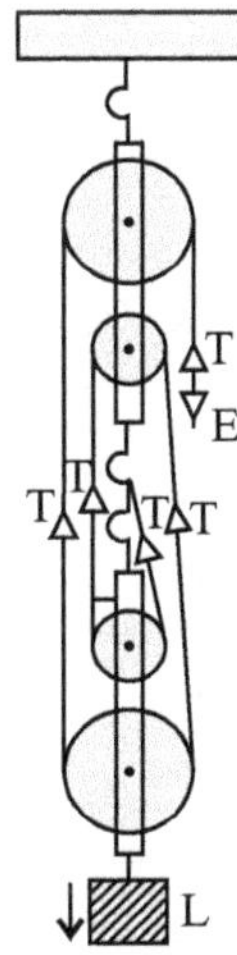

(ii) If weight of movable pulley is doubled there will be no change in the velocity ratio.

Q. 2. The diagram below shows a pulley arrangement:

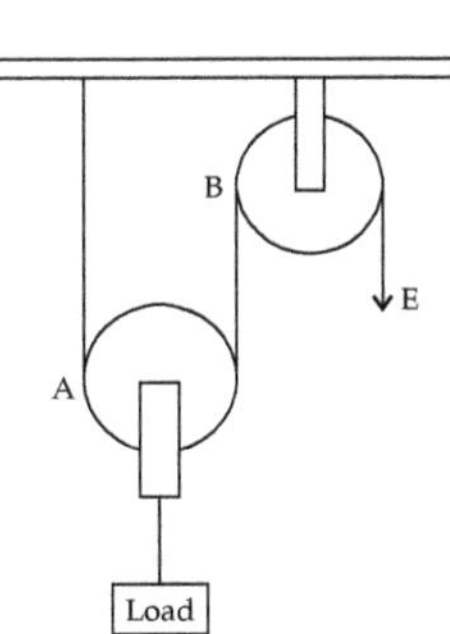

(i) Copy the diagram and mark the direction of tension on each strand of the string.

(ii) What is the velocity ratio of the arrangement?

(iii) If the tension acting on the string is T, then what is the relationship between T and effort E?

(iv) If the free end of the string moves through a distance x, find the distance by which the load is raised. **[2019]**

Marking Scheme

(i)

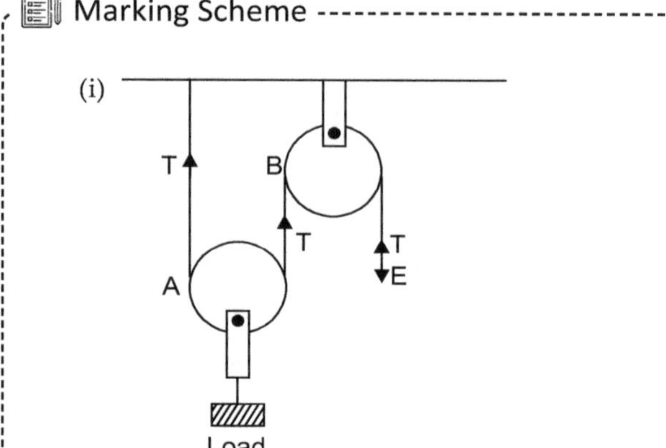

(ii) V.R. = No. of stands supporting load = 2

(iii) E = T

(iv) V.R. $= \dfrac{d_E}{d_L} \therefore 2 = \dfrac{x}{d_L} \therefore d_L = \dfrac{x}{2}$

Ans. **(i)** The diagram with direction of tension on each strand is shown below.

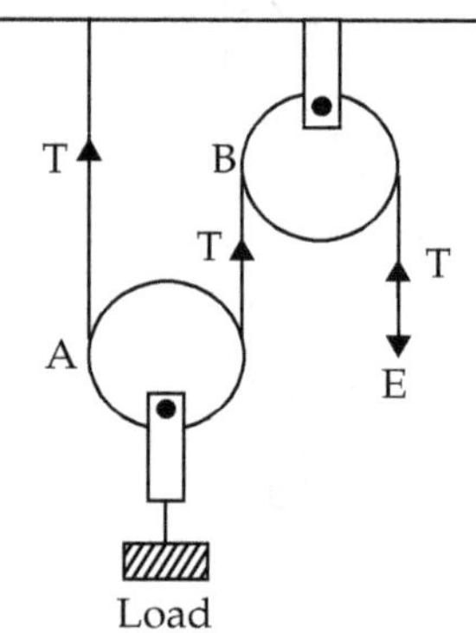

(ii) Velocity ratio = 2

(iii) E = T

(iv) Load is raised by a distance $\dfrac{x}{2}$.

Q. 3. **(i)** Draw a diagram to show a block and tackle pulley system having a velocity ratio of 3 marking the direction of load (L), effort (E) and tension (T).

(ii) The pulley system drawn lifts a load of 150 N when an effort of 60 N is applied. Find its mechanical advantage.

(iii) Is the above pulley system an ideal machine or not? **[2018]**

Ans. **(i)** The diagram is shown below:

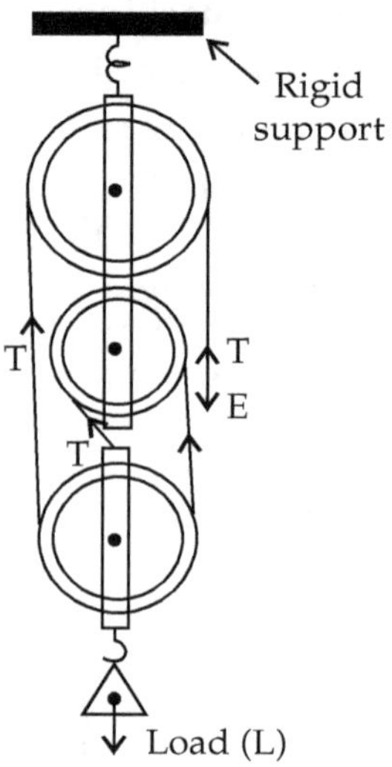

(ii) M.A. $= \dfrac{\text{Load}}{\text{Effort}} = \dfrac{150}{60} = 2.5$

(iii) No, the pulley system is not ideal because M.A. < V.R.

Q. 4. A pulley system with V.R. = 4 is used to lift a load of 175 kgf through a vertical height of 15 m. The effort required is 50 kgf in the downward direction. (g = 10 N kg⁻¹)

Calculate:

(i) Distance moved by the effort.

(ii) Work done by the effort.

(iii) M.A. of the pulley system.

(iv) Efficiency of the pulley system. **[2017]**

Ans. Given: Velocity Ratio (V.R.) = 4

$$\text{Load (L)} = 175 \text{ kgf}$$
$$= 175 \times 10 \text{ N} = 1750 \text{ N}$$

Displacement of load (d_2)
$$= 15 \text{ m}$$

$\therefore$ Effort (E) = 50 kgf
$$= 50 \times 10 \text{ N} = 500 \text{ N}$$
$$g = 10 \text{ N kg}^{-1}.$$

(i) V.R. $= \dfrac{\text{Distance moved by effort } (d_E)}{\text{Distance moved by load } (d_L)}$

or $\quad 4 = \dfrac{d_E}{15}$

$\therefore$ Distance moved by effort (d_E)
$$= 4 \times 15 \text{ m} = 60 \text{ m}$$

(ii) Work done by the effort
$$= E \times d_E$$
$$= 500 \times 60 \text{ J} = 30000 \text{ J}$$

(iii) M.A. $= \dfrac{L}{E} = \dfrac{1750}{500} = 3.5$

(iv) Efficiency (η) $= \dfrac{\text{M.A.}}{\text{V.R.}} \times 100\%$
$$= \dfrac{3.5}{4} \times 100\% = 87.5\%$$

Q. 5. A pulley system has three pulleys. A load of 120 N is overcome by applying an effort of 50 N. Calculate the Mechanical Advantage and Efficiency of this system. **[2016]**

Ans. Mechanical advantage (M.A.)

$$= \frac{\text{Load}}{\text{Effort}} = \frac{120}{50} = 2.4$$

$$\text{Efficiency} = \frac{\text{M.A.}}{\text{V.R.}} \times 100\%$$

Since, Velocity ratio (V.R.)

$$= \text{Number of pulleys} = 3$$

$$\therefore \quad \text{Efficiency} = \frac{2.4}{3} \times 100 = 80\%$$

Q. 6. **(i)** Name the physical quantity measured in terms of horse power.

(ii) A nut is opened by a wrench of length 20 cm. If the least force required is 2 N, find the moment of force needed to loosen the nut.

(iii) Explain briefly why the work done by a fielder when he takes a catch in a cricket match is negative. **[2015]**

Ans. **(i)** The physical quantity is power.

$$1 \text{ H.P.} = 746 \text{ W}$$

(ii) Given: Distance = 20 cm

$$= \frac{20}{100} = 0.2 \text{ m}$$

$$\text{Force} = 2 \text{ N}$$

Moment of the force

$$= \text{Force} \times \text{Distance}$$
$$= 2 \times 0.2 \text{ Nm}$$
$$= 0.4 \text{ Nm}$$

(iii) Here, the fielder uses a force to oppose the motion of the ball.

Thus, $\theta = 180°$

We know,

$$\text{work done} = \text{force (F)} \times$$
$$\text{displacement } (d) \times \cos 180°$$
$$= - \text{F} \times d$$
$$(\because \cos 180° = -1)$$

Thus, work done is negative.

Q. 7. A block and tackle system has V.R. = 5.

(i) Draw a neat labelled diagram of a system indicating the direction of its load and effort.

(ii) Rohan exerts a pull of 150 kgf. What is the maximum load he can raise with this pulley system if its efficiency = 75%? **[2015]**

Ans. **(i)**

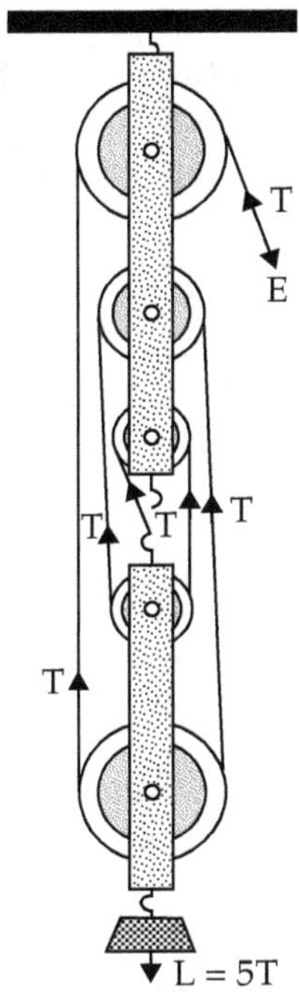

(ii)

$$\text{Efficiency} = 75\%$$
$$\text{V.R.} = 5$$
$$\text{Efficiency} = \frac{\text{M.A.}}{\text{V.R.}}$$

Thus, $\quad \dfrac{75}{100} = \dfrac{\text{M.A.}}{5}$

Or $\quad \text{M.A.} = 3.75$

Now, $\quad \text{M.A.} = \dfrac{\text{Load}}{\text{Effort}}$

$$3.75 = \frac{\text{Load}}{150}$$

Thus, $\quad \text{Load} = 3.75 \times 150$

$$= 562.5 \text{ kgf.}$$

Q. 8. **(i)** A man having a box on his head, climbs up a slope and another man having an identical box walks the same distance on a levelled road. Who does more work against the force of gravity and why?

(ii) Two forces each of 5 N act vertically upwards and downwards respectively on the two ends of a uniform metre rule which is placed at its mid-point as shown in the diagram. Determine the magnitude of the resultant moment of these forces about the midpoint. **[2014]**

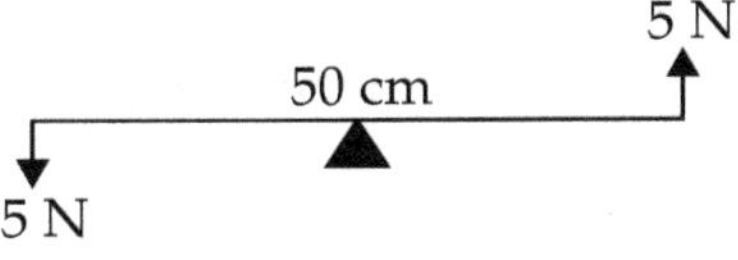

Ans. **(i)** Man having a box on his head who climbs up a slope does more work against the force of gravity because he has more potential energy by virtue of his position *i.e.,* height.

As, $\quad$ P.E. $=$ Work done $=$ F $\times$ S

$$= mg \times h$$

(ii) The two forces each of 5 N form a couple.

$\therefore \quad$ Moment of the couple

$$= \text{Either force}$$
$$\times \text{ Perpendicular distance}$$
$$\text{between the two forces}$$
$$= 5 \times 1$$
$$= 5 \text{ Nm (anti-clockwise)}$$

Q. 9. A block and tackle system of pulleys has a velocity ratio 4.

(i) Draw a labelled diagram of the system indicating clearly the points of application and directions of load and effort.

(ii) What is the value of the mechanical advantage of the given pulley system if it is an ideal pulley system? **[2013]**

Ans. **(i)**

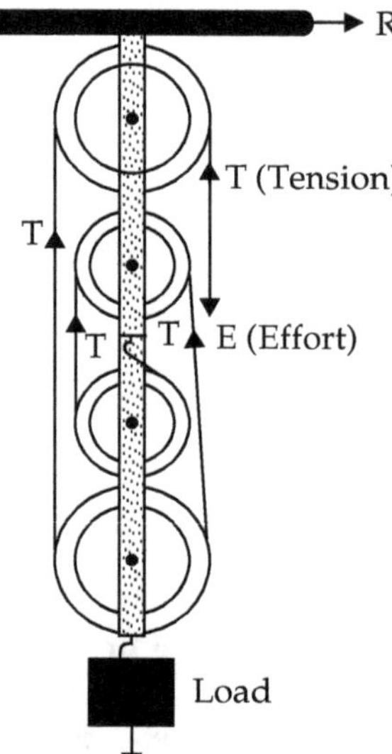

(ii) M.A. $=$ V.R. $=$ 4, for an ideal pulley system.

Q. 10. A moving body weighing 400 N possesses 500 J of kinetic energy. Calculate the velocity with which the body is moving. (g $=$ 10 ms^{-2}) **[2012]**

Ans. $\quad$ Given: Weight $=$ 400 N

$$W = mg$$
$$400 = m \times 10$$
$$m = 40 \text{ kg}$$

Now, Kinetic Energy

$$= \frac{1}{2} mv^2$$
$$500 = \frac{1}{2} \times 40 \times v^2$$

$$v = 5 \text{ m/s}$$

Q. 11. **Give two reasons as to why the efficiency of a single movable pulley system is always less than 100%.** **[2010**

Ans. $\quad$ The efficiency of a single movable pulley system is always less than 100% because of the friction of the pulley and also the weight of the pulley.

Q. 12. **An object of mass 'm' is allowed to fall freely from point A as shown in the figure. Calculate the total mechanical energy of the object at:**

(i) Point A

(ii) Point B

(iii) Point C

(iv) State the law which is verified by your calculations in parts (i), (ii) and (iii). **[2009]**

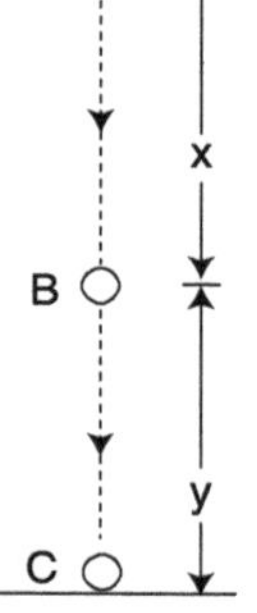

Ans. **(i)** Since at point A, height is $x + y$ and velocity $= 0$

$\therefore$ Total energy at A $=$ P.E. at A $+$ K.E. at A

$$= mg (x + y) + \frac{1}{2} \times m \times 0^2$$
$$= mg (x + y)$$

(ii) At point B, height is y and velocity $= v_1$

Total energy at B $=$ P.E. at B $+$ K.E. at B

$$= mg\, y + \frac{1}{2} mv_1^2$$

But $\qquad v_1^2 = u^2 + 2\, gh$
$$v_1^2 = 2\, gx$$
$$[\because u = 0 \text{ during free fall}]$$

$\therefore$ Total energy at B $= mg\, y + \frac{1}{2} m \times 2\, gx$
$$= mg (x + y)$$

(iii) At point C, height $= 0$ and velocity $= v_2$.

Total energy at C $=$ P.E. at C $+$ K.E. at C

$$= 0 + \frac{1}{2} mv_2^2$$

But $\qquad v_2^2 = u^2 + 2\, gh$
$$v_2^2 = 0 + 2g (x + y)$$
$$v_2^2 = 2g (x + y)$$

$\therefore$ Total energy at C $= \frac{1}{2} m \times 2g(x + y)$
$$= mg (x + y)$$

(iv) Low of conservation of mechanical energy.

Q. 13. **(i)** Draw a labelled diagram of a block and tackle system of pulleys with two pulleys in each block. Indicate the directions of the load, effort and tension in the string.

(ii) Write down the relation between the load and the effort of the pulley system. **[2008]**

Ans. **(i)** A labelled diagram of a block and tackle system with two pulleys in each block is shown alongside. Load, effort and tension are marked in the diagram.

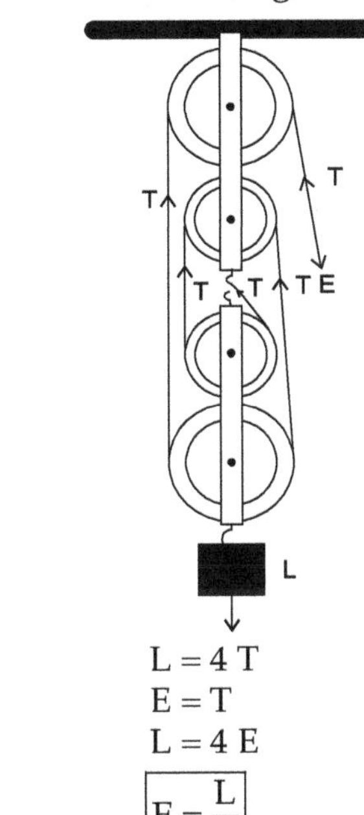

(ii)   L = 4 T
                 E = T
So,   L = 4 E

or $$E = \dfrac{L}{4}$$

Q. 14. A block and tackle pulley system has a velocity ratio 3.

(i) Draw a labelled diagram of this system. In your diagram, indicate clearly the points of application and the directions of the load and effort.

(ii) Why should the lower block of this pulley system be of negligible weight? **[2007]**

Ans. **(i)** Figure is shown below.

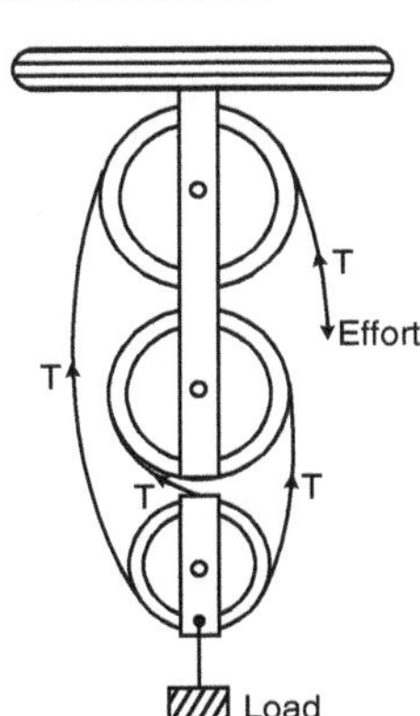

(ii) For greater efficiency.

Q. 15. Show that for the free fall of a body, the sum of the mechanical energy at any point in its path is constant. **[2006]**

Ans. Let a body of mass m falls freely under gravity from height h above ground.

Let A, B and C be the positions of body.

Let x be the distance fallen from A to B

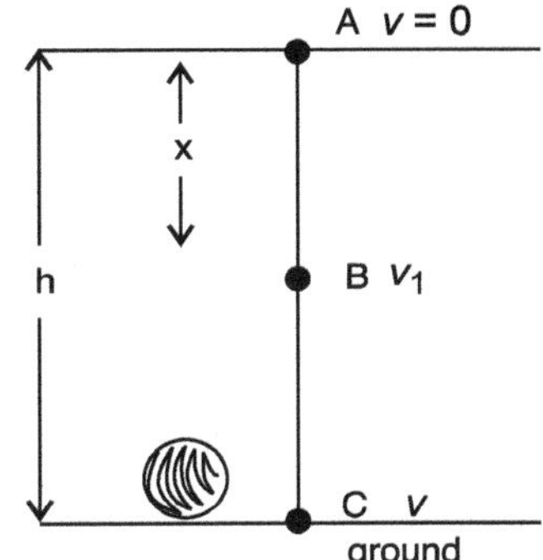

At position A:

$$\text{K.E.} = 0 \qquad \text{(body is at rest)}$$

and $$\text{P.E.} = mgh$$

$\therefore$ Total energy $= 0 + mgh = mgh$ …(i)

At position B:

Let v_1 be velocity of body, then $u = 0$, $s = x$.

From equation $\qquad v^2 = u^2 + 2as$

$$v_1^2 = 0 + 2gx = 2gx$$

Since $\qquad \text{K.E.} = \dfrac{1}{2} mv^2$

$$= \dfrac{1}{2} m \times 2gx$$

$$= mgx$$

and $\qquad \text{P.E.} = mg\,(h - x)$

$$= mgh - mgx$$

$\therefore$ Total energy $= mgx + mgh - mgx$

$$= mgh \qquad …(ii)$$

At position C:

Let velocity of body be v, then $u = 0$, $s = h$.

From equation $\qquad v^2 = u^2 + 2gs$

$$v^2 = 0 + 2gh$$

$$= 2gh$$

Science $\qquad \text{K.E.} = \dfrac{1}{2} mv^2$

$$= \dfrac{1}{2} m \times 2gh = mgh$$

and $\qquad \text{P.E.} = 0 \text{ (body at ground)}$

$\therefore$ Total energy $= mgh + 0 = mgh$ …(iii)

$\therefore$ From (i), (ii) and (iii) it is clear that sum of mechanical energy remains same at any point in the path of free fall of a body.

Refraction of Light

? Short Answer Type Questions-I

Q. 1. A ray of light falls normally on a rectangular glass slab.

Draw a ray diagram showing the path of the ray till it emerges out of the slab. **[2020]**

Ans.

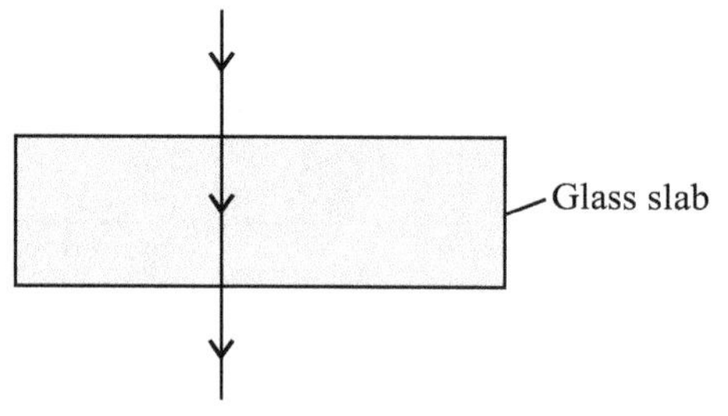

Q. 2. Complete the path of the monochromatic light ray AB incident on the surface PQ of the equilateral glass prism PQR till it emerges out of the prism due to refraction.

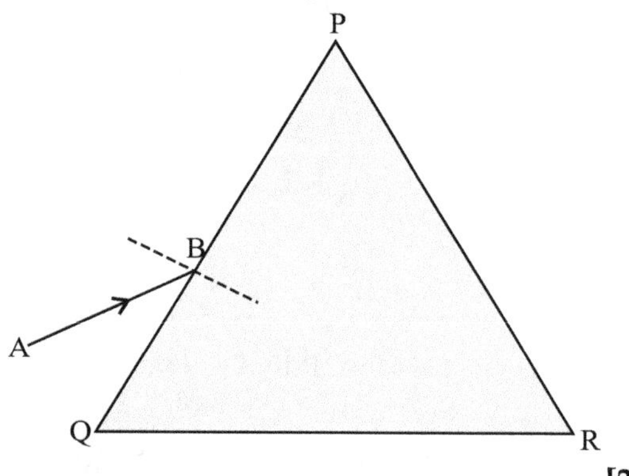

[2020]

Ans. AB → Incident Ray
BC → Refracted Ray
CD → Emergent Ray.

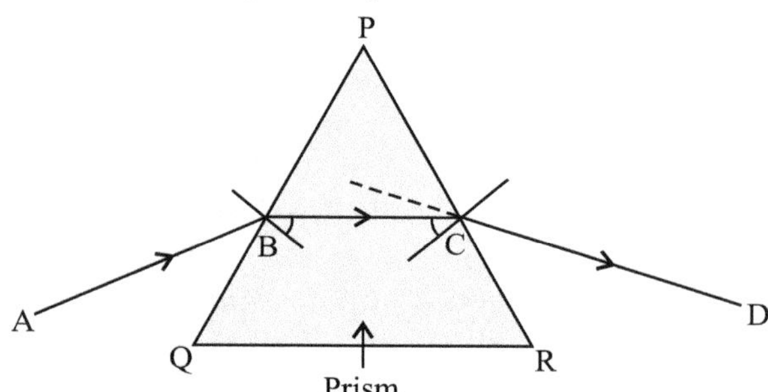

Q. 3. A pond appears to be 2.7 m deep. If the refractive index of water is $\dfrac{4}{3}$, find the actual depth of the pond. **[2020]**

Ans. Apparent depth = 2.7 m

$$\mu_w = \frac{4}{3}$$

$$\because \qquad \mu_w = \frac{\text{Actual depth}}{\text{Apparent depth}}$$

$$\Rightarrow \qquad \frac{4}{3} = \frac{\text{Actual depth}}{2.7}$$

$$\Rightarrow \qquad \text{Actual depth} = \frac{4}{3} \times 2.7 \text{ m} = 3.6 \text{ m}$$

Q. 4. The wave lengths for the light of red and blue colours are nearly 7.8×10^{-7} m and 4.8×10^{-7} m respectively.

(i) Which colour has the greater speed in a vacuum ?

(ii) Which colour has a greater speed in glass ? **[2020]**

Ans. (i) Both colours of light have same speed in vacuum.

(ii) In glass speed of red light is more than that of blue light.

Q. 5. (i) Define critical angle.

(ii) State one important factor which affects the critical angle of a given medium.

[2019]

Ans. (i) The angle of incidence in the denser medium corresponding to which the angle of refraction in the rarer medium is 90° is called critical angle

$$\text{Critical angle } (i_c) = \sin^{-1}\left(\frac{1}{\mu}\right)$$

(ii) Critical angle for a given pair of media depends on their refractive indices.

Q. 6. (i) What is the relation between the refractive index of water with respect to air $(_a\mu_w)$ and the refractive index of air with respect to water $(_w\mu_a)$.

(ii) If the refractive index of water with respect to air $(_a\mu_w)$ is $\dfrac{5}{3}$. Calculate the refractive index of air with respect to water $(_w\mu_a)$. **[2019]**

Ans. **(i)**

$$_a\mu_w = \frac{\mu_w}{\mu_a}$$

$$_w\mu_a = \frac{\mu_a}{\mu_w}$$

$$_a\mu_w = \frac{1}{_w\mu_a}$$

$\therefore$

(ii) Given,

$$_a\mu_w = \frac{5}{3}$$

$\therefore$

$$_w\mu_a = \frac{1}{_a\mu_w} = \frac{3}{5}$$

Q. 7. **The diagram below shows a light source P embedded in a rectangular glass block ABCD of critical angle 42°. Complete the path of the ray PQ till it emerges out of block. [Write necessary angles.]** **[2019]**

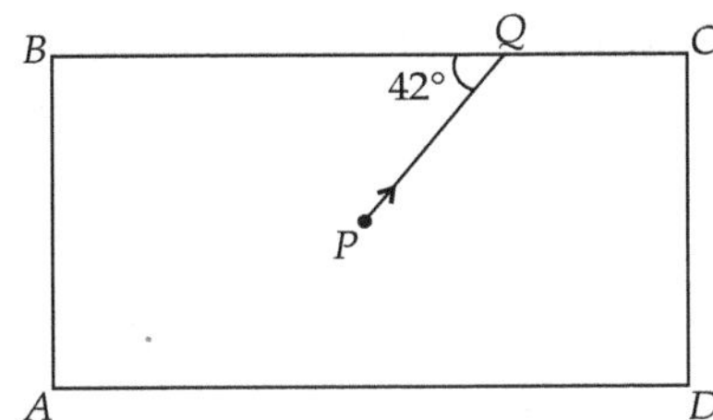

Ans. The complete ray diagram with necessary angles is as follows:

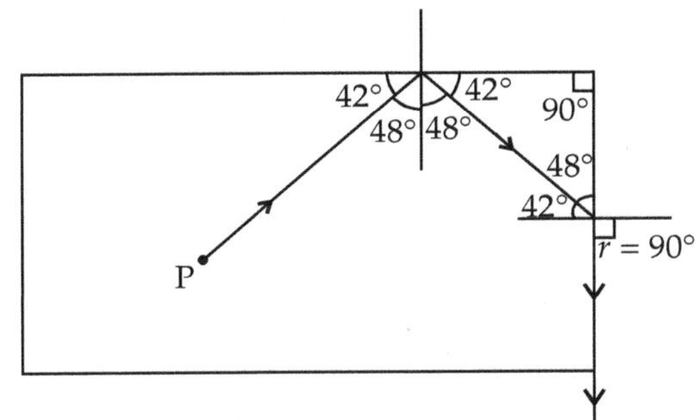

Q. 8. **(i) Why is the ratio of the velocities of light of wavelengths 4000 Å and 8000 Å in vacuum 1 : 1?**

(ii) Which of the above wavelengths has a higher frequency? **[2018]**

Ans. **(i)** In vacuum, the velocity of light is always constant *i.e.*, 3×10^8 ms^{-1} and it does not depend on wavelength or frequency.

(ii) We know that,

$$c = \lambda \nu$$

or

$$\nu = \frac{c}{\lambda}$$

$\therefore$

$$\nu \propto \frac{1}{\lambda} \quad \text{(As } c \text{ is always constant)}$$

Hence, lower wavelength *i.e.*, 4000 Å has higher frequency.

Q. 9. **(i) State the relation between the critical angle and the absolute refractive index of a medium.**

(ii) Which colour of light has a higher critical angle? Red light or Green light. **[2018]**

Ans. **(i)**

$$\mu = \frac{1}{\sin C} = \operatorname{cosec} C$$

where 'μ' is the absolute refractive index of medium and 'C' is the critical angle.

(ii) Critical angle increases with the increase in wavelength of light, since, red light has a longer wavelength than green light, thus it has a higher critical angle.

Q. 10. **The following diagram shows a 60°, 30°, 90° glass prism of critical angle 42°. Copy the diagram and complete the path of incident ray AB emerging out of the prism marking the angle of incidence on each surface.[2018]**

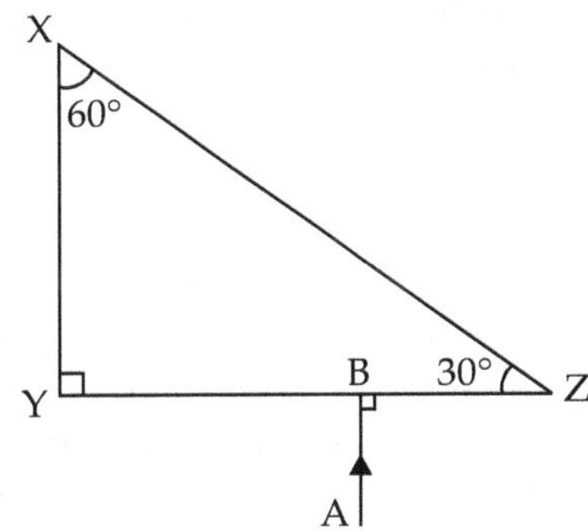

Ans. CD is the emergent ray as shown in the figure. Angle of incidence on the surface YZ is 0° and on surface XZ is 30°.

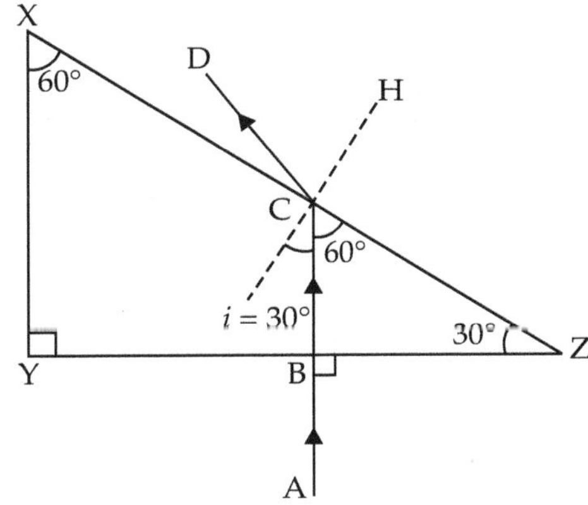

Q. 11. **How is the refractive index of a material related to:**

(i) real and apparent depth?

(ii) velocity of light in vacuum or air and the velocity of light in a given medium?

[2017]

Ans. Let μ be the refractive index of the material.

(i) $\mu = \dfrac{\text{Real depth}}{\text{Apparent depth}}$

(ii) $\mu = \dfrac{\text{Speed of light in vacuum or air }(c)}{\text{Speed of light in medium }(v)}$

Q. 12. State the conditions required for total internal reflection of light to take place. **[2017]**

Ans. (i) The light must travel from a denser to a rarer medium.

(ii) The angle of incidence must be greater than the critical angle for the given pair of media.

Q. 13. A boy uses blue colour of light to find the refractive index of glass. He then repeats the experiment using red colour of light. Will the refractive index be the same or different in the two cases? Give a reason to support your answer. **[2016]**

Ans. The index of refraction is a function of the wavelength of the light. The wavelength of red light is longer than the wavelength of blue light. Therefore, blue light bends more when it passes from air to glass. As the angle of deviation in both cases will be different, the refractive index will also be different. It will be more in case of blue light than in red light.

Q. 14. Copy the diagram given below and complete the path of light ray till it emerges out of the prism. The critical angle of glass is 42°. In your diagram mark the angles wherever necessary. **[2016]**

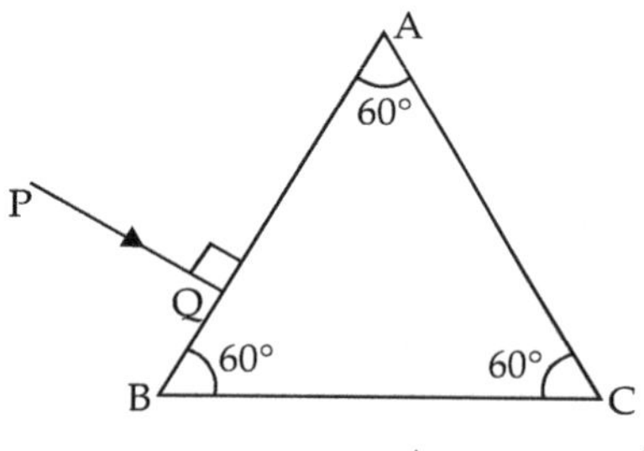

Ans.

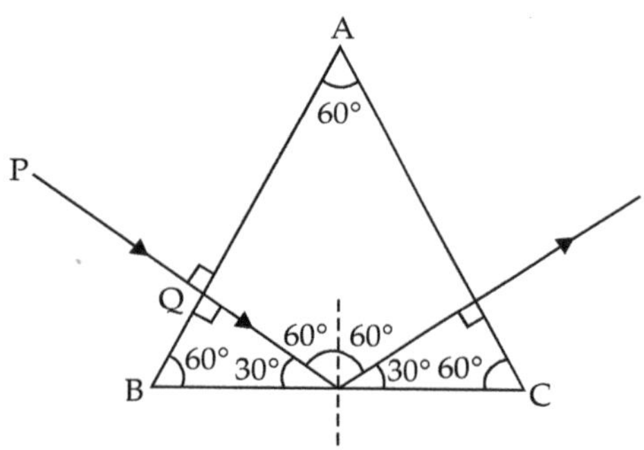

Q. 15. State the dependence of angle of deviation:

(i) On the refractive index of the material of the prism.

(ii) On the wavelength of light. **[2016]**

Ans. (i) If the refractive index of the material increases, the angle of deviation also increases.

(ii) Lesser the wavelength of light, greater is the angle of deviation.

Q. 16. Name one factor that affects the lateral displacement of light as it passes through a rectangular glass slab. **[2015]**

Ans. The thickness of glass slab affects the lateral displacement of light as it passes through a rectangular glass slab.

Q. 17. The speed of light in glass is 2×10^5 km/s. What is the refractive index of glass? **[2015]**

Ans. Given,

Speed of light in glass $= 2 \times 10^5$ km/s

$= 2 \times 10^5 \times 10^3$ m/s

$= 2 \times 10^8$ m/s

Refractive index of glass

$= \dfrac{\text{Speed of light in vacuum}}{\text{Speed of light in glass}}$

$= \dfrac{3 \times 10^8}{2 \times 10^8} = 1.5$

Q. 18. Draw the diagram given below and clearly show the path taken by the emergent ray: **[2014]**

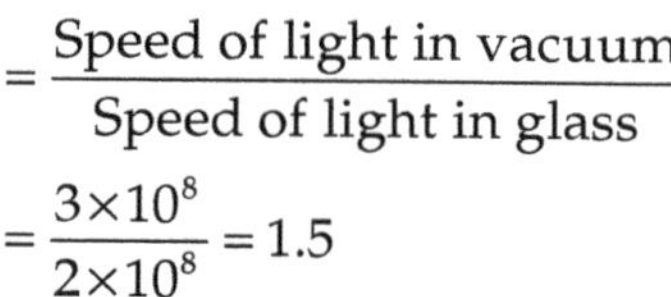

Ans.

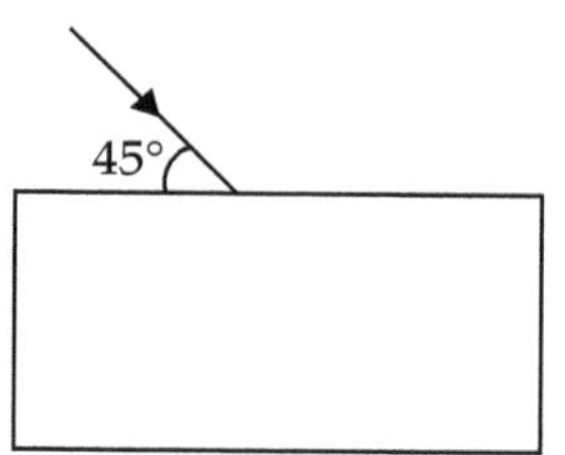

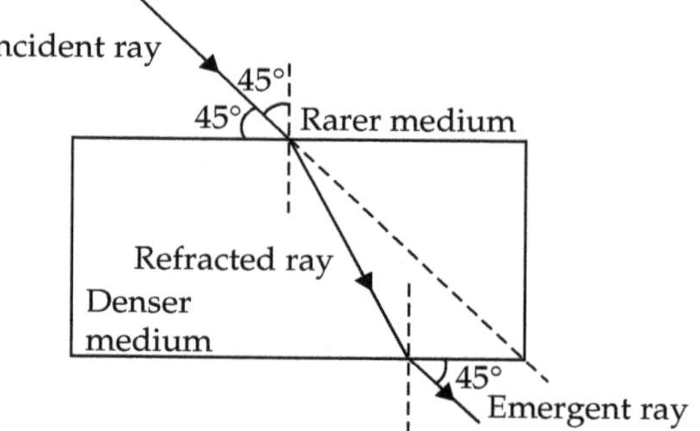

Q. 19. (i) A ray of light passes from water to air How does the speed of light change? **[2014]**

Ans. (i) When light passes from water to air *i.e.*, from denser to rarer medium, its speed increases.

Q. 20. Name the factors affecting the critical angle for the pair of media. **[2014]**

Ans. Factors affecting the critical angle:

(i) Wavelength of light.

(ii) Temperature (on changing the temperature of medium, its refractive index changes).

Q. 21. A ray of light is moving from a rarer medium to a denser medium and strikes a plane mirror placed at 90° to the direction of the ray as shown in the diagram.

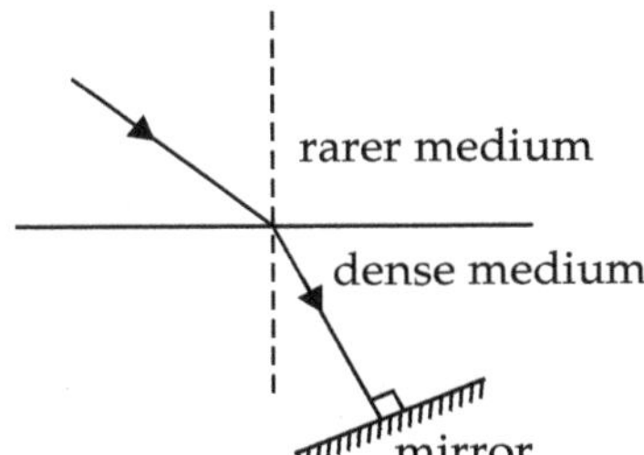

(i) Copy the diagram and mark arrows to show the path of the ray of light after it is reflected from the mirror.

(ii) Name the principle you have used to mark the arrows to show the direction of the ray. **[2013]**

Ans. **(i)**

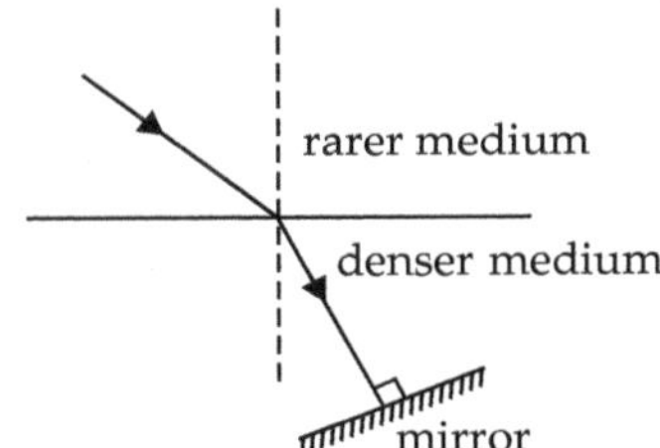

(ii) Principle of reversibility of light.

Q. 22. **(i)** The refractive index of glass with respect to air is 1.5. What is the value of the refractive index of air with respect to glass?

(ii) A ray of light is incident as a normal ray on the surface of separation of two different mediums. What is the value of the angle of incidence in this case? **[2013]**

Ans. **(i)**

$$_a\mu_g = 1.5$$

$$_g\mu_a = \frac{1}{_a\mu_g}$$

$$= \frac{1}{1.5} = 0.666 = 0.67$$

(ii) $\angle i = 0°$

Q. 23. **(i)** Define the term refractive index of a medium in terms of velocity of light.

(ii) A ray of light moves from a rarer medium to a denser medium as shown in the diagram below. Write down the number of the ray which represents the partially reflected ray. **[2012]**

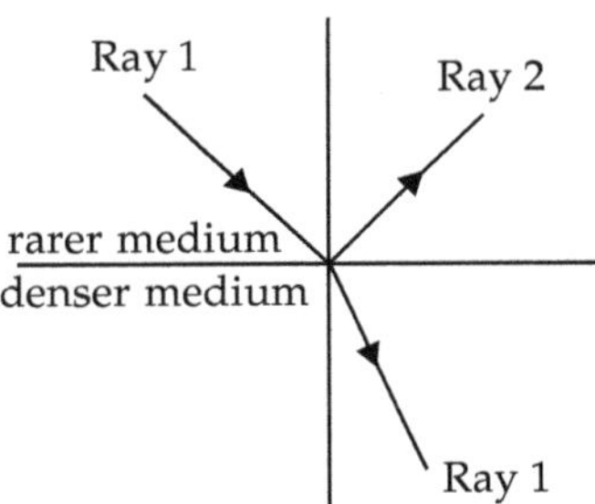

Ans. **(i)** **Refractive Index:** It is defined as the ratio of velocity of light in medium 1 to the velocity of light in medium 2.

(ii) Ray 2 shows partially reflected ray.

Q. 24. In the diagram below, PQ is a ray of light incident on a rectangular glass block.

(i) Copy the diagram and complete the path of the ray of light through the glass block. In your diagram, mark the angle of incidence by letter '*i*' and the angle of emergence by the letter '*e*'.

(ii) How are the angles '*i*' and '*e*' related to each other? **[2011]**

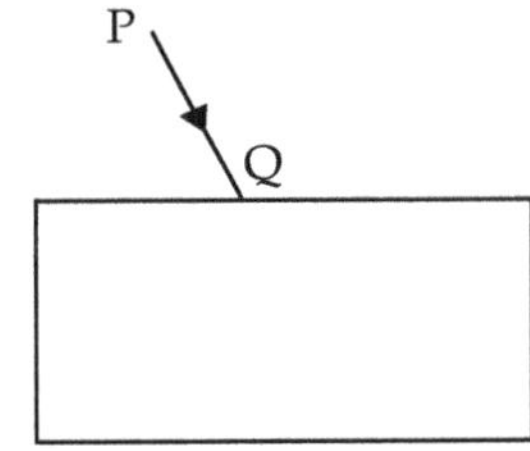

Ans. **(i)**

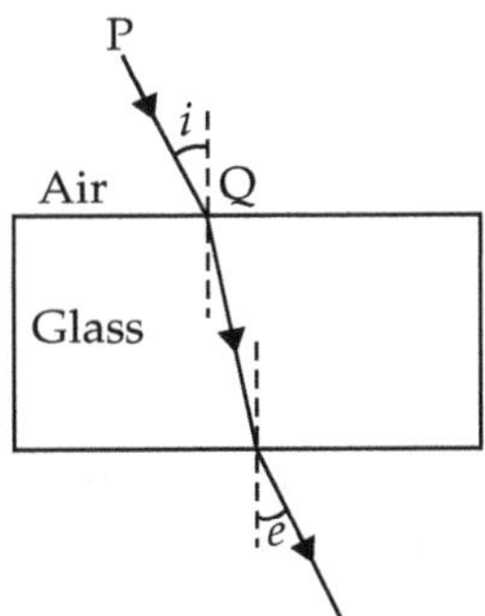

(ii) When the incident ray is undergoing minimum deviation, the angle of incidence is equal to angle of emergence, *i.e.,*

$$\angle i = \angle e$$

Q. 25. A ray of monochromatic light enters a liquid from air as shown in the diagram given below:

(i) Copy the diagram and show in the diagram the path of the ray of light after it strikes the mirror and reenters the medium of air.

(ii) Mark in your diagram the two angles on the surface of separation when the ray of light moves out from the liquid to air. **[2011]**

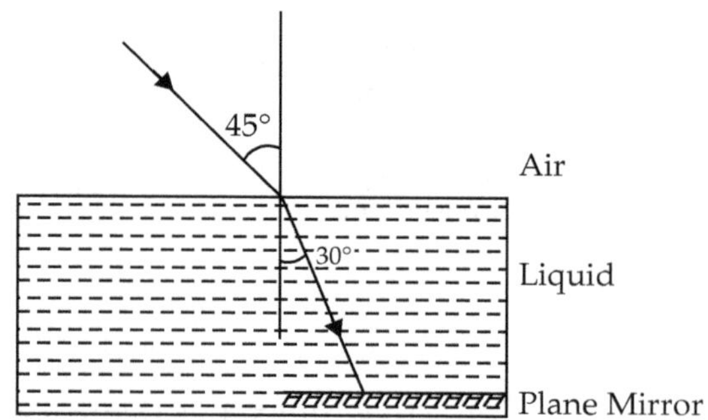

**Ans.** **(i)**

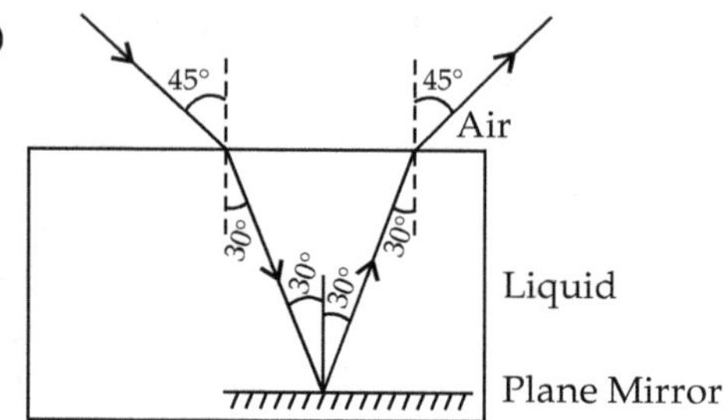

(ii) Angles are marked in the diagram.

Q. 26. How is the refractive index of a medium related to its real depth and apparent depth? **[2011]**

Ans. Refractive index $= \dfrac{\text{Real Depth}}{\text{Apparent Depth}}$

Q. 27. (i) What is meant by refraction of light?
(ii) What is the cause of refraction of light?
[2010]

Ans. **(i)** Refraction of light: The phenomenon in which a ray of light deviates from its original path while travelling from one optical medium to another medium having different optical densities is called refraction of light.
(ii) Cause of refraction: Speed of light changes as it passes from one medium to another medium, therefore, light shows refraction.

Q. 28. 'The refractive index of diamond is 2.42'. What is meant by this statement? **[2010]**

Ans. The velocity of light in diamond is 2.42 times less than that in air.

Q. 29. A ray of light enters a glass slab PQRS, as shown in the diagram. The critical angle of the glass is 42°. Copy this diagram and complete the path of the ray till it emerges from the glass slab.

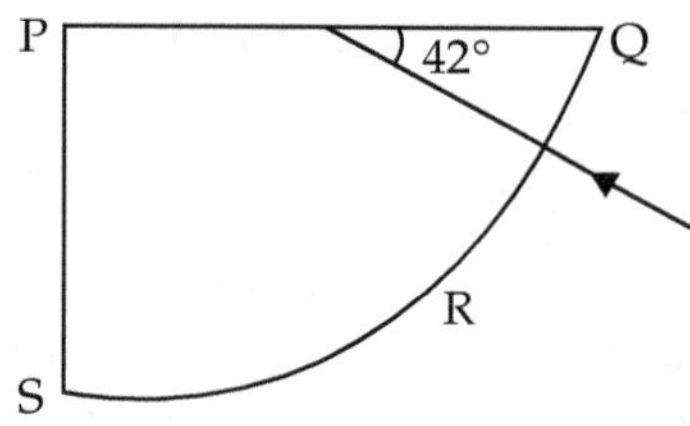

Mark the angles in the diagram wherever necessary. **[2010]**

Ans. The diagram along with the complete path of ray is as shown below:

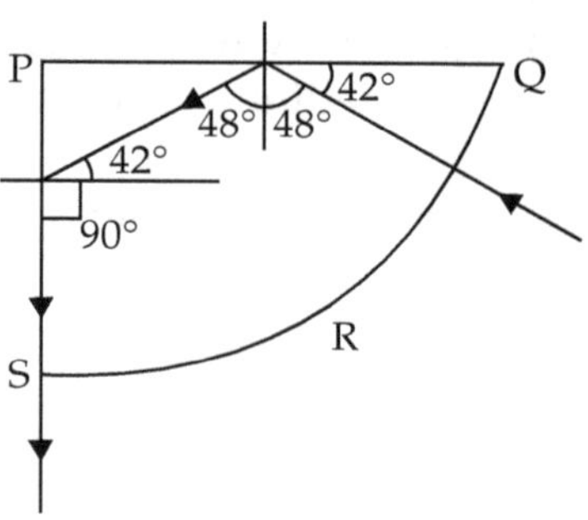

Q. 30. A ray of light strikes the surface of a rectangular glass block such that the angle of incidence is (i) 0° (ii) 42°. Sketch a diagram to show the approximate path taken by the ray in each case as it passes through the glass block and emerges from it. **[2009]**

Ans. **(i)**

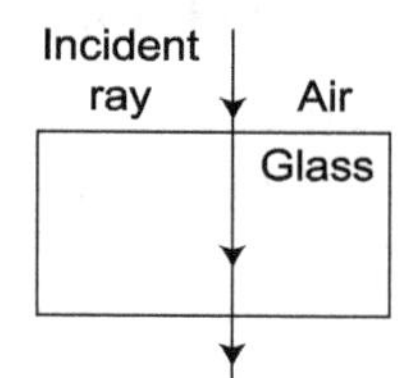

(ii) For rectangular glass block,
$n = 1.5$
We know that,
$$n = \frac{\sin i}{\sin r}$$
$$\Rightarrow \quad 1.5 = \frac{\sin 42°}{\sin r}$$
$$\Rightarrow \quad r = 26.5°$$

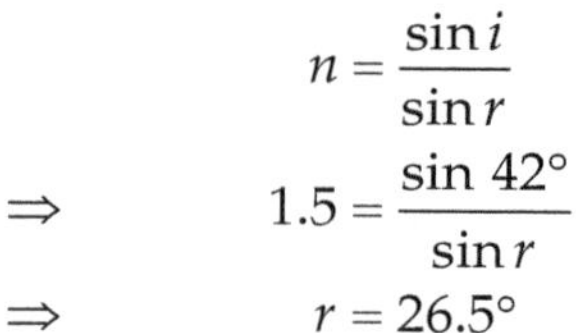

Q. 31. State the conditions required for total internal reflection of light to take place. **[2009]**

Ans. Conditions necessary for total internal reflection to take place are:
(i) Angle of incidence must be greater than critical angle for the given pair of media.
(ii) The ray should travel from denser medium to rarer medium.

Q. 32. (i) A monochromatic beam of light of wavelength λ passes from air into a glass block. Write an expression to show the relation between the speed of light in air and the speed of light in glass.

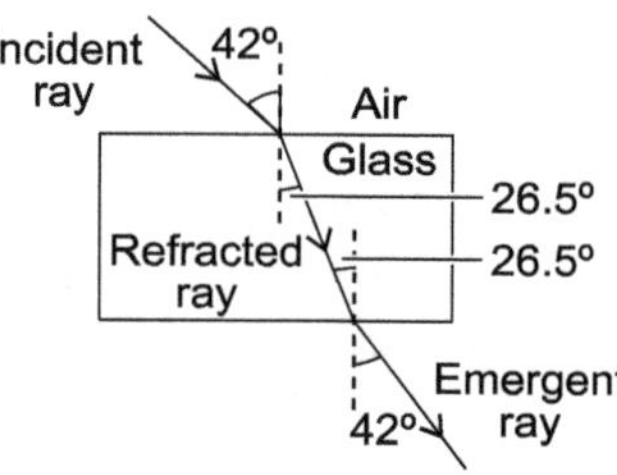

(ii) As the ray of light passes from air to glass, state how the wavelength of light changes. Does it increase, decrease or remain constant? **[2008]**

Ans. **(i)** Relation between the speed of light in air and speed of light in glass is given by the following expression:

$$_a\mu_g = \frac{\text{Speed of light in air}}{\text{Speed of light in glass}}$$

(ii) Wavelength of the light decreases as it passes from air to glass.

Q. 33. State Snell's Law of Refraction of light. **[2007]**

Ans. Snell's law states that the ratio of sine of the angle of incidence to the sine of the angle of refraction is constant for a pair of media. This constant is called refractive index of second media with respect to first media.

Where, μ = refractive index

$$\mu = \frac{\sin i}{\sin r}$$

Q. 34. Mention one difference between reflection of light from a plane mirror and total internal reflection of light from a prism. **[2007]**

Ans. In reflection of light from a plane mirror, light reflects partially, some part is refracted and transmitted also.

In total internal reflection through a prism there occurs 100% reflection of light.

Short Answer Type Questions-II

Q. 1. A diver in water looks obliquely at an object AB in air.

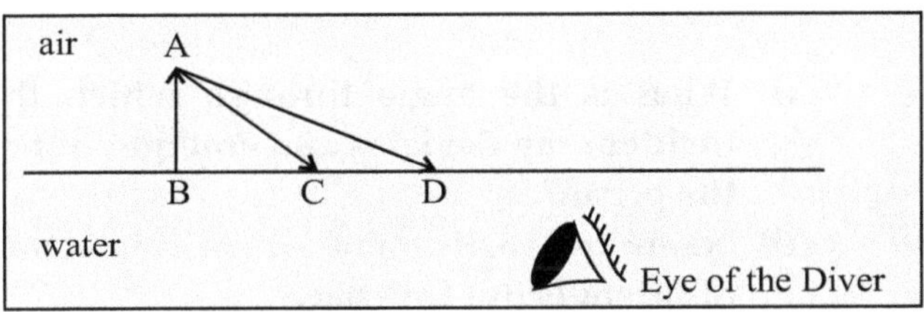

(i) Does the object appear taller, shorter or of the same size to the diver ?

(ii) Show the path of two rays AC and AD starting from the tip of the object as it travels towards the diver in water and hence obtain the image of the object. **[2020]**

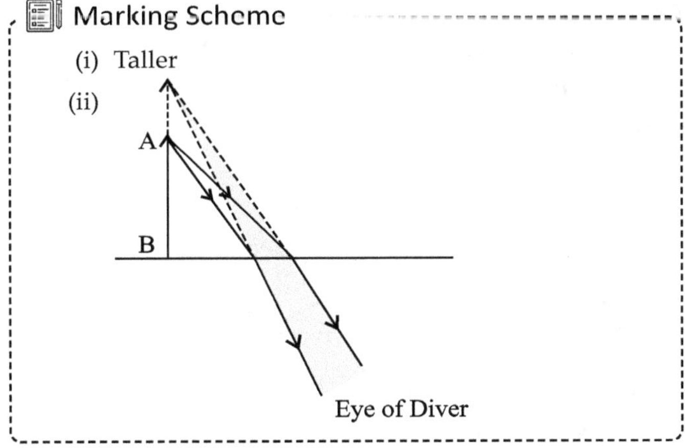

Ans. **(i)** The object will appear taller.

(ii) A'B is the image formed of the object AB.

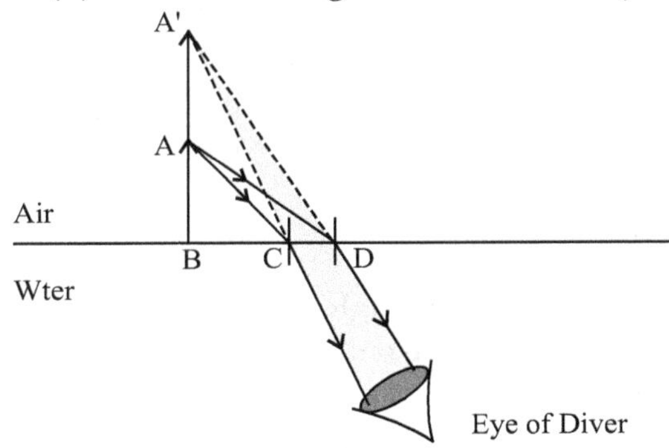

Q. 2. Complete the path of the ray AB through the glass prism in PQR till it emerges out of the prism. Given the critical angle of the glass as 42°. **[2020]**

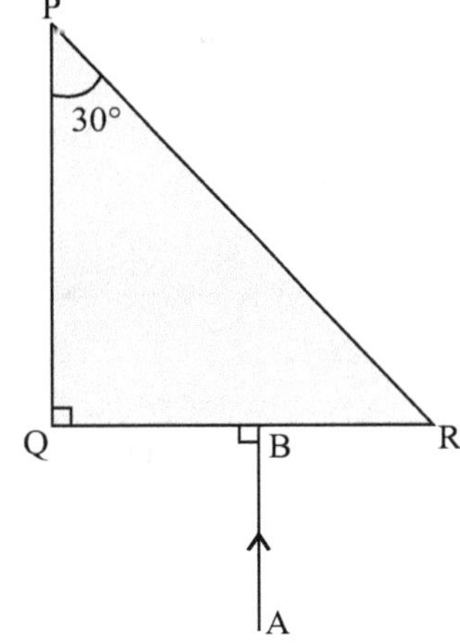

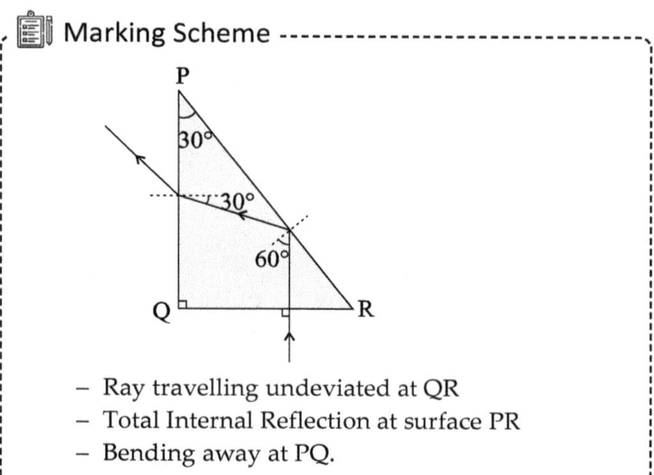

– Ray travelling undeviated at QR
– Total Internal Reflection at surface PR
– Bending away at PQ.

Ans. The path of the ray till it emerges out of the prism is ABCDE.

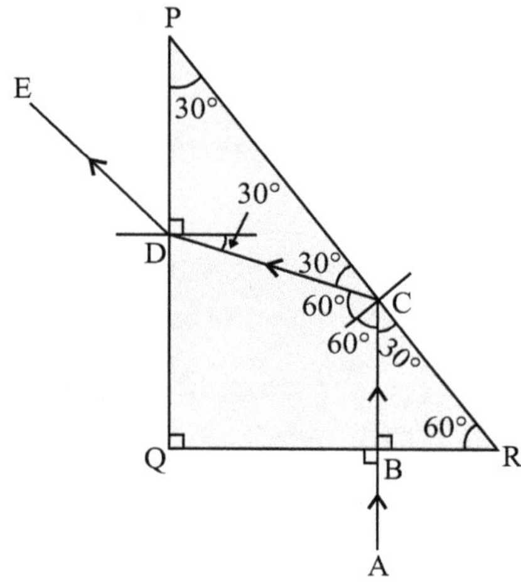

Q. 3. How does the angle of deviation formed by a prism change with the increase in the angle of incidence?

Draw a graph showing the variation in the angle of deviation with the angle of incidence at a prism surface. [2019]

Angle of deviation decreases, reaches to minimum value and then increases.

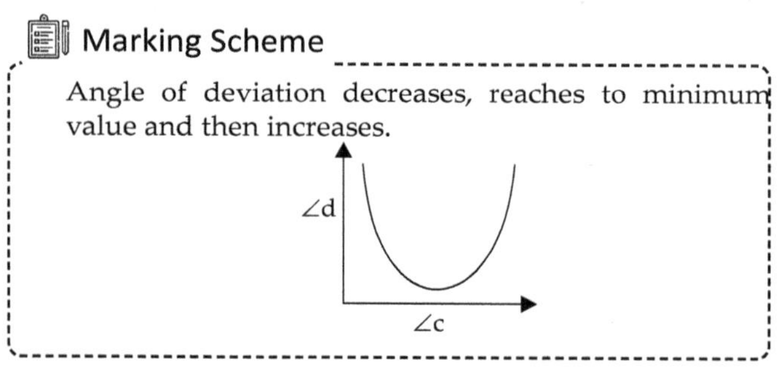

Ans. Experimentally it has been observed that as the angle of incidence increases, the angle of deviation first decreases, reaches to a minimum value for a certain angle of incidence and then

an further increasing the angle of incidence, the angle of deviation begins to increase.

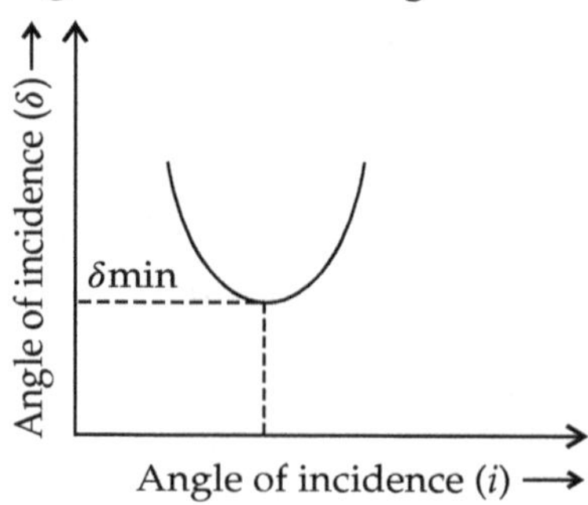

Q. 4. A ray of light XY passes through a right angled isosceles prism as shown below:

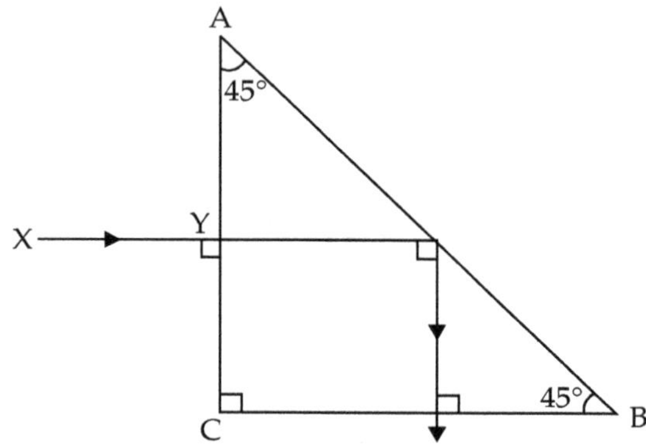

(i) What is the angle through which the incident ray deviates and emerges out of the prism?
(ii) Name the instrument where this action of prism is put into use.
(iii) Which prism surface will behave as a mirror? [2018]

Ans. (i) The angle through which the incident ray deviates and emerges out of the prism is 90°.
(ii) Refracting Periscope.
(iii) The surface AB of the prism behaves as a mirror.

Q. 5. Draw the diagram of a right angled isosceles prism which is used to make an inverted image erect. [2018]

Ans. The diagram is shown below:

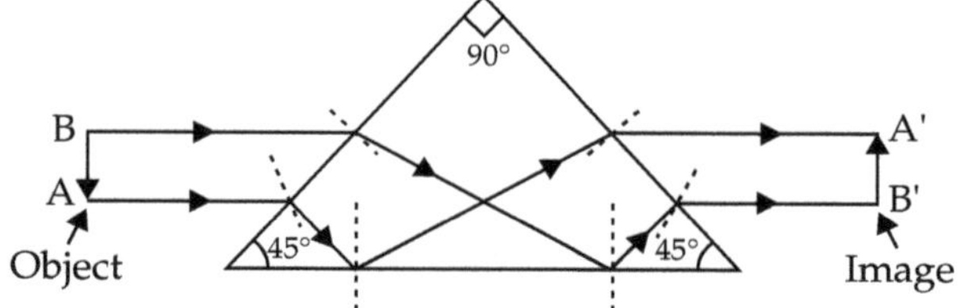

Q. 6. A ray of light travels from water to air as shown in the diagram given below:

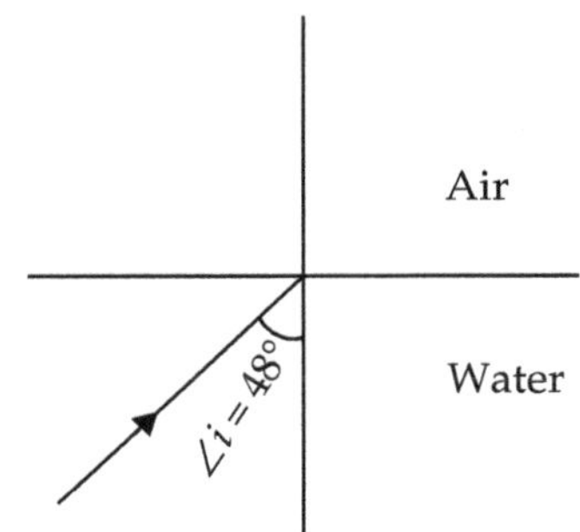

(i) Copy the diagram and complete the path of the ray. Given the critical angle for water is 48°.

(ii) State the condition so that total internal reflection occurs in the above diagram.

[2017]

Ans. **(i)**

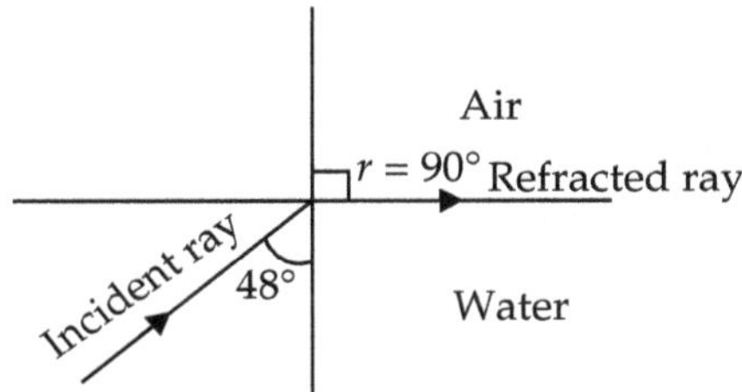

(ii) For total internal reflection to occur in the above diagram, the angle of incidence must be greater than 48°.

Q. 7. **(i) Write a relationship between angle of incidence and angle of refraction for a given pair of media.**

(ii) When a ray of light enters from one medium to another having different optical densities, it bends. Why does this phenomenon occur?

(iii) Write one condition where it does not bend when entering a medium of different optical density. **[2016]**

Ans. **(i)** The ratio of the sine of the angle of incidence i to the sine of the angle of refraction r is constant for a given pair of media. This constant is called refractive index.

$$\Rightarrow \qquad \frac{\sin i}{\sin r} = {}_1\mu_2 \text{ or } {}_1n_2$$

(ii) When a ray of light passes from one medium to another medium, its direction (or path) changes because of change in speed of light while travelling from one medium to another.

(iii) The ray of light which is incident normally on the surface separating the two media, passes undeviated (does not bend). Thus, if angle of incidence $\angle i = 0°$, then angle of refraction $\angle r = 0°$. The deviation of the ray is zero.

Q. 8. **(i) Can the absolute refractive index of a medium be less than one?**

(ii) A coin placed at the bottom of a beaker appears to be raised by 4.0 cm. If the refractive index of water is 4/3, find the depth of the water in the beaker. **[2013]**

Ans. **(i)** No, the absolute refractive index of a medium cannot be less than one because speed of light in any medium is always less than that of in vacuum.

(ii) Let Real depth $= x$

Refractive Index,

$$\mu = \frac{\text{Real depth}}{\text{Apparent depth}}$$

$$\Rightarrow \qquad \frac{4}{3} = \frac{x}{x-4}$$

$$\Rightarrow \qquad 4x - 16 = 3x$$

$$\therefore \qquad x = 16 \text{ cm.}$$

Q. 9. **(i) What is meant by the term 'critical angle'?**

(ii) How is it related to the refractive index of the medium?

(iii) Does the depth of a tank of water appear to change or remain the same when viewed normally from above? **[2012]**

Ans. **(i) Critical angle:** It is the angle of incidence in the denser medium corresponding to which the angle of refraction in the rarer medium is 90°.

(ii)
$$n = \frac{1}{\sin i_c}$$

where, n = refractive index, i_c = critical angle.

(iii) Depth of the tank remains the same when viewed normally from above.

Q. 10. **A ray of light PQ is incident normally on the hypotenuse of a right angled prism ABC as shown in the diagram given below:**

(i) Copy the diagram and complete the path of the ray PQ till it emerges from the prism.

(ii) What is the value of the angle of deviation of the ray?

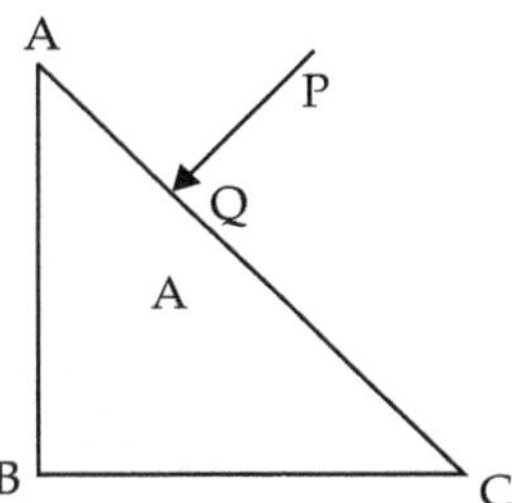

(iii) Name an instrument where this action of the prism is used. **[2012]**

Ans. **(i)**

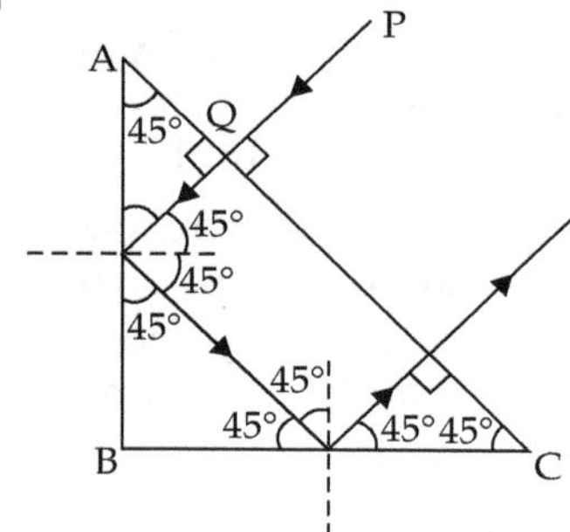

(ii) Angle of deviation of the ray $= 180°$.

(iii) Prism binoculars.

Q. 11. **(i)** State the laws of refraction of light.

(ii) Write a relation between the angle of incidence (i), angle of emergence (e), angle of prism (A) and angle of deviation (d) for a ray of light passing through an equilateral prism. **[2011]**

Ans. **(i)** Laws of refraction of light:

(1) The incident ray, refracted ray and normal at the point of incidence all lie in the same plane.

(2) The ratio of sine of angle of incidence to the sine of angle of refraction is a constant for a given pair of media and is known as refractive index of medium 2 with respect to medium 1.

It is generally represented by the Greek letter $_1\mu_2$.

$$\boxed{_1\propto_2 = \frac{\sin i}{\sin r}}$$

(ii) $i + e = A + d$.

Q. 12. A stick partly immersed in water appears to be bent. Draw a ray diagram to show the bending of the stick when placed in water and viewed obliquely from above. **[2010]**

Ans.

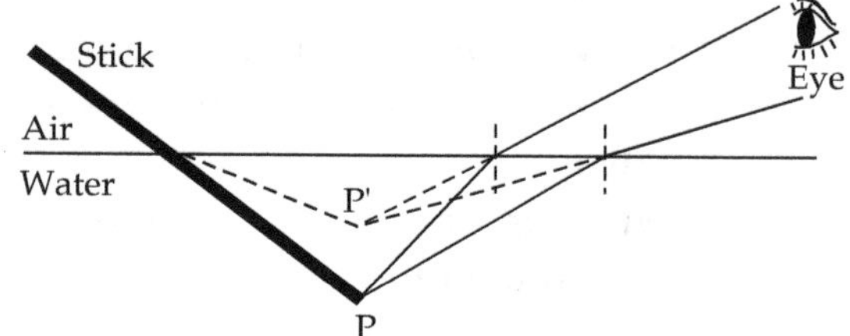

Q. 13. A ray of monochromatic light is incident from air on a glass slab:

(i) Draw a labelled ray diagram showing the change in the path of the ray till it emerges from the glass slab.

(ii) Name the two rays that are parallel to each other.

(iii) Mark the lateral displacement in your diagram. **[2010]**

Ans. **(i)**

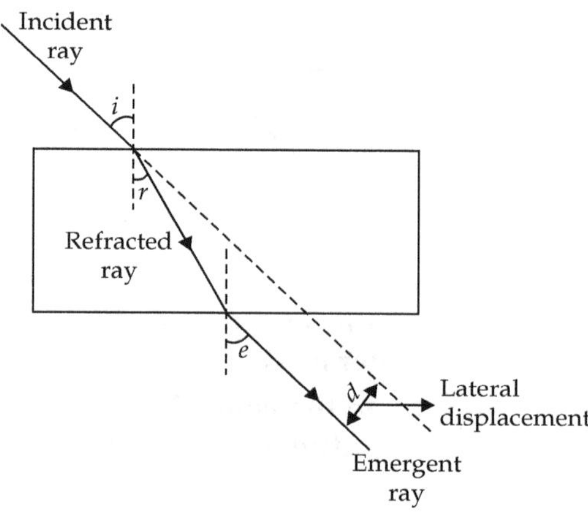

(ii) Incident ray and emergent rays are parallel to each other.

(iii) Lateral displacement is marked by d in the diagram.

Q. 14. Two parallel rays of Red and Violet travelling through air, meet the air-glass boundary as shown in the below figure:

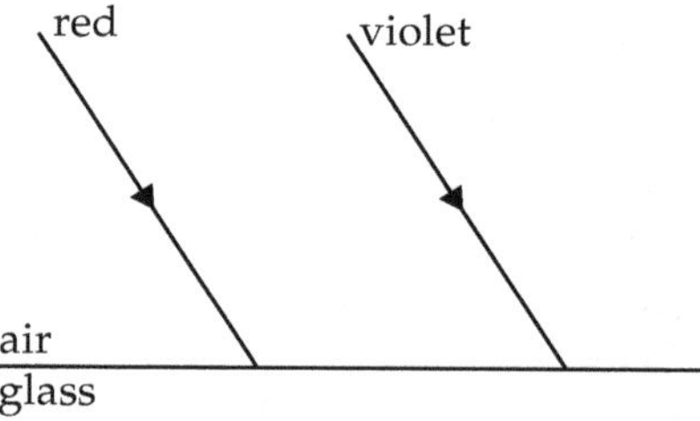

(i) Will their paths inside the glass be parallel? Give a reason for your answer.

(ii) Compare the speeds of the two rays inside the glass. **[2010]**

Ans. **(i)** No, the paths inside the glass will not be parallel.

Reason: Deviation suffered by each ray will be different because refractive index is different for different colours of light.

(ii) $v_R > v_V$. In glass, the speed of red ray is greater than violet ray.

Q. 15. How does the value of angle of deviation produced by a prism change with an increase in the:

(i) Value of angle of incidence.

(ii) Wavelength of incident light? **[2009]**

Ans. **(i)**

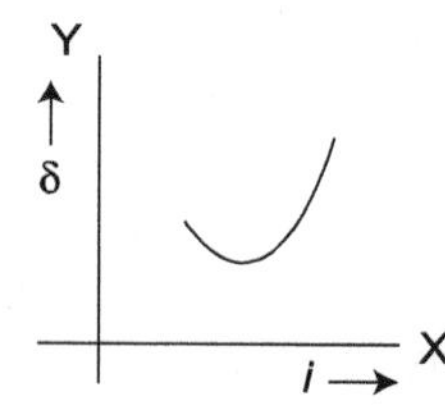

As the angle of incidence increases, initially angle of deviation decreases and later it increases after achieving to a minimum value.

(ii) As wavelength increases, angle of deviation decreases.

Q. 16. **(i)** The diagram below shows a ray of white light PQ coming from an object P and incident on the surface of a thick glass plane mirror. Copy the diagram and complete it to show the formation of three images of the object P as formed by the mirror.

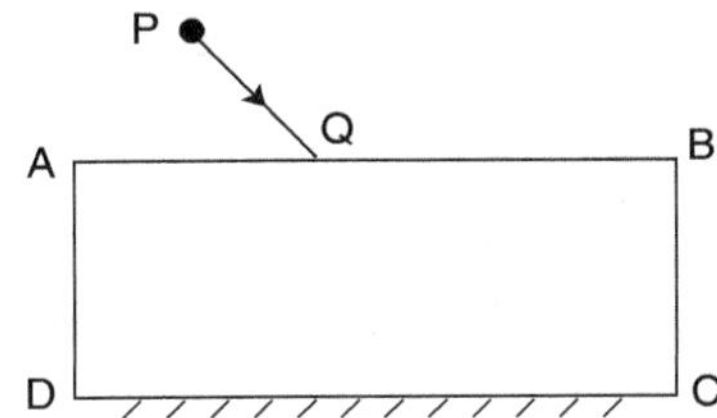

(ii) Which image will be the brightest image?

[2009]

Ans. **(i)**

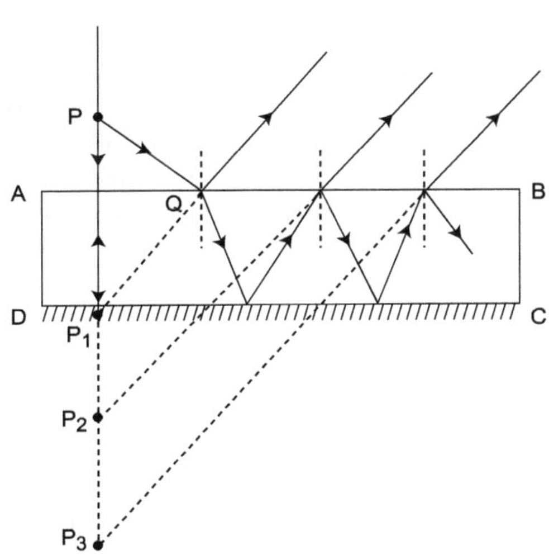

(ii) Second image will be the brightest.

Q. 17. **(i)** Draw a labelled ray diagram to illustrate: (1) critical angle, (2) total internal

reflection, for a ray of light moving from one medium to another.

(ii) Write a formula to express the relationship between refractive index of the denser medium with respect to rarer medium and its critical angle for that pair of media. [2008]

Ans. **(i)** **(1)** Ray diagram to illustrate critical angle is given below:

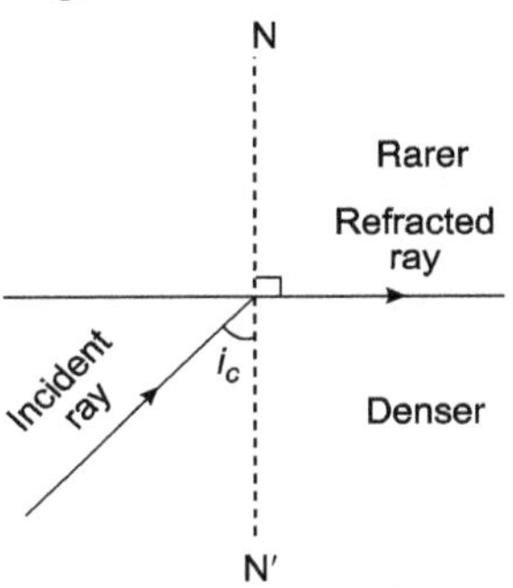

(2) Ray diagram to illustrate total internal reflection is given below:

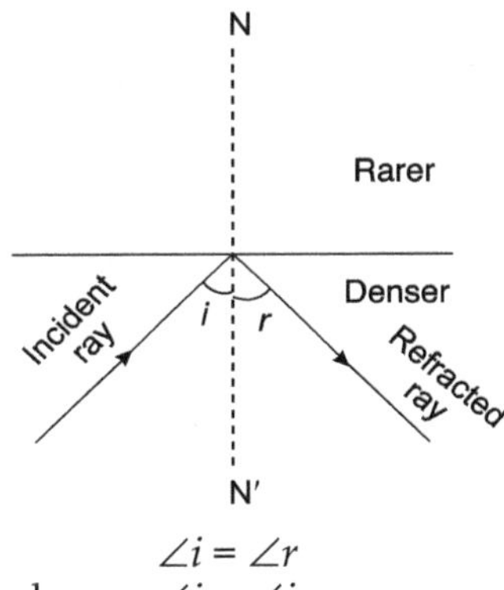

$$\angle i = \angle r$$
and $\quad \angle i > \angle i_c.$

(ii) The relationship between refractive index of the denser medium (glass) with respect to the rarer medium (air) and its critical angle is given by

$$_a\mu_g = \frac{1}{\sin i_c}$$

Long Answer Type Questions-I

Q. 1. The diagram below shows a point source P inside a water container. Four rays A, B, C, D starting from the source P are shown up to the water surface.

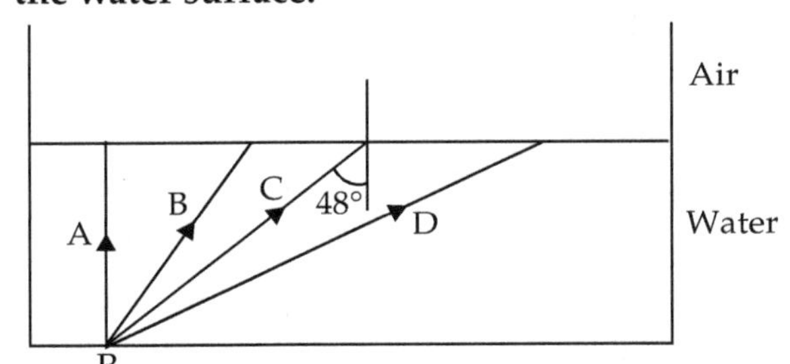

(i) Show in the diagram the path of these rays after striking the water surface. The critical angle for water air surface is 48°.

(ii) Name the phenomenon which the rays B and D exhibit. [2017]

Ans. **(i)**

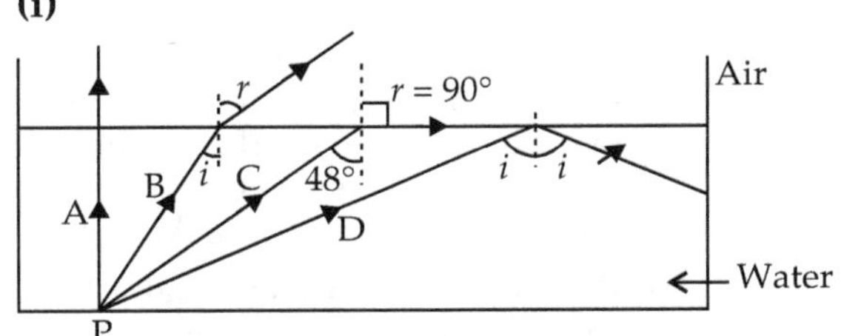

(ii) The ray B exhibits the phenomenon of refraction.

The ray D exhibits the phenomenon of total internal reflection.

Q. 2. Jatin puts a pencil into a glass container having water and is surprised to see the pencil in a different state.

(i) What change is observed in the appearance of the pencil?

(ii) Name the phenomenon responsible for the change.

(iii) Draw a ray diagram showing how the eye sees the pencil. **[2015]**

Ans. **(i)** He sees that the pencil appears to be bent.

(ii) Refraction of light

(iii)

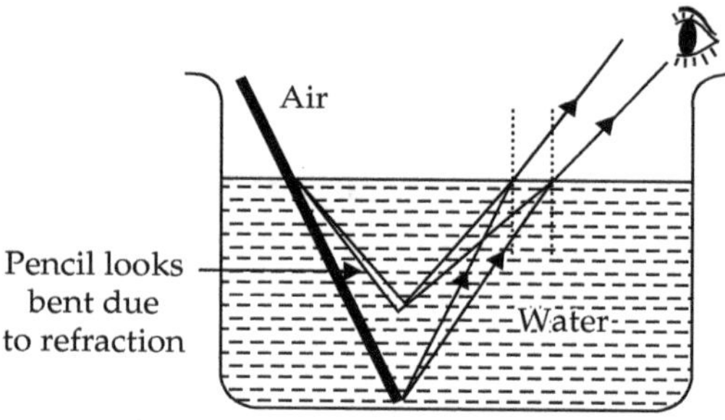

Q. 3. Light passes through a rectangular glass slab and through a triangular glass prism. In what way does the direction of the two emergent beams differ and why? **[2014]**

Ans.

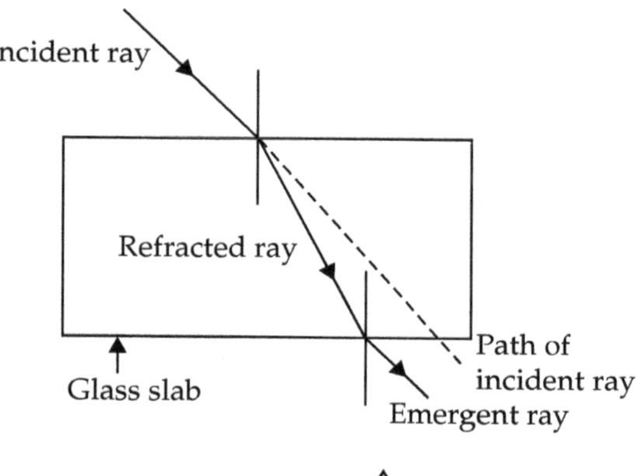

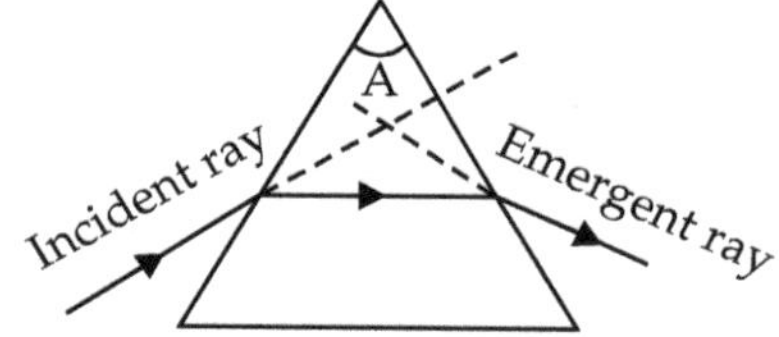

In a glass slab, the emergent ray is laterally displaced because the two refracting surfaces are parallel to each other whereas in case of prism, the emergent ray is deviated because two refracting surfaces are inclined at an angle A.

Q. 4. **(i)** With the help of a well-labelled diagram show that the apparent depth of an object, such as a coin, in water is less than its real depth.

(ii) How is the refractive index of water related to the real depth and the apparent depth of a column of water? **[2007]**

Ans. **(i)** AB = Apparent depth

AC = Real depth

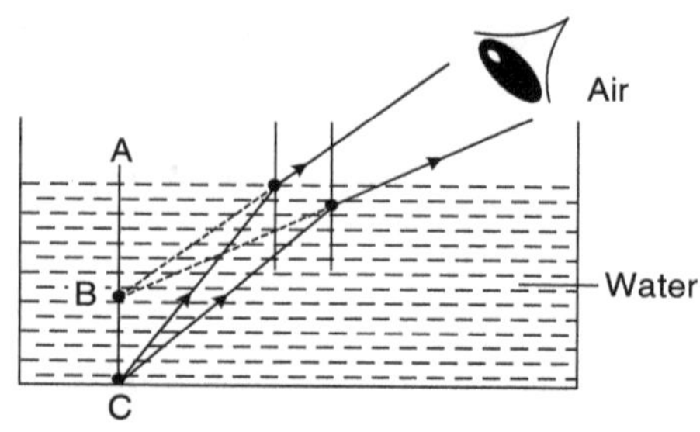

(ii) Relation between refractive index of water, real depth and apparent depth.

$$_a\mu_w = \frac{\text{Real depth}}{\text{Apparent depth}}$$

Q. 5. PQ and PR are two light rays emerging from the object P as shown in the figure below:

(i) What is the special name given to the angle of incidence ($\angle$PQN) of ray PQ?

(ii) Copy the ray diagram and complete it to show the position of the image of the object P when seen obliquely from above.

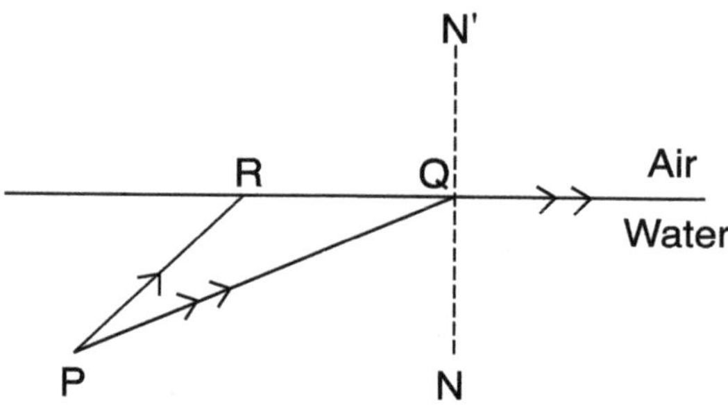

(iii) Name the phenomenon that occurs if the angle of incidence $\angle$PQN is increased still further. **[2006]**

Ans. **(i)** Critical angle

(ii) Diagram is completed as below:

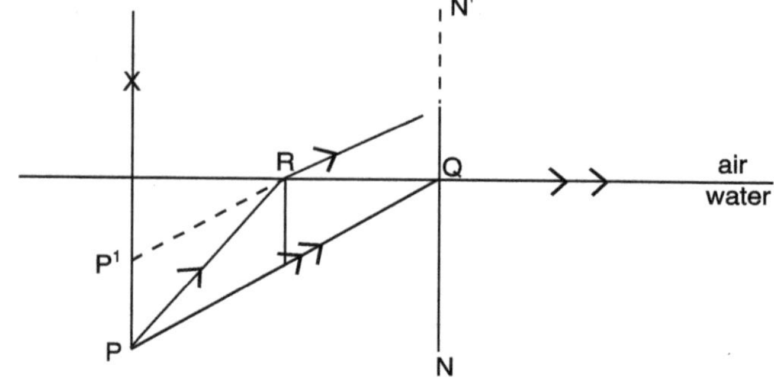

(iii) Total internal reflection of light.

4 Lenses

Short Answer Type Questions-I

Q. 1. Where should an object be placed in front of a convex lens in order to get :
(i) an enlarged real image
(ii) enlarged virtual image ? **[2020]**

Ans. (i) Object must be placed between first focal point (F_1) and the centre of curvature ($2F_1$) of the lens.
(ii) Object must be placed between the first focal point (F_1) and the lens.

Q. 2. (i) If the lens is placed in water instead of air, how does its focal length change?
(ii) Which lens, thick or thin has greater focal length? **[2019]**

Ans. (i) The focal length of the lens will increase in water (Focal length of the lens depends on the refractive index of the material of lens relative to its surrounding medium)
(ii) Thin lens will have greater focal length.

Q. 3. State the position of the object in front of a converging lens if:
(i) It produces a real and same size image of the object.
(ii) It is used as a magnifying lens. **[2018]**

Ans. (i) The object is placed on the principal axis at a distance equal to twice the focal length of the lens (or At $2F_1$).
(ii) The object is placed between the first principal focal point (F_1) and the optical centre of lens.

Q. 4. You are provided with a printed piece of paper. Using this paper how will you differentiate between a convex lens and a concave lens? **[2012]**

Ans. First we place the lens on a piece of printed paper. Then we lift it slowly. If the words of the printed paper, seen through the lens becomes bigger or magnified then it is convex lens otherwise concave lens.

Q. 5. (i) When does a ray of light falling on a lens pass through it undeviated?
(ii) Which lens can produce a real and inverted image of an object? **[2011]**

Ans. (i) A ray of light falling on the lens passes through it undeviated when it passes through optical centre of the lens.

(ii) Convex lens.

Q. 6. We can burn a piece of paper by focussing the sun rays by using a particular type of lens.
(i) Name the type of lens used for the above purpose.
(ii) Draw a ray diagram to support your answer. **[2010]**

Ans. (i) Convex lens.
(ii) Ray diagram:

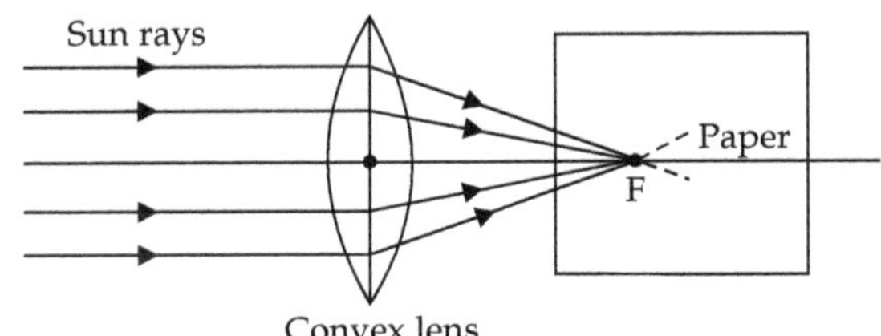

Q. 7. Copy and complete the following table: **[2009]**

Types of lens	Position of Object	Nature of Image	Size of Image
Convex	At F		
Concave	At infinity		

Ans.

Type of lens	Position of object	Nature of image	Size of image
Convex	At F	Real and Inverted	Highly magnified
Concave	At infinity	Virtual and Erect	Diminished to a point.

Q. 8. An object is placed in front of a converging lens at a distance greater than twice the focal length of the lens. Draw at a ray diagram to show the formation of the image. **[2007]**

Ans.

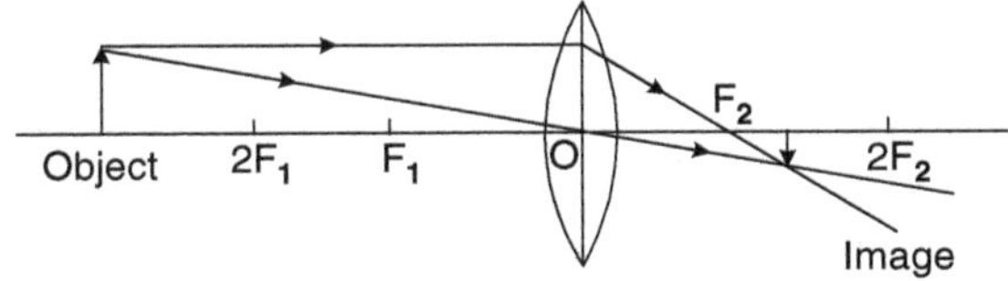

Q. 9. An object is placed in front of a convex lens such that the image formed has the same size as that of the object. Draw a ray diagram to illustrate this. **[2006]**

Ans.

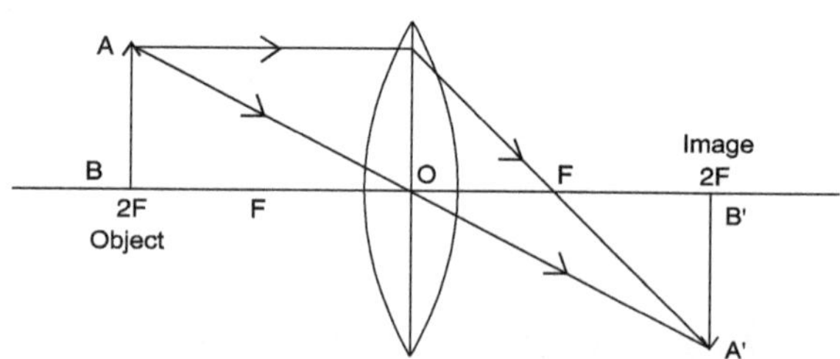

Short Answer Type Questions-II

Q. 1. A virtual, diminished image is formed when an object is placed between the optical centre and the principal focus of a lens.
  (i) Name the type of lens which forms the above image.
  (ii) Draw a ray diagram to show the formation of the image with the above stated characteristics. **[2019]**

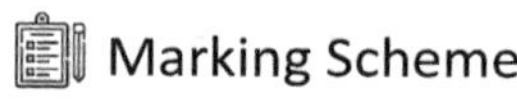

Marking Scheme

  (i) Concave lens

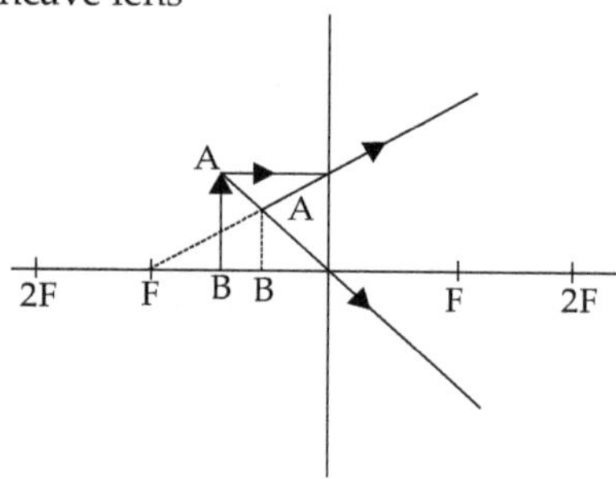

  (ii) Correct ray diagram with one ray passing through optical centre which goes undeviated Another ray parallel to the principle axis undergoing refraction and appears to pass through the principle focus. (Dotted line for virtual image and extended refracted rays & arrows marked on the rays)

Ans.   (i) A concave lens forms the given image.

  (ii) Ray diagram to show the formation of image (A'B') is given below.

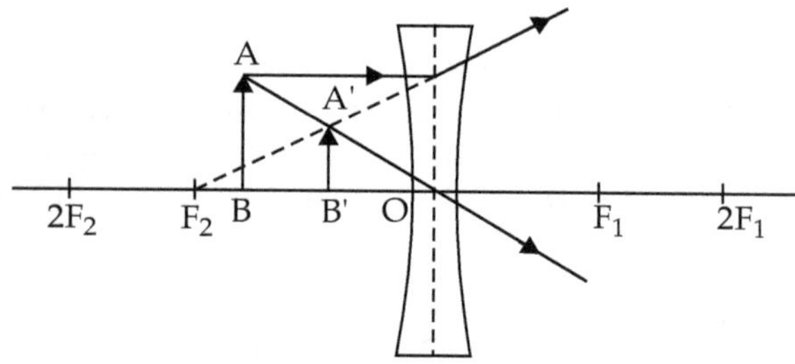

Q. 2. An object AB is placed between O and F_1 on the principal axis of a converging lens as shown in the diagram.

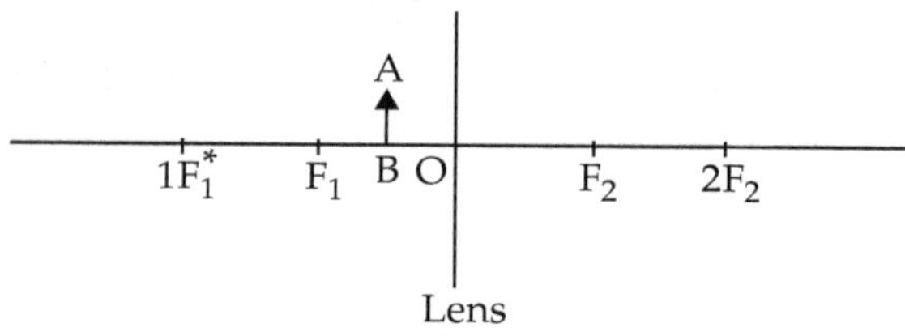

* Mark is an error by the Council. We suggest you to use '$2F_1$' instead of '$1F_1$'.
Copy the diagram and by using three standard rays starting from point A, obtain an image of the object AB. **[2018]**

Ans. A_1B_1 is the image formed.

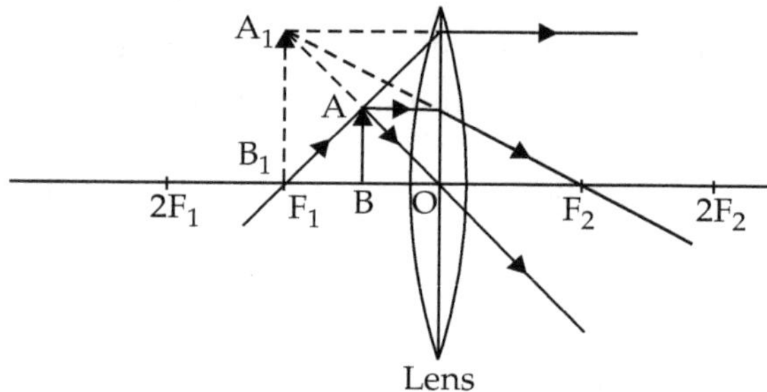

Q. 3. A lens forms an upright and diminished image of an object when the object is placed at the focal point of the given lens.
  (i) Name the lens.
  (ii) Draw a ray diagram to show the image formation. **[2017]**

Ans.   (i) Concave lens.
  (ii)

Q. 4. A lens produces a virtual image between the object and the lens.
  (i) Name the lens.
  (ii) Draw a ray diagram to show the formation of this image. **[2016]**

Ans. **(i)** Concave lens.

(ii)

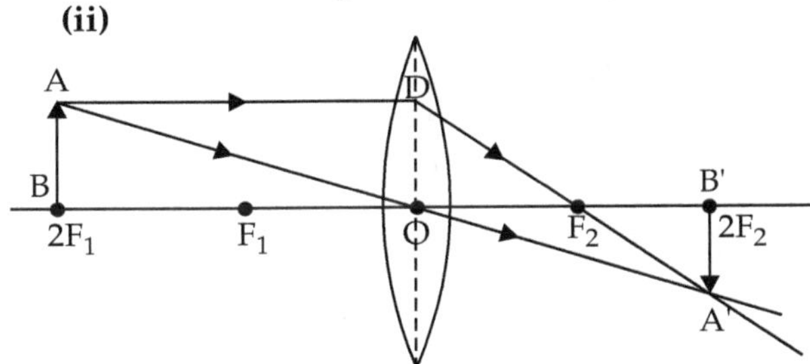

Q. 5. **(i)** Where should an object be placed so that a real and inverted image of the same size as the object is obtained using a convex lens?

(ii) Draw a ray diagram to show the formation of the image as specified in the part a (i). **[2015]**

Ans. **(i)** The object must be placed on the principal axis of a convex lens at a distance twice the focal length of the lens *i.e.*, at $2F_1$.

(ii)

Q. 6. A lens forms an erect, magnified and virtual image of an object.

(i) Name the lens.

(ii) Draw a labelled ray diagram to show the image formation. **[2014]**

Ans. **(i)** Convex lens.

(ii)

Q. 7. Define the power of a lens.

Ans. Power of a lens is defined as the measure of deviation produced in the path of light when it passes through the lens.

Or

The power of a lens is defined as the reciprocal of its focal length in metres. The S.I. unit of power is dioptre (D).

Power of lens (in D)

$$= \frac{1}{\text{Focal length (in metre)}}$$

Q. 8. **(i)** Copy and complete the diagram to show the formation of the image of the object AB.

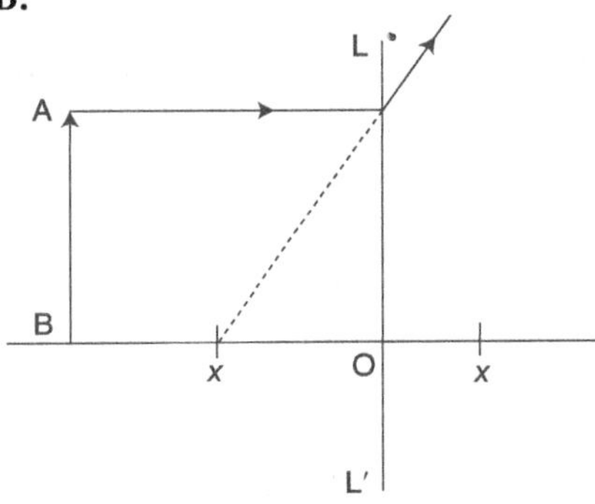

(ii) What is the name given to x? **[2009]**

Ans. **(i)**

(ii) The name of x is principal focus.

Q. 9. A linear object is placed on the axis of a lens. An image is formed by refraction in the lens. For all positions of the object on the axis of the lens, the positions of the image are always between the lens and the object.

(i) Name the lens.

(ii) Draw a ray diagram to show the formation of the image of an object placed in front of the lens at any position of your choice except infinity. **[2008]**

Ans. **(i)** The lens is a concave lens.

(ii) Ray diagram is shown below:

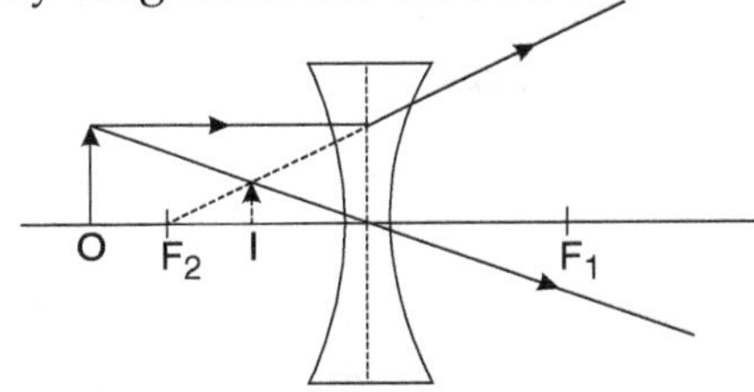

'O' is the object.

'I' is its image.

 **Long Answer Type Questions-I**

Q. 1. A lens of focal length 20 cm forms an inverted image at a distance 60 cm from the lens.
   (i) Identify the lens.
   (ii) How far is the lens present in front of the object ?
   (iii) Calculate the magnification of the image. **[2020]**

 Marking Scheme

   (i) Convex lens
   (ii) $f = 20$ cm, $v = 60$ cm
$$\frac{1}{f} = \frac{1}{v} - \frac{1}{u}$$
$$\therefore \quad \frac{1}{20} = \frac{1}{60} - \frac{1}{u}$$
$$\therefore \quad \frac{1}{u} = \frac{1}{60} - \frac{1}{20}$$
$$= \frac{1-3}{60} = \frac{-2}{60}$$
$$\therefore \quad u = -30 \text{ cm}$$
   (iii)
$$m = \frac{v}{u}$$
$$= \frac{60}{-30} = -2$$

Ans. (i) Convex lens
   (ii) $f = +20$ cm, $v = +60$ cm
$$\because \quad \frac{1}{f} = \frac{1}{v} - \frac{1}{u}$$
$$\Rightarrow \quad \frac{1}{20} = \frac{1}{60} - \frac{1}{u}$$
$$\Rightarrow \quad \frac{1}{u} = \frac{1}{60} - \frac{1}{20}$$
$$= \frac{1-3}{60} = -\frac{2}{60} = -\frac{1}{30}$$
$$\therefore \quad u = -30 \text{ cm}$$
   The lens is at a distance 30 cm in front of the object.
   (iii) $m = \dfrac{v}{u} = \dfrac{+60}{-30} = -2$

   [– ve sign because image is real]

Q. 2. An object is placed at a distance 24 cm in front of a convex lens of focal length 8 cm.
   (i) What is the nature of the image so formed?
   (ii) Calculate the distance of the image from the lens.
   (iii) Calculate the magnification of the image. **[2019]**

Marking Scheme

   (i) Rea, inverted diminished
   (ii) $1/v - 1/u = 1/f$
       $1/v = 1/8 + 1/(-24)$
       $1/v = 3 - 1/24$
       $v = 24/2 = 12$ cm
   (iii) $m = +v/-u = 12/-24 = -1/2 = -0.5$

Ans. (i) A real, inverted and diminished image is formed.
   (ii) Given: $u = -24$ cm, $f = +8$ cm

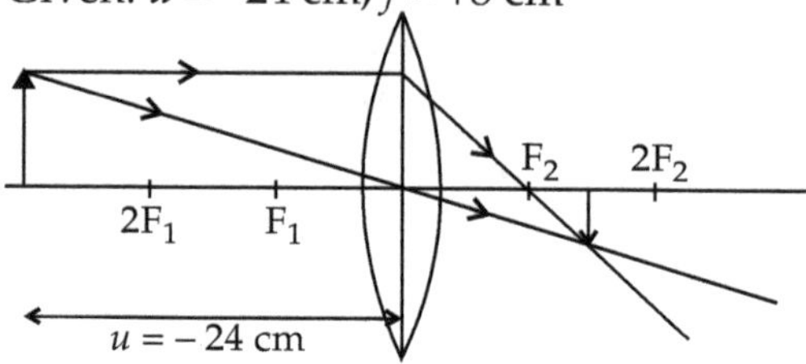

   From the relation,
$$\frac{1}{v} - \frac{1}{u} = \frac{1}{f}$$
$$\Rightarrow \quad \frac{1}{v} = \frac{1}{u} + \frac{1}{f}$$
$$= \frac{1}{-24} + \frac{1}{8}$$
$$= -\frac{1}{24} + \frac{1}{8}$$
$$= \frac{-1+3}{24} = \frac{1}{12}$$
   or $v = 12$ cm

   Thus, the image is at a distance 12 cm behind the lens.

   (iii) Magnification $(m) = \dfrac{v}{u} = \dfrac{12}{-14} = -\dfrac{1}{2}$
   Negative sign signifies inverted image.

Q. 3. An object is placed at a distance of 12 cm from a convex lens of focal length 8 cm. Find:
   (i) the position of the image
   (ii) nature of the image. **[2018]**

Ans. (i) Given: Object distance $(u) = -12$ cm
   Focal length $(f) = +8$ cm (convex lens)
   Using the relation,
$$\frac{1}{v} - \frac{1}{u} = \frac{1}{f}$$
   or $$\frac{1}{v} - \frac{1}{(-12)} = \frac{1}{8}$$

or $$\frac{1}{v}+\frac{1}{12}=\frac{1}{8}$$

or $$\frac{1}{v}=\frac{1}{8}-\frac{1}{12}=\frac{3-2}{24}=\frac{1}{24}$$

or $$v=+24 \text{ cm}$$

Therefore, the image is formed at a distance of 24 cm behind the lens (or on the other side).

(ii) The image is real, inverted and magnified.

Q. 4. **(ii) Ranbir claims to have obtained an image twice the size of the object with a concave lens. Is he correct? Give a reason for your answer.** **[2014]**

Ans. (ii) No, he is not correct because concave lens always forms virtual, erect and diminished image.

Q. 5. **An object AB is placed between $2F_1$ and F_1 on the principal axis of a convex lens as shown in the diagram:**

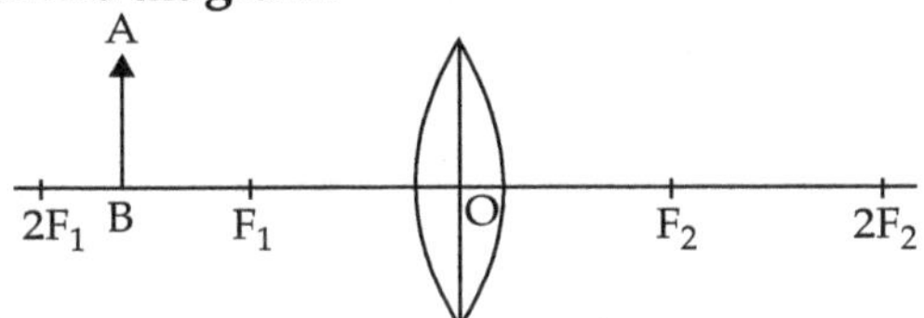

Copy the diagram and using three rays starting from point A, obtain the image of the object formed by the lens. **[2013]**

Ans.

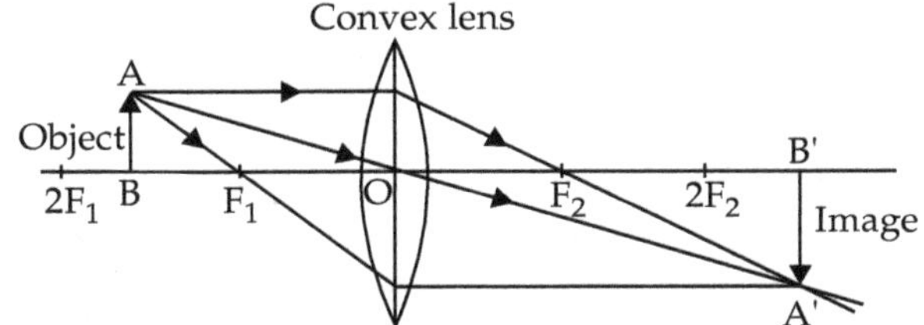

Q. 6. **A converging lens is used to obtain an image of an object placed in front of it. The inverted image is formed between F_2 and $2F_2$ of the lens.**

(i) **Where is the object placed?**

(ii) **Draw a ray diagram to illustrate the formation of the image obtained.** **[2012]**

Ans. (i) Object is beyond $2F_1$.

(ii)

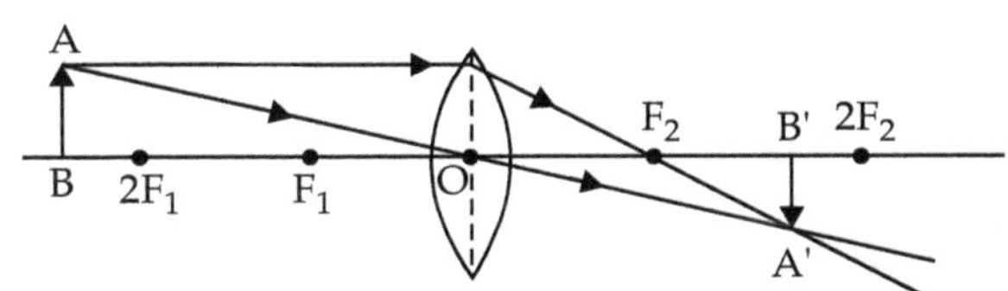

Q. 7. **An object is placed in front of a lens between its optical centre and the focus and forms a virtual, erect and diminished image.**

(i) **Name the lens which formed this image.**

(ii) **Draw a ray diagram to show the formation of the image with the above stated characteristics.** **[2011]**

Ans. (i) Concave lens.

(ii)

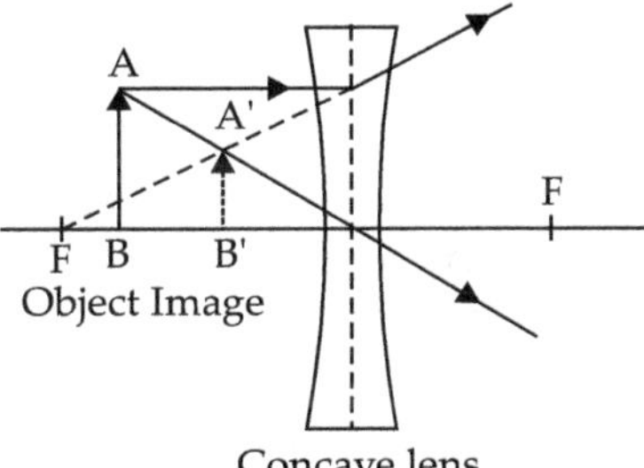

Q. 8. **An erect, magnified and virtual image is formed, when an object is placed between the optical centre and principal focus of a lens.**

(i) **Name the lens.**

(ii) **Draw a ray diagram to show the formation of the image with the above stated characteristics.** **[2010]**

Ans. (i) The lens is convex.

(ii)

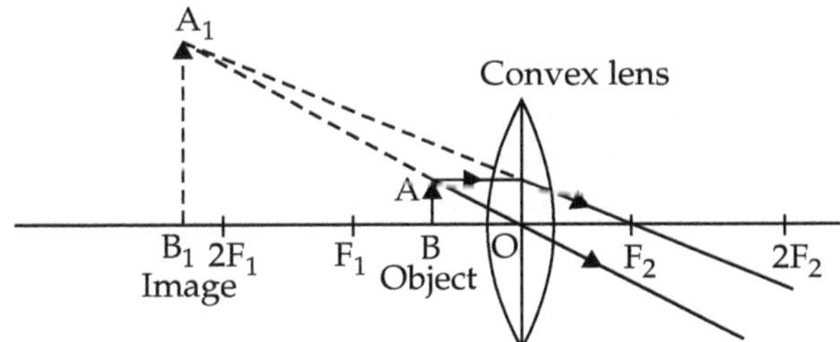

Spectrum of Light

Short Answer Type Questions-I

Q. 1. An electromagnetic radiation is used for photography in fog.
  (i) Identify the radiation.
  (ii) Why is this radiation mentioned by you, ideal for this purpose? **[2019]**

Ans. (i) Infrared radiation.
  (ii) They have low frequency, the energy associated with them is also low so they do not scatter much and can penetrate appreciably through it.

Q. 2. Draw a ray diagram to show the refraction of a monochromatic ray through a prism when it suffers minimum deviation. **[2017]**

Ans. For minimum deviation, refracted ray (BC) must be parallel to the base of the prism.

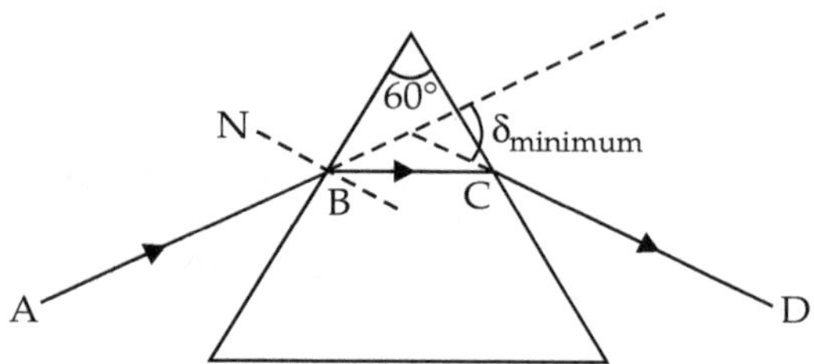

Q. 3. (i) Name the high energetic invisible electromagnetic waves which help in the study of the structure of crystals.
  (ii) State an additional use of the waves mentioned in part (i). **[2015]**

Ans. (i) X-rays
  (ii) They are used for the detection of fracture in bones.

Q. 4. (ii) Which colour of light travels fastest in any medium except air? **[2014]**

Ans. (ii) Red light travels fastest.

Q. 5. (i) Name a prism required for obtaining a spectrum of ultraviolet light.
  (ii) Name the radiations which can be detected by a thermopile. **[2014]**

Ans. (i) Quartz prism
  (ii) Infra-red radiations.

Q. 6. Why is the colour red used as a sign of danger? **[2014]**

Ans. Red colour is used as a sign of danger due to its longest wavelength and lesser deviation (scattering). Therefore, it can reach to a longer distance.

Q. 7. What is meant by 'Dispersion of light'?

Ans. Dispersion of light: When a beam of white light falls on a prism, it splits into the rays of constituent colours. This is known as dispersion of light.

Q. 8. A ray of light incident at an angle of incidence 'i' passes through an equilateral glass prism such that the refracted ray inside the prism is parallel to its base and emerges from the prism at an angle of emergence 'e'.
  (i) How is the angle of emergence 'e' related to the angle of incidence 'i'?
  (ii) What can you say about the value of the angle of deviation in such a situation? **[2012]**

Ans. (i) Angle of emergence $\angle e$
            = Angle of incidence $\angle i$
  (ii) Angle of deviation becomes minimum in this situation.

Q. 9. (i) Why is white light considered to be polychromatic in nature?
  (ii) Give the range of the wavelength of those electromagnetic waves which are visible to us. **[2009]**

Ans. (i) White light is made up of seven colours i.e., VIBGYOR that is why it is considered to be polychromatic.
  (ii) Range of wavelength which are visible to us are 4000 Å to 8000 Å.

Q. 10. Complete the path of the light ray entering the first isosceles right-angled glass prism till it emerges from the second identical prism. **[2008]**

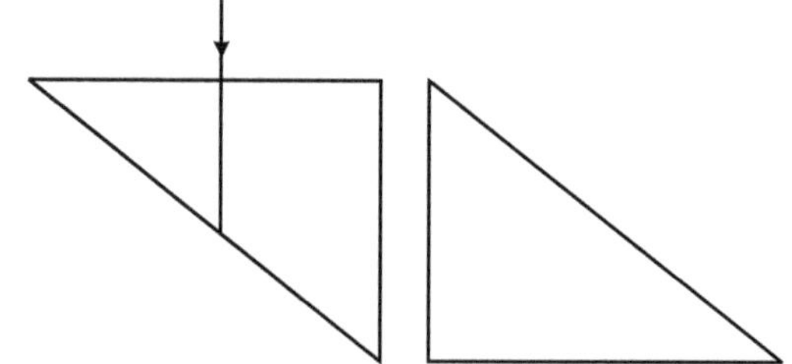

Ans.

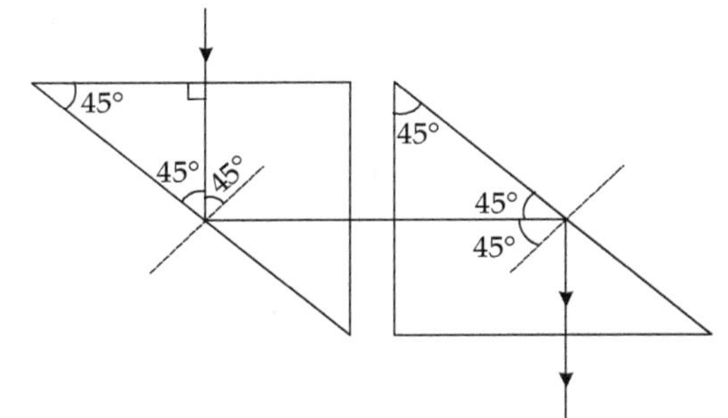

Q. 11. Why are infra-red radiations preferred over ordinary visible light for taking photographs in fog? [2007]

Ans. Infra-red radiations scattere less so they can penetrate appreciably through fog and better photographs can be taken in comparison to visible light.

Short Answer Type Questions-II

Q. 1. Name the radiations:

(i) that are used for photography at night.

(ii) used for detection of fracture in bones.

(iii) whose wavelength range is from 100 Å to 4000 Å (or 10 nm to 400 nm). [2013]

Ans. (i) Infrared radiations.

(ii) X-rays.

(iii) UV radiations.

Q. 2. (i) Suggest one way, in each case, by which we can detect the presence of:

(1) Infra-red radiations

(2) Ultraviolet radiations

(ii) Give one use of Infra-red radiations.

[2011]

Ans. (i) **(1) Infra-red radiations:** These are detected by a thermopile.

(2) Ultraviolet radiation: When a silver chloride solution is taken in a test tube and is passed from red to violet light no change is seen. But beyond the violet end, the solution first turns violet and then it turns dark brown.

(ii) Infrared radiations are used in remote control of television.

Q. 3. (i) A particular type of high energy invisible electromagnetic rays help us to study the structure of crystals. Name these rays and give another important use of these rays.

(ii) How does the speed of light in glass change on increasing the wavelength of light? [2007]

Ans. (i) X-rays

Use: X-rays are used for detection of fracture in bones, teeth, etc.

(ii) The speed of light increases on increasing the wavelength of light.

Q. 4. The diagram given below shows a right-angled prism with a ray of light incident on the side AB. (The critical angle for glass in 42°)

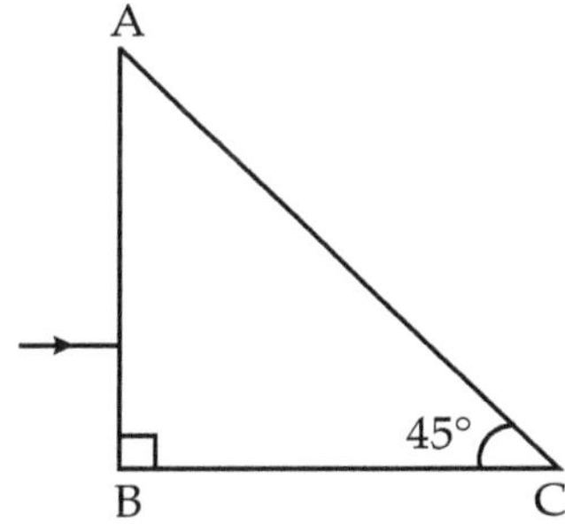

(i) Copy the diagram and complete the path of the ray of light in and out of the glass prism.

(ii) What is the value of the angle of deviation shown by the ray? [2007]

Ans. (i) Figure.

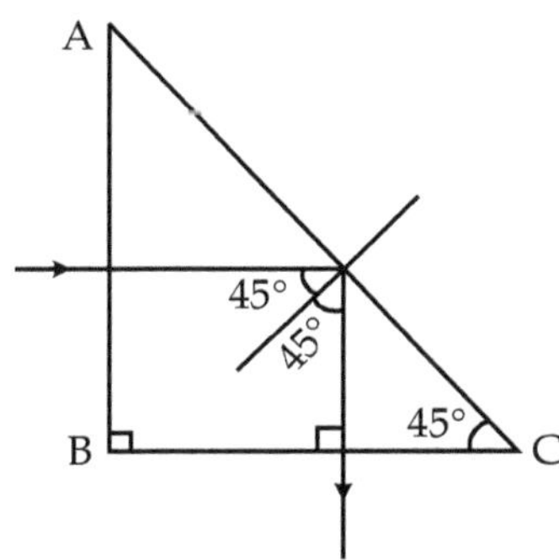

(ii) 90°

 Long Answer Type Questions -I

Q. 1. **(i)** The diagram below shows a ray of light incident on an equilateral glass prism placed in minimum deviation position.

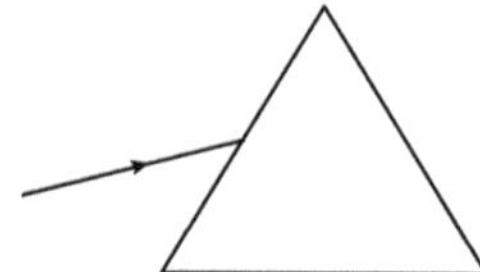

Copy the diagram and complete it to show the path of the refracted ray and the emergent ray.

(ii) How are angle of incidence and angle of emergence related to each other in this position of the prism? [2008]

Ans. **(i)**

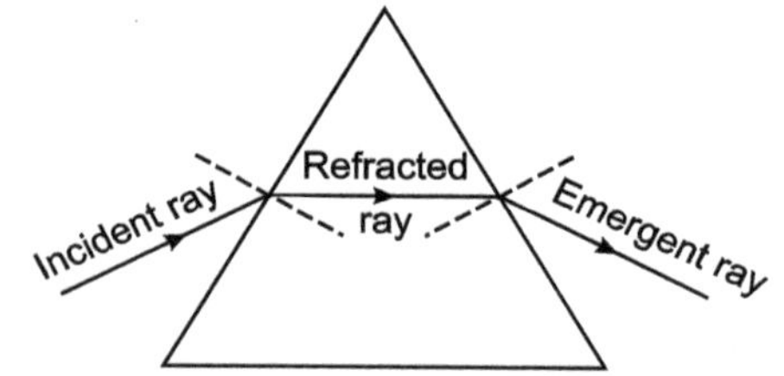

(ii) Angle of incidence = Angle of emergence, when the prism is in the position of minimum deviation.

? Short Answer Type Questions-I

Q. 1. Draw a graph between displacement from mean position and time for a body executing free vibration in a vacuum. **[2020]**

Ans.

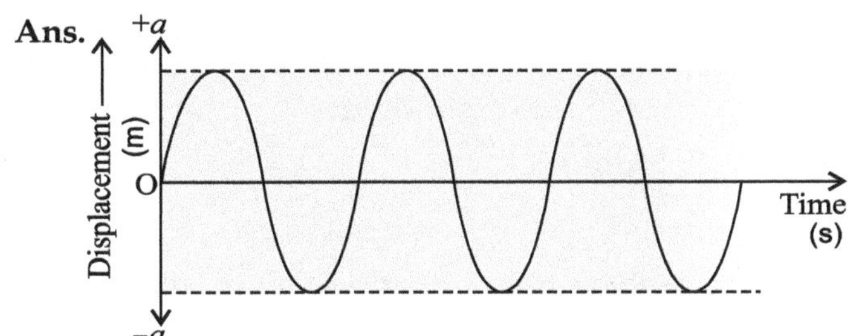

Q. 2. A sound wave travelling in water has wavelength 0.4 m.

Is this wave audible in air ? (The speed of sound in water = 1400 ms⁻¹) **[2020]**

Ans. Given:

$$\lambda = 0.4 \text{ m}$$
$$V = 1400 \text{ ms}^{-1}$$

$\because \qquad V = f\lambda \Rightarrow f = \dfrac{V}{\lambda} = \dfrac{1400}{0.4} \text{ Hz}$

$$= 3500 \text{ Hz}$$

∵ Frequency remains unchanged in air, the wave is audible in air because 3500 Hz falls in the audible range of frequency.

Q. 3. A man playing a flute is able to produce notes of different frequencies. If he closes the holes near his mouth, will the pitch of the note produced, increase or decrease? Give a reason. **[2019]**

Ans. If the man closes the holes in a flute near his mouth a sound of lower frequency note will be produced because the length of vibrating air column increases and the frequency of vibrating air column is inversely proportional to the length of vibrating air column.

Q. 4. Two waves of the same pitch have amplitudes in the ratio 1 : 3. What will be the ratio of their:
  (i) intensities and
  (ii) frequencies? **[2019]**

Ans. **(i)** Same pitch

$$\dfrac{A_1}{A_2} = \dfrac{1}{3}$$

Intensities, $I \propto A^2$

$\therefore \qquad \dfrac{I_1}{I_2} = \left(\dfrac{A_1}{A_2}\right)^2 = \dfrac{1}{9}$

(ii) Pitch is same ⇒ frequency is same.

Q. 5. **(i)** Define resonant vibrations.
  (ii) Which characteristic of sound, makes it possible to recognize a person by his voice without seeing him? **[2019]**

Ans. **(i)** When the frequency of the externally applied periodic force on a body is equal to its natural frequency, the body readily begins, to vibrate with an increased amplitude. Such large amplitude vibrations are called resonant vibrations.
  (ii) Quality of sound or Timbre.

Q. 6. Displacement distance graph of two sound waves A and B, travelling in a medium, are as shown in the diagram below:

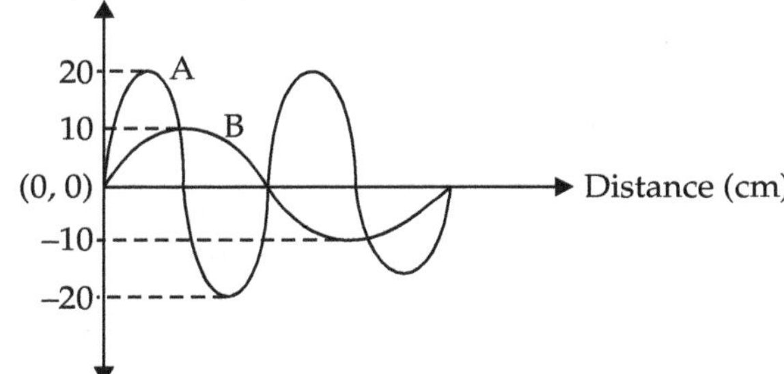

Study the two sound waves and compare their:
  (i) Amplitudes
  (ii) Wavelengths **[2018]**

Ans. **For wave A:** Amplitude (a_1) = 20 cm, Wavelength $(\lambda_1) = \lambda$ cm (say)
For wave B: Amplitude (a_2) = 10 cm, Wavelength $(\lambda_2) = 2\lambda$ cm

(i) $\dfrac{a_1}{a_2} = \dfrac{20}{10} = \dfrac{2}{1}$

The amplitude of wave A is two times of the amplitude of wave B.

(ii) $\dfrac{\lambda_1}{\lambda_2} = \dfrac{\lambda}{2\lambda} = \dfrac{1}{2}$

The wavelength of wave A is half of the wavelength of wave B.

Q. 7. **(i)** **What do you understand by free vibrations of a body?**

(ii) **Why does the amplitude of a vibrating body continuously decrease during damped vibrations?** **[2018]**

Ans. **(i)** The periodic vibrations of a body in the absence of any external periodic force on it, are called free (or natural) vibrations.

(ii) The amplitude of a vibrating body continuously decreases during damped vibrations because of the frictional (resistive) force due to the surrounding medium causes the energy loss.

Q. 8. **The human ear can detect continuous sounds in the frequency range from 20 Hz to 20000 Hz. Assuming that the speed of sound in air is 330 ms⁻¹ for all frequencies, calculate the wavelengths corresponding to the given extreme frequencies of the audible range.**
[2017]

Ans. For the lower extreme frequency of audible range:

$$\text{Frequency } (f_1) = 20 \text{ Hz}$$
$$\text{Speed of sound in air } (v) = 330 \text{ ms}^{-1}$$

$$\therefore \quad \text{Wavelength } (\lambda_1) = \frac{v}{f_1}$$
$$= \frac{330}{20} \text{ m} = 16.5 \text{ m}$$

For the upper extreme frequency of audible range:

$$\text{Frequency } (f_2) = 20{,}000 \text{ Hz}$$
$$\text{Speed of sound in air } (v) = 330 \text{ ms}^{-1}$$

$$\therefore \quad \text{Wavelength } (\lambda_2) = \frac{v}{f_2}$$
$$= \frac{330}{20{,}000} \text{ m}$$
$$= 0.0165 \text{ m}$$

Q. 9. **An enemy plane is at a distance of 300 km from a radar. In how much time the radar will be able to detect the plane? Take velocity of radio waves as 3×10^8 ms⁻¹.** **[2017]**

Ans. Given: Distance $(d) = 300 \text{ km} = 300 \times 10^3 \text{ m}$
$$= 3 \times 10^5 \text{ m}$$

Velocity (v) of radio waves $= 3 \times 10^8 \text{ ms}^{-1}$

Time taken by radar to detect the plane,

$$t = \frac{2d}{v} = \frac{2 \times 3 \times 10^5}{3 \times 10^8} \text{ s}$$
$$= 2 \times 10^{-3} \text{ s}$$

Q. 10. **How is the frequency of a stretched string related to:**

(i) **its length?**

(ii) **its tension?** **[2017]**

Ans. **(i)** The frequency of vibration of a stretched string is inversely proportional to its length, $\left(f \propto \dfrac{1}{l} \right)$.

(ii) The frequency of vibration of a stretched string is directly proportional to the square root of the tension applied on the string, $\left(f \propto \sqrt{T} \right)$.

Q. 11. **The ratio of amplitude of two waves is 3 : 4. What is the ratio of their:**

(i) **loudness?**

(ii) **frequencies?** **[2016]**

Ans. It is given that the ratio of amplitude of two waves is 3 : 4.

(i) As loudness is directly proportional to the square of the amplitude. So, the ratio of the two waves' loudness is 9 : 16.

(ii) As frequency does not depend upon amplitude. So, the ratio of frequency of the two waves is 1 : 1.

Q. 12. **State two ways by which the frequency of transverse vibrations of a stretched string can be increased.** **[2016]**

Ans. The frequency of transverse vibrations of a stretched string can be increased:

(i) by increasing the tension in the string.

(ii) by decreasing the length of the vibrating string.

Q. 13. **(i)** **Draw a graph between displacement and the time for a body executing free vibrations.**

(ii) **Where can a body execute free vibrations?**
[2015]

Ans. **(i)**

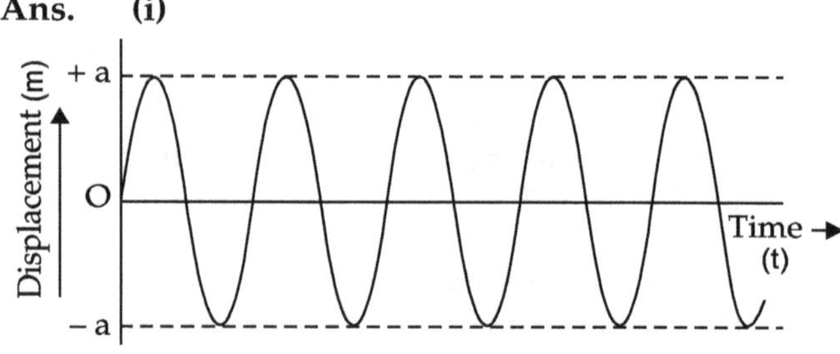

(ii) A body can execute free vibrations in vacuum because the presence of any medium offers some resistance, as a result of which the amplitude of vibrations does not remain constant.

Q. 14. (i) State the safe limit of sound level in terms of decibel for human hearing.

(ii) Name the characteristic of sound in relation to its waveform. [2015]

Ans. (i) The safe limit of sound level for human hearing is in the range of 0 to 80 dB.

(ii) The characteristic of sound in relation to its waveform is quality or timbre.

Q. 15. (i) What are mechanical waves?

(ii) Name one property of waves that do not change when the wave passes from one medium to another. [2014]

Ans. (i) Mechanical waves are waves which requires medium for their propagation. *E.g.*– sound waves

(ii) Property of wave that does not change when it passes from one medium to another is frequency.

Q. 16. A bucket kept under a running tap is getting filled with water. A person sitting at a distance is able to get an idea when the bucket is about to be filled.

(i) What change takes place in the sound to give this idea?

(ii) What causes the change in the sound? [2013]

Ans. (i) As the bucket is filled, the sound becomes shriller due to decrease in length of air column and increase in frequency.

(ii) The change in sound takes place due to change in frequency of sound due to decrease in the length of the air column.

Q. 17. A sound made on the surface of a lake takes 3 s to reach a boatman.

How much time will it take to reach a diver inside the water at the same depth?

Velocity of sound in air = 330 ms^{-1}

Velocity of sound in water = 1450 ms^{-1} [2013]

Ans. Given, depth *i.e.*, distance is same in both the cases.

Now,
$$s = \frac{d}{t}$$

$$\Rightarrow \quad 330 = \frac{d}{3}$$

$$\Rightarrow \quad d = 990 \text{ m}$$

Now for the diver inside water

$$s' = \frac{d}{t'}$$

or
$$t' = \frac{d}{s'} = \frac{990}{1450}$$

$$\therefore \quad t' = 0.682 \text{ sec.}$$

Q. 18. Which characteristics of sound will change if there is a change in

(i) its amplitude (ii) its waveform. [2012]

Ans. (i) If there is a change in amplitude of sound then its loudness will change.

(ii) If there is a change in waveform of sound then its quality will change.

Q. 19. (i) Name one factor which affects the frequency of sound emitted due to vibrations in an air column.

(ii) Name the unit used for measuring the sound level. [2012]

Ans. (i) Length of the air column.

(ii) Decibel.

Q. 20. When acoustic resonance takes place, a loud sound is heard. Why does this happen? Explain. [2011]

Ans. When acoustic resonance takes place, a loud sound is heard. This is because the natural frequency of the vibrating body becomes equal to the frequency of external applied force due to which amplitude becomes large and hence loud sound is heard.

Q. 21. (i) Three musical instruments give out notes at the frequencies listed below. Flute : 400 Hz; Guitar : 200 Hz; Trumpet : 500 Hz. Which one of these has the highest pitch?

(ii) With which of the following frequencies does a tuning fork of 256 Hz resonate : 288 Hz, 314 Hz, 333 Hz, 512 Hz? [2011]

Ans. (i) Trumpet (500 Hz) will have the highest pitch.

(ii) Tuning fork will resonate with 512 Hz.

Q. 22. Name the subjective property:

(i) of sound related to its frequency.

(ii) of light related to its wavelength. [2010]

Ans. (i) The subjective property of sound related to its frequency is pitch.

(ii) The subjective property of light related to its wavelength is colour.

Q. 23. State two differences between light waves and sound waves. **[2010]**

Ans. The two differences between light waves and sound waves are:

Light waves	Sound waves
1. Light waves do not require a medium for propagation.	1. Sound waves require a medium for propagation.
2. Light waves travel with a speed of 3×10^8 m/s.	2. Sound waves travel with a speed of 332 m/s.

Q. 24. Two waves of the same pitch have their amplitudes in the ratio 2 : 3.

   (i) What will be the ratio of their loudness?

   (ii) What will be the ratio of their frequencies?

   [2010]

Ans. **(i)** Given: Amplitude ratio, $a_1 : a_2 = 2 : 3$

$\because$ Loudness $\propto$ (Amplitude)^2

i.e., $L \propto a^2$

$\therefore$ $\dfrac{L_1}{L_2} = \dfrac{a_1^2}{a_2^2}$

$= \dfrac{2^2}{3^2} = \dfrac{4}{9}$

$\Rightarrow$ $L_1 : L_2 = 4 : 9$

(ii) The pitch of the two waves is same.

And Frequency $\propto$ Pitch

Hence, the frequency of the two waves is also same.

$\therefore$ Ratio of frequencies $= 1 : 1$

Q. 25. An ultrasonic wave is sent from a ship towards the bottom of the sea. It is found that the time interval between the sending and the receiving of the wave is 1.5 seconds. Calculate the depth of the sea if the velocity of sound in sea water is 1400 ms^{-1}. **[2009]**

Ans. Given: $v = 1400$ m/sec.

We know that, $v = \dfrac{2d}{t}$

$\Rightarrow$ $1400 = \dfrac{2d}{1.5}$

$\Rightarrow$ $d = \dfrac{1400 \times 1.5}{2}$

$= 1050$ m

Q. 26. A stringed musical instrument, such as the Sitar, is provided with a number of wires of different thicknesses. Explain the reason for this. **[2009]**

Ans. String instruments such as sitar is provided with number of wires of different thickness so that frequency of vibration could be altered thereby changing the pitch of the sound produced.

Q. 27. A radar sends a signal to an aeroplane at a distance 45 km away with a speed of 3×10^8 ms^{-1}. After how long is the signal received back from the aeroplane? **[2008]**

Ans. Given: Distance = 45 km.

          Speed = 3×10^8 m/sec.

$$\text{Speed} = \dfrac{\text{Distance}}{\text{Time}}$$

$$3 \times 10^8 = \dfrac{45 \times 1000}{t}$$

$$t = 0.00015 \text{ sec.}$$

Time taken to receive back the signal will be $2t$.

So,   T $= 0.00015 \times 2 = 0.0003$ sec.

Q. 28. Define the terms:

   (i) Amplitude

   (ii) Frequency (as applied to sound waves). **[2007]**

Ans. **(i)** Amplitude: During vibration the maximum displacement from mean position of a wave is called amplitude.

(ii) Frequency: The number of vibrations per second taken by a wave is called its frequency.

Q. 29. Explain why musical instruments like the guitar are provided with a hollow box. **[2006]**

Ans. Musical instruments like guitar are provided with a hollow box so that when the strings are set into vibration, forced vibrations are produced in box. Since the box has a large area, it sets a large volume of air into vibration which produces a loud sound of same frequency as that of the string.

Short Answer Type Questions-II

Q. 1. **(i)** Name the system which enables us to locate underwater objects by transmitting ultrasonic waves and detecting the reflecting impulse.
(ii) What are acoustically measurable quantities related to pitch and loudness ? **[2020]**

 **Marking Scheme**
(i) SONAR/Sound Navigation and Ranging.
(ii) For pitch—it is frequency.
For loudness—it is intensity of sound.

Ans. **(i)** SONAR or sound navigation and ranging.
(ii) The acoustically measurable quantities related to pitch is frequency or wavelength and for loudness, it is intensity of sound.

Q. 2. It is observed that during march-past we hear a base drum distinctly from a distance compared to the side drums.
(i) Name the characteristics of sound associated with the above observation.
(ii) Give a reason for the above observation. **[2019]**

 **Marking Scheme**
(i) Loudness.
(ii) Base drum has greater surface area compared to the side drums. Loudness is increased with the increase area of vibration

Ans. **(i)** Loudness.
(ii) The sound produced from the base drum is louder than the sound produced by the side drums, hence it can be heard distinctly from a distance as compared to the side drums.

Q. 3. A pendulum has a frequency of 4 vibrations per second. An observer starts the pendulum and fires a gun simultaneously. He hears the echo from the cliff after 6 vibrations of the pendulum. If the velocity of sound in air is 340 m/s, find the distance between the cliff and the observer. **[2019]**

Marking Scheme
$\because$ 4 vibrations in I s
$\therefore$ 6 vibrations = ? $\therefore$ $t = \dfrac{6}{4} = \dfrac{3}{2} = 1.5s$
$$V = \frac{2d}{t} \quad \therefore \quad 340 = \frac{2d}{1.5}$$
$$\therefore \quad d = \frac{340 \times 1.5}{2} = 255\, m$$

Ans. Time taken to complete 4 vibrations = 1 second
Time taken to complete 1 vibration = $\dfrac{1}{4}$ second
$\therefore$ Time taken to complete 6 vibrations
$$= \frac{1}{4} \times 6 \text{ second}$$
$$= 1.5 \text{ second}$$
Time $(t) = 1.5$ s
Velocity $(v) = 340$ m/s
$\therefore$ Distance between the cliff and observer
$$d = \frac{v \times t}{2}$$
$$= \frac{340 \times 1.5}{2} \text{ m}$$
$$= 255 \text{ m}$$

Q. 4.

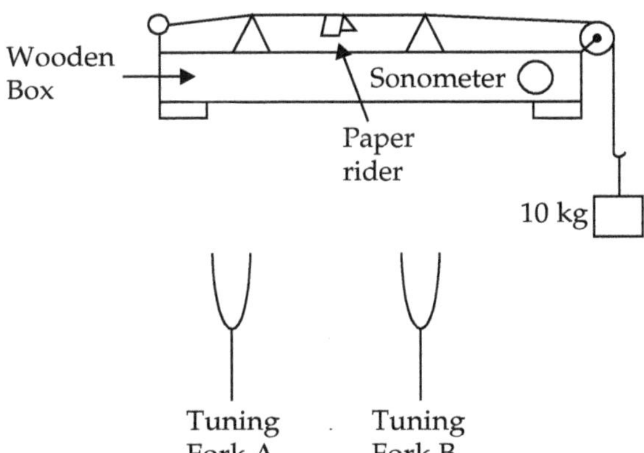

The diagram above shows a wire stretched over a sonometer. Stems of two vibrating tuning forks A and B are touched to the wooden box of the sonometer. It is observed that the paper rider (a small piece of paper folded at the centre) present on the wire flies off when the stem of vibrating tuning fork B is touched to the wooden box but the paper just vibrates when the stem of vibrating tuning fork A is touched to the wooden box.
(i) Name the phenomenon when the paper rider just vibrates.
(ii) Name the phenomenon when the paper rider flies off.
(iii) Why does the paper rider fly off when the stem of tuning fork B is touched to the box? **[2018]**

Ans. **(i)** Forced vibration.
(ii) Resonance.
(iii) The paper rider flies off when the stem of the tuning fork B is touched to the box because the frequency of vibration of tuning fork B is equal to the natural frequency of vibration of the stretched wire holding the paper rider and resonance occurs.

Q. 5. Name the factor that determines:
  (i) Loudness of the sound heard.
  (ii) Quality of the note.
  (iii) Pitch of the note. [2017]
Ans. **(i)** Amplitude.
  (ii) Waveform.
  (iii) Frequency.

Q. 6. **(i)** What are damped vibrations?
  (ii) Give one example of damped vibrations.
  (iii) Name the phenomenon that causes a loud sound when the stem of a vibrating tuning fork is kept pressed on the surface of a table. [2017]
Ans. **(i)** The periodic vibrations of decreasing amplitude in the presence of resistive force are called damped vibrations.
  (ii) A tuning fork when stroked on a rubber pad, executes damped vibrations in air.
  (iii) Forced vibrations.

Q. 7. **(i)** Name the waves used for echo depth sounding.
  (ii) Give one reason for their use for the above purpose.
  (iii) Why are the waves mentioned by you not audible to us? [2016]
Ans. **(i)** Ultrasonic waves.
  (ii) The ultrasonic waves are used because they can travel undeviated through a long distance.
  (iii) The ultrasonic waves are not audible to us because they have frequency of more than audible range of frequency 20000 Hz.

Q. 8. **(i)** What is an echo?
  (ii) State two conditions for an echo to take place. [2016]
Ans. **(i)** The clear and distinct sound heard after reflection from a distant obstacle (cliff, wall etc.) after the original sound has ceased, is called an echo.
  (ii) Conditions for an echo to take place are:
  (1) The minimum distance between the source of sound and the reflector in air must be 17 m. It is different in different medium depending upon the speed of sound in that medium.
  (2) The size of the reflector must be large enough as compared to the wavelength of sound wave.

Q. 9. A person standing between two vertical cliffs and 480 m from the nearest cliff shouts. He hears the first echo after 3 s and the second echo 2 s later.
  Calculate:
  (i) The speed of sound.
  (ii) The distance of the other cliff from the person. [2015]

Ans. The first echo is heard from the nearest cliff. The total distance travelled by sound to reach the first cliff and then come back = 2 × 480 m = 960 m, Time taken = 3 second

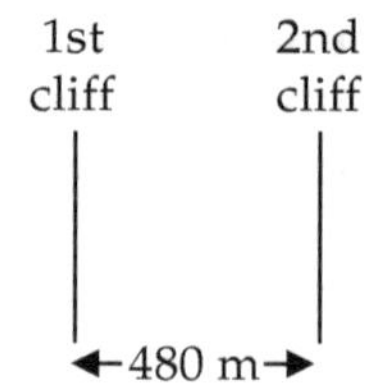

(i) Speed of sound
$$= \frac{\text{Total distance travelled}}{\text{Time taken}}$$
$$= \frac{960}{3} \text{m/s}$$
$$= 320 \text{ m/s}$$

(ii) Time taken for the second echo
$$= (3 + 2) \text{ second}$$
$$= 5 \text{ second}$$
Distance of the second cliff from the observer
$$= \frac{(\text{speed} \times \text{time})}{2}$$
$$= \frac{(320 \times 5)}{2} = 800 \text{ m}$$

Q. 10. A type of electromagnetic wave has wavelength 50 Å.
  (i) Name the wave.
  (ii) What is the speed of the wave in vacuum?
  (iii) State one use of this type of wave. [2014]
Ans. **(i)** X-rays.
  (ii) Speed of the wave in vacuum is 3×10^8 m/s.
  (iii) X-rays are used for determining fracture of bones, hidden objects in customs at airports.

Q. 11. **(i)** State one important property of waves used for echo depth sounding.
  (ii) A radar sends a signal to an aircraft at a distance of 30 km away and receives it back after 2×10^{-4} second. What is the speed of the signal? [2014]
Ans. **(i)** An important property of such type of waves is that they travel undeviated through long distances.

  (ii) Speed, $v = \dfrac{2d}{t}$
$$\Rightarrow \quad v = \frac{2 \times 30 \times 10^3}{2 \times 10^{-4}}$$
$$\Rightarrow \quad v = \frac{30 \times 10^3}{10^{-4}}$$
$$\Rightarrow \quad v = 3 \times 10^4 \times 10^4$$
$\therefore$ Speed of the signal,
$$v = 3 \times 10^8 \text{ m/s}$$

Q. 12. **(i)** What is the principle on which SONAR is based?

(ii) An observer stands at a certain distance away from a cliff and produces a loud sound. He hears the echo of the sound after 1.8 s. Calculate the distance between the cliff and the observer if the velocity of sound in air is 340 ms⁻¹. **[2013]**

Ans. **(i)** SONAR is based on the principle of reflection of sound *i.e.*, echo.

(ii) Here,
$$s = \frac{2d}{t}$$
$$\Rightarrow \quad 2d = s \times t$$
$$\Rightarrow \quad d = \frac{340 \times 1.8}{2}$$
$$\therefore \quad d = 306 \text{ m.}$$

Q. 13. A vibrating tuning fork is placed over the mouth of a burette filled with water. The tap of the burette is opened and the water level gradually starts falling. It is found that the sound from the tuning fork becomes very loud for a particular length of the water column.

(i) Name the phenomenon taking place when this happens.

(ii) Why does the sound become very loud for this length of the water column? **[2013]**

Ans. **(i)** Resonance.

(ii) The frequency of the tuning fork and the natural frequency of the vibrating air column become equal. The air column vibrates with larger amplitude thus producing a loud sound.

Q. 14. **(i)** What is meant by Resonance?

(ii) State two ways in which Resonance differs from Forced vibrations. **[2012]**

Ans. **(i)** **Resonance:** When the frequency of an externally applied periodic force on a body is equal to the natural frequency of the body, the body vibrates with increased amplitude thus producing a loud sound. This phenomenon is called resonance.

(ii) **(1)** In resonance, it is necessary that frequency of externally applied force should be equal to natural frequency of the body whereas, it is not necessary for forced vibrations.

(2) In forced vibrations, the amplitude of oscillations is small whereas, in resonance, the amplitude of vibration is large.

Q. 15. **(i)** A man standing between two cliffs produces a sound and hears two successive echoes at intervals of 3 s and 4 s respectively. Calculate the distance between the two cliffs.

The speed of sound in the air is 330 ms⁻¹.

(ii) Why will an echo not be heard when the distance between the source of sound and the reflecting surface is 10 m? **[2012]**

Ans. **(i)** First echo is heard from the nearest cliff so let its distance be d_1.

∴ Speed of sound
$$= \frac{\text{Total distance travelled, } 2d_1}{\text{Time taken, } t_1}$$
$$\therefore \quad d_1 = \frac{v \times t_1}{2} = \frac{330 \times 3}{2} = 495 \text{ m}$$

and second echo is heard from farther cliff so let its distance be d_2.
$$\therefore \quad d_2 = \frac{v \times t_2}{2} = \frac{330 \times 4}{2} = 660 \text{ m}$$

∴ Total distance = 660 + 495 = 1155 m.

(ii) Echo will not be heard because to hear an echo, the minimum distance between the source and the reflecting surface should be 17 m.

Q. 16. **(i)** Name the type of waves which are used for sound ranging.

(ii) Why are these waves mentioned in (i) above, not audible to us?

(iii) Give one use of sound ranging. **[2011]**

Ans. **(i)** Ultrasonic waves.

(ii) These waves are not audible to us because their frequency lies beyond the limits of audibility (20 Hz – 20000 Hz).

(iii) These are used in determining the depth of a sea.

Q. 17. A man standing 25 m away from a wall produces a sound and receives the reflected sound.

(i) Calculate the time after which he receives the reflected sound if the speed of sound in air is 350 ms⁻¹.

(ii) Will the man be able to hear a distinct echo? Give a reason for your answer. **[2011]**

Ans. **(i)** We know that, $v = \dfrac{2d}{t}$
$$\Rightarrow \quad 350 = \frac{50}{t}$$
$$\therefore \quad t = \frac{1}{7} \sec = 0.14 \sec.$$

(ii) Echo will be heard because the conditions required for the formulation of echo are fulfilled *i.e.*, the distance is more than 17 m and time period is more than 0.1 second.

Q. 18. **(i)** A man stands at a distance of 68 m from a cliff and fires a gun. After what time interval will he hear the echo, if the speed of sound in air is 340 ms⁻¹?

(ii) If the man had been standing at a distance of 12 m from the cliff would he have heard a clear echo? **[2010]**

Ans. (i) Given: Distance (d) = 68 m, Speed (v) = 340 ms^{-1}.

$$\therefore \quad \text{Time taken} = \frac{\text{Total distance}}{\text{Speed}}$$

$$= \frac{68}{340} = \frac{1}{5} = 0.2 \text{ sec}$$

So echo will be heard after a time interval of $2t$ i.e.

$$0.2 \times 2 = 0.4 \text{ sec.}$$

(ii) If man had been standing at a distance of 12 m, then

$$t = \frac{2d}{v} = \frac{2 \times 12}{340}$$

$$= \frac{24}{340}$$

$$= 0.07 \text{ sec}$$

which is less than 0.1 sec.

Hence, man can not hear a clear echo.

Q. 19. (i) **What is the principle on which sonar is based?**

(ii) **Calculate the minimum distance at which a person should stand in front of a reflecting surface so that he can hear a distinct echo. (Take speed of sound in air = 350 ms^{-1}.)** **[2009]**

Ans. (i) Sonar is based on the principle of echo.

(ii) The minimum time taken to hear an echo is given by

$$t = 0.1 \text{ sec.}$$

We know that, speed, $v = \dfrac{2d}{t}$

$$d = \frac{v \times t}{2}$$

$$= \frac{350 \times 0.1}{2}$$

$$= 17.5 \text{ m}$$

Q. 20. (i) **Name the characteristic of sound which enables a person to differentiate between two sounds with equal loudness but having different frequencies.**

(ii) **Define the characteristic named by you in (i).**

(iii) **Name the characteristic of sound which enables a person to differentiate between two sounds of the same loudness and frequency but produced by different instruments.** **[2009]**

Ans. (i) Pitch enables a person to differentiate between two sounds with equal loudness but having different frequencies.

(ii) Pitch: It is that characteristic of sound by which an acute note can be distinguished from a grave or flat note.

(iii) Quality of the sound enables a person to differentiate between two sounds of same loudness and frequency but produced by different instruments.

Q. 21. (i) **What is meant by an echo? Mention one important condition that is necessary for an echo to be heard distinctly.**

(ii) **Mention one important use of echo.** **[2008]**

Ans. (i) Echo: The sound heard after reflection from a rigid obstacle is called an echo.

For an echo to be heard distinctly the distance between the reflecting surface and the listener should be approximately 17 m.

(ii) Echo is used in SONAR.

Q. 22. **A man standing in front of a vertical cliff fires a gun. He hears the echo after 3 seconds. On moving closer to the cliff by 82.5 m, he fires again. This time, he hears the echo after 2.5 seconds. Calculate:**

(i) **The distance of the cliff from the initial position of the man.**

(ii) **The velocity of sound.** **[2007]**

Ans. (i) Let the distance between initial position of man and cliff be x meter

$\therefore$ Time taken in travelling $2x$ distance by sound = 3 sec

$$\therefore \quad \text{Speed of sound,} = \frac{\text{Distance}}{\text{Time}}$$

$$S = \frac{2x}{3} \qquad \text{...(i)}$$

When he moves 82.5 meter closer to cliff,

$$\text{Distance} = 2(x - 82.5)$$
$$\text{time} = 2.5 \text{ sec.}$$

$$\text{Speed of sound} = \frac{2(x - 82.5)}{2.5} \qquad \text{...(ii)}$$

Now $$\frac{2x}{3} = \frac{2(x - 82.5)}{2.5}$$

$$\Rightarrow \qquad 5x = 6x - 495.0$$

$$\therefore \qquad x = 495 \text{ meter}$$

$$\therefore \quad \text{Speed of sound} = \frac{2 \times 495}{3}$$

$$= 2 \times 165 = 330 \text{ m/s.}$$

Q. 23. **When a tuning fork, struck by a rubber pad, is held over a length of air column in a tube, it produces a loud sound for a fixed length of the air column.**

(i) **Name the above phenomenon.**

(ii) **How does the frequency of the loud sound compare with that of the tuning fork?**

(iii) **State the unit for measuring loudness.** **[2006]**

Ans. (i) Resonance

(ii) Frequency of loud sound is either equal to or an integer multiple of the natural frequency of tuning fork.

(iii) Decibel.

 Long Answer Type Questions-I

Q. 1. **(i)** When a tuning fork [vibrating] is held close to ear, one hears a faint hum. The same [vibrating tuning fork] is held such that its stem is in contact with the table surface, then one hears a loud sound. Explain.

(ii) A man standing in front of a vertical cliff fires a gun. He hears the echo after 3.5 seconds. On moving closer to the cliff by 84 m, he hears the echo after 3 seconds. Calculate the distance of the cliff from the initial position of the man. **[2020]**

Marking Scheme

(i) A tuning fork held close to ear, disturbs a small volume of air and hence, sound heard is faint. When the handle of the vibrating tuning fork is held against table it sets up forced vibrations in the tabletop. As tabletop has a large surface area large volume of air is set into vibration transmitting more energy thereby producing loud sound.

(ii) Let the distance between cliff and initial position of the man be x m.

Total distance travelled by the sound = $2x$

Time taken = 3.53

$$\text{Speed of sound} = \frac{2x}{3.5} \qquad \dots 1$$

When the moves 84 m closer to cliff

Distance travelled = $2(x - 84)$

Time taken to hear echo = 3 s

$$\text{Speed of sound} = \frac{2(x-84)}{3} \qquad \dots 2$$

From eqn. 1 and 2

$$\frac{2x}{3.5} = \frac{2(x-84)}{3}$$

$$7x - 588 = 6x$$

$$x = 588 \text{ m}$$

The required distance = 588 m

Ans. **(i)** A tuning fork held close to ear, disturb a small volume of air and hence, sound heard is faint, when the handle of vibrating tuning fork is held against table, it set up forced vibrators in the tabletop. As tabletop has a large surface area, large volume of the air is set into vibration transmitting more energy thereby producing loud sound.

(ii) Let the initial position of man from the cliff be d metre

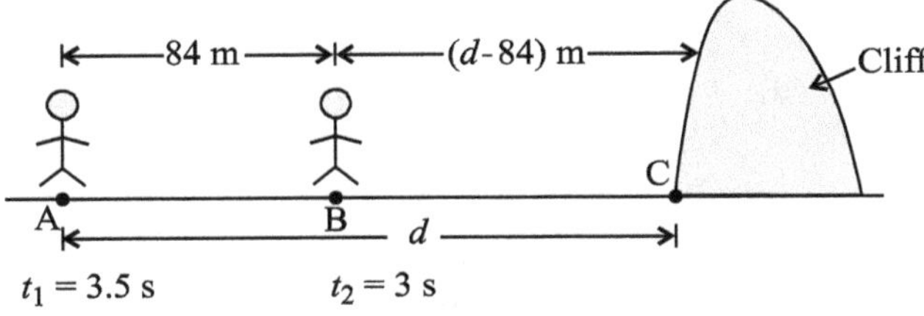

At Position A

$d_1 = d$ metre

$t_1 = 3.5$ s

At Position B

$d_2 = (d - 84)$ m

$t_2 = 3$ s

$$\text{Speed of sound} = \frac{2d}{t}$$

$$\Rightarrow \qquad \frac{2d_1}{t_1} = \frac{2d_2}{t_2}$$

$$\Rightarrow \qquad \frac{2d}{3.5} = \frac{2(d-84)}{3}$$

$$\Rightarrow \qquad 6d = 7d - 588$$

$$\Rightarrow \qquad d = 588 \text{ m}$$

∴ Distance of cliff from initial position of man = 588 m.

Q. 2. Two pendulums **C** and **D** suspended from a wire as shown in the figure given below. Pendulum C is made to oscillate by displacing it from its mean position. It is seen that D also starts oscillating.

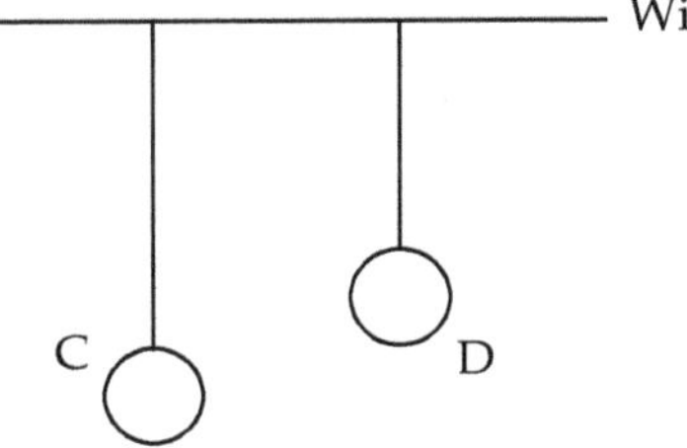

(i) Name the type of oscillation, C will execute.

(ii) Name the type of oscillation, D will execute.

(iii) If the length of D is made equal to C then what difference will you notice in the oscillations of D?

(iv) What is the name of the phenomenon when the length of D is made equal to C? **[2019]**

Marking Scheme

(i) Free vibration / damped vibrations

(ii) Forced vibrations.

(iii) D vibrates with the same amplitude as C or C and D vibrate with maximum amplitude alternately.

(iv) Resonance

Ans. **(i)** C will execute free or natural oscillations.

(ii) D will execute forced oscillations.

(iii) The amplitude of oscillations of D will increase and it will oscillate is same phase as that of C.

(iv) Resonance.

Q. 3. A person is standing at the sea shore. An observer on the ship which is anchored in between a vertical cliff and the person on the shore fires a gun. The person on the shore hears two sounds, 2 seconds and 3 seconds after seeing the smoke of the fired gun. If the speed of sound in the air is 320 ms^{-1}, then calculate:

(i) The distance between the observer on the ship and the person on the shore.

(ii) The distance between the cliff and the observer on the ship. **[2018]**

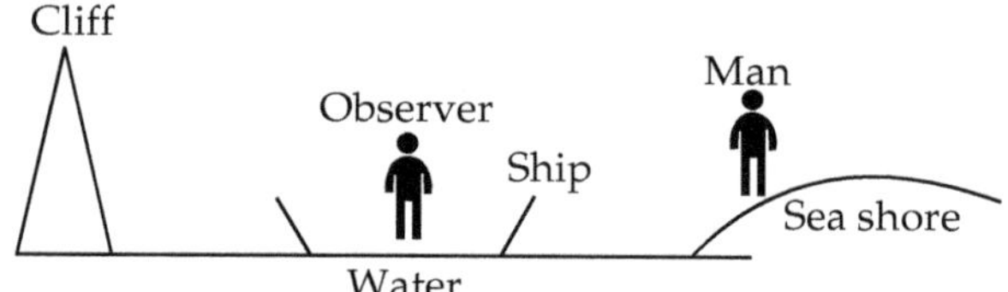

Ans. **(i)** The person on the shore hears the first direct sound after 2 s from the observer.

∴ Distance between observer on ship and man on shore

$$= v \times t_1$$
$$= 320 \times 2 = 640 \text{ m}$$

(ii) Let the distance between the cliff and the observer be d metre.

Therefore, the second sound heard by the man on the shore travels a total distance of

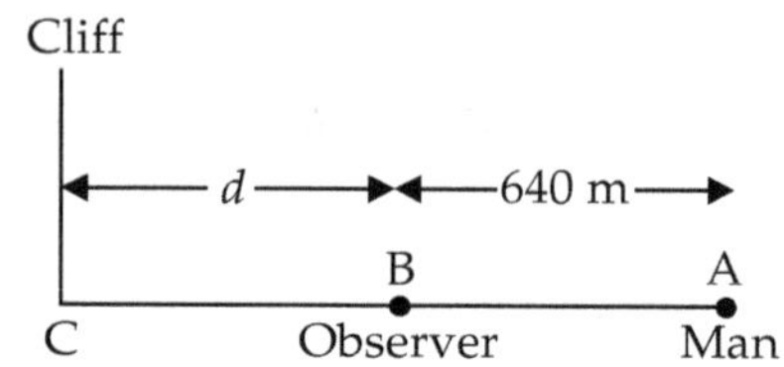

$(d + d + 640) \text{ m} = (2d + 640) \text{ m}$

Time taken, $t_2 = 3$ s

∴ Speed of sound

$$= \frac{\text{Total distance travelled}}{\text{Time taken}}$$

or $\quad 320 = \dfrac{2d + 640}{3}$

or $\quad 960 = 2d + 640$

or $\quad 2d = 960 - 640 = 320$

∴ $\quad d = \dfrac{320}{2} = 160 \text{ m}$

Q. 4. **(i)** A wire of length 80 cm has a frequency of 256 Hz. Calculate the length of a similar wire under similar tension, which will have frequency 1024 Hz.

(ii) A certain sound has a frequency of 256 hertz and a wavelength of 1.3 m.

(1) Calculate the speed with which this sound travels.

(2) What difference would be felt by a listener between the above sound and another sound travelling at the same speed, but of wavelength 2.6 m? **[2017]**

Ans. **(i)** Given: $f_1 = 256$ Hz, $l_1 = 80$ cm, $f_2 = 1024$ Hz, $l_2 = ?$

Since, $\qquad f \propto \dfrac{1}{l}$

∴ $\qquad fl = $ constant

or $\qquad f_1 l_1 = f_2 l_2$

or $\quad 256 \times 80 = 1024 \times l_2$

∴ $\qquad l_2 = \dfrac{256 \times 80}{1024} \text{ cm}$

$\qquad\qquad = 20 \text{ cm}$

The length of wire which will have frequency 1024 Hz under similar conditions is 20 cm.

(ii) Given: $f = 256$ hertz, $\lambda = 1.3$ m

(1) Speed of sound (v)

$$= f\lambda$$
$$= 256 \times 1.3 \text{ ms}^{-1}$$
$$= 332.8 \text{ ms}^{-1}$$

(2) Given: $v = 332.8$ ms^{-1}, $\lambda = 2.6$ m

∴ Frequency, $f = \dfrac{v}{\lambda}$

$$= \dfrac{332.8}{2.6}$$
$$= 128 \text{ hertz.}$$

The second sound of wavelength 2.6 m will have low pitch and sound will be flat compared to the fixed sound of wavelength 1.3 m.

Q. 5. **(i)** Name the phenomenon involved in tuning a radio set to a particular station.

(ii) Define the phenomenon named by you in part (i) above.

(iii) What do you understand by loudness of sound?

(iv) In which units is the loudness of sound measured? **[2016]**

Ans. **(i)** Resonance.

(ii) When the frequency of an externally applied periodic force on a body is equal to its natural frequency, the body readily begins to vibrate with an increased amplitude. This phenomenon is known as resonance.

(iii) Loudness is the property by virtue of which a loud sound can be distinguished from a faint one, both having the same pitch and quality.

(iv) The unit of loudness is decibel (dB).

Q. 6. The adjacent diagram shows three different modes of vibrations P, Q and R of the same string.

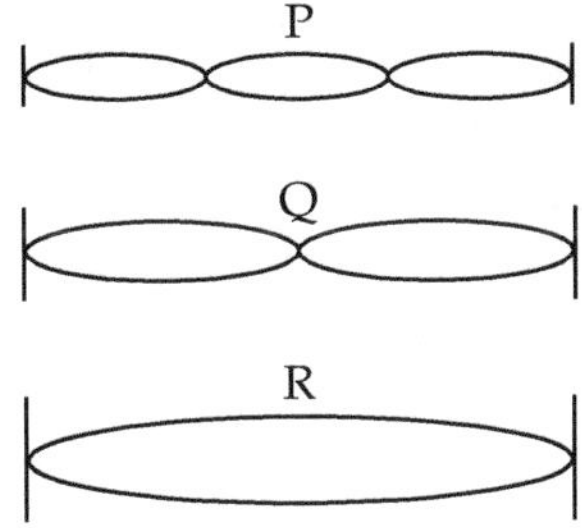

(i) Which vibration will produce a louder sound and why?

(ii) The sound of which string will have maximum shrillness?

(iii) State the ratio of wavelengths of P and R. **[2014]**

Ans. **(i)** Vibration R, as its amplitude is high.

(ii) Sound of string 'P' will have maximum shrillness as its frequency is maximum.

(iii) Let the frequency of the principal note in vibration R be f.

Then, the frequency of vibration P is $3f$.

$$\therefore \qquad f_R = f \text{ and } f_P = 3f$$

$$\Rightarrow \qquad f_R : f_P = 1 : 3$$

But $\qquad f \propto \dfrac{1}{\lambda}$

So, $\qquad \dfrac{\lambda_P}{\lambda_R} = \dfrac{f_R}{f_P} = \dfrac{1}{3}$

$$\therefore \qquad \lambda_P : \lambda_R = 1 : 3$$

Q. 7. **(i)** What is meant by the terms (1) amplitude (2) frequency, of a wave?

(ii) Explain why stringed musical instruments, like the guitar, are provided with a hollow box. **[2013]**

Ans. **(i)** **(1) Amplitude:** Maximum displacement of the vibrating particle on either side of the mean position is called amplitude.

(2) Frequency: Number of oscillations completed by the wave in one second is called frequency.

(ii) When the strings vibrate, the air column inside the box is set into forced vibrations. Since the sound box has a large area, it sets a large volume of air into vibration of the same frequency as that of the string, thereby producing resonance.

Q. 8. The diagram below shows the displacement-time graph for a vibrating body.

(i) Name the type of vibrations produced by the vibrating body.

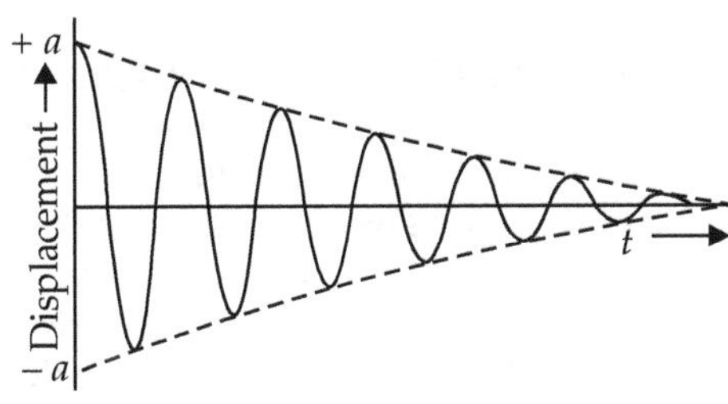

(ii) Give one example of a body producing such vibrations.

(iii) Why is the amplitude of the wave gradually decreasing?

(iv) What will happen to the vibrations of the body after some time? **[2012]**

Ans. **(i)** The diagram shows damped vibrations.

(ii) A tuning fork vibrating in air.

(iii) The amplitude of the wave decreases due to energy loss against frictional force which the surrounding medium exerts on the vibrating body.

(iv) After some time the amplitude gradually decreases and finally the body stops vibrating.

Q. 9. **(i)** A person is tuning his radio set to particular station. What is the person trying to do to tune it?

(ii) Name the phenomenon involved in tuning the radio set.

(iii) Define the phenomenon named by you in part (ii). **[2009]**

Ans. **(i)** The person is trying to change the values of the electronic components to produce vibrations of frequency equal to that of the incoming radio waves which he wants to receive.

(ii) The phenomenon involved in tuning the radioset is resonance.

(iii) Resonance: When the frequency of the externally applied periodic force is equal to the natural frequency of the body, the body starts vibrating with large amplitude, producing a loud sound.

Q. 10. **(i)** Sometimes when a vehicle is driven at a particular speed, a rattling sound is heard. Explain briefly, why this happens and give the name of the phenomenon taking place.

(ii) Suggest one way by which the rattling sound could be stopped. **[2008]**

Ans. **(i)** The phenomenon taking place is resonance. This occurs because the frequency of external force applied by the engine becomes equal to the frequency of some parts of the vehicle due to which resonance takes place.

(ii) Rattling sound can be stopped by altering the speed of the vehicle.

 Long Answer Type Questions-II

Q. 1. In the diagram below, A, B, C, D are four pendulums suspended from the same elastic string PQ. The length of A and C are equal to each other while the length of pendulum B is smaller than that of D. Pendulum A is set into a mode of vibrations.

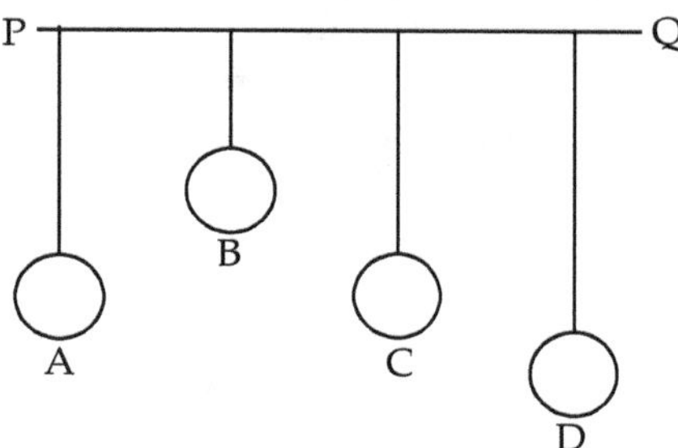

(i) Name the type of vibrations taking place in pendulums B and D?

(ii) What is the state of pendulum C?

(iii) State the reason for the type of vibrations in pendulums B and C.   [2015]

Ans.   (i) Forced vibration

(ii) Pendulum C is in a state of resonance with Pendulum A. Also they are in the same phase.

(iii) This is because the time period of pendulum B is different from that of C (since length of the pendulums B and C are different).

Current Electricity

Short Answer Type Questions-I

Q. 1. Why is it not advisable to use a piece of copper wire as fuse wire in an electric circuit ? **[2020]**

Ans. Copper wire should not be used as a fuse wire because it has high melting point and its specific resistance is much less than a normal fuse wire. (Normal fuse wire should have low melting point and high resistivity.)

Q. 2. Calculate the total resistance across AB :

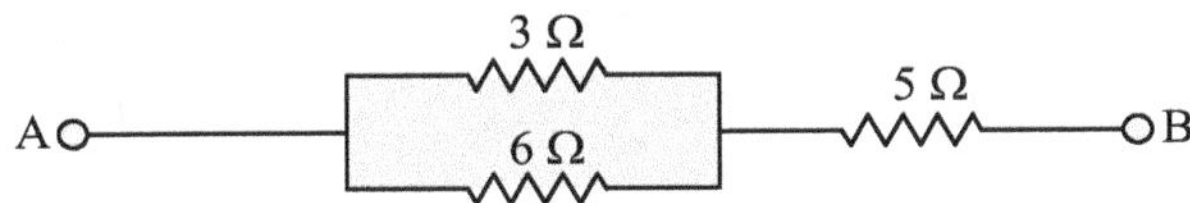

[2020]

Ans. Equivalent resistance of 3 Ω and 6 Ω in parallel is,

$$R_1 = \frac{3 \times 6}{6+3} = \frac{18}{9} = 2\ \Omega$$

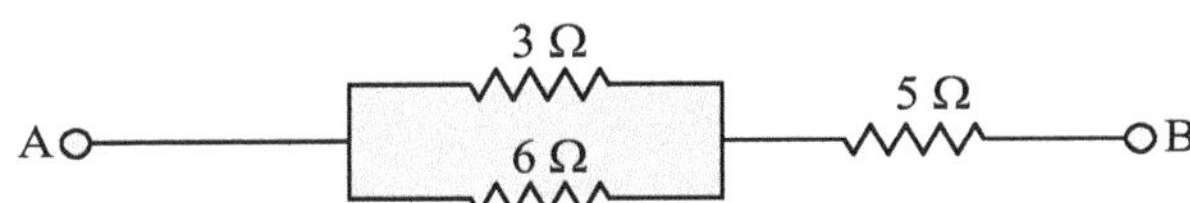

Total resistance across AB is $R_1 + R_2 = (5 + 2) = 7\ \Omega$.

Q. 3. Calculate the effective resistance across AB: **[2019]**

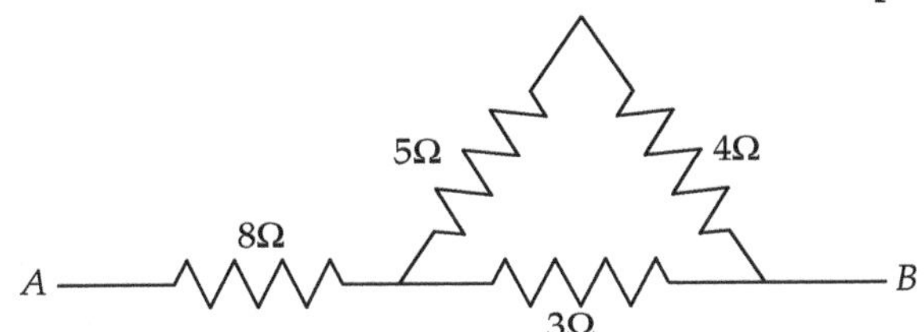

Ans. Given: 5 Ω and 4 Ω in series

$$\therefore \qquad R_1 = (5 + 4)\ \Omega = 9\ \Omega$$

Diagram can be simplified as follows:

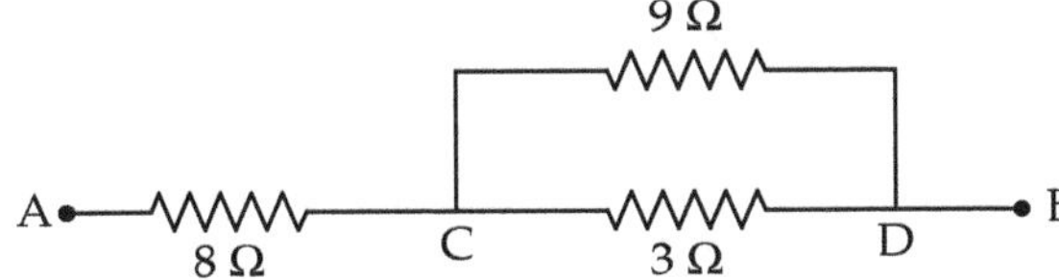

Now, 9 Ω and 3 Ω are in parallel.

$$\therefore \qquad R_2 = \frac{9 \times 3}{9+3} = \frac{27}{12} = \frac{9}{4}\ \Omega$$

Now, 8 Ω and R_2 are in series

A •—⎰⎰⎰— • —⎰⎰⎰— • B
   8 Ω $\frac{9}{4}$ Ω

$$\therefore \qquad R_3 = 8 + \frac{9}{4} = \frac{41}{4}\ \Omega = 10.25\ \Omega$$

Q. 4. You have three resistors of values 2 Ω, 3 Ω and 5 Ω. How will you join them so that the total resistance is more than 7 Ω?

(i) Draw a diagram for the arrangement.

(ii) Calculate the equivalent resistance. **[2018]**

Ans. 2 Ω, 3 Ω and 5 Ω have to be joined in series to obtain the total resistance more than 7 Ω.

(i) A•—⎰⎰⎰—•—⎰⎰⎰—•—⎰⎰⎰—•B
    2 Ω   3 Ω   5 Ω

(ii) $R_{eq.} = (2 + 3 + 5)\ \Omega = 10\ \Omega$

Q. 5. Identify the following wires used in a household circuit:

(i) The wire is also called as the phase wire.

(ii) The wire is connected to the top terminal of a three pin socket. **[2018]**

Ans. (i) Live wire.

(ii) Earth wire.

Q. 6. Define specific resistance and state its S.I. unit. **[2017]**

Ans. The specific resistance of a material is the resistance of a wire of that material of unit length and unit area of cross-section.

Its S.I. unit is ohm-metre (Ω m).

Q. 7. An electric bulb of resistance 500 Ω, draws a current of 0.4 A. Calculate the power of the bulb and the potential difference at its end. **[2017]**

Ans. Given: Resistance (R) = 500 Ω, Current (I) = 0.4 A

$$\text{Power (P)} = I^2 R$$
$$= (0.4)^2 \times 500\ \text{W} = 80\ \text{W}$$

Potential difference at its ends (V)

$$= IR$$
$$= 0.4 \times 500\ \text{V} = 200\ \text{V}$$

Q. 8. The V-I graph for a series combination and for a parallel combination of two resistors is shown in the figure below. Which of the two A or B represents the parallel combination? Give a reason for your answer.   [2016, 2007]

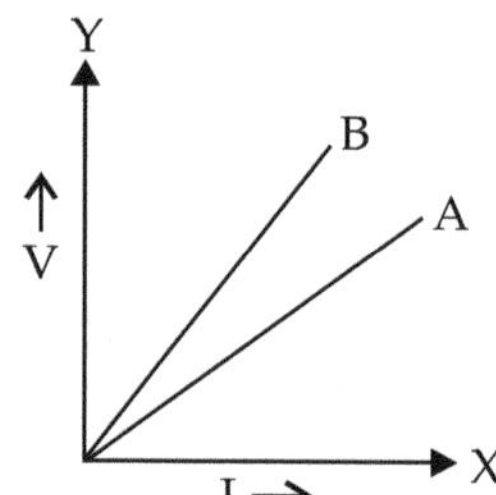

Ans. Since the straight line A is less steeper than B, so the straight line A represents small resistance. In a parallel combination, the equivalent resistance is less than in series combination. So, A represents the parallel combination.

Q. 9. A music system draws a current of 400 mA when connected to a 12 V battery.
  (i) What is the resistance of the music system?
  (ii) The music system is left playing for several hours and finally the battery voltage drops and the music system stops playing when the current drops to 320 mA. At what battery voltage does the music system stop playing?   [2016]

Ans.   Current $(I) = 400$ mA
$$= 400 \times 10^{-3} A$$

    Voltage $(V) = 12$ V

  (i) $V = IR$

$\therefore$ Resistance $(R) = \dfrac{V}{I} = \dfrac{12}{400 \times 10^{-3}} = 30\ \Omega$

  (ii) $R = 30\ \Omega$
$$I = 320 \text{ mA} = 320 \times 10^{-3} A$$
$$V = IR = 320 \times 10^{-3} \times 30 = 9.6 \text{ V}$$

Q. 10. State the characteristics required in a material to be used as an effective fuse wire.   [2016]

Ans. Characteristics required in a material to be used as an effective fuse wire are:
  (i) high resistivity   **(ii)** low melting point.

Q. 11. **(ii)** 1 kWh = ...J.   [2015]

Ans. **(ii)** 3.6×10^6

Q. 12. **(i)** What happens to the resistivity of semiconductors with the increase of temperature?
  (ii) For a fuse, higher the current rating......... is the fuse wire.   [2015]

Ans. **(i)** The resistivity of semiconductors decreases with increase in temperature.
  (ii) Thicker

Q. 13. Find the equivalent resistance between points A and B.   [2015]

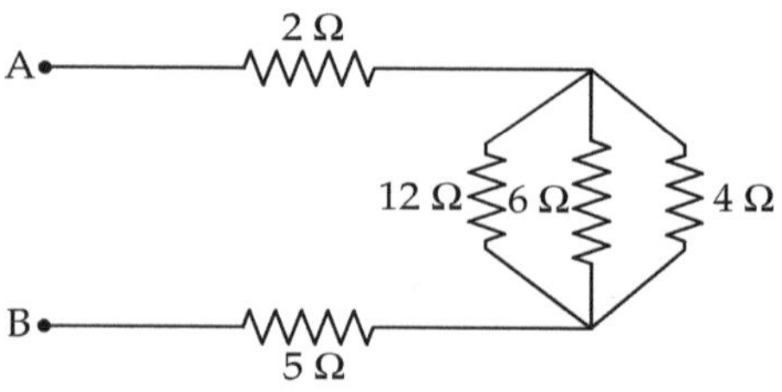

Ans. Three resistances 12 Ω, 6 Ω and 4 Ω are connected in parallel.

$\therefore$ The equivalent resistance in parallel is given by

$$\frac{1}{R_p} = \frac{1}{12} + \frac{1}{6} + \frac{1}{4}$$

$$\frac{1}{R_p} = \frac{1+2+3}{12}$$

$$R_p = \frac{12}{(1+2+3)} = 2\ \Omega$$

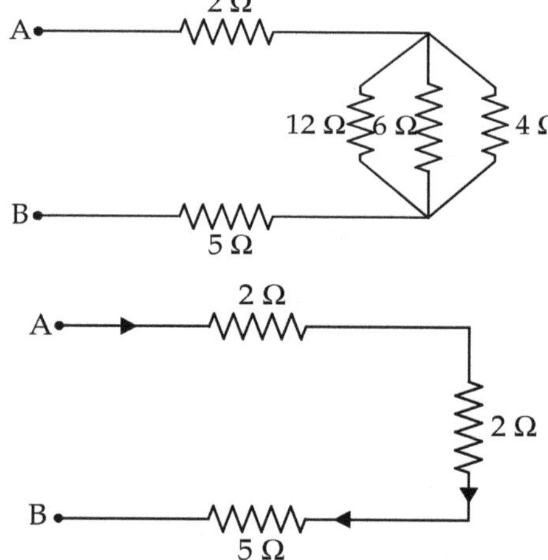

Now, $2\ \Omega$, R_p and $5\ \Omega$ are in series.

Thus, the equivalent resistance between A and
$$B = 2\ \Omega + 2\ \Omega + 5\ \Omega = 9\ \Omega.$$

Q. 14. What is consumed using different electrical appliances, for which electricity bills are paid?   [2014]

Ans. Electrical energy in kWh which is commercially known as unit.
$$1 \text{ kWh} = 1 \text{ kW} \times 1 \text{ h}$$
$$= 1 \text{ unit of electricity}$$

Q. 15. Find the equivalent resistance between points A and B.   [2014]

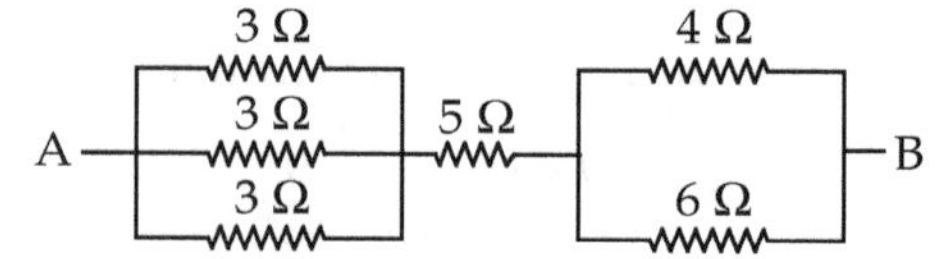

Ans.
$$\frac{1}{R_1} = \left(\frac{1}{3} + \frac{1}{3} + \frac{1}{3}\right)$$

$\Rightarrow \qquad \frac{1}{R_1} = 1$

$\Rightarrow \qquad R_1 = 1\,\Omega$

$\qquad R_2 = 5\,\Omega$

$$\frac{1}{R_3} = \frac{1}{4} + \frac{1}{6} = \frac{10}{24}$$

$\Rightarrow \qquad R_3 = \frac{24}{10}\,\Omega$

Now, these resistances are connected in series.

∴   Equivalent resistance between A and B is

$$R_{eq.} = R_1 + R_2 + R_3$$
$$= 1 + 5 + \frac{24}{10}$$
$$R_{eq.} = 8.4\,\Omega$$

Q. 16. Calculate the equivalent resistance between the points A and B for the following combination of resistors: **[2013]**

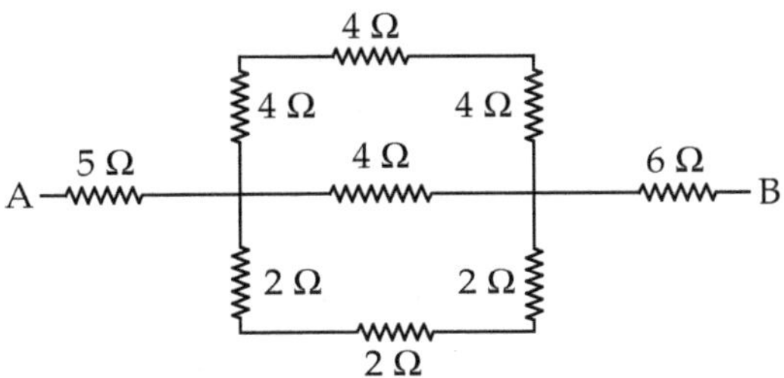

Ans.   In the given circuit, 4 Ω, 4 Ω and 4 Ω in series gives $R_1 = 4 + 4 + 4 = 12\,\Omega$

and 2 Ω, 2 Ω and 2 Ω in series gives
$$R_2 = 2 + 2 + 2 = 6\,\Omega.$$

Now, $R_1 = 12\,\Omega$, $R_2 = 6\,\Omega$ and $R_3 = 4\,\Omega$ are in parallel.

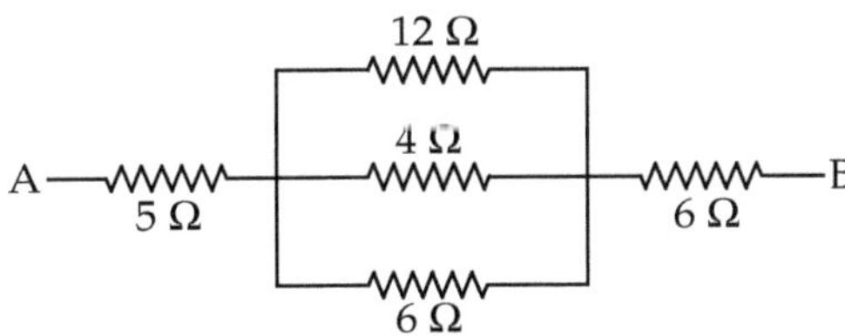

The equivalent resistance R′ is given by

$$\frac{1}{R'} = \frac{1}{12} + \frac{1}{4} + \frac{1}{6}$$
$$= \frac{1+3+2}{12} = \frac{6}{12}$$
$$\frac{1}{R'} = \frac{1}{2}$$
$$R' = 2\,\Omega$$

A —www— www— www— B
5 Ω   2 Ω   6 Ω

Total resistance $= 5 + 2 + 6 = 13\,\Omega$.

Q. 17. (i) Name the device used to protect the electric circuits from overloading and short circuits.

(ii) On what effect of electricity does the above device work? **[2013]**

Ans.   (i) Fuse.

(ii) Heating effect of electric current.

Q. 18. An electrical appliance is rated at 1000 KVA, 220 V. If the appliance is operated for 2 hours, calculate the energy consumed by the appliance in:

(i) kWh **(ii) joule** **[2012]**

Ans.   Given: V = 220 volt, P = 1000 kVA,

Time = 2 hrs

(i) Energy consumed $= Pt$
$$= 2000 \text{ kWh}$$

(ii) We know, $1 \text{ kWh} = 3.6 \times 10^6 \text{ J}$

So, $2000 \text{ kWh} = 2000 \times 3.6 \times 10^6 \text{ J}$
$$= 7.2 \times 10^9 \text{ J}$$

Q. 19. Calculate the equivalent resistance between P and Q from the following diagram: **[2012]**

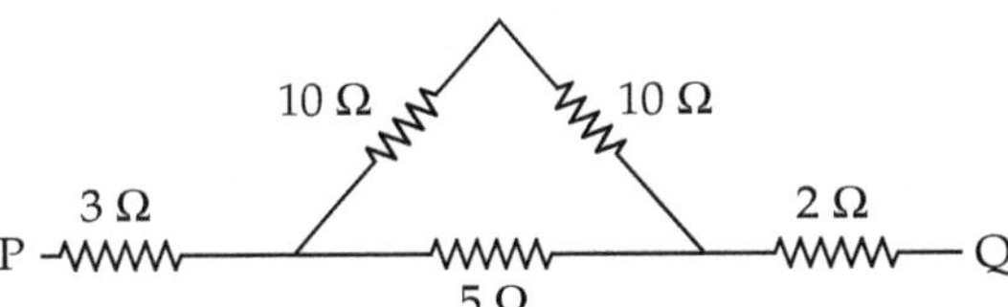

Ans.   In the given circuit, two 10 Ω resistances are in series.

∴ $R_S = 10\,\Omega + 10\,\Omega = 20\,\Omega.$

Now, 20 Ω and 5 Ω resistances are in parallel.

∴ $$\frac{1}{R_p} = \frac{1}{20} + \frac{1}{5}$$
$$\frac{1}{R_p} = \frac{1+4}{20} = \frac{5}{20}$$
$$R_P = 4\,\Omega$$

The equivalent resistance between P and Q is given by

$$R = 3 + 4 + 2 = 9\,\Omega$$

Q. 20. Two bulbs are marked 100 W, 220 V and 60 W, 110 V. Calculate the ratio of their resistances. **[2011]**

Ans. Given:

Ist Bulb	IInd Bulb
$P_1 = 100$ W	$P_2 = 60$ W
$V_1 = 220$ V	$V_2 = 110$ V

We know, $\quad P = \dfrac{V^2}{R}$

or $\quad R = \dfrac{V^2}{P}$

$\therefore \quad \dfrac{R_1}{R_2} = \dfrac{\dfrac{V_1^2}{P_1}}{\dfrac{V_2^2}{P_2}}$

$$= \dfrac{V_1^2 \times P_2}{P_1 \times V_2^2} = \dfrac{(220)^2 \times 60}{100 \times (110)^2}$$

$$= \dfrac{12}{5}$$

$$R_1 : R_2 = 12 : 5$$

Q. 21. (i) What is the colour code for the insulation on the earth wire?

(ii) Write an expression for calculating electrical power in terms of current and resistance. [2011]

Ans. **(i)** The colour code for the insulation of earth wire is green or yellow.

(ii) Electrical power in terms of current and resistance is

$$P = I^2 R.$$

Q. 22. Calculate the equivalent resistance between A and B from the following diagram: [2011]

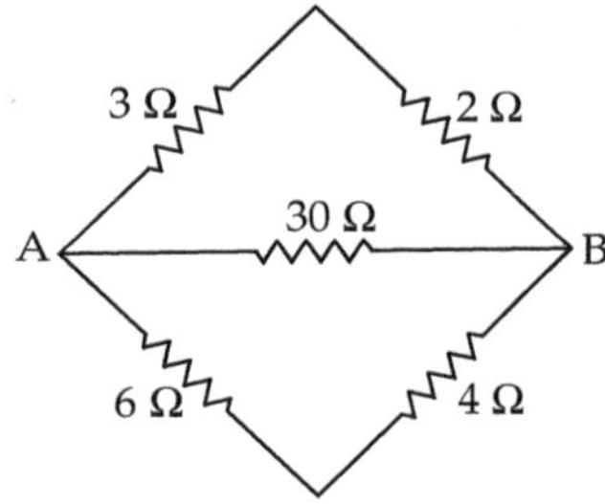

Ans.

$$\dfrac{1}{R} = \dfrac{1}{5} + \dfrac{1}{30} + \dfrac{1}{10}$$

$$\dfrac{1}{R} = \dfrac{6+1+3}{30}$$

$$R = \dfrac{30}{10} = 3 \; \Omega$$

Q. 23. Six resistances are connected together as shown in the figure. Calculate the equivalent resistance between the points A and B. [2010]

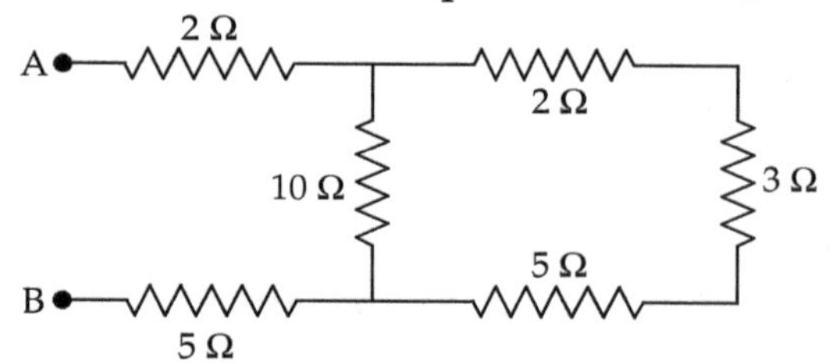

Ans. In the given circuit, the resistors 2 Ω, 3 Ω and 5 Ω are connected in series.

$\therefore \quad R' = 2 + 3 + 5 = 10 \; \Omega$

Now, R' and 10 Ω are in parallel.

$\therefore \quad \dfrac{1}{R''} = \dfrac{1}{R'} + \dfrac{1}{10}$

$$= \dfrac{1}{10} + \dfrac{1}{10} = \dfrac{2}{20} = \dfrac{1}{5}$$

$\therefore \quad R'' = 5 \Omega$

Now, 2 Ω, R'' and 5 Ω are connected in series between the points A and B. The equivalent resistance between A and B is

$$R = 2 + R'' + 5$$

$$= 2 + 5 + 5 = 12 \; \Omega$$

Q. 24. (i) Which part of an electrical appliance is earthed?

(ii) State a relation between electrical power, resistance and potential difference in an electrical circuit. [2010]

Ans. **(i)** Metal body of an electrical appliance is earthed.

(ii) In an electrical circuit, the electrical power is given by

$$P = \dfrac{V^2}{R}$$

where V = potential difference and R = resistance.

Q. 25. The equivalent resistance of the following circuit diagram is 4 Ω. Calculate the value of x. [2009]

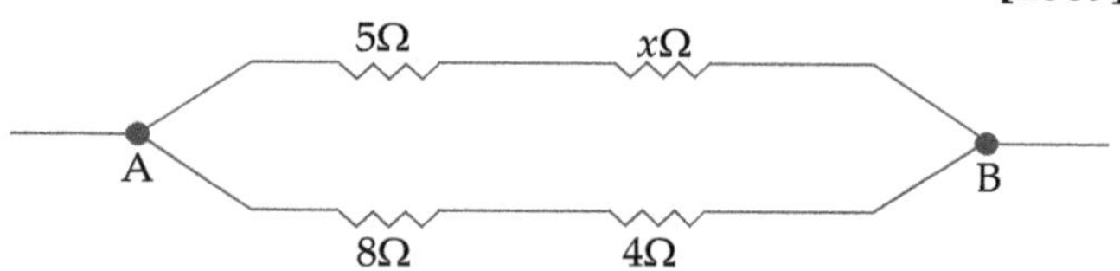

Ans. By the formula, we have,

$$\dfrac{1}{4} = \dfrac{1}{12} + \dfrac{1}{5+x}$$

$\Rightarrow \quad \dfrac{1}{5+x} = \dfrac{1}{4} - \dfrac{1}{12}$

$\Rightarrow \quad \dfrac{1}{5+x} = \dfrac{1}{6}$

$\Rightarrow \quad 5 + x = 6$

$\Rightarrow \quad x = 1 \; \Omega$

Q. 26. An electric heater is rated 1000 W – 200 V. Calculate:

(i) the resistance of the heating element.

(ii) the current flowing through it. [2009]

Ans. (i) We have, $\quad P = \dfrac{V^2}{R}$

$$\Rightarrow \qquad 1000 = \dfrac{200^2}{R}$$

$$\Rightarrow \qquad R = 40\ \Omega$$

(ii) We know that, $\quad V = IR$

$$\Rightarrow \qquad 200 = I \times 40$$

$$\Rightarrow \qquad I = 5\ A.$$

Q. 27. (i) **Give two characteristic properties of copper wire which make it unsuitable for use as fuse wire.**

(ii) **Name the material which is used as a fuse wire?** **[2009]**

Ans. (i) Two characteristics which make Cu wire unsuitable for using as a fuse wire are (a) low resistivity and (b) high melting point.

(ii) The material used for fuse wire is an alloy of lead and tin.

Q. 28. (i) **Sketch a graph to show the change in potential difference across the ends of an ohmic resistor and the current flowing in it. Label the axis of your graph.**

(ii) **What does the slope of the graph represent?** **[2008]**

Ans. (i)

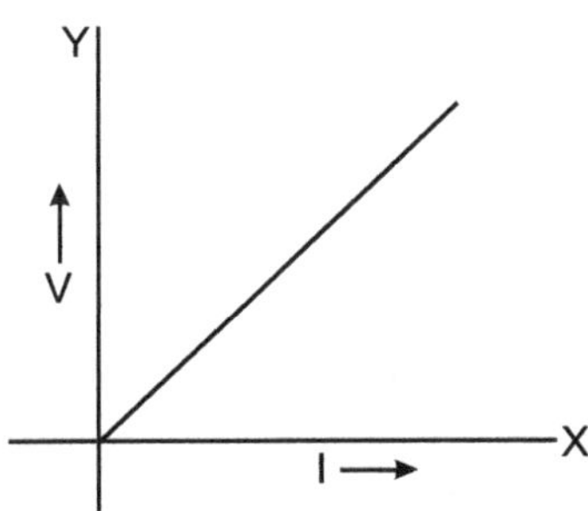

(ii) The slope of the graph represents resistance.

Q. 29. The electrical gadgets used in a house such as bulbs, fans, heater, etc, are always connected in parallel, NOT in series. Give two reasons for connecting them in parallel. **[2008]**

Ans. Two reasons for connecting electrical gadgets in a house in parallel are (1) As potential difference across each appliance connected in parallel remains the same so every appliance works with its maximum capacity. (2) Every appliance can be operated by an independent switch.

Q. 30. An electrical heater is rated 4 kW, 220 V. Find the cost of using this heater for 12 hours if one kWh of electrical energy costs ₹ 3.25. **[2008]**

Ans. $\quad$ Energy consumed $= P \times t$

$$= 4 \times 12 = 48\ kWh$$

Given; $\quad$ Cost of 1 kW $= ₹\ 3.25$

So, $\qquad$ Total cost $= 48 \times 3.25 = ₹\ 156$

Q. 31. Of the three connecting wires in a household circuit:

(i) **Which two of the three wires are at the same potential?**

(ii) **In which of the three wires should the switch be connected?** **[2007]**

Ans. (i) Neutral wire and Earth wire.

(ii) Live wire.

Q. 32. Calculate the value of the resistance which must be connected to a 15 Ω resistance to provide an effective resistance of 6 Ω. **[2007]**

Ans. Resistance decreases in parallel combination. So let R resistance is connected to 15 Ω resistance in parallel to make resultant 6 Ω.

Now, $\quad \dfrac{1}{6} = \dfrac{1}{15} + \dfrac{1}{R}$

or $\quad \dfrac{1}{R} = \dfrac{1}{6} - \dfrac{1}{15} = \dfrac{5-2}{30} = \dfrac{3}{30} = \dfrac{1}{10}$

∴ $\qquad R = 10\ \Omega.$

Q. 33. A wire of uniform thickness with a resistance of 27 Ω is cut into three equal pieces and they are joined in parallel. Find the resistance of the parallel combination. **[2006]**

Ans. Resistance of given wire $= 27\ \Omega$

∴ Resistance of each small wire $= \dfrac{27}{3} = 9$

Let R_P be equivalent resistance for parallel combination.

Then $\quad \dfrac{1}{R_P} = \dfrac{1}{R_1} + \dfrac{1}{R_2} + \dfrac{1}{R_3} = \dfrac{1}{9} + \dfrac{1}{9} + \dfrac{1}{9}$

$$\dfrac{1}{R_P} = \dfrac{3}{9}$$

or $\qquad R_P = \dfrac{9}{3}\ \Omega$

∴ $\qquad R_P = 3\ \Omega$

Q. 34. Draw a labelled diagram of a three-pin socket. **[2006]**

Ans.

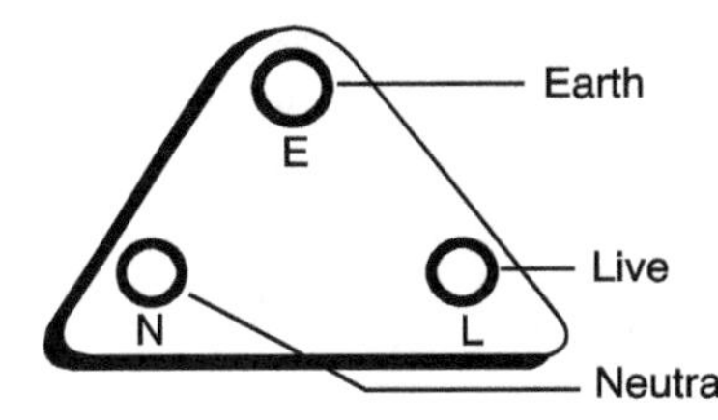

Q. 35. **Mention two factors on which the resistance of a wire depends.** **[2006]**

Ans. Resistance of a wire depends on:
(i) Length of wire
(ii) Area of cross-section of wire.

 ## Short Answer Type Questions-II

Q. 1. (i) **What are superconductors ?**
(ii) **Calculate the current drawn by an appliance rated 110 W, 220 when connected across 220 V supply.**
(iii) **Name a substance whose resistance decreases with the increase in temperature.** **[2020]**

Marking Scheme

(i) A superconductor is a substance whose resistance is zero at temperature closer to absolute zero.
(ii) P = VI
110 = 220 × I
$$I = \frac{110}{220} = \frac{1}{2} = 0.5 \text{ A}$$
(iii) Carbon/silicon/germanium or a semi-conductor.

Ans. (i) Superconductors are substances of zero resistance at temperatures closer to absolute zero.
(ii) P = 110 W V = 220 volt
$$\therefore \quad \text{Current I} = \frac{P}{V} = \frac{110}{220} \text{ A}$$
$$= 0.5 \text{ A}$$
(iii) For semiconductors such as silicon, germanium or carbon, resistance decreases with the increase in temperature.

Q. 2. (i) **Write one advantage of connecting electrical appliances in parallel combination.**
(ii) **What characteristics should a fuse wire have?**
(iii) **Which wire in a power circuit is connected to the metallic body of the appliance?** **[2019]**

Marking Scheme

(i) Each appliance will be working at the same potential; each appliance can operate independently.
(ii) high resistivity and low melting point.
(iii) earth wire.

Ans. (i) Each appliance gets connected to 220 V supply for its normal working.
(ii) A fuse wire must have low melting point and its specific resistance must be more than that of copper or aluminium.
(iii) Earth wire.

Q. 3. (i) **A fuse is rated 8 A. Can it be used with an electrical appliance rated 5 kW, 200 V? Give a reason.**
(ii) **Name two safety devices which are connected to the live wire of a household electric circuit.** **[2018]**

Ans. (i) Given: Power (P) = 5 kW = 5000 W,
V = 200 volt
$$\therefore \quad \text{Current (I)} = \frac{P}{V}$$
$$= \frac{5000}{200} = 25 \text{ A}$$
The 8 A fuse cannot be used with the above appliance because it draws a current of 25 A and the fuse will blow off.
(ii) (1) Fuse, (2) Switch.

Q. 4. (i) **Find the equivalent resistance between A and B.**

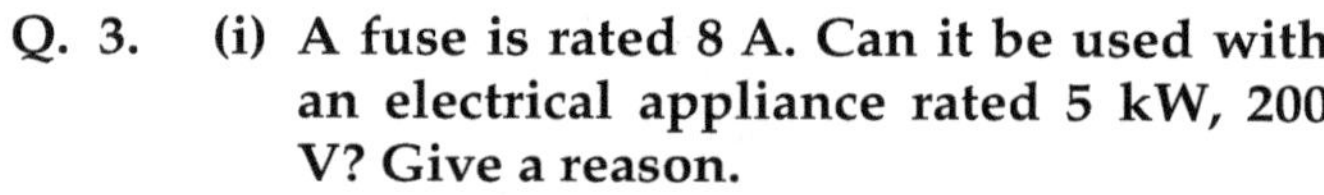

(ii) **State whether the resistivity of a wire changes with the change in the thickness of the wire.** **[2018]**

Ans. (i) 6 Ω and 3 Ω resistances are connected in parallel.
$$\therefore \quad \frac{1}{R_1} = \frac{1}{6} + \frac{1}{3}$$
$$= \frac{1+2}{6} = \frac{3}{6} = \frac{1}{2}$$
or $\quad R_1 = 2 \, \Omega$

4 Ω and 12 Ω resistances are connected in parallel.
$$\therefore \quad \frac{1}{R_2} = \frac{1}{4} + \frac{1}{12}$$
$$= \frac{3+1}{12} = \frac{4}{12} = \frac{1}{3}$$
or $\quad R_2 = 3 \, \Omega$

Now, R_1 and R_2 are connected in series.
∴ Equivalent resistance between A and B = (2 + 3) Ω = 5 Ω.

(ii) Resistivity of a substance is its characteristic property and it does not change with the change in the thickness of the wire.

Q. 5. **Name the colour code of the wire which is connected to the metallic body of an appliance.**

Ans. The colour code of the earth wire is green or yellow.

Q. 6. **(i) Which particles are responsible for current in conductors?**

(ii) To which wire of a cable in a power circuit should the metal case of a geyser be connected?

(iii) To which wire should the fuse be connected? **[2017, 2016]**

Ans. **(i)** Free Electrons

(ii) Earth wire

(iii) Live wire

Q. 7. **(i) What type of current is transmitted from the power station?**

(ii) At what voltage is this current available to our household? **[2016]**

Ans. **(i)** Alternating current

(ii) 220 V

Q. 8. **(i) At what frequency is A.C. supplied to residential houses?**

(ii) Name the wire in a household electrical circuit to which the switch is connected. **[2015]**

Ans. **(i)** 50 hertz

(ii) Live wire

Q. 9. **The relationship between the potential difference and the current in a conductor is stated in the form of a law.**

(i) Name the law.

(ii) What does the slope of V-I graph for a conductor represent?

(iii) Name the material used for making the connecting wire. **[2015]**

Ans. **(i)** Ohm's law

(ii) The slope of the graph represent resistance of the conductor.

(iii) Copper

Q. 10. **(i) What is an Ohmic resistor?**

(ii) Two copper wires are of the same length, but one is thicker than the other.

(1) Which wire will have more resistance?

(2) Which wire will have more specific resistance? **[2014]**

Ans. **(i)** An ohmic resistor is a resistor which obeys ohm's law. Examples are all metallic conductors such as silver, aluminium, copper, etc.

(ii) **(1)** Thinner wire will have more resistance because the resistance is inversely proportional to the area of cross-section.
(2) Specific resistance of both wire is same because specific resistance depends on the nature of the material which is same in both cases.

Q. 11. **(i) Two sets A and B, of three bulbs each, are glowing in two separate rooms. When one of the bulbs in set A is fused, the other two bulbs also cease to glow. But in set B, when one bulb fuses, the other two bulbs continue to glow. Explain why this phenomenon occurs.**

(ii) Why do we prefer arrangements of Set B for house circuiting? **[2014]**

Ans. **(i)** In set A, bulbs are in series so if one gets fused, others are also affected.
In set B, bulbs are in parallel so if one goes off, others continue to glow.

(ii) For house circuiting, we use the set B arrangement *i.e.*, all the appliances are connected in parallel because in this arrangement, each appliance operates at the same voltage and works independently without being affected whether the other appliance is switched on or off.

Q. 12. **(i) State Ohm's law.**

(ii) A metal wire of resistance 6 Ω is stretched so that its length is increased to twice its original length. Calculate its new resistance. **[2013]**

Ans. **(i)** **Ohm's law:** It states that the current flowing in a conductor is directly proportional to the potential difference across its ends provided the physical conditions and the temperature of the conductor remains constant *i.e.*, V $\propto$ I or V = IR

where R is a constant called resistance of conductor.

(ii)
$$R' = n^2 R$$
$$= 2^2 \times 6 = 24 \ \Omega.$$

Q. 13. **(i) An electrical gadget can give an electric shock to its user under certain circumstances. Mention any two of these circumstances.**

(ii) What preventive measure provided in a gadget can protect a person from an electric shock? **[2013]**

Ans. **(i)** **(1)** When the live wire comes in contact with the wet hand of the user.
(2) Due to short circuit in the electrical gadget.

(ii) Earthing can protect a person from electric shock.

Q. 14. (i) A cell is sending current in an external circuit. How does the terminal voltage compare with the e.m.f. of the cell?

(ii) What is the purpose of using a fuse in an electrical circuit?

(iii) What are the characteristic properties of fuse wire? **[2012]**

Ans. **(i)** E.m.f. of a cell is greater than terminal voltage.

(ii) Fuse is a safety device which is used to limit the current in an electric circuit.

(iii) Characteristic properties of a fuse wire:

(1) It is made up of an alloy of lead and tin.

(2) It has high resistivity and low melting point.

Q. 15. (i) Write an expression for the electrical energy spent in the flow of current through an electrical appliances in terms of I, R and t.

(ii) At what voltage is the alternating current supplied to our houses?

(iii) How should the electric lamps in a building be connected? **[2012]**

Ans. **(i)** Electrical energy = I^{2}Rt.

(ii) 220 volt.

(iii) Electric lamps should be connected in parallel.

Q. 16. (i) Draw a graph of Potential difference (V) versus Current (I) for an ohmic resistor.

(ii) How can you find the resistance of the resistor from this graph?

(iii) What is a non-ohmic resistor? **[2011]**

Ans. **(i)**

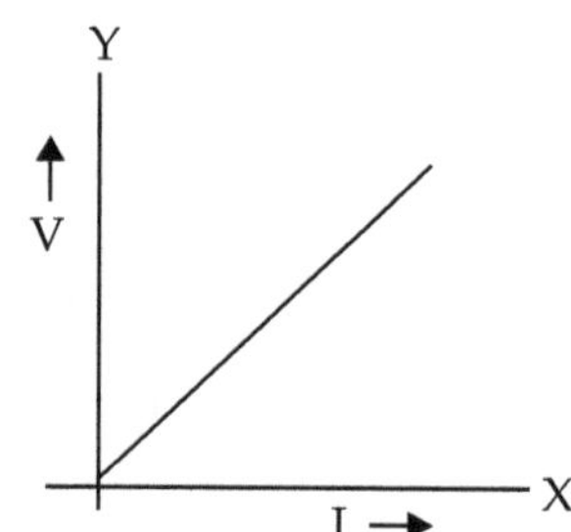

(ii) We can find resistance by finding the slope of the graph.

(iii) Non-ohmic Resistor: This is a resistor which does not obey Ohm's Law. V-I graph for non-ohmic resistor is not a straight line.

Q. 17. (i) An electric bulb is marked 100 W, 250 V. What information does this convey?

(ii) How much current will the bulb draw if connected to a 250 V supply? **[2011]**

Ans. **(i)** Given: 100 W, 250 V.

Information:

(1) It conveys that when the bulb is connected to a 250 V supply it consumes 100 J of energy in 1 second or 100 W power.

(2) It will work at its maximum capacity at 250 V.

(ii) Given: V = 250 V, I =?

We know, $P = VI$

$\Rightarrow \qquad 100 = 250 \times I$

$\therefore \qquad I = \dfrac{100}{250} = 0.4$ A.

Q. 18. Calculate the quantity of heat that will be produced in a coil of resistance 75 Ω if a current of 2 A is passed through it for 2 minutes. **[2010]**

Ans. Given: R = 75 Ω, i = 2 A, t = 2 minutes = 2 × 60 s = 120 s

Heat energy produced in the coil,

$$H = i^2Rt$$
$$= 2^2 \times 75 \times 120$$
$$= 300 \times 120 = 36000 \text{ J}$$

Q. 19. (i) A substance has nearly zero resistance at a temperature of 1 K. What is such a substance called?

(ii) State any two factors which affect the resistance of a metallic wire. **[2010]**

Ans. **(i)** Superconductor.

(ii) Length of wire and area of cross-section of the wire.

Q. 20. State Ohm's Law.

Ans. Ohm's Law: If physical conditions of the conductor remains the same and temperature is constant then potential difference across the conductor is directly proportional to the current flowing in it. This is known as Ohm's law.

Q. 21. Three resistors of 6.0 Ω, 2.0 Ω and 4.0 Ω respectively are joined together as shown in the figure. The resistors are connected to an ammeter and to a cell of e.m.f. 6.0 V. Calculate:

(i) the effective resistance of the circuit.

(ii) the current drawn from the cell. **[2008]**

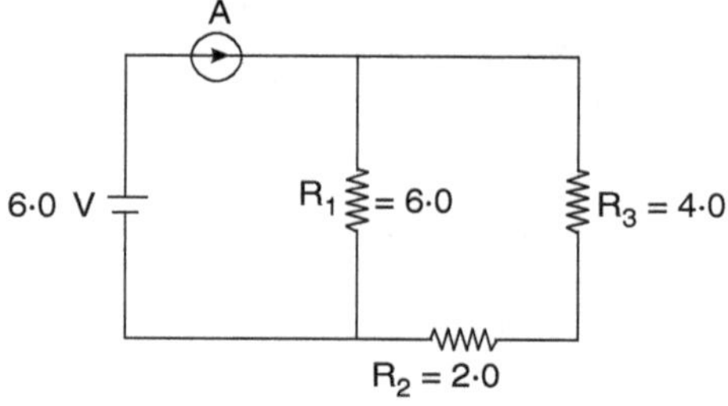

Ans. **(i)** Resistances R_2 and R_3 are in series so their effective resistance is

$$R' = 4 + 2$$
$$= 6\,\Omega$$

R' and R_1 are in parallel. So

$$\frac{1}{R} = \frac{1}{R'} + \frac{1}{R_1}$$
$$= \frac{1}{6} + \frac{1}{6}$$
$$\frac{1}{R} = \frac{2}{6}$$

∴ $\qquad R = 3\,\Omega.$

(ii) $\qquad V = IR$
$$6 = I \times 3$$
$$I = 2\,A.$$

Q. 22. **(i) What is meant by earthing of an electrical appliance? Why is it essential?**

(ii) What will be the effect on the working of an electric bell if instead of a direct current, an alternating current us used? **[2007]**

Ans. **(i)** Earthing of an electrical appliance means the outer metallic case of appliance is connected with earth wire which is welded to the end of a copper rod and it is buried in the ground.

It saves the appliance during short circuit by passing excessive current to earth.

(ii) If electric bell is connected to *a.c.* instead of *d.c.* then bell will ring intermittently.

Q. 23. **Find the cost of operating an electric toaster for two hours, if it draws 8 A current on a 110 volt circuit. The cost of electrical energy is ₹ 2.50 per kWh.** **[2006]**

Ans. Given that: Time = 2 hrs, I = 8A, V = 110 Volt

∴ $\qquad$ Power = IV = $8 \times 110 = 880$ Watt

$$\frac{\text{Electrical energy}}{\text{(in kWh)}} = \frac{\text{Power (in Watt)} \times \text{Time (in hrs)}}{1000}$$
$$= \frac{880 \times 2}{1000}$$
$$= 1.76\ \text{kWh}$$

Cost of 1 kWh energy = ₹ 2.50

∴ Cost of 1.76 kWh energy = 2.50×1.76
$$= \text{₹}\ 4.40$$

Long Answer Type Questions- I

Q. 1.

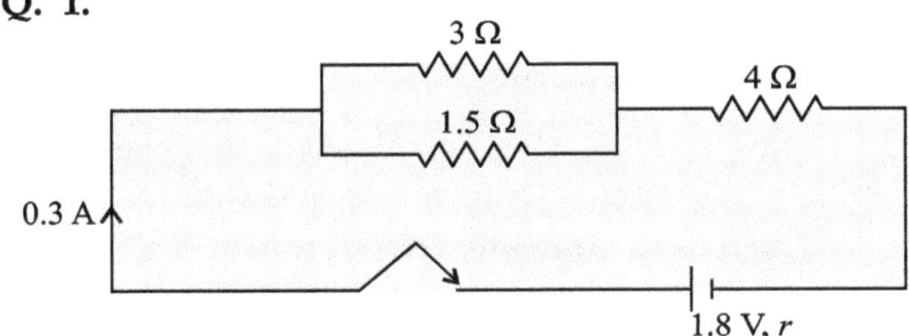

The diagram above shows three resistors connected across a cell of *e.m.f.* 1.8 V and internal resistance r. Calculate :
(i) Current through 3 Ω resistor.
(ii) The internal resistance r. **[2020]**

 **Marking Scheme**

(i) $\qquad I_{3\,\Omega} = \dfrac{0.3 \times 1.5}{3 + 1.5} = \dfrac{0.45}{4.5}$

∴ $\quad I_{3\,\Omega} = 0.1\ A$

(ii) $\qquad R_1 = \dfrac{1.5 \times 3}{1.5 + 3} = 1\,\Omega \qquad E = I\,(R + r)$

∴ $\quad 1.8 = 0.3\,(5 + r)$

$$r = \frac{1.8}{0.3} - 5 = 6 - 5 = 1\,\Omega$$

Or Terminal voltage $= 0.3\left[\dfrac{(0.3 \times 1.5)}{(3 + 1.5)} + 4\right]$

$$= 1.5\ V$$

∴ $\qquad 1.8 - 1.5 = 0.3 \times r$

∴ $\qquad r = 1\,\Omega$

Ans. **(i)** Equivalent resistance of 3 Ω and 1.5 Ω in parallel,

$$R_1 = \frac{3 \times 1.5}{3 + 1.5}\,\Omega = 1\,\Omega$$

Potential difference, across R_1

⇒ $\qquad V_1 = IR_1$
$$= 0.3 \times 1 = 0.3V$$

∴ Current through 3W resistor,

$$I_1 = \frac{V_1}{3} = \frac{0.3}{3} = 0.1A$$

(ii) Total external resentence R = 1 + 4 = 5Ω

∵ $\qquad E = I\,(R + r)$
⇒ $\qquad 1.8 = 0.3\,(5 + r)$

⇒ $\qquad \dfrac{1.8}{0.3} = 5 + r \Rightarrow 6 = 5 + r$

∴ $\qquad r = 6 - 5 = 1\,\Omega$

Q. 2.

The diagram above shows a circuit with the key k open. Calculate:

(i) the resistance of the circuit when the key k is open.

(ii) the current drawn from the cell when the key k is open.

(iii) the resistance of the circuit when the key k is closed.

(iv) the current drawn from the cell when the key k is closed. **[2019]**

 Marking Scheme

(i) $R = 5 + 0.5 = 5.5\,\Omega$

(ii) $I = \dfrac{3.3}{5.5} = \dfrac{3}{5} = 0.6\,A$

(iii) $R_1 = \dfrac{5 \times 5}{5 + 5} = 2.5\,\Omega$

$\therefore R = 2.5 + 0.5 = 3\,\Omega$

(iv) $I = \dfrac{3.3}{3} = 1.1\,A$

Ans. **(i)** When the key k is open:

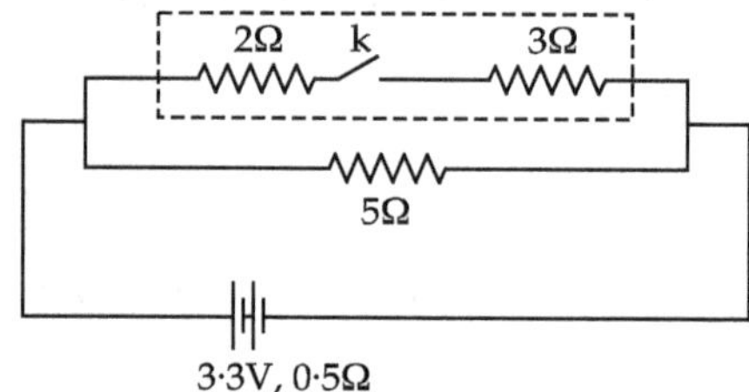

Resistance (R_1) of the circuit $= (5 + 0.5)\,\Omega$
$= 5.5\,\Omega$

(ii) Current (I_1) drawn when key k is open:

$$I_1 = \frac{V}{R_1} = \frac{3.3}{5.5}\,A$$

$$= \frac{3}{5}\,A = 0.6\,A$$

(iii) When the key k is closed:

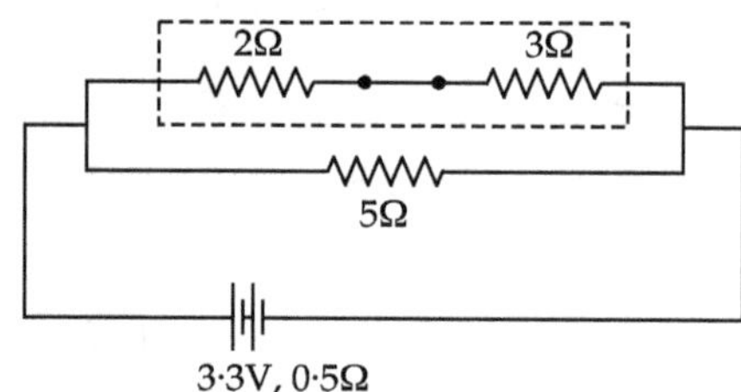

$2\,\Omega$ and $3\,\Omega$ are in series and their equivalent resistance $= (2 + 3)\Omega = 5\,\Omega$

$5\,\Omega$ and $5\,\Omega$ are in parallel

$$\frac{1}{R_P} = \frac{1}{5} + \frac{1}{5} = \frac{1+1}{5} = \frac{2}{5}$$

$$R_P = \frac{5}{2}\,\Omega = 2.5\,\Omega$$

Resistance of circuit (R_2) when key k is closed

$= (R_P + 0.5)\,\Omega$
$= (2.5 + 0.5)\,\Omega$
$= 3.0\,\Omega$

(iv) Current (I_2) drawn when key k is closed

$$= \frac{V}{R_2}$$

$$= \frac{3.3}{3}\,A = 1.1\,A$$

Q. 3. An electric iron is rated 220 V, 2 kW.

(i) If the iron is used for 2 h daily find the cost of running it for one week if it costs ₹ 4.25 per kWh.

(ii) Why is the fuse absolutely necessary in a power circuit? **[2018]**

Ans. **(i)** Electrical energy consumed daily
$= \text{Power} \times \text{Time} = 2\,kW \times 2\,h = 4\,kWh$

Electrical energy consumed in one week
$= 4\,kWh \times 7 = 28\,kWh$

$\therefore$ Total cost for running it for one week
$= ₹\,4.25 \times 28 = ₹\,119$

(ii) Fuse is necessary in power circuits to limit threats to human life and property damage due to excessive current or faulty appliance that may get connected to the power circuit.

Q. 4. **(i)** Explain the meaning of the statement 'current rating of a fuse is 5 A'.

(ii) In the transmission of power the voltage of power generated at the generating stations is stepped up from 11 kV to 132 kV before it is transmitted. Why? **[2017]**

Ans. **(i)** The current rating of a fuse is 5 A means that if current exceeds 5 A in the circuit, the fuse wire will melt.

(ii) The voltage is stepped up from 11 kV to 132 kV to minimise the loss of energy in the form of heat in the live wires used for transmission.

Q. 5. A battery of emf 12 V and internal resistance $2\,\Omega$ is connected with two resistors A and B of resistance $4\,\Omega$ and $6\,\Omega$ respectively joined in series.

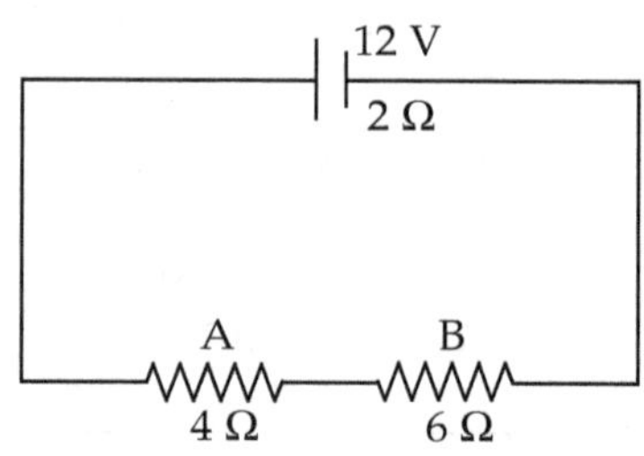

Find:
(i) Current in the circuit.
(ii) The terminal voltage of the cell.
(iii) The potential difference across $6\,\Omega$ resistor.
(iv) Electrical energy spent per minute in $4\,\Omega$ resistor. **[2016]**

Ans. (i) Total resistance $= 4 + 6 + 2 = 12\,\Omega$

$$I = \frac{\text{Emf}}{\text{Total resistance}}$$

$$= \frac{12}{12} = 1\,A$$

(ii)
$$V = E - Ir$$
$$= 12 - (1 \times 2) = 10\ V$$

(iii)
$$V = IR = 1 \times 6 = 6\ V$$

(iv) Electrical energy spent
$$= I^2Rt$$
$$= 1 \times 1 \times 4 \times 60 = 240\ J.$$

Q. 6. A cell of emf 2 V and internal resistance $1.2\,\Omega$ is connected with an ammeter of resistance $0.8\,\Omega$ and two resistors of $4.5\,\Omega$ and $9\,\Omega$ as shown in the diagram below:

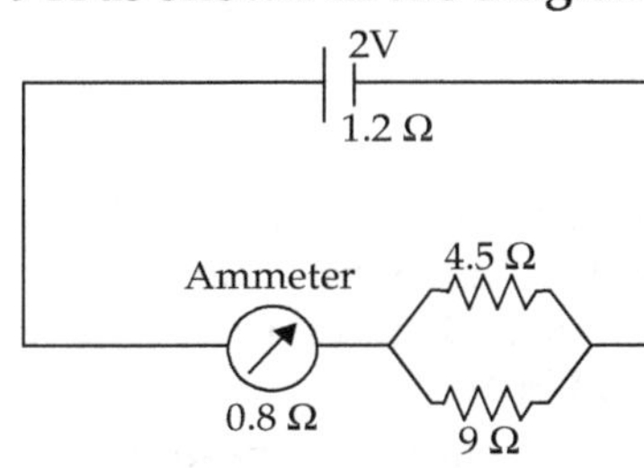

(i) What would be the reading on the Ammeter?
(ii) What is the potential difference across the terminals of the cell? **[2015]**

Ans. The resistance of $4.5\,\Omega$ and $9\,\Omega$ are connected in parallel.

∴ Equivalent resistance,

$$R_1 = \frac{(4.5 \times 9)}{(4.5 + 9)} = \frac{40.5}{13.5} = 3\,\Omega$$

Total resistance in the circuit (R)
$$= 1.2 + 0.8 + 3 = 5\,\Omega$$

(i) Reading of the ammeter
$$= \text{Current in the circuit (I)}$$
$$= \frac{\text{Total e.m.f. (E)}}{\text{Total resis}\tan\text{ce (R)}}$$
$$= \frac{2}{5} = 0.4\ \text{ampere}$$

(ii) Potential difference across the terminals of the cell (V)
$$= \text{Total p.d. in the external circuit}$$
$$= E - Ir$$
$$= 2 - (0.4 \times 1.2)$$
$$= 2 - 0.48 = 1.52\ \text{volts}$$

Q. 7. Two resistors of $4\,\Omega$ and $6\,\Omega$ are connected in parallel to a cell to draw 0.5 A current from the cell.
(i) Draw a labelled circuit diagram showing the above arrangement.
(ii) Calculate the current in each resistor. **[2014]**

Ans. (i)

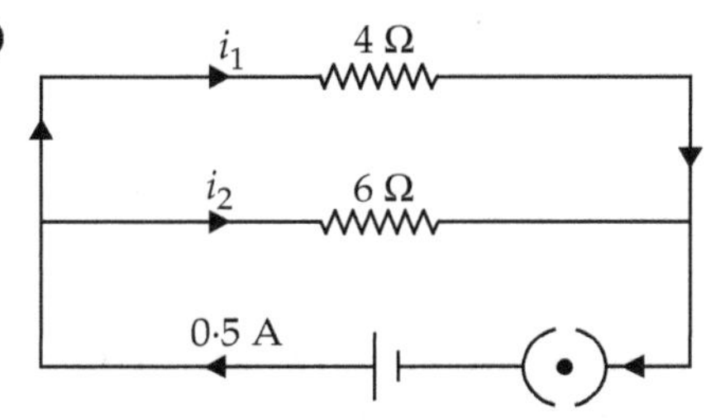

(ii)
$$\frac{1}{R} = \frac{1}{4} + \frac{1}{6}$$
$$R = 2.4\,\Omega$$

Now,
$$V = IR$$
$$V = 0.5 \times 2.4 = 1.2\ V$$
$$i_1 = \frac{V}{R_1} = \frac{1.2}{4} = 0.3\ A$$
$$i_2 = \frac{1.2}{6} = 0.2\ A$$

Q. 8. The figure shows a circuit. When the circuit is switched on, the ammeter reads 0.5 A.

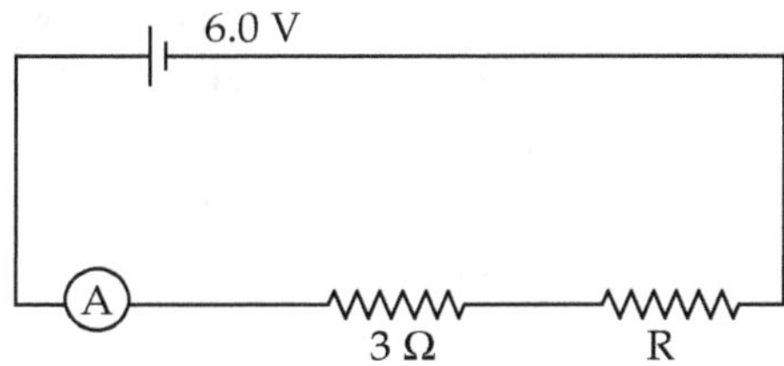

(i) Calculate the value of the unknown resistor R.
(ii) Calculate the charge passing through the $3\,\Omega$ resistor in 120 s.
(iii) Calculate the power dissipated in the $3\,\Omega$ resistor. **[2013]**

Ans. (i) We know, $V = IR'$
$\Rightarrow \qquad 6 = 0.5 \times R'$
$\Rightarrow \qquad R' = 12\,\Omega$
∵ $\qquad R' = 3 + R$
$\Rightarrow \qquad 12 = 3 + R$
∴ $\qquad R = 9\,\Omega$

(ii) $\qquad$ Charge, $q = It$
$\Rightarrow \qquad q = 0.5 \times 120 = 60\ \text{coulomb}$

(iii) Power dissipation,
$$P = I^2R$$
$$P = 0.5^2 \times 3 = 0.75\ W.$$

Q. 9. Three resistors are connected to a 6 V battery as shown in the figure given below:

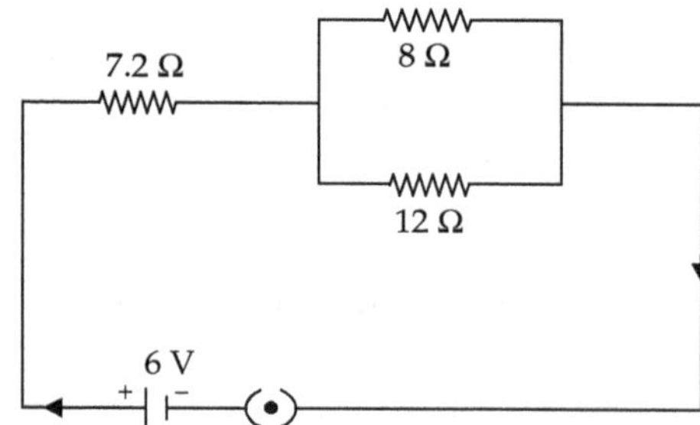

Calculate:

(i) the equivalent resistance of the circuit.

(ii) total current in the circuit.

(iii) potential difference across the 7.2 Ω resistor. **[2012]**

Ans. (i) In the given circuit, 8 Ω and 12 Ω are connected in parallel.

$$\therefore \quad \frac{1}{R_1} = \frac{1}{8} + \frac{1}{12} = \frac{3+2}{24} = \frac{5}{24}$$

$$R_1 = 4.8 \text{ ohm.}$$

Total resistance $= 4.8 + 7.2 = 12$ ohm

(ii)
$$V = IR$$
$$\Rightarrow \quad 6 = I \times 12$$
$$\Rightarrow \quad I = 0.5 \text{ A}$$

(iii)
$$V = IR = 0.5 \times 7.2 = 3.6 \text{ V.}$$

Q. 10. (i) Name two safety devices which are connected to the live wire of a household electrical circuit.

(ii) Give one important function of each of these two devices. **[2011]**

Ans. (i) (1) Switch (2) Fuse.

(ii) **(1)** Functions of Switch: It is an on-off device which is used to either connect or disconnect an electric appliance in a circuit. It is connected in the live wire.

(2) Function of Fuse: It is used to limit the current in the electric circuit.

Q. 11. Three resistors are connected to a 12 V battery as shown in the figure given below:

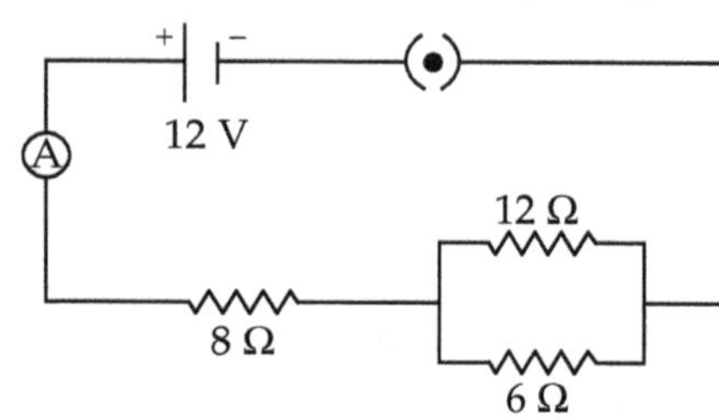

(i) What is the current through the 8 ohm resistor?

(ii) What is the potential difference across the parallel combination of 6 ohm and 12 ohm resistor?

(iii) What is the current through the 6 ohm resistor? **[2011]**

Ans. (i) 6 ohm and 12 ohm resistances are connected in parallel.

So,
$$\frac{1}{R_1} = \frac{1}{6} + \frac{1}{12} = \frac{2+1}{12} = \frac{3}{12}$$

$$\Rightarrow \quad \frac{1}{R_1} = \frac{1}{4}$$

$$\Rightarrow \quad R_1 = 4 \text{ ohm}$$

∴ Total Resistance, $R = 8 + 4 = 12$ ohm

Now, $V = IR$
$$\Rightarrow \quad 12 = I \times 12$$
$$\therefore \quad I = 1 \text{ A}$$

(ii)
$$V' = IR_1 = 1 \times 4 = 4 \text{ V}$$

(iii)
$$V' = I_1 R'$$
$$\Rightarrow \quad 4 = I_1 \times 6$$
$$\therefore \quad I_1 = \frac{4}{6} = 0.67 \text{ A}$$

Q. 12. (i) In what unit does the domestic electric meter measure the electrical energy consumed? State the value of this unit in S.I. Unit.

(ii) Why should switches always be connected to the live wire?

(iii) Give one precaution that should be taken while handling switches. **[2010]**

Ans. (i) The domestic electric meter measures the electrical consumption in kilowatt-hour (kWh).

$$1 \text{ kWh} = 1 \text{ kilowatt} \times 1 \text{ hour}$$
$$= 1000 \text{ js}^{-1} \times (60 \times 60) \text{ s}$$
$$= 3.6 \times 10^6 \text{ J.}$$

(ii) The switch should always be connected to the live wire, so that when it is 'off', no current flow through the appliance as the circuit is open. If the switch is connected to the neutral wire, then even in the 'off' position the appliance remains connected to high potential through the live wire. If anyone tries to touch the appliance he will get a shock which may be dangerous.

(iii) A switch should not be touched with wet hands.

Q. 13. Five resistors of different resistances are connected together as shown in the figure. A 12 V battery is connected to the arrangement.

Calculate:
 (i) the total resistance in the circuit.
(ii) the total current flowing in the circuit.
[2010]

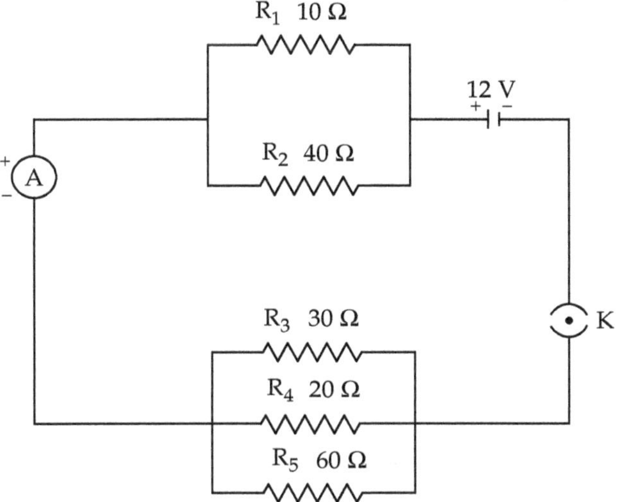

Ans. **(i)** From figure, R_1 and R_2 are parallel.

$$\frac{1}{R'} = \frac{1}{R_1} + \frac{1}{R_2}$$

$$= \frac{1}{10} + \frac{1}{40}$$

$$= \frac{5}{40}$$

$$= \frac{1}{8}$$

$$\therefore \qquad R' = 8\,\Omega$$

Resistances R_3, R_4 and R_5 are also parallel,

$$\therefore \qquad \frac{1}{R''} = \frac{1}{R_3} + \frac{1}{R_4} + \frac{1}{R_5}$$

$$= \frac{1}{30} + \frac{1}{20} + \frac{1}{60}$$

$$= \frac{6}{60}$$

$$= \frac{1}{10}$$

$$\therefore \qquad R'' = 10\,\Omega$$

$\therefore$ Total resistance in the circuit

$$= R' + R''$$

$$= 8 + 10 = 18\,\Omega$$

(ii) Given: V = 12 volt

$\therefore$ Total current flowing in the circuit

$$I = \frac{V}{R}$$

$$= \frac{12}{18}$$

$$= \frac{2}{3}$$

$$= 0.667\ \text{A}.$$

Q. 14. (i) The diagrams (a) and (b) given below are of a plug and a socket with arrows marked as 1, 2, 3 and 4, 5, 6 respectively on them. Identify and write Live (L), Neutral (N) and Earth (E) against the correct number.

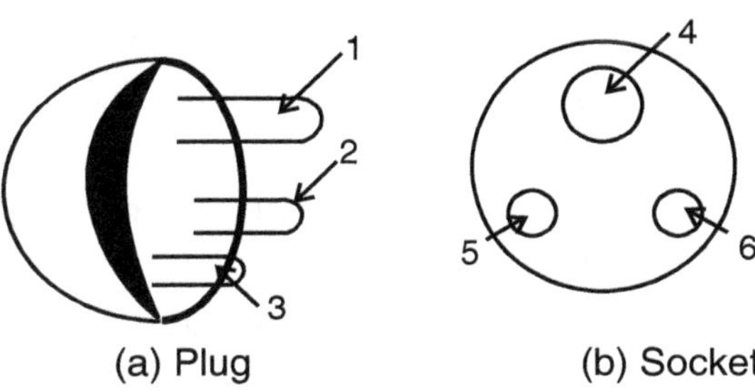

(a) Plug   (b) Socket

(ii) Calculate the electrical energy consumed when a bulb of 40 W is used for 12.5 hours everyday for 30 days. **[2009]**

Ans. **(i)**   Plug $1 \to$ Earth   Socket $4 \to$ Earth

$2 \to$ Neutral $\qquad\qquad 6 \to$ Live

$3 \to$ Live $\qquad\qquad\quad 5 \to$ Neutral

(ii)   Electrical energy consumed $= Pt$

$$= 40 \times 12.5 \times 30 = 15000\ \text{watt-hour.}$$

Q. 15. A cell of e.m.f. 1.5 V and internal resistance 1.0 Ω is connected to two resistors of 4.0 Ω and 20.0 Ω in series as shown in the figure:

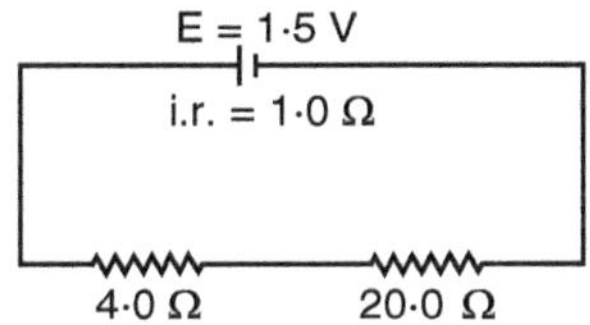

Calculate the:

(i) Current in the circuit.

(ii) Potential difference across the 4.0 ohm resistor.

(iii) Voltage drop when the current is flowing.

(iv) Potential difference across the cell.

[2007]

Ans.   E.m.f. of cell = 1.5 Volt,

Internal resistance = 1.0 ohm

External resistance $= r_1 + r_2$ (in series)

$$= 4 + 20 = 24\,\Omega$$

$$\text{Current (I)} = \frac{E}{r + R}$$

or

$$I = \frac{1.5}{1 + 24} = \frac{1.5}{25}$$

$$= .06\ \text{Amp.}$$

(ii) $\therefore$ P.D. across 4 Ω resistor $= r_1 I = 4 \times .06$

$$= .24 \text{ Volt}$$

(iii) Voltage drop $= Ir = .06 \times 1$

$$= .06 \text{ Volt.}$$

(iv) $\therefore$ Potential across cell $= RI = 24 \times .06$

$$= 1.44 \text{ Volt.}$$

Q. 16. In the figure below, the ammeter A reads 0.3 A. Calculate:

(i) The total resistance of the circuit.

(ii) The value of R.

(iii) The current flowing through R.   **[2006]**

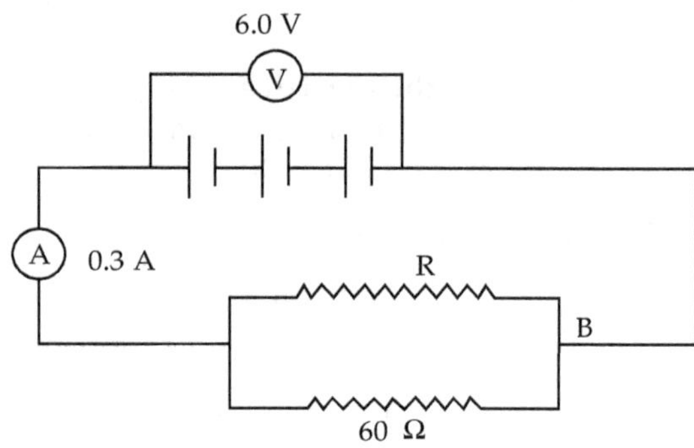

Ans. **(i)** Since $V = IR$

$$\therefore \qquad R = \frac{V}{I} = \frac{6.0}{0.3} = 20 \ \Omega$$

(ii) Total resistance $= 20 \ \Omega$

Given that resistances are in parallel

$$\therefore \qquad \frac{1}{20} = \frac{1}{R} + \frac{1}{60}$$

$$\text{or} \qquad \frac{1}{R} = \frac{1}{20} - \frac{1}{60}$$

$$\frac{1}{R} = \frac{3 - 1}{60}$$

Therefore, $\qquad R = \frac{60}{2} = 30 \ \Omega$

(iii) Since $\qquad V = IR$

and potential (V) is equal at the two ends *i.e.,* A and B.

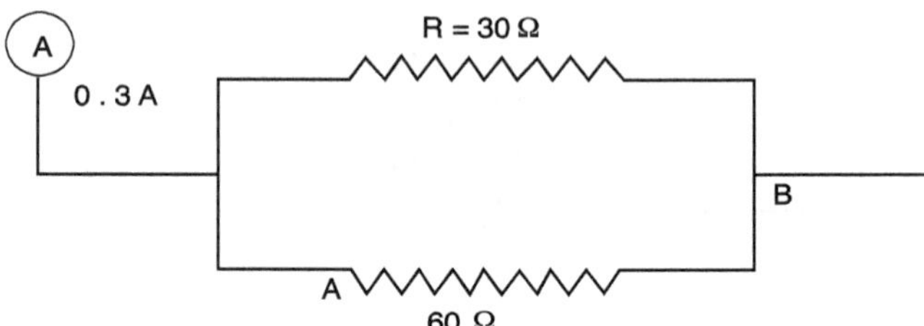

Let I_1 be current flowing through R, then $(0.3 - I_1)$ is current flowing through 60 Ω resistance.

Now $\qquad V = V \Rightarrow I_1 R_1 = I_2 R_2$

$$I_1 \times 30 = (0.3 - I_1) \times 60$$

$$I_1 = 0.6 - 2I_1$$

$$3I_1 = 0.6$$

$$I_1 = \frac{0.6}{3} = 0.2 \text{ A}$$

$\therefore$ Current flowing through R $= 0.2$ A

Magnetic Effect of Current

 ## Short Answer Type Questions-I

Q. 1. When a current carrying conductor is placed in a magnetic field, it experiences a mechanical force. What should be the angle between the magnetic field and the length of the conductor so that the force experienced is :
  (i) Zero
  (ii) Maximum ? **[2020]**

Ans. (i) 0°
  (ii) 90°

Q. 2. The diagram below shows a loop of wire carrying current I :

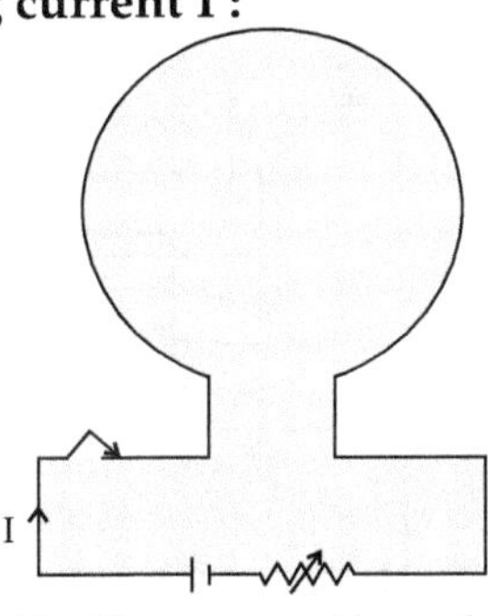

  (i) What is the magnetic polarity of the loop that faces us ?
  (ii) With respect to the diagram how can we increase the strength of the magnetic field produced by this loop ? **[2020]**

Ans. (i) South
  (ii) By increasing the strength of the current.

Q. 3. A magnet kept at the centre of two coils A and B is moved to and fro as shown in the diagram. The two galvanometers show deflection. **[2019]**

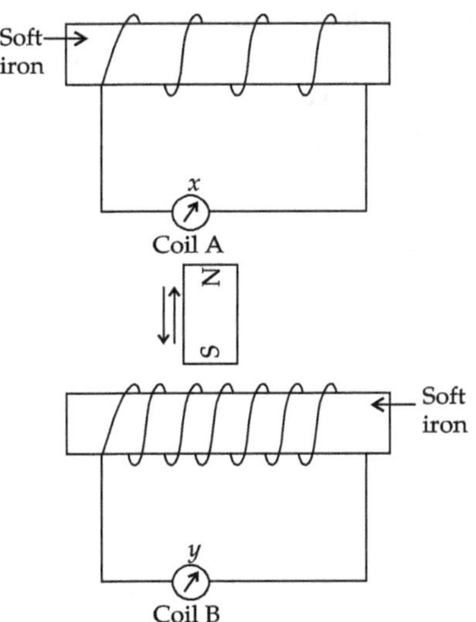

State with a reason whether:

$$x > y$$
or
$$x < y.$$

[x and y are magnitudes of deflection]

Ans. $x < y$ because coil B has more number of turns hence there will be a greater change in magnetic flux linked with the coil B.

Q. 4. State any two advantages of electromagnets over permanent magnets. **[2018]**

Ans. The advantages of electromagnets over permanent magnets are:

  (i) The strength of magnetic field of an electromagnet can easily be changed by changing the magnitude of current or the number of windings in its solenoid.

  (ii) The polarity of the electromagnet can be reversed easily by reversing the direction of current in its solenoid.

Q. 5. On reversing the direction of the current in a wire, the magnetic field produced by it gets......... **[2015]**

Ans. Reversed in direction.

Q. 6. (i) Why does a current carrying, freely suspended solenoid rest along a particular direction?
  (ii) State the direction in which it rests. **[2015]**

Ans. (i) This is because the current carrying freely suspended solenoid behaves like a bar magnet.
  (ii) It rests in the geographic North-South direction.

Q. 7. Name a common device that uses electro-magnets. **[2014]**

Ans. Electromagnets are used in electric bell, door alarm, electric motor, etc.

Q. 8. You have been provided with a solenoid AB.
  (i) What is the polarity at end A?
  (ii) Give one advantage of an electromagnet over a permanent magnet. **[2013]**

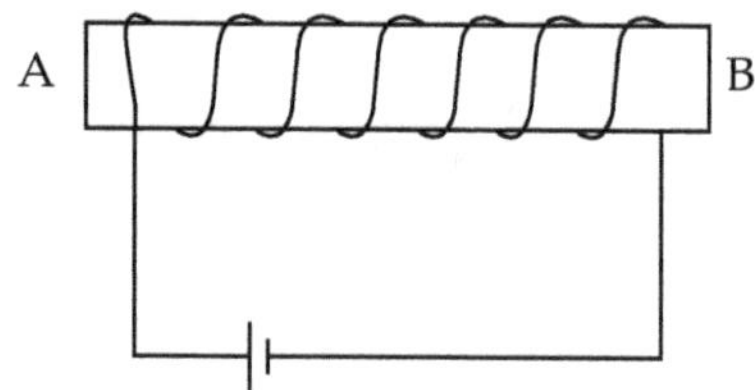

Ans. **(i)** North pole.

(ii) The strength of the magnetic field of an electromagnet can be changed according to its use and it will be a magnet till the time current passes through it whereas, the strength of permanent magnet can not be increased and can not be magnetized and demagnetized in an instance.

Q. 9. The figure below shows an electromagnet.
(i) What will be the polarity at the end X?
(ii) Suggest a way by which the strength of the electromagnet referred to in the question, may be increased. **[2009]**

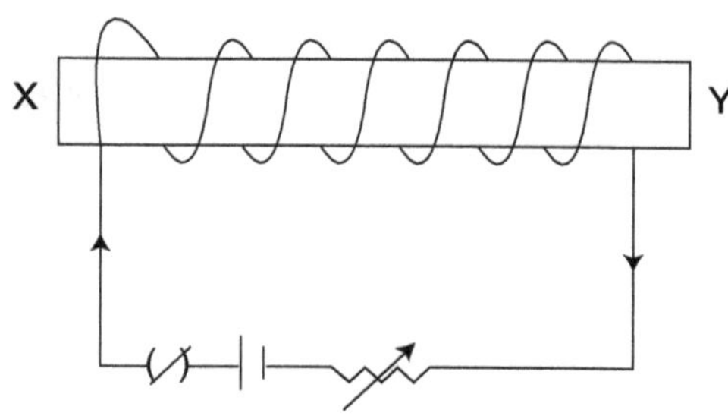

Ans. **(i)** The polarity at the end X is North.

(ii) By increasing the current.

Q. 10. State two advantages of an electromagnet over a permanent magnet. **[2006]**

Ans. **(i)** An electromagnet can produce a stronger magnetic field than permanent magnet.

(ii) The polarity of an electromagnet can be reversed whereas that of a permanent magnet cannot be reversed.

Short Answer Type Questions-II

Q. 1. The diagram shows a coil wound around a U shape soft iron bar AB.

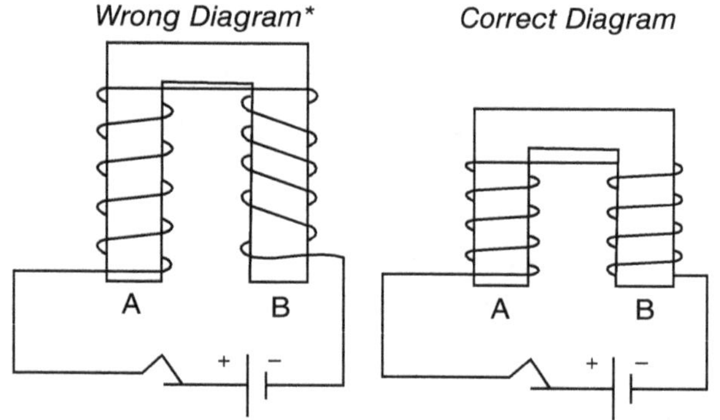

* **Mark is an error by the Council. We suggest you to use 'Correct Diagram' instead of 'Wrong Diagram'.**

(i) What is the polarity induced at the ends A and B when the switch is pressed?

(ii) Suggest one way to strengthen the magnetic field in the electromagnet.

(iii) What will be the polarities at A and B if the direction of current is reversed in the circuit? **[2018]**

Ans. **(i)** Polarity induced at end A is south pole (S) and at end B is north pole (N).

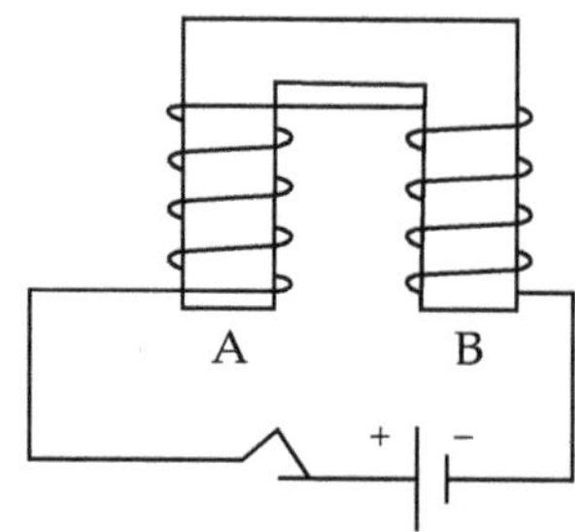

(ii) The strength of magnetic field can be increased by increasing the magnitude of current or by increasing the number of windings in the electromagnet.

(iii) If direction of current is reversed, the polarities at A and B will also be reversed. End A will become north pole (N) and end B will become south pole (S).

Q. 2. The diagram below shows a current carrying loop or a circular coil passing through a sheet of cardboard at the points M and N. The sheet of cardboard is sprinkled uniformly with iron filings.

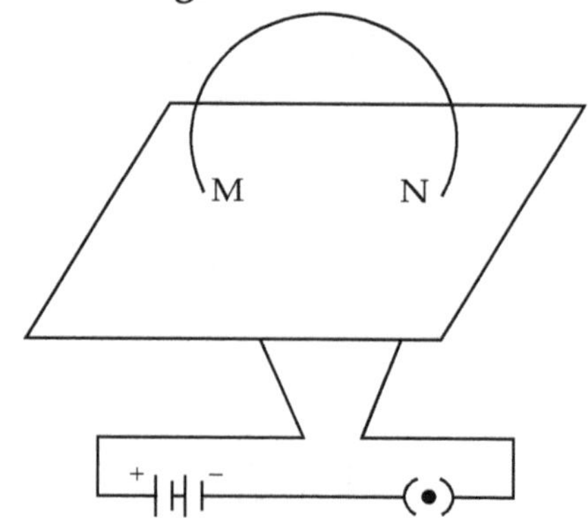

(i) Copy the diagram and draw an arrow on the circular coil to show the direction of current flowing through it.

(ii) Draw the pattern of arrangement of the iron filings when current is passed through the loop. **[2012]**

Ans. **(i)**

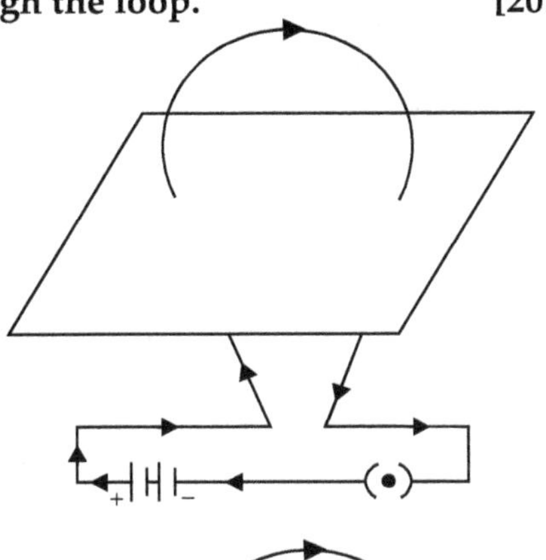

(ii)

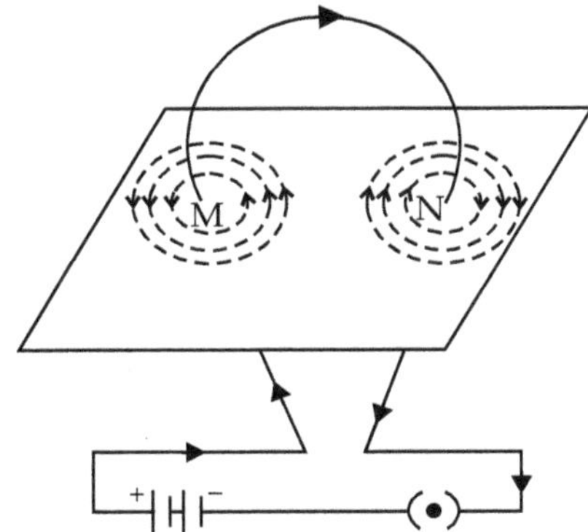

Q. 3. **(i)** A straight wire conductor passes vertically through a piece of cardboard sprinkled with iron filings. Copy the diagram and show the setting of iron filings when a current is passed through the wire in the upward direction and the cardboard is tapped gently. Draw arrows to represent the direction of the magnetic field lines.

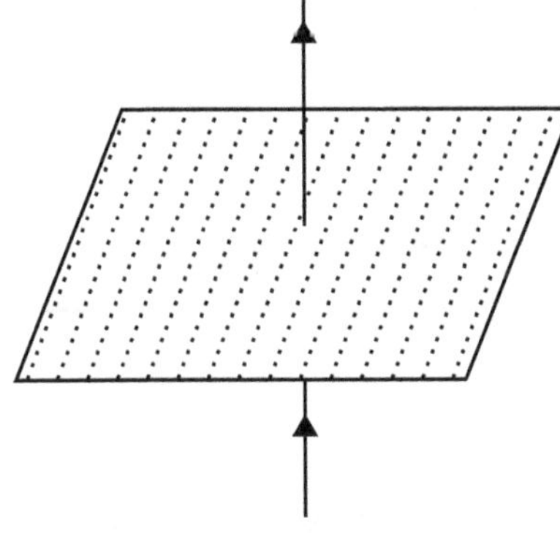

(ii) Name the law which helped you to find the direction of the magnetic field lines. **[2010]**

Ans. **(i)**

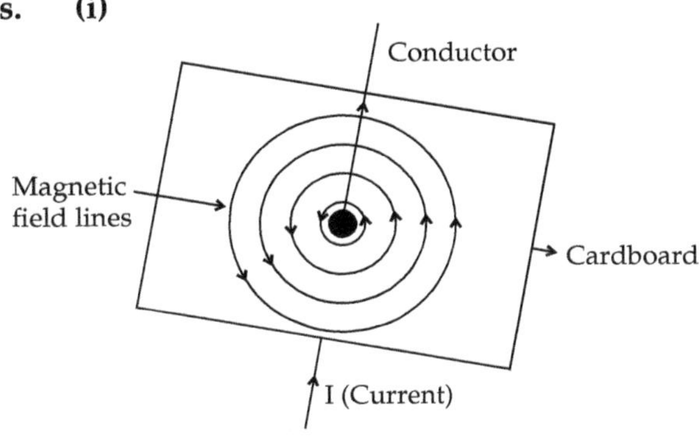

(ii) Right hand thumb rule helped to find the direction of magnetic field lines.

Q. 4. **(i)** What is the name given to a cylindrical coil whose diameter is less in comparison to its length?

(ii) If a piece of soft iron is placed inside the current carrying coil, what is the name given to the device?

(iii) Give one use of the device named by you in (ii) above. **[2008]**

Ans. **(i)** Cylindrical coil whose diameter is less in comparison to its length is a solenoid.

(ii) Electromagnet.

(iii) Electromagnet is used in an electric bell.

Q. 5. **(i)** Why does a magnetic needle show a deflection when brought close to a current carrying conductor?

(ii) A wire bent into a circle carries current in an anticlockwise direction. What polarity does this face of the coil exhibit? **[2008]**

Ans. **(i)** Magnetic needle shows deflection when brought closer to a current carrying conductor because it experiences a magnetic field around it.

(ii) This coil shows North polarity.

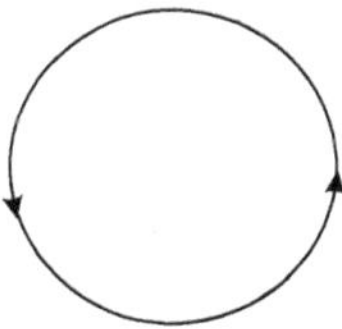

Q. 6. **(i)** State two factors on which the strength of an induced current depends.

(ii) When a solenoid that is carrying current is freely suspended, it comes to rest along a particular direction. Why does this happen? **[2007]**

Ans. **(i)** Two factors on which the strength of an induced current depends:

(1) The change in magnetic flux.

(2) The rate of change of magnetic flux.

(ii) Current carrying solenoid behaves like a bar magnet. At the end in which direction of current is anticlockwise, behaves as north pole and where current is in clockwise direction behaves as south pole. Therefore on suspending it freely, it sets itself in North-south direction as bar magnet does.

Q. 7. Give one use each of the electromagnetic radiations given below:

(i) Microwaves

(ii) Ultraviolet radiation

(iii) Infrared radiation. **[2006]**

Ans. **(i)** Microwaves are used for communication.

(ii) Ultraviolet radiations are used for sterilising purposes.

(iii) Infrared radiations are used as signals during war.

Q. 8. What will happen to a compass needle when the compass is placed below a wire and a current is made to flow through the wire? Give a reason to justify your answer.

Ans. The compass needle will show deflection. This happens because when a current is passed through a conductor (here, wire) a magnetic field is produced around the conductor due to which the compass needle gets deflected.

Long Answer Type Questions-I

Q. 1. The diagram below shows a magnetic needle kept just below the conductor AB which is kept in North-South direction. **[2019]**

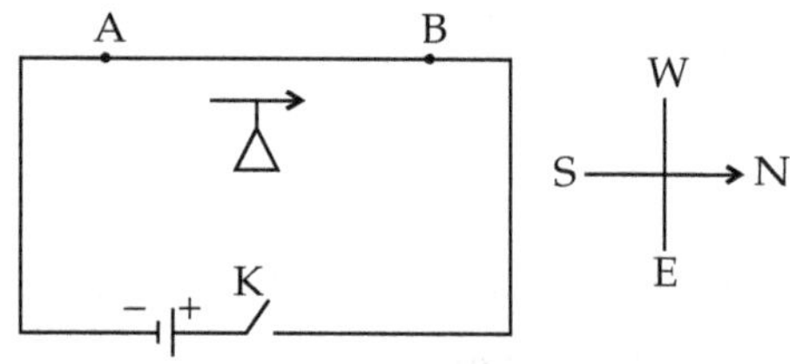

(i) In which direction will the needle deflect when the key is closed?

(ii) Why is the deflection produced?

(iii) What will be the change in the deflection if the magnetic needle is taken just above the conductor AB?

(iv) Name one device which works on this principle.

 Marking Scheme

(i) Towards east

(ii) Magnetic effect of current

(iii) Deflection in the opposite direction / towards west

(iv) Electric Bell, Electromagnet

Ans. **(i)** Needle deflects towards the east.

(ii) On passing current in the wire AB, a magnetic field is produced around it and the magnetic needle experiences a torque in this magnetic field, so it deflects to align itself in the direction of magnetic field at that point.

(iii) Needle will deflect towards the west.

(iv) Electric motor.

Q. 2. **(i)** Name two factors on which the magnitude of an induced e.m.f. in the secondary coil depends.

(ii) In the following diagram an arrow shows the motion of the coil towards the bar magnet.

(1) State in which direction the current flows, A to B or B to A?

(2) Name the law used to come to the conclusion.

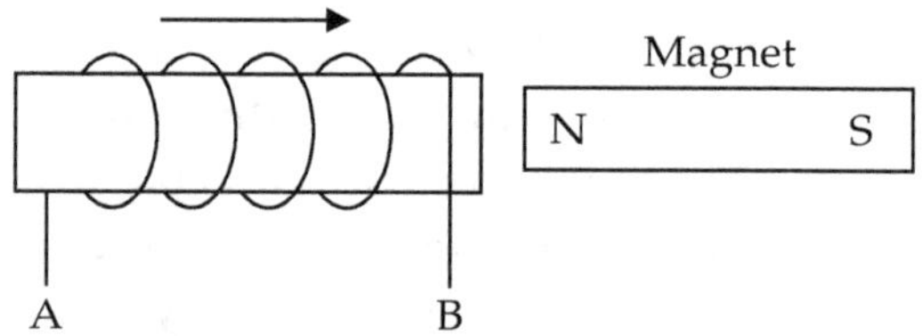

[2014]

Ans. **(i)** Magnitude of induced e.m.f. depends on

(1) the magnitude of e.m.f. applied in the primary coil.

(2) the number of turns in the coil.

(ii) **(1)**

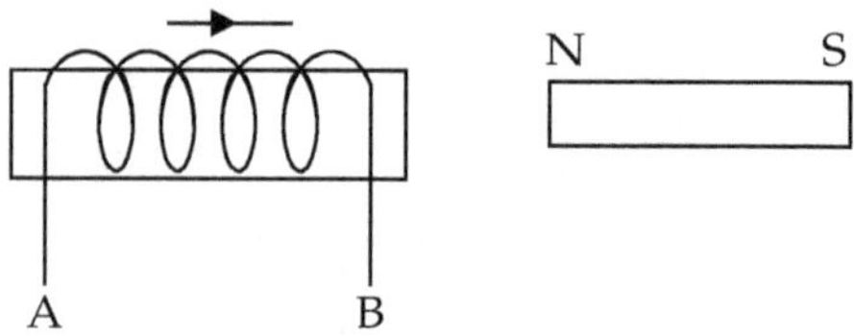

Current flows from A to B as the coil moves towards the magnet and induced e.m.f. always opposes the motion.

(2) Lenz's law

Q. 3. State one advantage of a.c. over d.c.   **[2013]**

Ans. Advantage of a.c. over d.c. is that it is able to travel long distance without much power loss.

Q. 4. **(i)** State two ways by which the magnetic field of a solenoid can be made stronger.
(ii) What material is used for making the armature of an electric bell? Give a reason for using this material.   **[2010]**

Ans. **(i)** The magnetic field of a solenoid can be made stronger by the following two ways:

(1) By increasing the current through the solenoid.

(2) By increasing number of turns of windings of the solenoid.

(ii) A soft iron metal piece is used for making the armature of an electric bell.
Reason: Soft iron can be easily magnetized and demagnetized.

Q. 5. How does the heat produced in a wire or a conductor depend upon the:

(1) current passing through the conductor.

(2) resistance of the conductor?

Ans. Heat produced in a wire:

(1) Is directly proportional to the square of the current.

(2) Is directly proportional to the resistance of the conductor.

❓ Short Answer Type Questions-I

Q. 1. Why does stone lying in the sun get heated up much more than water lying for the same duration of time ? [2020]

Ans. The specific heat capacity of stone is much less than the specific heat capacity of water, hence for the same heat supplied the temperature of stone rises much more than water for the same duration and gets heated up much more.

Q. 2. Two metallic blocks P and Q having masses in ratio 2 : 1 are supplied with the same amount of heat. If their temperatures rise by same degree, compare their specific heat capacities. [2020]

Ans. Let specific heat capacity of block P and block Q be C_P and C_Q respectively.

Metallic block P	Metallic block B
$m_1 = 2\ m$	$m_2 = m$
$c_1 = C_P$	$c_2 = C_Q$
$\Delta T = \Delta T$	$\Delta T = \Delta T$
$H_1 = m_1 c_1\ \Delta T$	$H_2 = m_2 c_2\ \Delta T$
$= 2m\ C_P\ \Delta T$	$= m\ C_Q\ \Delta T$

$\because$ $H1 = H2$

$\Rightarrow$ $2m\ C_P\ \Delta T = mC_Q\ \Delta T$

$\therefore$ $\dfrac{C_P}{C_Q} = \dfrac{m \times \Delta T}{2m \times \Delta T} = \dfrac{1}{2}$

$\therefore$ Ratio of specific heat capacities of block P and block Q is 1 : 2.

Q. 3. (i) Name the physical quantity which is measured in calories.

(ii) How is calorie related to the S.I. unit of that quantity? [2019]

Ans. (i) Heat energy is measured in calories.

(ii) 1 calorie = 4.186 joule.

Q. 4. The specific heat capacity of a substance A is 3,800 $Jkg^{-1}K^{-1}$ and that of a substance B is 400 $Jkg^{-1}K^{-1}$. Which of the two substances is a good conductor of heat? Give a reason for your answer. [2019]

Ans. Substance B with specific heat capacity 400 $Jkg^{-1}\ K^{-1}$ is good conductor of heat because for the same heat energy and same mass, the rise in temperature of B will be more.

Q. 5. How does an increase in the temperature affect the specific resistance of a: [2019]
(i) Metal and
(ii) Semiconductor?

Ans. (i) Specific resistance of a metal increases with the increase in temperature.

(ii) Specific resistance of a semiconductor decreases with the increase in temperature.

Q. 6. (i) State whether the specific heat capacity of a substance remains the same when its state changes from solid to liquid.

(ii) Give one example to support your answer. [2019]

Ans. (i) No, specific heat capacity of a substance is different in its different phases (states).

(ii) Specific heat capacity of water is 4200 $Jkg^{-1}\ K^{-1}$ and that of ice is 2100 $Jkg^{-1}\ K^{-1}$.

Q. 7. (i) How can a temperature in degree Celsius be converted into S.I. unit of temperature?

(ii) A liquid X has the maximum specific heat capacity and is used as a coolant in car radiators. Name the liquid X. [2018]

Ans. (i) The S.I. unit of temperature is Kelvin (K). To convert temperature in degree Celsius to Kelvin, 273.15 is added to degree Celsius.

$$T\ (K) = {}^\circ C + 273.15$$

(ii) The liquid 'X' is water because water has highest specific heat capacity.

Q. 8. A solid metal weighing 150 g melts at its melting point of 800°C by providing heat at the rate of 100 W. The time taken for it to completely melt at the same temperature is 4 min. What is the specific latent heat of fusion of the metal? [2018]

Ans. Given: $m = 150$ g, Power (P) = 100 W, Time (t) = 4 minute = 4 × 60 = 240 s

Heat energy supplied to melt the metal
$$= P \times t$$
$$= 100 \times 240 \text{ joule}$$
Heat energy required by the metal to melt
$$= mL$$
$$= 150 \times L \text{ joule}$$

If there is no exchange of heat energy with the surrounding, then
$$150 \times L = 100 \times 240$$
or
$$L = \frac{100 \times 240}{150}$$
$$= 160 \text{ J g}^{-1}.$$

Q. 9. Define heat capacity and state its S.I. unit. **[2017]**

Ans. The amount of heat energy needed to raise the temperature of a body by 1°C (or 1 K) is called the heat capacity or thermal capacity of the body. Its S.I. unit is JK^{-1}.

Q. 10. Why is the base of a cooking pan generally made thick? **[2017]**

Ans. The base of a cooking pan is made thick to increase its heat capacity so that it gets heated slowly and imparts sufficient heat energy at a slow rate to the food for its cooking. It also helps to keep the cooked food warm for a long time.

Q. 11. A solid of mass 50 g at 150°C is placed in 100 g of water at 11°C, when the final temperature recorded is 20°C. Find the specific heat capacity of the solid. **[2017]**
(Specific heat capacity of water = 4.2 J/g°C)

Ans. Given: For solid (Hot body): $m_1 = 50$ g, $T_1 = 150$°C, $T = 20$°C

Fall in temperature of solid,
$$\Delta T_1 = (150 - 20)°C$$
$$= 130°C$$
$$c_1 = ?$$

For water (Cold body): $m_2 = 100$ g, $T_2 = 11$°C, $T = 20$°C

Rise in temperature of water,
$$\Delta T_2 = (20 - 11)°C$$
$$= 9°C$$
$$c_2 = 4.2 \text{ Jg}^{-1}°C^{-1}$$

Heat lost by hot body
$$= m_1 c_1 \Delta T_1$$
$$= 50 \times c_1 \times 130 \text{ joule}$$

Heat gained by cold body
$$= m_2 c_2 \Delta T_2$$
$$= 100 \times 4.2 \times 9 \text{ joule}$$

From the principle of calorimetry, if the system is fully insulated, then,

Heat lost by hot body
$$= \text{Heat gained by cold body}$$
or
$$50 \times c_1 \times 130 = 100 \times 4.2 \times 9$$
or
$$c_1 = \frac{100 \times 4.2 \times 9}{50 \times 130} \text{Jg}^{-1}°C^{-1}$$
$$= 0.58 \text{ Jg}^{-1}°C^{-1}$$

Q. 12. Calculate the mass of ice required to lower the temperature of 300 g of water at 40°C to water at 0°C.
(Specific latent heat of ice = 336 J/g, Specific heat capacity of water = 4.2 J/g°C) **[2016]**

Ans. Mass of water = 300 g
Specific heat of water = 4.2 J/g °C
Specific heat of ice = 336 J/g
Fall in temperature, $\theta_F = 40 - 0 = 40$°C
Heat gained by ice
$$= \text{Heat lost by water}$$
∴ Mass of ice × Specific heat of ice
$$= \text{Mass of water} \times \text{Specific heat of water}$$
$$\times \text{Fall in temperature}$$

$$\text{Mass of ice} = \frac{\text{Mass of water} \times \text{Specific heat of water} \times \theta_F}{\text{Specific heat of ice}}$$
$$= \frac{300 \times 4.2 \times 40}{336} = 150 \text{ g}$$

Q. 13. What do you understand by the following statements: **[2016]**
(i) The heat capacity of the body is 60 JK^{-1}.
(ii) The specific heat capacity of lead is 130 $Jkg^{-1}K^{-1}$.

Ans. (i) The heat capacity of the body is 60 JK^{-1}. This means that the amount of heat energy required to raise the body's temperature by 1 K without going through a change of state is 60 J.
(ii) The specific heat capacity of lead is 130 Jkg^{-1} K^{-1}. This means that the amount of heat energy needed to raise the temperature of 1 kg of lead through 1 K is 130 J.

Q. 14. State two factors upon which the heat absorbed by a body depends. **[2016]**

Ans. Two factors upon which the heat absorbed by a body depends are:
(i) the change in the temperature of the body.
(ii) the mass of the body.

Q. 15. Calculate the quantity of heat produced in a 20 Ω resistor carrying 2.5 A current in 5 minutes. **[2016]**

Ans. Current $(I) = 2.5$ A

Resistance $= 20\ \Omega$

Time $(t) = 5$ min $= 5 \times 60$ sec

$= 300$ sec

Quantity of heat produced (H)

$= I^2Rt$

$= (2.5)^2 \times 20 \times 300$

$= 37500$ J $= 37.5$ kJ

Q. 16. Rishi is surprised when he sees water boiling at 115°C in a container. Give reasons as to why water can boil at the above temperature. **[2015]**

Ans. Water boils at higher temperature because of the increase in pressure or the presence of some impurity. More the impurity or pressure, more will be the boiling point.

Q. 17. Which property of water makes it an effective coolant? **[2015]**

Ans. High specific heat capacity (4200 Jkg^{-1}K^{-1}) of water makes it an effective coolant.

Q. 18. 50 g of metal piece at 27°C requires 2400 J of heat energy so as to attain a temperature of 327°C. Calculate the specific heat capacity of the metal. **[2014]**

Ans. Given, $m = 50$ g or $\dfrac{50}{1000}$ kg

$Q = 2400$ J

$T_1 = 27°C$

$T_2 = 327°C$

We know, $Q = mc\Delta t$

or $c = \dfrac{Q}{m\Delta t}$

$= \dfrac{2400}{\dfrac{50}{1000} \times (327 - 27)}$

$(\because\ \Delta t°C = \Delta tK)$

$= \dfrac{2400}{\dfrac{50}{1000} \times (300)}$

$= \dfrac{2400}{15} = 160$ Jkg^{-1} K^{-1}

Q. 19. Define the term 'Heat capacity' and state its S.I. unit. **[2013]**

Ans. **Heat capacity:** Heat capacity of the body is the amount of heat energy required to raise its temperature by 1°C or 1 K.

The S.I. unit of heat capacity is joule per kelvin (JK^{-1}).

Q. 20. How much heat energy is released when 5 g of water at 20°C changes to ice at 0°C?
[Specific heat capacity of water = 4.2 J g^{-1}°C^{-1}
Specific latent heat of fusion of ice = 336 J g^{-1}]
[2013]

Ans. Heat energy required

$= mc\Delta t + mL$

$= 5 \times 4.2 \times (20 - 0) + 5 \times 336$

$= 420 + 1680 = 2100$ J

Q. 21. A hot solid of mass 60 g at 100°C is placed in 150 g of water at 20°C. The final steady temperature recorded is 25°C. Calculate the specific heat capacity of the solid. [Specific heat capacity of water = 4200 J kg^{-1} °C^{-1}]
[2012]

Ans. Given:

Mass of hot solid, $m_1 = 60$ g at 100°C

Mass of water, $m_2 = 150$ g at 20°C

Final temperature $= 25°C$

By principle of calorimetry,

Heat given = Heat taken

$\Rightarrow \quad m_1c_1\Delta t_1 = m_2c_2\Delta t_2$

$\Rightarrow 60 \times c \times (100 - 25) = 150 \times 4.2 \times (25 - 20)$

$\therefore$ Required specific heat capacity,

$c = 0.7$ J g^{-1} °C^{-1}

Q. 22. Differentiate between heat and temperature.
[2011]

Ans.

	Heat		Temperature
1.	It is a form of energy.	1.	It is the sensation of hotness and coldness.
2.	Unit of heat is joule.	2.	Unit of temperature is °C or kelvin.

Q. 23. 200 g of hot water at 80°C is added to 300 g of cold water at 10°C. Calculate the final temperature of the mixture of water. Consider the heat taken by the container to be negligible. [specific heat capacity of water is 4200 J kg^{-1} °C^{-1}]
[2011]

Ans. Given: Mass of hot water $m = 200$ g

Temperature $= 80°C$

Mass of cold water, $m = 300$ g

Temperature $= 10°C$

Let the final temperature of mixture $= \theta$.

By the principle of calorimetry,

Heat given = Heat taken

$200 \times c \times (80 - \theta) = 300 \times c \times (\theta - 10)$

or $\quad 200 \times 80 - 200\ \theta = 300\ \theta - 300 \times 10$

or $\quad 16000 - 200\ \theta = 300\ \theta - 3000$

or $\qquad 19000 = 500\,\theta$

$\therefore \qquad \theta = 38°C$

Q. 24. **(i)** Which material is the calorimeter commonly made of?

(ii) Give one reason for using this material. **[2010]**

Ans. **(i)** Copper

(ii) It is good conductor of heat, so the vessel soon acquires the temperature of its contents.

Q. 25. Why do pieces of ice added to a drink cool it much faster than ice cold water added to it? **[2009]**

Ans. Ice needs an amount of heat, equal to its specific latent heat (336×10^3 J/kg) of fusion to melt and form water at 0°C. Hence each kilogram of ice is able to withdraw 336×10^3 J more heat than ice-cold water of 0°C. Pieces of ice therefore produce more effective cooling than ice-cold water.

Q. 26. 40 g of water at 60°C is poured into a vessel containing 50 g of water at 20°C. The final temperature recorded is 30°C. Calculate the thermal capacity of the vessel. (Take specific heat capacity of water as 4.2 J g^{-1}°C^{-1}). **[2009]**

Ans. Given: $m_1 = 40$ g, $t_1 = 60°C$, $m_2 = 50$ g, $t_2 = 20°C$, $t = 30°C$.

Heat lost by hot water = Heat gained by cold water + Heat gained by vessel

$40 \times 4.2 \times (60° - 30°) = 50 \times 4.2 \times (30° - 20°)$
$$+ \,C' \times (30° - 20°)$$

$$5040 = 2100 + 10\,C'$$

$$10\,C' = 2940$$

Heat capacity, $C' = \dfrac{2940}{10}$

$$= 294 \text{ J/°C}$$

Q. 27. A certain quantity of ice at 0°C is heated till it changes into steam at 100°C. Draw a time-temperature heating curve to represent it. Label the two phase changes in your graph. **[2008]**

Ans.

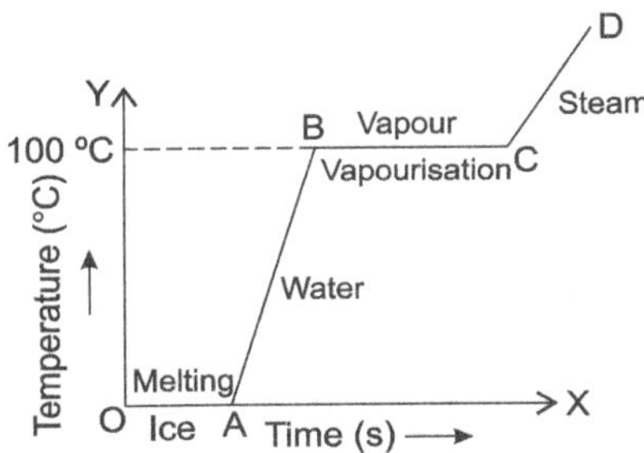

Ist phase change $\rightarrow$ O to A

IInd phase change $\rightarrow$ B to C.

Q. 28. Some hot water was added to three times its mass of cold water at 10°C and the resulting temperature was found to be 20°C. What was the temperature of the hot water? **[2007]**

Ans. Let the temperature of hot water be t°C and mass of hot water $= m$ g

$\therefore \qquad$ Mass of cold water $= 3\,m$ g

Temperature of cold water $= 10°C$

Final temperature of mixture $= 20°C$

Heat taken by cold water $= 3m \times c \times (20 - 10)$

Heat given by hot water $= m \times c \times (t - 20)$

Heat given = Heat taken

$m \times c \times (t - 20) = 3m \times c \times 10$

$$t - 20 = 30$$

$\therefore \qquad t = 30 + 20 = 50°C$

Q. 29. Why are burns caused by steam more severe than those caused by boiling water at the same temperature? **[2007]**

Ans. Steam has specific latent heat 2,268 joule/gm therefore first it burns by this heat in condensing to 100°C water.

Q. 30. Give two reasons as to why copper is preferred over other metals for making calorimeters. **[2006]**

Ans. Copper is preferred over other metals for making calorimeters because:

(i) It has a low specific heat capacity.

(ii) It takes negligible amount of heat from its contents to attain the temperature of the contents.

Q. 31. Calculate the amount of heat released when 5.0 g of water at 20°C is changed into ice at 0°C.

(Specific heat capacity of water $= 4.2$ J/g°C

Specific latent heat of fusion of ice $= 336$ J/g). **[2006]**

Ans. 5 g water at 20°C $\xrightarrow{\ mc\theta\ }$ 5 g water at 0°C

$\xrightarrow{\ mL\ }$ 5 g ice at 0°C.

$\therefore$ Amount of heat released $= mc\theta + mL$

$$= 5 \times 4.2 \times (20° - 0°) + 5 \times 336$$

$$= 21.0 \times 20 + 1680$$

$$= 420 + 1680$$

$$= 2100 \text{ joule}$$

 ## Short Answer Type Questions-II

Q. 1. (i) Define heat capacity of a substance.
(ii) Write the SI unit of heat capacity.
(iii) What is the relationship between heat capacity and specific heat capacity of a substance ? **[2020]**

 **Marking Scheme**

(i) The amount of heat energy absorbed to raise the temperature of a body by unit degree is called as heat capacity.
(ii) unit - J K^{-1}
(iii) Heat capacity = mass × specific heat capacity

Ans. (i) Heat capacity of a body is the amount of heat energy required to raise its temperature by 1 Kelvin.

(ii) SI Unit of heat capacity is joule per Kelvin (JK^{-1}).

(ii) Heat capacity = Mass × Specific heat capacity

Q. 2. The diagram below shows the change of phases of a substance on a temperature vs time graph on heating the substance at a constant rate.

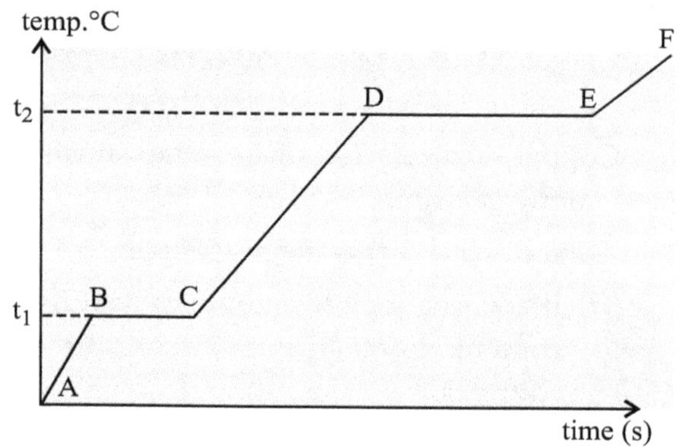

(i) Why is the slope of CD less than slope of AB ?
(ii) What is the boiling and melting point of the substance ? **[2020]**

 **Marking Scheme**

(i) Specific heat capacity in liquid state is greater than specific heat capacity in solid state.
(ii) Boiling point t_2°C
Melting point t_1°C

Ans. (i) The slope of CD is less than slope of AB because specific heat capacity of liquid phase of same material can be different from that of solid phase of same material.

(ii) Boiling point is t_2°C and melting point is t_1°C.

Q. 3. (i) Define Calorimetry.
(ii) Name the material used for making a Calorimeter.
(iii) Why is a Calorimeter made up of thin sheets of the above material answered in (ii)? **[2019]**

 **Marking Scheme**

(i) The measurement of the quantity of heat is called Calorimetry.
(ii) Copper
(iii) Specific heat capacity of copper is low and by making the vessel thin its mass and heat capacity becomes low therefore it taken a negligible amount of heat form the contents to attain the temperature.

Ans. (i) The measurement of the quantity of heat is called calorimetry.

(ii) Copper.

(iii) Calorimeter is made up of thin sheet of copper because copper is a good conductor of heat and so the calorimeter will soon acquire the temperature of its constants and also copper has low specific heat capacity so the heat capacity of the calorimeter remains low and it takes very less amount of heat energy from the contents to acquire its temperature.

Q. 4. The melting point of naphthalene is 80°C and the room temperature is 30°C. A sample of liquid naphthalene at 100°C is cooled down to the room temperature. Draw a temperature time graph to represent this cooling. In the graph, mark the region which corresponds to the freezing process. **[2019]**

 **Marking Scheme**

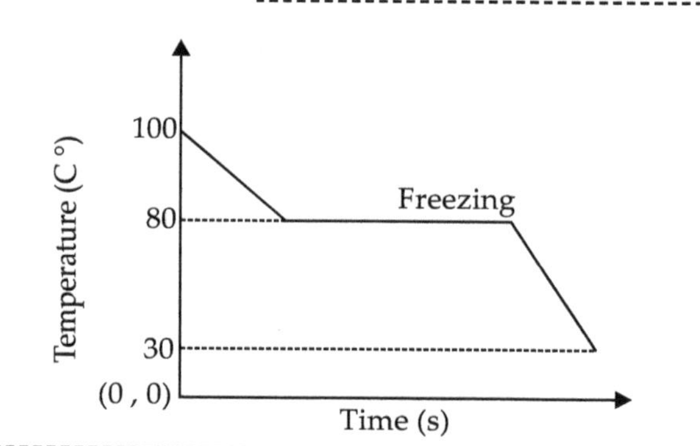

Ans. BC represents the freezing process in the graph.

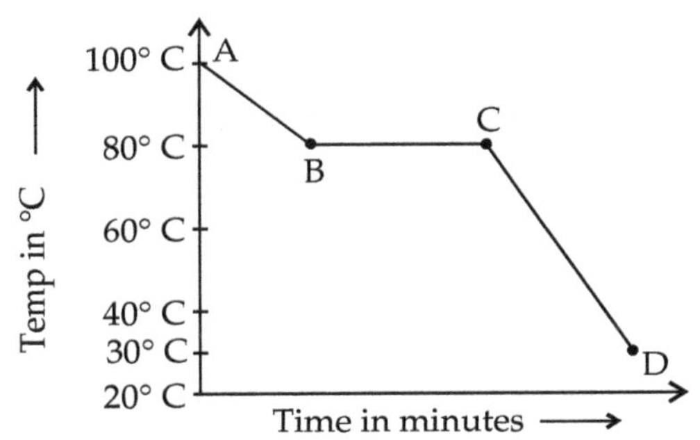

Q. 5. **(i)** **Heat supplied to a solid changes it into liquid. What is this change in phase called?**

(ii) **During the phase change does the average kinetic energy of the molecules of the substance increase?**

(iii) **What is the energy absorbed during the phase change called?** **[2018]**

Ans. **(i)** The change from solid state to a liquid state at a constant temperature is called melting.

(ii) Since, temperature remains constant during change of phase, the average kinetic energy does not change.

(iii) The energy absorbed during phase change is called latent heat of fusion.

Q. 6. **(i)** **State two differences between 'Heat Capacity' and 'Specific Heat Capacity'.**

(ii) **Give a mathematical relation between Heat Capacity and Specific Heat Capacity.** **[2018, 2012]**

📋 Marking Scheme -

(i)

Heat capacity	Specific heat capacity
Heat absorbed by the mass of a body to raise its temperature by 1°C.	Heat absorbed by unit mass of a body to raise its temperature by 1°C.
S.I. Unit is $J\ K^{-1}$	S.I. unit is $J\ kg^{-1}\ K^{-1}$
Depends on mass and (specific Heat capacity/ material)	Does not depend on mass (but depends on material)

(Any two points)

(ii) Heat capacity(C') = mass of the body(m) × specific heat capacity (c)

- -

Ans. **(i)** Difference between heat capacity and specific heat capacity:

Heat Capacity		Specific Heat Capacity	
1.	It is the amount of heat energy required to raise the temperature of entire body by 1°C.	1.	It is the amount of heat energy required to raise the temperature of unit mass of body by 1°C.
2.	Its S.I. unit is JK^{-1}.	2.	Its S.I. unit is $Jkg^{-1}\ K^{-1}$.

(ii) Heat capacity of a body

= Mass of the body

× Specific heat capacity

or $\qquad C' = m \times c$

$$c = \frac{C'}{m}$$

Q. 7. **(i)** **How is the transference of heat energy by radiation prevented in a calorimeter?**

(ii) **You have a choice of three metals A, B and C, of specific heat capacities 900 Jkg^{-1}°C^{-1}, 380 Jkg^{-1}°C^{-1} and 460 Jkg^{-1}°C^{-1} respectively, to make a calorimeter. Which material will you select? Justify your answer.** **[2017]**

Ans. **(i)** The outer and the inner surfaces of a calorimeter are highly polished to prevent the transfer of heat by radiation.

(ii) The metal B of specific heat capacity 380 J kg–1 °C–1 should be used because it will take the least amount of heat from the contents to attain the temperature of the contents.

Q. 8. **Calculate the mass of ice needed to cool 150 g of water contained in a calorimeter of mass 50 g at 32°C such that the final temperature is 5°C.**

Specific heat capacity of calorimeter = 0.4 J/g°C

Specific heat capacity of water = 4.2 J/g°C

Latent heat capacity of ice = 330 J/g. **[2017]**

Ans. Heat energy imparted by calorimeter and water contained in it in cooling from 32°C to 5°C is used in melting ice and then raising the temperature of melted ice from 0°C to 5°C.

For cold body: Ice at 0°C to water at 5°C.

$$\begin{aligned}
\text{Heat gained} &= mL + mc\Delta T \\
&= m \times 330 + m \times 4.2 \times (5 - 0) \\
&= 330\,m + m \times 4.2 \times 5 \\
&= 330\,m + 21\,m \\
&= 351m \text{ joule.}
\end{aligned}$$

For hot body: (Water + Calorimeter) at 32°C to 5°C.

$$\begin{aligned}
\text{Heat lost} &= m_1 c_1 \Delta T_1 + m_2 c_2\,\Delta T_2 \\
&= 150 \times 4.2 \times (32 - 5) \\
&\quad + 50 \times 0.4 \times (32 - 5) \\
&= 150 \times 4.2 \times 27 + 50 \times 0.4 \times 27 \\
&= 17010 + 540 = 17550 \text{ joule.}
\end{aligned}$$

From the principle of calorimetry, if the system is fully insulated then,

Heat gained by cold body

= Heat lost by hot body

$$351\,m = 17550$$

or $\qquad m = \dfrac{17550}{351}\,g$

$$= 50 \text{ g.}$$

∴ The mass of ice needed = 50 g.

Q. 9. **(i)** What is the principle of method of mixtures?

(ii) What is the other name given to it?

(iii) Name the law on which the principle is based. **[2016]**

Ans. **(i)** According to the principle of mixtures, when a hot body is mixed with a cold body, heat energy passes from the hot body to the cold body, till both the bodies attain the same temperature.

If no heat energy is lost to the surroundings *i.e.,* the system is perfectly insulated then Heat energy lost by the hot body

= Heat energy gained by cold body.

(ii) Principle of calorimetry.

(iii) It is based on the law of conservation of energy.

Q. 10. Some ice is heated at a constant rate, and its temperature is recorded after every few seconds, till steam is formed at 100°C. Draw a temperature time graph to represent the change. Label the two phase changes in your graph. **[2016]**

Ans.

250 200 150 100 50 0 -50 Temperature (°C) — Melting — (Liquid) Water — Ice (Solid) — Boiling — Steam — 0 10 20 30 40 50 60 70 80 90 100 110 120 Time (s)

Q. 11. Specific heat capacity of substance A is $3.8 \, J \, g^{-1} \, K^{-1}$ whereas the specific heat capacity of substance B is $0.4 \, J \, g^{-1} \, K^{-1}$.

(i) Which of the two is a good conductor of heat?

(ii) How is one led to the above conclusion?

(iii) If substances A and B are liquids then which one would be more useful in car radiators? **[2014]**

Ans. Specific heat capacity of A is $3.8 \, Jg^{-1} \, K^{-1}$.

Specific heat capacity of B is $0.4 \, Jg^{-1} \, K^{-1}$.

(i) 'B' is a good conductor of heat.

(ii) The specific heat capacity of B is lower than A. This means that less heat is required to raise the temperature of 1 g of B by 1 K than the heat required for A.

(iii) 'A' will be preferred as it absorbs large amount of heat energy without raising its own temperature much as its specific heat capacity is high.

Q. 12. **(i)** It is observed that the temperature of the surroundings starts falling when the ice in a frozen lake starts melting. Give a reason for the observation.

(ii) How is the heat capacity of the body related to its specific heat capacity? **[2013]**

Ans. **(i)** Temperature of the surroundings starts falling when the ice starts melting because every 1 gm of ice requires 336 J to convert it into water at 0°C so it extracts a great amount of heat from the atmosphere.

(ii) Heat capacity $= \dfrac{\Delta\theta}{\Delta T} = \dfrac{mc\Delta T}{\Delta T} = mc$

i.e., Heat capacity = mass × specific heat capacity

Q. 13. **(i)** Why does a bottle of soft drink cool faster when surrounded by ice cubes than by ice cold water, both at 0°C?

(ii) A certain amount of heat Q will warm 1 g of material X by 3°C and 1 g of material Y by 4°C. Which material has a higher specific heat capacity? **[2013]**

Ans. **(i)** Bottles of soft drink cools faster when surrounded by ice cubes because every 1 g of ice on melting requires 336 J. So, it extracts a large amount of heat from the bottle hence, they cool faster.

(ii) Specific heat capacity,

$$c = \dfrac{\text{Heat taken}}{\text{Mass} \times \text{Rise in temperature}}$$

$\therefore \qquad c_X = \dfrac{Q}{1 \times 3}$ and $c_Y = \dfrac{Q}{1 \times 4}$

$\therefore \qquad c_X > c_Y$

Hence, X has higher specific heat capacity.

Q. 14. **(i)** Write an expression for the heat energy liberated by a hot body.

(ii) Some heat is provided to a body to raise its temperature by 25°C. What will be the corresponding rise in temperature of the body as shown on the Kelvin scale?

(iii) What happens to the average kinetic energy of the molecules as ice melts at 0°C? **[2012]**

Ans. **(i)** Expression for the heat energy liberated by hot body $= mc\Delta T$

i.e., $\qquad H = mc\Delta T$

where m is the mass, c is the specific heat capacity and ΔT is the change in temperature.

(ii) Temperature rise of the body on the Kelvin scale will be 25 K.

(iii) Average K.E. of the molecules remain the same.

Q. 15. A piece of ice at 0°C is heated at a constant rate and its temperature recorded at regular intervals till steam is formed at 100°C. Draw a temperature-time graph to represent the change in phase. Label the different parts of your graph. **[2012]**

Ans.

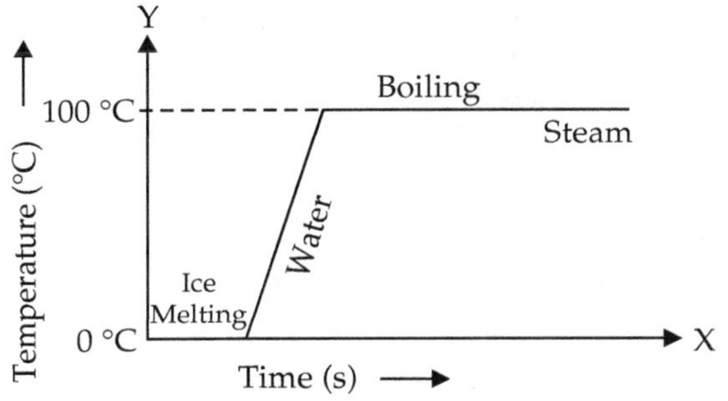

Q. 16. (i) Explain why the weather becomes very cold after a hail storm.

(ii) What happens to the heat supplied to a substance when the heat supplied causes no change in the temperature of the substance? **[2011]**

Ans. (i) It becomes very cold after the hail storm because ice begins to melt by absorbing heat energy from the surroundings. This decreases the temperature of the surroundings which leads to the cooling of atmosphere.

(ii) This heat supplied is used in the change of state. This heat is known as latent heat.

Q. 17. (i) When 1 g of ice at 0°C melts to form 1 g of water at 0°C then, is the latent heat absorbed by the ice or given out by it?

(ii) Give one example where high specific heat capacity of water is used as a heat reservoir.

(iii) Give one example where high specific heat capacity of water is used for cooling purposes. **[2011]**

Ans. (i) Latent heat is absorbed by the melting ice.

(ii) Water is used as heat reservoir in cold countries for preservation of juice bottle to avoid their freezing.

(iii) In car radiators.

Q. 18. (i) Define the term 'specific latent heat of fusion' of a substance.

(ii) Name the liquid which has the highest specific heat capacity.

(iii) Name two factors on which the heat absorbed or given out by a body depends. **[2010]**

Ans. (i) Specific latent heat of fusion: The specific latent heat of fusion of a substance is the heat energy released when a unit mass of substance converts from liquid to solid state without the change in temperature.

(ii) Water has the highest specific heat capacity.

(iii) The mass and specific heat capacity are two factors on which the heat absorbed or given out by a body depends.

Q. 19. (i) An equal quantity of heat is supplied to two substances A and B. The substance A shows a greater rise in temperature. What can you say about the heat capacity of A as compared to that of B?

(ii) What energy change would you expect to take place in the molecules of a substance when it undergoes:

(1) a change in its temperature?

(2) a change in its state without any change in its temperature? **[2010]**

Ans. (i) Heat capacity of substance B is more than that of substance A.

(ii) **(1)** Intermolecular space changes, kinetic energy increases.

(2) Intermolecular space increases, potential energy increases.

Q. 20. State in brief, the meaning of each of the following:

(i) The heat capacity of a body is 50 $J °C^{-1}$.

(ii) The specific latent heat of fusion of ice is 336000 $J\ kg^{-1}$.

(iii) The specific heat capacity of copper is 0.4 $J\ g^{-1}\ °C^{-1}$. **[2009]**

Ans. (i) Heat capacity of a body is 50 J/°C → It means 50 joule of heat energy is required to raise the temperature of a body by 1°C.

(ii) Amount of heat required to melt one kilogram of ice is 336000 J.

(iii) 0.4 J of heat is required to raise the temperature of one gram of copper by 1°C.

Q. 21. (i) What is the principle of method of mixtures?

(ii) Name the law on which this principle is based. **[2009]**

Ans. (i) When a hot body is mixed with a cold body, heat energy passes from the hot body to the cold body, till both the bodies attain the same temperature. If no heat energy is lost to the surroundings then

Heat energy lost by the hot body = Heat energy gained by the cold body.

(ii) Law of conservation of energy.

Q. 22. (i) Define heat capacity of a given body. What is its SI unit?

(ii) What is the relation between heat capacity and specific heat capacity of a substance? **[2008]**

Ans. (i) Heat capacity of the body is the amount of heat energy required to raise its temperature by 1°C (or 1 K). Its S.I. unit is J/K.

(ii) Heat capacity = Mass × specific heat capacity.

Q. 23. (i) What is meant by specific heat capacity of a substance?
(ii) Why does the heat supplied to a substance during its change of state not cause any rise in its temperature? [2007]

Ans. **(i)** Specific heat capacity of a substance is the amount of heat energy required to raise the temperature of unit mass of that substance through 1°C.

(ii) During the state change, heat supplied increases potential energy of molecules as distance between molecules increases, work is done by heat supplied against attractive force.

Q. 24. (i) Define specific latent heat of vaporization of a substance.
(ii) What is the principle of calorimetry?
[2006]

Ans. **(i)** Specific latent heat of vapourization is the quantity of heat required to convert unit mass of a substance from liquid to vapour state without change of temperature.

(ii) Principle of calorimetry states that when a hot body is mixed with a cold body, then heat passes from hot body to cold body till both attain same temperature, *i.e.*,
Heat lost by hot body = Heat gained by cold body
(when the system is fully insulated)

Q. 25. Explain why water is used in hot water bottles for fomentation and also as a universal coolant. **[2006]**

Ans. Hot water bottles are used for fomentation since water does not cool quickly due to its large specific heat capacity.

Water is used as an effective coolant because of its large specific heat capacity due to which it can extract more heat.

Long Answer Type Questions- I

Q. 1. **A piece of ice of mass 60 g is dropped into 140 g of water at 50°C.**
Calculate the final temperature of water when all the ice has melted.
(Assume no heat is lost to the surrounding)
Specific heat capacity of water = 4.2 Jg^{-1}k^{-1}
Specific latent heat of fusion of ice = 336 Jg^{-1}
[2020]

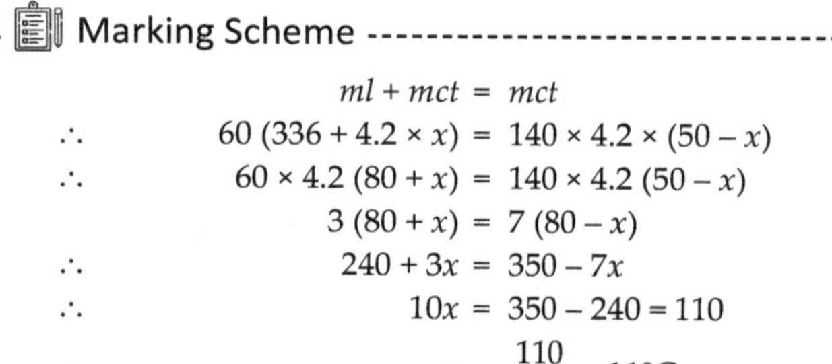

 Marking Scheme

$$ml + mct = mct$$
$$\therefore \quad 60\,(336 + 4.2 \times x) = 140 \times 4.2 \times (50 - x)$$
$$\therefore \quad 60 \times 4.2\,(80 + x) = 140 \times 4.2\,(50 - x)$$
$$3\,(80 + x) = 7\,(80 - x)$$
$$\therefore \quad 240 + 3x = 350 - 7x$$
$$\therefore \quad 10x = 350 - 240 = 110$$
$$\therefore \quad x = \frac{110}{10} = 11°C$$

Ans. Let final temperature of water = $x°C$

Ice	Water
$m_1 = 60$ g	$m_2 = 140$ g
$T_1 = 0°C$	$T_1 = 50°C$
$T_2 = x°C$	$T_2 = x°C$
Rise in temp.	fall in temp.
$(\Delta T) = (x - 0)°C = x°C$	$(\Delta T) = (50 - x)°C$

Heat gained by ice $= M_1L + m_1c\Delta T$
$$= (60 \times 336 + 60 \times 4.2 \times x)\ J$$
Heat lost by water $= m_2c\Delta T$
$$= 140 \times 4.2 \times (50 - x)\ J$$

Applying, the principle of mixtures,
$$140 \times 4.2 \times (50 - x) = 60 \times 336 + 60 \times 4.2 \times x$$
$$\Rightarrow \quad 4.2\,(7000 - 140x - 60x) = 60 \times 336$$
$$\Rightarrow \quad 7000 - 200x = \frac{60 \times 336}{4.2}$$
$$= \frac{60 \times 336}{42} \times 10$$
$$= 4800$$
$$\Rightarrow \quad 200x = 2200$$
$$\Rightarrow \quad x = 11°C$$
∴ Final temperature of water = 11°C

Q. 2. **104 g of water at 30°C is taken in a calorimeter made of copper of mass 42 g. When a certain mass of ice at 0°C is added to it, the final steady temperature of the mixture after the ice has melted, was found to be 10°C. Find the mass of ice added. [Specific heat capacity of water = 4.2 Jg^{-1} °C^{-1}; Specific latent heat of fusion of ice = 336 Jg^{-1}; Specific heat capacity of copper = 0.4 Jg$^{-1°}$ C^{-1}]** **[2019]**

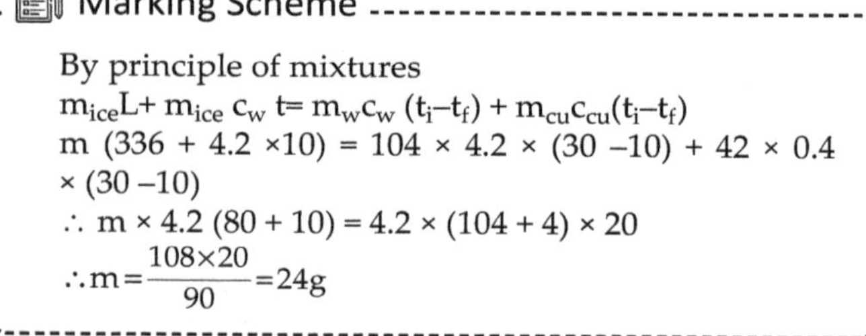

 Marking Scheme

By principle of mixtures
$$m_{ice}L + m_{ice}\,c_w\,t = m_w c_w\,(t_i - t_f) + m_{cu} c_{cu}(t_i - t_f)$$
$$m\,(336 + 4.2 \times 10) = 104 \times 4.2 \times (30 - 10) + 42 \times 0.4 \times (30 - 10)$$
$$\therefore\ m \times 4.2\,(80 + 10) = 4.2 \times (104 + 4) \times 20$$
$$\therefore m = \frac{108 \times 20}{90} = 24g$$

Ans. Given: $m_w = 104$ g $= T_w = 30°C$

$m_c = 42$ g, T = 10°C

$m_i = ?$

By calorimetry,

$$\text{Heat lost} = \text{Heat gained}$$

$$m_w S_w (T_w - T) + m_c S_c (T_w - T) = m_i \alpha + m_i S_w (T - T_i)$$

$$\Rightarrow (104)(4.2)(30 - 10) + (42)(0.4)(30 - 10)$$
$$= m_i(336) + m_i(4.2)(10 - 0)$$

$$\Rightarrow \quad m_i = \frac{(104)(4.2)(20) + (42)(0.4)(20)}{(336 + 42)}$$

$m_i = 24$ g

Q. 3. **The temperature of 170 g of water at 50°C is lowered to 5°C by adding certain amount of ice to it. Find the mass of ice added. Given: Specific heat capacity of water = 4200 J kg⁻¹ °C⁻¹ and Specific latent heat of ice = 336000 J kg⁻¹.** **[2018]**

Ans. Given:

For hot body:

170 g water at 50°C changes to water at 5°C.

$m = 170$ g $= \dfrac{170}{1000}$ kg, $c = 4200$ J kg⁻¹ °C⁻¹,

$\Delta T = (50 - 5)°C = 45°C$

$\therefore$ Heat lost by water

$$= mc\Delta T$$
$$= \frac{170}{1000} \times 4200 \times 45 \, J$$
$$= 32130 \, J$$

For cold body:

Let mass of ice be x kg.

x kg ice at 0°C changes to water at 5°C.

Mass $(m) = x$ kg, $L = 336000$ J kg⁻¹,

$c = 4200$ J kg⁻¹ °C⁻¹, $\Delta T = (5 - 0)°C = 5°C$

$\therefore$ Heat gained by ice

$$= mL + mc\Delta T$$
$$= (x \times 336000 + x \times 4200 \times 5) \, J$$
$$= (336000\,x + 21000\,x) \, J$$
$$= 357000\,x \, J.$$

When no heat energy is lost to the surroundings,

$$\text{Heat gained} = \text{Heat lost}$$

or $357000\,x = 32130$

$\therefore \qquad x = \dfrac{32130}{357000}$ kg

$$= 0.09 \text{ kg} = 90 \text{ g}.$$

$\therefore$ Mass of ice added = 90 g.

Q. 4. **Name two factors on which the heat energy liberated by a body depends.** **[2017]**

Ans. The heat energy liberated by a body depends on mass, specific heat capacity and change in temperature of the body.

Q. 5. **A copper vessel of mass 100 g contains 150 g of water at 50°C. How much ice is needed to cool to 5°C?**

Given:
Specific heat capacity of copper = 0.4 Jg⁻¹ °C⁻¹
Specific heat capacity of water = 4.2 Jg⁻¹ °C⁻¹
Specific latent heat of fusion of ice = 336 Jg⁻¹ **[2016]**

Ans. Heat energy imparted by vessel

$$= 100 \times 0.4 \times (50 - 5)$$
$$= 1800 \, J$$

Heat energy imparted by water

$$= 150 \times 4.2 \times (50 - 5)$$
$$= 28350 \, J$$

Let m gram of ice be used.

Heat energy taken by ice to melt

$$= m \times 336 \, J$$

Heat energy taken by the melted ice to raise its temperature from 0°C to 5°C

$$= m \times 4.2 \times (5 - 0) = 21m \, J$$

By law of conservation of energy,

Heat energy imparted by vessel and water

$$= \text{Heat energy taken by ice}$$
$$\text{and melted ice}$$

i.e., $1800 + 28350 = 336m + 21m$

or $\qquad 30150 = 357m$

$\therefore \qquad m = \dfrac{30150}{375} = 84.45\,g$

Thus, 84.45 g of ice is used.

Q. 6. **(i) Water in lakes and ponds do not freeze at once in cold countries. Give a reason in support of your answer.**
(ii) What is the principle of Calorimetry?
(iii) Name the law on which this principle is based.
(iv) State the effect of an increase of impurities on the melting point of ice. **[2015]**

Ans. **(i)** This is because of high specific latent heat of fusion of ice (equal to 336000 J/kg). So to freeze water, a large quantity of heat has to be taken out from water to freeze it.

(ii) The principle of calorimetry states that heat energy lost by a hot body is equal to the heat energy gained by the cold body, provided no heat is lost to the surrounding.

(iii) It is based on the law of conservation of energy.

(iv) The melting point of ice decreases with the increase in impurities in it.

Q. 7. **A refrigerator converts 100 g of water at 20°C to ice at –10°C in 35 minutes.**

Calculate the average rate of heat extraction in terms of watts.

Given: Specific heat capacity of ice = 2.1 J g⁻¹ °C⁻¹

Specific heat capacity of water = 4.2 J g^{-1} °C^{-1}

Specific Latent heat of fusion of ice = 336 J g^{-1}

[2015]

Ans. Heat lost by water when the refrigerator converts 100 g of water at 20°C to water at 0°C = mass of water × specific heat capacity of water × fall in temperature

= 100 × 4.2 × (20 − 0) = 8400 J

Heat energy extracted to convert 100 g of water at 0°C to ice at 0°C

= mass of water × specific latent heat of fusion of ice = 100 × 336 = 33600 J

Heat energy extracted to convert 100 g of ice at 0°C to ice at −10°C

= mass of ice × specific heat capacity of ice
$$\times \text{ fall in temperature}$$

= 100 × 2.1 × [0 − (− 10)] =100 × 2.1 × 10 = 2100 J

Total heat extracted = 8400 + 33600 + 2100
$$= 44100 \text{ J}$$

Let the average rate of extraction of heat be P watt.

Energy extracted by the refrigerator in t seconds
$$= \text{P} \times t$$

Thus, $\text{P} \times t = 44100 \text{ J}$

or $\text{P} \times 35 \times 60 = 44100$

$$(\because 35 \text{ minute} = 35 \times 60 \text{ second})$$

$$\therefore \qquad \text{P} = \frac{44100}{35 \times 60}$$

$$= 21 \text{ watt}$$

Q. 8. **Heat energy is supplied at a constant rate to 100 g of ice at 0°C. The ice is converted into water at 0°C in 2 minutes. How much time will be required to raise the temperature of water from 0°C to 20°C?**

[Given: sp. heat capacity of water 4.2 g^{-1}°C^{-1}, sp. latent heat of ice = 336 Jg^{-1}] **[2014]**

Ans. Given,

Mass of ice, m = 100 g = 0.1 kg

Heat energy required to raise the temperature of water from 0°C to 20°C,

$$Q = mc\Delta t$$

$$= 0.1 \text{ kg} \times 4200 \text{ Jkg}^{-1}°\text{C}^{-1}$$
$$\times 20°\text{C}$$

$$= 420 \times 20 = 8400 \text{ J}$$

Heat energy required for conversion of ice into water at 0°C = mL

$$= 0.1 \text{ kg} \times 336000 \text{ J/kg}$$

$$= 33600 \text{ J}$$

Now, Power, $\text{P} = \dfrac{W}{t}$

$$\text{P} = \frac{33600}{120}$$

$$= \frac{3360}{12} = 280 \text{ W}$$

Also, $\text{P} \times t' = Q$

$$t' = \frac{Q}{\text{P}}$$

$$= \frac{8400}{280} = 30 \text{ sec}.$$

Q. 9. **A calorimeter of mass 50 g and specific heat capacity 0.42 J g^{-1} °C^{-1} contains some mass of water at 20°C. A metal piece of mass 20 g at 100°C is dropped into the calorimeter. After stirring, the final temperature of the mixture is found to be 22°C. Find the mass of water used in the calorimeter.**

[specific heat capacity of the metal piece = 0.3 J g^{-1} °C^{-1}

specific heat capacity of water = 4.2 J g^{-1} °C^{-1}]

[2013]

Ans. Heat given = Heat taken

let mass of water used be m, then
$$mc\Delta\text{T} = m'c'\Delta t + m_1 c_1 \Delta t$$

$$\Rightarrow \quad 20 \times 0.3 \times (100 - 22)$$
$$= 50 \times 0.42 \times (22 - 20)$$
$$+ m \times 4.2 \times (22 - 20)$$

$$\Rightarrow \quad 468 = 42 + 8.4 \, m$$

$$\Rightarrow \quad 8.4 \, m = 426$$

$$\therefore \quad m = 50.71 \text{ g}.$$

Q. 10. **40 g of ice at 0°C is used to bring down the temperature of a certain mass of water at 60°C to 10°C. Find the mass of water used.**

[Specific heat capacity of water = 4200 J kg^{-1} °C^{-1}]

[Specific latent heat of fusion of ice = 336 × 10^3 J kg^{-1}] **[2012]**

Ans. Let mass of water used = m g

By principle of calorimetry,

Heat given = Heat taken

$$m_1 c_1 \Delta t_1 = mL + m_2 c_2 \Delta t_2$$

or $m \times 4.2 \times (60 - 10) = 40 \times 336 + 40 \times 4.2$
$$\times (10 - 0)$$

or $m \times 4.2 \times 50 = 40 \times 336 + 1680$

$$\therefore \qquad m = 72 \text{ g}$$

Q. 11. **250 g of water at 30°C is present in a copper vessel of mass 50 g. Calculate the mass of ice required to bring down the temperature of the vessel and its contents to 5°C.**

Specific latent heat of fusion of ice = 336 × 10^3 J kg^{-1}

Specific heat capacity of copper vessel = 400 J kg^{-1} °C^{-1}

Specific heat capacity of water = 4200 J kg^{-1} °C^{-1}. **[2011]**

Ans. Given:

$$\text{Mass of water} = 250 \text{ g}$$
$$\text{Temperature of water} = 30°C$$
$$\text{Mass of vessel} = 50 \text{ g}$$
$$\text{Final temperature} = 5°C$$

Let mass of ice = m g

By the principle of calorimetry,

$$\text{Heat given} = \text{Heat taken}$$

or $\quad 250 \times 4.2 \times (30 - 5) + 50 \times 0.4 \times (30 - 5)$

$$= m \times 336 + m \times 4.2 \times 5$$

or $\qquad 26250 + 500 = 336m + 21m$

or $\qquad 26750 = 357m$

$\therefore \qquad\qquad m = 74.9 \text{ g}$

Q. 12. 50 g of ice at 0°C is added to 300 g of a liquid at 30°C. What will be the final temperature of the mixture when all the ice has melted? The specific heat capacity of the liquid is 2.65 Jg⁻¹°C⁻¹ while that of water is 4.2 J g⁻¹°C⁻¹. Specific latent heat of fusion of ice = 336 J g⁻¹. **[2010]**

Ans. Given:

$m_1 = 50$ g, $t_1 = 0°C$, $m_2 = 300$ g, $t_2 = 30°C$.

Heat energy taken by ice to melt

$$= m_1 L$$
$$= 50 \times 336 \text{ J} = 16800 \text{ J}$$

By law of conservation of energy,

Heat energy given by liquid

$$= \text{Heat taken by water}$$

$$300 \times 2.65 \times (30 - t)$$
$$= 16800 + 50 \times t \times 4.2$$

$\Rightarrow \qquad 23850 - 795\,t = 16800 + 210\,t$

$\Rightarrow \qquad -795\,t - 210\,t = 16800 - 23850$

$\Rightarrow \qquad -1005\,t = -7050$

$\Rightarrow \qquad t = \dfrac{7050}{1005} = 7.014°C$

Q. 13. Calculate the amount of ice which is required to cool 150 g of water contained in a vessel of mass 100 g at 30°C, such that the final temperature of the mixture is 5°C. (Take specific heat capacity of material of vessel as 0.4 J g⁻¹ °C⁻¹, specific latent heat of fusion of ice = 336 J g⁻¹, specific heat capacity of water = 4.2 J g⁻¹ °C⁻¹) **[2009]**

Ans. Given: 150 g cold water at 30°C

100 g of vessel at 30°C.

$$\text{Heat given} = \text{Heat taken}$$

$\Rightarrow 150 \times 4.2 \times 25 + 100 \times 0.4 \times 25 = m \times 336 + m$
$$\times 4.2 \times 5$$

$\Rightarrow \qquad 15750 + 1000 = 357\,m$

$$m = 46.91 \text{ g}$$

Q. 14. A piece of ice of mass 40 g is dropped into 200 g of water at 50°C.

Calculate the final temperature of water after all the ice has melted.

(specific heat capacity of water = 4200 J/kg/°C, specific latent heat of fusion of ice = 336 × 10³ J/kg). **[2008]**

Ans. Given: $\qquad\qquad$ Mass = 40 g

$$\text{Mass of water} = 200 \text{ g}$$
$$\text{Temperature of water} = 50°C$$

Specific heat capacity of water = 4200 J/kg/°C

Specific latent heat of fusion of ice = 336 × 10³

$$\text{J/kg}$$

Let, $\quad$ Final temperature of water $= x$

By principle of calorimetry,

$$\text{Heat given} = \text{Heat taken}$$

$$\text{Heat given} = mc\Delta t = \frac{200}{1000} \times 4200\,(50 - x)$$

$$\text{Heat taken} = mL + mc\Delta t$$

$$= \frac{40}{1000} \times 336 \times 10^3 + \frac{40}{1000}$$
$$\times 4200\,(x - 0)$$

So, $\quad$ Heat given = Heat taken

$$\frac{200}{1000} \times 4200\,(50 - x) = \frac{40}{1000} \times 336 \times 10^3 + \frac{40}{1000}$$
$$\times 4200\,(x - 0)$$

$$42000 - 840x = 13440 + 168x$$
$$42000 - 13340 = 168x + 840x$$
$$28660 = 1008x$$
$$x = 28.43°C.$$

Q. 15. A substance is in the form of a solid at 0°C. The amount of heat added to this substance and the temperature of the substance are plotted on the following graph:

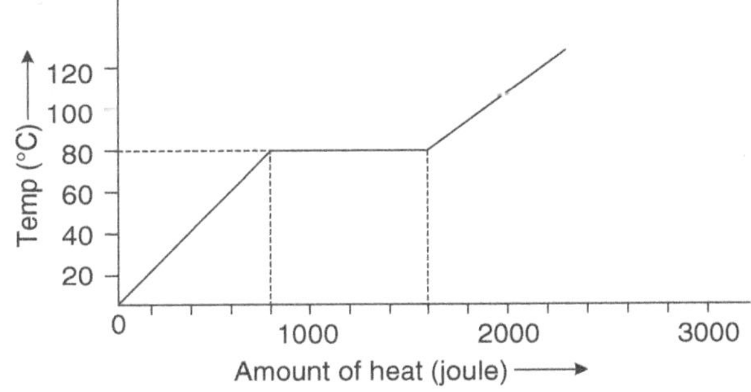

If the specific heat capacity of the solid substance is 500 J/kg°C, find from the graph:

(i) The mass of the substance;

(ii) The specific latent heat of fusion of the substance in the liquid state. **[2007]**

Ans. **(i)** From graph heat supplied is 800 joule during change in temperature from 0 to 80°C

$$\text{Heat} = \text{Mass} \times \text{Specific heat capacity} \times \text{Rise in temperature}$$

$$800 = m \times 500 \times 80$$

$$m = \frac{1}{50}\,\text{kg} = 20\,\text{g}$$

(ii) From graph heat required in changing the state is:

$$1600 - 800 = 800 \text{ joule}$$

$$\text{Heat} = m\text{L where L is specific latent heat}$$

$$\Rightarrow \quad 800 = \frac{1}{50} \times \text{L}$$

$$\therefore \quad \text{L} = 40{,}000 \text{ joule/Kg.}$$

Q. 16. A piece of iron of mass 2.0 kg has a thermal capacity of 966 J/°C.

(i) How much heat is needed to warm it by 15°C?

(ii) What is its specific heat capacity in S.I. units? **[2006]**

Ans. **(i)** Given that: $m = 2.0$ kg, Thermal capacity = 966 J/°C

and Rise in temperature = 15°C

$$\text{Thermal capacity, C} = \frac{\text{Heat required}}{\text{Rise in temp.}}$$

$$\therefore \quad \text{Heat needed} = 966 \times 15$$

$$= 14490 \text{ J}$$

(ii) Specific heat capacity,

$$C = \frac{\text{Amount of heat}}{\text{Mass} \times \text{Rise in temp.}}$$

$$= \frac{14490}{2.0 \times 15} = \frac{14490}{30} = 483 \text{ J/kg-°C}$$

10 Radioactivity and Nuclei

Short Answer Type Questions-I

Q. 1. A nucleus $_{84}X^{202}$ of an element emits an alpha particle followed by a beta particle. The final nucleus is $_aY^b$. Find a and b. **[2020]**

Ans. $_{84}X^{202} \longrightarrow _{82}X_1^{198} + 2He^4$

$_{82}X_1^{198} \longrightarrow _{83}Y^{198} + _{-1}\beta^0$

$\therefore$ a = 83, b = 198

Q. 2. Is it possible for a hydrogen $(_1^1H)$ nucleus to emit an alpha particle? Give a reason for your answer. **[2019]**

Ans. No, it is not possible because an alpha particle $(_2^4He)$ consists of two protons and two neutrons.

Q. 3. (i) What are isobars?

(ii) Give one example of isobars. **[2018]**

Ans. (i) Isobars are atoms of different elements which have the same mass number A, but different atomic number Z.

(ii) $_6^{14}C$ and $_7^{14}N$ are isobars.

Q. 4. When does the nucleus of an atom tend to be radioactive? **[2017]**

Ans. The nucleus of an atom becomes radioactive if the nucleus is large (*i.e.*, atomic number > 82) or if the number of neutrons is much more than the number of protons as compared to a normal stable atom.

Q. 5. An element $_ZS^A$ decays to $_{85}R^{222}$ after emitting 2α particles and 1β particle. Find the atomic number and atomic mass of the element S. **[2016]**

Ans. $S_Z^A \xrightarrow{2\alpha} X_{Z-4}^{A-8} \xrightarrow{\beta} R_{Z-4+1}^{A-8}$

Given: $R_{Z-3}^{A-8} = R_{85}^{222}$

$\therefore$ $Z - 3 = 85$; $A - 8 = 222$

$\Rightarrow$ $Z = 88$; $A = 230$

$\therefore$ Atomic number of S = 88

Atomic mass of S = 230

Q. 6. A radioactive substance is oxidized. Will there be any change in the nature of its radioactivity? Give a reason for your answer. **[2016]**

Ans. When a radioactive substance is oxidized, there will be no change in the nature of its radioactivity. This is because radioactivity is a property of the nucleus and the nucleus of a substance does not get changed if it gets oxidized. (Oxidation is a chemical change involving only the extra nuclear electrons.)

Q. 7. (i) What is nuclear energy? **[2014]**

(ii) Name the process used for producing electricity using nuclear energy. **[2014]**

Ans. (i) Nuclear energy is the energy released by the atom's nucleus during a nuclear reaction.

(ii) Nuclear fission.

Q. 8. State one important advantage and disadvantage each of using nuclear energy for producing electricity. **[2014]**

Ans.

Advantage	Disadvantage
Tremendous amount of electrical energy can be produced by using a very small amount of nuclear fuel.	The nuclear waste produced by it is the source of harmful radiations and also causes environmental pollution.

Q. 9. Which of the radioactive radiations:
(i) can cause severe genetical disorders.
(ii) are deflected by an electric field? **[2013]**

Ans. (i) γ-radiations.
(ii) α and β radiations are deflected by an electric field.

Q. 10. A radioactive nucleus undergoes a series of decays according to the sequence.

$$X \xrightarrow{\beta} X_1 \xrightarrow{\alpha} X_2 \xrightarrow{\alpha} X_3.$$

If the mass number and atomic number of X_3 are 172 and 69 respectively, what is the mass number and atomic number of X? **[2013]**

Ans.

$$_Z^A X \xrightarrow{\beta} _{Z+1}^A X_1 \xrightarrow{\alpha} _{Z+1-2}^{A-4} X_2 \xrightarrow{\alpha} _{Z+1-2-2}^{A-4-4} X_3$$

Given, Atomic number of X_3 = 69
Mass number of X_3 = 172

$\therefore$ $A - 8 = 172$ $\Rightarrow$ A = 180

And $\qquad Z - 3 = 69 \Rightarrow Z = 72$

Q. 11. What is the value of the speed of gamma radiations in air or vacuum? [2012]

Ans. Speed of γ radiation $= 3 \times 10^8$ m/s in air or vacuum.

Q. 12. Give any two important sources of background radiation. [2012]

Ans. Two sources of background radiations are:

(i) The radioactive substances such as potassium (K-40), Carbon (C-14) and radium present inside our body.

(ii) Cosmic rays, solar radiations coming from outer space and naturally occuring radioactive elements such as radon-222 etc.

Q. 13. Fill in the blanks in the following sentences with appropriate words:

(i) During the emission of a beta particle, the .... number remains the same.

(ii) The minimum amount of energy required to emit an electron from a metal surface is called .... [2011]

Ans. **(i)** During the emission of a beta particle, the mass number remains the same.

(ii) The minimum amount of energy required to emit an electron from a metal surface is called work function.

Q. 14. A mixture of radioactive substances gives off three types of radiations:

(i) Name the radiation which travels with the speed of light.

(ii) Name the radiation which has the highest ionizing power. [2011]

Ans. **(i)** γ-rays.

(ii) α-particles.

Q. 15. Complete the following nuclear changes:

(i) $^{24}_{11}Na \rightarrow ....Mg + ^{0}_{-1}\beta$

(ii) $^{238}_{92}U \rightarrow ^{234}_{90}Th + ... + Energy.$ [2010]

Ans. **(i)** $^{24}_{11}Na \rightarrow ^{24}_{12}Mg + ^{0}_{-1}\beta$

(ii) $^{238}_{92}U \rightarrow ^{234}_{90}Th + ^{4}_{2}He + Energy$

Q. 16. (i) Which radiation produces maximum biological damage?

(ii) What happens to the atomic number of an element when the radiation named by you in part (i) above, are emitted? [2010]

Ans. **(i)** Gamma radiation produces maximum biological damage.

(ii) No change in the atomic number of an element takes place when the gamma radiations are emitted.

Q. 17. Give two important precautions that should be taken while handling radioactive materials. [2009]

Ans. Two important precautions while handling radioactive materials are:

(i) One should wear lead lined aprons and lead gloves.

(ii) One should handle the radioactive materials with long lead tongs.

Q. 18. (i) What is the name given to atoms of a substance which have the same atomic number but different mass numbers?

(ii) What is the difference in the atomic structure of such atoms? [2009]

Ans. **(i)** Substances which have the same atomic number but different mass numbers are isotopes.

(ii) Such atoms have same number of protons but different number of neutrons.

Q. 19. What is radioactivity? [2008]

Ans. Radioactivity: It is a nuclear phenomenon. It is the process of spontaneous emission of α, β and γ radiations from the nuclei of atoms during decay.

Q. 20. Mention any two differences between nuclear energy and chemical energy. [2008]

Ans. Two differences between nuclear energy and chemical energy are given below:

Nuclear energy	Chemical energy
(i) Nuclear energy is released in the formation of nucleus from the constituent nucleons.	This takes place due to change in orbital electrons of the atom.
(ii) This takes place due to the loss in mass *i.e.*, due to mass defect.	In these reactions, nucleus is not affected at all. No mass defect occurs.

Q. 21. What will an alpha particle change into when it absorbs:

(i) One electron;

(ii) Two electrons? [2007]

Ans. **(i)** Single ionised Helium (He$^+$).

(ii) Helium atom.

Q. 22. Mention two important properties of a metal that make it a good thermionic emitter. [2007]

Ans. **(1)** Low work function

(2) High melting point.

Q. 23. A certain radioactive nucleus emits a particle that leaves its mass unchanged but increases its atomic number by one. Identify the particle and write its symbol. [2006]

Ans. Particle is beta. Symbol – β

Short Answer Type Questions-II

Q. 1. State one safety precaution in the disposal of nuclear waste. [2020]

Marking Scheme

Should be disposed in thick lead casks away from colonies and deep into the earth.

Ans. For disposal of nuclear waste, they must be first kept in thick casks and then buried in specially constructed deep underground stores and also while handling nuclear waste, we should wear special lined lead aprons and lead gloves.

Q. 2. Name the process used for producing electricity using nuclear energy. [2017]

Ans. Electricity is produced using nuclear energy by carrying out controlled chain reaction of nuclear fission in a nuclear reactor.

Q. 3. Arrange α, β and γ rays in ascending order with respect to their
(i) Penetrating power
(ii) Ionising power
(iii) Biological effect. [2016]

Ans. (i) $\alpha < \beta < \gamma$
(ii) $\gamma < \beta < \alpha$
(iii) $\alpha < \beta < \gamma$

Q. 4. An atomic nucleus A is composed of 84 protons and 128 neutrons.
(i) The nucleus A emits an alpha particle and is transformed into nucleus B. What is the composition of nucleus B?
(ii) The nucleus B emits a beta particle and is transformed into a nucleus C. What is the composition of nucleus C?
(iii) Does the composition of nucleus C change if it emits gamma radiations? [2015]

Ans. (i) Atomic number of A
$$= \text{Number of protons}$$
$$= 84$$
Number of neutrons in A = Mass number of A – Atomic number of A
Thus, Mass number of A
$$= \text{Number of neutrons in A} + \text{Atomic number of A}$$
$$= 128 + 84$$
$$= 212$$
When an alpha particle is emitted,
Atomic number of B = Atomic number of A–2
$$= 84 – 2 = 82$$
Thus, Number of protons in B
$$= \text{Number of electrons in B}$$

$$= \text{Atomic number}$$
$$= 82$$
Mass number of B = 212 – 4
$$= 208$$
Number of neutrons in B
$$= \text{Mass number of B} -$$
$$\text{Atomic number of B}$$
$$= 208 – 82$$
$$= 126$$

$$^{212}_{84}A \longrightarrow {}^{4}_{2}He + {}^{208}_{82}B$$

(ii) Atomic number of C is one more than the mass number of B due to beta emission i.e., 82 + 1 = 83, whereas mass number remains the same i.e., 208.

$$^{208}_{82}B \longrightarrow e^{0}_{-1} + {}^{208}_{83}C$$

So, Number of electrons in C
$$= \text{Number of protons in C}$$
$$= \text{Atomic number}$$
$$= 83$$
Number of neutrons
$$= \text{Mass number of C}$$
$$- \text{Atomic number of C}$$
$$= 208 – 83 = 125$$

(iii) If C emits gamma radiation, then there is no change in the composition of C.

Q. 5. A nucleus $_{11}Na^{24}$ emits a beta particle to change into Magnesium (Mg).
(i) Write the symbolic equation for the process.
(ii) What are numbers 24 and 11 called?
(iii) What is the general name $^{24}_{12}Mg$ with respect to $^{24}_{11}Na$? [2014]

Ans. (i) $_{11}Na^{24} \longrightarrow {}_{12}Mg^{24} + {}_{-1}e^{0} + energy$
(ii) 24 is the mass number (number of protons and neutrons).
11 is the atomic number (number of protons).
(iii) Isobars.

Q. 6. (i) What is meant by Radioactivity?
(ii) What is meant by nuclear waste?
(iii) Suggest one effective way for the safe disposal of nuclear waste. [2013]

Ans. (i) **Radioactivity:** The process of spontaneous emission of α, β and γ radiations from the nuclei of atoms during their decay is known as radioactivity.
(ii) After disintegration, the radioactive material finally converts into lead and still it holds some radioactivity. This is called nuclear waste.

(iii) Delay and decay method is the effective way for the safe disposal of nuclear waste.

Q. 7. When an alpha particle gains two electrons it becomes neutral and becomes an atom of an element which is a rare gas. What is the name of this rare gas? [2011]

Ans. Helium gas.

Q. 8. (i) Define radioactivity.
(ii) What happens inside the nucleus that causes the emission of beta particle?
(iii) Express the above change in the form of an equation. [2011]

Ans. **(i) Radioactivity:** It is the process of spontaneous emission of α, β and γ radiations from the nuclei of atoms during their decay.

(ii) In an unstable nucleus, number of neutrons are more than number of protons. In such a case, a neutron may change to a proton to achieve stability by emitting an electron called beta particle.

(iii) $_0n^1 \rightarrow {_1}p^1 + {_{-1}}e^0$
$\qquad\quad \downarrow \qquad \downarrow$
$\qquad$ Proton $\quad$ β-particle

Q. 9. (i) Name the radioactive radiations which have the least penetrating power.
(ii) Give one use of radio isotopes.
(iii) What is meant by background radiation? [2010]

Ans. **(i)** α-radiations have the least penetrating power.

(ii) Radio isotopes are used to cure many diseases such as leukaemia, cancer etc. by radiation therapy.

(iii) Background radiations are the radioactive radiations to which we all are exposed even in the absence of an actual visible radioactive source. Its total dose is not very large, so it does not cause any serious biological damage to us.

Q. 10. (i) When does the nucleus of an atom become radioactive?
(ii) How is the radioactivity of an element affected when it undergoes a chemical change to form a chemical compound?

Ans. **(i)** The nucleus of an atom becomes radioactive when the nucleus is unstable. Either the nuclei are large or their neutron to proton ratio is higher than what is required for stability.

(ii) Radioactivity of an element remains unaffected when it undergoes a chemical change to form a chemical compound.

Q. 11. (i) Mention one use and one harmful effect of radioactivity.
(ii) Give one source of background radiation. [2008]

Ans. **(i) One use of radioactivity:** Radioisotopes are used as fuels for atomic energy reactors.
Harmful effect: They cause harmful effect on genes.

(ii) One source of background radiations is cosmic rays.

Q. 12. Name the three main parts of a hot cathode ray tube. Mention one important function of each of the three main parts. [2007]

Ans. Three main parts of hot cathode ray tube:
(i) The electron gun,
(ii) The deflecting system,
(iii) The fluorescent screen
Functions:
(i) Electron gun gives out fine beam of electrons.
(ii) The deflecting system deflects electron beam in horizontal and vertical directions.
(iii) The fluorescent screen gives bright spot on striking of electron.

Q. 13. (i) Define thermionic emission.
(ii) Mention one use of thermionic emission.
(iii) Name a substance which is a good thermionic emitter. [2006]

Ans. **(i)** The emission of electrons from a metal surface when heat energy is imparted to it, is called thermionic emission.
(ii) Thermionic emission is used in hot cathode ray tube.
(iii) Tungsten.

Q. 14. State three properties that are common to and shown by both beta rays and cathode rays. [2006]

Ans. **(i)** Both beta rays and cathode rays carry a negative charge.
(ii) Both the rays are deflected by electric and magnetic fields.
(iii) Both the rays produce fluorescence on striking a fluorescent material.

Long Answer Type Questions-I

Q. 1. An atomic nucleus A is composed of 84 protons and 128 neutrons. The nucleus A emits and alpha particle and is transformed into a nucleus B.

(i) What is the composition of B ?

(ii) The nucleus B emits a beta particle and is transformed into a nucleus C. What is the composition of C ?

(iii) What is mass number of the nucleus A ?

(iv) Does the composition of C change if it emits gamma radiations ? **[2020]**

 Marking Scheme

(i) The composition of B is:
Number of proton = 82
Number of neutron = 126

(ii) The composition of C is:
Number of proton = 83
Number of neutron = 125

(iii) Mass number of the nucleus A = 212.

(iv) Nnumber, the composition of a nucleus does not change if it emits gamma radiation.

Ans. For nucleus A
Atomic no. (Z) = 84
Mass no. (A) = 84 + 128 = 212

(i) $_{84}A^{212} \xrightarrow{\alpha} {}_{82}B^{208}$ Nucleus B will have 82 protons and (208 − 82) = 126 neutrons.

(ii) $_{82}B^{208} \xrightarrow{\beta} {}_{83}C^{208}$ Nucleus C will have 83 protons and (208 − 83) = 125 neutrons

(iii) Mass number of nucleus, A = 212

(iv) No, the composition of nucleus C does not change due to emission of gamma radiations.

Q. 2. Radiations given out from a source when subjected to an electric field in a direction perpendicular to their path are shown below in the diagram. The arrows show the path of the radiation A, B and C. Answer the following questions in terms of A, B and C.

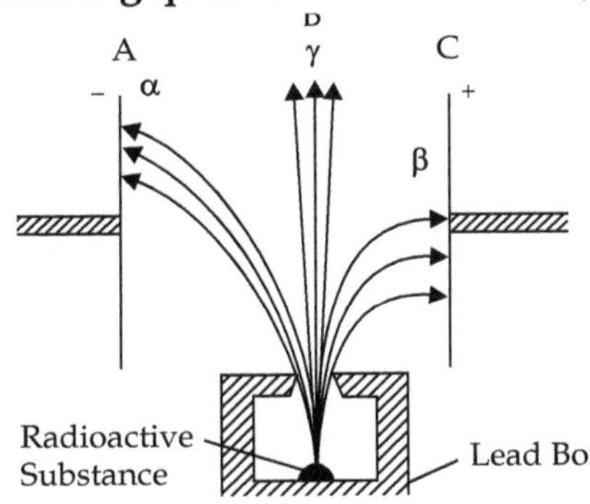

(i) Name the radiation B which is unaffected by the electrostatic field.

(ii) Why does the radiation C deflect more than A?

(iii) Which among the three causes the least biological damage externally?

(iv) Name the radiation which is used in carbon dating. **[2018]**

Ans. (i) γ - radiation.

(ii) The deflection of radiation C (or β-particle) is more than that of radiation A (or α-particle) because β-particles have less mass than α-particles.

(iii) Radiation A (or α-radiations) causes least biological damage.

(iv) The radiation which is used in carbon dating is radiation C (or β-radiation).

Q. 3. (i) Name the radiations which are absorbed by greenhouse gases in the earth's atmosphere. **[2017]**

(ii) A radiation X is focused by a particular device on the bulb of a thermometer and mercury in the thermometer shows a rapid increase. Name the radiation X. **[2017]**

Ans. (i) The radiations absorbed by the greenhouse gases are infra-red radiations of long wavelength.

(ii) The radiation X is infra-red radiation.

Q. 4. (i) Represent the change in the nucleus of radioactive element when a β particle is emitted.

(ii) What is the name given to elements with same mass number and different atomic number?

(iii) Under which conditions does the nucleus of an atom tend to be radioactive? **[2016]**

Ans. (i) In emitting a β-particle, the number of nucleons in the nucleus remains same, but the number of neutrons is decreased by one and the number of protons is increased by one.

$$\underset{\substack{\text{(Parent}\\\text{nucleus)}}}{{}_{Z}^{A}P} \longrightarrow \underset{\substack{\text{(daughter}\\\text{nucleus)}}}{{}_{Z+1}^{A}Q} + \underset{(\beta\text{-particle})}{{}_{-1}^{0}e}$$

(ii) Isobars

(iii) When the number of neutrons is 1.3 to 1.5 times the number of protons in the nucleus of an atom, nucleus has more mass or nucleus has excess energy under such condition it tends to be radioactive.

Q. 5. A certain nucleus X has a mass number 14 and atomic number 6. The nucleus X changes to $_7Y^{14}$ after the loss of a particle.

(i) Name the particle emitted.

(ii) Represent this change in the form of an equation.

(iii) A radioactive substance is oxidized. What change would you expect to take place in the nature of its radioactivity? Give a reason for your answer.   [2012]

Ans. (i) Particle emitted is β-particle.

(ii) $_6^{14}X \rightarrow _7^{14}Y + _{-1}^{0}e$.

(iii) Radioactivity is a nuclear phenomenon. Hence, oxidation has no effect on the nucleus of the substance.

Q. 6. (ii) The nucleus $_{84}^{202}X$ emits an alpha particle and forms the nucleus Y. Represent this change in the form of an equation.

(iii) What changes will take place in the mass number and atomic number of the nucleus Y if it emits gamma radiations?   [2011]

Ans. (ii) $_{84}X^{202} \rightarrow _{82}Y^{198} + _2He^4$.

(iii) No change in mass number and atomic number when γ radiations are emitted out.

Q. 7. (i) What happens to the atomic number of an element when it emits:

(1) An alpha particle;   (2) A beta particle.

(ii) Explain why alpha and beta-particles are deflected in an electric or a magnetic field but gamma rays are not deflected in such a field.   [2007]

Ans. (i) (1) $_Z^A X \xrightarrow{\alpha} _{Z-2}^{A-4} Y + _2^4 He$

(2) $_Z^A X \xrightarrow{\beta} _{Z+1}^{A} P + _{-1}\beta^0$

(ii) α and β are positive and negative charged particles respectively, therefore these are deflected in electric or magnetic field whereas γ radiations are not charged particles so does not deflect.

Long Answer Type Questions-II

Q. 1. (i) Complete the diagram as given above by drawing the deflection of radioactive radiations in an electric field.

(ii) State any two precautions to be taken while handling radioactive substances.   [2015]

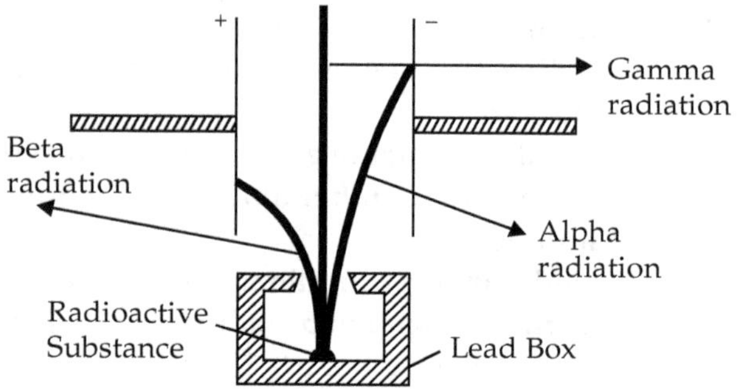

(ii) Two precautions to be taken while handling radioactive substances are:

(1) Special lead lined aprons and lead gloves should be used.

(2) The radioactive materials should be handled with long lead tongs.

Ans. (i)

CHEMISTRY

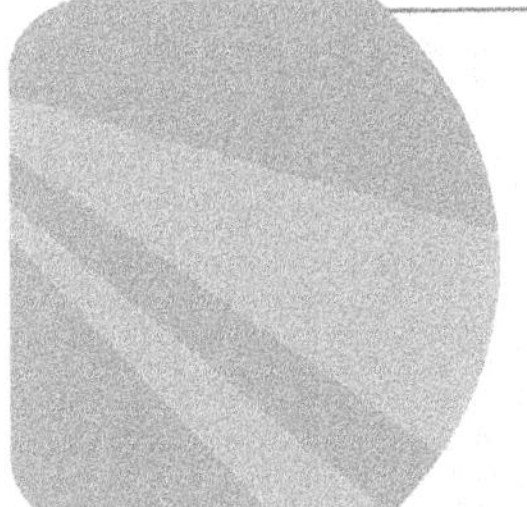

Section-I YEARWISE

 Very Short or One word Answer Type Questions

Q. 1. Choose the correct answer from the options given below:

   (i) The element with highest ionization potential, is:
     (A) Hydrogen   (B) Caesium
     (C) Radon   (D) Helium

   (ii) The inert electrode used in the electrolysis of acidified water, is:
     (A) Nickel   (B) Platinum
     (C) Copper   (D) Silver

   (iii) A compound with low boiling point, is:
     (A) Sodium chloride
     (B) Calcium chloride
     (C) Potassium chloride
     (D) Carbon tetrachloride

   (iv) The acid which can produce carbon from cane sugar, is:
     (A) Concentrated Hydrochloric acid
     (B) Concentrated Nitric acid
     (C) Concentrated Sulphuric acid
     (D) Concentrated Acetic acid

   (v) The organic compound having a triple carbon-carbon covalent bond, is:
     (A) C_3H_4 (B) C_3H_6
     (C) C_3H_8 (D) C_4H_{10} **[2020]**

Ans. **(i)** (D) Helium
   (ii) (B) Platinum
   (iii) (D) Carbon tetrachloride
   (iv) (C) Concentrated Sulphuric acid
   (v) (A) C_3H_4

Q. 2. State one relevant observation for each of the following reactions:

   (i) Action of concentrated nitric acid on copper.

   (ii) Addition of excess ammonium hydroxide into copper sulphate solution.

   (iii) A piece of sodium metal is put into ethanol at room temperature.

   (iv) Zinc carbonate is heated strongly.

   (v) Sulphide ore is added to a tank containing oil and water, and then stirred or agitated with air.   **[2020]**

Ans. **(i)** Action of concentrated nitric acid on copper:
Reddish brown fumes of NO_2 are produced when copper reacts with conc. nitric acid :

$$Cu\ (s) + 4HNO_3 \rightarrow Cu(NO_3)_2 + 2H_2O + 2NO_2$$

   (ii) Addition of excess ammonium hydroxide into copper sulphate solution leads to formation of a deep blue coloured solution.

When ammonium hydroxide is added in the solution of copper sulphate drop-wise, a pale blue precipitate of copper hydroxide is obtained. The equation for this follows:

$$CuSO_4 + 2NH_4OH \rightarrow Cu(OH)_2 + (NH_4)_2SO_4 + 4H_2O$$

When ammonium hydroxide is added in excess, the precipitate dissolves and gives a deep blue solution of tetraammine copper (II) sulphate. The equation for this follows:

$$Cu(OH)_2 + (NH_4)2SO_4 + 2NH_4OH \rightarrow [Cu(NH_3)_4]SO_4 + H_2O$$

Hence, the product formed is a complex named as tetraammine copper (II) sulphate.

   (iii) When a piece of sodium metal is put into ethanol at room temperature hydrogen gas is produced which can be identified by a pop sound and it extinguishes a burning splinter.

$$2Na(s) + 2C_2H_5OH(l) \rightarrow 2C_2H_5ONa(l) + H_2(g)$$

Sodium + Ethanol → Sodium ethoxide + Hydrogen

   (iv) White coloured zinc carbonate is heated strongly to give pale yellow zinc oxide and carbon dioxide gas which extinguishes wooden splinter.

$$ZnCO_3 \rightarrow ZnO + CO_2 \uparrow$$

   (v) Sulphide ore is added to a tank containing oil and water and then stirred or agitated with air to generate a froth.

This is known as froth floatation where the sulphide ore particles are preferentially wetted by oil while gangue particles are preferentially wetted by water. A mixture of water and pine oil is taken in the tank. The powdered Sulphide ore is dropped in. Compressed air is blown in through the agitator. The agitator is rotated several times. Froth containing ore starts rising up.

Q. 3. Write a balanced chemical equation for each of the following reactions:

   (i) Reaction of carbon powder and concentrated nitric acid.

   (ii) Reaction of excess ammonia with chlorine.

   (iii) Reaction of lead nitrate solution with ammonium hydroxide.

   (iv) Producing ethane from bromo ethane using Zn/Cu couple in alcohol

   (v) Complete combustion of ethane. **[2020]**

Ans. **(i)** Carbon powder reacts with concentrated nitric acid to give carbon dioxide, nitrogen dioxide and water.

$$C(s) + 4HNO_3(l) \rightarrow CO_2(g) + 4NO_2(g) + 2H_2O(l)$$

(ii) Excess of ammonia reacts with chlorine to give nitrogen and ammonium chloride.

$$8NH_3(g) + 3Cl_2(g) \rightarrow N_2(g) + 6NH_4Cl$$
Solid white fog

(iii) Lead nitrate solution reacts with ammonium hydroxide to give lead hydroxide and ammonium nitrate.

$$Pb(NO_3)_2 + 2NH_4OH \rightarrow Pb(OH)_2 + 2NH_4NO_3$$

(iv) Production of ethane from bromoethane using Zn/Cu couple in ethanol gives H_2 gas for the reaction.

$$\underset{\text{Bromoethane}}{C_2H_5Br} + H_2 \xrightarrow{Zn/Cu,\ C_2H_5OH} \underset{\text{Ethane}}{C_2H_6} + HBr$$

(v) Complete combustion of ethane gives carbon dioxide and water.

$$\underset{\text{Ethane}}{2C_2H_6} + \underset{\text{Oxygen}}{7O_2} \longrightarrow \underset{\text{Carbon dioxide}}{4CO_2} + \underset{\text{Water}}{6H_2O}$$

Q. 4. **(i)** Draw the structural formula for each of the following:

   1. **2, 2 dimethyl pentane**

   2. **Methanol**

   3. **Iso propane**

   (ii) Write the IUPAC name for the following compounds :

   1. **Acetaldehyde**

   2. **Acetylene** **[2020]**

Ans. **(i)** 1. 2, 2-Dimethyl pentane

$$CH_3-\underset{\underset{CH_3}{|}}{\overset{\overset{CH_3}{|}}{C}}-CH_2-CH_2-CH_3$$

   2. Methanol

$$H-\underset{\underset{H}{|}}{\overset{\overset{H}{|}}{C}}-O-H$$

3. Isopropane

$$H_3C-\underset{\underset{CH_3}{|}}{CH}-CH_3$$

(ii) 1. IUPAC name of acetaldehyde (CH_3CHO) is Ethanal.

   2. IUPAC name of acetylene ($HC \equiv CH$) is Ethyne.

Q. 5. State one relevant reason for each of the following

   (i) Graphite anode is preferred to platinum in the electrolysis of molten lead bromide.

   (ii) Soda lime is preferred to sodium hydroxide in the laboratory preparation of methane.

   (iii) Hydrated copper sulphate crystals turn white on heating.

   (iv) Concentrated nitric acid appears yellow, when it is left for a while in a glass bottle.

   (v) Hydrogen chloride gas fumes in moist air. **[2020]**

Ans. **(i)** Graphite anode is preferred in the electrolysis of molten lead bromide, because graphite remains unaffected by the reactive bromine vapours which are released at the anode.

(ii) Soda lime is preferred to sodium hydroxide in the laboratory preparation for methane because Sodium hydroxide is deliquescent and absorbs water from atmosphere.

$$CH_3COONa \xrightarrow{NaOH/CaO} CH_4 + Na_2CO_3$$

(iii) Hydrated copper sulphate crystals turn white on heating due to the loss of water molecules upon heating.

$$CuSO_4 . 5H_2O \underset{\text{add } H_2O}{\overset{\Delta}{\rightleftharpoons}} CuSO_4 + 5H_2O$$

(iv) Concentrated nitric acid appears yellow, when it is left for a while in a glass bottle because Nitric acid has tendency to decompose slowly in presence of sunlight and produce nitrogen dioxide gas, which is reddish brown in colour. This liberated NO_2 gas dissolves in nitric acid and gives it a yellowish colour.

$$4HNO_3 \rightarrow 4NO_2 + 2H_2O + O_2$$

(v) Hydrogen chloride gas fumes in moist air because it is highly soluble in water and when it comes in contact with air containing water droplets it dissolves in water and forms mist, which appears as white fumes.

Q. 6. Calculate:
 (i) The amount of each reactant required to produce 750 ml of carbon dioxide, when two volumes of carbon monoxide combine with one volume of oxygen to produce two volumes of carbon dioxide:
$$2CO + O_2 \rightarrow 2CO_2$$
 (ii) The volume occupied by 80 g of carbon dioxide at STP.
 (iii) Calculate the number of molecules in 4.4 gm of CO_2.
 [Atomic mass of C = 12, O = 16]
 (iv) State the law associated in question no. (f) (i) above. **[2020]**

Ans. (i) $2CO + O_2 \rightarrow 2CO_2$
 Here, 2 moles of CO react with 1 mole of O_2
 At STP, 1 mole of any ideal gas takes up 22.4 L.
 So, 44.8 L of CO reacts with 22.4 L of O_2 to give 44.8 L of CO_2.
 So, 750 ml of CO_2 production will need 750 ml of CO and 375 ml of O_2.
 (ii) Molecular weight of CO_2 = 44 g
 So, weight of one mole CO_2 gas is 44 g
 Or, 44 g of CO_2 occupies 22.4 L at STP
 $$80 \text{ g will occupy} = \frac{22.4}{44} \times 80$$
 $$= 40.72 \text{ L or} = 40720 \text{ mL}$$
 (iii) Weight of one mole CO_2 gas is 44 g
 Or, 44 g CO_2 contains 6.023×10^{23} CO_2 molecules.
 So, 4.4 g of CO_2 will contain 6.023×10^{22} CO_2 molecules.
 (iv) Gay Lussac's law of combining volumes of gases. When gases react, they do so in volumes which bears a simple whole number ratio to one another and to the volumes of the products, if gaseous, provided the temperature and pressure of the reacting gases and their products remain constant.

Q. 7. Give one word or a phrase for the following statements:
 (i) The chemical bond formed by a shared pair of electrons, each bonding atom contributing one electron to the pair.
 (ii) Electrode used as cathode in electrorefining of impure copper.
 (iii) The substance prepared by adding other metals to a base metal in appropriate proportions to obtain certain desirable properties.
 (iv) The tendency of an atom to attract electrons to itself when combined in a compound.

 (v) The reaction in which carboxylic acid reacts with alcohol in the presence of conc. H_2SO_4 to form a substance having a fruity smell. **[2020]**

Ans. (i) Covalent bond.
 (ii) Pure (thin block) of copper.
 (iii) Alloys
 (iv) Electronegativity
 (v) Esterification

Q. 8. Fill in the blanks from the choices given in brackets: **[2020]**
 (i) The polar covalent compound in gaseous state that does not conduct electricity is .... (carbon tetra chloride, ammonia, methane)
 (ii) A salt prepared by displacement reaction is .... (ferric chloride, ferrous chloride, silver chloride)
 (iii) The number of moles in 11 gm of nitrogen gas is .... (0.39, 0.49, 0.29) [atomic mass of N = 14]
 (iv) An alkali which completely dissociates into ions is .... (ammonium hydroxide, calcium hydroxide, lithium hydroxide)
 (v) An alloy used to make statues is .... (bronze, brass, fuse metal)

Ans. (i) ammonia
 (ii) ferric chloride
 (iii) 0.39
 (iv) calcium hydroxide
 (v) bronze

Q. 9. Choose the correct answer from the options given below:
 (i) An electrolyte which completely dissociates into ions is:
 (A) Alcohol
 (B) Carbonic acid
 (C) Sucrose
 (D) Sodium hydroxide
 (ii) The most electronegative element from the following elements is:
 (A) Magnesium (B) Chlorine
 (C) Aluminium (D) Sulphur
 (iii) The reason for using aluminium in the alloy duralumin is:
 (A) Aluminium is brittle.
 (B) Aluminium gives strength.
 (C) Aluminium brings lightness.
 (D) Aluminium lowers melting point.
 (iv) The drying agent used to dry HCl gas is:
 (A) Conc. H_2SO_4 (B) ZnO
 (C) Al_2O_3 (D) CaO

(v) A hydrocarbon which is a greenhouse gas is:

(A) Acetylene (B) Ethylene

(C) Ethane (D) Methane [2019]

Ans. (i) (D) sodium hydroxide

(ii) (B) Chlorine

(iii) (C) Aluminium brings lightness

(iv) (A) Conc. H_2SO_4

(v) (D) Methane (CH_4)

Q. 10. Fill in the blanks with the choices given in brackets:

(i) Conversion of ethanol to ethene by the action of concentrated sulphuric acid is an example of ....
(dehydration/dehydrogenation/dehydrohalogenation)

(ii) When sodium chloride is heated with concentrated sulphuric acid below 200°C, one of the products formed is .... (sodium bisulphate/sodium sulphate/chlorine)

(iii) Ammonia reacts with excess chlorine to form .... (nitrogen/nitrogen trichloride/ammonium chloride)

(iv) Substitution reaction are characteristic reactions of .... (alkynes/alkenes/alkanes)

(v) In period 3, the most metallic element is .... (Sodium/magnesium/aluminium) [2019]

Ans. (i) dehydration

(ii) sodium bisulphate or sodium hydrogen Sulphate

(iii) ammonium chloride or Nitrogen trichloride

(iv) Alkanes

(v) Sodium or Nitrogen trichloride

Q. 11. Write a balanced chemical equation for each of the following reactions:

(i) Reduction of copper (II) oxide by hydrogen.

(ii) Action of dilute sulphuric acid on sodium hydroxide.

(iii) Action of dilute sulphuric acid on zinc sulphide.

(iv) Ammonium hydroxide is added to ferrous sulphate solution.

(v) Chlorine gas is reacted with ethene. [2019]

Ans. (i) Reduction of copper (II) oxide by hydrogen-

$$CuO\ (s) + H_2\ (g) \rightarrow Cu\ (s) + H_2O\ (g)$$

(ii) Action of dilute sulphuric acid on sodium hydroxide-

$$H_2SO_4\ (aq) + 2NaOH\ (aq) \rightarrow Na_2SO_4\ (aq) + 2H_2O\ (l)$$

(iii) Action of dilute sulphuric acid on zinc sulphide-

$$ZnS + H_2SO_4 \rightarrow ZnSO_4 + H_2S\uparrow$$

(iv) Ammonium hydroxide is added to ferrous sulphate solution –

$$FeSO_4 + 2NH_4OH \rightarrow (NH_4)_2SO_4 + Fe(OH)_2$$

(v) Chlorine gas is reacted with ethene :

$$\underset{\text{Ethene}}{H_2C=CH_2} + \underset{\text{Chlorine}}{Cl-Cl} \longrightarrow \underset{\text{Dichloroethane}}{H_2ClC-CClH_2}$$

Q. 12. State one observation for each of the following:

(i) Concentrated nitric acid is reacted with sulphur.

(ii) Ammonia gas is passed over heated copper (II) oxide.

(iii) Copper sulphate solution is electrolysed using copper electrodes.

(iv) A small piece of zinc is added to dilute hydrochloric acid.

(v) Lead nitrate is heated strongly in a test tube. [2019]

Ans. (i) Concentrated nitric acid is reacted with sulphur to give reddish brown nitrogen dioxide gas.

$$6HNO_3(Conc.) + S\ (s) \rightarrow H_2SO_4\ (g) + 6NO_2\uparrow(g) + 2H_2O\ (l)$$

(ii) When ammonia gas is passed over heated copper (II) oxide, the black copper (II) oxide turns into a pink or reddish-brown substance.

$$2NH_3 + 3CuO \xrightarrow{\text{Heat}} 3Cu + 3H_2O + N_2$$

(iii) Copper sulphate solution is electrolysed using copper electrodes and the cathode increases in size due to deposition of copper metal, whereas the copper anode gets thin due to loss of copper metal into the solution as Cu^{2+} ions.

(iv) A small piece of zinc is added to dilute hydrochloric acid to give bubbles in solution due to evolution of hydrogen gas.

$$Zn(s) + 2HCl(aq) \rightarrow ZnCl_2(s) + H_2(g)\uparrow$$

(v) Lead nitrate is heated strongly in a test tube to give a decrepitating sound and a reddish brown gas (NO_2).

$$2Pb(NO_3)_2(s) \xrightarrow{\text{Heat}} 2PbO + \underset{\text{Reddish brown gas}}{4NO_2}\uparrow + O_2(g)$$

Q. 13. **(i) Calculate:**

    1. **The number of moles in 12g of oxygen gas.** **[O = 16]**

    2. **The weight of 1022 atoms of carbon.** **[C = 12, Avogadro's No. = 6 × 10²³]**

(ii) Molecular formula of a compound is $C_6H_{18}O_3$. Find its empirical formula.

[2019]

Ans. **(i) 1.** The number of moles in 12 g of oxygen gas can be calculated as below-

Given atomic mass of oxygen is 16 g,

Hence molar mass of O_2 gas = 16 × 2

              = 32 g

That is, 32 g oxygen gas has one molecule of O_2 molecules.

Therefore, 12 g of oxygen gas would contain = (1/32) × 12 = 0.375 moles

2. The weight of 10^{22} atoms of carbon can be calculated as follows –

Given – atomic weight of carbon = 12, and Avogadro's number = 6.023 × 10²³

Weight of one mole of carbon is 12 g,

Weight of 6.023 × 10²³ carbon atoms is 12 g

Hence, weight of 10^{22} carbon atoms is (12 g/6.023 × 10²³) × 10²² = 0.199

              ≈ 0. 2 g

(ii) Empirical formula can be obtained by dividing the number of atoms in molecule by the smallest number in the molecular formula-

Given molecular formula – $C_6H_{18}O_3$

Smallest number in formula is 3

Dividing all the atoms by 3,

Empirical formula comes to be – C_2H_6O

Q. 14. **(i) Give the IUPAC name of the following organic compounds :**

    1. $H-\overset{\overset{\displaystyle H}{|}}{\underset{\underset{\displaystyle H}{|}}{C}}-C \equiv C-H$

    2. $H-\overset{\overset{\displaystyle H}{|}}{\underset{\underset{\displaystyle H}{|}}{C}}-\overset{\overset{\displaystyle O}{||}}{C}-H$

(ii) What is the special feature of the structure of ethyne ?

(iii) Name the saturated hydrocarbon containing two carbon atoms.

(iv) Give the structural formula of acetic acid. **[2019]**

Ans. **(i) IUPAC name-**

    1. $H-\overset{\overset{\displaystyle H}{|}}{\underset{\underset{\displaystyle H}{|}}{C}}-C \equiv CH$ **2.** $H-\overset{\overset{\displaystyle H}{|}}{\underset{\underset{\displaystyle H}{|}}{C}}-\overset{\overset{\displaystyle O}{||}}{C}H$

      Propyne   Ethanal

(ii) Special feature of ethyne structure is that ethyne (C_2H_2) contains a triple bond between the two carbon atoms and it is linear in shape due to sp hybridisation in carbon atoms.

(iii) The saturated hydrocarbon containing two carbon atoms is Ethane, C_2H_6.

(iv) The structural formula of acetic acid is –

$$H_3C-\overset{\overset{\displaystyle O}{\diagup\!\!\diagdown}}{C}\diagdown_{OH}$$

Ethanoic acid (acetic acid)

Q. 15. **Give the appropriate term defined by the statements given below:**

    (i) **The formula that represents the simplest ratio of the various elements present in one molecule of the compound.**

    (ii) **The substance that releases hydronium ion as the only positive ion when dissolved in water.**

    (iii) **The tendency of an atom to attract electrons towards itself when combined in a covalent compound.**

    (iv) **The process by which certain ores, specially carbonates are converted to oxide in the absence of air.**

    (v) **The covalent bond in which the electrons are shared equally between the combining atoms.** **[2019]**

Ans. **(i)** The formula that represents the simplest ratio of various elements present in one molecule of a compound is known as **Empirical formula**.

    (ii) The substance that releases hydronium ion as the only positive ion when dissolved in water is **protic acid**.

    (iii) The tendency of an atom to attract electrons towards itself when combined in a covalent compound is known as **electronegativity**.

    (iv) The process by which certain ores, specially carbonates, are converted to oxides in absence of air is known as **calcination**.

    (v) The covalent bond in which the electrons are shared equally between the combining atoms is known as **Non-polar covalent bond**.

Q. 16. Arrange the following according to the instructions given in brackets:

(i) K, Pb, Ca, Zn. (In the increasing order of the reactivity)

(ii) Mg^{2+}, Cu^{2+}, Na^+, H^+ (In the order of preferential discharge at the cathode)

(iii) Li, K, Na, H (In the decreasing order of their ionization potential)

(iv) F, B, N, O (In the increasing order of electron affinity)

(v) Ethane, methane, ethene, ethyne. (In the increasing order of the molecular weight) [H = 1, C = 12]　　　[2019]

Ans. (i) The given elements can be arranged in increasing order of reactivity as follows–
$$Pb < Zn < Ca < K$$

(ii) In the order of preferential discharge at the cathode–
$$Na^+ > Mg^{2+} > H^+ > Cu^{2+}$$

(iii) In the decreasing order of their ionization potential–
$$H > Li > Na > K$$

(iv) In the increasing order of electron affinity–
$$B < N < O < F$$

(v) In the increasing order of molecular weight–
Methane (CH_4) < ethyne (C_2H_2) < ethene (C_2H_4) < ethane (C_2H_6)

Q. 17. Choose the correct answer from the options given below:

(i) The salt solution which does not react with ammonium hydroxide is:

(A) Calcium nitrate　(B) Zinc nitrate

(C) Lead nitrate　　(D) Copper nitrate

(ii) The organic compound which undergoes substitution reaction is:

(A) C_2H_2　　　　(B) C_2H_4

(C) $C_{10}H_{18}$　　　(D) C_2H_6

(iii) The electrolysis of acidified water is an example of:

(A) Reduction　　(B) Oxidation

(C) Redox reaction (D) Synthesis

(iv) The IUPAC name of dimethyl ether is :

(A) Ethoxy methane

(B) Methoxy methane

(C) Methoxy ethane

(D) Ethoxy ethane

(v) The catalyst used in the Contact Process is:

(A) Copper

(B) Iron

(C) Vanadium pentoxide

(D) Manganese dioxide　　　[2018]

Ans. (i) **(A)** Calcium nitrate

(ii) **(D)** C_2H_6 [As saturated hydrocarbons undergo substitution reaction.]

(iii) **(C)** Redox reaction

(iv) **(B)** Methoxy methane

(v) **(C)** Vanadium pentoxide

Q. 18. Give one word or a phrase for the following statements:

(i) The energy released when an electron is added to a neutral gaseous isolated atom to form a negatively charged ion.

(ii) Process of formation of ions from molecules which are not in ionic state.

(iii) The tendency of an element to form chains of identical atoms.

(iv) The property by which certain hydrated salts, when left exposed to atmosphere, lose their water of crystallization and crumble into powder.

(v) The process by which sulphide ore is concentrated.　　　[2018]

Ans. (i) Electron affinity

(ii) Ionization

(iii) Catenation

(iv) Efflorescence or Efflorescent

(v) Froth floatation method

Q. 19. Write a balanced chemical equation for each of the following:

(i) Action of concentrated sulphuric acid on carbon.

(ii) Reaction of sodium hydroxide solution with iron (III) chloride solution.

(iii) Action of heat on aluminium hydroxide.

(iv) Reaction of zinc with potassium hydroxide solution.

(v) Action of dilute hydrochloric acid on magnesium sulphite.　　　[2018]

Ans. (i) $C + 2H_2SO_4 \text{ (conc.)} \rightarrow CO_2 + 2SO_2 + 2H_2O$

(ii) $FeCl_3 + 3NaOH \rightarrow \underset{\text{Iron (III) hydroxide}}{Fe(OH)_3} + 3NaCl$

(iii) Aluminium hydroxide on heating decomposes into aluminium oxide along with water.
$$2Al(OH)_3 \rightarrow \underset{\substack{\text{Aluminium} \\ \text{oxide}}}{Al_2O_3} + 3H_2O$$

(iv) Zinc reacts with potassium hydroxide solution to form potassium zincate
$$Zn + 2KOH \rightarrow \underset{\substack{\text{Potassium} \\ \text{Zincate}}}{K_2ZnO_2} + H_2$$

(v) Magnesium sulphite reacts with dilute hydrochloric acid to give magnesium chloride :
$$MgSO_3 + 2HCl \rightarrow MgCl_2 + H_2O + SO_2\uparrow$$

Q. 20. **(i)** Give the IUPAC name for each of the following :

(1) H—C=O with H below

(2)
$$H-\overset{H}{\underset{H}{C}}-\overset{H}{\underset{H}{C}}-\overset{H}{\underset{H}{C}}-OH$$

(3) $H_3C-\overset{H}{C}=\overset{H}{C}-CH_3$

(ii) Write the structural formula of the two isomers of butane. **[2018]**

Ans. **(i)** **(1)** Methanal

(2) Propan-1-ol

(3) But-2-ene

(ii) H_3C ⌒⌒ CH_3

n-Butane

$CH_3-CH-CH_3$ with CH_3 below

Iso-Butane

Q. 21. State one relevant observation for each of the following reactions :

(i) Lead nitrate solution is treated with sodium hydroxide solution drop wise till it is in excess.

(ii) At the anode, when molten lead bromide is electrolyzed using graphite electrodes.

(iii) Lead nitrate solution is mixed with dilute hydrochloric acid and heated.

(iv) Anhydrous calcium chloride is exposed to air for some time.

(v) Barium chloride solution is slowly added to sodium sulphate solution. **[2018]**

Ans. **(i)** On dropwise addition of sodium hydroxide solution to lead nitrate solution it first gives a white precipitate and then on adding excess of sodium hydroxide solution, a clear solution is obtained due to formation of sodium plumbate (Na_2PbO_2) which is colourless and soluble.

$$Pb(NO_3)_2 + 2NaOH \longrightarrow Pb(OH)_2 (\downarrow) + 2NaNO_3$$

$$Pb(OH)_2 + 2NaOH(Excess) \longrightarrow Na^2PbO_2$$

(ii) At the anode, when lead bromide is electrolyzed using graphite electrodes following reaction occurs at the anode during electrolysis and red brown vapours are evolved at anode.

$$2Br^- - 2e^- \rightarrow 2Br$$
$$2Br \rightarrow Br_2(\uparrow)$$

(iii) Lead nitrate solution is mixed with dilute hydrochloric acid and heated to give lead chloride and nitric acid :

$$Pb(NO_3)_2 + 2HCl \rightarrow PbCl_2 \downarrow + 2HNO_3$$

Lead chloride is a white precipitate solution in warm water but on heating colourless solution is observed.

(iv) Anhydrous calcium chloride is exposed to air for some time and it absorbs moisture from air as it has a strong affinity for water.

$$CaCl_2 + 2H_2O \rightarrow Ca(OH)_2 + 2HCl$$

(v) Barium chloride solution is slowly added to sodium sulphate solution to obtain white precipitate of barium sulphate :

$$BaCl_2(aq) + Na_2SO_4(aq) \rightarrow BaSO_4(s) + 2NaCl(aq)$$

Q. 22. Give a reason for each of the following :

(i) Ionic compounds have a high melting point.

(ii) Inert gases do not form ions.

(iii) Ionisation potential increases across a period, from left to right.

(iv) Alkali metals are good reducing agents.

(v) Conductivity of dilute hydrochloric acid is greater than that of acetic acid. **[2018]**

Ans. **(i)** Ionic compounds have high melting points because the ionic bonds are formed by transfer of electrons which are held by strong electrostatic force of attraction and require a great deal of energy to break the bond.

(ii) Inert gases do not form ions because their outermost shell is complete and they have a stable electronic configuration.

(iii) Ionisation potential increases across a period from left to right because size of atom decreases and effective nuclear charge increases per electron, hence making it difficult to remove electron.

(iv) Alkali metals are good reducing agents because alkali metals have ns^1 outer electron configuration and they achieve the nearest stable configuration by losing one electron, hence they have a great tendency to loose electrons or get oxidized therefore, they are good reducing agents.

(v) Conductivity of dilute hydrochloric acid is greater than that of acetic acid because hydrochloric acid is a strong acid and it dissociates completely in aqueous solution to form H^+ and Cl^- ions (a higher concentration of ions). Acetic acid, on the other hand, is a weak acid and it partially dissociates forming H^+ and CH_3COO^- ions (concentration of ions is low).

Q. 23. Name the gas that is produced in each of the following cases :

    (i) Sulphur is oxidized by concentrated nitric acid.

    (ii) Action of dilute hydrochloric acid on sodium sulphide.

    (iii) Action of cold and dilute nitric acid on copper.

    (iv) At the anode during the electrolysis of acidified water.

    (v) Reaction of ethanol and sodium. **[2018]**

Ans. **(i)** H_2SO_4 and NO_2 are produced when sulphur reacts with conc. HNO_3.

$$S + 6HNO_3(conc.) \rightarrow H_2SO_4 + 6NO_2\uparrow + 2H_2O$$

    (ii) Hydrogen sulphide (H_2S) gas is produced when dilute hydrochloric acid reacts with sodium sulphide.

$$Na_2S(aq) + 2HCl(aq) \rightarrow H_2S(g) + 2NaCl(aq)$$

    (iii) NO gas is evolved when cold and dilute nitric acid reacts with copper.

$$3Cu(s) + 8HNO_3(aq) \rightarrow 3Cu(NO_3)_2(aq)\uparrow$$
$$+ 2NO(g)\downarrow + 4H_2O(l)$$

    (iv) Oxygen is evolved at the anode during the electrolysis of acidified water.

$$OH^- - 1e^- \rightarrow OH$$
$$4OH \rightarrow 2H_2O + O_2\uparrow$$

    (v) Hydrogen gas is produced during the reaction of ethanol and sodium.

$$C_2H_5OH + Na \rightarrow C_2H_5ONa + \frac{1}{2}H_2(g)\uparrow$$

Q. 24. Fill up the blanks with the correct choice given in brackets :

    (i) Ionic or electrovalent compounds do not conduct electricity in their __________ state. (fused/solid)

    (ii) Electrolysis of aqueous sodium chloride solution will form __________ at the cathode. (hydrogen gas/sodium metal)

    (iii) Dry hydrogen chloride gas can be collected by__________ displacement of air. (downward/upward)

    (iv) The most common ore of iron is __________. (calamine/haematite)

    (v) The salt prepared by the method of direct combination is __________ (iron (II) chloride/iron (III) chloride). **[2018]**

Ans. **(i)** solid   **(ii)** hydrogen gas

    (iii) upward (HCl gas is heavy than air)

    (iv) haematite   **(v)** iron (III) chloride

Q. 25. Fill in the blanks with the choices given in brackets.

    (i) The energy required to remove an electron from a neutral isolated gaseous atom and convert it into a positively charged gaseous ion is called __________. (electron affinity, ionisation potential, electronegativity)

    (ii) The compound that does not have a lone pair of electrons is __________ . (water, ammonia, carbon tetra chloride).

    (iii) When a metallic oxide is dissolved in water, the solution formed has a high concentration of __________ ions. (H^+, H_3O^+, OH^-).

    (iv) Potassium sulphite on reacting with hydrochloric acid releases __________ gas. (Cl_2, SO_2, H_2S).

    (v) The compound formed when ethene reacts with hydrogen is __________ . (CH_4, C_2H_6, C_3H_8). **[2017]**

Ans. **(i)** The energy required to remove an electron from a neutral isolated gaseous atom and convert it into a positively charged gaseous ion is called ionisation potential.

    (ii) The compound that does not have a lone pair of electron is carbon tetrachloride.

    (iii) When a metallic oxide is dissolved in water, the solution formed has a high concentration of OH^- ions.

    (iv) Potassium sulphite on reacting with hydrochloric acid releases SO_2 gas.

    (v) The compound formed when ethene reacts with hydrogen is C_2H_6.

Q. 26. Choose the correct answer from the options given below :

    (i) A chloride which forms a precipitate that is soluble in excess of ammonium hydroxide, is :

      (A) Calcium chloride

      (B) Ferrous chloride

      (C) Ferric chloride   **(D)** Copper chloride

    (ii) If the molecular formula of an organic compound is $C_{10}H_{18}$ it is :

      (A) alkene

      (B) alkane

      (C) alkyne

      (D) not a hydrocarbon

    (iii) Which of the following is a common characteristic of a covalent compound ?

      (A) high melting point

      (B) consists of molecules

      (C) always soluble in water

      (D) conducts electricity when it is in the molten state

(iv) To increase the pH value of neutral solution, we should add :
    (A) an acid   **(B)** an acid salt
    (C) an alkali   **(D)** a salt

(v) Anhydrous iron (III) chloride is prepared by :
    (A) direct combination
    (B) simple displacement
    (C) decomposition
    (D) neutralization   [2017]

Ans. **((i)** **(D)** Copper chloride
(ii) **(C)** Alkyne
(iii) **(B)** Consists of molecules
(iv) **(C)** an alkali
(v) **(A)** Direct combination

Q. 27. Identify the substance underlined, in each of the following cases :

(i) Cation that does not form a precipitate with ammonium hydroxide but forms one with sodium hydroxide.

(ii) The electrolyte used for electroplating an article with silver.

(iii) The particles present in a liquid such as kerosene, that is a non-electrolyte.

(iv) An organic compound containing — COOH functional group.

(v) A solid formed by reaction of two gases, one of which is acidic and the other basic in nature.   [2017]

Ans. **(i)** Cation that does not form a precipitate with ammonium hydroxide but forms one with sodium hydroxide — Ca^{2+}

(ii) The electrolyte used for electroplating an article with silver — Solution of sodium argentocyanide *i.e.,* $Na[Ag(CN)_2]$

(iii) The particles present in a liquid such as kerosene, that is a non-electrolyte — Free Molecules

(iv) An organic compound containing — COOH functional group — Carboxylic acid

(v) A solid formed by reaction of two gases, one of which is acidic and the other basic in nature — Ammonium chloride (NH_4Cl) (formed by combining vapours of ammonia with hydrogen chloride gas)

Q. 28. Write a balanced chemical equation for each of the following :

(i) Action of cold and dilute nitric acid on copper.

(ii) Reaction of ammonia with heated copper oxide.

(iii) Preparation of methane from iodomethane.

(iv) Action of concentrated sulphuric acid on sulphur.

(v) Laboratory preparation of ammonia from ammonium chloride.   [2017]

Ans. **(i)** Copper reacts with cold and dilute nitric acid to form copper nitrate, water and nitric oxide.

$$3Cu + 8HNO_3 \longrightarrow$$
Copper   Nitric acid
$$3Cu(NO_3)_2 + 4H_2O + 2NO\uparrow$$
Copper   Water   Nitric oxide

(ii) $$3CuO + 2NH_3 \longrightarrow 3Cu + N_2 + 3H_2O$$
Copper   Ammonia
oxide

(iii) $$CH_3I + 2H \xrightarrow[\text{Alcohol}]{\text{Zn/Cu}} CH_4 + HI$$
                 Methane

(iv) $$S + 2H_2SO_4 \longrightarrow 3SO_2 + 2H_2O$$

(v) $$2NH_4Cl + Ca(OH)_2 \xrightarrow{\text{Heat}} CaCl_2 + 2NH_3 + 2H_2O$$

Q. 29. State one relevant observation for each of the following reactions :

(i) Addition of ethyl alcohol to acetic acid in the presence of concentrated sulphuric acid.

(ii) Action of dilute hydrochloric acid on iron (II) sulphide.

(iii) Action of sodium hydroxide solution on ferrous sulphate solution.

(iv) Burning of ammonia in air.

(v) Action of concentrated sulphuric acid on hydrate copper sulphate.   [2017]

Ans. **(i)** Ethanoic or acetic acid reacts with ethanol in the presence of concentrated sulphuric acid to produce the ester, ethyl ethanoate having a fruity smell and turns blue litmus paper red.

(ii) Iron sulphide reacts with hydrochloric acid, releasing a highly toxic gas hydrogen sulphide having rotten egg smell and turns blue litmus paper red.

(iii) A dirty green precipitate of ferrous hydroxide is formed which is insoluble in excess of NaOH solution.

(iv) Ammonia burns in air to form greenish-yellow vapours of nitric oxide.

(v) The blue crystals are changed into white powder as water is removed. Concentrated sulphuric acid takes away the water molecules and the copper sulphate becomes anhydrous.

Q. 30. **(i)** Draw the structural formula for each of the following :

1. 2, 3-dimethyl butane

2. diethyl ether

3. propanoic acid

(ii) From the list of terms given, choose the most appropriate term to match the given description.

(calcination, roasting, pulverisation, smelting).

1. Crushing of the ore into a fine powder.

2. Heating of the ore in the absence of air to a high temperature. **[2017]**

Ans. **(i) 1.** 2, 3-dimethyl butane

$$
\begin{array}{c}
\ \ \ \ \text{H} \ \ \ \text{H} \ \ \ \text{H} \ \ \ \text{H} \\
\ \ \ \ | \ \ \ \ \ | \ \ \ \ \ | \ \ \ \ \ | \\
\text{H}-\text{C}-\text{C}-\text{C}-\text{C}-\text{H} \\
\ \ \ \ | \ \ \ \ \ | \ \ \ \ \ | \ \ \ \ \ | \\
\ \ \ \ \text{H} \ \ \ \text{CH}_3 \ \text{CH}_3 \ \text{H}
\end{array}
$$

2. Diethyl ether

$$
\begin{array}{c}
\text{H} \ \ \ \text{H} \ \ \ \ \ \ \ \text{H} \ \ \ \text{H} \\
| \ \ \ \ \ | \ \ \ \ \ \ \ \ \ | \ \ \ \ \ | \\
\text{H}-\text{C}-\text{C}-\text{O}-\text{C}-\text{C}-\text{H} \\
| \ \ \ \ \ | \ \ \ \ \ \ \ \ \ | \ \ \ \ \ | \\
\text{H} \ \ \ \text{H} \ \ \ \ \ \ \ \text{H} \ \ \ \text{H}
\end{array}
$$

3. Propanoic acid

$$
\begin{array}{c}
\text{H} \ \ \ \text{H} \\
| \ \ \ \ \ | \ \ \ \ \ \ \ \ \nearrow^{\text{O}} \\
\text{H}-\text{C}-\text{C}-\text{C} \\
| \ \ \ \ \ | \ \ \ \ \ \ \ \ \searrow_{\text{OH}} \\
\text{H} \ \ \ \text{H}
\end{array}
$$

(ii) 1. Pulverisation

2. Calcination

Q. 31. **(i)** Calculate the number of gram atoms in 4.6 grams of sodium (Na = 23).

(ii) Calculate the percentage of water of crystalization in $CuSO_4.5H_2O$

(H = 1, O = 16, S = 32, Cu = 64)

(iii) A compound of X and Y has the empirical formula XY_2. Its vapour density is equal to its empirical formula weight. Determine its molecular formula. **[2017]**

Ans. **(i)** 1 g atom is the mass of 1 mole of monoatomic element.

1 mole of Na is equal to 23 g atom of Na.

23 g of Na $= 1$ mole of Na

4.6 g of Na $= 4.6 \times 1/23 = 0.2$ mole

So, number of gram atoms

$$= 0.2 \times 6.022 \times 10^{23} \text{ atoms}$$

$$= 1.204 \times 10^{23} \text{ atoms}$$

(ii) Molar mass of $CuSO_4.5H_2O$

$$= [64 + 32 + (16 \times 4) + 5 (2 \times 1 + 16)]$$

$$= 250$$

Mass of water of crystallisation

$$= 5 (2 \times 1 + 16) = 90$$

$\therefore$ Percentage of water of crystallisation

$$= \frac{90}{250} \times 100 = 36\%$$

(iii) Molecular weight $= 2 \times$ Vapour density

$$= 2 \times \text{Empirical formula weight}$$

(Given, Vapour density

$$= \text{empirical formula weight})$$

Also,

Molecular Weight = Empirical formula

$$\text{weight} \times n$$

Therefore, $2 \times$ Empirical formula weight

$$= \text{Empirical formula weight} \times n$$

$$n = 2$$

Now, Molecular Formula

$$= (\text{Empirical Formula}) \times n$$

$$= (XY_2)_2$$

$$= X_2Y_4$$

Q. 32. Match the atomic number 2, 4, 8, 15 and 19 with each of the following :

(i) A solid non-metal belonging to the third period.

(ii) A metal of valency 1.

(iii) A gaseous element with valency 2.

(iv) An element belonging to Group 2.

(v) A rare gas. **[2017]**

Ans. **(i)** Z = 15   **(ii)** Z = 19

(iii) Z = 8   **(iv)** Z = 4

(v) Z = 2

Q. 33. Fill in the blanks with the choices given in brackets.

(i) Metals are good _________ .

(oxidizing agents/ reducing agents) because they are electron_________ .

(acceptors/donors).

(ii) Electrovalent compounds have _________ (high/low) melting points.

(iii) Higher the pH value of a solution, the more _________ (acidic/ alkaline) it is.

(iv) _______(AgCl/PbCl₂), a white precipitate is soluble in excess NH_4OH.

(v) Conversion of ethene to ethane is an example of _________.

(hydration/hydrogenation) **[2016]**

Ans. **(i)** Reducing agents, donors

(ii) High

(iii) Alkaline

(iv) AgCl

(v) Hydrogenation

Q. 34. Choose the correct answer from the options given below :

(i) An element with the atomic number 19 will most likely combine chemically with the element whose atomic number is :

(A) 17   **(B)** 11

(C) 18   **(D)** 20

    (ii) The ratio between the number of molecules in 2 g of hydrogen and 32 g of oxygen is :
        (A) 1 : 2
        (B) 1 : 0.01
        (C) 1 : 1
        (D) 0·01 : 1 [Given that H = 1, O = 16]

    (iii) The two main metals in bronze are :
        (A) Copper and zinc
        (B) Copper and lead
        (C) Copper and nickel
        (D) Copper and tin

    (iv) The particles present in strong electrolytes are :
        (A) only molecules (B) mainly ions
        (C) ions and molecules (D) only atoms

    (v) The aim of the fountain experiment is to prove that :
        (A) HCl turns blue litmus red
        (B) HCl is denser than air
        (C) HCl is highly soluble in water
        (D) HCl fumes in moist air   [2016]

Ans.   (i) (A) 17
     (ii) (C) 1 : 1
     (iii) (D) Copper and tin
     (iv) (B) Mainly ions
     (v) (C) HCl is highly soluble in water.

Q. 35. Write balanced chemical equations for each of the following :
    (i) Action of warm water on AlN.
    (ii) Action of hot and concentrated nitric acid on copper.
    (iii) Action of hydrochloric acid on sodium bicarbonate.
    (iv) Action of dilute sulphuric acid on sodium sulphite.
    (v) Preparation of ethanol from ethyl chloride.   [2016]

Ans.   (i) $AlN + 3H_2O \longrightarrow Al(OH)_3 + NH_3 \uparrow$
                          Ammonia gas
     (ii) $Cu + 4HNO_3 \longrightarrow Cu(NO_3)_2 + 2NO_2 \uparrow + 2H_2O$
     (iii) $NaHCO_3 + HCl \longrightarrow NaCl + H_2O + CO_2 \uparrow$
     (iv) $Na_2SO_3 + H_2SO_4 \longrightarrow Na_2SO_4 + H_2O + SO_2 \uparrow$
     (v) $C_2H_5Cl + KOH \xrightarrow{\Delta} C_2H_5OH + KCl$

Q. 36. State your observations when :
    (i) Dilute hydrochloric acid is added to lead nitrate solution and the mixture is heated.
    (ii) Barium chloride solution is mixed with sodium sulphate solution.
    (iii) Concentrated sulphuric acid is added to sugar crystals.
    (iv) Dilute hydrochloric acid is added to copper carbonate.
    (v) Dilute hydrochloric acid is added to sodium thiosulphate.   [2016]

Ans.   (i) When dilute hydrochloric acid is added to lead nitrate and the mixture is heated, insoluble white precipitate of lead chloride is formed but is soluble on heating.
$$Pb(NO_3)_2 + 2HCl \xrightarrow{\Delta} 2HNO_3 + PbCl_2 \downarrow$$
                              (white ppt.)

    (ii) When barium chloride is added to sodium sulphate, the products are sodium chloride (which remains in the solution) and barium sulphate precipitate (which settles down as a white precipitate).
$$BaCl_2 + Na_2SO_4 \longrightarrow BaSO_4 \downarrow + 2NaCl$$
                         (white ppt.)

    (iii) When concentrated sulphuric acid is added to sugar crystals, it leaves behind residue of black carbon.
$$C_{12}H_{22}O_{11} \xrightarrow[H_2SO_4]{Conc.} 12C + 11H_2O$$

    (iv) When dilute hydrochloric acid is added to copper carbonate, a brisk effervescence is seen due to the evolution of CO2, with the formation of copper chloride and it turns lime water milky.
$$CuCO_3(s) + 2HCl\,(aq) \longrightarrow CuCl_2(aq) + H_2CO_3(aq)$$
$$\longrightarrow CuCl_2\,(aq) + H_2O(l) + CO_2(g) \uparrow$$

    (v) Sodium thiosulphate reacts with dilute hydrochloric acid to produce sodium chloride, gas of sulphur dioxide, water and sulphur in a yellow solid form.
$$Na_2S_2O_3 + 2HCl \longrightarrow 2NaCl + S \downarrow + H_2O + SO_2 \uparrow$$

Q. 37. Identify the term/substance in each of the following :
    (i) The tendency of an atom to attract electrons to itself when combined in a compound.
    (ii) The method used to separate ore from gangue by preferential wetting.
    (iii) The catalyst used in the conversion of ethyne to ethane.
    (iv) The type of reactions alkenes undergo.
    (v) The electrons present in the outermost shell of an atom.   [2016]

Ans.   (i) Electronegativity
     (ii) Froth Floatation

(iii) Nickel or Platinum

(iv) Addition reaction or hydrogenation reaction

(v) Valence electrons

Q. 38. **(i) A gas of mass 32 gm has a volume of 20 litre at S.T.P. Calculate the gram molecular weight of the gas.**

(ii) How much calcium oxide is formed when 82 g of calcium nitrate is heated? Also find the volume of nitrogen dioxide evolved :

$$2Ca(NO_3)_2 \rightarrow 2CaO + 4NO_2 + O_2$$

(Ca = 40, N = 14, O = 16)

[2016]

Ans. **(i)** Given,

Mass of 20 l of a gas at STP = 32 g

∴ Mass of 1 l of gas at STP would be

$$= \frac{32}{20} g$$

We know that,

Gas at STP has volume

$$= 22.4\ l$$

∴ Gram molecular weight of the gas

$$= \frac{32}{20} \times 22.4$$

$$= 35.84\ g$$

(ii) $2Ca(NO_3)_2 \longrightarrow 2CaO + 4NO_2 + O_2$

(2×164) g $\qquad (2 \times 56)$g 4 vol. 1 vol.

From the above given chemical reaction

328 g of $Ca(NO_3)_2$ decomposes to form 112 g of CaO

∴ 1 g of $Ca(NO_3)_2$ will decompose

$$= \frac{112}{328} g$$

And thus 82 g of Ca $(NO_3)_2$ will decompose

$$= \frac{112}{328} \times 82\ g$$

$$= 28\ g\ of\ CaO$$

From given chemical equation :

328 g of $Ca(NO_3)_2$ gives 4 vol. of NO_2

And we know that a gas at STP has volume

$$= 22{\cdot}4\ l$$

∴ Volume of NO_2 evolved when 82 g of Ca $(NO_3)_2$ is heated

$$= \frac{4 \times 22.4}{328} \times 82$$

$$= 22.4\ l$$

Q. 39. **Match the salts given in column I with their method of preparation given in column II :**

	Column I		Column II
(i)	$Pb(NO_3)_2$ from PbO	**(A)**	Simple displacement
(ii)	$MgCl_2$ from Mg	**(B)**	Titration
(iii)	$FeCl_3$ from Fe	**(C)**	Neutralization
(iv)	$NaNO_3$ from NaOH	**(D)**	Precipitation
(v)	$ZnCO_3$ from $ZnSO_4$	**(E)**	Combination

[2016]

Ans.

	Column I		Column II
(i)	$Pb(NO_3)_2$ from PbO	**(C)**	Neutralization
(ii)	$MgCl_2$ from Mg	**(A)**	Simple displacement
(iii)	$FeCl_3$ from Fe	**(E)**	Combination
(iv)	$NaNO_3$ from NaOH	**(B)**	Titration
(v)	$ZnCO_3$ from $ZnSO_4$	**(D)**	Precipitation

Q. 40. **(i) Write the IUPAC names of each of the following :**

$$
1.\quad H-C=C-C-H \text{ (with H atoms attached)}
$$

$$
2.\quad H-C-C\equiv C-C-H \text{ (with H atoms attached)}
$$

$$
3.\quad H-C-C=O \text{ (with H atoms attached)}
$$

(ii) Rewrite the following sentences by using the correct symbol > (greatert than) or < (less than) in the blanks given :

1. The ionization potential of potassium is —————— that of sodium.

2. The electronegativity of iodine is —————— that of chlorine.

[2016]

Ans. **(i) 1.** Propene   **2.** But-2-yne

         3. Ethanal

(ii) 1. less than (<)   **2.** less than (<)

Q. 41. **Select from the list the gas that matches the description given in each case:**

[ammonia, ethane, hydrogen chloride, hydrogen sulphide, ethyne]

(i) This gas is used as a reducing agent in reducing copper oxide to copper.

(ii) This gas produces dense white fumes with ammonia gas.

(iii) This gas is used for welding purposes.

(iv) This gas is also a saturated hydrocarbon.

(v) This gas has a characteristic rotten egg smell. **[2015]**

Ans. (i) Ammonia (ii) Hydrogen chloride

(iii) Ethyne   (iv) Ethane

(v) Hydrogen sulphide.

Q. 42. Choose the most appropriate answer for each of the following :

(i) Among the elements given below, the element with the least electronegativity is :

(A) Lithium   (B) Carbon

(C) Boron   (D) Fluorine

(ii) Identify the statement which does not describe the property of alkenes :

(A) They are unsaturated hydrocarbons

(B) They decolourise bromine water

(C) They can undergo addition as well as substitution reactions.

(D) They undergo combustion with oxygen forming carbon dioxide and water.

(iii) This is not an alloy of copper :

(A) Brass   (B) Bronze

(C) Solder   (D) Duralumin

(iv) Bonding in this molecule can be understood to involve coordinate bonding :

(A) Carbon tetrachloride

(B) Hydrogen

(C) Hydrogen chloride

(D) Ammonium chloride

(v) Which of the following would weigh the least ?

(A) 2 gram atoms of Nitrogen

(B) 1 mole of silver

(C) 22.4 litre of oxygen gas at 1 atmospheric pressure and 273 K

(D) 6.02×10^{23} atoms of carbon

[Atomic masses : Ag = 108, N = 14, O = 16, C = 12]

[2015]

Ans. (i) **(A)** Lithium

(ii) **(C)** They can undergo addition as well as substitution reactions.

(iii) **(C)** Solder

(iv) **(D)** Ammonium chloride

(v) **(D)** 6.02×10^{23} atoms of carbon

Q. 43. Complete the following calculations. Show working for complete credit :

(i) Calculate the mass of calcium that will contain the same number of atoms as are present in 3.2 gm of sulphur.

[Atomic masses : S = 32, Ca = 40]

(ii) If 6 litre of hydrogen and 4 litre of chlorine are mixed and exploded and if water is added to the gases formed, find the volume of the residual gas.

(iii) If the empirical formula of a compound is CH and it has a vapour density of 13, find the molecular formula of the compound. **[2015]**

Ans. (i) 32 g of sulphur contain

$$= 6.023 \times 10^{23} \text{ atoms}$$

$\therefore$ 3.2 g of sulphur contain

$$= \frac{6.023 \times 10^{23}}{32} \times 3 \cdot 2$$

$$= 6.023 \times 10^{22}$$

Now, 6.023×10^{23} atom of calcium have mass

$$= 40 \text{ g}$$

$\therefore$ 6.023×10^{22} atoms of calcium have mass

$$= \frac{40}{6.023 \times 10^{23}} \times 6.023 \times 10^{22}$$

$$= 4 \text{ g}$$

Hence, the mass of calcium is 4 g.

(ii) $H_2 + Cl_2 \longrightarrow HCl$

1 vol. 1 vol.   2 vols.

Since, 1 volume of chlorine reacts with 1 volume of hydrogen.

$\therefore$ 4 litre of chlorine will react with only 4 volumes of hydrogen.

$\therefore$ $(6 - 4)$ *i.e.*, 2 litre of hydrogen will remain unreacted.

HCl formed will get dissolved in water.

$\therefore$ Volume of residual gas hydrogen is 2 litre.

(iii) Given,

Empirical formula = CH

Now, Empirical formula mass

$$= 12 \times 1 + 1 \times 1 = 13$$

Molecular mass = 2 × Vapour density

$$= 2 \times 13 = 26$$

Molecular formula mass

$$= n \times \text{Empirical formula mass}$$

$\therefore$ $n = \dfrac{\text{Molecular formula mass}}{\text{Empirical formula mass}}$

$$= \frac{26}{13} = 2$$

$$\text{Molecular formula} = n \times \text{Empirical formula}$$
$$= 2 \times (CH)$$
$$= C_2H_2$$

Hence, the molecular formula of the compound is C_2H_2.

Q. 44. State one relevant observation for each of the following :

    (i) When crystals of copper nitrate are heated in a test tube.

    (ii) When the gaseous product obtained by dehydration of ethyl alcohol is passed through bromine water.

    (iii) When hydrogen sulphide gas is passed through lead acetate solution.

    (iv) When ammonia gas is burnt in an atmosphere of excess oxygen.

    (v) At the anode when aqueous copper sulphate solution is electrolysed using copper electrodes. **[2015]**

Ans.   **(i)** The blue coloured copper nitrate crystals changes into black powdery residue CuO with the release of reddish brown NO_2 gas.

    (ii) The reddish brown colour of bromine water disappears.

    (iii) Lead acetate solution becomes black due to the formation of lead sulphide.

    (iv) Ammonia burns with a yellowish green flame in the atmosphere of excess oxygen.

    (v) The copper of the anode dissolves and, therefore, it becomes thin gradually.

Q. 45. Identify the acid which matches the following description (i) to (v) :

    (i) The acid which is used in the preparation of a non-volatile acid.

    (ii) The acid which produces sugar charcoal from sugar.

    (iii) The acid which is prepared by catalytic oxidation of ammonia.

    (iv) The acid on mixing with lead nitrate solution produces a white precipitate which is insoluble even on heating.

    (v) The acid on mixing with silver nitrate solution produces a white precipitate which is soluble in excess ammonium hydroxide. **[2015]**

Ans.   **(i)** Conc. nitric acid

    (ii) Conc. sulphuric acid

    (iii) Conc. nitric acid

    (iv) Dil. sulphuric acid

    (v) Dil. hydrochloric acid.

Q. 46. Give appropriate scientific reasons for the following statements :

    (i) Zinc oxide can be reduced to zinc by using carbon monoxide, but aluminium oxide cannot be reduced by a reducing agent.

    (ii) Carbon tetrachloride does not conduct electricity.

    (iii) During electrolysis of molten lead bromide graphite anode is preferred to other electrodes.

    (iv) The electrical conductivity of acetic acid is less in comparison to the electrical conductivity of dilute sulphuric acid at a given concentration.

    (v) Electrolysis of molten lead bromide is considered to be a redox reaction. **[2015]**

Ans.   **(i)** This is because of the fact that aluminium has great affinity towards oxygen than zinc and so aluminium oxide cannot be reduced by reducing agents such as carbon monoxide or carbon or hydrogen.

    (ii) This is because of the absence of free ions in the carbon tetrachloride molecule.

    (iii) This is because graphite rod is unaffected by the reactive bromine vapours formed during electrolysis at anode. Graphite is inert in nature.

    (iv) This is because acetic acid being a weak acid partially dissociates and produces less ions in solution whereas sulphuric acid being a strong acid completely dissociates and produces more free ions in solution. Hence, conduction of electric current in acetic acid is less as compared to dil. H_2SO_4 at given concentration.

    (v) This is because of the fact that during electrolysis of molten lead bromide, both reduction (at cathode) and oxidation (at anode) takes place. At cathode, Pb^{2+} ions gain electrons and get reduced while at anode, Br^- ions lose electrons and get oxidised.

$$PbBr_2 \rightleftharpoons Pb^{2+} + 2Br^-$$
(Lead Bromide)

Cathode : $Pb^{2+} + 2e^- \longrightarrow Pb$

Anode : $2Br^- - 2e^- \longrightarrow 2Br$

Q. 47.   **(i)** Give balanced chemical equations for the following conversions A, B and C :

$$Fe \xrightarrow{A} FeCl_3 \xrightarrow{B} FeCO_3$$
$$\xrightarrow{C} Fe(NO_3)_2$$

    (ii) Differentiate between the terms strong electrolyte and weak electrolyte. (stating any two differences) **[2015]**

Ans. **(i)**

$$2Fe + 3Cl_2 \longrightarrow 2FeCl_3$$

Chlorine gas   Iron (III) Chloride
(Dry) (A)

$$2FeCl_3 + 3Na_2CO_3 \longrightarrow Fe_2(CO_3)_3 + 6NaCl$$

Sodium carbonate solution (B)

$$FeCO_3 + 2HNO_3 \longrightarrow Fe(NO_3)_2 + H_2O + CO_2$$

Nitric acid (C)

(ii)

Strong Electrolyte	Weak Electrolyte
They allow a large amount of electricity to flow through them *i.e.*, they are good conductors of electricity.	They allow small amount of electricity to flow through them *i.e.*, they are poor conductors of electricity.
They are completely dissociated into the fused or aqueous solution state and contains only free mobile ions.	They are partially dissociated into their fused or aqueous solution state and contain ions as well as molecules.

Q. 48. **Answer the following questions :**

(i) Explain the bonding in methane molecule using electron dot structure.

(ii) The metals of Group 2 from top to bottom are Be, Mg, Ca, Sr, and Ba.

(1) Which one of these elements will form ions most readily and why ?

(2) State the common feature in the electronic configuration of all these elements. **[2015]**

Ans. **(i)** To attain the stable electronic configuration of the nearest noble gas, carbon needs four electrons and hydrogen needs one electron. Therefore, in the methane molecule formation, one atom of carbon shares four electron pairs, one with each of the four atoms of hydrogen resulting in the formation of four single covalent bond between them. The electron sharing can be illustrated using electron dot structure which is as follows :

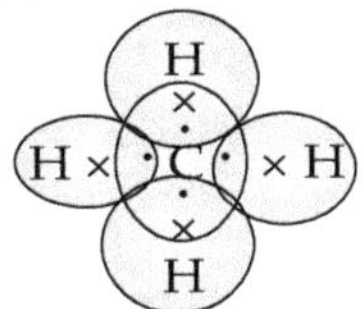

Electron dot structure of methane molecule

where × = electron of carbon atom

· = electron of hydrogen atom

(ii) **(1)** Barium (Ba) will form ions most readily because its ionisation potential is lowest in the group. Hence, the removal of electrons is easy.

(2) All these elements have two electrons in their valence or outer most shell.

Q. 49. **Choose the correct answer from the options given below :**

(i) Ionization potential increases over a period from left to right because the :

(A) Atomic radius increases and nuclear charge increases

(B) Atomic radius decreases and nuclear charge decreases

(C) Atomic radius increases and nuclear charge decreases

(D) Atomic radius decreases and nuclear charge increases.

(ii) A compound X consists of only molecules. Hence X will have :

(A) A crystalline hard structure.

(B) A low melting point and low boiling point.

(C) An ionic bond.

(D) A strong force of attraction between its molecules.

(iii) When fused lead bromide is electrolyzed we observe :

(A) a silver grey deposit at anode and a reddish brown deposit at cathode.

(B) a silver grey deposit at cathode and a reddish brown deposit at anode.

(C) a silver grey deposit at cathode and reddish brown fumes at anode.

(D) silver grey fumes at anode and reddish brown fumes at cathode.

(iv) The main ore used for the extraction of iron is :

(A) Haematite   (B) Calamine
(C) Bauxite   (D) Cryolite

(v) Heating an ore in a limited supply of air or in the absence of air at a temperature just below its melting point is known as:

(A) smelting   (B) ore dressing
(C) calcination   (D) bessemerisation

(vi) If an element A belongs to Period 3 and Group II then it will have :

(A) 3 shells and 2 valence electrons.

(B) 2 shells and 3 valence electrons.

(C) 3 shells and 3 valence electrons.

(D) 2 shells and 2 valence electrons.

(vii) The molecule containing a triple covalent bond is :

(A) ammonia   (B) methane
(C) water   (D) nitrogen

(viii) The electrolyte used for electroplating an article with silver is :
(A) silver nitrate solution
(B) silver cyanide solution
(C) sodium argentocyanide solution
(D) nickel sulphate solution.

(ix) Aluminium powder is used in thermite welding because :
(A) it is a strong reducing agent.
(B) it is a strong oxidising agent.
(C) it is corrosion resistant.
(D) it is a good conductor of heat.

(x) The I.U.P.A.C. name of acetylene is :
(A) propane   (B) propyne
(C) ethene   (D) ethyne.   [2014]

Ans.
(i) (D) Atomic radius decreases and nuclear charge increases.
(ii) (B) A low melting point and low boiling point.
(iii) (C) A silvery grey deposit at cathode and reddish brown fumes at anode.
(iv) (A) Haematite
(v) (C) Calcination
(vi) (A) 3 shells and 2 valence electrons.
(vii) (D) Nitrogen.
(viii) (C) Sodium argentocyanide solution.
(ix) (A) It is a strong reducing agent.
(x) (D) Ethyne.

Q. 50. Fill in the blanks from the choices given within brackets
(i) The basicity of acetic acid is ....(3, 1, 4).
(ii) The compound formed when ethanol reacts with sodium is .... (sodium ethanoate, sodium ethoxide, sodium propanoate).
(iii) Quicklime is not used to dry HCl gas because.........(CaO is alkaline, CaO is acidic, CaO is neutral).
(iv) Ammonia gas is collected by .... (an upward displacement of air, a downward displacement of water, a downward displacement of air).
(v) Cold, dilute nitric acid reacts with copper to form............(Hydrogen, nitrogen dioxide, nitric oxide).   [2014]

Ans.
(i) 1
(ii) Sodium ethoxide
(iii) CaO is alkaline
(iv) A downward displacement of air
(v) Nitric oxide.

Q. 51. Give one word or phrase for the following :
(i) The ratio of the mass of a certain volume of gas to the mass of an equal volume of hydrogen under the same conditions of temperature and pressure.
(ii) Formation of ions from molecules.
(iii) Electrolytic deposition of a superior metal on a baser metal.
(iv) Hydrocarbons containing a $-\overset{\overset{\textstyle O}{\|}}{C}-$ functional group.
(v) The amount of energy released when an atom in the gaseous state accepts an electron to form an anion.   [2014]

Ans.
(i) Vapour density   (ii) Ionization
(iii) Electroplating   (iv) Ketones
(v) Electron affinity.

Q. 52. Match the options A to E with the statements (i) to (v) :

A	alkynes	(i)	No. of molecules in 22.4 dm^3 of carbon dioxide at S.T.P.
B	alkane	(ii)	An element with electronic configuration 2, 8,8,3.
C	iron	(iii)	$C_n H_{2n+2}$
D	6.023 $\times 10^{23}$c	(iv)	$C_n H_{2n-2}$
E	metal	(v)	The metal that forms two types of ions.

[2014]

Ans.
(A) (iv)   (B) (iii)   (C) (v)
(D) (i)   (E) (ii)

Q. 53. Write balanced equations for the following :
(i) Action of heat on a mixture of copper and concentrated nitric acid.
(ii) Action of warm water on magnesium nitride.
(iii) Action of concentrated sulphuric acid on carbon.
(iv) Action of dilute hydrochloric acid on sodium sulphide.
(v) Preparation of ethane from sodium propionate.   [2014]

Ans.
(i) $Cu + 4HNO_3 \xrightarrow{\Delta} Cu(NO_3)_2 + 2H_2O$
   Copper   Conc.   Copper
         nitric acid   nitrate
                     $+ 2NO_2\uparrow$

(ii) $Mg_3N_2 + 6H_2O \longrightarrow 3Mg(OH)_2$
   Magnesium   Warm   Magnesium
   nitride   hydroxide
                     $+ 2NH_3\uparrow$
                 Ammonia gas

(iii) $C + 2H_2SO_4 \rightarrow CO_2 + 2H_2O + 2SO_2\uparrow$
      Conc.   Carbon   Sulphur
               dioxide   dioxide

(iv) $Na_2S + 2HCl \rightarrow 2NaCl + H_2S \uparrow$

Sodium   Dil.   Sodium   Hydrogen

sulphide   chloride   sulphide gas

(v) $C_2H_5COONa + NaOH \xrightarrow[300°C]{CaO} C_2H_6$

Sodium   Ethane

propionate $+ Na_2CO_3$

                     Sodium

                     carbonate

Q. 54. Distinguish between the following pairs of compounds using the test given within brackets :

(i) **Iron (II) sulphate and iron (III) sulphate (using ammonium hydroxide).**

(ii) **A lead salt and a zinc salt (using excess ammonium hydroxide).**

(iii) **Sodium nitrate and sodium sulphite (using dilute sulphuric acid).**

(iv) **Dilute sulphuric acid and dilute hydrochloric acid (using barium chloride solution).**

(v) **Ethane and ethene (using alkaline potassium permanganate solution).**

[2014]

Ans. (i) **Using ammonium hydroxide :**

Iron (II) Sulphate	Iron (III) Sulphate
Dirty green precipitate.	Reddish Brown precipitate.

(ii) **Using excess ammonium hydroxide :**

Lead Salt	Zinc Salt
White precipitate, insoluble in excess of NH4OH solution.	Gelatinous white ppt., dissolves in excess of NH4OH solution.

(iii) **Using dilute sulphuric acid :**

Sodium Nitrate	Sodium Sulphite
No effect.	Colourless gas i.e., SO_2 with smell of burning sulphur is liberated which turns moist blue litmus paper red.

(iv) **Using barium chloride solution :**

Dilute Sulphuric acid	Dilute hydrochloric acid
Thick white precipitate is obtained which remains insoluble in nitric acid.	No effect.

(v) **Using alkaline potassium permanganate solution :**

Ethane	Ethene
No effect as potassium permanganate remain purple	Solution of potassium permanganate gets decolourised. The purple colour gets decolourised.

Q. 55. (i) **Oxygen oxidizes ethyne to carbon dioxide and water as shown by the equation :**

$$2C_2H_2 + 5O_2 \longrightarrow 4CO_2 + 2H_2O$$

What volume of ethyne gas at S.T.P. is required to produce 8·4 dm3 of carbon dioxide at S.T.P. ?

[H = 1, C = 12, O = 16]

(ii) **A compound made up of two elements X and Y has an empirical formula X_2Y. If the atomic weight of X is 10 and that of Y is 5 and the compound has a vapour density 25, find its molecular formula.**

[2014]

Ans. (i) Given,

$$2C_2H_2 + 5O_2 \rightarrow 4CO_2 + 2H_2O$$

     2 vol.   4 vol.

$\therefore$ 1 vol.   2 vol.

According to Gay Lussac's law :

2 volume of CO_2 is produced from 1 vol. of C_2H_2

$\therefore$ 8.4 dm^3 of CO_2 at S.T.P. produced from

$$= \frac{1 × 8.4}{2}$$

$$= 4.2 \ dm^3 \ of \ C_2H_2$$

At s.t.p. 4.2 dm^3 of ethyne is required.

Empirical formula weight

$$= X_2Y = 2 × 10 + 5$$

$$= 25$$

(ii)   Molecular formula

$$= (\text{Empirical formula}) × n$$

$$n = \frac{\text{Molecular formula weight}}{\text{Empirical formula weight}}$$

$$= \frac{2 × V.D.}{(2 × 10 + 5)}$$

(V.D. = Vapour Density)

$$= \frac{2 × 25}{25} = 2$$

$\therefore$ Molecular formula

$$= (X_2Y) × 2 = X_4Y_2$$

Q. 56. From the list given below, select the word(s) required to correctly complete blanks (i) to (v) in the following passage. The words from the list are to be used only once. Write the answers as (a) (i), (ii), (iii) and so on. Do not copy the passage.

[ammonia, ammonium carbonate, carbon dioxide, hydrogen, hydronium, hydroxide, precipitate, salt, water]

(i) A solution M turns blue litmus red, so it must contain (i) _______ ions; another solution O turns red litmus blue and hence, must contain (ii) _______ ions.

(ii) When solutions M and O are mixed together, the products will be (iii) _______ and (iv) _______ .

(iii) If a piece of magnesium was put into a solution M, (v) _________ gas would be evolved. [2013]

Ans. (i) Hydronium   (ii) Hydroxide
(iii) Salt   (iv) Water
(v) Hydrogen

Q. 57. Identify the gas evolved in the following reactions when :

(i) Sodium propionate is heated with soda lime.

(ii) Potassium sulphite is treated with dilute hydrochloric acid.

(iii) Sulphur is treated with concentrated nitric acid.

(iv) A few crystals of KNO_3 are heated in a hard glass test tube.

(v) Concentrated hydrochloric acid is made to react with manganese dioxide. [2013]

Ans. (i) Ethane   (ii) Sulphur dioxide
(iii) Nitrogen dioxide (iv) Oxygen
(v) Chlorine

Q. 58. State one appropriate observation for each of the following :

(i) Concentrated sulphuric acid is added drop wise to a crystal of hydrated copper sulphate.

(ii) Copper sulphide is treated with dilute hydrochloric acid.

(iii) Excess of chlorine gas is reacted with ammonia gas.

(iv) A few drops of dilute hydrochloric acid are added to silver nitrate solution, followed by addition of ammonium hydroxide solution.

(v) Electricity is passed through molten lead bromide. [2013]

Ans. (i) Crystals of hydrated copper sulphate turn into white amorphous copper sulphate powder.

(ii) Rotten egg smell of hydrogen sulphide gas will be given out. Hydrogen sulphide gas will be given out which smells like rotten eggs and turns moist blue litmus paper red.

(iii) Yellow coloured highly explosive liquid nitrogen trichloride and hydrogen chloride gas is given out.

(iv) A white precipitate of silver chloride is formed which dissolves in NH_4OH.

(v) Red coloured bromine vapours with high irritating smell evolve at anode and a white lead metal deposits at cathode.

Q. 59. Give suitable chemical terms for the following :

(i) A bond formed by a shared pair of electrons with both electrons coming from the same atom.

(ii) A salt formed by incomplete neutralization of an acid by a base.

(iii) A reaction in which hydrogen of an alkane is replaced by a halogen.

(iv) A definite number of water molecules bound to some salts.

(v) The process in which a substance absorbs moisture from the atmospheric air to become moist, and ultimately dissolves in the absorbed water. [2013]

Ans. (i) Co-ordinate bond
(ii) Acid salt
(iii) Halogenation
(iv) Water of crystallisation
(v) Deliquescence

Q. 60. Give a chemical test to distinguish between the following pairs of compounds :

(i) Sodium chloride solution and sodium nitrate solution.

(ii) Hydrogen chloride gas and hydrogen sulphide gas.

(iii) Ethene gas and ethane gas.

(iv) Calcium nitrate solution and zinc nitrate solution.

(v) Carbon dioxide gas and sulphur dioxide gas. [2013]

Ans. (i)

Test	Sodium Chloride Solution	Sodium Nitrate Solution
On adding silver nitrate solution.	White ppt. of AgCl is formed which dissolves in NH_4OH.	No reaction takes place.

(ii)

Test	Hydrogen Chloride Gas	Hydrogen Sulphide Gas
A rod dipped in ammonium hydroxide is brought near the gas.	Dense white fumes of ammonium chloride are formed.	No reaction takes place.

(iii)

Test	Ethene	Ethane
On pouring few drops of bromine solution in carbon tetrachloride with the hydrocarbon.	The reddish brown bromine solution gets decolourised.	No change is observed.

(iv)

Test	Calcium Nitrate Solution	Zinc Nitrate Solution
Ammonium hydroxide is added first dropwise and then in excess.	No precipitation of $Ca(OH)_2$ occurs even with addition of excess of NH_4OH.	Gelatinous white ppt. of $Zn(OH)_2$ is formed which is soluble in excess of NH_4OH.

(v)

Test	Calcium Nitrate Solution	Zinc Nitrate Solution
The gas is passed into acidified solution of orange coloured $K_2Cr_2O_7$ solution.	No change is observed.	Orange solution of $K_2Cr_2O_7$ turns green.

Q. 61. Choose the most appropriate answer from the following options :

(i) Among the period 2 elements, the element which has high electron affinity is :
(A) Lithium   (B) Carbon
(C) Chlorine   (D) Fluorine

(ii) Among the following compounds identify the compound that has all three bonds (ionic, covalent and coordinate bond).
(A) Ammonia
(B) Ammonium chloride
(C) Sodium hydroxide
(D) Calcium chloride.

(iii) Identify the statement that is incorrect about alkanes :
(A) They are hydrocarbons.
(B) There is a single covalent bond between carbon and hydrogen.
(C) They can undergo both substitution as well as addition reactions.
(D) On complete combustion they produce carbon dioxide and water.

(iv) Which of these will act as a non-electrolyte ?
(A) Liquid carbon tetrachloride
(B) Acetic acid
(C) Sodium hydroxide aqueous solution acid
(D) Potassium chloride aqueous solution

(v) Which one of the following will not produce an acid when made to react with water ?
(A) Carbon monoxide
(B) Carbon dioxide
(C) Nitrogen dioxide
(D) Sulphur trioxide

(vi) Identify the metallic oxide which is amphoteric in nature :
(A) Calcium oxide
(B) Barium oxide
(C) Zinc oxide
(D) Copper(II) oxide

(vii) In the given equation identify the role played by concentrated sulphuric acid
$$S + 2H_2SO_4 \longrightarrow 3SO_2 + 2H_2O :$$
(A) Non-volatile acid
(B) Oxidising agent
(C) Dehydrating agent
(D) None of the above

(viii) Nitrogen gas can be obtained by heating :
(A) Ammonium nitrate
(B) Ammonium nitrite
(C) Magnesium nitride
(D) Ammonium chloride

(ix) Which of the following is not a typical property of an ionic compound ?
(A) High melting point
(B) Conducts electricity in the molten and in the aqueous solution state.
(C) They are insoluble in water.
(D) They exist as oppositely charged ions even in the solid state.

(x) The metals zinc and tin are present in the alloy :
(A) Solder   (B) Brass
(C) Bronze   (D) Duralumin

[2013]

Ans. (i) **(D)** Fluorine

(ii) **(B)** Ammonium chloride

(iii) **(C)** They can undergo both substitution as well as addition reactions.

(iv) **(A)** Liquid carbon tetrachloride

(v) **(A)** Carbon monoxide

(vi) **(C)** Zinc oxide

(vii) **(B)** Oxidising agent

(viii) **(B)** Ammonium nitrite

(ix) **(C)** They are insoluble in water

(x) **(C)** Bronze

Q. 62. Solve the following :

(i) **What volume of oxygen is required to burn completely 90 dm3 of butane under similar conditions of temperature and pressure ?**

$$2C_4O_{10} + 13O_2 \rightarrow 8CO_2 + 10H_2O$$

(ii) **The vapour density of a gas is 8. What would be the volume occupied by 24.0 g of the gas at STP ?**

(iii) **A vessel contains X number of molecules of hydrogen gas at a certain temperature and pressure. How many molecules of nitrogen gas would be present in the same vessel under the same conditions of temperature and pressure ?** **[2013]**

Ans. There is printing error in the question paper : Instead of C_4O_{10} in the equation formula, it should be C_4H_{10}

(i) $2C_4H_{10} + 13O_2 \longrightarrow 8CO_2 + 10H_2O$

    2 vol.   13 vol.

∵ 2 vol. of butane require 13 vol. of oxygen (according to Gay Lussac's Law)

∴ 90 dm3 of butane require $= \dfrac{13 \times 90}{2}$

$= 585 \text{ dm}^3$

585 dm^3 of oxygen is required to burn 90 dm^3 of butane.

(ii) Given,

(Vapour Density) V.D. = 8

∴ Molecular weight $= 2 \times$ V.D.

$= 2 \times 8 = 16$

Number of moles in 24.0 g of gas

$= \dfrac{\text{Wt.}}{\text{Mol.wt}} = \dfrac{24.0}{16}$

= 1.5 moles

At S.T.P., 1 mole of a gas occupies 22.4 l.

∴ 1.5 moles (or 24.0 g) of the gas will occupy $= \dfrac{22.4 \times 1.5}{1} = 33.6 \, l.$

(iii) 'X' number of molecules. (According to Avogadro's law)

Q. 63. Name the gas in each of the following :

(i) **The gas evolved on reaction of aluminium with boiling concentrated caustic alkali solution.**

(ii) **The gas produced when excess ammonia reacts with chlorine.**

(iii) **A gas which turns acidified potassium dichromate clear green.**

(iv) **The gas produced when copper reacts with concentrated nitric acid.**

(v) **The gas produced on reaction of dilute sulphuric acid with a metallic sulphide.** **[2012]**

Ans. (i) Hydrogen gas

(ii) Nitrogen gas

(iii) Sulphur dioxide gas

(iv) Nitrogen dioxide gas

(v) Hydrogen sulphide gas

Q. 64. State one observation for each of the following :

(i) **Excess ammonium hydroxide solution is added to lead nitrate solution.**

(ii) **Bromine vapours are passed into a solution of ethyne in carbon tetrachloride.**

(iii) **A zinc granule is added to copper sulphate solution.**

(iv) **Zinc nitrate crystals are strongly heated.**

(v) **Sodium hydroxide solution is added to ferric chloride solution at first a little and then in excess.** **[2012]**

Ans. (i) A white ppt. of lead hydroxide is formed which is soluble in excess of NH_4OH.

(ii) A colourless solution is obtained and brown colour of bromine vapours disappears.

(iii) A red metal starts precipitating and the blue colour of the copper sulphate solution fades due to the formation of colourless zinc sulphate.

(iv) A reddish brown gas is liberated.

(v) A reddish brown ppt. of ferric hydroxide is formed which remains insoluble in excess of sodium hydroxide.

Q. 65. Some word/words are missing in the following statements. You are required to rewrite the statements in the correct form using the appropriate word/words :

(i) **Ethyl alcohol is dehydrated by sulphuric acid at a temperature of about 170°C.**

(ii) **Aqua regia contains one part by volume of nitric acid and three parts by volume of hydrochloric acid.**

(iii) **Magnesium nitride reacts with water to liberate ammonia.**

(iv) **Cations migrate during electrolysis.**

(v) **Magnesium reacts with nitric acid to liberate hydrogen gas.** [2012]

Ans. (i) Ethyl alcohol is dehydrated by concentrated sulphuric acid at a temperature of about 170°C to form ethylene.

(ii) Aqua regia contains a mixture of one part by volume of concentrated nitric acid and three parts by volume of concentrated hydrochloric acid.

(iii) Magnesium nitride reacts with warm water to liberate ammonia.

(iv) Cations migrate to cathode during electrolysis.

(v) Magnesium reacts with very dilute and cold nitric acid to liberate hydrogen gas.

Q. 66. **Choose the correct answer from the options given below :**

(i) **An element in period-3 whose electron affinity is zero.**

    (A) **Neon**   (B) **Sulphur**

    (C) **Sodium**   (D) **Argon**

(ii) **An alkaline earth metal.**

    (A) **Potassium**   (B) **Calcium**

    (C) **Lead**   (D) **Copper**

(iii) **The vapour density of carbon dioxide [C = 12, O = 16]**

    (A) **12**   (B) **16**

    (C) **44**   (D) **22**

(iv) **Identify the weak electrolyte from the following :**

    (A) **Sodium chloride solution**

    (B) **Dilute hydrochloric acid**

    (C) **Dilute sulphuric acid**

    (D) **Aqueous acetic acid**

(v) **Which of the following metallic oxides cannot be reduced by normal reducing agents ?**

    (A) **Magnesium oxide**

    (B) **Copper(II) oxide**

    (C) **Zinc oxide**

    (D) **Iron(III) oxide** [2012]

Ans. (i) **(D)** Argon (ii) **(B)** Calcium

(iii) **(D)** 22

(iv) **(D)** Aqueous acetic acid

(v) **(A)** Magnesium oxide

Q. 67. **Match the following :**

Column A		Column B	
1.	Acid salt	A.	Ferrous ammonium sulphate
2.	Double salt	B.	Contains only ions
3.	Ammonium hydroxide solution	C.	Sodium hydrogen sulphate
4.	Dilute hydrochloric acid	D.	Contains only molecules
5.	Carbon tetrachloride	E.	Contains ions and molecules

[2012]

Ans. 1. (C), 2. (A), 3. (E), 4. (B), 5. (D)

Q. 68. **Give the structural formula for the following :**

(i) **Methanoic acid**   (ii) **Ethanal**

(iii) **Ethyne**   (iv) **Acetone**

(v) **2-methyl propane.** [2012]

Ans.

(i)
$$\text{H}\overset{\overset{\displaystyle O}{\|}}{\underset{}{-\text{C}-}}\text{OH}$$

Methanoic acid

(ii)
$$\text{H}-\underset{\underset{\displaystyle H}{|}}{\overset{\overset{\displaystyle H}{|}}{\text{C}}}-\text{C}\overset{\displaystyle O}{\underset{\displaystyle H}{<}}$$

Ethanal

(iii) $\text{H}-\text{C} \equiv \text{C}-\text{H}$

Ethyne

(iv)
$$\text{H}-\underset{\underset{\displaystyle H}{|}}{\overset{\overset{\displaystyle H}{|}}{\text{C}}}-\overset{\overset{\displaystyle O}{\|}}{\text{C}}-\underset{\underset{\displaystyle H}{|}}{\overset{\overset{\displaystyle H}{|}}{\text{C}}}-\text{H}$$

Acetone

(v)
$$\text{H}-\underset{\underset{\displaystyle H}{|}}{\overset{\overset{\displaystyle H}{|}}{\text{C}}}-\underset{\underset{\displaystyle H}{|}}{\overset{\overset{\displaystyle \underset{|}{\overset{|}{\text{C}}-\text{H}}}{}}{\text{C}}}-\underset{\underset{\displaystyle H}{|}}{\overset{\overset{\displaystyle H}{|}}{\text{C}}}-\text{H}$$

2-methyl propane

Q. 69. **Concentrated nitric acid oxidises phosphorus to phosphoric acid according to the following equation :**

$$P + 5HNO_3(\text{conc.}) \rightarrow H_3PO_4 + H_2O + 5NO_2$$

If 9.3 g of phosphorus was used in the reaction, calculate :

   (i) Number of moles of phosphorus taken.

   (ii) The mass of phosphoric acid formed.

   (iii) The volume of nitrogen dioxide produced at S.T.P.

   [H = 1, N = 14, P = 31, O = 16]   **[2012]**

Ans. **(i)** Number of moles

$$= \frac{\text{Given weight}}{\text{Molecular wt. of substance}}$$

$$= \frac{9.3}{31} = 0.3$$

0·3 moles of phosphorus is taken.

   (ii) Molecular weight of H_3PO_4

$$= (1 \times 3) + (31) + (4 \times 16)$$

$$= 3 + 31 + 64 = 98 \text{ g}$$

$\because$ 31 g of phosphorus gives 98 g of phosphoric acid

$\therefore$ 9.3 g of phosphorus gives

$$= \frac{98 \times 9.3}{31}$$

$$= 29.4 \text{ g of phosphoric acid}$$

   (iii) From the equation :

1 mole of phosphorus liberates 5 moles of nitrogen dioxide

0·3 mole of phosphorus liberates

$$= 5 \times 0.3$$

$$= 1.5 \text{ moles of } NO_2$$

Now, at S.T.P. 1 mole of NO_2 occupies 22.4 l.

$\therefore$ 1.5 mole of NO_2 occupies

$$= 22.4 \times 1.5 = 33.6 \, l$$

Q. 70. Give reasons for the following :

   (i) Iron is rendered passive with fuming nitric acid.

   (ii) An aqueous solution of sodium chloride conducts electricity.

   (iii) Ionization potential of the element increases across a period.

   (iv) Alkali metals are good reducing agents.

   (v) Hydrogen chloride gas cannot be dried over quick lime.   **[2012]**

Ans. **(i)** Due to the formation of a thin protective layer of insoluble iron oxide (Fe_3O_4) which stops the reaction.

   (ii) An aqueous solution of sodium chloride conducts electricity because in aqueous solution, Na^+ and Cl^- ions become free and mobile.

   (iii) Ionization potential of the elements increases across a period because across a period, atomic size decreases and nuclear charge increases, so more energy is required to remove a valence electron.

   (iv) Alkali metals are good reducing agents because they combine exothermically with electronegative elements to form very stable compounds. That is why, alkali metals are strong reducing agent.

   (v) Hydrogen chloride gas cannot be dried over quick lime because quick lime is basic in nature and combines with moist hydrogen chloride gas to form calcium chloride.

Q. 71. Choose from the following list of substances, as to what matches the description from (i) to (v) given below :

[Acetylene gas, aqua fortis, coke, brass, barium chloride, bronze, platinum].

   (i) An aqueous salt solution used for testing sulphate radical.

   (ii) A catalyst used in the manufacture of nitric acid by Ostwald's process.

   (iii) A black powdery substance used for the reduction of zinc oxide during its extraction.

   (iv) A gaseous hydrocarbon commonly used for welding purposes.

   (v) The substance is an alloy of zinc, copper and tin.   **[2011]**

Ans. **(i)** Barium Chloride   **(ii)** Platinum

   (iii) Coke   **(iv)** Acetylene

   (v) Bronze

Q. 72. What would you observe in each of the following cases ?

   (i) Ammonium hydroxide is first added in a small quantity and then in excess to a solution of copper sulphate.

   (ii) Sugar crystals are added to a hard glass test tube containing concentrated sulphuric acid.

   (iii) Copper is heated with concentrated nitric acid in a hard glass test tube.

   (iv) Water is added to the product formed, when aluminium is burnt in a jar of nitrogen gas.

   (v) When carbon monoxide is passed over heated copper oxide.   **[2011]**

Ans. **(i)** First a light blue ppt. appears then ppt. dissolves and solution turns inky blue.

   (ii) Sugar crystals first turn brown then to a black spongy mass. Steam is also evolved.

   (iii) A reddish brown pungent smelling gas is evolved.

   (iv) A colourless gas with characteristic pungent smell of ammonia is formed.

   (v) Black powdery copper oxide changes to red shiny copper metal.

Q. 73. Give reasons as to why :

   (i) the electrolysis of acidulated water is considered to be an example of catalysis.

   (ii) almost 90% of all known compounds are organic in nature.

(iii) **it is dangerous to burn methane in an insufficient supply of air.**

(iv) **hydrogen chloride can be termed as a polar covalent compound.**

(v) **the oxidising power of elements increases on moving from left to right along a period in the periodic table.** [2011]

Ans. (i) It is because during electrolysis of acidulated water, quantity of acid present remains unchanged throughout and the rate of electrolysis of water gets increased.

(ii) It is because in all the living world compounds are mainly made of carbon and hydrogen. And carbon has the ability to form maximum number of compounds than those of other elements put together.

(iii) It is because it will form carbon monoxide which is poisonous in nature.

(iv) It is because there is large difference between electro negativities of H and Cl.

(v) It is because on moving from left to right along a period in the periodic table, the electron affinity of elements increases.

Q. 74. Fill in the blanks from the choices given below :

(i) **In covalent compounds, the bond is formed due to the .... (sharing/transfer) of electrons.**

(ii) **Electrovalent compounds have a.................. (low/high) boiling point.**

(iii) **A molecule of...............contains a triple bond. (hydrogen, ammonia, nitrogen).**

(iv) **Across a period, the ionization potential........ (increases, decreases, remains same).**

(v) **Down the group, electron affinity............(increases, decreases, remains same).** [2011]

Ans. (i) Sharing (ii) High

(iii) Nitrogen (iv) Increases

(v) Decreases

Q. 75. (i) **Calculate the volume of 320 g of SO_2 at S.T.P. (Atomic mass : S = 32 and O = 16).**

(ii) **State Gay-Lussac's Law of combining volumes.**

(iii) **Calculate the volume of oxygen required for the complete combustion of 8.8 g of propane (C_3H_8). (Atomic mass : C = 14, O = 16, H = 1, Molar Volume = 22.4 dm^3 at S.T.P).** [2011]

Ans. (i) Gram molar mass of SO_2
$$= 32 + (2 \times 16) = 64 \text{ g.}$$
No. of moles in 64 g = 1 mole

$\therefore$ No. of moles in 320 g of SO_2
$$= = 5 \text{ moles}$$
At S.T.P. 1 mole of SO_2 occupies 22.4 l

$\therefore$ 5 moles of SO_2 will occupy $5 \times 22.4 = 112$ l

(ii) **Gay-Lussac's Law of combining volumes :** Under same conditions of temperature and pressure, the volume of gases taking part in a chemical reaction show simple whole number ratio to one another and to the volume of products if gaseous.

(iii) Chemical equation for the complete combustion of propane is :
$$C_3H_8 + 5O_2 \rightarrow 3CO_2 + 4H_2O$$
1 mole   5 mole

1 mole $5 \times 22{\cdot}4$ l at S.T.P.

$(12 \times 3) + (1 \times 8) = 44$ g

Molecular weight of C_3H_8
$$= 12 \times 3 + 1 \times 8$$
$$= 44 \text{ g}$$
44 g of C_3H_8 requires $= 5 \times 22.4$ l of oxygen

1 g of C_3H_8 requires =

$\therefore$ 8.8 g of propane would require
$$= \frac{5 \times 22.4 \times 8.8}{44} \, 22.4 \, l \text{ of oxygen.}$$

Q. 76. Choose the correct answer from the options given below :

(i) **This metal is a liquid at room temperature :**
(A) **Potassium** (B) **Zinc**
(C) **Gold** (D) **Mercury**

(ii) **Hydroxide of this metal is soluble in sodium hydroxide solution :**
(A) **Magnesium** (B) **Lead**
(C) **Silver** (D) **Copper**

(iii) **In the periodic table alkali metals are placed in the group :**
(A) **1** (B) **11**
(C) **17** (D) **18**

(iv) **Hydrogen chloride gas being highly soluble in water is dried by :**
(A) **Anhydrous calcium chloride**
(B) **Phosphorous penta oxide**
(C) **Quick lime**
(D) **Concentrated sulphuric acid**

(v) **The brown ring test is used for detection of :**
(A) CO^{2-}_3 (B) NO^-_3
(C) SO^{2-}_3 (D) Cl^-

(vi) When dilute sulphuric acid reacts with iron sulphide, the gas evolved is :

(A) Hydrogen sulphide

(B) Sulphur dioxide

(C) Sulphur trioxide

(D) Vapour of sulphuric acid

(vii) The functional group present in acetic acid is :

(A) Ketonic $>C = O$

(B) Hydroxyl $-OH$

(C) Aldehydic $-CHO$

(D) Carboxyl $-COOH$

(viii) The unsaturated hydrocarbons undergo :

(A) a substitution reaction

(B) an oxidation reaction

(C) an addition reaction

(D) none of the above

(ix) The number of C–H bonds in ethane molecule are :

(A) Four (B) Six

(C) Eight (D) Ten

(x) Which of the following properties do not match with elements of the halogen family ?

(A) They have seven electrons in their valence shell.

(B) They are highly reactive chemically.

(C) They are metallic in nature.

(D) They are diatomic in their molecular form. **[2011]**

Ans. (i) **(D)** Mercury

(ii) **(B)** Lead

(iii) **(A)** 1

(iv) **(D)** Concentrated sulphuric acid

(v) **(B)** NO_3^-

(vi) **(A)** Hydrogen sulphide

(vii) **(D)** Carboxyl $-COOH$

(viii) **(C)** An addition reaction

(ix) **(B)** Six

(x) **(C)** They are metallic in nature.

Q. 77. Write the balanced chemical equation for each of the following reactions :

(i) Sodium thiosulphate is reacted with dilute hydrochloric acid.

(ii) Calcium bicarbonate reacts with dilute hydrochloric acid.

(iii) Dilute sulphuric acid is poured over sodium sulphite.

(iv) Lead nitrate solution is added to sodium chloride solution.

(v) Zinc is heated with sodium hydroxide solution. **[2011]**

Ans. (i) $Na_2S_2O_3 + 2HCl \rightarrow 2NaCl + SO_2\uparrow$
(Dil.) Sodium chloride
$+ H_2O + S\downarrow$

(ii) $Ca(HCO_3)_2 + 2HCl \rightarrow CaCl_2 + 2H_2O$
(Dil.) Calcium chloride
$+ 2CO_2\uparrow$

(iii) $Na_2SO_3 + H_2SO_4 \rightarrow Na_2SO_4 + H_2O$
Sodium sulphate
$+ SO_2\uparrow$

(iv) $Pb(NO_3)_2 + 2NaCl \rightarrow PbCl_2\downarrow + 2NaNO_3$
Lead chloride

(v) $Zn^{2+} + NaOH \rightarrow Za(OH)_2 + 2Na^+$

OR

$Zn + 2NaOH \rightarrow Na_2ZnO_2 + H_2$

Periodic Properties and Variation of Properties— Physical and Chemical

Short Answer Type Questions-I

Q. 1. Fill in the blanks by selecting the correct word from the brackets:

(i) If an element has a low ionization energy then it is likely to be______ (metallic/non-metallic).

(ii) If an element has seven electrons in its outermost shell then it is likely to have the______ (largest/smallest) atomic size among all the elements in the same period. **[2016, 2008]**

Ans. (i) Metallic (ii) Smallest

Q. 2. Define the following terms:

(i) Ionization potential.

(ii) Electron affinity. **[2010]**

Ans. (i) **Ionization potential:** It is the amount of energy required to remove an electron from the outermost (valence) shell of an isolated gaseous atom in its ground state.

(ii) **Electron affinity:** It is the amount of energy released when an electron is added to the outermost (valence) shell of an isolated gaseous atom to form gaseous negative ion.

Short Answer Type Questions-II

Q. 1. The following table represent the elements and the atomic number :

With reference to this, answer the following using only the alphabets given in the table.

Element	Atomic number
P	13
Q	7
R	10

(i) Which element combines with hydrogen to form a basic gas ?

(ii) Which element has an electron affinity zero ?

(iii) Name the element, which forms an ionic compound with chlorine. **[2020]**

 **Marking Scheme**

(i) Q/7

(ii) R/10

(iii) P with Z = 13

Ans. (i) Q (QH_3 is the basic gas) with Z = 7

(ii) R with Z = 10

(iii) P with Z = 13

Q. 2. Name the following elements :

(i) An alkaline earth metal present in group 2 and period 3.

(ii) A trivalent metal used to make light tools.

(iii) A monovalent non-metal present in fluorspar. **[2020]**

Marking Scheme

(i) Magnesium or Mg

(ii) Aluminium or Al

(iii) Fluorine or F

Ans. (i) Magnesium or Mg

(ii) Aluminium or Al

(iii) Fluorine or F

Q. 3. In Period 3 of the Periodic Table, element B is placed to the left of element A. On the basis of this information, choose the correct word from the brackets to complete the following statements:

(i) The element B would have (lower/higher) metallic character than A.

(ii) The element A would probably have (lesser/higher) electron affinity than B.

(iii) The element A would have (greater/smaller) atomic size than B. **[2018]**

Ans. (i) The element **B** would have *higher* metallic character than element **A**.

(ii) The element **A** would have probably *higher* electron affinity than element **B**.

(iii) The element **A** would have *smaller* atomic size than element **B**.

Q. 4. An element has an atomic number 16. State:

(i) the period to which it belongs.

(ii) the number of valence electrons.

(iii) whether it is a metal or non-metal. **[2010]**

Ans. (i) 3rd period (ii) Six electrons

(iii) Non-metal

Q. 5. (i) The metals of Group 2 from top to bottom are: Be, Mg, Ca, Sr, Ba. Which of these metals will form ions most readily and why?

(ii) What property of an element is measured by electronegativity? **[2008]**

Ans. (i) Ba will form ions most readily because its ionisation potential is lowest in the group.

(ii) Ability of the element to attract the shared pair of electron in a covalent bond towards itself.

 ## Short Answer Type Questions-III

Q. 1. Arrange the following as per the instruction given in the brackets:

(i) He, Ar, Ne (Increasing order of the number of electron shells)

(ii) Na, Li, K (Increasing Ionisation Energy)

(iii) F, Cl, Br (Increasing electronegativity)

(iv) Na, K, Li (Increasing atomic size) **[2017]**

Ans. (i) He < Ne < Ar (ii) K < Na < Li

(iii) Br < Cl < F (iv) Li < Na < K

Q. 2. Use the letters only written in the Periodic Table given below to answer the questions that follow:

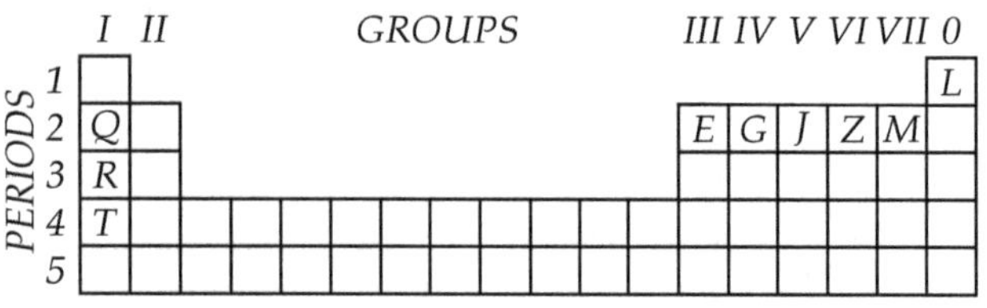

(i) State the number of valence electrons in atom J.

(ii) Which element shown forms ions with a single negative charge?

(iii) Which metallic element is more reactive than R?

(iv) Which element has its electrons arranged in four shells? **[2016]**

Ans. (i) Five valence electrons

(ii) M

(iii) T

(iv) T

Q. 3. Arrange the following as per the instructions given in the brackets:

(i) Cs, Na, Li, K, Rb (increasing order of metallic character).

(ii) Mg, Cl, Na, S, Si (decreasing order of atomic size).

(iii) Na, K, Cl, S, Si (increasing order of ionization energy)

(iv) Cl, F, Br, I (increasing order of electron affinity) **[2015]**

Ans. (i) Li < Na < K < Rb < Cs

(ii) Na > Mg > Si > S > Cl

(iii) K < Na < Si < S < Cl

(iv) I < Br < F < Cl

Long Answer Type Questions-I

Q. 1. An element Z has atomic number 16. Answer the following questions on Z:

(i) State the period and group to which Z belongs.

(ii) Is Z a metal or a non-metal?

(iii) State the formula between Z and hydrogen.

(iv) What kind of a compound is this? **[2014]**

Ans. (i) 3rd period, 16th group.

(ii) Z is a non-metal.

(iii) H_2Z

(iv) Covalent compound.

Q. 2. Consider the section of the periodic table given below:

Group numbers	I A 1	II A 2	III A 13	IV A 14	V A 15	VI A 16	VII A 17	0 18
	Li		D			O	J	Ne
	A	Mg	E	Si		H	K	
	B	C		F	G			L

Note: In this table B does not represent boron
C does not represent carbon
F does not represent fluorine
H does not represent hydrogen

K does not represent potassium

You must see the position of the element in the periodic table.

Some elements are given in their own symbol and position in the periodic table, while others are shown with a letter. With reference to the table:

  (i) Which is the most electronegative?

 (ii) How many valence electrons are present in G?

(iii) Write the formula of the compound between B and H.

 (iv) In the compound between F and J, what type of bond will be formed?

  (v) Draw the electron dot structure for the compound formed between C and K.

[2009]

Ans.   (i) Element J   (ii) Five

(iii) B_2H (iv) Covalent

  (v) $[C^{2+}] [:\!\overset{\times}{\underset{\bullet}{K}}\!:]_2$

Electron dot structure of CK_2

Q. 3. The following questions refer to the Periodic Table.

  (i) Name the first and last element in period 2.

 (ii) What happens to the atomic size of elements moving from top to bottom of a group?

(iii) Which of the elements has the greatest electron affinity among the halogens?

 (iv) What is the common feature of the electronic configurations of the elements in group 7?   [2008]

Ans.   (i) First element $\longrightarrow$ Lithium.
Last element $\longrightarrow$ Neon.

 (ii) Increases

(iii) Chlorine

 (iv) Seven electrons in the valence shell.

Q. 4. A group of elements in the Periodic Table are given below (Boron is first member of the group and Thallium is the last).

Boron

Aluminium

Gallium

Indium

Thallium

Answer the following questions in relation to the above group of elements:

  (i) Which element has the most metallic character?

 (ii) Which element would be expected to have the highest electronegativity?

(iii) If the electronic configuration of Aluminium is 2, 8, 3, how many electrons are there in the outer shell of Thallium?

 (iv) The atomic number of Boron is 5. Write the chemical formula of the compound formed when Boron reacts with Chlorine.

  (v) Will the elements in the group to the right of this Boron group be more metallic or less metallic in character? Justify your answer.   [2007]

Ans.   (i) Thallium,   (ii) Boron,

(iii) Three,   (iv) BCl_3,

  (v) Less metallic because the metallic character decreases from left to right on the periodic table.

Q. 5. From the list of characteristics given below, select the five which are relevant to non-metals and their compounds:

A. Ductile

B. Conduct electricity

C. Brittle

D. Acidic oxides

E. Basic oxides

F. Discharged at anode

G. Discharged at cathode

H. Ionic Chlorides

I. Covalent Chlorides

J. Reaction with dilute Sulphuric acid yields hydrogen.

K. 1, 2, or 3 valence electrons

L. 5, 6 or 7 valence electrons

(Write the five letters corresponding to the correct characteristics)   [2007]

Ans.   C, D, F, I, L

Q. 6. The elements of one short period of the Periodic Table are given below in order from left to right:

Li, Be, B, C, O, F, Ne

  (i) To which period do these elements belong?

 (ii) One element of this period is missing. Which is the missing element and where should it be placed?

(iii) Which one of the elements in this period shows the property of catenation ?

 (iv) Place the three elements fluorine, beryllium and nitrogen in the order of increasing electronegativity.

  (v) Which one of the above elements belongs to the halogen series?   [2006]

Ans.   (i) 2nd period

 (ii) Nitrogen. It should be placed between carbon and oxygen.

(iii) Carbon

 (iv) Beryllium < Nitrogen < Fluorine

  (v) Fluorine

 # Long Answer Type Questions-II

Q. 1.

Group number	IA 1	IIA 2	IIIA 13	IVA 14	VA 15	VIA 16	VIIA 17	0 18
2nd period	Li		D			O	J	Ne
	A	Mg	E	Si		H	M	
	R	T	I		Q	u		y

- In this table H does not represent hydrogen.
- Some elements are given in their own symbol and position in the periodic table.
- While others are shown with a letter.

With reference to the table answer the following questions:

(i) Identify the most electronegative element.

(ii) Identify the most reactive element of group 1.

(iii) Identify the element from period 3 with least atomic size.

(iv) How many valence electrons are present in Q?

(v) Which element from group 2 would have the least ionization energy?

(vi) Identify the noble gas of the fourth period.

(vii) In the compound between A and H what type of bond would be formed and give the molecular formula for the same. [2013]

Ans.

(i) J (ii) R

(iii) M (iv) Five

(v) T (vi) y-Krypton

(vii) Ionic bond. Molecular formula $\longrightarrow A_2H$

Chemical Bonding

 ## Short Answer Type Questions-I

Q. 1. State the type of Bonding in the following molecules:
   (i) Water
   (ii) Calcium oxide **[2017]**

Ans. (i) Covalent bonding
   (ii) Ionic or electrovalent bonding

Q. 2. By drawing an electron dot diagram show the formation of Ammonium Ion [Atomic No. : N = 7 and H = 1] **[2016]**

Ans.

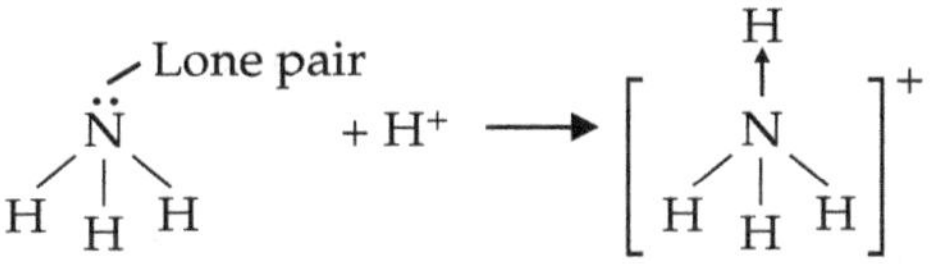

Ammoniumion

Q. 3. An element L consists of molecules:
   (i) What type of bonding is present in the particles that make up L?
   (ii) When L is heated with iron metal, it forms a compound FeL. What chemical term would you use to describe the change undergone by L? **[2015]**

Ans. (i) Covalent bonding since L consists of molecules.
   (ii) L is getting reduced.

Q. 4. Compare the compounds carbon tetrachloride and sodium chloride with regard to solubility in water and electrical conductivity. **[2013]**

Ans.

S. No.	Carbon Tetrachloride (forms covalent bond)	Sodium Chloride (forms ionic bond)
Solubility in water	Insoluble in water.	Soluble in water.
Electrical conductivity	Non-conductor of electricity.	Good conductor of electricity in molten state and in aqueous solution.

 ## Short Answer Type Questions-II

Q. 1. Draw the electron dot diagram for the compounds given below. Represent the electrons by (.) and (x) in the diagram :
[Atomic No. Ca = 20, O = 8, Cl = 17, H = 1]
   (i) Calcium oxide
   (ii) Chlorine molecule
   (iii) Water molecule **[2020]**

 Marking Scheme

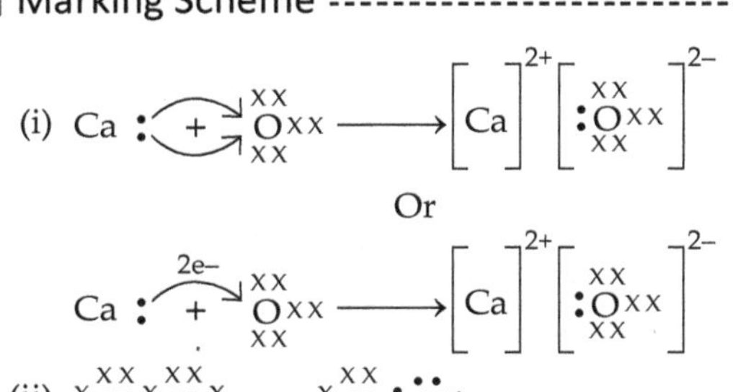

Ans. (i) Electron dot diagram for Calcium oxide

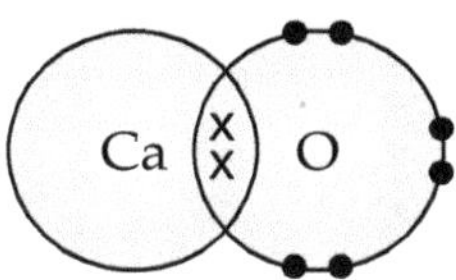

(ii) Electron dot diagram for chlorine molecule

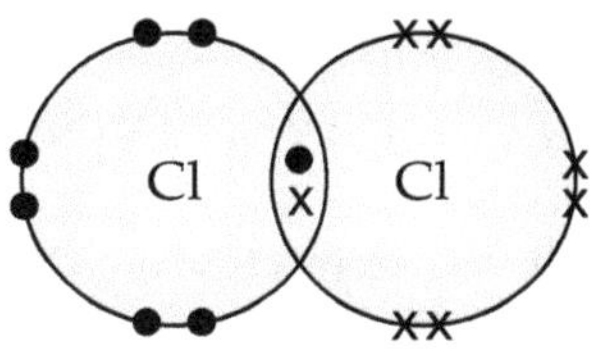

(iii) Electron dot diagram for water molecule

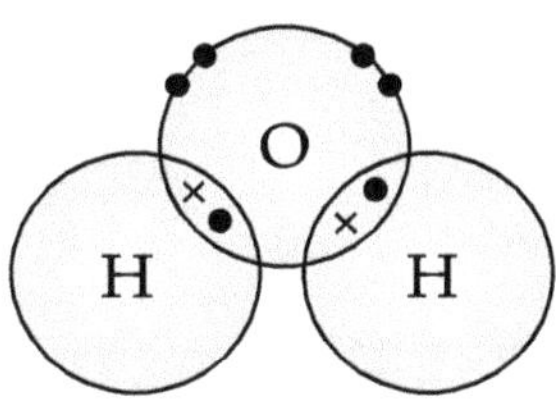

Q. 2. Draw the electron dot structure of:
  (i) Nitrogen molecule [N = 7]
  (ii) Sodium chloride [Na = 1, Cl = 17]
  (iii) Ammonium ion [N = 7, H = 1] **[2019]**

📋 Marking Scheme

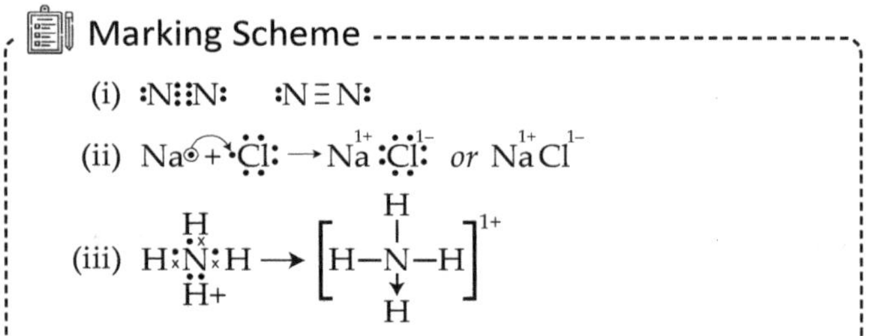

Ans. **(i)** Electron dot structure of nitrogen molecule –

$$:N\overset{..}{:}N: \quad or \quad :N\equiv N:$$

  (ii) Electron dot structure of Sodium chloride –

$$Na\times \overset{+}{\longrightarrow} :\overset{..}{\underset{..}{Cl}}: \longrightarrow Na^+ \ :\overset{..}{\underset{..}{Cl}}\times^-$$

  (iii) Electron dot structure of Ammonium ion –

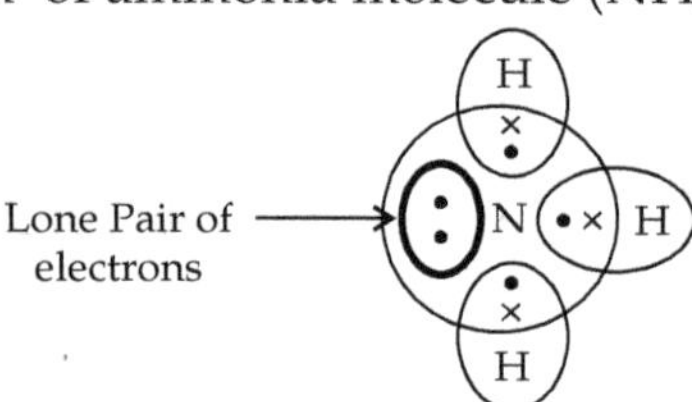

Q. 3. **(i)** What do you understand by a lone pair of electrons?
  (ii) Draw the electron dot diagram of hydronium ion. (H = 1; O = 8) **[2018]**

Ans. **(i)** A lone pair is an electron pair in the outermost shell of an atom that is not shared or bonded to another atom. Below is the example of lone pair on nitrogen atom of ammonia molecule (NH₃).

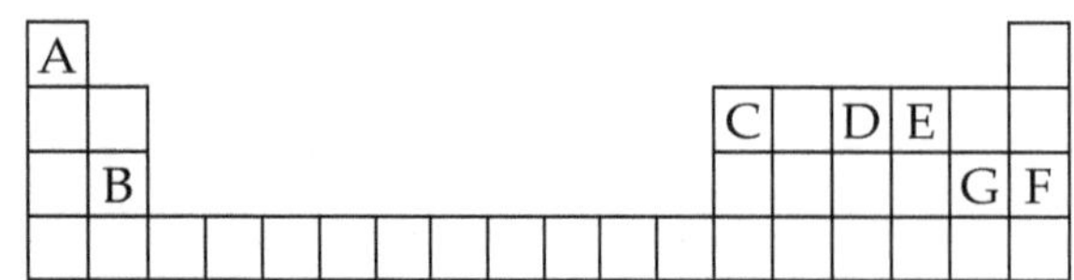

  (ii) Electron dot diagram of hydronium ion:

$$H^+ + :\overset{..}{\underset{..}{O}}: H \longrightarrow \left[H\times\overset{..}{\underset{..}{O}}: H \right]^+$$

Q. 4. Draw an electron dot diagram to show the structure of hydronium ion. State the type of bonding present in it. **[2012]**

Ans.

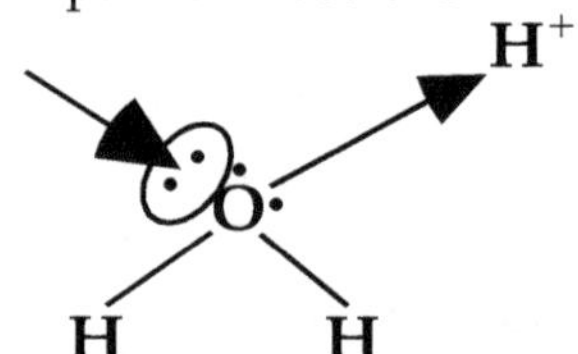

Structure of hydronium ion

The type of bonding in hydronium ion is coordinate bonding.

Q. 5. Differentiate between electrical conductivity of copper sulphate solution and copper metal. **[2011]**

Ans. Difference between electrical conductivity of copper sulphate solution and copper metal:

	Copper sulphate solution	Copper metal
1.	Electric current is by flow of ions.	Electric current is by flow of electrons.
2.	It is aqueous solution of ionic compound.	It is a metal in solid state.
3.	Copper sulphate undergoes a chemical change.	Copper metal remains unchanged chemically.

Q. 6. **(i)** What is a lone pair of electrons?
  (ii) Draw an electron dot diagram of a hydronium ion and label the lone pair of electrons.
  (iii) Name a neutral covalent molecule which contains one lone pair of electrons. **[2006]**

Ans. **(i)** The pair of electrons which do not participate in bond formation is known as lone pair.
  (ii) Lone pair of electrons

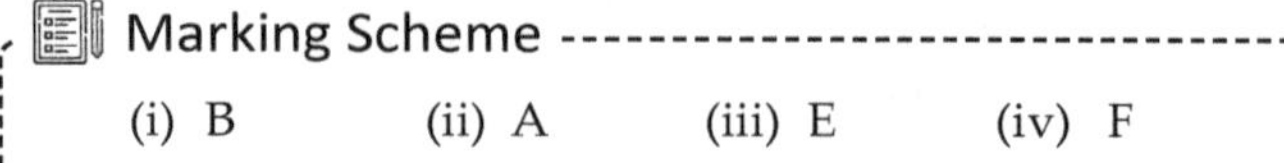

  (iii) Carbon monoxide

💬 ## Short Answer Type Questions-III

Q. 1. Study the extract of the Periodic Table given below and answer the questions that follow. Give the alphabet corresponding to the elements in question. DO NOT repeat an element.

A																	
												C		D	E		
B																G	F

  (i) Which element forms electrovalent compound with G?
  (ii) The ion of which element will migrate towards the cathode during electrolysis?
  (iii) Which non-metallic element has the valency of 2?
  (iv) Which is an inert gas? **[2019]**

📋 Marking Scheme

(i) B   (ii) A   (iii) E   (iv) F

Ans (i) A would form electrovalent compound with G.

(ii) B ion would travel to cathode during electrolysis.

(iii) E has valency of 2.

(iv) F is an inert gas.

Q. 2. Draw an electron dot diagram to show the formation of each of the following compounds:

(i) Methane

(ii) Magnesium Chloride

$$[H = 1, C = 6, Mg = 12, Cl = 17]$$

[2017]

Ans. (i)

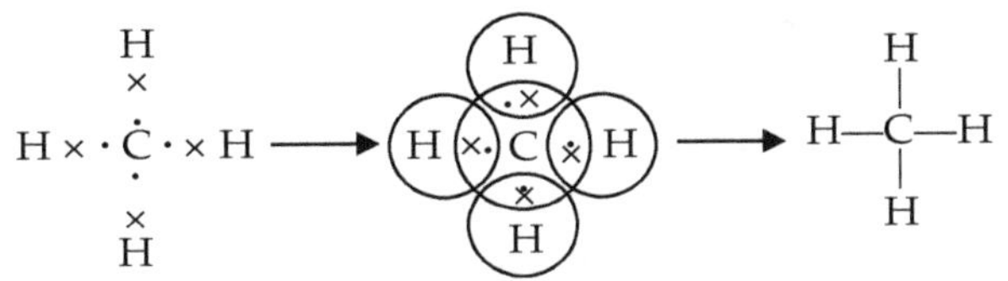

Methane

(ii) Magnesium chloride

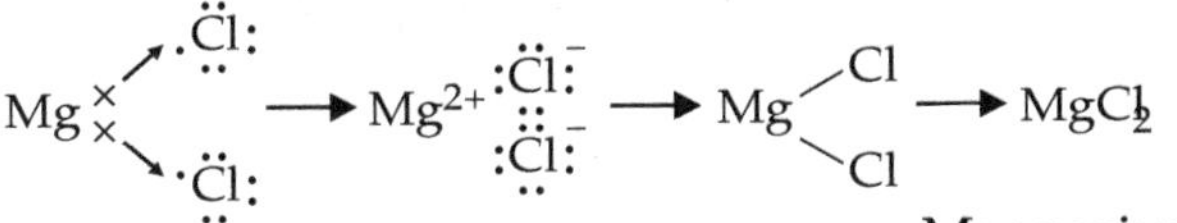

Magnesium chloride

Q. 3. There are three elements E, F, G with atomic numbers 19, 8 and 17 respectively.

(i) Classify the elements as metals and non-metals.

(ii) Give the molecular formula of the compound formed between E and G and state the type of chemical bond in this compound. **[2012]**

Ans: (i) 19 E is a metal.

8 F and 17 G are non-metals.

(ii) Molecular formula—EG.

Type of bond—Ionic bond.

Long Answer Type Questions-I

Q. 1. Match the column A with column B.

Column A	Column B
(i) Sodium chloride	Increases
(ii) Ammonium ion	Covalent bond
(iii) Electronegativity across the period	Ionic bond
(iv) Non metallic character down the group	Covalent and coordinate bond
(v) Carbon tetrachloride	Decreases

Answer as follows:

(i) Correct item from B matching sodium chloride.

(ii) Correct item from B matching ammonium ion, and so on. **[2010]**

Ans. (i) Ionic bond

(ii) Covalent and coordinate bond

(iii) Increases

(iv) Decreases

(v) Covalent bond

Q. 2. (i) Name the charged particles which attract one another to form electrovalent compounds.

(ii) In the formation of electrovalent compounds, electrons are transferred from one element to another. How are electrons involved in the formation of a covalent compound?

(iii) The electronic configuration of nitrogen is 2, 5. How many electrons in the outer shell of a nitrogen atom are not involved in the formation of a nitrogen molecule?

(iv) In the formation of magnesium chloride (by direct combination between magnesium and chlorine), name the substance that is oxidized and the substance that is reduced. **[2007]**

Ans. (i) Cation and anion.

(ii) Electrons are shared.

(iii) Two electrons.

(iv) Magnesium is oxidized and chlorine is reduced.

Short Answer Type Questions-I

Q. 1. Three solutions P, Q and R have pH value of 3.5, 5.2 and 12.2 respectively. Which one of these is a:
(i) Weak acid? (ii) Strong alkali? **[2018]**

Ans. (i) Solution Q is a weak acid as its pH is 5.2
(ii) Solution R is a strong alkali as its pH is 12.2.

Q. 2. State what would you observe when:
(i) Washing soda crystals are exposed to the atmosphere.
(ii) The salt ferric chloride is exposed to the atmosphere. **[2016]**

Ans. (i) When crystals of washing soda are exposed to air, they lose 9 water molecules of crystallisation and becomes monohydrate forming a white powder. Thus, shows the phenomenon of efflorescence.
$$Na_2CO_3 \cdot 10H_2O \xrightarrow{\text{Dry air}} Na_2CO_3 \cdot H_2O + 9H_2O$$
(ii) The salt ferric chloride, when exposed to the atmosphere, absorbs water molecules to become moist and show the phenomenon of deliquescence.

Q. 3. Draw the structure of the stable positive ion formed when an acid dissolves in water. **[2014]**

Ans. (i)
$$\left[H - \overset{\cdot\cdot}{\underset{\underset{H}{|}}{O}} \to H \right]^{+}$$

(H_3O^+) Hydronium ion.

Q. 4. (i) Name the other ion formed when ammonia dissolves in water.
(ii) Give one test that can be used to detect the presence of the ion produced. **[2014]**

Ans. (i) Hydroxide ion.
(ii) It will turn moist red litmus to blue.

Q. 5. Select the correct answer from the choices A, B, C and D which are given.
Write only the letter corresponding to the correct answer:
(i) Select the acid which contains four hydrogen atoms in it.
(A) Formic acid
(B) Sulphuric acid
(C) Nitric acid
(D) Acetic acid
(ii) Carbon dioxide and sulphur dioxide gas can be distinguished by using:
(A) Moist blue litmus paper
(B) Lime water
(C) Acidified potassium dichromate paper
(D) None of the above **[2009]**

Ans. (i) (D)   (ii) (C)

Q. 6. Write balanced chemical equations for the following reactions:
(i) Carbon and carbon dioxide
(ii) Iron (III) oxide and carbon monoxide **[2006]**

Ans. (i) $C + CO_2 \longrightarrow 2CO$
(ii) $Fe_2O_3 + 3CO \longrightarrow 2Fe + 3CO_2$

Short Answer Type Questions-II

Q. 1. Complete the following by selecting the correct option from the choices given :
(i) pH of acetic acid is greater than dilute sulphuric acid. So acetic acid contains .... concentration of H⁺ ions. (greater, same, low)
(ii) The indicator which does not change colour on passage of HCl gas is .... (methyl orange, moist blue litmus, phenolphthalein)
(iii) The acid which cannot act as an oxidizing agent is ....(conc. H_2SO_4, conc. HNO_3, conc. HCl) **[2020]**

 Marking Scheme
(i) low or less
(ii) Phenolphthalein
(iii) concentrated HCl

Ans. (i) low (ii) phenolphthalein (iii) conc. HCl

Q. 2. The pH values of three solution, A, B and C are given in the table. Answer the following questions:

Solution	pH value
A	12
B	2
C	7

   (i) Which solution will have no effect on litmus solution?

   (ii) Which solution will liberate CO_2 when reacted with sodium carbonate?

   (iii) Which solution will turn red litmus solution blue? **[2019]**

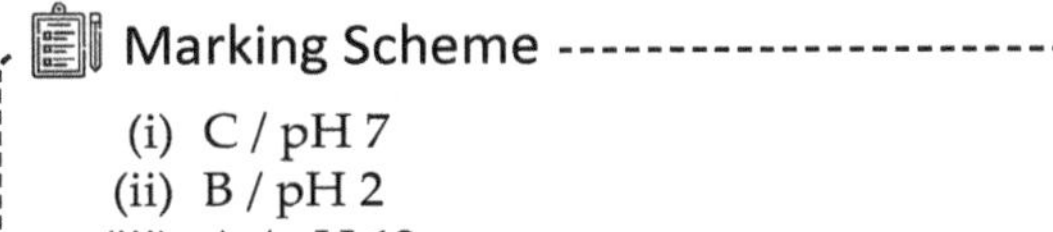

Marking Scheme

   (i) C / pH 7
  (ii) B / pH 2
 (iii) A / pH 12

Ans. **(i)** Solution C would have no effect on litmus solution as its pH is 7 and hence it is neutral.

   (ii) Solution B would liberate CO_2 when reacted with sodium carbonate as it is acidic solution and has pH 2.

   (iii) Solution A would turn red litmus solution blue as it is basic in nature and has pH 12.

Q. 3. Identify the anion present in each of the following compounds:

   (i) A salt M on treatment with concentrated sulphuric acid produces a gas which fumes in moist air and gives dense fumes with ammonia.

   (ii) A salt D on treatment with dilute sulphuric acid produces a gas which turns lime water milky but has no effect on acidified potassium dichromate solution.

   (iii) When barium chloride solution is added to salt solution E a white precipitate insoluble in dilute hydrochloric acid is obtained. **[2015]**

Ans. **(i)** Cl^- **(ii)** CO_3^{2-} or HCO_3^-

   (iii) SO_4^{2-}

Q. 4. Solution A is a sodium hydroxide solution. Solution B is a weak acid. Solution C is dilute sulphuric acid. Which solution will.

   (i) liberate sulphur dioxide from sodium sulphite.

   (ii) give a white precipitate with zinc sulphate solution.

   (iii) contain solute molecules and ions? **[2010]**

Ans. **(i)** C   **(ii)** A   **(iii)** B

Q. 5. Mention the colour changes observed when the following indicators are added to acids:

   (i) Alkaline phenolphthalein solution

   (ii) Methyl orange solution

   (iii) Neutral litmus solution **[2006]**

Ans. **(i)** From pink to colourless

   (ii) From orange to pink (red)

   (iii) From colourless to red

Short Answer Type Questions-III

Q. 1. From the list of the following salts choose the salt that most appropriately fits the description given in the following:

[AgCl, $MgCl_2$, $NaHSO_4$, $PbCO_3$, $ZnCO_3$, KNO_3, $Ca(NO_3)_2$]

   (i) A deliquescent salt.

   (ii) An insoluble chloride.

   (iii) On heating, this salt gives a yellow residue when hot and white when cold.

   (iv) On heating this salt, a brown coloured gas is evolved. **[2015]**

Ans. **(i)** $MgCl_2$ **(ii)** AgCl

   (iii) $ZnCO_3$ **(iv)** $Ca(NO_3)_2$.

Q. 2. Solution A is a strong acid

   Solution B is a weak acid

   Solution C is a strong alkali

   (i) Which solution contains solute molecules in addition to water molecules?

   (ii) Which solution will give a gelatinous white precipitate with zinc sulphate solution? The precipitate disappears when an excess of the solution is added.

   (iii) Which solution could be a solution of glacial acetic acid?

   (iv) Give an example of a solution which is a weak alkali. **[2009]**

Ans. **(i)** Solution B

   (ii) Solution C

   (iii) Solution B

   (iv) Ammonium hydroxide solution.

 **Long Answer Type Questions-I**

Q. 1. Give balanced chemical equations to prepare the following salts:
 (i) Lead sulphate from lead carbonate.
 (ii) Sodium sulphate using dilute sulphuric acid.
 (iii) Copper chloride using copper carbonate. **[2014]**

Ans. (i) $PbCO_3 + 2HNO_3 \longrightarrow Pb(NO_3)_2 + H_2O + CO_2\uparrow$
 Lead carbonate · · · Lead nitrate

$Pb(NO_3)_2 + H_2SO_4 \longrightarrow PbSO_4\downarrow + 2HNO_3$
 Lead nitrate · Dil. · Lead sulphate

(ii) $2NaOH + H_2SO_4 \longrightarrow Na_2SO_4 + H_2O + CO_2\uparrow$
 Sodium hydroxide · Dil. · Sodium sulphate

(iii) $CuCO_3 + 2HCl \longrightarrow CuCl_2 + H_2O + CO_2\uparrow$
 Copper carbonate · · Copper chloride

Q. 2. (i) Give the number of the group and the period, of the element having three shells with three electrons in valence shell.
 (ii) By drawing an electron dot diagram, show the lone pair effect leading to the formation of ammonium ion from ammonia gas and hydrogen ion.
 (iii) What happens to the crystals of washing soda when exposed to air? Name the phenomenon exhibited. **[2011]**

Ans. (i) Thirteenth group, third period.

(ii)

(iii) When exposed to air, washing soda crystals lose their water of crystallisation and become monohydrate forming a white powder. The phenomenon is called efflorescence.

Q. 3. Select from the list given (A to E) one substance in each case which matches the description given in parts (i) to (v). (Note:

Each substance is used only once in the answer.)
(A) Nitroso Iron(II) sulphate (B) Iron(III) chloride (C) Chromium sulphate (D) Lead(II) chloride (E) Sodium chloride.
 (i) A compound which is deliquescent.
 (ii) A compound which is insoluble in cold water, but soluble in hot water.
 (iii) The compound responsible for the brown ring during the brown ring test of nitrate ion.
 (iv) A compound whose aqueous solution is neutral in nature.
 (v) The compound which is responsible for the green colouration when sulphur dioxide is passed through acidified potassium dichromate solution. **[2010]**

Ans. (i) (B) (ii) (D)
 (iii) (A) (iv) (E)
 (v) (C)

Q. 4. The action of heat on the blue crystalline solid L gives a reddish brown gas M, a gas which re-lights a glowing splint and leaves a black residue. When gas N, which has a rotten egg smell, is passed through a solution of L a black precipitate is formed:
 (i) Identify L, M and N (Name or formula)
 (ii) Write the equation for the action of heat on L.
 (iii) Write the equation for the reaction between the solution of L and the gas N. **[2010]**

Ans. (i) L is copper nitrate.
 M is nitrogen dioxide gas.
 N is hydrogen sulphide gas.

(ii) $2\,Cu(NO_3)_2 \overset{\Delta}{\longrightarrow} 2CuO + 4NO_2 + O_2$
 Copper (II) oxide

(iii) $Cu(NO_3)_2 + H_2S \longrightarrow CuS + 2HNO_3$.
 Copper sulphide

Chapter 4

Analytical Chemistry—Uses of Ammonium Hydroxide and Sodium Hydroxide

Short Answer Type Questions-I

Q. 1. Answer the following questions:

(i) How will you distinguish between ammonium hydroxide and sodium hydroxide using copper sulphate solution?

(ii) How will you distinguish between dilute hydrochloric acid and dilute sulphuric acid using lead nitrate solution? **[2017]**

Ans. (i) When ammonium hydroxide solution is added drop by drop to copper sulphate solution, a pale blue or bluish white precipitate is formed which is soluble in excess of ammonium hydroxide and a deep blue or inky blue solution is formed with excess of ammonium hydroxide.

$$CuSO_4 + 2NH_4OH \longrightarrow Cu(OH)_2 \downarrow$$
$$+ (NH_4)_2SO_4$$

$$Cu(OH)_2 + 4NH_4OH \longrightarrow [Cu(NH_3)_4](OH)_2$$
$$+ 4H_2O$$

Copper solution forms a blue precipitate with sodium hydroxide solution. It is insoluble in excess of NaOH.

$$CuSO_4 + 2NaOH \longrightarrow Cu(OH)_2 + Na_2SO_4$$

| Copper sulphate | Sodium hydroxide | Copper hydroxide | Sodium sulphate |

(ii) On adding lead nitrate to both acids, we will get a white precipitate. On heating the solution, the one whose precipitate will redissolve will be dil. HCl and the one with insoluble precipitate will be dil. H_2SO_4.

Actually on adding lead nitrate to HCl, $PbCl_2$ precipitates out and on heating the solution it redissolves. But in case of H_2SO_4, $PbSO_4$ is formed which is insoluble even on heating it and white in colour.

$$Pb(NO_3)_2 + 2HCl \longrightarrow PbCl_2 + 2HNO_3$$
$$\text{(dil.)}$$

$$Pb(NO_3)_2 + H_2SO_4 \longrightarrow PbSO_4 + 2HNO_3$$
$$\text{(dil.)}$$

Q. 2. State your observations when ammonium hydroxide solution is added drop by drop and then in excess to each of the following solutions:

(i) Copper sulphate solution.

(ii) Zinc sulphate solution. **[2016]**

Ans (i) A pale blue precipitate is formed and the precipitate dissolves when excess of ammonium hydroxide is added, giving clear deep blue solution of tetra amine copper sulphate.

(ii) White gelatinous precipitate of $Zn(OH)_2$ is formed and the ppt. dissolves in excess of ammonium hydroxide to give a clear transparent solution.

Q. 3. State two relevant observations for each of the following:

(i) Ammonium hydroxide solution is added to copper (II) nitrate solution in small quantities and then in excess.

(ii) Ammonium hydroxide solution is added to zinc nitrate solution in minimum quantities and then in excess.

(iii) Lead nitrate crystals are heated in a hard glass test tube. **[2013]**

Ans. (i) Initially a light blue ppt. is formed which on addition of excess of ammonium hydroxide dissolves and a deep inky blue solution is formed.

(ii) Initially a white ppt. is formed which disappears (dissolves) in excess of ammonium hydroxide.

(iii) A reddish brown gas is evolved and a yellow residue is left in the test tube.

 ## Short Answer Type Questions-II

Q. 1. Distinguish between the following pairs of compounds using a reagent as a chemical test :
  (i) Calcium nitrate and Zinc nitrate solution.
  (ii) Ammonium sulphate crystals and Sodium sulphate crystals.
  (iii) Magnesium chloride and Magnesium nitrate solution. **[2020]**

 Marking Scheme

(i) **Add NaOH / KOH / dil H$_2$SO$_4$** to both the solutions
Calcium nitrate forms a white **precipitate** which is **insoluble** in excess of NaOH while Zinc nitrate forms a gelatinous white **precipitate soluble in excess.**
With (dilute) Sulphuric acid ... Calcium nitrate forms a white precipitate while Zinc nitrate **does not form precipitate.**
Or
With NH$_4$OH - Calcium nitrate no **reaction** or **no precipitate** while with Zinc nitrate it forms a (gelatinous white) **precipitate** soluble in excess / or **white** gelatinous precipitate with zinc nitrate

(ii) Add **any alkali / base**
Ammonium sulphate produces a **pungent colourless gas** or colourless gas is released which turns red litmus blue. While there is **no reaction** with sodium sulphate. Or **no pungent gas released.**

(iii) Add **silver nitrate / lead nitrate** solution to both / or perform brown ring test for nitrates
Magnesium chloride forms a white **precipitate** while there is **no reaction** with magnesium nitrate.
Or
Magnesium chloride **does not** form brown ring with Brown ring test while magnesium nitrate **forms a brown ring.**

Ans. **(i)** Calcium nitrate and Zinc nitrate solutions can be distinguish by reacting with ammonium hydroxide solution :
  1. On adding ammonium hydroxide gelatinous white precipitates of zinc hydroxide are formed.
$$Zn(NO_3)_2 + 2NH_4OH \longrightarrow Zn(OH)_2 + 2NH_4NO_3$$
  2. On adding excess of ammonium hydroxide, the precipitates dissolve forming a soluble complex.
$$Zn(NO)_2 + 2NH_4NO_3 \longrightarrow 2NH_4OH$$
$$[Zn(NH_3)_4](NO_3)_2 + 4H_2O$$
No visible reaction occurs when we add calcium nitrate to ammonium hydroxide.
$$CaNO_3 + NH_4OH \longrightarrow No\ reaction$$

(ii) Ammonium sulphate crystals give pungent colourless gas Ammonia (NH$_3$) when heated. When NH$_3$ gas comes in contact with a glass rod dipped in HCl white fumes of NH$_4$Cl are produced. Sodium sulphate crystals do no undergo the above reaction sequence, hence can be differentiated from ammonium sulphate crystals.

(iii) Magnesium chloride reacts with silver nitrate solution to give precipitate of silver chloride, whereas magnesium nitrate does not react with silver nitrate solution to give a precipitate.
$$MgCl_2\ (aq) + 2AgNO_3\ (aq) \longrightarrow Mg(NO_3)_2\ (aq)$$
$$+ 2AgCl\ (s)\downarrow$$
$$MgNO_3 + AgNO_3 \longrightarrow No\ reaction$$

Q. 2. Identify the salts P, Q, R from the following observations
  (i) Salt P has light bluish green colour. On heating, it produces a black coloured residue. Salt P produces brisk effervescence with dil. HCl and the gas evolved turns lime water milky, but no action with acidified potassium dichromate solution.
  (ii) Salt Q is white in colour. On strong heating, it produces buff yellow residue and liberates reddish brown gas Solution of salt Q produces chalky white insoluble precipitate with excess of ammonium hydroxide
  (iii) Salt R is black in colour. On reacting with concentrated HCl, it liberates a pungent greenish yellow gas which turns moist starch iodide paper blue black. **[2020]**

 Marking Scheme

(i) CuCO$_3$ or copper carbonate or copper(II) carbonate
(ii) Pb(NO$_3$)$_2$ or lead nitrate or lead(II) nitrate
(iii) MnO$_2$ or manganese dioxide or manganese (IV) oxide ....

Ans. **(i)** P is Copper carbonate.
$$CuCO_3(s) \rightarrow CuO(s)$$
Copper II carbonate $\rightarrow$ Copper (II) oxide
Bluish green   Black
$$+ CO_2(g)$$
Carbon dioxide(g)
$$CuCO_3 + HCl \rightarrow CuCl_2 + CO_2 + H_2O$$
(P)   Effervescence
$$CuCO_3 + K_2Cr_2O_7 \rightarrow No\ reaction$$

(ii) The salt Q is Lead nitrate

$$2Pb\,(NO_3)_2(s) \xrightarrow{\text{heat}} 2PbO(s) \ + \ 4NO_2(g)$$

Lead nitrate	Lead monoxide	Nitrogen
Colourless	Yellow	dioxide
(Q)		Reddish
		brown
		$+ O_2(g)$
		Oxygen

When reacted with ammonium hydroxide solution it gives a chalky white precipitate of lead hydroxide :

$$Pb(NO_3)_2 + 2NH_4OH \rightarrow 2NH_4NO_3 + Pb(OH)_2\downarrow$$

(Q)	Chalky
	white ppt.

(iii) The salt R is MnO_2, which is black in colour and reacts with HCl to give Cl_2 gas

$$MnO_2(s) + 4HCl(aq) \rightarrow MnCl_2(aq) + 2H_2O(l)$$
$$+ Cl_2(g)$$

Chlorine gas is pungent and greenish yellow in colour. The chlorine gas oxidizes some of the iodide ions in the starch iodide paper to create iodine diatomic molecules. These molecules react with the iodide ions and the starch to form a charge-transfer complex of blue colour.

Q. 3. Write balanced chemical equations, for the preparation of the given salts :

(i) to (iii) by using the methods A to C respectively :

A : Neutralization   B : Precipitation   C : Titration

(i) Copper sulphate

(ii) Zinc carbonate

(ii) Ammonium sulphate [2020]

Marking Scheme

(i) $CuO + H_2SO_4 \rightarrow CuSO_4 + H_2O$
Or $Cu(OH)_2 + H_2SO_4 \rightarrow CuSO_4 + 2H_2O$
Or $CuCO_3 + H_2SO_4 \rightarrow CuSO_4 + H_2O + CO_2$
Or $Cu(HCO_3)_2 + H_2SO_4 \rightarrow$
$$CuSO_4 + 2H_2O + 2CO_2$$

(ii) $ZnCl_2 + Na_2CO_3 \rightarrow ZnCO_3 + 2NaCl$

(or any soluble salts of zinc along with carbonates of sodium, potassium or ammonium as reactants)

(iii) $2NH_4OH + H_2SO_4 \rightarrow (NH_4)_2SO_4 + 2H_2O$
Or $2NH_3 + H_2SO_4 \rightarrow (NH_4)_2SO_4$

Ans.   (i) Copper sulphate by neutralization

$$Cu(OH)_2 \ + H_2SO_4 \rightarrow \ CuSO_4\downarrow \ + 2H_2O$$

Copper	Sulphuric	Copper
hydroxide	acid	sulphate

(ii) Zinc carbonate by precipitation

$$Zn(NO_3)_2\,(aq) + 2NaCO_3\,(aq) \rightarrow Zn(CO_3)_2$$

Zinc nitrate	Sodium
	carbonate

$$+ 2NaNO_3\,(aq)$$
Zinc carbonate

(iii) Ammonium sulphate can be prepared by titration of NH_3 solution with dil. H_2SO_4 solution.

$$2NH_4OH(aq) + H_2SO_4\,(aq) \longrightarrow$$
$$(NH_4)_2SO_4 + 2H_2O\,(l)$$
White powder

Q. 4. **Copper sulphate solution reacts with sodium hydroxide solution to form a precipitate of copper hydroxide according to the equation:**

$$2NaOH + CuSO_4 \longrightarrow Na_2SO_4 + Cu(OH)_2\downarrow$$

(i) What mass of copper hydroxide is precipitated by using 200 gm of sodium hydroxide?

[H = 1, O = 16, Na = 23, S = 32, Cu = 64]

(ii) What is the colour of the precipitate formed? [2019]

Marking Scheme

(i) RMW of NaOH = 40, $Cu(OH)_2$ = 98
∴ 2 × 40 g precipitate = 98 g

∴ 200 g precipitate = $\dfrac{98 \times 200}{80}$ = 245 g

(ii) Pale blue

Ans.   (i) The given equation is
$$2NaOH + CuSO_4 \longrightarrow Na_2SO_4 + Cu(OH)_2\downarrow$$
Molecular weight of NaOH, Sodium hydroxide = 23 + 16 + 1 = 40
Molecular weight of $Cu(OH)_2$, Copper hydroxide = 64 + 16 + 1 + 16 + 1 = 98
2 × 40 g = 80 g of NaOH is used to precipitate 98 g of $Cu(OH)_2$
Hence, 200 g of NaOH will be used to precipitate = (98/80) × 200 g of $Cu(OH)_2$ = 245 g of $Cu(OH)_2$
So, 490 g of copper hydroxide would be prepared using 200 g of sodium hydroxide.

(ii) The precipitate of copper hydroxide is bluish green solid or pale blue solid.

Q. 5. **Complete the following by selecting the correct option from the choices given :**

(i) The metal which does not react with water or dilute H_2SO_4 but reacts with concentrated H_2SO_4 is——.

(Al/Cu/Zn/Fe)

(ii) The metal whose oxide, which is amphoteric, is reduced to metal by carbon reduction——. **(Fe/Mg/Pb/Al)**

(iii) **The divalent metal whose oxide is reduced to metal by electrolysis of its fused salt is——.** (Al/Na/Mg/K)
[2017]

Ans. **(i)** The metal which does not react with water or dilute H_2SO_4 but reacts with concentrated H_2SO_4 is Cu.

(ii) The metal whose oxide, which is amphoteric, is reduced to metal by carbon reduction Pb.

(iii) The divalent metal whose oxide is reduced to metal by electrolysis of its fused salt is Mg.

Q. 6. **Sodium hydroxide solution is added to the solutions containing the ions mentioned in List X. List Y gives the details of the precipitate. Match the ions with their coloured precipitates.** **[2011]**

	List X		List Y
(i)	Pb^{2+}	A.	Reddish brown
(ii)	Fe^{2+}	B.	White insoluble in excess
(iii)	Zn^{2+}	C.	Dirty green
(iv)	Fe^{3+}	D.	White soluble in excess
(v)	Cu^{2+}	E.	White soluble in excess
(vi)	Ca^{2+}	F.	Blue

Ans.

	List X		List Y
(i)	Pb^{2+}	D.	White soluble in excess.
(ii)	Fe^{2+}	C.	Dirty green.
(iii)	Zn^{2+}	E.	White soluble in excess.
(iv)	Fe^{3+}	A.	Reddish brown.
(v)	Cu^{2+}	F.	Blue.
(vi)	Ca^{2+}	B.	White insoluble in excess.

Q. 7. **Give one chemical test to distinguish between the following pairs of compounds.**

(i) **Zinc sulphate solution and Zinc chloride solution.**

(ii) **Iron (II) chloride solution and Iron (III) chloride solution.**

(iii) **Calcium nitrate solution and Calcium chloride solution.** **[2009]**

Ans. **(i)** When $BaCl_2$ solution is added to the given solution, $ZnSO_4$ gives a white ppt. while no ppt. is obtained with $ZnCl_2$ solution.

(ii) When NaOH solution is added to the given solution, Iron (II) chloride gives dirty green ppt. while reddish brown ppt. is obtained with Iron (III) chloride.

(iii) When $AgNO_3$ solution is added to the given solution, $CaCl_2$ solution will give a white ppt. while no change is observed with calcium nitrate solution.

Short Answer Type Questions-III

Q. 1. **Match the gases given in column I to the identification of the gases mentioned in column II :**

Column I	Column II
(i) Hydrogen sulphide	A. Turns acidified potassium dichromate solution green.
(ii) Nitric oxide	B. Turns lime water milky.
(iii) Carbon dioxide	C. Turns reddish brown when it reacts with oxygen.
(iv) Sulphur dioxide	D. Turns moist lead acetate paper silvery black.

[2020]

Marking Scheme

(i) D or turns moist lead acetate paper silvery black.

(ii) C or turns reddish brown when it reacts with oxygen.

(iii) B or turns lime water milky.

(iv) A or turns acidified potassium dichromate solution green / **B** or turns lime water milky or **A and B**

Ans.

Column I	Column II
(i) Hydrogen sulphide	D. Turns moist lead acetate paper silvery black.
(ii) Nitric oxide	C. Turns reddish brown when reacts with oxygen.
(iii) Carbon dioxide	B. Turns lime water milky.
(iv) Sulphur dioxide	A. Turns acidified potassium dichromate solution green.

Q. 2. **Choose the most appropriate answer from the following list of oxides which fit the description. Each answer may be used only once:**

$[SO_2, SiO_2, Al_2O_3, MgO, CO, Na_2O]$

(i) **A basic oxide.**

(ii) **An oxide which dissolves in water forming an acid.**

(iii) **An amphoteric oxide.**

(iv) **A covalent oxide of a metalloid.** **[2015]**

Ans. **(i)** Na_2O, MgO   **(ii)** SO_2
(iii) Al_2O_3 **(iv)** SiO_2.

Q. 3. The following table shows the tests a student performed on four different aqueous solutions which are X, Y, Z and W. Based on the observations provided, identify the cation present:

Chemical test	Observation	Conclusion
To solution X, ammonium hydroxide is added in minimum quantity first and then in excess.	A dirty white precipitate is formed which dissolves in excess to form a clear solution.	(i)
To solution Y, ammonium hydroxide is added in minimum quantity first and then in excess.	A pale blue precipitate is formed which dissolves in excess to form a clear inky blue solution.	(ii)
To solution W, a small quantity of sodium hydroxide solution is added and then in excess.	A white precipitate is formed which remains insoluble.	(iii)
To a salt Z, calcium hydroxide solution is added and then heated.	A pungent smelling gas turning moist red litmus paper blue is obtained.	(iv)

[2015]

Ans. **(i)** $X - Zn^{2+}$ **(ii)** $Y - Cu^{2+}$ **(iii)** $W - Ca^{2+}$ or Mg^{2+} **(iv)** $Z - NH_4^+$

Mole Concept and Stoichiometry

 ## Short Answer Type Questions-I

Q. 1. The percentage composition of a gas is:
Nitrogen 82.35%, Hydrogen 17.64%.
Find the empirical formula of the gas.
[N = 14, H = 1]   **[2018]**

Ans. Nitrogen: 82.35% and Hydrogen: 17.64%

Element	N	H
Percentage	82.35	17.64
Relative Ratio	82.35/14 = 5.88	17.64/1 = 17.64
Simple Ratio	$\dfrac{5.88}{5.88} = 1$	$\dfrac{17.64}{5.88} = 3$

So, the empirical formula of the gas would be NH_3.

 ## Short Answer Type Questions-II

Q. 1. A gaseous hydrocarbon contains 82.76% of carbon. Given that its vapour density is 29, find its molecular formula. [C = 12, H = 1]
[2016]

Ans.

Element	Percentage	Molecules	Simple ratio	Simple whole ratio
C	82.76	$\dfrac{82.76}{12} = 6.89$	$\dfrac{6.89}{6.89} = 1$	2
H	17.24	$\dfrac{17.24}{1} = 17.24$	$\dfrac{17.24}{6.89} = 2{\cdot}5$	5

$\therefore$ Empirical formula $= C_2H_5$

Empirical formula mass $= (12 \times 2) + (1 \times 5)$
$$= 24 + 5 = 29$$

Vapour density $\longrightarrow 29$ (Given)

Molecular mass $= \text{V.D.} \times 2 = 29 \times 2 = 58$ g

Molecular formula mass $= n \times$ Empirical formula mass

$\Rightarrow \quad n = \dfrac{\text{Molecular Formula mass}}{\text{Empirical Formula mass}}$

$$= \dfrac{58}{29} = 2$$

Molecular formula $= n \times$ Empirical formula
$$= 2 \times C_2H_5$$
$$= C_4H_{10}$$

Q. 2. An organic compound with vapour density = 94 contains
C = 12.67%, H = 2.13%, and Br = 85.11%. Find the molecular formula.
[Atomic mass: C = 12, H = 1, Br = 80]   **[2011]**

Ans.

Elements	Percentage ratio	Atomic mass	Relative number of atoms	Simplest ratio
C	12.67	12	12.67/12 = 1.055	$\dfrac{1.055}{1.055} = 1$
H	2.13	1	2.13/1 = 2.13	$\dfrac{2.13}{1.055} \approx 2$
Br	85.11	80	85.11/80 = 1.063	$\dfrac{1.063}{1.055} = 1$

$\therefore$ Empirical formula of the compound is CH_2Br

Molecular formula $= $ (Empirical formula) $\times n$

$$n = \dfrac{\text{M.W.}}{\text{Empirical formula Weight}}$$

$$= \dfrac{2 \times \text{V.D}}{\text{Empirical formula weight}}$$

$$= \dfrac{2 \times 94}{(12 + 2 + 80)}$$

$$= \dfrac{2 \times 94}{94} = 2$$

$\therefore$ Molecular formula $= (CH_2Br) \times 2$
$$= C_2H_4Br_2$$

 ## Short Answer Type Questions-III

Q. 1. Find the *empirical formula* and the *molecular formula* of an organic compound from the data given below:

$C = 75.92\%$, $H = 6.32\%$ and $N = 17.76\%$
The vapour density of the compound is 39.5
$[C = 12, H = 1, N = 14]$ **[2019]**

 **Marking Scheme**

Element	% composition	Atomic weight	Relative no. of atoms	Simplest Ratio
C	75.92	12	$\dfrac{75.92}{12} = 6.32$	$\dfrac{6.32}{1.26} = 5$
H	6.32	1	$\dfrac{6.32}{1} = 6.32$	$\dfrac{6.32}{1.26} = 5$
N	17.76	14	$\dfrac{17.76}{14} = 1.26$	$\dfrac{1.26}{1.26} = 1$

Empirical formula is: C_5H_5N
Empirical formula weight = 60+5+14 = 79

$$n = \frac{molecular\ weight}{empirical\ formula\ weight} = \frac{2 \times 39.5}{79} = \frac{79}{79} = 1$$

Molecular formula = C_5H_5N

Ans. Given: $C = 75.92\%$, $H = 6.32\%$ and $N = 17.76\%$
Let us assume that the weight of compound is 100 g. So, in that 100 g C is 75.92 g, H is 6.32 g and N is 17.76 g.
Now, lets calculate the moles of each element present in the compound-
75.92 g C × (1 mol C/12 g C) = 6.32
6.32 g H × (1 mol H/1 g H) = 6.32
17.76 g N × (1 mol N/14 g N) = 1.26

Next, dividing all the mole numbers by the smallest among them, which is 1.26. This division yields –

5 mol C, 5 mol H and 1 mol N

So, the compound has the empirical formula – C_5H_5N.
Now, we know that
Molecular mass of a gas = 2 × vapour density of the gas
= 2 × 39.5
= 79
So, Molecular mass of the given compound is 79.
Empirical formula mass = $(12 \times 5) + (1 \times 5) + (14 \times 1) = 79$
As, Empirical formula mass = Molecular mass
So, in this case
Empirical formula = Molecular formula
= C_5H_5N.

 ## Long Answer Type Questions-I

Q. 1. A compound X consists of 4.8% carbon and 95.2% bromine by mass.

(i) Determine the empirical formula of this compound working correct to one decimal place (C = 12; Br = 80).

(ii) If the vapour density of the compound is 252, what is the molecular formula of the compound?

(iii) Name the type of chemical reaction by which X can be prepared from ethane.
[2007]

Ans. (i) Empirical formula:

Elements	% Composition	At. Mass	Relative Number of Atoms	Simplest Ratio
Carbon	4.8	12	$\dfrac{4.8}{12} = 0.4$	$\dfrac{0.4}{0.4} = 1$
Bromine	95.2	80	$\dfrac{95.2}{80} = 1.19$	$\dfrac{1.19}{0.4} = 3$

Empirical formula of substance is CBr_3
Empirical mass = $12 + 80 \times 3 = 252$
Molecular mass = 2 × V.D = 2 × 252 = 504
∴ $$n = \frac{Molecular\ mass}{Empirical\ formula\ mass}$$

$$= \frac{504}{252} = 2$$

(ii) Molecular formula $= n \times$ Empirical formula

$$2 \times CBr_3 = C_2Br_6$$

(iii) This substance can be prepared by substitution method.

Q. 2. **(i)** Determine the empirical formula of a compound containing 47.9% potassium, 5.5% beryllium and 46.6% fluorine by mass.

(Atomic weight of Be = 9; F = 19; K = 39). Work to one decimal place.

(ii) Given that the relative molecular mass of copper oxide is 80, what volume of ammonia (measured at S.T.P.) is required to completely reduce 120 g of copper oxide?

The equation for the reaction is:

$$3CuO + 2NH_3 \longrightarrow 3Cu + 3H_2O + N_2$$

(Volume occupied by 1 mole of gas at S.T.P. is 22.4 litres). **[2006]**

Ans. **(i)** Solution: Determination of Empirical formula

Element	%	Atomic mass	Relative number of atoms	Simplest Ratio
K	47.9	39	$\dfrac{47.9}{39} = 1.2$	$\dfrac{1.2}{0.6} = 2$
Be	5.5	9	$\dfrac{5.5}{9} = 0.6$	$\dfrac{0.6}{0.6} = 1$
F	46.6	19	$\dfrac{46.6}{19} = 2.4$	$\dfrac{2.4}{0.6} = 4$

Empirical formula $= K_2BeF_4$

(ii) $3CuO \ + \ 2NH_3 \longrightarrow 3Cu + 3H_2O + N_2$

3 moles   2 moles

3×80 g 2×22.4 l

$= 240$ g   44.8 l

120 g   ?

$\because$ For 240 g of CuO, volume of NH_3 consumed $= 44.8$ l

$\therefore$ For 120 g of CuO, volume of NH_3

consumed $= \dfrac{44.8}{240} \times 120 = 22.4$ l

Long Answer Type Questions-II

Q. 1. **(i)** A compound has the following percentage composition by mass: carbon 14.4%, hydrogen 1.2% and chlorine 84.5%. Determine the empirical formula of this compound. Work correct to 1 decimal place.

(H = 1; C = 12; Cl = 35.5).

(ii) The relative molecular mass of this compound is 168, so what is its molecular formula?

(iii) By what type of reaction could this compound be obtained from ethyne?

[2008]

Ans. **(i)**

Element	% Composition	No. of Atoms	Simplest Ratio
Carbon	14.4	14.4/12 = 1.2	1.2/1.2 = 1
Hydrogen	1.2	1.2/1 = 1.2	1.2/1.2 = 1
Chlorine	84.5	84.5/35.5 = 2.4	2.4/1.2 = 2

Empirical formula $= CHCl_2$.

(ii) Molecular formula = (Empirical formula) $\times n$

$$n = \frac{\text{Molecular mass}}{\text{Empirical formula mass}} = \frac{168}{84} = 2$$

$\therefore$ Molecular formula = $(CHCl_2) \times 2 = C_2H_2Cl_4$.

(iii) Addition reaction with chlorine.

 **Short Answer Type Questions-I**

Q. 1. Select the ion in each case, that would get selectively discharged from the aqueous mixture of the ions listed below:
  (i) SO_4^{2-}, NO_3^- and OH^-
  (ii) Pb^{2+}, Ag^+ and Cu^{2+} **[2017]**

Ans.   (i) OH^- ions
    (ii) Ag^+ ions

Q. 2.   (i) Name the product formed at the anode during the electrolysis of acidified water using platinum electrodes.
    (ii) Name the metallic ions that should be present in the electrolyte when an article made of copper is to be electroplated with silver.   **[2016]**

Ans.   (i) O_2 (oxygen) gas
    (ii) Ag^+ ions and Cu^+ ions

Q. 6. Differentiate between the terms strong electrolyte and weak electrolyte. (stating any two differences)   **[2015]**

Ans.

Strong Electrolyte	Weak Electrolyte
1. They allow a large amount of electricity to flow through them *i.e.*, they are good conductors of electricity.	They allow small amount of electricity to flow through them *i.e.*, they are poor conductors of electricity.
2. They are completely dissociated into the fused or aqueous solution state and contains only free mobile ions.	They are partially dissociated into their fused or aqueous solution state and contain ions as well as molecules.

Q. 3. Aqueous solution of Nickel sulphate contains Ni^{2+} and SO_4^{2-} ions.
    (i) Which ion moves towards the cathode?
    (ii) What is the product at the anode?
        [2009]

Ans.   (i) Ni^{2+} ion
    (ii) When anode is inert in nature oxygen gas is the product obtained.

 **Short Answer Type Questions-II**

Q. 1. Differentiate between the following pairs based on the information given in the brackets :
    (i) Conductor and electrolyte (conducting particles)
    (ii) Cations and anions (formation from an atom)
    (iii) Acid and Alkali (formation of type of ions)   **[2020]**

Marking Scheme
  (i) Conductor – conduction due to electrons.
     Electrolyte – conduction due to ions.
  (ii) Cations are formed by the **loss of electrons** from an atom / or **oxidation** of an atom / **donating electrons**.
     Anions are formed by the **gain of electrons** by an atom / **reduction** of an atom/ **accepting electrons**.
  (iii) Acid – forms H^+ ions or hydronium (ions in solution) or H_3O^+ or hydrogen ions.
     Alkali – forms hydroxyl (ion) or OH^- (in solution) or hydroxide ion/hydroxide.

Ans.   (i) Conductor has electrons as the conduction particles whereas ions are the conducting species in electrolyte.

    (ii) Cations are formed when a neutral atom loses electrons whereas anions are formed when a neutral atom gains electron.

    (iii) An acid dissociates to furnish H^+ ions and the conjugate base which is negatively charged and a base dissociates to give OH^- ions and a conjugate acid which is positively charged.

Q. 2. Identify the substance underlined in each of the following :

    (i) The <u>electrode</u> that increases in mass during the electrorefining of silver.

    (ii) The <u>acid</u> that is a dehydrating as well as a drying agent.

    (iii) The <u>catalyst</u> used to oxidize ammonia into nitric oxide.   **[2020]**

 **Marking Scheme**

> (i) cathode or negative electrode or reducing electrode or **pure silver** or **pure silver** strip or **pure silver** metal or pure Ag.
> (ii) concentrated sulphuric acid or conc. H_2SO_4.
> (iii) Platinum or Pt or Cu (copper) or Ni (Nickel) or Rh (Rhodium).

Ans. (i) Cathode

(ii) conc. H_2SO_4

(iii) Platinum Rhodium catalyst in Ostwald's process.

Q. 3. **Name the particles present in:**
  (i) **Strong electrolyte**
  (ii) **Non-electrolyte**
  (iii) **Weak electrolyte**   **[2019]**

 **Marking Scheme**

> (i) Only ions
> (ii) Only molecules
> (iii) Both molecules and ions

Ans. (i) The particles present in strong electrolyte are molecules which easily and completely dissociate into ions. Example: Strong electrolyte such as NaCl which dissociates strongly into Na^+ and Cl^- ions.

(ii) The particles present in non-electrolyte are molecules which do not dissociate into ions. Example: Non-electrolyte such as urea. NH_2CONH_2 which do not dissociate.

(iii) The particles present in weak electrolyte are both molecules and ions which dissociate into ions to a very less extent. Example: CH_3COOH which dissociates feebly into CH_3COO^- and H^+ ions.

Q. 4. **Name the gas evolved in each of the following cases:**

(i) **Alumina undergoes electrolytic reduction.**

(ii) **Ethene undergoes hydrogenation reaction.**

(iii) **Ammonia reacts with heated copper oxide.**   **[2019]**

 **Marking Scheme**

> (i) Oxygen gas or O_2
> (ii) Ethane gas or C_2H_6
> (iii) Nitrogen or N_2

Ans. (i) Oxygen gas (O_2) is evolved when alumina undergoes electrolysis.

$$Al_2O_3 \rightleftharpoons 2Al^{3+} + 3O^{2-}$$

(ii) Ethane gas (C_2H_6) is evolved when ethene undergoes hydrogenation reaction.

$$\underset{\text{Ethene}}{\ce{H2C=CH2}} \text{ (g) } + \text{ H–H (g) } \rightarrow \underset{\text{Ethane}}{\ce{H3C-CH3}} \text{ (g)}$$

(iii) Nitrogen (N_2) gas is evolved when ammonia is treated with copper oxide.

$$\underset{\text{Ammonia}}{2NH_3} + 3CuO \xrightarrow{\Delta} 3\,Cu + 3H_2O + \underset{\substack{\text{Nitrogen} \\ \text{gas}}}{N_2}$$

Q. 5. **Give reasons why:**
  (i) **Sodium chloride will conduct electricity only in fused or aqueous solution state.**
  (ii) **In the electroplating of an article with silver, the electrolyte sodium argento-cyanide solution is preferred over silver nitrate solution.**
  (iii) **Although copper is a good conductor of electricity, it is a non-electrolyte.** **[2016]**

Ans. (i) NaCl is an ionic compound. Sodium chloride ions in the solid state are held by the electrostatic force of attraction, thus are not free to move and conduct electricity but in the fused state, the crystal lattice breaks down and the charged particles (ions) are free to move and thus are able to conduct electricity.

(ii) In aqueous solution of sodium argento-cyanide, silver ions migrate slowly as compared to that in silver nitrate. Thereby, ensuring even deposition of silver metal on the articles to be electroplated.

(iii) Copper is a good conductor of electricity but it is a non-electrolyte because it is a solid metal and has no mobile ions which act as charge carriers to conduct electricity.

Q. 6. **Identify the cations in each of the following case:**
  (i) **NaOH solution when added to the solution (A) gives a reddish brown precipitate.**
  (ii) **NH₄OH solution when added to the solution (B) gives white ppt. which does not dissolve in excess.**
  (iii) **NaOH solution when added to solution (C) gives white ppt. which is insoluble in excess.** **[2016]**

Ans. (i) Fe^{3+} (ii) Pb^{2+} (iii) Ca^{2+}

Q. 7. (i) **Copy and complete the following table:**

	Anode	Electrolyte
Purification of copper		

(ii) **Write the equation taking place at the anode.** **[2015]**

Ans. (i)

	Anode	Electrolyte
Purification of copper	Impure copper	Copper sulphate solution with little amount of sulphuric acid

(ii) $Cu \longrightarrow Cu^{2+} + 2e^-$ (At anode)

$Cu - 2e^- \longrightarrow Cu^{2+}$ (At anode)

Q. 8. (i) **Why do covalent compounds exist as gases, liquids or soft solids?**

(ii) **Which electrode: anode or cathode is the oxidising electrode? Why?** **[2014]**

Ans: (i) Covalent compounds exists as gases, liquids or soft solids because they are held by relatively weaker forces that are known as van der waal's forces.

(ii) Anode is the oxidising electrode because anions lose electrons at anode.

Q. 9. **Three different electrolytic cells A, B and C are connected in separate circuits. Electrolytic cell A contains sodium chloride solution. When the circuit is completed a bulb in the circuit glows brightly. Electrolytic cell B contains acetic acid solution and in this case the bulb in the circuit glows dimly. The electrolytic cell C contains sugar solution and the bulb does not glow. Give a reason for each of these observations.** **[2010]**

Ans. In Cell A: Sodium chloride being strong electrolyte dissociates completely and therefore current flows better.

In Cell B: Acetic acid being weak electrolyte ionises only partially and therefore, only a weak current flows.

In Cell C: Sugar being a covalent compound does not ionise at all and therefore, no current flows.

Q. 10. **Identify the following reactions as either oxidation or reduction:**

(i) $O + 2e^- \longrightarrow O^{2-}$

(ii) $K - e^- \longrightarrow K^+$

(iii) $Fe^{3+} + e^- \longrightarrow Fe^{2+}$ **[2006]**

Ans. (i) Reduction.

(ii) Oxidation.

(iii) Reduction.

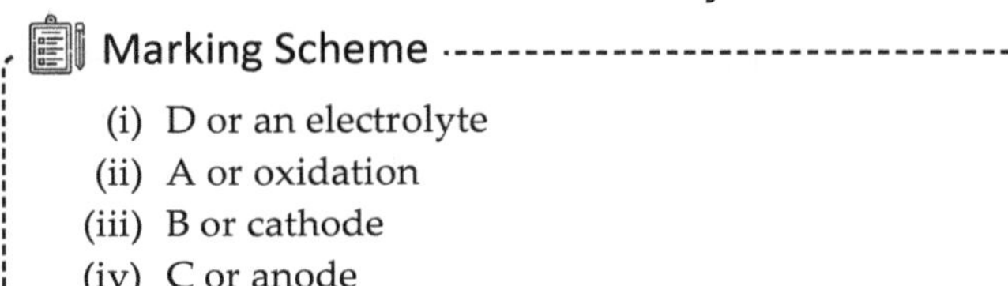 Short Answer Type Questions-III

Q. 1. **Choose the correct word which refers to the process of electrolysis from A to E, to match the description (i) to (iv) :**

A : Oxidation B : Cathode C : Anode

D : An electrolyte E : Reduction

(i) **Conducts electricity in aqueous or in molten state.**

(ii) **Loss of electron takes place at anode.**

(iii) **A reducing electrode.**

(iv) **Electrode connected to the positive end or terminal or the battery.** **[2020]**

Marking Scheme

(i) D or an electrolyte
(ii) A or oxidation
(iii) B or cathode
(iv) C or anode

Ans. (i) Conducts electricity in aqueous or in molten state – D : An electrolyte

(ii) Loss of electron takes place at anode – A. Oxidation

(iii) A reducing electrode – B : Cathode

(iv) Electrode connected to the positive end or terminal of the battery – C : Anode

Q. 2. **An aqueous solution of nickel (II) sulphate was electrolyzed using nickel electrodes. Observe the diagram and answer the questions that follow :**

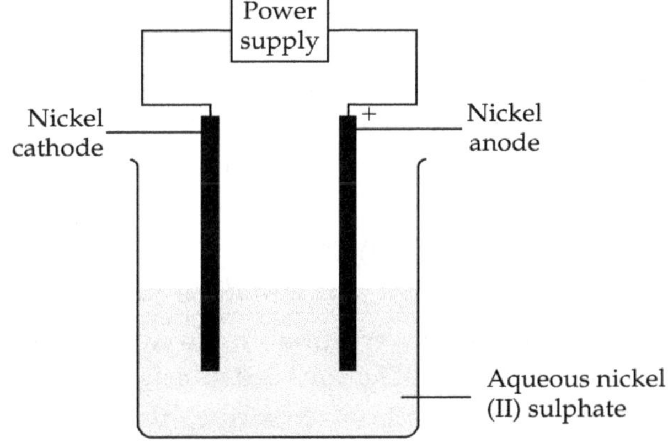

(i) **What do you observe at the cathode and anode respectively ?**

(ii) **Name the cation that remains as a spectator ion in the solution.**

(iii) **Which equation for the reaction at the anode is correct ?**

1. $Ni \rightarrow Ni^{2+} + 2e^-$ 2. $Ni + 2e^- \rightarrow Ni^{2+}$

3. $Ni^{2+} \rightarrow Ni + 2e^-$ 4. $Ni^{2+} + 2e^- \rightarrow Ni$

[2020]

 **Marking Scheme**

(i) **Cathode** – silvery metal **deposited or coated** or sticks / nickel or **metal is deposited** or **coated** or **sticks** / silvery deposit/increases in size or mass Anode – Size decreases / reduction in mass / Anode dissolves / Anode Diminishes/ Anode loses weight.

(ii) Hydrogen ion or H⁺ or hydrogen.

(iii) 1 or Ni → Ni²⁺ + 2e⁻ Or Ni - 2e⁻ → Ni²⁺

Ans. **(i)** At cathode reduction takes place and deposition of Ni takes place as Ni^{2+} ions from solution convert to Ni metal.

$$Ni^{2+} + 2e^- \rightarrow Ni$$

At anode oxidation takes place and Ni metal converts to Ni^{2+} ions.

$$Ni \rightarrow Ni^{2+} + 2e^-$$

(ii) H^+ is the spectator cation.

(iii) 1. $Ni \rightarrow Ni^{2+} + 2e^-$

Q. 3. Copy and complete the following table which refers to the conversion of ions to neutral particles:

Conversion	Ionic Equation	Oxidation/ Reduction
Chloride ion to chlorine molecule	(i) _______	(ii) _______
Lead (II) ion to lead	(iii) _______	(iv) _______

[2018]

Ans.

Conversion	Ionic Equation	Oxidation/ Reduction
Chloride ion to chlorine molecule	(i) $Cl^- - e^- \longrightarrow \frac{1}{2} Cl_2(g)$	(ii) Oxidation
Lead (II) ion to lead	(iii) $Pb^{2+} + 2e^- \longrightarrow Pb(s)$	(iv) Reduction

Q. 4. State the observations at the anode and at the cathode during the electrolysis of:

(i) fused lead bromide using graphite electrodes.

(ii) copper sulphate solution using copper electrodes. [2017]

Ans. **(i)** At anode, the Br^- ion gives up electrons. Red brown bromine gas bubbles can be seen. At cathode, the Pb^{2+} ion accepts electrons. The electrolysis of lead bromide using graphite electrodes produces lead metal at the cathode as silvery grey deposits and bromine gas at the anode.

At the cathode: $Pb^{2+} + 2e^- \longrightarrow Pb$

At the anode: $2Br^- - 2e^- \longrightarrow 2Br$

$$2Br \longrightarrow Br_2\uparrow$$

(ii) At the cathode, Cu^{2+} ions are discharged and deposited on the cathode. At the anode, however, copper ions go into solution in preference to the discharge of either OH^- or SO_4^{2-} ions. As the electrolysis continues, the cathode increases in thickness by reddish brown deposit of copper while the anode slowly dissolves away.

At the cathode: $Cu^{2+} + 2e^- \longrightarrow Cu$

At the anode: $Cu - 2e^- \longrightarrow Cu^{2+}$

Q. 5. Write equations for the reactions taking place at the two electrodes (mentioning clearly the name of the electrode) during the electrolysis of:

(i) Acidified copper sulphate solution with copper electrodes.

(ii) Molten lead bromide with inert electrodes. [2016]

Ans. **(i)** $CuSO_4 \longrightarrow Cu^{2+} + SO_4^-$

∴ $CuSO_4$ undergoes dissociation reaction.

Cathode: $Cu^{2+} + 2e^- \longrightarrow Cu$ (Reduction)

Anode: $Cu - 2e^- \longrightarrow Cu^{2+}$ (Oxidation)

(ii) $PbBr_2 \longrightarrow Pb^{2+} + 2Br^-$

Cathode: $Pb^{2+} + 2e^- \longrightarrow Pb$ (Reduction)

Anode: $2Br^- - 2e^- \longrightarrow Br_2$ (Oxidation)

Q. 6. The following questions relate to the extraction of aluminium by electrolysis:

(i) Name the other aluminium containing compound added to alumina and state its significance.

(ii) Give the equation for the reaction that takes place at the cathode.

(iii) Explain why is it necessary to renew the anode periodically? [2013]

Ans. **(i)** Cryolite

Molten cryolite acts as solvent for alumina and also lowers the fusion temperature from 2050°C to 950°C and enhances conductivity and thereby saves electrical energy.

(ii) $2Al^{3+} + 6e^- \longrightarrow 2Al$.

(iii) During electrolysis oxygen gas is formed at anode which oxidises graphite or carbon anode to carbon dioxide, so it is necessary to replace anode periodically.

Q. 7. During the electrolysis of copper (II) sulphate solution using platinum as cathode and carbon as anode:

(i) What do you observe at the cathode and at the anode?

(ii) What change is noticed in the electrolyte?

(iii) Write the reactions at the cathode and at the anode. **[2011]**

Ans. **(i)** At cathode, reddish brown shiny metal deposits are seen. At anode, bubbles of a colourless, odourless gas seens to come out.

(ii) Colour of electrolyte gradually fades from blue to colourless because effective concentration of copper ions in solution decreases.

(iii) At cathode:
$$Cu^{2+} + 2e^- \longrightarrow Cu\downarrow$$

At anode:
$$OH^- - e^- \longrightarrow OH$$
$$4OH \longrightarrow 2H_2O + O_2\uparrow$$

 Long Answer Type Questions-I

Q. 1. M is a metal above hydrogen in the activity series and its oxide has the formula M_2O. This oxide when dissolved in water forms the corresponding hydroxide which is a good conductor of electricity. In the above context answer the following:

   (i) What kind of combination exists between M and O?

   (ii) How many electrons are there in the outermost shell of M?

   (iii) Name the group to which M belongs.

   (iv) State the reaction taking place at the cathode.

   (v) Name the product at the anode. **[2014]**

Ans. **(i)** Electrovalent bond exists between M and O.

   (ii) One electron is there in the outermost shell.

   (iii) M belongs to first group or alkali metals.

   (iv) $M^+ + e^- \longrightarrow M$ (at cathode).

   (v) Oxygen gas is liberated at anode.

Q. 2. Copper sulphate solution is electrolysed using copper electrodes.

Study the diagram given below and answer the question that follows:

   (i) Which electrode to your left or right is known as the oxidising electrode and why?

   (ii) Write the equation representing the reaction that occurs.

   (iii) State two appropriate observations for the above electrolysis reaction.

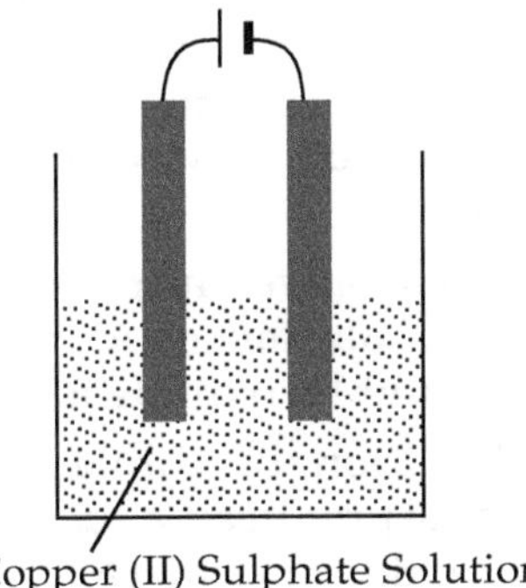

Copper (II) Sulphate Solution **[2013]**

Ans. **(i)** Electrode on the left side is the oxidising electrode because copper atoms lose electrons at this electrode. *i.e.*, it is called anode.

   (ii) At anode: $Cu - 2e^- \longrightarrow Cu^{2+}$

   At cathode: $Cu^{2+} + 2e^- \longrightarrow Cu$

   (iii) 1. Reddish brown copper metal is deposited at cathode so anode becomes thin and cathode grows thick gradually.

     2. Blue colour of aqueous copper (II) sulphate solution remains unchanged because the effective concentration of copper ions in solution remains the same.

Q. 3. Select the correct answer from the list given in brackets:

   (i) An aqueous electrolyte consists of the ions mentioned in the list, the ion which could be discharged most readily during electrolysis. [Fe^{2+}, Cu^{2+}, Pb^{2+}, H^+].

   (ii) The metallic electrode which does not take part in an electrolytic reaction. [Cu, Ag, Pt, Ni].

   (iii) The ion which is discharged at the cathode during the electrolysis of copper sulphate solutions using copper electrodes as anode and cathode. [Cu^{2+}, OH^-, SO_4^{2-}, H^+].

   (iv) When dilute sodium chloride is electrolysed using graphite electrodes, the cation is discharged at the cathode most readily. [Na^+, OH^-, H^+, Cl^-]

   (v) During silver plating of an article using potassium argentocyanide as an electrolyte, the anode material should be [Cu, Ag, Pt, Fe]. **[2012]**

Ans. **(i)** Cu^{2+} **(ii)** Pt

   (iii) Cu^{2+} at cathode   **(iv)** H^+

   (v) Ag (Pure silver)

Q. 4. Mr. Ramu wants to electroplate his key chain with nickel to prevent rusting. For this electroplating:

   (i) Name the electrolyte

   (ii) Name the cathode

   (iii) Name the anode

   (iv) Give the reaction at the cathode

   (v) Give the reaction at the anode. **[2010]**

Ans. **(i)** Nickel sulphate   **(ii)** Key chain

   (iii) Pure nickel plate   **(iv)** $Ni^{2+} + 2e^- \longrightarrow Ni$

   (v) $Ni - 2e^- \longrightarrow Ni^{2+}$

Q. 5. A metal article is to be electroplated with silver. The electrolyte selected is sodium argentocyanide.

   (i) What kind of salt is sodium argentocyanide?

   (ii) Why is it preferred to silver nitrate as an electrolyte?

   (iii) State one condition to ensure that the deposit is smooth, firm and long lasting.

   (iv) Write the reaction taking place at the cathode.

   (v) Write the reaction taking place at the anode. **[2009]**

Ans. **(i)** Sodium argentocyanide is a complex salt.

   (ii) It is preferred over silver nitrate because it gives a smooth and firm silver plating over article as its conversion is slowly that leads to even deposition of silver on cathode.

   (iii) A low voltage current passed for a longer time.

   (iv) $Ag^+ + e^- \longrightarrow Ag$

   (v) $Ag - e^- \longrightarrow Ag^+$.

Q. 6. **(i)** Here is an electrode reaction:

$$Cu \longrightarrow Cu^{2+} + 2e.$$

   At which electrode (anode or cathode) would such a reaction take place? Is this an example of oxidation or reduction?

   (ii) A solution contains magnesium ions (Mg^{2+}) iron (II) ions (Fe^{2+}) and copper ions (Cu^{2+}). On passing an electric current through this solution which ions will be the first to be discharged at the cathode? Write the equation for the cathode reaction.

   (iii) Why is carbon tetrachloride, which is a liquid, a non-electrolyte? **[2008]**

Ans. **(i)** At anode. It is oxidation.

   (ii) Cu^{2+} ions will discharge first.

$$Cu^{2+} + 2e^- \longrightarrow Cu$$

   (iii) Carbon tetrachloride is a liquid and a non- electrolyte because it is a covalent compound which does not contain ions.

Q. 7. The following is a sketch of an electrolytic cell used in the extraction of aluminium:

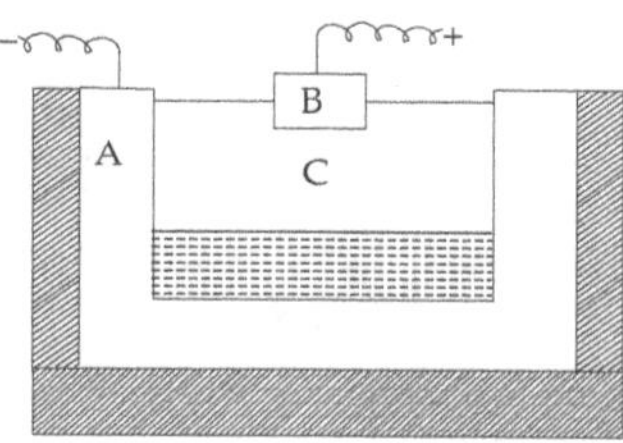

   (i) What is the substance of which the electrodes A and B are made?

   (ii) At which electrode (A or B) is the aluminium formed?

   (iii) What are the two aluminium compounds in the electrolyte C?

   (iv) Why is it necessary for electrode B to be continuously replaced? **[2008]**

Ans. **(i)** Carbon

   (ii) A (cathode)

   (iii) Alumina, *i.e.,* Al_2O_3 and Cryolite *i.e.,* Na_3AlF_6.

   (iv) It is necessary for electrode B to be continuously replaced because it gets burnt by hot oxygen formed at B.

Q. 8. Choose A, B, C or D to match the descriptions **(i)** to **(v)** below. Some alphabets may be repeated.

A. non-electrolyte

B. strong electrolyte

C. Weak electrolyte

D. metallic conductor

   (i) Molten ionic compound

   (ii) Carbon tetrachloride

   (iii) An aluminium wire

   (iv) A solution containing solvent molecules, solute molecules and ions formed by the dissociation of solute molecules.

   (v) A sugar solution with sugar molecules and water molecules. **[2007]**

Ans. **(i)** B,   **(ii)** A,   **(iii)** D,

   (iv) C,   **(v)** A.

Q. 9. Salts A, B, C, D and E undergo reactions (i) to (v) respectively. Identify the anion present in these salts on the basis of these reactions. Tabulate your answers in the format given below:

   (i) When silver nitrate solution is added to a solution of A, a white precipitate, insoluble in dilute nitric acid, is formed.

   (ii) Addition of dilute hydrochloric acid to B produces a gas which turns lead acetate paper black.

(iii) When a freshly prepared solution of ferrous sulphate is added to a solution of C and concentrated sulphuric acid is gently poured from the side of the test-tube, a brown ring is formed.

(iv) When dilute sulphuric acid is added to D, a gas is produced which turns acidified potassium dichromate solution from orange to green.

(v) Addition of dilute hydrochloric acid to E produces an effervescence. The gas produced turns lime water milky but does not affect acidified potassium dichromate solution.

Salt	Anion
A	
B	
C	
D	
E	

[2007]

Ans. **(i)** A—Chloride, **(ii)** B—Sulphide,

(iii) C—Nitrate, **(iv)** D—Sulphite,

(v) E—Carbonate.

Q. 10. **(i)** **Study the diagram given below and answer the questions that follows:**

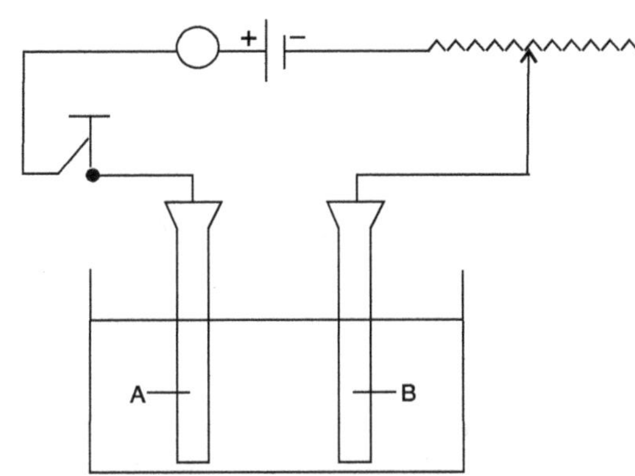

1. Give the names of the electrodes A and B.
2. Which electrode is the oxidizing electrode?

(ii) A strip of copper is placed in four different colourless salt solutions. They are KNO_3, $AgNO_3$, $Zn(NO_3)_2$, $Ca(NO_3)_2$. Which one of the solutions will finally turn blue?

(iii) Write the equations of the reactions which take place at the cathode and anode when acidified water is electrolysed. [2006]

Ans. **(i)** (1) A—Anode   B—Cathode

(2) A

(ii) $AgNO_3$ solution

(iii) Cathode reaction—

$$2H^+ + 2e^- \longrightarrow 2H \longrightarrow H_2$$

Anode reaction—

$$2OH^- - 2e^- \longrightarrow 2OH \longrightarrow H_2O + O$$
$$O + O \longrightarrow O_2$$

Chapter 7

Metallurgy

 Short Answer Type Questions-I

Q. 1. For the electrorefining of copper:
    (i) What is the cathode made up of?
    (ii) Write the reaction that takes place at the anode. **[2018]**

Ans. (i) For electro-refining of copper the cathode is made up of a strip of pure copper metal.
    (ii) The reaction taking place at anode (made up of impure copper) is:
$$Cu - 2e^- \longrightarrow Cu^{+2}$$

Q. 2. Name the main component of the following alloys:
    (i) Brass
    (ii) Duralumin **[2018]**

Ans. (i) Main components of brass are copper and zinc.
    (ii) Main components of duralumin are aluminium (95%), copper (4%), manganese (0.5%) and magnesium (0.5%).

Q. 3. Identify the gas evolved and give the chemical test in each of the following cases:
    (i) Dilute hydrochloric acid reacts with sodium sulphite.
    (ii) Dilute hydrochloric acid reacts with iron (II) sulphide. **[2016]**

Ans. (i) **Gas evolved:** SO_2 (Sulphur dioxide)
    Chemical test: It changes orange acidified potassium dichromate green.
    (ii) **Gas evolved:** H_2S (Hydrogen sulphide)
    Chemical test: Turns lead acetate paper silvery black and turns moist blue litmus paper red.

Q. 4. State the property of the metal being utilized in the following:

Use of metal	Property
Zinc in Galvanization Aluminium in Thermite welding	

[2009]

Ans.

Use of metal	Property
Zinc in Galvanization	Not affected by air and moisture
Aluminium in Thermite welding	Stronger affinity for oxygen as compared to iron.

 Short Answer Type Questions-II

Q. 1. Baeyer's process is used to concentrate bauxite ore to alumina. :
Give balanced chemical equations for the reaction taking place for its conversion from bauxite to alumina. **[2020]**

Marking Scheme

(i) $Al_2O_3.2H_2O + 2NaOH \xrightarrow{150°-200°C} 2NaAlO_2 + 3H_2O$

(ii) $NaAl_2 + 2H_2O \xrightarrow{50°-60°C} NaOH + Al(OH)_3$

(iii) $2Al(OH)_3 \xrightarrow[Alumina]{Heat} Al_2O_3 + 3H_2O$

Ans. Chemical reactions related to Baeyer's process for the conversion from bauxite to alumina:

1. $Al_2O_3.2H_2O(s) + 2NaOH \xrightarrow{150°-200°C} 2NaAlO_2 + 3H_2O$

2. $NaAl_2 + 2H_2O \xrightarrow{50°-60°C} Al(OH)_3 + NaOH$

3. $2Al(OH)_3 \xrightarrow[Alumina]{Heat} Al_2O_3 + 3H_2O$

Q. 2. Give the chemical formula of:
    (i) Bauxite
    (ii) Cryolite
    (iii) Sodium aluminate. **[2019]**

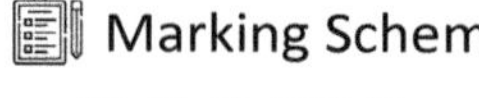 Marking Scheme

(i) $Al_2O_3.2H_2O$
(ii) Na_3AlF_6
(iii) $NaAlO_2$

Ans. (i) The chemical formula of Bauxite is $Al_2O_3.2H_2O$ [where, $0 < x < 1$]

    (ii) The chemical formula of Cryolite is Na_3AlF_6.

    (iii) The chemical formula of Sodium aluminate is $NaAlO_2$.

Q. 3. Answer the following question based on the extraction of aluminium from alumina by Hall-Heroult's Process:

   (i) **What is the function of cryolite used along with alumina as the electrolyte?**

   (ii) **Why is powdered coke sprinkled on top of the electrolyte?**

   (iii) **Name the electrode, from which aluminium is collected.** **[2019]**

📋 Marking Scheme -------------------------------------

   (i) Cryolite reduces the fusion temperature of the mixture/Cryolite increases the mobility of the ions/increases the conductivity of the electrolyte/Acts as solvent for alumina.

   (ii) Powdered coke protects the graphite rods of the anode from oxidation by oxygen released at the anode/Powdered coke prevents the loss of heat from the electrolyte.

   (iii) Cathode

Ans. **(i)** Cryolite (Na_3AlF_6) is mixed with alumina to bring down the melting point of electrolyte mixture and to increase its electrical conductivity.

   (ii) The electrolytic mixture is sprinkled with coke to prevent the anode's oxidation by the oxygen evolved.

   (iii) Aluminium is collected at cathode which is carbon lining covering the inside portion of vessel.

Q. 4. **Answer the following questions with respect to the electrolytic process in the extraction of aluminium:**

   (i) **Identify the components of the electrolyte other than pure alumina and the role played by each.**

   (ii) **Explain why powdered coke is sprinkled over the electrolytic mixture.** **[2017]**

Ans. **(i)** The electrolyte is a solution of aluminium oxide (Al_2O_3) dissolved in cryolite (sodium hexafluoroaluminate(III), Na_3AlF_6). The use of cryolite reduces the melting point of alumina and fluorspar increases the conductivity of solution.

   (ii) To prevent the heat loss due to radiation from molten electrolyte. It also prevents carbon anode from burning in air.

Q. 5. **State the main components of the following alloys:**

   (i) **Brass.**   **(ii)** **Duralumin.**

   (iii) **Bronze.** **[2014]**

Ans. **(i)** Copper and zinc.

   (ii) Aluminium and copper.

   (iii) Copper and tin.

Q. 6. **Name the following:**

   (i) **The property possessed by metals by which they can be beaten into sheets.**

   (ii) **A compound added to lower the fusion temperature of electrolytic bath in the extraction of aluminium.**

   (iii) **The ore of zinc containing its sulphide.** **[2014]**

Ans. **(i)** Malleability

   (ii) Cryolite or Na_3AlF_6

   (iii) Zinc blende.

Q. 7. **The following questions are relevant to the extraction of aluminium:**

   (i) **State the reason for addition of caustic alkali to bauxite ore during purification of bauxite.**

   (ii) **Give a balanced chemical equation for the above reaction.**

   (iii) **Along with cryolite and alumina, another substance is added to the electrolyte mixture. Name the substance and give one reason for the addition** **[2012]**

Ans. **(i)** **Caustic alkali:** Caustic soda or sodium hydroxide dissolves aluminium oxide forming soluble sodium aluminate while impurities remain insoluble and precipitate as red mud.

   (ii) $Al_2O_3 \cdot 2H_2O + 2NaOH \xrightarrow{\Delta} 2NaAlO_2$
     Bauxite ore   Sodium
                      Aluminate
                       $+ 3H_2O$

   (iii) The name of substance is Fluorspar (CaF_2) and it increases conductivity of the electrolyte, since alumina is almost a non-conductor of electricity.

Q. 8. **Name the main constituent metal in the following alloys:**

   (i) **Duralumin.**

   (ii) **Brass**

   (iii) **Stainless steel.** **[2010]**

Ans. **(i)** Aluminium

   (ii) Copper

   (iii) Iron

 ## Short Answer Type Questions-III

Q. 1. Match the alloys given in column I to the uses given in column II.

Column I	Column II
(i) Duralumin	A. Electrical fuse
(ii) Solder	B. Surgical instrument
(iii) Brass	C. Aircraft body
(iv) Stainless Steel	D. Decorative articles

[2019]

 Marking Scheme ----------------------------

(i) Duralumin: C or Aircraft body.
(ii) Solder: A or Electrical fuse
(iii) Brass: D or Decorative articles
(iv) Stainless Steel: B or surgical instruments

Ans.
(i) Duralumin — C. Aircraft body
(ii) Solder — A. Electrical fuse
(iii) Brass — D. Decorative articles
(iv) Stainless steel — B. Surgical instruments

Q. 2. (i) Name the most common ore of the metal aluminium from which the metal is extracted. Write the chemical formula of the ore.

(ii) Name the process by which impure ore of aluminium gets purified by using concentrated solution of an alkali.

(iii) Write the equation for the formation of aluminium at the cathode during the electrolysis of alumina. [2018]

Ans. (i) Most common ore of aluminium metal is bauxite, $Al_2O_3.2H_2O$.

(ii) The process by which impure ore of aluminium gets purified by using concentrated solution of an alkali is known as 'Baeyer's process'.
$$Al_2O_3.2H_2O + 2NaOH \longrightarrow 2NaAlO_2 + 3H_2O$$

(iii) During electrolysis of alumina, the cathode reaction is :
$$Al^{3+} (melt) + 3e^- \longrightarrow Al \text{ (Pure Al)}$$

Q. 3. Name the following:
(i) The process of coating of iron with zinc.
(ii) An alloy of lead and tin that is used in electrical circuits.
(iii) An ore of zinc containing its sulphide.
(iv) A metal oxide that can be reduced by hydrogen. [2017]

Ans. (i) Galvanisation (ii) Solder
(iii) Zinc blende (iv) Copper oxide

Q. 4. Fill in the blanks with the substances given in the box:

Carbon monoxide, carbon dioxide, coal, coke, lime iron (II) oxide, iron (III) oxide, limestone

The raw-materials required for the extraction of iron from haematite are (i) .... (ii) .... and hot air. The mineral present in haematite is (iii) .... which is reduced by (iv) .... to iron. [2006]

Ans. (i) Limestone
(ii) Coke
(iii) Iron (III) oxide
(iv) Carbon monoxide

Long Answer Type Questions-I

Q. 1. (i) Name the solution used to react with bauxite as a first step in obtaining pure aluminium oxide, in the Baeyer's process.

(ii) Write the equation for the reaction where the aluminium oxide for the electrolytic extraction of aluminium is obtained by heating aluminium hydroxide.

(iii) Name the compound added to pure alumina to lower the fusion temperature during the electrolytic reduction of alumina.

(iv) Write the equation for the reaction that occurs at the cathode during the extraction of aluminium by electrolysis.

(v) Explain why it is preferable to use a number of graphite electrodes as anode instead of a single electrode, during the above electrolysis. [2016]

Ans. (i) NaOH (sodium hydroxide)

(ii) $2Al(OH)_3 \xrightarrow[1000°C]{\Delta} Al_2O_3 + 3H_2O$

(iii) Cryolite and fluorspar

(iv) **At cathode:** $2Al^{3+} + 3e^- \longrightarrow 2Al$

(v) During the electrolysis process, aluminium is deposited at the cathode and oxygen is liberated at the anode. Some of the oxygen reacts with the carbon in the graphite to form carbon dioxide, by consuming the anode slowly.

Thus, the anodes have to be replaced periodically or a number of graphite electrode as anodes have to be used.

Q. 2. **(i)** **For each of the substance listed below, describe the role played in the extraction of aluminium:**

   (1) Cryolite

   (2) Sodium hydroxide

   (3) Graphite

(ii) **Explain why:**

   (1) **In the electrolysis of alumina using the Hall Heroult's process the electrolyte is covered with powdered coke.**

   (2) **Iron sheets are coated with zinc during galvanization.** **[2015]**

Ans. **(i) (1)** Cryolite acts as a solvent for the electrolytic mixture and also lowers the fusion temperature from 2050°C to 950°C which saves electrical energy. It increases the electrical conductivity and it acts as a solvent.

   (2) Sodium hydroxide is used to remove insoluble impurities from the ore. When bauxite ore is treated with sodium hydroxide, it dissolves and forms sodium aluminate leaving behind insoluble impurities called red mud (consists of ferric oxide, sand etc.)

   (3) Graphite is used as an electrode in the extraction of aluminium because it has a very high melting point, good conductor of electricity and it prevent formation of O_2 otherwise Aluminium will get oxidised.

   (ii) (1) To reduce the heat loss by radiation and to prevent burning of anode in air at the point above the electrolyte. It also prevents the oxidation of the anode.

   (2) Iron sheets are coated with zinc during galvanisation to prevent them from rusting as zinc is more reactive than iron.

Q. 3. **Match the properties and uses of alloys in List 1 with the appropriate answer from List 2:**

List 1	List 2
(i) The alloy contains Cu and Zn, is hard, silvery and is used in decorative articles.	A. Duralumin
(ii) It is stronger than aluminium, light and is used in making light tools.	B. Brass
(iii) It is lustrous, hard, corrosion resistant and used in surgical instruments.	C. Bronze
(iv) Tin lowers the melting point of the alloy and is used for soldering purpose.	D. Stainless steel
(v) The alloy is hard, brittle, takes up polish and is used for making statues.	E. Solder

[2012]

Ans. **(i)** B   **(ii)** A
   (iii) D   **(iv)** E
   (v) C

Q. 4. **Answer the following questions:**

   (i) **Name a metal which is found abundantly in the earth's crust.**

   (ii) **What is the difference between calcination and roasting?**

   (iii) **Name the process used for the enrichment of sulphide ore.**

   (iv) **Write the chemical formulae of one main ore of iron and aluminium.**

   (v) **Write the constituents of electrolyte for the extraction of aluminium.** **[2011]**

Ans. **(i)** Aluminium.

   (ii) Calcination is used in the decomposition of hydroxide and carbonate ores generally by heating them in absence of air whereas Roasting is the oxidation of sulphide ores generally by heating them in excess of air.

   (iii) Froth floatation process.

   (iv) Main ore of iron $\longrightarrow$ Haematite – Fe_2O_3. Main ore of aluminium $\longrightarrow$ Bauxite – $Al_2O_3.2H_2O$.

   (v) Molten alumina, cryolite and fluorspar.

Q. 5. **Name the following:**

   (i) **A metal which is a liquid at room temperature.**

   (ii) **A compound which is added to lower the fusion temperature of the electrolytic bath in the extraction of aluminium.**

   (iii) **The process of heating an ore to a high temperature in the presence of air.**

   (iv) **The compound formed by the reaction between calcium oxide and silica.**

   (v) **The middle region of the blast furnace.** **[2006]**

Ans. **(i)** Mercury
   (ii) Cryolite
   (iii) Roasting
   (iv) Calcium silicate
   (v) Zone of heat absorption

8 Study of Compounds

Short Answer Type Questions-I

Q. 1. Write a balanced chemical equation for each of the following reactions:

    (i) Action of dilute sulphuric acid on sodium hydroxide.

    (ii) Action of dilute sulphuric acid on zinc sulphide. **[2019]**

Ans. (i) Action of dilute sulphuric acid on sodium hydroxide

$$H_2SO_4 \, (aq) + 2NaOH \, (aq) \longrightarrow Na_2SO_4 \, (aq) + H_2O \, (l)$$

    (ii) Action of dilute sulphuric acid on zinc sulphide

$$ZnS + 4H_2SO_4 \longrightarrow ZnSO_4 + 4SO_2 + 4H_2O$$

Q. 2. For the preparation of hydrochloric acid in the laboratory:

    (i) Why is direct absorption of hydrogen chloride gas in water not feasible?

    (ii) What arrangement is done to dissolve hydrogen chloride gas in water? **[2018]**

Ans. (i) Hydrogen chloride gas is not directly absorbed in water because hydrogen chloride gas is higly soluble in water and causes back suction.

    (ii) Hydrogen chloride gas is produced by reacting sodium chloride and sulphuric acid in a reaction vessel, the outlet from the vessel containing hydrogen chloride gas is put into another vessel containing sulphuric acid which helps to obtain dry hydrogen chloride gas. The dry gas then reaches to the vessel containing water through an empty vessel (this empty vessel is kept for accommodation of any back suction of water during absorption of hydrogen chloride gas in water). After travelling the empty vessel, hydrogen chloride gas is introduced to the vessel containing water through a pipe fitted with a funnel at the end and over the water vessel, this ensures maximum surface area for hydrochloric acid gas absorption in water.

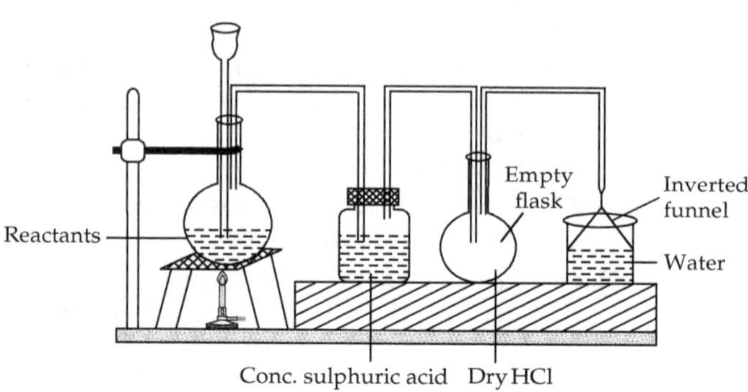

Q. 3. Write a balanced equation for the preparation of each of the following salts:

    (i) Copper sulphate from copper carbonate.

    (ii) Zinc carbonate from zinc sulphate. **[2018]**

Ans. (i) Preparation of copper sulphate from copper carbonate can be done by reacting copper carbonate with sulphuric acid.

$$CuCO_3 + H_2SO_4 \longrightarrow CuSO_4 + CO_2\uparrow + H_2O$$

    (ii) Zinc carbonate from zinc sulphate can be prepared by reacting zinc sulphate with sodium carbonate.

$$ZnSO_4 + Na_2CO_3 \longrightarrow ZnCO_3 + Na_2SO_4$$

Q. 4. (i) What is the type of salt formed when the reactants are heated at a suitable temperature for the preparation of nitric acid?

    (ii) State why for the preparation of nitric acid, the complete apparatus is made up of glass. **[2018]**

Ans. (i) Sodium sulphate is formed if the reactants (sodium hydrogen sulphate and sodium nitrate) for the preparation of nitric acid are heated above 200°C. The sodium sulphate formed deposits as a hard crust and is difficult to remove.

$$NaNO_3 + NaHSO_4 \xrightarrow{>200°C} Na_2SO_4 + HNO_3$$

    (ii) All glass apparatus should be used while preparing nitric acid as the nitric acid vapours are highly corrosive and they corrode the cork or rubber fittings used in the apparatus.

Q. 5. **Which property of sulphuric acid is shown by the reaction of concentrated sulphuric acid with:**
  (i) Ethanol?
  (ii) Carbon? **[2018]**
Ans. (i) Reaction of concentrated sulphuric acid with ethanol leads to formation of ethene, which shows that it is dehydrating in nature.
$$C_2H_5OH \xrightarrow[\text{Dehydration}]{H_2SO_4} C_2H_4 + H_2O$$
  (i.e. Ethanol → Ethene)

  (ii) Reaction of concentrated sulphuric acid with carbon shows its oxidizing nature, where it oxidizes carbon to carbon dioxide.
$$C + 2H_2SO_4 \longrightarrow CO_2 + 2H_2O + 2SO_2$$

Q. 6. **Write a balanced chemical equation for the preparation of each of the following salts:**
  (i) Copper carbonate
  (ii) Ammonium sulphate crystals **[2017]**
Ans. (i) $CuCl_2 + Na_2CO_3 \longrightarrow CuCO_3 + 2NaCl$
  (ii) $2NH_4OH + H_2SO_4 \longrightarrow (NH_4)_2SO_4 + 2H_2O$

Q. 7. **Write balanced chemical equations to show how SO_3 is converted to sulphuric acid in the contact process.** **[2017,]**
Ans. Conversion of sulphur trioxide into sulphuric acid:

  1. $SO_3 + H_2SO_4 \longrightarrow H_2S_2O_7$
  (Sulphur trioxide) (conc.) (Oleum)

  2. Dilution of oleum:
  $H_2S_2O_7 + H_2O \longrightarrow 2H_2SO_4$
  (Oleum) (Sulphuric acid)

Q. 8. **Write balanced chemical equations for each of the following:**
  (i) When excess of ammonia is treated with chlorine.
  (ii) An equation to illustrate the reducing nature of ammonia. **[2016]**
Ans. (i) $8NH_3 + 3Cl_2 \longrightarrow 6NH_4Cl + N_2\uparrow$
  (ii) $2NH_3 + 3CuO \longrightarrow 3Cu + 3H_2O + N_2\uparrow$

Q. 9. **Fill in the blanks using the appropriate words given below:**

  (Sulphur dioxide, Nitrogen dioxide, Nitric oxide, Sulphuric acid)

  (i) Cold, dilute nitric acid reacts with copper to give ———.
  (ii) Hot, concentrated nitric acid reacts with sulphur to form ———. **[2016]**
Ans. (i) Nitric oxide (ii) Sulphuric acid

Q. 10. **Name the gas evolved when the following mixtures are heated:**
  (i) Calcium hydroxide and ammonium chloride.
  (ii) Sodium Nitrite and ammonium chloride. **[2016]**
Ans. (i) Ammonia: $2NH_4Cl + Ca(OH)_2 \longrightarrow CaCl_2 + 2H_2O + 2NH_3\uparrow$
  (ii) Nitrogen: $NH_4Cl + NaNO_2 \longrightarrow NaCl + 2H_2O + N_2\uparrow$

Q. 11. **Give balanced chemical equations for the action of sulphuric acid on each of the following:**
  (a) (i) Potassium hydrogen carbonate.
  (ii) Sulphur.
  (b) In the contant process for the manufacture of sulphuric acid. given the equations for the conversion of sulphur trioxide to sulphuric acid. **[2015]**

Ans. (a) (i) $2KHCO_3 + H_2SO_4 \longrightarrow K_2SO_4$
  (Potassium hydrogen carbonate) (Sulphuric acid) (dil.) (Potassium sulphate)
  $+ 2H_2O + 2CO_2\uparrow$
  (Water) (Carbon dioxide)

  (ii) $S + 2H_2SO_4 \longrightarrow 3SO_2\uparrow + 2H_2O$
  (Sulphur) (Sulphuric acid (conc.)) (Sulphur dioxide) (Water)

  (b) Conversion of sulphur trioxide into sulphuric acid:
  $SO_3 + H_2SO_4 \longrightarrow H_2S_2O_7$
  (Sulphur trioxide) (conc.) (Oleum)
  Dilution of oleum :
  $H_2S_2O_7 + H_2O \longrightarrow 2H_2SO_4$
  (Oleum) (Sulphuric Acid)

Q. 12. **(i) What is the special feature of the apparatus that is used in the laboratory preparation of nitric acid?**
  (ii) Why should the temperature of the reaction mixture of nitric acid not be allowed to rise above 200°C? **[2011]**
Ans. (i) It is an all glass retort. The apparatus is made of glass because vapours of nitric acid are corrosive.
  (ii) The temperature of the reaction mixture of nitric acid should not be allowed to rise above 200° C because above 200°C, nitric acid will decompose and glass apparatus may break.

Q. 13. **Correct the following statements.**
  For example: 'Chlorine is a bleaching agent'.
  Should read as: 'Moist chlorine is a bleaching agent'.
  (i) Copper reacts with nitric acid to produce nitrogen dioxide.

(ii) Hydrochloric acid is prepared in the laboratory by passing hydrogen chloride directly through water. [2009]

Ans. (i) Copper reacts with concentrated nitric acid to produce nitrogen dioxide.

(ii) Hydrochloric acid is prepared in the laboratory by dissolving hydrogen chloride in water using antisuction device like inverted funnel arrangement.

Q. 14. Write the equation for the following reactions:
(i) Aluminium nitride and water.
(ii) Sulphur dioxide and water. [2008]

Ans. (i) $$AlN + 3H_2O \longrightarrow Al(OH)_3 + NH_3$$
$$\text{aluminium hydroxide}$$

(ii) $$SO_2 + H_2O \longrightarrow H_2SO_3$$
$$\text{Sulphurous acid}$$

Q. 15. Write a balanced equation for a reaction in which ammonia is oxidized by:
(i) A metal oxide,
(ii) A gas which is not oxygen. [2007]

Ans. (i) $2NH_3 + 3CuO \longrightarrow 3Cu + N_2 + 3H_2O$
(ii) $2NH_3 + 3Cl_2 \longrightarrow N_2 + 6HCl$

Q. 16. (i) Explain why only all glass apparatus should be used for the preparation of nitric acid by heating concentrated sulphuric acid and potassium nitrate.

(ii) Write a chemical equation to illustrate the acidic nature of nitric acid. [2006]

Ans. (i) Nitric acid is highly corrosive and therefore destroys rubber and cork of the apparatus.

(ii) $$CaCO_3 + \text{dil. } 2HNO_3 \longrightarrow$$
$$Ca(NO_3)_2 + H_2O + CO_2$$
$$\text{Calcium nitrate}$$

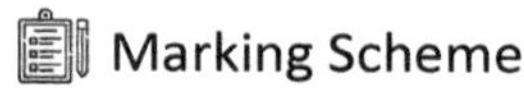

Short Answer Type Questions-II

Q. 1. Distinguish between the following pairs of compounds using the reagent given in the bracket.
(i) Manganese dioxide and copper (II) oxide. (using concentrated HCl)
(ii) Ferrous sulphate solution and ferric sulphate solution. (using sodium hydroxide solution)
(iii) Dilute hydrochloric acid and dilute sulphuric acid. (using lead nitrate solution) [2019]

Marking Scheme

(i) On adding concentrated hydrochloric acid if a greenish yellow gas is evolved it is Manganese dioxide.
If no gas is evolved it is CuO.

(ii) On adding sodium hydroxide solution if a dirty green precipitate is formed it is ferrous sulphate solution.
If a reddish-brown precipitate is formed, it is Ferric sulphate solution.

(iii) On adding lead nitrate solution, if white precipitate is formed which dissolves on heating, then it is dilute HCl.
If white precipitate formed does not dissolve on heating, it is dilute H_2SO_4.

Ans. (i) Manganese dioxide reacts with concentrated hydrochloric acid to give chlorine gas, which is greenish yellow in colour, whereas copper (II) oxide reacts with concentrated hydrochloric acid to give $CuCl_2$, but no chlorine gas is evolved.
$$MnO_2 + 4HCl \rightarrow MnCl_2 + Cl_2\uparrow + 2H_2O$$

(ii) A reddish precipitate of Iron(III) hydroxide is obtained when ferric sulphate reacts with sodium hydroxide solution, whereas dirty green precipitate is obtained when ferrous sulphate is mixed with sodium hydroxide.
$$Fe_2(SO_4)_3(aq) + 6NaOH(aq) \rightarrow 2Fe(OH)_3(s)$$
$$+ 3Na_2SO_4(aq)$$

(iii) Lead nitrate reacts with dilute HCl to form the insoluble salt lead chloride, which appears as the white precipitate. The insoluble lead chloride reacts with excess Cl^- ions (of HCl) to form a soluble complex, the tetrachloroplumbate(II) ion,
$$Pb(NO_3)_2 + 2HCl \rightarrow PbCl_2\downarrow + 2HNO_3$$
$$PbCl_2 + 2HCl \rightarrow [PbCl_4]^{2-} + 2H^+(aq)$$
Soluble
Lead nitrate solution reacts with H_2SO_4 to give lead sulphate precipitate, which does not dissolve further in sulphuric acid solution.
$$Pb(NO_3)_2 + H_2SO_4 \rightarrow PbSO_4\downarrow + HNO_3$$

Q. 2. Complete the following equations:
(i) S + conc. $HNO_3 \longrightarrow$
(ii) C + conc. $H_2SO_4 \longrightarrow$
(iii) Cu + dil. $HNO_3 \longrightarrow$ [2019]

Marking Scheme

(i) $S + 6HNO_3 \rightarrow H_2SO_4 + 6NO_2 + 2H_2O$
(ii) $C + 2H_2SO_4 \rightarrow CO_2 + 2SO_2 + 2H_2O$
(iii) $3Cu + 8HNO_3 \rightarrow 3Cu(NO_3)_2 + 2NO + 4H_2O$

Ans. (i) $S + 6HNO_3 \rightarrow H_2SO_4 + 6NO_2 + 2H_2O$

(ii) $C + 2H_2SO_4 \rightarrow CO_2 + 2SO_2 + 2H_2O$

(iii) $3Cu + 8HNO_3 \rightarrow 3Cu(NO_3)_2 + 2NO + 4H_2O$

Q. 3. **Study the flow chart given and give balanced equations to represent the reactions A, B and C:**

$$\boxed{Mg_3N_2} \xrightarrow{A} \boxed{NH_3} \underset{C}{\overset{B}{\rightleftarrows}} \boxed{NH_4Cl}$$

[2019]

📋 Marking Scheme ----------------------------

A. $Mg_3N_2 + 6H_2O \longrightarrow 3Mg(OH)_2 + 2NH_3$
B. $NH_3 + HCl \longrightarrow NH_4Cl$
          Or
  $8NH_3 + 3Cl_2 \longrightarrow 6NH_4Cl + N_2$
C. $NH_4Cl + NaOH \longrightarrow NaCl + NH_3 + H_2O$ Or with any other alkali.

Ans. The flow chart can be completed as follows-

$$\boxed{Mg_3N_2} \xrightarrow{H_2O(A)} \boxed{NH_3} \underset{Ca(OH)_2(C)}{\overset{HCl(B)}{\rightleftarrows}}$$

$$\boxed{NH_4Cl}$$

The full reactions are as follows-

$Mg_3N_2 + 6H_2O \longrightarrow 3Mg(OH)_2 + 2NH_3$
           (A)

$NH_3 + HCl \longrightarrow NH_4Cl$
     (B)

$2NH_4Cl + Ca(OH)_2 \longrightarrow 2NH_3 + 2H_2O + CaCl_2$
         (C)

Q. 4. **(i)** **Write the balanced chemical equation to prepare ammonia gas in the laboratory by using an alkali.**

(ii) **State why concentrated sulphuric acid is not used for drying ammonia gas.**

(iii) **Why is ammonia gas not collected over water?** **[2018]**

Ans. **(i)** Preparation of NH_3 gas using alkali can be done by reacting ammonium sulphate with sodium hydroxide.

$(NH_4)_2SO_4 + 2NaOH \longrightarrow 2NH_3 + 2H_2O$
$\qquad\qquad\qquad\qquad\qquad\qquad + Na_2SO_4$

(ii) Concentrated sulphuric acid is not used for drying ammonia gas because concentrated sulphuric acid (H_2SO_4) being acidic in nature reacts with basic ammonia gas to give ammonium sulphate $[(NH_4)_2SO_4]$.

(iii) Ammonia gas is not collected over water because it has a high solubility in water and it dissolves in water to give a basic solution.

$NH_3(g) + H_2O(l) \longrightarrow NH_4^+(aq) + OH^-(aq)$

Q. 5. **(i)** **Name the acid used for the preparation of hydrogen chloride gas in the laboratory. Why is this particular acid preferred to other acids?**

(ii) **Write the balanced chemical equation for the laboratory preparation of hydrogen chloride gas.** **[2018]**

Ans. **(i)** Conc. sulphuric acid is used for preparation of hydrogen chloride gas in laboratory. This is preferred over other acids because of the following reasons:

1. It has low volatility than HCl gas (so that the produced HCl gas is collected easily).

2. It has dehydrating properties, so the HCl gas produced can be effectively dehydrated to remove traces of water.

(ii) Laboratory preparation of hydrogen chloride gas can be done by heating NaCl with concentrated sulphuric acid:

$$NaCl + H_2SO_4 \xrightarrow{420\,K\ or\ <200°C} NaHSO_4$$
$$(conc.) \qquad\qquad\qquad Sodium$$
$$hydrosulphate$$
$$+ HCl\ (\uparrow)$$

Q. 6. **Write balanced chemical equations to show:**

(i) **The oxidizing action of conc. Sulphuric acid on Carbon.**

(ii) **The behavior of H_2SO_4 as an acid when it reacts with magnesium.**

(iii) **The dehydrating property of conc. Sulphuric acid with sugar.** **[2017]**

Ans. **(i)** $C + 2H_2SO_4 \longrightarrow CO_2\uparrow + 2SO_2\uparrow + 2H_2O$

(ii) $Mg + H_2SO_4 \longrightarrow MgSO_4 + H_2\uparrow$

(iii) $C_{12}H_{22}O_{11} \xrightarrow{conc.\ H_2SO_4} 12C + 11H_2O$
    (Cane sugar)

Q. 7. **A, B, C and D summarize the properties of sulphuric acid depending on whether it is dilute or concentrated.**

A = Typical acid property

B = Non-volatile acid

C = Oxidizing agent

D = Dehydrating agent

Choose the property (A, B, C or D) depending on which is relevant to each of the following:

(i) **Preparation of hydrogen chloride gas.**

(ii) **Preparation of copper sulphate from copper oxide.**

(iii) **Action of conc. sulphuric acid on sulphur.** **[2016]**

Ans. **(i)** B = Non-volatile acid

(ii) A = Typical acid property

(iii) C = Oxidizing agent

Q. 8. **Explain the following:**

(i) Dilute nitric acid is generally considered a typical acid but not so in its reaction with metals.

(ii) Concentrated nitric acid appears yellow when it is left standing in a glass bottle.

(iii) An all glass apparatus is used in the laboratory preparation of nitric acid.

[2015]

Ans. **(i)** Dilute nirtic acid is generally considered a typical acid but not so in its reaction with metals because it does not liberate hydrogen with all metals except Mg and Mn. It is a powerful oxidising agent and the nascent oxygen formed oxidises the hydrogen to water.

(ii) Concentrated nitric acid appears yellow when it is left standing in a glass bottle because when nitric acid is left standing in a glass bottle, it decomposes to give reddish brown NO_2 gas which dissolves in undecomposed nitric acid to give a yellow colour.

(iii) An all glass apparatus is used in the laboratory preparation of nitric acid because nitric acid vapours are corrosive and destroy materials like rubber, cork or metal.

Q. 9. **Give balanced chemical equations for each of the following:**

(i) Lab preparation of ammonia using an ammonium salt.

(ii) Reaction of ammonia with excess chlorine.

(iii) Reaction of ammonia with sulphuric acid. **[2015]**

Ans. **(i)** $2NH_4Cl(s) + Ca(OH)_2 \xrightarrow{\Delta} CaCl_2(s)$
Ammonium salt   Slaked lime   Calcium chloride

$+ 2H_2O + 2NH_3\uparrow$
Water   Ammonia

(ii) $NH_3 + 3Cl_2 \longrightarrow 3HCl + NCl_3$
Hydrochloric acid   Nitrogen chloride

(iii) $2NH_3 + H_2SO_4 \longrightarrow (NH_4)_2SO_4$
Ammonium sulphate

Q. 10. **Study the figure given below and answer the questions that follow:**

(i) Identify the gas Y.

(ii) What property of gas Y does this experiment demonstrate?

(iii) Name another gas which has the same property and can be demonstrated through this experiment.

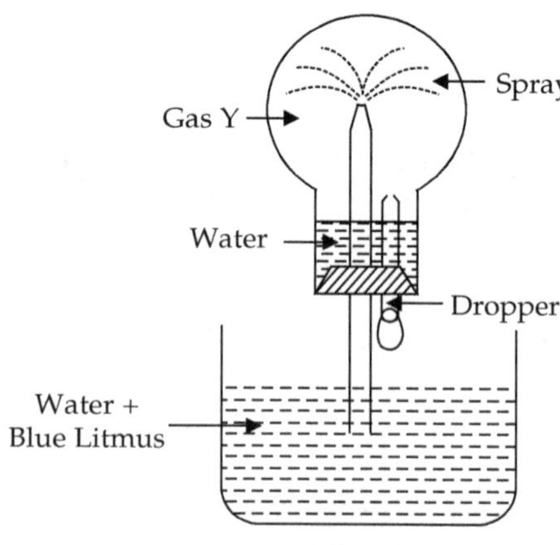

[2014]

Ans. **(i)** Y is hydrochloride (HCl) gas.

(ii) Gas Y is highly soluble in water.

(iii) Ammonia gas.

Q. 11. **Give one equation each to show the following properties of sulphuric acid:**

(i) Dehydrating property.

(ii) Acidic nature.

(iii) As a non-volatile acid. **[2014]**

Ans. **(i)** $CuSO_4.5H_2O \xrightarrow[H_2SO_4]{Conc.} CuSO_4 + 5H_2O$

or $C_{12}H_{22}O_{11} \xrightarrow{Conc. H_2SO_4} 12C + 11H_2O$
Sucrose

(ii) $H_2SO_4 + Na_2CO_3 \longrightarrow Na_2SO_4 + CO_2\uparrow + H_2O$
Dil.   Sodium carbonate   Sodium sulphate

(iii) $NaCl + H_2SO_4 \xrightarrow[\Delta]{<200°C} NaHSO_4 + HCl\uparrow$
Sodium chloride   Conc.   Sodium hydrogen sulphate

Q. 12. **Copy and complete the following table relating to important industrial process:**

Name of the process	Temperature	Catalyst	Equation for the catalyzed reaction
Haber's process			

[2013]

Ans.

Name of the process	Temperature	Catalyst	Equation for the catalyzed reaction
Haber's process	(450–500)°C	Finely divided iron	$N_2 + 3H_2 \rightleftharpoons 2NH_3 + $ Heat

Q. 13. **State one chemical test between each of the following pairs:**

(i) **Sodium carbonate and sodium sulphite.**
(ii) **Ferrous nitrate and lead nitrate**
(iii) **Manganese dioxide and copper (II) oxide.** [2012]

Ans. (i) Sodium carbonate when treated with dil. H_2SO_4 will liberate colourless odourless gas with brisk effervescence. The gas will turn lime water milky and will have no effect on acidified potassium permanganate solution.

Sodium sulphite when treated with dil. H_2SO_4 will liberate a colourless gas having suffocating smell of burning sulphur. The gas will turn acidified potassium permanganate solution from pink to colourless.

(ii) Aqueous ferrous nitrate when treated with NaOH solution gives a dirty green ppt. and is insoluble in excess of NaOH.

Aqueous lead nitrate when treated with NaOH solution gives a white ppt. which dissolves in excess of NaOH.

(iii) When manganese dioxide is heated with conc. HCl, a pungent smelling greenish yellow chlorine gas is evolved which turns iodide paper blue-black.

When copper oxide is heated with conc. HCl, no such gas is evolved.

Q. 14. Name the following metals:
(i) **A metal present in cryolite other than sodium.**
(ii) **A metal which is unaffected by dilute or concentrated acids.**
(iii) **A metal present in period 3, group 1 of the periodic table.** [2012]

Ans. (i) Aluminium
(ii) Platinum
(iii) Sodium

Q. 15. Write balanced chemical equations for the following:
(i) **Chlorine reacts with excess of ammonia.**
(ii) **Ferric hydroxide reacts with nitric acid.**
(iii) **Zinc oxide dissolves in sodium hydroxide.** [2011]

Ans. (i) $3Cl_2 + 8NH_3 \longrightarrow 6NH_4Cl + N_2$
Ammonium chloride
(ii) $Fe(OH)_3 + 3HNO_3 \longrightarrow Fe(NO_3)_3 + 3H_2O$
Iron (III) nitrate
(iii) $ZnO + 2NaOH \longrightarrow Na_2ZnO_2 + H_2O$
Sodium zincate

Q. 16. The diagram shows a simple arrangement of the fountain experiment: [2010]

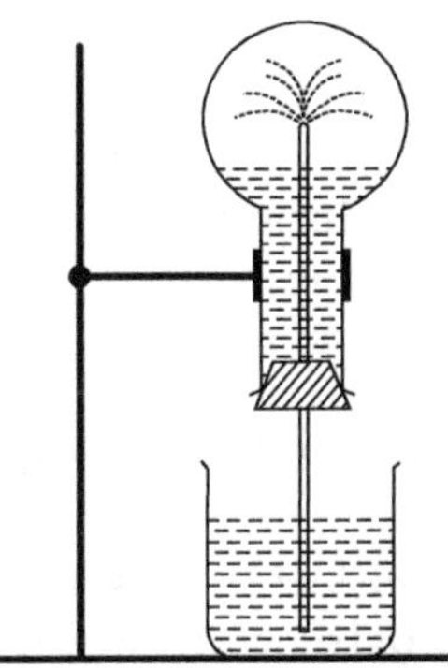

(i) **Name the two gases you have studied which can be used in this experiment.**
(ii) **What is the common property demonstrated by this experiment?**

Ans. (i) Hydrogen chloride gas and ammonia gas.
(ii) High solubility of the gas in water.

Q. 17. Name the gas evolved in each case (formula is not acceptable).
(i) **The gas produced by the action of dilute nitric acid on copper.**
(ii) **The gas that burns in oxygen with a greenish yellow flame.**
(iii) **The gas that can be oxidised to sulphur.** [2009]

Ans. (i) Nitric oxide   (ii) Ammonia
(iii) Hydrogen sulphide

Q. 18. (i) **Of the two gases, ammonia and hydrogen chloride, which is more dense? Name the method of collection of this gas.**
(ii) **Give one example of a reaction between the above two gases which produces a solid compound.** [2007]

Ans. (i) Hydrogen chloride is more dense. Since HCl is heavier than air, it is collected by upward displacement of air.
(ii) $NH_3 + HCl \longrightarrow NH_4Cl$ (Solid)
Ammonium chloride

Q. 19. Give one test each to distinguish between the following pairs of chemicals:
(i) **Zinc nitrate solution and Calcium nitrate solution.**
(ii) **Sodium nitrate solution and sodium chloride solution.**
(iii) **Iron (III) chloride solution and Copper Chloride solution.** [2006]

Ans. (i) Add NaOH solution in excess to the two solutions. The one in which white precipitate initially formed dissolves in excess of NaOH solution is $Zn(NO_3)_2$ solution and the other is $Ca(NO_3)_2$ solution.
(ii) Add freshly prepared ferrous sulphate solution to the two solutions. Then by

the side of the test tube, pour conc. sulphuric acid to each slowly. The one in which brown ring appears is sodium nitrate solution while the other is sodium chloride solution.

(iii) Add NaOH solution to both the solutions. The one which gives a reddish brown precipitate is iron (III) chloride solution and the one which gives blue precipitate is copper chloride solution.

Short Answer Type Questions-III

Q. 1. Hydrogen chloride gas is prepared in the laboratory using concentrated sulphuric acid and sodium chloride. Answer the questions that follow based on this reaction :

(i) Give the balanced chemical equation for the reaction with suitable conditions(s if any.

(ii) Why is concentrated sulphuric acid used instead of concentrated nitric acid ?

(iii) How is the gas collected ?

(iv) Name the drying agent not used for drying the gas. **[2020]**

 Marking Scheme

(i) $NaCl + (conc.) H_2SO_4 \xrightarrow{< 200°C \text{ or less than } 200} NaHSO_4 + HCl$

(ii) **Concentrated H_2SO_4 is non-volatile / least volatile / less volatile/ has high boiling point** and (hence can displace the more volatile HCl gas from the salt)

OR

Concentrated nitric acid is **a volatile** acid / **low boiling** point and (will displace out itself along with HCl gas)

(iii) Upward displacement of air / downward delivery / downward delivery of gas

(iv) Quick lime / calcium oxide / phosphorus pentoxide

Ans. **(i) 1.** $NaCl + H_2SO_4 \xrightarrow[\text{conc.}]{\text{below } 200°C} NaHSO_4 + HCl\uparrow$

2. $2NaCl + H_2SO_4 \xrightarrow[\text{conc.}]{\text{Heated above } 200°C} Na_2SO_4 + 2HCl\uparrow$

(ii) Concentrated nitric acid is not used for preparation of HCl gas as it is very strong oxidising agent and will end up oxidising HCl produced to H_2 gas.

(iii) HCl is collected by the upward displacement of air.

(iv) Calcium oxide.

Q. 2. Copy and complete the following table which refers to the industrial method for the preparation of ammonia and sulphuric acid.

Name of the compound	Name of the process	Catalytic equation (with the catalyst)
Ammonia	(i)..............	(ii)..............
Sulphuric acid	(iii)..............	(iv)..............

[2019]

Marking Scheme

(i) Haber's Process

(ii) $N_2 + 3H_2 \xrightarrow{Fe} 2NH_3$

(iii) Contact Process

(iv) $2SO_2 + O_2 \xrightarrow{V_2O_5} 2SO_3$

Or

$2SO_2 + O_2 \quad N_2 + 3H_2 \xrightarrow{Pt} 2SO_3$

Ans. Details of industrial processes

Name of the compound	Name of the process	Catalytic equation (with the catalyst)
Ammonia	(i) **Haber's Process**	(ii) $N_2(g) + 3H_2(g) \xrightleftharpoons[K_2O + Al_2O_3]{\text{Iron oxide}} 2NH_3(g)$ Ammonia
Sulphuric acid	(iii) **Contact process**	(iv) $2SO_2 + O_2(g) \xrightarrow{V_2O_5} 2SO_3(g) \xrightarrow{H_2SO_4} H_2S_2O_7$ Oleum

Q. 3. Give a chemical test to distinguish between the following pairs of chemicals:

(i) **Lead nitrate solution and zinc nitrate solution.**

(ii) **Sodium chloride solution and sodium nitrate solution.**

[2018]

Ans. (i) Add aqueous hydrochloric acid solution to the solution of lead nitrate and solution of zinc nitrate prepared separately. The solution of lead nitrate would give a white precipitate of $PbCl_2$ whereas there would be no precipitate formed with zinc nitrate solution.

$$Pb^{2+} + 2Cl^- \longrightarrow PbCl_2(\downarrow)$$

$$Pb(NO_3)_2 + 2HCl \longrightarrow PbCl_2(\downarrow) + 2HNO_3$$
$$Zn(NO_3)_2 + 2HCl \longrightarrow ZnCl_2(\downarrow) + 2HNO_3$$

   (ii) Add aqueous solution of silver nitrate ($AgNO_3$) to the solution of sodium chloride and solution of sodium nitrate prepared separately. The solution of sodium chloride would give a white precipitate of $AgCl$ whereas there would be no precipitate, only a colourless solution is formed with sodium nitrate solution.

Q. 4. **Give a balanced chemical equation for each of the following:**
   (i) Action of conc. nitric acid on sulphur.
   (ii) Catalytic oxidation of ammonia.
   (iii) Laboratory preparation of nitric acid.
   (iv) Reaction of ammonia with nitric acid.
                                   [2017]

Ans.
(a)

   (i) $\underset{\text{Sulphur}}{S(s)} + \underset{\text{Nitric acid}}{6HNO_3(aq)} \longrightarrow \underset{\text{Water}}{2H_2O(l)}$
$$+ \underset{\underset{\text{acid}}{\text{Sulphuric}}}{H_2SO_4(aq)} + \underset{\underset{\text{dioxide}}{\text{Nitrogen}}}{6NO_2(g)}$$

   (ii) The equation for catalytic oxidation of ammonia is:

$$\underset{\text{Ammonia}}{4NH_3} + 5O_2 \xrightarrow[700-800°C]{Pt} \underset{\text{Nitric oxide}}{4NO} + 6H_2O + \text{Heat}$$

Catalyst is a wire mesh consisting of platinum and rhodium.

   (iii) $\underset{\underset{\text{nitrate}}{\text{Potassium}}}{KNO_3(s)} + \underset{\underset{\text{acid}}{\text{Conc. sulphuric}}}{H_2SO_4(l)} \longrightarrow \underset{\text{Nitric acid}}{HNO_3(l)}$
$$+ \underset{\underset{\text{sulphate}}{\text{Potassium hydrogen}}}{KHSO_4(s)}\ (T < 200°C)$$

   (iv) Ammonia reacts with nitric acid to produce ammonium nitrate

$$\underset{\text{Ammonia}}{NH_3(g)} + \underset{\text{Nitric acid}}{HNO_3(aq)} \longrightarrow \underset{\underset{\text{nitrate}}{\text{Ammonium}}}{NH_4NO_3(s)}$$

Q. 5. **The following questions are pertaining to the laboratory preparation of hydrogen chloride gas:**
   (i) Write the equation for its preparation mentioning the condition required.
   (ii) Name the drying agent used and justify your choice.
   (iii) State a safety precaution you would take during the preparation of hydrochloric acid.
                                   [2015]

Ans. **(i)**

$$\underset{\underset{\text{chloride}}{\text{Sodium}}}{NaCl} + \underset{\underset{\text{acid (conc.)}}{\text{Sulphuric}}}{H_2SO_4} \xrightarrow{<200°C} \underset{\underset{\text{sulphate}}{\text{Sodium hydrogen}}}{NaHSO_4}$$
$$+ \underset{\text{Hydrogen chloride}}{HCl \uparrow}$$

When metal chlorides react with conc. H_2SO_4, hydrogen chloride gas is liberated. The temperature is kept less than 200°C, because if temperature increases then sodium sulphate is formed.

   (ii) It is dried by passing through conc. sulphuric acid because it does not react with hydrogen chloride gas.

   (iii) While preparing hydrochloric acid, HCl gas is dissolved in water by inverted funnel arrangement as HCl gas is highly soluble in water and causes back suction. Back suction is undesired as it breaks the apparatus. It is prevented by using funnel arrangement.

Q. 6. **State the inference drawn from the following observations:**
   (i) On carrying out the flame test with a salt P a brick red flame was obtained. What is the cation in P?
   (ii) A gas Q turns moist lead acetate paper silvery black. Identify the gas Q.
   (iii) pH of liquid R is 10. What kind of substance is R?
   (iv) Salt S is prepared by reacting dilute sulphuric acid with copper oxide. Identify S.
                                  [2014]

Ans. **(i)** Cation in P is Ca^{2+}.
   (ii) Gas Q is hydrogen sulphide (H_2S).
   (iii) Substance R is alkaline.
   (iv) Salt S is copper sulphate ($CuSO_4$).

Q. 7. **Choosing the substances from the list given below, write balanced chemical equations for the reactions which would be used in the laboratory to obtain the following salts:**

Dilute Sulphuric acid	Copper	Copper(II) carbonate
	Iron	Sodium carbonate
	Sodium	Sodium chloride
		Zinc nitrate

   (i) Sodium sulphate
   (ii) Zinc carbonate
   (iii) Copper(II) sulphate
   (iv) Iron(II) sulphate.   **[2013]**

Ans. **(i)** $\underset{\underset{\text{carbonate}}{\text{Sodium}}}{Na_2CO_3} + \underset{\underset{\text{sulphuric acid}}{\text{Dil}}}{H_2SO_4} \longrightarrow \underset{\underset{\text{sulphate}}{\text{Sodium}}}{Na_2SO_4}$
$$+ H_2O + CO_2 \uparrow$$

   (ii) $\underset{\text{Zinc nitrate}}{Zn(NO_3)_2} + \underset{\underset{\text{carbonate}}{\text{Sodium}}}{Na_2CO_3} \longrightarrow \underset{\underset{\text{carbonate}}{\text{Zinc}}}{ZnCO_3}$
$$+ \underset{\underset{\text{nitrate}}{\text{Sodium}}}{2NaNO_3}$$

(iii) $\underset{\substack{\text{Copper} \\ \text{Carbonate}}}{CuCO_3} + \underset{\substack{\text{Dil.} \\ \text{sulphuric acid}}}{H_2SO_4} \longrightarrow \underset{\substack{\text{Copper (II)} \\ \text{Sulphate}}}{CuSO_4} + H_2O + CO_2\uparrow$

(iv) $\underset{\text{Iron}}{Fe} + \underset{\substack{\text{Dil.} \\ \text{Sulphuric acid}}}{H_2SO_4} \longrightarrow \underset{\substack{\text{Iron (II)} \\ \text{sulphate}}}{FeSO_4} + H_2$

Q. 8. Identify the anion present in the following compounds:

(i) Compound X on heating with copper turnings and concentrated sulphuric acid liberates a reddish brown gas.

(ii) When a solution of compound Y is treated with silver nitrate solution a white precipitate is obtained which is soluble in excess of ammonium hydroxide solution.

(iii) Compound Z which on reacting with dilute sulphuric acid liberates a gas which turns lime water milky, but the gas has no effect on acidified potassium dichromate solution.

(iv) Compound L on reacting with barium chloride solution gives a white precipitate insoluble in dilute hydrochloric acid or dilute nitric acid. **[2012]**

Ans. (i) NO_3^- ion,   (ii) Cl^- ion,

(iii) CO_3^{2-} ion,   (iv) SO_4^{2-} ion

Q. 9. The following questions are based on the preparation of ammonia gas in the laboratory:

(i) Explain why ammonium nitrate is not used in the preparation of ammonia.

(ii) Name the compound normally used as a drying agent during the process.

(iii) How is ammonia gas collected?

(iv) Explain why it is not collected over water? **[2012]**

Ans. (i) Ammonium nitrate is not used in the preparation of ammonia because ammonium nitrate is explosive in nature and dissociates into nitrous oxide and water on heating.

(ii) Quick lime or calcium oxide (CaO).

(iii) By downward displacement of air.

(iv) Ammonia gas is not collected over water because it is highly soluble in water.

Q. 10. Refer to the flow chart diagram below and give balanced equations with conditions, if any, for the following conversions A to D.

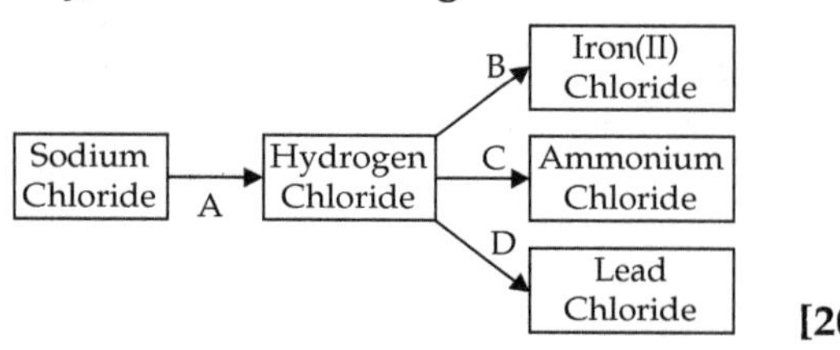

Ans. A. $\underset{\text{conc.}}{NaCl} + H_2SO_4 \xrightarrow{\Delta < 200°C} Na_2SO_4 + \underset{\text{Hydrogen chloride}}{HCl\uparrow}$

B. $2HCl(g) + Fe \longrightarrow \underset{\substack{\text{Iron (II)} \\ \text{chloride}}}{FeCl_2} + H_2\uparrow$

C. $HCl(g) + NH_3(g) \longrightarrow \underset{\text{Ammonium chloride}}{NH_4Cl}$

D. $\underset{\text{dil.}}{2HCl} + \underset{\text{aq.}}{Pb(NO_3)_2} \longrightarrow \underset{\text{Lead chloride}}{PbCl_2}\downarrow + 2HNO_3$

Q. 11. State how the following conversions can be carried out:

(i) Ethyl chloride to Ethyl alcohol.

(ii) Ethyl chloride to Ethene.

(iii) Ethene to Ethyl alcohol.

(iv) Ethyl alcohol to Ethene. **[2009]**

Ans. (i) By treating ethyl chloride with aqueous KOH.

(ii) By heating ethyl chloride with alcoholic KOH.

(iii) By passing ethene into concentrated H_2SO_4 at 80°C and high pressure.

(iv) By heating ethyl alcohol with conc. H_2SO_4 at 170°C.

Q. 12. (i) Name the process used for the large scale manufacture of sulphuric acid.

(ii) Which property of sulphuric acid accounts for its use as a dehydrating agent?

(iii) Concentrated sulphuric acid is both an oxidizing agent and a non-volatile acid. Write one equation each to illustrate the above mentioned properties of sulphuric acid. **[2006]**

Ans. (i) Contact process.

(ii) Sulphuric acid's high affinity for water accounts for its use as a dehydrating agent.

(iii) Oxidizing agent. $S + 2H_2SO_4 \xrightarrow{\text{conc.}} 3SO_2 + 2H_2O$

Non volatile acid. $2NaNO_3 + H_2SO_4 \longrightarrow Na_2SO_4 + 2HNO_3$

Q. 13. (i) Name the substance used for drying ammonia.

(ii) Write an equation to illustrate the reducing nature of ammonia.

(iii) With reference to Haber's process for the preparation of ammonia, write the equation and the conditions required. **[2006]**

Ans. (i) Quick lime.

(ii) $3CuO + 2NH_3 \longrightarrow 3Cu + N_2 + 3H_2O$

(iii) $N_2 + 3H_2 \underset{\substack{\text{Fine iron powder catalyst} \\ \text{with Mo as promoter}}}{\overset{\substack{\text{Temp. 450–500 °C and} \\ \text{Press. 200–1000 atm.}}}{\rightleftharpoons}} 2NH_3 + \Delta$

💬 Long Answer Type Questions-I

Q. 1. Certain blank spaces are left in the following table and these are labelled as A, B, C, D and E. Identify each of them

	Lab preparation of	Reactants used	Products formed	Drying agent	Method of collection
(i)	HCl gas	$NaCl^+$ H_2SO_4	A ____	conc. H_2SO_4	B ____
(ii)	NH_3 gas	C	$Mg(OH)_2$ NH_3 ____	D	E

[2017]

Ans. (i) (A) $NaHSO_4 + HCl$
   (B) Upward displacement of air
(ii) (C) $Mg_3N_2 + H_2O$
   (D) CaO
   (E) Downward displacement of air.

Q. 2. State your observation in each of the following cases:
   (i) When dilute hydrochloric acid is added to sodium carbonate crystals.
   (ii) When excess sodium hydroxide is added to calcium nitrate solution.
   (iii) At the cathode when acidified aqueous copper sulphate solution is electrolyzed with copper electrodes.
   (iv) When calcium hydroxide is heated with ammonium chloride crystals.
   (v) When moist starch iodide paper is introduced into chlorine gas. [2014]

Ans. (i) A colourless, odourless gas with brisk effervescence is evolved and when tested turns moist blue litmus red and lime water milky.
   (ii) A chalky white ppt. is obtained which is insoluble in excess sodium hydroxide.
   (iii) Cathode becomes thick due to deposition of red copper metal.
   (iv) A colourless gas with characteristic pungent smell of ammonia is evolved.
   (v) Starch iodide paper turns blue-black.

Q. 3. State the conditions required for the following reactions to take place:
   (i) Catalytic hydrogenation of ethyne.
   (ii) Preparation of ethyne from ethylene dibromide.
   (iii) Catalytic oxidiation of ammonia to nitric oxide.
   (iv) Any two conditions for the conversion of sulphur dioxide to sulphur trioxide. [2014]

Ans. (i) In the presence of catalyst like finely divided nickel, platinum, etc., and on heating upto 473 K or about 300°C hydrogenation takes place.

(ii) Hot and concentrated ethanolic solution of potassium hydroxide.
(iii) Platinum gauze is used as catalyst at 800°C in presence of oxygen.
(iv) Vanadium pentoxide acts as catalyst and temperature 450°C / 2 atm. pressure.

Q. 4. Identify the following substances which are underlined:
   (i) An alkaline gas which produces dense white fumes when reacted with hydrogen chloride gas.
   (ii) An acid which is present in vinegar.
   (iii) A gas which does not conduct electricity in the liquid state but conducts electricity when dissolved in water.
   (iv) A dilute mineral acid which forms a white precipitate when treated with barium chloride solution.
   (v) The element which has the highest ionization potential. [2013]

Ans. (i) Ammonia
   (ii) Acetic acid
   (iii) Hydrogen chloride gas
   (iv) Dilute sulphuric acid
   (v) Helium

Q. 5. Some properties of sulphuric acid are listed below. Choose the role played by sulphuric acid as A, B, C or D which is responsible for the reactions (i) to (v). Some role/s may be repeated.
   (A) Dilute acid
   (B) Dehydrating agent
   (C) Non-volatile acid
   (D) Oxidising agent.
   (i) $CuSO_4 \cdot 5H_2O \xrightarrow{\text{Conc. } H_2SO_4} CuSO_4 + 5H_2O$
   (ii) $S + H_2SO_4 \text{ (conc.)} \longrightarrow 3SO_2 + 2H_2O$
   (iii) $NaNO_3 + H_2SO_4 \text{ (conc.)} \xrightarrow{< 200°C} NaHSO_4 + HCl$
   (iv) $MgO + H_2SO_4 \longrightarrow MgSO_4 + H_2O$
   (v) $Zn + 2H_2SO_4 \text{ (conc.)} \longrightarrow ZnSO_4 + SO_2 + 2H_2O$
[2012]

Ans. (i) (B) Dehydrating agent
   (ii) (D) Oxidising agent
   (iii) (C) Non-volatile acid
   (iv) (A) Dilute acid
   (v) (D) Oxidising agent

Q. 6. Give balanced equations for the following reactions:
   (i) Dilute nitric acid and copper carbonate.
   (ii) Concentrated hydrochloric acid and potassium permanganate solution.

(iii) Ammonia and oxygen in the presence of a catalyst.

(iv) Silver nitrate solution and sodium chloride solution.

(v) Zinc sulphide and dilute sulphuric acid. **[2012]**

Ans. **(i)** $CuCO_3 + 2HNO_3 \longrightarrow Cu(NO_3)_2 + H_2O$
Copper nitrate
$+ CO_2\uparrow$

(ii) $2KMnO_4 + 16HCl \longrightarrow$
Potassium   conc.
permanganate
$2MnCl_2 + 2KCl + 8H_2O + 5Cl_2$
Manganese   Potatssium
chloride   chloride

(iii) $4NH_3 + 5O_2 \xrightarrow{Pt,\ 800°C} 4NO + 6H_2O$
Nitric oxide
$+ Heat$
Or $4NH_3 + 3O_2 \xrightarrow{Cu\ catalyst} 2N_2 + 6H_2O$

(iv) $AgNO_3 + NaCl \longrightarrow AgCl\downarrow + NaNO_3$
Silver   Silver   Sodium
nitrate   chloride   Nitrate

(v) $ZnS + H_2SO_4 \longrightarrow ZnSO_4 + H_2S\uparrow$
Zinc   Zinc   Hydrogen
sulphide   sulphate sulphide gas

Q. 7. In the laboratory preparation of hydrochloric acid, HCl gas is dissolved in water.

(i) Draw a diagram to show the arrangement used for the absorption of HCl in water.

(ii) Why is such an arrangement necessary? Give two reasons.

(iii) Write the chemical equations for the laboratory preparation of HCl gas when the reactants are:
(A) below 200°C
(B) above 200°C **[2011]**

Ans. **(i)** HCl gas

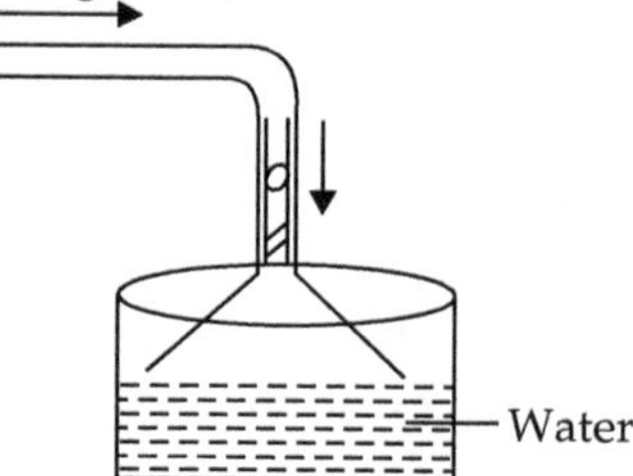

Inverted funnel arrangement.

(ii) 1. The funnel arrangement provides a large surface area, which checks back suction.

2. To check its escape in the air.

(iii) (A) $NaCl + H_2SO_4 \xrightarrow[below\ 200°C]{\Delta}$
(conc.)
$NaHSO_4 + HCl\uparrow$

(B) $NaCl + NaHSO_4 \xrightarrow{T > 200°}$
Sodium
Hydrosulphate
$Na_2SO_4(aq) + HCl\uparrow$
Sodium

sulphate

Q. 8. The diagram shows an experimental set up for the laboratory preparation of a pungent smelling gas. The gas is alkaline in nature.

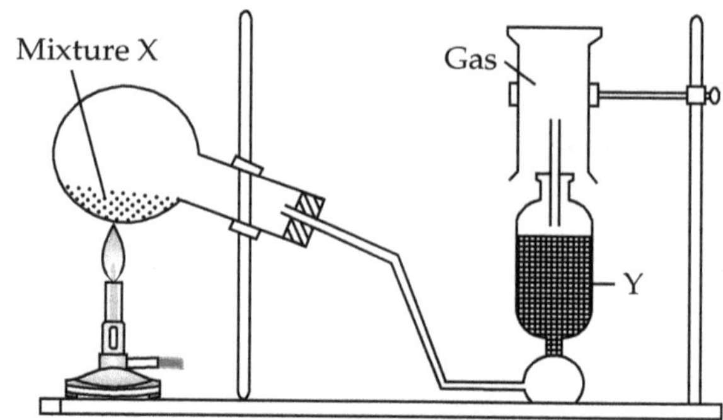

(i) Name the gas collected in the jar.

(ii) Write the balanced equation for the above preparation.

(iii) How is the gas being collected?

(iv) Name the drying agent used.

(v) How will you find that the jar is full of gas? **[2011]**

Ans. **(i)** Ammonia.

(ii) $Ca(OH)_2 + 2NH_4Cl \xrightarrow{\Delta} CaCl_2$
Calcium   Ammonium   Calcium
hydroxide   chloride   chloride
$+ 2H_2O + 2NH_3\uparrow$
Ammonia
gas

(iii) By downward displacement of air because it is lighter than air.

(iv) Quick lime (CaO).

(v) By bringing a wet red litmus paper near the brim (mouth) of the gas jar. When jar is full of gas, litmus will turn blue.

Q. 9. **(i)** With the help of equations, give an outline for the manufacture of sulphuric acid by the contact process.

(ii) What property of sulphuric acid is shown by the reaction of concentrated sulphuric acid when heated with
(A) Potassium nitrate
(B) Carbon? **[2011]**

Ans. **(i)** $S + O_2 \longrightarrow SO_2$
Sulphur
dioxide
$2SO_2 + O_2 \xrightarrow[450°C]{V_2O_5} 2SO_3$
Sulphur   Sulphur
dioxide   trioxide
$SO_3 + H_2SO_4 \longrightarrow H_2S_2O_7$
(Conc.)   Oleum
$H_2S_2O_7 + H_2O \longrightarrow 2H_2SO_4$
Sulphuric acid

(ii) (A) Less volatile nature.
(B) Oxidising property.

Q. 10. Give the equation for the preparation of each of the following salts from the starting material given:
  (i) Copper sulphate from copper(II) oxide.
  (ii) Iron(III) chloride from Iron.
  (iii) Potassium sulphate from potassium hydroxide solution.
  (iv) Lead chloride from lead carbonate (two equations). **[2010]**

Ans. (i) $CuO + H_2SO_4 \longrightarrow CuSO_4 + H_2O$
Copper
sulphate
(Neutralisation acid of acid on insoluble oxides)

(ii) $2Fe + 3Cl_2 \longrightarrow 2FeCl_3$
Iron (III) chloride
(direct combination)

(iii) $2KOH + H_2SO_4 \longrightarrow K_2SO_4 + 2H_2O$
Potassium
Sulphate
(Titration)

(iv) $PbCO_3 + 2HNO_3 \longrightarrow Pb(NO_3)_2 + H_2O$
Lead nitrate
$+ CO_2$
$Pb(NO_3)_2 + 2HCl \longrightarrow PbCl_2 + 2HNO_3$
Lead chloride

Q. 11. Give the equations for the following conversions A to E.

$$ZnSO_4 \xrightarrow{A} ZnSO_3 \xrightarrow{B} Zn(NO_3)_2$$

with $\xrightarrow{E}$ from ZnO, $\xrightarrow{C}$ to Zn(OH)$_2$, and $ZnO \xleftarrow{D} Zn(OH)_2$ **[2010]**

Ans. (A) $ZnSO_4 + Na_2CO_3 \longrightarrow ZnCO_3 + Na_2SO_4$
(B) $ZnCO_3 + 2HNO_3 \longrightarrow Zn(NO_3)_2 + H_2O + CO_2 \uparrow$
(C) $Zn(NO_3)_2 + 2NaOH \longrightarrow Zn(OH)_2 + 2NaNO_3$
(D) $Zn(OH)_2 \xrightarrow{\Delta} ZnO + H_2O$
(E) $ZnO + H_2SO_4 \longrightarrow ZnSO_4 + H_2O$

Q. 12. Write the equation for each of the following reactions:
  (i) Sulphur is heated with concentrated sulphuric acid.
  (ii) Zinc oxide is treated with sodium hydroxide solution.
  (iii) Ammonium chloride is heated with sodium hydroxide.
  (iv) Concentrated sulphuric acid is poured over sugar.
  (v) Magnesium sulphate solution is mixed with barium chloride solution. **[2010]**

Ans. (i) $S + 2H_2SO_4 \longrightarrow 2H_2O + 3SO_2$
Sulphur dioxide

(ii) $ZnO + 2NaOH \longrightarrow Na_2ZnO_2 + H_2O$
Sodium zincate

(iii) $NH_4Cl + NaOH \longrightarrow NaCl + H_2O + NH_3 \uparrow$
Sodium
chloride

(iv) $C_{12}H_{22}O_{11} \xrightarrow[\text{Conc.}]{H_2SO_4} 12C + 11H_2O$
Carbon

(v) $MgSO_4 + BaCl_2 \longrightarrow MgCl_2 + BaSO_4$

Q. 13. The questions below are related to the manufacture of ammonia.
  (i) Name the process.
  (ii) In what ratio must the reactants be taken?
  (iii) Name the catalyst used.
  (iv) Give the equation for the manufacture of ammonia.
  (v) Ammonia can act as a reducing agent — write a relevant equation for such a reaction. **[2010]**

Ans. (i) Haber's process.
(ii) Nitrogen one part, hydrogen three parts.
(iii) Iron and molybdenum.
(iv) $N_2 + 3H_2 \longrightarrow 2NH_3 + Heat$
(v) $2NH_3 + 3CuO \longrightarrow 3Cu + 3H_2O + N_2 \uparrow$
Copper Copper
oxide

Q. 14. The diagram shows an apparatus for the laboratory preparation of hydrogen chloride.

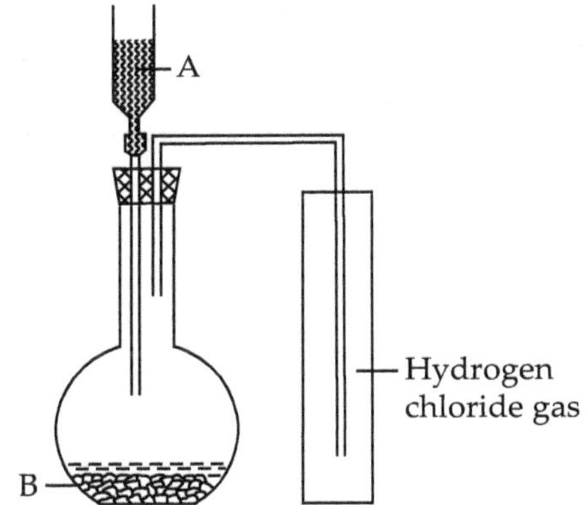

(i) Identify A and B.
(ii) Write the equation for the reaction.
(iii) How would you check whether or not the gas jar is filled with hydrogen chloride?
(iv) What does the method of collection tell you about the density of hydrogen chloride? **[2010]**

Ans. (i) $A \longrightarrow$ Conc. H_2SO_4, $B \longrightarrow NaCl$
(ii) $NaCl + H_2SO_4 \xrightarrow{< 200°C} NaHSO_4 + HCl \uparrow$
Sodium hydrogen
sulphate

(iii) If a moist blue litmus paper is brought near the mouth of gas jar turns red, the gas jar is filled with HCl.

(iv) Hydrogen chloride is denser than air.

Q. 15. Write a fully balanced equation for each of the following cases:

(i) Red lead is warmed with concentrated hydrochloric acid.

(ii) Magnesium metal is treated with dilute hydrochloric acid.

(iii) Magnesium nitride is treated with warm water.

(iv) Acetic acid is warmed with ethanol in the presence of concentrated sulphuric acid. **[2009]**

Ans. **(i)** $Pb_3O_4 + 8HCl \longrightarrow 3PbCl_2 + 4H_2O + Cl_2$

(ii) $Mg + 2HCl \longrightarrow MgCl_2 + H_2 \uparrow$
Magnesium chloride

(iii) $Mg_3N_2 + 6H_2O \longrightarrow 3Mg(OH)_2 + 2NH_3$
Magnesium hydroxide

(iv) $C_2H_5OH + CH_3COOH \xrightarrow[\Delta]{conc.\ H_2SO_4}$
$$CH_3COOC_2H_5 + H_2O$$
Ethyl acetate

Q. 16. Find the odd one out and explain at your choice. (note: valency is not a criterion):

(i) $Al(OH)_3$, $Pb(OH)_2$, $Mg(OH)_2$, $Zn(OH)_2$

(ii) C_3H_8, C_5H_{10}, C_2H_6, CH_4

(iii) Sulphur, Phosphorus, Carbon, Iodine

(iv) Copper, Lead, Zinc, Mercury

(v) Formic acid, Nitric acid, Acetic acid, Propanoic acid. **[2009]**

Ans. **(i)** $Mg(OH)_2$: It is basic while rest are amphoteric.

(ii) C_5H_{10}: It is an alkene while rest are alkanes.

(iii) Carbon: It forms very large number of compounds while rest do not.

(iv) Mercury: It is a liquid metal while rest are solid.

(v) Nitric acid: It is a mineral acid while the rest are organic acids.

Q. 17. Identify the substances P, Q, R, S and T in each case based on the information given below:

(i) The deliquescent salt P, turns yellow on dissolving in water, and gives a reddish brown precipitate with sodium hydroxide solution.

(ii) The white crystalline solid Q is soluble in water. It liberates a pungent smelling gas when heated with sodium hydroxide solution.

(iii) The pale green solid R turns reddish brown on heating. Its aqueous solution gives a white precipitate with barium chloride solution. The precipitate is insoluble in mineral acids.

(iv) The reddish brown liquid S is dissolved in water. When Ethyne gas is passed through it, turns colourless.

(v) The nitrate T does not leave any residue on heating. **[2009]**

Ans. **(i)** P is Ferric chloride

(ii) Q is an Ammonium salt

(iii) R is Ferrous sulphate

(iv) S is Bromine

(v) T is Ammonium nitrate

Q. 18. The diagram given below is to prepare Iron (III) chloride in the laboratory:

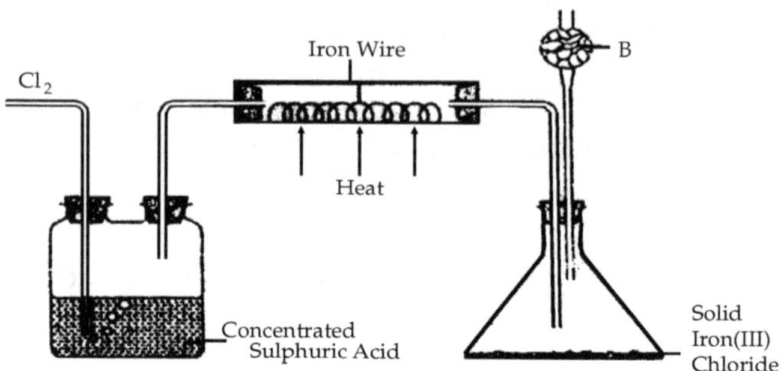

(i) What is substance B?

(ii) What is the purpose of B?

(iii) Why is iron (III) chloride to be stored in a closed container?

(iv) Write the equation for the reaction between iron and chlorine. **[2009]**

Ans. **(i)** B is a drying agent like anhydrous calcium chloride.

(ii) B absorbs moisture from the receiver.

(iii) Because iron (III) chloride is deliquescent.

(iv) $2Fe + 3Cl_2 \longrightarrow 2FeCl_3$
Ferric chloride

Q. 19. Identify the following substances:

(i) An alkaline gas A which gives dense white fumes with hydrogen chloride.

(ii) A dilute acid B which does not normally give hydrogen when reacted with metals but does give a gas when it reacts with copper.

(iii) Gas C has an offensive smell like rotten eggs.

(iv) Gas D is a colourless gas which can be used as a bleaching agent.

(v) Liquid E can be dehydrated to produce ethene. **[2008]**

Ans. **(i)** A is Ammonia gas.

(ii) B is dilute nitric acid.

(iii) C is Hydrogen sulphide

(v) E is Ethanol.

Q. 20. **(i)** What is the property of concentrated sulphuric acid which allows it to be used in the preparation of hydrogen chloride and nitric acid?

(ii) What property of hydrogen chloride is demonstrated when it is collected by downward delivery (upward displacement)?

(iii) Why is hydrogen chloride not collected over water?

(iv) What is the property of nitric acid which allows it to react with copper?

(v) What property of concentrated sulphuric acid is in action when sugar turns black in its presence? **[2008]**

Ans. **(i)** It is a non-volatile acid.

(ii) It is denser than air.

(iii) Because it is highly soluble in water.

(iv) Oxidising property.

(v) Dehydrating property.

Q. 21. Write the equations for the following reactions:

(i) Dilute nitric acid and copper.

(ii) Dilute sulphuric acid and barium chloride.

(iii) Dilute hydrochloric acid and sodium thiosulphate.

(iv) Dilute hydrochloric acid and lead nitrate solution.

(v) Dilute sulphuric acid and sodium sulphide. **[2008]**

Ans. **(i)** $3Cu + 8HNO_3 \longrightarrow 3Cu(NO_3)_2 + 4H_2O + 2NO$
Copper (II) nitrate

(ii) $H_2SO_4 + BaCl_2 \longrightarrow BaSO_4 + 2HCl$
Barium Sulphate

(iii) $2HCl + Na_2S_2O_3 \longrightarrow 2NaCl + SO_2 + H_2O + S$

(iv) $2HCl + Pb(NO_3)_2 \longrightarrow PbCl_2 + 2HNO_3$
Lead chloride

(v) $H_2SO_4 + Na_2S \longrightarrow H_2S + Na_2SO_4.$

Q. 22. Some properties of Sulphuric acid are listed below. Choose the property A, B, C or D which is responsible for the reactions (i) to (v). Some properties may be repeated:

A. Acid

B. Dehydrating agent

C. Non-volatile acid

D. Oxidizing agent

(i) $C_{12}H_{22}O_{11} + nH_2SO_4 \longrightarrow 12C + 11H_2O + nH_2SO_4$

(ii) $S + 2H_2SO_4 \longrightarrow 3SO_2 + 2H_2O$

(iii) $NaCl + H_2SO_4 \longrightarrow NaHSO_4 + HCl$

(iv) $CuO + H_2SO_4 \longrightarrow CuSO_4 + H_2O$

(v) $Na_2CO_3 + H_2SO_4 \longrightarrow Na_2SO_4 + H_2O + CO_2$ **[2007]**

Ans. **(i)** B, **(ii)** D, **(iii)** C, **(iv)** A and **(v)** A

Q. 23. Write balanced equation for the following reactions:

(i) Lead sulphate from lead nitrate solution and dilute sulphuric acid.

(ii) Copper sulphate from copper and concentrated sulphuric acid.

(iii) Lead chloride from lead nitrate solution and sodium chloride solution.

(iv) Ammonium sulphate from ammonia and dilute sulphuric acid.

(v) Sodium chloride from sodium carbonate solution and dilute hydrochloric acid. **[2007]**

Ans. **(i)** $Pb(NO_3)_2 + H_2SO_4 \longrightarrow PbSO_4 + 2HNO_3$
Lead sulphate

(ii) $Cu + 2H_2SO_4 \longrightarrow CuSO_4 + SO_2 + 2H_2O$
Copper sulphate

(iii) $Pb(NO_3)_2 + 2NaCl \longrightarrow PbCl_2 + 2NaNO_3$
Lead chloride

(iv) $2NH_3 + H_2SO_4 \longrightarrow (NH_4)_2SO_4$
Ammonium Sulphate

(v) $Na_2CO_3 + 2HCl \longrightarrow 2NaCl + CO_2 + H_2O$

Q. 24. Write balanced equations for the reaction of dilute hydrochloric acid with each of the following:

(i) Iron

(ii) Sodium hydrogen carbonate

(iii) Iron (II) sulphide

(iv) Sodium sulphite

(v) Sodium thiosulphate solution. **[2007]**

Ans. **(i)** $Fe + 2HCl \longrightarrow FeCl_2 + H_2$
Iron (II) chloride

(ii) $NaHCO_3 + HCl \longrightarrow NaCl + H_2O + CO_2$

(iii) $FeS + 2HCl \longrightarrow FeCl_2 + H_2S$

(iv) $Na_2SO_3 + 2HCl \longrightarrow 2NaCl + SO_2 + H_2O$

(v) $Na_2S_2O_3 + 2HCl \longrightarrow 2NaCl + H_2O + SO_2 + S.$

Q. 25. The figure given below illustrates the apparatus used in the laboratory preparation of nitric acid.

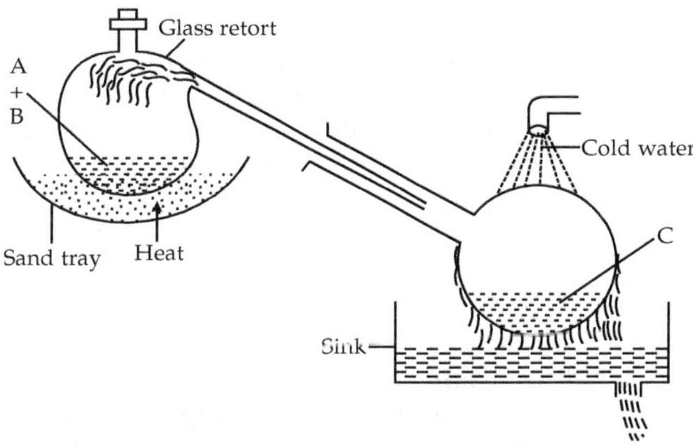

(i) Name A (a liquid), B (a solid) and C (a liquid). (Do not give the formulae)

(ii) Write an equation to show how nitric acid undergoes decomposition.

(iii) Write the equation for the reaction in which copper is oxidized by concentrated nitric acid. **[2007]**

Ans. **(i)** A-Conc. Sulphuric acid, B-Potassium nitrate or Sodium nitrate, C-Nitric acid.

(ii) $4HNO_3 \longrightarrow 2H_2O + 4NO_2 + O_2$

(iii) $Cu + 4HNO_3 \longrightarrow Cu(NO_3)_2 + 2H_2O + 2NO_2$
Copper (II) nitrate

Q. 26. **The following is an extract from 'Metals in the Service of Man. Alexander and Street/ Pelican 1976'.**

"Alumina (aluminium oxide) has a very high melting point of over 2,000°C so that it cannot readily be liquefied. However, conversion of alumina to aluminium and oxygen, by electrolysis, can occur when it is dissolved in some other substance.'

(i) **Which solution is used to react with bauxite as a first step in obtaining pure aluminium oxide?**

(ii) **The aluminium oxide for the electrolytic extraction of aluminium is obtained by heating aluminium hydroxide. Write the equation for this reaction.**

(iii) **Name the element which serves both as the anode and the cathode in the extraction of aluminium.**

(iv) **Write the equation for the reaction that occurs at the cathode during the extraction of aluminium by electrolysis.**

(v) **Give the equation for the reaction which occurs at the anode when aluminium is purified by electrolysis.** **[2007]**

Ans. **(i)** Sodium hydroxide

(ii) $2Al(OH)_3 \xrightarrow[1500°C]{\Delta} Al_2O_3 + 3H_2O$

(iii) Carbon

(iv) $[Al^{3+} + 3e^- \longrightarrow Al] \times 2$

(v) $Al - 3e^- \longrightarrow Al^{3+}$

Q. 27. **(i)** **HCl, HNO$_3$ and H$_2$SO$_4$ are the formulae of three compounds. Which of these compounds has the highest boiling point and which has the lowest?**

(ii) **Dilute hydrochloric acid and dilute sulphuric acid are both colourless solutions. How will the addition of barium chloride solution to each help to distinguish between the two?**

(iii) **You enter in a laboratory after a Class has completed the Fountain Experiment. How will you be able to tell whether the gas used in the experiment was hyrdogen chloride or ammonia?** **[2007]**

Ans. **(i)** Hydrochloric Acid has the lowest and sulphuric acid has the highest boiling point.

(ii) Dilute sulphuric acid will give a white precipitate of barium sulphate with barium chloride solution whereas no visible reaction occurs with dilute hydrochloric acid.

(iii) Hydrogen chloride has a choking smell whereas ammonia has characteristic pungent smell. If the gas is hydrogen chloride, solution in flask will be red and if the gas is ammonia, solution in flask will be blue.

Q. 28. **Select from the list given below (A to F), the one substance in each case which matches the descriptions given in parts (ii) to (vi). Copy and complete the given grid with your answers as shown for part (i).**

(i)	(ii)	(iii)	(iv)	(v)	(vi)
A					

A Ammonia

B Copper oxide

C Copper sulphate

D Hydrogen chloride

E Lead bromide

(i) **Although this compound is not a metal hydroxide, its aqueous solution is alkaline in nature.**

(ii) **A solution of this compound is used as the electrolyte when copper is purified.**

(iii) **When this compound is electrolysed in the molten state, lead is obtained at the cathode.**

(iv) **This compound can be oxidized to chlorine.**

(v) **This compound can be reduced to copper when heated with coke.** **[2006]**

Ans.

(i)	(ii)	(iii)	(iv)	(vi)
A	C	E	D	B

Q. 29. **Match the following:**

	Column A		Column B
1.	A substance that turns moist starch iodide paper blue.	A.	Ammonium sulphate
2.	A compound which releases a reddish brown gas on reaction with concentrated sulphuric acid and copper turnings.	B.	Lead carbonate
3.	A solution of this compound gives a dirty green precipitate with sodium hydroxide.	C.	Chlorine

| 4. | A compound which on heating with sodium hydroxide produces a gas which forms dense white fumes with hydrogen chloride. | D. | Copper nitrate |
| 5. | A white solid which gives a yellow residue on heating. | E. | Ferrous sulphate |

[2006]

Ans.

Column A	1	2	3	4	5
Column B	C	D	E	A	B

Q. 30. State what is observed when:
   (i) Copper sulphate solution is electrolysed using a platinum anode.
   (ii) Hydrochloric acid is added to silver nitrate solution.
   (iii) Nitric acid is kept in a reagent bottle for a long time.
   (iv) Excess of ammonia is passed through an aqueous solution of lead nitrate.

[2006]

Ans.   **(i)** Blue colour of the solution disappears.

   (ii) A curdy white precipitate is seen.

   (iii) Brown vapours are seen in the bottle and the nitric acid turns yellowish in colour.

   (iv) A white ppt. which remains insoluble in excess of ammonia.

 **Long Answer Type Questions-II**

Q. 1. Copy and complete the following table relating to important industrial processes. Output refers to the product of the process not the intermediate steps.

Name of Process	Inputs	Catalyst	Equation for catalyzed reaction	Output
Haber Process	Hydrogen + ______			
	Ammonia + air			Nitric acid
Contact Process	Sulphur dioxide + oxygen			

[2008]

Ans.

Name of Process	Inputs	Catalyst	Equation for catalyzed reaction	Output
Haber Process	Hydrogen + Nitrogen	Iron powder	$3H_2 + N_2 \xrightleftharpoons{\text{Fe powder}} 2NH_3$	Ammonia
Ostwald's Process	Ammonia + Air	Platinum	$4NH_3 + 5O_2 \xrightarrow{\text{Pt}} 4NO + 6H_2O$	Nitric acid
Contact Process	Sulphur dioxide + Oxygen	V_2O_5	$2SO_2 + O_2 \xrightleftharpoons{V_2O_5} 2SO_3$	Sulphuric acid

Organic Chemistry

Short Answer Type Questions-I

Q. 1. Draw the structural formula for each of the following:
1. 2, 3-dimethyl butane
2. diethyl ether
3. propanoic acid [2017]

Ans. (1) 2, 3-dimethyl butane

$$H-\underset{\underset{H}{|}}{\overset{\overset{H}{|}}{C}}-\underset{\underset{CH_3}{|}}{\overset{\overset{H}{|}}{C}}-\underset{\underset{CH_3}{|}}{\overset{\overset{H}{|}}{C}}-\underset{\underset{H}{|}}{\overset{\overset{H}{|}}{C}}-H$$

(2) Diethyl ether

$$H-\overset{\overset{H}{|}}{\underset{\underset{H}{|}}{C}}-\overset{\overset{H}{|}}{\underset{\underset{H}{|}}{C}}-O-\overset{\overset{H}{|}}{\underset{\underset{H}{|}}{C}}-\overset{\overset{H}{|}}{\underset{\underset{H}{|}}{C}}-H$$

(3) Propanoic acid

$$H-\overset{\overset{H}{|}}{\underset{\underset{H}{|}}{C}}-\overset{\overset{H}{|}}{\underset{\underset{H}{|}}{C}}-C\overset{O}{\underset{OH}{}}$$

Q. 2. Equation for the reaction when compound A is bubbled through bromine dissolved in carbon tetrachloride is as follows:

$$A \xrightarrow{Br_2/CCl_4} \begin{array}{c} CH_2Br \\ | \\ CH_2Br \end{array}$$

(i) Draw the structure of A.
(ii) State your observation during this reaction. [2016]

Ans. (i)

$$H-\overset{\overset{H}{|}}{C}=\overset{\overset{H}{|}}{C}-H$$

(ii) Bromine solution in CCl_4 has an reddish-brown colour. When added dropwise to ethene, the reddish-brown colour of bromine disappears, due to the formation of the colourless ethylene dibromide.

$$\underset{H}{\overset{H}{}}\!\!C=C\!\!\underset{H}{\overset{H}{}} + Br_2 \xrightarrow{CCl_4} H-\overset{\overset{H}{|}}{\underset{\underset{Br}{|}}{C}}-\overset{\overset{H}{|}}{\underset{\underset{Br}{|}}{C}}-H$$

(Ethene) (Bromine solution) (Ethylene Dibromide) [Colourless]

Q. 3. Using their structural formulae identify the functional group by circling them:
(i) Dimethyl ether   (ii) Propanone. [2015]

Ans. (i)

$$H-\overset{\overset{H}{|}}{\underset{\underset{H}{|}}{C}}-\boxed{O}-\overset{\overset{H}{|}}{\underset{\underset{H}{|}}{C}}-H$$

Functional Group

(ii)

$$H-\overset{\overset{H}{|}}{\underset{\underset{H}{|}}{C}}-\overset{\overset{O}{\parallel}}{C}-\overset{\overset{H}{|}}{\underset{\underset{H}{|}}{C}}-H$$

Functional Group

Q. 4. Draw the structural formula for each of the following:
(i) Ethanoic acid   (ii) But-2-yne [2010]

Ans. (i)

$$H-\overset{\overset{H}{|}}{\underset{\underset{H}{|}}{C}}-\overset{\overset{O}{\parallel}}{C}-OH$$

Ethanoic acid

(ii)

$$H-\overset{\overset{H}{|}}{\underset{\underset{H}{|}}{C}}-C\equiv C-\overset{\overset{H}{|}}{\underset{\underset{H}{|}}{C}}-H$$

But-2-yne

Q. 5. (i) Write the equation(s) for the reaction(s) to prepare lead sulphate from lead carbonate.

(ii) Methane is the first member of alkane, when it is treated with excess of chlorine in the presence of diffused sunlight forms carbon tetra-chloride. Draw the appropriate structural formula of carbon tetra-chloride and state the type of bond present in it. [2009]

Ans. (i) $PbCO_3 + 2HNO_3 \longrightarrow Pb(NO_3)_2 + H_2O + CO_2$

$Pb(NO_3)_2 + H_2SO_4 \longrightarrow PbSO_4 + 2HNO_3$
Lead sulphate

(ii)

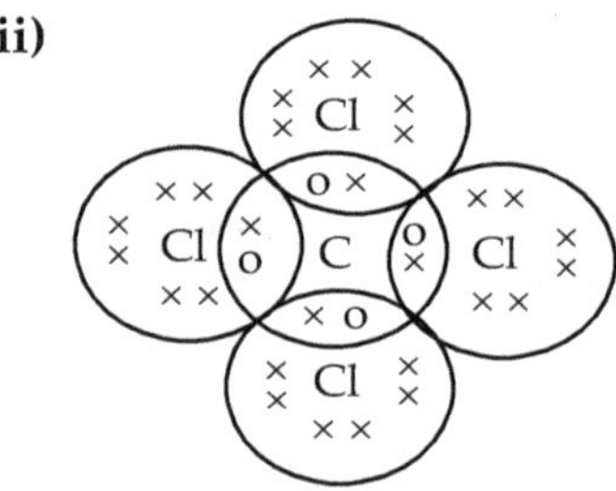

Structural formula of CCl_4. The type of bond present in CCl_4 is covalent bond.

Q. 6. **(i)** Define isomerism.

(ii) Give the IUPAC name of the isomer C_4H_{10} which has a branched chain.

[2009]

Ans. **(i)** **Isomerism:** When two or more compounds having the same molecular formula but different arrangement of atoms in space are called isomers and the phenomenon is called isomerism.

(ii) IUPAC name of branched isomer of butane is 2-methyl propane

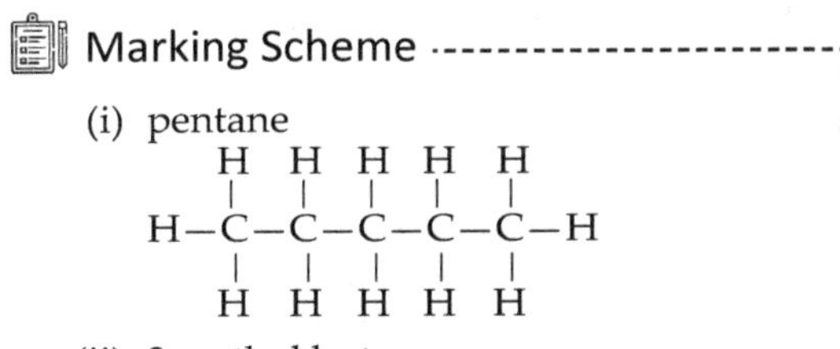

Q. 7. Distinguish between the saturated hydrocarbon ethane and the unsaturated hydrocarbon ethene by drawing their structural formulae. **[2008]**

Ans. Ethane has single covalent bond between two carbon atoms while ethene has a double covalent bond.

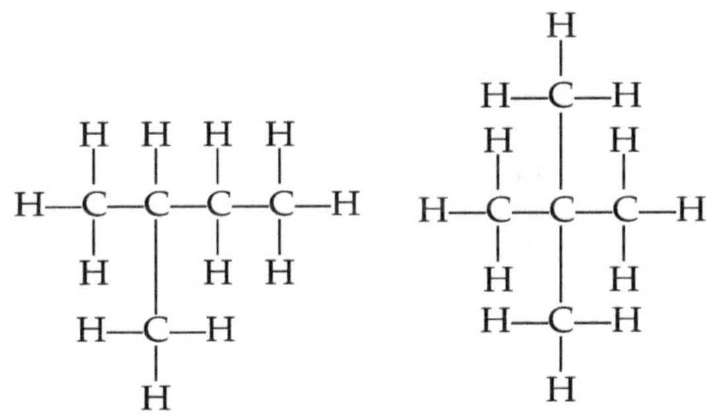

Q. 8. Addition reactions and substitution reactions are types of organic reactions. Which type of reaction is shown by:

(i) ethane   **(ii)** ethene   **[2008]**

Ans. **(i)** Substitution reaction.

(ii) Addition reaction.

Short Answer Type Questions-II

Q. 1. Draw the structures of isomers of pentane. **[2020]**

> **Marking Scheme**
>
> (i) pentane
>
> (ii) 2 methyl butane
>
> (iii) 2, 2 dimethyl propane

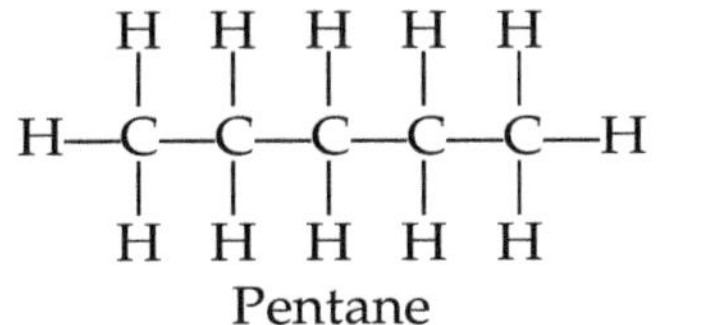

Q. 2. Write a balanced chemical equation for the preparation of

(i) Ethene from bromoethane.

(ii) Ethyne using calcium carbide.

(iii) Methane from sodium acetate. **[2019]**

> **Marking Scheme**
>
> (i) $C_2H_5Br + KOH \longrightarrow C_2H_4 + KBr + H_2O$
>   (alc.)
> (ii) $CaC_2 + 2H_2O \longrightarrow C_2H_2 + Ca(OH)_2$
> (iii) $CH_3COONa + NaOH \longrightarrow CH_4 + Na_2CO_3$

Ans. Structures of isomers of pentane are as follows :

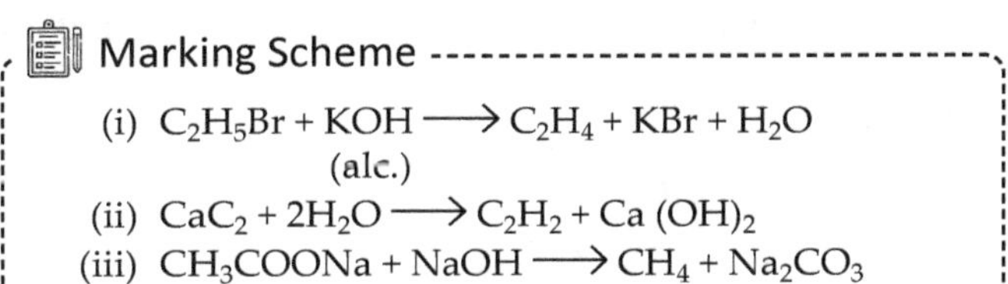

Ans. **(i)** Ethene from bromoethane

$H_2CBr\text{-}CH_3 + KOH \longrightarrow$

Bromoethane $H_2C{=}CH_2 + KBr + H_2O$

                    Ethene

(ii) Ethyne using calcium carbide

$CaC_2 + 2H_2O \longrightarrow HC \equiv CH + Ca(OH)_2$

Calcium   Ethyne

Carbide

(iii) Methane from sodium acetate

$$CH_3COONa + NaOH \xrightarrow[CaO]{\Delta} CH_4 + Na_2CO_3$$

Sodium   Sodium   Methane Sodium
acetate   Hydroxide   carbonate

Q. 3. **Identify the substances underlined.**

(i) The <u>catalyst</u> used to oxidise ammonia.

(ii) The <u>organic compound</u> which when solidified, forms an ice like mass.

(iii) The <u>dilute acid</u> which is an oxidizing agent. **[2019]**

📋 Marking Scheme

(i) Platinum or Pt.
(ii) Acetic acid or ethonoic acid or CH_3COOH
(iii) HNO_3 or nitric acid

Ans. **(i)** Platinum

(ii) Acetic acid or ethanoic acid (CH_3COOH)

(iii) Dilute nitric acid

Q. 4. **Give a balanced chemical equation for each of the following:**

(i) Preparation of ethane from sodium propionate.

(ii) Action of alcoholic KOH on bromoethane. **[2017]**

Ans. **(i)** $C_2H_5COONa + NaOH \xrightarrow[\Delta]{CaO} C_2H_6$

Sodium   Sodium   Ethane
propionate hydroxide

$$+ Na_2CO_3$$

Sodium
carbonate

(ii) $CH_3CH_2Br + alc. KOH \xrightarrow{\Delta} C_2H_4$

Bromo ethane   Ethene

$$+ KBr \qquad + H_2O$$

Potassium Bromide

Q. 5. **Give the structural formulae of each of the following:**

(i) 2-methyl propane

(ii) Ethanoic acid

(iii) Butan-2-o1 **[2016]**

Ans. **(i)** 2-methyl propane

(ii) Ethanoic acid

(iii) Butan-2-ol

Q. 6. **Give balanced chemical equations for the following conversions:**

(i) Ethanoic acid to ethyl ethanoate.

(ii) Calcium carbide to ethyne

(iii) Sodium ethanoate to methane. **[2015]**

Ans. **(i)** $CH_3COOH(l) + C_2H_5OH(l)$

Ethanoic acid   Ethanol

$$\xrightarrow{Conc.\ H_2SO_4} CH_3COOC_2H_5(l) + H_2O(l)$$

Ethyl ethanoate   Water
(ester)

(ii) $CaC_2(s) + 2H_2O(l) \longrightarrow Ca(OH)_2(s)$

Calcium   Calcium
carbide   hydroxide

$$+ C_2H_2(g)$$

Ethyne

(iii) $CH_3COONa(s) + NaOH(s) \xrightarrow[300°C]{CaO}$

Sodium   Sodium
ethanoate   hydroxide
(from soda lime)

$$Na_2CO_3(s) \quad + \quad CH_4(g)$$

Sodium   Methane
carbonate

Q. 7. **Name the kind of particles present in:**

(i) Sodium Hydroxide solution.

(ii) Carbonic acid.

(iii) Sugar solution. **[2014]**

Ans. **(i)** NaOH-Ions only.

(ii) Carbonic acid-Ions and molecules both.

(iii) Sugar solution-Molecules only.

Q. 8. **Give the structural formulae for the following:**

(i) An isomer of *n*-butane.

(ii) 2-propanol.

(iii) Diethyl ether. **[2013]**

Ans. **(i)**

2-methyl propane (an isomer of *n*-butane)

(ii)

2-propanol

(iii)

Diethyl ether

Q. 9. **Give reasons for the following:**

(i) Methane does not undergo addition reactions, but ethene does.

(ii) Ethyne is more reactive than ethane.

(iii) Hydrocarbons are excellent fuels.

[2013]

Ans. **(i)** Methane does not undergo addition reaction but ethene does because methane is saturated hydrocarbon while ethene is an unsaturated hydrocarbon. Addition reactions are characteristic properties of unsaturated hydrocarbons.

(ii) Ethane is a saturated hydrocarbon, while ethyne is an unsaturated hydrocarbon with triple bond which can undergo addition reaction, hence is more reactive than ethane.

(iii) Hydrocarbons are excellent fuels because they ignite easily at low temperature and liberate large amount of heat without leaving any residue.

Q. 10. Write the equation for the following reactions:

(i) Calcium carbide and water.

(ii) Ethene and water (steam)

(iii) Bromoethane and an aqueous solution of sodium hydroxide. **[2008]**

Ans. **(i)** $CaC_2 + 2H_2O \longrightarrow C_2H_2 + Ca(OH)_2$
   ethene

(ii) $C_2H_4 + H_2O \longrightarrow C_2H_5OH$
   ethanol

(iii) $C_2H_5Br + NaOH(aq) \longrightarrow C_2H_5OH + NaBr$
   ethanol

Q. 11. Give the correct IUPAC name and the functional group for each of the compounds whose structural formulae are given below:

[2006]

(i)

$$
\begin{array}{ccc}
 & H & H & O \\
 & | & | & \| \\
H- & C- & C- & C-H \\
 & | & | & \\
 & H & H &
\end{array}
$$

(ii)

$$
\begin{array}{cccc}
 & H & H & H \\
 & | & | & | \\
H- & C- & C- & C-OH \\
 & | & | & | \\
 & H & H & H
\end{array}
$$

Ans. **(i)** IUPAC name $\longrightarrow$ Propanal
   Functional group $\longrightarrow$ – CHO

(ii) IUPAC name $\longrightarrow$ Propanol
   Functional group $\longrightarrow$ – OH

Q. 12. **(i) Draw the structural formulae of the two isomers of Butane. Give the correct IUPAC name of each isomer.**

(ii) State one use of acetylene. **[2006]**

Ans. **(i)** IUPAC name – normal butane

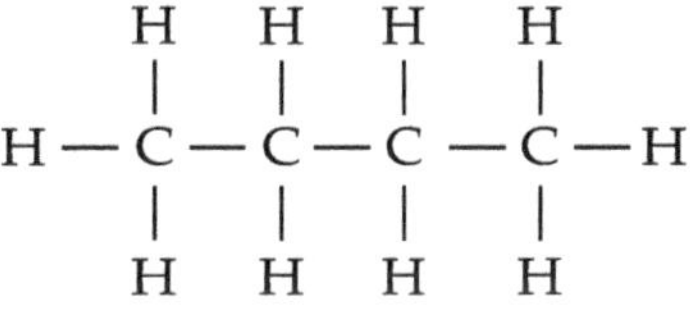

IUPAC name – 2 methyl propane

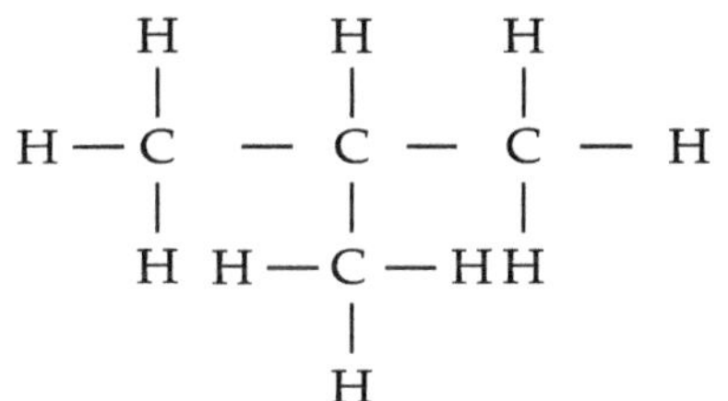

(ii) Artificial ripening of fruits.

Short Answer Type Questions-III

Q. 1. **Copy and complete the following paragraph using the options given in brackets :**

Alkenes are a homologous series of **(i)** .... **(saturated / unsaturated)** hydrocarbons characterised by the general formula **(ii)** .... **(C_nH_{2n+2}/C_nH_{2n}).** Alkenes undergo **(iii)** .... **(addition/ substitution)** reactions and also undergo **(iv)** .... **(hydrogenation / dehydrogenation)** to form alkanes. **[2020]**

Marking Scheme

(i) Unsaturated
(ii) C_nH_{2n}
(iii) Addition
(iv) Hydrogenation

Ans. **(i)** unsaturated

(ii) C_nH_{2n}

(iii) addition

(iv) hydrogenation

Q. 2. **Name the following organic compounds:**

(i) The compound with 3 carbon atoms functional group is a carboxyl.

(ii) The first homologue whose general formula is C_nH_{2n}.

(iii) The compound that reacts with acetic acid to form ethyl ethanoate.

(iv) The compound formed by complete chlorination of ethyne. **[2019]**

 **Marking Scheme**

(i) Propanoic acid
(ii) Ethene or ethylene
(iii) Ethanol or ethyl alcohol
(iv) 1, 1, 2, 2 – tetra chloro ethane

Ans. (i) The compound with three carbon atoms whose functional group is carboxyl-

Propanoic acid, CH_3CH_2COOH

(ii) The first homologue whose general formula is C_nH_{2n} is C_2H_4 that is Ethene.

(iii) The compound that reacts with acetic acid to form ethyl ethanoate is ethanol-

$$H_3C-\overset{\displaystyle O}{\underset{\displaystyle OH}{C}} + C_2H_5OH \longrightarrow H_3C-\overset{\displaystyle O}{\underset{\displaystyle OC_2H_5}{C}}$$

Ethanoic acid   Ethyl ethanoate
(acetic acid)

(iv) The compound formed by complete chlorination of ethyne is tetrachloroethane, $C_2H_2Cl_4$.

Q. 3. A compound X (having vinegar like smell) when treated with ethanol in the presence of the acid Z, gives a compound Y which has a fruity smell. The reaction is:

$$C_2H_5OH + X \xrightarrow{Z} Y + H_2O$$

(i) Identify Y and Z.
(ii) Write the structural formula of X.
(iii) Name the above reaction. **[2018]**

Ans. (i) Compound X is acetic acid (CH_3COOH) as it has vinegar like smell. Compound Y is a ester *i.e.*, $CH_3COOC_2H_5$ ethyl ethanoate.
Z is a protic acid for example HCl (aq) or conc. H_2SO_4.

(ii) The structural formula of X is CH_3COOH acetic acid.

(iii) The above reaction is known as 'Esterification' reaction.

$$\underset{\text{Ethanol}}{C_2H_5OH} + \underset{\text{Acetic acid}}{CH_3COOH} \xrightarrow[\text{Esterification}]{H_3O^+}$$

$$\underset{\text{Ethyl acetate}}{CH_3COOC_2H_5}$$

Q. 4. Identify the term or substance based on the descriptions given below:
(i) Ice like crystals formed on cooling an organic acid sufficiently.
(ii) Hydrocarbon containing a triple bond used for welding purposes.
(iii) The property by virtue of which the compound has the same molecular formula but different structural formulae.

(iv) The compound formed where two alkyl groups are linked by $-\overset{\displaystyle O}{\underset{\displaystyle \|}{C}}-$ group. **[2017]**

Ans. (i) Glacial acetic acid
(ii) Acetylene or ethyne
(iii) Isomerism
(iv) Ketone

Q. 5. The following table shows the electronic configuration of the elements W, X, Y, Z:

Element	W	X	Y	Z
Electronic configurations	2, 8, 1	2, 8, 7	2, 5	1

Answer the following questions based on the table above:
(i) What type of Bond is formed between:
1. W and X
2. Y and Z
(ii) What is the formula of the compound formed between:
1. X and Z
2. W and X **[2016]**

Ans. (i) 1. Ionic bond   2. Covalent Bond
(ii) 1. ZX   2. WX

Q. 6. Give the structural formula of the following:
(i) ethanol   (ii) 1-propanal
(iii) ethanoic acid   (iv) 1, 2-dichloroethane. **[2014]**

Ans. (i)

$$H-\underset{\underset{\displaystyle H}{|}}{\overset{\overset{\displaystyle H}{|}}{C}}-\underset{\underset{\displaystyle H}{|}}{\overset{\overset{\displaystyle H}{|}}{C}}-OH$$

Ethanol

(ii)

$$H-\underset{\underset{\displaystyle H}{|}}{\overset{\overset{\displaystyle H}{|}}{C}}-\underset{\underset{\displaystyle H}{|}}{\overset{\overset{\displaystyle H}{|}}{C}}-\overset{\overset{\displaystyle H}{|}}{C}=O$$

1-Propanal

(iii)

$$H-\underset{\underset{\displaystyle H}{|}}{\overset{\overset{\displaystyle H}{|}}{C}}-\overset{\overset{\displaystyle O}{\|}}{C}-OH$$

Ethanoic acid

(iv)

$$H-\underset{\underset{\displaystyle H}{|}}{\overset{\overset{\displaystyle Cl}{|}}{C}}-\underset{\underset{\displaystyle H}{|}}{\overset{\overset{\displaystyle Cl}{|}}{C}}-H$$

1,2-dichloroethane

Q. 7. Give balanced equations for the laboratory preparations of the following organic compounds:

(i) **A saturated hydrocarbon from iodomethane.**

(ii) **An unsaturated hydrocarbon from an alcohol.**

(iii) **An unsaturated hydrocarbon from calcium carbide.**

(iv) **An alcohol from ethyl bromide.** [2013]

Ans. (i) $CH_3I \quad +2[H] \xrightarrow[C_2H_5OH]{Zn/Hg} CH_4 \quad +HI$
Iodomethane   Methane
or methyl
iodide

(ii) $C_2H_5OH \xrightarrow[Conc.\ H_2SO_4]{170°C} C_2H_4 + H_2O$
Ethanol   Ethene

(iii) $CaC_2 \quad + 2H_2O \longrightarrow Ca(OH)_2 + C_2H_2$
Calcium   Ethyne
carbide

(iv) $C_2H_5Br + KOH(aq) \longrightarrow C_2H_5OH + KBr$
Ethyl bromide   Ethanol

Q. 8. **From the following organic compounds given below, choose one compound in each case which relates to the description [i] to [iv]:**

[Ethyne, ethanol, acetic acid, ethene, methane]

(i) **An unsaturated hydrocarbon used for welding purposes.**

(ii) **An organic compound whose functional group is carboxyl.**

(iii) **A hydrocarbon which on catalytic hydrogenation gives a saturated hydrocarbon.**

(iv) **An organic compound used as a thermometric liquid.** [2012]

Ans. (i) Ethyne (ii) Acetic acid

(iii) Ethene (iv) Ethanol

Q. 9. **Give chemical equation for:**

(i) **The laboratory preparation of methane from sodium acetate.**

(ii) **The industrial preparation of methanol from water gas.**

(iii) **The reaction of one mole of ethene with one mole of chlorine gas.**

(iv) **The preparation of ethyne from 1, 2-dibromoethane.** [2009]

Ans. (i) $CH_3COONa + NaOH \xrightarrow[\Delta]{CaO}$
$CH_4 \quad + Na_2CO_3.$
Methane

(ii) $CO + 2H_2 \xrightarrow[350°C]{Cr_2O_3,\ ZnO} CH_3OH$

(iii) $CH_2=CH_2 + Cl_2 \xrightarrow{200\ atm.,\ 350°C} CH_2Cl.CH_2Cl.$
1, 2-dichloroethane

(iv) $CH_2Br.CH_2Br + 2KOH \longrightarrow$
$CH \equiv CH + 2KBr + 2H_2O.$
ethyne

Q. 10. **Fill in the blanks with the correct words from the brackets:**

Generally ionic compounds exist in (i)..................... (solid / liquid / gas) state. Melting and boiling points of covalent compounds are generally (ii)........... (low / high). The general formula for alkane is (iii) .... (C_nH_{2n}/C_nH_{2n-2}/C_nH_{2n+2}). For alkynes the general formula is (iv) .... (C_nH_{2n}/C_nH_{2n-2}/C_nH_{2n+2}).

[2009]

Ans. (i) solid, (ii) low,

(iii) C_nH_{2n+2}, (iv) C_nH_{2n-2}.

Q. 11. (i) **Write the equation for the complete combustion of ethane.**

(ii) **Using appropriate catalysts, ethane can be oxidized to an alcohol, an aldehyde and an acid. Name the alcohol, aldehyde and acid formed when ethane is oxidized.** [2008]

Ans. (i) $2C_2H_6 + 7O_2 \longrightarrow 4CO_2 + 6H_2O$

(ii) Ethane $\xrightarrow{(O)}$ Ethanol $\xrightarrow{(O)}$ Ethanal $\xrightarrow{(O)}$ Ethanoic acid.

Q. 12. **Fill in the blanks with the correct words from the brackets:**

Alkenes are the (i) .... (analogous/ homologous) series of (ii) .... (saturated/ unsaturated) hydrocarbons. They differ from alkanes due to the presence of (iii) .... (double/single) bonds. Alkenes mainly undergo (iv) .... (addition/substitution) reactions. [2006]

Ans. (i) Homologous (ii) Unsaturated

(iii) Double (iv) Addition

 ## Long Answer Type Question-I

Q. 1. Complete the following table which relates to the homologous series of hydrocarbons:

General formula	IUPAC name of the homologous series	Characteristic bond type	IUPAC name of the first member of the series
C_nH_{2n-2}	(A)	(B)	(C) ....
C_nH_{2n+2}	(D)	(E)	(F) ....

[2018]

Ans.

General formula	IUPAC names of the homologous series	Characteristic bond type	IUPAC name of the first member of the series
C_nH_{2n-2}	(A) Alkyne	(B) Triple covalent bond $-C \equiv C-$	(C) Ethyne
C_nH_{2n+2}	(D) Alkane	(E) Single covalent bond $-C-C-$	(F) Methane

Q. 2. Name the following:

(i) Process by which ethane is obtained from ethene.

(ii) A hydrocarbon which contributes towards the greenhouse effect.

(iii) Distinctive reaction that takes place when ethanol is treated with acetic acid.

(iv) The property of elements by virtue of which atoms of the element can link to each other in the form of a long chain or ring structure.

(v) Reaction when an alkyl halide is treated with alcoholic potassium hydroxide. **[2015]**

Ans. (i) Hydrogenation

(ii) Methane (CH_4)

(iii) Esterification

(iv) Catenation

(v) Dehydrohalogenation

Q. 3. State the conditions required for the following reactions to take place:

(i) Catalytic hydrogenation of ethyne.

(ii) Preparation of ethyne from ethylene dibromide.

(iii) Catalytic oxidiation of ammonia to nitric oxide.

(iv) Any two conditions for the conversion of sulphur dioxide to sulphur trioxide. **[2014]**

Ans. (i) In the presence of catalyst like finely divided nickel, platinum, etc., and on heating upto 473 K or about 300°C hydrogenation takes place.

(ii) Hot and concentrated ethanolic solution of potassium hydroxide.

(iii) Platinum gauze is used as catalyst at 800 °C in presence of oxygen.

(iv) Vanadium pentoxide acts as catalyst and temperature of 450 °C-500 °C and atm. pressure.

Q. 4. Write balanced chemical equations for the following:

(i) Monochloroethane is hydrolysed with aqueous KOH.

(ii) A mixture of sodalime and sodium acetate is heated.

(iii) Ethanol under high pressure and low temperature is treated with acidified potassium dichromate.

(iv) Water is added to calcium carbide.

(v) Ethanol reacts with sodium at room temperature. **[2011]**

Ans. (i) $C_2H_5Cl + KOH(aq) \longrightarrow \underset{\text{Ethanol}}{C_2H_5OH} + KCl$

(ii) $CH_3COONa + NaOH \xrightarrow[\text{300°C (soda lime)}]{\text{CaO}} \underset{\text{Methane}}{CH_4 + Na_2CO_3}$

(iii) $CH_3CH_2OH + 2[O] \xrightarrow[K_2Cr_2O_7]{\text{Acidified}} \underset{\text{Acetic acid}}{CH_3COOH + H_2O\uparrow}$

(iv) $CaC_2 + 2H_2O \longrightarrow \underset{\substack{\text{Calcium} \\ \text{hydroxide}}}{Ca(OH)_2} + \underset{\text{Ethyne}}{C_2H_2\uparrow}$

(v) $2C_2H_5OH + 2Na \longrightarrow \underset{\text{Sodium ethoxide}}{2C_2H_5ONa} + H_2\uparrow$

Q. 5. Choose the correct word/phrase from within the brackets to complete the following sentences: **[2011]**

(i) The catalyst used for conversion of ethene to ethane is commonly .... (nickel/iron/cobalt).

(ii) When acetaldehyde is oxidized with acidified potassium dichromate, it forms...... (ester/ethanol/acetic acid).

(iii) Ethanoic acid reacts with ethanol in presence of concentrated H_2SO_4, so as

(i) **A saturated hydrocarbon from iodomethane.**

(ii) **An unsaturated hydrocarbon from an alcohol.**

(iii) **An unsaturated hydrocarbon from calcium carbide.**

(iv) **An alcohol from ethyl bromide.** [2013]

Ans.

(i) $CH_3I \quad +2[H] \xrightarrow[C_2H_5OH]{Zn/Hg} CH_4 \quad +HI$
Iodomethane $\qquad$ Methane
or methyl
iodide

(ii) $C_2H_5OH \xrightarrow[Conc.\ H_2SO_4]{170°C} C_2H_4 + H_2O$
Ethanol $\qquad$ Ethene

(iii) $CaC_2 \quad + 2H_2O \longrightarrow Ca(OH)_2 + C_2H_2$
Calcium $\qquad\qquad$ Ethyne
carbide

(iv) $C_2H_5Br + KOH(aq) \longrightarrow C_2H_5OH + KBr$
Ethyl bromide $\qquad$ Ethanol

Q. 8. **From the following organic compounds given below, choose one compound in each case which relates to the description [i] to [iv]:**

[Ethyne, ethanol, acetic acid, ethene, methane]

(i) **An unsaturated hydrocarbon used for welding purposes.**

(ii) **An organic compound whose functional group is carboxyl.**

(iii) **A hydrocarbon which on catalytic hydrogenation gives a saturated hydrocarbon.**

(iv) **An organic compound used as a thermometric liquid.** [2012]

Ans. (i) Ethyne $\qquad$ (ii) Acetic acid

(iii) Ethene $\qquad$ (iv) Ethanol

Q. 9. **Give chemical equation for:**

(i) **The laboratory preparation of methane from sodium acetate.**

(ii) **The industrial preparation of methanol from water gas.**

(iii) **The reaction of one mole of ethene with one mole of chlorine gas.**

(iv) **The preparation of ethyne from 1, 2-dibromoethane.** [2009]

Ans. (i) $CH_3COONa + NaOH \xrightarrow[\Delta]{CaO}$
$\qquad\qquad CH_4 + Na_2CO_3.$
$\qquad\qquad$ Methane

(ii) $CO + 2H_2 \xrightarrow[350°C]{Cr_2O_3,\ ZnO} CH_3OH$

(iii) $CH_2=CH_2 + Cl_2 \xrightarrow{200\ atm.,\ 350°C} CH_2Cl.CH_2Cl.$
$\qquad\qquad\qquad\qquad$ 1, 2-dichloroethane

(iv) $CH_2Br.CH_2Br + 2KOH \longrightarrow$

$\qquad CH \equiv CH + 2KBr + 2H_2O.$
$\qquad$ ethyne

Q. 10. **Fill in the blanks with the correct words from the brackets:**

Generally ionic compounds exist in (i).................... (solid / liquid / gas) state. Melting and boiling points of covalent compounds are generally (ii)........... (low / high). The general formula for alkane is (iii) .... (C_nH_{2n}/C_nH_{2n-2}/C_nH_{2n+2}). For alkynes the general formula is (iv) .... (C_nH_{2n}/C_nH_{2n-2}/C_nH_{2n+2}).

[2009]

Ans. (i) solid, $\qquad$ (ii) low,

(iii) C_nH_{2n+2}, $\qquad$ (iv) C_nH_{2n-2}.

Q. 11. (i) **Write the equation for the complete combustion of ethane.**

(ii) **Using appropriate catalysts, ethane can be oxidized to an alcohol, an aldehyde and an acid. Name the alcohol, aldehyde and acid formed when ethane is oxidized.** [2008]

Ans. (i) $2C_2H_6 + 7O_2 \longrightarrow 4CO_2 + 6H_2O$

(ii) Ethane $\xrightarrow{(O)}$ Ethanol $\xrightarrow{(O)}$ Ethanal
$\xrightarrow{(O)}$ Ethanoic acid.

Q. 12. **Fill in the blanks with the correct words from the brackets:**

Alkenes are the (i) .... (analogous/ homologous) series of (ii) .... (saturated/ unsaturated) hydrocarbons. They differ from alkanes due to the presence of (iii) .... (double/single) bonds. Alkenes mainly undergo (iv) .... (addition/substitution) reactions. [2006]

Ans. (i) Homologous $\qquad$ (ii) Unsaturated

(iii) Double $\qquad$ (iv) Addition

 **Long Answer Type Question-I**

Q. 1. Complete the following table which relates to the homologous series of hydrocarbons:

General formula	IUPAC name of the homologous series	Characteristic bond type	IUPAC name of the first member of the series
C_nH_{2n-2}	(A)	(B)	(C) ....
C_nH_{2n+2}	(D)	(E)	(F) ....

[2018]

Ans.

General formula	IUPAC names of the homologous series	Characteristic bond type	IUPAC name of the first member of the series
C_nH_{2n-2}	(A) Alkyne	(B) Triple covalent bond $-C\equiv C-$	(C) Ethyne
C_nH_{2n+2}	(D) Alkane	(E) Single covalent bond $-C-C-$	(F) Methane

Q. 2. Name the following:

(i) Process by which ethane is obtained from ethene.

(ii) A hydrocarbon which contributes towards the greenhouse effect.

(iii) Distinctive reaction that takes place when ethanol is treated with acetic acid.

(iv) The property of elements by virtue of which atoms of the element can link to each other in the form of a long chain or ring structure.

(v) Reaction when an alkyl halide is treated with alcoholic potassium hydroxide. [2015]

Ans.
(i) Hydrogenation
(ii) Methane (CH_4)
(iii) Esterification
(iv) Catenation
(v) Dehydrohalogenation

Q. 3. State the conditions required for the following reactions to take place:

(i) Catalytic hydrogenation of ethyne.

(ii) Preparation of ethyne from ethylene dibromide.

(iii) Catalytic oxidiation of ammonia to nitric oxide.

(iv) Any two conditions for the conversion of sulphur dioxide to sulphur trioxide. [2014]

Ans.
(i) In the presence of catalyst like finely divided nickel, platinum, etc., and on heating upto 473 K or about 300°C hydrogenation takes place.

(ii) Hot and concentrated ethanolic solution of potassium hydroxide.

(iii) Platinum gauze is used as catalyst at 800 °C in presence of oxygen.

(iv) Vanadium pentoxide acts as catalyst and temperature of 450 °C-500 °C and atm. pressure.

Q. 4. Write balanced chemical equations for the following:

(i) Monochloroethane is hydrolysed with aqueous KOH.

(ii) A mixture of sodalime and sodium acetate is heated.

(iii) Ethanol under high pressure and low temperature is treated with acidified potassium dichromate.

(iv) Water is added to calcium carbide.

(v) Ethanol reacts with sodium at room temperature. [2011]

Ans.
(i) $C_2H_5Cl + KOH(aq) \longrightarrow C_2H_5OH + KCl$
Ethanol

(ii) $CH_3COONa + NaOH \xrightarrow[\text{300°C (soda lime)}]{\text{CaO}}$
$CH_4 + Na_2CO_3$
Methane

(iii) $CH_3CH_2OH + 2[O] \xrightarrow[K_2Cr_2O_7]{\text{Acidified}}$
$CH_3COOH + H_2O\uparrow$
Acetic acid

(iv) $CaC_2 + 2H_2O \longrightarrow Ca(OH)_2 + C_2H_2\uparrow$
Calcium   Ethyne
hydroxide

(v) $2C_2H_5OH + 2Na \longrightarrow 2C_2H_5ONa + H_2\uparrow$
Sodium ethoxide

Q. 5. Choose the correct word/phrase from within the brackets to complete the following sentences: [2011]

(i) The catalyst used for conversion of ethene to ethane is commonly .... (nickel/iron/cobalt).

(ii) When acetaldehyde is oxidized with acidified potassium dichromate, it forms...... (ester/ethanol/acetic acid).

(iii) Ethanoic acid reacts with ethanol in presence of concentrated H_2SO_4, so as to form a compound and water. The chemical reaction which takes place is called......... .

(dehydration/ hydrogenation/ esterification)

(iv) Write the equation for the reaction taking place between 1, 2-dibromoethane and alcoholic potassium hydroxide.

(v) The product formed when ethene gas reacts with water in the presence of sulphuric acid is.........

(ethanol/ethanal/ethanoic acid).

Ans. (i) Nickel

(ii) Acetic acid

(iii) Esterification

(iv) $CH_2BrCH_2Br + 2KOH \longrightarrow C_2H_2$
        (alc.)   Ethyne
                                  $+ 2KBr + 2H2O$

(v) Ethanol

Q. 6. Compound A is bubbled through bromine dissolved in carbon tetrachloride and the product is $CH_2Br - CH_2Br$.

$$A \xrightarrow{Br_2/CCl_4} CH_2Br\text{-}CH_2Br$$

(i) Draw the structural formula of A.

(ii) What type of reaction has A undergone?

(iii) What is your observation?

(iv) Name (not formula) the compound formed when steam reacts with A in the presence of phosphoric acid.

(v) What is the procedure for converting the product of (b)(iv) back to A?   [2010]

Ans. (i) $\underset{H}{\overset{H}{\diagdown}}C = C\underset{H}{\overset{H}{\diagup}}$

(ii) Addition reaction.

(iii) Bromine solution gets decolourised forming dibromoethane.

(iv) Ethanol

(v) By heating it (ethanol) with concentrated sulphuric acid at 170°C.

Q. 7. Give the IUPAC names of the following compounds numbered (i) to (v). The IUPAC names of the compounds on the left are to guide you into giving the correct IUPAC names of the compounds on the right.

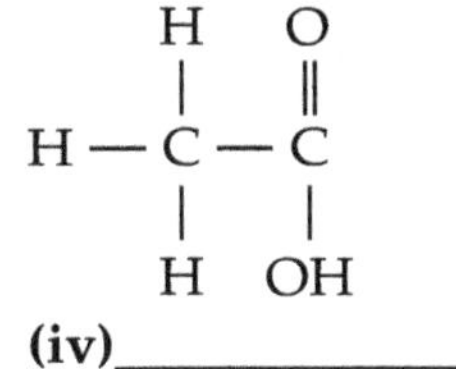

Propene

(i)_____________

Pentan-2-ol

(ii)_____________

2, 2-dimethylpropane

(iii)_____________

Propanoic acid   **1, 2-dibromoethane**

(iv)_____________   **(v)**_____________

[2007]

Ans. (i) Propyne (ii) Pentan-3-ol
(iii) 2-methyl propane
(iv) Ethanoic acid and
(v) 1, 2-dichloroethane.

Q. 9. Name the organic compound prepared by each of the following reactions:
(i) $C_2H_5COONa + NaOH \longrightarrow$

(ii) $CH_3I + 2H \longrightarrow$
(iii) $C_2H_5Br + KOH$ (alcoholic solution) $\longrightarrow$
(iv) $CO + 2H_2$ (Zinc oxide catalyst) $\longrightarrow$
(v) $CaC_2 + 2H_2O \longrightarrow$ [2008]

Ans. (i) Ethane   (ii) Methane
(iii) Ethene   (v) Ethyne or Acetylene

 **Long Answer Type Questions-II**

Q. 1. Copy and complete the following table which relates to three homologous series of Hydrocarbons:

General Formula	C_nH_{2n}	C_nH_{2n-2}	C_nH_{2n+2}
IUPAC name of the homologous series			
Characteristic bond type			Single bond
IUPAC name of the first member of the series			
Type of reaction with chlorine.		Addition	

[2007]

Ans.

General Formula	C_nH_{2n}	C_nH_{2n-2}	C_nH_{2n+2}
IUPAC name of the homologous series	Alkenes	Alkynes	Alkanes
Characteristic bond type	Double bond	Triple bond	Single bond
IUPAC name of the first member of the series	Ethene	Ethyne	Methane
Type of reaction with chlorine.	Addition	Addition	Substitution

BIOLOGY

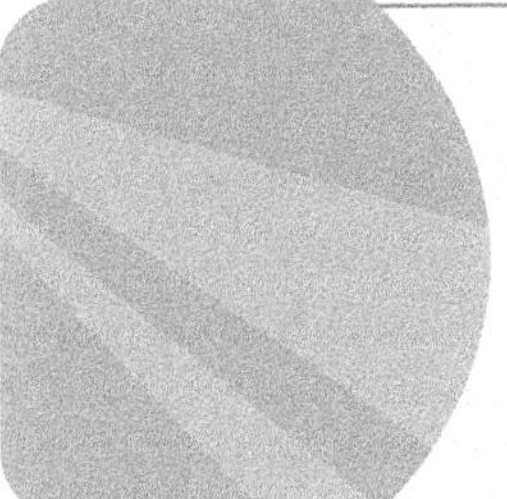

Section-I YEARWISE

Very Short or One word Answer Type Questions

Q. 1. Name the following:
  (i) The process of transformation of several glucose molecules into one molecule of starch.
  (ii) The point of attachment of two chromatids.
  (iii) The iron containing pigment in erythrocytes.
  (iv) The duct which transports urine from the kidney to the urinary bladder.
  (v) The part of the brain which is concerned with memory. **[2020]**

Ans. (i) Polymerisation   (ii) Centromere
  (iii) Haemoglobin   (iv) Ureter
  (v) Cerebrum

Q. 2. Explain the following terms:
  (i) **Allele**   (ii) **Diffusion**
  (iii) **Photolysis**   (iv) **Phenotype**
  (v) **Population density** **[2020]**

Ans. (i) Allele is the alternative forms of a gene occupying the same position on the homologous chromosomes, affecting the same characteristic but in different ways.
  (ii) Diffusion is the free movement of molecules of a substance from the region of their higher concentration to the region of their lower concentration when two are in direct contact.
  (iii) Photolysis is the process of splitting of water molecules into hydrogen ions and oxygen in presence of sunlight inside grana.
  (iv) Phenotype refers to the observable characteristics which are controlled genetically.
  (v) Population density is defined as the number of individuals per square kilometre at any given time.

Q. 3. Given below are certain groups of terms. In each group the first pair indicates a relationship between the two terms. Rewrite and complete the second pair on a similar basis.
Example: Cytoplasm: Cytokinesis :: Nucleus: Karyokinesis.
  (i) Widening of hips: Oestrogen :: Deepening of voice in males:
  (ii) Brain : Meninges :: Heart :
  (iii) Insulin : Beta-cells :: Glucagon :
  (iv) Kidney : Renal artery :: Liver :
  (v) Uterus : Implantation :: Fallopian tube : **[2020]**

Ans. (i) Testosterone   (ii) Pericardium
  (iii) Alpha cells   (iv) Hepatic artery
  (v) Fertilisation

Q. 4. Given below are sets of five terms each. Rewrite the terms in correct order in a logical sequence beginning with the first word that is underlined:
  (i) **Stimulus, Response, Receptor, Effector, Spinal cord.**
  (ii) **Root hair, Endodermis, Epidermis, Xylem, Cortex.**
  (iii) **Conjunctiva, Yellow spot, Pupil, Vitreous Humour, Aqueous Humour.**
  (iv) **Australopithecus, Cro-Magnon Man, Homo erectus, Neanderthal Man, Homo sapiens.**
  (v) **Artery, Capillaries, Venule, Vein, Arteriole.** **[2020]**

Ans. (i) Stimulus, receptor, spinal cord, effector, response
  (ii) Root hair, epidermis, cortex, endodermis, xylem
  (iii) Conjunctiva, aqueous humour, pupil, vitreous humour, yellow spot
  (iv) Australopithecus, Homo erectus, Neanderthal man, Cro-Magnon man, Homo sapiens
  (v) Artery, arteriole, capillaries, venule, vein

Q. 5. Choose the correct answer from the four options given below :
  (i) The fusion of the sperm and ovum is termed as:
    (a) Reproduction   (b) Development
    (c) Fertilization   (d) Embryo
  (ii) Agranulocytes are:
    (a) Lymphocytes, Monocytes
    (b) Lymphocytes, Basophils
    (c) Eosinophils, Basophils
    (d) Eosinophils, Monocytes

(iii) Which of the following is not a natural reflex action?
(a) Knee-jerk
(b) Blinking of eyes due to strong light
(c) Salivation at the sight of food
(d) Sneezing when any irritant enters the nose

(iv) The structural and functional units of excretion in the human kidney is the:
(a) Ureter   (b) Bowman's capsule
(c) Renal pelvis (d) Nephron

(v) In a human female, ovum consists of:
(a) 23 pair of autosomes
(b) 22 pairs of autosomes and 1 pair of sex chromosomes
(c) 22 autosomes and 1 Y-chromosome
(d) 22 autosomes and 1 X-chromosome
[2020]

Ans. **(i)** C. Fertilization
(ii) A. Lymphocytes, Monocytes
(iii) C. Salivation at the sight of food
(iv) D. Nephron
(v) D. 22 autosomes and 1 X chromosome

Q. 6. Identify the ODD term in each set and name the CATEGORY to which the remaining three belong:
(i) Auxin, Ethylene, Adrenaline, Cytokinin
(ii) Tympanum, Ear ossicles, Auditory canal, Pinna
(iii) Syringes, Soiled dressings, Discarded needles, Houshold detergents
(iv) Exophthalmic Goitre, Simple Goitre, Cretinism, Myxoedema
(v) Adenine, Guanine, Creatinine, Cytosine
[2020]

Ans. **(i)** Odd- Adrenaline;
Category- Plant hormones
(ii) Odd- Ear ossicles
Category- Parts of outer ear
(iii) Odd- Household detergents
Category- Biomedical wastes
(iv) Odd- Exophthalmic goitre
Category- Conditions due to Hypothyroidism
(v) Odd- Creatinine
Category- Nitrogenous bases

Q. 7. Match the items given in column A with the most appropriate ones in Column B and Rewrite the correct matching pairs:

Column A	Column B
(i) Biston betularia	– Calcium
(ii) Testes	– Balance of the body
(iii) Clotting of blood	– Light independent reaction
(iv) Stroma	– diffusion of gases
(v) Stomata	– gonad
	– Peppered moth
	– Light dependent reaction
	– Chlorophyll

[2020]

Ans.

Column A		Column B
(i) Biston betularia	–	Peppered moth
(ii) Testes	–	Gonad
(iii) Clotting of blood	–	Calcium
(iv) Stroma	–	Light independent reaction
(v) Stomata	–	diffusion of gases

Q. 8. Name the following:
(i) The layer of eyeball that provides nourishment to the eye.
(ii) One gaseous compound which depletes the ozone layer.
(iii) The structure which connects the placenta and the foetus.
(iv) A pair of corresponding chromosomes of the same shape and size and derived one from each parent.
(v) The compound formed when haemoglobin combines with carbon dioxide in blood. [2019]

Marking Scheme
(i) Choroid
(ii) Chlorofluorocarbon (CFC) or carbon tetrachloride
(iii) Umbilical cord
(iv) Homologous chromosomes
(v) Carbaminohaemoglobin/$HbCO_2$

Ans. **(i)** Choroid layer
(ii) CFCs [Chlorofluorocarbons] or CCl_4
(iii) Umbilical cord
(iv) Homologous chromosomes
(v) Carbamino-haemoglobin / $HbCO_2$

Q. 9. Correct and rewrite the statement by changing the biological term that is underlined for each statement:
(i) The theory of Inheritance of Acquired characters was proposed by <u>Watson and Crick</u>.
(ii) The protective sac which develops around the developing embryo is called the <u>Pericardium</u>.
(iii) Maintaining balance of the body and coordinating muscular activities is carried out by the <u>cerebrum</u>.

(iv) The kidney is composed of number of <u>neurons</u>.

(v) The part of the eye which can be donated from a clinically dead person is the <u>Retina</u>. **[2019]**

📋 Marking Scheme ------------------------------

(i) Jean-Baptiste Lamarck

(ii) Amnion
(iii) Cerebellum
(iv) Nephrons/Uriniferous tubules
(v) Cornea

Ans. **(i)** The theory of Inheritance of Acquired characters was proposed by Lamarck.

(ii) The protective sac which develops around the developing embryo is called the Amnion.

(iii) Maintaining balance of the body and coordinating muscular activities is carried out by the Cerebellum.

(iv) The kidney is composed of number of Nephrons Uriniferous tubules.

(v) The part of the eye which can be donated from a clinically dead person is the Cornea.

Q. 10. Give suitable biological reasons for the following statements:
(i) The birth rate in India is very high.
(ii) Carbon monoxide is dangerous when inhaled.
(iii) Root hairs become flaccid and droop when excess fertilizers are added to the moist soil around them.
(iv) Acid rain is harmful to the environment.
(v) All life on Earth is supported by Photosynthesis. **[2019]**

📋 Marking Scheme ------------------------------

(i) Illiteracy, children are a gift of God, sign of prosperity, due to high infant mortality, more helping hands for family income, do not accept family planning methods, desire for a male child, lack of recreation.
(ii) Easily combines with haemoglobin to form carboxyhaemoglobin which cuts off supply of oxygen to tissues.
(iii) Formation of hypertonic solution which results in plasmolysis/exosmosis.
(iv) Pollutes soil, damages vegetation, buildings, statues, monuments, kills fish and aquatic animals.
(v) All organisms depend directly or indirectly on green plants for food, beginning of all food chains, provides oxygen for respiration.
(Any alternate correct answer)

Ans. **(i)** Most of the people who belong to rural area are illiterate, superstitious and ignorant. They don't know much about the function of reproductive system and use of contraceptives which is the major reason for population explosion in India. They consider children as the gift of god and a sign of prosperity. Desire for a male child is another important reason.

(ii) Haemoglobin has a very strong affinity for Carbon monoxide and a stable compound called Carboxy-haemoglobin HbCO is formed when carbon monoxide is inhaled. It cuts down the capacity of blood to transport oxygen which may lead to death. Hence it is very dangerous to inhale carbon monoxide.

(iii) When excess fertilizers are added to moist soil, solute concentration increases, making the soil a hypertonic solution, in turn outward flow of water occurs from cells of root hair causing plasmolysis of cell. Hence root hairs become flaccid and droop down.

(iv) Acid rain has oxides of nitrogen and sulphur dissolved in it which decreases its pH value thus making it acidic. This damages vegetation, corrodes monuments, statues, buildings etc., and also causes harm to human health, aquatic life and crops and pollutes soil.

(v) Our food chain starts with producers *i.e.,* green plants as they are the only organisms which can prepare their own food by photosynthesis process. All other living organisms depend upon them directly or indirectly for food. Photosynthesis is thus the process by which oxygen is released to our atmosphere which is a life supporting gas. So we can say that directly or indirectly all life on Earth is supported by photosynthesis.

Q. 11. Match the items given in Column A with the most appropriate ones in Column B and Rewrite the correct matching pairs:

	Column A	Column B
(i)	Cranial nerves	Testosterone
(ii)	Leydig cells	Natural reflex
(iii)	Acetylcholine	12 pairs
(iv)	Spinal nerves	Prolactin
(v)	Sneezing	Neurotransmitter
		18 pairs
		31 pairs
		Conditioned reflex

[2019]

 **Marking Scheme**

(i) Cranial nerves – 12 pairs
(ii) Leydig cells – Testosterone
(iii) Acetylchlorine – Neuro transmitter
(iv) Spinal nerves – 31 pairs
(v) Sneezing – Natural reflex

Ans.

	Column A	Column B
(i)	Cranial nerves	12 pairs
(ii)	Leydig cells	Testosterone
(iii)	Acetylcholine	Neurotransmitter
(iv)	Spinal nerves	31 pairs
(v)	Sneezing	Natural reflex

Q. 12. Choose the correct answer from the four options given below:

(i) While recording the pulse rate, where exactly does a doctor press on our wrist?
 (a) Nerve (b) Vein
 (c) Artery (d) Capillary

(ii) In a human male, a sperm will contain:
 (a) Both X and Y chromosomes
 (b) Only Y chromosome
 (c) Only X chromosome
 (d) Either X or Y chromosome

(iii) A muscular wall is absent in :
 (a) Capillary (b) Venule
 (c) Arteriole (d) Vein

(iv) On which day of the menstrual cycle does ovulation take place?
 (a) 5th day (b) 28th day
 (c) 14th day (d) 1st day

(v) Which one of the following does not affect the rate of transpiration?
 (a) Light (b) Humidity
 (c) Wind (d) Age of the plan
 [2019]

 **Marking Scheme**

(i) C. Artery
(ii) D. Either X or Y chromosome
(iii) A. Capillary
(iv) C. 14th day
(v) D. Age of the plant

Ans. (i) **(c)** Artery

(ii) **(d)** Either X or Y chromosome

(iii) **(a)** Capillary

(iv) **(c)** 14th day

(v) **(d)** Age of the plant

Q. 13. Identify the ODD term in each set and name the CATEGORY to which the remaining three belong:

Example : glucose, starch, cellulose, calcium

Odd term : calcium

Category : others are different types of carbohydrates.

(i) Addison's disease, Cushing's Syndrome, Acromegaly, Leukemia

(ii) Insulin, Adernaline, Pepsin, Thyroxine.

(iii) Axon, Dendron, Photon, Cyton.

(iv) Chicken, Pox, Colour blindness, Haemophilia, Albinism.

(v) Polythene bag, Crop residue, Animal waste, Decaying vegetable. **[2019]**

 **Marking Scheme**

(i) O – Leukemia
 C – Hormonal / Endocrinal disorders
(ii) O – Pepsin
 C – Hormones
(iii) O – Photon
 C – Parts of neuron / nerve cell
(iv) O – Chicken pox
 C – Genetic diseases
(v) O – Polythene bag
 C – Biodegradable wastes

Ans. (i) **Odd** : Leukemia

 Category : The rest are Hormonal disorders.

(ii) **Odd** : Pepsin

 Category : Others are Hormones while pepsin is an enzyme.

(iii) **Odd** : Photon

 Category : The rest are parts of a neuron.

(iv) **Odd** : Chicken pox

 Category : Others are genetic disorders.

(v) **Odd** : Polythene bag

 Category : Others are Biodegradable pollutants.

Q. 14. Expand the following biological abbreviations.
 (i) ABA (ii) IAA
 (iii) ATP (iv) DNA
 (v) TSH **[2019]**

Marking Scheme

(i) Abscisic acid
(ii) Indole 3-acetic acid
(iii) Adenosine triphosphate
(iv) Deoxyribo nucleic acid
(v) Thyroid stimulating hormone

Ans. (i) Abscisic Acid

(ii) Indole 3-Acetic Acid

(iii) Adenosine Triphosphate

(iv) Deoxyribonucleic Acid

(v) Thyroid Stimulating Hormone

Q. 15. Name the following:

  (ii) The blood vessel which supplies blood to the liver.

  (iii) The number of chromosomes present in a nerve cell of a human being.

  (iv) The layer of the eyeball that forms the transparent Cornea.

  (v) The wax-like layer on the epidermis of leaves which reduces transpiration.

  [2018]

Marking Scheme

  (ii) Hepatic artery/Hepatic Portal Vein
  (iii) 46 or 23 pairs
  (iv) Sclera/Sclerotic layer
  (v) Cuticle/cutin

Ans. (ii) Hepatic artery (iii) 46

  (iv) Sclera/sclerotic layer (v) Cuticle

Q. 16. Choose the correct answer from each of the four options given below:

  (i) The number of Spinal nerves in a human being are:

  (a) 31 pairs (b) 10 pairs

  (c) 21 pairs (d) 30 pairs

  (ii) Which one of the following is non-biodegradable?

  (a) DDT (b) Vegetable peel

  (c) Cardboard (d) Bark of trees

  (iii) Aqueous humour is present between the:

  (a) Lens and Retina (b) Iris and Lens

  (c) Cornea and Iris

  (d) Cornea and Lens

  (v) Which one of the following is a Greenhouse gas?

  (a) Oxygen (c) Methane

  (b) Sulphur dioxide (d) Nitrogen **[2018]**

Marking Scheme

  (i) A. 31 pairs
  (ii) A. DDT
  (iii) D. Cornea and Lens
  (v) B. Methane/CH_4

Ans. (i) (a) 31 pairs (ii) (a) DDT

  (iii) (d) Cornea and lens (v) (b) Methane

Q. 17. Match the items given in Column A with the most appropriate ones in Column B and rewrite the correct matching pairs.

	Column A	Column B
(i)	Cretinism	(a) Hypersecretion of adrenal cortex
(ii)	Diabetes insipidus	(b) Hyposecretion of Thyroxine
(iii)	Exophthalmic Goitre	(c) Hyposecretion of growth hormone
(iv)	Adrenal virilism	(d) Hyposecretion of Vasopressin
(v)	Dwarfism	(e) Hyposecretion of adrenal cortex
		(f) Hypersecretion of Growth hormone
		(g) Hypersecretion of Thyroxine

[2018]

Marking Scheme

  (i) Cretinism - (b) Hyposecretion of thyroxine

  (ii) Diabetes insipidus - (d) Hyposecretion of Vasopressin

  (iii) Exophthalmic Goitre - (g) Hypersecretion of thyroxine

  (iv) Adrenal virilims - (a) Hypersecretion of adrenal cortex

  (v) Dwarfism - (c) Hyposecretion of growth hormones

Ans.

	Column A	Column B
(i)	Cretinism	(b) Hyposecretion of Thyroxine
(ii)	Diabetes insipidus	(d) Hyposecretion of Vasopressin
(iii)	Exophthalmic Goitre	(g) Hypersecretion of Thyroxine
(iv)	Adrenal virilism	(a) Hypersecretion of adrenal cortex
(v)	Dwarfism	(c) Hyposecretion of growth hormone

Q. 18. Correct the following statements by changing the underlined words:

  (i) Normal pale yellow colour of the urine is due to the presence of the pigment <u>Melanin</u>.

  (ii) The outermost layer of Meninges is <u>Pia mater</u>.

  (iii) The cell sap of root hair is <u>Hypotonic</u>.

  (iv) <u>Xylem</u> transports starch from the leaves to all parts of the plant body.

  (v) <u>Nitrogen</u> bonds are present between the complementary nitrogenous bases of DNA. **[2018]**

Marking Scheme

  (i) Urochrome/Urobilin
  (ii) Duramater
  (iii) Hypertonic/Concentrated
  (iv) Phloem
  (v) Hydrogen/ H

Ans. (i) Normal pale yellow colour of the urine is due to the presence of the pigment **Urochrome.**

(ii) The outermost layer of Meninges is **Dura mater.**

(iii) The cell sap of root hair is **Hypertonic.**

(iv) **Phloem** transports starch from the leaves to all parts of the plant body.

(v) **Hydrogen** bonds are present between the complementary nitrogenous bases of DNA.

Q. 19. Choose between the two options to answer the question specified in the brackets for the following:

An example is illustrated below.

Example : Corolla or Calyx (Which is the outer whorl?)

Answer : Calyx

(i) **Blood in the renal artery or renal vein (Which one has more urea?)**

(ii) **Perilymph or endolymph (Which one surrounds the organ of Corti?)**

(iii) **Lenticels or stomata (Which one remains open always?)**

(iv) **Sclerotic layer or choroid layer (Which one forms the Iris?)**

(v) **Blood in the pulmonary artery or pulmonary vein (Which one contains less oxyhaemoglobin?)** [2018]

📋 **Marking Scheme**
(i) Renal artery
(ii) Endolymph
(iii) Lenticels
(iv) Choroid
(v) Pulmonary artery

Ans. (i) Blood in renal artery
(ii) Endolymph
(iii) Lenticels
(iv) Choroid layer
(v) Blood in the pulmonary artery

Q. 20. Choose the ODD one out from the following terms given and name the Category to which the others belong:

Example : Nose, Tongue, Arm, Eye.

Answer : Odd Term – Arm, Category – Sense organs

(i) **Detergents, X-rays, sewage, oil spills.**

(ii) **Lumen, muscular tissue, connective tissue, pericardium.**

(iii) **Dendrites, Medullary Sheath, Axon, Spinal cord.**

(iv) **Centrosome, Cell wall, Cell membrane, Large vacuoles.**

(v) **Prostate gland, Cowper's gland, seminal vesicle, seminiferous tubules.** [2018]

📋 **Marking Scheme**
(i) X-rays - water pollutants
(ii) Pericardium - parts of artery and vein/blood vessels
Lumen - Parts of heart/tissues of heart
(iii) Spinal Cord - parts of neuron/nerve cell
(iv) Centrosome - parts of plant cell
(v) Seminiferous tubules - accessory or reproductive glands of male

Ans. (i) **Odd one** : X-rays

Category : Water pollutants.

(ii) **Odd one** : Lumen

Category : Type of tissues

(iii) **Odd one** : Spinal cord

Category : Parts of neuron.

(iv) **Odd one** : Centrosome

Category : Parts of a plant cell.

(v) **Odd one** : Seminiferous tubules

Category : Accessory glands of human male reproductive system.

Q. 21. Name the following:

(i) **The process by which root hairs absorb water from the soil.**

(ii) **The organ which produces urea.**

(iii) **The kind of lens required to correct Myopia.**

(iv) **The pituitary hormone which stimulates contraction of uterus during child birth.** [2017]

Ans. (i) Osmosis [Endosmosis] (ii) Liver

(iii) Concave lens (iv) Oxytocin

Q. 22. Choose the correct answer from each of the four options given below:

(i) **The prime source of chlorofluorocarbons is:**

(a) **Vehicular emissions**

(b) **Industrial effluents**

(c) **Domestic sewage**

(d) **Refrigeration equipments**

(iii) **Marine fish when placed in tap water bursts because of:**

(a) **Endosmosis** (b) **Exosmosis**

(c) **Diffusion** (d) **Plasmolysis**

(iv) **Surgical method of sterilization in a woman involves cutting and tying of:**

(a) **Ureter** (b) **Uterus**

(c) **Urethra** (d) **Oviduct**

(v) **Synthesis phase in the cell cycle is called so, because of the synthesis of more :**

(a) **RNA** (b) **RNA and proteins**

(c) **DNA** (d) **Glucose** [2017]

Ans. **(i)** **(d)** Refrigeration equipments

(iii) **(a)** Endosmosis

(iv) **(d)** Oviduct

(v) **(c)** DNA

Q. 23. **The statements given below are incorrect. Rewrite the correct statement by changing the underlined words of the statements:**

(i) **The Graafian follicle after ovulation turns into a hormone producing tissue called Corpus callosum.**

(ii) **Deafness is caused due to the rupturing of the Pinna.**

(iii) **Gyri and Sulci are the folds of Cerebellum.**

(iv) **Free movement of solutes in and out of the cell takes place across the cell membrane.**

(v) **The solvent used to dissolve the chlorophyll pigments while testing a leaf for starch is Soda lime.** **[2017]**

Ans. **(i)** The Graafian follicle after ovulation turns into a hormone producing tissue called **Corpus luteum**.

(ii) Deafness is caused due to the rupturing of the **ear drum/tympanum**.

(iii) Gyri and Sulci are the folds of **Cerebrum**.

(iv) Free movement of solutes in and out of the cell takes place across the **cell wall**.

(v) The solvent used to dissolve the chlorophyll pigments while testing a leaf for starch is **methylated spirit**.

Q. 24. **Given below are sets of five terms each. Rewrite the terms in correct order in a logical sequence.**

Example : Large intestine, Stomach, Mouth, Small intestine, Oesophagus.

Answer : Mouth → Oesophagus → Stomach → Small intestine → Large intestine.

(i) **Fibrin, Platelets, Thromboplastin, Fibrinogen, Thrombin.**

(ii) **Cochlea, Malleus, Pinna, Stapes, Incus.**

(iii) **Receptor, Spinal cord, Effector, Motor neuron, Sensory neuron.**

(iv) **Uterus, Parturition, Fertilisation, Gestation, Implantation.**

(v) **Caterpillar, Snake, Owl, Frog, Green leaves.** **[2017]**

Ans. **(i)** Platelets → Thromboplastin → Thrombin → Fibrinogen → Fibrin

(ii) Pinna → Malleus → Incus → Stapes → Cochlea

(iii) Receptor → Sensory neuron → Spinal cord → Motor neuron → Effector

(iv) Fertilisation → Uterus → Implantation → Gestation → Parturition

(v) Green leaves → Caterpillar → Frog → Snake → Owl

Q. 25. **Choose the odd one out of the following terms given and name the category to which the others belong:**

(i) **Aqueous humour, Vitreous humour, Iris, Central canal**

(iii) **ACTH, TSH, ADH, FSH**

(iv) **Phosphate, RNA, Sugar, Nitrogenous base**

(v) **Bile, Urea, Uric acid, Ammonia** **[2017]**

Ans. **(i)** **Odd one :** Central canal

Category : Rest are found in our eye whereas central canal is seen in spinal cord.

(iii) **Odd one :** ADH

Category : Rest are hormones secreted from anterior pituitary whereas ADH is secreted from posterior pituitary.

(iv) **Odd one :** RNA

Category : Rest are components of a nucleotide whereas RNA is a nucleic acid.

(v) **Odd one :** Bile

Category : Rest are nitrogenous metabolic waste whereas bile is produced in liver and stored in gall bladder and play an important role in digestion i.e., emulsification of fats.

Q. 26. **Given below are group of terms. In each group the first pair indicates the relationship between the two terms. Rewrite and complete the second pair on a similar basis.**

Example : Oxygen : Inspiration : : Carbon dioxide : Expiration

(i) **Eye : Optic nerve : : Ear : __________.**

(ii) **Cytoplasm : Cytokinesis : : Nucleus : __________.**

(iii) **TT : Homozygous : : Tt : __________.**

(iv) **Foetus : Amnion : : Heart : __________.**

(v) **Adenine : Thymine : : Cytosine : __________.** **[2017]**

Ans. **(i)** Eye : Optic nerve : : Ear : <u>Auditory nerve</u>.

(ii) Cytoplasm : Cytokinesis : : Nucleus : <u>Karyokinesis</u>.

(iii) TT : Homozygous : : Tt : <u>Heterozygous</u>.

(iv) Foetus : Amnion : : Heart : <u>Pericardium</u>.

(v) Adenine : Thymine : : Cytosine : <u>Guanine</u>.

Q. 27. Match the items given in Column A with the most appropriate ones in Column B and rewrite the correct matching pairs:

	Column A	Column B
(i)	Sacculus	Dynamic body balance
(ii)	Birth rate	Hyperglycemia
(iii)	DNA and histones	Hypoglycemia
(iv)	Euro norms	Natality
(v)	Diabetes mellitus	Static body balance
		Vehicular standards
		Nucleosome

[2017]

Ans.

Column A	Column B
(i) Sacculus	— Static body balance
(ii) Birth rate	— Natality
(iii) DNA and histones	— Nucleosome
(iv) Euronorms	— Vehicular standards
(v) Diabetes mellitus	— Hyperglycemia

Q. 28. Name the following:
   (i) The exchange of chromatid parts between the maternal and the paternal chromatids of a pair of homologous chromosomes during meiosis.
   (ii) The number of individuals inhabiting per unit area.
   (iv) The pollutants that cannot be broken down to simple and harmless products.
   (v) The part of the brain that carries impulses from one hemisphere of the cerebellum to the other. [2016]

Ans.   (i) Crossing over
   (ii) Population density
   (iv) Non-biodegradable pollutants
   (v) Pons varolii

Q. 29. Choose the correct answer from each of the four options given below:
   (i) A plant cell may burst when :
      (a) Turgor pressure equalises wall pressure
      (b) Turgor pressure exceeds wall pressure
      (c) Wall pressure exceeds turgor pressure
      (d) None of the above
   (ii) The individual flattened stacks of membranous structures inside the chloroplasts are known as:
      (a) Grana   (b) Stroma
      (c) Thylakoids   (d) Cristae

   (iii) The nephrons discharge their urine at the:
      (a) Urinary bladder (b) Urethra
      (c) Renal pelvis   (d) Renal pyramid
   (iv) Gigantism and Acromegaly are due to:
      (a) Hyposecretion of Thyroxine
      (b) Hyposecretion of Growth hormone
      (c) Hypersecretion of Thyroxine
      (d) Hypersecretion of Growth hormone
   (v) The mineral ion needed for the formation of blood clot is :
      (a) Potassium   (b) Sodium
      (c) Calcium   (d) Iron   [2016]

Ans.   (i) (b) Turgor pressure exceeds wall pressure
   (ii) (c) Thylakoids
   (iii) (c) Renal pelvis
   (iv) (d) Hypersecretion of growth hormone
   (v) (c) Calcium

Q. 30. In each set of terms given below, there is an odd one and cannot be grouped in the same category to which the other three belong. Identify the odd term in each set and name the category to which the remaining three belong.
   Example: Ovary, Fallopian tube, Ureter, Uterus.
   Odd term: Ureter
   Category: Parts of female reproductive system.
   (i) Sewage, Newspaper, Styrofoam, Hay.
   (ii) Thymine, Cytosine, Adenine, Pepsin.
   (iii) Malleus, Iris, Stapes, Incus.
   (iv) Cortisone, Somatotropin, Adrenocortico-tropic hormone, Vasopressin.
   (v) Typhoid, Haemophilia, Albinism, Colour blindness. [2016]

Ans.   (i) **Odd term** : Styrofoam
   Category : Biodegradable materials
   (ii) **Odd term** : Pepsin
   Category : Nitrogenous bases of DNA
   (iii) **Odd term** : Iris
   Category : Ear ossicles
   (iv) **Odd term** : Cortisone
   Category : Hormones secreted by pituitary gland
   (v) **Odd term** : Typhoid
   Category : Genetic disorders

Q. 31. Complete the following paragraph by filling in the blanks (i) to (v) with appropriate words:

The amount of urine output is under the regulation of a hormone called

(i) _______ secreted by the (ii) _______ lobe of the pituitary gland. If this hormone secretion is reduced, there is an increased production of urine. This disorder is called (iii) __________ . Sometimes excess glucose is passed with urine due to hyposecretion of another hormone called (iv)______ leading to the cause of a disease called (v) __________ . [2016]

Ans. (i) Antidiuretic hormone (ADH) or Vasopressin

(ii) Posterior   (iii) Diabetes insipidus

(iv) Insulin   (v) Diabetes mellitus

Q. 32. State the exact location of the following structures:

(i) **Centromere**   (ii) **Chordae tendinae**

(iii) **Thyroid gland**   (iv) **Ciliary body**

(v) **Proximal convoluted tubule** [2016]

Ans. (i) **Centromere**: A part of chromosome is marked by a primary constriction which divides the chromosome into two arms. In this region of primary constriction, lies the centromere, which joins the two sister chromatids.

(ii) **Chordae tendinae**: Between bicuspid/tricuspid valves and papillary muscles of the heart.

(iii) **Thyroid gland**: Thyroid gland is present below larynx over the upper part of the trachea in the neck region.

(iv) **Ciliary body**: At the junction of choroid and iris.

(v) **Proximal convoluted tubule**: At the cortex of the kidney, just below the Bowman's capsule.

Q. 33. Given in the box below are a set of 14 biological terms. Of these, 12 can be paired into 6 matching pairs. Out of the six pairs, one has been done for you as an example.

Example : Endosmosis — Turgid cell.

> Cushing's syndrome, Turgid cell, Iris, Free of rod and cone cells, Colour of eyes, Hypoglycemia, Active transport, Acrosome, Addison's disease, Blind spot, Hyperglycemia, Spermatozoa, Endosmosis, Clotting of blood.

[2016]

Ans.

1.	Cushing's syndrome	Hyperglycemia
2.	Iris	Colour of the eyes
3.	Free of rod and cone cells	Blind spot
4.	Hypoglycemia	Addison's disease
5.	Acrosome	Spermatozoa

Q. 34. State the main function of the following:

(i) **Lymphocytes of blood**

(ii) **Leydig cells**

(iii) **Guard cells**

(iv) **Eustachian tube**

(v) **Corpus luteum** [2016]

(h) (i) **Lymphocytes of blood**: These are the defense cells of our body. These produce antibodies for immobilizing the foreign particles and their toxins. They are thus, the immunity arsenals of our body.

(ii) **Leydig cells**: Also called 'Interstitial cells'. Secrete male sex hormone testosterone.

(iii) **Guard cells**: Regulates the opening and closing of stomata in leaf to facilitate transpiration and exchange of gases.

(iv) **Eustachian tube**: Balances air pressure on either sides of eardrum, so that eardrum can vibrate freely.

(v) **Corpus luteum**: Secretes hormones oesterogen, progesterone and relaxin.

Q. 35. Name the following:

(i) The process of uptake of mineral ions against the concentration gradient using energy from cell.

(ii) The form in which glucose is stored in liver.

(iii) The vein that carries oxygenated blood.

(iv) The cross between two parents having one pair of contrasting characters.

(v) The structure formed by the villi of the embryo and the uterus of the mother. [2015]

Ans. (i) Active Transport

(ii) Glycogen

(iii) Pulmonary veins

(iv) Monohybrid cross

(v) Placenta

Q. 36. The statements given below are False. Rewrite the correct form of the statement by changing the word which is underlined:

(i) Alpha cells of pancreas secrete **Insulin**.

(iii) **CNG** is mainly responsible for the formation of acid rain.

(v) Cretinism is caused due to deficiency of **Adrenaline**. [2015]

Ans. (i) Glucagon   (iii) SO_2

(v) Thyroxine

Q. 37. Choose the correct answer from the four options given below:

(i) A single highly coiled tube where sperms are stored, gets concentrated and mature is known as:

(a) Epididymis

(b) Vas efferentia

(c) Vas deferens

(d) Seminiferous tubule.

(ii) Chromosomes get aligned at the centre of the cell during:

(a) Metaphase   (b) Anaphase

(c) Prophase   (d) Telophase

(iv) Which one of the following is mainly associated with the maintenance of the posture?

(a) Cerebrum   (b) Cerebellum

(c) Thalamus   (d) Pons

(v) An example of non-biodegradable waste is:

(a) Vegetable peels   (b) Sewage

(c) Livestock waste   (d) DDT   [2015]

Ans. (i) (a) Epididymis   (ii) (b) Metaphse

(iv) (b) Cerebellum   (v) (d) DDT

Q. 38. Mention the exact location of the following structures:

(i) Thylakoids   (ii) Organ of Corti

(iii) Lenticels   (iv) Bicuspid Valve

(v) Loop of Henle   [2015]

Ans. (i) Present in each granum of the chloroplast.

(ii) Present in the cochlea of internal ear.

(iii) Present in the epidermis of the stems of woody plants.

(iv) Present in between the left atrium and left ventricle.

(v) Present in the medulla region of the kidney and conncets PCT with DCT.

Q. 39. Given below is an example of a certain structure and its special functional activity. On a similar pattern fill in the blanks with suitable functions:

Example: Chloroplast and Photosynthesis:

(i) Xylem and ....

(ii) Ciliary Body and ....

(iii) Seminiferous Tubule and ....

(iv) Thyroid Gland and ....

(v) Eustachian Tube and ....   [2015]

Ans. (i) Xylem and Water transport.

(ii) Ciliary body and accommodation of eye lens.

(iii) Seminiferous tubule and Spermatogenesis

(iv) Thyroid gland and Secretion of thyroxine

(v) Eustachian tube and Equalising air pressure.

Q. 40. Rewrite and complete the following sentences by inserting the correct word in the space indicated:

(i) The phenomenon of loss of water through a cut stem or injured part of plant is called ....

(ii) .... is the scientific name of garden pea, which Mendel used for his experiments.

(iii) A fluid that occupies the larger cavity of the eye ball behind the lens is ....

(iv) Oxygen combines with haemoglobin present in RBC and forms ....

(v) .... causes corrosion of the marble or brick surface.   [2015]

Ans. (i) Bleeding

(ii) Pisum sativum

(iii) Vitreous humour

(iv) Oxy-haemoglobin

(v) Acid rain

Q. 41. Match the items in Column 'A' with those which are most appropriate in Column 'B'. Rewrite the matching pairs as shown in the example:

Example: Fibrinogen–Clotting of blood.

	Column A	Column B
(i)	Allele	(a) Control of automobile exhaust
(ii)	Leydig cells	(b) Tourniquet
(iii)	Utriculus	(c) Alternate forms of genes
(v)	Euro IV norms	(d) Dynamic equilibrium
		(e) Testosterone
		(f) Sudden change in genes
		(g) Static equilibrium

[2015]

Ans.

	Column A	Column B
(i)	Allele	(c) Alternate forms of genes
(ii)	Leydig cells	(e) Testosterone
(iii)	Utriculus	(g) Static equilibrium
(v)	Euro IV norms	(a) Control of automobile exhaust

Q. 42. Name the following:

(i) The part of the brain associated with memory.

(ii) The ear ossicle which is attached to the tympanum.

(iii) The type of gene, which in the presence of a contrasting allele is not expressed.

(iv) The hormone secreted by islets of langerhans.

(v) The process of conversion of ADP into ATP during photosynthesis.   [2014]

Ans. (i) Cerebrum   (ii) Malleus
(iii) Recessive   (iv) Insulin/Glucagon
(v) Photophosphorylation

Q. 43. **State the main function of the following:**
(i) **Cerebrospinal fluid**
(ii) **Eustachian tube**
(iii) **Suspensory ligament of the eye**
(iv) **Sperm duct**
(v) **Lenticels**   **[2014]**

Ans. (i) It acts as a cushion to protect the brain from jerks and shocks.
(ii) It equalizes air pressure on both sides of the ear drum helping it to vibrate freely.
(iii) It helps to suspend the lens in the eye ball cavity.
(iv) It carries sperms from the epididymis to the urethra.
(v) They allow diffusion of gases for respiration and photosynthesis.

Q. 44. **Given below are six sets with four terms each. In each set one term is odd and cannot be grouped in the same category to which the other three belong. Identify the odd one in each set and name the category to which the remaining three belong. The first one has been done as an example.**
Example: Calyx, Corolla, Stamens, Midrib
Odd term: Midrib
Category: Parts of a flower.
(i) **Haemoglobin, Glucagon, Iodopsin, Rhodopsin.**
(ii) **Urethra, Uterus, Urinary bladder, Ureter.**
(iii) **Transpiration, Photosynthesis, Phagocytosis, Guttation.**
(iv) **Cyton, Photon, Axon, Dendron.**
(v) **Oxytocin, Insulin, Prolactin, Progesterone.**   **[2014]**

Ans. (i) **Odd** : Glucagon
Category : Pigments
(ii) **Odd** : Uterus
Category : Excretory organs
(iii) **Odd** : Phagocytosis
Category : Plant processes
(iv) **Odd** : Photon
Category : Parts of neuron
(v) **Odd** : Insulin
Category : Female hormones.

Q. 45. **Match the items given in Column A with the most appropriate ones in Column B and rewrite the correct matching pairs from Column A and Column B:**

S. No.	Column A	Column B
1.	Pituitary gland	(a) Testosterone
2.	Sulphur dioxide	(b) Calcium
3.	Seminiferous tubules	(c) Growth hormone
4.	Clotting of blood	(d) Acid rain
5.	Guttation	(e) Sperms
		(f) Global warming
		(g) Magnesium
		(h) Hydathodes

[2014]

Ans.

S. No.	Column A	Column B
1.	Pituitary gland	(c) Growth hormone
2.	Sulphur dioxide	(d) Acid rain
3.	Seminiferous tubules	(e) Sperms
4.	Clotting of blood	(b) Calcium
5.	Guttation	(h) Hydathodes

Q. 46. **Choose the correct answer from the options given below:**
(i) **Cretinism and Myxoedema are due to:**
(a) **Hypersecretion of thyroxin**
(b) **Hypersecretion of growth hormone**
(c) **Hyposecretion of thyroxin.**
(d) **Hyposecretion of growth hormone.**
(ii) **Which of the following is not a natural reflex action?**
(a) **Knee-jerk.**
(b) **Blinking of eyes due to strong light.**
(c) **Salivation at the sight of food.**
(d) **Sneezing when any irritant enters the nose.**
(iii) **After mitotic cell division, a female human cell will have:**
(a) **44 + xx chromosome.**
(b) **44 + xy chromosome.**
(c) **22 + x chromosome.**
(d) **22 + y chromosome.**
(v) **The site of maturation of human sperms is the:**
(a) **Seminiferous tubule**
(b) **Interstitital cells**
(c) **Epididymys**
(d) **Prostate gland**   **[2014]**

Ans. (i) (c) Hyposecretion of thyroxin.
(ii) (c) Salivation at the sight of food.

(iii) **(a)** 44 + xx chromosome

(v) **(c)** Epididymis

Q. 47. **State the exact location of the following:**

(i) **Tricuspid valve** **(ii)** **Amnion**

(iii) **Yellow spot** **(iv)** **Seminal vesicle**

(v) **Adrenal gland** **[2014]**

Ans. **(i)** **Tricuspid valve**—Between right auricle and right ventricle.

(ii) **Amnion**—Around the embryo in uterus and inner to chorion.

(iii) **Yellow spot**—On the horizontal median axis of eye ball in retina.

(iv) **Seminal vesicle**—Lobulated glands located between the posterior surface of the urinary bladder and the rectum.

(v) **Adrenal gland**—On top of each kidney as a cap.

Q. 48. **Copy and complete the following by filling in the blanks 1 to 5 with appropriate words:**

The human female gonads are ovaries. A maturing egg in the ovary is present in a sac of cells called............(1). As the egg grows larger, the follicle enlarges and gets filled with a fluid and is now called the............ (2) follicle. The process of releasing the egg from the ovary is called...............(3). The ovum is picked up by the oviduct funnel and fertilisation takes place in the............(4). In about a week the blastocyst gets fixed in the endometrium of the uterus and this process is called............(5). **[2014]**

Ans. **(1)** Follicle. **(2)** Graafian

(3) Ovulation **(4)** Oviduct

(5) Implantation

Q. 49. **Name the following:**

(i) **The cell body of a nerve cell.**

(ii) **The waxy layer on the epidermis of the leaf meant to reduce transpiration.**

(iii) **A non-biodegradable pesticide.**

(iv) **The physical expression of genes in an individual.**

(v) **Knot-like mass of blood capillaries inside the Bowman's capsule.** **[2013]**

Ans. **(i)** Cyton **(ii)** Cuticle

(iii) DDT **(iv)** Phenotype

(v) Glomerulus

Q. 50. **State the exact location of the following:**

(i) **Chloroplast** **(ii)** **Incus**

(iii) **Corpus callosum** **(iv)** **Guard cells**

(v) **Pulmonary semilunar valve.** **[2013]**

Ans. **(i)** **Chloroplast:** In mesophyll cells, located between upper and lower epidermis.

(ii) **Incus:** In middle ear inside tympanic cavity between malleus and stapes.

(iii) **Corpus callosum:** Thick band of nerve fibres joining two cerebral hemispheres of cerebrum.

(iv) **Guard cells:** Pair of guard cells surround the stomata on the upper and lower epidermis of leaf.

(v) **Pulmonary semilunar valve:** In right ventricle which guards the opening of pulmonary trunk.

Q. 51. **Given below are six sets with four terms each. In each set a term is an odd one and cannot be grouped in the same category to which the other three belong. Identify the odd one in each set and name the category to which the remaining three belong. The first one has been done as an example:**

Example: **Fructose, Sucrose, Glucose, Calcium.**

Odd term: Calcium

Category: Carbohydrates.

(ii) **Saliva, bile, sweat, tears.**

(iii) **Cretinism, myxedema, simple goitre, acromegaly.**

(iv) **Sneezing, coughing, blinking, typing.**

(v) **Semicircular canals, cochlea, tympanum, utriculus.** **[2013]**

Ans. **(ii)** **Odd term :** Bile

Category : Germ killing secretions

(iii) **Odd term :** Acromegaly

Category : Effects of abnormal thyroxine secretion

(iv) **Odd term :** Typing

Category : Unconditioned reflex

(v) **Odd term :** Tympanum

Category : Parts of inner ear.

Q. 52. **Match the items in Column A with that which is most appropriate in Column B. Rewrite the matching pair.**

Column A	Column B
(1) Testis	**(a) Kidney**
(3) Transpiration	**(b) Water vapour**
(4) Clotting of blood	**(c) Prostate gland**
(5) Uriniferous tubule	**(d) Iron**
	(e) Uterus
	(f) Gonad
	(g) Salk's vaccine
	(h) Water droplet
	(i) Calcium
	(j) TAB vaccine

[2013]

Ans.

Sr. No.	Column A	Column B
(1)	Testis	(f) Gonad
(3)	Transpiration	(b) Water vapour
(4)	Clotting of blood	(i) Calcium
(5)	Uriniferous tubule	(a) Kidney

Q. 53. Choose the correct answer from the four options given below:

(i) The cell component visible only during cell division:

    (a) Mitochondria   (b) Chloroplast

    (c) Chromosome   (d) Chromatin

(ii) Pulse wave is mainly caused by the:

    (a) Systole of atria

    (b) Diastole of atria

    (c) Systole of the left ventricle

    (d) Systole of the right ventricle

(iii) The recessive gene is one that expresses itself in :

    (a) Heterozygous condition

    (b) Homozygous condition

    (c) F_2 generation

    (d) Y-linked inheritance.

(iv) A gland which secretes both hormone and enzyme is the:

    (a) Pituitary   (b) Pancreas

    (c) Thyroid   (d) Adrenal

(v) The ventral root ganglion of the spinal cord contains cell bodies of the:

    (a) Motor neuron

    (b) Sensory neuron

    (c) Intermediate neuron

    (d) Association neuron.   [2013]

Ans. (i) (c) Chromosome

(ii) (c) Systole of left ventricle

(iii) (b) Homozygous condition

(iv) (b) Pancreas

(v) (a) Motor neuron

Q. 54. Given below is an example of certain structures and their special functional activities.

For example : Eye and vision, On a similar pattern complete the following:

(i) Neutrophils : ....

(ii) Ureter : ....

(iii) Neurotransmitters : ....

(iv) Iris of the eye : ....

(v) Placenta : .... [2013]

Ans. (i) **Neutrophils**: Engulf microbes (phagocytosis)

(ii) **Ureter**: Carries urine from kidneys to the urinary bladder.

(iii) **Neurotransmitters**: Carry nerve impulse.

(iv) **Iris of the eye**: Regulate the amount of light entering into the eye by controlling the size of pupil.

(v) **Placenta** Transfer nutrients, oxygen, etc. from materal blood to foetus.

Q. 55. Given below are five groups of terms. In each group arrange and rewrite the terms in the correct order so as to be in a logical sequence.

For example:

Question: Implantation, Parturition, Ovulation, Gestation, Fertilization.

Answer: Ovulation, Fertilization, Implantation, Gestation, Parturition.

(i) Spongy cells, Upper epidermis, Stoma, Palisade tissue, Substomatal space.

(ii) Spinal cord, Motor neuron, Receptor, Effector, Sensory neuron.

(iii) Endodermis, Cortex, Soil water, Xylem, Root hair.

(iv) Metaphase, Telophase, Prophase, Anaphase, Cytokinesis.

(v) Intestine, Liver, Intestinal artery, Hepatic Vein, Hepatic Portal Vein.   [2013]

Ans. (i) Upper epidermis, palisade tissue, spongy cells, substomatal space, stoma.

(ii) Receptor, sensory neuron, spinal cord, motor neuron, effector.

(iii) Soil water, root hair, cortex, endodermis, xylem.

(iv) Prophase, metaphase, anaphase, telophase, cytokinesis.

(v) Intestinal artery, intestine, hepatic portal vein, liver, hepatic vein.

Q. 56. Name the following:

(i) The phenomenon by which living or dead plant cells absorb water by surface attraction.

(ii) The phase of cardiac cycle in which the auricles contract.

(iii) The organ where urea is produced.

(iv) The hormone that helps increase the reabsorption of water from the kidney tubules.   [2012]

Ans. (i) Imbibition

(ii) Atrial systole

(iii) Liver

(iv) Vasopressin or Antidiuretic Hormone (ADH)

Q. 57. Choose the correct answer from the four options given below each statement:

(ii) A plant is kept in a dark cupboard for about 48 hours before conducting any experiment on photosynthesis to:

(a) **Remove starch from the plant.**

(b) **Ensure that starch is not translocated from the leaves.**

(c) **Remove chlorophyll from the leaf of the plant.**

(d) **Remove starch from the experimental leaf.**

(iii) **The part of the human eye where rod cells and cone cells are located is the:**

(a) **Retina**   (b) **Cornea**

(c) **Choroid**   (d) **Sclera.**

(iv) **A reflex arc in man is best described as movement of stimuli from :**

(a) **Receptor cell, sensory neuron, relaying neuron, effector muscles.**

(b) **Receptor cell, efferent nerve, relaying neuron, muscles of the body.**

(c) **Receptor cell, spinal cord, motor neuron, relaying neuron.**

(d) **Receptor cell, synapse, motor neuron, relaying neuron.**

(v) **NADP is expanded as:**

(a) **Nicotinamide adenosine dinucleotide phosphate.**

(b) **Nicotinamide adenine dinucleotide phosphate**

(c) **Nicotinamide adenine dinucleous phosphate**

(d) **Nicotinamide adenosine dinucleous phosphate.**   [2012]

Ans. (ii) (a) Remove starch from the plant.

(iii) (a) Retina

(iv) (a) Receptor cell, sensory neuron, relaying neuron, effector muscles.

(v) (b) Nicotinamide adenine dinucleotide phosphate

Q. 58. State the main function of the following:

(i) **Chordae tendinae**

(iii) **Seminiferous tubule**

(iv) **Thylakoids**

(v) **Beta cells of pancreas**   [2012]

Ans. (i) **Chordae tendinae**: Keeps the valves in position and prevents the backflow of blood in the atria.

(iii) **Seminiferous tubule**: Formation of sperms by spermatogenesis.

(iv) **Thylakoids**: Absorb sunlight for the photosynthesis process to occur.

(v) **Beta cells of pancreas**: Produce insulin.

Q. 59. Give the exact location of the following:

(i) **Lenticels**   (ii) **Prostate gland**

(iii) **Thyroid gland**   (iv) **Centrosome**

(v) **Mitral valve.**   [2012]

Ans. (i) **Lenticels**: Loose aggregation of cells in the bark of the stems and roots of certain plants for gaseous exchange.

(ii) **Prostate gland**: At the base of urinary bladder.

(iii) **Thyroid gland**: In the neck region at the base of larynx.

(iv) **Centrosome**: Situated close to the nucleus in Eukaryotic cell.

(v) **Mitral valve or bicuspid valve**: Present in the left atrio-ventricular aperture within the heart.

Q. 60. Given below are sets of five terms each. In each case rewrite the terms in logical sequence as directed at the end of each statement. An example has been done for you:

Example : Cortical cells, Root hair, xylem, Soil water, endodermis (absorption of water by the plants)

Answer : Soil water, Root hair, cortical cells, endodermis, xylem.

(ii) **Implantation, Parturition, Ovulation, Gestation, Fertilization (stages leading to formation of foetus and birth).**

(iii) **Oval window, Tympanum, Cochlea, Auditory canal, Ear ossicles (path through which a vibration of sound is transferred in the human ear).**

(iv) **Karyokinesis, S-phase, Cytokinesis, G_1-phase, G_2-phase (cell cycle).**

(v) **Renal vein, Renal artery, Afferent arteriole, Efferent arteriole, Glomerulus (pathway of blood through glomerulus).**   [2012]

Ans. (ii) Ovulation, fertilization, implantation, gestation, parturition.

(iii) Auditory canal, tympanum, ear ossicles, oval window, cochlea.

(iv) G_1-phase, S-phase, G_2-phase, Karyokinesis, Cytokinesis.

(v) Renal artery, afferent arteriole, glomerulus, efferent arteriole, renal vein.

Q. 61. Match the items in Column A with that which is most appropriate in Column B. Rewrite the matching pairs:

Column A	Column B
(1) Potometer	(a) Antiseptic
(2) Hypothalamus	(b) Disinfectants
(4) Contraception in males	(c) Vasectomy
(5) Mutation	(d) Sudden change in genes
	(e) Pituitary gland
	(f) Tubectomy
	(g) Transpiration

	(h)	Thyroid gland
	(i)	Alleles
	(j)	Photosynthesis

[2012]

Ans.

Column A	Column B
(1) Potometer	(g) Transpiration
(2) Hypothalamus	(e) Pituitary gland
(4) Contraception in males	(c) Vasectomy
(5) Mutation	(d) Sudden change in genes

Q. 62. Given below are six sets with four terms each. In each set a term is an odd one and cannot be grouped in the same category to which the other three belong. Identify the odd one in each set and name the category to which the remaining three belong. The first has been done for you as an example.

No.	Set	Odd one	Category
e.g. :	Cell wall, large vacuole, plastids, centrosome	Centrosome	Parts of plant cell
(i)	Cerebrum, cerebellum, thalamus, hypothalamus		
(ii)	Ovary, ureter, fallopian tube, uterus		
(iii)	Adrenal gland, liver, thyroid gland, pituitary gland		
(iv)	Malleus, pinna, incus, stapes		
(v)	Haemophilia, colour blindness, albinism, night blindness		

[2012]

Ans.

	Odd one	Category
(i)	Cerebellum	Parts of forebrain
(ii)	Ureter	Parts of female reproductive system
(iii)	Liver	Endocrine glands
(iv)	Pinna	Ear ossicles
(v)	Night blindness	Sex-linked inheritance

Q. 63. Name the following:
  (i) The mineral element essential for the clotting of blood.
  (ii) The cells of the testes that produce male hormones.
  (iii) The nutritive layer of the eye which also prevents reflection of light.
  (iv) The structural and functional unit of the kidney.
  (v) The part of the chloroplast where the light reaction of photosynthesis takes place. [2011]

Ans. (i) Calcium
  (ii) Interstitial cells/Leydig cells
  (iii) Choroid
  (iv) Nephron/Uriniferous tubule
  (v) Thylakoids

Q. 64. State the main function of the following:
  (i) Yellow spot   (ii) Coronary artery
  (iii) Medulla oblongata (iv) Thrombocytes
  (v) Vitreous humour. [2011]

Ans. (i) It is the region of best, clearest and sharpest vision.
  (ii) It carries oxygenated blood to the muscles of heart.
  (iii) It controls involuntary functions of the body like heart beat, breathing etc.
  (iv) Thrombocytes help in clotting of blood.
  (v) It maintains the shape of eyeball.

Q. 65. Give the exact location of:
  (i) Hydathodes   (ii) Organ of corti
  (iii) Mitral valve   (iv) Pituitary gland
  (v) Amnion [2011]

Ans. (i) At the tip and margins of leaves.
  (ii) In the endolymph, present in the middle canal of cochlea.
  (iii) Between the opening of left auricle and left ventricle.
  (iv) At the base of brain.
  (v) Around the embryo in the uterus.

Q. 66. State whether the following statements are True or False. If False rewrite the correct form of the statement by changing the first or last word only:
  (i) Lysosomes is a part of the cell in which chromosomes are present.
  (ii) Urethra carries urine from kidney to the urinary bladder.
  (iii) Centromere is the organelle of the cell that initiates cell division.
  (iv) Gestation is the process of fixing of the zygote to the uterine wall. [2011]

Ans. (i) False. Nucleus is a part of the cell in which chromosomes are present.

(ii) False. Ureter carries urine from kidney to the urinary bladder.

(iii) False. Centrosome is the organelle of the cell that initiates cell division.

(iv) False. Implantation is the process of fixing of the zygote to the uterine wall.

Q. 67. Rewrite and complete the following sentences by inserting the correct word in the space indicated:

    (ii) Phenotype is the observable characteristic which is............controlled.

    (iii) Wooden doors swell up in rainy season due to..........

    (iv) The blood vessel that begins and ends in capillaries is the.............

    (v) .... is the phenomenon of contraction of the cytoplasm from the cell wall. **[2011]**

Ans. **(ii)** Phenotype is the observable characteristic which is genetically controlled.

    (iii) Wooden doors swell up in rainy season due to imbibition.

    (iv) The blood vessel that begins and ends in capillaries is the portal vein.

    (v) Plasmolysis is the phenomenon of contraction of the cytoplasm from the cell wall.

Q. 68. Match the items in Column I with that which is most appropriate in Column II.

Column I	Column II
(1) Pacemaker	(a) Associated with static body balance
(2) Stroma	(b) Chordae tendinae
(3) Afferent nerve	(c) Site of light reaction
(4) Prolactin	(d) Motor neuron
(5) Saccules	(e) S A node
	(f) Stimulates production of milk by the mammary gland
	(g) Site of dark reaction
	(h) Transmits impulses from receptor organ to spinal cord
	(i) Secreted by anterior lobe of Pituitary gland
	(j) Transfers impulses from spinal cord to muscles.

[2011]

Ans.

Column I	Column II
(1) Pacemaker	(e) SA node
(2) Stroma	(g) Site of dark reaction
(3) Afferent nerve	(h) Transmists impulses from receptor organ to spinal cord
(4) Prolactin	(f) Stimulates production of milk by the mammary gland
(5) Saccules	(a) Associated with static body balance

Q. 69. Name the following :

    (i) The type of cell division which occurs in the cells of the reproductive organs.

    (ii) A plant with sunken stomata.

    (iii) The place where fertilization occurs in the female reproductive system. **[2010]**

Ans. **(i)** Meiosis   **(ii)** Nerium

    (iii) Oviduct

Q. 70. State whether the following statements are true or false. If false, rewrite the correct form of the statement by changing the first or last word only.

    (i) Tubectomy is the surgical method of sterilization in males.

    (ii) Mitosis is the type of cell division occurring in the cells of injured parts of the body.

    (iii) Photolysis is the process of splitting of water molecules in the presence of grana and temperature.

    (iv) Dilation of the pupil is brought about by the sympathetic nervous system.

    (v) Chromosomes other than the pair of sex chromosome are called alleles. **[2010]**

Ans. **(i)** False, **Vasectomy** is the surgical method of sterilisation in males.

    (ii) True.

    (iii) False, Photolysis is the process of splitting of water molecules in the presence of grana and **light**.

    (iv) True.

    (v) False, Chromosomes other than the pair of sex chromosomes are called **autosomes**.

Q. 71. Given below are five sets of five terms each. In each case, rewrite the terms in logical sequence as directed at the end of each statement.

One has been done for you as an example.

Example: Anaphase, Telophase, Prophase, Metaphase, Interphase. (sequential order of Karyokinesis)

Answer : Interphase, Prophase, Metaphase, Anaphase, Telophase.

(i) Vagina, Ovary, Uterus, Oviduct, Cervix (pathway of egg after ovulation)

(ii) Motor Neuron, Receptor, Sensory Neuron, Effector, Association Neuron. (pathway of a nerve impulse)

(iii) Pupil, Yellow Spot, Cornea, Lens, Aqueous humour. (path of entry of light into the eye from an object)

(iv) Stoma, Mesophyll cells, Xylem, Substomatal space, Intercellular space (loss of water due to transpiration)

(v) Cortical cells, root hair, soil, water, endodermis, xylem. (entry of water into the plant from the soil) **[2010]**

Ans. Ovary, Oviduct, Uterus, Cervix, Vagina.

(ii) Receptor, Sensory Neuron, Association Neuron, Motor Neuron, Effector.

(iii) Cornea, Aqueous Humour, Pupil, Lens, Yellow Spot.

(iv) Xylem, Mesophyll Cells, Intercellular Space, Substomatal Space, Stoma.

(v) Soil, Water, Root Hair, Cortical Cells, Endodermis, Xylem.

Q. 72. There are five sets consisting of five terms given below. In each set there is a word which is an odd one. For each of these sets write down the category of the group having identified the odd one out, as shown in the example :

Example : (0) cell wall, vacuole, centrosome, plastids, mitochondria.

S. No.	Category	Odd One
0	Organelles of Plant Cell	Centrosome

(i) Blinking, Knitting without looking, Smiling, Blushing, Crying.

(ii) Myopia, Cataract, Hypermetropia, Squint, Cretinism.

(iii) Cowper's gland, Urethral gland, Lacrimal gland, Seminal vesicles, Prostrate gland.

(iv) Vasopressin, Growth hormone, TSH, ACTH, FSH.

(v) Cresol, DDT, Lime, Mercurochrome, Bordeaux mixture.** **[2010]**

Ans.

S. No.	Category	Odd one
(i)	Simple reflexes	Knitting without looking
(ii)	Diseases of eye	Cretinism
(iii)	Associated with male reproductive parts	Lacrimal gland

(iv)	Hormones from anterior pituitary	Vasopressin

Q. 73. Choose the correct answer to the following statements out of the three choices given after each statement.

(i) A point of contact between two neurons is termed :

(A) Synapsi

(B) Neuro motor junction

(C) Synapse.

(ii) Loss of water as droplets from hydathodes is called :

(A) Transpiration   (B) Bleeding

(C) Guttation

(iii) The technical term for the fertilized egg is :

(A) Placenta   (B) Zygote

(C) Morula

(iv) The photo receptor cells of the retina sensitive to colour are :

(A) Cones   (B) Rods

(C) Organ of Corti   **[2010]**

Ans. (i) 3. Synapse   (ii) 3. Guttation

(iii) 2. Zygote   (iv) 1. Cones

Q. 74. Given below is an example of a certain structure and its special functional activity : Example : (0) Ribosomes and <u>Protein synthesis</u>. On a similar pattern complete the following:

(i) Hypothalamus and ---------------.

(ii) Suspensory ligaments and -------------.

(iii) Semi-circular canals and --------------.

(iv) Mitochondria and ---------------.

(v) Seminiferous tubules and ---------------. **[2010]**

Ans. (i) Controlling pituitary gland.

(ii) Holding eye lens in position.

(iii) Dynamic balance.

(iv) Cellular respiration.

(v) Spermatogenisis.

Q. 75. Explain the following terms :

(i) Hormones   (ii) Diffusion

(iii) Destarched plant   **[2010]**

Ans. (i) **Hormones** : These are the chemicals produced by ductless glands into the blood and which act on target organs.

(ii) **Diffusion** : It is the movement of molecules of any type, from their high to their low concentration.

(iii) **Destarched plant :** It is the plant in which starch has been removed from the leaves completely by keeping the plant in dark for 24-48 hours.

Chapter 1

Cell Cycle, Cell Division and Structure of Chromosome

Q. 1. Given below is a diagram representing a stage during the mitotic cell division. Study the diagram and answer the following question:

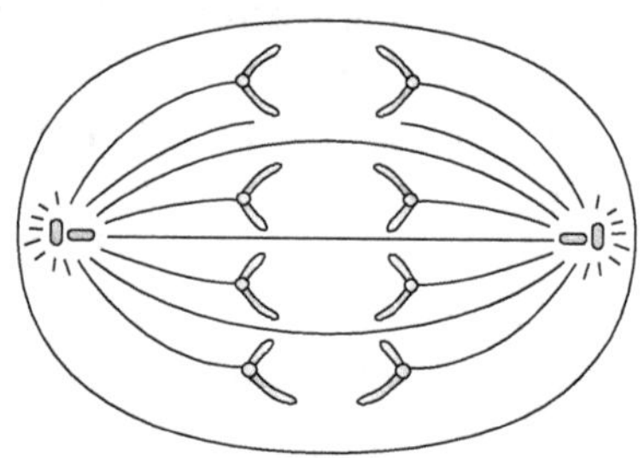

(i) Identify the stage by giving a suitable reason.

(ii) Is it a plant or an animal cell ? Give a reason to support your answer.

(iii) Draw a neat, labelled diagram of the stage which follows the one shown in the diagram.

(iv) How many chromosomes will each daughter cell have after the completion of the above division?

(v) Name of the nitrogenous bases. [2019]

Marking Scheme

(i) Anaphase
Chromatids are being pulled towards the opposite poles.

(ii) Animal cell
Cell wall is absent, centrioles are present, asters are present.

(iii)

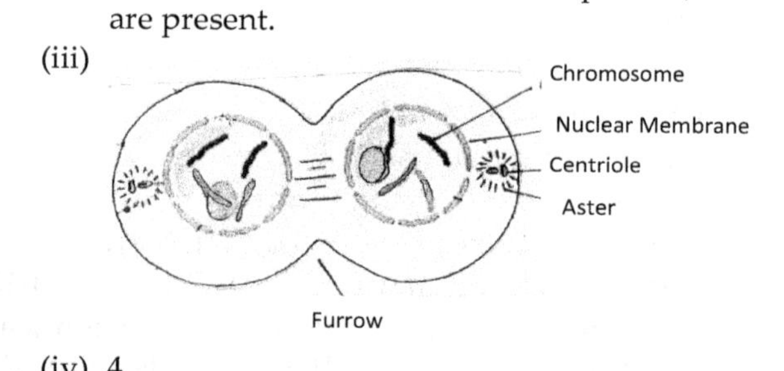

(iv) 4

(v) Adenine, Thymine, Cytosine, Guanine.

Ans. (i) It is anaphase stage of mitosis as the two sister chromatids are separated from each other and moving towards opposite poles by contraction of spindle fibres.

(ii) It is an animal cell as there is presence of centrioles and formation of aster, also cell wall is absent.

(iii) Telophase

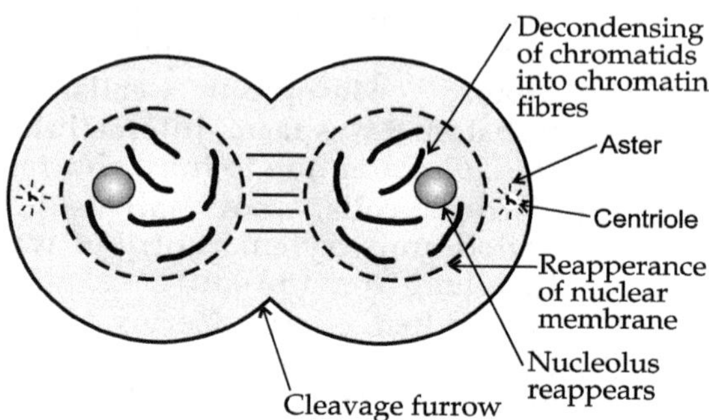

(iv) Each daughter cell shall have 4 chromosomes as in mitosis process, the number of chromosome remains constant.

(v) Adenine, Guanine, Cytosine, Thymine.

Q. 2. The diagram given below represents a stage during cell division.
Study the same and answer the questions that follow:

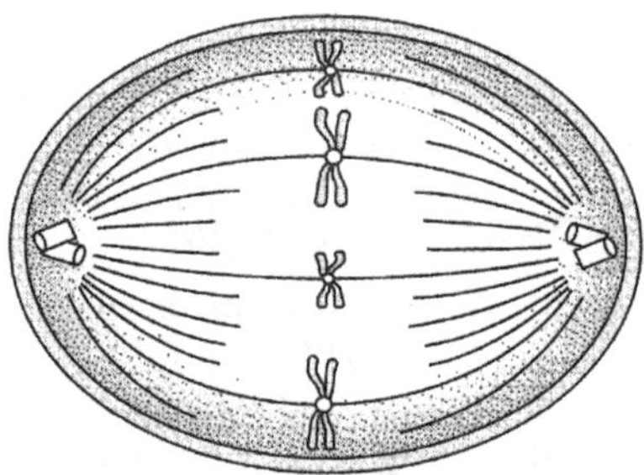

(i) Identify whether it is a plant cell or an animal cell.
Give a reason in support of your answer.

(ii) Name the stage depicted in the diagram. What is the unique feature observed in this stage?

(iii) Name the type of cell division that occurs during:
(1) Replacement of old leaves by new ones.
(2) Formation of gametes.

(iv) What is the stage that comes before the stage shown in the diagram?

(v) Draw a neat, labelled diagram of the stage mentioned in (iv) above keeping the chromosome number constant.

[2018]

📋 **Marking Scheme** ----------------------------------

   (i) Plant cell/cell wall present, Aster absent, Aster present Animal cell, Centrioles/Centrosome present

  (ii) Metaphase, Chromosomes are in the equatorial plane.

 (iii) 1. Mitosis   2. Meosis

 (iv) Prophase

  (v)

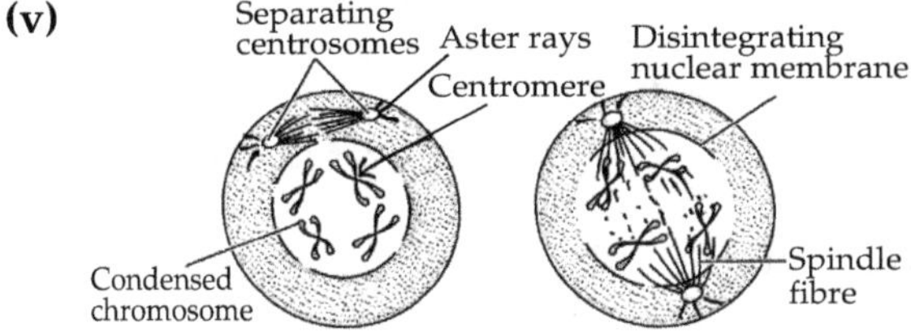

Ans.   **(i)** It is an animal cell as centrioles are present and aster is also present.

   (ii) Metaphase of mitosis

     All the duplicated chromosomes are aligned on the equatorial plane and the chromosomes are attached to the spindle fibres through centromere.

 (iii) **(1)** Mitosis   **(2)** Meiosis

  (iv) Prophase

   (v)

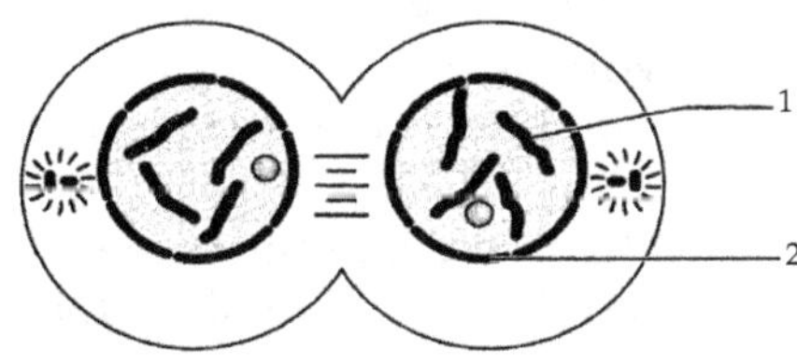

Q. 3. Study the diagram given below which represents a stage during the mitotic cell division and answer the questions that follow:

(i) Identify the stage giving suitable reasons.

(ii) Name the parts numbered 1 and 2.

(iii) What is the technical term for the division of nucleus?

(iv) Mention the stage the comes before the stage shown in the diagram. Draw a neat labelled diagram of the stage mentioned.

(v) Which is the cell division that results in half the number of chromosomes in daughter cells? **[2017]**

Ans.   **(i)** The stage shown in the figure is telophase due to the following reasons:

     1. Nuclear membrane and nucleolus have reappeared.

     2. Spindle fibres are disappearing.

     3. Furrows have been formed for the division of cytoplasm.

     4. Sister chromatids reach opposite poles.

     5. The two sets of daughter chromosomes have reached the opposite poles.

  (ii) 1- Chromatin fibres 2- Nuclear membrane

 (iii) The division of nucleus is called Karyokinesis.

  (iv) The stage comes before telophase is anaphase as shown in the diagram given below:

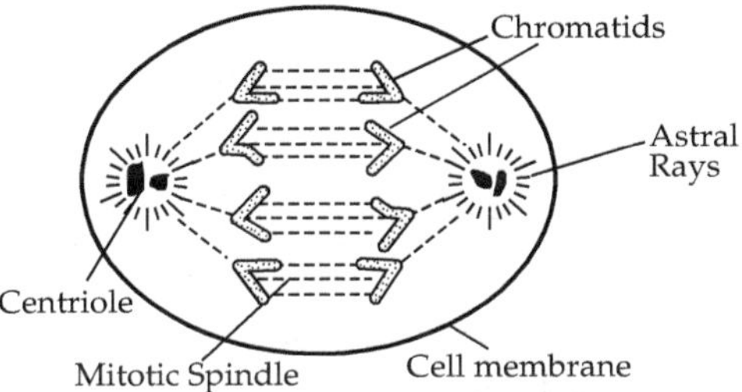

   (v) Meiosis is the cell division that results in half of the number of chromosomes in daughter cells.

Q. 4. The given diagram shows a stage during mitotic division in an animal cell:

(i) Identify the stage. Give a reason to support your answer.

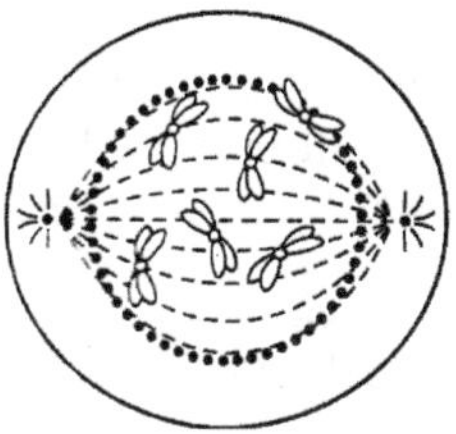

(ii) Draw a neat labelled diagram of the cell as it would appear in the next stage. Name the stage.

(iii) In what two ways is mitotic division in an animal cell different from the mitotic division in a plant cell?

(iv) Name the type of cell division that occurs during:

(1) Growth of a shoot.

(2) Formation of pollen grains. **[2016]**

Ans.   **(i)** The diagram represents the Prophase stage (Late prophase stage).

     The stage is Late prophase as there is no nucleolus and cell organelles like

Golgi body, endoplasmic reticulum have become inconspicuous, nuclear envelope is shown disintegrated into small vesicles and the two asters have reached the two poles.

(ii) Metaphase stage

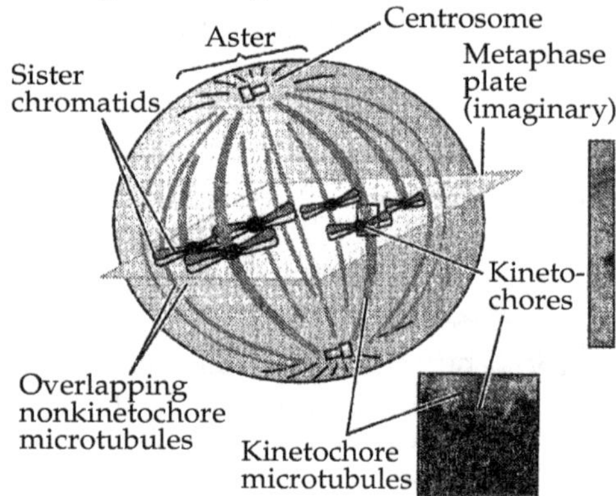

(iii) Any two differences from those given below:

Animal cell mitosis	Plant cell mitosis
1. It occurs in almost all type of somatic cells of the organism.	It occurs in the growing tips or meristems.
2. An animal cell becomes rounded before cell division.	There is no change in the shape of plant cell before division.
3. Presence of centrosome is essential.	Centrosome is not present.
4. Asters are present.	Asters are absent.
5. Cytokinesis occurs by cleavage wherein a furrow is formed dividing the mother cell into two daughter cells.	Cytokinesis occurs commonly by the cell plate method wherein a solid middle lamella develops dividing the mother cell into two daughter cells.

(iv) (1) Mitosis

   (2) Meiosis

Q. 5. The diagram given below represents a certain stage of mitosis:

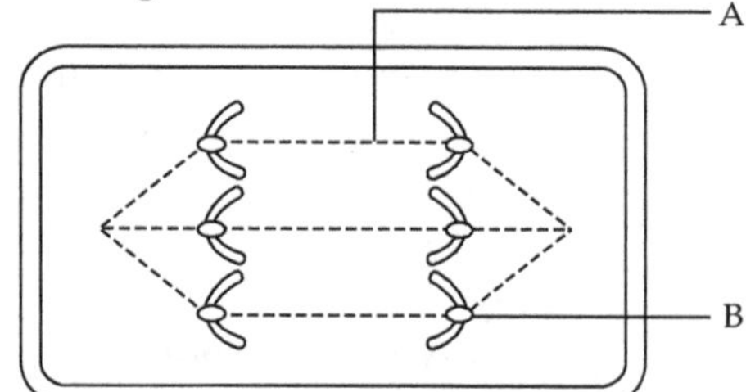

(i) Identify the stage of cell division.

(ii) Name the parts labelled A and B.

(iii) What is the unique feature observed in this stage?

(iv) How many daughter cells are formed from this type of cell division? **[2015]**

Ans. **(i)** Anaphase

(ii) A—Spindle fibre   B—Centromere

(iii) Two sister chromatids of each chromosome separate and are drawn apart towards opposite poles.

(iv) Two daughter cells are formed from mitosis .

Q. 6. **Given below is a diagram representing a stage during mitotic cell division. Study it carefully and answer the questions that follow:**

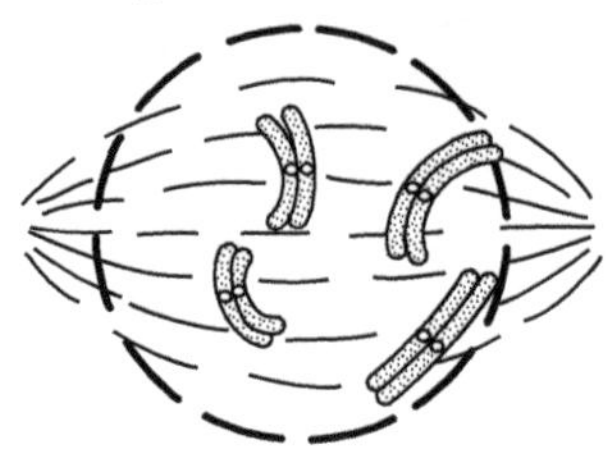

(i) Is it a plant cell or an animal cell? Give a reason to support your answer.

(ii) Identify the stage shown.

(iii) Name the stage that follows the one shown here. How is that stage identified?

(iv) How will you differentiate between mitosis and meiosis on the basis of the chromosome number in the daughter cells?

(v) Draw a duplicated chromosome and label its parts. **[2014]**

Ans. **(i)** It is plant cell because centrosome is absent and spindle apparatus is not connected to it.

(ii) Prophase.

(iii) Metaphase: In this stage, the chromosomes lies in one plane at equator and gets attached to a spindle fibre by its centromere.

(iv) Mitosis : Chromosome number of the daughter cells is same as that of parent cell.

Meiosis : Chromosome number of the daughter cells is half as that of the parent cell.

(v)

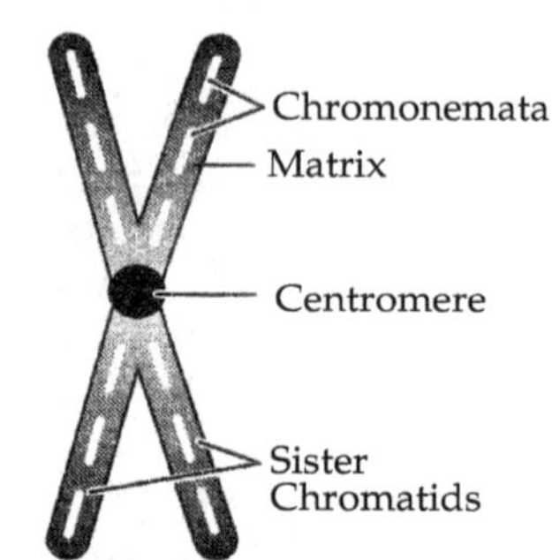

Structure of Chromosome

Q. 7. The diagram below represents a stage during cell division. Study the same and then answer the questions that follow:

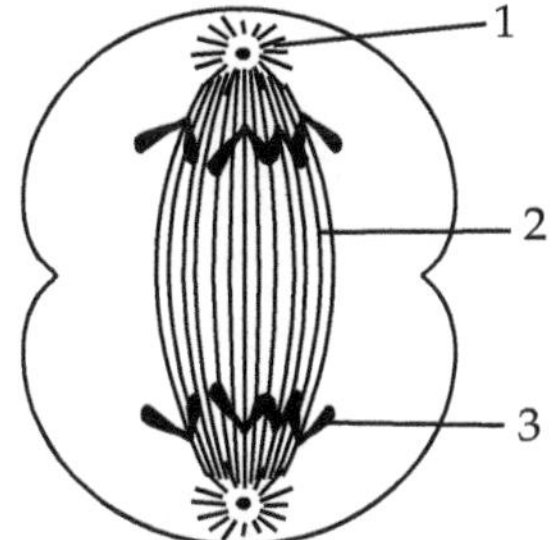

(i) Name the parts labelled 1, 2 and 3.

(ii) Identify the above stage and give a reason to support your answer.

(iii) Mention where in the body this type of cell division occurs.

(iv) Name the stage prior to this stage and draw a diagram to represent the same.

[2011]

Ans. (i) **1.** Aster rays

2. Spindle fibre

3. Chromatid

(ii) **Anaphase:** The two sister chromatids of each chromosome separate and move apart towards opposite poles.

(iii) Cell division takes place in the somatic cells of the body.

(iv) Metaphase

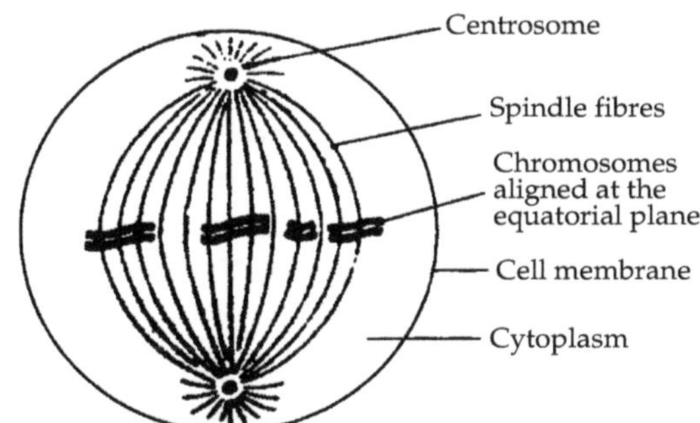

Q. 8. Given below is a diagram representing a stage during mitotic cell division in an animal cell:

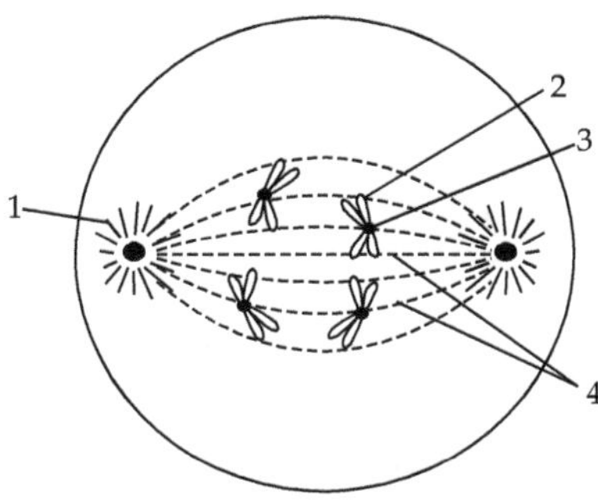

(i) Identify the above stage. Give a reason to support your answer.

(ii) Name the parts labelled 1, 2, 3 and 4.

(iii) What is the function of part 3?

(iv) Name the stage that comes just after the stage shown in the diagram. Draw a well labelled diagram of this stage.

[2010]

Ans. (i) Prophase.

The nuclear membrane is disappearing.

(ii) **1.** Asters   **2.** Chromatid

3. Centromere   **4.** Spindle fibres

(iii) Part '3' *i.e.,* centromere joins the two chromatids of the chromosome. The spindle fibres also attach it to the centromere at the time of cell division.

(iv) Metaphase.

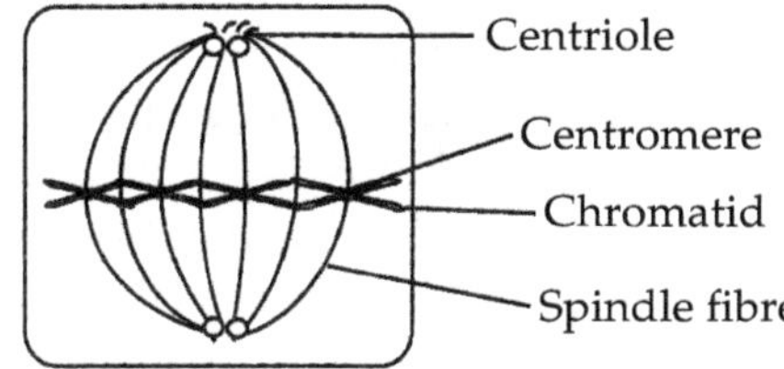

Short Answer Type Questions

Q. 1. A homozygous dominant tall pea plant bearing red flowers (TTRR) is crossed with a hormozygous recessive dwarf pea plant bearing white flowers (ttrr).

  (i) What is the phenotype and genotype of F_1 individuals?

  (ii) Write the possible combination of gametes that are obtained when two F_1 hybrid plants are crossed.

  (iii) Mention the phenotypic ratio of the F_2 generation.

  (iv) State Mendel's Law of Independent Assortment. **[2020]**

Ans. **(i)** Phenotype is tall pea plants bearing red flowers.

    Genotype is TtRr

  (ii) Possible combination of gametes is TR, tR, Tr, tr.

  (iii) Phenotypic ratio is 9:3:3:1

  (iv) Law of Independent Assortment states that the two pairs of factors in a dihybrid cross are segregated independently during gamete formation and are randomly combined in F_2 generation. Inheritance of factors controlling a particular trait in an organism is independent of the other.

Q. 2. In Mendel's experiments, tall pea plants (T) are dominant over dwarf pea plants (t).

  (i) What is the phenotype and genotype of the F_1 generation if a homozygous tall plant is crossed with a homozygous dwarf plant?

  (ii) Draw a punnett square board to show the gametes and offspring when both the parents are heterozygous for tallness.

  (iii) What is the phenotypic ratio and genotypic ratio of the above cross in (ii)?

  (iv) State Mendel's Law of Dominance.

      [2019]

Ans. **(i)** In F_1 generation, phenotype of the plants will be Tall and genotype is Tt.

Parental Generation → Pure Tall Pea Plant TT × Pure Dwarf Pea Plant tt

Gametes → T × t

F_1 generation — Tt [Tall]

  (ii) Tt [Tall] × Tt [Tall]

Gametes — T t × T t

Tt	T	t
T	TT	Tt
t	Tt	tt

  (iii) Phenotypic ratio is 3 : 1

    Genotypic ratio is 1 : 2 : 1

  (iv) **Law of Dominance :** It states that in a cross between pure breeding lines out of the pair of contrasting characters, the one that is expressed in first generation is dominant and the one that is not expressed is recessive. Only dominant trait is expressed in first generation.

Q. 3. A pea plant which is homozygous for Green pods which are inflated [GGII] is crossed with a homozygous plant for yellow pods which are constricted [ggii]. Answer the following questions:

(i) Give the phenotype and genotype of the F_1 generation.

Which type of pollination has occurred to produce F_1 generation ?

(ii) Write the phenotypic ratio of the F_2 generation.

(iii) Write the possible combinations of the gametes that can be obtained if two F_1 hybrid plants are crossed.

(iv) State Mendel's law of 'Segregation of Gametes'.

(v) What is the scientific name of the plant which Mendel used for his experiments on inheritance? **[2018]**

📋 Marking Scheme ------------------------------------

(i) Phenotype: All have green, inflated pods. Genotype: GgIi, Cross pollination

(ii) $9 : 3 : 3 : 1$

(iii) GI, Gi, gI, gi

(iv) Two members of a pair of factors separate during gamete formation./The two alleles of a trait separate during gamate formation.

(v) Pisum Sativum

Ans. **(i)**

Parental Generation →	Pure pea plants with green, inflated pods GGII [GI]	× Pure pea plants with yellow, constricted pods ggii [gi]

F_1 **generation** → GgIi [pea plants with green inflated pods]

Phenotype : Inflated, green pods
Genotype : GgIi.
Cross pollination has occurred to produce F_1 generation.

(ii) F_2 generation : $9 : 3 : 3 : 1$

(iii)

Gametes ⇒ ⇓	GI	Gi	gI	gi
GI	GGII	GGIi	GgII	GgIi
Gi	GGIi	GGii	GgIi	Ggii
gI	GgII	GgIi	ggII	ggIi
gi	GgIi	Ggii	ggIi	ggii

So, the possible combination of gametes in F_2 generation are GI, Gi, gI, gi.

(iv) Law of segregation states that the two members of a pair of factors separate during the formation of gametes. They do not blend but segregate into different gametes.

(v) *Pisum sativum.*

Q. 4. In a homozygous pea plant, axial flowers (A) are dominant over terminal flowers (a).

(i) What is the phenotype and genotype of the F_1 generation if a plant bearing pure axial flowers is crossed with a plant bearing pure terminal flowers?

(ii) Draw a Punnett square board to show the gametes and offsprings when both the parent plants are heterozygous for axial flowers.

(iii) What is the phenotypic ratio and genotypic ratio of the above cross shown in (ii)?

(iv) State Mendel's Law of Dominance. **[2017]**

Ans. **(i)** The phenotype of the F_1 generation is plants with axial flowers that will be produced. The genotype of F_1 generation plants is Aa, *i.e.*, all plants are heterozygous dominant for axial flowers.

(ii)

Aa ×	A	a
A	AA	Aa
a	Aa	aa

(iii) From the above cross, 3 plants with axial flowers (AA, Aa, Aa) and 1 plant with terminal flower (aa) is produced. So, phenotypic ratio is 3 : 1 and Genotypic ratio is 1 : 2 : 1 *i.e.*, 1AA : 2Aa : 1aa

(iv) Mendel's Law of Dominance states that "Out of a pair of contrasting characters present together, only one is able to express itself while the other remains suppressed. The one that expresses itself is the dominant character and the one unexpressed is the recessive. The recessive character can express only when the pair is homozygous recessive."

Q. 5. A homozygous tall plant (T) bearing red coloured (R) flowers is crossed with a homozygous dwarf (t) plant bearing white (r) flowers:

(i) Give the genotype and phenotype of the plants of F_1 generation.

(ii) Mention the possible combinations of the gametes that can be obtained from the F_1 hybrid plant.

(iii) State the Mendel's law of Independent Assortment.

(iv) Mention the phenotypes of the offsprings obtained in F_2 generation.

(v) What is the phenotypic ratio obtained in F_2 generation? **[2016]**

Ans.

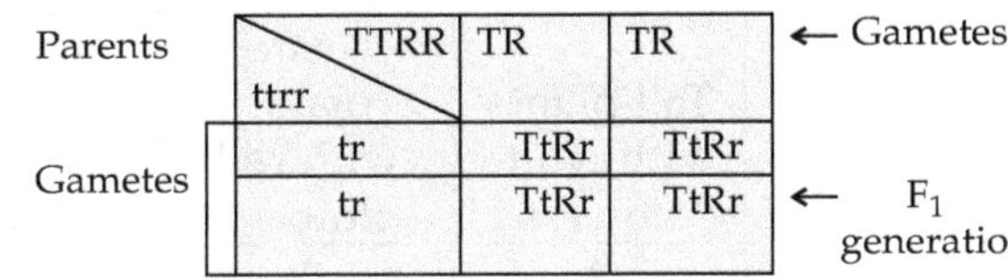

Parents		TTRR	TR	TR	← Gametes
	ttrr				
Gametes		tr	TtRr	TtRr	
		tr	TtRr	TtRr	← F_1 generation

(i) Genotype of F_1 generation: TtRr
Phenotype of F_1 generation: Tall plants bearing red flowers

(ii) The selfing of F_1 generation – TtRr will yield following gametes –TR, Tr, tR, tr
The possible combinations of these gametes are given in the following Punnett square:

TtRr \ TtRr	TR	Tr	tR	tr
TR	TTRR Tall plants with red flowers	TTRr Tall plants with red flowers	TtRR Tall plants with red flowers	TtRr Tall plants with red flowers
Tr	TTRr Tall plants with red flowers	TTrr Tall plants with white flowers	TtRr Tall plants with red flowers	Ttrr Tall plants with white flowers
tR	TtRR Tall plants with red flowers	TtRr Tall plants with red flowers	ttRR Dwarf plants with red flowers	ttRr Dwarf plants with red flowers
tr	TtRr Tall plants with red flowers	Ttrr Tall plants with white flowers	ttRr Dwarf plants with red flowers	ttrr Dwarf plants with white flowers

(iii) Mendel's law of independent assortment: This law was deduced from a dihybrid cross, where simultaneous inheritance of two different characters were considered. According to this law, the alleles of two different characters assort or separate independently from one another at the time of gamete formation. The alleles are thus free to recombine and form new combinations in the subsequent generations.

(iv) The F_2 generation phenotypes would be –
1. Tall plants with red flowers
2. Tall plants with white flowers
3. Dwarf plants with red flowers
4. Dwarf plant with white flowers

Out of these, tall plants with white flowers and dwarf plants with red flowers are the recombinants.

(v) The phenotypic ratio of F_2 generation would be $9 : 3 : 3 : 1$

Tall plants with red flowers	Tall plants with white flowers	Dwarf plants with red flowers	Dwarf plant with white flowers
9	3	3	1

Q. 6. In a homozygous plant, round seeds (R) are dominant over wrinkled seeds (r):

(i) Draw a Punnett square to show the gametes and offspring when both the plants have heterozygous round seeds (Rr).

(ii) Mention the Phenotype and Genotype ratios of the offsprings in F_2 generation.

(iii) Name the sex chromosomes in human males and females.

(iv) Briefly explain the term 'Mutation'.

(v) What is the number of chromosomes in the gametes of human beings?   [2015]

Ans. **(i)** Homozygous round seed — RR
Homozygous wrinkled seed — rr
$$RR \times rr$$
Gametes: — Rr

F_1 generation — All Round seeds

♀ \ ♂	R	r
R	RR (Round)	Rr (Round)
r	Rr (Round)	rr (Wrinkled)
F_2 generation		

(ii) F_2 generation:
Phenotypic ratio – 3 : 1
Genotypic ratio – 1 : 2 : 1

(iii) Sex chromosomes in human males and females are known as allosomes.
Males: XY   Females: XX

(iv) A chemical change in the gene which may produce new traits that can be inherited, is known as mutation.

(v) Number of chromosomes in the gametes of human beings is 23.

Q. 7. Given below is a schematic diagram showing Mendel's experiment on sweet pea plants having axial flowers with round seeds (AARR) and terminal flowers with wrinkled seeds (aarr). Study the same and answer the questions that follow:

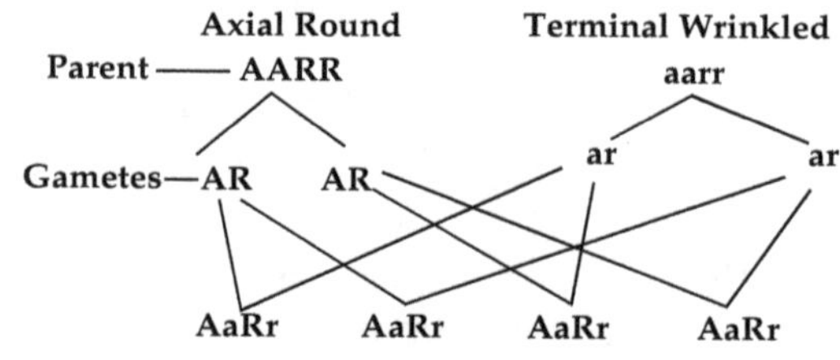

(i) Give the phenotype of F_1 progeny.

(ii) Give the phenotypes of F_2 progeny produced upon by the self-pollination of F_1 progeny.

(iii) Give the phenotypic ratio of F_2 progeny.

(iv) Name and explain the law induced by Mendel on the basis of the above observation. **[2013]**

Ans. **(i)** Axial flowers and round seeds.

(ii) 1. Axial flowers and round seeds.

2. Axial flowers and wrinkled seeds.

3. Terminal flowers and round seeds.

4. Terminal flowers and wrinkled seeds.

(iii) 9 : 3 : 3 : 1

(iv) Law of independent assortment: When there are two pairs of contrasting characters, the distribution of factors of each pair in the gametes is independent of the distribution of other pair of characters.

Q. 8. A homozygous plant having round (R) and yellow (Y) seed is crossed with homozygous plant having wrinkled (r) and green (y) seeds:

(i) Give the scientific name of the plant on which Mendel conducted his hybridization experiments.

(ii) Give the genotype of the F_1 generation.

(iii) Give the dihybrid phenotypic ratio and the phenotype of the offsprings of the F_2 generation when two plants of the F_1 generation are crossed.

(iv) Name and state the law which explains the dihybrid ratio.

(v) Give the possible combinations of gametes that can be obtained from F_1 hybrid. **[2012]**

Ans. **(i)** *Pisum sativum.*

(ii) RrYy

(iii) 9 : 3 : 3 : 1—Yellow round (9), green round (3), yellow wrinkled (3), green wrinkled (1).

(iv) Law of independent assortment, which states that when there are two pairs of contrasting characters, the distribution of factors of each pair in the gametes is independent of the distribution of other pair of character.

(v) YR, Yr, yR, yr.

Q. 9. **(i) State Mendel's Law of Dominance.**

(ii) A pure tall plant (TT) is crossed with a pure dwarf plant (tt).
Draw Punnett squares to show (1) F_1 generation (2) F_2 generation.

(iii) Give the Phenotype of the F_2 generation.

(iv) Give the Phenotypic and Genotypic ratio of the F_1 and F_2 generation. **[2010]**

Ans. **(i)** The one which expresses itself in F1 generation is dominant trait while the other which is suppressed is known as recessive trait.

(ii) Parents   Tall plant   Dwarf plant
         TT   ×   tt

(1) F_1 generation

	t	t
T	Tt	Tt
T	Tt	Tt

(2) F_2 generation   Tt   ×   Tt

	T	t
T	TT	Tt
t	Tt	tt

(iii) In F_2 generation 75% plants will be tall and 25% dwarf.

(iv) F_1 Phenotypic ratio—All tall plants, 1 : 1
Genotypic ratio—All hybrids, 1 : 1

F_2 Phenotypic ratio—3 : 1 (3 tall : 1 dwarf)
Genotypic ratio—1 : 2 : 1

(1 TT : 2 Tt : 1 tt)

Q. 10. Given below is a diagram of a double helical structure of DNA:

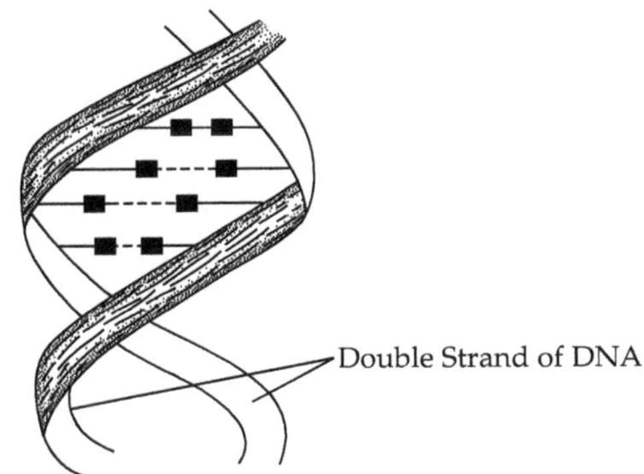

(i) Name the four nitrogenous bases that form a DNA molecule.

(ii) Give the full form of DNA.

(iii) Name the unit of heredity.

(iv) Mention two points of difference between Mitosis and Meiosis. **[2010]**

Ans. **(i)** Guanine, thymine, adenine, Cytosine.

(ii) Deoxyribonucleic acid.

(iii) Gene

(iv)

Mitosis	Meiosis
1. Two daughter cells are produced.	Four daughter cells are produced.
2. Diploid cells are produced.	Haploid cells are produced.

Absorption by Roots

Short Answer Type Questions

Q. 1. The diagram given represents a plant cell after being placed in a strong sugar solution. Study the diagram and answer the questions that follow:

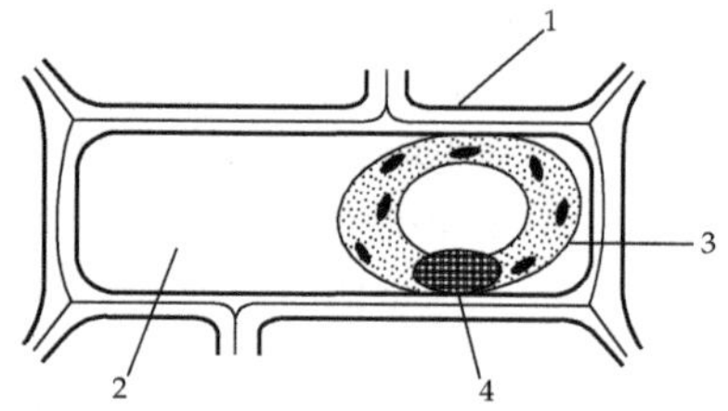

(i) What is the state of the cell shown in the diagram?

(ii) Name the structure that acts as a selectively permeable membrane.

(iii) Label the parts numbered 1 to 4 in the diagram.

(iv) How can the above cell be brought back to its original condition? Mention the scientific term for the recovery of the cell.

(v) State any two features of the above plant cell which is not present in animal cells. [2017]

Ans. (i) The cell shown in the diagram is in flaccid [plasmolysed] state.

(ii) Plasma membrane acts as a selectively permeable membrane.

(iii) 1. Cell wall

2. Strong sugar solution

3. Cell membrane

4. Nucleus

(iv) If this flaccid or plasmolysed cell is placed in water, its protoplasm again swells up and cell can retain back its original condition. This recovery of the cell is termed as deplasmolysis.

(v) In plant cell, cell wall, a large vacuole in the centre and chloroplasts are present which are not seen in an animal cell.

Q. 2. The figure given below is a diagrammatic representation of a part of the cross section of the root in the root hair zone. Study the same and then answer the questions that follow:

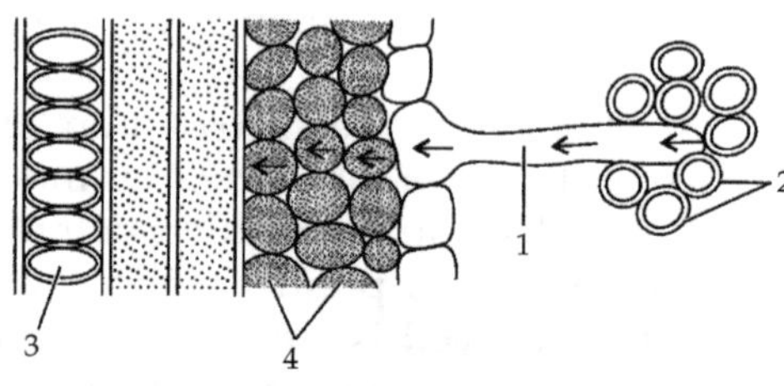

(i) Name the parts indicated by 1 to 4.

(ii) Which is the process that enables the passage of water from the soil into the root hair?

(iii) Name the pressure that is responsible for the movement of water in the direction indicated by the arrows. Define it.

(iv) Due to an excess of this pressure sometimes drops of water are found along the leaf margins of some plants especially in the early mornings. What is the phenomenon called?

(v) Draw a well labelled diagram of the root hair cell as it would appear if an excess of fertilizer is added to the soil close to it. [2016]

Ans. (i) 1. Root hair cell (Epiblema cell)

2. Soil particles   3. Xylem vessel

4. Cortex cells

(ii) The process that enables the passage of water from the soil into the root hair is called osmosis.

(iii) The pressure that is responsible for the movement of water in the direction indicated in the figure is known as root pressure. Root pressure is a positive pressure found in the xylem channel of some plants due to inflow of water.

(iv) This phenomenon is called guttation.

(v) Diagram of root hair cell when excessive fertilisers are added:

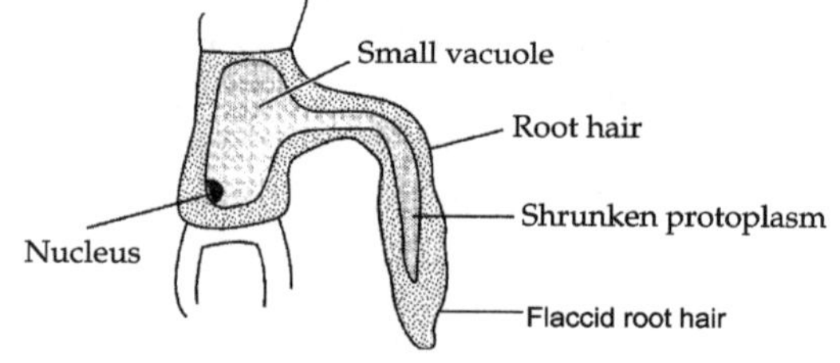

The excessive fertilisers when added to soil create hypertonic conditions near the root hair and leads to the movement of water from the root hair cell to the outside environment. This causes the root hair to shrink.

Q. 3. **A candidate in order to study the process of osmosis has taken 3 potato cubes and put them in 3 different beakers containing 3 different solutions. After 24 hours, in the first beaker the potato cube increased in size, in the second beaker the potato cube decreased in size and in the third beaker there was no change in the size of the potato cube. The following diagram shows the result of the same experiment:**

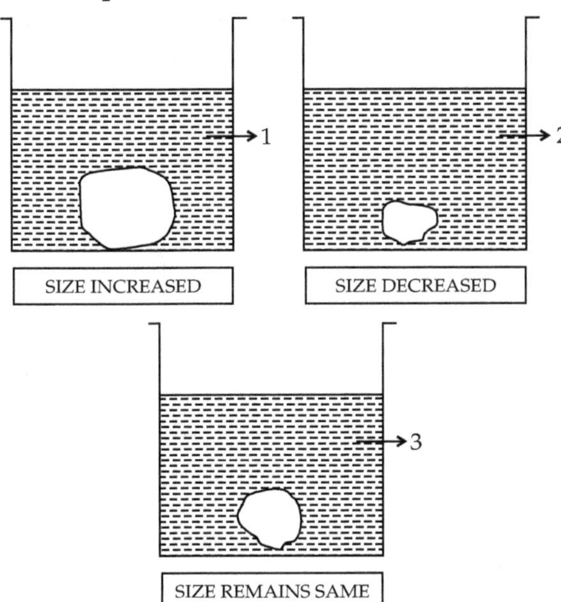

(i) Give the technical terms of the solutions used in beakers 1, 2 and 3.

(ii) In beaker 3 the size of the potato cube remains the same. Explain the reason in brief.

(iii) Write the specific feature of the cell sap of root hairs which helps in absorption of water.

(iv) What is osmosis?

(v) How does a cell wall and a cell membrane differ in their permeability?

[2014]

Ans. **(i) Beaker 1:** Hypotonic solution

Beaker 2: Hypertonic solution

Beaker 3: Isotonic solution

(ii) In beaker 3 the size of potato cube remains the same because of isotonic solution which has same concentration of solutes as that of potato cells. So, water is neither lost nor gained by the potato cells.

(iii) Cell sap of root hair is much more concentrated than the soil solution and

this causes entry of water into the root cells.

(iv) Osmosis is the movement of water molecules from a more dilute solution having high water potential to a less dilute solution having low water potential, through a semi-permeable membrane.

(v) Cell wall is freely permeable while cell membrane is selectively permeable.

Q. 4. **The figure given below shows the epidermal cells of an onion bulb. This cell was then transferred to a drop of sugar solution.**

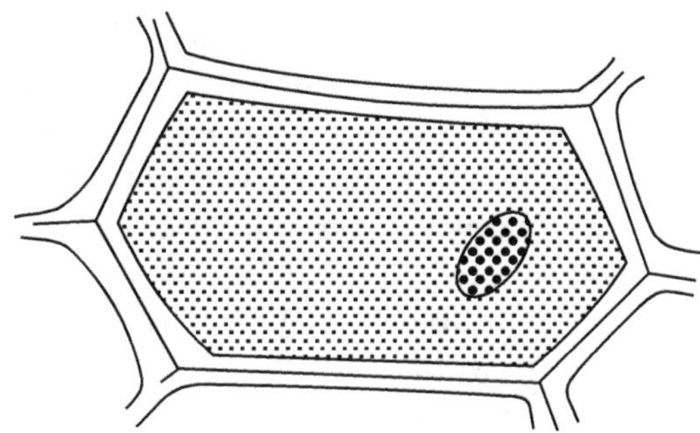

(i) Draw a well labelled diagram of the epidermal cell as it would appear after immersion in a strong sugar solution.

(ii) What scientific term is used for the changes as shown in (i) above?

(iii) What should be done to restore the cell back to its original condition?

(iv) Give the scientific term for the recovery of the cell as a result of the step taken in (iii) above.

(v) Define the term osmosis. **[2013]**

Ans. **(i)**

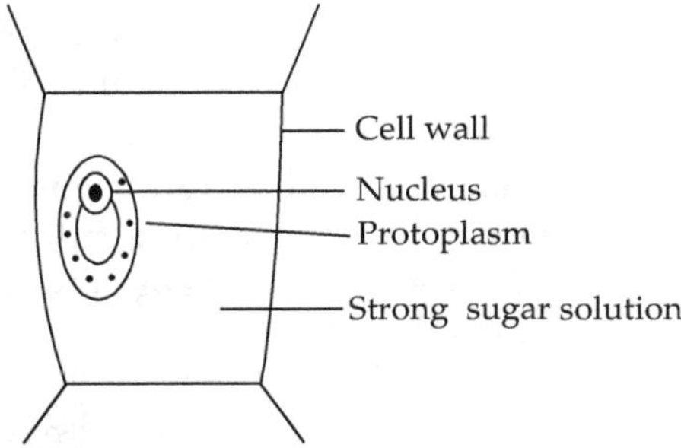

(ii) Plasmolysis or flaccidity.

(iii) Cell has to be placed in a hypotonic solution so, that water will enter the cell by endosmosis and the cell will regain its original shape.

(iv) Deplasmolysis.

(v) Osmosis is the diffusion of water molecules through a semi-permeable membrane from a region of high concentration of water molecules to a region of low concentration of water molecules.

Q. 5. Given below is the diagram of a cell as seen under the microscope after having been placed in a solution:

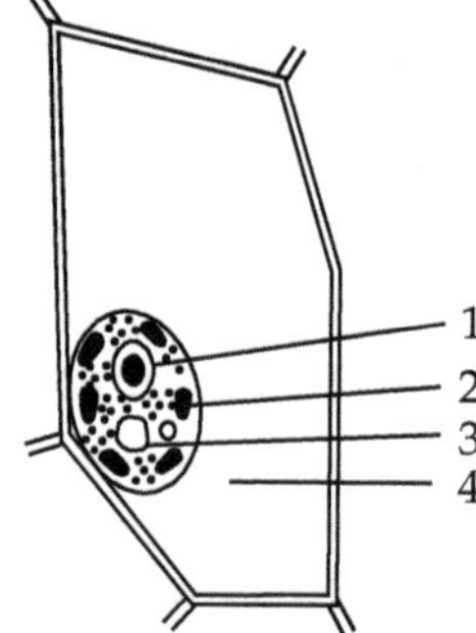

(i) What is the technical term used for the state/condition of the cell given above?

(ii) Give the technical term for the solution in which the cell was placed.

(iii) Name the parts numbered 1 to 4.

(iv) Is the cell given above a plant cell or an animal cell? Give two reasons in support of your answer as evident from the diagram.

(v) What would you do to bring this cell back to its original condition? **[2012]**

Ans. **(i)** Plasmolysed

(ii) Hypertonic solution

(iii) **1.** Nucleus, **2.** Chloroplast, **3.** Vacuole, **4.** Hypertonic solution.

(iv) Plant cell

Reasons for identification of cell:

1. Presence of cell wall,

2. Presence of large vacuole.

(v) It has to be placed in a hypotonic solution so, that water will enter the cell by endosmosis and the cell will regain its original shape.

Q. 6. The diagram below represents a layer of epidermal cells showing a fully-grown root hair. Study the diagram and answer the questions that follow:

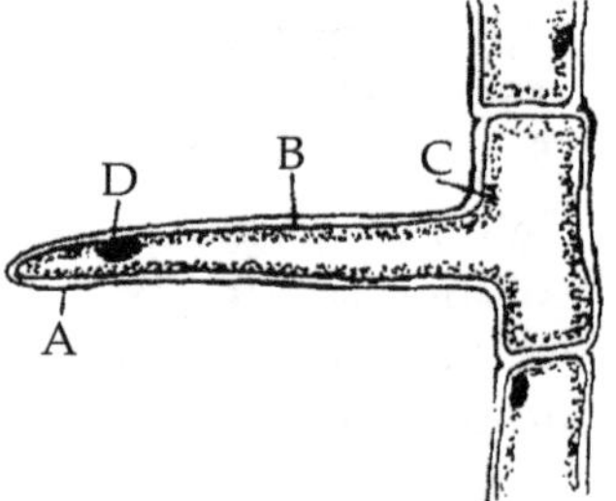

(i) Name the parts labelled A, B, C and D.

(ii) The root hair cell is in a turgid state. Name and explain the process that caused this state.

(iii) Mention one distinct difference between the parts labelled A and B.

(iv) Draw a diagram of the above root hair cell as it would appear when a concentrated solution of fertilizers is added near it. **[2011]**

Ans. **(i)** A– Cell wall   B– Cell membrane
C–Cytoplasm   D– Nucleus

(ii) The process is called endosmosis and is defined as the movement of solvent (water) from outside to inside of the cell.

(iii)

A (Cell wall)	B (Cell membrane)
It is freely permeable.	It is semi-permeable.

(iv) Refer to Short Answer type Questions Answer 2(v).

Q. 7. Given below is the diagram of an apparatus set up to study a very important physiological process:

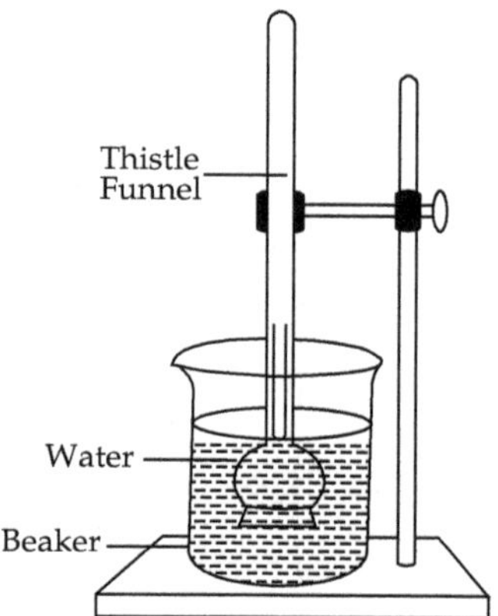

(i) Name the process being studied.

(ii) Explain the process.

(iii) What change would you observe in the thistle funnel containing sugar solution after about 10 minutes?

(iv) Is sugar solution hypertonic or hypotonic?

(v) Name the part of the plant cell which is represented by the sugar solution.

(vi) Explain why much salt is added to pickles. **[2010]**

Ans. **(i)** Osmosis.

(ii) Oswosis is the movement of solvent molecules from a region of their high concentration to the region of their low concentration through a semi-permeable membrane.

(iii) Level of solution will rise.

(iv) Hypertonic solution.

(v) Cell sap.

(vi) Much salt is added to pickles so that a hypertonic solution is formed around the vegetable pieces. Any fungi etc., attacking the preserved food will die due to plasmolysis by the solution.

Short Answer Type Questions

Q. 1. The diagram below represents an experiment to demonstrate a certain phenomenon in a green plant:

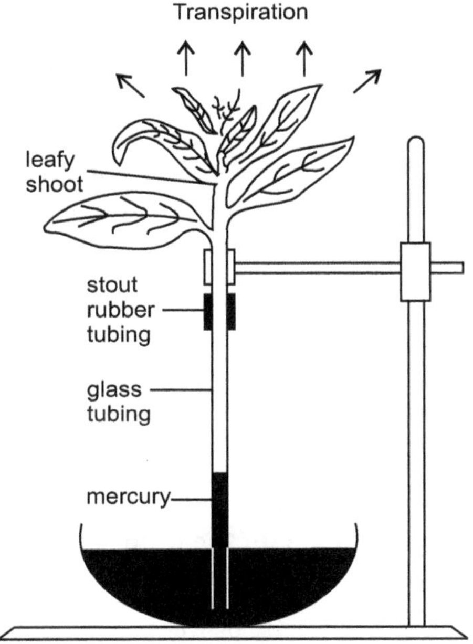

(i) Will the level of mercury in the glass tubing rise or fall?

Which conducting tissue of the plant does the glass-tubing represent?

(ii) Define Transpiration.

(iii) How will the rate of the above process differ if the environment of the plant has:

1. Less humidity

2. High temperature?

(iv) State any two advantages of transpiration to the plant.

(v) Draw a neat labelled diagram of a Plasmolysed cell. **[2020]**

Ans. **(i)** Mercury in the glass tube will rise.

Xylem

(ii) Transpiration is the loss of water in the form of water vapours from the leaves and other aerial parts of the plant.

(iii) 1. Less humidity increases the rate of transpiration.

2. High temperature increases the rate of transpiration.

(iv) Two advantages of transpiration are:

1. It provides cooling effect to the plant.

2. It provides a suction force which helps in ascent of sap.

(v)

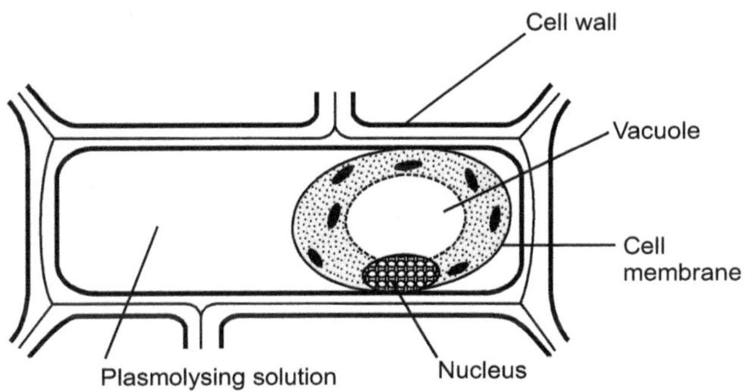

Q. 2. Given below is an apparatus which was setup to investigate a physiological process in plants. The setup was placed in bright sunlight. Answer the questions that follow:

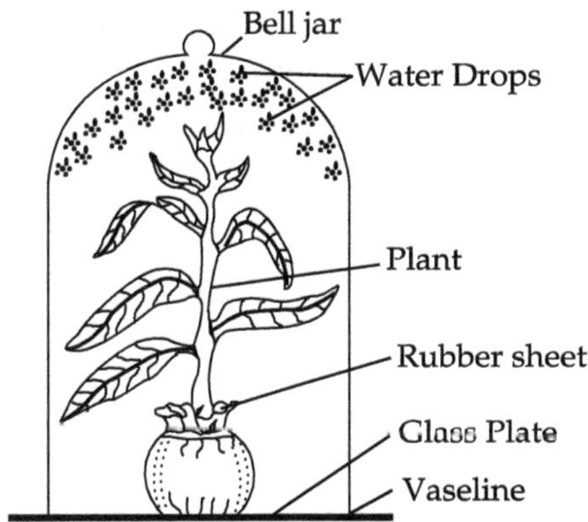

(i) Name the process being studied. Define the process.

(ii) Why was the pot enclosed in a rubber sheet?

(iii) Mention two external factors which can accelerate the above process.

(iv) List two adaptations in plants to reduce the above process.

(v) Draw a neat, labelled diagram of a stomatal apparatus. **[2019]**

 Marking Scheme --------------------------------

  (i) Transpiration
It is the loss of water as water vapour from the aerial parts of the plant.

 (ii) To prevent evaporation of water from the pot/soil.

(iii) Bright sunlight, high temperature, high velocity of wind, low humidity.

(iv) Thick cuticle, loss of leaves, narrow leaves, fewer stomata, sunken stomata, leaves modified into spines, multiple layers of epidermal cells.

 (v)

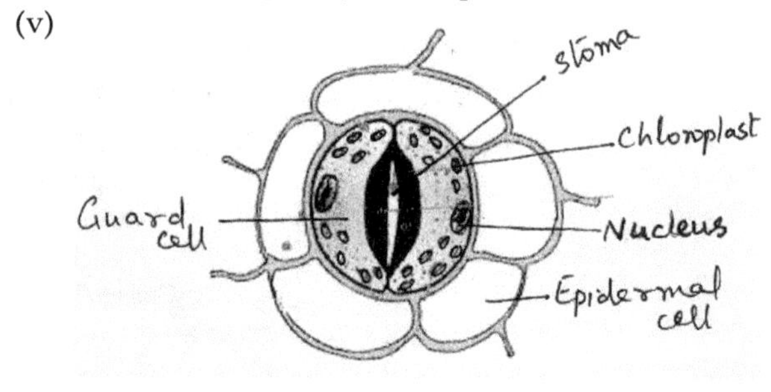

Ans.   **(i)** Transpiration is being studied. It is the process by which water is lost in the form of water vapour from leaves and other aerial parts of the plant.

  (ii) The pot was enclosed in a rubber sheet to prevent the escape of water in the form of vapours from the pot.

(iii) Temperature and velocity of wind. If both temperature and wind velocity are high then process of transpiration increases.

(vi) Adaptations in plants to reduce transpiration are:

  1. The stomata may be sunken or covered by hairs or their number may be reduced.

  2. The leaves may become narrower.

  3. The leaves may be covered with thick cuticle.

  (v)

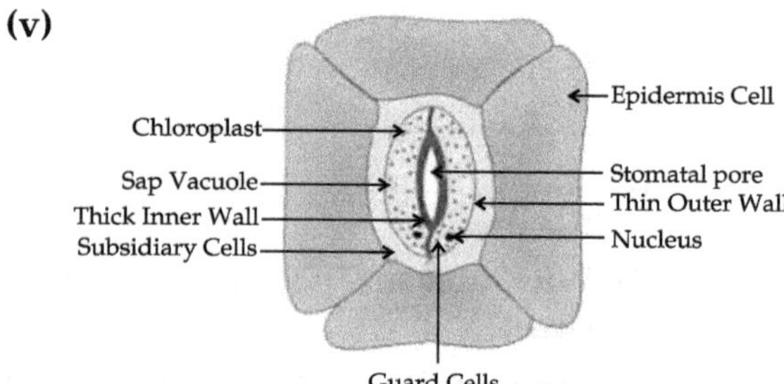

Stomatal Apparatus

Q. 3. **The diagram below represents a process in plants.**

The setup was placed in bright sunlight. Answer the following questions:

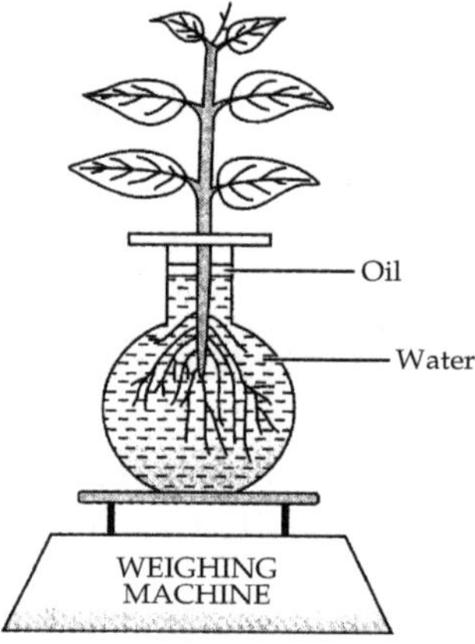

  (i) **Name the physiological process depicted in the diagram.**
Why was oil added to the water?

 (ii) **When placed in bright sunlight for four hours, what do you observe with regard to the initial and final weight of the plant?**
Give a suitable reason for your answer.

(iii) **What happens to the level of water when this setup is placed in:**
1. Humid conditions?
2. Windy conditions?

(iv) **Mention any three adaptations found in plants to overcome the process mentioned in (i).**

 (v) **Explain the term 'Guttation'.**   **[2018]**

Marking Scheme --------------------------------

  (i) Absorption of water by roots, Transpiration by leaves. To prevent evaporation of water.

 (ii) Weight of the plant reduces. Rate of transpiration is more than the rate of absorption of water./ Final weight is less than initial weight because leaves transpire

(iii) 1. Remains same
2. Reduces

(iv) Sunken stomata, fewer stomata, narrow leaves, Rolled or folded leaves, loss of leaves, leaves modified to spines, thick cuticle on leaves./small leaves/needle like leaves/hair on leaves/multiple epidermis.

 (v) Loss of water (as droplets) from the margins/hydathodes of leaves./apex, tips of leaves.

Ans.   **(i)** Absorption of water by roots and transpiration through the leaves.
Oil was added to the water to prevent loss of water through evaporation.

  (ii) The final weight of the plant will be less than its initial weight since the rate of transpiration is more than the rate of absorption of water. Hence leaves transpire, causing reduction in the weight of the plant.

(iii) 1. In humid conditions, transpiration rate is very low so the level of water in the jar will not show any change.

2. On a windy day, transpiration rate increases so the level of water in the jar will fall rapidly.

(iv) 1. Sunken stomata

2. Modification of leaves into spines.

3. Presence of thick layer of cuticle on the leaf surface.

(v) Guttation is the process of loss of water in the form of droplets from special openings called hydathodes present on the margins of leaves.

Q. 4. **The diagram of an apparatus given below demonstrates a particular process in plants. Study the same and answer the questions that follow:**

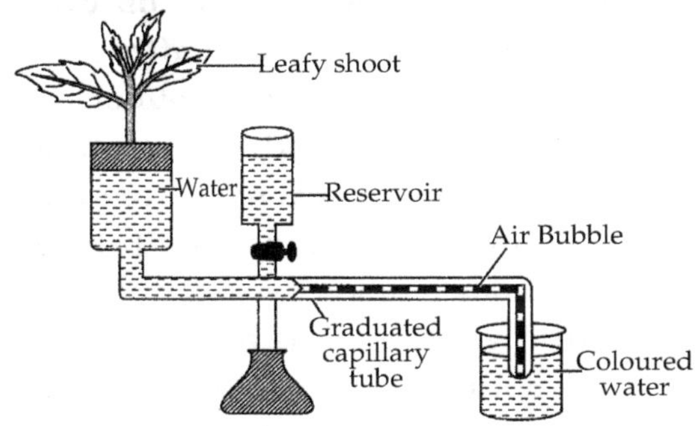

(i) Name the apparatus.

(ii) Which phenomenon is demonstrated by this apparatus?

(iii) Explain the phenomenon mentioned in (ii) above.

(iv) State two limitations of using this apparatus.

(v) What is the importance of the air bubble in the experiment?

(vi) Name the structure of plant through which the above process takes place.

[2016]

Ans. **(i)** The apparatus is called Ganong's Potometer.

(ii) The potometer demonstrates the phenomenon of transpiration.

(iii) The loss of water in the form of water vapour from the aerial parts of the plants is called 'Transpiration'.

(iv) Limitations of using this apparatus are:

1. Potometer cannot measure the rate of transpiration precisely as not all of the water taken up by plant is used for transpiration.

2. Potometer only measures the rate of uptake of water.

3. Introducing an air bubble is difficult.

4. Twig may not be active for a long time.

(v) The movement of air bubble along the scale gives a measure of water absorbed by the plant over a period of time and hence indicates the rate of transpiration. *(Any two of the above can be used)*

(vi) Stomata

Q. 5. **An apparatus as shown below was setup to investigate a physiological process in plants. The setup was kept in sunlight for two hours. Droplets of water were then seen inside the bell jar. Answer the questions that follow:**

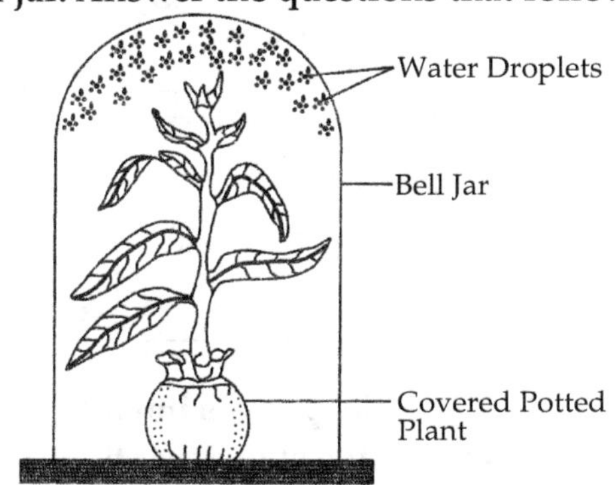

(i) Name the process being studied.

(ii) Explain the process named above in Q. 4. (a) (i).

(iii) Why was the pot covered with a plastic sheet?

(iv) Suggest a suitable control for this experiment.

(v) Mention two ways in which this process is beneficial to plants.

(vi) List three adaptations in plants to reduce the above mentioned process. **[2015]**

Ans. **(i)** Transpiration.

(ii) Transpiration is the evaporative loss of water from the aerial parts (leaves and stems) of the plant.

(iii) To prevent evaporation of water from the soil, pot is covered with a plastic sheet.

(iv) An empty polythene bag with its mouth tied and kept in sunlight will show no droplets of water inside.

(v) Benefits of transpiration are:

1. Excess water is removed by plants which creates a suction force in the stem. This helps to pull up absorbed water and minerals from roots.

2. The release of water from plant, transpiration contributes towards the lowering of the temperature.

(vi) Adaptations in plants to reduce transpiration are:

1. The stomata may be sunken or covered by hairs or their number may be reduced.

2. The leaves may become narrower.

3. The leaves may be covered with thick cuticle.

Q. 6. The figure given below represents an experimental set up with a weighing machine to demonstrate a particular process in plants. The experimental set up was placed in bright sunlight. Study the diagram and answer the following questions:

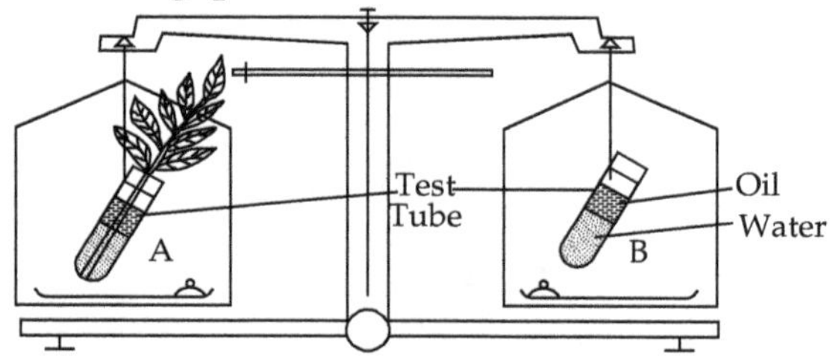

(i) Name the process intended for study.

(ii) Define the above mentioned process.

(iii) When the weight of the test tube (A and B) is taken before and after the experiment, what is observed? Give reasons to justify your observation in A and B.

(iv) What is the purpose of keeping the test tube B in the experimental set up? [2014]

Ans. **(i)** Transpiration

(ii) Transpiration is the loss of water in the form of water vapours from the aerial parts of the plant.

(iii) Weight of test tube A will decrease after the experiment because water will be lost from it through the leaves by transpiration. Weight of test tube B will remain same after the experiment because water will not be lost by transpiration as there is no plant in it and nor by evaporation as oil is spread over it, which will not allow evaporation.

(iv) It is a controlled experiment where the purpose of using test tube B is to compare

the level of water in both the test tubes. Test tube B is used here as a control.

Q. 7. **Given below is an experimental set up to demonstrate a particular process. Study the same and answer the questions that follow:**

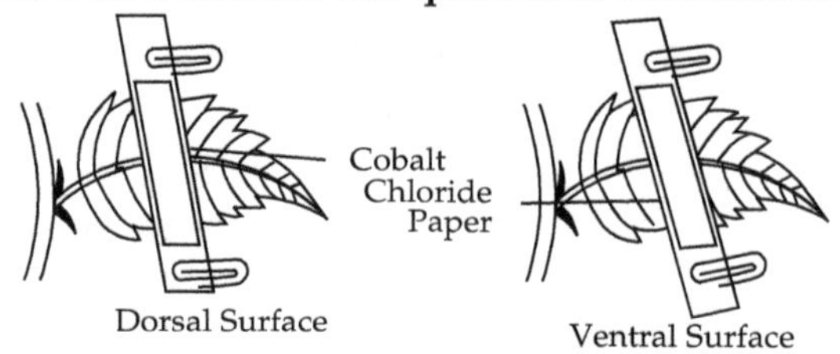

(i) Name the physiological process being studied.

(ii) Explain the process mentioned above.

(iii) What is the aim of the above experiment?

(iv) What would you observe in the experimental set-up after an hour? Give a reason to support your answer.

(v) Mention any three adaptations found in plants to overcome the physiological process mentioned in (i) above. [2012]

Ans. **(i)** Transpiration

(ii) Transpiration is the loss of water in the form of water vapours from the aerial parts of the plant.

(iii) To show that more transpiration occurs from the under surface of the leaf.

(iv) Cobalt chloride paper in the lower surface will turn pink faster because of presence of more stomata present on the under surface.

(v) **1.** Sunken stomata, **2.** Presence of thick cuticle, **3.** Fewer stomata.

Q. 8. **Study the diagram given below and answer the questions that follow:**

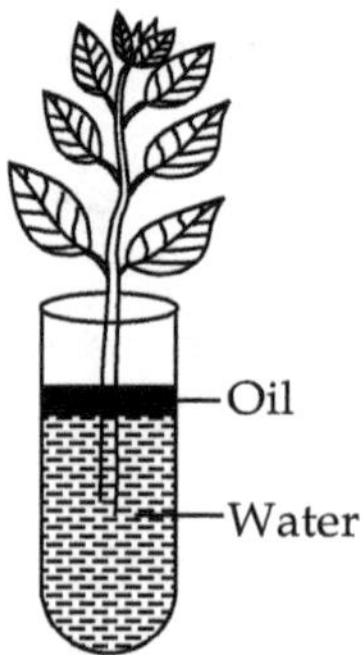

(i) Name the process being studied in the above experiment.

(ii) Explain the process mentioned in (i) above.

(iii) Why is oil placed over water?

(iv) What do we observe with regard to the level of water when this set up is placed in (1) bright sunlight, (2) humid conditions, (3) windy day?

(v) Mention any three adaptations found in plants to overcome the process mentioned in (ii) above. **[2011]**

Ans. **(i)** Absorption by the roots and transpiration by leaves.

(ii) It is the process by which plants lose water as vapours through the aerial parts.

(iii) To prevent direct evaporation of water from the test tube.

(iv) 1. In bright sunlight, the level of water decreases quickly.

2. In humid conditions, transpiration rate is very low so level of water in jar will not show much change.

3. On a windy day, transpiration rate increases so level of water in the jar will fall rapidly.

(v) 1. The number of stomata may be reduced.

2. Leaves may become narrow as modification of leaves into spines.

3. A thick layer of cuticle on the leaf surface helps to decrease transpiration.

Short Answer Type Questions

Q. 1. The diagram given below represents an experiment to prove the importance of a factor in photosynthesis. Answer the questions that follow:

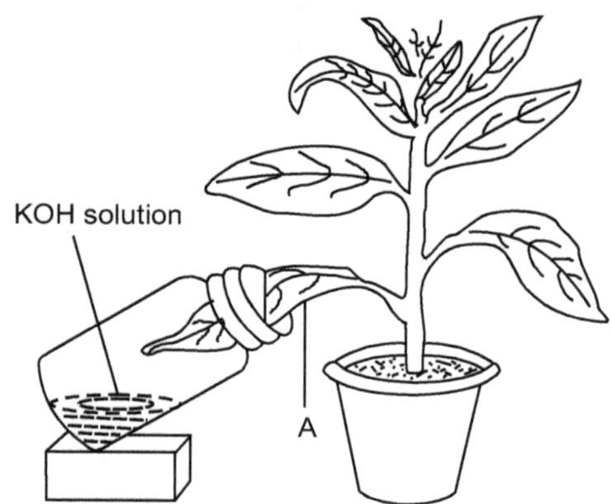

(i) Which factor is being studied here?

(ii) What is the purpose of keeping KOH in the flask?

(iii) Explain the term Photosynthesis.

(iv) What will you observe when the leaf A is tested for starch?

(v) Write a well balanced chemical equation for the process of photosynthesis.

[2020]

Ans. **(i)** Carbon dioxide is necessary for photosynthesis.

(ii) KOH absorbs carbon dioxide.

(iii) Photosynthesis is the process by which cells containing chlorophyll using carbon dioxide and water in presence of light energy produce glucose and release oxygen as by-product.

(iv) When leaf A is tested for starch for the portion inside the flask, it does not show blue-black colour indicating absence of starch whereas the portion that is outside will show blue-black colour.

(v) $6CO_2 + 12H_2O \xrightarrow[\text{Sunlight}]{\text{Chlorophyll}} C_6H_{12}O_6 + 6H_2O + 6O_2$

Q. 2. The diagram given below represents an experiment to prove the importance of a factor in photosynthesis. Answer the questions that follow:

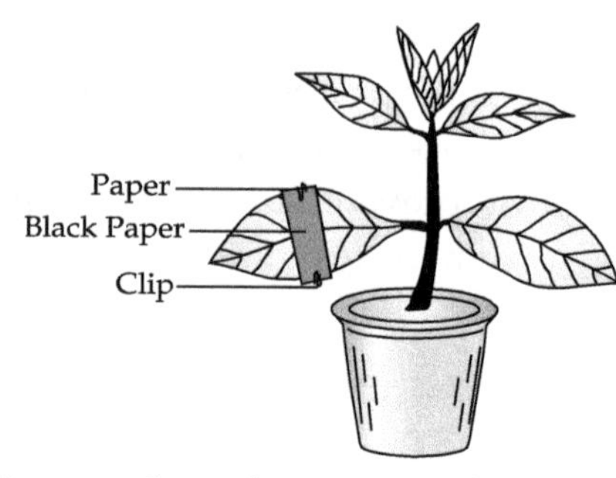

(i) Name the factor studied in this experiment.

(ii) What will you observe in the experimental leaf after the starch test?

(iii) Explain the process of Photosynthesis.

(iv) Give a balanced chemical equation to represent the process of photosynthesis.

(v) Draw a neat, labelled diagram of an experimental setup to show that oxygen is released during photosynthesis. [2019]

(i) Sunlight

(ii) – Part of leaf covered by black paper turns brown, absence of starch.
– Parts of leaf exposed to sunlight turns blue black, presence of starch.

(iii) Plant cells having chlorophyll, use water and carbon dioxide to produce glucose in the presence of sunlight.

(iv) $6CO_2 + 12H_2O \xrightarrow[\text{Chlorophyll}]{\text{Sunlight}} C_6H_{12}O_6 + 6H_2O + 6O_2$

(v)

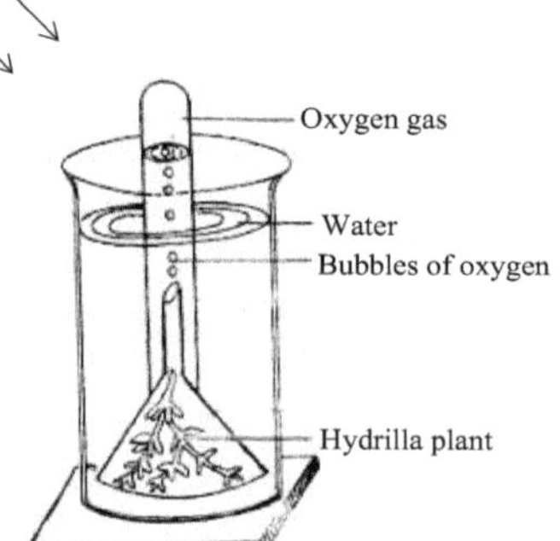

Ans. **(i)** Sunlight

(ii) After the starch test, we observe that the parts of leaf which remains uncovered will turn to blue-black colour indicating the presence of starch, but the covered portion of the leaf will turn brown in colour which indicates the absence of starch.

(iii) Photosynthesis is the process by which chlorophyll containing cells in the presence of suitable factors like water, carbon dioxide, sunlight prepare glucose and release oxygen gas into the atmosphere as a byproduct.

(iv) The balanced chemical equation representing photosynthesis process is as follows:

$$6CO_2 + 12H_2O \xrightarrow[\text{chlorophyll}]{\text{light energy}} C_6H_{12}O_6 + 6H_2O + 6O_2$$

(v) Oxygen is released during photosynthesis.

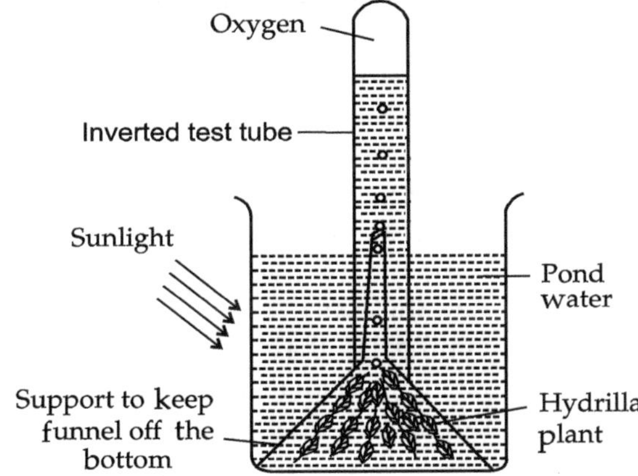

Q. 3. Complete the following paragraph by filling in the blanks (i) to (v) with appropriate words:

To test a leaf for starch, the leaf is boiled in water to (i) _________. It is then boiled in Methylated spirit to (ii) ________. The leaf is dipped in warm water to soften it. It is placed in a petri dish, and (iii) ______ solution is added. The region of the leaf which contains starch, turns (iv) ______ and the region which does not contain starch, turns (v) ________. **[2018]**

 Marking Scheme ------------------------

(i) kill the cells

(ii) remove chlorophyll/decolourise the leaf

(iii) Iodine/Potassium iodide/KI/I_2

(iv) blue black/blackish blue/dark blue/Indigo

(v) yellowish brown/reddish brown/yellow/golden brown

Ans. (i) Kill the cells   (ii) Remove chlorophyll
(iii) Iodine   (iv) Blue-black
(v) Yellowish Brown

Q. 4. A potted plant with variegated leaves was taken in order to prove a factor necessary for photosynthesis. The potted plant was kept in the dark for 24 hours and then placed in bright sunlight for a few hours. Observe the diagrams and answer the questions.

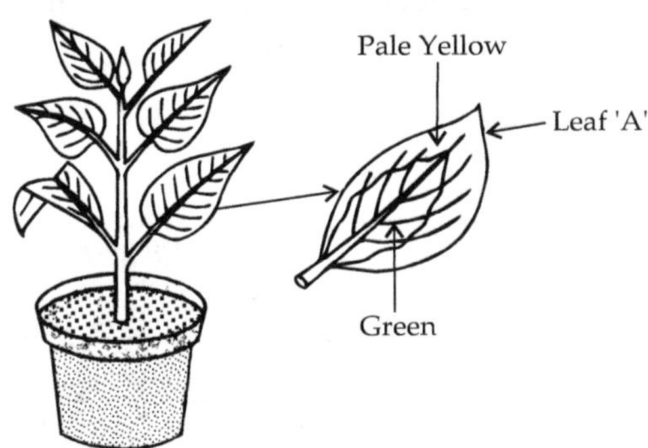

(i) What aspect of photosynthesis is being tested in the above diagram?

(ii) Represent the process of photosynthesis in the form of a balanced equation.

(iii) Why was the plant kept in the dark before beginning the experiment?

(iv) What will be the result of the starch test performed on leaf 'A' shown in the diagram? Give an example of a plant with variegated leaves.

(v) Draw a neat labelled diagram of a chloroplast. **[2018]**

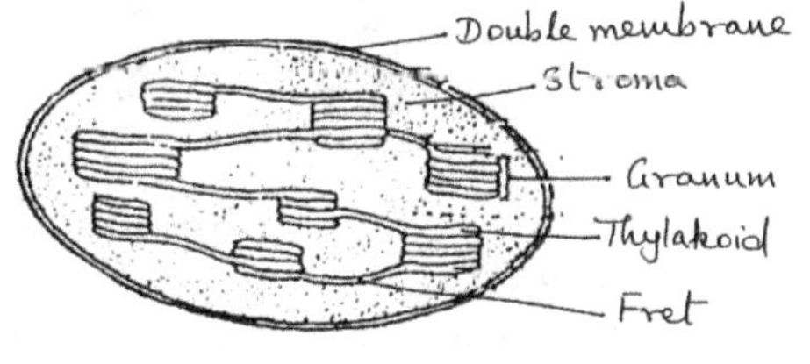 Marking Scheme ------------------------

(i) Chlorophyll is necessary for photosynthesis.

(ii) $6CO_2 + 12H_2O \xrightarrow[\text{Chlorophyll}]{\text{Sunlight}} C_6H_{12}O_6 + 6H_2O + 6O_2$

(iii) to destarch the leaves.

(iv) Green part – blue black/blackish/dark blue/indigo

(v) Yellow part – brown/yellowish brown/golden yellow

Ans. (i) Chlorophyll is necessary for the photosynthesis.

(ii) $6CO_2 + 12H_2O \xrightarrow[\text{Chlorophyll}]{\text{Sunlight}} C_6H_{12}O_6 + 6H_2O + 6O_2$

(iii) Plant was kept in the dark to destarch the leaves so that the starch already present in the plant does not interfere with the results of the experiment.

(iv) The green portion of the leaf will turn blue-black, indicating the presence of starch and the pale yellow portion of the leaf will turn brown, indicating the absence of starch.

Example of plant with variegated leaves: Croton.

(v)

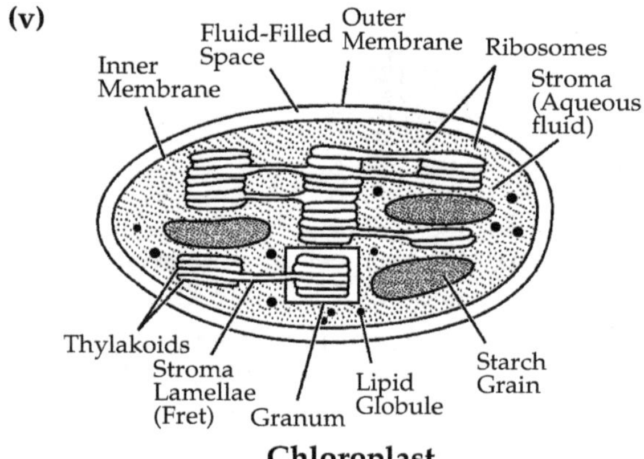

Chloroplast

Q. 5. The diagrams given below represent the relationship between a mouse and a physiological process that occurs in green plants. Study the diagram and answer the questions that follow:

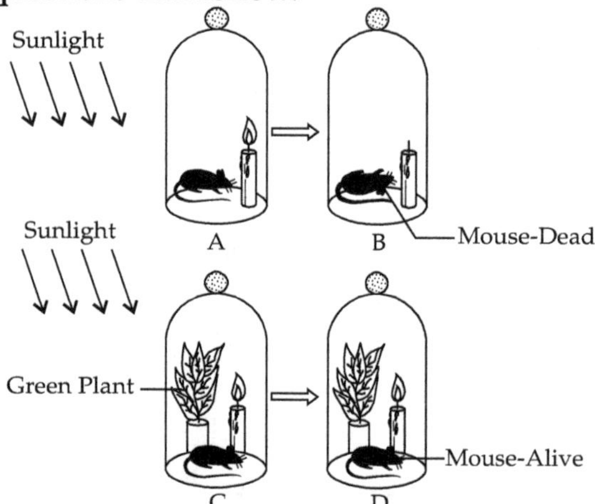

(i) Name the physiological process occurring in the green plant that has kept the mouse alive.

(ii) Explain the physiological process mentioned above.

(iii) Why did the mouse die in bell jar B?

(iv) What is the significance of the process as stated in (i) for life on earth?

(v) Represent the above mentioned physiological process in the form of a chemical equation. **[2017]**

Ans. **(i)** Photosynthesis is the physiological process that is occurring in the green plant. It releases oxygen which kept the mouse alive.

(ii) Photosynthesis is the process by which living plant cells containing chlorophyll produce food substances like glucose and starch from carbon dioxide and water by using light energy. Plants release oxygen gas during this process which is a life supporter for the living organisms on the earth's surface.

(iii) In bell jar B, there was no green plant so no oxygen was produced by photosynthesis process. The oxygen gas present in the bell jar had already been consumed by the mouse and the burning candle. So due to lack of oxygen, the mouse died and also the candle got extinguished.

(iv) The significance of photosynthesis process is that it is the only biological process which releases oxygen into the atmosphere that supports all life forms on the earth's surface. Green plants synthesise their food by photosynthesis. All organisms are directly or indirectly dependent on green plants for their food.

(v) $6CO_2 + 12H_2O \xrightarrow[\text{Chlorophyll}]{\text{Light energy}}$
$$C_6H_{12}O_6 + 6H_2O + 6O_2$$

Q. 6. The following diagram demonstrates a physiological process taking place in green plants. The whole set up was placed in bright sunlight for several hours. Study the diagram and answer the questions that follow:

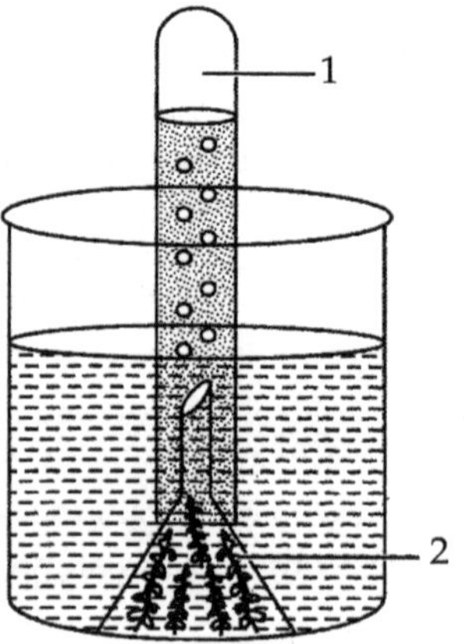

(i) What aspect of the physiological process is being examined?

(ii) Explain the physiological process mentioned in (i) above.

(iii) Label the parts numbered 1 and 2 in the diagram.

(iv) Write a well-balanced chemical equation for the physiological process explained in (ii) above.

(v) What would happen to the rate of bubbling of the gas if a pinch of sodium bicarbonate is added to the water in the beaker? Explain your answer. **[2016]**

Ans. **(i)** The apparatus is set to examine the release of oxygen gas during photosynthesis.

(ii) Photosynthesis is the process by which green plants utilise CO_2 and H_2O as raw materials in the presence of sunlight and chlorophyll, to synthesize food in the form of glucose. This process releases oxygen as a byproduct.

(iii) 1. Oxygen getting filled in the empty space in test tube

2. Hydrilla plant

(iv) A well-balanced chemical equation for photosynthesis is as follows:

$$6CO_2 + 12H_2O \xrightarrow[\text{Chlorophyll}]{\text{Sunlight}} C_6H_{12}O_6 + 6O_2 + 6H_2O$$

(v) The rate of bubbling of the gas will increase.

If a pinch of $NaHCO_3$ (sodium bicarbonate) is added to the water, the reaction results in the release of CO_2. This CO_2 is then utilised for photosynthesis. The increased amount of CO_2 will increase the rate of photosynthesis, which subsequently will increase the rate of release of oxygen bubbles.

Q. 7. The diagram below shows two test-tubes A and B. Test-tube A contains a green water plant. Test-tube B contains both a green water plant and a snail. Both Test-tubes are kept in sunlight. Answer the questions that follow:

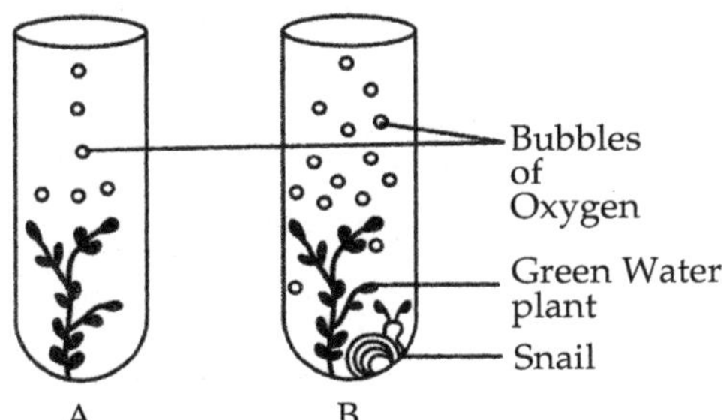

(i) Name the physiological process that releases the bubbles of oxygen.

(ii) Explain the physiological process as mentioned above in Q. 7 (a) (i).

(iii) What is the purpose of keeping a snail in test-tube 'B'?

(iv) Why does test-tube 'B' have more bubbles of oxygen?

(v) Give an example of a water plant that can be used in the above experiment.

(vi) Write the overall chemical equation for the above process. **[2015]**

Ans. **(i)** Photosynthesis

(ii) Photosynthesis is the process by which living plant cells, containing chlorophyll, produce food substances (glucose and starch) from CO_2 and water by using light energy and releases oxygen as a byproduct.

(iii) The purpose to put snail in the test tube is to increase the rate of photosynthesis by releasing CO_2 by the snail. This also suggests that both respiration and photosynthesis are needed to maintain O_2 and CO_2 concentration in the atmosphere.

(iv) When snail respires, concentration of CO_2 increases which enhances the rate of photosynthesis. Hence, oxygen is much released.

(v) Hydrilla

(vi) $6CO_2 + 12H_2O \xrightarrow[\text{Chlorophyll}]{\text{light energy}} C_6H_{12}O_6 + 6H_2O + 6O_2 \uparrow$

Q. 8. A potted plant was taken in order to prove a factor necessary for photosynthesis. The potted plant was kept in the dark for 24 hours. One of the leaves was covered with black paper in the centre. The potted plant was then placed in sunlight for a few hours.

(i) What aspect of photosynthesis was being tested?

(ii) Why was the plant placed in the dark before beginning the experiment?

(iii) During the starch test why was the leaf:

   (1) boiled in water

   (2) boiled in methylated spirit.

(iv) Write a balanced chemical equation to represent the process of photosynthesis.

(v) Draw a neat diagram of a chloroplast and label its parts. **[2014]**

Ans. **(i)** The aspect for the test is that light is necessary for photosynthesis.

(ii) To remove all pre-existing starch from the leaves of the plant.

(iii) (1) The leaf was boiled in water to destroy enzymes so that further chemical changes do not take place in the leaf.

(2) To dissolve the chlorophyll.

(iv) $6CO_2 + 12H_2O \xrightarrow[\text{Chlorophyll}]{\text{Sunlight}} C_6H_{12}O_6$
$$+ 6H_2O + 6O_2$$

(v) Refer to short answer type question Answer. 6 (v)

Q. 9. The figure given below represents an experiment to demonstrate a particular aspect of photosynthesis. The alphabet 'A' represents a certain condition inside the flask.

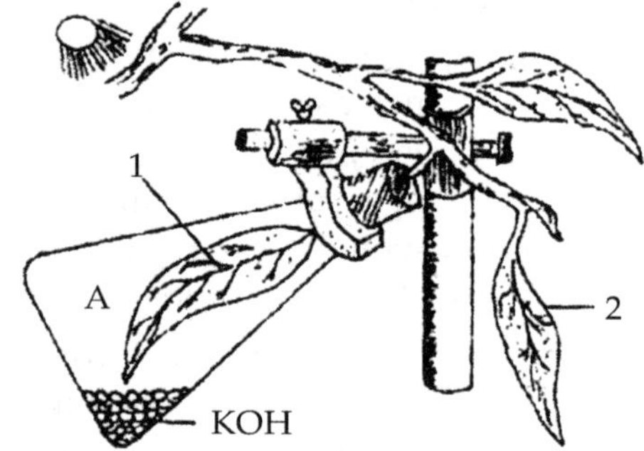

(i) What is the aim of the experiment?

(ii) Identify the special condition inside the flask.

(iii) Name an alternative chemical that can be used instead of KOH.

(iv) In what manner do the leaves 1 and 2 differ at the end of the starch test?

[2013]

Ans. **(i)** Aim was to prove that CO_2 is necessary for photosynthesis.

(ii) No CO_2 in the flask.

(iii) CaO (limestone), potassium pyrogallate.

(iv) Leaf 1 will turn brown indicating absence of starch.

Leaf 2 will turn blue-black at the end of starch test indicating presence of starch.

Q. 10. The diagram given below is an experiment conducted to study a factor necessary for Photosynthesis. Observe the diagrams and then answer the following questions:

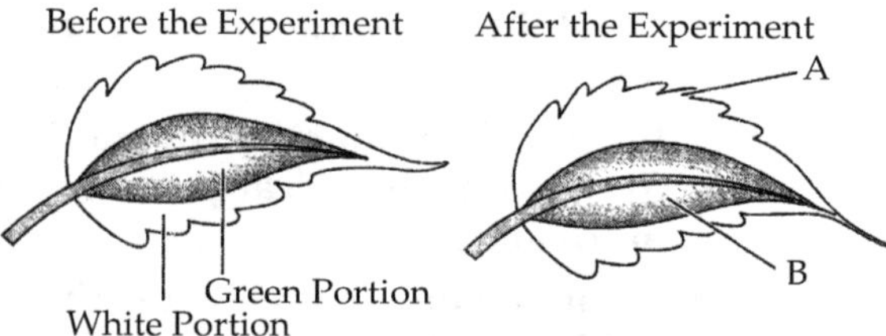

(i) What is the aim of the experiment?

(ii) Name the test performed on the leaf and the solution used for the test.

(iii) What type of leaf was used for the experiment? Give an example.

(iv) What is the expected result of the above test on the parts labelled A and B?

(v) Give a balanced chemical equation to represent the process of Photosynthesis.

[2012]

Ans. **(i)** To show that chlorophyll is necessary for photosynthesis.

(ii) Starch test, and the solution used was iodine solution.

(iii) Variegated leaf, example—croton

(iv) Green part (B) will turn blue-black, part (A) will turn brown

(v) $6CO_2 + 12\,H_2O \xrightarrow[\text{Chlorophyll}]{\text{Sunlight}} C_6H_{12}O_6$
$$+ 6O_2\uparrow + 6\,H_2O$$

Q. 11. Copy and complete the following by filling in the blanks 1 to 5 with appropriate words/terms/phrases:

To test the leaf for starch, the leaf is boiled in water to………(1). It is next boiled in methylated spirit to…………(2). The leaf is placed in warm water to soften it. It is then placed in a dish and…………(3) solution is added. The region, which contains, starch, turns…………(4) and the region, which does not contain starch, turns…………(5). [2011]

Ans. **1.** Kill the cells

2. Remove chlorophyll

3. Iodine

4. Blue-black

5. Yellowish Brown

Chapter 6
Circulatory System

Short Answer Type Questions

Q. 1. The diagram given below represents the simplified pathway of the circulation of blood. Answer the questions that follow:

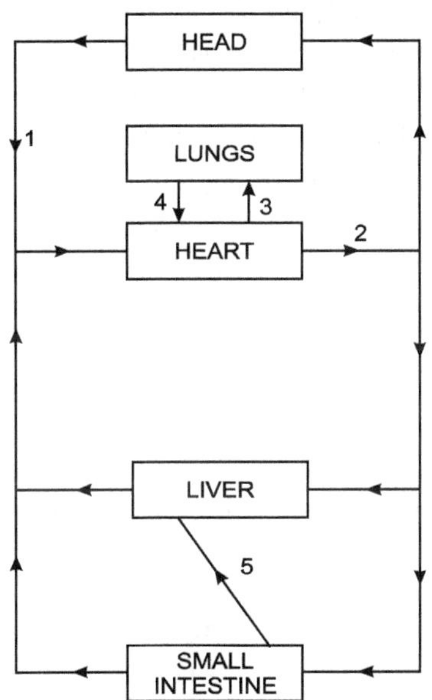

(i) Name the blood vessels labelled 1 to 4.

(ii) Which blood vessel supplies oxygenated blood to the muscles of the heart?

(iii) What is the importance of blood vessel labelled 5?

(iv) What is the type of blood circulation that takes place between the heart and the lungs?

(v) Draw a diagram of the different blood cells as seen in a smear of human blood.

[2020]

Ans. **(i)** 1. Superior vena cava;
2. Aorta;
3. Pulmonary artery;
4. Pulmonary vein

(ii) Coronary artery

(iii) Hepatic portal vein carries the blood from stomach and intestine to liver where the excess sugar is stored as glycogen. If any toxins are present in blood, they are detoxified in liver. In this way, the quantity of nutrients flowing in the blood is regulated and circulation of toxic substances in the blood is prohibited.

(iv) Pulmonary circulation

(v)

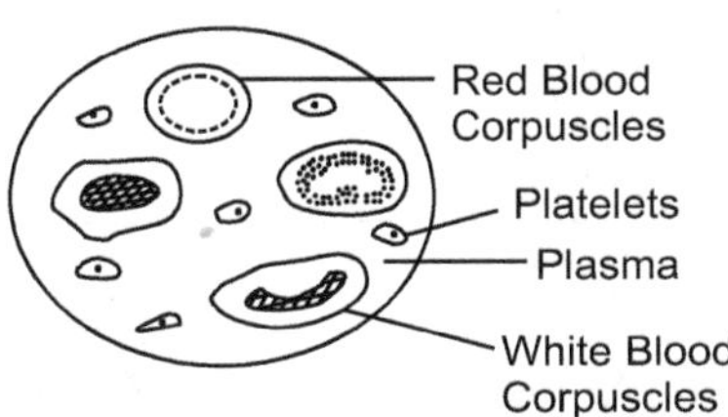

Q. 2. Given below is a diagram of a human blood smear.
Study the diagram and answer the questions that follow:

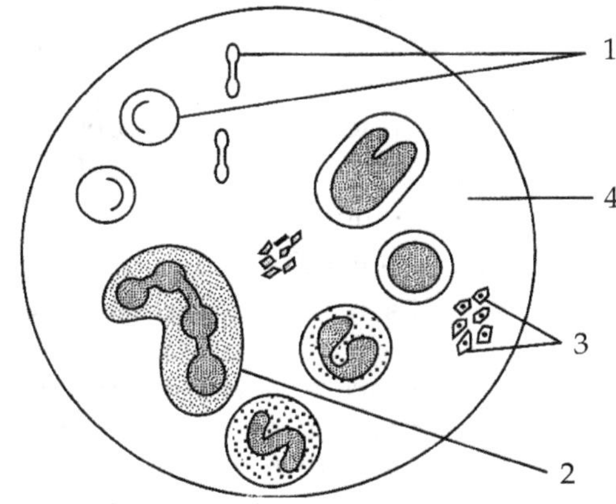

(i) Name the components numbered '1' to '4'.

(ii) Mention two structural differences between the parts '1' and '2'.

(iii) Name the soluble protein found in part '4' which forms insoluble threads during clotting of blood.

(iv) What is the average lifespan of the component numbered '1' ?

(v) Component numbered '1' do not have certain organelles but are very efficient in their function. Explain. **[2018]**

Marking Scheme

(i) 1. RBCs/Erythrocytes
2. WBC/Leucocytes/named WBC
3. Platelets/Thrombocytes
4. Plasma

(ii) 1. RBC
- Biconcave disc like
- Nucleus absent
- Haemoglobin present

    2. WBC
        - Irregular, amoeboid
        - Nucleus present
        - Haemoglobin absent
(iii) Fibrinogen
(iv) 120 days
 (v) Absence of nucleus increases the surface area for absorbing more oxygen / more RBCs can be accommodated.

Absence of mitochondria means they do not use oxygen for respiration, hence all the transported to tissues.

Absence of endoplasmic reticulum increases the flexibility to move through narrow capillaries.

Ans. **(i)** 1. RBCs,   2. WBC,

    3. Platelets,   4. Plasma.

(ii)

RBC	WBC
1. These are biconcave disc shaped.	These are irregular, amoeboid shaped.
2. RBCs do not have the nucleus.	They are characterised by the presence of a large central nucleus.

(iii) Fibrinogen

(iv) About 120 days

(v) Absence of nucleus in RBCs make them biconcave shaped. This increases their surface area for absorbing more oxygen. They do not have mitochondria so they are unable to use oxygen for themselves, so all oxygen is transported and delivered to cells and tissues. Absence of endoplasmic reticulum make them flexible due to which these can easily move through narrow capillaries.

Q. 3. The diagram given below represents a section of the human heart. Answer the questions that follow:

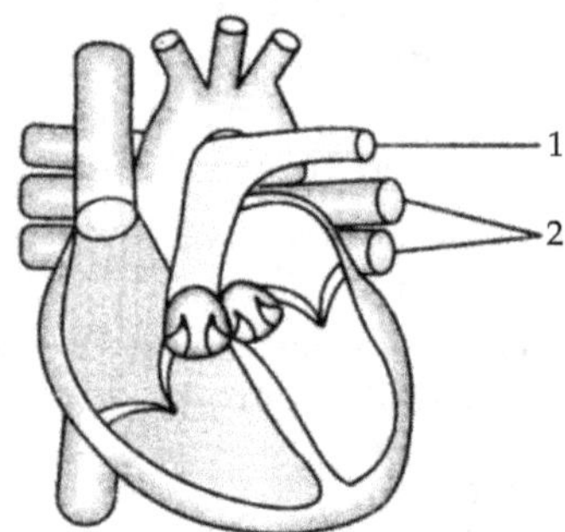

(i) Which parts of heart are in the diastolic phase? Give a reason to support your answer.

(ii) Label the parts numbered 1 and 2 in the diagram. What type of blood flows through them?

(iii) What causes the heart sounds 'LUBB' and 'DUP'?

(iv) Name the blood vessels that supply oxygenated blood to the heart muscles.

(v) Draw neat labelled diagrams of a cross section of an artery and a vein.   [2017]

Ans. **(i)** Ventricles are in the diastolic phase as semilunar valves at the root of aorta and pulmonary artery are closed and bicuspid and tricuspid valves are open. Blood enters from atria to ventricles through atrio-ventricular valves.

(ii) 1. Pulmonary artery

2. Pulmonary vein

Deoxygenated blood flows through pulmonary artery and oxygenated blood flows through pulmonary veins.

(iii) LUBB sound is caused by the closure of atrio-ventricular valves *i.e.,* tricuspid and bicuspid valves. Due to closure of semilunar valves located at the root of pulmonary artery and aorta, DUP sound is produced.

(iv) Coronary artery supplies oxygenated blood to the heart muscles.

(v)

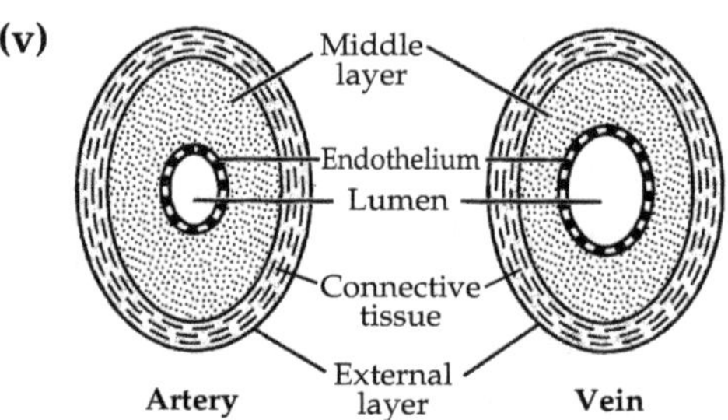

Q. 4. The diagram given below are cross-sections of blood vessels:

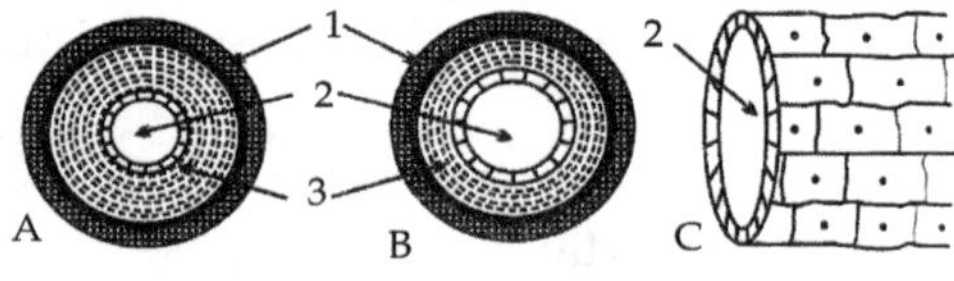

(i) Identify the blood vessels A, B and C.

(ii) Name the parts labelled 1 to 3.

(iii) Name the type of blood that flows through A.

(iv) Mention one structural difference between A and B.

(v) In which of the above vessels does exchange of gases actually take place?   [2015]

Ans. **(i)** A– Artery   B– Vein

C– Capillary

(ii) 1. Tunica externa/connective tissue layer

    2. Lumen

    3. Tunica media/Muscular layer

(iii) Oxygenated blood flows through A.

(iv) Arteries are thick-walled and do not have valves. Veins are thin-walled and have valves.

(v) The exchange of gases takes place in C (capillaries).

Q. 5. The diagram below represents the human heart in one phase of its functions.

Study the diagram carefully and answer the questions that follows:

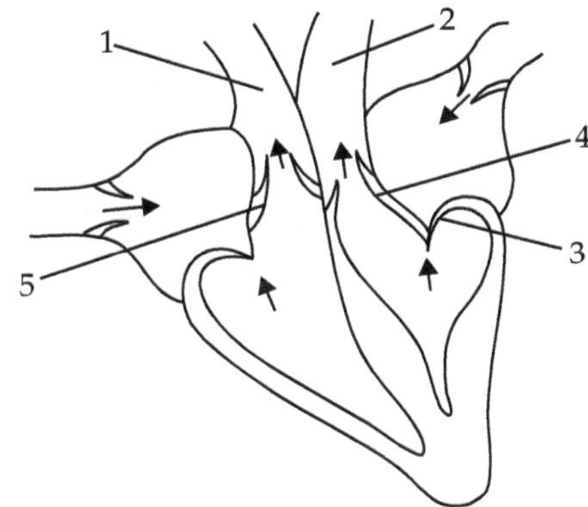

(i) Name the phase.

(ii) Which part of the heart is contracting in this phase? Give a reason to support your answer.

(iii) Name the parts labelled 1 to 4.

(iv) What type of blood flows through '2'?

(v) State the function of the part numbered '5'.

(vi) Name the membrane that covers the heart. **[2015]**

Ans. **(i)** Ventricular systole

(ii) Both ventricles are contracting in this phase, because both bicuspid and tricuspid valves are closed in order to prevent the backflow of blood into atria and the semilunar valves are open.

(iii) 1. Pulmonary artery

    2. Aorta

    3. Aortic Bicuspid valve

    4. Semilunar valve

(iv) '2' carries oxygenated blood.

(v) Part 5 is pulmonary semilunar valve through which blood passes into pulmonary artery and prevents the backflow of blood into the right ventricle.

(vi) Pericardium.

Q. 6. The diagram below represents the simplified pathway of the circulation of blood. Study the same and answer the questions that follow:

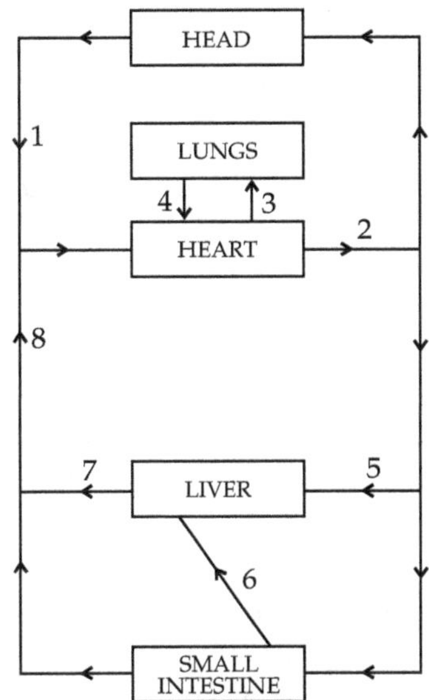

(i) Name the blood vessels labelled 1 and 2.

(ii) State the function of blood vessels labelled 5 and 8.

(iii) What is the importance of the blood vessel labelled 6?

(iv) Which blood vessel will contain a high amount of glucose and amino acids after a meal?

(v) Draw a diagram of the different blood cells as seen in a smear of human blood.

[2014]

Ans. **(i)** 1. Anterior vena cava   2. Aorta

(ii) Blood vessel 5 carries oxygenated blood to the liver.

Blood vessels 8 brings deoxygenated blood from lower parts of the body to the heart.

(iii) It brings all the digested food and deoxygenated blood from parts of alimentary canal to the liver.

(iv) Blood vessel number 6. *i.e.*, hepatic portal vein.

(v)

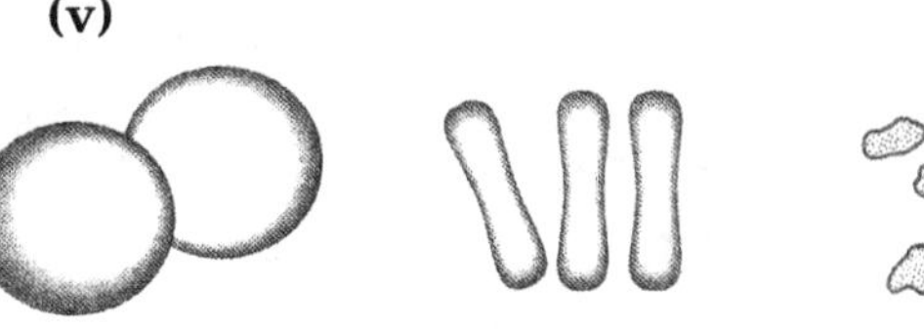

Red blood cells   White blood cells   Platelets

Q. 7. The diagram given below represents the human heart in one phase of its functional activities. Study the same and answer the questions that follow:

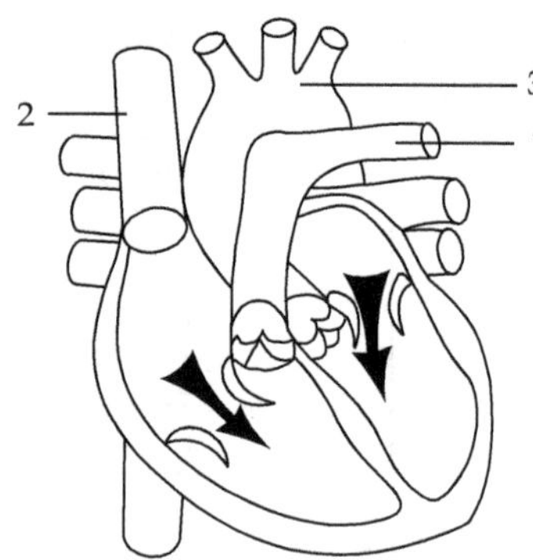

(i) Name the phase.

(ii) Label the parts 1, 2 and 3.

(iii) Which part of the heart is contracting in this phase? Give a reason to support your answer.

(iv) Draw well labelled diagrams of part 1 and 2 to show the structural differences between them. [2013]

Ans. **(i)** Atrial systole

(ii) **1.** Left pulmonary artery

2. Superior vena cava

3. Aorta

(iii) Both atria are contracting in this phase because the cuspid valves are open, allowing blood to flow into the ventricles.

(iv)

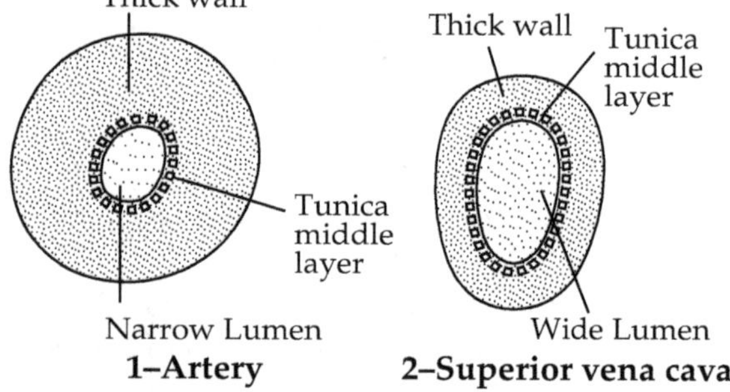

Q. 8. The diagrams given below show the cross section of two kinds of blood vessels:

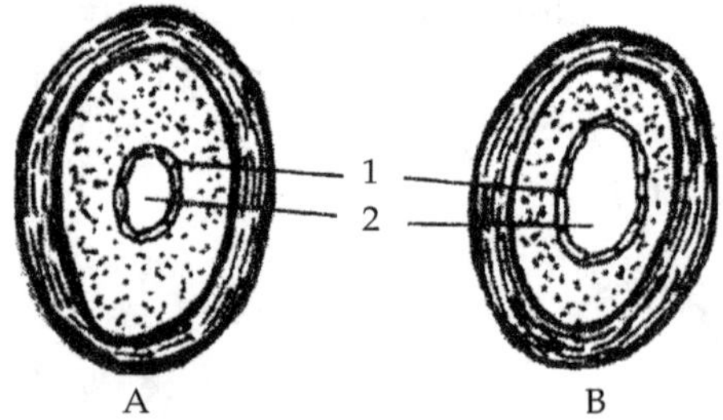

(i) Identify the blood vessels A and B. In each case give a reason to support your answer.

(ii) Name the parts numbered 1 and 2.

(iii) When are the sounds "LUBB" and "DUPP" produced during a heartbeat?

(iv) Name the blood vessel that:

(1) begins and ends in capillaries.

(2) supplies blood to the walls of the heart. [2012]

Ans. **(i)** A—Artery, B—Vein, because in A lumen is narrow, in B lumen is wide.

(ii) **1.** Endothelium, **2.** Lumen.

(iii) "LUBB" sound is produced when ventricles contract and atrio-ventricular valves get closed at the beginning of ventricular systole.

"DUPP" sound is produced by the closure of semilunar valves at the beginning of ventricular diastole.

(iv) **1.** Hepatic portal vein

2. Coronary artery

Q. 9. The diagram below represents circulation in the human body. Answer the questions that follow:

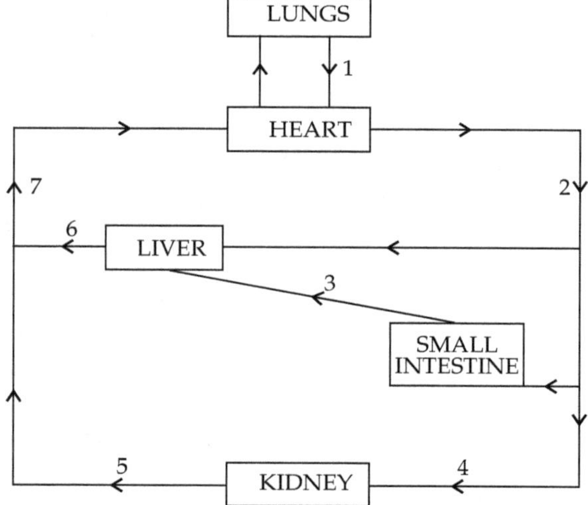

(i) Name the blood vessels labelled 1, 3, 6 and 7.

(ii) Name the blood vessel that supplies the walls of the heart with oxygen.

(iii) Draw a neat labelled diagram of the blood vessel numbered '2' as seen in a cross section.

(iv) Mention one structural difference between blood vessels numbered 4 and 5. [2011]

Ans. **(i)** **1.** Pulmonary vein

3. Hepatic portal vein

6. Hepatic vein

7. Inferior vena cava.

(ii) Coronary arteries

(iii) Cross-sectional diagram of Artery

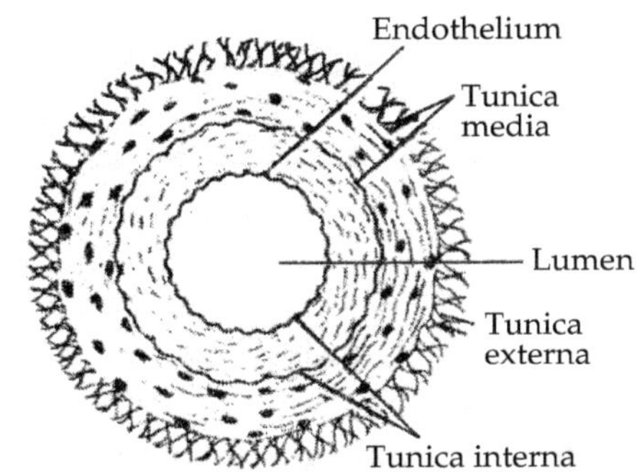

(i) Name the cell labelled 1.

(ii) Identify the phenomenon occurring in A.

(iii) Mention two structural differences between 1 and 2.

(iv) Name the process occurring in B and C and state the importance of this process in the human body.　　　**[2011]**

(iv)	4 (Renal Artery)	5 (Renal Vein)
	Wall thick and more muscular.	Wall thin and less muscular.

Q. 10. **Study the following diagram carefully and then answer the questions that follow:**

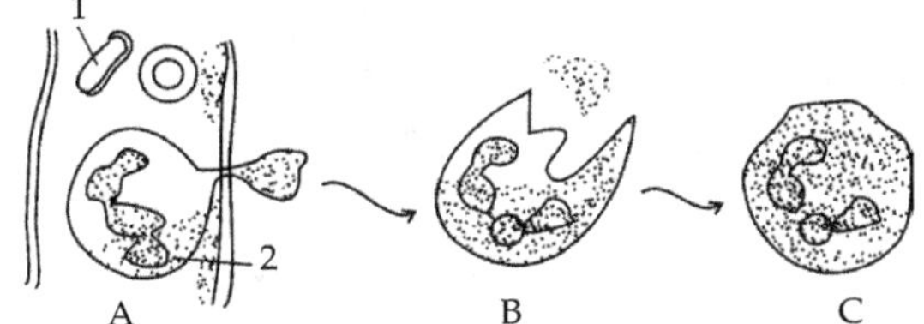

Ans. **(i)** 1-Red blood cell or Erythrocyte

(ii) Diapedisis

(iii)		1	2
	(a)	Non-nucleated.	Nucleated.
	(b)	Round, disc shaped.	Amoeboid, irregular in shape.

(iv) **Phagocytosis:** By this process, the WBCs destroy the germs coming into the body.

Chapter 7

Excretory System

Short Answer Type Questions

Q. 1. The figure given below shows a part of a nephron.

Answer the questions that follow:

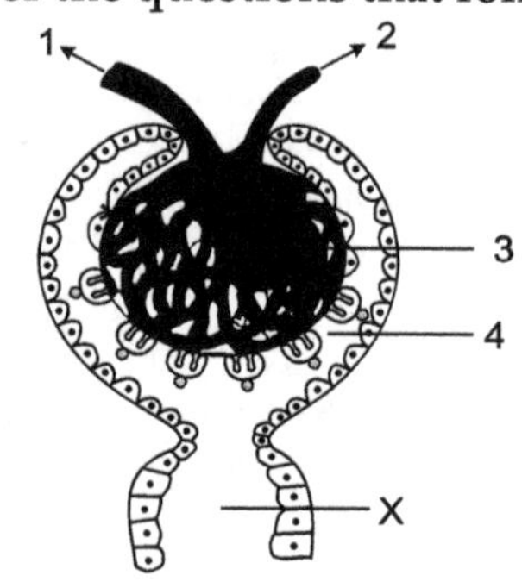

(i) In which region of the kidney is the above structure present?

(ii) Label the parts numbered 1 to 4.

(iii) What is the technical terms for the process that occurs in part 3?

(iv) Why is fluid X not called urine? Justify your answer.

(v) Draw a neat, labelled diagram of the urinary system of man. **[2020]**

Ans. **(i)** Cortex region of kidney.

(ii) **1.** Afferent arteriole; **2.** Efferent arteriole; **3.** Glomerulus; **4.** Bowman's capsule

(iii) Ultrafiltration

(iv) Fluid X is called glomerular filtrate but not urine because it is a very dilute solution that contains not only harmful wastes but also many useful substances like water, salts, glucose etc. which needs to be reabsorbed in the different parts of the nephron.

(v)

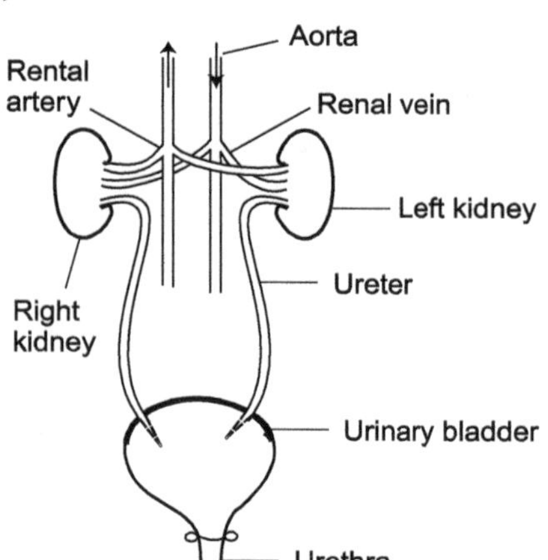

Q. 2. The diagram given below represents an organ system in the human body. Study the same and answer the questions that follow:

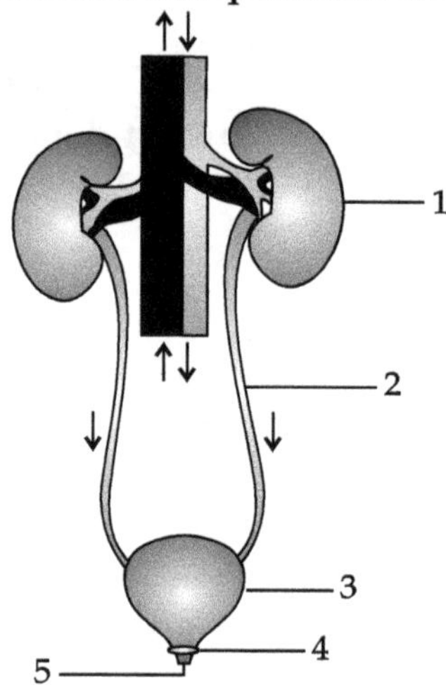

(i) Identify the system.

(ii) Label the parts marked 2 and 4. Mention the function of part 5.

(iii) Name the structural and functional units of the part marked 1.

(iv) What is the fluid that accumulates in part 3?

Which is the main nitrogenous waste present in it?

(v) Draw a neat, labelled diagram showing the longitudinal section of part 1.

[2019]

Marking Scheme

(i) Excretory system/Urinary system

(ii) 2 – Ureter

4 – Sphincter

5 – Expels urine

(iii) Nephrons

(iv) Urine

Urea

(v)

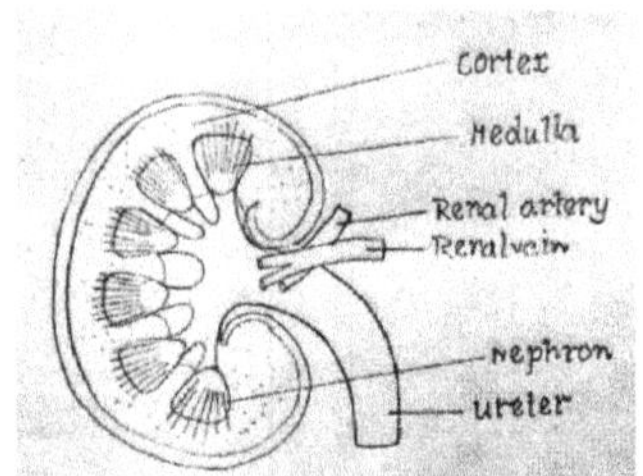

(Any other correct labelling)

Ans. **(i)** Excretory system

(ii) 2. Ureter; 4. Sphincter Muscle,

The structure labelled as 5 is urethra.

Urethra empties the urinary bladder at regular intervals *i.e.,* carries the urine from the bladder to outside of the body.

(iii) The structure labelled as 1 is kidney.

The structural and functional unit of kidney is a nephron.

(iv) Urine gets accumulated in urinary bladder [part 3]. Urea is the main nitrogenous waste present in urine.

(v) Diagram of longitudinal section of kidney.

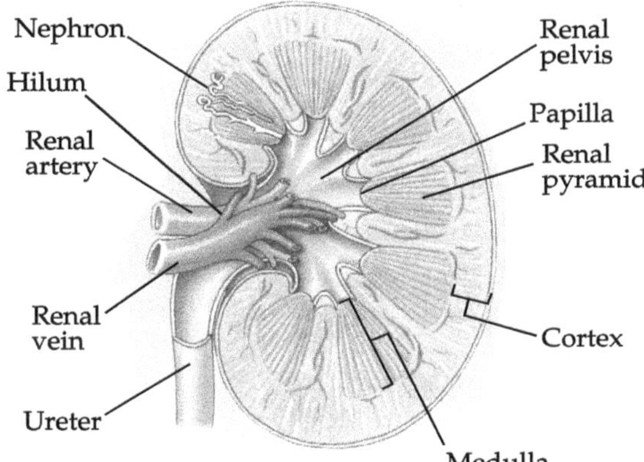

Q. 3. The diagram given below is that of a structure present in a human kidney.

Study the same and answer the questions that follow:

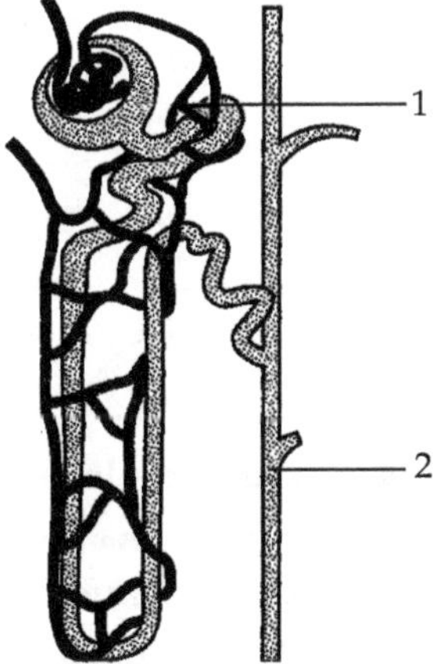

(i) Name the structure represented in the diagram.

(ii) What is the liquid entering part '1' called?

Name two substances present in this liquid that are reabsorbed in the tubule.

(iii) What is the fluid that comes to part '2' called?

Name the main nitrogenous waste in it.

(iv) Mention the three main steps involved in the formation of the fluid mentioned in (iii) above.

(v) Name the substance which may be present in the fluid in part '2' if a person suffers from Diabetes mellitus. **[2018]**

📋 Marking Scheme ------------------------------

(i) Nephron/Uriniferous tubule/Renal tubule/Kidney tubule

(ii) Glomerular filtrate, water/glucose/Sodium Chloride/Na ions/chloride ions/amino acids/ultrafiltrate/Nephric filtrate

(iii) Urine, Urea

(iv) Ultrafiltration, selective reabsorption, tubular secretion, Glomerular filtration.

(v) Glucose/Sugar/Ketones

Ans. **(i)** Nephron/uriniferous tubule/renal tubule.

(ii) Glomerular filtrate

Two substances present in glomerular filtrate are water and glucose.

(iii) Urine

Urea is the main nitrogenous waste in urine.

(iv) Ultrafiltration, selective reabsorption, tubular secretion and Glomerular fillration.

(v) Glucose

Q. 4. The diagram given below shows a section of a human kidney. Study the diagram carefully and answer the questions that follow:

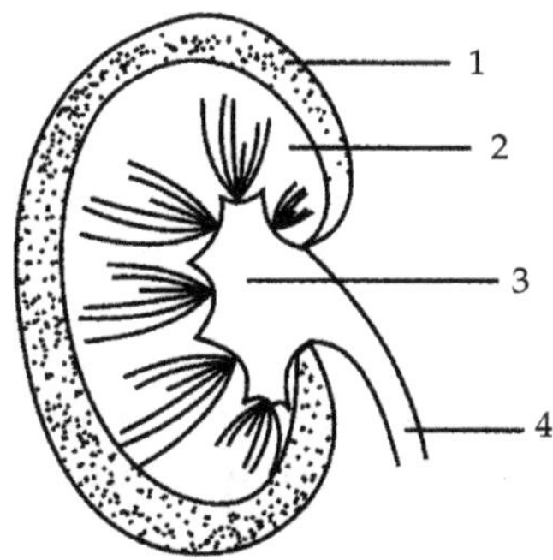

(i) Label the parts numbered 1 to 4.

(ii) Why does part '2' have a striped appearance?

(iii) What is the fluid that passes down part '4'? Name the main nitrogenous waste present in it.

(iv) Mention the structural and functional units of kidneys.

(v) Name the two major steps in the formation of the fluid mentioned in 3 (iii). **[2015]**

Ans. **(i)** 1. Cortex   2. Medulla

3. Pelvis   4. Ureter

(ii) Medulla has a striped appearance because the straight tubules and blood vessels are associated with the renal pyramids, present in the renal medulla.

(iii) Fluid that passes down the ureter is urine. Its main nitrogenous waste is urea.

(iv) Nephron

(v) 1. Ultrafiltration

    2. Tubular reabsorption

Q. 5. The diagram given below shows the male urinogenital system of a human being. Study the diagram and answer the questions that follow:

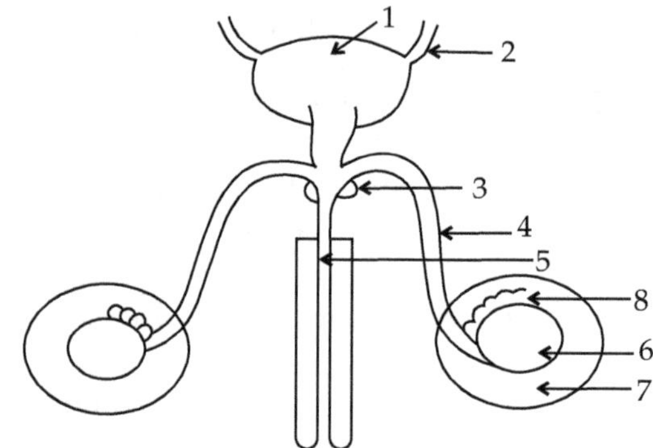

(i) Label the parts numbered 1 to 8.

(ii) Name the corresponding structure of part (4) in female reproductive system.

(iii) What is the role of part 7? [2015]

Ans. **(i) 1.** Urinary Bladder   **2.** Ureter

    3. Prostate glands   **4.** Vas deferens

    5. Urethra   **6.** Testis

    7. Scrotum   **8.** Epididymis

(ii) Fallopian tube or oviduct.

(iii) The high temperature of body does not permit maturation of sperms. Thus the scrotum suspends the testis outside the body at a lower temperature suitable for spermatogenesis.

Q. 6. The given diagram represents a nephron and its blood supply. Study the diagram and answer the following questions:

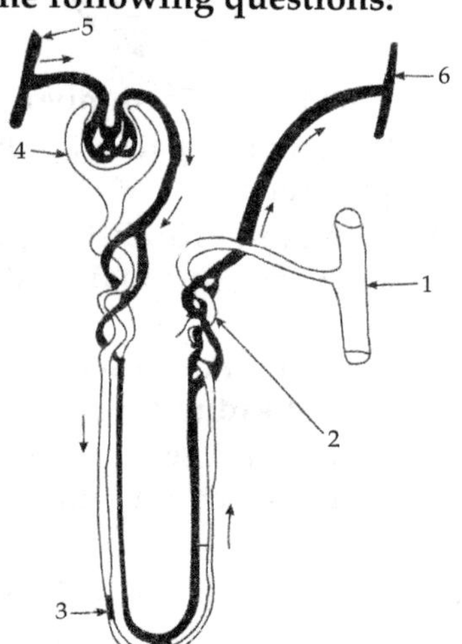

(i) Label parts 1, 2, 3 and 4.

(ii) State the reason for the high hydrostatic pressure in the glomerulus.

(iii) Name the blood vessel which contains the least amount of urea in this diagram.

(iv) Name the two main stages of urine formation.

(v) Name the part of the nephron which lies in the renal medulla. [2014]

Ans. **(i) 1.** Collecting duct

    2. Distal convoluted tubule

    3. Descending limb of Loop of Henle

    4. Bowman's capsule

(ii) The afferent arteriole entering the Bowman's capsule is wider than the efferent arteriole which leaves it. So more blood is entering and less blood is moving out of the glomerulus which creates high hydrostatic pressure in the glomerulus.

(iii) Renal vein.

(iv) Ultrafiltration and reabsorption.

(v) Loop of Henle.

Q. 7. The diagram below shows the excretory system of a human being. Study the same and then answer the questions that follow:

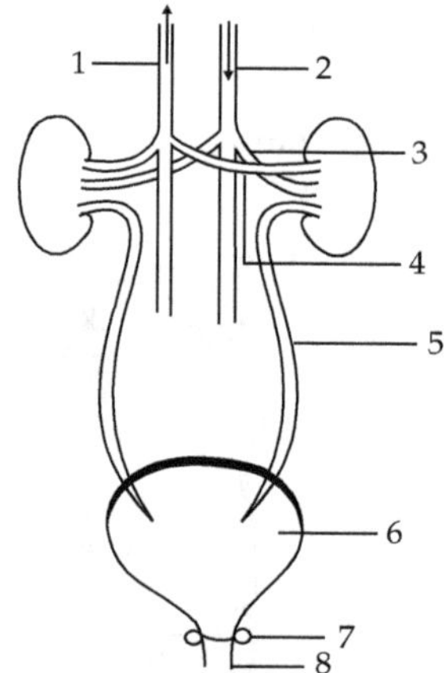

(i) Name the parts labelled 1, 2, 3, and 4.

(ii) Give the main function of the parts labelled 5, 6, 7 and 8.

(iii) Name the endocrine gland which could be added in the diagram and state its location/position. [2012]

Ans. **(i) 1.** Posterior vena cava,

    2. Aorta,

    3. Renal artery,

    4. Renal vein

(ii) 5. Ureter : Carries urine to the bladder from the kidney.

6. Urinary bladder: Temporarily stores urine.

7. Sphincter muscle: Controls the voiding of urine.

8. Urethra: Release urine periodically.

(iii) Adrenal gland : At the top of each kidney.

Q. 8. Study the diagram given below and then answer the questions that follow:

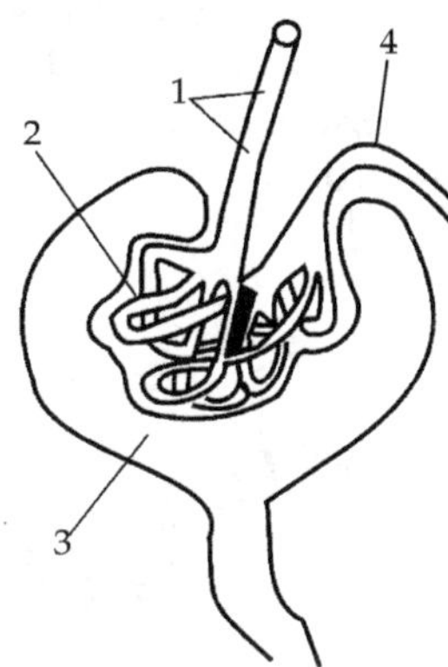

(i) Name the region in the kidney where the above structure is present.

(ii) Name the parts labelled 1, 2, 3 and 4.

(iii) Name the stages involved in the formation of urine.

(iv) What is the technical term given to the process occurring in 2 and 3? Briefly describe the process. [2011]

Ans. **(i)** Renal cortex

(ii) 1. Afferent arteriole

2. Glomerulus

3. Bowman's capsule

4. Efferent arteriole

(iii) Ultrafiltration, reabsorption and tubular secretion.

(iv) Ultrafiltration: In it, blood entering the glomerulus under great pressure is filtered. The reason for this greater pressure is that the efferent arteriole is narrower than the afferent arteriole. The liquid part of the blood filters through the walls of glomerular capillaries and Bowman's capsule and enters into the nephron where it is called the glomerular filtrate.

Short Answer Type Questions

Q. 1. The diagram given below depicts a defect of the human eye which has been corrected by using a suitable lens.

Answer the following questions:

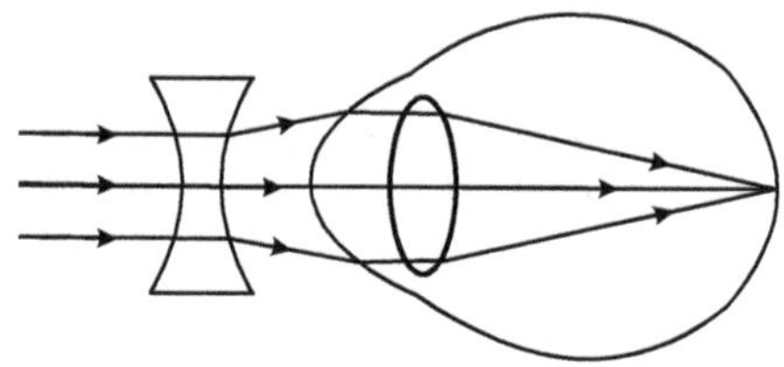

- **(i)** Name the defect that has been corrected Which type of lens has been used for the correction?
- **(ii)** Mention one cause for the above defect.
- **(iii)** Where would the image have formed if the above lens was not used for correction?
- **(iv)** Name the three concentric layers of the eyeball.
- **(v)** Draw a neat, labelled diagram of a neuron. **[2020]**

Ans.
- **(i)** Myopia, Concave lens
- **(ii)** The cause of myopia is lengthening of eyeball from front to back.
- **(iii)** The image would have formed in front of the retina.
- **(iv)** The three concentric layers of the eyeball are sclera, choroid and retina.
- **(v)**

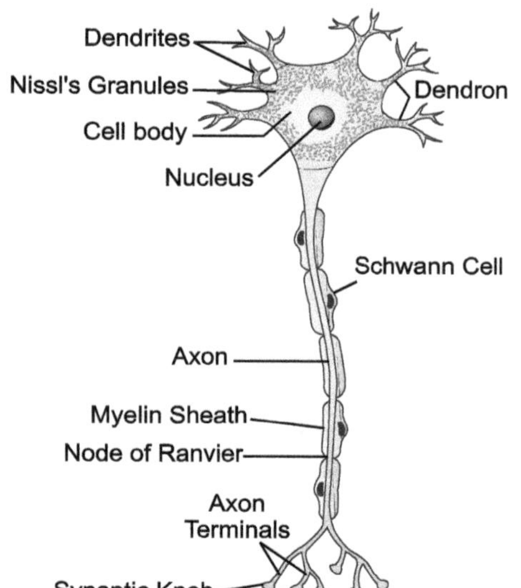

Q. 2. The diagram given below shows the internal structure of a spinal cord depicting a phenomenon. Study the diagram and answer the questions:

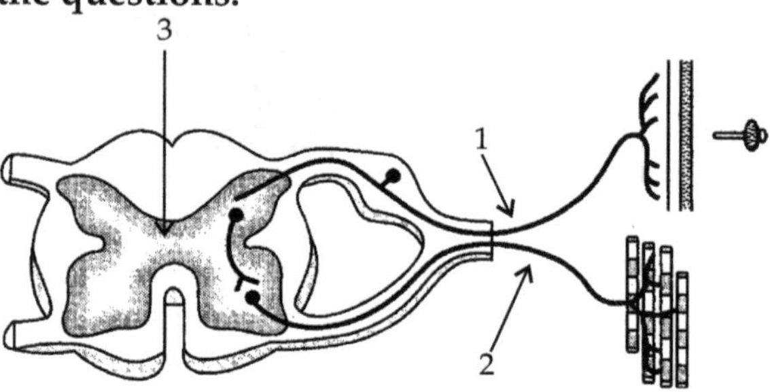

- **(i)** Name the phenomenon that is depicted in the diagram. Define the phenomenon.
- **(ii)** Give the technical term for the point of contact between the two nerve cells.
- **(iii)** Name the parts numbered 1, 2 and 3.
- **(iv)** How does the arrangement of neurons in the spinal cord differ from that of the brain?
- **(v)** Mention two ways by which the spinal cord is protected in our body. **[2018]**

📋 Marking Scheme ----------------

- **(i)** Reflex action, /Simple reflex/Reflex act
  It is an automatic, [spontaneous, quick] involuntary response to a stimulus.
- **(ii)** Synapse
- **(iii)** 1. Sensory neuron/afferent fibre/Axon of sensory neuron
  2. Motor neuron/efferent fibre/Axon of motor neuron
  3. Grey matter/central canal
- **(iv)** Spinal Cord – Cytons in the inner grey matter and axons in the outer white matter. /Cytons are inside & Axons are outside
  Brain – Cytons in the outer grey matter and axons in the inner white matter. /Cytons inside, Axons outside
- **(v)** Meninges, Cerebrospinal fluid, Vertebral column/backbone.

Ans.
- **(i) Reflex action:** It is an automatic, quick and involuntary action in the body brought about by a stimulus.
- **(ii)** Synapse
- **(iii)** 1. Sensory neuron,
  2. Motor neuron,
  3. Gray matter.

(iv) In spinal cord, the gray matter containing the cell bodies of neurons lies on inner side and white matter containing myelinated axons on outer side, whereas in the brain, gray matter is outside and white matter lies on the inner side.

(v) 1. Spinal cord is covered by three membranous layer of meninges which protects it and also its central canal is filled with cerebrospinal fluid which absorbs shocks.

2. It is also protected by the vertebrae of backbone.

Q. 3. **The diagram given below is an external view of the human brain. Study the same and answer the questions that follow:**

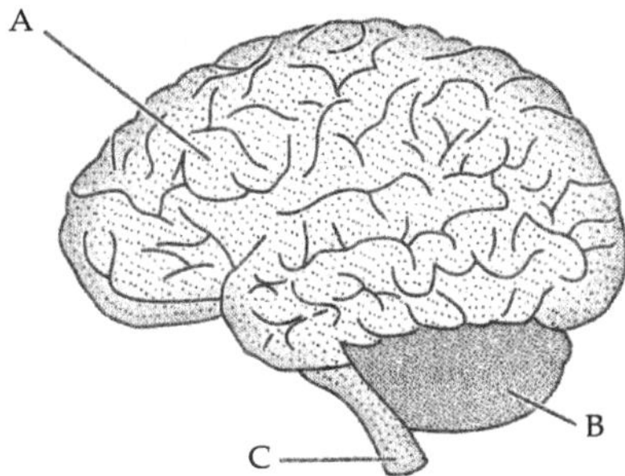

(i) **Name the parts labelled A, B and C in the diagram.**

(ii) **State the main functions of the parts labelled A and B.**

(iii) **What are the structural and functional units of the brain ? How are the parts of these units arranged in A and B?**

(iv) **Mention the collective term for the membranes covering the brain.**

(v) **What is the function of Cerebrospinal fluid?** **[2017]**

Ans. **(i)** A – Cerebrum

B – Cerebellum

C – Spinal cord

(ii) Cerebrum is the seat of intelligence, consciousness and will power. It controls all the voluntary activities. Cerebellum coordinates muscular activities and maintains balance of the body.

(iii) Neuron is the structural and functional unit of the brain. In cerebrum, outer portion contains cell bodies of the neuron whereas inner portion contains axons of the neurons. Whereas in spinal cord, outer portion contains axons and inner portion contains cell bodies of neurons.

(iv) The membranes covering the brain are meninges which are a three membranous covering.

(v) Cerebrospinal fluid is a watery fluid found within the space of the covering membrane and also in the ventricles of brain and the central canal of spinal cord. It acts as a cushion to protect the brain from mechanical shocks. It also acts as a medium for the exchange of food materials, waste products and respiratory gases with neurons.

Q. 4. **Given below is a diagram depicting a defect of the human eye. Study the same and then answer the questions that follow:**

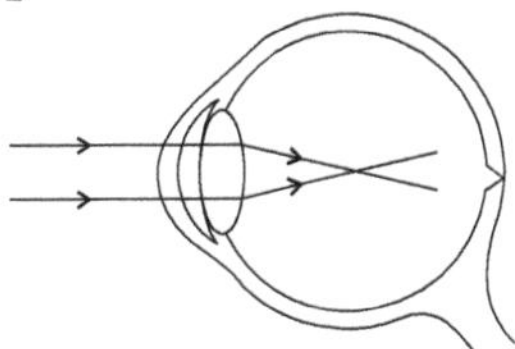

(i) **Name the defect shown in the diagram.**

(ii) **What are the two possible reasons that cause this defect?**

(iii) **Name the type of lens used to correct this defect.**

(iv) **With the help of a diagram show how the defect shown above is rectified using a suitable lens.** **[2016]**

Ans. **(i)** The defect shown in the diagram is called Short-sightedness or Myopia.

(ii) This defect may arise due to:

1. Excessive curvature of the eye lens.

2. Elongation of the eyeball.

(iii) The defect can be corrected by using spectacles with concave or divergent lenses.

(iv) Diagram showing rectification of the defect:

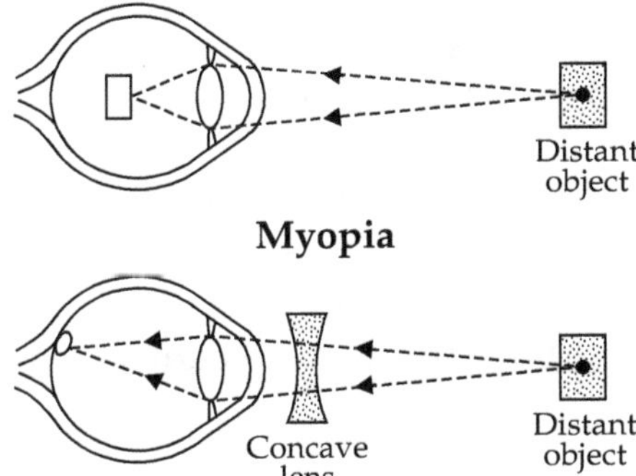

Myopia with correction

Q. 5. **(i)** **Draw a well labelled diagram of the membranous labyrinth found in the inner ear.**

(ii) **Based on the diagram drawn above in (i) give a suitable term for each of the following descriptions:**

1. **The sensory cells that helps in hearing.**

2. The part that is responsible for static balance of the body.

3. The membrane covered opening that connects the middle ear to the inner ear.

4. The fluid present in the middle chamber of cochlea.

5. The structure that maintains dynamic equilibrium of the body.

[2016]

Ans. (i) Diagram showing membranous labyrinth found in the inner ear:

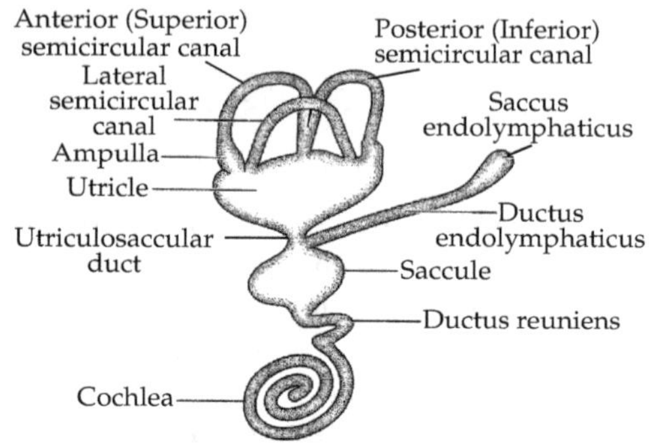

(ii) 1. Sensory cells that help in hearing are called **organ of corti.**

2. The **utricle and saccule part of the inner ear** have presence of gravity receptors that aid in maintaining static balance of the body.

3. **Oval window or fenestra ovalis** is the membrane covered opening that connects the middle ear to the inner ear.

4. **Endolymph** is the fluid present in the middle chamber of cochlea.

5. **Ampulla region of semi circular canal** maintains dynamic balance of the body.

Q. 6. Draw neat and labelled diagrams of the following:

(i) Malpighian Capsule.

(ii) A Myelinated Neuron. [2015]

Ans. (i)

(ii)

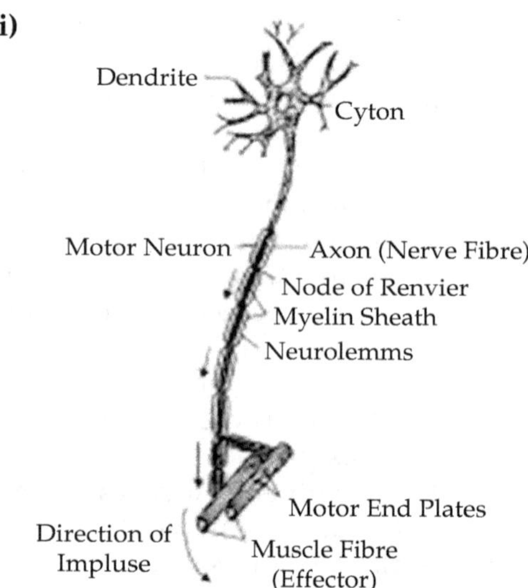

Myelinated Neuron

Q. 7. The diagram given below is a representation of a certain phenomenon pertaining to the nervous system. Study the diagram and answer the following questions:

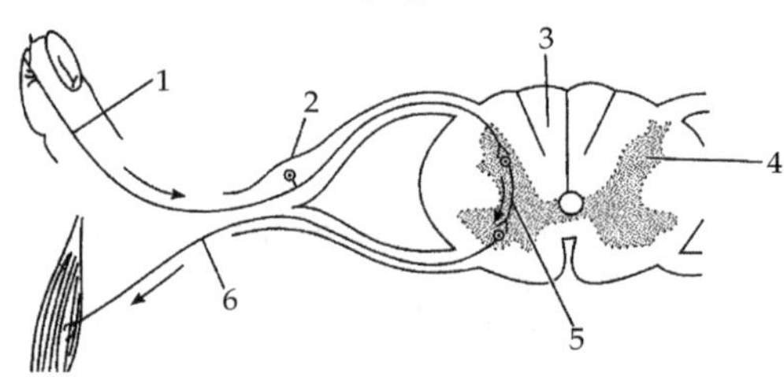

(i) **Name the phenomenon that is being depicted.**

(ii) **Give the technical term for the point of contact between the two nerve cells.**

(iii) **Name the parts 1, 2, 3 and 4.**

(vi) **Write the functions of parts 5 and 6.**

(v) **How does the arrangement of neurons in the spinal cord differ from that of the brain?** [2014]

Ans. (i) Pathway of reflex action or reflex arc

(ii) Synapse

(iii) 1. Sensory neuron

2. Dorsal root ganglions

3. White matter

4. Gray matter

(iv) Function of interneuron: –It receives messages from sensory neuron and passes it to the motor neuron.

Function of motor neuron: It passes impulses from the main nervous system to the effector organ.

(v) In the brain, the cell bodies of neurons lie in the cortex *i.e.,* the outer region (gray matter) and axons lie on the inner region (white matter). In the spinal cord, the cell bodies lie in the medulla region (inner gray matter) and axons lie on the outer side *i.e.*, cortex (outer white matter).

Q. 8. Draw a diagram of the human eye as seen in a vertical section and label the parts which suits the following descriptions relating to the:

   (i) Photosensitive layer of the eye.

   (ii) Structure which is responsible for holding the eye lens in its position.

   (iii) Structure which maintains the shape of the eye ball and the area of no vision.

   (iv) Anterior chamber seen in front of the eye lens.

   (v) Outermost transparent layer seen in front of the eye ball. **[2013]**

Ans.

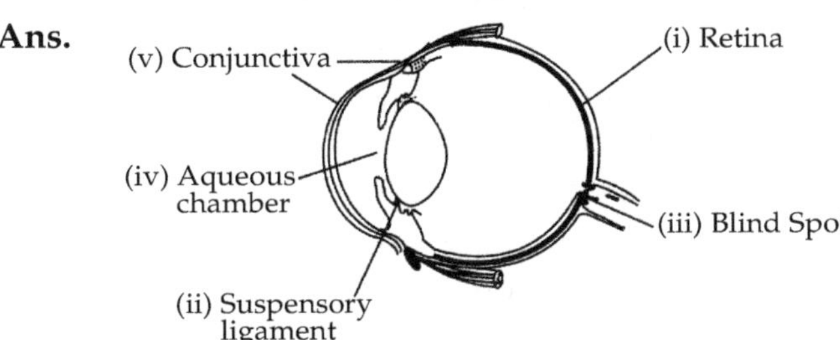

Vertical Section of Eye

Q. 9. Study the following diagram carefully and then answer the questions that follow. The diagram is depicting a defect of the human eye:

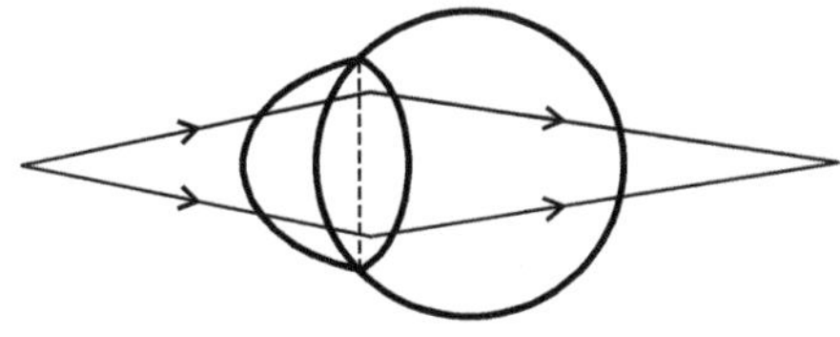

   (i) Identify the defect shown in the diagram.

   (ii) Give two possible reasons for the above defect.

   (iii) Draw a neat labelled diagram to show how the above defect can be rectified. **[2012]**

Ans.   **(i)** Far sightness or hypermetropia.

   (ii) 1. Lens is flattened or less convex.

     2. Eyeball is short from front to back.

   (iii)

Q. 10. Answer the following:

   (i) Draw a well labelled diagram of a 'Neuron' and name the following parts:

     (1) Node of Ranvier

     (2) Nissl granules

     (3) Cyton

   (ii) Name the part of the human brain which is concerned with the following:

     (1) Seat of memory

     (2) Coordinates muscular activity. **[2012]**

Ans.   **(i)**

Neuron

   (ii) (1) Cerebrum   **(2)** Cerebellum

Q. 11. With reference to the human ear, answer the questions that follow:

   (i) Give the technical term for the structure found in the inner ear.

   (ii) Name the three small bones present in the middle ear. What is the biological term for them collectively?

   (iii) Name the part of the ear associated with (1) static balance, (2) hearing, (3) dynamic balance.

   (iv) Name the nerve, which transmits messages from the ear to the brain. **[2011]**

Ans.   **(i)** Membranous labyrinth

   (ii) Malleus, incus, stapes. Collectively called ear ossicles.

   (iii) (1) Utriculus and sacculus

     (2) Cochlea

     (3) Semi-circular canals

   (iv) Auditory nerve.

Q. 12. With reference to the functioning of the eye, answer the questions that follow:

   (i) What is meant by power of accommodation of the eye?

   (ii) What is the shape of the lens during (1) near vision, (2) distant vision?

   (iii) Name the two structures in the eye responsible for bringing about the change in the shape of the lens.

   (iv) Name the cells of the retina and their respective pigments which get activated (1) in the dark, (2) in light. **[2011]**

Ans.   **(i)** It is the ability of the body to focus clearly on objects, both close and distant from the eye.

   (ii) (1) More convex or almost round

     (2) Less convex or almost flat

   (iii) Ciliary muscles and suspensory ligaments.

(iv) (1) Rods, rhodopsin

   (2) Cones, iodopsin

Q. 13. During a street fight between two individuals, mention the effects on the following organs by the autonomous nervous system, in the table given below : (one has been done for you as an example)

Organ	Sympathetic system	Parasympathetic system
e.g. Lungs	Dilates bronchi and bronchioles	Constricts bronchi and bronchioles
1. Heart		
2. Pupil of the eye		
3. Salivary gland		

[2011]

Ans.

1. Increases heart beat.	Return heart beat to normal.
2. Dilates.	Constricts.
3. Secretion of the salivary gland decreases.	Increases.

Q. 14. (i) Draw a well labelled diagram of a Neuron showing the following parts:

Perikaryon, Dendrites, Axon, Node of Ranvier and Myelin sheath.

   (ii) State the function of sensory neuron and a motor neuron.

  (iii) What is a nerve made up of?   [2010]

Ans.   (i)

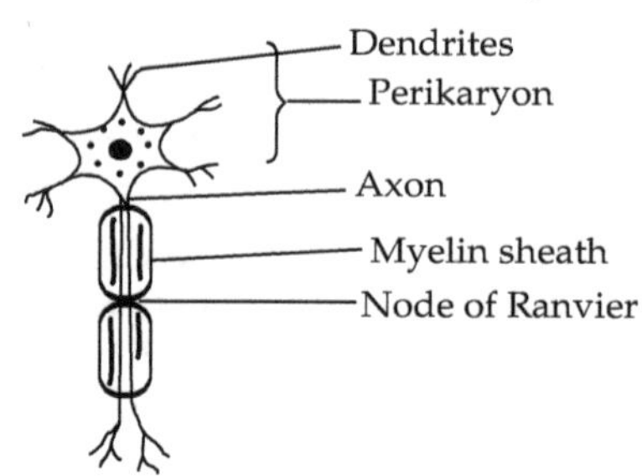

   (ii) Sensory neuron transmits impulses from sense organs to the central nervous system.

Motor neuron carries impulses from the central nervous system to the effector organs.

  (iii) Nerve is made up of a bundle of nerve fibres enclosed in a sheath.

Chapter 9

Endocrine System

Short Answer Type Questions

Q. 1. Complete the table:

Name of the Hormone	Endocrine Gland	Function
(i)	(ii)	Deposits extra glucose of blood as glycogen
Growth Hormone	(iii)	(iv)
(v)	Thyroid	(vi)
(vii)	(viii)	Prepare body for any emergency
Oxytocin	(ix)	(x)

[2020]

Ans. (i) Insulin (ii) Pancreas
(iii) Anterior Pituitary gland
(iv) It promotes the normal growth of the whole body.
(v) Thyroxine
(vi) It regulates the basal metabolism of the body.
(vii) Adrenaline (viii) Adrenal gland
(ix) Posterior Pituitary gland
(x) It stimulates contraction of uterus during child birth and stimulates milk ejection.

Q. 2. The diagram given below represents an endocrine gland in the human body. Study the diagram and answer the following questions:

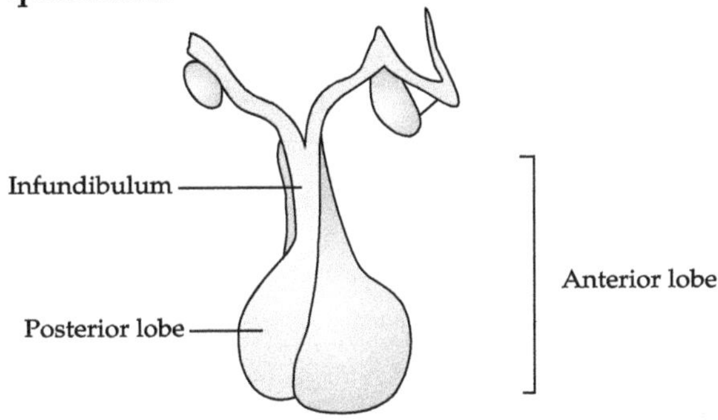

(i) Identify the endocrine gland. Where is it located?
(ii) Why is the above gland referred to as the 'Master gland'?
(iii) Name the hormone which in deficiency causes Diabetes Insipidus.
How does this disorder differ from Diabetes Mellitus?
(iv) Explain the term 'Hormone'.
What is the role of Tropic hormones in the human body?
(v) Which lobe of the above gland secretes:
1. Oxytocin 2. ACTH
3. Growth hormone [2019]

Marking Scheme

(i) Pituitary gland
Hangs from hypothalamus
(ii) Controls the secretions of other endocrine glands/regulates the activities of other endocrine glands.
(iii) Vasopressin/ADH
Diabetes mellitus is due to deficiency of insulin/high level of sugar in blood, urine has sugar.
Diabetes insipidus: Normal sugar in blood, urine free of sugar/urine loaded with water.
(iv) It is the secretion of an endocrine gland, which is transported by blood and acts on target organs or cells.
Secreted by pituitary gland and stimulates other endocrine glands to secrete their hormones.
(v) 1 – Posterior/neurohypophysis
2 – Anterior/adenohypophysis
3 – Anterior/adenohypophysis

Ans. (i) It is pituitary gland. It is located in the brain between hypothalamus and pineal gland.
(ii) Pituitary gland is called the master gland as it controls the functions of other endocrine glands and the main body functions such as growth.
(iii) Hormone is ADH/Vasopressin.
In Diabetes insipidus there is no sugar in urine but it is pale in Diabetes mellitus sugar is present in urine and there is deficiency of insulin.
(iv) Hormones are chemical secretions from specific glands which are poured directly into blood stream and produce effect in one or more target organs only.
Tropic hormones stimulate other glands for the production of some other hormones. For example–TSH [Thyroid stimulating hormone] stimulates thyroid gland to secrete thyroxine.
(v) 1. Posterior lobe/ Neurohypophysis

2. Anterior lobe/ Adenohypophysis

3. Anterior lobe/ Adenohypophysis

Q. 3. The diagram given below represents the location and structure of an endocrine gland. Study the same and answer the questions that follow:

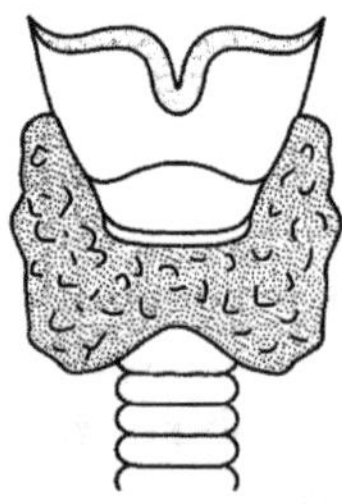

(i) Name the endocrine gland shown in the diagram.

(ii) Name the secretion of the gland which regulates basal metabolism.

(iii) Name the mineral element required for the synthesis of the above mentioned hormone.

(iv) Name the disease caused due to undersecretion of the above mentioned hormone in children.

(v) Name the disease caused due to hypersecretion of the above mentioned hormone. **[2017]**

Ans. (i) The endocrine gland shown in the diagram is thyroid gland.

(ii) The secretion of this gland is thyroxine which regulates basal metabolism.

(iii) The mineral element required for the synthesis of thyroxine is iodine.

(iv) Cretinism is caused due to undersecretion of thyroxine in children.

(v) Exophthalmic goitre is caused due to hypersecretion of thyroxine.

Q. 4. Given below is the outline of the human body showing the important glands:

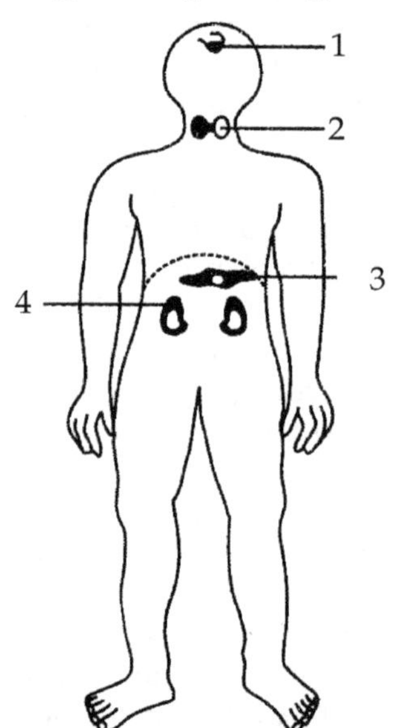

(i) Name the glands marked 1 to 4.

(ii) Name the hormone secreted by part 2. Give one important function of this hormone.

(iii) Name the endocrine part of the part numbered 3.

(iv) Why is the part labelled 1 called the master gland? Which part of the forebrain controls the gland labelled 1?

(v) Name the gland that secretes the 'emergency hormone'. **[2016]**

Ans. (i) 1. Pituitary gland 2. Thyroid gland
3. Pancreas 4. Adrenal gland

(ii) The hormone secreted by part 2 is thyroxine. Thyroxine controls the Basal Metabolic Rate (BMR) of the body and maintains temperature by regulating production of energy.

(iii) The endocrine part of the gland numbered 3 is called Islet of Langerhans.

(iv) The part labelled 1 is the pituitary gland and it is called the 'Master gland' because it secretes hormones which controls the secretions of other endocrine glands of our body.

The hypothalamus part of the forebrain controls the pituitary gland and is thus called the 'Master of master gland'.

(v) Adrenal gland secretes the emergency hormone *i.e.,* adrenaline.

Q. 5. Complete the following table by filling in the blanks from 1 to 10 with appropriate terms:

S. No.	Gland	Secretion	Function / Effect on body
1.	Thyroid	1	2
2.	3	Vasopressin	4
3.	5	6	Promotes glucose utilization by the body cells.
4.	Lacrimal gland	7	8
5.	Adrenal medulla	9	10

[2013]

Ans. 1–Thyroxine.

2–Regulates basal metabolism.

3–Posterior lobe of pituitary gland.

4–Increases reabsorption of water from urinary filtrate by kidney tubules.

5–Pancreas.

6–Insulin.

7–Tears.

8–Lubricates eyeball, keeps the eyes clean and protects the eyes from bacterial infection.

9–Adrenaline.

10–Increases heart rate and blood pressure.

Q. 6. Study the diagram given below and then answer the questions that follow:

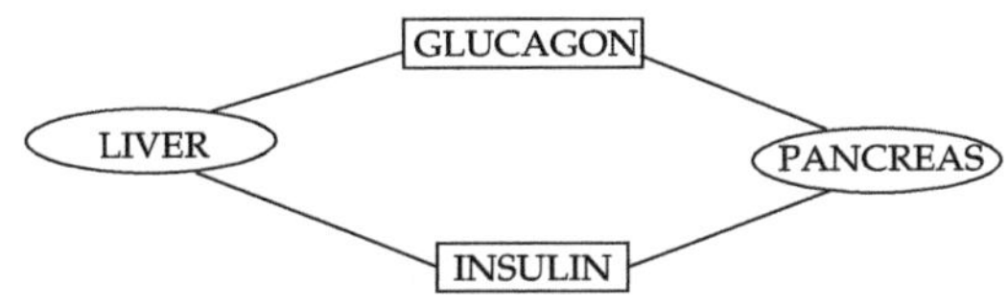

(i) Name the cells of the pancreas that produce (1) glucagon, (2) insulin.

(ii) State the main function of (1) glucagon, (2) insulin.

(iii) Why is the pancreas referred to as an exo-endocrine gland?

(iv) Why is insulin not given orally but is injected into the body?

(v) What is the technical term for the cells of the pancreas that produce endocrine hormones?

(vi) Where in the body is the pancreas located? [2011]

Ans. **(i) (1)** Alpha cells of islet of Langerhans

(2) Beta cells of islet of Langerhans.

(ii) (1) In case of low blood sugar levels, glucagon stimulates the breakdown of glycogen into glucose in the liver and raises blood sugar level.

(2) Insulin controls high blood sugar level in the body. It promotes conversion of glucose to glycogen in the liver.

(iii) Pancreas produces pancreatic juice which is carried by pancreatic duct into the duodenum. It also produces hormones which are poured into blood. Because of this dual activity, it is called an exo-endocrine gland.

(iv) If insulin is given orally, it will be digested by the protein digesting enzymes in the stomach. Hence, it has to be injected.

(v) Islets of Langerhans.

(vi) Below the stomach.

Q. 7. Given below is an outline of the human body showing the important glands.

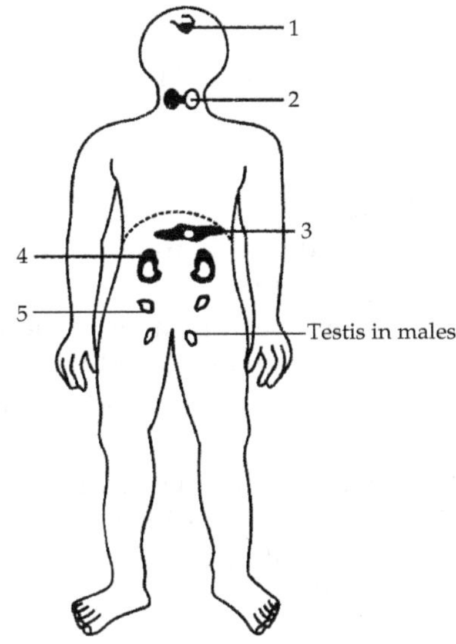

(i) Name the glands marked 1 to 5.

(ii) Name the hormone secreted by 2.

Give one important function of this hormone.

(iii) Name the endocrine cells present in part 3.

(iv) Name the hormone secreted by part 4.

Give one important function of this hormone. [2010]

Ans. **(i)** 1. Pituitary   2. Thyroid

2. Pancreas   4. Adrenal

5. Ovary

(ii) Thyroxine.

It regulates the basal metabolism.

(iii) Islets of Langerhans.

(iv) Adrenaline.

It prepares the body for some emergency by causing production of glucose from glycogen in liver, and releasing it into blood.

Short Answer Type Questions

Q. 1. **Give the biological reasons for the following statements:**
  (i) **It is advisable to keep green plants in an aquarium.**
  (ii) **Water pollution is a major cause of concern in our country.**
  (iii) **We cannot distinguish colours in dim light.**
  (iv) **Medical discoveries such as antibiotics and vaccinations have indirectly contributed to the sharp rise in human population.**
  (v) **Homo sapiens sapiens is the most highly evolved form of man.** **[2020]**

Ans. **(i)** Green plants undergo photosynthesis by which oxygen gas is released which can be utilised by fishes for respiration. So, it is advisable to keep green plants in an aquarium.

  (ii) Water pollution is the major cause of concern in our country because most of the wastes from households, industries, power plants etc., are dumped into water bodies without prior treatment. Agricultural activities, oil spills, untreated sewage water also contribute to water pollution. This leads to degradation in water quality, making it unfit for human consumption and other uses and lead to several infectious diseases. Further, decrease in oxygen level in the polluted water harm the aquatic life, leading to loss of biodiversity. All the factors results in water scarcity and making it difficult to sustain the basic needs of the large population of the country.

  (iii) In dim light, only rod cells of our eyes function, which do not respond to colour. So we cannot distinguish colours in dim light.

  (iv) Due to medical discoveries of vaccine and antibiotics, many diseases have been controlled, increasing the lifespan of the inviduals and decrease in the mortality rate. Thus, they have indirectly contributed to sharp rise in human population.

  (v) Homo sapiens sapiens is the most highly evolved form of man because they developed a logical and syllabic speech in order to communicate, can cultivate plants and domesticated animals, prepared tools, ornaments, used advanced agricultural techniques. They developed cities; create new survival challenges for themselves as well as other species.

Q. 2. **Differentiate between the following pairs on the basis of what is mentioned in the brackets:**
  (i) **Transpiration and Guttation (place of occurrence)**
  (ii) **Biodegradable waste and Non-biodegradable waste (One example)**
  (iii) **Population control and Swachh Bharat Abhiyan (One objective)**
  (iv) **Osmosis and Active Transport (Substances undergoing movement)**
  (v) **Metaphase and Anaphase (Position of chromosomes)** **[2020]**

Ans. **(i)** Transpiration occurs mainly through the stomata of the leaves.

  Guttation occurs through hydathodes present along the margins of the leaves.

  (ii) Example of biodegradable waste is kitchen left overs like peels of vegetables and fruits. Example of non-biodegradable waste is plastics.

  (iii) One objective of population control is to make people aware of the advantages of having small family so that they can get proper food, clothing, education, medical facilities.

  One objective of Swachh Bharat Abhiyan is to clean streets, roads, infrastructure of country's cities and towns.

  (iv) Osmosis is the movement of water molecules. Active transport is the movement of salts or ions.

  (v) In metaphase, chromosomes are lined up in one plane at equator of the cell.

  In Anaphase, chromosomes move towards opposite poles of the cell.

Q. 3. Give appropriate biological/technical terms for the following:

(i) The sensory organ in Cochlea.

(ii) Number of live births per 1000 people per year.

(iii) The point of contract between two neurons.

(iv) The accessory gland in human males whose secretion neutralises the acid in the vagina.

(v) Condition when blood sugar level is lowered in the blood.

(vi) Structure which helps in the adjustment of the size of the pupil.

(vii) A surgical method of fertility control in human males.

(viii) Process by which leucocytes migrate through the walls of capillaries.

(ix) A sudden inheritable change in one or more genes.

(x) A non-dividing phase of the cell cycle where more DNA is synthesised. **[2020]**

Ans. (i) Organ of Corti   (ii) Natality

(iii) Synapse   (iv) Prostate gland

(v) Hypoglycemia   (vi) Iris

(vii) Vasectomy   (viii) Diapedesis

(ix) Mutation

(x) Synthesis phase of Interphase

Q. 4. State two functions of:

(i) Ear   (ii) Ethylene

(iii) Tears   (iv) Testis

(v) Cerebellum   **[2020]**

Ans. (i) **Ear- 1.** It acts as a hearing organ.

2. It helps in maintaining the dynamic as well as static balance the body.

(ii) **Ethylene- 1.** It helps in ripening of fruits.

2. It accelerates senescence.

(iii) **Tears- 1.** It serves as a lubricant for the surface of eye.

2. It contains an enzyme lysozyme which kills germs.

(iv) **Testis- 1.** They produce sperms.

2. They produce male hormone testosterone.

(v) **Cerebellum- 1.** It maintains balance of the body.

2. It coordinates muscular activity.

Q. 5. Mention the exact location of the following:

(i) Testis   (ii) Incus

(iii) Thylakoids   (iv) Amniotic fluid

(v) Corpus callosum   **[2019]**

Ans. (i) Testes are located in thin walled sac like structure called scrotal sac.

(ii) Incus is the middle of the three bones of ear ossicles which is connected to malleus on one end and stapes on other end and is present in the middle ear of human beings.

(iii) Thylakoids are closely packed flattened sacs found in the stroma of chloroplast.

(iv) Amniotic fluid is found in the amnion. It fills the space between amnion and embryo.

(v) Corpus callosum is a bridge of nerve fibres which connects the two cerebral hemispheres.

Q. 6. State the main function of the following:

(i) Medulla Oblongata (ii) Cytokinins

(iii) Tears   (iv) Coronary Artery

(v) Seminal Vesicles.   **[2019]**

Ans. (i) Medulla oblongata controls the activity of internal organs and other involuntary functions like heart beats, peristaltic movement, breathing movement etc.

(ii) Cytokinins stimulate plant growth by cell division and cell enlargement. They inhibit apical dominance.

(iii) Tears clean the front surface of our eye by removing dust particles and the enzyme lysozyme present in tears, kills the germs.

(iv) Coronary artery supplies oxygenated blood to heart muscles.

(v) The secretion from seminal vesicles activates the sperms and helps in their transportation.

Q. 7. **Answer the following questions briefly:**

(i) How are the cytons and axons placed in the brain and the spinal cord?

(ii) Which part of the human ear gives 'Dynamic balance' and 'Static balance' to the body?

(iii) Explain how the human eye adapts itself to bright light and dim light.

(iv) What is Parthenocarpy? Give one example.

(v) Mention any two objectives of 'Swachh Bharat Abhiyan'. **[2019]**

Marking Scheme

(i) Brain - Outer, grey matter has cytons and inner white matter has axons.
Spinal Cord - Outer, white matter has axons and inner grey matter has cytons.

(ii) Dynamic - semi-circular canals/ducts/tubes
Static - utriculus, sacculus, utricle, saccule, vestibule

(iii) Bright light - Pupils constrict, Rhodopsin is bleached.
Dim light - Pupils dilate, Rhodopsin is regenerated.

(iv) Formation of fruit without fertilisation

(v) – To clean roads, streets and buildings in cities and towns.
– To eliminate open defecation
– To build and monitor the use of latrines
– To manage solid and liquid waste
e.g. grapes, water melon, banana, papaya

Ans. **(i)** Axons are placed in the inner portion whereas cytons are placed in the outer portion of brain but in the spinal cord, axons are placed in outer side and cell bodies/cytons are placed in the inner portions.

(ii) Sensory cells in semi-circular canals are concerned with dynamic balance of the body.

Sensory patches in Utriculus and Sacculus are concerned with static balance of the body.

(iii) When we move from a brightly lighted area to a dark room *i.e.,* in dim light, we experience difficulty in seeing objects for some time. Slowly, our vision is improved. This is called dark adaptation. The pupil dilates to allow more light to enter the eyes and rhodopsin/visual purple is generated.

When we enter a brightly lighted area after being in a dimly lighted area for a period of time, we experience a dazzling light for short period after which our vision improves. This is called the light adaptation. Pupil constricts to allow less light to enter our eyes and rhodopsin pigment is degenerate.

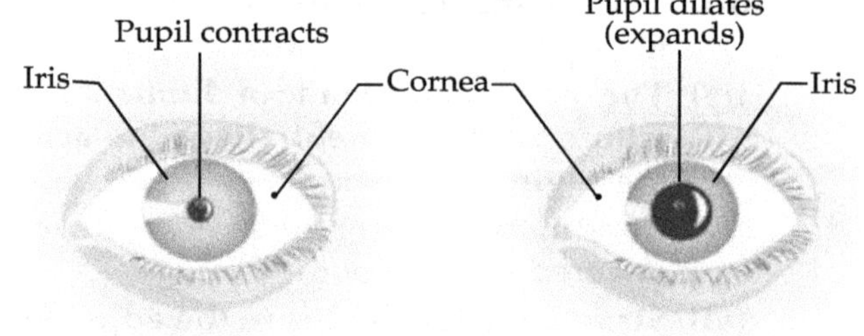

(iv) Development of fruits without fertilization is called Parthenocarpy. Example- Banana, Apple.

(v) Two objectives of Swachh Bharat Abhiyan are:
1. To eliminate open defecation by building individual and public toilets even in the remotest areas.
2. To make our villages, cities and towns clean by removing wastes from streets, roads, parks, gardens, houses etc.

Q. 8. **Mention the exact location of the following:**
(i) Epididymis
(ii) Lacrimal gland
(iii) Malleus
(iv) Hydathodes
(v) Pulmonary semilunar valve **[2018]**

Marking Scheme

(i) on top of the testis/head, dorsal ride, back, rear of testis

(ii) upper sideward portion of orbit/upper outer part of eye/upper lateral region of eye

(iii) middle ear/between eardrum and incus. /inner surface of eardrum

(iv) Tips/margins of leaves/in leaves. /ends or apex of veins/apex of leaves/Epidermis of leaves

(v) In the right ventricle at the base of pulmonary artery. /at the opening of Pulmonary Artery

Ans. **(i) Epididymis:** Inside the scrotum and on upper pole of testis.

(ii) Lacrimal glands: At the upper sideward portion of the orbit of eyes.

(iii) Malleus: In the middle ear between the tympanic membrane and the incus.

(iv) Hydathodes: On the edges and tips of leaves.

(v) Pulmonary semilunar valves: At the opening of right ventricle into the pulmonary artery.

Q. 9. Give appropriate biological or technical terms for the following:

(i) Process of maintaining water and salt balance in the blood.

(ii) Hormones which regulate the secretion of other endocrine glands.

(iii) Movement of molecules of a substance from their higher concentration to lower concentration when they are in direct contact.

(iv) The condition in which a pair of chromosomes carry similar alleles of a particular character.

(v) The complex consisting of a DNA strand and a core of histones.

(vi) The onset of menstruation in a young girl.

(vii) Squeezing out of white blood cells from the capillaries into the surrounding tissues.

(viii) The fluid which surrounds the foetus.

(ix) The relaxation phase of the heart.

(x) The difference between the birth rate and the death rate. **[2018]**

Marking Scheme

(i) Osmoregulation/Osmotic regulation
(ii) Tropic hormones
(iii) Diffusion
(iv) Homozygous
(v) Nucleosome
(vi) Menarche
(vii) Diapedesis
(viii) Amniotic fluid
(ix) Diastole
(x) Growth rate of population

Ans.
(i) Osmoregulation
(ii) Tropic hormones
(iii) Diffusion   (iv) Homozygous
(v) Nucleosome   (vi) Menarche
(vii) Diapedesis   (viii) Amniotic fluid
(ix) Diastole
(x) Growth rate of population

Q. 10. Differentiate between the following pairs on the basis of what is indicated in the brackets:

(i) Leaf and Liver [form in which glucose is stored]

(ii) ATP and AIDS [expand the abbreviations]

(iii) Testosterone and Oestrogen [organ which secretes]

(iv) Ureter and Urethra [function]

(v) Hypotonic solution and Hypertonic solution [condition of a plant cell when placed in them] **[2018]**

Marking Scheme

(i) Leaf – Starch, Liver – Glycogen
(ii) ATP – Adeosine triphosphate, AIDS – Acquired immune deficiency syndrome.
(iii) Testosterone – testis, Oestrogen – Ovary
(iv) Ureter – conducts urine from the kidney to the urinary bladder/transports urine from Renal pelvis to bladder
Urethra – expulsion of urine from the urinary bladder/eliminates urine from body/expels urine and semen.
(v) Hypotonic – Turgid/Turgidity
Hypertonic – Flaccid/Plasmolysed/Flaccidity

Ans. (i)

Leaf	Liver
Glucose is stored in the form of starch.	Glucose is stored in the form of glycogen.

(ii)

ATP	AIDS
Adenosine triphosphate	Acquired immune deficiency syndrome.

(iii)

Testosterone	Oestrogen
Testosterone is secreted by leydig cells, present in the testes.	Oestrogen is secreted by ovaries.

(iv)

Ureter	Urethra
Ureter carries urine from kidneys to the urinary bladder.	Urethra carries urine from urinary bladder to the outside of the body.

(v)

Hypotonic solution	Hypertonic solution
When a cell is placed in hypotonic solution, it gets swollen up and the condition is called turgidity.	When a cell is placed in hypertonic solution, it shrinks and the condition is called flaccidity.

Q. 11. Give biological explanations for the following:

(i) Education is very important for population control.

(ii) The placenta is an important structure for the development of a foetus.

(iii) All the food chains begin with green plants.

(iv) Plants growing in fertilized soil are often found to wilt if the soil is not adequately watered.

(v) We should not put sharp objects into our ears. [2018]

🗒 Marking Scheme ------------------------------

(i) Desire for a male child, ignorance regarding the functioning of reproductive system, gender inequality, etc can be eliminated with education and population increase can be checked./to create awareness for birth control measures/vital for growth of nation/Food, water, environmental pollution, lack of job opportunities can be eliminated/to improve quality of life.

(ii) – Transport of oxygen/digested foods/hormones /antibodies from maternal blood to foetal blood/nutrients/glucose etc.
– Elimination of nitrogenous wastes/carbon dioxide from foetal blood to maternal blood./ urea, uric acid, creatinine
– Secretes oestrogen and progesterone
– Acts as a barrier to germs.

(iii) All animals/organisms depend on green plant for oxygen and directly or indirectly depend for food.

(iv) Soil medium becomes hypertonic. Roots lose water by exosmosis/plasmolysis and the plants wilt.

(v) Can damage eardrum/tympanum leading to deafness

Ans. **(i)** Education makes people aware about the advantages of having a small family and birth control measures which in turn help in controlling the population of the country. Thus, education is very important for population control.

(ii) Placenta is a disc-like structure which connects foetus with mother. It delivers food, oxygen to the foetus and removes carbon dioxide, nitrogenous waste from foetus. It acts as barrier to germs and helps in secretion of oestrogen and Progesterone. Thus, placenta is an important structure for the development of foetus.

(iii) Green plants are the only autotrophs which prepare their own food. All other living beings depend upon green plants for their food. So, all the food chains begin with green plants.

(iv) If the soil is fertilised and not watered properly, then the concentration of the fertilizer in soil becomes high. As a result, soil becomes hypertonic as compared to the root cells of the plant, so exosmosis takes place which may result in drop of water level in plant and thus plant wilts.

(v) Sharp objects when put into the ears may rupture the eardrum, leading to deafness. So, we should not put sharp objects into our ears.

Q. 12. Differentiate between the following pairs on the basis of what is mentioned in brackets:

(i) Active Transport and Diffusion (significance in plants)

(ii) Demography and Population density (Definition)

(iv) Renal cortex and Renal medulla (Parts of the nephrons present)

(v) NADP and ATP (Expand the abbreviation) [2017]

Ans. **(i)**

Active Transport	Diffusion
In plants, the mineral nutrients like nitrates, sulphates, potassium etc. are taken up by root hairs from the soil by active transport.	Gaseous exchange during respiration and photosynthesis in plants occurs by diffusion process.

(ii)

Demography	Population Density
Statistical study of human population specially with reference to size and density, distribution and other vital statistics is called demography.	Population density is the number of individuals per square kilometre at any given time.

(iv)

Renal Cortex	Renal Medulla
Bowman's capsule, proximal convoluted tubule, distal convoluted tubule lies in the renal cortex.	Loop of Henle which is the U-shaped part of nephron lies in renal medulla along with the collecting duct.

(v)

NADP	ATP
NADP is Nicotinamide Adenine Dinucleotide Phosphate.	ATP is Adenosine Triphosphate.

Q. 13. Give biological reasons for the following statements:

(i) Some women have facial hair like beard and moustache.

(ii) Cutting of trees should be discouraged.

(iii) In some xerophytes leaves are modified into spines.

(iv) There is frequent urination in winter than in summer.

(v) The left ventricle of the heart has a thicker wall than the right ventricle. **[2017]**

Ans. **(i)** When women have high level of androgens in their blood or if there is an overgrowth of adrenal cortex in a mature woman, she develops certain male characteristics such as a beard, moustaches and deep male voice. This condition is known as adrenal virilism.

(ii) Cutting of trees should be discouraged because if there were no green plants, all life on the earth would come to an end. Trees provides food and oxygen to all by the process of photosynthesis. Oxygen is the life supporting gas. They release water in the form of vapours by transpiration process which helps in bringing rain, so they also affect our climate. They also absorb carbon dioxide from the atmosphere for the process of photosynthesis. This helps in controlling global warming.

(iii) In some xerophytes, leaves are modified into spines to reduce transpiration process as xerophytes are mainly found in deserts where there is water scarcity. As leaves are modified into spines, their surface area is reduced hence transpiration will be less.

(iv) During winter, surrounding temperature is low and there is almost no sweating. So water is not lost by perspiration. Hence, water along with waste substances is mainly removed through urine. So, we urinate frequently in winter than in summer.

(v) The left ventricle pumps blood to the farthest points of the body like toes, feet, brain and other parts of the body whereas right ventricle pumps blood only up to the lungs. So walls of the left ventricle are thicker than the walls of right ventricle.

Q. 14. Give appropriate biological/technical terms for the following:

(ii) The suppressed allele of a gene.

(iii) The accessory gland in human males whose secretion activates the sperms.

(iv) An apparatus that measures the rate of water uptake in a cut shoot due to transpiration.

(v) The kind of twins formed from two fertilised eggs.

(vi) A pair of corresponding chromosomes of the same size and shape, one from each parent.

(vii) The type of waste generated in hospitals and pathological laboratories.

(ix) The antiseptic substance in tears.

(x) Cellular components of blood containing haemoglobin. **[2017]**

Ans. **(ii)** Recessive allele

(iii) Seminal vesicles

(iv) Ganong's potometer

(v) Fraternal twins

(vi) Homologous chromosomes

(viii) Biomedical waste

(ix) Lysozyme

(x) RBCs/ Erythrocytes

Q. 15. Briefly explain the following terms:

(i) Reflex action

(ii) Power of accommodation

(iii) Photophosphorylation

(iv) Hormone

(v) Synapse **[2016]**

Ans. **(i)** **Reflex action:** A reflex action is a nerve mediated spontaneous, automatic, involuntary response to a stimulus acting on a specific receptor. The route of every reflex passes through an aggregation of nervous tissue, either brain or spinal cord. Brain or spinal cord aids in transfer of sensory stimulus to motor response.

(ii) **Power of accommodation:** It refers to the ability of the eye lens to adjust its focal length to see objects at different distances clearly. The ciliary muscles contract and make the lens thicker to view nearby objects clearly, whereas they relax and make the lens thinner to focus on distant objects. The least distance of distinct vision for a normal eye is 25 cm and the maximum distance is infinity.

(iii) **Photophosphorylation:** It is the process of formation of ATP from ADP and inorganic phosphate in chloroplasts with the help of energy obtained from solar radiations.

(iv) **Hormone:** A hormone is a chemical substance produced by the cells of endocrine gland which are transported by circulatory system to other parts of the body, where they regulate one or more physiological processes.

(v) Synapse: A synapse is referred as an area of specialised activity between the terminal ends of axon of one neuron and the dendrites or cell body of adjacent neuron. It facilitates transmission of nerve impulse from one neuron to another. Conduction of nerve impulse across a synapse can be of two types *i.e.*, electrical and chemical.

Q. 16. Give scientific reasons for the following statements:

  (i) Colour blindness is more common in men than in women.

  (ii) Injury to medulla oblongata leads to death.

  (iii) When an ovum gets fertilized, menstrual cycle stops temporarily in a woman.

  (iv) Mature erythrocytes in humans lack nucleus and mitochondria.

  (v) Blood flows in arteries in spurts and is under pressure. **[2016]**

Ans. **(i)** Colour blindness is more common in men than in women because it is an X-linked recessive disorder. Men have just one X-chromosome and if that single X-chromosome has the allele for colour blindness, it get expressed while in women there are 2 copies of X-chromosome in which defective allele of X-chromosome get masked by the effects of other X-chromosome.

  (ii) Medulla oblongata forms the innermost part of the brain. It controls various involuntary movements of the body like rate of heart beat, respiration, etc. Thus, any injury to medulla oblongata will hamper these involuntary activities and thus might result in death due to stoppage of heart beat and breathing.

  (iii) In case of fertilisation of an ovum by a sperm, the corpus luteum persists and continues to secrete progesterone. Progesterone maintains endometrial lining and prevents maturation of another ovum, thus temporarily stopping the menstrual cycle.

  (iv) Mature erythrocytes in humans lack a nucleus, so as to provide more surface area for transport of oxygen to haemoglobin in blood. They also lack mitochondria which prevents the use of oxygen for themselves in cellular respiration, thus transporting all oxygen absorbed.

  (v) As the ventricles of the heart contract, they push blood into the small lumen of the arteries with a great force, thus making the blood in arteries flow in spurts and under pressure.

Q. 17. Differentiate between the following pairs on the basis of what is mentioned within brackets:

  (i) Human skin cell and human ovum (number of chromosomes)

  (ii) Sperm duct and fallopian tube (function).

  (iv) Rod cells and cone cells (pigment).

  (v) LUBB and DUPP (names of the valves whose closure produce the sound). **[2016]**

Ans. **(i)**

Human skin cell	Human ovum
Human skin cell is a somatic cell with diploid number of chromosomes, *i.e.*, 46.	Human ovum is female gamete bearing haploid number of chromosomes, *i.e.*, 23.

(ii)

Sperm duct	Fallopian tube
Sperm duct, also known as vas deferens, receives the sperms from the epididymis and transports them along with secretions of seminal vesicles, prostate gland and cowper's gland to the tip of the urethra.	Also known as oviduct, it receives the secondary oocyte from the ovary and also act as the site of fertilisation of egg and sperm.

(iv)

Rod cells	Cone cells
Photoreceptor cells with a visual purple pigment called 'Rhodopsin' that aids in twilight vision (dim light or night vision).	In cone cells, the photosensitive pigment is visual violet or 'Iodopsin' which facilitates vision in day light or bright artificial light.

(v)

LUBB	DUPP
It is the first heart sound produced by the closure of the bicuspid and tricuspid atrioventricular valves.	It is the second heart sound produced by the closure of pulmonary and aortic semilunar valves.

Q. 18. Give the Biological/technical term for the following:

(i) Complete stoppage of menstrual cycle in females.

(ii) Pigment providing colour to urine.

(iii) The vein which drains the blood from the intestine to the liver.

(iv) The canal through which has testes descend into the scrotum just before the birth of a male baby.

(v) The process causing an undesirable change in the environment.

(vi) The removal of nitrogenous wastes from the body.

(vii) The repeating components of each DNA strand lengthwise.

(viii) An alteration in the genetic material that can be inherited.

(ix) The process of uptake of mineral ions against the concentration gradient using energy from the cell.

(x) Blood vessels carrying blood to the left atrium. **[2016]**

Ans. (i) Menopause (ii) Urochrome

(iii) Hepatic portal vein

(iv) Inguinal canal

(v) Pollution (vi) Excretion

(vii) Nucleotides (viii) Mutation

(ix) Active transport (x) Pulmonary veins

Q. 19. Give the biological/technical terms for the following:

(i) A mixture of smoke and fog.

(iii) Fixing of developing zygote on the uterine wall.

(iv) The permanent stoppage of menstruation at about the age of 45 years in a female.

(v) The hormone increasing reabsorption of water by kidney tubules.

(vi) A thin membrane covering the entire front part of the eye.

(vii) The lens of eye losing flexibility resulting in a kind of long-sightedness in middle aged people.

(viii) The number of persons living per square kilometre at any given time.

(ix) The sound produced when the atrio-ventricular valves close in the heart.

(x) The process by which white blood cells engulf bacteria. **[2015]**

Ans. (i) Smog (iii) Implantation

(iv) Menopause

(v) Antidiuretic Hormone (ADH)

(vi) Conjunctiva (vii) Presbyopia

(viii) Population density (ix) LUBB

(x) Phagocytosis

Q. 20. Briefly answer the following questions :

(i) State two reasons for the increase of population in India.

(ii) What is the significance of amniotic fluid ?

(iii) What is the function of ear ossicles ?

(v) State Mendel's law of Dominance. **[2015]**

Ans. (i) Reasons for the increase of population in India :

1. Low marriage age.

2. Illiteracy.

3. Most Indian families desire to have at least one male child. Hence, a couple produces several children till a son is born.

(ii) Amniotic fluid acts as shock absorber and protects the embryo from mechanical jerks. It also maintains even pressure all around the embryo.

(iii) Ear ossicles transmit vibrations to the oval window which sets the cochlear fluid into vibration.

(v) Mendel's Law of Dominance : Out of a pair of contrasting characters present together in an offspring, one dominates over the other or one character is expressed while other remains suppressed.

Q. 21. Differentiate between the following pairs on the basis of what is mentioned within brackets:

(i) Diffusion and Osmosis (Definition)

(ii) RBC and WBC (Shape)

(iii) Tubectomy and Vasectomy (Part cut and tied)

(iv) Vasopressin and Insulin (Deficiency disorder)

(v) Rods and Cones of Retina (Type of Pigment). **[2015]**

Ans. (i)

Diffusion	Osmosis
It is the movement of the molecules of a substance from higher concentration towards the lower concentration when the two substances are in direct contact.	It is the movement of solvent molecules through a semipermeable membrane from a less concentrated solution to a more concentrated solution.

(ii)

RBC	WBC
Biconcave disc, non-nucleated.	Irregular (amoeboid), nucleated.

(iii)

Tubectomy	Vasectomy
Cutting of the fallopian tubes and tied the cuts ends to prevent the passage of ova down the fallopian tube.	Sperm duct is cut and tied at both cut ends in male to block the path of the sperms from the testes.

(iv)

Vasopressin	Insulin
Diabetes insipidus	Diabetes mellitus

(v)

Rods	Cones
Rhodopsin	Iodopsin

Q. 22. Explain the following terms:
 (i) Greenhouse effect
 (ii) Turgor pressure
 (iii) Selective reabsorption
 (iv) Natality
 (v) Pulse **[2015]**

Ans. **(i) Greenhouse effect:** Certain gases especially CO_2, methane (CH_4) and nitrogen oxides accumulating in the atmosphere prevent the escape of heat, thus warming the air. This is known as greenhouse effect.

 (ii) Turgor pressure: It is the pressure of the cell contents on the cell wall. It results due to the movement of water into the cell through osmosis.

 (iii) Selective reabsorption: The reabsorption of water and some other usable substances from the glomerular filtrate in the renal tubule. This reabsorption occurs only to the extent that the normal concentration of blood is undisturbed.

 (iv) Natality: It is the number of children born per 1000 people of population in a year.

 (v) Pulse: It is the throb in the arteries caused due to the contraction of left ventricle of the heart.

Q. 23. Give scientific reasons for the following statements:
 (i) Use of CFC is banned in many countries.
 (ii) We cannot distinguish colours in moonlight.
 (iii) Balsam plants wilt during mid-day even if the soil is well watered.
 (iv) Carbon monoxide is highly dangerous when inhaled.
 (v) A person after consuming alcohol walks clumsily. **[2014]**

Ans. **(i)** Chlorine from CFC breaks ozone molecules into oxygen and nascent oxygen. CFC reacts with ozone in the atmosphere and decreases its concentration. This has resulted in a thinner layer of ozone in the air specially over the polar region. Harmful ultraviolet rays would be able to enter the earth's atmosphere through this thin ozone layer and cause damage to life and diseases like skin cancer in humans. Therefore, its use is banned in many countries.

 (ii) In dim light, colours cannot be distinguished because the rod cells are working in dim light but they do not detect colours. Cone cells detect colours but they do not work in dim light like that of moon.

 (iii) Transpiration rate in such plants is very high during mid-day and exceeds the water absorption rate of the roots. So, more water is lost than absorbed. This water deficiency in cells causes them to loose turgidity and the plants get wilted.

 (iv) Carbon monoxide combines with haemoglobin of RBCs and forms a stable and irreversible complex compound known as carboxyhaemoglobin. This decreases the oxygen carrying capacity of blood, sometimes resulting in the death of person.

 (v) Alcohol affects the cerebellum which is the center of body balance and co-ordination. Due to the alcohol affect, the cerebellum is unable to co-ordinate muscular movements properly and hence person after consuming alcoh walks clumsily.

Q. 24. Differentiate between the following pairs on the basis of what is mentioned within brackets:
 (i) Spinal nerves and Cranial nerves (Number of nerves).
 (ii) Near vision and Distant Vision (shape of the eye lens)
 (iii) Corpus callosum and Corpus luteum. (function).
 (iv) Turgor pressure and wall pressure. (Explain). **[2014]**

Ans. **(i)**

Spinal nerve	Cranial nerve
31 pairs	12 pairs

 (ii)

Near vision	Distant vision
More convex or rounded.	More flattened.

(iii)	Corpus callosum	Corpus luteum
	Transfer information from one cerebral hemisphere to the other.	It secretes progesteron and oestrogen.

(iv)	Turgor pressure	Wall pressure
	It is the outward pressure exerted by the contents of a turgid cell on its cell wall.	It is the inward pressure exerted by the cell wall on its contents (protoplasm).

Q. 25. Briefly explain the following terms:
   (i) monohybrid cross.
   (ii) Biomedical waste.
   (iv) Diapedesis.
   (v) Hormones. **[2014]**

Ans **(i) Monohybrid cross** is a cross between two pure breeding different varieties of organisms taking the alternative traits of a single character e.g., cross between pure tall and pure dwarf variety.

   (ii) Biomedical waste is the waste that is generated in the hospitals, nursing homes etc. like used bottles, syringes, plastic, bandages etc.

   (iv) Diapedesis is the movement of the blood cells, especially white blood cells, through intact capillary walls into surrounding body tissue.

   (v) Hormones are the chemical messengers produced by endocrine glands which move through blood to reach their target organs.

Q. 26. Give technical terms for the following:
   (i) A method of contraception in which the sperm duct is cut and ligated.
   (ii) Statistical study of human population.
   (iii) The protective covering of the heart.
   (iv) A sudden heritable change in the gene.
   (v) Repeated units of DNA molecule.
   (vi) The fluid portion of blood.
   (vii) The nerve that transmits impulses from the ear to the brain.
   (viii) Group of hormones which influence other endocrine glands to produce hormones.
   (ix) Thin walled sac of skin that covers the testes.
   (x) The permanent stoppage of the menstrual cycle in a woman aged 50 years. **[2014]**

Ans. **(i)** Vasectomy   **(ii)** Demography
   (iii) Pericardium   **(iv)** Mutation
   (v) Nucleotides   **(vi)** Plasma

   (vii) Auditory nerve   **(viii)** Tropic hormones
   (ix) Scrotum   **(x)** Menopause

Q. 27. (ii) Give one example of each of the following :
   1. A water pollutant.
   2. An aquatic plant used in the lab to demonstrate O_2 liberation during photosynthesis.
   4. A nitrogenous base in DNA.
   (iii) Expand the following biological abbreviations :
   1. ATP   **2.** TSH   **3.** DNA   **[2014]**

Ans. **(ii)** 1. Pesticides/Sewage
   2. Hydrilla
   4. Adenine
   (iii) 1. Adenosine triphosphate
   2. Thyroid stimulating hormone
   4. Deoxyribo Nucleic Acid

Q. 28. (i) State any two harmful effects of noise pollution on human health.
   (iii) Write any two major reasons for the population explosion in India.
   (iv) State Mendel's law of segregation. [2014]

Ans. **(i)** 1. It causes hypertension.
   2. It causes hearing impairment.
   (iii) 1. Desire for a male child.
   2. Economic reasons as children are considered to be helping hands to increase the family income.
   (iv) Law of segregation states that the two members of a pair of factors separate during formation of gametes and are rejoined at random, one from each parent during fertilisation.

Q. 29. Give the _biological/technical_ terms for the following:
   (ii) A constituent that causes pollution.
   (iii) The onset of menstruation in a young girl.
   (iv) Structure which connects the placenta with the foetus.
   (v) The fluid present between the layers of meninges.
   (vi) Permanently open structures seen on the bark of an old woody stem.
   (vii) The biological process which is the starting point of the food chain.
   (iii) The change in an organism resulting due to stimulus.
   (ix) An Antiseptic substance present in tears.
   (x) A solution in which the relative concentration of water molecules and the solute on either side of the cell membrane is the same. **[2013]**

Ans. **(ii)** Pollutant   **(iii)** Menarche
(iv) Umbilical cord   **(v)** Cerebrospinal fluid
(vi) Lenticels   **(vii)** Photosynthesis
(viii) Response   **(ix)** Lysozyme
(x) Isotonic

Q. 30. **Differentiate between the following pairs on the basis of what is mentioned within brackets:**

(i) **Photolysis and Photophosphorylation. (Definition)**

(ii) **Bicuspid valve and Tricuspid valve. (Function)**

(iii) **Vasectomy and Tubectomy. (Explain)**

(iv) **Cerebrum and Spinal cord. (Arrangement of nerve cells)**

(v) **Bowman's capsule and Malpighian capsule. (Parts included)**   **[2013]**

Ans. **(i)**

Photolysis	Photophosphorylation
The light energy absorbed by chlorophyll splits water into hydrogen and oxygen and releases two electrons.	The energy rich electrons released during photolysis of water are used in the synthesis of ATP from ADP.

(ii)

Bicuspid valve	Tricuspid valve
Prevents backflow of blood from right ventricle to right atrium.	Prevents backflow of blood from left ventricle to left atrium.

(iii)

Vasectomy	Tubectomy
Sperm duct is cut and tied at both cut ends in male to block the path sperms from the testes.	Cutting of the fallopian tubes and tied the cut ends to prevent the passage of ova down the fallopian tube.

(iv)

Cerebrum	Spinal cord
Outer gray matter that forms the cortex, contains cell bodies of neurons. Inner white matter contains nerve fibres.	Outer white matter contains axons. Inner gray matter contains cell bodies of motor and association neurons.

(v)

Bowman's capsule	Malpighian capsule
Epithelial cells, glomerulus (blood capillaries).	Glomerulus, Bowman's capsule.

Q. 31. **Give biological reasons for the following:**

(i) **The wall of the ventricle is thicker than the auricles.**

(ii) **The renal cortex has a dotted appearance.**

(iii) **Wooden frames of doors get jammed during the monsoon season.**

(iv) **Throat infections can lead to ear infections.**

(v) **The hand automatically shows the direction to turn a cycle without thinking.**   **[2013]**

Ans. **(i)** Ventricles pump blood against force of gravity, which requires a great force. To apply this large force without any damage to the walls of ventricles, they are thicker.

(ii) Because of the presence of malpighian capsules.

(iii) Lignified dead cells imbibe moisture and thus swell up during the monsoon season.

(iv) Because eustachian tube connects middle ear with the throat, so infection can be passed.

(v) Because of conditioned reflex which we learn by experience and gradually responds to it unconsciously.

Q. 32. **Briefly explain the following terms:**

(i) **Genes**

(ii) **Cytokinesis in plant cells**

(iii) **Guttation**

(iv) **Diabetes insipidus**   **[2013]**

Ans. **(i)** **Genes:** Gene is a basic unit of inheritance for a given character. Genes are specific sequence of nucleotides located in a chromosome which code for a particular protein which is expressed in the form of a visible character of the body.

(ii) **Cytokinesis in plant cells:** Process in which the cytoplasmic content of the cell is divided into two new daughter cells by formation of a cell plate which extends from centre to periphery of the cell is called cytokinesis.

(iii) **Guttation:** In herbs, when root pressure is high and transpiration low, water is forced out in the form of drops from the margins or tips of leaves through special pores called hydathodes. This process is known as guttation.

(iv) **Diabetes insipidus:** It is a disease caused due to the deficiency of ADH (antidiuretic hormone) in which large amount of urine is secreted, resulting loss of water from the body.

Q. 33. (i) Draw a well labelled diagram to show the anaphase stage of mitosis in a plant cell having four chromosomes.

(ii) State any two harmful effects of acid rain.

(iii) Expand the following biological abbreviations :

(1) NADP   (2) ACT   [2013]

Ans. (i)

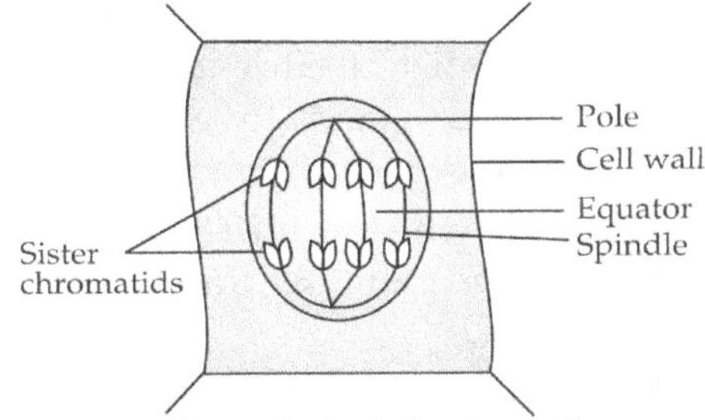

Anaphase of mitosis in plant cell

(ii) 1. Acid rain destroys the soil as well as the crop.

2. Acid rain corrodes the buildings, statues, etc.

(iii) 1. NADP → Nicotinamide Adenine Dinucleotide Phosphate.

2. ACT → Adreno Cortico Tropin.

Q. 34. (i) Write any two major reasons for the population explosion in the world.

(ii) Write the names of four nitrogenous bases in a DNA molecule.   **[2013]**

Ans. (i) 1. Economic reasons: Children are considered to be helping hands to increase the family income.

2. Desire for a male child: In the desire of having a son, people give birth to many children.

(ii) Adenine, Guanine, Cytosine, Thymine.

Q. 35. Give the biological/technical terms for the following:

(i) A membrane which allows the passage of molecules selectively.

(ii) The suppressed allele of a gene.

(iii) Structure that carries visual stimuli from retina to the brain.

(iv) WBCs squeeze through the walls of the capillaries into the tissue.

(v) Protective coverings located round the human brain and spinal cord.

(vi) Eye lens losing flexibility resulting in a kind of long sightedness in elderly people.

(vii) Hormones which stimulate other endocrine glands to produce their specific hormones.

(viii) The phase in the menstrual cycle in which the remnant of follicle in the ovary turns to Corpus luteum.

(ix) Statistical study of human population.   **[2012]**

Ans. (i) Semi-permeable membrane

(ii) Recessive allele

(iii) Optic nerve   **(iv)** Diapedesis

(v) Meninges   **(vi)** Presbyopia

(vii) Tropic hormones   **(viii)** Luteal phase

(ix) Demography

Q. 36. Differentiate between the following pairs on the basis of what is mentioned in brackets:

(i) Natality and Mortality (definition)

(ii) Stoma and Stroma (describe its structure)

(iii) Acromegaly and Cretinism (symptoms)

(iv) Transpiration and Guttation (structures involved)

(v) Diabetes mellitus and Diabetes insipidus (reason/cause)   **[2012]**

Ans. (i)

Natality	Mortality
It is the number of live births per 1000 individuals of a population per year.	It is the number of deaths per 1000 individuals of a population per year.

(ii)

Stoma	Stroma
There are minute openings surrounded by guard cells present in the epidermal layers of the leaf.	There are ground substance of chloroplast containing ribosome and DNA.

(iii)

Acromegaly	Cretinism
Elongation, enlargement of bones and jaws.	Poor physical and mental development, delayed growth, short hands and feet, dry skin.

(iv)

Transpiration	Guttation
Stomata, cuticles and lenticels.	Hydathodes, present on the leaf margin.

(v)

Diabetes Mellitus	Diabetes Insipidus
Insufficient secretion of insulin.	Deficiency of antidiuretic hormone.

Q. 37. **Briefly explain the following:**
(i) **Osmosis**   (ii) **Allele**
(iii) **Pulse**   (iv) **Reflex action**
(v) **Synapse.**   [2012]

Ans. (i) **Osmosis:** It is the diffusion of water molecules through a semi-permeable membrane from a region of higher concentration of water to a region of its low concentration.

(ii) **Allele:** It is one of the alternative form of the same gene responsible for determining contrasting characteristics.

(iii) **Pulse:** Rhythmic contraction of heart and elastic recoil of the wall of the artery during ventricular systole is called pulse.

(iv) **Reflex action:** Reflex action is the automatic, quick and involuntary action initiated by external stimulus at the level of spinal cord without the involvement of brain.

(v) **Synapse:** It is the point of contact between the axon ending of one neuron and dendrites of the other neuron for the transmission of impulse signal.

Q. 38. **Give reasons for the following:**
(i) **Photosynthesis is considered as a process supporting all life on earth.**
(ii) **A matured mammalian erythrocyte lacks nucleus and mitochondria.**
(iii) **Potato cubes when placed in water become firm and increase in size.**
(iv) **Urine is slightly thicker in summer than in winter.**
(v) **People living in hilly regions usually suffer from simple goitre.**   [2011]

Ans. (i) Photosythesis is the process which produces food and releases oxygen, both of which are necessary to maintain life on earth.

(ii) Absence of nucleus gives the RBCs a biconcave shape which increases its surface area for absorption and transportation of oxygen. Lack of mitochondria ensures anaerobic respiration in them so that the oxygen they transport will not be used by them.

(iii) Cells of potato are hypertonic and water enters into them due to endosmosis. This more water increases the size of the cells of the potato cubes. At this time due to turgor pressure and wall pressure, the potato becomes firm.

(iv) In summer, water is lost from the body through sweating. To compensate for the loss, much water is reabsorbed by the kidney tubules and put back in blood and this makes the urine concentrated. In winter, all this water is lost from the body through urine only, that is why, is thinner.

(v) In hilly regions, soil is deficient in iodine. people thus have deficiency of iodine in their diet. Deficiency of iodine causes thyroid gland to enlarge in effort to produce more hormone.

Q. 39. **Write down the difference between the following pairs as indicated within the brackets:**
(ii) **Erythrocytes and leucocytes (function).**
(iii) **Guttation and bleeding in plants (cause)**
(iv) **NADP and AIDS (expand the abbreviation).**
(v) **Monohybrid and Dihybrid cross (phenotypic ratio).**   [2011]

Ans. (ii)

Erythrocytes	Leucocytes
Carry oxygen from lungs to all body tissues.	Defend the body from germs by destroying them.

(iii)

Guttation	Bleeding
Caused due to high hydrostatic pressure in the plant body and warm, humid conditions around it.	Defend the body from germs by destroying them.

(iv)

NADP	AIDS
Nicotinamide Adenine Dinucleotide Phosphate	Acquired Immune Deficiency Syndrome.

(v)

Monohybrid	Dihybrid cross
3 : 1	9 : 3 : 3 : 1

Q. 40. (i) **Draw a well labelled diagram to show the metaphase stage of mitosis in an animal cell having four chromosomes.**

(ii) **Mention any two reasons for the population explosion in INDIA.**

(iii) **Give biological reasons for the following:**

(1) **Pituitary gland is also known as the master gland.**

(2) **Gametes have a haploid number of chromosomes.**   [2012]

Ans. **(i)**

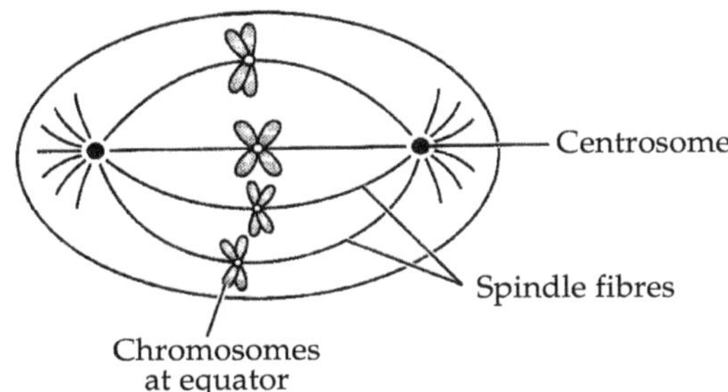

(ii) **(1)** Strong urge among people to have male children.

   (2) Children are considered to be helping hands to increase the family income.

(iii) **(1)** As pituitary gland controls the secretion of the hormones of other endocrine glands.

   (2) Gametes have haploid number of chromosomes because after sexual reproduction, the diploid number of chromosome is maintained.

Q. 41. **Account for the following:**

   (i) **Wilted lettuce leaves become crisp/firm when placed in cold water for a while.**

   (ii) **One feels blinded for a short time while coming out of a dark room.**

   (iii) **The leaves of certain plants roll up on a bright sunny day.**

   (iv) **An alcoholic person walks unsteadily when drunk.**

   (v) **Sleeping under a tree at night is not advisable.** **[2010]**

Ans. **(i)** Wilted lettuce leaves have hypertonic cell sap. When placed in cold water, endosmosis occurs in them and the plasmolysed cells become turgid and the leaves become crisp.

   (ii) In the dark, the pupil is wide open to let in more light. Also the pigment visual purple is built up in more amount. As we come out in bright light, the visual purple is bleached and iris muscles contract to diminish the pupil. Till this happens, one feels blinded in light.

   (iii) On a bright sunny day, leaves roll up to decrease the area of leaf. This helps to reduce transpiration from the reduced surface.

   (iv) Alcohol affects the cerebellum which co-ordinates muscular activities. Due to alcohol, the cerebellum is not able to function properly and the leg movements appear unsteady.

   (v) At night, photosynthesis does not take place and so plants do not absorb CO_2 and release O_2. Only respiration occurs in plants and during respiration, they release carbon dioxide. This makes the air under the trees stale. Hence it is not advisable to sleep under the trees.

Q. 42. **Explain the following terms:**

   (i) **Reflex action**

   (ii) **Turgidity**

   (iii) **Bleeding in plants**

   (iv) **Cataract.** **[2010]**

Ans. **(i)** **Reflex action:** It is a quick, automatic and spontaneous action in the body caused by a stimulus.

   (iii) **Turgidity:** It is the condition of cell in which it is fully distended and filled with water.

   (iv) **Bleeding in plants:** It is the loss of sap from a cut or injured part of a plant.

   (v) **Cataract:** It is a condition when, in old age, the eye lens turns opaque causing blindness.

Q. 43. **Give one point of difference between the following on the basis of what is given in the brackets :**

   (i) **Myopia and Hypermetropia. (cause of the defect)**

   (ii) **Cerebrum and Spinal cord.(arrangement of cytons and axons of neuron)**

   (iii) **Genotype and Phenotype. (definition)**

   (iv) **Karyokinesis and Cytokinesis. (explain the term)**

   (v) **Light reaction and Dark reaction. (site of occurrence)** **[2010]**

Ans. (i)

Myopia	Hypermetropia
Eye ball lengthened from front to back.	Eye ball shortened from front to back.

(ii)

Cerebrum	Spinal Cord
Cyton outside and axons inside.	Axons outside and cytons inside.

(iii)

Genotype	Phenotype
It is the genetic constitution.	These are the observable characters controlled by genes.

(iv)

Karyokinesis	Cytokinesis
It is the division of nucleus.	It is the division of cytoplasm during cell division.

(v)

Light reaction	Dark reaction
In grana.	In stroma of chloroplast.

Q. 44. Give the biological/technical term for the following:

(i) Cessation of menstruation in females.

(ii) An eye defect in which the cornea becomes uneven.

(iii) The period of complete intrauterine development of the embryo.

(iv) Inflammation of meninges.

(v) Non-identical twins produced by the fertilisation of two eggs.

(vi) Membrane that protects the foetus and secretes a protective fluid.

(vii) Process of conversion of several molecules of glucose to one molecule of starch.

(viii) The photosensitive pigment present in the cone cells of the retina.

(ix) The fluid present in the anterior part in front of the eye lens. [2010]

Ans.

(i) Menopause   (ii) Astigmatism

(iii) Gestation   (iv) Meningitis

(v) Fraternal twins   (vi) Amnion

(vii) Polymerisation   (viii) Iodopsin

(ix) Aqueous humour

COMPUTER APPLICATIONS

Revision of Class IX Syllabus

Short Answer Type Questions

Q. 1. Define Java byte code. **[2020]**

Ans. It is a machine instruction for java processor chip called JVM.

Q. 2. Name the following:
   (i) The keyword which converts variabl into constant.
   (ii) The method which terminates the entire program from any stage. **[2020]**

Ans. (i) final
   (ii) System.exit(0)

Q. 3. What is an operator? Name any two types of operators used in Java. **[2020]**

Ans. Operator is a symbol which specifies the type of operation to be performed on the operands.
Ex: Arithmetic Operator (+,-,*,/,%)
or Relational operator(>,<,>=,<=, ==, !=) etc.

Q. 4. What is the use of import statement in Java? **[2020]**

Ans. Import keyword is used to include predefined classes and functions in our program which are available in java.
import java.util.*; will include all the classes of util package in our program.

Q. 5. What is an infinite loop? Give an example. **[2020]**

Ans. Non terminating loop whose test condition is always true is called infinite loop.
for(i=1 ; i > 0 ; i++)
{
     System.out.println("This is Infinite
                              Loop");
}

Q. 6. Write a Java expression for the following:

$$\sqrt{b^2 - 4ac}$$ **[2020]**

Ans. Math.sqrt(b*b − 4*a*c)

Q. 7. Evaluate the following if the value of
x = 7, y = 5
x + = x++ + x+ ++ y **[2020]**

Ans. x = 28 , y = 6

Q. 8. Write the output of the following statement:
System.out.println("A picture is worth \t \"A thousand words.\" "); **[2020]**

Ans. A picture is worth "A thousand words."

Q. 9. Give the output of the following program segment and mention how many times the loop will execute:
int k;
for (k = 5 ; k < = 20; k + = 7)
if (k% 6==0)
continue;
System.out.println (k); **[2020]**

Ans. Loop will execute 3 times output 19.

Q. 10. Rewrite the following program segment using logical operators:
if (x > 5)
if (x > y)
System.out.println (x+y); **[2020]**

Ans. if(x > 5 && x > y)
          System.out.println(x + y);

Q. 11. Convert the following if else if construct into switch case: **[2020]**
if (ch== 'c' || ch=='C')
System.out.print("COMPUTER");
else if (ch== 'h' || ch=='H')
System.out.print("HINDI");
else
System.out.print("PHYSICAL
                              EDUCATION");

Ans. switch(ch)
{
case 'c' :
case 'C' : System.out.print(" COMPUTER ") ;
          break;
case 'h' :
case 'H' : System.out.print(" HINDI"); break;
default: System.out.print
("PHYSICAL EDUCATION");
}

Q. 12. Give the output of the following:
   (i) Math.pow (36,0.5) + Math.cbrt (125)
   (ii) Math.ceil (4.2) + Math.floor (7.9) **[2020]**

Ans. (i) 6.0 + 5.0 = 11.0
   (ii) 5.0 + 7.0 = 12.0

Q. 13. Rewrite the following using ternary operator:
if(n1>n2)
r = true;
else
r = false; **[2020]**

Ans.   r = n1 > n2 ? true : false;

Q. 14. Write a difference between unary and binary operator. **[2019]**

Ans.

Unary Operator	Binary Operator
1. The operator that acts on a single operand is called a unary operator.	The operator that acts on two operands is called a binary operator.
2. E.g., ++,– –	E.g., +, –, *, /

Q. 15. Identify and name the following tokens:
   (i) public
   (ii) 'a'
   (iii) ==
   (iv) { } **[2019]**

Ans.   (i) public — Keyword.
   (ii) 'a' — Character Literal.
   (iii) == — Operator.
   (iv) { } — Separator.

Q. 16. Differentiate between if else if and switch-case statements. **[2019]**

Ans.

If Else If	Switch Case
1. It can work with all relational operators.	It can only test for equality.
2. It can work with any data type.	It can only work with byte, short, int, long char and string data types.

Q. 17. Write a Java expression for the following:
$|x^2 + 2xy|$ **[2019]**

Ans.   Math.abs(x * x + 2 * x * y)

Q. 18. If the value of basic = 1500, what will be the value of tax after the following statement is executed?

tax = basic > 1200? 200 : 100; **[2019]**

Ans.   200

Q. 19. Give the output of the following:
Math.sqrt(Math.max(9, 16)) **[2019]**

Ans.   4.0

Q. 20. Write the output for the following:
String s1 = "phoenix"; String s2 = "island";
System.out.println(s1.substring(0).concat
(s2.substring(2)));
System.out.println(s2.toUpperCase()); **[2019]**

Ans.   phoenixland
   ISLAND

Q. 21. Evaluate the following expression if the value of x = 2, y = 3 and z = 1.
v = x + – –z + y++ + y **[2019]**

Ans.   9

Q. 22. Write a Java expression for the following:
$$\frac{\sqrt{3x + x^2}}{a + b}$$ **[2018]**

Ans.   Math.sqrt((3 * x) + (x * x))/(a + b);

Q. 23. What is the value of y after evaluating the expression given below?
y += ++y + y– – + – –y; when int y = 8 **[2018]**

Ans.   33

Q. 24. Give the output of the following:
   (i) Math.floor(–4.7)
   (ii) Math.ceil(3.4) + Math.pow(2, 3) **[2018]**

Ans.   (i) –5.0   (ii) 12.0

Q. 25. Convert the following if else if construct into switch case
if(var == 1)
   System.out.println("good");
else if(var == 2)
   System.out.println("better");
elseif(var == 3)
   System.out.println("best");
else
   System.out.println("invalid"); **[2018]**

Ans.   switch(var)
   {
      case 1: System.out.println("good");
      break;
      case 2: System.out.println("better");
      break;
      case 3: System.out.println("best");
      break
      default: System.out.println("invalid");
   }

Q. 26. Write the output for the following:
System.out.println("Incredible"+
"\n"+"world"); **[2018]**

Ans.   Incredible
   world

Q. 27. Rewrite the following using ternary operator:
   if(bill > 1000)
      discount = bill * 10.0/100;
   else
      discount = bill * 5.0/100; **[2018]**

Ans.   discount = bill > 10000? (bill * 10.0 / 100): (bill * 5.0 / 100);

Q. 28. What is inheritance? **[2017]**

Ans.   **Inheritance** allows a class to use the properties and methods of another class. In other words, the derived class **inherits** the states and behaviors from the base class. The derived class is also called subclass and the base class is also known as super-class OR Inheritance is the process by which one object acquires the properties of another object.

Q. 29. Name the operators listed below:
   (i) <   (ii) ++
   (iii) &&   (iv) ? :   [2017]

Ans.   (i) < is a Relational / Comparison operator.
   (ii) ++ is an Unary increment operator.
   (iii) && is a Logical operator.
   (iv) ? : is a Conditional / Ternary operator.

Q. 30. State the number of bytes occupied by char and int data types.   [2017]

Ans.   char occupies 2 bytes and int occupies 4 bytes.

Q. 31. Write one difference between '/' and '%' operator.   [2017]

Ans.

'/' operator	'%' operator
'/' It is the division operator that returns the quotient of two operands when divided.	% It is the modulas operator that returns the remainder of two operands when divided.

Q. 32. Name the following:
   (i) A keyword used to call a package in the program.
   (ii) Any one reference data type.   [2017]

Ans.   (i) import
   (ii) class / object

Q. 33. Write a Java expression for the following:
$ax^5 + bx^3 + c$ [2017]

Ans.   a * Math.pow(x, 5) + b * Math.pow (x, 3) + c.

Q. 34. What is the value of x1 if x = 5?
x1 = ++x − x++ + − − x   [2017]

Ans.   x1 = 6

Q. 35. Give the output of the following expression:
a+= a++ + ++a + − −a + a−−;
when a = 7   [2016]

Ans.   a = 7 + 7 + 9 + 8 + 8 = 39

Q. 36. Write the return type of the following library functions:
   (i) isLetterOrDigit(char)
   (ii) replace(char, char)   [2016]

Ans.   (i) boolean   (ii) String

Q. 37. Evaluate the value of n if value of p = 5, q = 19.
int n = (q − p) > (p − q)? (q − p) : (p − q);
         [2015]

Ans.   n = 14.

Q. 38. Which of the following are valid comments?
   (i) /* comment */
   (ii) /* comment
   (iii) // comment
   (iv) */ comment */   [2014]

Ans.   (i) /*comment */
   (iii) //comment
   are valid comments.

Q. 39. Operators with higher precedence are evaluated before operators with relatively lower precedence. Arrange the operators given below in order of higher precedence to lower precedence:
   (i) &&   (ii) %
   (iii) >=   (iv) ++   [2014]

Ans.   (iv) ++,   (ii) %,   (iii) >= , (i) &&

Q. 40. What is meant by precedence of operators?
         [2013]

Ans.   The order in which operators of an expression are evaluated in a predetermined order is called operator precedence. It is also called hierarchy of operators.

Q. 41. What are the types of casting shown by the following examples?
   (i) double x = 15.2;
       int y = (int)x;
   (ii) int x = 12;
       long y = x;   [2013]

Ans.   (i) Explicit type casting.
   (ii) Implicit type casting.

Q. 42. Name the Java keyword that:
   (i) indicates that a method has no return type
   (ii) stores the address of the currently - calling object.   [2013]

Ans.   (i) void   (ii) this

Q. 43. What is an exception?   [2013]

Ans.   It is the anomalous (unexpected) situation which occurs during program execution.

Q. 44. How many times will the following loop execute? What value will be returned?
```
int x = 2, y = 50;
do
{
++x;
y − = x++;
} while(x <= 10);
return y;
```
         [2013]

Ans.   Loop will execute 5 times and y will be returned as 15.

Q. 45. Write a Java expression for
$ut + \dfrac{1}{2} ft^2$ [2013]

Ans.   u * t + 1.0/2 * f * Math.pow(t, 2)

                OR

   u * t + 1.0/2 * f * t * t

Class as the Basis of all Computation

 ## Very Short Answer Type Questions

Q. 1. Name the keyword which:

(i) makes the variable as a class variable. **[2019]**

Ans. (i) static

 ## Short Answer Type Questions

Q. 1. Write a difference between class and an object. **[2020]**

Ans. Class is a set of objects that shares common characteristics and behaviour whereas object is an instance of a class.

Q. 2. Which of the following are primitive data types?

(i) double   (ii) String

(iii) Char   (iv) Integer   **[2020]**

Ans. (i) double , char are primitive data types.

Q. 3. Name any two basic principles of Object-oriented Programming. **[2019]**

Ans. Encapsulation and Abstraction.

Q. 4. Define abstraction. **[2018]**

Ans. Abstraction refers to the act of representing essential features without including the background details. For example switchboard. We only press certain switches according to our requirement without knowing what is happening inside and how it is happening.

Q. 5. Why is an object called an instance of a class? **[2017]**

Ans. Since an object contains all the necessary information (Data members and member functions) specified inside the class, therefore, it is known as the instance of a class.

Q. 6. What are keywords? Give an example. **[2016]**

Ans. Keywords are the tokens which convey a special meaning to the java compiler. These are reserved for special purpose and must not be used as normal identifiers.

e.g., for, while, class, return.

Q. 7. Write one difference between primitive data types and composite data types. **[2016]**

Ans.

Primitive Data Types	Composite Data Types
1. All primitive types have fixed sizes.	The size of composite types depends upon its constituent members.
2. Primitive data type is passed by value.	Composite data type is passed by reference.

Q. 8. What are identifiers? **[2015]**

Ans. Identifiers are a sequence of characters used to name variables, objects, classes, etc.

Q. 9. What are the default values of the primitive data type int and float? **[2015]**

Ans. Default value of int is 0 and float is 0.0f.

Q. 10. Arrange the following primitive data types in an ascending order of their size:

(i) char   (ii) byte

(iii) double   (iv) int   **[2015]**

Ans. (i) byte,   (ii) char,

(iii) int,   (iv) double.

Q. 11. State the data type and value of y after the following is executed:

char x = '7';

y = Character.isLetter(x); **[2015]**

Ans. Data type of y will be boolean and value of y = false.

Q. 12. Name the keyword which is used to resolve the conflict between method parameter and instance variables/fields. **[2015]**

Ans. This keyword is used to differentiate between local/parameters and global/instance variables.

Q. 13. Name the primitive data type in Java that is:

   (i) a 64-bit integer and is used when you need a range of values wider than those provided by int.

   (ii) a single 16-bit Unicode character whose default value is '\u0000' **[2014]**

Ans.   (i) long

    (ii) char

Q. 14. List the variables from those given below that are composite data types:

   (i) static int x;

   (ii) arr [i] = 10;

   (iii) obj.display();

   (iv) boolean b;

   (v) private char chr;

   (vi) String str; **[2014]**

Ans. The variables those can be categorized under composite data types are as follows:

   (ii) arr[i] = 10;

   (iii) obj.display();

   (vi) String str;

Q. 15. State the output of the following program segment:

```
String str 1 = "great"; String str2 = "minds";
System.out.println(str1.substring(0, 2).
                concat(str2.substring(1)));
System.out.println(("WH"+(str1.substring(2).
                toUpperCase())));    [2014]
```

Ans. grinds

   WHEAT

Q. 16. What are the final values stored in variable x and y below?

```
double a = – 6.35;
double b = 14.74;
double x = Math.abs(Math.ceil(a));
double y = Math.rint(Math.max(a, b));
                                    [2014]
```

Ans. $x = 6.0$

   $y = 15.0$

Q. 17. Rewrite the following program segment using if-else statements instead of the ternary operator.

```
String grade = (mark >= 90)? "A": (mark >=
80)?\"B": "C";               [2014]
```

Ans.
```
String grade;
if(mark >= 90)
      grade = "A";
else if( mark >= 80)
      grade = "B";
else
      grade = "C";
```

Q. 18. Give the output of the following method:

```
public static void main (String [] args)
{
      int a = 5;
      a++;
      System.out.println(a);
      a – = (a– –) – (– –a);
      System.out.println(a);
}                            [2014]
```

Ans. 6

   4

Q. 19. What is the data type returned by the library functions:

   (i) compareTo()

   (ii) equals() **[2014]**

Ans.   (i) int

     Ex.: int result = "computer".

        compareTo("applications");

    (ii) boolean

     Ex.: boolean result = "ritesh".equals

        ("jhansi");

Q. 20. State the value of characteristic and mantissa when the following code is executed.

```
String s = "4.3756";
int n = s.indexOf('.');
int characteristic = Integer.parseInt(s.substring
                                    (0,n));
int mantissa = Integer.valueOf (s.substring
                                    (n + 1));
                                    [2014]
```

Ans. characteristic = 4

   mantissa = 3756

Q. 21. Consider the following class:

```
public class myClass
{
      public static int x = 3, y = 4;
      public int a = 2, b = 3;
}
```

   (i) Name the variable for which each object of the class will have its own distinct copy.

   (ii) Name the variable that are common to all objects of the class. **[2014]**

Ans.   (i) a, b since they are instance variables.

    (ii) x, y since they are class variables.

Q. 22. What will be the output when the following code segments are executed?

(i) String s = "1001";
int x = Integer.valueOf(s);
double y = Double.valueOf(s);
System.out.println("x = "+x);
System.out.println("y = "+y);

(ii) System.out.println("The king said "Begin at the beginning!"to me.");
[2014]

Ans. **(i)** x = 1001

y = 1001.0

(ii) The king said "Begin at the beginning!" to me.

Q. 23. State one difference between the floating point literals float and double. [2014]

Ans.

Float	Double
Float occupies 4 bytes of storage.	Double occupies 8 bytes of storage.

Q. 24. What is a literal? [2013]

Ans. A literal is the data or a sequence of characters used in a program to represent a constant that never changes its value during the execution of a program.

Q. 25. State the Java concept that is implemented through:

(i) a superclass and a subclass

(ii) the act of representing essential features without including background details. [2013]

Ans. **(i)** Inheritance.

(ii) Abstraction.

Q. 26. Write a Java statement to create an object mp4 of class digital. [2013]

Ans. digital mp4 = new digital();

Q. 27. What does a class encapsulate? [2013]

Ans. A class encapsulates the data members and the member functions. Data members represent the state of an object and member functions represent the behaviour of an object.

Constructors

 Short Answer Type Questions ______________

Q. 1. What is constructor overloading? [2020]

Ans. Defining more than one constructors having same name but different signature is called constructor overloading.

```
class Overload
{
    String s;
    public Overload()
    {
        s="DPC Jhansi";
    }
    public Overload( String s1)
    {
        s=s1;
    }
}
```

Q. 2. Write two characteristics of a constructor. [2018]

Ans. (i) Constructors have the same name as that of the class.
(ii) They do not have any return type not even void.

Q. 3. Differentiate between constructor and function. [2017]

Ans.

Constructor	Function
1. It has the same name as that of the class.	It has a different name as that of the class.
2. It has no return type, not even void data type.	It has void or a valid return data type.

Q. 4. What is a parameterized constructor? [2016]

Ans. A constructor which accepts some values through parameters *i.e.,* take arguments are called parameterized constructors.

e.g.:
```
class Test
{
    int n;
```
```
    public Test(int n1)  // Parameterized
                          constructor
    {
        n = n1;
    }
}
```

Q. 5. Name the two types of constructors. [2015]

Ans. Two types of constructors are:
(i) Non Parameterized Constructor.
(ii) Parameterized Constructor.

e.g.:
```
class Computer
{
    String teacher, coaching;
    public Computer() // Non Para-
                      meterized Constructor
    {
        teacher ="Ritu Sharma";
        coaching = "Destination Point
        Computers, MP";
    }
    public Computer(String t, String c) //
                       Parameterized Constructor
    {
        teacher = t;
        coaching = c;
    }
}
```

Q. 6. What is a constructor? When is it invoked? [2014]

Ans. Constructor is a member function that has the same name as the class and it has no return type, not even void.

It is automatically invoked at the time of object creation.

 ## Very Short Answer Type Questions

Q. 1. Name the keyword which:

    (i) indicates that a method has no return type. **[2019]**

Ans. **(i)** void

 ## Short Answer Type Questions

Q. 1. State a difference between call by value and call by reference. **[2019]**

Ans.

Call By Value	Call By Reference
1. In this, local copy of parameters are created and whatever changes are made inside the function gets reflected in the local copies while the original copy remains unaffected.	In this, no local copy of parameters are created therefore whatever changes are made inside the function gets reflected in the original copies.
2. In this primitive data types are passed.	In this non-primitive data types are passed.

Q. 2. Write a difference between the functions isUpper Case( ) and toUpperCase( ). **[2018]**

Ans.

isUpperCase()	toUpperCase()
1. This function is used to check whether a character is in upper case.	This function is used to convert a character to upper case.
2. Return type is boolean.	Return type is char.

Q. 3. What are the two ways of invoking functions? **[2017]**

Ans. Two ways of invoking functions are:

    (i) Call by value

    (ii) Call by reference.

Q. 4. Identify the literals listed below:

    (i) 0.5   **(ii)** 'A'

    (iii) false   **(iv)** "a". **[2015]**

Ans. **(i)** 0.5 is a double/floating point literal.

    (ii) 'A' is a character literal.

    (iii) false is a boolean literal.

    (iv) "a" is a string literal.

Q. 5. What is the value stored in variable res given below:

double res = Math.pow("345".indexOf('5'), 3); **[2015]**

Ans. res = 8.0

Q. 6. What is the function of catch block in exception handling? Where does it appear in a program? **[2015]**

Ans. Catch block is a group of Java statements that are used to handle a raised exception. We can put the code to deal with the execution that might arise in this block. Catch block appears just after the try block.

Q. 7. If int n[ ] = {1, 2, 3, 5, 7, 9, 13, 16}, what are the values of x and y?

x = Math.pow(n[4], n[2]);

y = Math.sqrt(n[5] + n[7]); **[2013]**

Ans. x = 343.0 and y = 5.0

 Long Answer Type Questions

Q. 1. Design a class to overload a function series( ) as follows:

(a) void series(int x, int n) – To display the sum of the series given below:

$x^1 + x^2 + x^3 + \dots\dots\dots x^n$ terms

(b) void series(int p) – To display the following series:

0, 7, 26, 63 …………… p terms

(c) void series() – To display the sum of the series given below:

$$\frac{1}{2} + \frac{1}{3} + \frac{1}{4} \dots\dots\dots \frac{1}{10}$$

[2019]

Marking Scheme

```
class Overload
{
public static void series (int x , int n)
{
        double sum=0.0;
        for (int i=1;i<=n;i++)
        {
        sum=sum+ Math.pow(x,i);
        }
        System.out.println(sum);
}
        public static void series (int p)
        {
            for (int i=1; i<=p; i++)
            System.out.println((i*i*i)-1);
        }
        public static void series ()
        {
        double sum=0.0;
        for (int i=2; i<=10;i++)
        {
        sum=sum+(double)1/i;
        }
        System.out.print("Sum= "+sum);
        }//end of function
}
```

Ans.
```
class Overload
{
        double s = 0;
        int i;
        void series(int x, int n)
            for(i = 1; i <= n; i++)
            {
                s = s + Math.pow(x, i);
            }
            System.out.println("Sum of the
                                series is" + s);
        }
        void series(int p)
        {
            for(i = 1; i <= p; i++)
```

```
            {
                System.out.print((i * i * i) – 1+ ", ");
            }
        }
        void series()
        {
            for(i = 2; i <= 10; i++)
            {
                s = s + 1.0/i;
            }
            System.out.println("Sum of the
                                series is" + s);
        }
}
```

Name	Type	Description
i	int	for loop variable.
s	double	To store the sum of the series.
x, n, p	int	To store the terms of the series.

Q. 2. Design a class to overload a function volume () as follows:

(i) double volume (double R) – with radius (R) as an argument, returns the volume of sphere using the formula.
$V = 4/3 \times 22/7 \times R^3$.

(ii) double volume(double H, double R) – with height(H) and radius(R) as the arguments, returns the volume of a cylinder using the formula.
$V = 22/7 \times R^2 \times H$

(iii) double volume(double L, double B, double H) – with length(L), breadth(B) and Height(H) as the arguments, returns the volume of a cuboid using the formula.
$V = L \times B \times H$

[2018]

Marking Scheme

```
class Overload{
    public static double volume(double r){
        return 4.0 / 3 * 22.0 / 7 * r * r * r;
    }
    public static double volume(double h, double r){
        return 22.0 / 7 * r * r * h;
    }
    public static double volume(double l, double b,
                               double h){
        return l * b * h;
    }
}
```

Ans.
```
class Overload
{// class beginning
```

```
double V;
double volume(double R)
{
    V = (4.0/3) * (22/7) *(R * R * R);
    return(V);
}
double volume(double H, double R)
{
    V = (22/7) * (R * R) * H;
    return(V);
}
double volume(double L, double B, double H)
{
    V = L * B * H;
    return(V);//returning the value of V
}
}
```

Name	Type	Description
V	double	To store volume.
R	double	To store radius.
H	double	To store height.
L	double	To store length.
B	double	To store breadth.

Q. 3. Design a class to overload a function SumSeries() as follows:

(i) void SumSeries(int n, double x) – with one integer argument and one double argument to find and display the sum of the series given below:

$$s = \frac{x}{1} - \frac{x}{2} + \frac{x}{3} - \frac{x}{4} + \frac{x}{5} \ \dots\dots\dots \text{ to n terms}$$

(ii) void SumSeries() – To find and display the sum of the following series:

$$s = 1 + (1 \times 2) + (1 \times 2 \times 3)$$
$$+ \dots\dots\dots + (1 \times 2 \times 3 \times 4 \dots\dots\dots \times 20)$$

[2016]

Ans.

```
class Overload
{
    double s = 0.0d;
    void SumSeries(int n, double x)
    {
        int i, sign = 1;
        for(i = 1; i <= n; i++)
        {
            s = s + x /i * sign;
            sign = sign * –1;
        }
        System.out.println(s);
    }
    void SumSeries()
    {
        int i, j, f;
        for(i = 1; i <= 20; i++)
        {
            f = 1;
            for(j = 1; j <= i; j++)
            {
                f = f * j;
            }
            s = s + f;
        }
        System.out.println(s);
    }
}
```

Name	Type	Description
s	double	To store the sum.
f	int	To store the factorial.
i, j	int	Counter variables.

Q. 4. Design a class to overload a function area() as follows:

(i) double area (double a, double b, double c) with three double arguments, returns the area of a scalene triangle using the formula:

$$area = \sqrt{s(s - a)(s - b)(s - c)}$$
$$\text{where } s = \frac{a + b + c}{2}$$

(ii) double area (int a, int b, int height) with three integer arguments, returns the area of a trapezium using the formula.

$$area = \frac{1}{2} \text{ height } (a + b)$$

(iii) double area (double diagonal 1, double diagonal 2) with two double arguments, returns the area of a rhombus using the formula:

$$area = \frac{1}{2} \text{ (diagonal 1} \times \text{diagonal 2)}$$ [2014]

Ans.

```
class Overload
{
    double ar;
    double area(double a, double b, double c)
    {
        double s = (a + b + c)/2;
        ar = Math.sqrt(s * (s – a) * (s – b) * (s – c));
        return(ar);
    }
    double area(int a, int b, int height)
    {
        ar = 0.5 * height * (a + b);
        return(ar);
    }
    double area(double diagonal1, double diagonal2)
    {
        ar = 0.5 * diagonal1 * diagonal2;
        return(ar);
    }
}
```

Name	Type	Description
a	double	To store a double argument.
b	double	To store a double argument.
c	double	To store a double argument.
ar	double	To calculate area.
s	double	As a variable used to calculate area of a scalene triangle.
height	int	To store height of trapezium.
diagonal 1	double	To store the value of the diagonal of a rhombus.
diagonal 2	double	To store the value of the diagonal of the rhombus.

Q. 5. **Design a class to overload a function series() as follows:**

(i) double series(double n) with one double argument and returns the sum of the series,

$$\text{sum} = \frac{1}{1} + \frac{1}{2} + \frac{1}{3} + \dots + \frac{1}{n}$$

(ii) double series(double a, double n) with two double arguments and returns the sum of the series,

$$\text{sum} = \frac{1}{a^2} + \frac{4}{a^5} + \frac{7}{a^8} + \frac{10}{a^{11}} + \dots \text{ to } n \text{ terms.}$$

[2013]

Ans.
```
class Overload
{ // class beginning
    double s = 0;
    double series(double n)
    {
        int i;
        for(i = 1; i <= n; i++)
        {
            s = s + 1.0/i;
        }
        return(s);
    }
    double series(double a, double n)
    {
        int i, c = 1;
        for(i = 1; i <= n; i++)
        {
            s = s + c/Math.pow(a, c + 1);
            c = c + 3;
        }
        return(s); // returns the value of s
    }
}
```

Name	Type	Description
n	double	To store value of n.
s	double	To store sum.
i	int	Loop counter.
c	Int	To store exponent value.

Q. 6. **Design a class to overload a function check( ) as follows:**

(i) void check(String str, char ch) – to find and print the frequency of a character in a string.

Example:

Input	Output
str = "success"	number of s present is = 3
ch = 's'	

(ii) void check(String s1) – to display only vowels from string s1, after converting it to lower case.

Example: Input:
s1 = "computer"   Output: o u e [2017]

Ans.
```
class Overload
{ // class beginning
    int i;
    void check(String str, char ch)
    {
        int c = 0;
        str = str.toLowerCase();
        for(i = 0; i < str.length(); i++)
        {
            if(ch == str.charAt(i))
            {
                c++;
            }
        }
        System.out.println("number of" +
                ch + " present is " +c);
    }
    void check(String s1)
    {
        char ch;
        s1 = s1.toLowerCase();
        for(i = 0; i < s1.length(); i++)
        {
            ch = s1.charAt(i);
            if(ch == 'a' || ch == 'e' || ch == 'i'
                    || ch == 'o' || ch == 'u')
            {
                System.out.print(ch + " ");
            }
        }
    }
} // class ending
```

Name	Type	Description
str	String	To store the given string.
c	int	To store the count value.
ch	char	To store the given character.
i	int	For loop variable.
s1	string	To store a string.

Short Answer Type Questions

Q. 1. Write the memory capacity (storage size) of short and float data type in bytes. **[2019]**

Ans. Short requires 16 bits or two(2) bytes of storage whereas float requires 32 bits or four(4) bytes of storage.

Q. 2. State the data type and value of res after the following is executed:

char ch = '9';

res = Character.isDigit(ch); **[2019]**

Ans. Data type of **res** is boolean and it's value is true.

Q. 3. (i) int res = 'A';

What is the value of res?

(ii) Name the package that contains wrapper classes. **[2018]**

Ans. (i) res = 65

(ii) java.lang

Q. 4. What are the types of casting shown by the following examples:

(i) char c = (char)120;

(ii) int x = 't'; **[2016]**

Ans. (i) Explicit type casting.

(ii) Implicit type casting.

Q. 5. Write a function prototype of the following:

A function *PosChar* which takes a string argument and a character argument and returns an integer value. **[2016]**

Ans. int PosChar(String s, char c)

Q. 6. Name the wrapper classes of char type and boolean type. **[2015]**

Ans. For char it is Character and for boolean it is Boolean.

Q. 7. State the output when the following program segment is executed:

String a = "Smartphone",

b = "Graphic Art";

String h = a.substring(2, 5);

String k = b.substring(8).toUpperCase( );

System.out.println.(h);

System.out.println(k.equalsIgnoreCase(h)); **[2015]**

Ans. art

true

Q. 8. Write the output of the following program code:

char ch;

int x = 97;

do

{

ch = (char) x;

System.out.print(ch +" ");

if(x%10 = 0)

break;

++x;

} while(x <= 100); **[2015]**

Ans. a b c d

Q. 9. Name any two wrapper classes. **[2013]**

Ans. Integer, Double.

Q. 10. State the values stored in the variables str1 and str2

String s1 = "good"; String s2 = "world matters";

String str1 = s2.substring(5), replace('t', 'n');

String str2 = s1.concat(str1); **[2013]**

Ans. str1 = manners and str2 = good manners

Q. 11. What is the data type that the following library functions return?

(i) isWhitespace(char ch)

(ii) Math.random() **[2013]**

Ans. (i) boolean

(ii) double

 # Long Answer Type Questions

Q. 1. A private Cab service company provides service within the city at the following rates:
[2020]

	AC CAR	NON-AC CAR
Up to 5 K\km	₹ 150/-	₹ 120/-
Beyond 5 km	₹ 10/- Per km	₹ 08/- Per km

Design a class CabService with the following description:

Member variables /data members:

String Car-type : **To store the type of car (AC or NON AC)**

double km : **To store the kilometer travelled**

double bill : **To calculate and store the bill amount**

Member methods:

CabService() – **Default constructor to initialize data members.**
String data members to " " and double data members to 0.0.

void accept() – **To accept car_type and km (using Scanner class only).**

void calculate() – **To calculate the bill as per the rules given above.**

void display() – **To display the bill as per the following format**
CAR TYPE:
KILOMETER TRAVELLED:
TOTAL BILL:

Create an object of the class in the main method and invoke the member methods.

Ans.

```java
import java.util.*;
class CabServices
{
    String car_type;
    double km,bill;
    public CabServices()
    {
        car_type="";
        km=bill=0.0;
    }
    void accept()
    {
        Scanner sc = new Scanner(System.in);
        System.out.println("Enter Car Type
                           and no. of Km");
        car_type=sc.nextLine();
        km=sc.nextDouble();
    }
    void calculate()
    {
        if(car_type.equalsIgnoreCase
                           ("AC"))
        {
            if(km<=5)
            {
                bill=150;
            }
            else
            {
            bill=150 + (km − 5) * 10;
            }
        }
        elseif(car_type.equalsIgnoreCase
                           ("NON AC"))
        {
            if(km<=5)
            {
                bill=120
            }
            else
            {
                bill=120 + (Km − 5) * 8;
            }
        }
        else
        {
            System.out.println("Wrong
                                Type");
        }
    }
    void display()
    {
        System.out.println("CAR TYPE :
                           "+ car_type);
        System.out.println("KILOMETER
                           TRAVELLED : " + km);
        System.out.println("TOTAL BILL:
                           "+ bill);
    }
}
```

Q. 2. Design a class to overload a method number()
as follows : **[2020]**

   (i) void Number
   (int num, int d) – To count and display the frequency
of a digit in a num-
ber.

   Example:
   num = 2565685
   d = 5
   Frequency of digit 5 = 3

(ii) void Number
   (int n1) – To find and display
the sum of even
digits of a number.

   Example:
   n1 = 29865
   Sum of even digits = 16

Write a main method to create an object and
invoke the above methods.

Ans. (i)class Overload

```
{
 void Number(int num,int d)
 {
     int c=0,d1;
     while(num>0)
     {
         d1=num%10;
         if(d1==d)
         {
             c++;
         }
         num=num/10;
     }
     System.out.println("Frequency of digit
                        " + d + " = " + c);
 }
(ii) void Number(int n1)
 {
 int d,s=0;
 while(n1>0)
 {
     d=n1%10;
     if(d%2==0)
     {
         s=s+d;
     }
     n1=n1/10;
 }
     System.out.println("Sum of Even Digits =
                        " + s);
 }
}
```

Q. 3. Write a program to input a sentence and
convert it into uppercase and count and
display the total number of words starting
with a letter 'A'.

Example:

Sample Input: ADVANCEMENT AND
APPLICATION OF INFORMATION
TECHNOLOGY ARE EVER CHANGING.

Sample Output: Total number of words
starting with letter 'A' = 4. **[2019]**

Marking Scheme

```
import java.util.*;
class loop
{
    public static void main (String args[])
    {
    Scanner sc=new Scanner (System.in);
    String str; char ch, ch1; int c=0;
    System.out.println("Enter a sentence");
    str= sc.nextLine();
    str=str.toUpperCase();
    int len= str.length();
    for (int i=0; i<len-1;i++)
    {
        ch= str.charAt(i);
        ch1=str.charAt(i+1);
        if (i==0 && ch=='A')
        c++;
        else if (ch==' ' && ch1=='A')
            c++;
    }
        System.out.println("Number
        of words started with letter 'A' ="+c);
    }
}
```

Ans.

```
import java.util.*;
class Count
{
    String s;
    int l, i, c = 0;
    void display()
    {
        Scanner sc = new Scanner(System.in);
        System.out.println("Enter a sentence");
        s = sc.nextLine();
        s = s.toUpperCase();
        s = " " + s;
        l = s.length();
        for(i = 0; i < l; i++)
        {
            if(s.charAt(i) == ' ' && s.charAt(i + 1)
```

                                    == 'A')
                {

          c++;

                }

            }
        System.out.println("Total number of
            words starting with letter A = " + c);

        }

    }

Name	Type	Description
s	String	To store a sentence.
l	int	To store the length.
i	int	For loop variable.
c	int	Counter variable.

Q. 4. Design a class *RailwayTicket* with following description:

Instance variables/data members:

String name : To store the name of the customer

String coach : To store the type of coach customer wants to travel

long mobno : To store customer's mobile number

int amt : To store basic amount of ticket

int totalamt : To store the amount to be paid after updating the original amount

Member methods:

void accept() – To take input for name, coach, mobile number and amount.

void update() – To update the amount as per the coach selected (extra amount to be added in the amount as follows)

Type of Coaches	Amount
First_AC	700
Second_AC	500
Third_AC	250
Sleeper	None

void display() – To display all details of a customer such as name, coach, total amount and mobile number.

Write a main method to create an object of the class and call the above member methods.

[2018]

Marking Scheme

```
import java.io.*;
class RailwayTicket
{
    String name;
    String coach;
    long mobno;
    int amt;
    int totalamt;
    public void accept()throws IOException
    {
        InputStreamReader in = new
                    InputStreamReader(System.in);
        BufferedReader br = new BufferedReader(in);
        BufferedReader br = new BufferedReader(in);
        System.out.print("Name:");
        name = br.readLine();
        System.out.print("Coach:");
        coach = br.readLine();
        System.out.print("Mobile number:");
        mobno = Long.parseLong(br.readLine());
        System.out.print("Amount:");
        amt = Integer.parseInt(br.readLine());
    }
    public void update()
    {
        if(coach.equalsIgnoreCase("First_AC"))
            totalamt = amt + 700;
        else if(coach.equalsIgnoreCase("Second_AC"))
            totalamt = amt + 500;
        else if(coach.equalsIgnoreCase("Third_AC"))
            totalamt = amt + 250;
    }
    public void display()
    {
        System.out.println("Name:" + name);
        System.out.println("Coach:" + coach);
        System.out.println("Total Amount:" + totalamt);
        System.out.println("Mobile number:" + mobno);
    }
    public static void main(String args[])
    throws IOException
    {
        RailwayTicket obj = new RailwayTicket();
        obj.accept();
        obj.update();
        obj.display();
    }
}
```

Ans.
```
import java.util.*;//importing package
class RailwayTicket
{
    String name, coach;
    long mobno;
    int amt, totalamt;
    void accept()
    {
        Scanner sc = new
            Scanner(System.in);
        System.out.println("Enter the Details");
```

```
        name = sc.next();
        coach = sc.next();
        mobno = sc.nextLong();
        amt = sc.nextInt();
    }
    void update()
    {
        if(coach.equalsIgnoreCase
                          ("First_AC"))
        {
            totalamt = amt + 700;
        }
        else if(coach.equalsIgnoreCase
                          ("Second_AC"))
        {
            totalamt = amt + 500;
        }
        else if(coach.equalsIgnoreCase
                          ("Third_AC"))
        {
            totalamt = amt + 250;
        }
        else
        {
            totalamt = amt;
        }
    }
    void display()
    {
        System.out.println("Name : " + name);
        System.out.println("Coach : " + coach);
        System.out.println("Mobile no. : "
                          + mobno);
        System.out.println("Total Amt :
                          " + totalamt);
    }
    public static void main(String args[])
    {
        RailwayTicket ob = new
                          RailwayTicket();
        ob.accept();//function call
        ob.update();
        ob.display();
    }
}
```

Name	Type	Description
name	String	To store the name of the customer.
coach	String	To store name of coach.
mobno	long	To store customer's mobile number.
amt, totalamt	int	To store amount and total amount.

Q. 5. **Write a program to input a number and check and print whether it is a Pronic number or not. (Pronic number is the number which is the product of two consecutive integers).**

Example:

$12 = 3 \times 4$

$20 = 4 \times 5$

$42 = 6 \times 7$

[2018]

> 📋 **Marking Scheme**
>
> ```
> import java.io.*;
> class Pronic
> {
>     public static void main(String args[])
>     throws IOException
>     {
>         InputStreamReader in = new
>                   InputStreamReader(System.in);
>         BufferedReader br = new BufferedReader(in);
>                   S t t i t("E t th b ")
>         System.out.print("Enter the number: ");
>         int n = Integer.parseInt(br.readLine());
>         int i = 1;
>         while(i * (i + 1) < n)
>             i++;
>         if(i * (i + 1) == n)
>             System.out.println(n + " is a Pronic
>                          Number.");
>         else
>             System.out.println(n + " is not a Pronic
>                          Number.");
>     }
> }
> ```

Ans.

```
import java.util.*;//importing package
class Pronic
{
    int n, i = 1, p = 0;
    void display()
    {
        Scanner sc = new Scanner(System.in);
        System.out.println("Enter a number");
        n = sc.nextInt();
        int flag = 0;
        for(i = 0; i < n; i++)
        {
            if(i * (i + 1) == n)
            {
                flag = 1;
                break;
            }
        }
        if(flag == 1)
            System.out.println("It is a pronic
                          number");
        else
            System.out.println("It is not a
                          pronic number");
    }
}
```

Name	Type	Description
n	int	To store a number.
i	int	Loop variable.
p	int	To store product.
flag	int	Flag variable.

Q. 6. **Write a program in Java to accept a string in lower case and change the first letter of every word to upper case. Display the new string.**
Sample input: we are in cyber world.
Sample output: We Are In Cyber World.

[2018]

📋 Marking Scheme ------------------------------------

```java
import java.io.*;
class TitleCase
{
    public static void main(String args[])
    throws IOException
    {
        InputStreamReader in = new
                    InputStreamReader(System.in);
        BufferedReader br = new BufferedReader(in);
        System.out.print("Enter the string: ");
        String s = br.readLine();
        s = s.toLowerCase();
        String t = new String();
        for(int i = 0; i < s.length(); i++)
        {
            if(i == 0 || s.charAt(i - 1) == ' ')
                t += Character.toUpperCase(s.charAt(i));
            else
                t += s.charAt(i);
        }
        System.out.println(t);
    }
}
```

Ans.
```java
import java.util.*;//importing package
class Demo
{
    String s,w;
    char ch;
    int i, l;
    void display()
    {
        Scanner sc = new Scanner(System.in);
        System.out.println("Enter a Sentence");
        s = sc.nextLine();
        s = s + " ";
        l = s.length();
        for(i = 0; i < l; i++)
        {
            w = "";
            while(s.charAt(i) != ' ')
            {
                w = w + s.charAt(i);
                i++;
            }//while loop ending
            ch = w.charAt(0);
            ch = 32;
```

```java
            w = ch + w.substring(1);
            System.out.print(w + " ");
        }
    }
}
```

Name	Type	Description
s	String	To store a string.
w	String	To store a word.
ch	char	To store a character.
i	int	For loop variable.
l	int	To store length of the string.

Q. 7. **Write a menu driven program to display the pattern as per user's choice.**

Pattern 1	Pattern 2
ABCDE	B
ABCD	LL
ABC	UUU
AB	EEEE
A	

For an incorrect option, an appropriate error message should be displayed. [2018]

📋 Marking Scheme ------------------------------------

```java
import java.io.*;
class Menu{
    public static void main(String args[])
    throws IOException{
        InputStreamReader in = new
                    InputStreamReader(System.in);
        BufferedReader br = new BufferedReader(in);
        System.out.println("1. Pattern 1");
        System.out.println("2. Pattern 2");
        System.out.print("Enter your choice: ");
        int choice = Integer.parseInt(br.readLine());
        switch(choice){
            case 1:
            String s = "ABCDE";
            for(int i = s.length(); i >= 0; i--)
                System.out.println(s.substring(0, i));
            break;
            case 2:
            s = "BLUE";
            for(int i = 0; i < s.length(); i++){
                char ch = s.charAt(i);
                for(int j = 0; j <= i; j++)
                    System.out.print(ch);
                System.out.println();
            }
            break;
            default:
            System.out.println("Invalid choice!");
        }
    }
}
```

Ans.
```
import java.util.*;
class series
{
    public static void main(String arg[])
    {
        Scanner sc = new Scanner(System.in);
        System.out.println("1 for Pattern 1 and
                            2 for Pattern 2");
        System.out.println("enter the choice");
        int ch = sc.nextInt();
        switch(ch)
        {
            case 1: String s = "ABCDE";
                    for(int i = s.length(); i > 0; i−−)
                    {
                        System.out.println
                            (s.substring(0, i));
                    }
                    break;
            case 2: String s1 = "BLUE";
                    for(int i = 0; i < s1.length(); i++)
                    {
                        for(int j = 0; j <= i; j++)
                        {
                            System.out.print
                                (s1.charAt(i));
                        }
                        System.out.println();
                    }
                    break;
            default: System.out.println("invalid
                                        choice");
        }
    }
}
```

Name	Type	Description
ch	int	To store the choice.
i, j	int	For loop variables.
s	String	To store the string.
s1	String	To store the string.

Q. 8. <u>Special words</u> **are those words which starts and ends with same letter.**

Examples:

EXISTENCE

COMIC

WINDOW

<u>Palindrome words</u> are those words which read the same from left to right and vice-versa.

Examples:

MALAYALAM

MADAM

LEVEL

ROTATOR

CIVIC

All palindromes are special words, but all special words are not palindromes.

Write a program to accept a word check and print whether the word is a palindrome or only special word. **[2016]**

Ans.
```
import java.util.*;
class check
{
    String s, rev = "";
    int i, l;
    void display()
    {
        Scanner obj = new Scanner(System.in);
        System.out.println("Enter a word");
        s = obj.nextLine();
        s = s.toUpperCase();
        l = s.length();
        for(i = l − 1; i >= 0; i−−)
        {
            rev = rev + s.charAt(i);
        }
        if(s.equals(rev))
        {
            System.out.println("Palindrome
                                word");
        }
        else if(s.charAt(0) == s.charAt(l − 1))
        {
            System.out.println("Special
                                word");
        }
        else
        {
            System.out.println("Not a
                Palindrome or a Special word");
        }
    }
}
```

Name	Type	Description
s	String	To store a string.
rev	String	To store the reverse of a string.
i	int	Counter variables.
l	int	To store the length of string.

Q. 9. **Write a program to accept a number and check and display whether it is a Niven number or not.**

(Niven number is that number which is divisible by its sum of digits).

Examples:

Consider the number 126.

Sum of its digits is 1 + 2 + 6 = 9 and 126 is divisible by 9. **[2016]**

Ans.
```java
import java.util.*;
class Niven
{
    int n, d, t, s = 0;
    void display(String args[])
    {
        Scanner sc = new Scanner(System.in);
        System.out.println("Enter a no.");
        n = sc.nextInt();
        t = n;
        while(n > 0)
        {
            d = n % 10;
            s = s + d;
            n = n/10;
        }
        if(t % s == 0)
        {
            System.out.println("Niven no.");
        }
        else
        {
            System.out.println("Not a Niven no.");
        }
    }
}
```

Name	Type	Description
n, t	int	To store the number.
d	int	To extract the digits.
s	int	To store the sum of digits.

Q. 10. Write a program to initialize the seven Wonders of the World along with their locations in two different arrays. Search for a name of the country input by the user. If found, display the name of the country along with its Wonder, otherwise display "Sorry Not Found !"

Seven wonders	–	CHICHEN ITZA, CHRIST THE REDEEMER, TAJMAHAL, GREAT WALL OF CHINA, MACHU PICCHU, PETRA, COLOSSEUM
Locations	–	MEXICO, BRAZIL, INDIA, CHINA, PERU, JORDAN, ITALY
Example	–	Country Name: INDIA Output: INDIA – TAJMAHAL Country Name: USA Output: Sorry Not Found!

[2016]

Ans.
```java
import java.util.*;
class Search
{
    String w[] = {"CHICHEN ITZA",
    "CHRIST THE REDEEMER", "TAJMAHAL",
    "GREAT WALL OF CHINA",
     "MACHU PICCHU", "PETRA",
                        "COLOSSEUM"};
    String c[] = {"MEXICO", "BRAZIL",
    "INDIA", "CHINA", "PERU", "JORDAN",
                        "ITALY"};
    String s;
    int i, flag = 0, index;
    void display(String args[])
    {
        Scanner br = new Scanner(System.in);
        System.out.println("Enter name to be searched");
        s = br.nextLine();
        for(i = 0; i < 7; i++)
        {
            if(s.equalsIgnoreCase(c[i]))
            {
                flag = 1;
                index = i;
                break;
            }
        }
        if(flag == 1)
        {
            System.out.println(c[index] + "–"
                            + w[index]);
        }
        else
        {
            System.out.println("Sorry Not Found!");
        }
    }
}
```

Name	Type	Description
w[], c[]	String array	To store 7 wonders and their countries.
s	String	To store name to be searched.
i	int	Counter variable.
flag	int	To check the status.
index	int	To store the index number.

Q. 11. A special two-digit number is such that when the sum of its digits is added to the product of its digits, the result is equal to the original two-digit number.

Example: Consider the number 59.

Sum of digits = 5 + 9 = 14

Product of its digits = 5 × 9 = 45

Sum of the sum of digits and product of digits = 14 + 45 = 59

Write a program to accept a two-digit number. Add the sum of its digits to the product of its digits. If the value is equal to the number input, output the message "Special 2-digit number" otherwise, output the message "Not a special 2-digit number".

[2014]

Ans.

```java
import java.io.*;
class Special
{
    int n, b, s = 0, p = 1;
    void display()throws IOException
    {
        BufferedReaderbr = new BufferedReader
            (new InputStreamReader(System.in));
        System.out.println("Enter a two digit
                                        no.");
        n = Integer.parseInt(br.readLine());
        if(n >= 10 && n <= 99)
        {
            while(n > 0)
            {
                b = n % 10;
                s = s + b;
                p = p * b;
                n = n/10;
            }
            if(s + p == n)
            {
                System.out.println("Special  2 -
                            digit number");
            }
            else
            {
                System.out.println("Not a
                    Special 2 - digit number");
            }
        }
    }
}
```

Name	Type	Description
n	int	To store a two-digit number.
b	int	To extract digits from the number.
s	int	To calculate sum of digits.
p	int	To calculate product of digits.

Q. 12. Write a program that encodes a word into Piglatin. To translate word into a Piglatin word, convert the word into uppercase and then place the first vowel of the original word as the start of the new word along with the remaining alphabets. The alphabets present before the vowel being shifted towards the end followed by "AY".

Sample input (1): London,

Sample output (1): ONDONLAY

Sample input (2): Olympics,

Sample output (2): OLYMPICSAY

[2013]

Ans.

```java
import java.io.*; // importing package
class Piglatin
{
    int l, i;
    String s, p;
    char ch;
    public Piglatin()
    {
        s = "ComputerWorld";
    }
    void display()throws IOException
    {
        BufferedReader br = new
        BufferedReader(new InputStream
                        Reader (System.in));
        System.out.println("Enter a string");
        s = br.readLine();
        s = s.toUpperCase();
        l = s.length();
        for(i = 0; i < l; i++)
        {
            ch = s.charAt(i);
            if(ch == 'A' || ch == 'E' || ch == 'I'
                    || ch == 'O' || ch == 'U')
            {
                p = s.substring(i) + s.substring(0, i)
                                        + "AY";
                System.out.println(p);
                break;
            }
        }
    }
} // class ending
```

Name	Type	Description
s, p	String	To store words.
ch	char	To store a character.
l	int	To store length of string.
i	int	Counter variable.

 6 Iterations

Short Answer Type Questions

Q. 1. Give the output of following code and mention how many times the loop will execute?

```
int i;
for(i = 5; i >= 1; i--)
{
    if(i%2 == 1)
        continue;
    System.out.print(i+"");
}                                   [2019]
```

Ans. 4 2

The loop will get executed 5 times.

Q. 2. State the difference between while and do while loop. **[2018]**

Ans.

while	do while
1. The loop does not execute if the condition is false.	The loop executes at least once even if the condition is false.
2. It is an entry controlled loop.	It is an exit controlled loop.
3. Minimum repetition is 0.	Minimum repetition is 1.

Q. 3. Give the output of the following program segment and also mention how many times the loop is executed:

```
int i;
    for(i = 5; i > 10; i ++)
    System.out.println(i);
    System.out.println(i * 4);      [2018]
```

Ans. Loop will be executed 0 times since the test condition is initially false.

Output will be: 20.

Q. 4. Give the output of the following program segment and also mention the number of times the loop is executed:

```
int a, b;
for(a = 6, b = 4; a <= 24; a = a + 6)
{
    if(a % b == = 0)
        break;
}
System.out.println(a);              [2017]
```

Ans. 12

The loop will be executed 2 times.

Q. 5. Convert following do-while loop into for loop.

```
    int i = 1;
    int d = 5;
    do
    {
        d = d * 2;
        System.out.println(d);
        i++;
    } while(i <= 5);                 [2017]
```

Ans.
```
int i, d = 5;
for(i = 1; i <= 5; i++)
{
    d = d * 2;
    System.out.println(d);
}
```

Q. 6. Analyze the given program segment and answer the following questions:

(i) Write the output of the program segment.

(ii) How many times does the body of the loop gets executed?

```
for(int m = 5; m <= 20; m += 5)
{
    if(m % 3 == 0)
        break;
    else if(m % 5 == 0)
    System.out.println(m);
        continue;
}                                   [2016]
```

Ans. (i) 5
10

(ii) Loop body will be executed 3 times.

Q. 7. What is an infinite loop? Write an infinite loop statement. **[2014]**

Ans. A non terminating loop is known as an infinite loop.

```
e.g.: for(i = 1; i > 0; i++)
    {
        System.out.println("Destination");
    }
```

Q. 8. Give two differences between the switch statement and the if-else statement. **[2014]**

Ans.

Switch	If - Else
1. It can only test for equality.	It can work with all relational/logical operators.
2. It cannot handle floating points.	It can handle floating/ integers as well as characters and strings.

Q. 9. What is the difference between a break statement and a continue statement when they occur in a loop? **[2013]**

Ans.

Break Statement	Continue Statement
The break statement is used to quit from the loop without executing any of the remaining statements in the loop and the execution begins at the next statement following the loop.	The continue statement skips the current iteration of the loop and moves to the next iteration skipping all the remaining instructions within the loop.

Q. 10. Rewrite the following program segment using the if - else statement

comm = (sale > 15000)? sale × 5/100 : 0;   **[2013]**

Ans.
```
if(sale > 15000)
{
    comm = sale * 5/100;
}
else
{
    comm = 0;
}
```

 Long Answer Type Questions

Q. 1. A tech number has even number of digits. If the number is split in two equal halves, then the square of sum of these halves is equal to the number itself. Write a program to generate and print all <u>four digit tech numbers</u>.

Example:

Consider the number 3025

Square of sum of the halves of 3025

$= (30 + 25)^2$

$= (55)^2$

$= 3025$ is a tech number.   **[2019]**

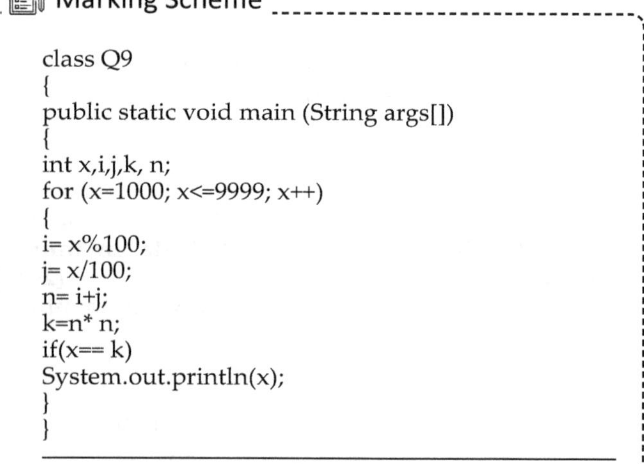 Marking Scheme

```
class Q9
{
public static void main (String args[])
{
int x,i,j,k, n;
for (x=1000; x<=9999; x++)
{
i= x%100;
j= x/100;
n= i+j;
k=n* n;
if(x== k)
System.out.println(x);
}
}
```

STEPS
Declaration of variables
loop
Finding the first half and second half of the number
Adding the two halves
Finding the square
Checking the original number with the square
Displaying the output
Mnemonic codes / Variable description

Ans.
```
class Tech
{
    int i, a, b, s;
    void display()
    {
        for(i = 1000; i <= 9999; i++)
        {
            a = i % 100;
            b = i/100;
            s = a + b;
            if(s * s == i)
            {
                System.out.println(i);
            }
        }
    }
}
```

Name	Type	Description
a	int	To store the last two digits.
b	int	To store the first two digits.
s	int	To store the sum.
i	int	For loop variable.

Q. 2. Using switch statement, write a menu driven program for the following:

(i) To find and display the sum of the series given below:

$$S = x^1 - x^2 + x^3 - x^4 + x^5 \ldots\ldots - x^{20}$$

(where $x = 2$)

(ii) To display the following series:

1 11 111 1111 11111

For an incorrect option, an appropriate error message should be displayed.

[2017]

Ans.
```
import java.util.*;
class series   {
public static void main(String arg[])   {
System.out.println("1.series_1 2.series_2 ");
Scanner sc=new
Scanner(System.in);
System.out.println("enter your choice");
int choice=sc.nextInt();
switch(choice)   {
case 1: double sum=0.0;
int x=2;
for (int i=1;i<=20;i++)
{
if (i%2==0)
sum =sum-Math.pow(x,i);
else
sum =sum+Math.pow(x,i);
}
System.out.println("sum is ="+sum);
break;
case 2: int s=0;
for(int i=1 ;i<=5 ;i++)
{
s=s*10+1 ;
System.out.print(s +" " );
}
break;
default:System.out.println("invalid choice");
}
}
}
```

STEPS

Display of menu
Choice input and switch(choice)
Case 1: Declaration and Initialisation of
variables sum and x
for loop
if else and sum calculation
Displaying sum
Case 2: Declaration and initialization of variable s
for loop
Calculation of s
Display of s
default
Variable description

Name	Type	Description
ch	int	To enter choice.
x	int	Variable of the given expression.
i	int	For loop.
sign	int	To store sign of the expression.
s	double	To store the sum.

Q. 3. **Using the switch statement, write a menu driven program to calculate the maturity amount of a Bank Deposit.**

   The user is given the following options:

   (i) Term Deposit

   (ii) Recurring Deposit

   For option (i) accept principal (P), rate of interest (r) and time period in years(n). Calculate and output the maturity amount (A) receivable using the formula

$$A = P\left[1 + \frac{r}{100}\right]^n$$

For option (ii) accept Monthly Installment (P), rate of interest (r) and time period in months (n). Calculate and output the maturity amount (A) receivable using the formula:

$$A = P \times n + P \times \f(n\,(n+1),\,2) \times \frac{r}{100} \times \frac{1}{12}$$

For an incorrect option, an appropriate error message should be displayed. **[2014]**

Ans.
```
import java.io.*; //import java.util.*;

public class bank

{ public void sampleMethod()throws IOE x
ception // throwsInputMismatchException

{ double P,A=0,r,n,x; int choice;

BufferedReader br=new BufferedReader(new
                InputStreamReader(System.in));

//Scanner sc=new Scanner(System.in);

System.out.println("Enter Choice(1) Term
                Deposit(2) Recurring Deposit ");

choice=Integer.parseInt(br.readLine());//
sc.nextInt();

switch(choice)

{

case 1:

System.out.println(" Enter Principal:");

P=Double.parseDouble(br.readLine());//
sc.nextDouble();

System.out.println(" Enter rate of interest:");
r=Double.parseDouble(br.readLine());

System.out.println(" Enter time period in
                years:");

n=Double.parseDouble(br.readLine());//
                sc.nextDouble();

x=1.0+r/100.0;
```

```
A=P*(Math.pow(x,n));

break;

case 2:

System.out.println(" Enter Monthly Instal-
ment:");

P=Double.parseDouble(br.readLine());//
                        sc.nextDouble();

System.out.println(" Enter rate of interest:");
        r=Double.parseDouble(br.readLine());

System.out.println(" Enter time period in
months:");

n=Double.parseDouble(br.readLine());//
                        sc.nextDouble();

x=P*n;

A=x+ P*(n*(n+1)/2.0)*(r/100.0)*(1.0/12.0);

break;

default: System.out.println("Invalid input");

} System.out.print("Amount = Rs."); System.
out.                    printf("%.2f",A); } }

OR Sytem.out.println("Amount = Rs." +A)
```

STEPS

Output menu

Input option

switch statement

case 1 and break

Input 3 parameters (any data type)

Compute Amount for term deposit (ignore data types)

case 2 and break

Input 3 parameters (any data type)

Computing Amount for recurring deposit (ignore data types)

default statement with appropriate message

Output Amount (ignore formatting)

Description of variables/ comments/ mnemonics

Name	Type	Description
ch	int	To input user's choice.
r	double	To enter rate.
P	double	To enter principal amount.
n	double	To enter time period.
A	double	To calculate maturity amount.

Q. 4. **Using the switch statement, write a menu driven program:**

(i) To check and display whether a number input by the user is a composite number or not (A number is said to be a composite, if it has one or more than one factor excluding 1 and the number itself).

Example: 4, 6, 8, 9 ...

(ii) To find the smallest digit of an integer that is input.

Sample input: 6524

Sample output: Smallest digit is 2

For an incorrect choice, an appropriate error message should be displayed. [2013]

Ans.

```
import java.io.*;// importing package
class Menu
{
    int n, ch, i, c = 0, d, min = 10;
    void display()throws IOException
    {
        BufferedReader br = new
                    BufferedReader(new
            InputStreamReader(System.in));
        System.out.println("1.Composite");
        System.out.println("2. Minimum Digit");
        System.out.println("Enter Your Choice");
        ch = Integer.parseInt(br.readLine());
        System.out.println("Enter a no.");
        n = Integer.parseInt(br.readLine());
        switch(ch)
        {
            case 1: for(i = 1; i <= n; i++)
                {
                    if(n % i == 0)
                    {
                        c++;
                    }
                }
                if(c > 2)
                {
                    System.out.println(n + "is
                        composite no.");
                }
                else
                {
                    System.out.println(n + " is not
                        a composite no.");
                }
```

```
            }
        break;
case 2: mid = d % 10;
        while(n > 0)
        {
            d = n%10;
            if(d < min)
            {
                min = d;
            }
            n = n/10;
        }
        System.out.println("Smallest
                    Digit is: " + min);
```

```
            break;
        default: System.out.println("Wrong
                            Choice");
        } // switch case ending
    }
}
```

Name	Type	Description
n	int	To store value of n.
ch	int	To store choice.
i	int	Loop counter.
c	int	To store exponent value.
d	int	To store digit.
min	int	To store the smallest digit.

Short Answer Type Questions

Q. 1. What is autoboxing in Java? Give an example. [2020]

Ans. Converting primitive types to corresponding wrapper class object is called Autoboxing. For eg: int to Integer, double to Double type etc.

Q. 2. Give the output of the following code:
String P = "20", Q = "19";
int a = Integer.parseInt(P);
int b = Integer.valueOf(Q);
System.out.println(a+""+ b); [2019]

Ans. 2019

Q. 3. What are the various types of errors in Java? [2019]

Ans. Compile time errors, Runtime errors and Logical errors.

Q. 4. Write the return data type of the following functions:
(i) startsWith( )
(ii) random( ) [2019]

Ans. (i) boolean
(ii) double

Q. 5. Classify the following as primitive or non-primitive datatypes:
(i) char
(ii) arrays
(iii) int
(iv) classes [2018]

Ans. primitive: (i) char, (iii) int
non-primitive: (ii) arrays, (iv) classes

Q. 6. Write the prototype of a function check which takes an integer as an argument and returns a character. [2018]

Ans. char check(int n)

Q. 7. Write the return data type of the following function:
(i) endsWith( )
(ii) log( ) [2018]

Ans. (i) boolean
(ii) double

Q. 8. State the data type and value of res after the following is executed:
char ch = 't';
res = Character.toUpperCase(ch); [2017]

Ans. Data type of res is char and value of res = 'T'.

Q. 9. Write the output:
char ch = 'F';
int m = ch;
m = m + 5;
System.out.println(m+ " " + ch); [2017]

Ans. 75 F

Q. 10. Write the output for the following:
String s = "Today is Test";
System.out.println(s.indexOf('T'));
System.out.println(s.substring
(0, 7) +" " + "Holiday"); [2017]

Ans. 0
Today i Holiday

Q. 11. What are the values stored in variables r_1 and r_2;
(i) double r_1 = Math.abs
(Math.min(–2.83, –5.83));
(ii) double r_2 = Math.sqrt
(Math.floor(16.3)); [2017]

Ans. (i) r_1 = 5.83   (ii) r_2 = 4.0

Q. 12. Name any two library packages. [2016]

Ans. java.io, java.util

Q. 13. Name the type of error (syntax, runtime or logical error) in each case given below:
(i) Math.sqrt (36 – 45)
(ii) int a;b;c; [2016]

Ans. (i) It's a runtime error since we cannot obtain the square root of – 9.
(ii) It's a syntax error as comma must be used instead of semicolon.

Q. 14. If int x[ ] = {4, 3, 7, 8, 9, 10}; what are the values of p and q?
(i) p = x.length
(ii) q = x[2] + x[5] * x[1] [2016]

Ans. (i) p = 6
(ii) q = 37

Q. 15. State the difference between == operator and equals () method. [2016]

Ans.

== operator	equals() method
== is a relational operator, used to check the equality of two primitive types.	equals() is a string function, used to check the equality of two strings.

Q. 16. Give the output of the following string functions:
    (i) "MISSISSIPPI".indexOf('S') +
             "MISSISSIPPI".lastIndexOf('I')
    (ii) "CABLE".compareTo("CADET") [2016]

Ans. **(i)** 2 + 10 = 12   **(ii)** − 2

Q. 17. Give the output of the following math functions:
    (i) Math.ceil(4.2)   **(ii)** Math.abs(– 4) [2016]

Ans. **(i)** 5.0   **(ii)** 4

Q. 18. Write down java expression for:

$$T = \sqrt{A^2 + B^2 + C^2}$$ [2016]

Ans. T = Math.sqrt(A * A + B * B + C * C);
                  OR
    T = Math.sqrt(Math.pow(A, 2) + Math.pow(B, 2) + Math.pow(C, 2));

Q. 19. Rewrite the following using ternary operator:
```
if(x % 2 == 0)
    System.out.print("EVEN");
else
    System.out.print("ODD");
```
[2016]

Ans. System.out.print(x % 2 == 0? "EVEN": "ODD");

Q. 20. **(i)** Name the mathematical function which is used to find sine of an angle given in radians.
    (ii) Name a string function which removes the blank spaces provided in the prefix and suffix of a string. [2015]

Ans. **(i)** Math.sin()
    (ii) trim()

Q. 21. What will this code print?
```
int arr [ ] = new int [5];
System.out.println(arr);
```
    (a) 0   **(b)** value stored in arr [0]
    (c) 0000   **(d)** garbage value
[2015]

Ans. **(d)** garbage value

Q. 22. Write the Java expressions for:

$$\frac{a^2 + b^2}{2ab}$$ [2015]

Ans. (a * a + b * b)/(2 * a * b)

Q. 23. What is meant by a package? Name any two java Application Programming Interface packages. [2014]

Ans. Package is the collection of related classes and interfaces having common functionality.
    e.g.: java.io, java.lang

Long Answer Type Questions

Q. 1. Design a class name ShowRoom with the following description:

Instance variables/Data members:

String name	:	To store the name of the customer
long mobno	:	To store the mobile number of the customer
double cost	:	To store the cost of the items purchased.
double dis	:	To store the discount amount
double amount	:	To store the amount to be paid after discount.

Member methods:

ShowRoom()	–	default constructor to initialize data members
void input()	–	To input customer name, mobile number, cost
void calculate()	–	To calculate *discount* on the *cost* of purchased items, based on the following criteria:

Cost	Discount (in percentage)
Less than or equal to ₹ 10,000	5%
More than ₹ 10,000 and less than or equal to ₹ 20,000	10%
More than ₹ 20,000 and less than or equal to ₹ 35,000	15%
More than ₹ 35,000	20%

void display() – To display customer name, mobile number, amount to be paid after discount.

Write a main method to create an object of the class and call the above member methods. [2019]

Marking Scheme

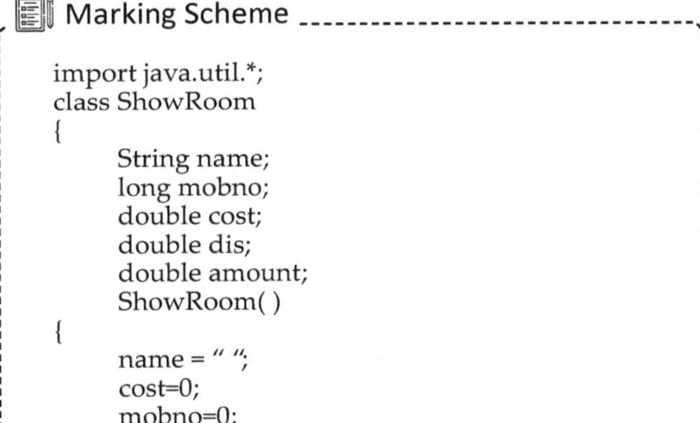

```
            dis = 0.0;
            amount=0.0;
    }
    void input()
    {
            Scanner sc = new Scanner(System.in);
            System.out.println("enter name, mobile no and
            cost");
            name=sc.next();
            mobno=sc.nextLong();
            cost=sc.nextDouble();
    }
    void calculate()
    {
            if(cost <=10000)
            {
                dis=0.05*cost;
            }
            else if(cost >10000 && cost <=20000)
            {
                dis=0.1*cost;
            }
            else if(cost >20000 && cost <=35000)
            {
                dis=0.15*cost;
            }
            else
            {
                dis=0.2*cost;
            }
    amount = cost - dis;
    }
    void display()
    {
```

STEPS

Class name
Declaration of Variables
Default constructor
void input ()
3 Inputs
4 conditions and calculations
amount = cost – dis
void display () with Output statements
Object creation & function call
Mnemonic code / Variable description

Ans.

```java
import java.util.*;
class ShowRoom
{
    String name;
    long mobno;
    double cost; dis; amount;
    public ShowRoom()
    {
        name = "";
        mobno = 0L;
        cost = 0.0;
        dis = 0.0;
        amount = 0.0;
    }
    void input()
    {
        Scanner sc = new Scanner(System.in);
        System.out.println("Enter the details");
        name = sc.next();
        mobno = sc.nextLong();
        cost = sc.nextDouble();
    }
    void calculate()
    {
        if(cost <= 10000)
        {
            dis = 0.05 * cost;
        }
        else if(cost > 10000 && cost <= 20000)
        {
            dis = 0.1 * cost;
        }
        else if(cost > 20000 && cost <= 35000)
        {
            dis = 0.15 * cost;
        }
        else
        {
            dis = 0.2 * cost;
        }
        amount = cost – dis;
    }
    void display()
    {
System.out.println("Customer Name :
                                "+ name);
System.out.println("Customer Mobile no:
                                "+mobno);
System.out.println("Amount to be paid:
                                "+ amount);
    }
    public static void main(String args[])
    {
        ShowRoom ob = new ShowRoom();
        ob.input();
        ob.calculate();
        ob.display();
    }
}
```

Name	Type	Description
name	String	To store the name of the customer.
mobno	long	To store the mobile number of the customer.
cost	double	To store the cost of the item purchased.
dis	double	To store the discount on the item purchased.
amount	double	To store the final amount to be paid.

Q. 2. Define a class ElectricBill with the following specifications:

Class: ElectricBill

Instance variables/data member:

String n – to store the name of the customer

int units – to store the number of units consumed

double bill – to store the amount to be paid

Member methods:

void accept() – to accept the name of the customer and number of units consumed

void calculate() – to calculate the bill as per the following tariff:

Number of units	Rate per unit
First 100 units	₹ 2.00
Next 200 units	₹ 3.00
Above 300 units	₹ 5.00

A surcharge of 2.5% charged if the number of units consumed is above 300 units.

Void print( ) –

To print the details as follows:

Name of the customer: ....

Number of units consumed: ......

Bill amount: ....

Write a main method to create an object of the class and call the above member methods.

[2017]

Ans.
```java
import java.util.*;
public class ElectricBill    {
int units;
String n;
double bill;
Scanner ob = new Scanner (System.in);
void accept()        {
System.out.println("Enter Name of the
                                customer");
n=ob.next();
System.out.println("Enter  Number  of  units
                                consumed");
units=ob.nextInt();        }
void calculate()    {
if (units<=100)
bill=units*2;
else
if (units >100 && units <=300)
bill=100*2+(units-100)*3;
else
bill=100*2+200*3+(units-300)*5;
if (units>300)
bill=bill+2.5/100*bill;        }
void print()        {
System.out.println("Name of the
customer:"+n);
System.out.println("Number of Units
                                consumed:"+units);
System.out.println("Bill Amount:"+bill);    }
public static void main(String args[])        {
ElectricBill obj=new ElectricBill();
obj.accept();
obj.calculate();
obj.print();    }    }
```

STEPS

class name

Declaration of variables

void accept()

Two inputs

void calculate()

Calculation of bill amount (3 conditions

With 3 calculations)

Calculation of surcharge with condition

void print()

Three Outputs

Object creation

Variable description /Mnemonic codes

Q. 3. Write a program to assign a full path and file name as given below. Using library functions, extract and output the file path, file name and file extension separately as shown.

Input   : C:\Users\admin\Pictures\ flower.jpg

Output   : path: C:\users\admin\ Pictures\

File name : flower

Extension : jpg   **[2014]**

Ans.
```java
public class stringHandling
{
  public void sampleMethod()
    {
        String       s="C:\\users\\admin\\
        pictures\\flower.jpg";
        int len,i, pos=0; char c; String
        fpath="", fname="", fextn="";
        len=s.length();
        for(i=len-1;i>=0;i--)
        {
            c=s.charAt(i);
        if(c=='.')
        {        fextn=s.substring(i+1);
                pos=i;
        }
        if(c=='\\')
        {        fname=s.substring(i+1,pos);
        fpath =
s.substring(0,i+1);
```

```
            break;
        }
    }
    System.out.println("Path: "+fpath);
      System.out.println("File name: "+fname);
        System.out.println("Extension: "+fextn);
      }
  }
```

STEPS

Assign value to String (accept single slash instead of double slash)

Declare variables (ignore initialisation)

Find length of string

Loop

Extract character

Check if character is '.'

Extract substring for file extension

store position of '.'

Check if character is '//' (accept single slash instead of double slash)

Extract substring for file name

Extract substring for file path

break to exit loop

Output file path, file name, file extension

Description of variables/ comments/ mnemonics

Name	Type	Description
s	String	To assign full path and file name.
pth	String	To extract the file path.
file	String	To extract the file name.
ext	String	To extract the file extension.
i	int	To find the last position of 'II'.
j	int	To find the last position of '.'
fname	String	To extract a part of string from the original string.

Q. 4. **The International Standard Book Number (ISBN) is a unique numeric book identifier which is printed on every book. The ISBN is based upon a 10-digit code. The ISBN is legal if:**

$1 \times digit_1 + 2 \times digit_2 + 3 \times digit_3 + 4 \times digit_4 + 5 \times digit_5 + 6 \times digit_6 + 7 \times digit_7 + 8 \times digit_8 + 9 \times digit_9 + 10 \times digit_{10}$ **is divisible by 11.**

Example: For an ISBN 1401601499

Sum $= 1 \times 1 + 2 \times 4 + 3 \times 0 + 4 \times 1 + 5 \times 6 + 6 \times 0 + 7 \times 1 + 8 \times 4 + 9 \times 9 + 10 \times 9 = 253$ **which is divisible by 11.**

Write a program to:

(i) Input the ISBN code as a 10-digit integer.

(ii) If the ISBN is not a 10-digit integer, output the message, "Illegal ISBN" and terminate the program.

(iii) If the number is 10-digit, extract the digits of the number and compute the sum as explained above.

If the sum is divisible by 11, output the message, "Legal ISBN". If the sum is not divisible by 11, output the message, "Illegal ISBN". **[2013]**

Ans.

```
import java.io.*; // importing package
class Number
{
    long n, t, rev = 0, d, s = 0;
    int c = 0, x = 1;
    void display()throws IOException
    {
        BufferedReader br = new
                BufferedReader(new
            InputStreamReader(System.in));
        System.out.println("Enter a no.");
        n = Long.parseLong(br.readLine());
        t = n;
        while(t > 0)
        {
            c++;
            t = t/10;
        }
        if(c != 10)
        {
            System.out.println("Illegal ISBN");
            System.exit(0);
        }
        else
        {
            while(n > 0)
            {
                d = n % 10;
                rev = rev * 10 + d;
                n = n/10;
```

```
}
while(rev > 0)
{
    d = rev % 10;
    s = s + x * d;
    x++;
    rev = rev/10;
} // while loop ending
if(s % 11 == 0)
{
    System.out.println("Legal ISBN");
}
else
    {
        System.out.println("Illegal ISBN");
    }
    }
}
}
```

Name	Type	Description
n, rev, s	long	To store ISBN and its reverse.
t, d	long	To store digits.
i	int	For loop counter.
c, x	int	To store counter value.

Chapter 8

Encapsulation

 ## Short Answer Type Questions

Q. 1. What is meant by a package? Give an example. [2019]

Ans. A package is a collection of inter-related classes and interfaces having common functionality. e.g., java.io, java.util, java.lang, etc.

Q. 2. How are private members of a class different from public members? [2018]

Ans. 1. Private members of a class are the most restricted members of a class whereas public members of a class are the least restricted members of a class.

2. Private members are accessible in their own class whereas public members are accessible in all parts of a java program.

Q. 3. Define Encapsulation. [2016]

Ans. The wrapping up of data members and member functions together into a single unit called class is known as encapsulation.

Q. 4. Convert the following while loop to the corresponding for loop:

```
int m = 5, n = 10;
while(n >= 1)
{
    System.out.println(m * n);
    n– –;
}
```
[2016]

Ans.
```
int m = 5, n;
for(n = 10; n >= 1; n– –)
{
    System.out.println(m * n);
}
```

Q. 5. Name any two OOP's principle. [2015]

Ans. Encapsulation and Abstraction.

Q. 6. What are the values of a and b after the following function is executed, if the values passed are 30 and 50;

```
void paws(int a, int b)
{
    a = a + b;
    b = a – b;
    a = a – b;
    System.out.println(a + ", "+b);
}
```
[2015]

Ans. Value of a = 50 and b = 30.

Q. 7. Identify the statements listed below as assignment, increment, method invocation or object creation statements:

(i) System.out.println("Java");

(ii) costPrice = 457·70;

(iii) Car hybrid = new Car();

(iv) petrolPrice++; [2014]

Ans.

(i) System.out.println ("Java"); → is method invocation statement.

(ii) costPrice = 457.50; → is assignment statement.

(iii) Car hybrid = new Car() → is object creation statement.

(iv) petrolPrice++; → is increment statement.

Long Answer Type Questions

Q. 1. Define a class named BookFair with the following description:

Instance variables/Data members:

String Bname	– Stores the name of the book.
double price	– Stores the price of the book.

Member methods:

(i) BookFair()	– Default constructor to initialize data members.
(ii) void Input()	– To input and store the name and the price of the book.

(iii) void calculate() – To calculate the price after discount. Discount is calculated based on the following criteria.

Price	Discount
Less than or equal to ₹ 1000	2% of price
More than ₹ 1000 and less than or equal to ₹ 3000	10% of price
More than ₹ 3000	15% of price

(iv) void display() – To display the name and price of the book after discount.

Write a main method to create an object of the class and call the above member methods.

[2016]

Ans.

```
import java.util.*;
class BookFair   {
    String Bname;
    double price;
    BookFair()   {
        Bname = "";
        price = 0.0d;  }
    void input()
    {
        Scanner sc = new Scanner(System.in);
        System.out.println("Enter Name
                        and Price");
        Bname = sc.next();
        price = sc.nextDouble();    }
    void calculate()  {
        if(price <= 1000)
            price = price – price* 2/100;
        else if(price <= 3000)
        {
            price = price price*10/100;
        }
        else
        {
            price = price – price* 15/100;    }
    void display()   {
        System.out.println("Name: " + Bname
                        + " Price: " + price);}
    public static void main(String args[])
    {
        BookFair obj = new BookFair();
        obj.input();
        obj.calculate();
        obj.display();
    }   }
```

Varible description / mnemonic codes

Name	Type	Description
Bname	String	To store the book name.
price	double	To store the price of the book.

Q. 2. Define a class called ParkingLot with the following description:

Instance variables/data members:

int vno – To store the vehicle number

int hours – To store the number of hours the vehicle is parked in the parking lot

double bill – To store the bill amount

Member methods:

void input( ) – To input and store the vno and hours.

void calculate( ) – To compute the parking charge at the rate of ₹ 3 for the first hour of part thereof, and ₹ 1.50 for each additional hour of part thereof.

void display( ) – To display the detail.

Write a main method to create an object of the class and call the above methods.

[2015]

Ans.

```
import java.util.*;
class ParkingLot
{
    int hours;
    int vno;
    double bill;
    Scanner sc = new Scanner(System.in);
    void input ()
        {
        System.out.println("Enter the vehicle
                        number and number of hours");
        vno = sc.nextInt();
        hours = sc.nextInt();
    }
    void calculate()
    {
        if(hours <= 1)

        bill = 3;

        else

        bill = 3 + (hours – 1)1.50*;
        }
    void display()
    {
        System.out.println("vehicle number:"+vno)
        System.out.println("Hours"+house);
        System.out.println("Bill"+bill);
    }
    public static void main(String args[])
    {
        ParkingLot pl = new ParkingLot();
        pl.input();
        pl.calculate();
        pl.display();
    }
}
```

Description of variables / comments / mnemonics

Name	Type	Description
vno	int	To store the vehicle number.
hours	int	To store the number of hours the vehicle is parked.
bill	double	To store the bill amount.

Q. 3. **Design a class to overload a function Joystring() as follows:**

(i) **void joystring (String s, char ch1, char ch2) with one string argument and two character arguments that replaces the character argument *ch1* with the character argument *ch2* in the given strings and prints the new string.**
Example:
Input value of s = "TECHNALAGY"
ch1 = 'A',
ch2 = 'O'
Output: "TECHNOLOGY"

(ii) **void Joystring (String s) with one string argument that prints the position of the first space and the last space of the given string s.**
Example:
Input value of ="Cloud computing means Internet based computing"
Output: First index: 5
Last index: 36

(iii) **void Joystring (String s1, String s2) with two string arguments that combines the two strings with a space between them and prints the resultant string.**
Example:
Input value of s1 =
"COMMONWEALTH"
Input value of s2="GAMES"
Output: "COMMONWEALTH GAMES"
(use library functions) [2015]

Ans.
```
import java. util.*;
class Quest_4
{
    void joystring(String s, char ch1, char ch2)
    {
        string str = s.replace(ch1, ch2);
        System.out.println(str);
    }
    void joystring(String s)
    {
        int First = s.index of (' ');
        System.out.println("First index: "+first);
        int last = S.lastIntexOf(' ') System.out
        println("Last index:"+last);
    }
    void joystring(String s1, String s2)
    {   String s3 = "   ";
        String str = s1   Concat (s3). Concat (s2)
        System.out.println(str);
    }
    public static void main(String args[])
    {
        Quest_4 obj = new Quest_4();
        obj.joystring("TECHNALAGY", 'A', 'O');
        obj.joystring("Cloud computing means
                    Internet based computing");
        obj.joystring("COMMONWEALTH",
                        "GAMES");
    }
}
```

Description of variable/ comments/ mnemonics

Name	Type	Description
s	String	To store a string argument.
ch1	char	To store a character argument.
ch2	char	To store another character argument.
f	int	To find the position of first space in the string.
l	int	To find position of last space in the string.
s1	String	To store a string argument.
s2	String	To store another string argument.

Q. 4. **Using the switch statement, write a menu driven program :**

(i) **To find and display all the *factors* of a number input by the user (including 1 and excluding number itself).**
Example:
Sample Input: n = 15
Sample Output: 1, 3, 5

(ii) **To find and display the *factorial* of a number input by the user (the factorial of a non-negative integer *n*, denoted by n!, is the product of all integers less than or equal to n.**
Example:
Sample Input: n = 5
Sample Output: 5! = 1 × 2 × 3 × 4 × 5 = 120.
For an incorrect choice, an appropriate error message should be displayed.
[2015]

Ans.
```
import java.util.*;
class question5
{
        public static void main(String args[])
        {
                Scanner sc=new Scanner(System.in);
                System.out.println("MENU");
                System.out.println("1.FACTORS OF
                A NUMBER");
                System.out.println("2.FACTORIAL
                OF A NUMBER");
                System.out.println("ENTER A
                NUMBER");
                int num=sc.nextInt();
                System.out.println("ENTER YOUR
                CHOICE");
                int choice=sc.nextInt();
                switch (choice)
                {
                    case 1:
                    System.out.print("FACTORS
                    ARE=");
                        for(int i=1;i<=num/2;i++)
                        {
                            if(num%i==0)
                            System.out.print(i+",");
                        }
                        break;
                    case 2:
                        int f=1;
                        for(int i=1;i<=num;i++)
                        {
                            f=f*i;
                        }
                System.out.println("FACTORIAL OF
                                "+num+"="+f);
                        break;
                        default:
                        System.out.rintln("Wrong
                        choice");
                        }
}}
```
Description of variables/ comments/mnemonics

Name	Type	Description
ch	int	To input user's choice.
n	int	To store a number.
i	int	As a loop variable.
f	int	Used as a variable to find factorial of number.

Q. 5. **Define a class named movieMagic with the following description:**

Instance variables/data members:

int year — to store the year of release of a movie

String title — to store the title of the movie

float rating — to store the popularity rating of the movie (**minimum rating = 0.0 and maximum rating = 5.0**)

Member methods:

 (i) movieMagic() Default constructor to initialize numeric data members to 0 and String data members to " ".

(ii) void accept() To input and store year, title and rating.

(iii) void display() To display the title of a movie and a message based on the rating as per the table below.

Rating	Message to be displayed
0.0 to 2.0	Flop
2.1 to 3.4	Semi-hit
3.5 to 4.5	Hit
4.6 to 5.0	Super Hit

Write a main method to create an object of the class and call the above member methods.

[2014]

Ans.
```
import java.io.*;//import java.util.*;
public class movieMagic
{
    int year; float rating; String title;
    BufferedReader     br=newBufferedReader
    (new InputStreamReader(System.in));
    //Scanner sc=new Scanner(System.in);
    public movieMagic()
    {
        year=0;
        rating=0.0f;
        title="";
    }
public void accept()throws IOException//
throws InputMismatchException
    {
        System.out.println("Enter year of
        rlease");
        year=Integer.parseInt(br.readLine());//
        sc.nextInt();
        System.out.println("Enter title");
        title=br.readLine(); // sc.next();
    do
```

```
{
System.out.println("Enter rating (minimum
0.0 and maximum 5.0)");
rating=Float.parseFloat(br.readLine());//
sc.nextInt();
}
while (!(rating>=0.0f && rating<=5.0.f)); OR
while (rating < 0.0f || rating > 5.0f );
}
public void display()
{
    System.out.print("Title:"+title+" Rating: ");
    if (rating <=2.0) System.out.println("Flop");
    else if (rating<=3.4) System.out println
    ("Semi Hit");
    else if (rating<=4.5) System.out println
    ("Hit");
    else System.out.println("Super Hit");
}
public static void main()throws IOException
    {
        movieMagic object = new movieMagic();
        object.accept();
        object.display()
    }
}
```

STEPS

Declaration of class and instance variables
Creating object of class BufferedReader/Scanner
Constructor properly declared and data members initialised
accept() method declaration (with exception handling if required)
3 Inputs correct
Output title in display() method
Decision for rating<=2.0 and output

Name	Type	Description
year	int	To store the year of release of a movie.
title	String	To store title of the movie.
rating	float	To store the popularity rating of a movie.

Q. 6. **Define a class named FruitJuice with the following description:**

Instance variables/data members:

int product_code	—	stores the product code number
String flavour	—	stores the flavour of the juice (E.g. orange, apple, etc.)
String pack_type	—	stores the type of packaging (E.g. tetra-pack, PET bottle, etc.)
int pack_size	—	stores package size (E.g. 200 ml, 400 ml, etc.)
int product_price	—	stores the price of the product

Member methods:

(i) FruitJuice()	—	Default constructor to initialize integer data members to 0 and String data members to " ".
(ii) void input()	—	To input and store the product code, flavour, pack type, pack size and product price.
(iii) void discount()	—	To reduce the product price by 10.
(iv) void display()	—	To display the product code, flavour, pack type, pack size and product price.

[2013]

Ans.

```
import java.io.*; // importing package
class FruitJuice
{
    int product_code, pack_size, product_price;
    String flavour, pack_type;
    public FruitJuice()
    {
        product_code = 0;
        pack_size = 0;
        product_price = 0;
        flavour = "";
        pack_type = "";
    }
    void input()throws IOException
    {
        BufferedReader br = new
                BufferedReader(new
            InputStreamReader(System.in));
        System.out.println("Enter Product
                Details");
        product_code = Integer.parseInt
                (br.readLine());
        flavour = br.readLine();
        pack_type = br.readLine();
        pack_size = Integer.parseInt(br.read
                Line());
        product_price = Integer.parseInt
                (br.readLine());
    }
```

```
    void discount()
    {
        product_price = product_price – 10;
    }
    void display()
    {
        System.out.println(product_code + " " +
        flavour + " " + pack_type + " " +
        pack_size + " " + product_price);
    }
} // class ending
```

Name	Type	Description
Product_code	int	To store product code number.
flavour	String	To store flavour.
pack_type	String	To Store type of packaging.
pack_size	int	To store package size.
product_price	int	To store price of product.

Short Answer Type Questions

Q. 1. State the difference between length and length() in Java. **[2020]**

Ans. Length is a variable used with arrays to find its size whereas length() is a function used with Strings to determine the no. of characters present in it.

If arr[] = {1,2,3,4,5} then arr.length will return 5.

If s="JAVA" the s.length() will return 4.

Q. 2. Write the output for the following: **[2020]**
```
String s1 = "Life is Beautiful";
System.out.println ("Earth" +
                    s1.substring(4));
System.out.println( s1.endsWith("L") );
```

Ans. Earth is Beautiful

false

Q. 3. What is the data type returned by the following library methods? **[2020]**

(i) isWhitespace()

(ii) compareToIgnoreCase()

Ans. (i) boolean

(ii) int

Q. 4. What is the difference between the linear search and the binary search technique? **[2019]**

Ans.

	Linear Search	Binary Search
1.	It can work with both sorted and unsorted arrays.	It can only work with sorted arrays.
2.	It takes more number of comparisons.	It takes less number of comparisons

Q. 5. String x[] = {"Artificial intelligence", "IOT", "Machine learning", "Big data"};

Give the output of the following statements:

(i) System.out.println(x[3]);

(ii) System.out.println(x.length); **[2019]**

Ans. (i) Big Data

(ii) 4

Q. 6. Differentiate between searching and sorting. **[2018]**

Ans.

	Searching	Sorting
1.	It is the process of checking whether the element is present in the array or not.	It is the process of arranging the data in ascending or descending order in the array.
2.	Examples of searching techniques are linear and binary search.	Examples of sorting techniques are Selection sort, bubble sort, etc.

Q. 7. Consider the following String array and give the output:
```
String arr[] = {"DELHI", "CHENNAI",
"MUMBAI", "LUCKNOW", "JAIPUR"};
System.out.println(arr[0].length()
                    > arr[3].length());
System.out.print(arr[4].substring(0, 3));
```
[2018]

Ans. false

JAI

Q. 8. String x[] = {"SAMSUNG", "NOKIA", "SONY","MICROMAX", "BLACKBERRY"};

Give the output of the following statements:

(i) System.out.println(x[1]);

(ii) System.out.println(x[3].length()); **[2017]**

Ans. (i) NOKIA

(ii) 8

Q. 9. Find the errors in the given program segment and rewrite the statements correctly to assign values to an integer array:
```
int a = new int (5);
for(int i = 0; i <= 5; i++) a [i]=i;
```
[2014]

Ans. (i) int a[] = new int[5]; (square brackets [] must be used.)

(ii) for(int i = 0; i < 5; i++) a[i] = i; (i must be less than 5)

Q. 10. Write statements to show how finding the length of a character array char[] differs from finding the length of a String object str. **[2013]**

Ans. To find the length of an array; the statement is:
char.length

To find the length of a string; the statement is:
```
String str = "abc";
str.length();
```

Long Answer Type Questions

Q. 1. Write a program to search for an integer value input by the user in the sorted list given below using binary search technique. If found display "Search Successful" and print the element, otherwise display "Search Unsuccessful" **[2020]**

{31, 36, 45, 50, 60, 75, 86, 90}

Ans.
```java
import java.util.*;
class Search
{
    int A[]={31,36,45,50,60,75,86,90};
    int n,low,high,mid,flag=0;
    void display()
    {
        low=0;
        high=A.length-1;
        Scanner sc=new Scanner(System.in);
System.out.println("Enter a no.");
n=sc.nextInt();
while(low<=high)
{
    mid=(low+high)/2;
    if(n>A[mid])
    {
        low=mid+1;
    }
    else if(n<A[mid])
        {
            high=mid-1;
        }
        else
        {
            flag=1;
            break;
        }
    }
    if(flag==1)
    {
        System.out.println("Search
                Successful"+n+"Found");
    }
    else
    {
        System.out.println("Search
                Unsuccessful ");
    }
}
}
```

Q. 2. Write a program to input a sentence and convert it into uppercase and display each word in a separate line. **[2020]**

Example:

Input : India is my country

Output : INDIA

       IS

       MY

       COUNTRY

Ans.
```java
import java.util.*;
class Sentence
{
    String s,w;
    int i,l;
    public Sentence()
    {
        s="Destination Point Computers";
    }
    void display()
    {
    Scanner sc=new Scanner(System.in);
    System.out.println("Enter a Sentence");
    s=sc.nextLine();
    s=s.toUpperCase();
    s=s+" ";
    l=s.length();
    for(i=0;i<l;i++)
    {
        w="";
        while(s.charAt(i)!=' ')
        {
            w=w+s.charAt(i);
            i++;
        }
        System.out.println(w);
    }
    }
}
```

Q. 3. Write a menu driven program to perform the following operations as per user's choice: **[2020]**

To print the value of c = a2 + 2ab, where a varies from 1.0 to 20.0 with increment of 2.0 and b = 3.0 is a constant.

Ans.
```java
import java.util.*;
class Menu
```

```
    {
        int ch;
        double a,b=3.0,c;
        char :i,j;
        void display()
        {
            Scanner sc=new Scanner(System.in);
            System.out.println("1. Value of c");
            System.out.println("2. Pattern");
            System.out.println("Enter Your
                                        Choice");
            ch=sc.nextInt();
            if(ch==1)
            {
                for(a=1.0;a<=20.0;a=a+2)
                {
                    c=a*a + 2*a*b;
                        System.out.println(c);
                }
            }
        }
```

Q. 4. **Write a program to accept name and total marks of N number of students in two single subscript array name[ ] and totalmarks[ ].**
   Calculate and print:

   (i) The average of the total marks obtained by *N* number of students.

   [average = (sum of total marks of all the students)/N]

   (ii) Deviation of each student's total marks with the average.

   [deviation = total marks of a student – average] **[2018]**

Ans.
```
import java.util.*;//importing package
class Student
{
    int n, i, s = 0;
    double avg, d;
    void display()
    {
        Scanner sc = new Scanner(System.in);
        System.out.println("Enter number
                                of students");
        n = sc.nextInt();
        String name[] = new String[n];
        int totalmarks[] = new int[n];
        for(i = 0; i < n; i++)
        {
            System.out.println("Enter
                    name and total marks");
            name[i] = sc.nextLine();
            totalmarks[i] = sc.nextInt();
            s = s + totalmarks[i];
        }
        avg = (double)s/n;
        System.out.println("Average = " + avg);
        for(i = 0; i < n; i++)
        {
            d = totalmarks[i] – avg;
            System.out.println(name[i]
                    + " Deviation is " + d);
        }
    }
} // class end
```

Name	Type	Description
n	int	To store number of students.
i	int	For loop variable.
s	int	To store sum.
avg	double	To store average.
d	double	To store deviation.

Q. 5. Write a program to input integer elements into an array of size 20 and perform the following operations:

   (i) Display largest number from the array.

   (ii) Display smallest number from the array.

   (iii) Display sum of all the elements of the array. **[2017]**

Ans.

```
import java.util.*;
class array
{
public static void main(String arg[])
{
Scanner sc =new Scanner(System.in);
System.out.println("enter numbers");
int a[ ]=new int [20];
for(int i=0;i<20;i++)
{
a[i]=sc.nextInt();
}
int max=a[0];
int min=a[0];
int sum= 0;
for(int i=0;i<20;i++)
{
if( a[i]>max)
max = a[i];
if(a[i]<min)
min=a[i];
sum=sum+ a[i];
}
System.out.println("largest number is"+ max);
System.out.println("smallest number is"+min);
System.out.println("sum is "+ sum);
}
}
```

STEPS

Creating an array

Loop for input

Taking input of array elements

Initialization of max and min

for loop

if condition and updating the value of max variable

If condition and updating the value of min variable

calculating sum of array elements

Display

Variable description

Name	Type	Description
A[]	int	Integer array.
l	int	To store the largest value.
i	int	For loop variable.
sum	int	To store sum of all the elements of the array.
s	int	To store the smallest value.

Q. 6. Write a program to input and store roll numbers, names and marks in 3 subjects of n number students in five single dimensional arrays and display the remark based on average marks as given below: (The maximum marks in the subject are 100)

Average marks = Total Marks/3

Average marks	Remark
85–100	EXCELLENT
75–84	DISTINCTION
60–74	FIRST CLASS
40–59	PASS
Less than 40	POOR

[2015]

Ans.

```
import java.util.*;
class Quest-5
{
    void grade()
    {
    Scanner br = new Scanner(System.in);
    System.out.println("Enter no. of students");
    int n = br.nextInt();
    int roll [] = new int[n];
    string name = new String[n];
    double m1 = new double[n];
    double m2 = new double[n];
    double m3 = new double[n];
    double avg [ ]= new double [n];
    for(i = 0; i < n; i++)
    {
        System.out.println("Enter roll number,
        name, marks in 3 subjects for"+(i+i) +"
                                        student);
        roll[i] = br.nextInt();
        name[i] = br.next();
        m1[i] = br.nextDouble();
        m2[i] = br.nextDouble();
        m3[i] = br.nextDouble();
        avg [i] = (m1[i] + m2[i] + m3[i]) / 3;
        if(avg [i] >= 85 && avg <= 100)
            System.out.println("EXCELLENT");
        else if(avg [i] >= 75 && avg [i] <= 84)
            System.out.println("DISTINCTION");
```

```
else if(avg [i] >= 60 && avg [i] <= 74)
    System.out.println("FIRST CLASS");
else if(avg [i] >= 40 && avg [i] <= 59)
    System.out.println("PASS");
else
    System.out.println("POOR");
}
}
}
```

Name	Type	Description
n	int	To input number of students.
rno[]	int	To store roll number of students in one array.
m1[]	int	To store marks of students in an array.
m2[]	int	To store marks of students in an array.
m3[]	int	To store marks of students in an array.
name[]	String	To store names of students in an array.
avg	double	To calculate average marks.
i	int	As a loop variable.

Q. 7. Write a program to accept the year of graduation from school as an integer value from the user. Using the Binary Search technique on the sorted array of integers given below,

Output the message "Record exists" If the value input is located in the array. If not, output the message "Record does not exist".
{1982, 1987, 1993, 1996, 1999,
2003, 2006, 2007, 2009, 2010}   **[2014]**

Ans.
```
import java.io.*; //import java.util.*;
public class BinarySearch {
    public static void main() throws IO
Exception
    {   int[] intArray = {1982, 1987, 1993,
        1996, 1999, 2003, 2006, 2007, 2009,
        2010};
        int searchValue = 0;
BufferedReader br=new BufferedReader(new
InputStreamReader(System.in));
//Scanner sc=new Scanner(System.in);
        System.out.print("Enter a number to
        search for: ");
        searchValue=Integer.parseInt(br
        readLine());//sc.nextInt();
        boolean b=false;
        int start, end, mid;
        start = 0;
        end = intArray.length - 1; // end=9
        while (start <= end) {
            mid = (start + end) / 2;
            if (intArray[mid] == searchValue)
                                        1 mark
            {System.out println
            ("Record exists"); b=true; break;}
            else if (intArray[mid] < search
            Value)
                start = mid + 1;
            else
                    end = mid - 1;
            }
            if (b==false) System.out
            println("Record does not
            exist");
    }
}
```

STEPS
Assign (or accept) values to integer array
Input number to be searched
Initialize boolean or integer value to check if search number exists in
array (Deduct mark if boolean/integer value status does not change when search number is located)
Initialise start index and end index of array
Condition statement while(start<=end)
Compute middle index
Check if array item at middle index equals search number
Output "Record exists", break to exit loop
Check if array item at middle index less than search number
start index = middle index +1
Check if array item at middle index greater than search number
end index = middle index - 1
Condition and output message "Record does not exist"
Description of variables/ comments/ mnemonics

Name	Type	Description
A [ ]	int	To store year of graduation in an array.
n	int	To enter year from user to find the mid term.
mid	int	To find the mid term in the array.
flag	int	As a variable to check whether the year is present in the record list.
d	int	To store a value.
n	in	To Store the length of the variable.

Input/Output

Short Answer Type Questions

Q. 1. System.out.print("BEST");
System.out.println("OF LUCK");
Choose the correct option for the output of the above statements
(i) BEST OF LUCK
(ii) BEST
OF LUCK **[2018]**

Ans. (i) BEST OF LUCK is the correct option.

Q. 2. Give the output of the following string functions:
(i) "ACHIEVEMENT".replace('E', 'A')
(ii) "DEDICATE"compareTo("DEVOTE") **[2018]**

Ans. (i) ACHIAVAMANT
(ii) –18

Q. 3. Give the output of the following code:
String A ="26", B = "100";
String D = A + B + "200";
int x = Integer.parseInt(A);
int y = Integer.parseInt(B);
int d = x + y;
System.out.println("Result 1 = " + D);
System.out.println("Result 2 = " + d); **[2017]**

Ans. Result 1 = 26100200
Result 2 = 126

Q. 4. Analyze the given program segment and answer the following questions:
for(int i = 3; i <= 4; i++)
{
    for(int j = 2; j < i; j++)
    {
        System.out.print(" ");
    }
    System.out.println("WIN");
}
(i) How many times does the inner loop execute?
(ii) Write the output of the program segment. **[2017]**

Ans. (i) Inner loop will be executed 3 times.
(ii) WIN
WIN

Q. 5. What is the difference between the Scanner class functions next( ) and nextLine( )? **[2017]**

Ans.

next()	nextLine()
It is used to accept a string input without any space.	It is used to accept a string input with spaces.

Q. 6. Differentiate between formal parameter and actual parameter. **[2016]**

Ans.

Formal Parameter	Actual Parameter
The parameter appearing in function definition statement is called formal parameter.	The parameter appearing in function calling statement is called actual parameter.

e.g.:
```
class Demo
{
    void f1(int n)//Formal parameter
    {
        System.out.println(n);
    }
    void call()
    {
        int a = 5;
        f1(a); //Actual parameter
    }
}
```

Q. 7. State the package that contains the class:
(i) BufferedReader
(ii) Scanner. **[2015]**

Ans. (i) Buffered Reader is stored in java.io package.
(ii) Scanner is stored in java.util package.

Q. 8. If int y = 10 then find int z = (++y * (y++ + 5)); **[2015]**

Ans. int z = (++y * (y++ + 5));
(11 * (11 + 5));
176

Q. 9. Name the methods of Scanner class that:
(i) is used to input an integer data from the standard input stream.
(ii) is used to input a String data from the standard input stream. **[2013]**

Ans. (i) scanner.nextInt();
(ii) scanner.next();

 Long Answer Type Questions

Q. 1. Write a program to accept a number and check and display whether it is a spy number or not. (A number is spy if the sum of its digits equals the product of its digits.)

Example: consider the number 1124,
Sum of the digits = 1 + 1 + 2 + 4 = 8
Product of the digits = 1 × 1 × 2 × 4 = 8

[2017]

Ans.
```
public class SpyNumber
{
void print (int n)
{
int i, s=0, p = 1,d;
while (n>0)
{
d=n%10;
n=n/10;
s+=d;
p*=d;
}
if (s==p)
System.out.println( "It is a spy number");
else
System.out.println( " It is not a spy number");
}
}
```

STEPS
Input
Declaration of variables
Initialization of variables s=0 & p=1
Loop
Extraction of digit
Updation
Sum
Product
Check
Output
Variable description

Name	Type	Description
n	int	To input a number.
d	int	To store a digit.
p	int	To store product of digits.
s	int	To store sum of digits.

CPSIA information can be obtained
at www.ICGtesting.com
Printed in the USA
LVHW021821050623
748890LV00005B/22